Your fully reengineered Microsoft Study Guide.

The all-new learning format of your Microsoft study guide delivers in-depth preparation for the exam—including full objective-by-objective review—along with great new study tools to help prepare you for the job. Features include:

- Relevant exam objectives highlighted at the start of each chapter

- "Why This Chapter Matters" and "Real World" sidebars on how you can apply learning concepts to the job

- Case scenario exercises where you work through a multi-step, real-world solution

- Troubleshooting labs on a simulated operating system for practical field experience

D0460735

❑ Create and modify user accounts by using the Active Directory Users and Computers MMC snap-in.
❑ Create and modify user accounts by using automation.
❑ Import user accounts.
- Manage local, roaming, and mandatory user profiles.
- Troubleshoot user accounts.
❑ Diagnose and resolve account lockouts.
❑ Diagnose and resolve issues related to user account properties.
- Troubleshoot user authentication issues.

Why This Chapter Matters

Before individuals in your enterprise can begin to access resources they require, you must enable authentication of those individuals. Of course, the primary component of that authentication is the user's identity, maintained as an account in Active Directory. In this chapter, you will review and enhance your knowledge related to the creation, maintenance, and troubleshooting of user accounts and authentication.

Each enterprise, and each day, brings with it a unique set of challenges related to user management. The properties you configure for a standard user account are likely to be different from those you apply to the account of a Help Desk team member, which are different still from those configured on the built-in Administrator account. Skills that are effective to create or modify a single user account become clumsy and inefficient when you are working with masses of accounts, for example when managing the accounts for a number of new hires.

To effectively address a diverse sampling of account management scenarios, we will examine a variety of user management skills and tools including the Active Directory Users & Computers snap-in and powerful command-line utilities.

3-1

Lesson 2: Creating Multiple User Objects

There occasionally situations that require you to create multiple user objects quickly, such as a new class of incoming students at a school, or a group of new hires at an organization. In these situations you need to know how to effectively facilitate or automate user object creation so that you are not approaching the task on an account-by-account basis. In Lesson 1, you learned how to create and manage user objects with Active Directory Users and Computers. This lesson will extend those concepts, skills, and tools to include user object creation through template objects, imported objects, and command line scripting of objects.

After this lesson, you will be able to
- Create and utilize user object templates
- Import user objects from comma-delimited files
- Leverage new command-line tools to create and manage user objects

Estimated lesson time: 15 minutes

Creating and Using User Templates

It is common for objects to share similar properties. For example, all sales representatives may belong to the same security groups, are allowed to log on to the network during the same hours, and have home folders and roaming profiles on the same server. In such cases, it is helpful when creating a user object for that object to be pre-populated with common properties. This can be accomplished by creating a generic user object—often called a *template*—and then copying that object to create new users.

To generate a user template, create a user and populate its properties. Put the user into appropriate groups.

 Security Alert Be certain to disable the user, since it is just a template, to ensure that the account is not used for access to network resources.

To create a new user based on the template, select the template and choose Copy from the Action menu. You will be prompted for properties similar to those when you create a new user: first and last name, initials, logon names, password, and account options. When the object is created, you will find that properties are copied from the template based on the following property page based descriptions:

- **General** No properties copied.
- **Address** All properties except Street address are copied.

 Note Be sure to configure share permissions allowing Everyone Full Control. The Windows Server 2003 default share permissions allow Read, which is not sufficient for a roaming profile share.

On the Profile tab of the user's Properties dialog box, type the Profile Path in the format: **<server>****<share>****%username%**. The *%username%* variable will automatically be replaced with the user's logon name.

It's that simple. The next time the user logs on to their system, the system will identify the roaming profile location.

 Exam Tip Roaming user profiles are nothing more than a shared folder and a path to the user's profile folder, within that share, entered into the user object's profile path property. Roaming profiles are not, in any way, a property of a computer object.

When the user logs *off* of their system, it will upload the profile to the profile server. The user can now log on to their system, or any other system in the domain, and the documents and settings that are part of the RUP will be applied.

 Note Windows Server 2003 introduces a new policy: Only allow local user profiles. This policy, linked to an OU containing computer accounts, will prevent roaming profiles from being used on those computers. Users will, instead, maintain local profiles.

When a user with an RUP logs on to a new system for the first time, the system does not copy its Default User profile. Instead, it downloads the RUP from the network location. When a user logs off, or when a user logs on to a system on which they've worked before, the system copies only files that have changed.

 Real World   Roaming Profile Synchronization
Unlike previous versions of Microsoft Windows, Windows 2000, Windows XP, and Windows Server 2003 do not upload and download the entire user profile at logoff and logon. Instead, the user profile is *synchronized*. Only files that have changed are transferred between the local system and the network RUP folder. This means that logon and logoff with RUPs are significantly faster than with earlier Windows systems. Organizations that have not implemented RUPs for fear of their impact on logon and network traffic should reevaluate their configuration in this light.

- "Off the Record" sidebars bridge the gap between how things *should* work and how they *do* work

- Security Alerts and Planning Tips you can apply in the real world

- Complete objective-by-objective review section

- Exam highlights—key points and terms you should know

- Exam tips written by industry insiders

Microsoft

MCSA/MCSE

Exams 70-292
and 70-296

UPGRADING YOUR CERTIFICATION
to Microsoft
WINDOWS
SERVER™ 2003

*Dan Holme and
Orin Thomas, Editors*

Self-Paced
Training Kit

PUBLISHED BY
Microsoft Press
A Division of Microsoft Corporation
One Microsoft Way
Redmond, Washington 98052-6399

Library of Congress Cataloging-in-Publication Data
Holme, Dan
    MCSA/MCSE Self-Paced Training Kit: Upgrading Your Certification to Microsoft
  Windows Server 2003: Managing, Maintaining, Planning, and Implementing a Microsoft
  Windows Server 2003 environment: Exams 70-292 and 70-296 / Dan Holme, Orin Thomas.
      p. cm.
    Includes index.
    ISBN 0-7356-1971-9
     1. Electronic data processing personnel--Certification.   2. Microsoft
  software--Examinations--Study guides.   3. Microsoft Windows server.   I. Thomas, Orin,
  1973-   II. Title.

    QA76.3.H669   2003
    005.4'4765--dc22   2003058833

Printed and bound in the United States of America.

1 2 3 4 5 6 7 8 9   QWT   8 7 6 5 4 3

Distributed in Canada by H.B. Fenn and Company Ltd.

A CIP catalogue record for this book is available from the British Library.

Microsoft Press books are available through booksellers and distributors worldwide. For further information about international editions, contact your local Microsoft Corporation office or contact Microsoft Press International directly at fax (425) 936-7329. Visit our Web site at www.microsoft.com/mspress. Send comments to *tkinput@microsoft.com*.

Microsoft, Microsoft Press, Active Directory, ActiveX, FrontPage, IntelliMirror, JScript, MS-DOS, NetMeeting, Outlook, PowerPoint, Visual Basic, Windows, Windows Media, Windows NT, and Windows Server are either registered trademarks or trademarks of Microsoft Corporation in the United States and/or other countries. Other product and company names mentioned herein may be the trademarks of their respective owners.
The example companies, organizations, products, domain names, e-mail addresses, logos, people, places, and events depicted herein are fictitious. No association with any real company, organization, product, domain name, e-mail address, logo, person, place, or event is intended or should be inferred.

Acquisitions Editor: Kathy Harding
Project Editor: Karen Szall
Technical Editor: Robert Lyon

Body Part No. X10-00025

Dan Holme

A graduate of Yale University and Thunderbird, the American Graduate School of International Management, Dan has spent 10 years as a consultant and a trainer, delivering solutions to tens of thousands of IT professionals from the most prestigious organizations and corporations around the world. His clients have included AT&T, Compaq, HP, Boeing, Home Depot, and Intel, and he has recently been involved supporting the design and implementation of Active Directory at enterprises including Raytheon, ABN AMRO, Johnson & Johnson, Los Alamos National Laboratories, and General Electric. Dan is the Director of Training Services for Intelliem, which specializes in boost-ing the productivity of IT professionals and end users by creating advanced, customized solutions that integrate clients' specific design and configuration into productivity-focused training and knowledge management services (info@intelliem.com). From his base in sunny Arizona, Dan travels to client sites around the world and then unwinds on his favorite mode of transportation—his snowboard. It takes a village to raise a happy geek, and Dan sends undying thanks and love to those, without whom, sanity would be out of reach: Lyman, Barb & Dick, Bob & Joni, Stan & Marylyn & Sondra, Mark, Kirk, John, Beth, Dan & June, Lena and the entire crazy commando crew.

Orin Thomas

Orin is a writer, an editor, and a systems administrator who works for the certification advice Web site Certtutor.net. His work in IT has been varied: he's done everything from providing first-level networking support to acting in the role of systems administrator for one of Australia's largest companies. He has authored several articles for technical publications as well as contributing to *The Insider's Guide to IT Certification*. He holds the MCSE, CCNA, CCDA, and Linux+ certifications. He holds a bachelor's degree in science with honors from the University of Melbourne and is currently working toward the completion of a Ph.D. in Philosophy of Science. Orin would like to thank his beautiful, amazing wife, Oksana, for being more wonderful and loving than he could ever have dreamed. Orin wants to thank their son, Rooslan, for making fatherhood so easy and fun. He would also like to thank the following friends and family: Ma, Mick, Lards, Gillian, Lee, Neil, Will, Jon, Alexander, Irina, Stas, and Kasia as well as the entire Certtutor.net tutor team, who offer great free advice to those who are interested in getting certified.

Contents at a Glance

Practices

Tables

Troubleshooting Labs

Case Scenario Exercises

Contents

3 Managing and Maintaining an Active Directory Implementation 3-1

5   Planning, Implementing, and Troubleshooting Group Policy   5-1

6   Managing the User Environment with Group Policy   6-1

13   Managing and Implementing Disaster Recovery   13-1

14   Clustering Servers   14-1

Part 2   Prepare for the Exam

15   Exam 70-292—Managing Users, Computers, and Groups (1.0)   15-1

16 Exam 70-292—Managing and Maintaining Access to Resources (2.0) — 16-1

17 Exam 70-292—Managing and Maintaining a Server Environment (3.0) — 17-1

18 Exam 70-292—Managing and Implementing Disaster Recovery (4.0) — 18-1

19 Exam 70-292—Implementing, Managing, and Maintaining Name Resolution (5.0) — 19-1

20 Exam 70-292—Implementing, Managing, and Maintaining Network Security (6.0)   20-1

21 Exam 70-296—Planning and Implementing Server Roles and Server Security (1.0)   21-1

22 Exam 70-296—Planning, Implementing, and Maintaining a Network Infrastructure (2.0)   22-1

23 Exam 70-296—Planning, Implementing, and Maintaining Server Availability (3.0)   23-1

About This Book

Welcome to *MCSA/MCSE Self-Paced Training Kit (Exams 70-292 and 70-296): Upgrading Your Certification to Microsoft Windows Server 2003.* We have designed this book to prepare you effectively for the MCSE upgrade examinations and, along the way, to share with you knowledge about what it takes to implement Windows Server 2003 in your enterprise network. We hope that by helping you understand the underlying technologies, the variety of options for configuring feature sets, and the complex interaction between components, you are better equipped to tackle the challenges that you face in the trenches of information technology (IT). We also hope to serve the community at large—to elevate the worth of the MCSE moniker—so that behind each certification is a knowledgeable, experienced, capable professional.

Note For more information about becoming a Microsoft Certified Professional, see the "The Microsoft Certified Professional Program" section later in this introduction.

Intended Audience

This book was developed for IT professionals who plan to take the related Microsoft Certified Professional exams 70-292 and 70-296 as well as IT professionals who administer computers running Windows Server 2003.

Note Exam skills are subject to change without prior notice and at the sole discretion of Microsoft.

Prerequisites

This training kit requires that students meet the following prerequisites:

- Twelve to eighteen months of experience administering Microsoft Windows technologies in a network environment
- Understanding of Active Directory directory services and related technologies, including Group Policy
- Existing Windows 2000 MCSA or MCSE certification

About the CD-ROM

For your use, this book includes a Supplemental CD-ROM, which contains a variety of informational aids to complement the book content, including:

- The Microsoft Press Readiness Review Suite Powered by MeasureUp. This suite of practice tests and objective reviews contains questions of varying degrees of complexity and offers multiple testing modes. You can assess your understanding of the concepts presented in this book and use the results to develop a learning plan that meets your needs.

- An electronic version of this book (eBook). For information about using the eBook, see the "The eBooks" section later in this introduction.

- An eBook of the *Microsoft Encyclopedia of Networking*, Second Edition, and an eBook of the *Microsoft Encyclopedia of Security*. These eBooks provide complete and up-to-date reference materials for networking and security.

- Sample chapters from several Microsoft Press books. These chapters give you additional information about Windows Server 2003 and introduce you to other resources that are available from Microsoft Press.

A second CD-ROM contains a 180-day evaluation edition of Microsoft Windows Server 2003, Enterprise Edition.

Caution The 180-day Evaluation Edition provided with this training kit is not the full retail product and is provided only for the purposes of training and evaluation. Microsoft Technical Support does not support this evaluation edition.

For additional support information regarding this book and the CD-ROM (including answers to commonly asked questions about installation and use), visit the Microsoft Press Technical Support Web site at *http://www.microsoft.com/mspress/support/*. You can also e-mail tkinput@microsoft.com or send a letter to Microsoft Press, Attention: Microsoft Press Technical Support, One Microsoft Way, Redmond, WA 98052-6399.

Features of This Book

This book has two parts. Use Part 1 to learn at your own pace and practice what you've learned with hands-on exercises. Part 2 contains questions and answers you can use to test yourself on what you've learned.

Part 1: Learn at Your Own Pace

Each chapter identifies the exam objectives that are covered within the chapter, provides an overview of why the topics matter by identifying how the information is applied in the real world, and lists any prerequisites that must be met to complete the lessons presented in the chapter.

The chapters contain a set of lessons. Lessons contain practices that include one or more hands-on exercises. These exercises give you an opportunity to use the skills being presented or explore the part of the application being described.

After the lessons, you are given an opportunity to apply what you've learned in a case scenario exercise. In this exercise, you work through a multistep solution for a realistic case scenario. You are also given an opportunity to work through a troubleshooting lab that explores difficulties you might encounter when applying what you've learned on the job.

Each chapter ends with a summary of key concepts and a short section listing key topics and terms you need to know before taking the exam. This section summarizes the key topics you've learned, with a focus on demonstrating that knowledge on the exam.

> **Real World   Helpful Information**
> You will find sidebars like this one that contain related information you might find helpful. "Real World" sidebars contain specific information gained through the experience of IT professionals just like you.

Part 2: Exam Preparation

Part 2 helps to familiarize you with the types of questions you will encounter on the MCP exam. By reviewing the objectives and sample questions, you can focus on the specific skills you need to improve on before taking the exam.

> **See Also**   For a complete list of MCP exams and their related objectives, go to *http://www.microsoft.com/traincert/mcp*.

Part 2 is organized by the exam's objectives. Each chapter covers one of the primary groups of objectives, referred to as *Objective Domains*. Each chapter lists the tested skills you need to master to answer the exam questions, and it includes a list of further readings to help you improve your ability to perform the tasks or skills specified by the objectives.

Within each Objective Domain, you will find the related objectives that are covered on the exam. Each objective provides you with several practice exam questions. The answers are accompanied by explanations of each correct and incorrect answer.

Note   These questions are also available on the Supplemental CD as an objective-by-objective review.

Informational Notes

Several types of reader aids appear throughout the training kit.

- **Tip** contains methods of performing a task more quickly or in a not-so-obvious way.
- **Important** contains information that is essential to completing a task.
- **Note** contains supplemental information.
- **Caution** contains valuable information about possible loss of data; be sure to read this information carefully.
- **Warning** contains critical information about possible physical injury; be sure to read this information carefully.
- **See also** contains references to other sources of information.
- **Planning** contains hints and useful information that should help you to plan the implementation.
- **On the CD** points you to supplementary information or files you need that are on the companion CD.
- **Security Alert** highlights information you need to know to maximize security in your work environment.
- **Exam Tip** flags information you should know before taking the certification exam.
- **Off the Record** contains practical advice about the real-world implications of information presented in the lesson.

Notational Conventions

The following conventions are used throughout this book:

- Characters or commands that you type appear in **bold** type.

- *Italic* in syntax statements indicates placeholders for variable information. *Italic* is also used for book titles.

- Names of files and folders appear in Title caps, except when you are to type them directly. Unless otherwise indicated, you can use all lowercase letters when you type a file name in a dialog box or at a command prompt.

- File name extensions appear in all lowercase.

- Acronyms appear in all uppercase.

- Monospace type represents code samples, examples of screen text, or entries that you might type at a command prompt or in initialization files.

- Square brackets [ ] are used in syntax statements to enclose optional items. For example, [*filename*] in command syntax indicates that you can choose to type a file name with the command. Type only the information within the brackets, not the brackets themselves.

- Braces { } are used in syntax statements to enclose required items. Type only the information within the braces, not the braces themselves.

Keyboard Conventions

- A plus sign (+) between two key names means that you must press those keys at the same time. For example, "Press ALT+TAB" means that you hold down ALT while you press TAB.

- A comma (,) between two or more key names means that you must press each of the keys consecutively, not together. For example, "Press ALT, F, X" means that you press and release each key in sequence. "Press ALT+W, L" means that you first press ALT and W at the same time, and then release them and press L.

Getting Started

This training kit contains hands-on exercises to help you learn about implementing, supporting, and troubleshooting Windows Server 2003 technologies. Use this section to prepare your self-paced training environment.

To complete some of these procedures, you must have two networked computers or be connected to a larger network. Both computers must be capable of running Windows Server 2003, Standard Edition or Enterprise Edition.

> **Caution**   Several exercises might require you to make changes to your servers. These changes might have undesirable results if you are connected to a larger network. Check with you Network Administrator before attempting these exercises.

Hardware Requirements

Each computer must have the following minimum configuration. All hardware should be in the Windows Server Catalog at *http://www.microsoft.com/windows/catalog/server/*, and should meet the requirements listed at *http://www.microsoft.com/windowsserver2003 /evaluation/sysreqs/*.

- Minimum CPU: 133 MHz for x86-based computers (733 MHz is recommended) and 733 MHz for Itanium-based computers

- Minimum RAM: 128 MB (256 MB is recommended)

- Disk space for setup: 2.0 GB for x86-based computers and 2.0 GB for Itanium-based computers

- Display monitor capable of 800 x 600 resolution or higher

- CD-ROM drive

- Microsoft Mouse or compatible pointing device

Software Requirements

The following software is required to complete the procedures in this training kit.

- Windows Server 2003, Enterprise Edition (A 180-day evaluation edition of Windows Server 2003, Enterprise Edition, is included on the CD-ROM.)

> **Caution**   The 180-day Evaluation Edition provided with this training is not the full retail prod-
> uct and is provided only for the purposes of training and evaluation. Microsoft Technical Sup-
> port does not support these evaluation editions. For additional support information regarding
> this book and the CD-ROMs (including answers to commonly asked questions about installation
> and use), visit the Microsoft Press Technical Support Web site at *http://www.microsoft.com
> /mspress/support/*. You can also e-mail tkinput@microsoft.com or send a letter to Microsoft
> Press, Attn: Microsoft Press Technical Support, One Microsoft Way, Redmond, WA 98502-6399.

Setup Instructions

Set up your computers according to the manufacturer's instructions.

The first computer should be configured as follows:

- Windows Server 2003, Enterprise Edition
- Computer name: Server01
- IP Address: 192.168.0.1
- Subnet Mask: 255.255.255.0
- The computer should be configured as a stand-alone (workgroup) server. It will be promoted to a domain controller in Chapter 2.

The second computer should be configured as follows:

- Windows Server 2003, Enterprise Edition
- Computer name: Server02
- IP Address: 192.168.0.2
- Subnet Mask: 255.255.255.0
- The computer should be configured as a stand-alone (workgroup) server. It will be promoted to a domain controller in Chapter 2. Server02 will be used as a member server and a domain controller for various exercises in the training kit.
- For the optional Automated System Recovery exercises in Chapter 13, you need about 2 GB of free disk space and a second physical hard disk.

Because most exercises require networked computers, you need to make sure the two servers can communicate with each other.

Caution   If your computers are part of a larger network, you *must* verify with your network administrator that the computer names, domain name, and other information used in setting up Windows Server 2003 as described in this section do not conflict with network operations. If they do conflict, ask your network administrator to provide alternative values and use those values throughout all of the exercises in this book.

The Readiness Review Suite

The CD-ROM includes a practice test made up of 300 sample exam questions and an objective-by-objective review with an additional 125 questions. Use these tools to reinforce your learning and to identify any areas in which you need to gain more experience before taking the exam.

▶ **To install the practice test and objective review**

1. Insert the Supplemental CD-ROM into your CD-ROM drive.

Note   If AutoRun is disabled on your machine, refer to the Readme.txt file on the CD-ROM.

2. Click Readiness Review Suite on the user interface menu.

The eBooks

The CD-ROM includes an electronic version of the training kit, as well as eBooks for both the *Microsoft Encyclopedia of Security* and the *Microsoft Encyclopedia of Networking*, Second Edition. The eBooks are in portable document format (PDF) and can be viewed using Adobe Acrobat Reader.

▶ **To use the eBooks**

1. Insert the Supplemental CD-ROM into your CD-ROM drive.

Note   If AutoRun is disabled on your machine, refer to the Readme.txt file on the CD-ROM.

2. Click Training Kit eBook on the user interface menu. You can also review any of the other eBooks that are provided for your use.

The Microsoft Certified Professional Program

The Microsoft Certified Professional (MCP) program provides the best method to prove your command of current Microsoft products and technologies. The exams and corresponding certifications are developed to validate your mastery of critical competencies as you design and develop, or implement and support, solutions with Microsoft products and technologies. Computer professionals who become Microsoft certified are recognized as experts and are sought after industry-wide. Certification brings a variety of benefits to the individual and to employers and organizations.

> **See Also**   For a full list of MCP benefits, go to *http://www.microsoft.com/traincert/mcp /mcp/benefits.asp*.

Certifications

The Microsoft Certified Professional program offers multiple certifications, based on specific areas of technical expertise:

- *Microsoft Certified Professional (MCP)*. Demonstrated in-depth knowledge of at least one Microsoft Windows operating system or architecturally significant platform. An MCP is qualified to implement a Microsoft product or technology as part of a business solution for an organization.

- *Microsoft Certified Solution Developer (MCSD)*. Professional developers qualified to analyze, design, and develop enterprise business solutions with Microsoft development tools and technologies, including the Microsoft .NET Framework.

- *Microsoft Certified Application Developer (MCAD)*. Professional developers qualified to develop, test, deploy, and maintain powerful applications using Microsoft tools and technologies, including Microsoft Visual Studio .NET and XML Web services.

- *Microsoft Certified Systems Engineer (MCSE)*. Qualified to effectively analyze the business requirements, and design and implement the infrastructure for business solutions based on the Microsoft Windows and Microsoft Server 2003 operating system.

- *Microsoft Certified Systems Administrator (MCSA)*. Individuals with the skills to manage and troubleshoot existing network and system environments based on the Microsoft Windows and Microsoft Server 2003 operating systems.

- *Microsoft Certified Database Administrator (MCDBA)*. Individuals who design, implement, and administer Microsoft SQL Server databases.

- *Microsoft Certified Trainer (MCT)*. Instructionally and technically qualified to deliver Microsoft Official Curriculum through a Microsoft Certified Technical Education Center (CTEC).

Requirements for Becoming a Microsoft Certified Professional

The certification requirements differ for each certification and are specific to the products and job functions addressed by the certification.

To become a Microsoft Certified Professional, you must pass rigorous certification exams that provide a valid and reliable measure of technical proficiency and expertise. These exams are designed to test your expertise and ability to perform a role or task with a product, and they are developed with the input of professionals in the industry. Questions in the exams reflect how Microsoft products are used in actual organizations, giving them "real-world" relevance.

- Microsoft Certified Product (MCPs) candidates are required to pass one current Microsoft certification exam. Candidates can pass additional Microsoft certification exams to further qualify their skills with other Microsoft products, development tools, or desktop applications.

- Microsoft Certified Solution Developers (MCSDs) are required to pass three core exams and one elective exam. (MCSD for Microsoft .NET candidates are required to pass four core exams and one elective.)

- Microsoft Certified Application Developers (MCADs) are required to pass two core exams and one elective exam in an area of specialization.

- Microsoft Certified Systems Engineers (MCSEs) are required to pass five core exams and two elective exams.

- Microsoft Certified Systems Administrators (MCSAs) are required to pass three core exams and one elective exam that provide a valid and reliable measure of technical proficiency and expertise.

- Microsoft Certified Database Administrators (MCDBAs) are required to pass three core exams and one elective exam that provide a valid and reliable measure of technical proficiency and expertise.

- Microsoft Certified Trainers (MCTs) are required to meet instructional and technical requirements specific to each Microsoft Official Curriculum course they are certified to deliver. The MCT program requires on-going training to meet the requirements for the annual renewal of certification. For more information about becoming a Microsoft Certified Trainer, visit *http://www.microsoft.com/traincert /mcp/mct/* or contact a regional service center near you.

Technical Support

Every effort has been made to ensure the accuracy of this book and the contents of the companion disc. If you have comments, questions, or ideas regarding this book or the companion disc, please send them to Microsoft Press using either of the following methods:

E-mail: tkinput@microsoft.com

Postal Mail: Microsoft Press
                 Attn: MCSE Training Kit (Exams 70-292 and 70-296): Upgrading Your
                 Certification to Microsoft Windows Server 2003, Editor
                 One Microsoft Way
                 Redmond, WA 98052-6399

For additional support information regarding this book and the CD-ROM (including answers to commonly asked questions about installation and use), visit the Microsoft Press Technical Support Web site at *http://www.microsoft.com/mspress/support/*. To connect directly to the Microsoft Press Knowledge Base and enter a query, visit *http://www.microsoft.com/mspress/support/search.asp*. For support information regarding Microsoft software, please connect to *http://support.microsoft.com/*.

Evaluation Edition Software Support

The 180-day Evaluation Edition provided with this training is not the full retail product and is provided only for the purposes of training and evaluation. Microsoft and Microsoft Technical Support do not support this evaluation edition.

Caution   The Evaluation Edition of Windows Server 2003, Enterprise Edition, included with this book should not be used on a primary work computer. The evaluation edition is unsupported. For online support information relating to the full version of Windows Server 2003, Enterprise Edition, that *might* also apply to the Evaluation Edition, you can connect to *http://support.microsoft.com/*.

Information about any issues relating to the use of this evaluation edition with this training kit is posted to the Support section of the Microsoft Press Web site (*http://www.microsoft.com/mspress/support/*). For information about ordering the full version of any Microsoft software, please call Microsoft Sales at (800) 426-9400 or visit *http://www.microsoft.com*.

Part 1
Learn at Your Own Pace

1 Introduction to Windows Server 2003

Exam Objectives in this Chapter:

- Plan a strategy for placing global catalog servers (Exam 70-296).
  - ❏ Evaluate network traffic considerations when placing global catalog servers.
  - ❏ Evaluate the need to enable universal group membership caching.

Why This Chapter Matters

As an MCSE or MCSA already certified on Microsoft Windows 2000, you already possess much of the core knowledge necessary to step into the world of Windows Server 2003. Although it includes a variety of new features aimed at improving availability, reliability, scalability, manageability, and security, Windows Server 2003 was ultimately developed using the best features of Windows 2000 as its foundation.

This chapter begins by introducing the new editions of Windows Server 2003, taking a look at their capabilities and requirements, as well as exploring the reasons why a company might choose one edition over another. Appreciating and understanding the basic differences between the editions is an important first step if you will be involved in planning, deploying, or managing Windows Server 2003 systems.

Although Windows Server 2003 builds on a foundation provided by Windows 2000, it provides a variety of new features and enhancements that you will need to be familiar with. This chapter provides a high-level overview of many new features in Windows Server 2003, with an emphasis on those that you will need to be familiar with for both the MCSE and MCSA upgrade exams.

Finally, the chapter finishes with an overview of Microsoft Active Directory directory service in Windows Server 2003 environments. This overview includes a review of important Active Directory concepts, as well as a look at planning the location of global catalog servers, and the implementation of a new feature, universal group membership caching.

Lessons in this Chapter:

Before You Begin

This chapter assumes that you have at least 18 months of experience working with Windows 2000 in environments that include Active Directory, and that you are comfortable working with common administrative tools and utilities. If you intend to complete the hands-on practice exercises in this chapter, you should have the following prepared:

- One Windows Server 2003 (Standard or Enterprise Edition) system installed as Server01. It is not required to be part of a domain.

- Access to the server using the built-in Administrator account or another account that is part of the Administrators local group.

Lesson 1: Overview of Windows Server 2003 Editions

The Windows Server 2003 family of operating systems consists of four editions, each designed with the particular needs of a different type of customer in mind. Although each edition is built on the same core architecture, editions differ in terms of scalability, services offered, and supported hardware platforms. The four editions of Windows Server 2003 are:

- Windows Server 2003, Standard Edition

- Windows Server 2003, Enterprise Edition

- Windows Server 2003, Datacenter Edition

- Windows Server 2003, Web Edition

> **Note**   The Windows Server 2003 family does not include a desktop operating system or "Professional" edition. Windows XP Professional is the operating system that now fills this role, marking a clear distinction between desktop- and server-based operating systems in the Microsoft Windows product line.

After this lesson, you will be able to

- Differentiate between the four editions of Windows Server 2003
- Describe the minimum hardware requirements for editions of Windows Server 2003
- Describe the reasons why a company might choose one edition of Windows Server 2003 over another
- Verify whether an existing computer is capable of running Windows Server 2003

Estimated lesson time: 30 minutes

Windows Server 2003 Editions

Much like the three different editions of Windows 2000 Server, Microsoft has developed different editions of Windows Server 2003 to better meet the needs of customers with specific scalability, service, and hardware platform requirements. In this way, the different editions of Window Server 2003 are capable of meeting the business needs of everyone from small businesses to large datacenter customers. A new edition within the Windows operating system family, Windows Server 2003, Web Edition, is the first to be provided with the needs of a specific application market in mind, namely those focused on Web services or hosting.

The following sections provide more detail about each of the four editions of Windows Server 2003, including their intended markets, uses, and capabilities.

Windows Server 2003, Standard Edition

Windows Server 2003, Standard Edition, is effectively the replacement product for Windows 2000 Server. Much like its predecessor, this product is aimed at small businesses and departmental use within larger organizations. Some common uses of Windows Server 2003, Standard Edition, include:

- File and printer sharing
- Secure Internet connectivity
- Centralized desktop application deployment

Windows Server 2003, Standard Edition, does support Active Directory and, as such, can fill the role of a domain controller. However, the product does have a few limitations, particularly with respect to scalability and availability. For example, some key features and limitations of Windows Server 2003, Standard Edition, are shown in Figure 1-1 and include:

- Provides symmetric multiprocessing (SMP) support for up to 4 CPUs
- Supports a maximum of 4 gigabytes (GB) of RAM
- Does not support clustering
- Does not provide support for Intel Itanium-based systems

For customers who require clustering capabilities, support for Itanium-based systems, or the ability to scale servers beyond 4 CPUs or 4 GB of RAM, the recommended operating system is Windows Server 2003, Enterprise Edition.

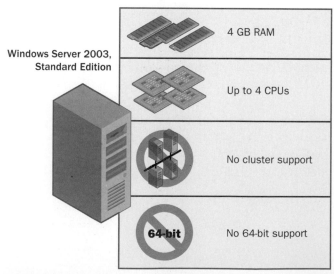

Figure 1-1   Key features of Windows Server 2003, Standard Edition

Windows Server 2003, Enterprise Edition

Windows Server 2003, Enterprise Edition, is the replacement product for Windows 2000 Advanced Server. This edition of Windows Server 2003 is built to meet the general-purpose needs of businesses of all sizes, and especially those that require a higher degree of availability and scalability. Like the Standard Edition, Enterprise Edition provides full support for Active Directory, including the ability to function as a domain controller. Some key features of Windows Server 2003, Enterprise Edition, are shown in Figure 1-2 and include:

- Provides symmetric multiprocessing (SMP) support for up to 8 CPUs

- Supports a maximum of 32 gigabytes (GB) of RAM

- Supports clustering up to 8 nodes

- Is available for Intel Itanium-based systems

- 64-bit version supporting Intel Itanium platforms with up to 8 CPUs and 64 GB of RAM

Although Windows Server 2003, Enterprise Edition, is likely to provide enough flexibility to meet the needs of almost all organizations, those requiring the highest levels of reliability, availability, and scalability should consider Windows Server 2003, Datacenter Edition.

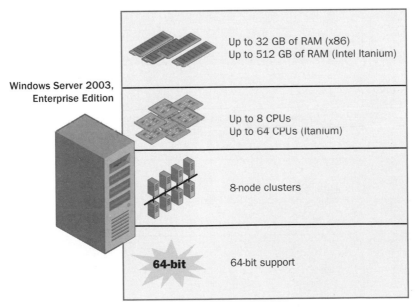

Figure 1-2   Key features of Windows Server 2003, Enterprise Edition

Windows Server 2003, Datacenter Edition

Windows Server 2003, Datacenter Edition, is the replacement product for Windows 2000 Datacenter Server. This edition of Windows Server 2003 is aimed at high-end data-processing environments consisting of business- and mission-critical applications demanding the highest levels of reliability, availability, and scalability. Like the Standard and Enterprise Editions, the Datacenter Edition provides full support for Active Directory, including the ability to function as a domain controller. Some key features of Windows Server 2003, Datacenter Edition, are shown in Figure 1-3 and include:

- Provides symmetric multiprocessing (SMP) support for up to 32 CPUs on 32-bit platforms, with an absolute minimum of 8 CPUs
- Supports a maximum of 64 gigabytes (GB) of RAM on 32-bit platforms
- Supports clustering up to 8 nodes
- 64-bit version supporting Intel Itanium platforms with up to 64 CPUs and 512 GB of RAM

Unlike the other editions of Windows Server 2003, the Datacenter Edition is always preinstalled on original equipment manufacturer (OEM) systems and cannot be acquired separately from Microsoft or through other software channels. This helps to ensure that the Datacenter Edition is distributed only with server configurations that have been thoroughly tested and are proven to be highly reliable.

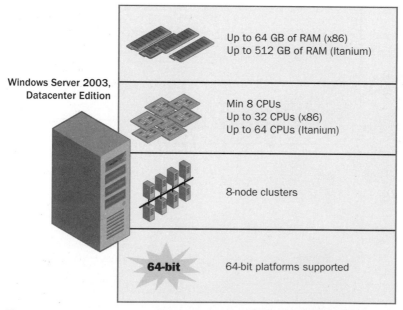

Figure 1-3   Key features of Windows Server 2003, Datacenter Edition

Windows Server 2003, Web Edition

Windows Server 2003, Web Edition, represents an entirely new product in the Windows server line and is not meant as a replacement for any previous edition. Instead, the Web Edition is clearly aimed at Web service and hosting functions and does not provide the complete functionality found in other Windows Server 2003 editions. For example, although the Web Edition can be made a member of an Active Directory domain, it cannot be configured to function as a domain controller. Similarly, Windows Server 2003, Web Edition, is not designed to act as a file or print server; it is limited to 10 inbound server message block (SMB) connections for the primary purpose of publishing content. Some key features of Windows Server 2003, Web Edition, are shown in Figure 1-4 and include:

- Provides symmetric multiprocessing (SMP) support for up to 2 CPUs

- Supports a maximum of 2 gigabytes (GB) of RAM

Optimized for Web-serving functions, Windows Server 2003, Web Edition, includes Internet Information Services (IIS) 6.0, ASP.NET, and the Microsoft .NET Framework. (IIS 6.0, ASP.NET, and the .NET Framework are included with all editions of Windows Server 2003.) Because it is not positioned as a file, print, or application server, client access licenses (CALs) do not apply to Windows Server 2003, Web Edition.

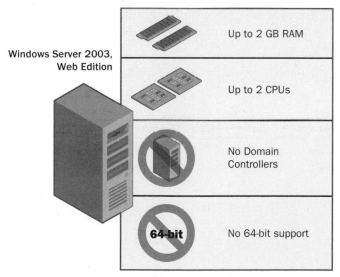

Figure 1-4   Key features of Windows Server 2003, Web Edition

Real World **Windows Server 2003, Web Edition**

Windows Server 2003, Web Edition, was developed specifically for the deployment of Web pages, Web sites, Web applications, and Web services. Based on its competitive pricing model, Web Edition provides a facility that gives Web-hosting providers and other organizations the ability to deploy cost-effective and scalable Web solutions that support the .NET Framework. For example, a company might decide to migrate existing intranet or internal Web servers to Web Edition, dedicating these servers to Web-serving functions. Under Windows 2000, the same customer would have been required to purchase the full edition of the product, even if additional services were not being utilized. Now even the smallest hosting companies can easily afford to provide clients with access to a platform that supports popular technologies such as Active Server Pages (ASP) and ASP.NET. For large companies, the ability to deploy dedicated Web servers in a cost-effective manner can result in substantial cost savings in the long term.

Windows Server 2003 Hardware Requirements

As with previous versions of Windows, Microsoft publishes both absolute minimum and recommended minimum hardware specifications for the various Windows Server 2003 editions. Although a server configured to meet the recommended minimum requirements will usually perform adequately, it should be noted that these numbers do represent minimums and, depending on the software and services installed, actual requirements might be much higher.

Table 1-1 outlines hardware requirements and capabilities for each Windows Server 2003 edition.

Table 1-1   Windows Server 2003 Hardware Requirements

	Standard Edition	Enterprise Edition	Datacenter Edition	Web Edition
Minimum CPU speed	133 MHz	133 MHz (x86) 733 MHz (Itanium)	400 MHz (x86) 733 MHz (Itanium)	133 MHz
Recommended Minimum CPU Speed	550 MHz	733 MHz	733 MHz	550 Mhz
Minimum RAM	128 MB	128 MB	512 MB	128 MB
Recommended Minimum RAM	256 MB	256 MB	1 GB	256 MB

Table 1-1   Windows Server 2003 Hardware Requirements

	Standard Edition	Enterprise Edition	Datacenter Edition	Web Edition
Maximum RAM	4 GB	32 GB (x86) 64 GB (Itanium)	64 GB (x86) 512 GB (Itanium)	2 GB
SMP Support	Up to 4	Up to 8	Minimum 8 Maximum 64	Up to 2
Disk Space for Setup	1.5 GB	1.5 GB (x86) 2.0 GB (Itanium)	1.5 GB (x86) 2.0 GB (Itanium)	1.5 GB

Upgrading to Windows Server 2003

As part of moving to the Windows Server 2003 platform, companies will generally take one of two paths—upgrading existing servers, or performing clean installations that involve migrating data, applications, and settings. The method that a company will choose depends largely on its business needs and functional requirements. Windows Server 2003 supports both deployment methods. Specifically, it allows both Windows NT Server 4.0 and Windows 2000 Server to be upgraded to Windows Server 2003 editions.

Advantages of Upgrading

Why would a company choose an upgrade over a migration or vice versa? Both have associated advantages, depending on the circumstances surrounding the deployment. The following bullet points outline some of the reasons a company might choose to upgrade to Windows Server 2003:

- Generally a simpler process, with existing user accounts, settings, groups, rights, and permissions retained

- Typically no need to reinstall applications, although vendor patches might ultimately need to be applied

In contrast, some of the reasons a company might opt for a clean installation and then migrate settings and data include:

- Disk efficiency might improve if a current disk is reformatted and then partitioned according to new requirements.

- A migration eliminates the chance that any previous problems with hardware or software settings will be carried over to the new operating system.

Supported Upgrade Paths

Although Windows NT Server 4.0 and Windows 2000 Server systems can be upgraded to Windows Server 2003, you need to be familiar with the supported upgrade paths. As a general rule, it is possible to upgrade from a previous version to its equivalent Windows Server 2003 edition, or to a higher edition. For example, you could choose to upgrade a Windows 2000 Server to Windows Server 2003, Standard Edition, or Windows Server 2003, Enterprise Edition. However, you cannot "downgrade" a server to a lower edition—for example, moving from Windows 2000 Advanced Server to Windows Server 2003, Standard Edition, is not supported.

Planning   Prior to attempting any upgrade to Windows Server 2003, you need to gather accurate information about a server's existing operating system and hardware settings. The best tool to accomplish this is the System Information utility found in the System Tools program group.

Table 1-2 outlines the possible upgrade paths from Windows NT Server 4.0 and Windows 2000 Server editions to Windows Server 2003 editions. Because Windows Server 2003, Web Edition, is a new edition, upgrades to it are not supported.

Table 1-2   Windows Server 2003 Supported Upgrade Paths

	Standard Edition	Enterprise Edition	Datacenter Edition
Windows NT Server 4.0	X	X	
Windows NT 4.0, Terminal Server Edition	X	X	
Windows NT Server 4.0, Enterprise Edition		X	
Windows 2000 Server	X	X	
Windows 2000 Advanced Server		X	
Windows 2000 Datacenter Server			X

Planning   To upgrade any edition of Windows NT 4.0 to Windows Server 2003, Service Pack 5 or later must be installed. Also note that direct upgrades from versions of Windows NT prior to 4.0 are no longer supported. As such, an upgrade from Windows NT 3.51 would involve first upgrading to Windows NT 4.0 or Windows 2000, and then upgrading again to Windows Server 2003. In such cases, a clean installation is almost always the better alternative.

Verifying System Compatibility

Prior to installing any edition of Windows Server 2003, you must ensure that your hardware meets at least the minimum requirements outlined earlier. However, it is also critical to check that other hardware and software to be installed on the server is capable of working with Windows Server 2003. To allow you to verify hardware compatibility, Microsoft publishes the Hardware Compatibility List (HCL), which is a list of hardware that has been tested and proven compatible with Windows Server 2003. If you plan to upgrade from a previous version of Windows, it is highly recommended that you first run the Microsoft Windows Upgrade Advisor tool from the Windows Server 2003 installation CD. This wizard-based tool will help you to determine whether any system compatibility issues relating to both hardware and software exist. Both of these resources are looked at in more detail in the following sections.

The Hardware Compatibility List

The role of the Hardware Compatibility List (HCL) in Windows Server 2003 is effectively the same as it was in Windows 2000—to provide a list of hardware devices that are supported under the new version of Windows (in this case, Windows Server 2003). This list is constantly updated over the life cycle of the operating system as new hardware is developed and then tested for compliance with Windows Server 2003.

Prior to installing any Windows Server 2003 edition, you should check to ensure that all your server's hardware appears on this list. An online and searchable version of the HCL can be found at *http://www.microsoft.com/whdc/hcl/default.mspx*.

Compatibility Tools and Resources

Windows Server 2003 also includes diagnostic and configuration utilities to help ensure that hardware and software is capable of functioning correctly on an upgraded server. Prior to upgrading any valid server to Windows Server 2003, you should first run the Microsoft Windows Upgrade Advisor tool, which analyzes the current settings on the server. This tool can be accessed from the graphical setup program that loads automatically when a Windows Server 2003 CD is inserted by following the Check System Compatibility link and then clicking the Check My System Automatically link. As in Windows 2000, this diagnostic tool can also be launched from the command line by issuing the d:\i386\winnt32.exe command with the /checkupgradeonly switch. The Microsoft Windows Upgrade Advisor tool will analyze the current hardware and software environment, and report back on any issues that might exist.

Although most programs run properly on Windows Server 2003, an application in your environment might not if it was specifically developed for a previous version of Windows. To help account for this scenario, Windows Server 2003 provides the Program Compatibility Wizard, an application that allows you to test programs in different modes (environments) that emulate the operating system for which they were originally developed. For example, on a Windows Server 2003 system, you could use the Program Compatibility Wizard to run an application in a mode that emulates Windows 2000, Windows XP, or even versions as old as Windows 95. You can start the Program Compatibility Wizard by clicking Start, clicking Run, and typing **hcp://system /compatctr/compatmode.htm**.

You can also manually set compatibility for a particular program. Program compatibility options can be configured from the Compatibility tab of an executable file or associated shortcut, as shown in Figure 1-5. Additional information on program compatibility can be found in the Help And Support Center, accessible from the Start menu.

Figure 1-5 Changing the compatibility mode of a program to emulate a previous version of Windows

Practice: Verifying System Compatibility with Windows Server 2003

In this practice, you will use the Microsoft Windows Upgrade Advisor tool to verify whether any Windows Server 2003 system compatibility issues exist, and then use the System Information tool to gather information about the current configuration of your server.

Exercise 1: Using the Microsoft Windows Upgrade Advisor Tool

1. Log on to Server01 as an administrator. Ensure that the Windows Server 2003 CD is inserted in your CD or DVD drive.

2. Click Start, and then click Run. In the Open text box, type **d:\i386\winnt32 /checkupgradeonly** and click OK. A Get Updated Setup Files window displays asking whether you want to get updated setup files for the Microsoft Windows Upgrade Advisor.

3. Depending on whether you have an Internet connection, select either Yes, Download The Updated Setup Files or No, Skip This Setup And Continue Installing Windows, and then click Next. After a moment, the Microsoft Windows Upgrade Advisor will begin analyzing your system.

4. Once step 3 is complete, click any items that appear in the Report System Compatibility window and click the Details button to obtain more information.

5. Click Finish to close the Microsoft Windows Upgrade Advisor window.

Exercise 2: Gathering System Information

1. Log on to Server01 as an administrator.

2. Click Start, select All Programs, select Accessories, select System Tools, and then click System Information.

3. Review the information provided by the System Summary node, including the operating system name, version, processor type, and total physical memory. Click the File menu item to view the available options.

> **Tip**   This information can be exported to a text file, or printed if necessary.

4. Expand the Components node, and then expand the Storage node. Click the Disks node. Review the information about the disk size, as well as information about any partitions that might exist.

5. Click the Drives node. Notice that this interface now displays not only the individual volumes configured on the disks, but also the size and amount of available free space on each.

6. Close the System Information window.

Lesson Review

The following questions are intended to reinforce key information presented in this lesson. If you are unable to answer a question, review the lesson materials and try the question again. You can find answers to the questions in the "Questions and Answers" section at the end of this chapter.

1. You have decided to upgrade one of the servers on your network from Windows 2000 Server to Windows Server 2003, Standard Edition. What are the recommended minimum hardware requirements for this edition, and what are the hardware and service limitations of Windows Server 2003, Standard Edition?

_____

_____

_____

_____

2. Which of the following are limitations associated with Windows Server 2003, Web Edition?

   a. It cannot be a member of a domain.

   b. It cannot run Active Directory.

   c. Each client requires a CAL.

   d. A maximum of 10 simultaneous SMB sessions are supported.

   e. It supports a maximum of 4 GB of RAM.

   f. It supports up to 2-way SMP.

3. Which of the following operating systems can be upgraded to Windows Server 2003, Standard Edition?

   a. Windows NT Server 4.0 SP6

   b. Windows NT Server 4.0, Enterprise Edition SP5

   c. Windows NT 3.51

   d. Windows 2000, Advanced Server

   e. Windows 2000 Server

   f. Windows 2000, Datacenter Server

Lesson Summary

■ The Windows Server 2003 family consists of four different editions—Standard Edition, Enterprise Edition, Datacenter Edition, and Web Edition. Each edition has different hardware, service, and application support capabilities to meet different business requirements.

■ Windows Server 2003 supports upgrades from both Windows 2000 Server and Windows NT Server 4.0 editions. For upgrades from Windows NT 4.0, Service Pack 5 or later must be installed or the upgrade will not be possible.

■ The Hardware Compatibility List (HCL) provides a list of hardware that has been tested and is known to work with editions of Windows Server 2003. All hardware installed in a server should be on this list to ensure maximum compatibility and, ultimately, availability.

■ The Microsoft Windows Upgrade Advisor is a diagnostic tool that should be run on a server prior to installing Windows Server 2003. The tool provides information relating to any hardware or software compatibility issues that might exist.

Lesson 2: New Features in Windows Server 2003

Although Windows Server 2003 is built on the foundation provided by Windows 2000, a number of new features and tools have been included in Microsoft's newest operating system release. In some cases, the changes are simply enhancements to existing tools that you are likely already familiar with, such as Active Directory Users And Computers. In others, completely new tools have been provided to simplify and enhance the administration of familiar elements, such as Group Policy.

One area in which Windows Server 2003 has changed significantly compared to Windows 2000 is with respect to its default security settings. For example, Windows Server 2003 does not install Internet Information Services (IIS) by default, thus ensuring that it is present only on systems where it is explicitly required. Further, once IIS 6.0 is installed, its default security settings are much more restrictive than in past versions.

Recognizing the challenges faced by organizations trying to stay current with security patches and critical updates in large environments, Microsoft designed Windows Server 2003 to support Microsoft Software Update Services (SUS). Software Update Services is a free tool that allows patches and updates to first be tested and then automatically deployed and installed throughout a Windows network. This tool helps to ensure that all necessary systems are patched and are therefore less prone to security threats, while at the same time making the management of critical updates much easier for administrators.

Windows Server 2003 also provides new features aimed at ensuring that systems and data can be recovered quickly in the event of system failures or even the accidental deletion of data by users. Automated System Recovery (ASR) provides a facility to get Windows Server 2003 systems back up and running quickly after a failure occurs. The Shadow Copies Of Shared Folders feature makes point-in-time backups of user data to ensure that previous versions are easily accessible in cases where a user has accidentally deleted a file.

Finally, Windows Server 2003 introduces a number of new features to Active Directory. Some of the major changes to Active Directory from Windows 2000 include new tools, new functions within existing tools, and new features aimed at making it easier to change names, restructure domains, and manage multiforest environments.

New Windows Server 2003 features and tools listed in this section are meant as an introduction rather than an in-depth analysis. Each of these elements will be looked at in more detail later in the book.

After this lesson, you will be able to

- Describe some of the enhancements to common administrative tools in Windows Server 2003
- Describe some of the ways in which Windows Server 2003 provides better security than previous versions
- Describe the basic purpose of some of the new administrative tools and features included in Windows Server 2003
- Describe the new disaster recovery features included in Windows Server 2003
- Describe some of the new key features of Active Directory in Windows Server 2003

Estimated lesson time: 40 minutes

Enhanced Administration Features

As an MCSE or MCSA, you are likely to already be familiar with many administration tools available in Windows Server 2003. For example, Active Directory Users And Computers is still the primary tool used to administer domain users, groups, and computers. While this tool is largely the same as in Windows 2000, a few enhancements make it more intuitive and easy to use. For example, the tool now provides the ability to select multiple objects simultaneously, and drag and drop them to a new location such as a different container or organizational unit (OU). By the same token, the common properties of multiple objects can also be changed at once—for example, you can now select multiple user accounts and simultaneously change the user profile location for all of them. Although some might consider these changes to be minor, they do help to speed up the administration of Active Directory objects, especially in large environments.

One of the most powerful features of Active Directory is the ability to quickly search for and find objects based on a wide range of criteria. While this capability has always existed via the Active Directory Users And Computers Find command, Windows Server 2003 introduces a new feature that makes it easier than ever before for administrators to quickly find what they are looking for. Active Directory Users And Computers now includes a new node named Saved Queries, which allows an administrator to create a number of predefined queries that are saved for future access. For example, a query could be defined that automatically searches a domain for all disabled users accounts, as illustrated in Figure 1-6. Then, when an administrator wants to determine exactly which accounts have been disabled (potentially across hundreds of OUs), she would simply need to click the saved query for the answer. In the long run, the ability to predefine and quickly access these queries can save administrators a great deal of time and administrative effort.

Figure 1-6   The Active Directory Users And Computers Saved Queries node

New Security Enhancements

In 2002, Microsoft announced its commitment to a new initiative known as Trustworthy Computing. Trustworthy Computing is a framework for developing hardware and software devices that are ultimately as secure as common household appliances. Although no such platform exists today, Microsoft has ensured that the Windows Server 2003 platform is a step toward this vision. Some ways in which Windows Server 2003 works toward providing better security than previous versions involve changes in the manner in which Internet Information Services (IIS) is deployed, methods for deploying critical software updates and security patches, and more.

Internet Information Services

Windows Server 2003 introduces a new version of Internet Information Services, IIS 6.0. Based on a new architectural model that includes features such as process isolation and a metabase stored in XML format, IIS 6.0 also implements a number of new security measures that makes it more secure than ever before.

First and foremost, unlike in Windows 2000 Server, IIS 6.0 is not installed by default during new operating system installations. This ensures that IIS is installed only on systems that actually require it and does not unintentionally present a security risk on systems where it is not explicitly being used. When a system running a previous version of IIS is upgraded to Windows Server 2003, IIS 6.0 is also upgraded and installed, but it is disabled by default. This approach helps to ensure that the upgrade does not present any initial security risks, giving an administrator the opportunity to properly configure IIS to organizational standards prior to it being enabled and servicing requests.

Even when IIS 6.0 is manually installed, its configuration is highly secured and locked down by default. For example, the default configuration of IIS serves only static content, such as traditional HTML pages. If any dynamic content needs to be served, the required features must be explicitly enabled. For example, features such as FrontPage Server Extensions, Active Server Pages, ASP.NET, the Indexing Service, server-side includes (SSI), and Web Distributed Authoring and Versioning (WebDAV) are disabled by default and must be individually enabled as required.

To give systems administrators a higher degree of control over where IIS is installed throughout an organization, Windows Server 2003 includes a new Group Policy setting named Prevent IIS From Installing. As the name suggests, this policy setting allows an administrator to prevent IIS from being installed on Windows Server 2003 systems altogether, using standard Group Policy application methods.

Internet Information Services security will be looked at in more detail later in this book.

Software Update Services

Managing security updates throughout an organization can be a daunting task for systems administrators, especially in very large environments. Although Windows client operating systems include the Windows Update feature, its use can lead to the inconsistent application of new security patches and critical updates throughout an environment. Adding to the problem is the fact that users might choose to install updates prior to them being thoroughly tested, which might lead to system stability or usability issues. Even in cases where an administrator can take the time to download and test new updates prior to distribution, the problem of how to then effectively deploy the updates has become an issue. Various methods exist, ranging from scripted installations, to using advanced software deployment tools, to time-consuming manual installations. Clearly the amount of time and administrative effort involved with managing updates and security patches can be overwhelming for systems administrators.

To help remedy this issue, Microsoft has introduced a new free tool known as Software Update Services (SUS). This server-based software is used to distribute security patches and critical updates in environments that include Windows 2000, Windows XP, and Windows Server 2003 systems. For example, the tool allows administrators to download any available updates to the SUS system, test the installation of these updates on one or more systems to ensure that they function correctly, and then automatically deploy the updates on a selective basis throughout their environment, as shown in Figure 1-7. Besides the obvious benefit in terms of reduced administrative effort, Software Update Services provides a much higher degree of control over the update process and helps to ensure that only tried and tested updates are distributed to the necessary network clients and servers.

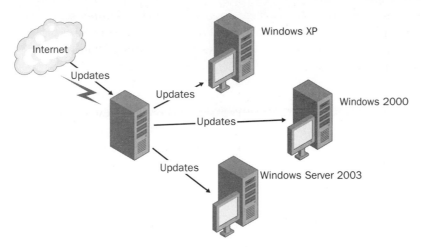

Figure 1-7   Microsoft Software Update Services

 Note   Software Update Services does not support the deployment of custom software packages or drivers, such as those you might have defined. Additionally, SUS cannot be used to deploy Service Packs.

New Administrative Tools and Utilities

Having worked with Windows 2000 in the past, you are already familiar with the vast majority of the Administrative Tools provided in Windows Server 2003. Certainly the capabilities of some of these tools have changed, such as the drag-and-drop functionality of Active Directory Users And Computers or the Saved Queries feature. In Windows Server 2003, a number of new tools have also been provided for the purpose of making it easier to plan, manage, and troubleshoot the deployment of features such as Group Policy and Terminal Server. As in Windows 2000, the Microsoft Management Console (MMC) still serves as the environment in which Administrative Tools are hosted. However, a number of new command-line utilities have also been included in Windows Server 2003, making it easier to automate administrative functions and manage servers remotely.

Group Policy Tools

In large Active Directory environments, planning, managing, and troubleshooting the application of Group Policy settings can be an unwieldy task. Not only can Group Policy objects be applied to different sites, domains, and OUs, but for any given user or computer, multiple (and sometimes conflicting) policy settings will often apply. When these Group Policy options are combined with the ability to block or filter certain policies, determining which settings actually apply can become a daunting task. To help alleviate some of these difficulties, Windows Server 2003 provides a variety of new Group Policy tools that make it easier to plan, deploy, manage, and troubleshoot Group Policy settings.

The Group Policy Management Console (GPMC) is a new a new tool for managing Group Policy in Windows Server 2003. While Group Policy–related elements have typically been found across a range of tools—such as Active Directory Users And Computers, the Group Policy MMC snap-in, and others—GPMC acts as a single consolidated environment for carrying out Group Policy–related tasks. For example, GPMC provides a single interface with drag-and-drop functionality to allow an administrator to manage Group Policy settings across multiple sites, domains, or even forests. Some of the capabilities of GPMC include the ability to back up, restore, import, and copy Group Policy objects, while providing an intuitive reporting interface on how Group Policy objects have been deployed. For example, using this tool an administrator can easily determine exactly which Group Policy objects apply to a given domain, how inheritance settings are configured, and which users or groups have been delegated the ability to manage these objects. The Group Policy Management Console is shown in Figure 1-8.

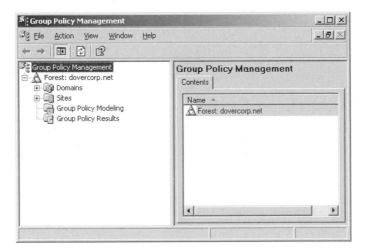

Figure 1-8   Group Policy Management Console

Note   The Group Policy Management Console tool was released shortly after Windows Server 2003. It can be downloaded from *http://www.microsoft.com/windowsserver2003 /gpmc/default.mspx.*

Another new administrative tool included with Windows Server 2003 related to Group Policy planning and troubleshooting is known as the Resultant Set of Policy (RSoP) tool. The main purpose of this tool is to allow an administrator to determine exactly which Group Policy settings apply to a given user or computer, based on the various levels at which Group Policy objects might have been defined. For example, it can quickly become difficult to determine the effective Group Policy settings for a user when Group Policy objects and related settings from a domain and various OUs apply to the user. By the same token, policies might be blocked at certain levels, have their No Override setting configured, or be filtered through the use of permissions. As such, it can be very difficult to understand and troubleshoot Group Policy application issues, even in small environments. The Resultant Set of Policy tool allows an administrator to obtain an accurate snapshot of the settings that will ultimately apply to a user or computer based on all these variables.

For example, imagine that an administrator wants to determine the effective Group Policy settings for a user in a particular OU. Using the RSoP tool, the administrator could generate a query that would process all the applicable Group Policy settings for that user for the local computer or another computer on the network. After processing the query, RSoP would present the exact Group Policy settings that apply to that user, as well as the source Group Policy object that was responsible for the setting. This information makes it easy to isolate and troubleshoot any policy processing issues that might exist. Far from being a tool to analyze only applicable settings, the Resultant Set of Policy tool also provides what is known as planning mode, allowing an administrator to perform a "what if"–style analysis to determine the impact of a potential policy change, without the need to deploy it. The Resultant Set of Policy tool is shown in Figure 1-9.

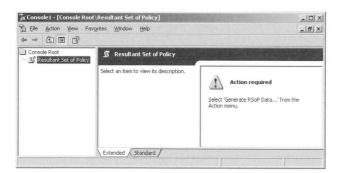

Figure 1-9   The Resultant Set of Policy (RSoP) MMC snap-in

For administrators who prefer working from the command line, Windows Server 2003 now includes a command-line tool known as Gpresult.exe. This tool, previously a Resource Kit utility, provides a function similar to the RSoP MMC snap-in, allowing you to specify a particular user or computer account for which Group Policy settings should be analyzed. For example, the command Gpresult /user contoso.com\Dan would provide a list of applicable Group Policy settings to the user named Dan in the contoso.com domain.

In Windows 2000 environments, the Secedit.exe utility was used to refresh Group Policy settings immediately, rather than waiting for the next update interval. In Windows Server 2003, this functionality is removed from the Secedit.exe command. Instead, a new utility named Gpupdate.exe is used to force an update of Group Policy settings. A variety of switches are available for use with the Gpupdate.exe command, allowing an administrator to force a logoff or reboot after the update, if desired. When the Gpupdate.exe command is issued without any switches, only new or updated user and computer policy settings are applied.

Exam Tip   Remember that the Secedit.exe command is no longer used to refresh Group Policy settings. The Gpupdate.exe command is now responsible for refreshing both user and computer Group Policy settings.

Server Management Tools

As in Windows 2000, most MMC-based Administrative tools in Windows Server 2003 provide the ability to manage both local and remote servers as necessary, by right-clicking a server object and selecting the Connect To Another Computer option. Windows 2000 also included Terminal Services Remote Administration mode to allow an administrator to connect to the desktop of a server using the Terminal Services client. In Windows Server 2003, Terminal Services Remote Administration mode is known as Remote Desktop. Remote Desktop connections are enabled via the Remote tab in the System applet in Control Panel, as shown in Figure 1-10.

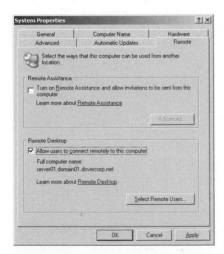

Figure 1-10   The Remote tab of the System program in Control Panel

Instead of using the Terminal Services client to connect to a server remotely, the client is now called Remote Desktop Connection, and is found in the Communications program group under Accessories. Remote Desktop Connection is installed on Windows

Server 2003 and Windows XP systems by default and can be downloaded to install on clients running operating systems such as Windows 2000 or Windows 98. Figure 1-11 illustrates a Remote Desktop connection to a server configured to accept incoming connections.

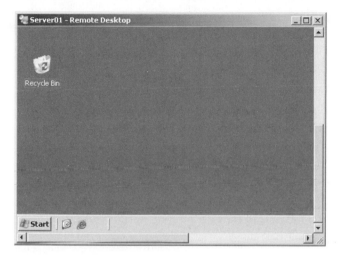

Figure 1-11   The Remote Desktop Connection software

Remote server management methods and tools will be looked at in more detail later in this book

Command-Line Tools

Windows Server 2003 provides a greater degree of flexibility for systems administrators through a number of new command-line tools. Some of the benefits of command-line administration include the ability to automate repetitive tasks and manage servers more efficiently over slow connections.

A variety of new tools have been provided in Windows Server 2003 to manage everything from Active Directory objects to individual services like IIS. For example, the Dsadd.exe utility allows an administrator to quickly add users, computers, groups, OUs, and other objects to the directory from the command line. Dsmod.exe allows the properties of directory services objects to be changed. The Bootcfg.exe utility allows you to configure, change, or query the contents of an existing Boot.ini file on a local or remote server. Other common tasks, such as backing up the configuration of IIS or creating a new Web site, can also be handled in a similar manner by using utilities like Iisback.vbs and Iisweb.vbs.

Many new command line utilities available in Windows Server 2003 will be looked at in more detail in later chapters.

New Disaster Recovery Tools and Features

In a manner similar to Windows 2000, Windows Server 2003 provides a number of tools and methods to be sure that a server or data can be recovered when necessary. While tools and features such as the Backup Utility, Last Known Good configuration, and Safe Mode are still provided, Windows Server 2003 goes further than previous versions to ensure that when server failures or data loss occurs, recovery procedures can be undertaken as quickly and painlessly as possible. For example, Windows Server 2003 provides a new feature known as Automated System Recovery (ASR), which allows a failed server to be returned to operation as quickly as possible without requiring extensive reconfiguration. For environments where users often lose or accidentally delete data files, Windows Server 2003 provides a new feature known as Shadow Copies Of Shared Folders. This feature creates point-in-time copies of all shared files on selected volumes, ultimately allowing a user to restore a previous version of the affected file without the need to contact an administrator. Shadow Copies Of Shared Folders makes users and administrators more productive by reducing the downtime and administrative effort typically associated with losing data files.

Automated System Recovery

The Automated System Recovery feature is new in Windows Server 2003. The purpose of this tool is not to act as a replacement for regular data backups, but rather to provide a method to restore a server and its related configuration settings as quickly and easily as possible in the event of system failure. Automated System Recovery is positioned as a last-resort recovery method, and familiar techniques such as using the Last Known Good configuration and Safe Mode to attempt to restore a server should always be tried first. If neither of these techniques is successful in restoring a Windows Server 2003 system to a working state, only then should Automated System Recovery be used.

Automated System Recovery is essentially a server recovery option made up of two parts—an ASR backup, and an ASR restore. An ASR backup is created using the Automated System Recovery Preparation Wizard in the Windows Server 2003 Backup Utility. The wizard produces a backup set including System State data, critical system files, and disk configuration. It also creates a floppy disk that contains information about the backup, including how a restore should proceed.

If a server does need to be restored by Automated System Recovery, you initiate the process by booting with the Windows Server 2003 CD-ROM and pressing F2 when prompted. Automated System Recovery will read the information from the floppy disk, restoring disk configuration. ASR then automatically begins to restore the ASR backup set. When this process is complete, Windows Server 2003 should be available in your original configuration. However, it is important to note that Automated System Recovery does not back up any data files. These files must be backed up and restored according to normal procedures.

> **Exam Tip**   Remember that an ASR backup set does not include data files. If required, data files must be restored through normal restore procedures once the ASR process is complete.

Automated System Recovery will be looked at in more detail later in this book.

Shadow Copies of Shared Folders

To reduce the amount of user time wasted and administrative effort required to restore files that have been deleted, corrupted, or incorrectly modified, Windows Server 2003 introduces a new feature known as Shadow Copies Of Shared Folders. This feature is meant to provide users with easy access to previous versions of files, both for cases where a file has been accidentally deleted and when a user needs to compare a current and previous version of a file while working.

Traditionally, if a user accidentally deleted a required file, he or she would need to contact an administrator and attempt to have the file restored from a backup set. In almost all cases, finding and then restoring a previous version from backup media such as a tape drive can be exceptionally time consuming for an administrator, and the user's productivity is adversely affected. Even in cases where the file is restored, the version might be older than expected, depending on the backup strategy and schedule in place.

To help circumvent this issue, the Shadow Copies Of Shared Folders feature can be enabled on a volume-by-volume basis on Windows Server 2003 systems. Once enabled, this feature makes point-in-time backups of all data stored on a volume, allowing a user to easily access previous versions of a file. For Shadow Copies Of Shared Folders to be used, it must first be enabled on required volumes, and then the associated client software must be installed on user systems. Shadow Copies Of Shared Folders works on a volume basis only—you cannot enable it for a single folder, for example. An administrator can specify the interval at which shadow copies should be created that best meets the needs of an organization. Figure 1-12 shows the Shadow Copies tab of a volume on a Windows Server 2003 system. Notice that only one volume has Shadow Copies enabled in this example.

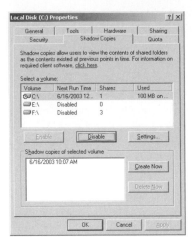

Figure 1-12   Shadow Copies Of Shared Folders enabled on a volume-by-volume basis

Shadow Copies Of Shared Folders will be looked at in more detail later in this book.

> **Note**   The Shadow Copies Of Shared Folders feature is not a replacement for implementing a regular backup procedure.

New Active Directory Features in Windows Server 2003

Windows Server 2003 introduces a number of new features to Active Directory aimed at making it more efficient, flexible, and secure. The following sections provide an overview of the key new features that you will need to be familiar with.

Domain and Forest Functional Levels

Windows Server 2003 Active Directory introduces a new feature that Windows 2000 MCSEs and MCSAs will already find somewhat familiar. Domain and forest functional levels provide a way to enable certain features of Active Directory on a per-domain or forest-wide basis. In Windows 2000 environments, Active Directory supported two different modes, mixed and native. In mixed mode, Windows NT 4.0 backup domain controllers (BDCs) were still supported, but features such as the ability to implement universal groups were not possible until a domain was switched to native mode. In native mode, all domain controllers in a given domain had to be running Windows 2000.

In Windows Server 2003, this concept extends to include not only domains, but also forests. In fact, the Windows Server 2003 version of Active Directory supports four different domain functional levels and three different forest functional levels. Each level allows certain new features to be deployed, and different levels of interoperability with existing domain controllers running Windows 2000 or Windows NT 4.0.

To use some of the new features listed in this chapter, a domain or forest must be configured to a specific functional level. These requirements are noted in both this lesson and the next, but domain and forest functional levels will be looked at in more detail in Chapter 2.

Cross-Forest Trust Relationships

Although the recommended deployment scenario for Active Directory has always involved creating a single forest consisting of one or more domains, this is not always practical or possible. For example, imagine a case where two large companies with existing Active Directory deployments merge. It might not be practical or financially feasible to attempt to reconfigure all the systems in one company to move them to the other's forest. Although a single forest is optimal, sometimes a variety of business reasons dictate that multiple forests must exist.

In the Windows 2000 version of Active Directory, it was possible to create an external trust relationship between domains in two different forests. While this capability made it possible for the users in a domain of one forest to access resources in a domain of another forest, Windows 2000 external trust relationships are intransitive. If users from a domain in one forest needed to access resources in multiple domains in another forest, multiple external trust relationships needed to be created, in various directions according to which users needed to access which resources.

Although the Windows Server 2003 version of Active Directory still supports external trust relationships between domains in separate forests, it also provides a new capability aimed at making multiple-forest Active Directory implementations easier to manage. Windows Server 2003 supports cross-forest transitive trust relationships to allow users in one forest to access resources in any domain in another, and vice versa. Cross-forest transitive trusts can be configured between two forests only. For example, if a cross-forest trust relationship is configured between Forest A and Forest B, and Forest B also has a cross-forest transitive trust relationship with Forest C, this does not mean that Forest A trusts Forest C. These relationships are illustrated in Figure 1-13.

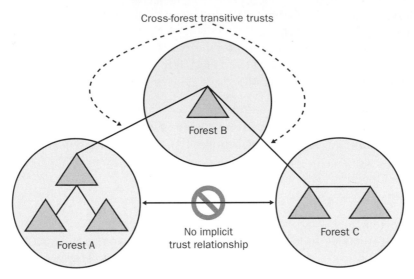

Figure 1-13 Cross-forest transitive trust relationships

For cross-forest transitive trust relationships to be created between two forests, both forests must be configured to the Windows Server 2003 forest functional levels. Functional levels will be looked at in more detail later in this book.

Domain Renaming

The Windows Server 2003 version of Active Directory also supports the ability to rename domains to accommodate issues such as acquisitions, mergers, name changes, and reorganizations. For example, a company might have originally chosen a domain name, and now it wants to change the name of that domain because it has merged with a second company. In Windows 2000, domains could not be renamed without first removing Active Directory completely. In Windows Server 2003, domain names cannot only be renamed, but individual domains can also be restructured to a different position within a forest. For example, if a company originally created a domain as a child domain and then decided that it wanted to instead make the domain the root of a new tree, it would now be possible. All domains in a Windows Server 2003 environment can be renamed, including the forest root domain. However, it is not possible to change the position of the forest root domain.

While Windows Server 2003 provides the ability to rename and move domains within a forest, it cannot do this until the forest is configured to the Windows Server 2003 forest functional level.

Domain Controller Renaming

In Windows 2000 Active Directory environments, it was not possible to change the name of a domain controller without first demoting the system back to a member server, changing the name, and then promoting it back to a domain controller. In

Windows Server 2003, it is possible to rename domain controllers without first demoting them. However, to do so, the domain in which the domain controller exists must be configured to the Windows Server 2003 domain functional level.

Universal Group Membership Caching

When a user attempts to log on to a domain in an Active Directory environment, a global catalog server must be available to provide universal group membership information. If a user attempts to log on to a domain for the first time and a global catalog server cannot be contacted, the logon request fails for all accounts except those that are part of the Domain Admins global group.

In Windows 2000 environments, it was highly recommended to place a global catalog server in each remote site to ensure that authentication queries for universal group membership information did not have to traverse a wide area network (WAN) link. Although having a local global catalog server at each remote site helped to reduce or eliminate authentication traffic over a WAN link, these links could still be adversely affected by global catalog replication traffic.

Windows Server 2003 introduces a new feature aimed at reducing the need for global catalog servers at all remote locations. Universal group membership caching is a new feature that can be enabled on selected domain controllers, making them capable of caching universal group information locally without being a full-fledged global catalog server. For example, if this feature were enabled on a domain controller in a branch site, the first time a user attempted to log on, the local domain controller would contact a global catalog server for the user's universal group membership information. After obtaining it, the local domain controller would cache the universal group membership information for this user. The next time the same user attempted to log on, the local domain controller would not need to contact the global catalog server because it would already hold a copy of the user's universal group membership information.

In Lesson 3, you will learn more about planning the placement of global catalog servers based on network traffic, as well as determining when universal group membership caching would be a more appropriate strategy.

Application Directory Partitions

The Active Directory database is composed of different partitions that serve specific purposes. For example, every domain controller in an Active Directory forest has a copy of the schema partition, which defines the object types that can be created, and their associated properties. Similarly, all domain controllers in the forest hold a copy of the configuration partition, which holds information about sites and services. Within a domain, all domain controllers hold a copy of the domain partition, which includes information about the objects within that particular domain only.

In Windows Server 2003, a new type of Active Directory partition is defined, known as an *application directory partition*. This new partition is unique in that it allows directory information to be replicated to certain domain controllers only, on an as-necessary basis. Specifically designed for directory-enabled applications and services, application directory partitions can contain any type of object, with the exception of security principals such as users, computers, or security group accounts.

In the past, directory-enabled application data was stored in the domain partition, meaning that it would be replicated to every domain controller within a domain. The benefit of using application directory partitions instead is that only the domain controllers that require access to the data have it replicated to them. Furthermore, an application directory partition is not limited to a single domain—it can be replicated to selected domain controllers in different domains throughout a forest as necessary, as shown in Figure 1-14.

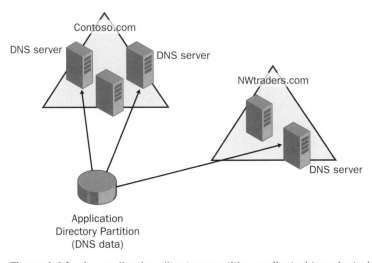

Figure 1-14   An application directory partition replicated to selected domain controllers

Consider the example of a company that has implemented an Active Directory integrated DNS topology. Although not every domain controller is configured as a DNS server, each domain controller stores a copy of the information relating to the integrated zone. In a very large domain environment, something as simple as a client updating DNS changes the directory, and then these changes need to be replicated. In this example, the environment would benefit from the use of application directory partitions, allowing the DNS information to be stored there and then forwarded to only the domain controllers running the DNS service.

Practice: Exploring Windows Server 2003 New Features

In this practice, you will install the Group Policy Management Console, use one of the new command-line utilities available in Windows Server 2003, and then enable and connect to your server using Remote Desktop.

Exercise 1: Downloading and Installing the Group Policy Management Tool

1. Open Internet Explorer, and browse to *http://www.microsoft.com/windowsserver 2003/gpmc/default.mspx*. Download the Group Policy Management Console MSI file, gpmc.msi, saving the file to your My Documents folder.

2. Open My Documents, and double-click the gpmc.msi file. At the Welcome screen, click Next.

3. At the License Agreement screen, click the I Agree option button and click Next.

4. Once the installation wizard completes, click Finish.

5. Click Start, select Administrative Tools, and then click Group Policy Management.

6. Browse through the available settings in the tool, noting that functionality is limited with Active Directory installed.

7. Close the Group Policy Management Console.

Exercise 2: Exploring the Bootcfg.exe Command-Line Utility

1. Click Start, and then click Run.

2. In the Open text box, type **cmd.exe** and press ENTER.

3. At the command prompt, type **bootcfg.exe /?** and press ENTER. Review the top-level switches associated with the Bootcfg.exe command and their purposes.

4. Type **bootcfg.exe /copy /?** to view the options associated with the /copy switch.

5. Type **bootcfg.exe /delete /?** to view the options associated with the /delete switch.

6. Type **bootcfg.exe /query /?** to view the options associated with the /query switch.

7. Type **bootcfg.exe /query /s** <servername> to view the contents of the boot.ini file on the server specified in the <servername> command.

8. Close the command-prompt window.

Exercise 3: Enabling and Connecting to a Server Using Remote Desktop

1. Click Start, select Control Panel, and click System.

2. Click the Remote tab.

3. In the Remote Desktop section, select the Allow Users To Connect Remotely To This Computer check box. If prompted by the Remote Sessions dialog box, click OK.

4. Click OK to exit System Properties.

5. Click Start, select All Programs, select Accessories, select Communications, and then click Remote Desktop Connection.

6. In the Remote Desktop Connection window, type Server01 in the Computer text box, and click Connect. Notice that a Remote Desktop connection has been initiated to your server with the Log On To Windows dialog box displayed.

7. Enter your password, and click OK. Notice that a new blank desktop appears, as though you were connected remotely.

8. Click Start, and then click Log Off. When the Log Off Windows dialog box appears, click Log Off. The Remote Desktop session closes.

Lesson Review

The following questions are intended to reinforce key information presented in this lesson. If you are unable to answer a question, review the lesson materials and try the question again. You can find answers to the questions in the "Questions and Answers" section at the end of this chapter.

1. Your network environment includes many servers running Windows 2000 and IIS 5.0. After upgrading one of these servers to Windows Server 2003, users are complaining that they can no longer access the corporate intranet site. What is most likely the cause of the problem?

    a. IIS is not installed by default in Windows Server 2003.

    b. IIS is installed, but has been disabled.

    c. IIS cannot be upgraded from version 5.0 to version 6.0.

    d. Users are likely attempting to connect to the wrong server.

2. Which of the following operating systems are supported by Microsoft Software Update Services?

   a. Windows 2000

   b. Windows 98

   c. Windows ME

   d. Windows Server 2003

   e. Windows XP

   f. Windows NT 4.0

3. Which of the following statements regarding Shadow Copies Of Shared Folders is true?

   a. Shadow Copies Of Shared Folders can be enabled on a volume-by-volume basis.

   b. Shadow Copies Of Shared Folders cannot be enabled for a specific shared folder.

   c. Shadow Copies Of Shared Folders cannot be enabled on a volume-by-volume basis.

   d. Shadow Copies Of Shared Folders can be enabled for a specific shared folder.

   e. Shadow Copies Of Shared Folders is an effective replacement for regular backups.

Lesson Summary

■ Windows Server 2003 provides a number of enhancements to existing administrative tools, including drag-and-drop and multiselect in Active Directory Users And Computers.

■ New security features in Windows Server 2003 include changes to the default settings of Internet Information Services, which is not installed by default. The Microsoft Software Update Service (SUS) makes managing network security easier by allowing an administrator to test and then automatically deploy critical software updates and security patches to network clients.

■ Windows Server 2003 includes a variety of new administrative tools and command-line utilities. Tools such as the Group Policy Management Console and Resultant Set of Policy make it easier to effectively manage, plan, and troubleshoot Group Policy settings. New command-line utilities such as Dsadd.exe make it possible to automate repetitive tasks and make it easy to manage servers remotely, especially over slow connections.

■ New disaster and data recovery tools in Windows Server 2003 include the Automated System Restore and Shadow Copies Of Shared Folders features.

■ The Windows Server 2003 version of Active Directory includes a number of new features and capabilities aimed at making it more efficient and flexible. Some important new Active Directory features include the ability to rename or reposition domains, rename domain controllers, enable universal group membership caching, configure application directory partitions, and create cross-forest transitive trust relationships.

Lesson 3: Planning an Active Directory Implementation

Originally introduced in Windows 2000, Active Directory continues to serve as the directory service of Windows Server 2003. Although the foundation directory service concepts from Active Directory in Windows 2000 remain largely unchanged, a number of new features have been implemented in the Windows Server 2003 version.

This section is meant as a review of some of the core concepts that you should be familiar with to effectively plan an Active Directory implementation, and as an introduction to new Windows Server 2003 Active Directory features aimed at providing more flexibility in the deployment of global catalog servers.

After this lesson, you will be able to

■ Describe the function of directory services, and specifically the role of Active Directory on a Windows Server 2003 network

■ Differentiate between the physical and logical components of Active Directory

■ Understand the elements involved in planning an Active Directory implementation, including reasons why companies might choose to deploy components differently based on their specific needs and requirements

■ Determine the appropriate placement of global catalog servers based on network traffic considerations

■ Determine where universal group membership caching should be implemented In an Active Directory environment

Estimated lesson time: 40 minutes

The Role of Directory Services

Much like a telephone book, a directory is essentially a store of information. In the case of Active Directory, this store is a hierarchical structure that contains information about objects on a network. Examples of objects include user accounts, computer accounts, shared printers, volumes, and more. To be uniquely defined, objects have properties that describe them. For example, a user account will have a variety of properties including a name, password, phone number, group membership information, and so forth. Ultimately, the purpose of a directory service like Active Directory is to store data and then make this data available to network users, administrators, and services.

For example, one function of the directory database in an Active Directory environment is to serve as the facility against which authentication occurs. When a user attempts to log on to a domain, the request is ultimately passed to a domain controller, which verifies the validity of the user's logon name and password.

However, as a store of information, a directory service also makes it possible for users to search for resources, even when only a limited number of properties are known. For example, a user in an Active Directory environment might choose to search the directory for a color printer, or more specifically a color printer located in the Chicago office. Through the use of object permissions, an administrator can control the directory objects to which users have access in a very granular fashion. So, if an administrator did not want a particular user or group of users to be able to find the Chicago color printer, the administrator could deny the user read permission for that object. In this case, the user's search would turn up empty.

When a sophisticated directory service such as Active Directory organizes information, it does so in a hierarchical fashion. This allows objects to be organized relative to one another in a manner that best meets the needs of an organization. For example, a user account object might exist within an organizational unit object, which subsequently exists within a domain object. Ultimately, this type of hierarchy allows an object to be organized, and ultimately found, through the use of queries. In many directory services, the protocol used to query a directory is the Lightweight Directory Access Protocol (LDAP), and Active Directory is no exception.

Although you are likely already familiar with many individual components of Active Directory, the following sections are meant to provide you with an overview of both the logical and physical components of Active Directory, as well as an introduction to some new features and capabilities provided by the Windows Server 2003 implementation.

Logical Components of Active Directory

As with Windows 2000, the logical components of Active Directory do not directly relate to any type of physical topology such as the layout of a network. Instead, the logical components of Active Directory are used to organize objects according to the administrative and security requirements of an organization. The logical components of Active Directory include forests, trees, domains, and organizational units (OUs). The following sections review each of these logical components in more detail.

Domains

As in Windows 2000, domains in a Windows Server 2003 Active Directory environment are logical groupings of resources that ultimately form units of replication. All domain controllers that are members of the same domain replicate their directory partition with one another, which typically includes (but is not limited to) information about user, group, and computer objects specific to that particular domain. So, when a new user account is created on one domain controller, it is ultimately replicated to all other domain controllers in the same domain.

In Windows Server 2003, domains continue to use the Domain Name System (DNS) to define their namespace. As such, domain names follow a convention similar to contoso.com. As in Windows 2000, domain names still have an associated NetBIOS name for the purpose of down-level clients and applications. Typically, the NetBIOS name chosen for a domain will closely resemble the DNS name—in this example, the NetBIOS name CONTOSO would likely be chosen.

Windows Server 2003 domains can span multiple physical locations and ultimately contain millions of objects. There is no direct relationship between domains and a network's physical topology. Defining the physical topology of a network in Active Directory is still handled through the use of sites, which will be looked at shortly.

In a Windows NT 4.0 domain environment, a domain was both a unit of replication and of security. Although a Windows Server 2003 domain does exhibit some characteristics of a security unit, a collection of domains, referred to as a *forest*, still forms the ultimate security boundary in Active Directory environments.

Some of the main benefits of domains include:

- The ability to organize objects into broad groupings that fall under common administrative control.

- The ability to define Group Policy settings that will apply to all users or computers within a domain.

- Authority over portions of a domain can be specified by delegating permissions to organizational units, making it unnecessary to create multiple domains to achieve administrative decentralization.

- Security policies and settings such as user rights and password policies do not cross from one domain to another. As such, distinct policies can be defined on a domain-by-domain basis.

- Each domain stores only information about the objects located in that domain, thus partitioning the directory into more manageable units and reducing unnecessary replication traffic.

Much like in Windows 2000, Windows Server 2003 domains are defined by promoting a server to the role of domain controller by using the Dcpromo.exe tool. Creating Windows Server 2003 domain controllers is looked at in detail in Chapter 2.

Trees

Although a single domain is often sufficient for even very large Active Directory implementations, many companies often choose to implement multiple domains for various purposes. Some common reasons for implementing multiple domains include:

- Different password requirements are defined for different divisions.

- Administration of specific domain-wide features, such as user account security policy, is decentralized.

- An extraordinarily large number of objects need to be created.

- More control over replication is required.

Although it is possible to give each and every domain a unique DNS name, many companies will instead choose to arrange domains into a logical hierarchy known as a *tree*. By definition, a tree is a collection of domains that share a single DNS namespace and are connected by transitive trust relationships. For example, assume that a company originally created a single domain named contoso.com. If that company then chose to create a second domain, it could be named *asia.contoso.com*. In this case, the Asia domain would be a subdomain of contoso.com, forming a parent/child relationship. Asia would be considered the child domain, while contoso.com would be its parent.

In this example, a tree is formed that consists of two domains: one child, and one parent. Ultimately, additional domains could be added to the tree. For example, if a third domain named *europe.contoso.com* were created, it would also be a child domain of contoso.com. By the same token, additional domains could be defined below the europe.contoso.com domain—for example, a domain named *spain.europe.contoso.com* would be a child of the europe.contoso.com domain, which in turn is a child of the contoso.com domain. In this example, the europe.contoso.com domain is a child domain of contoso.com, and is also the parent domain of spain.europe.contoso.com. This structure is illustrated in Figure 1-15.

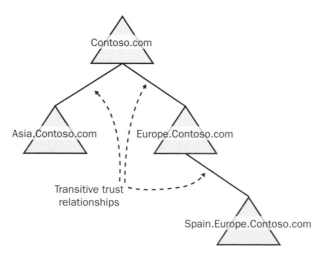

Figure 1-15   A single Active Directory tree that consists of four domains

When domains are arranged into a tree, transitive trust relationships are formed between each child domain and its parent domain. In Figure 1-15, three transitive trust relationships exist. Because these trusts are transitive, users in the spain.europe.contoso.com domain are able to access resources to which they have appropriate permissions in the asia.contoso.com domain, even through the two do not have an explicit trust relationship connecting them. By the same token, a user from the asia.contoso.com domain would be able to sit down at a computer located in the europe.contoso.com domain and still be authenticated as a user from asia.contoso.com.

Forests

As in Windows 2000 Active Directory, a forest in Windows Server 2003 is a collection of one or more domains that share a common schema and global catalog. The schema represents the definitions for all object types that can exist within Active Directory and their associated attributes. The Active Directory schema is stored on all domain controllers throughout a forest. The global catalog is a role held by domain controllers that store information about all objects in an Active Directory forest. The main role of a global catalog server is to help quickly find objects across domains, supply information about universal group membership, and authenticate users when user principal names (UPNs) are supplied, such as dan@contoso.com.

It is important to keep in mind that a forest does not necessarily consist of multiple domains. In fact, forests that consist of only one domain are common and are considered a forest nonetheless. However, a forest can also consist of multiple domains, arranged into either a single tree or multiple trees. An example of a forest that contains multiple domains is shown in Figure 1-16. In this example, the forest contains two trees, the contoso.com tree looked at earlier and a second tree named *nwtraders.com*.

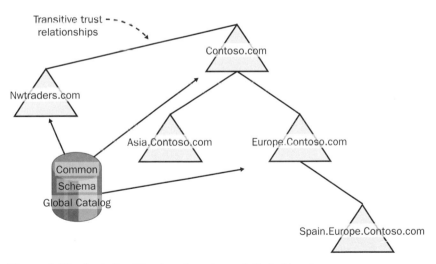

Figure 1-16   An Active Directory forest consisting of two trees

In this example, even though each tree uses a different DNS namespace, both trees are still part of the same forest, as shown by the common schema and global catalog. When multiple trees are configured as part of a common forest, the root of each tree forms a transitive trust relationship with the forest root domain. The forest root domain is simply the first domain that was defined when a new Active Directory forest was created. In this example, the contoso.com domain was defined first, making it the forest root domain for this Active Directory implementation.

Organizational Units

Organizational units (OUs) are Active Directory container objects that can store users, computers, groups, and other organizational units. As the name suggests, the main purpose of an OU is to organize objects. The two most common purposes for organizing objects in OUs are to delegate administration and to manage the application of Group Policy settings.

In most companies, an OU structure within a domain is usually designed along a combination of geographic and departmental lines. For example, a company might choose to create two parent OUs that represent the two major administrative teams within the company, one named East Coast and another named West Coast. Then, assuming that Group Policy settings are applied according to departments, each of these OUs might contain child OUs named Marketing, Finance, and Management. Figure 1-17 illustrates this example of an OU structure based first on the company's administrative model regions and then on group policy application by department.

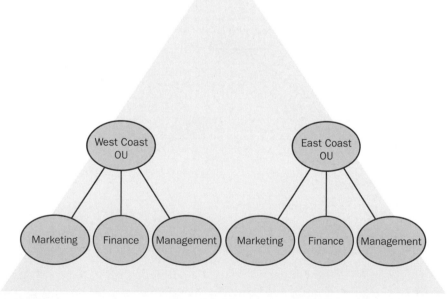

Figure 1-17   An OU based on both geographic and departmental considerations

In this example, administrative authority for the East Coast OU would be delegated to the East Coast IT staff, and administrative authority for the West Coast OU would be delegated to the West Coast IT staff. Then, each administrative team could define its own Group Policy settings for the individual departments that they look after. Certainly many different OU design possibilities exist, and what might work well for one company might not be appropriate for another. However, the key elements to keep in mind are that OU structures should be designed with the delegation of administrative authority and the application of Group Policy settings as the primary considerations.

Physical Components of Active Directory

The physical components of Active Directory include sites and domain controllers. Sites are used to represent the physical structure of a network, otherwise known as the *network topology*. A domain controller is a server running Windows Server 2003 (or Windows 2000/Windows NT 4.0) and configured to hold the Active Directory database. The following sections provide a review of both sites and domain controllers, outlining their purposes in an Active Directory environment.

Sites

A site is a physical component of Active Directory that is used to define and represent the topology of a network. More specifically, an Active Directory site is a collection of one or more well-connected Internet Protocol (IP) subnets. While the definition of *well-connected* is open to interpretation, the term is generally considered to mean subnets connected at LAN speeds, such as a network within a building. In cases where a network spans large geographic distances, WAN links tend to represent the boundaries between sites.

There are three main reasons for defining sites in Active Directory. These include:

- To control replication traffic
- To make authentication faster and more efficient
- To locate the nearest server providing directory-enabled services

Sites help to control Active Directory domain controller replication traffic by allowing you to specify the intervals at which replication occurs between sites. Because domain controllers within the same site are generally connected at high speeds, replication traffic is not a concern. However, when domain controllers that are part of the same domain are separated by a WAN link, regular replication traffic could overburden the link and have a negative impact on other network traffic. In contrast, if both locations were defined as Active Directory sites, a site link could be configured between the locations and replication over that link could be specified, as shown in Figure 1-18. For example, the replication schedule might allow replication to occur only at off-peak times or only at intervals that an administrator considered reasonable.

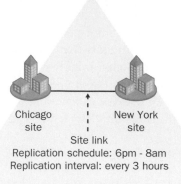

Chicago
site

New York
site

Site link
Replication schedule: 6pm - 8am
Replication interval: every 3 hours

Figure 1-18   A single Active Directory domain consisting of two sites

Sites help to make the user authentication process more efficient by allowing a client computer to locate a domain controller in the same site. Ultimately, this helps to reduce unnecessary WAN traffic because logon requests are handled locally. If individual sites are not defined, a logon request could conceivably cross many WAN links to contact a domain controller.

Finally, sites are used to help find the nearest server when directory-enabled services are being used. For example, if a company has implemented a distributed file system (DFS) architecture that uses replicas to store copies of data locally, the client would choose a replica from the same site rather than attempt to access the resource across a WAN link.

Active Directory sites are associated with IP subnets. An administrator defines the subnets within an enterprise and links those subnets to sites such that one subnet identifies one and only one site, while one site might be identified by multiple subnets. Active Directory clients are then assigned to sites based on the subnet object that corresponds to their configured IP address and subnet mask. Domain controllers are assigned to sites based on the location of their associated server object in Active Directory.

Domain Controllers

Domain controllers represent the second physical component of Active Directory. Any Windows Server 2003 system, with the exception of those running Web Edition, can be configured as a domain controller.

Domain controllers are the physical storage location for the Active Directory database, Ntds.dit. As in Windows 2000, Windows Server 2003 domain controllers use a multi-master replication model, meaning that each domain controller has a writable copy of the Active Directory database. Although a single domain controller is the absolute minimum required to implement Active Directory, it is highly recommended that each domain contain at least two domain controllers for redundancy. In Active Directory deployments that include multiple sites connected by slower WAN links, each site should include at least one domain controller to reduce authentication traffic over those links.

The first domain controller installed in an Active Directory forest takes on a special role and is known as a *global catalog server*. Global catalog servers contain information about every Active Directory object defined in a forest and are used for functions such as authenticating UPN-based logon requests, as well as holding universal group membership information. Only the first domain controller installed in a new forest is configured as a global catalog server by default. Other global catalog servers can be defined, but they must be configured manually.

In Windows 2000 Active Directory environments, it was highly recommended to deploy at least one global catalog server in each site. This structure is not necessarily the best one in Windows Server 2003 environments, where a new feature known as *universal group membership caching* can sometimes be used instead. This feature was introduced in Lesson 2 and will be looked at again later in this lesson.

Also similar to Windows 2000, certain domain controllers in a Windows Server 2003 Active Directory environment are assigned operations master roles. By default, the first domain controller installed in the forest root domain holds five roles, including:

- Schema Master
- Domain Naming Master
- Relative Identifier (RID) Master
- Primary Domain Controller (PDC) Emulator
- Infrastructure Master

Because the Schema Master and Domain Naming Master roles are found only in the forest root domain, the first domain controller installed in any subsequent domain is granted the three other roles as part of the installation process. As in Windows 2000, operations master roles can be moved to different servers once additional domain controllers have been installed.

Deploying Global Catalog Servers

Planning the location of global catalog servers throughout an Active Directory environment requires that you first understand the purpose of these servers. Much like in Windows 2000 Active Directory environments, the functions that a Windows Server 2003 global catalog server is responsible for include:

- Storing information about all Active Directory objects from all domains in a single forest. Although all the objects in a forest are stored on a global catalog server, only a subset of their attributes are stored for domains other than their home domain. When a user or application searches for directory information across all domains in a forest, a global catalog is queried for this information.

- Storing information about universal groups and their associated membership.

- Forwarding authentication requests to the appropriate domain when a user principal name (UPN) is used to log on.

- Validating object references within a forest. For example, when a domain controller in one domain stores an object that includes an attribute referencing an object in another domain, a global catalog server is used to validate the reference.

While Windows Server 2003 will define only one global catalog server automatically when Active Directory is installed, all implementations should have at least one additional global catalog server configured for fault tolerance, and possibly many more for load balancing and better traffic management in larger environments.

Locating Global Catalog Servers

Deciding where to deploy global catalog servers throughout an organization is a very important consideration in any Active Directory deployment. You have already learned that global catalog servers are necessary to carry out many key authentication and object location functions, especially in multiple-domain environments. Although having at least one global catalog server in every physical site is optimal to reduce authentication-related WAN traffic, this strategy ultimately leads to increased replication traffic—in other words, a tradeoff is always involved.

In Windows 2000 Active Directory environments, placing a global catalog server in each site was not strictly required but was highly recommended. For sites that included a domain controller but no global catalog server, all user authentication requests had to traverse a WAN link to contact a global catalog server to obtain universal group membership information. Furthermore, there were no guarantees as to which global catalog server would be chosen. Ultimately, the need for these requests to travel over a WAN link made the authentication process slower for users, resulting in longer logon times.

Similarly, in cases where users or applications need to query the entire directory when looking for an object, a global catalog server must be contacted. A few examples would be a user using the Windows XP Search feature to locate printers throughout the directory, or an application such as Microsoft Exchange 2000 providing users with access to the Global Address List (GAL). In situations where query traffic will be high, not having a global catalog server in each location can saturate WAN links, resulting in unacceptable performance.

While the benefits of having global catalog servers in each physical site might be obvious, potential disadvantages also apply. First, global catalog servers typically require more resources than normal domain controllers, and upgrades or replacements of existing domain controllers might not be financially feasible. Second, global catalog servers need to replicate with other global catalog servers, based on a replication topology generated by the Knowledge Consistency Checker (KCC). In multiple-domain forests that include many regular changes to data stored in the directory, replication can have a significant impact on WAN link utilization.

When making the decision on where to locate global catalog servers throughout an Active Directory site topology, you should consider current WAN utilization, the amount of expected query traffic, and whether domain controllers have sufficient resources to take on the role. For example, if WAN traffic is already very high to begin with, it is probably best to locate a global catalog server at each site, or consider implementing universal group membership caching instead. Authentication-related traffic generally has a greater impact on WAN utilization than replication traffic, which can be scheduled for off-peak hours if necessary. In environments where a high number of queries are expected, such as those running Microsoft Exchange Server 2000, local global catalog servers are the best choice. Whether a local domain controller can handle the function of a global catalog server is an issues that also needs to be considered, but this decision is affected by myriad factors—including any additional roles that the server might already be handling, the number of local users, and so on. As a general rule, companies should continue to implement global catalog servers in each site if possible, especially in cases where directory-enabled applications are heavily used and sufficient WAN bandwidth to handle replication exists.

Universal Group Membership Caching

Windows Server 2003 Active Directory provides a new feature that can help to reduce the number of required global catalog servers in multisite environments. Universal group membership caching helps to reduce the number of universal group membership queries that need to be forwarded across a WAN link when a user attempts to log on.

When a user attempts to log on to a Windows Server 2003 domain, a domain controller in the same site as the user will usually handle the request. Although the local domain controller will hold information about the global and domain local groups that the user is a member of, it does not store information about universal group membership. To build a complete security token for the user, the local domain controller must contact a global catalog server. If one is not present locally, the query will be sent across one or more WAN links, potentially resulting in long delays. Although having a global catalog server present in each site would help to avoid this problem, doing so is not always practical or feasible, as the previous section explained.

To make planning the placement of global catalog servers more flexible, Windows Server 2003 provides the ability to configure universal group membership caching on selected domain controllers. Once enabled, a local domain controller will query a global catalog server the first time it requires a user's universal group membership information during an authentication request, but it will then cache this information for subsequent logon attempts. By default, a domain controller with universal group membership caching enabled will update the cached universal group membership information for a user every 8 hours. Ultimately, this feature can help to dramatically reduce the impact of authentication traffic on WAN links, as well as reduce the need to define global catalog servers in every site. This feature is especially helpful in small branch offices where an existing domain controller might not be capable of handling the increased load associated with servicing global catalog requests, and in cases where a WAN link might not have sufficient bandwidth to handle replication and authentication traffic.

Note that universal group membership caching does not completely eliminate the need for global catalog servers in remote locations. A domain controller configured to use universal group membership caching will handle only this specific function and not the other roles of a global catalog server. For example, implementing universal group membership caching does not make a domain controller capable of handling directory-wide queries like a global catalog server. As such, any queries for objects outside the local domain would still need to be forwarded to a global catalog server, perhaps across a WAN link. The primary reasons for implementing universal group membership caching include:

- Faster user logon times, because a global catalog server does not need to be contacted for all logon requests

- Reducing the need to place global catalog servers in each site

- Reducing the WAN bandwidth usage associated with global catalog replication

In cases where a high number of directory queries are expected, placing a global catalog server at each site still represents the best possible solution. The configuration of universal group membership caching will be looked at in detail in Chapter 2.

> **Exam Tip** Universal group membership caching does not eliminate the need for global catalog servers. Instead, it helps to ensure faster logon times and potentially less authentication-related WAN traffic by locally caching universal group membership information.

Lesson Review

The following questions are intended to reinforce key information presented in this lesson. If you are unable to answer a question, review the lesson materials and try the question again. You can find answers to the questions in the "Questions and Answers" section at the end of this chapter.

1. Which of the following are considered to be logical components of Active Directory?

   a. Domain

   b. Tree

    c. Forest

    d. Site

    e. Organizational Unit

    f. Domain Controller

2. Which of the following is not a reason for defining sites in Active Directory?

    a. To control replication traffic

    b. To organize user accounts

    c. To make authentication more efficient

    d. To support a larger number of directory objects

3. Which of the following reduces the need for a global catalog server in small branch offices?

    a. Directory application partitions

    b. Cross-forest trust relationships

    c. Universal group membership caching

    d. The ability to rename domains

4. Which of the following would be good reasons for implementing universal group membership caching on a Windows Server 2003 domain controller?

    a. Faster user logon times

    b. To handle directory-wide queries

    c. To reduce replication bandwidth

    d. To eliminate the need for global catalog servers

5. Which of the following represent reasons why a global catalog server would need to be contacted?

    a. A user logs on to a domain for the first time

    b. A query is received for an object in the local domain

    c. A user searches the entire directory for a printer

    d. A user logs on using a user principal name (UPN)

Lesson Summary

- Active Directory is the directory service of Windows Server 2003. A directory stores information about network objects such as domains, OUs, users, computers, and groups in a hierarchical manner. A directory service makes this data available to network users and services.

■ Windows Server 2003 Active Directory consists of both logical and physical components. The logical components of Active Directory include domains, trees, forests, and organizational units. The physical components of Active Directory include sites and domain controllers.

■ When planning an Active Directory implementation, companies need to consider the domain structure to be used, how OUs will be organized, how sites will be defined, and more. The needs of specific companies will dictate the design.

■ Windows Server 2003 introduces a new feature known as universal group membership caching, which provides greater flexibility in the deployment of global catalog servers. While universal group membership caching does not handle the same functions as a global catalog server, it can make user logon faster and reduce replication across WAN links in sites where deploying a global catalog server might not be feasible.

Case Scenario Exercise

You are an external consultant helping Contoso to plan its intended deployment of Windows Server 2003. The company has provided you with a number of different requirements based on its current environment and planned purchases, which must be considered. Contoso currently has a number of existing servers with Windows 2000 Server and is running Active Directory. Some of these servers are configured as domain controllers, others as file and print servers, and some as Web servers. The current environments includes the following:

■ Seven branch offices, each configured as a unique site and including one Windows 2000 Server domain controller. Five of the offices are connected by 512 kilobits per second (Kbps) frame relay links, and in these offices the local domain controller functions as a global catalog server. Two offices use 64-Kbps ISDN connections, with no local global catalog. The domain controller in each office also functions as a file and print server for local users. Each of the existing domain controllers in these offices is a Pentium II 400-MHz system with 128 MB of RAM.

■ One head office location that includes 2 domain controllers running Windows 2000 Advanced Server on 4-way SMP systems with 1 GB of RAM. One of these domain controllers is configured as a global catalog server. 4 additional Windows 2000 Server systems with 1.2 GHz processors and 512 MB of RAM provide file, print, and Web services to head office users.

■ A new Itanium server that supports up to 8-way SMP, purchased to function as a new domain controller at the head office location.

■ The company does not run any directory-enabled applications and does not plan to install any in the near future.

- **Requirement 1**   Based on the current Windows 2000 Server implementation, Contoso would like you to plan an appropriate upgrade, migration, or installation strategy for all servers to Windows Server 2003. Where possible, the company wants to take advantage of the capabilities of its existing hardware with the appropriate Windows Server 2003 edition.

- **Requirement 2**   Contoso is also concerned about the fact that users in the offices connected by the 64-Kbps WAN links are complaining about very slow logon times. In the company's original Windows 2000 Active Directory implementation, these offices were considered too small to have a local domain controller, but one was eventually added to each to increase performance. Based on the low bandwidth available to these offices, Contoso decided not to configure these servers as global catalogs. However, as these offices have expanded, it is now clear that a new solution is required, and the company has asked for your input.

- **Requirement 3**   In the past, Contoso has relied on full server backups to recover from any failures that might occur. However, on the two occasions where a failure occurred, it took at least two days to get the associated servers back up and running. Contoso management finds this unacceptable and has dictated that any deployment should include a strategy to ensure that servers are restored to a functioning state in five hours or less in the event of a failure.

Requirement 1

Requirement 1 involves determining the appropriate edition of Windows Server 2003 to use based on both current and new servers at Contoso.

1. Which of the following Editions of Windows Server 2003 would be the best solution for upgrading the existing branch office domain controllers?

    a. Windows Server 2003, Web Edition

    b. Windows Server 2003, Enterprise Edition

    c. Windows Server 2003, Standard Edition

    d. Windows Server 2003, Datacenter Edition

2. Why should Contoso consider replacing or upgrading the domain controllers in each branch office?

    a. The existing servers do not meet the minimum hardware requirements for Windows Server 2003.

    b. The existing servers do not meet the recommended minimum hardware requirements for Windows Server 2003.

    c. The existing servers cannot be configured as Windows Server 2003 domain controllers.

    d. Active Directory domain controllers must be multiprocessor systems.

3. Contoso has asked whether the existing Windows 2000 file and print servers can be upgraded to or replaced by Windows Server 2003, Web Edition. Which of the following represent reasons this is not possible based on their current situation?

   a. Windows 2000 Server cannot be upgraded to Windows Server 2003, Web Edition.

   b. Windows Server 2003, Web Edition, cannot be a member of a domain.

   c. Windows Server 2003, Web Edition, cannot fill the role of a file and print server.

   d. The existing file and print servers do need meet the minimum hardware requirements for Windows Server 2003, Web Edition.

4. What version of Windows Server 2003 would be most appropriate for the new Itanium server to be deployed at the head office location?

   a. Windows Server 2003, Web Edition

   b. Windows Server 2003, Standard Edition

   c. Windows Server 2003, Enterprise Edition

   d. Windows Server 2003, Datacenter Edition

Requirement 2

Requirement 2 involves finding a solution for the slow user logon times at the Contoso branch office locations connected by 64-Kbps ISDN links.

1. Which of the following represent possible solutions to decrease the logon response time in the two branch offices connected by the 64-Kbps ISDN links?

   a. Remove the existing domain controllers at these two locations.

   b. Configure the domain controllers at each location as global catalog servers.

   c. Implement universal group membership caching on Windows Server 2003 domain controllers at each location.

   d. Make the two sites part of the head office site.

2. Which of the following would not be good reasons for implementing universal group membership caching at these two branch offices?

   a. Faster user queries are needed across the entire directory.

   b. The company plans to implement Exchange Server 2000.

   c. The company wants to make user logon faster.

   d. The company wants the local domain controller to authenticate users who log on using UPNs.

Requirement 3

Requirement 3 involves determining an appropriate server recovery solution that will allow the new Windows Server 2003 systems at Contoso to be recovered quickly in the event of failure.

1. Which of the following represents the best server recovery solution based on Contoso's requirements?

   a. Last Known Good

   b. Directory application partitions

   c. Shadow Copies Of Shared Folders

   d. Automated System Recovery

2. Which of the following need to be considered when using the restore method specified in question 1?

   a. Automated System Recovery does not restore user data.

   b. Automated System Recovery does not restore the operating system configuration.

   c. Shadow copies of shared folders are configured on all volumes by default.

   d. Last Known Good should be considered a last-resort recovery solution.

Chapter Summary

- The Windows Server 2003 family consists of four different editions—Standard Edition, Enterprise Edition, Datacenter Edition, and Web Edition. Each edition has different hardware, service, and application support capabilities to meet different business requirements.

- Windows Server 2003 supports upgrades from both Windows 2000 Server and Windows NT Server 4.0 editions. For upgrades from Windows NT 4.0, Service Pack 5 or later must be installed or the upgrade will not be possible.

- The Hardware Compatibility List (HCL) provides a list of hardware that has been tested and is known to work with editions of Windows Server 2003. All hardware installed in a server should be on this list to ensure maximum compatibility and, ultimately, availability.

- The Microsoft Windows Upgrade Advisor is a diagnostic tool that should be run on a server prior to installing Windows Server 2003. The tool provides information relating to any hardware or software compatibility issues that might exist.

- Windows Server 2003 provides a number of enhancements to existing administrative tools, including drag-and-drop and multiselect in Active Directory Users And Computers.

- New security features in Windows Server 2003 include changes to the default settings of Internet Information Services, which is not installed by default. The Microsoft Software Update Service (SUS) makes managing network security easier by allowing an administrator to test and then automatically deploy critical software updates and security patches to network clients.

- Windows Server 2003 includes a variety of new administrative tools and command-line utilities. Tools such as the Group Policy Management Console and Resultant Set of Policy make it easier to effectively manage, plan, and troubleshoot Group Policy settings. New command-line utilities such as Dsadd.exe make it possible to automate repetitive tasks and to easily manage servers remotely, especially over slow connections.

- New disaster and data recovery tools in Windows Server 2003 include Automated System Recovery and Shadow Copies Of Shared Folders.

- The Windows Server 2003 version of Active Directory includes a number of new features and capabilities aimed at making it more efficient and flexible. Some important new Active Directory features include the ability to rename or reposition domains, rename domain controllers, enable universal group membership caching, configure application directory partitions, and create cross-forest transitive trust relationships.

- Windows Server 2003 introduces a new feature known as universal group membership caching, which provides greater flexibility in the deployment of global catalog servers. While universal group membership caching does not handle the same functions as a global catalog server, it can make user logon faster and reduce replication across WAN links in sites where deploying a global catalog server might not be feasible.

Exam Highlights

Before taking the exam, review the key points and terms that are presented in the following sections to help you identify topics you need to review. Return to the lessons for additional practice, and review the "Further Readings" sections in Part 2 for pointers to more information about topics covered by the exam objectives.

Key Points

- The four editions of Windows Server 2003 provide customers with different capabilities based on supported hardware and services. Different editions each have different degrees of scalability in terms of support for SMP, maximum RAM, and clustering.

- The deployment of global catalog servers throughout an Active Directory site infrastructure involves factors such as the current speed and saturation of WAN links, the use of directory-enabled applications, and the impact of global catalog replication and authentication traffic.

- Universal group membership caching is a new Windows Server 2003 feature that allows a domain controller not functioning as a global catalog server to cache universal group membership information. This feature helps to reduce user authentication traffic being sent over WAN links, and ultimately makes logon faster for users in remote sites that do not include a global catalog server.

Key Terms

Global catalog server   A domain controller that stores a read-only copy of all Active Directory objects within a forest. Global catalog servers are used to respond to directory-wide queries, authenticate users when a UPN is used during logon, and hold universal group membership information.

Universal group membership caching   A new feature in Windows Server 2003 that allows a domain controller to cache universal group membership information, thus reducing the need for a global catalog server to be contacted during the user authentication process.

Software Update Services   A free server service used to centrally manage and deploy security patches and critical updates to Windows 2000, Windows XP, and Windows Server 2003 systems.

Automated System Recovery   A new Windows Server 2003 service designed to automate the restoration of the operating system and configured settings in the event of a server failure. Automated System Recovery does not restore user data as part of the process.

Functional level   The level to which a Windows Server 2003 domain or forest is configured based on whether Windows 2000 or Windows NT 4.0 domain controllers are still in use. The functional level of a domain or forest affects the ability to use certain new Active Directory features in Windows Server 2003.

Questions and Answers

Page
1-13

Lesson 1 Review

1. You have decided to upgrade one of the servers on your network from Windows 2000 Server to Windows Server 2003, Standard Edition. What are the recommended minimum hardware requirements for this edition, and what are the hardware and service limitations of Windows Server 2003, Standard Edition?

   The recommended minimum processor speed for Windows Server 2003, Standard Edition, is 550 MHz, and the recommended minimum amount of RAM is 256 MB. Choosing Windows Server 2003, Standard Edition, limits you to a maximum of 4-way SMP and 4 GB of RAM. This edition does not support clustering or Itanium-based servers.

2. Which of the following are limitations associated with Windows Server 2003, Web Edition?

   a. It cannot be a member of a domain.

   b. It cannot run Active Directory.

   c. Each client requires a CAL.

   d. A maximum of 10 simultaneous SMB sessions are supported.

   e. It supports a maximum of 4 GB of RAM.

   f. It supports up to 2-way SMP.

   b, d, f

3. Which of the following operating systems can be upgraded to Windows Server 2003, Standard Edition?

   a. Windows NT Server 4.0 SP6

   b. Windows NT Server 4.0, Enterprise Edition SP5

   c. Windows NT 3.51

   d. Windows 2000, Advanced Server

   e. Windows 2000 Server

   f. Windows 2000, Datacenter Server

   a, e

Lesson 2 Review

1. Your network environment includes many servers running Windows 2000 and IIS 5.0. After upgrading one of these servers to Windows Server 2003, users are complaining that they can no longer access the corporate intranet site. What is most likely the cause of the problem?

   a. IIS is not installed by default in Windows Server 2003.

   b. IIS is installed, but has been disabled.

   c. IIS cannot be upgraded from version 5.0 to version 6.0.

   d. Users are likely attempting to connect to the wrong server.

   b

2. Which of the following operating systems are supported by Microsoft Software Update Services?

   a. Windows 2000

   b. Windows 98

   c. Windows ME

   d. Windows Server 2003

   e. Windows XP

   f. Windows NT 4.0

   a, d, e

3. Which of the following statements regarding Shadow Copies Of Shared Folders is true?

   a. Shadow Copies Of Shared Folders can be enabled on a volume-by-volume basis.

   b. Shadow Copies Of Shared Folders cannot be enabled for a specific shared folder.

   c. Shadow Copies Of Shared Folders cannot be enabled on a volume-by-volume basis.

   d. Shadow Copies Of Shared Folders can be enabled for a specific shared folder.

   e. Shadow Copies Of Shared Folders is an effective replacement for regular backups.

   a, b

Lesson 3 Review

1. Which of the following are considered to be logical components of Active Directory?

    a. Domain

    b. Tree

    c. Forest

    d. Site

    e. Organizational Unit

    f. Domain Controller

    a, b, c, e

2. Which of the following is not a reason for defining sites in Active Directory?

    a. To control replication traffic

    b. To organize user accounts

    c. To make authentication more efficient

    d. To support a larger number of directory objects

    a, c

3. Which of the following reduces the need for a global catalog server in small branch offices?

    a. Directory application partitions

    b. Cross-forest trust relationships

    c. Universal group membership caching

    d. The ability to rename domains

    c

4. Which of the following would be good reasons for implementing universal group membership caching on a Windows Server 2003 domain controller?

    a. Faster user logon times

    b. To handle directory-wide queries

    c. To reduce replication bandwidth

    d. To eliminate the need for global catalog servers

    a, c

5. Which of the following represent reasons why a global catalog server would need to be contacted?

    a. A user logs on to a domain for the first time

    b. A query is received for an object in the local domain

    c. A user searches the entire directory for a printer

    d. A user logs on using a user principal name (UPN)

    a, c, d

Page
1-49
Case Scenario Exercise, Requirement 1

1. Which of the following Editions of Windows Server 2003 would be the best solution for upgrading the existing branch office domain controllers?

    a. Windows Server 2003, Web Edition

    b. Windows Server 2003, Enterprise Edition

    c. Windows Server 2003, Standard Edition

    d. Windows Server 2003, Datacenter Edition

    c

2. Why should Contoso consider replacing or upgrading the domain controllers in each branch office?

    a. The existing servers do not meet the minimum hardware requirements for Windows Server 2003.

    b. The existing servers do not meet the recommended minimum hardware requirements for Windows Server 2003.

    c. The existing servers cannot be configured as Windows Server 2003 domain controllers.

    d. Active Directory domain controllers must be multiprocessor systems.

    b

3. Contoso has asked whether the existing Windows 2000 file and print servers can be upgraded to or replaced by Windows Server 2003, Web Edition. Which of the following represent reasons this is not possible based on their current situation?

    a. Windows 2000 Server cannot be upgraded to Windows Server 2003, Web Edition.

    b. Windows Server 2003, Web Edition, cannot be a member of a domain.

    c. Windows Server 2003, Web Edition, cannot fill the role of a file and print server.

    d. The existing file and print servers do need meet the minimum hardware requirements for Windows Server 2003, Web Edition.

a, c

4. What version of Windows Server 2003 would be most appropriate for the new Itanium server to be deployed at the head office location?

    a. Windows Server 2003, Web Edition

    b. Windows Server 2003, Standard Edition

    c. Windows Server 2003, Enterprise Edition

    d. Windows Server 2003, Datacenter Edition

c

Page
1-50

Case Scenario Exercise, Requirement 2

1. Which of the following represent possible solutions to decrease the logon response time in the two branch offices connected by the 64-Kbps ISDN links?

    a. Remove the existing domain controllers at these two locations.

    b. Configure the domain controllers at each location as global catalog servers.

    c. Implement universal group membership caching on Windows Server 2003 domain controllers at each location.

    d. Make the two sites part of the head office site.

b, c

2. Which of the following would not be good reasons for implementing universal group membership caching at these two branch offices?

    a. Faster user queries are needed across the entire directory.

    b. The company plans to implement Exchange Server 2000.

    c. The company wants to make user logon faster.

    d. The company wants the local domain controller to authenticate users who log on using UPNs.

a, b, d

Page
1-51
Case Scenario Exercise, Requirement 3

1. Which of the following represents the best server recovery solution based on Contoso's requirements?

    a. Last Known Good

    b. Directory application partitions

    c. Shadow Copies Of Shared Folders

    d. Automated System Recovery

    d

2. Which of the following needs to be considered when using the restore method specified in question 1?

    a. Automated System Recovery does not restore user data.

    b. Automated System Recovery does not restore the operating system configuration.

    c. Shadow copies of shared folders are configured on all volumes by default.

    d. Last Known Good should be considered a last-resort recovery solution.

    a

2 Implementing an Active Directory Infrastructure

Exam Objectives in this Chapter:

- Implement an Active Directory directory service forest and domain structure (Exam 70-296).

    - ❑ Create the forest root domain.

    - ❑ Create a child domain.

    - ❑ Create and configure Application Data Partitions.

    - ❑ Install and configure an Active Directory domain controller.

    - ❑ Set an Active Directory forest and domain functional level based on requirements.

Why This Chapter Matters

As in Microsoft Windows 2000, Active Directory serves as the centralized directory service of Microsoft Windows Server 2003 environments. Although most core concepts associated with Active Directory remain similar to those you are already familiar with from Windows 2000, a number of new features are introduced in the Windows Server 2003 version that you will be expected to be familiar with for the MCSE and MCSA upgrade exams.

This chapter begins by explaining the various methods that can be used to promote a Windows Server 2003 system to the role of domain controller, outlining the benefits, limitations, and steps associated with each. Once the promotion of a new domain controller is complete, you have the option of configuring the system as a global catalog server or implementing universal group membership caching, a new Active Directory feature that was introduced in Chapter 1. The steps associated with both approaches are examined in this chapter, as is the process for demoting a domain controller back to the role of a member server.

Similar to the different domain modes that could be configured in Windows 2000 Active Directory environments, Windows Server 2003 introduces two new concepts known as domain and forest *functional levels*. The functional level of a domain or forest affects not only the versions of Microsoft Windows supported as domain controllers, but also the availability of many new Active Directory features. This chapter provides an explanation of the features and limitations associated with each functional level, as well as instructions on how the functional level of a domain or forest can be changed.

In Chapter 1, you were also introduced to the concept of an application directory partition, and how this Windows Server 2003 feature gives administrators a higher degree of control over how application data is stored and replicated throughout an Active Directory forest. This chapter not only outlines the purpose of application directory partitions, but also provides details of how these partitions can be configured, managed, and even removed if necessary.

 Note Application directory partitions may be referred to as application data partitions in the exam objectives. The two terms are synonymous.

Lessons in this Chapter:

Before You Begin

To complete the hands-on practices and exercises in this chapter, you should have the following prepared:

- Two Windows Server 2003 (Standard or Enterprise Edition) systems installed as Server01 and Server02, respectively. These servers should not yet be configured as domain controllers.

- Access to both servers using the built-in Administrator account or another account that is part of the Administrators local group.

Lesson 1: Installing and Configuring Domain Controllers

The process of implementing Active Directory in a Windows Server 2003 network environment is as simple as promoting a single server to the role of domain controller. Although this process can be handled in much the same way as in Windows 2000 (using Dcpromo.exe), Windows Server 2003 actually supports four methods of creating domain controllers. While the different methods provide administrators with greater flexibility than in Windows 2000, not every method is applicable to every situation. This lesson takes a look at each method and the situations in which that method is most appropriate, as well as additional domain controller configuration options such as implementing universal group membership caching or defining global catalog servers.

After this lesson, you will be able to

- Install Active Directory using various methods
- Configure a domain controller as a global catalog server
- Configure a site to use the new universal group membership caching feature
- Remove Active Directory, and demote domain controllers

Estimated lesson time: 45 minutes

Planning Your Active Directory Installation

While the processes for promoting a member server to the role of domain controller are relatively straightforward, it is critical that you plan your proposed Active Directory environment in advance. Examples of environment-related information that should already be documented and well understood prior to promoting any server to the role of domain controller include:

- The domain structure for the new or existing forest
- The domain naming scheme to be used
- How Domain Name System (DNS) will be configured to support Active Directory
- Whether the Active Directory environment will need to support servers running previous versions of Windows

Similarly, you will also need to ensure that the specific settings for the server to be promoted have been correctly configured, and that the information required during the promotion process has already been determined and documented. Some issues that need to be considered prior to promoting a domain controller include:

- Domain controllers require static IP address and subnet mask values
- The client DNS settings of the server must be configured correctly

- The storage location of the database and log files should be defined

- The location of the shared system volume folder should be defined

By properly planning and documenting the domain controller promotion process in advance, you greatly reduce the risk of misconfiguration or encountering errors during the installation process.

Installing Active Directory

Four different methods can be used to promote a Windows Server 2003 system to a domain controller. These include:

- Using the Active Directory Installation Wizard (to install Active Directory in most situations)

- Using an answer file to perform an unattended installation (to automate the installation process or install Active Directory remotely)

- Using the network or backup media (to install Active Directory on additional domain controllers in the network by using media rather than relying upon replication)

- Using the Configure Your Server Wizard (an additional way to install the first domain controller in a network only)

The following sections outline the specific steps and considerations associated with installing domain controllers using each of these four methods.

Installing Active Directory Using the Active Directory Installation Wizard

The Active Directory Installation Wizard (Dcpromo.exe) is the main tool used to install Active Directory. Information that must be provided as part of completing the wizard includes:

- Domain controller type, either the first domain controller for a new domain or a new domain controller added to an existing domain

- Domain type—a new domain in a new forest, a child domain in an existing domain tree, or a new domain tree in an existing forest

- Domain name

- NetBIOS name for the domain

- Storage location for the Active Directory database

- Storage location for the Active Directory transaction log files

- Storage location for the shared system volume

- Default Active Directory access permissions
- Directory services restore mode administrator password

After you input this information, the wizard installs Active Directory, creating the database, configuring associated services, and modifying security settings. If a DNS server is not available, you will be given the option to install DNS as part of the Active Directory installation.

One of the most fundamental choices presented by the wizard is whether you want the server to become the first domain controller for an entirely new domain, or to serve as an additional domain controller within an existing domain. Ultimately, the choice you make affects the structure of your Active Directory implementation.

Creating the First Domain Controller for a New Domain   If you choose to create the first domain controller for a new domain, you are actually defining both a new domain controller and a new domain. You will therefore be asked whether you want to create the new domain in a new forest, as a child domain in an existing domain tree, or as a new domain tree in an existing forest. These choices are illustrated in Figure 2-1.

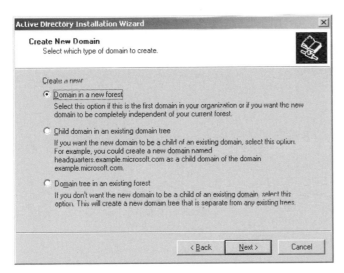

Figure 2-1   Creating a new domain using the Active Directory Installation Wizard

When you create a new domain in a new forest, the new domain is either the first domain in the organization or a new domain that you want to be completely independent from an existing forest. When you create a new child domain in an existing domain tree, the new domain becomes a subdomain of an existing domain, within the DNS namespace of its parent domain. If you choose to create a new domain tree in an existing forest, the new domain becomes the root domain of a new tree, with a DNS name that is not contiguous with any other existing domains in the forest.

Adding a New Domain Controller to an Existing Domain   If you use the Active Directory Installation Wizard to add an additional domain controller to an existing domain, you are effectively adding redundancy and authentication load-balancing to a domain in a forest that has already been created. In all cases, an absolute minimum of two domain controllers should be deployed per domain to provide redundancy. In most Active Directory implementations, the number of domain controllers that need to be deployed within a single domain is a function of the number of users that need to be serviced, as well as the number of physical sites that have been implemented.

Off the Record   When implementing Active Directory, each domain should include an absolute minimum of two domain controllers for the purpose of directory redundancy.

Using the Active Directory Installation Wizard   Issuing the Dcpromo.exe command from the Run dialog box or the command line starts the Active Directory Installation Wizard. To install Active Directory for a new domain in a new forest, complete the following steps:

1. Click Start and then click Run. In the Run dialog box, type **dcpromo** in the Open box and click OK.

2. At the Welcome To The Active Directory Installation Wizard page, click Next.

3. At the Operating System Compatibility page, click Next.

4. At the Domain Controller Type page, select Domain Controller For A New Domain, as shown in Figure 2-2. Click Next.

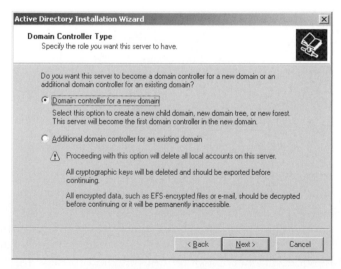

Figure 2-2   Active Directory Installation Wizard, Domain Controller Type page

5. On the Create New Domain page, ensure that Domain In A New Forest is selected, and then click Next.

6. If DNS is not configured for this computer, the Install Or Configure DNS page appears. Select No, Just Install And Configure DNS On This Computer, and click Next.

Note   If you choose to allow the Active Directory Installation Wizard to install and configure DNS, it will create an Active Directory-Integrated zone stored on an application directory partition.

7. On the New Domain Name page, type the name of your domain in the Full DNS Name For New Domain box, and click Next.

8. On the NetBIOS Domain Name page, the Active Directory Installation Wizard will suggest a NetBIOS name. Accept the default name provided by clicking Next.

Note   Clients running versions of Windows prior to Windows 2000 still use the NetBIOS name associated with a domain to access many domain-related functions.

9. On the Database And Log Folders page, type the location of the Active Directory database in the Database Folder box and the location of the Active Directory log in the Log Folder box, as shown in Figure 2-3. Similar to Windows 2000, it is recommended that you place the Active Directory database and associated log files on separate disks formatted with the NTFS file system. Click Next.

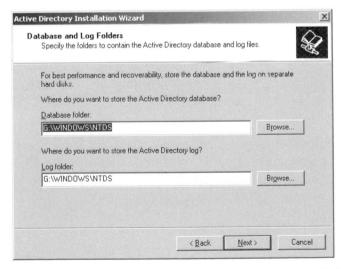

Figure 2-3   Active Directory Installation Wizard, Database And Log Folders page

10. On the Shared System Volume page, specify the location of the Sysvol folder in the Folder Location box. The Sysvol folder must reside on a partition or volume formatted with the NTFS file system. Click Next.

11. If DNS is configured for this computer and the wizard is unable to connect to the DNS server, the DNS Registration Diagnostics page appears. Select Install And Configure The DNS Server On This Computer, And Set This Computer To Use This DNS Server As Its Preferred DNS Server, and click Next.

12. On the Permissions page, read through the available options as shown in Figure 2-4. Click Next.

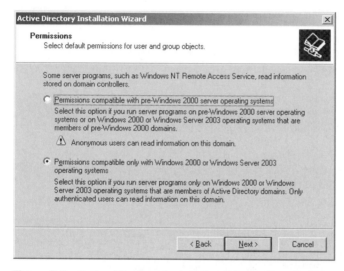

Figure 2-4   Active Directory Installation Wizard, Permissions page

13. On the Directory Services Restore Mode Administrator Password page, type the directory services restore mode password you want to assign to this server's Administrator account in the Restore Mode Password box. Confirm the password in the Confirm Password box. Click Next.

14. The Summary page displays the options that you have selected during the wizard, as shown in Figure 2-5. Review the contents of this page for accuracy, and then click Next. The wizard takes a few minutes to configure Active Directory components. You might be prompted for your Windows Server 2003 CD-ROM. If you did not configure this server with a static IP address prior to starting the wizard, you will be prompted to do so.

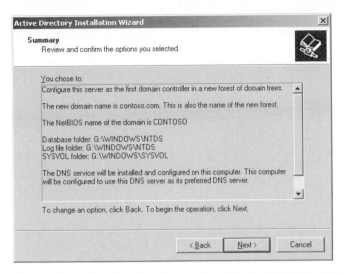

Figure 2-5   Active Directory Installation Wizard, Summary page

15. When the Completing The Active Directory Installation Wizard page appears, click Finish, and then click Restart Now.

Installing Active Directory Using an Answer File

The steps associated with the Active Directory Installation Wizard can also be automated through the use of an answer file. An *answer file* is simply a text file that contains answers to the questions normally asked when the wizard is completed manually. The answer file must contain all the parameters that the Active Directory Installation Wizard normally needs to complete the Active Directory installation process. Some benefits of promoting domain controllers by using answer files include:

- The ability to automate the domain controller installation process on remote servers that might be accessible only via low-bandwidth connections

- The ability to define and control the exact parameters to be configured during the promotion process, saving time and reducing the risk of misconfiguration

Figure 2-6 displays a sample answer file that could be used to promote a Windows Server 2003 system to a domain controller.

Figure 2-6   A sample answer file used to install Active Directory

To install Active Directory on a Windows Server 2003 system using an answer file, issue the command **dcpromo /answer:*answer file***, where *answer file* is the name of the text file that contains the necessary parameters to be passed to Dcpromo.exe.

> **Note**   To create an answer file for use with Dcpromo.exe, refer to the instructions located in "Microsoft Windows Preinstallation Reference" found in the Ref.chm file on the Windows Server 2003 CD. The Ref.chm file is located in the Deploy.cab file in the \Support\Tools folder. Use the Index tab to search for DCInstall, the help topic that explains each of the entries that can be specified in the [DCInstall] section of the file.

Installing Active Directory Using the Network or Backup Media

In Windows 2000, promoting a member server to become an additional domain controller in an existing domain required the entire directory database to be replicated to the new domain controller. In cases where low network bandwidth or exceptionally large directory databases were factors, this replication could take hours or sometimes even days to complete.

A new feature in Windows Server 2003 helps to make the process of adding a new domain controller to an existing domain more flexible in situations like those described. A Windows Server 2003 member server can be promoted to the role of domain controller using a backup of the directory database taken from an existing domain controller. This backup can be restored to the target server from different types of backup media or from a shared network folder. Ultimately, this approach helps to reduce much of the replication traffic associated with deploying new domain controllers, which is especially useful for domain controllers located in remote sites connected via WAN links. For example, if a new domain controller needs to be installed in a branch office connected over a low-speed WAN link, an administrator could back up the Active Directory database of an existing domain controller to removable media, and then ship that media to the branch office. The media could then be used to promote the member server to a domain controller locally, without the need for full replication of the directory database to take place over the WAN link. Of course, some replication will still be necessary to ensure that the remote domain controller is fully synchronized with existing domain controllers, but this typically amounts to much less traffic than full synchronization would incur.

The amount of replication that is ultimately required to fully synchronize the remote domain controller depends on the age of the backup used and the number of changes that have occurred since the backup was taken. The backup cannot be older than the tombstone lifetime for the domain, which is set to a default value of 60 days. To minimize the amount of replication that needs to occur after promotion, a very recent backup is always preferred. The process of backing up Active Directory will be looked at in more detail in Chapter 3.

> **Note**   If the domain controller from which the backup of Active Directory was created contained an application directory partition, the partition will not be restored to the new domain controller. For information about creating an application directory partition on a new domain controller, refer to Lesson 3 later in this chapter.

To install Active Directory using a network share or backup media, complete the following steps:

1. Click Start, click Run, type **dcpromo /adv** in the Open box, and then click OK.

> **Exam Tip**   To create an additional domain controller in an existing domain from backup media, remember that the Dcpromo.exe command must be issued with the /adv switch.

2. At the Operating System Compatibility page, click Next.

3. At the Domain Controller Type page, select Additional Domain Controller For An Existing Domain, and then click Next.

4. At the Copying Domain Information page shown in Figure 2-7, select one of the following options:

   ❑ Over The Network From A Domain Controller, to copy domain information to this server over the network

❑ From These Restored Backup Files, and then type the path to the backup files in the box to copy domain information to this server from backup files

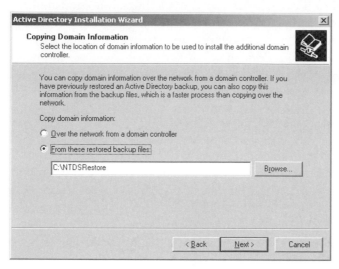

Figure 2-7   Active Directory Installation Wizard, Copying Domain Information page

5. On the Network Credentials page, specify your user name and password in the User Name and Password boxes, respectively. In the Domain box, type the domain name and then click Next.

6. On the Additional Domain Controller page, specify the domain name and then click Next.

7. On the Database And Log Folders page, ensure that the correct locations for the database folder and the log folder appear in the Database Folder box and the Log Folder box, respectively. Click Next.

8. On the Shared System Volume page, ensure that the correct location for the shared system volume folder appears in the Folder Location box. Click Next.

9. On the Directory Services Restore Mode Administrator Password page, type the password you want to assign to this server's Administrator account in the event the computer is started in directory services restore mode in the Restore Mode Password box. Confirm the password in the Confirm Password box. Click Next.

10. On the Summary page, review your selections and then click Next to proceed with the installation. Restart the computer when prompted.

Installing Active Directory Using the Configure Your Server Wizard

The Configure Your Server Wizard provides a centralized location from which you can install many server services, including Active Directory. The Configure Your Server Wizard is available from the Manage Your Server page, which opens automatically the first time you log on to a server. Figure 2-8 shows the Server Role page of the wizard. You can use the Configure Your Server Wizard to install Active Directory only on the first domain controller on a network. If you attempt to use the Configure Your Server Wizard to install additional domain controllers, the wizard will launch the Active Directory Installation Wizard to perform the installation.

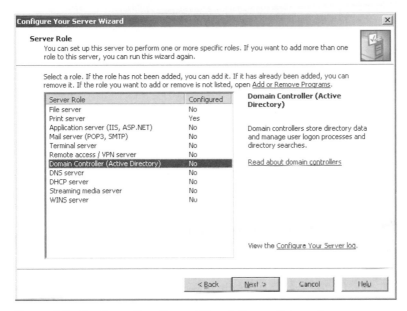

Figure 2-8   Configure Your Server Wizard, Server Role page

Although the Configure Your Server Wizard provides a simplified method for inexperienced users to install Active Directory, experienced users should take advantage of the higher degree of flexibility provided by the Active Directory Installation Wizard.

Configuring Global Catalog Servers

When a new Active Directory forest is created, only the first domain controller installed in the forest root domain will be configured as a *global catalog server* by default—any additional global catalog servers need to be configured manually. While a single global catalog server might suffice in very small environments, at least two are recommended as a minimum for the purposes of fault tolerance and load balancing. In environments that include multiple sites connected by WAN links, it is generally recommended that each remote location have at least one domain controller configured as a global catalog server, or that the site implement universal group membership caching.

Because of the importance of the global catalog in providing universal group membership information and authenticating logon requests that use user principal names (UPNs), you will almost certainly need to configure additional global catalog servers in any Active Directory environment. As in Windows 2000, global catalog servers are configured via the NTDS Settings object associated with a domain controller object in the Active Directory Sites And Services tool.

To configure a Windows Server 2003 domain controller as a global catalog server, follow these steps:

1. Click Start, select Administrative Tools, and then click Active Directory Sites And Services.

2. Click the plus sign (+) next to the Sites folder to expand it.

3. Expand Default-First-Site-Name, the Servers folder, and then the server object.

4. Right-click the NTDS Settings object, and click Properties.

5. On the General tab, select the Global Catalog check box, as shown in Figure 2-9.

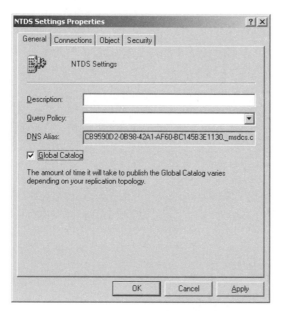

Figure 2-9   Configuring a global catalog server from the NTDS Settings Properties General tab

6. Click OK, and then close Active Directory Sites And Services.

Implementing Universal Group Membership Caching

Universal group membership caching is a Windows Server 2003 feature that can help to reduce the number of global catalog servers that need to be deployed as part of an Active Directory implementation. Recall from Chapter 1 that when a user attempts to log on to a Windows Server 2003 domain in a multiple domain environment, a global catalog server must be queried to obtain universal group membership information for that user. In the case of a branch office location that includes a domain controller that is not a global catalog server, this request must pass over a WAN link, resulting in longer logon times for the user. With universal group membership caching, domain controllers within a site will query a global catalog server for universal group membership information the first time it receives a logon request from a particular user, and then cache this information locally. Subsequent logon attempts from the same user would no longer result in query traffic for universal group membership information over a WAN link because the locally cached copy could be used instead.

> **Note**   By default, domain controllers in a site configured to use universal group membership caching will refresh the information contained in their cache every 8 hours.

Universal group membership caching is not enabled within a site by default. To enable universal group membership caching for domain controllers within a site running Windows Server 2003, you must be a member of the Domain Admins group in the forest root domain or a member of Enterprise Admins, or you must have been delegated the appropriate authority. Because universal group membership caching is site-specific, all Windows Server 2003 domain controllers within a site use the feature once it has been enabled.

> **Exam Tip**   Global catalog settings are configured on individual domain controllers. In contrast, universal group membership caching is configured at the site level, and applies to all domain controllers within a specific site.

In much the same way that you configure a domain controller to function as a global catalog server, you configure universal group membership caching using Active Directory Sites And Services. However, instead of configuring the NTDS Settings object of a particular domain controller, you configure universal group membership caching from the properties of the NTDS Site Settings for a particular site. The following list shows the steps to configure universal group membership caching within a site.

1. Click Start, select Administrative Tools, and then click Active Directory Sites and Services.

2. Click the plus sign (+) next to the Sites folder to expand it.

3. Click Default-First-Site-Name to view its contents.

4. Right-click NTDS Site Settings, and click Properties.

5. On the Site Settings tab, select the Enable Universal Group Membership Caching check box, as shown in Figure 2-10.

Figure 2-10   Configuring universal group membership caching

6. In the Refresh Cache From drop-down box, choose the site from which domain controllers in this site will attempt to locate a global catalog server. If the <Default> option is selected, domain controllers in this site will attempt to refresh their cache from the nearest site that has a global catalog server.

7. Click OK, and close Active Directory Sites And Services.

Removing Active Directory from a Domain Controller

Running Dcpromo.exe on an existing domain controller allows you to remove Active Directory from a system, demoting it to either a stand-alone server or a member server. If the system being demoted is the last domain controller in the domain, it becomes a stand-alone server because the domain will no longer exist. If other domain controllers remain in the domain, a demoted server will become a member server within the existing domain.

To remove Active Directory from existing domain controllers, you must be a member of certain groups, depending upon the specific situation that surrounds the demotion process. The following list outlines the requirements to remove Active Directory from domain controllers in different situations.

- To remove Active Directory from a system that is the last domain controller in any domain except the forest root, you must be a member of the Enterprise Admins group.

- To remove Active Directory from the last domain controller in a forest, you must be a member of the Domain Admins group.

- To remove Active Directory from a system that is not the last domain controller in the domain, you must be a member of either the Domain Admins group in that domain or a member of the Enterprise Admins group.

To remove Active Directory from a domain controller, complete the following steps:

1. Log on as the appropriate administrator.

2. Click Start, click Run, type **dcpromo** in the Open box, and then click OK.

3. On the Welcome To The Active Directory Installation Wizard page, click Next.

4. If the domain controller is a global catalog server, a message appears telling you to make sure other global catalogs are accessible to users of the domain before removing Active Directory from this computer. Click OK.

5. On the Remove Active Directory page, select the check box if the server is the last domain controller in the domain. Click Next.

6. If the server is the last domain controller in the domain, the Application Directory Partitions page appears. If you want to remove all application directory partitions listed on this page, click Next. Otherwise, click Back. If you click Next, the Confirm Deletion page appears. Select the check box if you want the wizard to delete all the application directory partitions on the domain controller, and then click Next.

> **Note**   Because removing the last replica of an application directory partition will result in the permanent loss of any data contained in the partition, the Active Directory Installation Wizard will not remove application directory partitions unless you confirm the deletion. You must decide when it is safe to delete the last replica of a particular partition. If the domain controller holds a Telephony Application Programming Interface (TAPI) application directory partition, you might need to use the Tapicfg.exe command-line tool to remove the TAPI application directory partition. For more information on using Tapicfg.exe, refer to Windows Server 2003 help.

7. On the Administrator Password page, type and confirm the administrator password, and then click Next.

8. On the Summary page, click Next. The Configuring Active Directory progress indicator appears as Active Directory is removed from the server. This process will take several minutes. Click Finish.

9. On the Active Directory Installation Wizard dialog box, click Restart Now to restart the computer and complete the removal of Active Directory from the computer.

Practice: Installing Active Directory, Configuring a Global Catalog Server, and Enabling Universal Group Membership Caching

In this practice, you install Active Directory on Server01 and Server02, configure Server02 as a global catalog server, and enable universal group membership caching for a site.

Exercise 1: Installing Active Directory

In this exercise, you install Active Directory on Server01, a stand-alone server, making it the first domain controller in the contoso.com domain. Server01 does not have a DNS server configured.

1. Click Start, and then click Run. In the Run dialog box, type **dcpromo** in the Open box and click OK.

2. On the Welcome To The Active Directory Installation Wizard page, click Next.

3. On the Operating System Compatibility page, click Next.

4. On the Domain Controller Type page, select Domain Controller For A New Domain, and click Next.

5. On the Create New Domain page, ensure that Domain In A New Forest is selected, and then click Next.

6. On the Install Or Configure DNS page, select No, Just Install And Configure DNS On This Computer and click Next.

7. On the New Domain Name page, type **contoso.com** in the Full DNS Name For New Domain box, and click Next.

8. On the NetBIOS Domain Name page, the Active Directory Installation Wizard will suggest the NetBIOS name CONTOSO. Accept this default name by clicking Next.

9. On the Database And Log Folders page, type the location of the Active Directory database in the Database Folder box and the location of the Active Directory log in the Log Folder box. Click Next.

10. On the Shared System Volume page, specify the location of the Sysvol folder in the Folder Location box. The Sysvol folder must reside on a partition or volume formatted with the NTFS file system. Click Next.

11. On the Permissions page, read through the available options, and click Next.

12. On the Directory Services Restore Mode Administrator Password page, type the directory services restore mode password you want to assign to this server's Administrator account in the Restore Mode Password box. Confirm the password in the Confirm Password box. Click Next.

13. The Summary page displays the options that you have selected during the wizard. Review the contents of this page for accuracy, and then click Next. The wizard takes a few minutes to configure Active Directory components. You might be prompted for your Windows Server 2003 CD-ROM. If you did not configure this server with a static IP address prior to starting the wizard, you will be prompted to do so.

14. When the Completing The Active Directory Installation Wizard page appears, click Finish, and then click Restart Now.

> **Note**   Once Server01 has been fully promoted to the role of domain controller, configure Server02 to use the IP address of Server01 as its preferred DNS server, and join Server02 to the contoso.com domain. Install Active Directory on Server02, configuring it as an additional domain controller in the contoso.com domain.

Exercise 2: Configuring a Global Catalog Server

Although Windows Server 2003 will automatically configure the first domain controller in a new Active Directory forest as a global catalog server, any additional global catalog servers need to be configured manually. In this exercise, you will configure Server02 as a global catalog server using the Active Directory Sites And Services tool.

1. On Server02, click Start, select Administrative Tools, and then click Active Directory Sites And Services.

2. Click the plus sign (+) next to the Sites folder to expand it.

3. Expand Default-First-Site-Name, the Servers folder, and then the Server02 object.

4. Right-click the NTDS Settings object, and click Properties.

5. On the General tab, select the Global Catalog check box, and then click OK.

6. Close Active Directory Sites And Services.

Exercise 3: Enabling Universal Group Membership Caching

Universal group membership caching is not enabled in any Active Directory sites by default. In this exercise, you will enable universal group membership caching in the default site, known as Default-First-Site-Name.

1. On either Server01 or Server02, click Start, select Administrative Tools, and then click Active Directory Sites And Services.

2. Click the plus sign (+) next to the Sites folder to expand it.

3. Click Default-First-Site-Name to view its contents.

4. Right-click NTDS Site Settings, and click Properties.

5. On the Site Settings tab, select the Enable Universal Group Membership Caching check box.

6. In the Refresh Cache From drop-down box, select Default-First-Site-Name. This will ensure that domain controllers using universal group membership caching will attempt to refresh cached information from global catalog servers located within the Default-First-Site-Name site.

7. Click OK, and close Active Directory Sites And Services.

Lesson Review

The following questions are intended to reinforce key information presented in this lesson. If you are unable to answer a question, review the lesson materials and try the question again. You can find answers to the questions in the "Questions and Answers" section at the end of this chapter.

1. What command must you use to install Active Directory using the network or backup media?

   _____

   _____

2. Which of the following items can be installed or configured as part of the Active Directory Installation Wizard? (Choose all that apply.)

   a. DNS

   b. Sysvol folder location

   c. RRAS

   d. Universal group membership caching

   e. NetBIOS domain name

3. What command is used to automate an Active Directory installation by using the contents of a file named Dcpromo.txt?

   _____

   _____

4. Which of the following commands is used to demote a domain controller?

   a. dcdemote

   b. dcinstall

   c. dcpromo

   d. dcremove

Lesson Summary

- The Active Directory Installation Wizard is the main tool used to install Active Directory. The Dcpromo.exe command is used to start the Active Directory Installation Wizard. The /answer switch is used to specify an answer file used to automate the installation process, while the /adv switch provides access to advanced features such as the ability to install a new domain controller by using a backed-up version of Active Directory from an existing domain controller.

- You can use the network or backup media to install Active Directory on additional domain controllers for an existing domain. Using backup media reduces bandwidth requirements for Active Directory installation.

- The Configure Your Server Wizard provides inexperienced administrators with a method to configure various network services, including Active Directory.

- Only the first domain controller installed in a new Active Directory forest is configured as a global catalog server by default. Additional global catalog servers can be configured via the NTDS Settings object associated with a domain controller in Active Directory Sites And Services.

- Universal group membership caching is a new Active Directory feature in Windows Server 2003 that allows a domain controller to cache universal group membership information for a user, eliminating the need to contact a global catalog server during the logon process. This feature is enabled on a site-wide basis by configuring the NTDS Site Settings object for a site in Active Directory Sites And Services.

- You can also remove Active Directory from an existing domain controller and dcmote it to either a stand-alone server or a member server by using the Dcpromo.exe command.

Lesson 2: Configuring Forest and Domain Functional Levels

This lesson walks you through two new features in Windows Server 2003 Active Directory, namely domain and forest functional levels. Much like a domain mode in Windows 2000 environments, the functional level of a domain or forest affects the versions of Windows that can be employed as domain controllers, as well as the availability of different Active Directory features.

After this lesson, you will be able to

■ Identify the Active Directory features that are available at different domain and forest functional levels

■ Identify the versions of Windows that can be used as domain controllers when a domain or forest is configured to different functional levels

■ Configure the functional level of a domain by using Active Directory Users And Computers

■ Configure the functional level of a forest by using Active Directory Domains And Trusts

Estimated lesson time: 30 minutes

Domain Functional Levels

The functional level at which a domain is configured affects an entire domain, but it affects that domain only. Within a Windows Server 2003 Active Directory forest, you can configure different domains to different domain functional levels, according to the versions of Windows deployed within that domain as domain controllers. As such, features that are available in a domain configured at one domain functional level might not be available in another domain within the same forest that is configured at a different domain functional level.

Windows Server 2003 Active Directory supports four domain functional levels, including:

■ Windows 2000 mixed (default)

■ Windows 2000 native

■ Windows Server 2003 interim

■ Windows Server 2003

Each of the four domain functional levels available in Windows Server 2003 is discussed in the following sections, including the capabilities and limitations associated with each.

Windows 2000 Mixed

After installing the first domain controller running Windows Server 2003 in a new domain, the domain functional level is set at Windows 2000 mixed by default. The Windows 2000 mixed domain functional level allows a Windows Server 2003 domain controller to interact with other domain controllers running Windows NT 4.0, Windows 2000, or Windows Server 2003, as illustrated in Figure 2-11. In this way, the Windows 2000 mixed domain functional level is similar to mixed mode in Windows 2000 Active Directory environments.

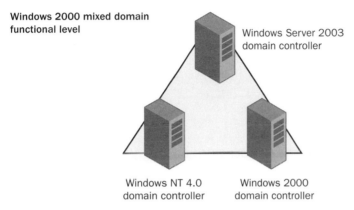

Windows 2000 mixed domain functional level

Windows Server 2003 domain controller

Windows NT 4.0 domain controller

Windows 2000 domain controller

Figure 2-11   Windows versions supported as domain controllers at the Windows 2000 mixed domain functional level

Although the Windows 2000 mixed domain functional level provides the flexibility to support different versions of Windows as domain controllers during the process of migrating a domain to Windows Server 2003 Active Directory, this functional level does not support many new or existing Active Directory features available when a domain is configured to the Windows 2000 native or Windows Server 2003 domain functional levels. For example, domains configured at the Windows 2000 mixed functional level do not support universal groups, the nesting of security groups, converting groups from one type to another, the ability to rename domain controllers, and more.

Note   Although the default domain functional level for Windows Server 2003 Active Directory is Windows 2000 mixed, the default domain functional level might be different if you are upgrading a domain from Windows 2000 to Windows Server 2003. For example, if the domain controller being upgraded is part of a Windows 2000 domain configured in native mode, the domain functional level after the upgrade will be Windows 2000 native rather than Windows 2000 mixed.

Windows 2000 Native

The Windows 2000 native domain functional level allows a domain controller running Windows Server 2003 to interact with other domain controllers running Windows 2000 or Windows Server 2003, as illustrated in Figure 2-12. Unlike the Windows 2000 mixed domain functional level, the Windows 2000 native domain functional level does not support domain controllers running Windows NT 4.0. In this way, the Windows 2000 native domain functional level is somewhat similar to native mode in Windows 2000 Active Directory environments.

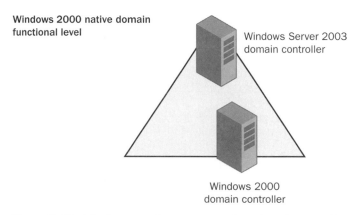

Windows 2000 native domain functional level

Windows Server 2003 domain controller

Windows 2000 domain controller

Figure 2-12   Windows versions supported as domain controllers at the Windows 2000 native domain functional level

Although the Windows 2000 native domain functional level provides the flexibility to support both Windows 2000 and Windows Server 2003 domain controllers during the process of migrating a domain to Windows Server 2003 Active Directory, this domain functional level does not support some of the new domain features available in Windows Server 2003. For example, while domains configured at the Windows 2000 native functional level do support universal groups, the nesting of security groups, and converting groups from one type to another, this domain functional level still lacks the ability to rename domain controllers, as well as other new features we will look at shortly.

Windows Server 2003 Interim

The Windows Server 2003 interim domain functional level is a special functional level that applies only to domains being upgraded from Windows NT 4.0 to Windows Server 2003 Active Directory. This domain functional level supports only domain controllers running Windows NT 4.0 and Windows Server 2003, as shown in Figure 2-13.

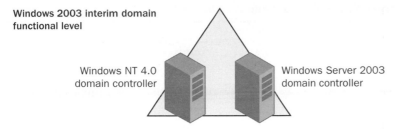

Windows 2003 interim domain
functional level

Windows NT 4.0
domain controller

Windows Server 2003
domain controller

Figure 2-13   Windows versions supported as domain controllers at the Windows Server 2003 interim domain functional level

> **Exam Tip**   The Windows Server 2003 interim domain functional level does not support domain controllers running Windows 2000.

The Windows Server 2003 interim functional level is subject to the same feature limitations as the Windows 2000 mixed domain functional level.

Windows Server 2003

Once all domain controllers in a domain are running Windows Server 2003, the domain can be raised to the Windows Server 2003 domain functional level. At the Windows Server 2003 domain functional level, neither Windows 2000 nor Windows NT 4.0 domain controllers are supported. The main advantage of the Windows Server 2003 domain functional level is that it allows you to use all the new domain features available in Windows Server 2003 Active Directory. Table 2-1 outlines the new domain features of Windows Server 2003 Active Directory and describes the level of support for each feature in the various domain functional levels.

> **Note**   Changing a domain functional level is a one-way process only; once you raise the functional level of a domain, you cannot return to a previously configured level.

Table 2-1 describes the status of domain-wide features in each domain functional level.

Table 2-1   Features Enabled by Domain Functional Level

Domain Feature	Windows 2000 Mixed/Windows Server 2003 Interim	Windows 2000 Native	Windows Server 2003
Domain controller rename tool	Disabled.	Disabled.	Enabled.
Update logon timestamp	Disabled.	Disabled.	Enabled.

Table 2-1   Features Enabled by Domain Functional Level

Domain Feature	Windows 2000 Mixed/Windows Server 2003 Interim	Windows 2000 Native	Windows Server 2003
User password on *InetOrgPerson* object	Disabled.	Disabled.	Enabled.
Universal Groups	Enabled for distribution groups. Disabled for security groups.	Enabled. Allows security and distribution groups.	Enabled. Allows security and distribution groups.
Group Nesting	Enabled for distribution groups. Disabled for security groups, except for domain local security groups that can have global groups as members.	Enabled. Allows full group nesting.	Enabled. Allows full group nesting.
Converting Groups	Disabled. No group conversions allowed.	Enabled. Allows conversion between security groups and distribution groups.	Enabled. Allows conversion between security groups and distribution groups.
SID History	Disabled.	Enabled. Allows migration of security principals from one domain to another.	Enabled. Allows migration of security principals from one domain to another.

Exam Tip   Ensure that you are familiar with the various domain functional levels in Windows Server 2003, including the versions of domain controllers supported in each and the capabilities available in one domain functional level versus another.

To change the domain functional level to Windows 2000 native or Windows Server 2003, complete the following steps:

1. Click Start, select Administrative Tools, and then click Active Directory Domains And Trusts.

2. Right-click the domain object whose domain functional level should be changed, and then click Raise Domain Functional Level.

> **Note**   To raise the functional level of a domain, you must be a member of either the Domain Admins group in that domain or the Enterprise Admins group in the forest root domain, or you must have been delegated the proper authority.

3. In the Select An Available Domain Functional Level drop-down box, select the domain functional level you want, as illustrated in Figure 2-14. Click Raise.

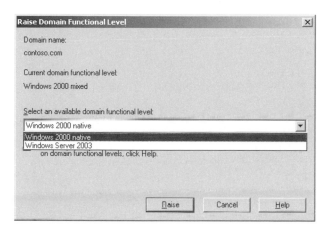

Figure 2-14   Raising the domain functional level

4. In the Raise Domain Functional Level message box, click OK.

Real World   Integration of Windows Server 2003 into Existing Domains

If you plan to install Windows 2003 Servers domain controllers into an existing Windows 2000 domain, or upgrade a Windows 2000 domain controller to Windows Server 2003, you first need to run the Adprep.exe utility on the Windows 2000 domain controllers currently holding the Schema Master and Infrastructure Master roles. This utility is located in the I386 directory of the Windows 2003 Server installation CD-ROM. The **adprep /forestprep** command must be issued on the Windows 2000 server holding the Schema Master role in the forest root domain to prepare the existing schema to support Windows Server 2003 Active Directory. The **adprep /domainprep** command must be issued on the server currently holding the Infrastructure Master role in the domain where the Windows Server 2003 domain controller will be deployed. Until these steps are completed, a Windows Server 2003 domain controller cannot be added to an existing Windows 2000 domain environment.

Forest Functional Levels

In much the same way as domain functional levels, forest functional levels affect the versions of Windows that can be employed as domain controllers throughout a forest, as well as the ability to implement forest-wide features of Windows Server 2003 Active Directory. While the two concepts are similar, the new Active Directory features enabled by changing the functional level of a forest are different than those enabled by changing the functional level of a domain.

Windows Server 2003 Active Directory supports three forest functional levels, including:

- Windows 2000 (default)
- Windows Server 2003 interim
- Windows Server 2003

Each of the three forest functional levels available in Windows Server 2003 is discussed in the following sections, including the capabilities and limitations associated with each.

Windows 2000

When you first install or upgrade a domain controller to a Windows Server 2003 operating system, the forest is configured to use the Windows 2000 forest functional level by default. At this forest functional level, domains within the forest that include domain controllers running Windows NT 4.0, Windows 2000, and Windows Server 2003 are all supported, as shown in Figure 2-15.

Windows 2000 forest functional level

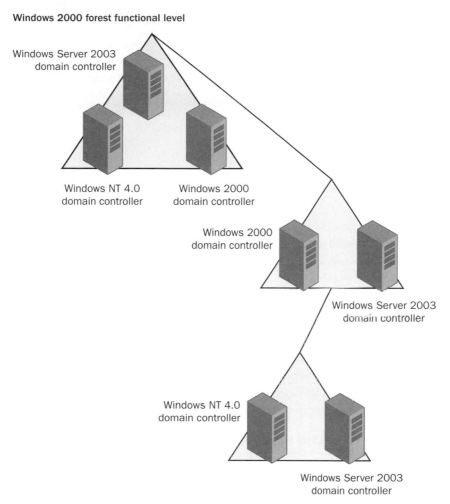

Figure 2-15   Windows versions supported as domain controllers at the Windows 2000 forest functional level

At the Windows 2000 forest functional level, almost all new forest-wide features associated with Windows Server 2003 Active Directory are disabled. The one exception is that any global catalog servers running Windows Server 2003 configured as replication partners can take advantage of the improved replication method used when new attributes are added to the global catalog. In Windows 2000 Active Directory, extending the partial attribute set maintained in the global catalog required a complete synchronization of the global catalog, which could lead to significant network traffic, especially in large environments. When the global catalog is extended to include a new attribute on domain controllers running Windows Server 2003, only the new attribute needs to be synchronized, rather than the entire global catalog.

Windows Server 2003 Interim

The Windows Server 2003 interim forest functional level is a special functional level used to support domain environments that are being upgraded from Windows NT 4.0 to Windows Server 2003 Active Directory. When the first domain controller in a Windows NT 4.0 domain is being upgraded to Windows Server 2003, the forest functional level is set to Windows Server 2003 interim by default. This forest functional level incurs the same limitations as those associated with the Windows 2000 forest functional level looked at in the previous section.

Windows Server 2003

The Windows Server 2003 forest functional level enables all the new forest-wide features of Windows Server 2003 Active Directory. To raise a forest to the Windows Server 2003 functional level, all domain controllers in all domains within the forest must be running Windows Server 2003. Prior to raising a forest to the Windows Server 2003 forest functional level, you must first raise each individual domain to at least the Windows 2000 native domain functional level. As part of the process of raising a forest to the Windows Server 2003 forest functional level, all domains within the forest are automatically raised to the Windows Server 2003 domain functional level.

Once the forest functional level has been raised, domain controllers running Windows 2000 or Windows NT 4.0 are no longer supported and cannot be introduced into the forest. Table 2-2 describes the forest-wide features introduced by Windows Server 2003 Active Directory and the status of these features at different forest functional levels.

Table 2-2   Features Enabled by Forest Functional Levels

Forest Feature	Windows 2000/Windows Server 2003 interim	Windows Server 2003
Global catalog replication improvements	Enabled if both replication partners are running Windows Server 2003. Otherwise, disabled.	Enabled.
Defunct schema objects	Disabled.	Enabled.
Forest trusts	Disabled.	Enabled.
Linked value replication	Disabled.	Enabled.
Domain rename	Disabled.	Enabled.
Improved Active Directory replication algorithms	Disabled.	Enabled.
Dynamic auxiliary classes.	Disabled.	Enabled.
InetOrgPerson objectClass change	Disabled.	Enabled.

> **Exam Tip**   Ensure that you are familiar with the various forest functional levels in Windows Server 2003, including the versions of domain controllers supported in each and the capabilities available in one forest functional level versus another.

To change the forest functional level to Windows Server 2003, complete the following steps:

1. Click Start, select Administrative Tools, and then click Active Directory Domains And Trusts.

2. Right-click the Active Directory Domains And Trusts node, and then click Raise Forest Functional Level. If any domains within the forest are not configured to at least the Windows 2000 native domain functional level, you will not be able to raise the functional level of the forest, as shown in Figure 2-16.

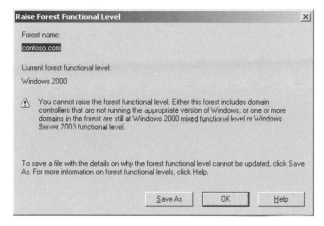

Figure 2-16   Error message encountered when attempting to raise the forest functional level to Windows Server 2003

> **Note**   To raise the functional level of a forest, you must be a member of either the Domain Admins group in the forest root domain or the Enterprise Admins group, or you must have been delegated the proper authority.

3. If all domains have already been raised to at least the Windows 2000 native domain functional level, click Raise.

4. In the Raise Forest Functional Level message box, click OK.

Practice: Raising Forest and Domain Functional Levels

In this practice, you will first raise the domain functional level of the contoso.com domain to Windows Server 2003, and then raise the forest functional level of the contoso.com forest to Windows Server 2003.

Exercise 1: Raising the Domain Functional Level

In this exercise, you will raise the domain functional level of the contoso.com domain from Windows 2000 mixed to Windows Server 2003.

1. On Server01, click Start, select Administrative Tools, and then click Active Directory Users And Computers.

2. Right-click the contoso.com domain object, and then click Raise Domain Functional Level.

3. In the Select An Available Domain Functional Level drop-down box, select Windows Server 2003 and click the Raise button.

4. In the Raise Domain Functional Level dialog box, click OK.

5. In the Raise Domain Functional Level dialog box, read the status message that appears and click OK.

6. Close Active Directory Users And Computers.

Exercise 2: Raising the Forest Functional Level

In this exercise, you will raise the forest functional level of the contoso.com forest from Windows 2000 to Windows Server 2003.

1. On Server01, click Start, select Administrative Tools, and then click Active Directory Domains And Trusts.

2. Right-click the Active Directory Domains And Trusts node, and then click Raise Forest Functional Level.

3. In the Raise Forest Functional Level window, notice that the Select An Available Forest Functional Level drop-down box contains only one choice, Windows Server 2003. Click the Raise button.

4. In the Raise Forest Functional Level dialog box, click OK.

5. In the Raise Forest Functional Level dialog box, read the status message that appears and click OK.

6. Close Active Directory Domains And Trusts.

Lesson Review

The following questions are intended to reinforce key information presented in this lesson. If you are unable to answer a question, review the lesson materials and try the question again. You can find answers to the questions in the "Questions and Answers" section at the end of this chapter.

1. Which domain functional level supports a combination of Windows NT 4.0, Windows 2000, and Windows Server 2003 domain controllers?

    a. Windows 2000 native

    b. Windows 2000 mixed

    c. Windows Server 2003 interim

    d. Windows Server 2003

2. If a Windows 2000 domain controller in a Windows 2000 Active Directory environment running in native mode is upgraded to Windows Server 2003, which Windows Server 2003 domain functional level will be configured by default?

    a. Windows 2000 mixed

    b. Windows Server 2003 interim

    c. Windows Server 2003

    d. Windows 2000 native

3. Which of the following must be true for a Windows Server 2003 Active Directory forest to be raised to the Windows Server 2003 forest functional level? (Choose all that apply.)

    a. All domains must be configured to the Windows Server 2003 domain functional level.

    b. All domains must be configured to at least the Windows 2000 native domain functional level.

    c. All domain controllers must be running either Windows 2000 or Windows Server 2003.

    d. All domain controllers must be running Windows Server 2003.

Lesson Summary

- Windows Server 2003 Active Directory supports four domain functional levels—Windows 2000 mixed, Windows 2000 native, Windows Server 2003 interim, and Windows Server 2003. The functional level of a domain dictates the versions of Windows supported as domain controllers, as well as the ability to use new domain-wide Active Directory features.

- The Windows 2000 mixed domain functional level supports domain controllers running Windows NT 4.0, Windows 2000, and Windows Server 2003. However, this functional level cannot take advantage of many new and existing features of Windows Server 2003 Active Directory.

- The Windows 2000 native domain functional level supports domain controllers running Windows 2000 and Windows Server 2003 only. While this domain functional level can implement many existing Active Directory features, such as universal groups, it cannot take advantages of new Windows Server 2003 features, such as the ability to rename domain controllers.

- The Windows Server 2003 interim domain functional level is a special functional level applicable to domains being upgraded from Windows NT 4.0 to Windows Server 2003. Only Windows NT 4.0 and Windows Server 2003 domain controllers are supported. This functional level is subject to the same limitations as the Windows 2000 mixed domain functional level.

- The Windows Server 2003 domain functional level supports domain controllers running Windows Server 2003 only, and it takes advantage of all the new domain-wide features in Windows Server 2003 Active Directory.

- Windows Server 2003 supports three forest functional levels—Windows 2000, Windows Server 2003 interim, and Windows Server 2003. The functional level of a forest dictates the versions of Windows supported as domain controllers, as well as the ability to use new forest-wide Active Directory features.

- The Windows 2000 forest functional level supports domain controllers running Windows NT 4.0, Windows 2000, and Windows Server 2003. However, this forest functional level offers very limited support for new forest-wide Active Directory features.

- The Windows Server 2003 interim forest functional level is a special functional level used to support domain environments that are being upgraded from Windows NT 4.0 to Windows Server 2003 Active Directory. It is subject to the same limitations as the Windows 2000 forest functional level with respect to new forest-wide Active Directory features.

Lesson 3: Creating and Configuring Application Directory Partitions

This lesson introduces you to application directory partitions, another new feature of Windows Server 2003 Active Directory. It also walks you through the tasks involved in configuring and managing application directory partitions.

After this lesson, you will be able to

- Explain the purpose of an application directory partition
- Configure an application directory partition by using Ntdsutil.exe
- Manage an application directory partition by using Ntdsutil.exe

Estimated lesson time: 30 minutes

Types of Application Directory Partitions

In Windows 2000 Active Directory environments, domain controllers could hold up to four types of partitions, depending on their configured role. The types of partitions included:

- The domain partition, which contained all objects associated with a particular domain. This partition was replicated to all domain controllers in the same domain.

- The schema partition, which contained a copy of the Active Directory schema for a given forest. This partition was replicated to all domain controllers in the same forest.

- The configuration partition, which contained information about Active Directory sites and services. This partition was replicated to all domain controllers in the same forest.

- The global catalog partition, which contained a subset of the attributes of all objects in an Active Directory forest. This partition was replicated to all domain controllers configured as global catalog servers in the same forest.

Windows Server 2003 continues to support all four types of Active Directory partitions found in Windows 2000, but it also introduces a new type of partition known as an *application directory partition*. An application directory partition is a partition that is replicated only to specific domain controllers throughout an Active Directory forest. Because an application directory partition is a feature specific to Windows Server 2003, only domain controllers running Windows Server 2003 can host a replica of an application directory partition.

Note   Although only domain controllers running Windows Server 2003 can host a replica of an application directory partition, these partitions can exist in Active Directory environments that still include Windows 2000 or Windows NT 4.0 domain controllers.

The main purpose of an application directory partitions is to store data (objects and attributes) related to Active Directory–integrated applications and services. For example, Windows Server 2003 automatically creates an application directory partition for data used by the TAPI service. Along the same lines, an application directory partition could also be used to store data relating to services such as DNS, as originally discussed in Chapter 1. Some benefits of using application directory partitions to store information include:

- Provides redundancy, availability, and fault tolerance by replicating data to specific domain controllers throughout a forest

- Might reduce replication traffic because the application or service data is only replicated to specific domain controllers (replicas) where the information is required

- Allows applications or services that use Lightweight Directory Access Protocol (LDAP) to store and access their data in Active Directory.

Note   Application directory partitions can hold any type of object *except* security principals such as users, computers, and security groups.

Application directory partitions are most commonly created by the applications that use them to store and replicate data. However, members of the Enterprise Admins group can manually create or manage application directory partitions by using the Ntdsutil.exe command-line tool.

Application Directory Partition Naming

An application directory partition is part of the overall forest namespace just like any domain directory partition. It follows the same DNS and distinguished name naming conventions as a domain partition did in Windows 2000 Active Directory. An application directory partition can appear anywhere in the forest namespace that a domain partition can appear.

An application directory partition can be placed in the following areas in the forest namespace:

- A child of a domain partition
- A child of an application directory partition
- A new tree in the forest

For example, if you created an application directory partition named app1 as a child of the contoso.com domain, the DNS name of the application directory partition would be app1.contoso.com. The distinguished name of the application directory partition would be dc=app1,dc=contoso,dc=com. If you then created an application directory partition named app2 as a child of app1.contoso.com, the DNS name of the application directory partition would be app2.app1.contoso.com and the distinguished name would be dc=app2,dc=app1,dc=contoso,dc=com.

However, if the domain contoso.com was the root of the only domain tree in your forest, and you created an application directory partition with the DNS name of app1 and the distinguished name of dc=app1, this application directory partition would not be in the same tree as the contoso.com domain. This application directory partition would be the root of a new tree in the forest.

Domain partitions cannot be children of an application directory partition. For example, if you created an application directory partition with the DNS name of app1.contoso.com, you could not create a domain with the DNS name domain1.app1.contoso.com.

Application Directory Partition Replication

The Knowledge Consistency Checker (KCC) automatically generates and maintains the replication topology for all application directory partitions in a forest. When an application directory partition has replicas in more than one site, those replicas follow the same intersite replication schedule as a domain partition. Unlike objects from a domain partition, objects stored in an application directory partition are never replicated to the global catalog. However, any domain controller running Windows Server 2003 can hold an application directory partition replica, including global catalog servers.

In addition, if an application requests data through the global catalog port (with LDAP, port 3268, or with LDAP/SSL, port 3269), that query will not return any objects from an application directory partition if the computer hosting the application directory partition is also hosting the global catalog. This structure was adopted so that LDAP queries to different global catalogs would not return inconsistent results because the application directory partition might be replicated only to certain global catalog servers.

Exam Tip   Objects stored in an application directory partition are never replicated to the global catalog. However, a domain controller functioning as a global catalog server can host a replica of an application directory partition.

Application Directory Partitions and Domain Controller Demotion

If you need to demote a domain controller that is hosting a replica of an application directory partition, you must consider the following:

- If a domain controller holds *a replica* of an application directory partition, you must remove the domain controller from the replica set or delete the application directory partition before you can demote the domain controller.

- If a domain controller holds *the last replica* of an application directory partition, before you can demote the domain controller you must do one of the following:

    - Specify that you want the Active Directory Installation Wizard to remove all replicas from the domain controller.

    - Remove the replica manually by using the utility provided by the application that installed it.

    - Remove the replica manually by using the Ntdsutil.exe command.

Before deleting an application directory partition, you should:

- **Identify the applications that use it**   To determine what application directory partitions are hosted on a computer, refer to the list on the Application Directory Partitions page of the Active Directory Installation Wizard, as shown in Figure 2-17.

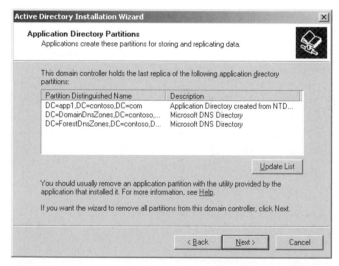

Figure 2-17   Active Directory Installation Wizard, Application Directory Partitions page

- **Determine whether it is safe to delete the last replica**   Removing the last replica of an application directory partition results in the permanent loss of any data contained in the partition. If you have identified the applications using the application directory partition, consult the documentation provided with those applications to determine whether there is any reason to keep the data. If the programs that use the application directory partition are no longer being used, it is probably safe to remove the partition. In cases where you must demote the last domain controller holding a replica but have determined that the application directory partition must not be permanently deleted, follow these steps:

1. Add a replica of the partition on another domain controller.

2. Force the replication of the contents of the application directory partition to the domain controller holding the new replica.

3. Remove the replica of the partition on the domain controller to be demoted.

- **Identify the partition deletion tool provided by the application**   Almost all programs that create application directory partitions provide a utility to manage and remove these partitions as necessary. When possible, always delete an application directory partition by using the utility provided by the program that created it. Refer to the program's documentation for information about removing application directory partitions that were created and used by that program. If you cannot identify the program that created the application directory partition, or if the program does not provide a means to delete any application directory partitions that it might have created, you can use the Ntdsutil.exe command-line tool. To do this, refer to the section "Creating or Deleting an Application Directory Partition" later in this lesson.

Note   If the domain controller holds a TAPI application directory partition, you can use the Tapicfg.exe command-line tool to remove the TAPI application directory partition. For more information about the Tapicfg.exe command-line tool, refer to the Windows Server 2003 help.

Security Descriptor Reference Domain

Every container and object in Active Directory has a set of access control information associated with it. Known as a *security descriptor*, this information controls the type of access allowed by users, groups, and computers. If the object or container is not assigned a security descriptor by the application or service that created it, it is assigned the default security descriptor for that object class as defined in the schema. This default security descriptor is ambiguous in that it might assign members of the Domain Admins group read permissions to the object, but it does not specify to what domain the domain administrators belong. When an object is created in a domain partition, that domain partition is used to specify which Domain Admins group is assigned the read permission. For example, if an object is created in domain1.contoso.com, members of the domain1 Domain Admins group would be assigned read permission.

When an object is created in an application directory partition, the definition of the default security descriptor is less clear because an application directory partition can have replicas on domain controllers in different domains. Because of this potential ambiguity, a default security descriptor reference domain is assigned when the application directory partition is created.

The default security descriptor reference domain defines which domain name should be used when an application directory partition needs to assign a domain value for the default security descriptor. If the application directory partition is a child of a domain partition, the parent domain partition becomes the security descriptor reference domain by default. If the application directory partition is a child object of another application directory partition, the security descriptor reference domain of the parent application directory partition becomes the reference domain of this new partition. If the new application directory partition is created as the root of a new tree, the forest root domain is used as the default security descriptor reference domain.

You can also manually specify a different security reference domain if that better meets your needs. However, if you plan to change the default security descriptor reference domain of a particular application directory partition, you should do so before creating the first instance of that partition. To do this, you must prepare what is known as a cross-reference object, and change the default security reference domain before creating the new application directory partition. The procedure for creating a cross-reference object is discussed later in this lesson.

Managing Application Directory Partitions

A variety of tools can be used to create, delete, or manage application directory partitions, including:

- Application-specific tools from the application vendor
- The Ntdsutil.exe command-line tool
- The LDP.exe utility
- Active Directory Service Interfaces (ADSI)

This lesson provides information about using Ntdsutil.exe to create and manage application directory partitions. To manage application directory partitions, you must first complete the following tasks:

- Create or delete an application directory partition
- Add or remove an application directory partition replica
- Display application directory partition information
- Set a notification delay
- Prepare a cross-reference object
- Set an application directory partition reference domain

Note   To perform these tasks, you must be a member of the Domain Admins group or the Enterprise Admins group in Active Directory, or you must have been delegated the appropriate authority.

To perform tasks related to creating and managing application directory partitions, the domain management command is issued from within Ntdsutil.exe. The following steps outline the procedure to access domain management functions with the Ntdsutil.exe utility.

1. Click Start, and then click Command Prompt.

2. At the command prompt, type **ntdsutil**.

3. At the ntdsutil prompt, type **domain management**.

4. At the domain management prompt, type **connection**.

5. At the server connections prompt, type **connect to server** *ServerName*, where *ServerName* is the DNS name of the domain controller to which you want to connect, as shown in Figure 12-18.

```
Command Prompt - ntdsutil                                    _ | □ | X |
C:\>ntdsutil
ntdsutil: domain management
domain management: connection
server connections: connect to server server01.contoso.com
Binding to server01.contoso.com ...
Connected to server01.contoso.com using credentials of locally logged on user.
server connections: _
```

Figure 2-18   Connecting to a domain controller to perform domain management functions

6. At the server connections prompt, type **quit**.

Creating or Deleting an Application Directory Partition

When you create an application directory partition, you are creating the first instance of this partition. When you delete an application directory partition, you are removing all replicas of that partition from your forest. The deletion process must replicate to all domain controllers that contain a replica of the application directory partition before the deletion process is complete. When an application directory partition is deleted, any data that is contained in it is lost. The following steps create or delete an application directory partition.

1. Type the appropriate commands to invoke the Ntdsutil.exe domain management command if necessary.

2. At the domain management prompt, do one of the following.

❑ To create an application directory partition, type: **create nc *Application-DirectoryPartition DomainController***, where *ApplicationDirectory-Partition* is the distinguished name of the application directory partition you want to create, such as dc=app1,dc=contoso,dc=com, and *DomainController* is the DNS name of the domain controller on which you want to create the application directory partition. To create the application directory partition on the domain controller you are currently connected to, you can use **null** for *DomainController*. This is illustrated in Figure 2-19.

❑ To delete an application directory partition, type: **delete nc *Application-DirectoryPartition***, where *ApplicationDirectoryPartition* is the distinguished name of the application directory partition you want to delete.

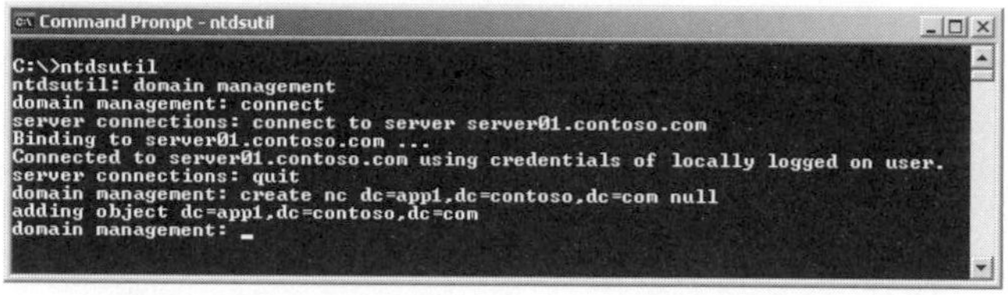

Figure 2-19   Creating an application directory partition with Ntdsutil.exe

Adding or Removing an Application Directory Partition Replica

An *application directory partition replica* is an instance of a partition on another domain controller, created for redundancy or load-balancing purposes. When you remove an application directory partition replica, any data that is contained in the replica is lost.

To add or remove an application directory partition replica:

1. Type the appropriate commands to invoke the Ntdsutil.exe domain management command.

2. At the domain management command prompt, do one of the following.

❑ To add an application directory partition replica, type: **add nc *Application-DirectoryPartition DomainController***, where *ApplicationDirectoryPartition* is the distinguished name of the application directory partition replica that you want to add, and *DomainController* is the DNS name of the domain controller on which you want to create the application directory partition replica. To add the application directory partition replica on the domain controller you are currently connected to, you can use **null** for *DomainController*.

❑ To remove an application directory partition replica, type: **remove nc** ***ApplicationDirectoryPartition DomainController***, where *Application-DirectoryPartition* is the distinguished name of the application directory partition replica that you want to delete, and *DomainController* is the DNS name of the domain controller on which you want to remove the application directory partition replica. To remove the application directory partition replica on the domain controller you are currently connected to, you can use **null** for *DomainController*.

Exam Tip   Remember that the *create nc* and *delete nc* Ntdsutil.exe domain management commands are used to create and delete application directory partitions, while the *add nc* and *remove nc* commands are used to add and remove application directory partition replicas.

Displaying Application Directory Partition Information

Any domain controller that holds a replica of a particular partition (including application directory partitions) is considered to be a member of the replica set for that directory partition. Ntdsutil.exe can be used to list the domain controllers that are members of a replica set for any directory partition, including application directory partitions.

To display information about different directory partitions, including application directory partitions:

1. Type the appropriate commands to invoke the Ntdsutil.exe domain management command.

2. At the domain management prompt, do one or more of the following.

   ❑ To show the distinguished names of known directory partitions, type **list**. This is illustrated in Figure 2-20.

   ❑ To show the reference domain and replication delays for an application directory partition, type **list nc information** ***DistinguishedName***, where *DistinguishedName* is the distinguished name of the application directory partition you want information about.

   ❑ To show the list of domain controllers in the replica set for an application directory partition, type **list nc replicas** ***DistinguishedName***, where *DistinguishedName* is the distinguished name of the application directory partition you want information about.

```
Command Prompt - ntdsutil                                           _ | □ | x |
C:\>ntdsutil
ntdsutil: domain management
domain management: connect
server connections: connect to server server01.contoso.com
Binding to server01.contoso.com ...
Connected to server01.contoso.com using credentials of locally logged on user.
server connections: quit
domain management: list
Note: Directory partition names with International/Unicode characters will only
display correctly if appropriate fonts and language support are loaded
Found 6 Naming Context(s)
0 - CN=Configuration,DC=contoso,DC=com
1 - DC=contoso,DC=com
2 - CN=Schema,CN=Configuration,DC=contoso,DC=com
3 - DC=DomainDnsZones,DC=contoso,DC=com
4 - DC=ForestDnsZones,DC=contoso,DC=com
5 - DC=app1,DC=contoso,DC=com
domain management:
```

Figure 2-20   The list of all known directory partitions, including application directory partitions

Setting Replication Notification Delays

Changes made to a particular directory partition on a domain controller are replicated to the other domain controllers that contain that directory partition. The domain controller on which the change was made notifies its replication partners that it has a change. You can configure how long the domain controller will wait to send the change notification to its first replication partner if necessary. Similarly, you can also configure how long a domain controller waits to send the subsequent change notifications to its remaining replication partners. These delays can be set for any directory partition (including domain directory partitions) on a particular domain controller.

To set a replication notification delay:

1. Type the appropriate commands to invoke the Ntdsutil.exe domain management command.

2. At the domain management command prompt, type **set nc replicate notification delay** *ApplicationDirectoryPartition DelayInSeconds AdditionalDelayInSeconds*, where *ApplicationDirectoryPartition* is the distinguished name of the application directory partition for which you want to set a notification delay, *DelayInSeconds* is the number of seconds to delay before sending the change notification to the first replication partner, and *AdditionalDelayInSeconds* is the number of seconds to delay before sending subsequent change notifications to the remaining replication partners.

Delegating the Creation of Application Directory Partitions

Two primary actions take place when a new application directory partition is created.

■ A cross-reference object is created.

■ The application directory partition root node is created.

Normally, only members of the Enterprise Admins group can create an application directory partition. However, a member of the Enterprise Admins group can prepare a cross-reference object for the application directory partition in order to delegate the rest of the process to a user with more limited permissions.

The *cross-reference object* for an application directory partition holds several valuable pieces of information, including the domain controllers that are to hold a replica of this partition and the security descriptor reference domain. The partition root node is the Active Directory object at the root of the partition.

An Enterprise Admin can create the cross-reference object and then delegate to a person or group with less permissions the right to create the application directory partition root node. Both the creation of the cross-reference object and the application directory partition root node can be accomplished using Ntdsutil.exe.

After using Ntdsutil.exe to create the cross-reference object, the enterprise administrator must modify the cross-reference object's access control list to allow the delegated user to modify this cross-reference. This will ultimately allow the delegated user to create the application directory partition and modify the list of domain controllers that hold replicas of the partition.

To prepare a cross-reference object:

1. Type the appropriate commands to invoke the Ntdsutil.exe domain management command.

2. At the domain management command prompt, type **precreate** *ObjectName DomainController*, where *ObjectName* is the distinguished name of the object you want to create and *DomainController* is the DNS name of the domain controller on which the object will reside.

Setting the Application Directory Partition Reference Domain

The security descriptor reference domain specifies a domain name for the default security descriptor for objects in an application directory partition. Recall that, by default, the security descriptor reference domain is the parent domain of the application directory partition. If the application directory partition is a child of another application directory partition, the default security descriptor reference domain is the security descriptor reference domain of the parent application directory partition. If the application directory partition has no parent, the forest root domain becomes the default security descriptor reference domain. You can use Ntdsutil.exe to change the default security descriptor reference domain.

To set an application directory partition reference domain:

1. Type the appropriate commands to invoke the Ntdsutil.exe domain management command.

2. At the domain management command prompt, type **set nc reference domain**
   ApplicationDirectoryPartition   ReferenceDomain, where *Application-
   DirectoryPartition* is the distinguished name of the application directory partition
   for which you want to set the reference domain, and *ReferenceDomain* is the distinguished name of the domain that you want to be the reference domain for the
   application directory partition.

> **Exam Tip**   Know how to create and configure application directory partitions by using the
> various Ntdsutil.exe commands looked at in this lesson.

Lesson Review

The following questions are intended to reinforce key information presented in this
lesson. If you are unable to answer a question, review the lesson and then try the question again. You can find answers to the questions in the "Questions and Answers" section at the end of this chapter.

1. What is an application directory partition?

   _____

   _____

   _____

2. Name the benefits of using an application directory partition.

   _____

   _____

   _____

   _____

   _____

   _____

3. What is a security descriptor, and how is it used in an application directory partition?

   _____

   _____

   _____

   _____

   _____

4. What considerations should you make before deleting an application directory partition?

_____

_____

_____

5. Which of the following tools can you use to delete an application directory partition? (Choose all that apply.)

   a. Ntdsutil.exe command-line tool

   b. Application-specific tools from the application vendor

   c. Active Directory Installation Wizard

   d. Active Directory Domains and Trusts console

   e. Active Directory Sites And Services console

Lesson Summary

■ An application directory partition is a directory partition that is replicated only to specific domain controllers throughout a forest. Only domain controllers running Windows Server 2003 can host a replica of an application directory partition. Application directory partitions are usually created by the applications that use them to store and replicate data.

■ An application directory partition can be a child of a domain partition, a child of an application directory partition, or a new tree in the forest.

■ The KCC automatically generates and maintains the replication topology for all application directory partitions in the enterprise. When an application directory partition has replicas in more than one site, those replicas follow the same intersite replication schedule as domain partitions.

■ If you must demote a domain controller, you must remove the domain controller from the replica set of the application directory partition, or delete the application directory partition before you can demote the domain controller.

■ For testing and troubleshooting purposes, members of the Enterprise Admins group can manually create and manage application directory partitions by using the Ntdsutil.exe command-line tool.

Case Scenario Exercise

As part of helping Contoso with its Windows Server 2003 Active Directory implementation, you have been asked to help its network team with the configuration of Windows Server 2003 domain controllers for both the head office and all branch office locations.

- **Requirement 1** The IT manager at Contoso has decided that all remote locations will have new domain controllers installed running Windows Server 2003. He would like the promotion process to be automated to reduce the risk of misconfiguration by staff members in those locations. At the head office location, the existing domain controllers should be upgraded to Windows Server 2003 to ensure that existing domain objects do not need to be re-created.

- **Requirement 2** Contoso is planning to merge with another organization within the next 6 to 12 months. This organization is currently running Windows Server 2003, and the IT manager has specified that complete interoperability with the other organization's Active Directory implementation is required immediately once the merger is finalized.

- **Requirement 3** The administration team at Contoso has decided to implement global catalog servers at the four branch office locations connected via the 512-Kbps frame relay links, but they will instead rely upon universal group membership caching at the locations connected by 64-Kbps ISDN links. You have been asked for your thoughts on this arrangement, and for help with the implementation.

Requirement 1

Requirement 1 involves determining an appropriate Active Directory installation strategy for remote locations and an upgrade strategy for the head office location.

1. Which of the following methods should be used to upgrade the Windows Server 2003 systems at the branch offices to the role of domain controller?

    a. The Configure Your Server Wizard

    b. The Active Directory Installation Wizard

    c. The Active Directory Installation Wizard in conjunction with an answer file

    d. The Active Directory Installation Wizard using a backup from an existing domain controller

2. On which of the following Windows 2000 domain controllers at the head office location will the Adprep.exe utility need to be run prior to upgrading or installing any domain controllers to Windows Server 2003? (Choose all that apply.)

   a. The Schema Master

   b. The PDC Emulator

   c. The Infrastructure Master

   d. The RID Master

3. If the current Windows 2000 domain environment is configured in native mode, which domain functional level will be configured by default when the first domain controller is upgraded?

   a. Windows 2000 mixed

   b. Windows 2000 native

   c. Windows Server 2003 interim

   d. Windows Server 2003

Requirement 2

Requirement 2 involves determining the required domain and forest functional levels for contoso.com to support a planned merger with another organization running Windows Server 2003 Active Directory.

1. Which forest or domain functional level will be required for Contoso to create a cross-forest trust relationship with this other organization?

   a. The Windows Server 2003 forest functional level

   b. The Windows 2000 native domain functional level

   c. The Windows 2000 forest functional level

   d. The Windows Server 2003 interim domain functional level

2. Which of the following are true once the domain functional level of contoso.com has been raised to Windows Server 2003? (Choose all that apply.)

   a. The Active Directory environment will support domain renaming.

   b. Windows 2000 domain controllers will no longer be supported.

   c. The domain will support the ability to rename domain controllers.

   d. Windows 2000 member servers will no longer be supported.

Requirement 3

Requirement 3 involves determining where global catalog servers and universal group caching should be implemented at branch offices, and how these services should be configured.

1. Which of the following are advantages of placing a Windows Server 2003 global catalog server at each branch office site?

    a. User authentication requests will not generate WAN traffic.

    b. Windows Server 2003 domain controllers can take advantage of new replication enhancements.

    c. Global catalog servers eliminate the need for replication over WAN links.

    d. Users can perform directory-wide queries without generating additional WAN traffic.

2. Which of the following represent reasons why individual domain controllers cannot be configured to use universal group membership caching?

    a. A forest must be configured to the Windows Server 2003 forest functional level before universal group membership caching can be implemented.

    b. Universal group membership caching can be configured at the domain level only.

    c. Universal group membership caching can be configured at the site level only.

    d. Universal group membership caching cannot be implemented in domains running at the Windows 2000 mixed domain functional level.

Chapter Summary

- Windows Server 2003 supports four methods of promoting servers to domain controllers. This includes using the Configure Your Server Wizard, as well as the Active Directory Installation Wizard either manually, using answer files, or using backup media.

- The Dcpromo.exe command is used to start the Active Directory Installation Wizard. The /answer switch allows the promotion process to be automated using an answer file, while the /adv switch allows a backup of an existing domain controller to be specified during the promotion process.

- Windows Server 2003 domain controllers can be configured as global catalog servers manually using the Active Directory Sites And Services tool. Universal group membership caching is also configured using Active Directory Sites And Services, but this setting is configured on a site-wide rather than per-server basis.

- Windows Server 2003 Active Directory supports four domain functional levels, including Windows 2000 mixed (default), Windows 2000 native, Windows Server 2003 interim, and Windows Server 2003. The functional level of a domain affects the versions of Windows that can be deployed as domain controllers, as well as the ability to use different Active Directory domain features.

- Windows Server 2003 Active Directory supports three forest functional levels, including Windows 2000 (default), Windows Server 2003 interim, and Windows Server 2003. The functional level of a forest affects the versions of Windows that can be deployed as domain controllers, as well as the ability to use different Active Directory forest features.

- Application directory partitions are a new feature in Windows Server 2003 Active Directory that allow application or service data to be replicated to selected domain controllers throughout an Active Directory forest.

- A variety of methods can be used to create, configure, manage, and delete application directory partitions, including utilities provided with programs that use these partitions, the Ntdsutil.exe command line tool, the LDP.exe utility, and ADSI.

Exam Highlights

Before taking the exam, review the following key points and terms to help you identify topics you need to review. Return to the lessons for additional practice, and review the "Further Readings" sections in Part 2 for pointers to more information about topics covered by the exam objectives.

Key Points

- Windows Server 2003 systems can be promoted to domain controllers using four methods. You should be familiar with how to initiate each method, as well as the types of information that need to be supplied for each.

- Windows Server 2003 Active Directory supports four domain functional levels and three forest functional levels. You should be familiar with the Windows versions supported as domain controllers at each functional level, as well as how to make use of different domain- and forest-wide features in each.

- When a Windows Server 2003 system is promoted to be the first domain controller in a new forest, only that server is automatically configured as a global catalog server. Other global catalog servers can be configured manually using the Active Directory Sites And Services tool.

- Universal group membership caching is a new Windows Server 2003 feature that is configured using the Active Directory Sites And Services tool. Universal group membership caching is configured on a site-wide basis rather than on individual domain controllers.

- Application directory partitions are a new feature of Windows Server 2003 Active Directory that allows application or service data to be replicated to specific domain controllers throughout an Active Directory forest. You should be familiar with application directory partition features, as well as how these partitions can be created, deleted, and managed using Ntdsutil.exe.

Key Terms

Application directory partition   A new type of directory partition introduced in Windows Server 2003 Active Directory. Application directory partitions store application and service data that is replicated to selected domain controllers throughout an Active Directory forest. Application directory partitions can contain any type of object with the exception of security principals such as users, computers, and security groups.

Domain functional level   The domain functional level to which a domain is configured affects its ability to support domain controllers running different versions of Windows, as well as its ability to support new domain-wide Active Directory features. Windows Server 2003 Active Directory supports four domain functional levels, including Windows 2000 mixed (default), Windows 2000 native, Windows Server 2003 interim, and Windows Server 2003.

Forest functional level   The forest functional level to which a forest is configured affects its ability to support domain controllers running different versions of Windows, as well as its ability to support new forest-wide Active Directory features. Windows Server 2003 Active Directory supports three forest functional levels, including Windows 2000 (default), Windows Server 2003 interim, and Windows Server 2003.

Global catalog server   A global catalog server is a domain controller that stores a read-only copy of all Active Directory objects in a forest, with the exception of objects stored in application directory partitions. Global catalog servers are used to store universal group membership information, authenticate users who log on using a UPN, and facilitate searches for objects across the entire forest.

Universal group membership caching   A new Windows Server 2003 Active Directory feature that allows the Windows Server 2003 domain controllers within a specific site to cache information about a user's universal group memberships, helping to reduce authentication query traffic to remote global catalog servers.

Questions and Answers

Lesson 1 Review

1. What command must you use to install Active Directory using the network or backup media?

   Use the dcpromo /adv command to install Active Directory using the network or backup media.

2. Which of the following items can be installed or configured as part of the Active Directory Installation Wizard? (Choose all that apply.)

   a. DNS

   b. Sysvol folder location

   c. RRAS

   d. Universal group membership caching

   e. NetBIOS domain name

   a, b, e

3. What command is used to automate an Active Directory installation by using the contents of a file named Dcpromo.txt?

   The command used to automate an Active Directory installation by using the contents of a file named Dcpromo.txt is dcpromo /answer:dcpromo.txt.

4. Which of the following commands is used to demote a domain controller?

   a. dcdemote

   b. dcinstall

   c. dcpromo

   d. dcremove

   c

Lesson 2 Review

1. Which domain functional level supports a combination of Windows NT 4.0, Windows 2000, and Windows Server 2003 domain controllers?

   a. Windows 2000 native

   b. Windows 2000 mixed

   c. Windows Server 2003 interim

   d. Windows Server 2003

   b

2. If a Windows 2000 domain controller in a Windows 2000 Active Directory environment running in native mode is upgraded to Windows Server 2003, which Windows Server 2003 domain functional level will be configured by default?

   a. Windows 2000 mixed

   b. Windows Server 2003 interim

   c. Windows Server 2003

   d. Windows 2000 native

   d

3. Which of the following must be true for a Windows Server 2003 Active Directory forest to be raised to the Windows Server 2003 forest functional level? (Choose all that apply.)

   a. All domains must be configured to the Windows Server 2003 domain functional level.

   b. All domains must be configured to at least the Windows 2000 native domain functional level.

   c. All domain controllers must be running either Windows 2000 or Windows Server 2003.

   d. All domain controllers must be running Windows Server 2003.

   b, d

Lesson 3 Review

1. What is an application directory partition?

   An application directory partition is a directory partition that is replicated only to specific domain controllers. Only domain controllers running Windows Server 2003 can host a replica of an application directory partition.

2. Name the benefits of using an application directory partition.

   Using an application directory partition provides redundancy, availability, or fault tolerance, by replicating data to a specific domain controller or any set of domain controllers anywhere in the forest; it reduces replication traffic because the application data is replicated only to specific domain controllers; and it allows applications or services that use LDAP to access and store their application data in Active Directory.

3. What is a security descriptor, and how is it used in an application directory partition?

   A security descriptor is a set of access control information attached to a container or object that controls the type of access allowed by users, groups, and computers. When an object is created in an application directory partition, a default security descriptor reference domain is assigned when the application directory partition is created.

4. What considerations should you make before deleting an application directory partition?

   Before deleting the application directory partition, you must identify the applications that use it, determine whether it is safe to delete the last replica, and identify the partition deletion tool provided by the application.

5. Which of the following tools can you use to delete an application directory partition? (Choose all that apply.)

   a. Ntdsutil.exe command-line tool

   b. Application-specific tools from the application vendor

   c. Active Directory Installation Wizard

   d. Active Directory Domains and Trusts console

   e. Active Directory Sites And Services console

   a, b, c

Case Scenario Exercise, Requirement 1

1. Which of the following methods should be used to upgrade the Windows Server 2003 systems at the branch offices to the role of domain controller?

   a. The Configure Your Server Wizard

   b. The Active Directory Installation Wizard

   c. The Active Directory Installation Wizard in conjunction with an answer file

   d. The Active Directory Installation Wizard using a backup from an existing domain controller

   c

2. On which of the following Windows 2000 domain controllers at the head office location will the Adprep.exe utility need to be run prior to upgrading or installing any domain controllers to Windows Server 2003? (Choose all that apply.)

   a. The Schema Master

   b. The PDC Emulator

   c. The Infrastructure Master

   d. The RID Master

   a, c

3. If the current Windows 2000 domain environment is configured in native mode, which domain functional level will be configured by default when the first domain controller is upgraded?

   a. Windows 2000 mixed

   b. Windows 2000 native

   c. Windows Server 2003 interim

   d. Windows Server 2003

   b

Case Scenario Exercise, Requirement 2

1. Which forest or domain functional level will be required for Contoso to create a cross-forest trust relationship with this other organization?

   a. The Windows Server 2003 forest functional level

   b. The Windows 2000 native domain functional level

   c. The Windows 2000 forest functional level

   d. The Windows Server 2003 interim domain functional level

   a

2. Which of the following are true once the domain functional level of contoso.com has been raised to Windows Server 2003? (Choose all that apply.)

   a. The Active Directory environment will support domain renaming.

   b. Windows 2000 domain controllers will no longer be supported.

   c. The domain will support the ability to rename domain controllers.

   d. Windows 2000 member servers will no longer be supported.

   b, c

Case Scenario Exercise, Requirement 3

1. Which of the following are advantages of placing a Windows Server 2003 global catalog server at each branch office site?

   a. User authentication requests will not generate WAN traffic.

   b. Windows Server 2003 domain controllers can take advantage of new replication enhancements.

   c. Global catalog servers eliminate the need for replication over WAN links.

   d. Users can perform directory-wide queries without generating additional WAN traffic.

   a, b, d

2. Which of the following represent reasons why individual domain controllers cannot be configured to use universal group membership caching?

    a. A forest must be configured to the Windows Server 2003 forest functional level before universal group membership caching can be implemented.

    b. Universal group membership caching can be configured at the domain level only.

    c. Universal group membership caching can be configured at the site level only.

    d. Universal group membership caching cannot be implemented in domains running at the Windows 2000 mixed domain functional level.

    c

3 Managing and Maintaining an Active Directory Implementation

Exam Objectives in this Chapter:

- Manage an Active Directory forest and domain structure (Exam 70-296).
    - ❑ Manage trust relationships.
    - ❑ Manage schema modifications.
    - ❑ Add or remove a user principal name (UPN) suffix.
- Implement an Active Directory forest and domain structure (Exam 70-296).
    - ❑ Establish trust relationships. Types of trust relationships include external trusts, shortcut trusts, and cross-forest trusts.
- Restore Active Directory directory services (Exam 70-296).
    - ❑ Perform an authoritative restore operation.
    - ❑ Perform a nonauthoritative restore operation.

Why This Chapter Matters

While Windows Server 2003 provides a stable, capable, and scalable directory service in Active Directory, unfortunately, organizations are typically not as stable: partnerships are formed and dissolved, mergers occur, new applications are rolled out, and occasionally, human or mechanical error can damage Active Directory. In this chapter, you will explore three key components of an Active Directory implementation. First, you will learn how to optimize trust relationships within a forest and establish trust relationships with external domains and forests. Then you will examine the Active Directory schema, which defines the types of objects and attributes that Active Directory can host, and the steps required to modify the schema. Finally, you will learn what it takes to back up and restore Active Directory.

Lessons in this Chapter:

Before You Begin

To complete the hands-on practices and exercises in this chapter, you need:

- Two Microsoft Windows Server 2003 (Standard or Enterprise Edition) systems installed as Server01 and Server02. Server01 should be a domain controller in the contoso.com domain. If Server02 is also a domain controller, consider removing Active Directory prior to beginning the exercises in this chapter.

Lesson 1: Understanding and Managing Trust Relationships and UPNs

This lesson introduces you to trust relationships and the tasks involved in the management of the different types of trusts available in Windows Server 2003 Active Directory. In Chapter 1, you learned that a trust relationship is a logical link between two domains, such as a child domain and its parent domain. In Windows Server 2003 Active Directory environments, trust relationships can be created automatically or manually. The trust relationships that Active Directory creates automatically do not need to be managed. In this lesson, you will learn how to plan, create, and administer the various types of trust relationships that can be configured manually.

After this lesson, you will be able to

- Name the protocols used in Active Directory trust relationships
- Describe the different types of trust relationships supported in Windows Server 2003 Active Directory
- Explain when it is necessary to create shortcut, realm, external, or forest trust relationships
- Create shortcut, realm, external, and forest trust relationships
- Administer shortcut, realm, external, and forest trust relationships
- Understand the purpose of UPN suffixes, as well as how to define additional UPN suffixes by using Active Directory Domains And Trusts

Estimated lesson time: 30 minutes

Trust Relationships

At the most basic level, a trust relationship is a logical link established between domains to allow pass-through authentication. There are two domains in every trust relationship—a trusting domain and a trusted domain. The trusting domain, which holds shared resources such as folders and printers, allows access by authenticated users of a trusted domain.

In Microsoft Windows NT, trust relationships were one-way and nontransitive by default. These trust relationships were limited to the two domains involved, and the relationship was one-way only. In other words, just because one domain trusted another, it didn't mean that the reverse was true. Similarly, if DomainA trusted DomainB, and DomainB trusted DomainC, that did not mean that DomainA trusted DomainC because Windows NT trust relationships were not transitive. In environments that included many domains that required trust relationships, the number of one-way trusts that needed to be created and managed could quickly become not only administratively overwhelming, but also confusing.

In Windows Server 2003 Active Directory, trust relationships have the following three main characteristics:

- Trust relationships can be created either manually or automatically.
- Trust relationships can be either transitive or nontransitive.
- Trust relationships can be either one-way or two-way.

A trust relationship is automatically configured between a parent domain and a child domain in Windows Server 2003 Active Directory, and a trust relationship is automatically configured between the root domain of each tree in a forest and the forest root domain. Within a forest, these trust relationships are automatically two-way, transitive trusts. These default forest trust relationships ensure that users in any domain in a forest have the ability to access resources in the other.

Authentication Protocols and Trust Relationships

Windows Server 2003 Active Directory authenticates users and applications by using one of two protocols—Kerberos version 5 or NT LAN Manager (NTLM). Kerberos version 5 is the default protocol used by computers running Windows Server 2003, Windows XP, and Windows 2000. If a computer involved in a transaction does not support Kerberos version 5, the NTLM protocol is used instead.

When a client running Kerberos version 5 logs on and then needs to access resources located on a server in its local domain, the following processes occur:

1. As part of the logon process, the authenticated user is granted what is known as a ticket-granting ticket (TGT) by a key distribution center (KDC). In a Windows Server 2003 Active Directory environment, a domain controller acts as the KDC.

2. When the user needs to access resources on a server in the same domain, the user must first obtain a valid service ticket for that server. The client presents the TGT to the KDC, requesting a service ticket to access the server on which the resources reside. The KDC checks its domain database for the service principal name (SPN) for the requested server. Because the requested server is in the same domain, a service ticket is passed back to the client.

3. After obtaining this service ticket from the KDC, the client presents it to the server and can then access resources on that server (according to the permissions associated with the requested resource).

Kerberos version 5 plays a similar role when a user needs to access resources on a server in another domain within an Active Directory forest. However, this process is somewhat more complex, as it involves crossing the trust path between the local and remote domains. For example, consider a situation where a user in domain01.contoso.com needs to access resources in domain02.contoso.com, another domain in the same tree. As illustrated in Figure 3-1, the request in this case must cross multiple trusts, specifically:

1. The parent-child trust relationship between domain01.contoso.com and contoso.com

2. The parent-child trust relationship between contoso.com and domain02.contoso.com

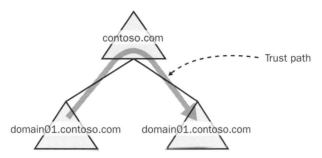

Figure 3-1   The trust path between two child domains

When the client running Kerberos version 5 logs on in the domain01.contoso.com domain and then needs to access resources located on a server in the domain02.contoso.com domain, the following processes occur:

1. As part of the logon process, the authenticated user's workstation is granted a TGT by a key distribution center (KDC), a domain controller in the domain01.contoso.com domain.

2. The client presents the TGT to the local KDC, requesting a ticket to access the server in domain02.contoso.com.

3. The KDC will check its domain database for the SPN of the requested server. Because the server does not exist in its domain, the KDC will query a global catalog server to see whether any domains in the forest contain this SPN. The global catalog server sends the requested information back to the KDC.

4. The KDC in domain01 then sends a referral back to the client for the contoso.com domain.

5. The client then contacts a KDC in the contoso.com domain, asking for a referral to a KDC (domain controller) in domain02.contoso.com. The KDC in contoso.com sends this referral back to the client.

6. The client workstation then contacts the KDC it was referred to in domain02.contoso.com, requesting a service ticket for the server on which the required resources reside. The KDC in domain02.contoso.com passes the service ticket to the client.

7. After obtaining this service ticket, the client presents it to the server in domain02.contoso.com and can then access resources on that server (according to the permissions associated with the requested resource).

This same process is used whenever a client in one domain within a forest wants to access resources in another. As you might imagine, the trust path between domains can become very long in Active Directory forests that include many trees and domains. Ways to circumvent long trust paths will be looked at shortly.

When a client tries to access resources on a server in another domain using NTLM authentication, the server containing the resource must contact a domain controller in the client's account domain to verify the user's credentials.

Trust Types

Windows Server 2003 Active Directory supports the following types of trust relationships:

- **Tree-root trust**   Tree-root trust relationships are automatically established when you add a new tree root domain to an existing forest. This trust relationship is transitive and two-way.

- **Parent-child trust**   Parent-child trust relationships are automatically established when you add a new child domain to an existing tree. This trust relationship is also transitive and two-way.

- **Shortcut trust**   Shortcut trusts are trust relationships that are manually created by systems administrators. These trusts can be defined between any two domains in a forest, generally for the purpose of improving user logon and resource access performance. Shortcut trusts can be especially useful in situations where users in one domain often need to access resources in another, but a long path of transitive trusts separates the two domains. Often referred to as cross-link trusts, shortcut trust relationships are transitive and can be configured as one-way or two-way as needs dictate.

- **Realm trust**   Realm trusts are manually created by systems administrators between a non–Windows Kerberos realm and a Windows Server 2003 Active Directory domain. This type of trust relationship provides cross-platform interoperability with security services in any Kerberos version 5 realm, such as a UNIX implementation. Realm trusts can be either transitive or nontransitive, and one-way or two-way as needs dictate.

- **External trust**   External trusts are manually created by systems administrators between Active Directory domains that are in different forests, or between a Windows Server 2003 Active Directory domain and a Windows NT 4.0 domain. These trust relationships provide backward compatibility with Windows NT 4.0 environments, and communication with domains located in other forests that are not configured to use forest trusts. External trusts are nontransitive and can be configured as either one-way or two-way as needs dictate.

- **Forest trust**   Forest trusts are trust relationships that are manually created by systems administrators between forest root domains in two separate forests. If a forest trust relationship is two-way, it effectively allows authentication requests from users in one forest to reach another, and for users in either forest to access resources in both. Forest trust relationships are transitive between two forests only and can be configured as either one-way or two-way as needs dictate.

> **Note**   When a user is authenticated, the presence of a trust relationship does not guarantee access to resources in another domain. Access to resources is determined solely by the rights and permissions granted to the user in the trusting domain.

The Windows Server 2003 New Trust Wizard, which is used to establish trust relationships, simplifies the process by allowing administrators on each side of the trust relationship to create their side of the trust and then to confirm the successful completion of the trust. Alternatively, one administrator with sufficient authority in each domain can complete both sides of the trust relationship using the wizard only once. Unfortunately, the wizard adds two new terms regarding trusts, and it is important to keep the distinction between the terms in mind:

- **Incoming Trust**   When an administrator in the trusted domain is establishing the trust relationship, the trust is considered incoming, meaning that prior to accessing resources in the trusting domain, users can be authenticated by passing authentication through to the trusted domain—into the trusted domain.

- **Outgoing Trust**   When an administrator in the trusting domain is establishing the trust relationship, the trust is considered outgoing, meaning that prior to accessing resources in the domain, users from the trusted domain can be authenticated by passing authentication through to the trusted domain—out to the trusted domain.

Understanding Forest Trusts

If users in one forest needed to access resources in another in Windows 2000 environments, administrators had to create an external trust relationship between two domains, one in each forest. Because external trusts are one-way and nontransitive, these relationships are limited to only the two domains specified and do not extend any type of trust path to other forest domains. For example, if an external trust relationship was configured between DomainA in Forest1 and DomainB in Forest2 as illustrated in Figure 3-2, users in DomainA could potentially access resources in DomainB but not in any other domains in Forest2. If users in a domain in Forest1 needed access to resources in many domains in Forest2, additional external trust relationships would need to be configured.

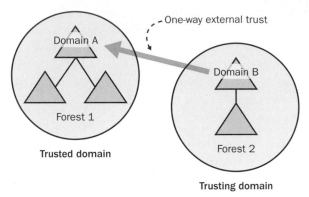

Figure 3-2   An external trust relationship

Forest trusts are a new feature in Windows Server 2003 Active Directory, extending transitive trusts beyond the scope of a single forest to a second Windows Server 2003 Active Directory forest. Forest trusts provide the following benefits:

■ Simplified management, because forest trusts reduce the number of external trusts necessary to share resources with a second forest.

■ Two-way transitive trust relationships between all domains in the two forests.

■ UPN authentication can be used across two forests.

■ Both the Kerberos and NTLM authentication protocols can be used to help improve the trustworthiness of authorization data transferred between forests.

■ Administrative flexibility, because administrators can choose to split collaborative delegation efforts with other administrators into forest-wide administrative units.

Forest trusts can be created between only two forests and are transitive between only two forests. Therefore, if a forest trust is created between Forest1 and Forest2, and a forest trust is also created between Forest2 and Forest3, Forest1 does not have a trust relationship with Forest3. If a transitive trust relationship were required between Forest1 and Forest3, an additional forest trust relationship would need to be created.

> **Note**   To create a forest trust relationship, both forests must be configured to the Windows Server 2003 forest functional level.

> **Real World   Forest Trusts**
>
> Forest trust relationships do not extend beyond two forests for a very good reason. Consider a scenario in which one company has created forest trust relationships with two different and unrelated partner organizations. If the transitive nature of forest trusts extended beyond two forests, users in the unrelated organizations could potentially be granted access to each other's forest via the trusted partner, which would present a serious security risk.

Planning Trust Relationships

As an administrator, you must plan trust relationships to provide users with access to the resources they require while at the same time maintaining proper security. When you add a Windows Server 2003 Active Directory domain to an existing Windows Server 2003 Active Directory forest, a tree-root or a parent-child trust relationship is established automatically. Both of these trust relationships are two-way and transitive, and are established automatically when the new domain is created. Once established, these trust relationships generally do not need to be managed.

While tree-root and parent-child trust relationships are created automatically, the four remaining types of trusts relationships looked at earlier do need to be manually configured. The following sections explore the details of when to create shortcut, realm, external, and forest trusts.

When to Create a Shortcut Trust

Shortcut trusts are transitive one-way or two-way trusts that can be used to optimize the authentication process between domains that are logically distant from each other. In an Active Directory forest, authentication requests must travel over an established trust path between domains. As mentioned earlier, a *trust path* is a series of transitive trust relationships that must be traversed to pass authentication requests between any two domains. In a large or complex forest, following the trust path can take time and affect performance; each time clients are referred to another domain controller, the chances of a failure or of encountering a slow link are increased. Windows Server 2003 Active Directory provides a means for improving query-response performance through the use of shortcut trusts. Shortcut trusts help to shorten the path that authentication requests must traverse between domains that are not already directly connected.

Figure 3-3 illustrates a shortcut trust created to shorten the trust path and improve query-response performance between DomainA and DomainF. If the shortcut trust were not created, the client in DomainA would have to "walk" the trust path through domains B, C, D, and E before being able to communicate with the domain controller in DomainF to verify the authentication request.

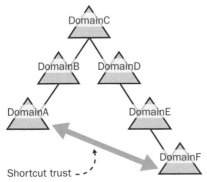

Figure 3-3   A shortcut trust relationship between two domains in the same forest

- **One-Way Shortcut Trusts**   When a one-way shortcut trust is established between two domains, the time needed to fulfill authentication requests is reduced, but only in one direction. If a one-way shortcut trust were established between DomainA and DomainF, for example, authentication requests made in DomainA to DomainF could take full advantage of the new one-way trust path. However, if authentication requests from DomainF to DomainA are made, they cannot use the one-way shortcut trust path that was created between the two domains and would default to crossing the existing trust path hierarchy.

- **Two-Way Shortcut Trusts**   When a two-way shortcut trust is established between two domains, it can help to optimize authentication requests made by users located in either domain. Therefore, authentication requests made from either DomainA to DomainF or from DomainF to DomainA could use the shortened shortcut trust path.

> **Important**   To create a shortcut trust, you must be a member of Enterprise Admins or Domain Admins in both domains, or you must have been delegated the proper authority.

When to Create a Realm Trust

A realm trust can be established between any non–Windows Kerberos version 5 realm and a Windows Server 2003 domain. This allows cross-platform interoperability with security services based on other Kerberos version 5 implementations. A common reason for creating a realm trust would be to grant Active Directory users the ability to access resources in a UNIX Kerberos version 5 realm, without requiring them to authenticate to those resources separately. Conversely, a realm trust could also be used to grant users in a UNIX Kerberos version 5 realm access to resources in a Windows Server 2003 Active Directory domain.

> **Important**   To create a realm trust, you must be a member of Enterprise Admins or Domain Admins in the Windows Server 2003 domain, or you must have been delegated the proper authority. You must also have appropriate administrative privileges in the target Kerberos realm.

When to Create an External Trust

You can create an external trust to form a one-way or two-way nontransitive trust relationship with another domain outside of your forest. External trusts are sometimes necessary when users need access to resources located in a Windows NT 4.0 domain or in any domain located in a different forest that is not configured with a forest trust.

When a trust is established between a domain in a forest and a domain outside of that forest, security principals from the external domain can access resources in the internal domain. Active Directory creates a foreign security principal object in the internal domain to represent each security principal from the trusted external domain that belongs to a group in the local domain. You can view foreign security principals in the Active Directory Users And Computers console when the Advanced Features option is enabled from the View menu.

Note If you upgrade a Windows NT 4.0 domain to a Windows Server 2003 Active Directory, existing trust relationships remain in the same state.

Accessing Resources Across Domains Joined by an External Trust

Using Active Directory Domains And Trusts, you can determine the scope of authentication between two domains that are joined by an external trust. You can set selective authentication differently for outgoing and incoming external trusts, which allows you to make flexible authentication decisions between external domains. You select domain-wide or selective authentication on the Outgoing Trust Authentication Level page when you set up an external trust using the New Trust Wizard.

If you apply domain-wide authentication to an external trust, users in the trusted domain have the same level of access to resources in the local domain as users who belong to the local domain. For example, if DomainA trusts DomainB and domain-wide authentication is used, any user from DomainB can access any resource in DomainA (assuming the user has the required permissions).

If you apply selective authentication to an external trust, you need to manually designate which users in the trusted domain can authenticate for specific computers in the trusting domain. To do this, use Active Directory Users And Computers to open the access control list (ACL) for each computer in the trusting domain that hosts resources that might be accessed by any users in the trusted domain. Grant users in the trusted domain (or groups that include users in the trusted domain) the access control right Allowed To Authenticate.

Off the Record   When a user authenticates across a trust with the Selective Authentication option enabled, an Other Organization security ID (SID) is added to the user's authorization data. The presence of this SID prompts a check on the resource domain to ensure that the user is allowed to authenticate to the particular service. Once the user is authenticated, the server to which the user authenticates adds the This Organization SID if it is not already present. Only one of these special SIDs can be present in an authenticated user's context.

Administrators in each domain can add objects from one domain to ACLs on shared resources in the other domain. You can use the Security tab of a resource to add or remove objects residing in one domain to resources in the other domain.

Important   To create an external trust, you must be a member of Enterprise Admins or Domain Admins in the local domain, or you must have been delegated the proper authority. Similar authority is required for the domain at the end of the external trust.

When to Create a Forest Trust

Creating a forest trust between two forest root domains creates a transitive trust relationship that allows users from any domain in either forest to access resources throughout both forests. Forest trusts are useful for application service providers, organizations undergoing mergers or acquisitions, collaborative business extranets, and organizations seeking solutions for administrative autonomy. To provide a higher degree of flexibility, forest trusts can be configured as both one-way and two-way trust relationships.

- **One-Way Forest Trusts**   In a one-way forest trust, all domains in the trusted forest can access resources in the trusting forest, but not vice versa. For example, if you create a one-way forest trust between Forest1 (the trusted forest) and Forest2 (the trusting forest), users in Forest1 can access resources in Forest2, assuming the Forest1 users have been granted appropriate permissions. However, users in Forest2 will not be able to access resources in Forest1 unless a second one-way forest trust is established.

- **Two-Way Forest Trusts**   In a two-way forest trust, every domain in one forest implicitly trusts every domain in its partner forest automatically. Users in either forest can access any resource located anywhere in both forests, again assuming the users have been granted appropriate permissions.

Accessing Resources Across Domains Joined by a Forest Trust

Using Active Directory Domains And Trusts, you can determine the scope of authentication between two forests that are joined by a forest trust. You can set selective authentication differently for outgoing and incoming forest trusts, which allows you to make flexible access-control decisions between forests. You select domain-wide or selective authentication on the Outgoing Trust Authentication Level page when you set up a forest trust using the New Trust Wizard.

If you use forest-wide authentication on a forest trust, users from the trusted forest have the same level of access to resources in the local forest as users who belong to the local forest. For example, if ForestA trusts ForestB (ForestB has an incoming trust from ForestA; ForestA has an outgoing trust to ForestB) and forest-wide authentication is used, any user from ForestB can access any resource in ForestA (assuming the user has the required permissions).

If you set selective authentication on a forest trust, you must manually designate which users in the trusted forest can authenticate for specific computers in the trusting forest. To do this, use Active Directory Users And Computers to open the access control list for each computer in the trusting forest that hosts resources that may be accessed by any users in the trusted forest's domains. Grant users in the trusted forest (or groups that include users in the trusted forest) the access control right Allowed To Authenticate.

Administrators in each forest can add objects from one forest to access control lists (ACLs) on shared resources in the other forest. You can use the Security tab of a resource to add or remove objects residing in one forest to resources in another forest.

> **Important**   To create a forest trust, you must be a member of Enterprise Admins (or have been delegated appropriate authority) in both forests. Before creating a forest trust, you need to verify that you have the correct DNS infrastructure in place and that the appropriate forest functional level for each has been configured. For more information on what to verify before creating a forest trust, refer to the "Creating a Forest Trust" section of this chapter.

> **Exam Tip**   Know when to create each type of Windows Server 2003 Active Directory trust relationship.

Creating Trust Relationships

Once you have determined the types of trust relationships that will meet the needs of your organization, it is time to actually implement the trusts. This section contains procedures for creating the shortcut, realm, external, and forest trust relationships looked at in this lesson. The tool used to create trust relationships on a Windows Server 2003 system is the New Trust Wizard, located in the Active Directory Domains And Trusts tool.

Creating a Shortcut Trust

A shortcut trust is a trust relationship between two domains in the same forest. Shortcut trusts are typically implemented to make user authentication and access to resources faster in forests that include long trust paths.

To create a shortcut trust, complete the following steps.

1. Click Start, point to Administrative Tools, and then click Active Directory Domains And Trusts.

2. In the console tree, right-click the domain for which you want to create a shortcut trust, and then click Properties.

3. In the Properties dialog box, click the Trusts tab.

4. In the Trusts tab shown in Figure 3-4, click New Trust to launch the New Trust Wizard.

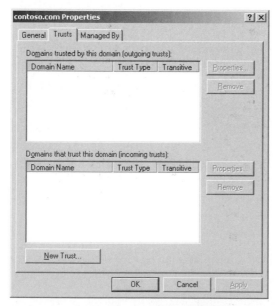

Figure 3-4   The Trusts tab on the Properties dialog box for a domain

5. On the Welcome To The New Trust Wizard page, click Next.

6. On the Trust Name page, type the DNS name of the target domain with which you want to establish a trust in the Name box, and then click Next.

7. On the Direction Of Trust page, shown in Figure 3-5, select one of the following choices:

❑ If you want all users in both domains to be able to access all resources in either domain, click Two-Way, and then click Next.

❑ If you want only users in this domain to be able to access resources in the other domain, click One-Way: Incoming, and then click Next.

Note By selecting the One-Way: Incoming option, users in the other domain will not be able to access any resources in this domain.

❑ If you want only users in the other domain to be able to access resources in this domain, click One-Way: Outgoing, and then click Next.

Note By selecting the One-Way: Outgoing option, users in this domain will not be able to access any resources in the other domain.

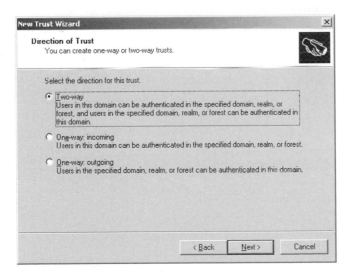

Figure 3-5   The Direction Of Trust page

8. On the Sides Of Trust page, shown in Figure 3-6, select one of the following choices:

❑ Select This Domain Only to create the trust relationship in the local domain. Click Next.

❑ Select Both This Domain And The Specified Domain to create a trust relationship in the local domain and a trust relationship in the specified domain. If you select this option, you must have trust creation privileges in the specified domain. Click Next.

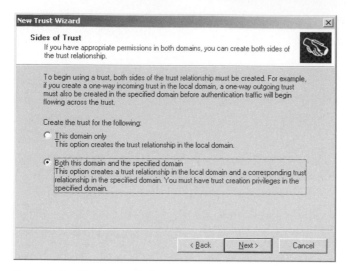

Figure 3-6   The Sides Of Trust page

9. Select one of the following paths, depending on your choices in steps 7 and 8:

   ❑ If you selected Two-Way or One-Way: Outgoing in step 7 and This Domain Only in step 8, the Outgoing Trust Authentication Level page appears, as shown in Figure 3-7. Select Domain-Wide Authentication to automatically authenticate all users in the specified domain for all resources in the local domain. Select Selective Authentication if you do not want to automatically authenticate all users in the specified domain for all resources in the local domain. Click Next. On the Trust Password page, type a password for the trust in the Trust Password and Confirm Trust Password boxes. Click Next.

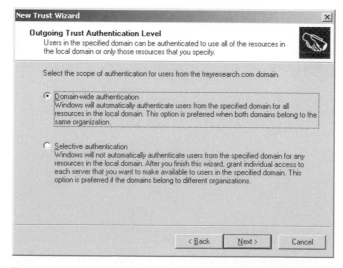

Figure 3-7   The Outgoing Trust Authentication Level page

❑ If you selected One-Way: Incoming in step 7 and This Domain Only in step 8, the Trust Password page appears. Type a password for the trust in the Trust Password and Confirm Trust Password boxes. Click Next.

❑ If you selected Both This Domain And The Specified Domain in step 8, the User Name And Password page appears, as shown in Figure 3-8. Type the user name and password of an account that has administrative privileges in the specified domain. Click Next.

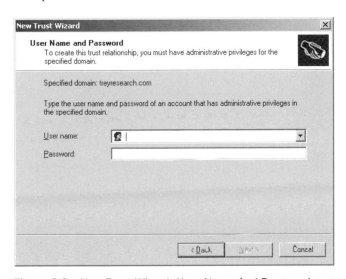

Figure 3-8 New Trust Wizard, User Name And Password page

10. On the Trust Selections Complete page, verify that the correct trust settings are configured, and then click Next. The wizard creates the trust.

11. On the Trust Creation Complete page, verify the settings, and then click Next.

12. On the Confirm Outgoing Trust page shown in Figure 3-9, select Yes, Confirm The Outgoing Trust if you created both sides of the trust. If you created only one side, choose No, Do Not Confirm The Outgoing Trust. Click Next.

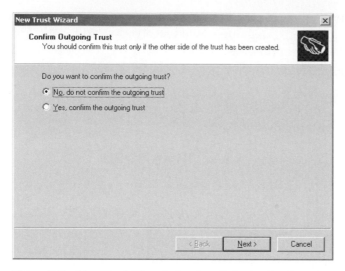

Figure 3-9   New Trust Wizard, Confirm Outgoing Trust page

13. On the Confirm Incoming Trust page shown in Figure 3-10, select Yes, Confirm The Incoming Trust if you created both sides of the trust. If you created only one side, choose No, Do Not Confirm The Incoming Trust. Click Next.

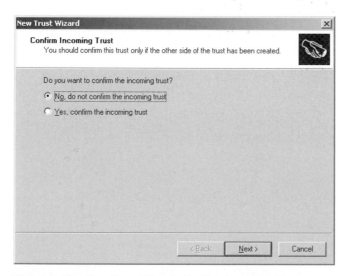

Figure 3-10   New Trust Wizard, Confirm Incoming Trust page

14. On the Completing The New Trust Wizard page, verify the settings, and then click Finish.

15. Note the presence of the shortcut trust you just set up in the Trusts tab of the Properties dialog box for the domain. An example is shown in Figure 3-11. Click OK.

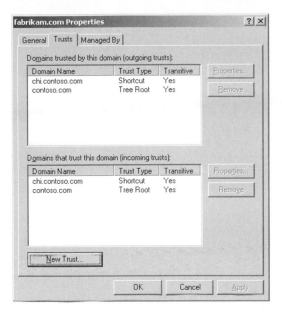

Figure 3-11   Trusts tab with shortcut trust configured

Creating a Realm Trust

A realm trust is a trust between a non–Windows Kerberos realm and a Windows Server 2003 domain, created to allow cross-platform interoperability with security services based on other Kerberos version 5 implementations.

To create a realm trust, complete the following steps.

1. Click Start, point to Administrative Tools, and then click Active Directory Domains And Trusts.

2. In the console tree, right-click the domain for which you want to create a realm trust, and then click Properties.

3. In the Properties dialog box, click the Trusts tab.

4. On the Trusts tab, click New Trust.

5. On the Welcome To The New Trust Wizard page, click Next.

6. On the Trust Name page, type the DNS name of the target realm with which you want to establish a trust in the Name box, and then click Next.

7. On the Trust Type page shown in Figure 3-12, select the Realm Trust option, and then click Next.

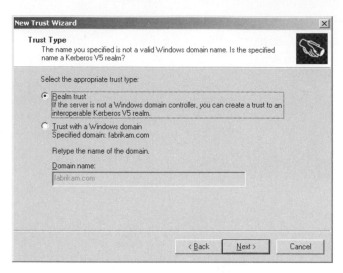

Figure 3-12   New Trust Wizard, Trust Type page

8. On the Transitivity Of Trust page shown in Figure 3-13, select one of the following choices.

   ❑ If you want only this domain and the specified realm to form a trust relationship, select Nontransitive, and then click Next.

   ❑ If you want this domain and all trusted domains to form a trust relationship with the specified realm and all trusted realms, select Transitive, and then click Next.

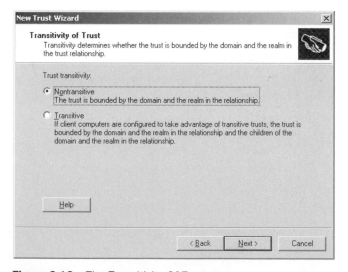

Figure 3-13   The Transitivity Of Trust page

9. On the Direction Of Trust page, select one of the following choices.

❑ If you want all users in both the domain and the realm to be able to access all resources in either the domain or the realm, select Two-Way, and then click Next.

❑ If you want only users in this domain to be able to access resources in the realm, select One-Way: Incoming, and then click Next.

Note   By selecting the One-Way: Incoming option, users in the realm will not be able to access any resources in this domain.

❑ If you want only users in the realm to be able to access resources in this domain, select One-Way: Outgoing, and then click Next.

Note   By selecting the One-Way: Outgoing option, users in this domain will not be able to access any resources in the realm.

10. On the Trust Password page, type the trust password in the Trust Password and Confirm Trust Password boxes. This password must match the password used in the realm. Click Next.

11. On the Trust Selections Complete page, verify that the correct trust settings appear, and then click Next.

12. On the Completing The New Trust Wizard page, verify the settings, and then click Finish.

13. Note the presence of the realm trust you just set up in the Trusts tab of the Properties dialog box for the domain. Click OK.

Creating an External Trust

An external trust is a trust relationship between a Windows Server 2003 domain and another domain outside of the same forest. External trusts are created to provide backward compatibility with Windows NT environments, or to facilitate communications with domains located in another forest not joined by a forest trust. Before you can create an external trust, you must configure a DNS forwarder *on both* of the DNS servers that are authoritative for the trusting domains.

To configure a DNS conditional forwarder, complete the following steps on both authoritative DNS servers:

1. Click Start, point to Administrative Tools, and then click DNS.

2. In the console tree, right-click the DNS server you want to configure, and then click Properties.

3. In the Properties dialog box for the DNS server, click the Forwarders tab.

4. On the Forwarders tab, specify the DNS domain names that require queries to be forwarded (conditional forwarding) in the DNS Domain box by clicking New and typing the domain name in the New Forwarder dialog box, as shown in Figure 3-14. Type the IP address or addresses of the server or servers to which the queries are forwarded in the Selected Domain's Forwarder IP Address List, and then click Add.

Figure 3-14   Configuring a new DNS forwarder for conditional forwarding

5. Click OK in the Forwarders tab, and close the DNS administrative tool.

To create an external trust, complete the following steps:

1. Click Start, point to Administrative Tools, and then click Active Directory Domains And Trusts.

2. In the console tree, right-click the domain for which you want to create an external trust, and then click Properties.

3. In the Properties dialog box, click the Trusts tab.

4. On the Trusts tab, click New Trust.

5. On the Welcome To The New Trust Wizard page, click Next.

6. On the Trust Name page, type the DNS name of the target domain in the second forest with which you want to establish a trust in the Name box, and then click Next.

7. If the forest functional level is set to Windows Server 2003, the Trust Type page appears, as shown in Figure 3-15. Select the External Trust option, and then click Next. Otherwise, skip to the next step.

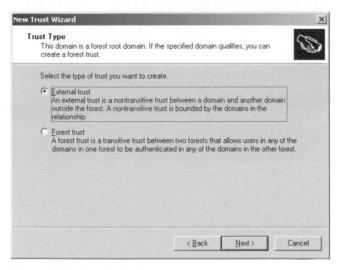

Figure 3-15   The Trust Type page

8. On the Direction Of Trust page, select one of the following choices:

❑ If you want all users in both domains to be able to access all resources in either domain, select Two-Way, and then click Next.

❑ If you want only users in this domain to be able to access resources in the second domain, select One-Way: Incoming, and then click Next.

Note   By selecting the One-Way: Incoming option, users in the domain in the second forest will not be able to access any resources in the domain in this forest.

❑ If you want only users in the second domain to be able to access resources in this domain, select One-Way: Outgoing, and then click Next.

Note   By selecting the One-Way: Outgoing option, users in the domain in this forest will not be able to access any resources in the domain in the second forest.

9. On the Sides Of Trust page, select one of the following choices:

❑ Select This Domain Only to create the trust relationship in the local domain. Click Next.

❑ Select Both This Domain And The Specified Domain to create a trust relationship in the local domain and a trust relationship in the specified domain. If you select this option, you must have trust creation privileges in the specified domain. Click Next.

10. Select one of the following paths, depending on your choices in steps 8 and 9:

    ❑ If you selected Two-Way or One-Way: Outgoing in step 8, and This Domain Only in step 9, the Outgoing Trust Authentication Level page appears. Select Domain-Wide Authentication to automatically authenticate all users in the specified domain for all resources in the local domain. Select Selective Authentication if you do not want to automatically authenticate all users in the specified domain for all resources in the local domain. Click Next. On the Trust Password page, type a password for the trust in the Trust Password and Confirm Trust Password boxes. Click Next.

    ❑ If you selected One-Way: Incoming in step 8 and This Domain Only in step 9, the Trust Password page appears. Type a password for the trust in the Trust Password and Confirm Trust Password boxes. Click Next.

    ❑ If you selected Both This Domain And The Specified Domain in step 9, the User Name And Password page appears. Type the user name and password of an account that has administrative privileges in the specified domain. Click Next.

11. On the Trust Selections Complete page, verify that the correct trust settings are configured, and then click Next. The wizard creates the trust.

12. On the Trust Creation Complete page, verify the settings, and then click Next.

13. On the Confirm Outgoing Trust page, select Yes, Confirm The Outgoing Trust if you created both sides of the trust. If you created only one side, choose No, Do Not Confirm The Outgoing Trust. Click Next.

14. On the Confirm Incoming Trust page select Yes, Confirm The Incoming Trust if you created both sides of the trust. If you created only one side, choose No, Do Not Confirm The Incoming Trust. Click Next.

15. On the Completing The New Trust Wizard page, verify the settings, and then click Finish.

16. Note the presence of the external trust you just set up in the Trusts tab of the Properties dialog box for the domain. An example is shown in Figure 3-16. Click OK.

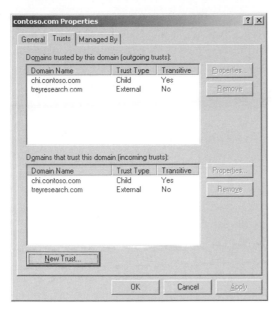

Figure 3-16   Properties dialog box for a domain, Trusts tab, showing an external trust

Creating a Forest Trust

A forest trust is a trust between two forest root domains, created to allow authentication requests made from one forest to reach another. The procedure for creating a forest trust is similar to the one used for creating an external trust. However, before you can create a forest trust, you must complete the following preliminary tasks.

■ Configure a DNS root server that is authoritative over both forest DNS servers that you want to form a trust with, or configure a DNS forwarder on both of the DNS servers that are authoritative for the trusting forests.

■ Ensure that the forest functional level for both forests is Windows Server 2003.

To configure a DNS forwarder, complete the following steps:

1. Click Start, point to Administrative Tools, and then click DNS.

2. In the console tree, right-click the DNS server you want to configure, and then click Properties.

3. In the Properties dialog box for the DNS server, click the Forwarders tab.

4. On the Forwarders tab, specify the DNS domain names that require queries to be forwarded (conditional forwarding) in the DNS Domain box by clicking New and typing the domain name in the New Forwarder dialog box. Type the IP address or addresses of the server or servers to which the queries are forwarded in the Selected Domain's Forwarder IP Address List, and then click Add.

5. Click OK in the Forwarders tab.

To create a forest trust, complete the following steps:

1. Click Start, point to Administrative Tools, and then click Active Directory Domains And Trusts.

2. In the console tree, right-click the domain node in the first forest for which you want to create a forest trust, and then click Properties.

3. In the Properties dialog box, click the Trusts tab.

4. On the Trusts tab, click New Trust.

5. On the Welcome To The New Trust Wizard page, click Next.

6. On the Trust Name page, type the DNS name of the target domain in the second forest with which you want to establish a trust in the Name box, and then click Next.

7. On the Trust Type page, select the Forest Trust option, and then click Next.

Note   If the Forest Trust option does not appear, you must confirm that you have completed the preliminary tasks for creating a forest trust.

8. On the Direction Of Trust page, select one of the following choices.

   ❑ If you want all users in both forests to be able to access all resources in either forest, click Two-Way, and then click Next.

   ❑ If you want only users in this forest to be able to access resources in the second forest, select One-Way: Incoming, and then click Next.

Note   By selecting the One-Way: Incoming option, users in the second forest will not be able to access any resources in this forest.

   ❑ If you want only users in the second forest to be able to access resources in this forest, select One-Way: Outgoing, and then click Next.

Note   By selecting the One-Way: Outgoing option, users in this forest will not be able to access any resources in the second forest.

9. On the Sides Of Trust page, select one of the following choices:

❑ Select This Domain Only to create the trust relationship in the local forest. Click Next.

❑ Select Both This Domain And The Specified Domain to create a trust relationship in the local forest and a trust relationship in the specified forest. If you select this option, you must have trust creation privileges in the specified forest. Click Next.

10. Select one of the following paths, depending on your choices in steps 8 and 9:

❑ If you selected Two-Way or One-Way: Outgoing in step 8 and This Domain Only in step 9, the Outgoing Trust Authentication Level page appears. Select Domain-Wide Authentication to automatically authenticate all users in the specified forest for all resources in the local forest. Select Selective Authentication if you do not want to automatically authenticate all users in the specified forest for all resources in the local forest. Click Next. On the Trust Password page, type a password for the trust in the Trust Password and Confirm Trust Password boxes. Click Next.

❑ If you selected One-Way: Incoming in step 8 and This Domain Only in step 9, the Trust Password page appears. Type a password for the trust in the Trust Password and Confirm Trust Password boxes. Click Next.

❑ If you selected Both This Domain And The Specified Domain in step 9, the User Name And Password page appears. Type the user name and password of an account that has administrative privileges in the specified forest. Click Next.

11. On the Trust Selections Complete page, verify that the correct trust settings are configured, and then click Next. The wizard creates the trust.

12. On the Trust Creation Complete page, verify the settings, and then click Next.

13. On the Confirm Outgoing Trust page, select Yes, Confirm The Outgoing Trust if you created both sides of the trust. If you created only one side, choose No, Do Not Confirm The Outgoing Trust. Click Next.

14. On the Confirm Incoming Trust page, select Yes, Confirm The Incoming Trust if you created both sides of the trust. If you created only one side, choose No, Do Not Confirm The Incoming Trust. Click Next.

15. On the Completing The New Trust Wizard page, verify the settings, and then click Finish.

16. Note the presence of the forest trust you just set up in the Trusts tab of the Properties dialog box for the domain. An example is shown in Figure 3-17. Click OK.

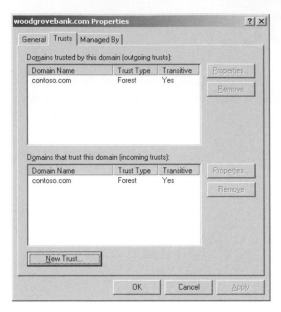

Figure 3-17   Properties dialog box for a domain, Trusts tab, showing a forest trust

Administering Trust Relationships

To administer trust relationships, you use Active Directory Domains And Trusts. Using this tool, you can verify and remove shortcut, realm, external, and forest trusts.

To verify a trust, complete the following steps:

1. Click Start, point to Administrative Tools, and then click Active Directory Domains And Trusts.

2. In the console tree, right-click one of the domains involved in the trust relationship that you want to verify, and then click Properties.

3. In the Properties dialog box, click the Trusts tab.

4. On the Trusts tab, click the trust to be verified in either the Domains Trusted By This Domain (Outgoing Trusts) box or the Domains That Trust This Domain (Incoming Trusts) box, and then click Properties.

5. In the Properties dialog box for the trust shown in Figure 3-18, click Validate.

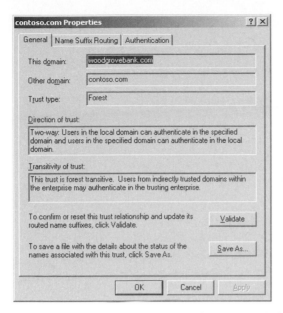

Figure 3-18   Properties dialog box for a trust relationship

6. In the Active Directory dialog box shown in Figure 3-19, select one of the following choices:

   ❑ Select No, Do Not Validate The Incoming Trust to validate only the outgoing trust, and then click OK.

   ❑ Select Yes, Validate The Incoming Trust to validate the outgoing and the incoming trust. Type the user name and password of an account with administrative privileges in the other domain in the User Name and Password boxes, respectively. Click OK.

Figure 3-19   Active Directory dialog box

7. In the Active Directory message box, a message indicates that the trust has been verified. Click OK.

8. In the Properties dialog box for the trust, click OK.

9. On the Trusts tab, click OK.

To remove a trust, complete the following steps:

1. Click Start, point to Administrative Tools, and then click Active Directory Domains And Trusts.

2. In the console tree, right-click one of the domain nodes involved in the trust you want to remove, and then click Properties.

3. In the Properties dialog box, click the Trusts tab.

4. On the Trusts tab, click the trust to be removed in the Domains Trusted By This Domain (Outgoing Trusts) box, and then click Remove.

5. In the Active Directory dialog box shown in Figure 3-20, select one of the following choices:

❑ Select No, Remove The Trust From The Local Domain Only to remove the trust from the local domain, and then click OK.

❑ Select Yes, Remove The Trust From Both The Local Domain And The Other Domain, to remove the trust from both domains. Type the user name and password of an account with administrative privileges in the other domain in the User Name and Password boxes, respectively. Click OK.

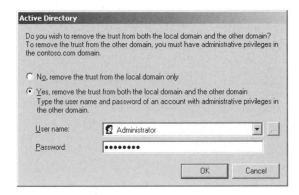

Figure 3-20   Active Directory dialog box

6. In the Active Directory message box, confirm that you want to remove the trust by clicking Yes.

7. On the Trusts tab, click the trust to be removed in the Domains That Trust This Domain (Incoming Trusts) box, and then click Remove.

8. Repeat steps 4 and 5 to remove the incoming trusts.

9. On the Trusts tab, note that the trusts have been removed, and then click OK.

Note   If you need to delete an external trust in a domain configured to the Windows 2000 mixed domain functional level, the trust relationship should always be deleted from a domain controller running Windows Server 2003. External trusts to Windows NT 4.0 or 3.51 domains can be deleted by an authorized administrator in those domains. However, only the trusted side of the relationship can be deleted on Windows NT 4.0 or 3.51 domain controllers. The trusting side of the relationship (created in the Windows Server 2003 domain) is not deleted, and although it will not be operational, the trust will continue to be displayed in the Active Directory Domains And Trusts console. To remove the trust completely, you must also delete the trust from a domain controller running Windows Server 2003 in the trusting domain. If an external trust is inadvertently deleted from a Windows NT 4.0 or 3.51 domain controller, re-create the trust from any domain controller running Windows Server 2003 in the trusting domain.

Note   It is not possible to remove the two-way transitive trust relationships created automatically between domains in the same forest. Only trusts created manually can be deleted.

Creating and Managing Trusts Using Netdom.exe

In addition to using Active Directory Domains And Trusts, you can also create and administer most types of trust relationships by using Netdom.exe, included with the Windows Support Tools on the Windows Server 2003 CD-ROM. You use the Netdom Trust command to create, verify, or reset trust relationships between domains.

Netdom Trust has the following syntax:

```
netdom trust TrustingDomainName /d: TrustedDomainName [/ud:[Domain\]User]
[/pd:{Password|*}] [/uo: User] [/po:{Password|*}] [/verify] [/reset]
[/passwordt: NewRealmTrustPassword] [/add [/realm]] [/remove [/force]]
[/twoway] [/kerberos] [/transitive[:{YES|NO}]] [/verbose]
```

The most common Netdom Trust command parameters are explained in Table 3-1.

Table 3-1   Netdom Trust Command Parameters

Parameter	Description
TrustingDomainName	Specifies the name of the trusting domain.
/d: *TrustedDomainName*	Specifies the name of the trusted domain. If the parameter is omitted, the domain that the current computer belongs to is used.
/uo: *User*	Specifies the user account that makes the connection with the trusting domain. If this parameter is omitted, the current user account is used.
/po:{*Password*|*}	Specifies the password of the user account that is specified in the */uo* parameter. Use * to be prompted for the password.
/verify	Verifies the secure channel secrets upon which a specific trust is based.

Table 3-1 Netdom Trust Command Parameters

Parameter	Description
/reset	Resets the trust secret between trusted domains or between the domain controller and the workstation.
/passwordt: *NewRealmTrustPassword*	Specifies a new trust password. This parameter is valid only with the */add* parameter and only if one of the domains specified is a non-Windows Kerberos realm. The trust password is set on the Windows domain only, which means that credentials are not needed for the non-Windows domain.
/add	Specifies to create a trust.
/realm	Indicates that the trust is created to a non-Windows Kerberos realm. The */realm* parameter is valid only with the */add* and */passwordt* parameters.
/remove	Specifies to break a trust.
/force	Removes both the trusted domain object and the cross-reference object for the specified domain from the forest. This parameter is used to clean up decommissioned domains that are no longer in use and could not be removed using the Active Directory Installation Wizard. This can occur if the domain controller for that domain was disabled or damaged and there were no domain controllers, or if it was not possible to recover the domain controller from backup media. This parameter is valid only when the */remove* parameter is specified.
/twoway	Specifies to establish a two-way trust relationship rather than a one-way trust relationship.
/kerberos	Specifies to exercise the Kerberos protocol between a workstation and a target domain. This parameter is valid only when the */verify* parameter is specified.
/transitive[:{YES | NO}]	Specifies whether to configure a transitive or nontransitive trust. This parameter is valid only for a non-Windows Kerberos realm. Non-Windows Kerberos trusts are created as nontransitive. If a value is omitted, the current transitivity state is displayed. Yes sets the realm to a transitive trust. No sets the realm to a nontransitive trust.
/verbose	Specifies verbose output. By default, only the result of the operation is reported. If */verbose* is specified, the output lists the success or failure of each transaction necessary to perform the operation as well as returns an error level based on the success (0) or failure (1) of the operation.
/?	Displays help for Netdom.exe, along with the default options and parameter values.

> **Note**   Netdom.exe cannot be used to create a forest trust. You can type the command **netdom query trust** to see a list of existing trust relationships.

For further information about using Netdom.cxe to create and administer trust relationships, refer to Windows Support Tools Help.

> **Off the Record**   The Nltest.exe tool can also be used to manage trust relationships. Nltest.exe is an older tool typically used for troubleshooting issues relating to Windows NT 4.0 clients and domains. However, you can use it with Windows Server 2003 computers and domains. For example, try typing the following command at a command prompt: **nltest /server:Server01 /trusted_domains**. For more information on the capabilities of Nltest.exe, see Windows Support Tools Help.

Adding or Removing UPNs

A *UPN suffix* is the part of a user principal name (UPN) to the right of the @ character. The default UPN suffix for a user account is the DNS domain name of the domain in which the user account was created. For example, if a new user named "mark" is created in the contoso.com domain, the UPN associated with this user account would be mark@contoso.com. Although the default UPN suffix for a domain is created automatically, you can also define alternative UPN suffixes to increase security and simplify the user logon process.

> **Note**   When users log on using a UPN, they do not specify a domain to log on to. Recall from Chapter 2 that a global catalog server directs all UPN-based authentication requests to appropriate domain controllers in the user's domain.

Using alternative domain names as UPN suffixes can provide additional logon security and simplify the user logon process. If your organization uses a deep domain tree, such as one organized by department or region, the UPN suffix associated with certain domains might be unreasonably long. For example, the default UPN suffix for a domain might be sales.chi.contoso.com. Creating a UPN suffix of "company.com" would allow a user in this domain to log on using the logon name of user@company.com rather than user@sales.chi.contoso.com.

Along the same lines, a company might choose to create a new UPN suffix that corresponds to a corporate domain name used for e-mail, which would allow users to log on using what they perceive to be their e-mail address. When new UPN suffixes are created, they are available in all domains throughout an Active Directory forest. As such, you cannot create more than one user account with the same UPN, regardless of the domain in which the user account is created. For example, two users in the same forest could not share the UPN mark@company.com, even if both "mark" user accounts were created in different domains in the forest.

> **Note**   When two Windows Server 2003 Active Directory forests are linked by a forest trust, the UPN suffixes used in one forest could directly come into conflict with those in the other. Ultimately, this conflict can lead to cases where users in one forest cannot access resources in another. For example, both companies might have created the additional UPN suffix "company.com" in their respective forests. If this is the case, the New Trust Wizard will detect and display the conflict when the forest trust is being created. UPN conflicts that exist can be viewed at any time via the Active Directory Domains And Trusts tool. See the "Routing name suffixes across forests" topic in the Help and Support Center for more information

To add or remove UPN suffixes, complete the following steps:

1. Click Start, select Administrative Tools, and then click Active Directory Domains And Trusts.

2. Right-click the Active Directory Domains And Trusts node, and then click Properties.

3. On the UPN Suffixes tab shown in Figure 3-21, do one of the following:

   ❏ To add a UPN suffix, type an alternative UPN suffix in the Alternative UPN Suffixes box, and then click Add.

   ❏ To remove a UPN suffix, select the suffix, and then click Remove. On the Active Directory Domains And Trusts message box, click Yes.

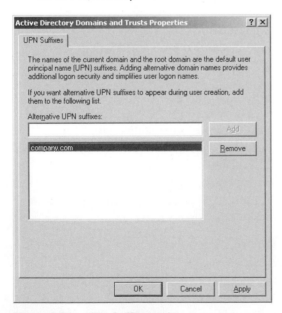

Figure 3-21   UPN Suffixes tab

4. Click OK, and close Active Directory Domains And Trusts.

Practice: Managing Trust Relationships and UPNs

In this practice, you will first manage trust relationships by creating, validating, and removing a forest trust, and then you will create an additional UPN suffix for the contoso.com forest.

Exercise 1: Creating an Additional Forest

In this exercise, you will create another forest in addition to the contoso.com forest you created in Chapter 2.

1. Use the procedure provided in Lesson 1 of Chapter 2 to create a new domain in a new forest on Server02. Note that you might need to remove Active Directory from Server02 if it is currently configured as an additional domain controller in the contoso.com domain. Name the new domain in the new forest nwtraders.com.

2. On Server01, click Start, point to Administrative Tools, and then click Active Directory Domains And Trusts. Note that the nwtraders.com domain is not visible.

Exercise 2: Creating, Validating, and Deleting a Forest Trust

In this exercise, you create, validate, and delete a forest trust between the contoso.com forest root domain you created in Chapter 2 and the nwtraders.com forest root domain that you created in Exercise 1.

1. Use the procedure provided earlier in this lesson to create a forest trust between the contoso.com forest root domain and the nwtraders.com forest root domain.

2. Use the procedure provided earlier in this lesson to validate the forest trust.

3. When you have finished exploring the forest trust, use the procedure provided earlier in this lesson to delete the forest trust.

Exercise 3: Adding and Removing a UPN Suffix

In this exercise, you will add and then remove a new UPN suffix named company.com to the contoso.com forest.

1. Click Start, select Administrative Tools, and then click Active Directory Domains And Trusts.

2. Right-click the Active Directory Domains And Trusts node, and then click Properties.

3. In the Alternative UPN Suffixes text box, type the new UPN name, and then click Add.

> **Note** After creating a new UPN suffix, you can use Active Directory Users And Computers to confirm that the UPN is available when creating a new user account. The new UPN suffix should be available from the drop-down box in the User Logon Name section of the New Object–User page once defined.

4. Click on the company.com UPN suffix, and then click Remove.

5. In the Active Directory Domains And Trusts dialog box shown in Figure 3-22, click Yes.

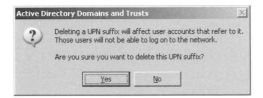

Figure 3-22   Removing a UPN suffix

6. Click OK, and close Active Directory Domains And Trusts.

Lesson Review

The following questions are intended to reinforce key information presented in this lesson. If you are unable to answer a question, review the lesson and try the question again. You can find answers to the questions in the "Questions and Answers" section at the end of this chapter.

1. Which type of trust provides a transitive trust relationship between two forests?

_____

_____

_____

2. What is the purpose of a shortcut trust?

_____

_____

_____

3. What preliminary tasks must you complete before you can create a forest trust?

_____

_____

_____

_____

_____

_____

4. Which of the following types of trust relationships are created automatically? Choose all that apply.

    a. Tree-root

    b. Parent child

    c. Shortcut

    d. Realm

    e. External

    f. Forest

_____

_____

_____

Lesson Summary

- A trust relationship is a logical link between two domains that allows users in one domain to gain access to resources in another.

- In Windows Server 2003 Active Directory, trusts can be created manually or automatically, can be transitive or nontransitive, and can be one-way or two-way.

- Windows Server 2003 operating systems support the following types of trust relationships: tree-root, parent-child, shortcut, realm, external, and forest.

- The New Trust Wizard is used to create trust relationships manually. This wizard is accessed from the Active Directory Domains And Trusts administrative tool.

- Windows Server 2003 Active Directory allows you to create additional UPN suffixes that can be used to increase security and simplify logon for users within a forest.

Lesson 2: Managing Schema Modifications

This lesson introduces you to concepts relating to modifying the Active Directory schema. It explores the different methods of schema modification possible in Windows Server 2003 Active Directory, as well as various reasons why a company might need to extend the schema. Concepts explored in this lesson also include group membership requirements for schema modification, transferring the schema master role to another domain controller, and replicating additional attributes to the global catalog. The primary tool for viewing and editing the schema, the Active Directory Schema snap-in, is also introduced.

After this lesson, you will be able to

- Understand the purpose of the Active Directory schema
- Identify the key considerations associated with making changes to the Active Directory schema
- Understand when to extended the Active Directory schema, as well as deactivate or reactivate existing classes and attributes
- Modify the Active Directory schema by using the Active Directory Schema snap-in

Estimated lesson time: 30 minutes

The Active Directory Schema

In Active Directory environments, the schema is the storage location for the definitions of all objects that can be created in the directory. All objects stored in Active Directory are associated with object classes and attributes. An object class is a category of directory objects that share a common set of characteristics, such as users, groups, or printers. Each object class is also associated with defined attributes that are used to describe instances of that class. For example, when you create a new computer account in Active Directory, that computer account becomes an instance of the *Computer* object class. The *Computer* object class has attributes associated with it, including location, operating system, and a DNS host name. In other words, when you are creating any Active Directory object, you are actually creating an instance of a particular object class that is already defined in the schema. The information that you enter about the object (such as its name) becomes an instance of that attribute. The only types of objects that can be created in Active Directory are ones that already have object classes and attributes present in the schema.

In Windows Server 2003 Active Directory, the schema is stored in a dedicated directory partition that is replicated to all domain controllers in the same forest. Although each domain controller stores a copy of this partition, changes to the schema can be made only on the domain controller designated as the schema master. By default, the schema master role is held on the first domain controller installed in a new Active Directory forest. However, the role can also be moved to a different domain controller using tools such as the Active Directory Schema snap-in. To make changes to the schema, a user must be a member of the Schema Admins group found in the forest root domain or have been delegated appropriate permissions.

> **Important**   Making changes to the schema has consequences across an entire forest. Because of this, membership in the Schema Admins group should be restricted. Microsoft recommends adding users to this group only for however long a schema modification will take, and then immediately removing the user from the group once the modification is completed. By default, only the Administrator account in the forest root domain is a member of the Schema Admins group.

Although the default schema installed with Windows Server 2003 Active Directory contains hundreds of common object classes and attributes, there might still be times when schema modification is necessary. For example, a company might want to associate additional custom attributes with existing object classes or define entirely new object classes to meet its needs. More commonly, the Active Directory schema is extended as part of installing a directory-enabled application, such as Microsoft Exchange.

The primary tool used to view and edit the Active Directory schema is the Active Directory Schema snap-in. However, the following tools and utilities can also be used to administer the schema:

- Ldifde.exe. This command-line tool is the preferred method for deploying tested extensions to the schema into a production environment.

- ADSI Edit snap-in. This MMC snap-in acts as a low-level editor for Active Directory.

- Ldp.exe. This GUI-based utility supports LDAP operations against any LDAP-compatible directory.

- Csvde.exe. This command-line utility is used to import and export data from Active Directory by using comma-separated text files.

Planning Schema Changes

Prior to making any changes to the Active Directory schema, you absolutely must consider all issues associated with schema modification. With a standard Active Directory installation, schema modifications are not generally required, except as dictated by directory-enabled applications in use. As a general rule, you should make changes to the schema only when absolutely necessary, keeping in mind that an incorrect configuration setting can potentially affect systems throughout an Active Directory forest.

The Windows Server 2003 Active Directory schema can be modified in a variety of ways. These include:

- Extending the schema to include new object classes or attributes

- Modifying existing classes or attributes

- Deactivating and reactivating existing classes or attributes

In each of these cases, the primary tool used to modify the schema is the Active Directory Schema snap-in. Considerations for each type of modification are listed in the following sections.

Extending the Schema

Extending the Active Directory schema involves defining new object classes or attributes when existing objects classes and attributes in the base Active Directory schema do not meet your needs. Prior to extending the Active Directory schema on a production network, it is highly recommended that you first implement and test your proposed schema extensions in a lab environment.

The following list outlines some key elements that should be considered prior to extending the Active Directory schema:

- Ensure that the base schema does not meet your needs prior to creating new object classes or attributes. In cases where an existing object class or attribute meets your needs, it is better to use these object classes or attributes rather than to define new ones unnecessarily.

- Review any available Active Directory schema documentation. If new object classes or attributes are randomly assigned properties, a conflict might occur. Schema documentation provides the best source of information about existing object classes and attributes.

- Remember that schema modifications are global. When you modify the schema, changes affect the entire forest.

- Understand that existing system classes in the schema cannot be modified.

- Understand that schema extensions are not reversible. Although object classes and attributes can be deactivated, you cannot delete them if an error was made or they are no longer required.

- Valid object identifiers (OIDs) will need to be obtained. All new objects and attributes should be assigned valid X.500 OID numbers. These numbers should not be randomly assigned.

- Once completed, all changes should be documented. Because the schema consists of many different object classes and attributes, any changes should be fully documented for future reference and troubleshooting purposes.

Modifying Existing Classes or Attributes

Modifying existing object classes and attributes does not extend the Active Directory schema, but rather changes various properties associated with those that already exist. For example, an administrator might decide to modify an existing object class by changing the description or security permissions associated with the class. Along the same lines, the goal might be to associate additional existing attributes with an object class.

Similarly, existing schema attributes can also be modified. Common examples of ways in which attributes are modified include changing their descriptions, configuring the attribute to be indexed in Active Directory, or configuring the attributes to be replicated to the global catalog. Recall from Chapter 2 that a domain controller acting as a global catalog holds information regarding all Active Directory objects in the forest, but only a subset of the attributes associated with those objects. If an administrator wanted additional attributes to be replicated to the global catalog, he or she would accomplish this by modifying the properties of an existing attribute, usually via the Active Directory Schema snap-in.

Deactivating and Reactivating Object Classes or Attributes

The Windows Server 2003 Active Directory schema does not allow you to delete object classes or attributes. However, both object classes and attributes can be deactivated if they are no longer required or were configured incorrectly. Once an object class or attribute has been disabled, it is considered to be defunct. Although instances of defunct object classes and attributes can no longer be created, a defunct object class or attribute can be reactivated if necessary.

Even after an object class or attribute has been deactivated, the ability to use that object class or attribute in the future is not necessarily lost. Because defunct object classes and attributes are never actually removed from the Active Directory schema, they can be reactivated if necessary, but only if a variety of conditions are met. For example, a defunct attribute can be reactivated only if the values of its *lDAPDisplayName*, *attributeID*, *governsID*, *schemaIDGUID*, and *mAPIID* do not conflict with other existing object classes or attributes that might have been subsequently created or modified.

 See Also   For more information about the constraints associated with reactivating a defunct object class or attribute, see the Windows Server 2003 Help and Support Center.

Active Directory Schema Snap-In

The primary tool used to manage the schema on a Windows Server 2003 system is the Active Directory Schema snap-in. This tool is not available on Windows Server 2003 domain controllers until it is manually installed. The process for installing the Active Directory Schema snap-in is as simple as registering the DLL file associated with the snap-in by using the Regsvr32.exe command, as outlined below:

```
regsvr32 schmmgmt.dll
```

Once this command is issued, the Active Directory Schema snap-in can be added to any new or existing custom MMC console as illustrated in Figure 3-23.

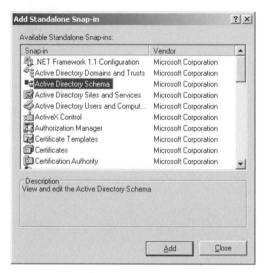

Figure 3-23   Adding the Active Directory Schema snap-in to the MMC

The Active Directory Schema snap-in can be used to carry out the following tasks:

- View and edit existing object classes and attributes
- Extend the schema by adding new object classes and attributes
- Deactivate and reactivate existing object classes and attributes
- Change the domain controller on which the schema master role resides
- Reload the schema

The following sections walk you through the process of installing the Active Directory Schema snap-in, extending and modifying the schema, replicating attributes to the global catalog, and finally transferring the schema master role to a different domain controller.

Installing the Active Directory Schema Snap-In and Adding It to an MMC Console

Perform the following steps to install the Active Directory Schema snap-in and then add it to a new MMC console:

1. Click Start, and then click Command Prompt.
2. At the command line, type **regsvr32 schmmgmt.dll** and press ENTER.

3. When the RegSvr32 dialog box appears, click OK.

4. Close the Command Prompt.

5. Click Start, and then click Run. In the Open text box, type **mmc** and click OK.

6. Click File, and then click Add/Remove Snap-In.

7. Click the Add button.

8. In the Add Standalone Snap-In window, click Active Directory Schema, and then click Add.

9. Click Close to close the Add Standalone Snap-In window.

10. On the Add/Remove Snap-In window, click OK.

11. Click File, and then click Save. Save the new custom MMC console to your desktop using a descriptive name.

Extending the Schema Using the Active Directory Schema Snap-In

Perform the following steps to extend the schema to include a new object class and attribute.

1. Double-click the custom MMC console that includes the Active Directory Schema snap-in to open it.

2. Click the plus sign next to the Active Directory Schema node to expand it.

3. Click the Classes node, as shown in Figure 3-24, to view the existing object classes defined in the schema.

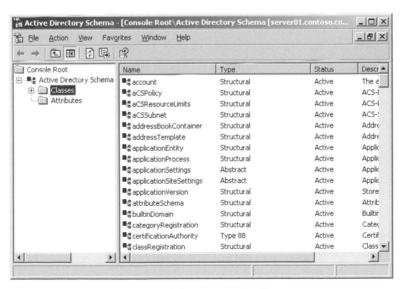

Figure 3-24   Active Directory Schema snap-in, Classes node

4. Right-click the Classes node, and click Create Class.

5. In the Schema Object Creation dialog box, shown in Figure 3-25, click Continue.

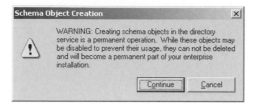

Figure 3-25   Schema Object Creation warning message

6. In the Create New Schema Class dialog box, shown in Figure 3-26, provide a Common Name, LDAP Display Name, Unique X500 Object ID, and Description. After defining the Parent Class of the object (if applicable) and the Class Type, click Next.

Warning   Because an object class cannot be deleted from the schema once it is created, you must be absolutely certain that the information entered here is correct and that it does not conflict with the properties of any existing or future object classes that might need to be defined. For more information about schema classes, attributes, identifiers, and syntax, search for Active Directory Schema on the MSDN Web site.

Figure 3-26   Creating a new schema class

7. Click the Add button next to the Mandatory and Optional sections to add any mandatory or optional attributes for the new object class. An example of the attributes that can be selected is shown in Figure 3-27. Once you have completed your selections, click Finish.

Figure 3-27   Adding an attribute to a new object class

> **Note**   To improve schema-related performance, each domain controller in a forest holds a cached copy of the schema in memory. This cached version is updated a short time after the schema is updated. However, the cached version can be updated immediately by right-clicking the Active Directory Schema node in the Active Directory Schema snap-in and selecting Reload The Schema.

8. Search for the LDAP display name that you gave the new object class in step 6. Double-click the object class to view its properties, and then click OK.

9. Click the Attributes node, as shown in Figure 3-28, to view the existing attributes defined in the schema.

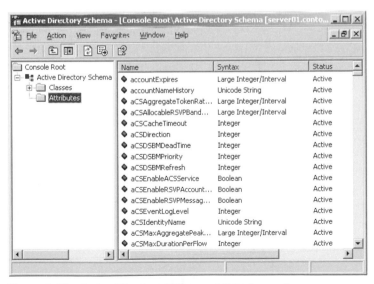

Figure 3-28   Active Directory Schema, Attributes node

10. Right-click the Attributes node, and click Create Attribute.

11. In the Schema Object Creation dialog box, click Continue.

12. In the Create New Attribute window shown in Figure 3-29, provide a Common Name, LDAP Display Name, Unique X500 Object ID, and Description. After defining the Syntax and Range information for the new attribute, click OK.

> **Warning**   Because an attribute cannot be deleted from the schema once it is created, you must be absolutely certain that the information entered here is correct, and that it does not conflict with the properties of any existing or future attributes that might need to be defined. For more information about schema classes, attributes, identifiers, and syntax, search for Active Directory Schema on the MSDN Web site.

Figure 3-29   Creating a new schema attribute

13. Search for the LDAP display name that you gave the new attribute in step 12. Double-click the attribute to view its properties, and then click OK.

14. Close the MMC console.

Deactivating or Reactivating a Class or Attribute Using the Active Directory Schema Snap-In

Perform the following steps to deactivate and then reactivate an existing schema object class:

1. Double-click the custom MMC console that includes the Active Directory Schema snap-in to open it.

2. Click the plus sign next to the Active Directory Schema node to expand it if necessary.

3. Click the Classes node to view the existing object classes defined in the schema.

> **Note**   You do not need to be a member of the Schema Admins group to view the properties of an object class or attribute. However, you do need to be a member of Schema Admins to make any changes to the Active Directory schema.

4. Right-click an existing object class, and then click Properties. The properties of the *Site* class object are displayed in Figure 3-30. Notice that this particular object class is a system object class; the Class Is Active check box cannot be cleared.

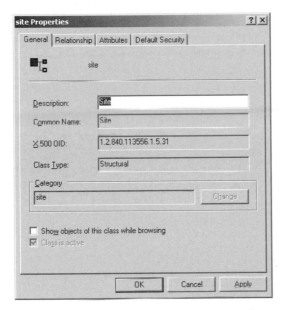

Figure 3-30   Viewing the properties of an existing class object

5. Right-click another existing object class that can be deactivated, such as *Document*, and then click Properties. To deactivate the object class, clear the Class Is Active check box. After doing so, you will be presented with the Active Directory Schema dialog box, as shown in Figure 3-31. Click Yes, and then click OK.

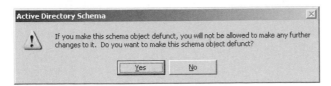

Figure 3-31   Warning message when deactivating an object class

6. Right-click the object class that was deactivated in step 5, and then click Properties. When the Active Directory Schema dialog box shown in Figure 3-32 appears, click OK.

Figure 3-32   Accessing the properties of a defunct object class

7. To reactivate the defunct object class, check the Class Is Active check box, and then click OK.

8. Close the Active Directory Schema MMC console.

> **Note**   To deactivate and subsequently reactivate an existing attribute, follow the previous steps, but access the properties of an existing attribute rather than an object class. Figure 3-33 shows the properties of the *associatedDomain* attribute, which can be deactivated by clearing the Attribute Is Active check box.

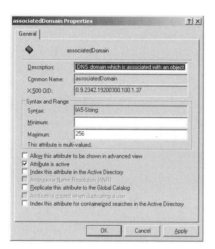

Figure 3-33   Viewing the properties of an existing attribute

Configuring an Attribute to Be Replicated to the Global Catalog

Perform the following steps to configure an existing attribute to be replicated to the global catalog:

1. Double-click the custom MMC console that includes the Active Directory Schema snap-in to open it.

2. Click the plus sign next to the Active Directory Schema node to expand it if necessary.

3. Click the Attributes node to view its contents.

4. Right-click an existing attribute, and click Properties.

5. Select the Replicate This Attribute To The Global Catalog check box if it isn't already checked, and click OK. Figure 3-34 shows an example of replicating the *accountExpires* attribute to the global catalog.

> **Note**   To add an attribute to the global catalog, you must be a member of Schema Admins or have been delegated the proper authority.

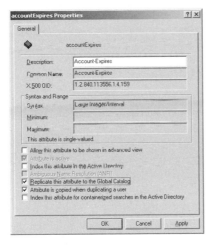

Figure 3-34   Replicating an attribute to the global catalog

6. Close the Active Directory Schema MMC console.

Transferring the Schema Master Role

Perform the following steps to transfer the schema master role to a different domain controller:

1. Double-click the custom MMC console that includes the Active Directory Schema snap-in to open it.

2. Right-click the Active Directory Schema node, and click Change Domain Controller.

3. In the Change Domain Controller window, click Specify Name and then enter the name of the domain controller that you ultimately want to transfer the schema master role to. Click OK.

4. Right-click the Active Directory Schema node, and click Operations Master. The Change Schema Master window appears, as shown in Figure 3-35.

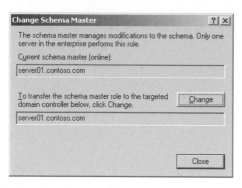

Figure 3-35   Transferring the schema master role

5. Click the Change button. This will transfer the schema master role to the domain controller specified in step 3.

6. Close the Active Directory Schema MMC console.

Practice: Installing and Using the Active Directory Schema Snap-In

In this practice, you will first review the membership of the Schema Admins group, then install the Active Directory Schema Snap-In, and finally review existing object class and attribute definitions.

Exercise 1: Adding a User to the Schema Admins Group

In this exercise, you will review the membership of the Schema Admins group in the forest root domain by using Active Directory Users And Computers.

1. Log on to Server01 as Administrator.

2. Click Start, select Administrative Tools, and then click Active Directory Users And Computers.

3. Click the plus sign next to the contoso.com node to expand it.

4. Click the Users node to view its contents.

5. Double-click the Schema Admins group to view its properties.

6. Click the Members tab. Notice that by default, only the Administrator account for the contoso.com domain is a member of Schema Admins.

7. Click OK, and then close Active Directory Users And Computers.

Exercise 2: Installing the Active Directory Schema Snap-In

In this exercise, you will install the Active Directory Schema Snap-In and then add it to a custom MMC console.

1. Follow steps 1 to 10 from the "Installing the Active Directory Schema Snap-In and Adding It to an MMC Console" section earlier in this lesson.

2. Click File, and then click Save As. Ensure that the Documents and Settings\All Users\Start Menu\Programs\Administrative Tools folder is selected in the Save In drop-down box. In the File Name box, name the custom console Active Directory Schema, and click Save. Close the MMC.

3. Click Start, and select Administrative Tools to verify that the Active Directory Schema console now exists in the Administrative Tools menu.

Exercise 3: Review Schema Object Class and Attribute Definitions

In this exercise, you will review existing schema object class and attribute definitions.

1. Click Start, select Administrative Tools, and click Active Directory Schema.

2. Click the plus sign next to the Active Directory Schema node to expand it if necessary.

3. Click on the Classes node to view its contents. Double-click various object classes to view their properties, including the contents of the General, Relationship, Attributes, and Default Security tabs. Do not make any changes to existing object class definitions.

4. Click the Attributes node to view its contents. Double-click various attributes to view their properties. Do not make any changes to existing attribute definitions.

5. Close the Active Directory Schema console.

Lesson Review

The following questions are intended to reinforce key information presented in this lesson. If you are unable to answer a question, review the lesson and try the question again. You can find answers to the questions in the "Questions and Answers" section at the end of this chapter.

1. To modify the Active Directory schema, what group must a user be a member of?

_____

_____

2. When the Active Directory schema is modified, to which domain controllers are the changes replicated?

_____

_____

3. Where is the Active Directory schema stored on a domain controller?

_____

_____

Lesson Summary

- The schema is the storage location for the definitions of all objects that can be created in Active Directory.

- One domain controller in an Active Directory forest holds the schema master role, but the schema partition is replicated to all domain controllers in a forest.

- The Active Directory schema can be extended to include new object classes and attributes. Existing object classes and attributes can be modified, deactivated, and reactivated, with the exception of system object classes and attributes.

- Only members of the Schema Admins group in the forest root domain can modify the Active Directory schema.

- The Active Directory Schema Snap-In is the primary tool used to view, edit, and create schema object classes and attributes. This tool can also be used to transfer the schema master role and reload the schema into memory.

Lesson 3: Backing Up and Restoring Active Directory

This lesson guides you through the steps required to back up Active Directory data. When you create a backup, you first need to conduct several preliminary tasks, and then perform a number of tasks using the Windows Server 2003 Backup Utility. In this lesson, you will learn how to back up Active Directory data, how to schedule and run an unattended backup, and how to restore Active Directory by using three different methods.

After this lesson, you will be able to

- Back up Active Directory data using the Windows Server 2003 Backup Utility
- Schedule and run an unattended backup of Active Directory data
- Understand the differences between restoring Active Directory using the primary, normal, and authoritative restore methods
- Restore Active Directory using the primary, normal, and authoritative methods

Estimated lesson time: 25 minutes

Preliminary Backup Tasks

An important part of backing up Active Directory data involves performing preliminary tasks to ensure that your backup device and media will function correctly. For example, if your backup method will involve using a removable media device such as a tape drive, you must ensure that

- The backup device is listed on the Windows Server 2003 Hardware Compatibility List (HCL).

- The backup device is attached to a computer on the network (or the network itself) and is turned on. If you are backing up to a tape drive using the Windows Server 2003 Backup Utility, the drive must be attached to the system running the Backup Utility.

- The appropriate media is loaded into the device. For example, if you are using a tape drive, ensure that the correct tape is loaded.

 Note   You must be a member of the Administrators or Backup Operators group to perform a backup.

Creating an Active Directory Backup

Windows Server 2003 provides the Backup Utility as its native tool for backing up system and user data files as well as Active Directory components. As part of the process of backing up Active Directory, the Backup Utility automatically backs up all system components and distributed services that Active Directory requires to function. Collectively, these components and services are known as *System State data*.

For all Windows Server 2003 operating systems, System State data includes the registry, COM+ Class Registration database, system boot files, files protected by Windows File Protection, and the Certificate Services database (if the server is configured as a certificate server). If a Windows Server 2003 system is functioning as a domain controller, Active Directory components and the Sysvol folder are also included as part of the System State backup. When using the Windows Server 2003 Backup Utility, you cannot back up individual System State components such as Active Directory or the system registry; all System State components are backed up as one logical group.

 Note   The Windows Server 2003 Backup Utility does not provide the ability to back up System State data for remote systems. Only local backups of System State data are supported with this tool.

To create an Active Directory backup, complete the following steps:

1. Log on to your domain as Administrator, click Start, point to All Programs, point to Accessories, point to System Tools, and click Backup.

2. At the Welcome To The Backup Or Restore Wizard page, click Next.

3. At the Backup Or Restore page, select Back Up Files And Settings, and then click Next.

4. At the What To Back Up page, select Let Me Choose What To Back Up, and then click Next.

5. At the Items To Back Up page, shown in Figure 3-36, expand the My Computer item, and then select System State. Click Next.

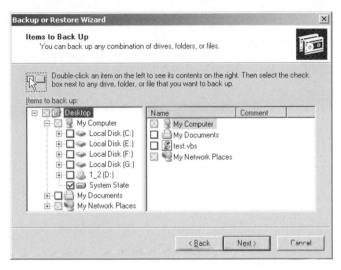

Figure 3-36   Items To Back Up page

6. At the Backup Type, Destination, And Name page, shown in Figure 3-37, complete the following steps:

   a. Select Tape in the Select The Backup Type list if you are using tape medium; otherwise, this box defaults to File target medium.

   b. In the Choose A Place To Save Your Backup list, choose the location where the Backup Utility will store the data. If you are saving to a tape, select the tape name. If you are saving to a file, browse to the path for the backup file location.

   c. In the Type A Name For This Backup box, enter a name for the backup.

   d. Click Next.

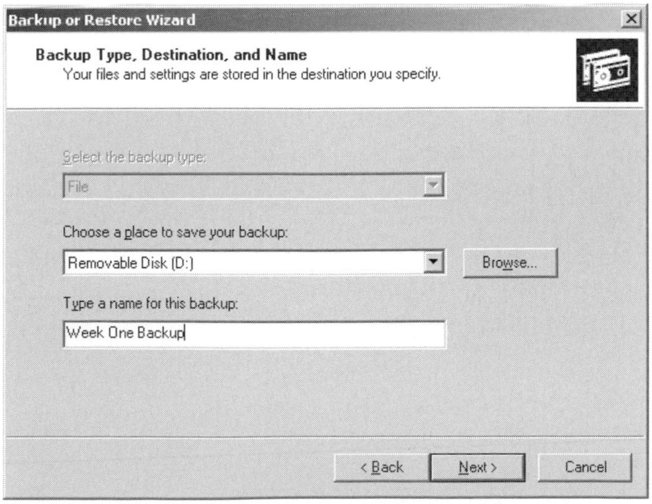

Figure 3-37   Backup Type, Destination, and Name page

7. At the Completing The Backup Or Restore Wizard page, click Advanced.

8. At the Type Of Backup page, select Normal as the backup type used for this backup job, as shown in Figure 3-38. The only backup type supported for System State data is Normal. If the Hierarchical Storage Manager (HSM) has moved data to remote storage and you want to back it up, select the Backup Migrated Remote Storage Data check box. Click Next.

> **Note** When performing a backup that includes System State data, the Windows Server 2003 Backup Utility will always perform a full backup of System State information, even if another option (such as Incremental or Differential) is chosen as the backup type. In cases where a method other than Full is chosen, files not included as part of the System State data will be backed up according to that method.

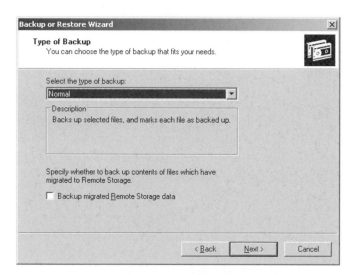

Figure 3-38 Type Of Backup page

9. At the How To Back Up page, select the Verify Data After Backup check box, shown in Figure 3-39. This option causes the backup process to take longer, but it confirms that files are correctly backed up. If you are using a tape device and it supports hardware compression, select the Use Hardware Compression, If Available check box to enable hardware compression. It's recommended that you do not select the Disable Volume Shadow Copy check box. By default, Backup creates a volume shadow copy of your data to create an accurate copy of the contents of the hard drive, including open files or files in use by the system. Click Next.

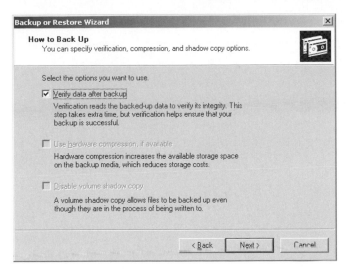

Figure 3-39   How To Back Up page

10. At the Backup Options page shown in Figure 3-40, select the Replace The Existing
Backups option, and then select the Allow Only The Owner And The Administrator Access To The Backup Data And To Any Backups Appended To This Medium
check box. This action saves only the most recent copy of Active Directory and
allows you to restrict who can gain access to the completed backup file or tape.
Click Next.

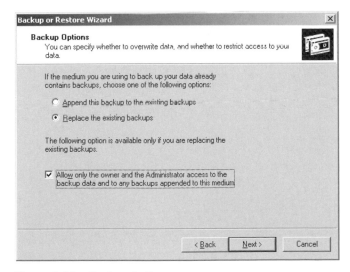

Figure 3-40   Backup Options page

11. On the When To Back Up page, select Now. Click Next.

12. On the Completing The Backup Or Restore Wizard page, click Finish to start the backup operation.

13. The Backup Progress window shows the progress of the backup.

14. When the backup operation is complete, the Backup Progress window shows that the backup is complete, as shown in Figure 3-41. You can click the Report button to see a report about the backup operation, as shown in Figure 3-42. The report is stored on the hard disk of the computer on which you are running the backup.

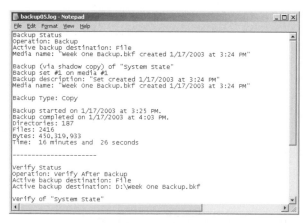

Figure 3-41   Backup Progress window showing completed backup

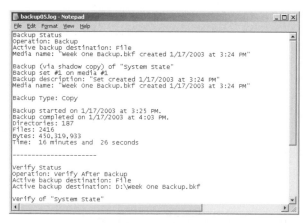

Figure 3-42   Backup operation report

15. Close the report when you have finished viewing it, and then click Close to close the backup operation.

> **Note** Windows Server 2003 automatically defaults to starting the Backup Or Restore Wizard when the Backup Utility is run. To access the Backup Utility in Advanced Mode (as shown in Figure 3-43), clear the Always Start In Wizard Mode check box at the Backup Or Restore Wizard Welcome page and click Cancel. The next time that the Backup Utility is started, it will open in Advanced Mode.

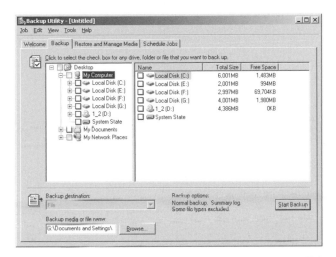

Figure 3-43 Backup Utility in Advanced Mode, Backup Tab

Scheduling Active Directory Backup Operations

The Windows Server 2003 Backup Utility allows backups to be automated and scheduled according to the needs of your environment. To make this possible, Windows Server 2003 integrates the Backup Utility with the Task Scheduler service. To schedule a backup operation, you need to access advanced backup settings as described in the following procedure.

To schedule an Active Directory backup operation, complete the following steps:

1. Follow steps 1 through 10 in the previous section, "Creating an Active Directory Backup."

2. At the When To Back Up page, select Later. Type a name in the Job name box, and click Set Schedule.

3. From the Schedule tab in the Schedule Job dialog box shown in Figure 3-44, select the frequency of the backup operation: Daily, Weekly, Monthly, Once, At System Startup, At Logon, or When Idle from the Schedule Task drop-down list. Indicate the time the backup operation will begin in the Start Time drop-down list. Indicate when the task will occur in the Schedule Task box for the selected frequency. Click Advanced.

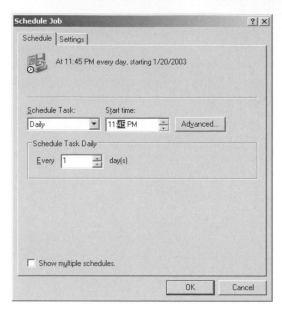

Figure 3-44 Schedule Job dialog box, Schedule tab

4. In the Advanced Schedule Options dialog box shown in Figure 3-45, you can specify when the backup operations should begin, end, or how often they should be repeated in the Start Date, End Date, and Repeat Task boxes, respectively. Enter information as necessary, and click OK.

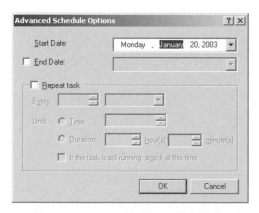

Figure 3-45 Advanced Schedule Options dialog box

5. From the Schedule tab in the Schedule Job dialog box, select the Show Multiple Schedules check box if you want to set up more than one schedule for the backup operation. Repeat steps 1 through 4 for each schedule. Click the Settings tab when you are finished setting up schedules.

6. From the Settings tab in the Schedule Job dialog box shown in Figure 3-46, specify whether to delete the task file from your computer's hard disk after the backup operation has finished running and is not scheduled to run again in the Scheduled

Task Completed box. Specify whether to start or stop the backup operation based on the computer's idle time in the Idle Time box. Specify whether to start or stop the backup operation based on the computer's power status in the Power Management box. Click OK.

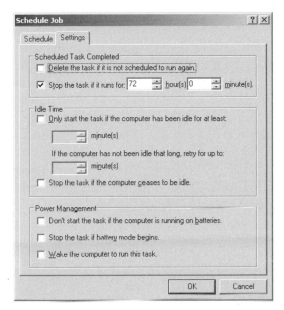

Figure 3-46   Schedule Job dialog box, Settings tab

7. On the When To Back Up page, click Next.

8. In the Set Account Information dialog box, type the password for the account shown in the Password box and confirm the password in the Confirm Password box. Click OK.

9. Confirm your selections on the Completing The Backup Or Restore Wizard page, and then click Finish to schedule the backup.

Restoring Active Directory

In the same way that System State components can be backed up only as a single logical group, individual components of the System State cannot be restored individually. As such, an administrator cannot choose to restore Active Directory without also restoring the registry, COM+ Class Registration database, system boot files, and so forth.

Different methods can be used to restore Active Directory on a domain controller. These include:

■ Normal restore (nonauthoritative restore)

■ Authoritative restore

■ Primary restore

Each of these methods is associated with a specific set of circumstances surrounding the need to restore Active Directory System State data. The following sections look at each restore method in more detail.

Normal Restore

During a *normal restore* operation (sometimes referred to as a *nonauthoritative restore*), the data and distributed services on a domain controller are restored from backup media, and then updated through normal replication. Each restored directory partition is updated via normal domain controller replication after you perform the restore process. For example, if the last backup was performed a week ago, and the System State is restored using a normal restore, any changes that were made after this backup was created will be replicated from the other domain controllers. So, if a restored backup in this situation includes a user object named *Mark*, and the *Mark* user object was deleted from Active Directory at some point after the backup was created, the *Mark* user object will also be deleted on the restored domain controller via the replication process. This occurs because the deletion of the *Mark* user object is considered more recent data in this case. If your specific goal was to restore the deleted *Mark* user object, an authoritative restore would need to be performed. To perform a normal restore of System State data, a domain controller must be started in Directory Services Restore Mode.

The primary reasons for performing a normal restore of System State data on a domain controller include:

- Restoring a single domain controller in an environment that includes multiple domain controllers

- Attempting to restore Sysvol or File Replication service (FRS) data on domain controllers other than the first in a replica set

Authoritative Restore

Another method that can be used to restore System State data is known as an *authoritative restore*. The main purpose of an authoritative restore is to undo or roll back changes that have been made to Active Directory, or to reset data stored in a distributed directory such as Sysvol. As you learned in the previous section, when System State data is restored using the normal restore method, the domain controller replication process will overwrite any changes that have occurred since the restored backup was taken. If your goal is to restore an object that was deleted or changed, an authoritative restore allows you to mark restored objects as being authoritative, thus disallowing the restored object to be deleted or updated according to the information currently stored on other domain controllers.

To perform an authoritative restore of System State data, a domain controller must be started in Directory Services Restore Mode. To authoritatively restore Active Directory data, you must run the *Ntdsutil.exe* utility after you have performed a normal restore of the System State data, but before you restart the server. The Ntdsutil utility allows you to mark Active Directory objects as authoritative. Marking objects as authoritative ultimately changes the update sequence number of an object, such that it is higher than any other update sequence number in the Active Directory replication system. This ensures that any replicated or distributed data that you have restored is properly replicated or distributed throughout your organization according to your intentions.

For example, suppose you back up the system on Monday, and then create a new user object named *Ben Smith* on Tuesday. This object will be replicated to all other domain controllers in the domain. On Wednesday, another user object named *Nancy Anderson* is accidentally deleted, a change which is replicated to other domain controllers as well. To authoritatively restore the *Nancy Anderson* object, you can start a domain controller in Directory Services Restore Mode and restore the backup created on Monday. Then, using Ntdsutil, you can mark the *Nancy Anderson* object as authoritative. After restarting the server normally, the *Nancy Anderson* object will be restored and replicated, without any impact on the *Ben Smith* object.

The primary reasons for performing a normal restore of System State data on a domain controller include:

- Rolling back or undoing changes to Active Directory objects and replica sets
- Resetting the data stored in the Sysvol folder

Primary Restore

A primary restore is used to rebuild a domain from a backup when all domain controllers (or the only domain controller) in a domain have failed. If a domain is lost, the first domain controller should be restored using a primary restore, and any subsequent domain controller should be restored using a normal restore. Like the other restore methods listed in this lesson, a server must be started in Directory Services Restore Mode to perform a primary restore. The primary reasons for performing a primary restore of System State data on a domain controller include:

- Restoring the only domain controller in an Active Directory environment
- Restoring the first of several domain controllers
- Restoring the first domain controller in a replica set

> **Exam Tip**   Know when to use a primary, normal, or authoritative restore for System State data.

Preliminary Restore Tasks

In a manner similar to the backup process, restoring System State data involves performing preliminary tasks to ensure that your restore device and media will function correctly. Common preliminary tasks associated with restoring System State data include:

- Ensuring that the appropriate device for the storage medium containing the data is attached to the computer on which the restore will be performed

- Ensuring that the medium containing the data to be restored is loaded in the device

Note   You can restore System State data only on a local computer when using the Windows Server 2003 Backup Utility. This program does not support restoring System State data to remote computers.

Performing a Normal Restore

To restore the System State data on a domain controller, you must first start the server in Directory Services Restore Mode. This mode allows you to restore the Sysvol folder and the Active Directory database without causing conflicts with other domain controllers. Remember that you can restore System State data only on a local computer when using the Windows Server 2003 Backup Utility.

While you cannot restore System State data to a remote computer, you can restore System State data to an alternate location—in other words, a destination folder of your choice. By restoring to an alternate location, you preserve the file and folder structure of the backed-up data, meaning that all folders and subfolders appear in the alternate folder you specify.

Note   If you restore System State data without designating an alternate location, the Windows Server 2003 Backup Utility will erase existing System State data and replace it with the data you are restoring. Also, if you restore the System State data to an alternate location, only the registry files, Sysvol folder files, Cluster database information files (if applicable), and system boot files are restored to the alternate location. The Active Directory database, Certificate Services database (if applicable), and COM+ Class Registration database are not restored if you designate an alternate location.

To perform a normal restore of System State data on a domain controller, complete the following steps:

1. Restart the computer.

2. During the phase of startup where the operating system is normally selected, press F8.

3. At the Windows Advanced Options Menu, select Directory Services Restore Mode (Windows domain controllers only) and press ENTER. This ensures that Active Directory on this domain controller is offline.

4. At the Please Select The Operating System To Start menu, select the appropriate Microsoft Windows Server 2003 operating system and press ENTER.

5. Log on using the local Administrator account.

> **Note** When you restart the computer in directory services restore mode, you must log on as an Administrator by using the valid Security Accounts Manager (SAM) account name and password, *not* the Active Directory Administrator's name and password. The password to be used when logging on is the Directory Services Restore Mode password that was supplied when the server was promoted to the role of a domain controller using the Active Directory Installation Wizard.

6. In the Desktop message box that warns you that Windows is running in safe mode, click OK.

7. Click Start, select All Programs, select Accessories, select System Tools, and then click Backup.

8. At the Welcome To The Backup Or Restore Wizard page, click Next.

9. At the Backup Or Restore page, select Restore Files And Settings. Click Next.

10. At the What To Restore page shown in Figure 3-47, expand the media type that contains the data that you want to restore in the Items To Restore box or click Browse. The media can be either tape or file. Expand the appropriate media set until the data that you want to restore is visible. Select the data you want to restore, such as System State, and then click Next.

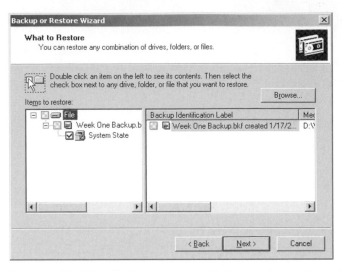

Figure 3-47   What To Restore page with System State data selected for restore

11. Ensure that the media containing the backup file is in the correct location.

12. At the Completing The Backup Or Restore Wizard page, do one of the following:

❑ Click Finish to start the restore process. The Backup Or Restore Wizard requests verification for the source of the restore data and then performs the restore. During the restore, the Backup Or Restore Wizard displays status information about the restore.

❑ Click Advanced to specify advanced restore options. The advanced restore options for a normal restore are discussed later in the section "Specifying Advanced Restore Settings for a Normal Restore."

13. In the Warning message box that warns you that restoring System State will always overwrite current System State, click OK.

14. The Restore Progress dialog box displays status information about the restore process. As with the backup process, when the restore is complete, you can choose to view the report of the restore. The report contains information about the restore, such as the number of files that have been restored and the duration of the restore process.

15. Close the report when you have finished viewing it, and then click Close.

16. When prompted to restart the computer, click Yes.

Real World   **Shutdown Event Tracker**

You've probably noticed that Windows 2003 Server includes a new feature that requires you to provide a reason each time you shut down or restart the server. This feature is known as the Shutdown Event Tracker. If you are working in a test environment, you might choose to disable this feature to avoid the hassle of typing in a reason each time you restart. To disable this feature, you can perform the following steps:

1. Click Start, click Run, type **gpedit.msc**, and press ENTER.

2. Expand the Computer Configuration and Administrative Templates objects. Click the System object. In the right-most pane, you'll see several settings.

3. Locate and double-click the Display Shutdown Event Tracker. The Display Shutdown Event Tracker Properties dialog box opens.

4. Click the Disabled option to disable the Shutdown Event Tracker. Click OK. Close the Group Policy Editor console.

Now when you shut down this server, you won't be asked to enter a reason.

Specifying Advanced Restore Settings for a Normal Restore

The advanced settings in the Backup Or Restore Wizard vary depending on the type of backup media from which you are restoring.

To specify advanced restore settings for a normal System State restore, complete the following steps:

1. At the Where To Restore page, select the target location for the data that you are restoring in the Restore Files To list. The choices in the list are:

   ❑ **Original location**   Replaces corrupted or lost data. This is the default option, and it must be selected to restore Active Directory.

   ❑ **Alternate location**   Restores an earlier version of a file to a folder you designate.

   ❑ **Single folder**   Consolidates the files from a tree structure into a single folder. For example, use this option if you want copies of specific files but do not want to restore the hierarchical structure of the files.

Note   If you select either the Alternate Location or Single Folder option, you must also provide a path to the location or folder.

2. Click Next.

3. At the How To Restore page, select how you want to restore the System State data. The options include:

   ❏ **Leave existing files (recommended)**   Prevents accidental overwriting of existing data. This is the default option.

   ❏ **Replace existing files if they are older than the backup files**   Verifies that the most recent copy exists on the computer.

   ❏ **Replace existing files**   Ensures that the Backup Utility does not provide a confirmation message if it encounters a duplicate file name during the restore operation.

4. Click Next.

5. At the Advanced Restore Options page, select whether or not to restore security or special system files. The options include:

   ❏ **Restore security settings**   Applies the original permissions to files that you are restoring to a Windows NTFS volume. Security settings include access permissions, audit entries, and ownership information. This option is available only if you have backed up data from an NFTS volume and are restoring to an NTFS volume.

   ❏ **Restore junction points, but not the folders and file data they reference**   Restores junction points on your hard disk, but not the data to which the junction points refer. If you have any mounted drives and you want to restore the data that mounted drives point to, you should *not* select this check box.

   ❏ **Preserve existing volume mount points**   Prevents the restore operation from writing over any volume mount points on the destination volume. If you are restoring data to a replacement drive, and you have partitioned and formatted the drive and restored volume mount points, you should select this option so your volume mount points are not restored. If you are restoring data to a partition or drive that you have just reformatted, and you want to restore the old volume mount points, you should not select this option.

   ❏ **Restore the Cluster Registry to the quorum disk and all other nodes**   Makes certain that the cluster quorum database is restored and replicated on all nodes in a server cluster. If selected, the Backup Or Restore Wizard will stop the Cluster service on all other nodes of the server cluster after the node that was restored reboots.

   ❏ **When restoring replicated data sets, mark the restored data as the primary data for all replicas**   Ensures that restored File Replication service (FRS) data is replicated to your other servers. If you are restoring FRS data, you should choose this option. If you do not choose this option, the FRS data that you are restoring might not be replicated to other servers because the restored data will appear to be older than the data already on the servers. This will cause the other servers to overwrite the restored data, preventing you from restoring the FRS data.

6. Click Next.

7. On the Completing The Backup Or Restore Wizard page, click Finish to start the restore process. The Backup Or Restore Wizard requests verification for the source of the restore data and then performs the restore. During the restore, the Backup Or Restore Wizard displays status information about the restore.

Performing an Authoritative Restore

An authoritative restore occurs after a normal restore and is used to designate that the entire directory, a distinct portion of the directory, or individual objects should be marked as authoritative. An authoritative restore is most commonly used to restore accidentally deleted objects or roll back any unwanted changes to Active Directory data.

To authoritatively restore a portion or all of Active Directory, complete the following steps:

1. Perform a normal restore as described previously, but do not restart the server once complete.

2. Click Start, and then click Command Prompt.

3. At the command line, type **ntdsutil** and press ENTER.

4. At the Ntdsutil prompt, type **authoritative restore** and press ENTER.

5. At the authoritative restore prompt

   ❑ To authoritatively restore the entire directory, type **restore database** and press ENTER.

   ❑ To authoritatively restore a portion or subtree of the directory, such as an OU, type **restore subtree** *subtree_distinguished_name* and press ENTER.

   For example, to restore the Marketing OU in the contoso.com domain, the commands would be:

   ```
   ntdsutil
   authoritative restore
   restore subtree OU=Marketing,DC=Contoso,DC=Com
   ```

   Similarly, to restore a user account named Mark stored in the Users container in the contoso.com domain, the commands would be:

   ```
   ntdsutil
   authoritative restore
   restore subtree CN=Mark,CN=Users,DC=Contoso,DC=Com
   ```

❑ To authoritatively restore the entire directory *and* override the version increase, type **restore database verinc** *version_increase* and press ENTER.

❑ To authoritatively restore a subtree of the directory *and* override the version increase, type **restore subtree** *subtree_distinguished_name* **verinc** *version_increase* and press ENTER.

After the Restore Subtree command is issued with correct parameters, the Authoritative Restore Confirmation Dialog window shown in Figure 3-48 will prompt you to confirm your decision.

Figure 3-48   Authoritative Restore Confirmation Dialog window

The authoritative restore opens the Ntds.dit file, increases version numbers, counts the records that need updating, verifies the number of records updated, and reports completion. If a version number increase is not specified, then one is automatically calculated.

6. Type **quit**, and press ENTER twice to exit the Ntdsutil utility. Then close the Command Prompt window.

7. Restart the domain controller normally. When the restored domain controller is online and connected to the network, normal replication brings the restored domain controller up to date with any changes from other domain controllers that were not overridden by the authoritative restore. Replication also propagates the authoritatively restored objects, such as any previously deleted objects, to other domain controllers. Because the objects that are restored have the same object globally unique identifier (GUID) and SID (if applicable), security remains intact, and object dependencies are maintained.

Practice: Backing Up Active Directory

In this practice, you back up Active Directory and perform tasks related to backup scheduling.

Exercise 1: Creating an Active Directory Backup

In this exercise, you will create a backup of Active Directory by backing up the System State data on Server01.

1. Log on to Server01 as Administrator.

2. Open the Active Directory Users And Computers console. Create a new, empty OU by right-clicking the contoso.com domain in the console tree, pointing to New, and then clicking Organizational Unit. In the New Object–Organizational Unit window, type **TEST1** in the Name box, and then click OK. Verify that the TEST1 OU appears in the console tree.

3. Use the procedure provided earlier in this lesson to back up System State data on Server01. Name this backup System State. If a tape drive is unavailable, save this backup to a file in an appropriate location on your hard drive.

4. When you have finished the backup operation, return to Active Directory Users And Computers and delete the TEST1 OU that you created in step 2.

> **Note**   In this exercise, you backed up System State data when it contained the TEST1 OU, and then deleted this OU. In Exercise 3, you perform an authoritative restore to restore the TEST1 OU.

Exercise 2: Scheduling an Active Directory Backup Operation

In this exercise, you will schedule a backup of System State data to ensure that daily backups of Active Directory data exist.

1. Use the procedure provided earlier in this lesson to automate and schedule the backup of System State data.

2. Name this backup System State 2.

3. Schedule this backup to occur daily at 12:00 A.M.

4. Choose an appropriate location for the backup based on the availability of a tape drive or hard disk space.

Exercise 3: Restoring Active Directory

In this exercise, you will perform an authoritative restore of Active Directory using the System State backup created in Exercise 1.

1. Use the procedure provided earlier in this lesson to authoritatively restore Active Directory using the System State backup created in Exercise 1. Hint: Use the **restore subtree** command parameter with **OU=TEST1,DC=contoso,DC=com** as the subtree distinguished name when marking the TEST1 OU as authoritative in Ntdsutil.

2. Verify that the TEST1 OU you created, backed up, and deleted in Exercise 1 has been restored in the Active Directory Users And Computers console.

Lesson Review

The following questions are intended to reinforce key information presented in this lesson. If you are unable to answer a question, review the lesson materials and try the question again. You can find answers to the questions in the "Questions and Answers" section at the end of this chapter.

1. What tasks should you complete before attempting to back up Active Directory data?

   _____

   _____

   _____

   _____

   _____

   _____

2. What is System State data, and why is it significant to backing up Active Directory?

   _____

   _____

   _____

   _____

   _____

   _____

3. Can you restrict who can gain access to a completed backup file or tape? If so, how?

   _____

   _____

   _____

   _____

   _____

   _____

4. When you specify the items you want to back up in the Backup Or Restore Wizard, which of the following should you select to successfully back up Active Directory data?

   a. System State data

   b. Shared system volume folder

    c. Database and log files

    d. Registry

Lesson Summary

- Active Directory can be backed up using the Windows Server 2003 Backup Utility. Active Directory cannot be backed up as an individual component; instead, it is backed up as part of the System State data on a domain controller.

- Windows Server 2003 supports three methods for restoring System State data: primary, normal, and authoritative restores. To restore System State data on a domain controller, the server must be started in Directory Services Restore Mode.

- When Active Directory objects that were deleted or misconfigured need to be restored or rolled back to previous settings, an authoritative restore must be performed. An authoritative restore involves using the Ntdsutil command-line utility to mark portions of the Active Directory database or individual objects as authoritative after a normal restore.

Case Scenario Exercise

The IT manager at Contoso has come to you with a number of concerns. He has just found out that management has decided to go ahead with a proposed merger with Northwind Traders. Management wants to be sure that the users in both companies will ultimately be able to access resources in the other. Another new project will involve the design of a directory-enabled application to support the needs of the Contoso sales staff. Finally, the IT manager wants to implement an Active Directory backup strategy to ensure that any objects that are accidentally deleted or misconfigured can be restored as quickly as possible.

- **Requirement 1**   Northwind Traders currently has a Windows 2000 Active Directory forest consisting of three domains running in native mode. Management wants to ensure that users in the contoso.com domain are immediately able to access resources in all three domains in the nwtraders.com forest, and that users in each of these domains can also access resources in the contoso.com domain. Within a few months of the merger, the company plans to upgrade the nwtraders.com forest to Windows Server 2003 Active Directory. The IT manager has asked for your help in planning the necessary trust relationships.

- **Requirement 2**   The new directory-enabled application being proposed will involve extensive schema modifications, including the creation of new object classes and attributes. The IT manager has asked for your input on what information will need to be gathered during this planning phase.

■ **Requirement 3**   An Active Directory backup and restore strategy needs to be developed for the contoso.com forest. Right now the company is unsure about how often Active Directory should be backed up, as well as how these back-up and restore procedures should be carried out using the Windows Server 2003 Backup Utility. The IT manager has asked you to develop a strategy for ensuring that backups are completed in a timely manner, using a method that will not require the purchase of additional backup software.

Requirement 1

Requirement 1 involves planning an appropriate trust relationship strategy to allow users in all domains in both forests to access resources across all domains.

1. Based on the fact that Contoso is running Windows Server 2003 Active Directory and Northwind Traders is running Windows 2000 Active Directory, what types of trust relationships will need to be configured?

   a. Shortcut trusts

   b. External trusts

   c. Forest trusts

   d. Realm trusts

2. How many trust relationships will need to be configured between Contoso and Northwind Traders based on the stated requirements?

   a. 1

   b. 2

   c. 3

   d. 6

3. Once both forests are configured to the Windows Server 2003 forest functional level, what method can be used to simplify the trust relationships between the two forests?

   a. Implement a forest trust

   b. Implement an external trust

   c. Implement a shortcut trust

   d. Implement a realm trust

Requirement 2

Requirement 2 involves planning an appropriate schema modification strategy for the proposed directory-enabled application.

1. Which of the following should Contoso consider doing prior to implementing schema changes on its production network?

    a. Ensure that existing object classes and attributes do not meet their needs.

    b. Test proposed changes on a test network.

    c. Obtain correct X.500 object identifiers (OIDs).

    d. Raise the forest to the Windows Server 2003 functional level.

2. An administrator at Contoso is attempting to implement schema changes on a test server but cannot access the Active Directory Schema snap-in. Of the following choices, which one is most likely the cause of the problem?

    a. She is not a member of the Schema Admins group.

    b. The forest is not configured to the Windows Server 2003 forest functional level.

    c. The associated DLL file has not been registered.

    d. The server does not hold the schema master role.

Requirement 3

Requirement 3 involves determining an appropriate Active Directory backup strategy using the Windows Server 2003 Backup Utility.

1. When the only domain controller in an Active Directory environment needs to be restored, what technique should be used?

    a. Authoritative restore

    b. Normal restore

    c. Primary restore

    d. Partial restore

2. What will happen when a deleted object is restored to Active Directory in an environment that includes multiple domain controllers?

    a. The restored object will be available on that domain controller only.

    b. The restored object will be replicated to all domain controllers.

    c. The restored object will be overwritten by replication.

Troubleshooting Lab

Over the course of the past two weeks, various administrators at Contoso have been adding, deleting, and editing Active Directory objects as part of their Windows Server 2003 deployment. When the IT manager at Contoso arrived at work yesterday morning, he noticed that one critical OU was no longer visible in Active Directory Users And Computers, and that all the computer objects stored in the container were also missing. Furthermore, one administrator misconfigured the user accounts of three different users. Knowing that a recent System State backup had been completed the previous morning when these objects still existed in their correct form, the IT manager attempted to restore System State data for the server, but after a brief period the objects were again missing. He has asked you to help troubleshoot the issue and restore the missing objects.

The missing objects include:

■ An OU named Desktops, which contained three computer accounts.

■ Three user accounts—named Mark, Bill, and Mary—that were stored in the Users container.

To replicate the circumstances leading to this scenario, you must:

1. Configure Server01 and Server02 as follows:

  ❑ Server01: Domain controller in contoso.com

  ❑ Server02: Domain controller in contoso.com

2. Create the following objects in Active Directory:

  ❑ Top-level OU: Desktops

  ❑ Computer accounts in the Desktops OU: Desktop01, Desktop02, Desktop03

  ❑ User accounts in the Users OU: Mark, Bill, Mary

3. Ensure that all objects have replicated to both Server01 and Server02, and then back up the System State on Server01 to a location of your choice, such as a file on Server01's hard drive.

4. After backing up the System State on Server01, delete the Desktops OU and change the Description attribute of the three user accounts.

To simulate the normal restore performed by the IT manager at Contoso.com:

1. Restart Server01 in Directory Services Restore Mode.

2. Open the Backup Utility, and restore the System State data using the steps outlined in Lesson 3.

3. Once the restore process is complete, reboot Server01 normally and log on as Administrator.

4. Open Active Directory Users And Computers on Server02. Notice that even after a number of minutes have passed, the restored objects have not been replicated to this domain controller.

You realize that to restore the Desktops OU and the three missing computer accounts, and to repair the changes to the user accounts, an authoritative restore must be performed.

1. Restart Server01 in Directory Services Restore Mode.

2. Open the Backup Utility, and restore the System State data using the steps outlined in Lesson 3.

3. When the System State restore has completed, *do not restart* Server01.

4. Once the System State information has been restored, open a Command Prompt and restore the Desktops OU, as well as all necessary computer and user accounts that are missing using Ntdsutil.

5. Once complete, restart Server01 normally, confirming that the objects have been restored.

6. Open Active Directory Users And Computers on Server02 to confirm that the restored objects have been replicated.

Chapter Summary

■ A trust relationship is a logical link between two domains that allows users in one domain to gain access to resources in another.

■ In Windows Server 2003 Active Directory, trusts can be created manually or automatically, can be transitive or nontransitive, and can be one-way or two-way. The following types of trust relationships can be created manually: shortcut, realm, external, and forest.

■ Windows Server 2003 Active Directory allows you to create additional UPN suffixes that can be used to increase security and simplify logon for users within a forest.

■ The schema is the storage location for the definitions of all objects that can be created in Active Directory. One domain controller in an Active Directory forest holds the schema master role, but the schema partition is replicated to all domain controllers in a forest.

■ The Active Directory schema can be extended to include new object classes and attributes. Existing object classes and attributes can be modified, deactivated, and reactivated, with the exception of system object classes and attributes. Only members of the Schema Admins group in the forest root domain can modify the Active Directory schema.

■ Active Directory can be backed up using the Windows Server 2003 Backup Utility. Active Directory cannot be backed up as an individual component; instead, it is backed up as part of the System State data on a domain controller.

■ Windows Server 2003 supports three methods for restoring System State data: primary, normal, and authoritative restores. To restore System State data on a domain controller, the server must be started in Directory Services Restore Mode.

■ When Active Directory objects that were deleted or misconfigured need to be restored or rolled back to previous settings, an authoritative restore must be performed. An authoritative restore involves using the Ntdsutil command-line utility to mark portions of the Active Directory database or individual objects as authoritative after a normal restore.

Exam Highlights

Before taking the exam, review the key points and terms that are presented in this section to help you identify topics you need to review. Return to the lessons for additional practice, and review the "Further Readings" sections in Part 2 for pointers to more information about topics covered by the exam objectives.

Key Points

■ Windows Server 2003 Active Directory supports various types of trust relationships. Be familiar with the circumstances under which each type should be created, as well as the characteristics associated with each.

■ Know when to create a forest trust, as well as the requirements and limitations associated with this type of trust relationship.

■ Understand how to create additional UPNs and why a company might choose to implement them.

■ Be familiar with the reasons why the Active Directory schema might need to be modified, as well as the different types of modifications supported.

■ Know how to back up Active Directory using the Windows Server 2003 Backup Utility, as well as the different restore processes and when each should be used.

Key Terms

Selective authentication   Windows Server 2003 external trust relationships can be limited to prevent uncontrolled authentication of users from the trusted domain by computers in the trusting domain. When selective authentication is applied to an external trust, administrators in the trusting domain specify the users in the trusting domain who can authenticate for specific computers in the trusting domain. Each computer object in Active Directory includes an Allow To Authenticate access control right, which must be granted to users (or groups that include users) from the trusted domain.

Domain-wide authentication   Windows Server 2003 external trust relationships can be limited to prevent uncontrolled authentication of users from the trusted domain by computers in the trusting domain. When domain-wide authentication is applied to an external trust, users in the trusted domain are able to authenticate against all computers in the trusting domain. All users in the trusted domain are members of the Authenticated Users and Everyone groups in the trusting domain.

Schema   The schema is the partition of Active Directory that defines attributes and object classes and therefore determines the types of objects that can be stored in the Active Directory directory service.

System State   The System State of a domain controller includes the Active Directory database. To back up Active Directory, you must select System State in the Backup Utility.

Authoritative restore   A normal restore of Active Directory restores the database as of the date of the backup. Upon rebooting, the domain controller replicates all of the updates that have occurred since the backup date. An authoritative restore, performed using the Ntdsutil tool immediately after restoring Active Directory, marks one or more objects, or the entire database, as authoritative, ensuring that the object or objects will be replicated from the restored domain controller to the other domain controllers in the forest. Authoritative restore is used to recover objects that have been deleted or changed since an Active Directory backup.

Questions and Answers

Page
3-36
Lesson 1 Review

1. Which type of trust provides a transitive trust relationship between two forests?

A forest trust.

2. What is the purpose of a shortcut trust?

A shortcut trust is a trust relationship between two domains in the same forest, created to improve user logon times and shorten a trust path.

3. What preliminary tasks must you complete before you can create a forest trust?

Before you can create a forest trust, you must

❑ Configure a DNS root server that is authoritative over both forest DNS servers that you want to form a trust with, or configure a DNS forwarder on both of the DNS servers that are authoritative for the trusting forests.

❑ Ensure that the forest functional level for both forests is Windows Server 2003.

4. Which of the following types of trust relationships are created automatically? Choose all that apply.

a. Tree-root

b. Parent-child

c. Shortcut

d. Realm

e. External

f. Forest

The correct answers are a and b. Shortcut, realm, external, and forest trusts must all be created manually.

Page
3-51
Lesson 2 Review

1. To modify the Active Directory schema, what group must a user be a member of?

Schema Admins

2. When the Active Directory schema is modified, to which domain controllers are the changes replicated?

All domain controllers in the same forest

3. Where is the Active Directory schema stored on a domain controller?

In the schema partition, a cached copy of which is stored in memory

Lesson 3 Review

1. What tasks should you complete before attempting to back up Active Directory data?

   Before attempting to back up Active Directory data, you must prepare the files that you want to back up, and if you are using a removable media device, you must prepare the device.

2. What is System State data, and why is it significant to backing up Active Directory?

   For Windows Server 2003 operating systems, the System State data is made up of the registry, COM+ Class Registration database, system boot files, files protected by Windows File Protection, and the Certificate Services database (if the server is a certificate server). If the server is a domain controller, Active Directory and the Sysvol directory are also contained in the System State data. To back up Active Directory, you must back up the System State data.

3. Can you restrict who can gain access to a completed backup file or tape? If so, how?

   You can restrict who can gain access to a completed backup file or tape by selecting the Replace The Existing Backups option and the Allow Only The Owner And The Administrator Access To The Backup Data And To Any Backups Appended To This Medium option on the Backup Options page in the Backup Or Restore Wizard.

4. When you specify the items you want to back up in the Backup Or Restore Wizard, which of the following should you select to successfully back up Active Directory data?

   a. System State data

   b. Shared system volume folder

   c. Database and log files

   d. Registry

   The correct answer is a. When you specify the items you want to back up in the Backup Or Restore Wizard, you must specify System State data to successfully back up Active Directory data.

Case Scenario Exercise, Requirement 1

1. Based on the fact that Contoso is running Windows Server 2003 Active Directory and Northwind Traders is running Windows 2000 Active Directory, what types of trust relationships will need to be configured?

   a. Shortcut trusts

   b. External trusts

   c. Forest trusts

   d. Realm trusts

   b

2. How many trust relationships will need to be configured between Contoso and Northwind Traders based on the stated requirements?

   a. 1

   b. 2

   c. 3

   d. 6

   d

3. Once both forests are configured to the Windows Server 2003 forest functional level, what method can be used to simplify the trust relationships between the two forests?

   a. Implement a forest trust

   b. Implement an external trust

   c. Implement a shortcut trust

   d. Implement a realm trust

   a

Page
3-75
Case Scenario Exercise, Requirement 2

1. Which of the following should Contoso consider doing prior to implementing schema changes on its production network?

   a. Ensure that existing object classes and attributes do not meet their needs.

   b. Test proposed changes on a test network.

   c. Obtain correct X.500 object identifiers (OIDs).

   d. Raise the forest to the Windows Server 2003 functional level.

   a, b, c

2. An administrator at Contoso is attempting to implement schema changes on a test server but cannot access the Active Directory Schema snap-in. Of the following choices, which one is most likely the cause of the problem?

   a. She is not a member of the Schema Admins group.

   b. The forest is not configured to the Windows Server 2003 forest functional level.

   c. The associated DLL file has not been registered.

   d. The server does not hold the schema master role.

   c

Page
3-75

Case Scenario Exercise, Requirement 3

1. When the only domain controller in an Active Directory environment needs to be restored, what technique should be used?

   a. Authoritative restore

   b. Normal restore

   c. Primary restore

   d. Partial restore

   c

2. What will happen when a deleted object is restored to Active Directory in an environment that includes multiple domain controllers?

   a. The restored object will be available on that domain controller only.

   b. The restored object will be replicated to all domain controllers.

   c. The restored object will be overwritten by replication.

   c

4 Managing Users, Groups, and Computers

Exam Objectives in this Chapter:

- Create and manage user accounts (Exam 70-292).

    - ❑ Create and modify user accounts by using the Active Directory Users And Computers snap-in.

    - ❑ Create and modify user accounts by using automation.

    - ❑ Import user accounts.

- Create and manage groups (Exam 70-292).

    - ❑ Identify and modify the scope of a group.

    - ❑ Find domain groups in which a user is a member.

    - ❑ Manage group membership.

    - ❑ Create and modify groups by using the Active Directory Users And Computers snap-in.

    - ❑ Create and modify groups by using automation.

- Plan a user authentication strategy (Exam 70-296).

    - ❑ Plan a smart card authentication strategy.

    - ❑ Create a password policy for domain users.

- Troubleshoot user authentication issues (Exam 70-292).

Why This Chapter Matters

To control user access to resources in a domain environment, a mechanism must first exist to identify users, and then rights and permissions must be associated with those identities. In Microsoft Windows Server 2003 Active Directory directory service, users are associated with individual user objects, which are ultimately used for authentication purposes and the configuration of user environment settings. In this chapter, you will not only learn the various ways in which user accounts can be created, but you will also learn how those accounts can be modified using a variety of tools included with Windows Server 2003.

To make the assignment of user rights, permissions to network resources, and e-mail distribution lists easier to manage, Windows Server 2003 Active Directory allows you to configure collections of objects into groups. Depending on the functional level of a domain, Active Directory supports two group types and three group scopes. These groups can then be used to aggregate user, computer, and even other group objects to lessen the administrative burden associated with managing multiple objects individually. For example, instead of assigning permissions to a resource multiple times for multiple users, you can make those users members of a single group, with permissions granted once instead. In this chapter, you will not only learn various methods used to create and manage Active Directory groups, but you will also learn the rules associated with changing the scope, type, or membership of a group.

Finally, this chapter takes a look at issues relating to planning and troubleshooting user authentication, including the configuration of account policy settings, methods of troubleshooting common authentication issues, and the implementation of smart cards.

Lessons in this Chapter:

Before You Begin

To complete the hands-on practices and exercises in this chapter, you need:

- Two Windows Server 2003 (Standard or Enterprise Edition) systems installed as Server01 and Server02, respectively. Both servers should currently be installed as domain controllers in the contoso.com domain.

- Access to both servers by using the built-in Administrator account or another account that is part of the Administrators local group.

Lesson 1: Creating and Modifying User Accounts

Before an individual can access network resources, Active Directory requires the verification of the individual's identity, a process more commonly referred to as authentication. The cornerstone of authentication is the user account, with its user logon name, password, and unique security identifier (SID). During logon, Active Directory authenticates a user by using the user name and password provided. Once successful authentication occurs, the Windows Server 2003 security subsystem builds the security access token that represents that user on the network. The access token contains the user account SID, as well as the SIDs of groups to which the user belongs. That token is then used to verify user rights assignments and to authorize access to resources secured by access control lists (ACLs).

A user is represented in Active Directory by a user object. A user object includes not just a user's name, password, and SID, but also contact information such as telephone numbers and addresses, group membership information, environment settings, and more. In this lesson, you will learn more about Active Directory user objects, including how to create and configure them using various methods.

After this lesson, you will be able to

- Create user objects in Active Directory by using the Active Directory Users And Computers snap-in
- Configure user object properties
- Modify properties of multiple user objects simultaneously
- Create and utilize user object templates
- Import user objects from comma-delimited files
- Leverage new command-line tools to create and manage user objects

Estimated lesson time: 40 minutes

Creating User Objects with Active Directory Users And Computers

The primary tool used to create user objects is Active Directory Users And Computers. Although user objects can be created in the root of a domain or in any of the default containers, it is usually best to locate user objects in organizational units (OUs) so that the ability to delegate administrative authority and deploy Group Policy settings can be fully leveraged.

To create a user object, right-click the container in which you want to create the object, select New, and then click User. The New Object–User dialog box appears, as shown in Figure 4-1. The first page of the New Object–User dialog box requests properties related to the user name. Table 4-1 describes the properties that appear on the first page of the dialog box.

Note   To create a new user object, you must be a member of the Enterprise Admins, Domain Admins, or Account Operators group, or you must have been delegated the necessary permissions for the container in which the account will be created.

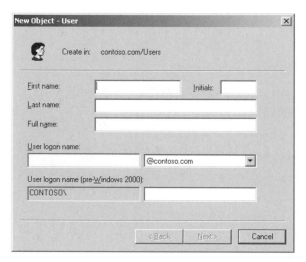

Figure 4-1   The New Object–User dialog box

Table 4-1   User Properties on the First Page of the New Object–User Dialog Box

Property	Description
First Name	The user's first name. Not required.
Initials	The middle initials of the user's name. Not required.
Last Name	The user's last name. Not required.
Full Name	The user's full name. If you enter values for the first or last name, the full name property is populated automatically. However, you can easily modify the suggested value. The field is required.
	The name entered here sets several user object properties, specifically *CN* (common name), *DN* (distinguished name), name, and *displayName*. Because *CN* must be unique within a container, the name entered here must be unique relative to all other objects in the OU (or other container) in which you create the user object.

Table 4-1   User Properties on the First Page of the New Object–User Dialog Box

Property	Description
User Logon Name	The user principal name (UPN) consists of a logon name and a UPN suffix which is, by default, the Domain Name System (DNS) name of the domain in which you create the object. The property is required, and the entire UPN, in the format *logon-name@UPN-suffix*, must be unique within the Active Directory forest. A sample UPN would be someone@contoso.com.
	The UPN can be used to log on from any Microsoft Windows system running Windows 2000, Windows XP, or Windows Server 2003.
User Logon Name (Pre–Windows 2000)	This logon name is used to log on from down-level clients, such as Microsoft Windows 95, Windows 98, Windows Millennium Edition (Windows Me), Windows NT 4.0, or Windows NT 3.51. This field is required and must be unique within the domain.

Once you have entered the values in the first page of the New Object–User dialog box, click Next. The second page of the dialog box, shown in Figure 4-2, allows you to enter the user password and to set account flags.

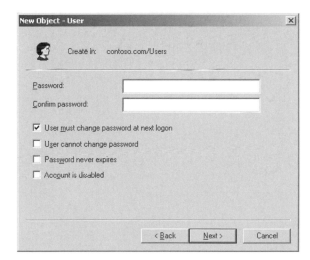

Figure 4-2   Second screen of the New Object–User dialog box

The properties available on the second page of the New Object–User dialog box are summarized in Table 4-2.

Table 4-2   User Properties on the Second Page of the New Object–User Dialog Box

Property	Description
Password	The password that is used to authenticate the user. For security reasons, you should always assign a password. The password is masked as you type it.
Confirm Password	Confirm the password by typing it a second time to make sure you typed it correctly.
User Must Change Password At Next Logon	Select this check box if you want the user to change the password you have entered the first time he or she logs on. You cannot select this option if you have selected Password Never Expires. Selecting this option will automatically clear the mutually exclusive option User Cannot Change Password.
User Cannot Change Password	Select this check box if you have more than one person using the same domain user account (such as Guest) or to maintain control over user account passwords. This option is commonly used to manage service account passwords. You cannot select this option if you have selected User Must Change Password At Next Logon.
Password Never Expires	Select this check box if you never want the password to expire. This option will automatically clear the User Must Change Password At Next Logon setting, as the two options are mutually exclusive. This option is commonly used to manage service account passwords.
Account Is Disabled	Select this check box to disable the user account—for example, when creating an object for a newly hired employee who does not yet need access to the network.

Some account options listed in Table 4-2 have the potential to conflict with settings configured in domain Group Policy objects. For example, the default domain policy disables the storing of passwords using reversible encryption. However, in the rare circumstances that require reversible encryption, the user account property Store Password Using Reversible Encryption will take precedence for that specific user object. Similarly, policies might specify a maximum password age or specify that users must change the password at next logon. If a user object is configured with the Password Never Expires option, this configuration will override the settings configured in any policy.

Managing User Objects with Active Directory Users And Computers

When creating a new user, you are initially prompted to configure the most common properties for the user object, including logon names and a password. However, user objects support numerous additional properties that you can configure at any time via Active Directory Users And Computers. These properties facilitate the administration of user objects, as well as the ability to search for objects by using LDAP queries.

To configure the properties of a user object, right-click it and choose Properties. The user's Properties dialog box appears, as shown in Figure 4-3.

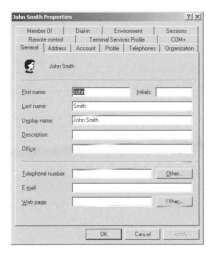

Figure 4-3   The user's Properties dialog box

The pages in the Properties dialog box expose configurable settings that fall into several broad categories:

- **Account properties: the Account tab**   This tab allows you to configure settings that were originally defined as part of creating a new user object, including logon names, password, and account flags.

- **Personal information: the General, Address, Telephones, and Organization tabs**   The General tab exposes the name properties that are configured when you create a user object. The Address, Telephones, and Organization tabs allow you to configure settings that you would expect on each of these tabs.

- **User configuration management: the Profile tab**   This tab is used to configure a profile path, logon script, and home folder location for a user.

- **Group membership: the Member Of tab**   This tab is used to configure the security groups that the user is a member of.

- **Terminal services: the Terminal Services Profile, Environment, Remote Control, and Sessions tabs**   These four tabs allow you to configure and manage user environment settings for Terminal Services sessions.

- **Remote access: the Dial-in tab**   This tab allows you to enable and configure remote access permission for a user.

- **Applications: the COM+ tab**   This tab, new in Windows Server 2003, facilitates the management of distributed applications by assigning Active Directory COM+ partition sets to the user.

Account Properties

When a new user object is created in Active Directory, the Account tab stores most of the settings originally configured via the New Object–User pages. Figure 4-4 displays the Account tab in the Properties dialog box of a user object.

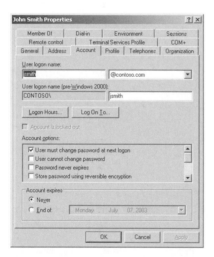

Figure 4-4   The Account tab of the user Properties dialog box

Several properties shown in Figure 4-4 were originally discussed in Table 4-2. Table 4-3 outlines some advanced properties that can be configured from the Account tab of a user object.

Table 4-3   User Account Properties

Property	Description
Logon Hours	This option is used to configure the hours during which a user is allowed to log on to the network.
Log On To	This option is used to limit the workstations to which the user can log on. You must have NetBIOS over TCP/IP enabled for this feature to function correctly.

Table 4-3   User Account Properties

Property	Description
Store Password Using Reversible Encryption	This option, which stores the user password in Active Directory without using the default nonreversible encryption algorithm, exists to support applications that require knowledge of the user password. If it is not explicitly required, do not enable this option because it weakens password security. Macintosh clients using the AppleTalk protocol require knowledge of the user password. If a user logs on using a Macintosh client, you will need to select the Store Password Using Reversible Encryption option.
Smart Card Is Required For Interactive Logon	This option is used to designate that the user must use a smart card during the authentication process. Smart cards are portable, tamper-resistant hardware devices that store unique identification information for a user. They are inserted into a card reader attached to a computer and provide an additional physical identification component to the authentication process.
Account Is Trusted For Delegation	This option enables a service account to impersonate a user to access network resources on behalf of a user. It is typically used for service accounts in multitier application infrastructures.
Account Expires	This option is used to specify when an account expires. For example, an account for a temporary employee or consultant could be set to expire on the day his or her contract is scheduled to finish.

Managing Properties on Multiple Accounts Simultaneously

Windows Server 2003 introduces a new feature in Active Directory Users And Computers that allows you to modify the properties of multiple user accounts simultaneously. To multiselect objects, hold down the CTRL key as you click each user object. Be certain that you select only objects of one object class, such as users. Once you have multiselected, click the Action menu and then choose Properties.

When you have multiselected user objects, a subset of properties is available for modification. Arranged by tab, these properties include:

- **General tab**   Description, Office, Telephone Number, Fax, Web Page, and E-mail
- **Account tab**   UPN Suffix, Logon Hours, Computer Restrictions (Logon Workstations), All Account Options, and Account Expires
- **Address tab**   Street, P.O. Box, City, State/Province, ZIP/Postal Code, and Country/Region
- **Profile tab**   Profile Path, Logon Script, and Home Folder
- **Organization tab**   Title, Department, Company, and Manager

Be sure to know which properties can be modified for multiple users simultaneously. Exam scenarios that suggest a need to change many user objects' properties as quickly as possible are often testing your understanding of multiselect.

Exam Tip There are still many properties that must be set on a user-by-user basis. Also, certain administrative tasks, including resetting passwords and renaming accounts, can be performed on only one user object at a time.

Moving a User

If a user is transferred to a different department or unit within an organization, you might need to move his or her user object to reflect administration or configuration changes. To move an object in Active Directory Users And Computers, first select the object and then choose Move from the Action menu. Alternatively, you can right-click the object and select Move from the shortcut menu. Once the Move dialog box appears, you can select the container the object should be moved to.

Tip Windows Server 2003 now allows drag-and-drop operations within many administrative tools, including Active Directory Users And Computers. For example, you can now move a user object from one container to another by simply clicking the object and dragging it to a new container, much like a file or folder in the Windows Explorer interface.

Creating and Using User Object Templates

In the previous section, you learned that it is not unusual for certain objects to share common properties. For example, all sales representatives might belong to the same groups, have the same logon restrictions, or have home folders on the same server. In such cases, it would be helpful to have a template to reduce some of the administrative burden associated with configuring objects with common properties.

To define a user template, you need to create a new user object and populate the properties that will be common to multiple users, such as group membership, logon hours, and so forth. Ultimately, this account will be used as the basis for creating new accounts that require the property settings you have configured.

Security Alert Be certain to *disable* any user object created for use as a template. Because this object is strictly a template, you need to ensure that the account cannot be used to log on and access network resources.

> **Tip**   When defining a template object, consider preceding the object name with the underscore (_) character. This will ensure that the template account appears at the top of the list when sorting by name in Active Directory Users And Computers.

To create new user accounts based on a defined template, right-click the template user object and then click Copy. You will be prompted to configure properties similar to those you configure when you create a new user object, such as first and last name, initials, logon names, password, and account options. The following list outlines the properties, arranged by tabs available in the properties of a user object, that will be copied from the template account:

- **General tab**   No properties are copied.
- **Address tab**   All properties except Street Address are copied.
- **Account tab**   All properties are copied, except for logon names, which you are prompted to enter when copying the template.
- **Profile tab**   All properties are copied, and the profile and home-folder paths are modified to reflect the new user's logon name.
- **Telephones tab**   No properties are copied.
- **Organization tab**   All properties are copied, except for Title.
- **Member Of tab**   All properties are copied.
- **Dial-In, Environment, Sessions, Remote Control, Terminal Services Profile, and COM+ tabs**   No properties are copied.

> **Exam Tip**   By default, a user object that has been created by copying a template has the same group membership settings as the template object. Permissions and rights that are assigned to the groups specified in the template will therefore apply to the new user. However, permissions or rights assigned directly to the template user object are *not* copied to the new object.   *Another good reason to use groups!*

Importing User Objects Using Csvde.exe

Csvde.exe is a command-line utility that allows you to import or export objects in Active Directory to or from a comma-delimited text file (also known as a comma-separated value text file). The command represents a powerful way to quickly generate new objects or extract information from Active Directory for use with other applications or databases. The basic syntax of the Csvde command is:

csvde [-i] [-f FileName] [-k]

- -i: Specifies import mode. If not specified, the default mode is export.

- -f *FileName*: Identifies the import file name.

- -k: Ignores errors including "object already exists," "constraint violation," and "attribute or value already exists" during the import operation, and continues processing.

The file used by Csvde is a comma-delimited text file (*.csv or *.txt), in which the first line is a list of Lightweight Directory Access Protocol (LDAP) names for the attributes to be imported, followed by one line for each individual object. Each object must contain the attributes listed on the first line, as shown in the following example:

```
DN,objectClass,sAMAccountName,sn,givenName,userPrincipalName
"CN=Scott Bishop,OU=Employees,DC=contoso,DC=com",
  user,sbishop,Bishop,Scott,scott.bishop@contoso.com
```

In this example, the text file used with Csvde would create a user object in the Employees OU named Scott Bishop. The file also configures the associated user logon name, first name, last name, and UPN.

> **See Also**   For more information about the powerful Csvde command, including details regarding its parameters and its usage to *export* directory objects, see the Windows Help and Support Center. More information about the Ldifde.exe command, which allows you to import and export accounts using LDAP formats, can also be found in the Help and Support Center. Ldifde is also discussed in Lesson 2.

Using Active Directory Command-Line Tools

For the purpose of automating the creation and management of Active Directory objects, Windows Server 2003 supports a number of powerful new command-line tools. The following list briefly describes some of these new tools and their basic capabilities:

- **Dsadd.exe**   Adds objects to the directory

- **Dsget.exe**   Displays or "gets" properties of objects in the directory

- **Dsmod.exe**   Modifies select attributes of an existing object in the directory

- **Dsmove.exe**   Moves an object from its current container to a new location

- **Dsrm.exe**   Removes an object or the complete subtree of an object

- **Dsquery.exe**   Queries Active Directory for objects that match specified search criteria

These tools use one or more of the following components in their command-line switches:

- **Target object type**   One of a predefined set of values that correlates with an object class in Active Directory. Common examples are: computer, user, OU, group, and server (domain controller).

- **Target object identity**   The distinguished name (DN) of the object against which the command is running. The DN of an object is an attribute of each object that represents the object's name and location within an Active Directory forest. For example, CN=Dan Holme, OU=Employees, DC=Contoso, DC=com.

> **Note**   When using distinguished names that include spaces in a command parameter, be sure to enclose the name in quotes.

- **Server**   You can specify the domain controller against which you want to run the command.

- **User**   You can specify a user name and password with which to run the command. This is useful if you are logged in with nonadministrative privileges and want to launch the command with elevated credentials.

- **Switches and parameters**   These are not case sensitive, and they can be prefixed with either a dash (-) or a forward slash (/).

Dsquery.exe

The Dsquery.exe command queries Active Directory for objects that match a specific criteria set. The command's basic syntax is:

```
dsquery object_type [{StartNode | forestroot | domainroot}]
[-o {dn | rdn | samid}] [-scope {subtree | onelevel | base}] [-name Name]
[-desc Description] [-upn UPN] [-samid SAMName] [-inactive NumberOfWeeks]
[-stalepwd NumberOfDays] [-disabled] [{-s Server | -d Domain}] [-u UserName]
[-p {Password | *}]
```

> **Tip**   Keep in mind that this command is usually used to generate a list of objects against which you will run other command-line utilities. This is accomplished by piping the output to a second command. For example, the following command first queries Active Directory for a user object name starting with "Dan" and then pipes the result set to *Dsmod*, which disables each object returned by *Dsquery*.
>
> dsquery user -name Dan* | dsmod user -disabled yes

The basic parameters of the Dsquery command are summarized in Table 4-4.

Table 4-4   Parameters for the Dsquery.exe Command

Parameter	Description
Query scope	
object_type	Required. The object type represents the object classes to be searched for. The object type can include computer, contact, group, OU, site, server, user, quota, partition, or the * wildcard character to represent any object class.
{*StartNode* | forestroot | domainroot}	Optional. Specifies the node from which the search should begin. You can specify the forest root (*forestroot*), domain root (*domainroot*), or a node's distinguished name (*StartNode*). If *forestroot* is specified, the search is performed against the global catalog. The default value is *domainroot*.
-scope {subtree | onelevel | base}	Specifies the scope of the search. A value of *subtree* indicates that the scope is a subtree rooted at *StartNode*. A value of *onelevel* indicates the immediate children of *StartNode* only. A value of base indicates the single object represented by *StartNode*. If *forestroot* is specified as *StartNode*, *subtree* is the only valid scope. By default, the *subtree* search scope is used.
How to display the result set	
-o {dn | rdn | samid}	Specifies the format in which the list of entries found by the search will be outputted or displayed. A *dn* value displays the distinguished name of each entry. An *rdn* value displays the relative distinguished name of each entry. A *samid* value displays the Security Accounts Manager (SAM) account name of each entry. By default, the *dn* format is used.
Query criteria	
-name *Name*	Searches for users whose name attributes (value of *CN* attribute) matches *Name*. You can use the * wildcard character—for example, "jon*" or "*ith", or "j*th".
-desc *Description*	Searches for users whose description attribute matches *Description*. You can also use wildcards to search for descriptions.
-upn *UPN*	Searches for users whose UPN attribute matches *UPN*.

Table 4-4   Parameters for the Dsquery.exe Command

Parameter	Description
-samid *SAMName*	Searches for users whose SAM account name matches *SAMName*. You can also use wildcards to search for *SAMName* values.
-inactive *NumberOfWeeks*	Searches for all users that have been inactive (stale) for the specified number of *weeks*.
-stalepwd *NumberOfDays*	Searches for all users who have not changed their passwords for the specified number of *days*.
-disabled	Searches for all disabled user accounts.
Domain controller and credentials used for the Dsquery.exe command	
{-s *Server* | -d *Domain*}	Connects to a specified remote server or domain.
-u *UserName*	Specifies the user name with which the user logs on to a remote server. By default, *-u* uses the user name with which the user logged on. You can use any of the following formats to specify a user name:
	user name (for example, Linda)
	domain\user name (for example, contoso\Linda)
	UPN (for example, Linda@contoso.com)
-p {*Password* | *}	Specifies to use either a password or an * to log on to a remote server. If you type *, you are prompted for a password.

> **Tip**   Inactivity is specified in weeks, but password changes are specified in days.

Dsadd.exe

The Dsadd.exe command enables you to create objects in Active Directory. When creating a user object, use the Dsadd User command. Dsadd parameters allow you to configure specific properties of an object. The parameters are self-explanatory; however, the Windows Server 2003 Help And Support Center provides more thorough descriptions of Dsadd command parameters if required. The command's basic syntax is:

dsadd user UserDN...

The *UserDN* parameter is used to specify one or more distinguished names for the new user object or objects. If a DN includes a space, surround the entire DN with quotation marks. The *UserDN* parameter can be entered in one of the following ways:

- By piping a list of DNs from another command, such as Dsquery.
- By typing each DN on the command line, separated by spaces.

- By leaving the *DN* parameter empty, at which point you can type the DNs one at a time from the command prompt. Press ENTER after each DN. Press CTRL+Z and ENTER after the last DN.

The Dsadd User command can take the following optional parameters after the DN parameter:

- -samid *SAMName*
- -upn *UPN*
- -fn *FirstName*
- -mi *Initial*
- -ln *LastName*
- -display *DisplayName*
- -empid *EmployeeID*
- -pwd {*Password* | *}, where * will prompt you for a password
- -desc *Description*
- -memberof *GroupDN*
- -office *Office*
- -tel *PhoneNumber*
- -email *Email*
- -hometel *HomePhoneNumber*
- -pager *PagerNumber*
- -mobile *CellPhoneNumber*
- -fax *FaxNumber*
- -iptel *IPPhoneNumber*
- -webpg *WebPage*
- -title *Title*
- -dept *Department*
- -company *Company*
- -mgr *ManagerDN*
- -hmdir *HomeDirectory*
- -hmdrv *DriveLetter*:
- -profile *ProfilePath*
- -loscr *ScriptPath*

- -mustchpwd {yes | no}

- -canchpwd {yes | no}

- -reversiblepwd {yes | no}

- -pwdneverexpires {yes | no}

- -acctexpires *NumberOfDays*

- -disabled {yes | no}

As with Dsquery, you can add *-s*, *-u*, and *-p* parameters to specify the domain controller against which Dsadd will run, along with a user name and password that will be used to execute the command.

- {-s *Server* | -d *Domain*}

- -u *UserName*

- -p {*Password* | *}

The special token *$username$* (case-insensitive) can replace the SAM account name in the value of the *-email, hmdir, -profile*, and *-webpg* parameters. For example, if a SAM account name is "Denise," the *-hmdir* parameter can be written in either of the following formats:

- -hmdir\users\Denise\home

- -hmdir\users\$username$\home

Dsmod.exe

The Dsmod.exe command modifies the properties of one or more existing objects.

```
dsmod user UserDN ... parameters
```

The Dsmod command handles the *UserDN* parameter in the same way as the Dsadd command, and it takes the same parameters. In this case, instead of adding a new object and specifying property values, you are modifying the properties of an existing object.

> **Note**   You cannot modify the *SAMName* (-samid parameter) or group membership (-memberof parameter) of a user object by using the Dsmod User command. Group membership information can be modified with the Dsmod Group command, a process that is looked at in more detail in Lesson 2 of this chapter.

The Dsmod command also accepts the *-c* parameter. This parameter puts Dsmod into "continuous operation mode," in which it reports errors but continues to modify the specified objects. Without the *-c* parameter, Dsmod will stop operation after the first error it encounters.

Dsget.exe

The Dsget.exe command is effectively a command-line query tool. Dsget first queries Active Directory to "get" properties associated with objects, and then outputs the properties requested.

```
dsget user UserDN ... parameters
```

The Dsget command handles the *UserDN* parameter exactly like the Dsadd command, and it accepts the same parameters. However, Dsget takes *only* the parameter and not an associated value. For example, Dsget takes the *-samid* parameter, not the *-samid SAMName* parameter and value. The main purpose of Dsget is to display properties, not add or modify them. In addition, Dsget does not support the *-password* parameter because it cannot display passwords. Dsget adds the *-dn* and *-sid* parameters, which display the user object's distinguished name and SID, respectively.

> **Exam Tip**   Keep track of the difference between Dsquery and Dsget. Dsquery finds and returns a result set of objects based on property-based search criteria. Dsget returns properties for one or more specified objects.

Dsmove.exe

The Dsmove.exe command allows you to move or rename an object within a domain. It cannot be used to move objects between domains. The basic syntax of the Dsmove command is:

```
dsmove ObjectDN [-newname NewName] [-newparent ParentDN]
```

Dsmove also supports the *-s*, *-u*, and *-p* parameters as described in the Dsquery section.

With Dsmove, an object is specified using its distinguished name via the *ObjectDN* parameter. To rename the object, specify its new common name using the *NewName* parameter. To move an object to a new location, specify the distinguished name of a container via the *ParentDN* parameter.

Dsrm.exe

Dsrm.exe is used to remove an Active Directory object, its subtree, or both. The basic syntax of the Dsrm command is:

```
dsrm ObjectDN ... [-subtree [-exclude]] [-noprompt] [-c]
```

Like the Dsquery command, Dsrm also supports the *-s*, *-u*, and *-p* parameters as described earlier.

The object to be removed from the directory is specified by providing its distinguished name in the *ObjectDN* parameter. The *-subtree* switch directs Dsrm to also remove child objects if a container object such as an OU is being removed. The *-exclude* switch excludes the object itself and can be used only in conjunction with *-subtree*. For example, specifying *-subtree* and *-exclude* would delete the subtree associated with an OU but leave the OU itself intact. Without the *-subtree* or *-exclude* switches supplied, only the specified object is deleted.

When Dsrm is used to remove an object from the directory, you will be prompted to confirm the deletion of each object unless you specify the *-noprompt* parameter. The *-c* switch puts Dsrm into continuous operation mode, in which errors are reported but the command continues to process additional objects. Without the *-c* switch, processing halts when Dsrm first encounters an error.

Practice: Creating and Managing User Objects

In this practice, you will create and modify user objects using Active Directory Users And Computers and the Active Directory command-line tools looked at in this lesson.

Exercise 1: Creating User Objects

1. Log on to Server01 as an administrator.
2. Open Active Directory Users And Computers.
3. Select the Users container.
4. Create a user account with the following information, ensuring that you use a strong password:

Text Box Name	Type
First Name	Andrew
Last Name	Manore
User Logon Name	andrew.manore
User Logon Name (Pre–Windows 2000)	amanore

5. Create a second user object with the following properties:

Property	Type
First Name	Mike
Last Name	Aubert
User Logon Name	mike.aubert
User Logon Name (Pre–Windows 2000)	maubert

6. Create a user object for yourself, following the same conventions for user logon names as you did for the first two objects.

Exercise 2: Modifying User Object Properties

1. Open the Properties dialog box for your user object.

2. Configure the appropriate properties for your user object on the General, Address, Profile, Telephones, and Organization tabs.

3. Examine the many properties associated with your user object, but do not change any other properties yet.

4. Click OK when finished.

Exercise 3: Modifying the Properties of Multiple User Objects

1. Click the Andrew Manore user object.

2. Hold down the CTRL key, and then click the Mike Aubert user object.

3. Click the Action menu, and then click Properties.

4. Notice the difference between the Properties dialog box here and the more extensive Properties dialog box viewed in Exercise 2. Examine the properties that are available when multiple objects are selected, but do not modify any properties yet.

5. Configure the following properties for the two user objects:

Property Page	Property	Type
General	Description	IT Department staff
General	Telephone Number	(416) 555-0175
General	Web Page	*http://www.contoso.com/*
Address	Street	2 Microsoft Way
Address	City	Redmond
Address	State/Province	Washington
Address	ZIP/Postal Code	98052
Organization	Title	Network Engineer
Organization	Company	Contoso

6. Click OK when you finish configuring the properties.

7. Open the properties of the Andrew Manore user object. Confirm that the properties you configured in step 5 now apply to the object. Click OK when you are finished.

8. Click the Mike Aubert user object.

9. Hold down the CTRL key, and click the Andrew Manore user object. Click the Action menu.

10. Notice that the Reset Password command is not available when you have selected more than one user object.

Exercise 4: Importing User Objects Using Csvde.exe

1. Open Notepad.

2. Type the following information on three lines:

```
DN,objectClass,sAMAccountName,sn,givenName,userPrincipalName
"CN=Valerie Whyte,CN=Users,DC=contoso,DC=com",
  user,vwhyte,Whyte,Valerie,valerie.whyte@contoso.com
"CN=Neman Syed,CN=Users,DC=contoso,DC=com",
  user,nsyed,Syed,Neman,neman.syed@contoso.com
```

3. Save the file as "**C:\Users.csv**". (Be sure to surround the filename with quotation marks. Without quotation marks, the file might be saved as C:\Users.csv.txt by default.)

4. Open a command prompt window, and type the following command:

csvde –i -f c:\users.csv

5. If the command output confirms that the command completed successfully, open Active Directory Users And Computers and view the Users container to confirm that the "Neman Syed" and "Valerie Whyte" objects were created. (If Active Directory Users And Computers is already open, you might need to refresh the display.) If the command output suggests that there were errors, open the Users.csv file in Notepad and correct the errors.

6. Because the users were imported without passwords, you must reset their passwords. Once the passwords have been configured, enable the accounts. Both the Reset Password and Enable Account commands can be found on either the Action or right-click shortcut menu.

7. If you have access to an application that can open comma-delimited text files, such as Microsoft Excel, open C:\Users.csv. You will be able to interpret its structure more easily in a columnar display than in Notepad's one-line, comma-delimited text file display.

Exercise 5: Using Active Directory Command-Line Tools

1. Open a command prompt window, and type the following command:

dsquery user "CN=Users, DC=Contoso,DC=Com" -stalepwd 7

2. The command, which finds user objects that have not changed their password in seven days, should list some of the objects you created in the previous exercises. If not, create one or two new user objects and then perform step 1.

3. Type the following command, and press ENTER:

dsquery user "CN=Users, DC=Contoso,DC=Com" -stalepwd 7 | dsmod user -mustchpwd yes

The command used the results of Dsquery as the input for the Dsmod command. Depending on the account options, the Dsmod command attempts to configure the User Must Change Password At Next Logon option for each object. Confirm your success by examining the Account tab of objects in the Users container.

Lesson Review

The following questions are intended to reinforce key information presented in this lesson. If you are unable to answer a question, review the lesson materials and try the question again. You can find answers to the questions in the "Questions and Answers" section at the end of this chapter.

1. You are creating a number of user objects for a team of your organization's temporary workers. They will work daily from 9:00 A.M. to 5:00 P.M. on a contract that is scheduled to begin in one month and end two months later. They will not work outside of that schedule. Which of the following properties should you configure initially to ensure maximum security for the objects?

   a. Password

   b. Logon Hours

   c. Account Expires

   d. Store Password Using Reversible Encryption

   e. Account Is Trusted For Delegation

   f. User Must Change Password At Next Logon

   g. Account Is Disabled

   h. Password Never Expires

2. Which of the following properties and administrative tasks can be configured or performed simultaneously on more than one user object?

    a. Last Name

    b. User Logon Name

    c. Disable Account

    d. Enable Account

    e. Reset Password

    f. Password Never Expires

    g. User Must Change Password At Next Logon

    h. Logon Hours

    i. Computer Restrictions (Logon Workstations)

    j. Title

    k. Direct Reports

3. What method would be most useful to generate 100 new user objects, each of which have identical profile path, home folder path, Title, Web Page, Company, Department, and Manager settings?

    _____

    _____

    _____

    _____

    _____

4. Which tool will allow you to identify accounts that have not been used for two months?

    a. Dsadd

    b. Dsget

    c. Dsmod

    d. Dsrm

    e. Dsquery

5. What variable can be used with the Dsmod and Dsadd commands to create user-specific home folders and profile folders?

   a. *%Username%*

   b. *$Username$*

   c. *CN=Username*

   d. *<Username>*

6. Which tools allow you to output the telephone numbers for all users in an OU?

   a. Dsadd

   b. Dsget

   c. Dsmod

   d. Dsrm

   e. Dsquery

Lesson Summary

■ To create user objects in an Active Directory domain, you must be a member of the Enterprise Admins, Domain Admins, or Account Operators group, or you must have been delegated the proper authority.

■ User objects include properties associated with user authentication requirements, including logon names, a password, and a unique SID. User objects also include properties related to the individuals they represent, including personal information, group membership, and administrative settings. Windows Server 2003 allows you to change some of these properties for multiple users simultaneously using the new multiselect feature.

■ The Csvde command enables you to import directory objects from a comma-delimited text file.

■ Windows Server 2003 supports powerful new command-line tools to create, manage, and delete directory objects, including Dsquery, Dsget, Dsadd, Dsmove, Dsmod, and Dsrm. Dsquery is typically used to produce a result set to pipe as input to other commands.

Lesson 2: Understanding, Creating, and Managing Groups

Groups are Active Directory objects that can contain users, computers, and even other groups as members. The main purpose of using groups is to simplify the administration of Windows Server 2003 Active Directory network environments. In this lesson, you will learn more about each type of group and the scope of each group found in Active Directory, including when each should be used. You will also learn how to create and manage groups by using both Active Directory Users And Computers and command-line utilities such as Ldifde.exe and Dsmod.exe.

After this lesson, you will be able to

- Identify the two types of groups supported by Active Directory, and identify when each should be used
- Identify the three group scopes supported by Active Directory, along with the membership rules associated with each
- Understand both the purpose of the default groups available in Active Directory and the purpose of special identities
- Create groups by using Active Directory Users And Computers
- Create and modify groups by using tools such as Ldifde.exe and Dsmod.exe

Estimated lesson time: 30 minutes

Introduction to Active Directory Groups

At the most basic level, an Active Directory group is nothing more than a collection of users, computers, and even other groups. In most network environments, groups are used to simplify the administration of objects that require common rights or permissions. For example, all users in a department might need the ability to print to a particular printer. Rather than granting each individual user object the print permission on the printer's access control list (ACL), an administrator could place the user objects for that department into a group, and then assign permissions for the group once rather than many times.

Similarly, groups can also be used to simplify the administration of user rights. For example, rather than granting an individual user object the individual rights associated with the ability to administer an Active Directory domain via Group Policy, the user object can instead be made a member of a group such as Domain Admins, which already has the necessary rights applied via its membership in the Administrators group. By applying rights to groups rather than individual user objects, an administrator simplifies the delegation of administrative authority, making an Active Directory environment more streamlined and manageable.

Windows Server 2003 Active Directory supports two main types of groups, as well as three group scopes. The following sections look at group types and scopes in more detail, outlining the situations in which each should be used, along with associated restrictions and limitations based on different Active Directory environments.

Group Types

Windows Server 2003 Active Directory supports two types of groups—security groups and distribution groups. Security groups are used for the purpose of assigning permissions and rights to shared resources, while distribution groups are used to create distribution lists for use with directory-enabled e-mail applications such as Microsoft Exchange Server 2003. Each group type is looked at in more detail in the following sections.

Security Groups

A security group is a security-related entity much like a user account. In the same way that user accounts have an associated security ID (SID), so do security groups. Because of this, members of a security group can be assigned rights and permissions to resources in an Active Directory environment.

It is very important to understand the differences between permissions and rights. Permissions grant users a certain level of access to shared network resources, such as the ability to read a file or manage documents for a particular printer. On the other hand, rights represent abilities throughout an Active Directory domain or forest. For example, the ability to log on locally to a domain controller would be a user right, as would the ability to back up files and folders. In Active Directory environments, rights are assigned to groups through the configuration of Group Policy settings.

Exam Tip   Be sure that you understand the difference between rights and permissions.

When a user is authenticated in an Active Directory environment, his or her access token not only includes information about the user identity, but also the security groups that the user belongs to. As such, rights or permissions assigned to a security group automatically apply to all members of that group.

Note   A user's access token is created after the user has been successfully authenticated. If a user is added to a new security group after he or she has been authenticated, the user will need to log off and then log back on to have the new security group SID associated with his or her access token. Until this happens, the user will not have access to the rights or permissions associated with the security group to which he or she was added.

Distribution Groups

Unlike security groups, distribution groups are created solely for the purpose of defining distribution lists for directory-enabled e-mail applications such as Exchange Server 2003. When an e-mail message needs to be sent to a large number of users simultaneously, the message can be sent to the distribution group rather than individual users. Distribution lists do not have an associated SID and, as such, cannot be used to assign rights or permissions in an Active Directory environment.

> **Exam Tip**   Although security groups are primarily defined for the purpose of assigning rights and permissions, they can also be used as an e-mail entity. This allows messages to be sent to members of a security group in a manner similar to sending messages to a distribution group.

Changing Group Types

When a domain is configured to the Windows 2000 native or Windows Server 2003 domain functional level, you can change the type of a group after it has been originally defined. For example, an administrator might have created a security group when he or she meant to create a distribution group, or vice versa. It is important to remember that when you change a group's type from security to distribution, any permissions or rights that were originally associated with the security group will be lost.

> **Note**   To change the type of an existing group, you must be a member of either the Account Operators, Enterprise Admins, or Domain Admins group, or you must have been delegated the proper authority.

Group Scope

Where a group's type identifies whether it can be assigned rights or permissions, the scope of a group is used to identify the extent to which a group can be applied throughout an Active Directory forest. In some cases, the scope of a group is limited to a single domain, while in other cases, the group can be used in domains throughout a forest. Windows Server 2003 supports the following three group scopes:

- Domain local scope
- Global scope
- Universal scope

The following sections look at each group scope in more detail, outlining the various capabilities and restrictions associated with each at different domain functional levels.

Domain Local Groups

Domain local groups, which were originally introduced in Windows 2000 Active Directory, are primarily used to assign rights and permissions within the domain in which they exist. Unlike local groups, domain local groups are defined in Active Directory and can be used on different Windows 2000, Windows XP, and Windows Server 2003 systems within a domain (depending on the domain functional level). These groups help to alleviate the administrative burden associated with the use of local groups, which can be used only to apply rights or permissions to the system on which they are created. Domain local groups:

- Exist in all forest and domain functional levels.

- Can be applied only to systems in the same domain in which the group exists. For example, you cannot apply permissions to a domain local group for resources outside of its home domain.

- Can be applied to any Windows 2000, Windows XP, or Windows Server 2003 system in a domain when the domain functional level is configured to Windows 2000 native or Windows Server 2003. When a domain is configured to the Windows 2000 mixed functional level, a domain local group can be used only on domain controllers, much like a local group.

- Can include members from global groups in the same domain or any trusted domain, universal groups from the same forest or any trusted forest, and other domain local groups in the same domain.

> **Note**   As a best practice, avoid adding user accounts directly to domain local groups. Instead, add individual users with common needs to global groups, and then make the global group a member of the domain local group. This ultimately makes domain local groups easier to maintain and manage.

Global Groups

Much like in Windows 2000 Active Directory, *global groups* are primarily used to aggregate user accounts with similar needs. Most often, global groups are used to collect users or computers from the same domain that share similar jobs, roles, or functions. For example, a company might create a global group to aggregate its entire sales staff or all users working on a particular project. Global groups:

- Exist in all domain and forest functional levels

- Can be used to assign rights or permissions for resources in any domain throughout a forest, as well as in any trusting domains outside the forest

- Can be made a member of any local group or domain local group in the same forest, as well as in any trusting domains outside of the forest

- Can be made a member of any universal group in the same forest

- Can contain other global groups from the same domain when the domain is configured to the Windows 2000 native or Windows Server 2003 domain functional levels

> **Note** As a best practice, avoid assigning permissions or rights directly to global groups. Instead, assign rights or permissions to domain local groups, and then add global groups as members. This ultimately makes Group Policy user rights assignments and resource ACLs easier to maintain and manage.

Universal Groups

Originally introduced in Windows 2000 Active Directory, *universal groups* are primarily used to aggregate users and groups from different domains with similar needs. Most often, universal groups are used to collect users or groups from the same forest that share similar jobs, roles, or functions. For example, a company might create a universal group to aggregate its entire finance staff. Unlike a global group, which contains members from the same domain only, a universal group can contain members from different domains. In this example, the finance universal group would likely contain all the finance global groups from the various domains in the same forest. Then, when permissions or rights need to be assigned to all finance users throughout the forest, they can be applied to the single universal group rather than to each individual global group, thus reducing administrative effort. Universal security groups:

- Exist only at the Windows 2000 native and Windows Server 2003 domain functional levels

- Can be used to assign rights or permissions to resources in any domain throughout a forest, as well as in any trusting domains outside the forest

- Can include members from any domain in the same forest, including global groups and other universal groups

- Are ultimately stored on global catalog servers in the forest where the group was defined

> **Note** As a best practice, avoid assigning permissions or rights directly to universal groups. Instead, assign rights or permissions to domain local groups, and then add universal groups as members. Along the same lines, avoid placing user accounts directly into universal groups. Instead, place user accounts in global groups, and then add the global group to the universal group. This ultimately helps to reduce global catalog replication traffic, and it makes universal groups easier to maintain and manage.

> **Exam Tip**   Remember that to create universal groups, the domain functional level must be set to Windows 2000 native or Windows Server 2003.

Group Membership Options and Changing Group Scopes

In the same manner as configuring a group type, the scope of an Active Directory group is configured as part of creating a new group. However, when a domain is configured to the Windows 2000 native or Windows Server 2003 domain functional level, the scope of a group can be changed, although the ability to do so depends on the group's current membership. For each group scope, rules exist as to the types of objects that are valid as members. Table 4-5 outlines the types of objects, arranged by domain functional level, that can be members of different group scopes.

Table 4-5   Group Scope and Allowed Objects

Group scope	Allowed objects
Windows 2000 native or Windows Server 2003 domain functional level	
Domain local	Users, computers, global groups, and universal groups from the same domain or any trusted domain. Domain local groups (nested) from the same domain.
Global	Users, computers, and other global groups (nested) from same domain.
Universal	Users, computers, global groups, and other universal groups (nested) from any domain in same forest.
Windows 2000 mixed or Windows Server 2003 interim domain functional level	
Domain local	Users, computers, and global groups from any domain in the same forest.
Global	Users and computers from same domain only.
Universal	Not available.

> **Exam Tip**   While both the Windows 2000 native and Windows Server 2003 domain functional levels support the nesting of groups (placing a global group within a global group, for example), the Windows 2000 mixed and Windows Server 2003 interim domain functional levels do not.

Once a domain is configured to the Windows 2000 native or Windows Server 2003 domain functional levels, you can change the scope of a group, but only if doing so does not break any of the membership rules outlined in Table 4-5. The following points outline the group scope conversions supported in Windows Server 2003, as well as the restrictions associated with each:

- **Global to universal**   A global group can be converted to a universal group, but only if it is not a member of any other global groups.

- **Domain local to universal**   A domain local group can be converted to a universal group, but only if it does not have any other domain local groups as members.

- **Universal to global**   A universal group can be converted to a global group, but only if it does not have any other universal groups as members.

- **Universal to domain local**   A universal group can be converted to a domain local group at any time without restrictions.

> **Note**   To change the type of an existing group, you must be a member of either the Account Operators, Enterprise Admins, or Domain Admins group, or you must have been delegated the proper authority.

> **Exam Tip**   Be familiar with the supported group scope conversions in Windows Server 2003. Remember that a domain must be configured to the Windows 2000 native or Windows Server 2003 domain functional levels for group scope conversions to be possible.

Default Groups

Windows Server 2003 automatically creates a number of security groups when Active Directory is installed on the first domain controller in a new domain. Administrators can use these default groups to control access to network resources or to assign rights to users and groups. Many of the default groups already have rights associated with them, according to common network functions. For example, members of the default Backup Operators group are preassigned the rights to back up files and directories, allow logon locally, restore files and directories, and shut down the system. Instead of granting these rights to an individual user, an administrator would be better off to simply make the user a member of the default Backup Operators group.

Default groups are stored in two different locations, namely the Builtin container and the Users container. Tables 4-6 and 4-7 outline the most commonly used groups found in each container and provide an overview of the purpose of each.

Table 4-6 Windows Server 2003 Default Groups, Builtin Container

Group name	Description
Account Operators	Members of this group can create, modify, and delete accounts for users, groups, and computers in all containers in the domain, with the exception of the Domain Controllers OU. Members cannot modify the membership of the Administrators or Domain Admins groups, but they can log on to domain controllers and shut them down.
Administrators	Members of this group have full control of domain resources. Default members include the Administrator account, along with Domain Admins and Enterprise Admins.
Backup Operators	Members of this group can back up and restore files on domain controllers, as well as log on to domain controllers and shut them down.
Guests	Members of this group have restricted access to the domain environment. By default, both the Domain Guests and built-in Guest account (disabled by default) are members.
Incoming Forest Trust Builders	Members of this group can create one-way incoming trust relationships to the forest root domain, allowing users in the same forest to access resources in another. This group exists only in the forest root domain and has no members by default.
Network Configuration Operators	Members of this group can change the TCP/IP settings on a domain controller. This group has no members by default.
Performance Log Users	Members of this group can manage performance counters, logs, and alerts for both local and remote domain controllers in the domain.
Performance Monitor Users	Members of this group can manage performance counters for both local and remote domain controllers in the domain. This group has no members by default.
Pre–Windows 2000 Compatible Access	Members of this group have the read permission for all user and group objects in the domain. This group is used for backward compatibility with Windows NT 4.0. The special identity Authenticated Users is a member of this group by default.
Print Operators	Members of this group can manage, create, add, and delete printers connected to any domain controller, and manage printer objects in Active Directory. Members of this group can also log on locally to a domain controller and shut it down. This group has no members by default.
Remote Desktop Users	Members of this group can remotely log on to domain controllers in the domain by using Remote Desktop. This group has no members by default.

Table 4-6   Windows Server 2003 Default Groups, Builtin Container

Group name	Description
Replicator	This group is used to support replication functions required by the File Replication Service (FRS). This group has no members by default, and users should not be added to this group.
Server Operators	Members of this group can create and delete shared resources, stop and start services, back up and restore files, format drives, and shut down domain controllers. This group has no members by default.
Users	Members of this group can perform common network tasks such as running applications and accessing shared resources. The Domain Users, Authenticated Users, and Interactive objects are members of this group by default.

Table 4-7   Windows Server 2003 Default Groups, Users Container

Group name	Description
Cert Publishers	Members of this group can publish certificates for both users and computers. This group has no members by default.
DnsAdmins (installed with DNS)	Members of this group have administrative access to the DNS service. This group has no members by default.
DnsUpdateProxy (installed with DNS)	Members of this group are DNS clients that can perform dynamic updates on behalf of other clients such as DHCP servers. This group has no members by default.
Domain Admins	Members of this group have full control of the domain. The only member of this group by default is the Administrator account. This group is a member of the Administrators group.
Domain Computers	This group contains all the computers added to the domain. When computers are added to the domain, they automatically become a member of this group.
Domain Controllers	This group contains all the domain controllers in the domain. When computers are promoted to domain controllers, they automatically become a member of this group.
Domain Guests	This group contains all domain guests.
Domain Users	This group contains all domain users. All new user accounts created in the domain automatically become a member of this group. This group is a member of the Users group by default.
Enterprise Admins	Members of this group, which exists in the forest root domain only, have full control of all domains in the same Active Directory forest. By default, only the Administrator account in the forest root domain is a member of this group. This group is a member of the Administrators group in all domains in the same forest.

Table 4-7   Windows Server 2003 Default Groups, Users Container

Group name	Description
Group Policy Creator Owners	Members of this group can modify Group Policy objects in the domain. The Administrator account is the only member by default.
IIS_WPG (installed with IIS)	This is the worker process group used with Internet Information Services (IIS) 6.0. Accounts added to this group are used to serve specific namespaces on an IIS server. Users should not be added to this group. This group has no members by default.
RAS and IAS Servers	Servers placed in this group have access to the remote access properties of user accounts.
Schema Admins	Members of this group, which exists in the forest root domain only, can modify the Active Directory schema. The Administrator account from the forest root domain is the only member of this group by default.
TelnetClients	Members of this group are able to access the Telnet service on the system. The group has no members by default.

Special Identities

Windows Server 2003 also supports a number of special groups, known as *special identities,* which are managed by the operating system. Special identities cannot be created or deleted, and their membership cannot be modified by administrators. Special identities do not appear in the Active Directory Users And Computers snap-in or in any other computer management tool, but they can be assigned permissions in an ACL. Table 4-8 details some of the special identities in Windows Server 2003.

Table 4-8   Windows Server 2003 Special Identities

Identity	Description
Everyone	Represents all current network users, including guests and users from other domains. Whenever a user logs on to the network, that user is automatically added to the Everyone group.
Network	Represents users currently accessing a given resource over the network (as opposed to users who access a resource by logging on locally). Whenever a user accesses a given resource over the network, the user is considered part of the Network group.

Table 4-8   Windows Server 2003 Special Identities

Identity	Description
Interactive	Represents all users currently logged on to a particular computer and accessing a resource located on that computer (as opposed to users who access the resource over the network). Whenever a user accesses a given resource on the computer to which he or she is logged on, the user is considered part of the Interactive group.
Anonymous Logon	The Anonymous Logon group refers to any user who is using network resources but did not go through the authentication process. In a Windows Server 2003 Active Directory environment, the Anonymous Logon group is not a member of the Everyone group.
Authenticated Users	The Authenticated Users group includes all users who are authenticated into the network by using a valid user account. When assigning permissions, you can use the Authenticated Users group in place of the Everyone group to prevent anonymous access to resources.
Creator Owner	The Creator Owner group refers to the user who created or has ultimately taken ownership of a resource. For example, if a user created a resource but the Administrator took ownership of it, the Creator Owner would be the Administrator.
Dialup	The Dialup group includes anyone who is connected to the network through a remote access connection.

Important   Special identities can be assigned permissions to network resources, although caution should be used when assigning permissions to some of these groups. For example, if you assign permissions for a shared folder to the Everyone group, users connecting from trusted domains will also have access to the resource.

Creating Security Groups

The primary tool used to create groups in Windows Server 2003 is Active Directory Users And Computers. Much like user objects, new group objects can be created in the root of the domain, any of the built-in containers, or defined OUs. To create a new group, simply right-click the container in which the group should be created, select New, and then click Group. The New Object–Group window is shown in Figure 4-5.

Figure 4-5   The New Object–Group window

When a domain is configured to the Windows 2000 native or Windows Server 2003 domain functional level, the New Object–Group window defaults to the global group scope and security group type automatically. If the domain functional level is set to Windows 2000 mixed or Windows Server 2003 interim, the universal group scope cannot be selected, as shown in Figure 4-6.

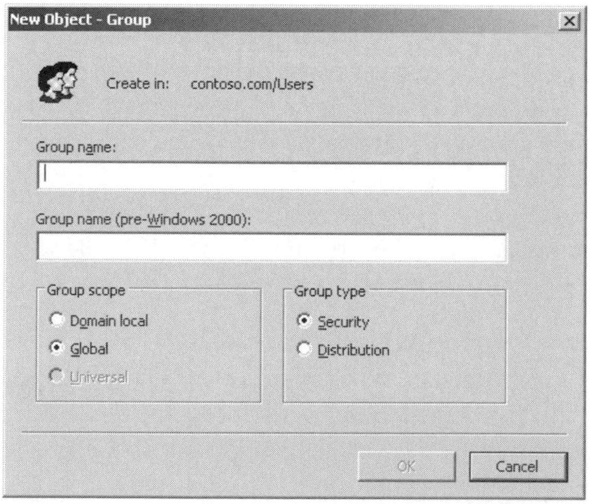

Figure 4-6   Security groups available at the Windows 2000 mixed or Windows Server 2003 interim domain functional level

When creating a new group of any type or scope, you must provide a name that is unique within the domain. As this name is typed into the Group Name field, the same name is automatically populated in the Group Name (Pre–Windows 2000) field.

Once a group has been created, access its properties to change configuration or membership settings as necessary. Notice in Figure 4-7 that the General tab of a global group allows the group type to be changed from security to distribution if necessary, but that the group scope can only be changed to universal. Windows Server 2003 does not allow you to convert a global group to a domain local group, as mentioned earlier in this lesson.

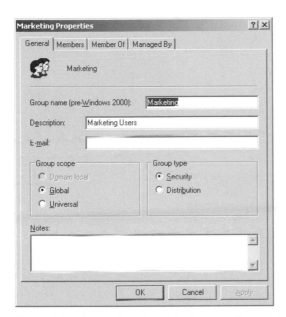

Figure 4-7   Properties of a global group, General tab

Modifying Group Membership

Once a new group has been created, members can be added to the group by using a variety of methods in Active Directory Users And Computers. Some common methods used to add members to groups include:

■ Right-clicking a user object and selecting Add To A Group

■ Accessing the properties of a user, computer, or group; selecting the Member Of tab; and then clicking Add

■ Accessing the properties of a group, selecting the Members tab, and then clicking Add

Figure 4-8 illustrates the Members tab for a global security group named Sales. Notice that this group includes not only users but also another global group.

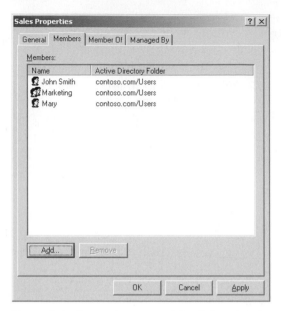

Figure 4-8   Properties page of the Sales global security group, Members tab

Figure 4-9 illustrates the Member Of tab for the Sales global security group. In this case, the tab displays that the Sales group is a member of the Enterprise Sales universal group.

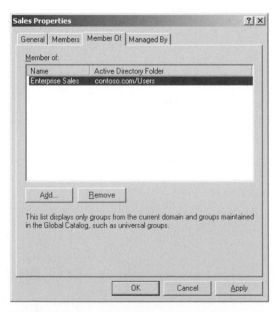

Figure 4-9   Properties page of the Sales security group, Member Of tab

Note   Although the Members and Member Of tabs in the properties of a group will display both the members of a group and its membership in other groups, the information provided by the interface is only one level deep. For example, if the Sales global group was a member of the Sales universal group, and then the Sales universal group was a member of the International universal group, the Members tab in the properties of the International universal group would show only the Sales universal group as a member. The Members and Member Of tabs do not display the multiple levels of nesting that might actually be configured in your environment.

Similarly, the properties of a user or computer object also include a Member Of tab. This allows administrators to quickly determine the groups in which a user or computer is a member and add or remove the object to or from groups as necessary. Figure 4-10 illustrates the Member Of tab for a computer object.

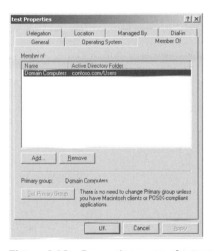

Figure 4-10   Properties page of a test computer object

Using Automation to Manage Group Accounts

Although Active Directory Users And Computers provides a convenient way to create and manage individual groups as necessary, it is not the most efficient method when a large number of groups need to be created at once. In these situations, the Ldifde.exe tool included with Windows Server 2003 would be a better choice. Ldifde.exe provides both import and export capabilities, allowing large numbers of security principals (including groups) to be created at once with the least possible administrative effort.

Using Ldifde.exe

The Lightweight Directory Access Protocol (LDAP) Data Interchange Format (LDIF) is a draft Internet standard for a file format used to perform batch operations against directories that conform to LDAP standards. LDIF can be used to both import and export data, allowing batch operations such as add, create, and modify to be performed against Active Directory. Ldifde is the command-line utility included in Windows Server 2003 to support batch operations based on the LDIF file format standard. The primary switches available for the Ldifde command are outlined in Table 4-9.

Table 4-9   Ldifde.exe Switches

Command	Usage
General parameters	
-i	Turn on Import mode. (The default is Export.)
-f *filename*	Input or Output *filename*.
-s *servername*	The server to bind to.
-c *FromDN ToDN*	Replace occurrences of *FromDN* to *ToDN*.
-v	Turn on Verbose mode.
-j *path*	Log File Location.
-t *port*	Port number (default = 389).
-?	Help.
Export specific parameters	
-d *RootDN*	The root of the LDAP search (defaults to Naming Context).
-r *Filter*	LDAP search filter (defaults to "(objectClass=*)").
-p *SearchScope*	Search Scope (Base/OneLevel/Subtree).
-l *list*	List of attributes (comma-separated) to look for in an LDAP search.
-o *list*	List of attributes (comma-separated) to omit from input.
-g	Disable Paged Search.
-m	Enable the Security Accounts Manager (SAM) logic on export.
-n	Do not export binary values.
Import specific parameters	
-k	The import will ignore "Constraint Violation" and "Object Already Exists" errors.
Credentials parameters	
-a *UserDN*	Sets the command to run using the supplied user distinguished name and password. For example: "cn=administrator,dc=contoso,dc=com password."
-b *UserName Domain*	Sets the command to run as username domain password. The default is to run using the credentials of the currently logged-on user.

When using the LDIF file to import data into Active Directory, the *changeType* value specifies the type of operation that needs to occur. The three valid *changeType* values are *add*, *modify*, and *delete*. As the names suggest, *add* will import new content into the directory, *modify* will change the configuration of existing content, and *delete* will remove the specified content. As an example, suppose that you wanted to use Ldifde to create two global groups named Marketing and Finance in the Users container of the contoso.com domain. The contents of the LDIF file would look similar to the following example:

```
DN: CN=Marketing,CN=Users,DC=Contoso,DC=Com
changeType: add
CN: Marketing
description: Marketing Users
objectClass: group
sAMAccountName: Marketing

DN: CN=Finance,CN=Users,DC=Contoso,DC=Com
changeType: add
CN: Finance
description: Finance Users
objectClass: group
sAMAccountName: Finance
```

Although doing so is not strictly required, this text file would usually be saved with a .LDF extension—for example, groups.ldf. To import the contents of this LDIF file from the command line, the command would be:

```
ldifde.exe -i -f groups.ldf
```

Once this command is issued, two new global groups named Marketing and Finance would be added to the Users container of the contoso.com domain.

Note   The Csvde.exe utility looked at in Lesson 1 can also be used to add group objects to Active Directory. However, Csvde.exe does not support the ability to modify or remove directory objects, while Ldifde.exe does.

Real World   Account Creation

Often, you will have a collection of data that already has a great deal of the information with which you will populate your Windows Server 2003 Active Directory. The data might currently be in an existing directory such as Windows NT 4.0, Windows 2000 Active Directory, Novell Directory Services (NDS), or some other type of database. (Human Resources departments are famous for compiling data, for example.)

> If you have this user data available, you can use it to populate Active Directory. There are many tools available to facilitate the extraction of data, such as Addusers.exe for Windows NT 4.0 and Ldifde.exe for Windows 2000. In addition, most database programs have the built-in capacity to export their data into a comma-separated value (CSV) file, which Csvde.exe can import.
>
> With a little editing, you could also add OU and group data to the import file and use Ldifde.exe to populate Active Directory much more quickly than manual methods would allow.

Adding, Modifying, and Deleting Groups from the Command Line

In Lesson 1, you learned that Windows Server 2003 includes a variety of new command-line utilities used to add, modify, delete, and query Active Directory objects. In the same way that tools such as Dsadd, Dsmod, Dsrm, and Dsquery can be used to perform tasks relating to user accounts, they can also be used to manage group accounts. The following sections give examples of how to use these tools to provide a variety of group management functions from the command line.

Dsadd Group   The Dsadd Group command allows you to create new group objects from the command line. As part of creating a new group, various configuration settings can also be specified, including the type and scope of the group. For example, to create a new global security group named Marketing in the Users container of the Contoso.com domain, the command would be:

```
dsadd group "CN=Marketing,CN=Users,DC=Contoso,DC=Com"
  -samid Marketing -secgrp yes -scope g
```

In this example, the Dsadd Group command is followed by the distinguished name of the new object. The *–samid* switch configures the Security Accounts Manager (SAM) name for the new group—in this case, Marketing. The *–secgrp yes* portion of the command specifies the group as a security group (whereas a value of *no* would create a distribution group), while the *–scope g* portion specifies that the group scope should be global. As you might have guessed, values of *l* or *u* after the *–scope* switch would be used to designate the new group as domain local or universal, respectively.

> **Note**   For a complete list of the switches available with the Dsadd Group command, see the Dsadd topic in the Help and Support Center.

Dsmod Group   The Dsmod Group command is used to modify existing groups. Modifying existing groups might entail changing the type or scope of a group, but more commonly it would involve changing the membership of a group or changing the groups that a particular group is a member of. The following example demonstrates how the Marketing group created in the previous section would be changed from a security group to a distribution group:

```
dsmod group "CN=Marketing,CN=Users,DC=Contoso,DC=Com" -secgrp no
```

However, if your goal was to add a used named Mike Jones in the Users container of contoso.com to the Marketing global security group, the proper Dsmod Group command would be:

```
dsmod group "CN=Marketing,CN=Users,DC=Contoso,DC=Com"
 -addmbr "CN=Mike Jones,CN=Users,DC=Contoso,DC=Com"
```

In Lesson 1, you also learned that the Dsget command is often used to pipe output to another command. In the following example, the Dsget command is used to get information about all the members of the Sales group and then to add those users to the Marketing group:

```
dsget group "CN=Sales,CN=Users,DC=Contoso,DC=Com" -members |
 dsmod group "CN=Marketing,CN=Users,DC=Contoso,DC=Com" -addmbr
```

Note   For a complete list of the switches available with the Dsmod Group command, see the Dsmod topic in the Help and Support Center.

Dsrm   The Dsrm command can be used to delete an existing group. The syntax of this command is very basic because it only requires the Dsrm command followed by the distinguished name of the group to be removed. For example, to delete the Marketing global security group created earlier, the command would be:

```
dsrm "CN=Marketing,CN=Users,DC=Contoso,DC=Com"
```

Note   For a complete list of the switches available with the Dsrm command, see the Dsrm topic in the Help and Support Center.

Dsquery Group   In the same way that the Dsquery command can be used to search for user objects within a portion of Active Directory, it can also be used to search for groups based on a range of different criteria. For example, to view a list of all groups that currently exist in the contoso.com domain, the command would be:

```
dsquery group "DC=Contoso,DC=Com"
```

Similarly, if you wanted to search for all groups within an Active Directory forest that start with the letters "market", the command would be:

```
dsquery group forestroot -name market*
```

Because this query searches for groups throughout a forest, a global catalog server would handle the query. If you are looking for an easy way to gather and document information about the various groups in an Active Directory environment, consider redirecting the output of the command to a text file. In the following example, all groups in the Sales OU (and any sub-OUs) would be redirected to a text file named salesgroups.txt:

```
dsquery group "OU=Sales,DC=Contoso,DC=Com"
  -scope subtree >> salesgroups.txt
```

Note   For a complete list of the switches available with the Dsquery Group command, see the Dsquery topic in the Help and Support Center.

Practice: Changing the Group Type and Scope

In this practice, you get hands-on experience creating and managing groups by using both Active Directory Users And Computers and the command-line tools outlined in this lesson.

Exercise 1: Creating Security and Distribution Groups

1. Click Start, select Administrative Tools, and click Active Directory Users And Computers.

2. Right-click the Users container, select New, and then click Group.

3. In the New Object–Group dialog box, type **Marketing** in the Group Name text box. Ensure that Global is selected under Group Scope and that Security is selected under Group Type. Click OK. Ensure that the Marketing global security group appears in the Users container.

4. Create two additional global security groups in the Users container, and name them **Sales** and **Finance**.

5. Right-click the Users container, select New, and then click Group.

6. In the New Object–Group dialog box, type **New York Users** in the Group Name text box. Ensure that Global is selected under Group Scope and that Distribution is selected under Group Type. Click OK. Ensure that the New York Users global distribution group appears in the Users container.

7. Right-click the Users container, select New, and then click Group.

8. In the New Object–Group dialog box, type **Enterprise Marketing** in the Group Name text box. Ensure that Universal is selected under Group Scope and that Security is selected under Group Type. Click OK. Ensure that the Enterprise Marketing universal group appears in the Users container.

9. Use Active Directory Users And Computers to create two domain local security groups, and name them **Marketing Local** and **Sales Local**.

Exercise 2: Managing Group Membership

1. In Active Directory Users And Computers, right-click the Andrew Manore user account created in Lesson 1 and click Add To A Group.

2. In the Select Group dialog box, type **Marketing** in the Enter The Object Name To Select text box and click OK.

3. In the Multiple Names Found dialog box, make sure Marketing is selected and click OK.

4. In the Active Directory dialog box, click OK.

5. Right-click the Andrew Manore user account, and click Properties.

6. Click the Member Of tab. Notice that the Andrew Manore user account is now a member of both the Domain Users and Marketing groups. Click OK.

7. Right-click the Marketing global security group, and click Properties.

8. Click the Members tab, and then click Add.

9. In the Select Users, Contacts, Computers, Or Groups dialog box, type **Sales** in the Enter The Object Names To Select text box. Click OK. Notice that the Sales global security group is now a member of the Marketing global security group. This nesting arrangement is possible only when the domain is configured to either the Windows Server 2003 or Windows 2000 native domain functional level.

10. Click OK to close the Properties dialog box.

Exercise 3: Changing Group Types and Scopes

1. In Active Directory Users And Computers, right-click the Marketing global security group created in Exercise 1 and click Properties.

2. On the General tab, notice that the group scope can be changed only to Universal and that the group type can be changed to Distribution. Active Directory does not allow global groups to be changed to domain local groups (or vice versa) under any circumstances. Click OK.

3. Right-click the Enterprise Marketing universal security group, and click Properties.

4. On the General tab, notice that the group scope can be changed to either Global or Domain Local. Change the group scope to Domain Local, and then click OK.

Exercise 4: Creating and Managing Groups from the Command Line

1. Click Start, and then click Run. Type **cmd.exe**, and then click OK.

2. To find the groups that Andrew Manore is a member of, type **dsget user "CN=Andrew Manore,CN=Users,DC=contoso,DC=com" –memberof –expand** and press ENTER. The list of groups in which Andrew Manore is a member will appear.

3. Using the Dsadd Group command looked at in this lesson, create a new domain local security group named Finance Resources.

4. Using the Dsmod Group command looked at in this lesson, change the scope of the Finance Resources group to Universal.

5. Using the Dsmod Group command looked at in this lesson, change the type of the Finance Resources group to Distribution.

6. Using the Dsrm command looked at in this lesson, delete the Finance Resources group.

Lesson Review

The following questions are intended to reinforce key information presented in this lesson. If you are unable to answer a question, review the lesson materials and try the question again. You can find answers to the questions in the "Questions and Answers" section at the end of this chapter.

1. Which of the following group scope changes are not supported in a domain configured to the Windows Server 2003 domain functional level?

   a. Global to domain local

   b. Domain local to universal

   c. Global to universal

   d. Domain local to global

2. Which of the following are requirements to create and assign permissions to a universal group?

   a. Universal group must be of the security type

   b. Domain must be configured to at least the Windows 2000 mixed domain functional level

   c. Domain must be configured to at least the Windows 2000 native domain functional level

   d. Universal group must be of the distribution type

3. Which of the following objects can be members of a domain local group in a domain configured to the Windows Server 2003 domain functional level?

   a. Universal groups from the same forest

   b. Global groups from the same forest

   c. Global groups from a trusted forest

   d. Domain local groups from a trusted forest

   e. Domain local groups from another domain

4. Which of the following objects can be a member of a global group in a domain configured to the Windows 2000 mixed domain functional level?

   a. Users in the same domain

   b. Computers in the same domain

   c. Other global groups from the same domain

   d. Domain local groups from the same domain

Lesson Summary

- Windows Server 2003 supports two types of groups: security and distribution. Security groups have a SID and can be assigned rights and permissions, while distribution groups do not have a SID and are used for e-mail distribution lists.

- Windows Server 2003 supports three group scopes: domain local, global, and universal. The ability to create universal groups requires that a domain be configured to the Windows 2000 native or Windows Server 2003 domain functional level.

- Groups can be nested when the domain in which they reside is set to either the Windows 2000 native or Windows Server 2003 domain functional level. If the domain is in the Windows 2000 mixed or Windows Server 2003 interim domain functional level, group nesting is not possible.

- The primary tool used to create and manage group accounts is Active Directory Users And Computers.

- Windows Server 2003 supports a number of utilities that can be used to automate the creation and management of groups, including Ldifde.exe, Csvde.exe, Dsadd.exe, Dsmod.exe, Dsrm.exe, and Dsquery.exe.

Lesson 3: Planning and Troubleshooting User Authentication

Once user objects have been created and enabled in Active Directory, individual users can begin using them for authentication purposes. Although user accounts represent a critical component of the authentication process, a number of other factors also need to be considered. For example, domain Group Policy settings affect various elements of user authentication, such as password complexity requirements, account lockout settings, and so forth. Similarly, the ability of users running down-level operating systems—such as Windows 98 or Windows NT—to log on to a Windows Server 2003 domain will also be affected by whether they have the Active Directory client software installed. Furthermore, in some environments users will log on using a traditional username and password, while in other environments smart cards will be used during the authentication process. Each of these factors needs to be considered as part of planning and troubleshooting authentication on a Windows Server 2003 network.

In this lesson, we will address a variety of issues related to user authentication. This overview includes a look at domain policies and how they affect the authentication process, the configuration of auditing to track user logon attempts, the effect of installing the Active Directory client on down-level operating systems, common authentication troubleshooting procedures, and how smart cards are used in Windows Server 2003 environments.

After this lesson, you will be able to

- Identify domain account policies and their effect on password requirements and authentication
- Configure auditing for logon events
- Modify authentication-related attributes of user objects
- Understand the capabilities provided by the Active Directory client software
- Troubleshoot common authentication-related problems using Windows Server 2003 administrative tools
- Understand and plan a smart card authentication strategy

Estimated lesson time: 35 minutes

Securing Authentication

Because of the security risks inherent in any network environment, administrators need to carefully consider how to secure not only resources but also access to user accounts. If an outside user is able to successfully authenticate against Active Directory using a guessed or stolen username and password combination, sensitive data on the network can more easily be compromised. To avoid such issues, Windows Server 2003 provides the ability to configure strict account policies that apply to all users within an Active Directory domain.

In Active Directory environments, account policy settings are implemented by the Group Policy object linked to the domain with the highest priority. With a default installation of Windows Server 2003, the Default Domain Policy controls the account policy settings for the domain. It would be possible to replace this Group Policy object, or to add a new Group Policy object linked to the domain with higher priority, and therefore override the Default Domain Policy. However, it is best practice to modify the account policy settings in the Default Domain Policy, and to use the Default Domain Policy only to control account policies—use other Group Policy objects to implement other policies at the domain level.

Exam Tip   Although the Account Policies node is available when configuring Group Policy objects at all levels, only account policy settings configured at the domain level will actually apply to domain users. On the exam, remember that account policies are implemented by the Default Domain Policy.

The three main areas within the Account Policies section of a Group Policy object include Password Policy, Account Lockout Policy, and Kerberos Policy, as illustrated in Figure 4-11. The policy settings configured in each of these areas affect all domain users and should be configured in line with the security objectives and requirements of the organization.

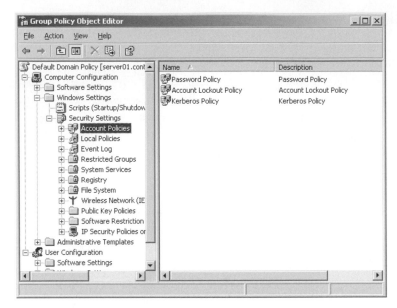

Figure 4-11 Default Domain Policy, Account Policies node

Real World Account Policies and Users

Even though it might initially seem like a good idea to configure all authentication-related security settings to the most secure levels possible, this seldom (if ever) works in practice. While requiring users to use a 14-character password is definitely more secure than an 8-character password, many users would ultimately have a hard time remembering their password. This in turn would likely lead to increased administrative effort as users forget their password and need to have them reset. Worse still, many users will write these passwords down instead of trying to remember them, presenting a huge security risk. At the end of the day, remember that truly effective policy settings require striking a balance between security and usability.

In the following sections, you'll learn more about the configurable security settings available in the Password Policy, Account Lockout Policy, and Kerberos Policy nodes of the Account Policies section of a Group Policy object.

Password Policy

The domain password policies enable you to protect your network against password compromise by enforcing best-practice password management techniques. The policies are described in Table 4-10.

Table 4-10   Password Policies

Policy	Description
Enforce Password History	When this policy is enabled, Active Directory maintains a list of recently used passwords and will not allow a user to create a password that matches a password in that history. The result is that a user, when prompted to change his or her password, cannot use the same password again and therefore cannot circumvent the password lifetime. The policy is enabled by default, using the maximum value of 24.
Maximum Password Age	This policy determines how long a password remains valid. Once the maximum password age has elapsed, the user will be forced to change his or her password The default value is 42 days.
Minimum Password Age	When users are required to change their passwords—even when a password history is enforced—they can simply change their passwords several times in a row to circumvent password requirements and return to their original passwords. The Minimum Password Age policy prevents this possibility by requiring the user to wait the specified number of days between password changes. An administrator or support person with sufficient permissions can reset a password at any time. The default value is 1 day.
Minimum Password Length	This policy specifies the minimum number of characters required in a password. The default in Windows Server 2003 is 7 characters.

Passwords Must Meet Complexity Requirements	This policy enforces complexity rules (sometimes referred to as filters) on new passwords. The default password filter in Windows Server 2003 (passfilt.dll) requires that a password:
	■ Is not based on the user's account name
	■ Is at least 6 characters long
	■ Contains characters from three of the following four character types:
	  ❏ Uppercase alphabet characters (A through Z)
	  ❏ Lowercase alphabet characters (a through z)
	  ❏ Arabic numerals (0 through 9)
	  ❏ Nonalphanumeric characters (for example, !, $, #, %)
	Windows Server 2003 enables this setting by default.

Store Passwords Using Reversible Encryption	This option causes Active Directory to store user passwords without using the default nonreversible encryption algorithm. The policy is disabled by default, as it critically weakens password security.

Note   Configuring password length and complexity requirements does not affect existing passwords. Any changes made to Password Policy settings will affect new accounts as well as any changes to existing passwords after the policy is applied.

Account Lockout Policy

Password Policy settings help an administrator to ensure that user passwords are changed regularly and meet minimum complexity requirements. In a similar vein, Account Lockout Policy settings are used to control what happens when any user attempts to log on using incorrect credentials. For example, an unauthorized user might attempt to gain access to the network by guessing user passwords or to automate the process via different hacking utilities. Through the configuration of Account Lockout Policy settings, an administrator can configure thresholds for invalid logon attempts that specify how many invalid attempts should result in an account being locked out, how long the lockout period should last, and whether locked-out accounts should be unlocked manually or automatically. Table 4-11 summarizes Account Lockout Policy settings available from the Account Policies node of a Group Policy object.

Table 4-11   Account Lockout Policies

Policy	Description
Account Lockout Duration	This policy determines the period of time that must pass after a lockout before Active Directory will automatically unlock a user's account. The policy is not enabled by default, as it is useful only in conjunction with a configured Account Lockout Threshold. Although the policy accepts values ranging from 0 to 99999 minutes (about 10 weeks), a low setting (5 to 15 minutes) is usually sufficient to reduce security risks without unreasonably affecting legitimate users. A value of 0 requires the user to contact an administrator to unlock the account manually.
Account Lockout Threshold	This policy configures the number of invalid logon attempts that will trigger account lockout. The value can be in the range of 0 to 999. A value that is too low might cause lockouts due to normal human error, such as a user temporarily forgetting or mistyping his or her password. A value of 0 (the default value) will result in accounts never being locked out.
Reset Account Lockout Counter After	This setting specifies the time that must pass after an invalid logon attempt before the counter resets to zero. The range is 1 to 99999 minutes and must be less than or equal to the account lockout duration.

Real World   Down-Level Clients and Active Directory

Many organizations still implement a mix of different client operating system platforms. In environments that include any combination of Windows 95, Windows 98, Windows Me, and Windows NT 4.0, the Active Directory client software will need to be installed on these systems in order to participate in an Active Directory domain. The Active Directory client can be downloaded from the Microsoft Web site. Administrators need to consider the Active Directory client's capabilities and limitations.

- The Active Directory client software enables systems running previous editions of Windows to take advantage of many Active Directory features, including:
  - ❑ Site awareness. A system with the Active Directory client installed will attempt to log on to a domain controller in its own site.
  - ❑ Active Directory Service Interfaces (ADSI). ADSI allows the use of scripting to manage Active Directory.
  - ❑ Distributed File System (DFS). Systems can access DFS shared resources on servers running Windows 2000 and Windows Server 2003.
  - ❑ NT LAN Manager (NTLM) version 2 authentication. Clients running the software can take advantage of improved authentication features in NTLM version 2.
  - ❑ Active Directory Windows Address Book (WAB). Clients can change the properties of user object properties pages, such as phone numbers or addresses.
  - ❑ Active Directory search capability integrated into the Start–Find or Start–Search commands.

While the Active Directory client software allows down-level operating systems to take advantage of many basic Active Directory features, it does not provide the following capabilities, available in both Windows 2000 Professional and Windows XP Professional:

- Kerberos V5 authentication
- Group Policy or Change And Configuration Management support
- Service principal name (SPN), or mutual authentication.

In addition, you should be aware of the following issues in mixed environments:

- Windows 98 supports passwords of up to 14 characters long. Windows 2000, Windows XP, and Windows Server 2003 can support 127-character passwords. Be aware of this difference when configuring passwords (or Password Policy settings) in environments where some users run Windows 98.

- Without the Active Directory client, users on systems using versions of Windows earlier than Windows 2000 can change their password only if the system can contact the domain controller holding the primary domain controller (PDC) emulator role. With the Active Directory client installed, users of down-level operating systems can change their password via any domain controller.

- As you learned earlier in this chapter, user objects maintain two user logon name properties. The Pre–Windows 2000 logon name, or SAM name, is equivalent to the user name in Windows 95, Windows 98, or Windows NT 4.0. When users log on, they enter their user name and must select the domain from the Log On To box. In other situations, the user name can be entered in the format *<Domain-Name>\<UserLogonName>*.

Kerberos Policy

In an Active Directory environment, systems running Windows 2000, Windows XP, and Windows Server 2003 all rely on Kerberos as their default authentication protocol. The Kerberos policy settings are configured via the Kerberos Policy node in the Account Policies section of a Group Policy object. Most administrators do not change the default settings. However, because Kerberos settings can affect the ability of users to authenticate and ultimately access resources, you should be familiar with these settings and their purpose. Table 4-12 outlines the purpose and default values of the Kerberos Policy settings in a Windows Server 2003 domain.

Table 4-12   Kerberos Policies

Policy	Description
Enforce User Logon Restrictions	This setting controls whether a key distribution center (KDC) validates every request for a session ticket against the user rights policy of a user account. Although the default setting of Enabled is more secure, it can also slow down the time it takes users to access resources.
Maximum Lifetime For Service Ticket	This setting determines the maximum amount of time (in minutes) that a session ticket can be used to access a particular resource. Once a user has authenticated to a resource, the session ticket lifetime no longer matters. The default value is 600 minutes.
Maximum Lifetime For User Ticket	This setting determines the maximum amount of time (in hours) that a user's ticket-granting ticket (TGT) can be used. When a TGT expires, a new one must be requested or the original one must be renewed. The default value is 10 hours.

Table 4-12 Kerberos Policies

Policy	Description
Maximum Lifetime For User Ticket Renewal	This setting determines the period of time (in days) in which a user's TGT can be renewed. The default value is 7 days.
Maximum Tolerance For Computer Clock Synchronization	This setting determines the maximum acceptable variance in minutes between the time configured on a client computer and the time configured on a domain controller. In cases where the variance is above the configured value, the client will not be able to obtain a valid ticket from the server. The default value is 5 minutes.

Auditing Authentication

Like Windows 2000, Windows Server 2003 provides the ability to track the success and failure of various authentication-related events by configuring Audit Policy settings. However, unlike Windows 2000, Windows Server 2003 domain controllers have a number of audit settings (including logon events) that are configured by default via the Default Domain Controllers Policy. This Group Policy object is applied to domain controllers automatically as part of the Active Directory installation process. When logon events specified in an audit policy occur, they are ultimately recorded in the Security log in Event Viewer.

> **Exam Tip** Keep in mind the difference between the Default Domain Policy (which is linked to the domain and determines password, lockout, and Kerberos policies) and the Default Domain Controller policy (which is linked to the Domain Controllers OU and is configured to enable security auditing by each of the domain controllers in the OU).

Audit Policies

The following authentication-related policy settings are located in the Computer Configuration\Windows Settings\Security Settings\Local Policies\Audit Policy node of Group Policy Object Editor (or the Local Security Policy snap-in). To audit logon events related to Active Directory authentication, you should configure settings in policies applied to the Domain Controllers OU. However, you can configure auditing for other domain computers, such as workstations or member servers, at any level that Group

Policy settings can normally be applied. The following list outlines the authentication-related Audit Policy settings available in Windows Server 2003.

- **Audit Account Logon Events**   This setting audits each instance of user logon that involves domain controller authentication. For domain controllers, this policy is defined in the Default Domain Controllers Policy Group Policy object. Note that this policy will create a Security log entry on a domain controller each time a user logs on interactively or over the network by using a domain account. Second, remember that to fully evaluate the results of the auditing, you must examine the Security logs on all domain controllers, because user authentication will be distributed among the various domain controllers in a site or domain. The Default Domain Controllers Policy has this setting configured to audit Success events by default. In other words, a Security log entry will be created only when a domain controller successfully authenticates a user. For security purposes, you should also consider configuring this policy to record Failure events.

- **Audit Account Management**   This setting configures auditing of activities including the creation, deletion, or modification of user, group, or computer accounts. This setting also includes configuring activities such as resetting passwords and is enabled by default in the Default Domain Controllers Policy for Success events.

- **Audit Logon Events**   Logon events include log on and log off, whether done interactively or through a network connection. If you have enabled the Audit Account Logon Events setting for successes on a domain controller, workstation logons will not generate logon audits. Only interactive and network logons to the domain controller itself generate logon events. Account logon events are generated on the local computer for local accounts and on the domain controller for network accounts. Logon events are generated wherever the logon occurs. This setting is enabled by default in the Default Domain Controllers Policy for Success events.

Security Event Log

Once you have configured auditing settings for logon events, the Security log in Event Viewer will begin to fill with messages according to the policy settings configured. You can view these messages by selecting Security from the Event Viewer snap-in and then double-clicking the event. Figure 4-12 illustrates an example of a Security log entry for a successful logon event recorded on Server01 in the contoso.com domain.

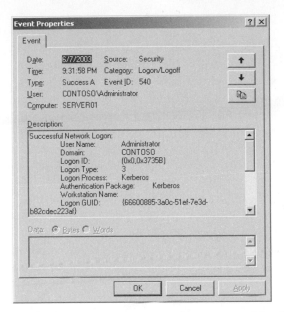

Figure 4-12   Security log entry for a successful authentication event

Administering User Authentication

When users forget their passwords or are transferred or terminated, you will have to manage their user objects appropriately. The most common administrative tasks related to user account security are unlocking accounts; resetting passwords; and disabling, enabling, renaming, and deleting user objects.

Unlocking a User Account

The Account Lockout Policy requires that when a user has exceeded the limit for invalid logon attempts, the account is locked and no further logons can be attempted for a specified period of time or until an administrator has unlocked the account.

To unlock a user, open Active Directory Users And Computers, select the user object and, from the Action menu, choose Properties. Click the Account tab, and clear the Account Is Locked Out check box.

Resetting User Passwords

If a user forgets his or her password, you must reset the password. You do not need to know the user's old password to do so. Simply right-click the user object in Active Directory Users And Computers, and select the Reset Password command. Enter the new password twice to confirm the change, and as a security best practice, select the User Must Change Password At Next Logon check box.

Disabling, Enabling, Renaming, and Deleting User Objects

Over time, changes in the status of personnel might require you to disable, enable, rename, or delete user accounts. For example, a user might be on maternity leave, in which case her account should be disabled until she returns. Similarly, another user might be leaving the company, with a new user being hired as his replacement. The ability to selectively enable, disable, rename, or delete user accounts not only helps an administrator to make an environment more secure but can also reduce administrative effort in the long term.

- **Disabling and Enabling a User** When a user does not require access to the network for an extended period of time, you should disable the account for security purposes. Then, when the user returns and needs access to the network again, enable the account. To perform either action, right-click the account in Active Directory Users And Computers and then click Enable Account or Disable Account. Note that only one of these two options will be available based on the current status of the account.

- **Deleting a User** When a user is no longer part of your organization and an account is no longer required, it can be deleted. Remember that by deleting a user the associated SID is also deleted, meaning that rights and permissions associated with the account are also lost. If you create a new user object with the same name, it will have a different SID, and you will have to reconfigure rights, permissions, and group membership information just as you would with any new account.

- **Renaming a User** In some cases, a user account will need to be renamed because of changes in a user's marital status. However, user accounts can also be renamed rather than deleted when one user replaces another, which will reduce administrative effort. Deleting an existing user account and then creating one for the new user usually requires more effort than simply renaming the existing user account. Renaming maintains the user account SID and all group membership settings, rights, and permissions of the old user. Renaming allows the new user to gain access to all the resources that the previous user required as part of his or her job function.

 Exam Tip Be certain to understand the difference between disabling and deleting an object, and between enabling and unlocking a user.

Troubleshooting User Authentication Problems

In any Active Directory environment, various issues can stop a user from being successfully authenticated. Although basic issues such as incorrect username and password combinations are common, other problems will require you to delve a little deeper into some of the possible configuration issues that might apply. Windows

Server 2003 includes a number of utilities—including Event Viewer and Active Directory Users And Computers—that can be used to troubleshoot authentication problems. The following sections outline some common authentication problems that occur in Active Directory environments and ways to resolve these issues.

Logon Issues

When a user cannot be successfully authenticated during the logon process, refer to the following bullet points for methods of troubleshooting the issue:

- Ensure that the user is attempting to log on using the correct username, password, and domain name. In many cases, users have simply forgotten their password or have not chosen the correct domain name as part of the logon process. Reset the user password in Active Directory Users And Computers if the user has forgotten it.

- Use Active Directory Users And Computers to be sure that the account has not been locked out because of multiple invalid logon attempts and that it has not been disabled. If the account has been disabled, re-enable it; and if it has been locked out, unlock it.

- If the user is logging on from a Windows 2000 or Windows XP workstation, ensure that the configured time on that workstation is within the Maximum Tolerance For Computer Clock Synchronization value (default 5 minutes) specified in the domain Kerberos Policy settings.

- If the user is logging on from a Windows 95, Windows 98, Windows Me, or Windows NT 4.0 system without the Active Directory client software installed, ensure that the domain controller holding the PDC emulator role is available. Consider installing the Active Directory client software on all down-level client operating systems in Active Directory environments.

- Ensure that the TCP/IP settings of the client system are configured correctly, including the address of the DNS server that will be queried for the address of a domain controller.

- If the user is logging on to the domain for the first time in a multiple-domain environment, ensure that a global catalog server is available, as the user's universal group membership information will be needed for the initial logon.

- If Audit Account Logon Events has been configured for Failure events in the Default Domain Controllers Policy, check the Security log in Event Viewer on domain controllers for messages that might help to decipher why the logon attempt failed.

- If the user is attempting to log on to a domain controller, ensure that the user has been granted sufficient rights in the Default Domain Controllers Policy.

- If the user is attempting to log on from a Windows 98 system, ensure that the user's password does not exceed the 14-character maximum that Windows 98 supports.

- If the user is attempting to log on using a UPN, ensure that a global catalog server is available to service the request.

- If the user cannot log on from certain workstations only, check the Log On To section of the Account tab in the user's object properties to determine whether workstation restrictions have been configured.

- If the user cannot log on during certain times of the day, check the Logon Hours section of the Account tab in the user's object properties to determine whether any logon hour restrictions have been configured.

- If the user cannot log on to a Terminal Server, ensure that the Allow Logon To Terminal Server check box is selected on the Terminal Services Profile tab in the properties of the user account.

- If the user cannot log on to the network remotely, ensure that the Dial-In tab in the properties of the user account is not configured to Deny Access in the Remote Access Permission section.

Resource Access Issues

When a user is able to successfully authenticate but subsequently cannot access required resources, perform the following steps as necessary:

- Ensure that the server or workstation hosting the resource is available, with network settings configured correctly.

- Check the access control lists associated with the resource that needs to be accessed to determine whether the user is a member of any group with sufficient permissions to access the resource. If not, add the user to a group with the appropriate permissions using Active Directory Users And Computers.

- Check the ACL of the object for any settings that might create a conflict. For example, a user might be a member of one group that is allowed the Read permission and a member of another group that is denied the same permission. As in Windows 2000, permissions explicitly denied override those explicitly allowed.

- Ensure that the user has sufficient rights to access servers and carry out tasks. For example, if a user should be able to back up and restore files and folders on a domain controller, you should add the user to the Backup Operators group. Similarly, you should use tools such as the Delegation Of Control Wizard in Active Directory Users And Computers to delegate the proper authority to users who need to perform tasks such as resetting passwords.

Using Smart Cards

Like Windows 2000, Windows Server 2003 also supports optional smart card authentication. A *smart card* is a credit card–sized device that is used with a personal identification number (PIN) to enable certificate-based authentication. Smart cards provide a more secure means of user authentication than traditional usernames and passwords. However, deploying and maintaining a smart card infrastructure requires additional overhead, including the configuration of Microsoft Certificate Services, smart card reader devices, and the smart cards themselves. A smart card contains a chip that stores the user's private key, logon information, and public key certificate. The user inserts the card into a smart card reader attached to the computer and types in a PIN (rather than a traditional password) when requested. Smart cards rely on the *public key infrastructure (PKI)* provided by Certificate Services in Windows Server 2003.

> **See Also**   For more information about implementing a Certificate Services public key infrastructure in Windows Server 2003, see Chapter 12.

Implementing Smart Cards

In addition to a correctly configured Certificate Services PKI and the physical smart cards themselves, user workstations require a smart card reader to support this authentication method. When implemented, at least one computer must be configured as a smart card enrollment station, and at least one user must be authorized to operate it. Although no extra hardware is required beyond a smart card reader, the user who operates the enrollment station needs to be issued an Enrollment Agent certificate. Because the holder of the Enrollment Agent certificate can generate a smart card for anyone in the organization, there must be strong security policies in place for issuing Enrollment Agent certificates.

> **Real World   Smart Card Benefit**
>
> The main problem with relying on traditional usernames and passwords during the authentication process is that the more secure a password, the more difficult it is to remember. For example, although a 32-character alphanumeric password is more secure, configuring such a policy would almost certainly lead users to write the password down, negating any security benefit. However, if you let your users choose any password they want, they will often pick something too simple that can be easily compromised. Smart cards offer a solution to this problem because users not only require their physical smart card during the logon process, but also the PIN number associated with it in order to authenticate successfully. Of course, you'll have to place smart card readers on every computer and issue smart cards to every user. However, once this is done, users won't have to remember passwords anymore. Smart cards make it much more difficult for remote attackers to compromise Active Directory user accounts.

Smart Card Deployment Considerations

Smart card logon is supported for the Windows 2000 family and the Windows Server 2003 family. To implement smart cards, you must deploy an enterprise certification authority rather than a stand-alone or third-party certification authority to support smart card logon to Windows Server 2003 domains. Windows Server 2003 supports industry-standard Personal Computer/Smart Card (PC/SC)–compliant smart cards and readers and provides drivers for commercially available plug-and-play smart card readers. Windows Server 2003 does not support non-PC/SC-compliant or non–plug-and-play smart card readers. Some manufacturers might provide drivers for non–plug-and-play smart card readers that work with Windows Server 2003; however, it is recommended that you purchase only plug-and-play PC/SC-compliant smart card readers.

The cost of administering a smart card program depends on several factors, including:

- The number of users enrolled in the smart card program and their location.

- Your organization's practices for issuing smart cards to users, including the requirements for verifying user identities. For example, will you require users to simply present a valid personal identification card or will you require a background investigation? Your policies affect the level of security provided as well as the actual cost.

- Your organization's practices for users who lose or misplace their smart cards. For example, will you issue temporary smart cards, authorize temporary alternate logon to the network, or make users go home to retrieve their smart cards? Your policies affect how much worker time is lost and how much help desk support is needed.

Your smart card authentication strategy must describe the network logon and authentication methods you use, including:

- Identify network logon and authentication strategies you want to deploy.

- Describe smart card deployment considerations and issues.

- Describe PKI certificate services required to support smart cards.

In addition to smart cards, third-party vendors offer a variety of security products to provide two-factor authentication, such as *security tokens* and biometric accessories. These accessories use extensible features of the Windows Server 2003 graphical logon user interface to provide alternate methods of user authentication.

See Also   The implementation of smart card authentication using a Windows Server 2003 Certificate Services PKI will be looked at in more detail in Chapter 12.

Practice: Securing and Troubleshooting Authentication

In this practice, you will configure new password and Account Lockout Policy settings for the contoso.com domain, configure additional auditing settings related to user logon, and then review Security log settings related to failed logon attempts.

Exercise 1: Configuring Password and Account Lockout Policy Settings

1. Click Start, select Administrative Tools, and then click Active Directory Users And Computers.

2. Right-click the contoso.com domain object, and then click Properties.

3. On the Group Policy tab, ensure that Default Domain Policy is selected and then click Edit.

4. Navigate to Computer Configuration\Windows Settings\Security Settings\Account Policies\Account Lockout Policy.

5. Double-click Account Lockout Duration.

6. Check the Define This Policy Setting check box.

7. Type **0** (zero) for the duration, and then click OK.

   The system will inform you that it will configure the account lockout threshold and reset counter policies.

8. Click OK to confirm the settings to close the dialog box.

9. Confirm that the Account Lockout Duration policy is 0 (zero), the Account Lockout Threshold is 5, and the Reset Account Lockout Counter After policy is 30 minutes.

10. Close the Group Policy Object Editor window.

11. Click OK to close the Properties dialog box for the Contoso.com domain.

12. In Active Directory Users And Computers, right-click the Domain Controllers OU and then click Properties.

13. On the Group Policy tab, ensure that Default Domain Controllers Policy is selected and click Edit.

14. Navigate to Computer Configuration\Windows Settings\Security Settings\Local Policies\Audit Policy.

15. Double-click the Audit Account Logon Events policy.

16. Check the Failure check box, and then click OK.

17. Double-click the Audit Logon Events policy.

18. Check the Failure check box, and then click OK.

19. Close the Group Policy Object Editor window.

20. Click OK to close the Properties dialog box for the Domain Controllers Properties dialog box.

21. Close Active Directory Users And Computers.

Exercise 2: Testing Account Lockout Settings

1. Click Start, select Administrative Tools, and then click Active Directory Users And Computers.

2. Using the steps learned in this chapter, add the Andrew Manore user account to the Domain Admins group.

3. Log off, and then attempt to log on as Andrew Manore six times using an incorrect password. When the Logon Message dialog box appears, click OK. The Andrew Manore user account has been locked out because it has exceeded the account lockout threshold configured in Exercise 1.

Exercise 3: Reviewing Failed Logon Events

1. Log on using the Administrator account.

2. Click Start, select Administrative Tools, and then click Event Viewer.

3. Click the Security log to view its contents.

4. Browse through the Security log to find a Failure event with an Event ID number of 529. Double-click the event to view its contents. Unless you have attempted to incorrectly log on as another user, this event should specify that the Andrew Manore user account attempted to log on using an unknown username or bad password. Click OK.

5. Close Event Viewer.

Lesson Review

The following questions are intended to reinforce key information presented in this lesson. If you are unable to answer a question, review the lesson materials and try the question again. You can find answers to the questions in the "Questions and Answers" section at the end of this chapter.

1. You enable the password complexity policy for your domain. Describe the requirements for passwords and when those requirements will take effect.

   _____

   _____

   _____

   _____

   _____

   _____

2. What would be the affect of configuring the Reset Account Lockout Counter After setting in the Account Lockout Policy section of a Group Policy object applied to an OU to a value of 4?

   a. The account lockout counter will be reset for domain user accounts in that OU after 4 minutes.

   b. The account lockout counter will be reset for domain users accounts in that OU after 4 attempts.

   c. The account lockout counter will be reset for domain user accounts in that OU after 4 hours.

   d. The account lockout counter settings will not apply to domain user accounts.

3. A user has forgotten his or her password and attempts to log on several times with an incorrect password. Eventually, the user receives a logon message indicating that the account is either disabled or locked out. The message suggests that the user contact an administrator. What must you do? (Choose all that apply.)

   a. Delete the user object and re-create it.

   b. Rename the user object.

   c. Enable the user object.

   d. Unlock the user object.

   e. Reset the password for the user object.

Lesson Summary

- The Account Policies section of a Group Policy object allows you to configure Password Policy, Account Lockout Policy, and Kerberos Policy settings for an Active Directory domain. Account Policies must be configured in Group Policy objects at the domain level to apply to domain users.

- Audit Policy settings allow you to track the success and failure of various authentication-related events. In a domain environment, these policy settings are usually configured in Group Policy objects applied to the Domain Controllers OU. Messages relating to audited logon events can be found in the Event Viewer Security log.

- Windows Server 2003 supports smart card authentication for a higher degree of authentication security. The use of smart cards requires the implementation of a Certificate Services public key infrastructure (PKI) as well as the purchase of smart cards and smart card readers.

Case Scenario Exercise

One of Contoso's competitors recently made the news as a recent victim of a breach of password security that exposed its sensitive data. You decide to audit Contoso's security configuration, and you set forth the following requirements:

- Requirement 1: Because you upgraded your domain controllers from Windows 2000 Server to Windows Server 2003, the domain account policy remained that of Windows 2000 Server. The domain account policies shall require:

  ❑ Password changes every 60 days

  ❑ 8-character passwords

  ❑ Password complexity

  ❑ Minimum password duration of one week

  ❑ Password history of 20 passwords

  ❑ Account lockout after five invalid logon attempts in a 60-minute period

  ❑ Administrator intervention to unlock locked-out accounts

- Requirement 2: In addition, ensure that these policies take effect within 24 hours. Password policies are implemented when a user changes his or her password—the policies do not affect existing passwords. So you require that users change their passwords as quickly as possible. You do not want to affect accounts used by services. Service accounts are stored in Contoso's Service Accounts OU. User accounts are stored in the Employees OU and 15 OUs located under the Employees OU.

- Requirement 3: The IT manager at Contoso wants to ensure that all users in the domain are authenticated by a domain controller in their own site, regardless of the operating system installed on the user's workstation. Contoso currently uses a combination of Windows 2000 Professional, Windows XP Professional, and Windows 98 on user desktop systems.

Requirement 1

The first requirement involves modifying password and account lockout settings.

1. What should be modified to achieve Requirement 1?

   a. The domain controller security template Hisecdc.inf

   b. The Default Domain policy

   c. The Default Domain Controller policy

   d. The domain controller security template Ssetup Security.inf

2. To configure account lockout so that users must contact the Help Desk to unlock their accounts, which policy should be specified?

   a. Account Lockout Duration: 999

   b. Account Lockout Threshold: 999

   c. Account Lockout Duration: 0

   d. Account Lockout Threshold: 0

Requirement 2

Requirement 2 indicates that you want to force users to change their password as quickly as possible. You know that user accounts include the option User Must Change Password At Next Logon.

1. What will be the fastest and most effective means to configure user accounts to require a password change at the next logon?

   a. Select a user account. Open its properties and, on the Account page, select User Must Change Password At Next Logon. Repeat for each user account.

   b. Press CTRL+A to select all users in the Employees OU. Choose the Properties command and, on the Account page, select User Must Change Password At Next Logon. Repeat for each OU.

   c. Use the Dsadd command.

   d. Use the Dsrm command.

   e. Use the Dsquery and Dsmod commands.

2. The Dsquery command allows you to create a list of objects based on those objects' location or properties, and to pipe those objects to the Dsmod command, which then modifies the objects. Open a command prompt, and type the following command:

```
dsquery user "OU=Employees,DC=Contoso,DC=Com"
```

The command will produce a list of all user objects in the Employees OU. An advantage of this command is that it would include users in sub-OUs of the Employees OU. The requirement indicates that you have 15 OUs under the Employees OU. All would be included in the objects generated by Dsquery.

Now, to meet the requirement, type the following command:

```
dsquery user "OU=Employees,DC=Contoso,DC=Com" | dsmod user -mustchpwd yes
```

Requirement 3

This requirement suggests that user workstations with Windows 98 installed will require the Active Directory client software to be installed.

1. Which of the following is not a capability provided by installing the Active Directory client software on a Windows 98 system?

   a. Support for NTLMv2 authentication

   b. Site awareness

   c. Ability to access DFS resources

   d. Support for Kerberos authentication

Troubleshooting Lab

Creating individual objects (such as users and groups) in Active Directory is a straightforward process, but finding objects and their associations after many objects have been created can present challenges. In a large, multiple-domain environment (or in a complicated smaller one), solving resource access problems can be difficult. For example, if Sarah can access some but not all of the resources that are intended for her, she might not have membership in the groups that have been assigned permissions to the resources.

If you have multiple domains with multiple OUs in each domain, and multiple, nested groups in each of those OUs, it could take a great deal of time to examine the membership of these many groups to determine whether the user has the appropriate membership. Active Directory Users And Computers would not be the best tool choice.

You will use the Dsget command to get a comprehensive listing of all groups of which a user is a member. For the purposes of this lab, the user is Ben Smith in the contoso.com domain and the Users OU will be used.

1. Choose a user in your Active Directory to use as a test case for the steps that follow. If you do not have a construction that is to your liking, create a number of nested groups across several OUs, making the user a member of only some of the groups.

2. Open a command prompt.

3. Type the following command (substituting your selected user name and OU for the account shown):

```
dsget user "CN=Ben Smith,CN=Users,DC=contoso,DC=com" -memberof -expand
```

The complete listing of all groups of which the user is a member is displayed. Use the Dsget command to view the settings of various objects in the contoso.com domain, including security and distribution groups.

Chapter Summary

- To create user objects in an Active Directory domain, you must be a member of the Enterprise Admins, Domain Admins, or Account Operators groups, or you must have been delegated the proper authority. The primary tool used to manage users and groups in a domain environment is Active Directory Users And Computers.

- User objects include properties associated with user authentication requirements, including logon names, a password, and a unique SID. User objects also include properties related to the individuals they represent, including personal information, group membership, and administrative settings. Windows Server 2003 allows you to change some of these properties for multiple users simultaneously using the new multiselect feature.

- The Csvde command enables you to import directory objects such as users or groups from a comma-delimited text file. The Ldifde utility allows you to add, modify, and delete directory objects according to the LDIF file format

- Windows Server 2003 supports powerful new command-line tools to create, manage, and delete directory objects, including Dsquery, Dsget, Dsadd, Dsmove, Dsmod, and Dsrm. Dsquery is typically used to produce a result set to pipe as input to other commands.

- Windows Server 2003 supports two types of groups: security and distribution. Security groups have a SID and can be assigned rights and permissions, while distribution groups do not have a SID and are used for e-mail distribution lists.

- Windows Server 2003 supports three group scopes: domain local, global, and universal. The ability to create universal groups requires that a domain be configured to the Windows 2000 native or Windows Server 2003 domain functional level.

- Groups can be nested when the domain in which they reside is set to either the Windows 2000 native or Windows Server 2003 domain functional level. If the domain is in Windows 2000 mixed or Windows Server 2003 interim domain functional level, group nesting is not possible.

- The Account Policies section of a Group Policy object allow you to configure Password Policy, Account Lockout Policy, and Kerberos Policy settings for an Active Directory domain. Account Policies must be configured in Group Policy objects at the domain level to apply to domain users.

- Audit Policy settings allow you to track the success and failure of various authentication-related events. In a domain environment, these policy settings are usually configured in Group Policy objects applied to the Domain Controllers OU. Messages relating to audited logon events can be found in the Event Viewer Security log.

- Windows Server 2003 supports smart card authentication for a higher degree of authentication security. The use of smart cards requires the implementation of a Certificate Services public key infrastructure (PKI) as well as the purchase of smart cards and smart card readers.

Exam Highlights

Before taking the exam, review the following key points and terms to help you identify topics you need to review. Return to the lessons for additional practice, and review the "Further Readings" sections in Part 2 for pointers to more information about topics covered by the exam objectives.

Key Points

- Be familiar with creating, managing, and changing the properties of users and groups by using Active Directory Users And Computers.

- Be familiar with the different group types and scopes available in Windows Server 2003, as well how the functional level of a domain affects the ability to create, convert, and nest groups.

- Be familiar with the various command-line tools and utilities that can be used to add, remove, query, or modify Active Directory users and groups.

- Be familiar with the various Account Policy settings used to manage passwords, account lockout, and authentication in Windows Server 2003 domain environments.

- Be familiar with some of the various methods that can be used to troubleshoot authentication issues in a Windows Server 2003 Active Directory environment.

Key Terms

Group scope   The scope of an Active Directory group determines where the group can exist within a forest, as well as the types of objects that can be configured as members. Windows Server 2003 supports three group scopes: domain local, global, and universal. The functional level of a domain dictates the possible members of each scope of group.

Group type   The type of an Active Directory group dictates its primary purpose. Security groups have a SID and are used to assign rights and permissions to members. Distribution groups do not have a SID and are used for e-mail distribution lists.

Smart card   A credit-card-sized plastic card that can be used to authenticate users in an Active Directory environment. A smart card holds a variety of user information, including their private key and associated public key certificate. When a user attempts to log on with a smart card, he or she must insert the card into a smart card reader and then provide the PIN number to be authenticated. Using smart cards requires the implementation of a Certificate Services public key infrastructure (PKI).

Questions and Answers

Page
4-22
Lesson 1 Review

1. You are creating a number of user objects for a team of your organization's temporary workers. They will work daily from 9:00 A.M. to 5:00 P.M. on a contract that is scheduled to begin in one month and end two months later. They will not work outside of that schedule. Which of the following properties should you configure initially to ensure maximum security for the objects?

   a. Password

   b. Logon Hours

   c. Account Expires

   d. Store Password Using Reversible Encryption

   e. Account Is Trusted For Delegation

   f. User Must Change Password At Next Logon

   g. Account Is Disabled

   h. Password Never Expires

   a, b, c, f, g

2. Which of the following properties and administrative tasks can be configured or performed simultaneously on more than one user object?

   a. Last Name

   b. User Logon Name

   c. Disable Account

   d. Enable Account

   e. Reset Password

   f. Password Never Expires

   g. User Must Change Password At Next Logon

   h. Logon Hours

   i. Computer Restrictions (Logon Workstations)

   j. Title

   k. Direct Reports

   c, d, f, g, h, i, j

3. What method would be most useful to generate 100 new user objects, each of which have identical profile path, home folder path, Title, Web Page, Company, Department, and Manager settings?

Dsadd will be the most useful method. You can enter one command line that includes all the parameters. By leaving the *UserDN* parameter empty, you can enter the users' distinguished names one at a time in the command console. A user object template does not allow you to configure options such as Title, Telephone Number, and Web Page. Generating a comma-delimited text file would be time-consuming in comparison, particularly when so many parameters are identical.

4. Which tool will allow you to identify accounts that have not been used for two months?

   a. Dsadd

   b. Dsget

   c. Dsmod

   d. Dsrm

   e. Dsquery

e

5. What variable can be used with the Dsmod and Dsadd commands to create user-specific home folders and profile folders?

   a. *%Username%*

   b. *$Username$*

   c. *CN=Username*

   d. *<Username>*

b

6. Which tools allow you to output the telephone numbers for all users in an OU?

   a. Dsadd

   b. Dsget

   c. Dsmod

   d. Dsrm

   e. Dsquery

The correct answers are b and e. Dsquery will produce a list of user objects within an OU and can pipe that list to Dsget, which in turn can output particular properties, such as phone numbers.

Lesson 2 Review

1. Which of the following group scope changes are not supported in a domain configured to the Windows Server 2003 domain functional level?

    a. Global to domain local

    b. Domain local to universal

    c. Global to universal

    d. Domain local to global

    a, d

2. Which of the following are requirements to create and assign permissions to a universal group?

    a. Universal group must be of the security type

    b. Domain must be configured to at least the Windows 2000 mixed domain functional level

    c. Domain must be configured to at least the Windows 2000 native domain functional level

    d. Universal group must be of the distribution type

    a, c

3. Which of the following objects can be members of a domain local group in a domain configured to the Windows Server 2003 domain functional level?

    a. Universal groups from the same forest

    b. Global groups from the same forest

    c. Global groups from a trusted forest

    d. Domain local groups from a trusted forest

    e. Domain local groups from another domain

    a, b, c

4. Which of the following objects can be a member of a global group in a domain configured to the Windows 2000 mixed domain functional level?

    a. Users in the same domain

    b. Computers in the same domain

    c. Other global groups from the same domain

    d. Domain local groups from the same domain

    a, b

Lesson 3 Review

1. You enable the password complexity policy for your domain. Describe the requirements for passwords and when those requirements will take effect.

   The password must not be based on the user's account name, and it must contain at least 6 characters, with at least one character from three of the four categories: uppercase, lowercase, Arabic numerals, and nonalphanumeric characters. The requirements will take effect immediately for all new accounts. Existing accounts will be affected when they next change their passwords.

2. What would be the affect of configuring the Reset Account Lockout Counter After setting in the Account Lockout Policy section of a Group Policy object applied to an OU to a value of 4?

   a. The account lockout counter will be reset for domain user accounts in that OU after 4 minutes.

   b. The account lockout counter will be reset for domain users accounts in that OU after 4 attempts.

   c. The account lockout counter will be reset for domain user accounts in that OU after 4 hours.

   d. The account lockout counter settings will not apply to domain user accounts.

   d

3. A user has forgotten his or her password and attempts to log on several times with an incorrect password. Eventually, the user receives a logon message indicating that the account is either disabled or locked out. The message suggests that the user contact an administrator. What must you do? (Choose all that apply.)

   a. Delete the user object and re-create it.

   b. Rename the user object.

   c. Enable the user object.

   d. Unlock the user object.

   e. Reset the password for the user object.

   The correct answers are d and e. Although the logon message text on Windows 2000 and other previous operating system versions indicates that the account is disabled, the account is actually locked. Windows Server 2003 displays an accurate message that the account is, in fact, locked out. However, you can recognize the problem by examining what caused the message: a user forgot his or her password. You must unlock the account and reset the password.

Page
4-67
Case Scenario Exercise, Requirement 1

1. What should be modified to achieve Requirement 1?

   a. The domain controller security template Hisecdc.inf

   b. The Default Domain policy

   c. The Default Domain Controller policy

   d. The domain controller security template Ssetup Security.inf

   b

2. To configure account lockout so that users must contact the Help Desk to unlock their accounts, which policy should be specified?

   a. Account Lockout Duration: 999

   b. Account Lockout Threshold: 999

   c. Account Lockout Duration: 0

   d. Account Lockout Threshold: 0

   c

Page
4-67
Case Scenario Exercise, Requirement 2

1. What will be the fastest and most effective means to configure user accounts to require a password change at the next logon?

   a. Select a user account. Open its properties and, on the Account page, select User Must Change Password At Next Logon. Repeat for each user account.

   b. Press CTRL+A to select all users in the Employees OU. Choose the Properties command and, on the Account page, select User Must Change Password At Next Logon. Repeat for each OU.

   c. Use the Dsadd command.

   d. Use the Dsrm command.

   e. Use the Dsquery and Dsmod commands.

   e

2. The Dsquery command allows you to create a list of objects based on those objects' location or properties, and to pipe those objects to the Dsmod command, which then modifies the objects. Open a command prompt, and type the following command:

```
dsquery user "OU=Employees,DC=Contoso,DC=Com"
```

The command will produce a list of all user objects in the Employees OU. An advantage of this command is that it would include users in sub-OUs of the Employees OU. The requirement indicates that you have 15 OUs under the Employees OU. All would be included in the objects generated by Dsquery.

Now, to meet the requirement, type the following command:

```
dsquery user "OU=Employees,DC=Contoso,DC=Com" | dsmod user -mustchpwd yes
```

Page
4-68

Case Scenario Exercise, Requirement 3

1. Which of the following is not a capability provided by installing the Active Directory client software on a Windows 98 system?

   a. Support for NTLMv2 authentication

   b. Site awareness

   c. Ability to access DFS resources

   d. Support for Kerberos authentication

   d

5 Planning, Implementing, and Troubleshooting Group Policy

Exam Objectives in this Chapter:

- Plan a Group Policy strategy (Exam 70-296).

    - Plan a Group Policy strategy by using Resultant Set of Policy (RSoP) Planning mode.

    - Plan a strategy for configuring the user environment by using Group Policy.

    - Plan a strategy for configuring the computer environment by using Group Policy.

- Troubleshoot the application of Group Policy security settings. Tools might include RSoP and the Gpresult command (Exam 70-296).

Why This Chapter Matters

The information in this chapter shows you how to plan, implement, and trouble-shoot group policies. Group Policy allows you to centralize the configuration of computers and user environments. In an environment managed by a well-executed Group Policy strategy, little or no configuration needs to be set by directly touching a desktop. All configuration is specified, enforced, and updated using settings in Group Policy objects (GPOs) that affect a portion of the enterprise as broad as an entire site or domain, or as narrow as a single organizational unit (OU). To achieve this vision, you must understand the nuances of Group Policy terminology and technologies—including the complex interactions of GPO link inheritance, exceptions, and filtering—so that you can anticipate the resultant set of policies that will effectively determine user and computer configuration. You must also be able to leverage the extensive Group Policy tools provided with Microsoft Windows Server 2003 to facilitate planning, logging, and troubleshooting GPO application.

Lessons in this Chapter:

Before You Begin

To complete the hands-on exercises in this chapter, you need

- Two Windows Server 2003 (Standard or Enterprise Edition) systems installed as Server01 and Server02, respectively. Both servers should currently be installed as domain controllers in the contoso.com domain.

- The contoso.com domain should be configured at the Windows 2000 Native domain functional level.

- Top-level OUs: East, West

- Second-level OUs in the East OU: New York

- Second-level OUs in the West OU: Seattle, Phoenix

- Users in the Phoenix OU: Danielle Tiedt

- Users in the Seattle OU: Lorrin Smith-Bates

- Users in the New York OU: Pat Coleman

 Note Keep track of the usernames and passwords you create for these user accounts; you will be logging on with these accounts.

In addition, the user accounts in the preceding list must have the right to log on locally to Server01. You can accomplish this by modifying the logon rights in the Default Domain Controller policy or by making users members of the Print Operators group, which already has the right to log on locally.

Lesson 1: Understanding Group Policy

Before attempting to implement Group Policy, you must be familiar with concepts that affect Group Policy operations. This lesson defines Group Policy, explains how GPOs work, and provides an overview of the settings in a GPO. It also shows you how Group Policy affects startup and logging on, how it is applied, and how security groups are used to filter Group Policy.

The Windows Server 2003 certification exams are deeper in their coverage of Group Policy than previous exams. Therefore, even if you are familiar with Group Policy as it applied to Windows 2000 and Windows XP, pay attention to this lesson, as the examination might surprise you with the detail it expects you to understand.

After this lesson, you will be able to

- Explain the function of group policies
- Explain the function of GPOs
- Explain the function of the Group Policy Object Editor
- Discuss Group Policy settings
- Explain the function of administrative templates
- Explain when Group Policy Objects are processed
- Describe how Group Policy Objects are applied, including the hierarchy of application, inheritance, Block Policy Inheritance, and No Override
- Explain how security groups and WMI filters can be used to modify the scope of a Group Policy Object

Estimated lesson time: 40 minutes

A Review and Overview of Group Policy Components

Group Policy is a feature of Active Directory that enables you to manage user and computer configuration from a single, central point of administration. The most granular component of Group Policy is an individual policy, or setting, that specifies a particular configuration. For example, a policy exists that removes the Run command from the Start menu. Another policy is available to configure the proxy server settings for computers. These two examples illustrate an important point: that policies can affect a user, regardless of the computer at which the user logs on, or can affect a computer, regardless of which user logs on.

A *group policy object (GPO)* is an object that contains or specifies one or more policies, and thereby affects one or more configuration settings for a user or computer. GPOs consist of two components: an Active Directory object and a folder stored in the SYS-VOL of domain controllers that contains a collection of files.

GPOs are modified using the Group Policy Object Editor snap-in, shown in Figure 5-1. The Group Policy Object Editor displays the hundreds of policies available in a GPO in an organized hierarchy that begins with a division between computer-based and user-based policies. As you drill down into a GPO, you will find policies listed in the details pane.

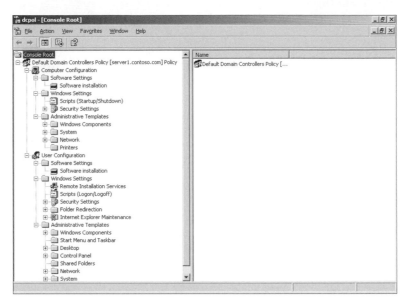

Figure 5-1   The Group Policy Object Editor snap-in

Every policy in a new GPO is Not Configured, meaning that the GPO will not modify the existing configuration for that particular setting. When you configure a policy, you can enable or disable the policy. For example, if you enable the policy that removes the Run command from the Start menu, that policy takes effect. If you disable the same policy, the result is that the Run command will appear in the Start menu. Each policy is accompanied by explanatory text that details the effect of enabling and disabling the policy. The policy that removes the Run command also enforces other restrictions to prevent users from running applications from certain interfaces such as Task Manager. Be certain to read the explanatory text and to test all policies prior to implementing them in a production environment.

Policies will always override a configuration made by a user or by a script. Because GPOs are regularly refreshed, GPOs not only set the initial configuration but also enforce the maintenance of that configuration. For example, a GPO might contain the policy that configures proxy server settings for a computer. If a user later modifies the proxy server settings on the computer, the group policy refresh will reset the settings to the standards that are specified in the policy.

When you configure policies within a GPO and then apply that GPO to a computer, site, domain, or OU, the policies you have specified will modify and maintain the configuration of the computer and the user environment. A GPO is applied by linking it to a site, domain, or OU. The computers and users underneath the container to which the GPO is linked fall under the scope of that GPO, and will be affected by the configurations specified by policies in the GPO. A single user or computer is likely to be under the scope of multiple GPOs linked to the sites, domain, or OUs in which the user or computer exists. The total or cumulative impact of the policies in the GPOs—the *Resultant Set of Policies (RSoP)*—depends on numerous factors, which will be examined later in this chapter.

By configuring policies within GPOs, you can deploy and configure a mind-boggling number of features and settings. Windows Server 2003 provides several tools, including Active Directory Users And Computers, the Group Policy Management console (a free and important download from the Microsoft Web site), the Resultant Set Of Policy snap-in, and the Group Policy Object Editor. Each will be explored in this chapter.

Tip   To download the Group Policy Management console, go to *http://www.microsoft.com /downloads/* and search for "Group Policy Management console."

What's In a Name? "Group" Policy?

As stated in this section, group policies apply to computer and user accounts. A common misconception is that group policies can be applied to groups. Although the name "Group Policy" suggests that you might set policies for global, domain local, or global groups, this is not the case. Instead, think of a GPO as a grouping of policies—a collection of configuration settings that is linked to sites, domains, or OUs. While *group policies do not apply to groups*, group membership can affect the application of Group Policy. For example, if a user or computer account belongs to a group that is specifically denied the ability to apply a GPO, that user or computer will not receive the settings in the GPO. This concept is known as *GPO filtering* with security groups, and it is discussed later in this chapter.

Understanding GPOs

To create a specific configuration for users and computers, you create *GPOs*, which are collections of policies. Each computer has one *local* GPO and can, in addition, be subject to any number of Active Directory–based GPOs.

Local GPOs

Each Windows 2000, Windows XP, and Windows Server 2003 computer has one *local GPO*, which can manage configuration of that system. The local GPO exists whether or not the computer is part of domain, workgroup, or a non-networked environment. It is stored in *%Systemroot%*\System32\GroupPolicy. The policies in the local GPO affect only the computer on which the GPO is stored. By default, only the Security Settings policies are configured on a system's local GPO. All other policies are Not Configured.

When a computer does not belong to an Active Directory domain, the local policy is useful to configure and enforce configuration on that computer. However, in an Active Directory domain, settings in GPOs that are linked to the site, domain, or OUs will override local GPO settings.

Active Directory–Based GPOs

Active Directory–based GPOs are created in Active Directory and stored on domain controllers, and they are used to centrally manage configuration for users and computers in the domain. The remainder of this lesson refers to Active Directory–based GPOs rather than local GPOs, unless otherwise specified.

When Active Directory is installed, two default GPOs are created:

- **Default Domain Policy**   This GPO is linked to the domain, and it affects all users and computers in the domain (including computers that are domain controllers) through Group Policy inheritance. For more information, refer to the "GPO Application" section later in this lesson.

- **Default Domain Controllers Policy**   This GPO is linked to the Domain Controllers OU and, by default, affects only domain controllers, because computer accounts for domain controllers are kept exclusively in the Domain Controllers OU.

> **Tip**   While you might want to modify existing policies in the default GPOs—such as changing the default Maximum Password Age (42 days)—it is not best practice to add new policies in the default GPOs. Instead, create one or more new GPOs to implement new policies in your environment.

GPO storage

Group Policy settings are represented by Group Policy objects (GPOs) in Active Directory. Like all Active Directory objects, each GPO includes a globally unique identifier (GUID) attribute that uniquely identifies the object within Active Directory. The files that are used by computers to apply Group Policy are stored on the domain controllers in *%Systemroot%* Sysvol*Domain Name*\Policies*GPO GUID*\Adm, where *GPO GUID* is the GPO's GUID.

> **Off the Record**   You can see a mapping of the Group Policy GUID and name in the Active Directory Replication Monitor (Replmon.exe). (Replmon.exe is a part of the Windows Support Tools on the Windows Server 2003 CD in the Support\Tools folder.) To see this, add a domain controller as the monitored server, and then right-click that domain controller and select Show Group Policy Object Status.

Creating GPOs

To create a GPO and link it to a domain or OU, open Active Directory Users And Computers, and from the properties of the domain or OU, click the Group Policy tab and click New. Enter a name for the GPO.

To create a GPO and link it to a site, open Active Directory Sites And Services, and from the properties of the site, click the Group Policy tab and click New. Enter a name for the GPO.

GPOs can also be created using the Group Policy Management console. Right-click the Group Policy Objects container, and choose New; or right-click a site, domain, or OU, and choose Create And Link A GPO Here.

Linking GPOs

A GPO is applied by *linking* the GPO to a site, domain, or OU. Computers within that container will be configured by computer policies in the GPO, and users within that container will be configured by user policies in the GPO.

GPO links can be managed on the Group Policy tab of the properties dialog box of a site, domain, or OU. When you click New, you create a new GPO and link it to that container. Click Add to link an existing OU to the container. Using the Group Policy Management console, right-click a site, domain, or OU and choose Link An Existing GPO.

Editing Group Policy Objects

You use the *Group Policy Object Editor* to configure policies in each GPO. The Group Policy Object Editor for the Default Domain Controllers Policy GPO is shown in Figure 5-1.

Note that the root node of the Group Policy Object Editor is displayed as the name of the GPO and the domain to which it belongs, in the format

`GPOName DomainName Policy`

Figure 5-1 provides an example of this: Default Domain Controllers Policy [server1.contoso.com] Policy.

You must open the Group Policy Object Editor focused on an existing GPO. To open the Group Policy Object Editor from the Group Policy Management console, right-click a GPO and choose Edit.

To open a GPO using the Active Directory administrative tools, open the properties of a site using Active Directory Sites And Services, or open the properties of a domain or OU using Active Directory Users And Computers. Click the Group Policy tab, and click Edit.

To open the Group Policy Object Editor for a computer's local GPO, complete the following steps:

1. Open Microsoft Management Console (MMC).

2. On the MMC's menu bar, click File and then click Add/Remove Snap-In.

3. In the Add/Remove Snap-In dialog box, in the Standalone tab, click Add.

4. In the Add Standalone Snap-In dialog box, click Group Policy Object Editor and then click Add.

5. In the Select Group Policy Object dialog box, ensure that Local Computer appears in the Group Policy Object box.

   To open the local GPO of a remote computer, browse to the remote computer in the Select Group Policy Object dialog box.

6. Click Finish, and then click Close in the Add Standalone Snap-In dialog box.

7. In the Add/Remove Snap-In dialog box, click OK.

Group Policy Settings

Group Policy settings, also known simply as *policies*, are contained in a GPO and are viewed and modified using the Group Policy Object Editor. There are two types of Group Policy settings: computer configuration settings and user configuration settings. They are contained in the Computer Configuration and User Configuration *nodes*, respectively, in a GPO.

Note   Group Policy settings override user profile settings.

Computer and User Configuration Nodes

The *Computer Configuration node* contains the settings that are applied to computers, regardless of who logs on to them. Computer configuration settings are applied when the operating system starts up and are updated at a refresh interval, by default every 90 minutes.

> **Exam Tip** GPOs can be applied only to Windows XP Professional, Windows 2000, or Windows Server 2003 operating systems and are not supported for Windows 95, Windows 98, Windows Millennium Edition (Windows Me), or Windows NT. To manage the configuration of those platforms, you must use System Policy. System Policy provides for centralized management of some settings for domain computers running those earlier versions of Windows. It does not provide the comprehensive and flexible management capabilities of Group Policy. System Policy is distributed by using System Policy Editor to create a policy file (called Ntconfig.pol for Windows NT and Config.pol for Windows 95, Windows 98, and Windows Me) that is placed in the Netlogon share of the domain controllers.

The *User Configuration node* contains the settings that are applied to users, regardless of which computer the user logs on to. User configuration settings are applied when users log on to the computer and are updated at a default refresh interval of every 90 minutes.

Both the Computer Configuration and User Configuration nodes include settings for installing software, settings for configuring and securing Windows, and registry settings. These settings are contained in the Software Settings, Windows Settings, and Administrative Templates nodes, respectively.

Software Settings Node

In both the Computer Configuration and User Configuration nodes, the Software Settings node (shown in Figure 5-2) contains only the Software Installation extension by default. The Software Installation extension helps you specify how applications are installed and maintained within your organization. It also provides a place for independent software vendors to add settings. Software deployment with Group Policy is discussed in Chapter 6.

Figure 5-2   Contents of the Software Settings node

Windows Settings Node

In both the Computer Configuration and User Configuration nodes, the Windows Settings node (shown in Figure 5-3) contains the Scripts extension and Security Settings node.

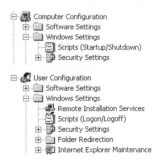

Figure 5-3   Contents of the Windows Settings node

The Scripts extension allows you to specify two types of scripts: startup/shutdown (in the Computer Configuration node) and logon/logoff (in the User Configuration node). Startup/shutdown scripts run at computer startup or shutdown. Logon/logoff scripts run when a user logs on or off the computer. When you assign multiple logon/logoff or startup/shutdown scripts to a user or computer, Windows Server 2003 executes the scripts from top to bottom. You can determine the order of execution for multiple scripts in the Properties dialog box. When a computer is shut down, Windows Server 2003 first processes logoff scripts, followed by shutdown scripts. By default, the time-out value for processing scripts is 10 minutes. If the logoff and shutdown scripts require more than 10 minutes to process, you must adjust the timeout value with a software policy. You can use any ActiveX scripting language to write scripts. Some possibilities include Microsoft Visual Basic, Scripting Edition (VBScript), Microsoft JScript, Perl, and MS-DOS style batch files (.bat and .cmd).

Note   Logon scripts on a shared network directory in another forest are supported for network logon across forests. This is a new feature of the Windows Server 2003 family.

The Security Settings node allows a security administrator to configure security using GPOs. This can be done after, or instead of, using a security template to set system security. For a detailed discussion of system security and the Security Settings node, refer to Chapter 9.

In the User Configuration node only, the Windows Settings folder contains the additional nodes Remote Installation Services, Folder Redirection, and Internet Explorer Maintenance. Remote Installation Services (RIS) is used to control the behavior of a remote operating system installation. Optionally, RIS can be used to provide customized packages for non–Windows Server 2003 clients of Active Directory. (Group policy requires a genuine Windows 2000 or Windows Server 2003 client, not merely a pre–Windows 2000 client of Active Directory, however.)

Folder Redirection allows you to redirect Windows Server 2003 special folders (Application Data, Desktop, My Documents, and Start Menu) from their default user profile location to an alternate location on the network, where they can be centrally managed. For details on folder redirection, refer to Chapter 6. Internet Explorer Maintenance allows you to administer and customize Microsoft Internet Explorer on computers running Windows 2000 and later.

Administrative Templates Node

In both the Computer Configuration and User Configuration nodes, the Administrative Templates node (shown in Figure 5-4) contains registry-based Group Policy settings. There are more than 550 of these settings available for configuring the user environment. As an administrator, you might spend a significant amount of time manipulating these settings. To assist you with the settings, a description of each policy setting is available in three locations:

- In the Explain tab in the Properties dialog box for the setting. In addition, the Setting tab in the Properties dialog box for the setting lists the required operating system or software for the setting.

- In Administrative Templates Help (a new feature for Windows Server 2003). Administrative Templates Help can be accessed by right-clicking the Administrative Templates node and clicking Help. In addition, Administrative Templates Help lists the required operating system or software for each setting.

- In the Extended tab (a new feature for Windows Server 2003, selected by default) in the Group Policy Object Editor. The Extended tab appears on the bottom of the right details pane. The Extended tab provides a description of each selected setting in a column between the console tree and the settings pane. The required operating system or software for each setting is also listed.

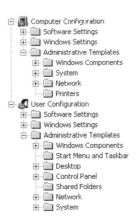

Figure 5-4   Contents of the Administrative Templates node

Each of the settings in the Administrative Templates node can be:

- **Not Configured**   The registry is not modified.
- **Enabled**   The registry reflects that the policy setting is selected.
- **Disabled**   The registry reflects that the policy setting is not selected.

Policies in the Administrative Templates node in the Computer Configuration modify registry values in the HKEY_LOCAL_MACHINE (HKLM) key. Policies in the Administrative Templates node in the User Configuration node modify registry values in the HKEY_CURRENT_USER (HKCU) key. Most of the registry values that are modified by the default polices are located in one of the following four reserved trees:

- HKEY_LOCAL_MACHINE\Software\Policies (computer settings)
- HKEY_CURRENT_USER\Software\Policies (user settings)
- HKEY_LOCAL_MACHINE\Software\Microsoft\Windows\CurrentVersion\Policies (computer settings)
- HKEY_CURRENT_USER\Software\Microsoft\Windows\CurrentVersion\Policies (user settings)

In the Computer Configuration and User Configuration nodes, the Administrative Templates node contains the Windows Components, System, and Network nodes.

Windows Components   The nodes in the Windows Components node enable you to administer Windows Server 2003 components, including Microsoft NetMeeting, Internet Explorer, Application Compatibility, Task Scheduler, Terminal Services, Microsoft Windows Installer, Microsoft Windows Messenger, Microsoft Windows Media Player, and Microsoft Windows Update. For the Computer Configuration node only, the Windows Components folder also includes the Internet Information Services and Windows Media Digital Rights Management node. For the User Configuration node only, the nodes in the Windows Components folder also include Help and Support Center, Microsoft Windows Explorer, and Microsoft Management Console (MMC).

System   The nodes in the System node are used to control how the Windows Server 2003 operating system is accessed and used, including settings for user profiles, scripts, logon and logoff functions, and Group Policy itself. For the Computer Configuration node only, the settings in the System node also include settings for disk quotas, the Net Logon service, remote assistance, system restore, error reporting, Microsoft Windows File Protection, Microsoft Remote Procedure Call, and Microsoft Windows Time Service. For the User Configuration node only, the settings in the System node also include settings for CTRL+ALT+DEL options and power management.

Network   The settings in the Network node enable you to control how the network is accessed and used, including settings for offline files and network and dial-up connections. For the Computer Configuration node only, the settings in the Network node also include settings for the Domain Name System (DNS) client, the quality of service (QoS) packet scheduler, and Simple Network Management Protocol (SNMP).

Printers   For the Computer Configuration node only, the Administrative Templates node contains additional registry-based Group Policy settings pertaining to printers in the Printers node.

Start Menu And Taskbar, Desktop, Control Panel, Shared Folders   For the User Configuration node only, the Administrative Templates node contains additional registry-based nodes for the Start menu and taskbar, the desktop, Control Panel, and shared folders. The settings in these nodes control a user's Start menu, taskbar, desktop, Control Panel, and shared folders.

Administrative Templates View Filtering   Because there are so many settings in the Administrative Templates node, a feature that filters the view of administrative templates has been developed in Windows Server 2003 in an effort to reduce screen clutter. This feature is known as *administrative templates view filtering*. You might want to filter your view of administrative templates if you are inconvenienced by seeing too many administrative template settings at once in the Group Policy Object Editor. Administrative templates view filtering simply selects the settings that are visible in the editor.

> **Note**   Administrative templates view filtering does not affect whether the settings apply to users or computers. Do not confuse this feature with the procedure for filtering GPO scope according to security group membership or Windows Management Instrumentation (WMI).

To filter the view provided by administrative templates, complete the following steps:

1. Open the Group Policy Object Editor, and in the console tree, right-click the folder under Administrative Templates that contains the policy settings you want to filter. Click View, and then click Filtering.

2. In the Filtering dialog box, shown in Figure 5-5, do any of the following to filter the settings you can view:

   ❑ If you want to remove any types of settings from the GPO display, select the Filter By Requirements Information check box, and then in the Select The Items To Be Displayed list, clear any categories you do not want to see. By default, all types of settings are selected (that is, are displayed).

   ❑ If you want to hide settings that are not configured, select the Only Show Configured Policy Settings check box. If you select this check box, only Enabled or Disabled settings are visible.

❑ If you want to hide Windows NT 4.0–style system policy settings, select the Only Show Policy Settings That Can Be Fully Managed check box. Microsoft recommends selecting this check box, and it is selected by default.

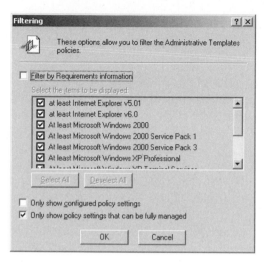

Figure 5-5   The Filtering dialog box

3. Click OK.

Administrative Templates

The previous section discussed the Administrative Templates node in a GPO, which contains the registry-based Group Policy settings you set on the Group Policy Object Editor. However, an administrative template is actually a text file used to generate the user interface for the Group Policy settings you can set using the Group Policy Object Editor.

In Windows Server 2003 operating systems, administrative templates have the .adm filename extension, as they did in Windows NT 4.0. In Windows NT 4.0 and earlier versions of Windows, administrative templates were text files using the American National Standards Institute (ANSI) character set. They created a namespace within the System Policy Editor for convenient editing of the registry, a friendlier user interface than the Registry Editor (Regedit.exe). In Windows Server 2003 and Windows 2000, administrative templates are Unicode-based text files. The Group Policy Object Editor replaces the System Policy Editor and gives you greater control over configuration settings. Administrative Templates is the only area of Group Policy (the other areas being software settings and Windows settings) that allows you to modify and extend the default policy setting options.

There are three types of administrative templates:

■ **Default**   Administrative templates provided with Windows Server 2003 operating systems, as described in Table 5-1.

- **Vendor-supplied**   Administrative templates provided with software applications designed to run on Windows Server 2003 operating systems. You might need to install these templates separately or download them from a Web site. For example, you can use the Microsoft Office policy templates (.adm files) to implement Microsoft Office Group Policy settings. The Office policy templates are included with the Office Resource Kit tools, which can be downloaded from the Microsoft Web site (*http://www.microsoft.com*).

- **Custom**   Templates created using the .adm language to further control computer or user settings. Custom templates are generally created by application developers.

> **Note**   A tutorial on creating custom administrative templates is beyond the scope of this training kit. You can find the details about creating your own administrative templates by searching for "Implementing Registry-Based Group Policy" on the Microsoft Web site (*http://www.microsoft.com*).

Table 5-1   Windows Server 2003 Default Administrative Templates

Administrative template	Description
System.adm	Installed in Group Policy by default; contains system settings
Inetres.adm	Installed in Group Policy by default; contains Internet Explorer policies
Wmplayer.adm	Contains Windows Media Player settings
Conf.adm[1]	Contains NetMeeting settings
Wuau.adm	Contains Windows Update settings

[1]This tool is not available on Windows XP 64-Bit Edition or the 64-bit versions of the Windows Server 2003 family.

Group Policy Processing

The following sequence shows the order in which computer configuration and user configuration settings are applied when a computer starts and a user logs on.

1. The network starts. Remote Procedure Call System Service (RPCSS) and Multiple Universal Naming Convention Provider (MUP) are started.

2. An ordered list of GPOs is obtained for the computer. The list contents depend on the following factors:

   ❑ Whether the computer is part of a Windows 2000 or Windows Server 2003 domain, and is therefore subject to Group Policy through Active Directory.

   ❑ The location of the computer in Active Directory.

3. Computer configuration settings are processed. This occurs synchronously by default and in the following order: local GPO, site GPOs, domain GPOs, and OU GPOs. See the section "GPO Application" for details about GPO processing.

4. Startup scripts run. This is hidden and synchronous by default; each script must complete or time out before the next one starts. The default timeout is 600 seconds (10 minutes). You can use several Group Policy settings to modify this behavior.

5. The user presses CTRL+ALT+DEL to log on.

6. After the user is validated, the user profile is loaded, governed by the Group Policy settings in effect.

7. An ordered list of GPOs is obtained for the user. The list contents depend on the following factors:

   ❏ Whether the user is part of a Windows 2000 or Windows Server 2003 domain, and is therefore subject to Group Policy through Active Directory.

   ❏ Whether loopback is enabled and the state (Merge or Replace) of the loopback policy setting. Refer to the section "GPO Application" for more information about loopback.

   ❏ The location of the user in Active Directory.

   ❏ If the list of GPOs to be applied has not changed, no processing is done. You can use a policy setting to change this behavior.

8. User configuration settings are processed. This occurs synchronously by default and in the following order: local GPO, site GPOs, domain GPOs, and OU GPOs. No user interface is displayed while user policies are being processed. See the section "GPO Application" for details about GPO processing.

9. Logon scripts run. Unlike Windows NT 4.0 scripts, Group Policy–based logon scripts are run hidden and asynchronously by default. The user object script runs last.

10. The operating system user interface prescribed by Group Policy appears.

> **Note** The following interactive logon tasks are supported across forests: applying Group Policy to user or computer objects across forests, and applying loopback processing across forests. This is a new feature of the Windows Server 2003 family.

GPO Application

Because GPOs are applied hierarchically, the user or computer's configuration is a result of the local GPO as well as GPOs applied to its site, domain, and OUs. Group Policy settings are applied in the following sequence:

1. Local GPO. Each computer running Windows Server 2003, Windows XP, and Windows 2000 has exactly one GPO stored locally.

2. Site GPOs. Any GPOs that have been linked to the site are applied next. GPO application is synchronous.

   A GPO linked to a site affects all computers in the site without regard to the domain to which the computers belong (so long as all computers belong to the same Active Directory forest). Therefore, by linking a GPO to a site, that GPO can be applied to multiple domains within a forest. Site-linked GPOs are stored on domain controllers in the forest root domain. Therefore, forest root domain controllers must be accessible for site-linked GPOs to be applied correctly. If you implement site-linked policies, you must consider policy application when planning your network infrastructure. Either place a forest root domain controller in the site to which the policy is linked, or ensure that WAN connectivity provides accessibility to a forest root domain controller.

> **Note**   When multiple GPOs are linked to a site, domain, or OU, an administrator determines the order of application. On the Group Policy tab of the Properties dialog box for a site, domain, or OU, the last policy on the list of GPO links is applied first. GPOs are then applied "up" the list, with the first GPO on the list applied last.

3. Domain GPOs. Multiple domain-linked GPOs are applied synchronously in the order specified for the GPO links.

4. OU GPOs. GPOs linked to the OU highest in the Active Directory hierarchy are applied first, followed by GPOs linked to its child OU, and so on. Finally, the GPOs linked to the OU that contains the user or computer are applied. At the level of each OU in the Active Directory hierarchy, one, many, or no GPOs can be linked. If several group policies are linked to an OU, they are applied synchronously in the order specified for the GPO links.

This sequence applies the local GPO first, followed by GPOs linked to the site, the domain, and the OUs containing the user or computer. GPOs linked to the OU of which the computer or user is a direct member are applied last. Policies contained in GPOs will, by default, overwrite policies of previously applied GPOs. For example, you might link a GPO to the domain that prevents users from running registry editing tools, and then link a second GPO to an OU containing administrative users and configure the second GPO to enable registry editing tools. Administrative users within the scope of the second GPO would then have access to registry editing tools.

> **Note**   Most policies are specific to either the User Configuration or Computer Configuration node. A small handful of policies appear in both nodes. While in most situations, the setting of the policy in the Computer Configuration node will override the setting of the policy in the User Configuration node, it is important to read the explanatory text accompanying the policy to understand the policy's effect and its application.

Figure 5-6 shows how Group Policy is applied for the contoso.com domain.

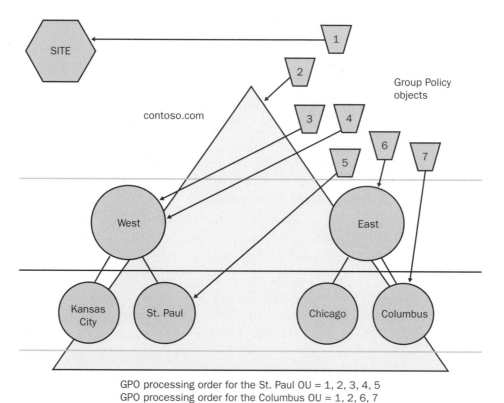

GPO processing order for the St. Paul OU = 1, 2, 3, 4, 5
GPO processing order for the Columbus OU = 1, 2, 6, 7

Figure 5-6   How Group Policy is applied for the contoso.com domain

Group Policy Inheritance

The ordered, hierarchical application of GPOs produces a result that resembles, and is called, *inheritance*. In the context of Group Policy, the term inheritance means that the policies that effectively determine the configuration for users and computers in an OU are the resultant set of policies inherited from the parent containers. Policies are, in effect, passed down from parent to child containers within a domain.

Exam Tip   Policies from a parent domain are *not* inherited by a child domain. Each domain maintains distinct policy links. However, computers in several domains might be within the scope of a GPO linked to a site.

A policy setting is inherited in the following ways:

- If a policy setting is configured (set to Enabled or Disabled) in a GPO linked to a parent OU, and the same policy setting is Not Configured in GPOs linked to its child OUs, the resultant set of policies that affect users and computers in the child OUs inherit the parent's policy setting.

- If a policy setting is configured (set to Enabled or Disabled) for a parent OU, and the same policy setting *is* configured for a child OU, the child OU's Group Policy setting overrides the setting inherited from the parent OU.

- If a policy setting of a parent OU is Not Configured, the child OU does not inherit that setting.

Exceptions to the Application Process

The default order for the application of Group Policy settings is subject to the following exceptions:

- **Workgroup members**   A computer that is a member of a workgroup processes only the local GPO.

- **Block Policy Inheritance**   A site, domain, or OU can be configured to Block Policy Inheritance using the check box on the container's Group Policy properties tab. Because Block Policy Inheritance is a property of the site, domain, or OU, it blocks *all* Group Policy settings from GPOs linked to parents in the Group Policy hierarchy. In Figure 5-7, Block Policy Inheritance has been applied to the East OU. As a result, GPOs 1 and 2, which are applied to the site and the domain, are blocked and do not apply to the East OU. Therefore, only GPOs 6 and 7 are processed for the Columbus OU.

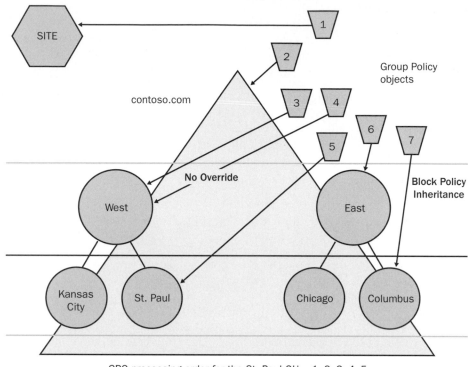

GPO processing order for the St. Paul OU = 1, 2, 3, 4, 5
GPO processing order for the Columbus OU = 6, 7

Figure 5-7   Applying No Override and Block Policy Inheritance for the contoso.com domain

■ **No Override**   The GPO link that applies a GPO to a site, domain, or OU can be set to No Override so that its policy settings will not be overridden by any other GPO during the processing of group policies. When more than one GPO has been set to No Override, the one highest in the Active Directory hierarchy (or higher in the hierarchy specified by the administrator at each fixed level in Active Directory) takes precedence. No Override is applied to the GPO link. In Figure 5-7, No Override has been applied to the GPO 4 link to the West OU. As a result, the policy settings in GPO 4 cannot be overwritten by other GPOs linked to OUs underneath the West OU. GPO links set to No Override are always applied and cannot be blocked by a child container's Block Policy Inheritance setting. Said another way, No Override always wins.

Note   Because No Override and Block Policy Inheritance have wide-ranging effects that can cause problems with other GPOs, you should use them sparingly.

Exam Tip   Know the difference between Block Policy Inheritance and No Override.

■ **Loopback setting**   By default, a user's settings come from a GPO list that depends on the user object's location in Active Directory. The ordered list goes from site-linked to domain-linked to OU-linked GPOs, with inheritance determined by the location of the user in Active Directory and in an order specified by the administrator at each level. Regardless of what computer the user logs on to, the resultant set of policies that determine the user's environment will be the same. There are situations, however, when you might want to configure a user differently depending on the computer in use. For example, you might want to lock down and standardize user desktops when users log on to computers in closely managed environments such as conference rooms, reception areas, laboratories, classrooms, and kiosks. Loopback achieves this goal by providing alternatives to the default method of obtaining the ordered list of GPOs that affect a user's configuration. Instead of user configuration being determined by the User Configuration node policies of GPOs that apply to the user object, user configuration can be determined by the User Configuration node policies of GPOs that apply to the *computer* object.

The User Group Policy Loopback Processing Mode policy, located in the Computer Configuration\Administrative Templates\System\Group Policy folder in Group Policy Object Editor can be, like all policy settings, set to Not Configured, Enabled, or Disabled. When enabled, the policy can specify Replace or Merge mode.

❑ Replace. In this case, the GPO list for the user is replaced in its entirety by the GPO list already obtained for the computer at computer startup (during step 2 in the "Group Policy Processing" section). The User Configuration policies of the computer's GPOs determine the configuration applied to the user. This mode would be useful in a situation, such as a classroom, where users should receive a standard configuration rather than the configuration applied to the users in a less managed environment.

❑ Merge. In this case, the GPO list is concatenated, or merged. The GPO list obtained for the computer at computer startup (step 2 in the "Group Policy Processing" section) is appended to the GPO list obtained for the user when logging on (step 7). Because the GPO list obtained for the computer is applied later, it has precedence if it conflicts with settings in the user's list. This mode would be useful to apply additional settings to users' typical configurations. For example, you might allow a user to receive his or her typical configuration when logging on to a computer in a conference room or reception area, but replace the wallpaper with a standard bitmap and disable the use of certain applications or devices.

Using Security Groups to Filter GPO Scope

By now you've learned that you can link a GPO to a site, domain, or OU. However, you might need to apply GPOs only to certain groups of users or computers rather than to all users or computers within the scope of the GPO. Although you cannot directly link a GPO to a security group, there is a way to apply GPOs to specific security groups. The policies in a GPO apply only to users who have Allow Read and Allow Apply Group Policy permissions to the GPO. Therefore, by setting the appropriate permissions for security groups, you can filter Group Policy to influence only the computers and users you specify. For more information on filtering GPO scope by using security groups, refer to Lesson 3 in this chapter.

Note   The Apply Group Policy permission is not available for the local GPO.

Using WMI Queries to Filter GPO Scope

Windows Management Instrumentation (WMI) is a management infrastructure technology that allows administrators to monitor and control managed objects in the network. A WMI query is capable of filtering systems based on characteristics including RAM, processor speed, disk capacity, IP address, operating system version and service pack level, installed applications, and printer properties. Because WMI exposes almost every property of every object within a computer, the list of attributes that can be used in a WMI query is virtually unlimited. WMI queries are written using WMI query language (WQL).

A new feature in Windows Server 2003, WMI filtering, enables you to use a WMI query to filter the scope of a GPO, similar to the way security groups can be used to filter GPO scope. The GPO is applied based on properties available in WMI that are contained in the query. A good way to understand the purpose of a WMI filter, both for the certification exams and for real-world implementation, is through example. Group Policy can be used to deploy software applications and service packs—a capability that is discussed in Chapter 6. You might create a GPO to deploy an application, and then use a WMI filter to specify that the policy should apply only to computers with a minimum amount of RAM and free disk space.

For more information about developing WMI queries for GPO filtering, see the Windows Management Instrumentation (WMI) software development kit (SDK), located at *http://www.microsoft.com/*.

Delegating Control of GPOs

There are different GPO-related tasks for which you can delegate control: GPO editing, GPO creation, and GPO linking.

By default, GPOs can be created only by members of the Domain Admins, Enterprise Admins, or Group Policy Creator Owner groups. You can give other users the ability to create GPOs by completing the following two steps:

1. Making them members of the Group Policy Creator Owners group.

2. Delegating them authority to control GPO linking to the site, domain, or OU in which they will create GPOs—a process described below.

GPOs can be edited by users who have Write permission to the GPO. GPO permissions can be set by selecting the GPO on the Group Policy tab, and then, as you would for permissions of a file or folder, clicking Properties and then clicking the Security tab.

Typically, the creation of GPOs is strictly limited in an enterprise, and those who can create GPOs are members of the Group Policy Creator Owners group. Selected administrators might be given Allow Write permission to one or more GPOs so that they can edit the policy settings contained in those GPOs. That privilege is also typically limited because of the broad-reaching effect of GPOs and the importance of understanding, testing, and documenting policies prior to implementing them in a production environment.

However, many organizations do allow administrators of divisional OUs to manage the policy links for those OUs. That allows those administrators to select which existing GPOs to apply to their portion of the enterprise. You delegate authority to control GPO links by using the Delegation Of Control Wizard and granting the Manage Group Policy Links permission.

Note   The Group Policy Management console allows you to easily manage and delegate GPO permissions on the Delegation tab of a GPO, site, domain, or OU.

Planning administrative control of GPOs is discussed in Lesson 2 of this chapter. Delegating administrative control when a GPO is implemented is discussed in Lesson 3 of this chapter.

Resultant Set of Policy (RSoP)

Because an object can be affected by multiple levels of GPOs, Group Policy inheritance, and exceptions, it's often difficult to determine just what policies apply. *Resultant Set of Policy (RSoP)* is a new tool in Windows Server 2003 operating systems that helps you anticipate and troubleshoot Group Policy settings. RSoP polls existing and planned policies and reports the results of those queries, listing the final set of applied policies and policy precedence for an object you specify. RSoP can help you manage and troubleshoot conflicting policies. For detailed information on using RSoP, refer to Lesson 4 later in this chapter.

Lesson Review

The following questions are intended to reinforce key information presented in this lesson. If you are unable to answer a question, review the lesson materials and try the question again. You can find answers to the questions in the "Questions and Answers" section at the end of this chapter.

1. What is a GPO?

   _____

   _____

   _____

   _____

2. What are the two primary groupings of policy settings, and how are they used?

   _____

   _____

   _____

   _____

   _____

   _____

   _____

3. In what order is Group Policy applied to components in the Active Directory structure?

   _____

   _____

   _____

4. What is the difference between Block Policy Inheritance and No Override?

   _____

   _____

   _____

   _____

   _____

   _____

_____

_____

_____

_____

_____

5. Which of the following nodes contains the registry-based Group Policy settings?

   a. Software Settings

   b. Windows Settings

   c. Administrative Templates

   d. Security Settings

_____

_____

_____

_____

_____

Lesson Summary

- Group Policy objects are collections of user and computer configuration settings that can be linked to computers, sites, domains, and OUs to specify and enforce the configuration of users and computers. You use the Group Policy Object Editor to organize and manage the Group Policy settings in each GPO.

- There are two types of Group Policy settings: computer configuration settings and user configuration settings. Computer configuration settings are used to configure computers, regardless of who logs on to them, and are applied when the operating system initializes. User configuration settings are used to configure the user environment, regardless of which computer the user logs on to, and are applied when the user log on to the computer.

- Group Policy objects are applied to users and computers based on their links in the following order: local computer, site, domain, and then OU.

■ Because of the ordered, hierarchical application of GPOs, Group Policy application is described as inheritance. If you have linked a GPO with a particular Group Policy setting to a parent container, that setting applies to all containers beneath the parent container, including the user and computer objects in the container. However, if you specify a Group Policy setting in a GPO linked to a child container, the child container's Group Policy setting overrides the setting inherited from the parent container.

■ The default order for the application of Group Policy settings is subject to the following exceptions: No Override, Block Policy Inheritance, the Loopback setting, and a computer that is a member of a workgroup.

Lesson 2: Group Policy Planning Strategies

Before implementing group policies, you should create a plan to manage them. You can plan your Group Policy settings, GPOs, and administrative control of GPOs to provide the most efficient Group Policy implementation for your organization. This lesson examines Group Policy planning strategies.

After this lesson, you will be able to

- Plan Group Policy settings
- Plan GPOs
- Plan administrative control of GPOs

Estimated lesson time: 15 minutes

Devising Group Policy Planning Strategies

There are three parts to planning Group Policy:

- Plan the Group Policy settings necessary for computers and users at each level (sites, domains, and OUs).

- Plan the GPOs necessary for computers and users at each level (sites, domains, and OUs).

- Plan administrative control of GPOs.

Document your Group Policy plans. Accurate and organized documentation of the Group Policy settings and GPOs needed by your organization and the administrators who control the GPOs can help when you need to revisit or modify your Group Policy configuration.

Plan Group Policy Settings

There are over 600 Group Policy settings in Windows Server 2003 operating systems. The best way to familiarize yourself with these settings is to look through them using the Group Policy Object Editor. You must plan the settings necessary for computers and users for each site, domain, and OU in your organization. Plan settings sparingly—justify the selection of each setting as you would the creation of a domain or OU. Choose settings based on their ability to help you simplify the administration of computers and users.

Planning GPOs

For each site, domain, and OU, you must determine how Group Policy settings should be arranged into GPOs. Base the arrangement of Group Policy settings on the users and computers that require them. You can arrange Group Policy settings in the following ways in a GPO:

- **Single-setting GPO**   Contains a single type of Group Policy setting—for example, a GPO that includes only security settings. This model is best suited for organizations in which administrative responsibilities are task-based and delegated among several individuals.

- **Multiple-setting GPO**   Contains multiple types of Group Policy settings—for example, a GPO that includes both software settings and application deployment, or a GPO that includes security and scripts settings. This model is best suited for organizations in which administrative responsibilities are centralized and an administrator might need to perform all types of Group Policy administration.

- **Dedicated-setting GPO**   Contains either computer configuration or user configuration Group Policy settings. This model increases the number of GPOs that must be applied when logging on, thereby lengthening logon time, but it can aid in troubleshooting. For example, if a problem with a computer configuration GPO is suspected, an administrator can log on as a user who has no user configuration GPO assigned so that user policy settings can be eliminated as a factor.

> **Exam Tip**   Be able to determine how Group Policy settings should be arranged into GPOs based on the needs and requirements of an organization.

Figure 5-8 illustrates these GPO types.

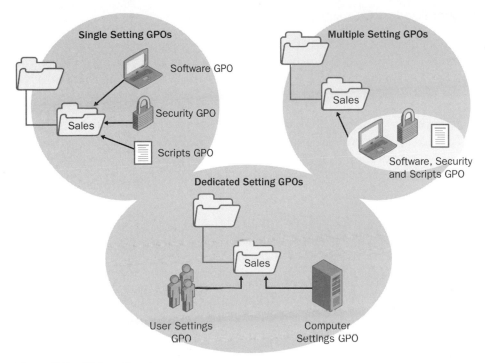

Figure 5-8   GPO setting types

Because sites and domains are the least restrictive components of Active Directory, it isn't too difficult to plan site and domain GPOs. Just remember that site and domain GPOs are applied to all child objects as a result of Group Policy inheritance, unless Block Policy Inheritance has been set for the child object.

The real challenge is determining the OU GPOs. To determine the OU GPOs, you must consider the OU hierarchy set up for the domain. In Chapter 1, you learned the main reasons for defining an OU: to organize objects, to delegate administration, and to manage the application of Group Policy. You were advised that because there is only one way to delegate administration and there are multiple ways to administer Group Policy, you must define OU structures to delegate administration first. The OU hierarchy structure can reflect administration handled by location, business function, object type, or a combination of the three elements.

After an OU structure is defined to handle delegation of administration, you can define additional OUs to hide objects and to administer Group Policy. So, if you've defined your OU structure to accurately reflect how your domain is administered, the next step is to determine which Group Policy settings must be applied to which users and computers in each OU. Basically, you can build GPOs by using a decentralized or a centralized design.

Decentralized GPO Design

With a decentralized GPO approach (see Figure 5-9), the goal is to include a specific policy setting in as few GPOs as possible. When a change is required, only one (or a few) GPO (or GPOs) has to be changed to enforce the change. Administration is simplified at the expense of a somewhat longer logon time (due to multiple GPO processing).

To achieve this goal, create a base GPO to be applied to the domain that contains policy settings for as many users and computers in the domain as possible. For example, the base GPO could contain corporate-wide security settings such as account and password restrictions. Next, create additional GPOs tailored to the common requirements of each OU, and apply them to the appropriate OUs.

This model is best suited for environments in which different groups in the organization have common security concerns and changes to Group Policy are frequent.

Centralized GPO Design

With a centralized GPO approach (shown in Figure 5-9), the goal is to use very few GPOs for any given user or computer. All of the policy settings required for a given site, domain, or OU should be implemented within a minimal number of GPOs. If the site, domain, or OU has groups of users or computers with different policy requirements, consider subdividing the container into OUs and applying separate GPOs to each OU rather than to the parent. A change to the centralized GPO design involves more administration than the decentralized approach because the settings might need to be changed in multiple GPOs, but logon time is shorter. This model is best suited for environments in which users and computers can be classified into a small number of OUs for policy assignment.

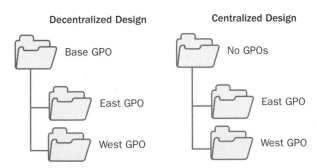

Figure 5-9   Decentralized and centralized GPO designs

> ### Real World   Group Policy Processing
>
> As mentioned in earlier chapters, planning your OU structure is key to the efficient application of Group Policy. Every additional policy that you apply increases the number of settings that the individual computers must evaluate. Planning your organizational structure so that you can apply as few group policies as possible to only those containers that require them is a key to improving startup and logon performance. You might even decide to create OUs for the purpose of applying a specific Group Policy. For example, if you have several computer accounts that require a specific configuration that is unique to only those systems, you might find it more efficient to create a separate OU to handle that special configuration.

Planning Administrative Control of GPOs

When you plan the Group Policy settings and GPOs to be used in your organization, you should also plan who will manage them. The appropriate level of administrative control can be delegated by using a centralized, decentralized, or task-based administrative control design.

Centralized Administrative Control Design

In the centralized design, administration of Group Policy is delegated only to top-level OU administrators. In the example shown in Figure 5-10, top-level OU administrators have the ability to manage all GPOs in the domain. Second-level OU administrators do not have the ability to manage GPOs. You can accomplish this by assigning Full Control permission to top-level OU administrators. This design is best suited for organizations that want to consolidate the administration of group policies.

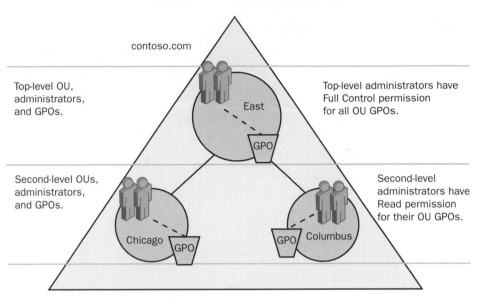

Figure 5-10   A centralized administrative control design

Decentralized Administrative Control Design

In the decentralized design, administration of Group Policy is delegated to top-level and second-level OU administrators. In the example shown in Figure 5-11, top-level OU administrators have the ability to manage GPOs in the top-level OU. Second-level OU administrators have the ability to manage GPOs in their second-level OUs. You can accomplish this by assigning Full Control permission to top-level OU administrators for the top-level OU GPOs and Full Control permission to second-level OU administrators for their second-level OU GPOs. This design is best suited for organizations that delegate levels of administration.

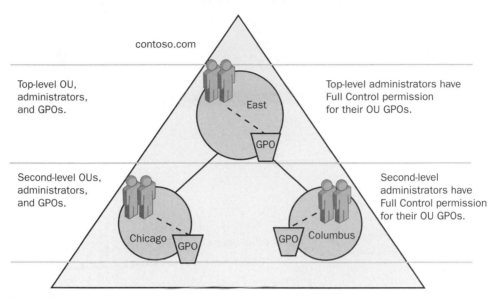

Figure 5-11   A decentralized administrative control design

Task-Based Administrative Control Design

In the task-based design, administration of specific group policies is delegated to administrators who handle the associated specific tasks, such as security or applications. In this case, the GPOs are designed to contain only a single type of Group Policy setting, as described earlier in this lesson.

In the example shown in Figure 5-12, security administrators have the ability to manage security GPOs in all OUs. Applications administrators have the ability to manage applications GPOs in all OUs. You can accomplish this by assigning Full Control permission to the security administrators for the security GPOs and Full Control permission to the applications administrators for the applications GPOs. This design is best suited for organizations in which administrative responsibilities are task-based and delegated among several individuals.

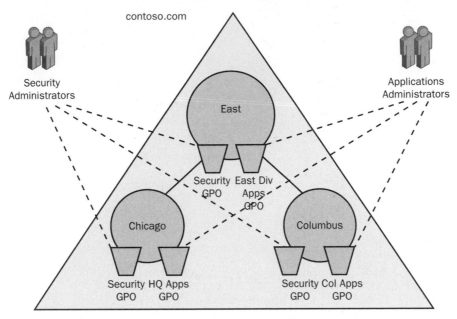

Figure 5-12 A task-based administrative control design

Lesson Review

The following questions are intended to reinforce key information presented in this lesson. If you are unable to answer a question, review the lesson materials and try the question again. You can find answers to the questions in the "Questions and Answers" section at the end of this chapter.

1. Describe a decentralized GPO design.

_____

_____

_____

_____

_____

_____

_____

2. If administrative responsibilities in your organization are task-based and delegated among several administrators, which of the following types of GPOs should you plan to create?

   a. GPOs containing only one type of Group Policy setting

   b. GPOs containing many types of Group Policy settings

   c. GPOs containing only computer configuration settings

   d. GPOs containing only user configuration settings

_____

_____

_____

_____

Lesson Summary

- There are three parts to planning Group Policy: plan the Group Policy settings, plan GPOs, and plan administrative control of GPOs.

- Plan Group Policy settings sparingly—justify the selection of each setting as you would the creation of a domain or OU. Choose settings based on their ability to help you simplify the administration of computers and users.

- You can build GPOs by using a decentralized or centralized design. A decentralized design uses a base GPO applied to the domain, which contains policy settings for as many users and computers in the domain as possible. Then this design uses additional GPOs tailored to the common requirements of each OU and applied to the appropriate OUs. A centralized design uses a single GPO containing all policy settings for the associated site, domain, or OU.

- Administrative control of GPOs can be delegated by using a centralized, decentralized, or task-based administrative control design. In the centralized design, administration of Group Policy is delegated only to top-level OU administrators. In the decentralized design, administration of Group Policy is delegated to top-level and second-level OU administrators. In the task-based design, administration of specific group policies is delegated to administrators that handle the associated specific tasks.

Lesson 3: Implementing a GPO

After you've familiarized yourself with the workings of Group Policy and planned your implementation strategy, you're ready to implement GPOs for your organization. This lesson walks you through the steps of implementing and modifying a GPO.

After this lesson, you will be able to

■ Implement a GPO

■ Modify a GPO

Estimated lesson time: 45 minutes

Implementing a GPO

The tasks for implementing a GPO are:

1. Creating a GPO

2. Creating an MMC for the GPO

3. Delegating administrative control of the GPO

4. Configuring Group Policy settings for the GPO

5. Disabling unused Group Policy settings

6. Indicating any GPO processing exceptions

7. Filtering the scope of the GPO with security groups

8. Linking the GPO to a site, domain, or OU

Creating a GPO

The first step in implementing a Group Policy is to create a GPO. Recall that a GPO is a collection of Group Policy settings.

To create a GPO, complete the following steps:

1. Determine whether the GPO you're creating will be linked to a site, domain, or OU. If the policy will be linked to a site, open Active Directory Sites And Services. If the policy will be linked to a domain or OU, open Active Directory Users And Computers.

2. Right-click the site, domain, or OU for which you want to create a GPO, and then click Properties.

3. In the Properties dialog box for the object, click the Group Policy tab. In the Group Policy tab, shown in Figure 5-13, click New, and then type the name you would like to use for this GPO. By default, the new GPO is linked to the site, domain, or OU in which it was created, and its settings will therefore apply to that site, domain, or OU.

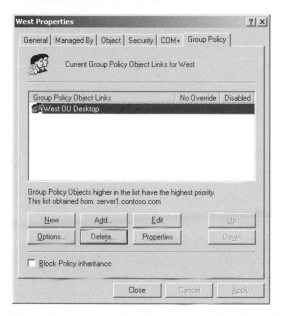

Figure 5-13   Properties dialog box for the West OU, Group Policy tab

4. Click Close.

Creating an MMC for a GPO

After you create a GPO, you can create an MMC to manage it. When you create an MMC for a GPO, you can open it whenever necessary from the Administrative Tools menu.

To create an MMC for a GPO, complete the following steps:

1. Click Start, and then click Run.

2. In the Run dialog box, type **mmc** in the Open box and then click OK.

3. In the new MMC, on the File menu, click Add/Remove Snap-In.

4. In the Add/Remove Snap-In dialog box, click Add.

5. In the Add Standalone Snap-In dialog box, select Group Policy Object Editor and then click Add.

6. In the Select Group Policy Object page, click Browse to find the GPO for which you want to create an MMC.

7. In the Browse For A Group Policy Object dialog box, click the All tab, click the GPO name, and then click OK.

8. In the Select Group Policy Object page, click Finish, and then in the Add Standalone Snap-In dialog box, click Close.

9. In the Add/Remove Snap-In dialog box, click OK.

10. In the MMC, on the File menu, click Save As.

11. In the Save As dialog box, type the GPO name in the File Name box and click Save. The GPO is now available on the Administrative Tools menu.

> **Note**   Windows Server 2003 has two Administrative Tools menus: one on the Start menu and one on the Start\All Programs menu. Where you save a newly created console will determine whether the console will appear in the Administrative Tools menus. If you save a console in the Documents and Settings\Administrator\Start Menu\Programs\Administrative Tools folder, the console will be available on the Start\All Programs\Administrative Tools menu. If you save a console in the Documents and Settings\All Users\Start Menu\Programs\Administrative Tools folder, the console will be available on both the Start\Administrative Tools menu and the Start\All Programs\Administrative Tools menu.

Delegating Control of a GPO

After you create a GPO, it is important to determine which groups of administrators have access permissions to the GPO. The default permissions on GPOs are shown in Table 5-2.

Table 5-2   Default GPO Permissions

Security group	Default settings
Authenticated Users	Read, Apply Group Policy, Special Permissions
Group Policy Creator Owners (also shown as CREATOR OWNER)	Special Permissions
Domain Admins	Read, Write, Create All Child Objects, Delete All Child Objects, Special Permissions
Enterprise Admins	Read, Write, Create All Child Objects, Delete All Child Objects, Special Permissions
ENTERPRISE DOMAIN CONTROLLERS	Read, Special Permissions
SYSTEM	Read, Write, Create All Child Objects, Delete All Child Objects, Special Permissions

By default, only the Domain Admins, Enterprise Admins, and Group Policy Creator Owner groups and the operating system can create new GPOs. Nonadministrative users or groups can be given the ability to create GPOs by adding the users or groups to the Group Policy Creator Owners security group. Membership in the Group Policy Creator Owners group gives a user full control of only the GPOs created by the user or explicitly delegated to the user. It does not give a nonadministrative user rights over any other GPOs. If an administrator creates a GPO, the Domain Admins group becomes the Creator Owner of the GPO.

By default, the Default Domain Policy GPO cannot be deleted by any administrator. This prevents the accidental deletion of this GPO, which contains important required settings for the domain.

GPO-related tasks for which you can delegate control are

- GPO editing
- GPO creation
- GPO linking

Note The Delegation Of Control Wizard is not available for automating and simplifying the process of setting administrative permissions directly for a GPO.

To delegate control of GPO editing, complete the following steps:

1. Access the Group Policy Object Editor for the GPO.

2. Right-click the root node of the GPO, and then click Properties.

3. In the Properties dialog box for the GPO, click the Security tab. In the Security tab, shown in Figure 5-14, click the security group for which you want to allow or deny administrative access to the GPO.

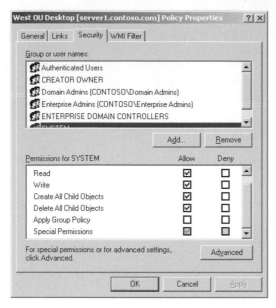

Figure 5-14   West OU Desktop GPO Properties dialog box, Security tab

If you need to change the list of security groups for which you want to allow or deny administrative access to the GPO, you can add or remove security groups using Add and Remove.

4. To provide administrative control of all aspects of the GPO, set both the Read permission and the Write permission to Allow.

> **Important**   A user or administrator who has Read permission for a GPO but does not have Write permission cannot use the Group Policy Object Editor to see the settings that it contains. Write access is required to open a GPO.

5. Click OK.

To delegate control of GPO creation, complete the following steps:

1. Click Start, point to Administrative Tools, and then click Active Directory Users And Computers.

2. In the console tree, click Users.

3. In the Name column in the details pane, double-click Group Policy Creator Owners.

4. In the Group Policy Creator Owners Properties dialog box, click the Members tab.

5. In the Members tab, click Add, and then type the name of each user or security group to whom you want to delegate creation rights in the Enter The Object Names To Select box. Click OK.

6. In the Group Policy Creator Owners Properties dialog box, click OK.

7. Execute the procedure for delegating control of GPO linking (shown next). By default, nonadministrators cannot manage links, and unless you execute the procedure for delegating GPO linking, they cannot use the Active Directory Users And Computers console to create a GPO.

To delegate control of GPO linking, complete the following steps:

1. Click Start, point to Administrative Tools, and then click Active Directory Users And Computers.

2. Right-click the OU to which you want to delegate the right to link GPOs, and then click Delegate Control.

3. On the Welcome To The Delegation Of Control Wizard page, click Next.

4. On the Users Or Groups page, click Add.

5. In the Select Users, Computers, Or Groups dialog box, type the user or group for which you want to delegate administration in the Enter The Object Names To Select box and then click OK. Click Next on the Users Or Groups page.

6. On the Tasks To Delegate page, click Delegate The Following Common Tasks, select the Manage Group Policy Links check box, and then click Next.

7. On the Completing The Delegation Of Control Wizard page, review your selections. Click Finish.

Important   Delegated control is inherited by all child containers below the container to which control is delegated.

Note   Delegation across forests is supported for managing GPO links. Other tasks—such as creating, deleting, or modifying GPOs across forests—are not supported. This is a new feature of the Windows Server 2003 family.

Configuring Group Policy Settings

After you create a GPO and determine the administrators who have access permissions to the GPO, you can configure the Group Policy settings.

To configure Group Policy settings for a GPO, complete the following steps:

1. Open the Group Policy Object Editor for the GPO, as shown in Figure 5-15.

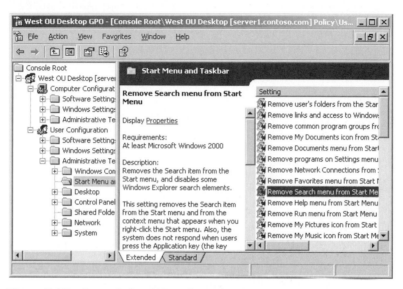

Figure 5-15 Group Policy Object Editor for the West OU Desktop GPO

2. In the console tree, expand the node that represents the policy setting you want to configure. For example, in Figure 5-15, the User Configuration, Administrative Templates, and Start Menu And Taskbar nodes are expanded.

3. In the details pane, right-click the setting that you want to configure and then click Properties.

4. In the Properties dialog box for the Group Policy setting (an example is shown in Figure 5-16), click Enabled to apply the setting to users or computers that are subject to this GPO and then click OK. Not Configured indicates that no change will be made to the setting. Disabled means that the registry will indicate that the setting does not apply to users or computers that are subject to this GPO.

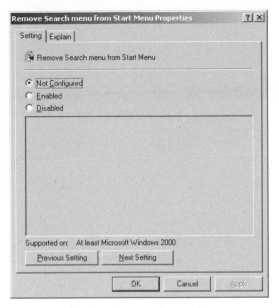

Figure 5-16   Configuring the Remove Search Menu From Start Menu Group Policy setting

Disabling Unused Group Policy Settings

If the Computer Configuration or User Configuration node for a GPO has only settings that are Not Configured, you can prevent the processing of those settings by disabling the node. Disabling unused Group Policy settings is recommended because it expedites startup and logging on for those users and computers subject to the GPO.

To disable the computer configuration or user configuration settings for a GPO, complete the following steps:

1. Access the Group Policy Object Editor for the GPO.

2. Right-click the root node, and then click Properties.

3. In the General tab in the Properties dialog box for the GPO, do one of the following:

   ❑ To disable the computer configuration settings, select the Disable Computer Configuration Settings check box.

   ❑ To disable the user configuration settings, select the Disable User Configuration Settings check box.

4. Click OK.

Exam Tip   Remember that disabling unused User Configuration or Computer Configuration nodes of GPOs will improve startup and logon times because the computer will not process disabled nodes.

Indicating GPO Processing Exceptions

As discussed in Lesson 1, GPOs are applied according to the Active Directory hierarchy: local GPO, site GPOs, domain GPOs, and OU GPOs. However, the default order of processing Group Policy settings can be changed by modifying the order of GPO links for an object, specifying the Block Policy Inheritance option, specifying the No Override option, or by enabling the Loopback setting. This section provides procedures for accomplishing these tasks.

To modify the order of GPO links for an object, complete the following steps:

1. Open the Active Directory Users And Computers console to set the order of GPOs for a domain or OU, or open the Active Directory Sites And Services console to set the order of GPOs for a site.

2. In the console, right-click the site, domain, or OU for which you want to modify the GPO order, click Properties, and then click the Group Policy tab.

3. In the Properties dialog box for the object, in the Group Policy tab, shown in Figure 5-17, select the GPO for which you want to modify the order in the Group Policy Object Links list. Click the Up button or the Down button to change the priority for the GPO for this site, domain, or OU. Windows Server 2003 operating systems process GPOs from the bottom of the list to the top of the list, with the topmost GPO having the final authority.

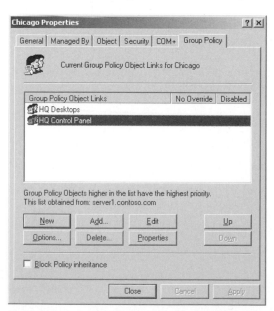

Figure 5-17   Modifying the order of GPOs in the Group Policy Object Links list

4. Click Close.

To specify the Block Policy Inheritance option, complete the following steps:

1. Open the Active Directory Users And Computers console to specify the Block Policy Inheritance option for a domain or OU, or open the Active Directory Sites And Services console to specify the Block Policy Inheritance option for a site.

2. In the console, right-click the site, domain, or OU for which you want to specify the Block Policy Inheritance option, click Properties, and then click the Group Policy tab.

3. In the Properties dialog box for the object, in the Group Policy tab, select the Block Policy Inheritance check box. By checking this box, you specify that all GPOs linked to higher level sites, domains, or OUs should be blocked from linking to this site, domain, or OU. You cannot block GPOs that use the No Override option.

4. Click Close.

To specify the No Override option, complete the following steps:

1. Open the Active Directory Users And Computers console to specify the No Override option for a domain or OU, or open the Active Directory Sites And Services console to specify the No Override option for a site.

2. In the console, right-click the site, domain, or OU to which the GPO is linked, click Properties, and then click the Group Policy tab.

3. In the Properties dialog box for the object, in the Group Policy tab, select the GPO and then click Options.

4. In the Options dialog box for the GPO, shown in Figure 5-18, select the No Override check box to specify that other GPOs should be prevented from overriding settings in this GPO and then click OK.

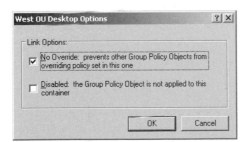

Figure 5-18   Options dialog box for a GPO link

5. In the Properties dialog box for the site, domain, or OU, click OK.

To enable the Loopback setting, complete the following steps:

1. Access the Group Policy Object Editor for the GPO.

2. In the console tree, expand Computer Configuration, Administrative Templates, System, and Group Policy.

3. In the Setting pane, double-click User Group Policy Loopback Processing Mode.

4. In the User Group Policy Loopback Processing Mode Properties dialog box, click Enabled.

5. Select one of the following modes in the Mode list:

   ❑ Replace, to replace the user settings normally applied to the user with the user settings defined in the computer's GPOs.

   ❑ Merge, to combine the user settings defined in the computer's GPOs with the user settings normally applied to the user. If the settings conflict, the user settings in the computer's GPOs take precedence over the user's normal settings.

6. Click OK.

Filtering GPO Scope with Security Groups

As discussed in Lesson 1, the policies in a GPO apply only to users who have the Read and Apply Group Policy permissions for the GPO set to Allow. However, by default, the Authenticated Users group has Allow Read and Allow Apply Group Policy permissions. This means that by default, *all* users and computers are affected by the GPOs set for their domain, site, or OU regardless of the other groups in which they might be members. Therefore, there are two ways of filtering GPO scope:

- Clear the Apply Group Policy permission (currently set to Allow) for the Authenticated Users group, but do not set this permission to Deny. Then determine the groups to which the GPO should be applied and set the Read and Apply Group Policy permissions for these groups to Allow.

- Determine the groups to which the GPO should not be applied, and set the Apply Group Policy permission for these groups to Deny.

Note   If you deny permission to an object, the user will not have that permission, even if you allow the permission for a group of which the user is a member.

To filter the scope of a GPO, complete the following steps:

1. Access the Group Policy Object Editor for the GPO.

2. Right-click the root node, and then click Properties.

3. In the Properties dialog box for the GPO, click the Security tab, previously shown in Figure 5-14, and then click the security group through which to filter this GPO. If you need to change the list of security groups through which to filter this GPO, you can add or remove security groups using Add and Remove.

4. Set the permissions as shown in Table 5-3, and then click OK.

Table 5-3   Permissions for GPO Scopes

GPO scope	Set these permissions	Result
Members of this security group should have this GPO applied to them.	Set Apply Group Policy to Allow. Set Read to Allow.	This GPO applies to members of this security group unless they are members of at least one other security group that has Apply Group Policy set to Deny, or Read set to Deny, or both.
Members of this security group are exempt from this GPO.	Set Apply Group Policy to Deny. Set Read to Deny. Note: Because denied permissions take precedence over all other permissions, you should use Deny sparingly.	This GPO never applies to members of this security group regardless of the permissions those members have in other security groups.
Membership in this security group is irrelevant to whether the GPO should be applied.	Set Apply Group Policy to neither Allow nor Deny. Set Read to neither Allow nor Deny.	This GPO applies to members of this security group if and only if they have both Apply Group Policy and Read set to Allow as members of at least one other security group. They also must not have Apply Group Policy or Read set to Deny as members of any other security group.

Linking a GPO

By default, a new GPO is linked to the site, domain, or OU in which it was created, as described earlier in this lesson in the procedure "Creating a GPO." Therefore, its settings apply to that site, domain, or OU. However, if you want to link a GPO to additional sites, domains, or OUs, you must use the Group Policy tab in the Properties dialog box for the site, domain, or OU.

To link a GPO to a site, domain, or OU, complete the following steps:

1. Open the Active Directory Users And Computers console to link a GPO to a domain or OU, or open the Active Directory Sites And Services console to link a GPO to a site.

2. In the console, right-click the site, domain, or OU to which the GPO should be linked. Click Properties, and then click the Group Policy tab.

3. In the Properties dialog box for the object, in the Group Policy tab, click Add.

4. In the Add A Group Policy Object Link dialog box, shown in Figure 5-19, click the All tab, click the desired GPO, and then click OK.

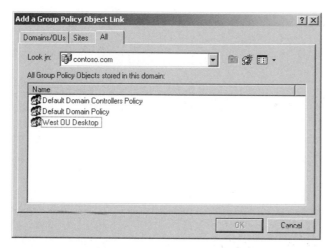

Figure 5-19   Add A Group Policy Object Link dialog box

5. In the Properties dialog box for the site, domain, or OU, click OK.

Modifying a GPO

The tasks for modifying a GPO are

- Removing a GPO link
- Deleting a GPO
- Editing a GPO and GPO settings
- Refreshing a GPO

Removing a GPO Link

Removing a GPO link simply unlinks the GPO from the specified site, domain, or OU. The GPO remains in Active Directory until it is deleted.

To remove a GPO link, complete the following steps:

1. Open the Active Directory Users And Computers console to unlink a GPO from a domain or OU, or open the Active Directory Sites And Services console to unlink a GPO from a site.

2. In the console, right-click the site, domain, or OU from which the GPO should be unlinked. Click Properties, and then click the Group Policy tab.

3. In the Properties dialog box for the object, in the Group Policy tab, select the GPO that you want to unlink and then click Delete.

4. In the Delete dialog box, shown in Figure 5-20, click Remove The Link From The List and then click OK. The GPO remains in Active Directory but is no longer linked.

Figure 5-20   Delete dialog box when removing a GPO link

Deleting a GPO

If you delete a GPO, it is removed from Active Directory, and any sites, domains, or OUs to which it is linked are no longer affected by it. You might want to take the less drastic step of removing the GPO link, which disassociates the GPO from its OU but leaves the GPO intact in Active Directory.

To delete a GPO, complete the following steps:

1. Open the Active Directory Users And Computers console to delete a GPO from a domain or OU, or open the Active Directory Sites And Services console to delete a GPO from a site.

2. In the console, right-click the site, domain, or OU from which the GPO should be deleted. Click Properties, and then click the Group Policy tab.

3. In the Properties dialog box for the object, in the Group Policy tab, select the GPO that you want to delete, and then click Delete.

4. In the Delete dialog box, click Remove The Link And Delete The Group Policy Object Permanently and then click OK. The GPO is removed from Active Directory.

Editing a GPO and GPO Settings

To edit a GPO or its settings, follow the procedures outlined earlier in this lesson for creating a GPO and for specifying Group Policy settings.

Refreshing a GPO

Each GPO is refreshed when you restart your computer. When you modify the settings in a GPO, they are refreshed every 90 minutes on a workstation or server and every five minutes on a domain controller. The settings are also refreshed every 16 hours, whether or not there are any changes. In Windows Server 2003 operating systems, you can refresh policy immediately by using the Gpupdate.exe command-line tool. Gpupdate replaces the Secedit.exe /refreshpolicy command used for refreshing GPOs in Windows 2000.

To refresh GPOs immediately, complete the following steps:

1. Click Start, and then click Run.

2. In the Run dialog box, type **gpupdate** in the Open box and then click OK. You briefly see the message "Refreshing Policy" on the command line while the policy is being refreshed.

Gpupdate also permits certain options to be specified on the command line. You can learn more about these options by searching for "gpupdate" in Help and Support Center.

Group Policy Best Practices

The following are the best practices for implementing Group Policy:

- **Disable unused parts of a GPO.**   If a GPO has, under the User Configuration or Computer Configuration node of the console, only settings that are Not Configured, disable the node to expedite startup and logging on.

- **Use the Block Policy Inheritance and No Override features sparingly.**   Routine use of these feature makes it difficult to troubleshoot Group Policy.

- **Do not use the same name for different GPOs.**   Although using the same GPO name doesn't affect GPO function, it can be confusing to administer.

- **Filter policy based on security group membership.**   Users who do not have permissions directing that a particular GPO be applied to them can avoid the associated logon delay, because the GPO is not applied for those users.

- **Use loopback only when necessary.**   Use loopback only if you need the desktop configuration to be the same regardless of who logs on.

- **Override Group Policy rather than System Policy.**   Use System Policy only to manage computers on an operating system earlier than Windows 2000 or if you need to manage desktops for multiple users on a stand-alone computer.

- **Avoid cross-domain GPO assignments.**   The processing of GPOs delays logging on and startup if Group Policy is obtained from another domain.

- **Do not link a GPO to the same OU more than once.**   When more than one link for the same OU is applied to a single object, the links might be interpreted differently and produce an unexpected RSoP.

Practice: Implementing and Testing a GPO

In this practice, you implement a GPO for contoso.com.

Exercise 1: Implementing a GPO

In this exercise, you implement a GPO for the West OU. You create a GPO, create an MMC for a GPO, specify Group Policy settings for the GPO, indicate a GPO processing exception, delegate administrative control of the GPO, filter the scope of the GPO, and link the GPO to an additional OU. Use the procedures provided earlier in this lesson to complete each step in the exercise.

1. Log on to Server01 as Administrator.

2. On Server01, create a GPO in the West OU. Name the GPO **Lockdown Desktop**.

3. Create an MMC for the Lockdown Desktop GPO. Name the console **Lockdown Desktop GPO**.

4. Specify the following Group Policy settings for the Lockdown Desktop GPO:

    ❑   In the User Configuration node, in the Administrative Templates node, in the Start Menu And Taskbar node, configure the Remove Search Menu From Start Menu setting to Enabled. Then configure the Remove Run Menu From Start Menu setting (still under User Configuration) to Enabled.

    ❑   In the User Configuration node, in the Administrative Templates node, in the System node, in the CTRL+ALT+DEL Options node, configure the Remove Lock Computer setting to Enabled.

5. For the Lockdown Desktop GPO link, set the No Override option in the Group Policy tab in the Properties dialog box for the West OU to prevent other GPOs from overriding the policies set in the Lockdown Desktop GPO.

6. Create a new Marketing domain local security group in the Seattle OU. Make Lorrin Smith-Bates and Danielle Tiedt members of the Marketing group.

7. For the Lockdown Desktop GPO, clear the Apply Group Policy permission (currently set to Allow) for the Authenticated Users group. Do not set this permission to Deny.

8. In the Lockdown Desktop GPO, add the Marketing domain local security group to the list of security groups.

9. Ensure that the Lockdown Desktop GPO applies to the Marketing group by setting the group's Apply Group Policy permission for the GPO to Allow.

10. By default the Lockdown Desktop GPO is linked to the West OU, and its settings apply to the West OU and its child OUs, Seattle and Phoenix. Link the Lockdown Desktop GPO to the New York OU.

Exercise 2: Testing a GPO

In this exercise, you view the effects of the GPO you implemented in Exercise 1.

1. Log on as Danielle Tiedt, a member of the Marketing security group.

2. Press CTRL+ALT+DEL. The Windows Security dialog box appears. Are you able to lock the workstation? Why?

   No, the Lock Computer option is not available. Danielle Tiedt is unable to lock the workstation because the Lockdown Desktop GPO applies to the Marketing security group, of which Danielle Tiedt is a member.

3. Click Cancel, and then click Start.

   Does the Search command appear on the Start menu?

   No.

   Does the Run command appear on the Start menu?

   No.

4. Log off as Danielle Tiedt, and then log on as Administrator.

5. Remove Danielle Tiedt from the Marketing security group.

6. Log off as Administrator, and then log on as Danielle Tiedt.

7. Press CTRL+ALT+DEL. Are you able to lock the workstation? Why?

   Yes, the Lock Computer option is available. Danielle Tiedt is able to lock the workstation because the Lockdown Desktop GPO applies only to members of the Marketing security group, of which Danielle Tiedt is no longer a member.

8. Log off as Danielle Tiedt, and then log on as Pat Coleman.

9. Press CTRL+ALT+DEL.

   Are you able to lock the workstation? Why or why not?

   Yes, because the Lock Computer option is available. Pat Coleman is able to lock the workstation because the Lockdown Desktop GPO applies only to the Marketing security group, of which Pat Coleman is not a member. This is true even though the Lockdown Desktop GPO is linked to the New York OU, in which Pat Coleman is contained.

10. Log off as Pat Coleman, and then log on as Administrator.

11. Make Pat Coleman a member of the Marketing security group.

12. Log off as Administrator, and then log on as Pat Coleman.

13. Press CTRL+ALT+DEL.

   Are you able to lock the workstation? Why or why not?

   No, because the Lock Computer option is not available. Pat Coleman is unable to lock the workstation because the Lockdown Desktop GPO is linked to the New York OU and applies only to the Marketing security group, of which Pat Coleman is now a member.

14. Log off as Pat Coleman, and then log on as Administrator.

15. Create a new GPO in the Seattle OU. Name the GPO **Lockdown Control Panel**. Create an MMC for the Lockdown Control Panel GPO. Name the console **Lockdown Control Panel GPO**.

16. In the User Configuration node, in the Administrative Templates node, in the Control Panel node, configure the Prohibit Access To The Control Panel setting to Enabled.

17. Set the Block Policy Inheritance option in the Group Policy tab in the Properties dialog box for the Seattle OU to block GPOs set in parent objects from applying to the Seattle OU.

18. In the Lockdown Control Panel GPO, add the Marketing domain local security group to the list of security groups.

19. Set the Apply Group Policy permission for the Marketing group to Allow. Clear the Apply Group Policy permission (currently set to Allow) for the Authenticated Users group. Do not set this permission to Deny.

20. Log off as Administrator, and then log on as Lorrin Smith-Bates. Which GPO applies and why?

   The Lockdown Desktop and Lockdown Control Panel GPOs both apply to Lorrin Smith-Bates because the Lockdown Desktop GPO has the No Override option set. The No Override option ensures that none of a GPO's settings can be overridden by any other GPO during the processing of group policies. Even though the Block Policy Inheritance option is set for the Seattle OU, the No Override option set for the Lockdown Desktop GPO link overrides the Seattle OU's Block Inheritance setting. Therefore, both GPOs apply to Lorrin Smith-Bates.

21. Log off as Lorrin Smith-Bates, and then log on as Pat Coleman. Which GPO applies and why?

   Only the Lockdown Desktop GPO applies to Pat Coleman. Because the Lockdown Control Panel GPO has not been linked to the New York OU (in which Pat Coleman is contained) or the East OU (parent OU of the New York OU), the Lockdown Control Panel GPO does not apply to Pat Coleman.

Lesson Review

The following questions are intended to reinforce key information presented in this lesson. If you are unable to answer a question, review the lesson materials and try the question again. You can find answers to the questions in the "Questions and Answers" section at the end of this chapter.

1. If you want to create a GPO for a site, what administrative tool should you use?

   _____

2. Why should you create an MMC for a GPO?

   _____

   _____

3. Besides Read permission, what permission must you assign to allow a user or administrator to see the settings in a GPO?

   _____

   _____

   _____

4. Why should you disable unused Group Policy settings?

   _____

   _____

5. How do you prevent a GPO from applying to a specific group?

   _____

   _____

6. What's the difference between removing a GPO link and deleting a GPO?

   _____

   _____

   _____

7. You want to deflect all Group Policy settings that reach the North OU from all of the OU's parent objects. To accomplish this, which of the following exceptions do you apply and where do you apply it?

   a. Block Policy Inheritance applied to the OU

   b. Block Policy Inheritance applied to the GPO

   c. Block Policy Inheritance applied to the GPO link

   d. No Override applied to the OU

   e. No Override applied to the GPO

   f. No Override applied to the GPO link

   _____

   _____

   _____

   _____

8. You want to ensure that none of the South OU Desktop settings applied to the South OU can be overridden. To accomplish this, which of the following exceptions do you apply and where do you apply it?

   a. Block Policy Inheritance applied to the OU

   b. Block Policy Inheritance applied to the GPO

   c. Block Policy Inheritance applied to the GPO link

   d. No Override applied to the OU

   e. No Override applied to the GPO

   f. No Override applied to the GPO link

   _____

   _____

   _____

Lesson Summary

- You use the Active Directory Users And Computers console to create a GPO for a domain or an OU. You use the Active Directory Sites And Services console to create a GPO for a site.

- You should create an MMC for a GPO because you can open it whenever necessary from the Administrative Tools menu, making it easier to administer.

- You should disable unused Group Policy settings to avoid the processing of those settings and expedite startup and logging on for the users and computers subject to the GPO.

- For a GPO to apply to a specific group, that group must have the Read and Apply Group Policy permissions for the GPO set to Allow. To prevent a GPO from applying to a specific group, that group must have the Apply Group Policy permission for the GPO set to Deny.

- When you remove a GPO link to a site, domain, or OU, the GPO still remains in Active Directory. When you delete a GPO, the GPO is removed from Active Directory, and any sites, domains, or OUs to which it is linked are no longer affected by it.

Lesson 4: Working with Resultant Set of Policy

Resultant Set of Policy (RSoP) is the sum of the group policies applied to a user or computer. Determining RSoP for a computer or user can be a complex task. In Windows Server 2003 operating systems, you can generate an RSoP query to determine the policies applied to a specified user or computer. This lesson introduces you to the tools used to generate RSoP queries, the ways to save RSoP queries, and the results provided by each of the RSoP generation tools.

After this lesson, you will be able to

- Define RSoP
- Describe the three tools available for generating an RSoP query
- Use the Resultant Set Of Policy Wizard to generate an RSoP query
- Save a query generated by the Resultant Set Of Policy Wizard
- View the results of an RSoP query generated by the Resultant Set Of Policy Wizard
- Use the Gpresult.exe command-line tool to generate an RSoP query
- View the results of an RSoP query generated by Gpresult.exe
- Use the Advanced System Information–Policy tool to generate an RSoP query
- View the results of an RSoP query generated by the Advanced System Information–Policy tool

Estimated lesson time: 40 minutes

Understanding RSoP

As you learned in Lesson 1, GPOs are cumulative as they are applied to a local computer, site, domain, and OU hierarchy. *RSoP* is the sum of the policies applied to a user or computer (including the application of filters), such as through security groups and Windows Management Instrumentation (WMI), and exceptions, such as No Override and Block Policy Inheritance. Because of the cumulative effects of GPOs, filters, and exceptions, determining a user's or computer's RSoP can be difficult. However, the ability to generate RSoP queries in Windows Server 2003 operating systems makes determining RSoP easier.

In Windows Server 2003, an RSoP query engine is available to poll existing GPOs and report the affects of GPOs on users and computers. The query engine also checks for security groups and WMI queries used to filter GPO scope, and it checks Software Installation for any applications that are associated with a particular user or computer and reports the affects of these settings as well. This information is gathered from the Common Information Management Object Model (CIMOM) database.

> **Note**   A detailed discussion of WMI is beyond the scope of this training kit. For detailed information about WMI, refer to the MSDN Library at *http://msdn.microsoft.com/library*. You can find information about WMI by pointing to Setup And System Administration, Windows Management Instrumentation (WMI), and finally Technical Articles.

Windows Server 2003 operating systems provide the following three tools for generating RSoP queries:

- Resultant Set Of Policy Wizard
- Gpresult.exe command-line tool
- Advanced System Information–Policy tool

Each tool uses a different interface and provides different levels of RSoP query information, as discussed in the sections that follow.

Generating RSoP Queries with the Resultant Set Of Policy Wizard

To help you analyze the cumulative effects of GPOs, Windows Server 2003 provides the Resultant Set Of Policy Wizard, which uses existing GPO settings to report the effects of GPOs on users and computers. You can also use the Resultant Set Of Policy Wizard in an entirely different manner to simulate the effects of planned GPOs. To accomplish polling of existing GPOs and the simulation of planned GPOs, the Resultant Set Of Policy Wizard uses two modes to create *RSoP queries*:

- *Logging mode* reports the existing GPO settings for a user or computer.
- *Planning mode* simulates the GPO settings that a user and computer might receive, and it enables you to change the simulation.

Logging Mode

RSoP logging mode enables you to review existing GPO settings, software installation applications, and security for a computer account or a user account. Use logging mode to

- Find failed or overwritten policy settings
- See how security groups affect policy settings
- Find out how local policy is affecting group policies

When you create an RSoP query in logging mode, each of the applications that are available for installation, the folders that will be redirected (and to where), and each policy setting that will be applied to the user or computer, as well as the security group's effect on those policies, are reported.

> **Note**   In RSoP logging mode, you can create an RSoP query only for user accounts and computer accounts. In addition, only users and computers that have logged on to the domain are available for an RSoP query.

Planning Mode

RSoP planning mode enables you to plan for growth and reorganization. Using RSoP planning mode, you can poll existing GPOs for policy settings, software installation applications, and security, and you can use WMI filter queries to read hardware and software properties. Then, you can use the results to construct a scenario to predict the effect of changes in policy settings. Use planning mode in the following situations:

- You want to test policy precedence in cases where
    - ❏ The user and the computer are in different security groups.
    - ❏ The user and the computer are in different OUs.
    - ❏ The user or the computer is moving to a new location.
- You want to simulate a slow link.
- You want to simulate loopback.

You can create an RSoP query in planning mode to see what will happen to a user or a group of users if they are moved to another location or security group, or even to another computer, by setting the RSoP planning mode options.

There are several RSoP planning mode options. Each option can be run separately or in conjunction with the other options, allowing for a wide range of simulation results. As you progress through the Resultant Set Of Policy Wizard, the planning mode options are presented to you in the following order:

1. **Slow-network connection.** This option simulates a slow connection. A connection is slow if the rate at which data is transferred (from the domain controller that provides a policy update to the computers in this group) is slower than the rate that is specified by this GPO. The system's response to a slow policy connection varies among policies.

2. **Loopback processing.** This option simulates enabling of the GPO setting User Group Policy Loopback Processing Mode, located in Computer Configuration, Administrative Templates, System, Group Policy. The simulation can be set to Merge or Replace. Select Merge to simulate the appending of the GPO list obtained for the computer at computer startup to the GPO list obtained for the user. Select Replace to simulate replacement of the GPO list for the user with the GPO list already obtained for the computer at computer startup.

3. **Site name.** This option simulates the application of alternate subnets for startup or logging on, enabling you to predict the RSoP if the subnet is changed.

4. **Alternate user and computer locations.** This option simulates the application of alternate locations for both users and computers, enabling you to predict the RSoP if the user, computer, or both are moved.

5. **Alternate user and computer security groups.** This option simulates the application of alternate security groups to both computer and user configurations, enabling you to predict the RSoP by using security groups to filter GPO scope.

6. **WMI filters for users and computers.** This option simulates the use of WMI filters to help define the policy settings that are applied, enabling you to predict the RSoP by using WMI queries to filter GPO scope.

Exam Tip   Make sure you understand the differences between using RSoP in logging mode and in planning mode.

Creating RSoP Queries

You create RSoP queries by first creating an RSoP query console and then configuring the RSoP query by using the Resultant Set Of Policy Wizard. You can also create an RSoP query from the Active Directory Users And Computers console (for domains, OUs, computer accounts, and user accounts) or the Active Directory Sites And Services console (for sites). However, if you create an RSoP query from the Active Directory Users And Computers or Active Directory Sites And Services consoles, you must remember to save the query to the Administrative Tools folder for the query to be available on the Administrative Tools menu.

Note   To create an RSoP query from the Active Directory Users And Computers or Active Directory Sites And Services consoles, open the console, right-click the site, domain, OU, user account, or computer account for which you want to create a query, click All Tasks, and click Resultant Set Of Policy (Planning) or Resultant Set Of Policy (Logging). Note that logging mode is available only for computer accounts and user accounts. Then run the Resultant Set Of Policy Wizard as described in the "To create an RSoP query with the Resultant Set Of Policy Wizard logging mode" and "To create an RSoP query with the Resultant Set Of Policy Wizard planning mode" procedures, which appear later in this section.

To create an RSoP query for an existing user and computer, you must either be logged on to the local computer as a user; be a member of the local Administrators, Domain Administrators, or Enterprise Administrators group; or have permission to generate RSoP for the domain or OU in which the user and computer accounts are contained.

You must be an enterprise administrator if the RSoP query includes site GPOs that cross domain boundaries in the same forest. This section describes how to create RSoP queries in logging mode and planning mode.

To create an RSoP query with the Resultant Set Of Policy Wizard logging mode, complete the following steps:

1. Click Start, and then click Run.

2. In the Run dialog box, type **mmc** in the Open box and then click OK.

3. In the MMC, from the File menu, click Add/Remove Snap-In.

4. In the Add/Remove Snap-In dialog box, click Add.

5. In the Add Standalone Snap-In dialog box, select Resultant Set Of Policy, click Add, and then click Close.

6. In the Add/Remove Snap-In dialog box, click OK.

7. In the MMC, right-click the Resultant Set Of Policy icon on the RSoP Wizard console, and then select Generate RSoP Data.

8. In the Welcome To The Resultant Set Of Policy Wizard page, click Next.

9. On the Mode Selection page, shown in Figure 5-21, select Logging Mode and then click Next.

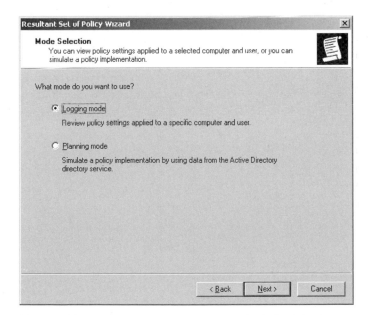

Figure 5-21   Resultant Set Of Policy Wizard, Mode Selection page

10. On the Computer Selection page in the Resultant Set Of Policy Wizard, shown in Figure 5-22, select This Computer, or to search for a different computer, click Another Computer, and then click Browse to select the appropriate computer. If you want to display user policy settings only, click the Do Not Display Policy Settings For The Selected Computer In the Results check box. Click Next.

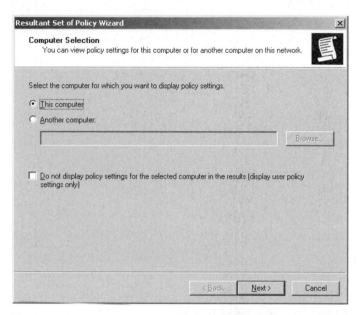

Figure 5-22   Resultant Set Of Policy Wizard, Computer Selection page

11. On the User Selection page, shown in Figure 5-23, select Current User to view policy settings for the current user, or to search for a different user, click Select A Specific User, and select a user in the list. If you want to display computer policy settings only, click the Do Not Display User Policy Settings In The Results check box. Click Next.

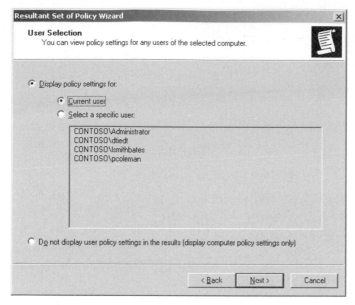

Figure 5-23   Resultant Set Of Policy Wizard, User Selection page

12. On the Summary Of Selections page, shown in Figure 5-24, review your selections. Click Next.

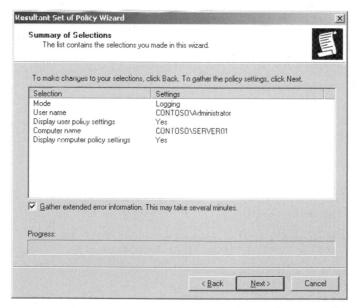

Figure 5-24   Resultant Set Of Policy Wizard, Summary Of Selections page

13. On the Completing The Resultant Set Of Policy Data Wizard page, click Finish.

14. The RSoP console opens. Click the folders in the console tree to view the data in the details pane.

To create an RSoP query with the Resultant Set Of Policy Wizard planning mode, complete the following steps:

1. Click Start, and then click Run.

2. In the Run dialog box, type **mmc** in the Open box and then click OK.

3. In the MMC, from the File menu, click Add/Remove Snap-In.

4. In the Add/Remove Snap-In dialog box, click Add.

5. In the Add Standalone Snap-In dialog box, select Resultant Set Of Policy, click Add, and then click Close.

6. In the Add/Remove Snap-In dialog box, click OK.

7. In the MMC, right-click the Resultant Set Of Policy icon on the RSoP Wizard console, and then select Generate RSoP Data.

8. In the Welcome To The Resultant Set Of Policy Wizard page, click Next.

9. On the Mode Selection page, shown in Figure 5-21, select Planning Mode and then click Next.

10. On the User And Computer Selection page, shown in Figure 5-25, type the name of the target user in the User Information box and the target computer in the Computer Information box. To search for a user or computer, click Browse. Click Next.

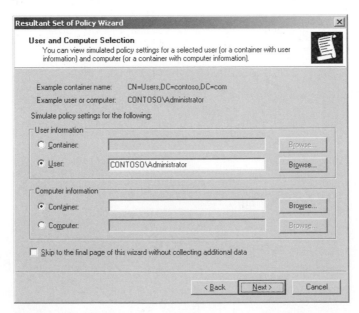

Figure 5-25   Resultant Set Of Policy Wizard, User And Computer Selection page

11. On the Advanced Simulation Options page, shown in Figure 5-26, select the Slow Network Connection check box if you want to simulate a slow network connection.

If you want to simulate the loopback processing mode, select the Loopback Processing check box, and then select one of the following:

❑ Click Replace Mode to indicate that the user policies that are defined in the computer's GPOs replace the user policies that are normally applied to the user.

❑ Click Merge Mode to indicate that the user policies that are defined in the computer's GPOs and the user policies that are normally applied to the user are combined. Recall that if the policy settings conflict, the user policies in the computer's GPOs take precedence over the user's normal policies.

12. In the Site list, select the site that the RSoP query uses, if you want. You select a site if you want to test policy where startup or logging on occurs on another subnet than the one on which the query is currently being run. Click Next.

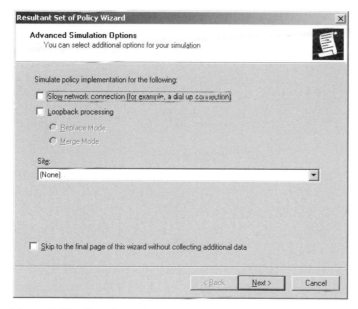

Figure 5-26   Resultant Set Of Policy Wizard, Advanced Simulation Options page

Note   If at any time while navigating the Resultant Set Of Policy Wizard you have finished entering information for your RSoP simulation, select the Skip To The Final Page Of This Wizard Without Collecting Additional Data check box and click Next.

13. On the Alternate Active Directory Paths page, shown in Figure 5-27, you can specify different locations for the selected user, computer of both, if you want. If you want to specify a different location for the user, enter the distinguished name of the location in the User Location box. If you want to specify a different location for a computer, enter the distinguished name of the location in the Computer Location box. Click Next.

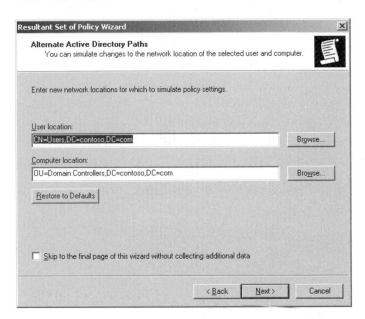

Figure 5-27   Resultant Set Of Policy Wizard, Alternate Active Directory Paths page

14. On the User Security Groups page, shown in Figure 5-28, in the Security Groups box, select the groups in which you want the user selected to be a member on the User And Computer Selection page. To add a security group, click Add, type the name of the target security group, and click OK. To remove a security group, select the security group and click Remove. Click Next.

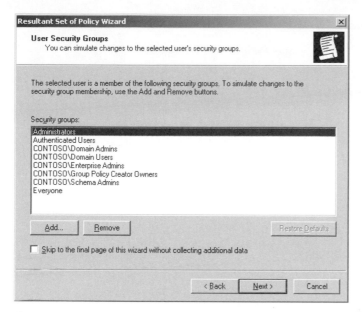

Figure 5-28   Resultant Set Of Policy Wizard, User Security Groups page

15. On the Computer Security Groups page, in the Security Groups box, select the groups in which you want the computer selected to be a member on the User And Computer Selection page. To add a security group, click Add, type the name of the target security group, and click OK. To remove a security group, select the security group and click Remove. Click Next.

16. On the WMI Filters For Users page, shown in Figure 5-29, select the WMI filters you want to use in the simulation. If a filter is not in the list and you want to add a WMI filter, click Only These Filters and then click List Filters. The system automatically searches for all true WMI filters. To remove WMI filters from the simulation, select the filter and click Remove. You should remove any filters that would be considered a false condition for the targeted user. Click Next.

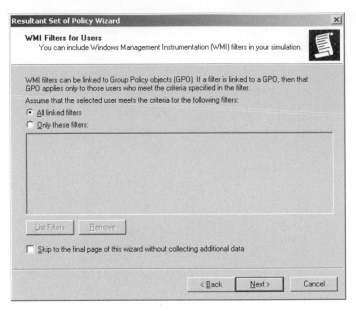

Figure 5-29   Resultant Set Of Policy Wizard, WMI Filters For Users page

17. On the WMI Filters For Computers page, select the WMI filters you want to use in the simulation. If a filter is not in the list and you want to add a WMI filter, click Only These Filters and then click List Filters. The system automatically searches for all true WMI filters. To remove WMI filters from the simulation, select the filter and click Remove. You should remove any filters that would be considered a false condition for the targeted computer. Click Next.

18. On the Summary Of Selections page, shown in Figure 5-30, verify the domain controller (click Browse, if necessary), click Next, and then wait for processing to complete.

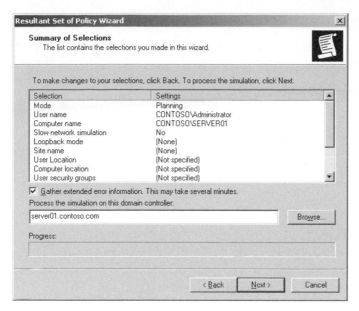

Figure 5-30   Resultant Set Of Policy Wizard, Summary Of Selections page

19. On the Completing The Resultant Set Of Policy Wizard page, click Finish.

20. The RSoP console opens. Click the folders in the console tree to view the data in the details pane.

Saving RSoP Queries and Query Data

After you create an RSoP query with the Resultant Set Of Policy Wizard, you can save the RSoP query and the RSoP query data. By saving the RSoP query, you can reuse it for processing another RSoP query later. The query is saved in the RSoP query console. By saving the RSoP query data, you can revisit the RSoP as it appeared for a particular query when the query was created. The query data is archived to an RSoP console, which you cannot use to process another RSoP query.

To save an RSoP query, complete the following steps:

1. After you have created an RSoP query, on the console for the RSoP query, in the File menu, select Save.

2. In the Save As dialog box, in the File Name box, type the name you want to use for the query console name, and then click Save. The saved RSoP query console has an .msc file name extension and appears on the Administrative Tools menu.

> **Note**   If you created an RSoP query from the Active Directory Users And Computers or Active Directory Sites And Services consoles, you must remember to save the query to the Administrative Tools folder for the query to be available on the Administrative Tools menu.

To save the data from an RSoP query in the console file, complete the following steps:

1. After you have created an RSoP query, on the console for the RSoP query, right-click the *user account*–RSoP or the *computer account*–RSoP node, point to View, and then select Archive Data In Console File.

2. On the File menu, click Save. (Click Save As if you want to save the RSoP console with a new name.)

3. In the Save As dialog box, in the File Name box, type the name you want to use for the RSoP console containing the archived data, and then click Save. The saved RSoP console containing the archived data has an .msc file name extension and appears on the Administrative Tools menu.

> **Note**   If you created an RSoP query from the Active Directory Users And Computers or Active Directory Sites And Services consoles, you must remember to save the archived query data to the Administrative Tools folder for the archived query data to be available on the Administrative Tools menu.

Viewing RSoP Queries

After you create an RSoP query with the Resultant Set Of Policy Wizard and save it, the query information appears in the RSoP query console, which looks like a Group Policy Object Editor console. The RSoP query console contains four types of information that you can view. They are

- Individual policy settings
- A list of GPOs associated with the query
- The scope of management associated with the query
- GPO revision information

Viewing Individual Policy Settings   You can view the RSoP query results for the various types of policy settings in the details pane of the RSoP query console. The details pane appears the same way that it does for the Group Policy Object Editor console, except only the settings that have been changed from the defaults appear and there might be extra columns, as described for each policy setting type in the following sections.

Software Settings Results   In the Software Settings details pane, the RSoP query results are listed in the columns described in Table 5-4.

Table 5-4   RSoP Query Results Column Descriptions for Software Settings

Column	Description
Name	Name of the deployed package
Version	Software version of the deployed package
Deployment State	Whether the package is assigned or published
Source	Source location of the deployed package
Origin	Name of the GPO that deployed the package

Windows Settings Results   Windows Settings contains the results for scripts settings, Internet Explorer Maintenance settings, and security settings. In the details pane for scripts, the RSoP query results are listed in the columns described in Table 5-5.

Table 5-5   RSoP Query Results Column Descriptions for Scripts

Column	Description
Name	Name of the script
Parameters	Any parameters that are assigned to the script
Last Executed	Date that the script was last run
GPO Name	Name of the GPO that assigned the script

The Internet Explorer Maintenance and security settings results appear in the same manner as they do on a Group Policy Object Editor console except that there is a Precedence tab, or sometimes more than one Precedence tab, indicating which GPOs affect the settings, in order from newest to oldest.

Administrative Templates Results   In the details pane for administrative templates, the RSoP query results are listed in the details pane and the GPO Name column, which provides the name of the last GPO affecting the policy setting. To view more information about a setting, double-click the setting in the details pane. A dialog box for the setting appears with three tabs, described in Table 5-6.

Table 5-6   RSoP Query Results Tab Descriptions for Administrative Templates

Tab	Description
Setting	Similar in appearance to Group Policy, but unavailable
Explain	Describes what this policy setting does
Precedence	Indicates GPO precedence, from newest to oldest

To view individual policy settings associated with an RSoP query, complete the following steps:

1. In the desired RSoP query console, in the console tree, double-click *user account–RSoP* or *computer account–RSoP*.

2. In the console tree, double-click the subfolders. The individual policy settings are visible in the details pane.

To view a list of GPOs associated with an RSoP query, complete the following steps:

1. In the desired RSoP query console, expand the *user account–RSoP* or the *computer account–RSoP* node. Right-click User Configuration or Computer Configuration, and then click Properties.

2. In the User Configuration Properties or Computer Configuration Properties dialog box, shown in Figure 5-31, in the General tab, select the Display All GPOs And Filtering Status check box. The list of GPOs associated with the RSoP query appears in the Group Policy Object column. Filtering status appears in the Filtering column as either Applied, Not Applied (Empty), or Not Applied (Unknown).

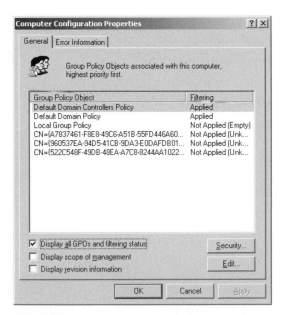

Figure 5-31 Computer Configuration Properties dialog box, displaying filtering status

To view the scope of management associated with an RSoP query, complete the following steps:

1. In the desired RSoP query console, expand the *user account*–RSoP or the *computer account*–RSoP node. Right-click User Configuration or Computer Configuration, and then click Properties.

2. In the User Configuration Properties or the Computer Configuration Properties dialog box, shown in Figure 5-32, in the General tab, select the Display Scope Of Management check box. The distinguished name of each GPO in Active Directory appears in the Scope Of Management column.

Figure 5-32   Computer Configuration Properties dialog box, displaying scope of management

To view GPO revision information associated with an RSoP query, complete the following steps:

1. In the desired RSoP query console, expand the *user account*–RSoP or the *computer account*–RSoP node. Right-click User Configuration or Computer Configuration, and then click Properties.

2. In the User Configuration Properties or the Computer Configuration Properties dialog box, shown in Figure 5-33, in the General tab, select the Display Revision Information check box. The location of the revision information for the GPOs appears in the Revision column.

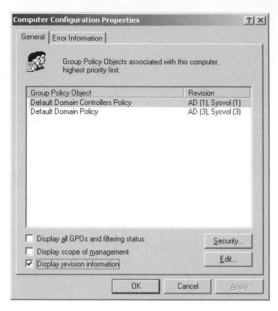

Figure 5-33   Computer Configuration Properties dialog box, displaying revision information

Reusing RSoP Queries Generated with the Resultant Set Of Policy Wizard

As discussed earlier in this lesson, you can reuse saved RSoP queries. To reuse an RSoP query, simply open the appropriate RSoP query console from the Administrative Tools menu. The query regenerates and displays the new query results on the console. If you open an RSoP console that contains archived data, you receive a message identifying the console as containing archived data.

> **Note**   If the query is generated in logging mode, and you change the settings in a GPO and then rerun the RSoP query, you do not see the new GPO settings reflected for a user unless the user logs on after the new GPO settings are implemented.

Generating RSoP Queries with the Gpresult.exe Command-Line Tool

The Gpresult.exe command-line tool enables you to create and display an RSoP query on the command line. In addition, Gpresult provides general information about the operating system, user, and computer. Gpresult provides the following information about Group Policy:

- The last time Group Policy was applied and the domain controller that applied policy—for the user and for the computer

- The complete list of applied GPOs and their details, including a summary of the extensions that each GPO contains

- Registry settings that are applied and their details
- Folders that are redirected and their details
- Software management information, including details about assigned and published applications
- Disk quota information
- Internet Protocol (IP) security settings
- Scripts

Gpresult has the following syntax:

```
gpresult [/s computer [/u domain\user /p password]] [/user username]
[/scope {user|computer}] [/v] [/z]
```

Each of the command parameters is explained in Table 5-7.

Table 5-7   Gpresult Command Parameters

Parameter	Function
/s computer	Specifies the name or IP address of a remote computer. The default is the local computer.
/u domain\user	Runs the command with the account permissions of the user that is specified by *user* or *domain\user*. The default is the permissions of the current logged-on user on the computer that issues the command.
/p password	Specifies the password of the user account that is specified in the */u* parameter.
/user username	Specifies the user name of the user whose RSoP data is to be displayed.
/scope {user|computer}	Displays either user or computer results. Valid values for the */scope* parameter are user or computer. If you omit the */scope* parameter, Gpresult displays both user and computer settings.
/v	Specifies that the output displays verbose policy information.
/z	Specifies that the output displays all available information about Group Policy. Because this parameter produces more information than the */v* parameter, redirect output to a text file when you use this parameter (for example, *gpresult /z > policy.txt*).

The following are examples of using the gpresult command:

- To display RSoP query computer information for User11 on the computer issuing the command, type

  gpresult /user User11 /scope computer

■ To display RSoP query user information for User11 on Server02 using the credentials of admin7, type

gpresult /s server02 /u contoso\admin7 /p p@ss314 /user User11 /scope user

■ To direct all available Group Policy information for User11 on Server02 to the text file Policy.txt using the credentials of admin7, type

gpresult /s server02 /u contoso.com\admin7 /p p@ss314 /user User11 /z > policy.txt

To create and display an RSoP query on the command line with Gpresult, complete the following steps:

1. Click Start, and then click Command Prompt.

2. At the command prompt, type **gpresult** and the appropriate parameters. In Figure 5-34, Gpresult has been used to display RSoP query computer information for Administrator on Server01.

Figure 5-34   Gpresult RSoP query information for Administrator on Server01

Tip   Gpotool.exe is a useful Resource Kit utility for obtaining information on group policies that exist on the domain. Gpotool.exe is part of the Windows Server 2003 Resource Kit Tools that can be downloaded from *http://www.microsoft.com*. After installing the Resource Kit, you can enter the command **gpotool /verbose > c:\gpotooloutput.txt** and open the text file to view a list of group policies, including friendly names, GUIDs, and information on when these GPOs were created.

Generating RSoP Queries with the Advanced System Information–Policy Tool

The *Advanced System Information–Policy tool* enables you to create an RSoP query and view the results in an HTML report that appears in the Help And Support Center window. This report can be printed, and it can be saved to an .htm file. Although this report does not contain as much information as the results of RSoP queries generated with the Resultant Set Of Policy Wizard or the Gpresult command-line tool, it can be run easily by novice users who have RSoP authority. The results of the Advanced System Information–Policy tool RSoP query are obtained from RSoP logging mode for the currently logged-on user on the computer on which the query is performed. The report generated displays policy-related information for the following categories:

- Computer name, associated domain, and current site
- User name and associated domain
- Applied GPOs for the computer and user
- Security group memberships for the computer and user
- Internet Explorer settings
- Scripts: logon, logoff, startup, shutdown
- Security settings
- Programs installed
- Folder redirection
- Registry settings

To create and display an RSoP query with the Advanced System Information–Policy tool, complete the following steps:

1. Click Start, and then click Help And Support.
2. Under Support Tasks, click Tools.
3. In the Tools pane, under Help And Support Center Tools, click Advanced System Information.

4. Under Advanced System Information, click View Group Policy Settings Applied. In Figure 5-35, the Advanced System Information–Policy tool has been used to display RSoP query computer information for Administrator on Server01. You can scroll to the results that you want to view and click the arrow in the upper-right corner of a category to hide details.

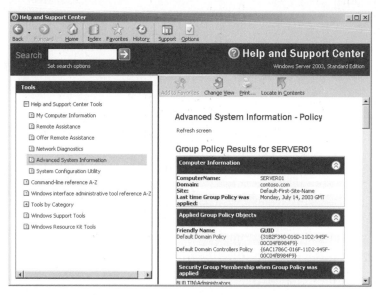

Figure 5-35   Advanced System Information–Policy RSoP query information for Administrator on Server01

Delegating Control of RSoP

Permission for generating an RSoP query is set for the domain or OU by selecting one of the Generate Resultant Set Of Policy Planning options in the Delegation Of Authority Wizard. You must be a member of the Enterprise Administrators group to delegate RSoP control at the domain and site level.

Important   Delegated control is inherited by all child containers below the container to which control is delegated.

To delegate control of RSoP, complete the following steps:

1. Click Start, point to Administrative Tools, and then click Active Directory Users And Computers.

2. In the console tree, right-click the domain or OU for which you want to delegate control of RSoP, and then click Delegate Control.

3. On the Welcome To The Delegation Of Control Wizard page, click Next.

4. On the Users Or Groups page, click Add.

5. In the Select Users, Computers, Or Groups dialog box, type the user or group for which you want to delegate administration in the Enter The Object Names To Select box and then click OK. Click Next on the Users Or Groups page.

6. On the Tasks To Delegate page, click Delegate The Following Common Tasks and select the Generate Resultant Set Of Policy (Logging) check box or the Generate Resultant Set Of Policy (Planning) check box, or both, and then click Next.

7. On the Completing The Delegation Of Control Wizard page, review your selections. Click Finish.

Practice: Generating RSoP Queries

In this practice, you generate three RSoP queries.

Exercise 1: Creating an RSoP Query with the Resultant Set Of Policy Wizard Logging Mode

In this exercise, you create an RSoP query with the Resultant Set Of Policy Wizard logging mode and view the results in the RSoP query console.

To create an RSoP query with logging mode:

1. Log on to Server01 as Administrator.

2. On Server01, use the procedure provided earlier in this lesson to create an RSoP query with the Resultant Set Of Policy Wizard logging mode. Create the query for the settings applied to Pat Coleman on Server01 (this computer).

3. View the results of the RSoP query on the RSoP query console in the User Configuration node, in the Administrative Templates node. The settings from the Lockdown Desktop GPO are shown.

4. Save the RSoP query console as Pat Coleman RSoP.

5. Open the Lockdown Desktop GPO. In the User Configuration node, in the Administrative Templates node, in the Desktop node, configure the Hide My Network Places Icon On Desktop setting to Enabled.

6. Open the Pat Coleman RSoP console. Is the new setting in the Lockdown Desktop GPO reflected in the RSoP? Why?

_____

_____

_____

7. Log off as Administrator, and then log on as Pat Coleman. Is the My Network Places icon visible on the desktop? Why?

_____

_____

8. Log off as Pat Coleman, and then log on as Administrator. Open the Pat Coleman RSoP console. Is the new setting in the Lockdown Desktop GPO reflected in the RSoP? Why?

_____

_____

_____

Exercise 2: Creating an RSoP Query with the Gpresult.exe Command-Line Tool

In this exercise, you create and view the results of an RSoP query on the command line with the Gpresult command-line tool.

To create an RSoP query with Gpresult:

1. On Server01, use the procedure provided earlier in this lesson to create and view the results of an RSoP query on the command line with the Gpresult command-line tool. Create the query for the settings applied to Lorrin Smith-Bates on Server01 (this computer). What did you type on the command line to achieve this?

_____

2. View the results of the RSoP query in the command line.

Exercise 3: Creating an RSoP Query with the Advanced System Information–Policy Tool

In this exercise, you create an RSoP query with the Advanced System Information–Policy tool and view the results in the Help And Support Center window.

To create an RSoP query with the Advanced System Information–Policy tool:

1. On Server01, use the procedure provided earlier in this lesson to create an RSoP query with the Advanced System Information–Policy tool. Create the RSoP query for Pat Coleman on Server01. How do you create the RSoP query for Pat Coleman?

   Log on to Server01 as Pat Coleman.

2. View the results in the Help And Support Center window. What registry key is used to hide the My Network Places icon on the desktop?

   Software\Microsoft\Windows\CurrentVersion\Policies\Explorer\NoNetHood

Lesson Review

The following questions are intended to reinforce key information presented in this lesson. If you are unable to answer a question, review the lesson materials and try the question again. You can find answers to the questions in the "Questions and Answers" section at the end of this chapter.

1. What is the purpose of generating RSoP queries?

_____

_____

_____

_____

_____

2. What are the three tools available for generating RSoP queries?

_____

_____

_____

3. What is the difference between logging mode and planning mode?

_____

_____

_____

4. What is the difference between saving an RSoP query and saving RSoP query data?

_____

_____

_____

5. Which RSoP query-generating tool provides RSoP query results on a console similar to a Group Policy Object Editor console?

    a. Resultant Set Of Policy Wizard

    b. Group Policy Wizard

    c. Gpupdate command-line tool

    d. Gpresult command-line tool

    e. Advanced System Information–Policy tool

    f. Advanced System Information–Services tool

_____

_____

_____

_____

_____

Lesson Summary

- RSoP is the sum of the policies applied to the user or computer, including the application of filters (security groups, WMI) and exceptions (No Override, Block Policy Inheritance).

- Windows Server 2003 provides three tools for generating RSoP queries: the Resultant Set Of Policy Wizard, the Gpresult.exe command-line tool, and the Advanced System Information–Policy tool.

- The Resultant Set Of Policy Wizard uses existing GPO settings to report the effects of GPOs on users and computers and can simulate the effects of planned GPOs. The wizard's logging mode reports the existing GPO settings for a user or computer. Its planning mode simulates the GPO settings that a user and computer might receive, and it enables you to change the simulation.

- The Gpresult.exe command-line tool enables you to create and display an RSoP query on the command line.

- The Advanced System Information–Policy tool enables you to create an RSoP query and view the results in an HTML report that appears in the Help And Support Center window.

Lesson 5: Troubleshooting Group Policy

To maintain an effective Group Policy configuration, you must be able to troubleshoot Group Policy. Troubleshooting Group Policy involves using the Resultant Set Of Policy Wizard, the Gpresult.exe and Gpupdate.exe command-line tools, the Event Viewer, and log files to solve policy-related problems. This lesson shows you how to work with these tools to troubleshoot Group Policy for Active Directory.

After this lesson, you will be able to

■ Troubleshoot Group Policy

Estimated lesson time: 20 minutes

Troubleshooting Group Policy

As an administrator, you will likely have the task of finding solutions to problems with Group Policy. If problems occur, you might need to perform some tests to verify that your Group Policy configuration is working properly, such as the following:

■ Verify that GPOs apply to the appropriate users and computers.

■ Verify that folders configured for redirection are redirected to the appropriate location.

■ Verify that files and folders configured to be available offline are available when a computer is offline.

You will also need to be able to diagnose and solve problems, including:

■ GPOs are not applied.

■ GPOs cannot be accessed.

■ GPO inheritance issues cause unexpected results.

■ Folders are not redirected or are redirected to an unexpected location.

■ Files and folders are not available offline.

■ Files are not synchronized.

Windows Server 2003 operating systems provide the following Group Policy trouble-shooting tools to assist you in verifying your configuration and in diagnosing and solving problems:

- Resultant Set Of Policy Wizard
- Gpresult.exe
- Gpupdate.exe
- Event Viewer
- Log files

Troubleshooting Group Policy with the Resultant Set Of Policy Wizard and Gpresult.exe

Recall that the Resultant Set Of Policy Wizard and the Gpresult.exe command-line tool are both used to generate RSoP queries and provide the RSoPs for users and computers you specify. In Windows Server 2003 operating systems, these tools can help you greatly reduce the amount of time you spend troubleshooting. Generating RSoP queries by using the Resultant Set Of Policy Wizard and Gpresult was discussed in detail in Lesson 4.

Troubleshooting Group Policy with Gpupdate.exe

Recall that the Gpupdate.exe tool, which is new in Windows Server 2003 (and also exists in Windows XP Professional), enables you to refresh policy immediately. Gpupdate replaces the Secedit /refreshpolicy command used for refreshing GPOs in Windows 2000. The Gpupdate tool was discussed in Lesson 3.

Troubleshooting Group Policy with Event Viewer

By examining the application event log in Event Viewer, you can view Group Policy failure and warning messages, such as the one shown in Figure 5-36. The application event log contains basic predetermined Group Policy events and is used to track problems, not for Group Policy planning. Event log records with the source Userenv pertain to Group Policy events.

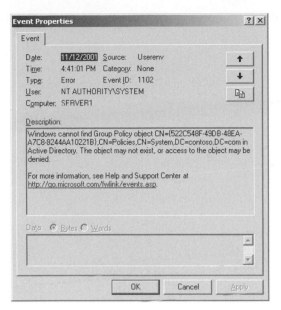

Figure 5-36   Properties for a Group Policy event log message

To avoid flooding the log, not all Group Policy failures and warnings are displayed in the event log. You can retrieve more detailed information about Group Policy processing by setting a switch in the registry to enable verbose logging for the event log.

> **Caution**   This section contains information about editing the registry. Using the Registry Editor incorrectly can cause serious damage to your operating system. Use the Registry Editor at your own risk.

To enable verbose logging for the event log, complete the following steps:

1. Log on as Administrator.

2. Click Start, and then click Run.

3. In the Run dialog box, in the Open box, type **regedit** and then click OK.

4. In the Registry Editor console, open the HKEY_LOCAL_MACHINE/Software /Microsoft/Windows NT/Current Version/ key, click Edit, select New, and then select Key on the toolbar.

5. Type **Diagnostics** as the name of the new key. Right-click the new key, select New, and select DWORD Value on the toolbar.

6. In the details pane, type **RunDiagnosticLoggingGroupPolicy** as the name of the new value. Right-click the new value, and select Modify.

7. In the Edit DWORD Value dialog box, type **1** in the Value Data box. Ensure that the Hexadecimal option is selected. Click OK.

8. Log off, and then log on again.

9. Open the Application Log in Event Viewer, and view the enhanced Group Policy event logging.

Troubleshooting Group Policy with Log Files

You can generate a diagnostic log to record detailed information about Group Policy processing to a log file named Userenv.log in the hidden folder *%system-root%*\Debug\Usermode. The generation of this diagnostic log is known as enabling verbose logging.

Caution   This section contains information about editing the registry. Using the Registry Editor incorrectly can cause serious damage to your operating system. Use the Registry Editor at your own risk.

To enable verbose logging to a log file, complete the following steps:

1. Log on as Administrator.

2. Click Start, and then click Run.

3. In the Run dialog box, in the Open box, type **regedit** and then click OK.

4. In the Registry Editor console, open the HKEY_LOCAL_MACHINE/Software /Microsoft/Windows NT/Current Version/Winlogon key, click Edit, select New, and then select DWORD Value on the toolbar.

5. In the details pane, type **UserenvDebugLevel** as the name of the new value. Right-click the new value, and select Modify.

6. In the Edit DWORD Value dialog box, type **30002** in the Value Data box. Ensure that the Hexadecimal option is selected. Click OK.

7. Log off, and then log on again.

8. Open the *%systemroot%*\Debug\Usermode\Userenv.log file, and view the enhanced Group Policy event logging.

Note   To read or copy the logs on the target machine, you must have local Administrator rights.

The Userenv.log file, shown in Figure 5-37, provides details of errors and warnings in Group Policy processing on the computer on which it is set. Reading from left to right, this log shows a process code, the time it was processed (the date is not displayed), the process name, followed by a short statement of the error. The Userenv.log file has a maximum size of 1 megabyte (MB). At system startup, if the log file exceeds 1 MB, the contents are copied into a file named Userenv.bak and a new Userenv.log file is created.

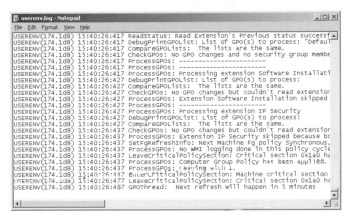

Figure 5-37   Contents of a Userenv.log file

Group Policy Troubleshooting Scenarios

Table 5-8 describes some troubleshooting scenarios related to the Group Policy Object Editor console.

Table 5-8   Group Policy Object Editor Console Troubleshooting Scenarios

Problem: **A user cannot open a GPO in the console even though he or she has Read access to it.**

Cause	Solution
A user must have both Read permission and Write permission for the GPO to open it in the Group Policy Object Editor console.	Make the user a member of a security group with at least Read and Write, and preferably Full Control, permission for the GPO. For example, a domain administrator can manage nonlocal GPOs. An administrator for a computer can edit the local GPO on that computer.

Problem: **When a user tries to edit a GPO, the Failed To Open The Group Policy Object message appears.**

Cause	Solution
A networking problem, specifically a problem with the Domain Name System (DNS) configuration.	Make sure DNS is working properly. Refer to help for details.

Table 5-8   Group Policy Object Editor Console Troubleshooting Scenarios

Problem: **When a user tries to edit a GPO, the Missing Active Directory Container message appears.**

Cause	Solution
This is caused by Group Policy attempting to link a GPO to an OU that it cannot find. The OU might have been deleted, or it might have been created on another domain controller but not replicated to the domain controller that you are using.	Limit the number of administrators who can make structural changes to Active Directory, or who can edit a GPO at any one time. Allow changes to replicate before making changes that affect the same OU or GPO.

Problem: **When a user tries to edit a GPO, the Snap-In Failed To Initialize message appears.**

Cause	Solution
This error can occur if Group Policy cannot find the file Framedyn.dll.	If you use installation scripts, make sure that your scripts place the %*systemroot*%\System32\Wbem directory in the system path. By default, %*systemroot*%\System32\Wbem is in the system path already; therefore, you are not likely to encounter this issue if you do not use installation scripts.

Table 5-9 describes some troubleshooting scenarios where Group Policy settings are not taking effect.

Table 5-9   Group Policy Settings Troubleshooting Scenarios

Problem: **Group Policy is not being applied to users and computers in a security group that contains those users and computers, even though a GPO is linked to an OU containing that security group.**

Cause	Solution
This is correct behavior. Group Policy affects only users and computers contained in sites, domains, and OUs. GPOs are not applied to security groups.	Link GPOs to sites, domains, and OUs only. Keep in mind that the location of a security group in Active Directory is unrelated to whether Group Policy applies to the users and computers in that security group.

Table 5-9   Group Policy Settings Troubleshooting Scenarios

Problem: **Group Policy is not affecting users and computers in a site, domain, or OU.**

Cause	Solution
Group Policy settings can be prevented, intentionally or inadvertently, from taking effect on users and computers in several ways. A GPO can be disabled from affecting users, computers, or both. It also needs to be linked either directly to an OU containing the users and computers or to a parent domain or OU so that the Group Policy settings apply through inheritance. When multiple GPOs exist, they are applied in this order: local, site, domain, OU. By default, settings applied later have precedence. In addition, Group Policy can be blocked at the level of any OU or enforced through a setting of No Override applied to a particular GPO link. Finally, the user or computer must belong to one or more security groups with appropriate permissions set.	Make sure that the intended policy is not being blocked. Make sure no policy set at a higher level of Active Directory has been set to No Override. If Block Policy Inheritance and No Override are both used, keep in mind that No Override takes precedence. Verify that the user or computer is not a member of any security group for which the Apply Group Policy access control entry (ACE) is set to Deny. Verify that the user or computer is a member of at least one security group for which the Apply Group Policy permission is set to Allow. Verify that the user or computer is a member of at least one security group for which the Read permission is set to Allow.

Problem: **Group Policy is not affecting users and computers in an Active Directory container.**

Cause	Solution
GPOs cannot be linked to Active Directory containers other than sites, domains, and OUs.	Link a GPO to an object that is a parent to the Active Directory container. Then, by default, those settings are applied to the users and computers in the container through inheritance.

Problem: **Local Group Policy is not taking effect on the computer.**

Cause	Solution
Local policies are the weakest. Any nonlocal GPO can overwrite them.	Check to see what GPOs are being applied through Active Directory and whether those GPOs have settings that are in conflict with the local settings.

Lesson Review

The following questions are intended to reinforce key information presented in this lesson. If you are unable to answer a question, review the lesson materials and try the question again. You can find answers to the questions in the "Questions and Answers" section at the end of this chapter.

1. In which Event Viewer log can you find Group Policy failure and warning messages? What type of event log records should you look for?

   _____

   _____

2. What diagnostic log file can you generate to record detailed information about Group Policy processing and in what location is this file generated?

   _____

   _____

   _____

3. Which of the following actions should you take if you attempt to open a Group Policy Object Editor console for an OU GPO and you receive the message Failed To Open The Group Policy Object?

   a. Check your permissions for the GPO.

   b. Check network connectivity.

   c. Check that the OU exists.

   d. Check that No Override is set for the GPO.

   e. Check that Block Policy Inheritance is set for the GPO.

   _____

   _____

   _____

4. Which of the following actions should you take if you attempt to edit a GPO and you receive the message Missing Active Directory Container?

   a. Check your permissions for the GPO.

   b. Check network connectivity.

   c. Check that the OU exists.

   d. Check that No Override is set for the GPO.

   e. Check that Block Policy Inheritance is set for the GPO.

_____

_____

_____

_____

Lesson Summary

- Windows Server 2003 provides the following Group Policy troubleshooting tools to assist you in verifying your configuration and in diagnosing and solving problems: Resultant Set Of Policy Wizard, Gpresult.exe and Gpupdate.exe command-line tools, Event Viewer, and log files.

- By using the application event log in Event Viewer, you can view Group Policy failure and warning messages. Event log records with the source Userenv indicate records pertaining to Group Policy events. You can retrieve more detailed information about Group Policy processing by enabling verbose logging for the event log.

- You can generate a diagnostic log to record detailed information about Group Policy processing to a log file named Userenv.log in the hidden folder %system-root%\Debug\Usermode. The generation of this diagnostic log is known as enabling verbose logging.

Case Scenario Exercise

You are a network administrator for Humongous Insurance. All domains are configured for a functional level of Windows 2000 Native. Figure 5-38 illustrates the current Humongous Insurance network infrastructure.

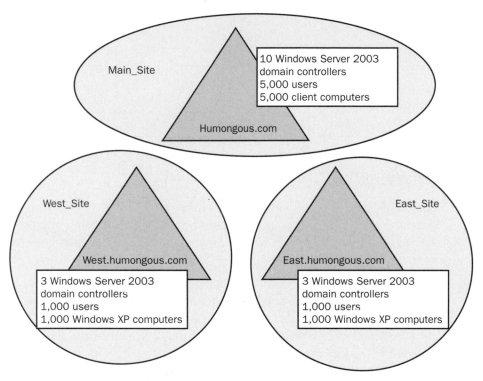

Figure 5-38   Humongous Insurance network structure

Five domain controllers in the Main_Site and two domain controllers in each of the other sites are configured as DNS servers. The DNS records are stored in, and replicated by, Active Directory. Each site has one global catalog server. The Humongous.com domain has five first-level OUs: Accounting, Administration, Claims, Executives, and Marketing. The West.humongous.com and East.humongous.com domains each have three OUs: Administration, Claims, and Regional Sales. This is depicted in Figure 5-39.

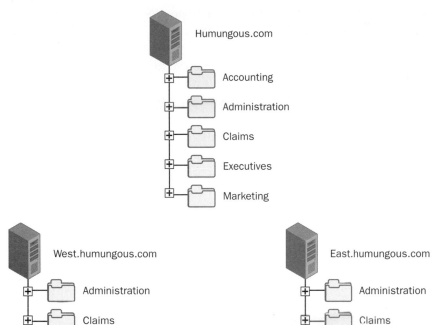

Figure 5-39   Humongous Insurance domain OU structure

You've been working with several other administrators to figure out how you can use Group Policy. Given this information, answer the following questions:

1. You link a GPO to the Humongous.com domain, but that policy isn't inherited by the East.humongous.com or West.humongous.com domains. Why is this happening and how can you make the policy apply to those two domains?

_____

_____

_____

_____

_____

_____

_____

_____

2. The East.humongous.com administrator, Sharon Salavaria, has configured a GPO, named Required_Set, that she says is mandatory for her entire domain. She also has several GPOs that she's configured at the domain, but she doesn't consider those policies mandatory. The Administration and Regional Sales OU administrators have blocked policy inheritance to their OUs. Sharon wants to be sure that they receive at least the Required_Set GPO. What should she do?

_____

_____

_____

3. Sharon realizes that three users in the Claims OU should not be receiving the Required_Set GPO, but she wants everyone else in the entire company, including other users in the Claims OU, to receive that policy. What are her options?

_____

_____

_____

_____

4. You've been asked to configure five public access computers that run the Windows XP Professional operating system in the Humongous Insurance lobby. You configure a GPO named LockDown that restricts the options that people have in operating these systems. However, you are concerned that some of your domain users might log on to these systems, which would change the appearance of the desktop. You want to be sure that the user settings that you've configured for the LockDown GPO apply to anyone who logs on to the public computers. What can you do?

_____

_____

_____

_____

_____

5. What tools could you use to document the policies and their effects once they are in place?

_____

_____

_____

_____

_____

_____

_____

_____

Troubleshooting Lab

You are a domain administrator for Contoso Pharmaceuticals. One of the desktop administrators calls to report some peculiar results with four user accounts. Users are not supposed to have the Run command in their Start menus, but three out of four have it. The desktop administrator is puzzled. You investigate the issue and document your results, as shown in Table 5-10.

Table 5-10   Results of Your Investigation

User account	Parent container	Group memberships
GPLabUser1	contoso.com	GPLabGroup1 Domain Users
GPLabUser2	contoso.com	GPLabGroup2 Domain Users
GPLabUser3	GPLab OU	GPLabGroup1 GPLabGroup2 Domain Users
GPLabUser4	GPLab OU	Domain Users

You learn that the GPO that doesn't seem to be working is named GPLabRemoveRun. You discover that someone has explicitly denied GPLabGroup2 the permission to Apply Group Policy for the GPLabRemoveRun policy. You also determined that GPLabRemoveRun is linked to the GPLab OU.

To experience this issue, complete the following steps:

1. Log on to Server01 as Administrator.

2. In the contoso.com domain container, create two users: GPLabUser1 and GPLabUser2.

Note   You will be logging on as these accounts—be certain to keep track of the user logon names and passwords that you configure.

3. In the contoso.com domain container, create a new OU in contoso.com named GPLab.

4. In the GPLab OU, create two universal security groups: GPLabGroup1 and GPLabGroup2.

5. In the GPLab OU, create two users: GPLabUser3, and GPLabUser4.

6. Add GPLabUser1, GPLabUser2, GPLabUser3, and GPLabUser4 as members of the Server Operators group. This allows these accounts to log on locally.

7. Add GPLabUser1 as a member of the GPLabGroup1 group.

8. Add GPLabUser2 as a member of the GPLabGroup2 group.

9. Add GPLabUser3 as a member of both GPLabGroup1 and GPLabGroup2.

> **Note**   GPLabUser4 was added only to the Server Operators group. By default, all new users are also members of Domain Users.

10. Create a new GPO for the GPLab OU. To do so, right-click GPLab and then click Properties.

11. In the GPLab Properties dialog box, click the Group Policy tab. Click New. Type **GPLabRemoveRun** as the new policy name, and press ENTER. Click Properties.

12. In the GPLabRemoveRun Properties dialog box, click the Security tab. Click Add.

13. Type **GPLabGroup1**, and click OK. You should see the GPLabGroup1 appear in the Group Or User Names list.

14. Look at the Permissions For GPLabGroup1 list. Notice that GPLabGroup1 has Read permissions (the Allow box is checked) for this GPO. Check the Allow box that corresponds to the Apply Group Policy entry in this list. Click Apply.

15. Click Add again. This time type **GPLabGroup2** and click OK. The GPLabGroup2 appears in the Group Or User Names list.

16. In the Permissions For GPLabGroup2 list, check the Deny box that corresponds to the Apply Group Policy entry and then click OK. The Security warning message box appears. Read the warning, and then click Yes.

> **Note**   You've now configured the GPLabRemoveRun GPO so that members of GPLabGroup1 can apply the policy but members of GPLabGroup2 cannot.

17. In the GPLab Properties dialog box, click Edit. The Group Policy Object Editor window opens.

18. Navigate to the following policy location: User Configuration, Administrative Templates, Start Menu And Taskbar.

19. Double-click the Remove Run Menu From Start Menu setting in the details pane.

20. In the Remove Run Menu From Start Menu Properties dialog box, click Enabled and then click OK. You've now enabled this setting, which removes the Run option from the Start menu of all affected users.

21. Close all open windows.

22. Click Start, click Run, type **gpupdate**, and then press ENTER. This ensures that the policy is immediately applied to the system.

23. Log off as Administrator. Log on as GPLabUser1. Click Start.

    Do you see the Run option in the Start menu?

    _____

24. Log off GPLabUser1, and log on as GPLabUser2. Do you see the Run option in the Start menu?

    _____

25. Log off GPLabUser2, and log on as GPLabUser3. Do you see the Run option in the Start menu?

    _____

26. Log off GPLabUser3, and log on as GPLabUser4. Do you see the Run option in the Start menu?

    _____

27. Why does the policy affect only GPLabUser4?

    _____

    _____

    _____

    _____

28. How could you configure your Active Directory objects to ensure that all four GPLabUser accounts were subject to the GPLabRemoveRun GPO?

    _____

    _____

    _____

    _____

    _____

Chapter Summary

- Group policies are collections of user and computer configuration settings that can be linked to computers, sites, domains, and OUs to specify the behavior of users' desktops. You use the Group Policy Object Editor to organize and manage the Group Policy settings in each GPO.

- There are two types of Group Policy settings: computer configuration settings and user configuration settings. Computer configuration settings are used to set group policies applied to computers, regardless of who logs on to them, and they are applied when the operating system initializes. User configuration settings are used to set group policies applied to users, regardless of which computer the user logs on to, and they are applied when users log on to the computer.

- Group Policy is applied to Active Directory components in the following order: local computer, site, domain, and then OU.

- Group Policy is passed down from parent to child containers within a domain. If you have assigned a separate Group Policy setting to a parent container, that Group Policy setting applies to all containers beneath the parent container, including the user and computer objects in the container. However, if you specify a Group Policy setting for a child container, the child container's Group Policy setting overrides the setting inherited from the parent container.

- The default order for the application of Group Policy settings is subject to the following exceptions: No Override, Block Policy Inheritance, the Loopback setting, and a computer that is a member of a workgroup.

- There are three parts to planning Group Policy: plan the Group Policy settings, plan GPOs, and plan administrative control of GPOs.

- You use the Active Directory Users And Computers console to create a GPO for a domain or an OU. You use the Active Directory Sites And Services console to create a GPO for a site. You can also use the new Group Policy Management console to perform all tasks related to Group Policy.

- RSoP is the sum of the policies applied to the user or computer, including the application of filters (security groups, WMI) and exceptions (No Override, Block Policy Inheritance).

- Windows Server 2003 provides three tools for generating RSoP queries: the Resultant Set Of Policy Wizard, the Gpresult.exe command-line tool, and the Advanced System Information–Policy tool.

- Windows Server 2003 provides the following Group Policy troubleshooting tools to assist you in verifying your configuration and in diagnosing and solving problems: Resultant Set Of Policy Wizard, Gpresult.exe and Gpupdate.exe command-line tools, Event Viewer, and log files.

Exam Highlights

Before taking the exam, review the following key points and terms to help you identify topics you need to review. Return to the lessons for additional practice, and review the "Further Readings" sections in Part 2 for pointers to more information about topics covered by the exam objectives.

Key Points

- Understand the key differences between group policy settings (*policies*), GPOs, and GPO links.

- Be prepared to plan, implement, and troubleshoot GPO application involving GPO link inheritance, No Override, Block Inheritance, GPO filtering with security groups and WMI filters, loopback processing, and disabling unused portions of a GPO.

- Know the effect of GPO permissions, and what permissions are required for a GPO to apply to a user or computer, what permissions are necessary to edit a GPO, and what permissions will prevent a GPO from applying to a user or computer.

- Remember that Group Policy does not apply to Windows 95, Windows 98, Windows Me, or Windows NT 4.0 computers. Those systems can be configured using System Policy.

- Know the functions of command-line Group Policy tools: Gpupdate.exe, Gpresult.exe, Gpotool.exe, and Secedit.exe. Gpupdate.exe is responsible for refreshing policies on Windows XP and Windows Server 2003 computers; Secedit.exe is able to refresh policies on Windows 2000 computers.

- You can generate RSoP queries by using three tools: the Resultant Set Of Policy Wizard, the Gpresult.exe command-line tool, and the Advanced System Information-Policy tool.

Key Terms

Group Policy Object (GPO)   A collection of user and computer configuration settings that specifies how programs, network resources, and the operating system work for users and computers in an organization. Group Policy Objects can be linked to computers, sites, domains, and OUs.

Resultant Set of Policy (RSoP)   A feature that simplifies Group Policy implementation and troubleshooting. RSoP has two modes: logging mode and planning mode. Logging mode determines the resultant effect of policy settings that have been applied to an existing user and computer based on a site, domain, and OU. Planning mode simulates the resultant effect of policy settings that are applied to a user and a computer.

Page
5-24

Lesson 1 Review

1. What is a GPO?

A GPO is a Group Policy object. Group Policy configuration settings, also known simply as *policies*, are contained within a GPO. Each computer running Windows Server 2003 has one local GPO and can, in addition, be subject to any number of Active Directory–based GPOs.

2. What are the two primary groupings of policy settings, and how are they used?

The two types of Group Policy settings are computer configuration settings and user configuration settings. Computer configuration settings are used to set group policies applied to computers, regardless of who logs on to them, and are applied when the operating system initializes. User configuration settings are used to set group policies applied to users, regardless of which computer the users log on to, and are applied when users log on to the computer. Policies are also updated based on refresh intervals.

3. In what order is Group Policy applied to components in the Active Directory structure?

Group Policy is applied to Active Directory components in the following order: local computer, site, domain, and then OU.

4. What is the difference between Block Policy Inheritance and No Override?

Block Policy Inheritance is applied directly to the site, domain, or OU. It is not applied to GPOs, nor is it applied to GPO links. Block Policy Inheritance prevents *all* settings from GPOs linked to parent containers from affecting the site, domain, or OU that is blocking inheritance.

Any GPO linked to a site, domain, or OU (not the local GPO) can be set to No Override so that its policy settings will not be overwritten by settings in any other GPO during the application of group policies. When more than one GPO has been set to No Override, the one highest in the Active Directory hierarchy (or higher in the hierarchy specified by the administrator at each fixed level in Active Directory) takes precedence. No Override is applied to the GPO link. GPO links set to No Override are always applied and cannot be blocked using the Block Policy Inheritance option.

5. Which of the following nodes contains the registry-based Group Policy settings?

    a. Software Settings

    b. Windows Settings

    c. Administrative Templates

    d. Security Settings

The correct answer is c. The Administrative Templates node contains the registry-based Group Policy settings. The Software Settings node contains only the Software Installation extension. The Windows Settings node contains the settings for configuring the operating system, such as scripts, security settings, folder redirection, and RIS. The Security Settings node contains settings for configuring security levels.

Lesson 2 Review

1. Describe a decentralized GPO design.

   With a decentralized GPO design, you create a base GPO to be applied to the domain that contains policy settings for as many users and computers in the domain as possible. Next, you create additional GPOs tailored to the common requirements of each OU, and apply them to the appropriate OUs. The goal of a decentralized GPO design is to include a specific policy setting in as few GPOs as possible. When a change is required, only one (or a few) GPO (GPOs) has to be changed to enforce the change.

2. If administrative responsibilities in your organization are task-based and delegated among several administrators, which of the following types of GPOs should you plan to create?

   a. GPOs containing only one type of Group Policy setting

   b. GPOs containing many types of Group Policy settings

   c. GPOs containing only computer configuration settings

   d. GPOs containing only user configuration settings

   The correct answer is a: GPOs containing a single type of Group Policy setting. For example, a GPO that includes only security settings is best suited for organizations in which administrative responsibilities are task-based and delegated among several individuals.

Lesson 3 Review

1. If you want to create a GPO for a site, what administrative tool should you use?

   Use the Active Directory Sites And Services console to create a GPO for a site.

2. Why should you create an MMC for a GPO?

   If you create an MMC for a GPO, it is easier to administer because you can open it whenever necessary from the Administrative Tools menu.

3. Besides Read permission, what permission must you assign to allow a user or administrator to see the settings in a GPO?

   Write permission. A user or administrator who has Read access but not Write access to a GPO cannot use the Group Policy Object Editor to see the settings that it contains.

4. Why should you disable unused Group Policy settings?

   Disabling unused Group Policy settings avoids the processing of those settings and expedites startup and logging on for the users and computers subject to the GPO.

5. How do you prevent a GPO from applying to a specific group?

   You can prevent a policy from applying to a specific group by denying that group the Apply Group Policy permission for the GPO.

6. What's the difference between removing a GPO link and deleting a GPO?

When you remove a GPO link to a site, domain, or OU, the GPO still remains in Active Directory. When you delete a GPO, the GPO is removed from Active Directory, and any sites, domains, or OUs to which it is linked are no longer affected by it.

7. You want to deflect all Group Policy settings that reach the North OU from all of the OU's parent objects. To accomplish this, which of the following exceptions do you apply and where do you apply it?

a. Block Policy Inheritance applied to the OU

b. Block Policy Inheritance applied to the GPO

c. Block Policy Inheritance applied to the GPO link

d. No Override applied to the OU

e. No Override applied to the GPO

f. No Override applied to the GPO link

The correct answer is a. You use the Block Policy Inheritance exception to deflect all Group Policy settings from the parent objects of a site, domain, or OU. Block Policy Inheritance can only be applied directly to a site, domain, or OU, not to a GPO or a GPO link.

8. You want to ensure that none of the South OU Desktop settings applied to the South OU can be overridden. To accomplish this, which of the following exceptions do you apply and where do you apply it?

a. Block Policy Inheritance applied to the OU

b. Block Policy Inheritance applied to the GPO

c. Block Policy Inheritance applied to the GPO link

d. No Override applied to the OU

e. No Override applied to the GPO

f. No Override applied to the GPO link

The correct answer is f. You use the No Override exception to ensure that none of a GPO's settings can be overridden by any other GPO during the processing of group policies. No Override can only be applied directly to a GPO link.

Page
5-79

Lesson 4, Practice, Exercise 1

6. Open the Pat Coleman RSoP console. Is the new setting in the Lockdown Desktop GPO reflected in the RSoP? Why?

No, the new setting in the Lockdown Desktop GPO is not reflected in the Pat Coleman RSoP because Pat Coleman has not logged on since the new GPO settings were implemented.

7. Log off as Administrator, and then log on as Pat Coleman. Is the My Network Places icon visible on the desktop? Why?

   No, the My Network Places icon is not visible on the desktop because the Lockdown Desktop GPO setting hides the icon.

8. Log off as Pat Coleman, and then log on as Administrator. Open the Pat Coleman RSoP console. Is the new setting in the Lockdown Desktop GPO reflected in the RSoP? Why?

   Yes, the new setting in the Lockdown Desktop GPO is reflected in the Pat Coleman RSoP because Pat Coleman has logged on since the new GPO settings were implemented.

Page 5-80

Lesson 4, Practice, Exercise 2

1. On Server01, use the procedure provided earlier in this lesson to create and view the results of an RSoP query on the command line with the Gpresult command-line tool. Create the query for the settings applied to Lorrin Smith-Bates on Server01 (this computer). What did you type on the command line to achieve this?

   Gpresult /user <Lorrin Smith-Bates' user logon name>

Page 5-81

Lesson 4 Review

1. What is the purpose of generating RSoP queries?

   RSoP is the sum of the policies applied to the user or computer, including the application of filters (security groups, WMI) and exceptions (No Override, Block Policy Inheritance). Because of the cumulative effects of GPOs, filters, and exceptions, determining a user or computer's RSoP can be difficult. The ability to generate RSoP queries in Windows Server 2003 operating systems makes determining RSoP easier.

2. What are the three tools available for generating RSoP queries?

   Windows Server 2003 provides three tools for generating RSoP queries: the Resultant Set Of Policy Wizard, the Gpresult.exe command-line tool, and the Advanced System Information–Policy tool.

3. What is the difference between logging mode and planning mode?

   Logging mode reports the existing GPO settings for a user or computer. Planning mode simulates the GPO settings that a user and computer might receive, and it enables you to change the simulation.

4. What is the difference between saving an RSoP query and saving RSoP query data?

   By saving an RSoP query, you can reuse it for processing another RSoP query later. By saving RSoP query data, you can revisit the RSoP as it appeared for a particular query when the query was created.

5. Which RSoP query-generating tool provides RSoP query results on a console similar to a Group Policy Object Editor console?

    a. Resultant Set Of Policy Wizard

    b. Group Policy Wizard

    c. Gpupdate command-line tool

    d. Gpresult command-line tool

    e. Advanced System Information–Policy tool

    f. Advanced System Information–Services tool

The correct answer is a. The Resultant Set Of Policy Wizard provides RSoP query results on a console similar to a Group Policy Object Editor console. There is no Group Policy Wizard. Gpupdate and Gpresult are command-line tools. The Advanced System Information tools provide results in an HTML report that appears in the Help And Support Center window.

Page 5-90 **Lesson 5 Review**

1. In which Event Viewer log can you find Group Policy failure and warning messages? What type of event log records should you look for?

You can find Group Policy failure and warning messages in the application event log. Event log records with the source Userenv pertain to Group Policy events.

2. What diagnostic log file can you generate to record detailed information about Group Policy processing and in what location is this file generated?

You can generate a diagnostic log to record detailed information about Group Policy processing to a log file named Userenv.log in the hidden folder %systemroot%\Debug\Usermode.

3. Which of the following actions should you take if you attempt to open a Group Policy Object Editor console for an OU GPO and you receive the message Failed To Open The Group Policy Object?

    a. Check your permissions for the GPO.

    b. Check network connectivity.

    c. Check that the OU exists.

    d. Check that No Override is set for the GPO.

    e. Check that Block Policy Inheritance is set for the GPO.

The correct answer is b. The message Failed To Open The Group Policy Object indicates a networking problem, specifically a problem with the Domain Name System (DNS) configuration.

4. Which of the following actions should you take if you attempt to edit a GPO and you receive the message Missing Active Directory Container?

   a. Check your permissions for the GPO.

   b. Check network connectivity.

   c. Check that the OU exists.

   d. Check that No Override is set for the GPO.

   e. Check that Block Policy Inheritance is set for the GPO.

   The correct answer is c. The message Missing Active Directory Container is caused by Group Policy attempting to link a GPO to an OU that it cannot find. The OU might have been deleted, or it might have been created on another domain controller but not replicated to the domain controller that you are using.

Page 5-93

Case Scenario Exercise

1. You link a GPO to the Humongous.com domain, but that policy isn't inherited by the East.humongous.com or West.humongous.com domains. Why is this happening and how can you make the policy apply to those two domains?

   GPOs linked to one domain aren't inherited by other domains. The only way to affect multiple domains with a single GPO is to link the GPO to a site that includes the resources of multiple domains. Because sites and domains are independent entities, you could only be sure that a GPO linked to the site applies to the computer and user accounts that are part of the site. At Humongous Insurance, each domain's resources are configured in three different sites. The only way to have a single GPO apply to the resources of multiple domains is to link the policy to all three domains (or all three sites).

2. The East.humongous.com administrator, Sharon Salavaria, has configured a GPO, named Required_Set, that she says is mandatory for her entire domain. She also has several GPOs that she's configured at the domain, but she doesn't consider those policies mandatory. The Administration and Regional Sales OU administrators have blocked policy inheritance to their OUs. Sharon wants to be sure that they receive at least the Required_Set GPO. What should she do?

   Sharon should configure the Required_Set GPO for No Override. The Required_Set GPO will be inherited by all the OUs, but the administrators of those OUs will not have to accept the other GPOs she has configured.

3. Sharon realizes that three users in the Claims OU should not be receiving the Required_Set GPO, but she wants everyone else in the entire company, including other users in the Claims OU, to receive that policy. What are her options?

   The most likely solution is for Sharon to create a group for those users who shouldn't receive the policy. She can then add specific users to that group and configure the group so that Apply Group Policy is denied. Her other options include moving the user accounts to another container that doesn't receive the GPO.

4. You've been asked to configure five public access computers that run the Windows XP Professional operating system in the Humongous Insurance lobby. You configure a GPO named LockDown that restricts the options that people have in operating these systems. However, you are concerned that some of your domain users might log on to these systems, which would change the appearance of the desktop. You want to be sure that the user settings that you've configured for the LockDown GPO apply to anyone who logs on to the public computers. What can you do?

Create a new OU named Public, and link the LockDown GPO to that OU. Move the computer accounts for each of those computers to the LockDown OU. Then, on the LockDown OU, enable the Computer Configuration, Administrative Templates, System, Group Policy, User Group Policy Loopback Processing Mode policy for Replace mode. This will ensure that everyone receives an identical desktop configuration.

5. What tools could you use to document the policies and their effects once they are in place?

Windows Server 2003 includes two tools that would be helpful in documenting the results of policy configurations. The Resultant Set Of Policy Wizard in planning mode will allow you to make RSoP queries based on chosen locations in the Active Directory structure. These queries include information on the effects of security group filtering, Block Policy Inheritance settings, No Override settings, and even GPOs that reverse earlier GPOs. RSoP queries can then be archived as documentation. Alternatively, Gpresult.exe can be used at the command line to generate RSoP queries. The result of these queries could then be saved to a text file.

Page
5-97

Troubleshooting Lab

23. Log off as Administrator. Log on as GPLabUser1. Click Start.

Do you see the Run option in the Start menu?

Yes, because the policy doesn't apply to this user.

24. Log off GPLabUser1, and log on as GPLabUser2. Do you see the Run option in the Start menu?

Yes, because the policy doesn't apply to this user.

25. Log off GPLabUser2, and log on as GPLabUser3. Do you see the Run option in the Start menu?

Yes, because the policy doesn't apply to this user.

26. Log off GPLabUser3, and log on as GPLabUser4. Do you see the Run option in the Start menu?

No, because the policy applies to this user.

27. Why does the policy affect only GPLabUser4?

GPLabUser4 is the only user account that is not specifically filtered from receiving the policy, and GPLabUser1 and GPLabUser2 are not in or subordinate to the container to which the policy is applied. GPLabUser3 is a member of a group that is specifically filtered from receiving the policy.

28. How could you configure your Active Directory objects to ensure that all four GPLabUser accounts were subject to the GPLabRemoveRun GPO?

First, you need to ensure that all user accounts are in a container that receives the GPO. You can do this by moving GPUser1 and GPUser2 to the GPLab OU. Second, you must ensure that the security filtering doesn't affect GPUser2 and GPUser3. To do this, either remove the security filtering by allowing GPLabGroup2 to apply the GPO, or remove GPUser2 and GPUser3 from GPLabGroup2.

6 Managing the User Environment with Group Policy

Exam Objectives in this Chapter:

- Configure the user environment by using Group Policy (Exam 70-296).
    - ❏ Distribute software using Group Policy.
    - ❏ Redirect folders using Group Policy.
    - ❏ Configure user security settings by using Group Policy.
- Troubleshoot issues related to Group Policy application deployment (Exam 70-296).

Why This Chapter Matters

Group Policy enables an organization to centralize the management of the user environment. This chapter shows you how to leverage Group Policy to redirect special folders such as My Documents so that user data is maintained on a server where it can be secured, backed up, and managed more efficiently. Using the Folder Redirection node in Group Policy, you can redirect Application Data, Desktop, My Documents, My Pictures, and Start Menu to other locations. Folder redirection does not mean, however, that users must be connected to the network to access their files—you will learn how to use Offline Files to cache network files so that they are available offline.

You will also learn how to deploy software with Group Policy, which is an essential skill for meeting the changing application needs of organizations. When you deploy software with Group Policy, users no longer need to look for a network share, use a CD-ROM, or install, fix, and upgrade software themselves. Best of all, deploying software with Group Policy reduces the time you must spend administering users' systems. You can also use Group Policy to redeploy, upgrade, or remove applications in the same manner in which they were deployed, which further reduces administrative time.

As you gain control of software distribution, you will also want to control which applications users run that are not in the scope of licensed and permitted software. Software restriction policies, new in Microsoft Windows XP and the Windows Server 2003 family, are available to help govern which software can be installed on users' computers, reducing the chance of hostile code being introduced to the environment.

Lessons in this Chapter:

Before You Begin

To complete the hands-on exercises in this chapter, you need:

- Two Windows Server 2003 (Standard or Enterprise Edition) systems installed as Server01 and Scrver02, respectively. Server01 should currently be installed as a domain controller in the contoso.com domain.

- The contoso.com domain should be configured at the Windows 2000 Native domain functional level.

■ Server02 should be configured as a member server in the contoso.com domain. Note this might require using Dcpromo.exe to demote Server02 if Server02 is currently a domain controller.

■ The following objects in Active Directory:

❑ Top-level OUs: East, West

❑ Second-level OUs in the East OU: New York

❑ Second-level OUs in the West OU: Seattle, Phoenix

❑ Users in the Phoenix OU: Danielle Tiedt

❑ Users in the Seattle OU: Lorrin Smith-Bates

❑ Users in the New York OU: Pat Coleman

❑ Domain local group in the Seattle OU: Marketing

❑ Members of the Marketing Group: Lorrin Smith-Bates, Danielle Tiedt, Pat Coleman

■ In addition, user accounts must have the right to log on locally and to install the Administrative Tools Pack on Server02. Add the Marketing group to the Administrators local group on Server02.

Note   Keep track of the usernames and passwords you create for these user accounts, as you will be logging on as these accounts.

Lesson 1: Managing Special Folders with Group Policy

Windows Server 2003 operating systems allow you to redirect the folders containing a user's profile to a location on the network by using the Folder Redirection node in the Group Policy Object Editor console. The Offline Files feature provides users with access to redirected folders even when they are not connected to the network, and it can be set up manually or by using the Offline Folder node in Group Policy. This lesson introduces special folder redirection and walks you through the steps for setting up folder redirection using Group Policy. It also introduces the Offline Files feature and walks you through the steps for setting up Offline Files manually.

After this lesson, you will be able to

- Explain the purpose of folder redirection
- Identify the folders that can be redirected
- Explain when to redirect My Documents to a home folder
- Redirect special folders
- Explain the purpose of the Offline Files feature
- Set up Offline Files

Estimated lesson time: 35 minutes

Folder Redirection

You redirect users' folders to provide a centralized location for key Microsoft Windows XP Professional folders on a server or servers. This centralized location, called a *sharepoint*, provides users with an access point for storing and finding information, and it provides administrators with an access point for managing information. The *Folder Redirection* node in the Group Policy Object Editor console enables you to redirect certain special folders to network locations, including file shares in other forests in which two-way forests trusts have been established. The Folder Redirection node is located under User Configuration\Windows Settings in the Group Policy Object Editor console. Special folders are folders such as My Documents and My Pictures, which are located in a user's profile.

Note   The default storage location for a user profile is *%systemdrive%*\Documents and Settings*username*, where *username* is the user logon name. If the computer was upgraded from Windows NT 4.0, Windows 95, Windows 98, or Windows Millennium Edition (Me), the profile will be in *%systemroot%*\Profiles*username*.

Windows Server 2003 allows the following special folders to be redirected:

- Application Data
- Desktop
- My Documents
- My Pictures
- Start Menu

Advantages of Redirecting Folders

The following benefits pertain to redirecting any folder, but redirecting My Documents can be particularly advantageous because this folder tends to become large over time.

- Even if a user logs on to various computers on the network, his or her documents are always available.

- When roaming user profiles are used, only the network path to the My Documents folder is part of the roaming user profile, not the My Documents folder itself. Therefore, its contents do not have to be copied back and forth between the client computer and the server each time the user logs on or off, and the process of logging on or off can be much faster than it was in Microsoft Windows NT 4.0.

- Offline File technology provides users with access to My Documents even when they are not connected to the network and is particularly useful for people who use portable computers.

- Data stored on a shared network server can be backed up as part of routine system administration. This approach is safer because it requires no action on the part of the user.

- The system administrator can use Group Policy to set disk quotas, limiting the amount of space taken up by users' special folders.

- Data specific to a user can be redirected to a different hard disk on the user's local computer from the hard disk holding the operating system files. This capability makes the user's data safer if the operating system needs to be reinstalled.

Redirecting My Documents to Home Folders

In Windows Server 2003 operating systems, a new feature enables you to redirect My Documents to a user's *home folder*. This option is intended only for organizations that have already deployed home folders and want to maintain compatibility with their existing home folder environment. The ability to redirect My Documents to a user's home folder requires a Windows XP Professional client and does not function for Microsoft Windows XP Home Edition, Microsoft Windows 2000, or Windows NT clients.

When you redirect My Documents to a user's home folder, the system assumes that the administrator has set the following items correctly:

- **Security**   Security is not checked and permissions are not changed when you redirect My Documents to a user's home folder.

- **Ownership**   No ownership checks are made when you redirect My Documents to a user's home folder. Normally, folder redirection fails if a user is not the owner of the folder to which he or she is being redirected.

- **Home directory property on the user object**   When you redirect My Documents to a user's home folder, the client computer finds the path for the user's home directory from the user object in Active Directory at logon time. If this path is not set correctly for the affected users, folder redirection fails.

This relaxed security environment is why redirecting My Documents to a user's home folder is recommended only for organizations that have already deployed home folders and want to provide backward compatibility.

> **Note**   Do not redirect My Documents to a home directory location that is subject to encryption by the Encrypting File System (EFS) because only you or a domain administrator will be able to decrypt it. The user whose My Documents folder is redirected there will not be able to decrypt it.

Setting Up Folder Redirection

There are two ways to set up folder redirection:

- Redirect special folders to one location for everyone in a site, domain, or OU.

- Redirect special folders to a location according to security group membership.

To redirect special folders to one location for everyone in the site, domain, or OU, complete the following steps:

1. Open a group policy object (GPO) linked to the site, domain, or OU containing the users whose special folders you want to redirect to a network location.

2. In User Configuration, open Windows Settings, and then double-click the Folder Redirection node to view the folder you want to redirect.

3. Right-click the folder you want to redirect (Application Data, Desktop, My Documents, or Start Menu), and then click Properties.

4. In the Target tab in the Properties dialog box for the redirected folder (shown in Figure 6-1), in the Setting list, select Basic–Redirect Everyone's Folder To The Same Location.

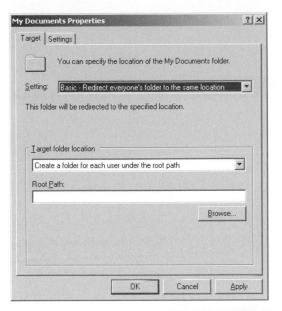

Figure 6-1   Target tab in the Properties dialog box for the redirected folder

Off the Record   Windows Server 2003 has more options for redirecting folders than Windows 2000 Server. In Windows 2000 Server, there are no selectable options for folder redirection in the target folder location section. Instead, there is only a text box where you can enter the location of the target folder. While Windows Server 2003 still offers the same features, in Windows 2000 you would have to use environment variables such as *%username%* or *%userprofile%* instead of being able to select from a drop-down list. Keep this in mind if you come across troubleshooting documents written for Windows 2000 folder redirection. You'll see one such example of this in the "Troubleshooting Lab" section near the end of this chapter.

5. In the Target Folder Location list, select the redirect location you want for this GPO from one of the following options:

  ❑ Create A Folder For Each User Under The Root Path (not available for the Start Menu folder), which creates a folder with the user's name in the root path. A new feature for Windows Server 2003 operating systems, folder redirection automatically appends the user name and the folder name when the policy is applied.

  ❑ Redirect To The Following Location, which enables you to redirect the folder to a location represented by the Uniform Naming Convention (UNC) path in the form \\servername\sharename or a valid path on the user's local computer.

❑ Redirect To The Local Userprofile Location, which enables you to redirect the folder to the default folder location in the absence of redirection by an administrator.

❑ Redirect To The User's Home Directory (available for the My Documents folder only), which enables you to redirect the user's My Documents folder to the user's home directory.

Note   Use the Redirect To The User's Home Directory option only if you have already deployed home directories in your organization. This option is intended only for organizations that want to maintain compatibility with their existing home directory environment.

6. If you have selected the Create A Folder For Each User Under The Root Path or Redirect To The Following Location option, enter the path to which the folder should be redirected, either the UNC path in the form \\servername\sharename or a valid path on the user's local computer.

7. Click the Settings tab (shown in Figure 6-2), and then set each of the following options (keeping in mind that the default settings are recommended):

❑ Grant The User Exclusive Rights To Special Folder Type (in this example, My Documents), which allows the user and the local system full rights to the folder—no one else, not even administrators, will have any rights. If this setting is disabled, no changes are made to the permissions on the folder. The permissions that apply by default remain in effect. This option is enabled by default.

Note   If you redirect My Documents to the home folder, domain administrators have Full Control permission over the user's My Documents folder, even if you enable the Grant The User Exclusive Rights To My Documents option.

❑ Move The Contents Of User's Current Special Folder Type (in this example, My Documents) To The New Location, which redirects the contents of the folder to the new location. This option is enabled by default.

Off the Record   Errors concerning Folder Redirection appear in the Application Log in the Event Viewer on the affected computers. For example, if you attempt to redirect a user's desktop and select the option Move The Contents Of Desktop To The New Location, but you fail to give the user permission to write to that folder, the user's desktop will not be redirected. If that happens, you can find errors in the Event Viewer where the user logged on indicating that the user didn't have permission to access the folder. To solve the issue, either give the user Write permission to the desktop or clear the Move The Contents Of Desktop To The New Location check box.

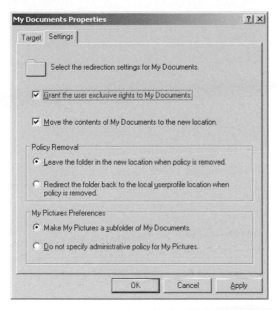

Figure 6-2   Settings tab in the Properties dialog box for the redirected folder

8. Choose one of the following options in the Policy Removal area (keeping in mind that the default setting is recommended):

   ❏ Leave The Folder In The New Location When Policy Is Removed, which leaves the folder in its new location even when the GPO no longer applies. This option is enabled by default.

   ❏ Redirect The Folder Back To The Local Userprofile Location When Policy Is Removed, which moves the folder back to its local user profile location when the GPO no longer applies.

Important   See the section "Policy Removal Considerations" later in this lesson for details on selecting a policy removal option.

9. Choose one of the following options (available for the My Documents folder only) in the My Pictures Preferences area:

   ❏ Make My Pictures A Subfolder Of My Documents, which redirects My Pictures automatically to remain a subfolder of My Documents. This option is enabled by default and is recommended.

   ❏ Do Not Specify Administrative Policy For My Pictures, which removes My Pictures as a subfolder of My Documents and has the user profile determine the location of My Pictures. With this option, the location of My Pictures is not dictated by Group Policy and a shortcut takes the place of the My Pictures folder in My Documents.

10. Click OK.

To redirect special folders to a location according to security group membership, complete the following steps:

1. Open a GPO linked to the site, domain, or OU containing the users whose special folders you want to redirect to a network location.

2. In User Configuration, open Windows Settings, and then double-click the Folder Redirection node to view the folder you want to redirect.

3. Right-click the folder you want (Application Data, Desktop, My Documents, or Start Menu), and then click Properties.

4. In the Target tab in the Properties dialog box for the folder (shown in Figure 6-1), in the Setting list, select Advanced–Specify Locations For Various User Groups and then click Add.

5. In the Specify Group And Location dialog box (shown in Figure 6-3), in the Security Group Membership box, click Browse.

Figure 6-3   Specify Group And Location dialog box

6. In the Select Group dialog box, type the name of the security group for which you want to redirect the folder and then click OK.

7. In the Specify Group And Location dialog box, in the Target Folder Location list, select the redirect location you want for this GPO from one of the following options:

❑ Create A Folder For Each User Under The Root Path (not available for the Start Menu folder), which creates a folder with the user's name in the root path. A new feature for Windows Server 2003 operating systems, folder redirection automatically appends the user name and the folder name when the policy is applied.

❑ Redirect To The Following Location, which enables you to redirect the folder to a location represented by the UNC path in the form \\servername\sharename or a valid path on the user's local computer.

❑ Redirect To The Local Userprofile Location, which enables you to redirect the folder to the default folder location in the absence of redirection by an administrator.

❑ Redirect To The User's Home Directory (available for the My Documents folder only), which enables you to redirect the user's My Documents folder to the user's home directory.

Note   Use the Redirect To The User's Home Directory option only if you have already deployed home directories in your organization. This option is intended only for organizations that want to maintain compatibility with their existing home directory environment.

8. If you have selected the Create A Folder For Each User Under The Root Path or Redirect To The Following Location option, enter the path to which the folder should be redirected, either the UNC path in the form \\servername\sharename or a valid path on the user's local computer.

9. In the Specify Group And Location dialog box, click OK.

10. If you want to redirect folders for members of other security groups, repeat steps 4 through 9 until all the groups have been entered.

11. Click the Settings tab (shown in Figure 6-2), and then set each of the following options (keeping in mind that the default settings are recommended):

❑ Grant The User Exclusive Rights To Special Folder Type, which allows the user and the local system full rights to the folder—no one else, not even administrators, will have any rights. If this setting is disabled, no changes are made to the permissions on the folder. The permissions that apply by default remain in effect. This option is enabled by default.

Note   If you redirect My Documents to the home folder, domain administrators have Full Control permission over the user's My Documents folder, even if you enable the Grant The User Exclusive Rights To My Documents option.

❑ Move The Contents Of User's Current Special Folder To The New Location, which redirects the contents of the folder to the new location. This option is enabled by default.

12. Choose one of the following options in the Policy Removal area (keeping in mind that the default setting is recommended):

❑ Leave The Folder In The New Location When Policy Is Removed, which leaves the folder in its new location even when the GPO no longer applies. This option is enabled by default.

❑ Redirect The Folder Back To The Local Userprofile Location When Policy Is Removed, which moves the folder back to its local user profile location when the GPO no longer applies.

Important   See the section "Policy Removal Considerations" later in this lesson for details on selecting a policy removal option.

13. Choose one of the following options (available for the My Documents folder only) in the My Pictures Preferences area:

❑ Make My Pictures A Subfolder Of My Documents, which redirects My Pictures automatically to remain a subfolder of My Documents. This option is enabled by default and is recommended.

❑ Do Not Specify Administrative Policy For My Pictures, which removes My Pictures as a subfolder of My Documents and has the user profile determine the location of My Pictures. With this option, the location of My Pictures is not dictated by Group Policy and a shortcut takes the place of the My Pictures folder in My Documents.

14. Click OK.

Off the Record   If you redirect a user's Application Data and the user encrypts files or folders using the Encrypting File System (EFS), the user might not be able to decrypt his or her EFS encrypted folders when he or she is not connected to the network. This occurs because the user's encryption keys are stored in the Application Data folder structure. For Windows 2000 Professional systems, network connectivity isn't an immediate issue because the encryption keys are stored in memory. However, if the user restarts, network connectivity can become an issue if it is still not available. For Windows XP Professional systems, loss of network connectivity could become an immediate issue for users trying to decrypt EFS encrypted files because the user's encryption keys are not stored in memory.

Exam Tip   Be sure you know the two ways to set up folder redirection.

Policy Removal Considerations

Table 6-1 summarizes what happens to redirected folders and their contents when a GPO no longer applies.

Table 6-1   Effects of Policy Removal Options

When the Move The Contents Of Special Folder Type To The New Location setting is...	And the Policy Removal option is...	Results when the policy is removed are...
Enabled	Redirect The Folder Back To The Local Userprofile Location When Policy Is Removed	The special folder returns to its user profile location. The contents are copied, not moved, back to the user profile location. The contents are not deleted from the location they were redirected to. The user continues to have access to the contents, but only on the local computer.
Disabled	Redirect The Folder Back To The User-profile Location When Policy Is Removed	The special folder returns to its user profile location. The contents are not copied or moved to the user profile location. *Caution*: If the contents of a folder are not copied to the user profile location, the user can no longer see them.
Either Enabled or Disabled	Leave The Folder In The New Location When Policy Is Removed	The special folder remains at the location it was redirected to. The contents remain at the location they were redirected to. The user continues to have access to the contents at the location they were redirected to.

Folder Redirection and Offline Files

As discussed earlier in this lesson, folder redirection provides users with a central network access point for storing and finding information, and it provides administrators with a central network access point for managing information. However, in the event of a network failure or for users who use portable computers, how will the users be able to access the information in redirected folders? The Offline Files feature provides users with access to redirected folders even when they are not connected to the network. *Offline Files* caches files accessed through folder redirection onto the hard drive of the local computer. When a user accesses a file in a redirected folder, the file is accessed and modified locally. When a user has finished working with the file and has logged off, only then does the file traverse the network for storage on the server.

Working Offline

If the status of your network connection changes, Offline Files provides notification by displaying an informational balloon over the notification area (lower right corner of the desktop). If the informational balloon notifies you that you are offline, you might or might not be able to continue to work with your files as you normally do. You can click the Offline Files icon in the notification area for more information about the status of your connection.

If you are working offline (either because you are disconnected from the network or because you undocked your portable computer), you can still browse network drives and shared folders in My Computer or My Network Places. A red *X* appears over any disconnected network drives. You can see only those files that you made available offline and any files that you created after the network connection was lost. Your permissions on the network files and folders remain the same whether you are connected to the network or working offline. When you are disconnected from the network, you can print to local printers, but you cannot print to shared printers on the network.

Once you reconnect to the network, the Synchronization Manager updates the network files with changes that you made while working offline. When you synchronize files, the files that you opened or updated while disconnected from the network are compared to the files that are saved on the network. As long as the files you changed haven't been changed by someone else while you were offline, your changes are copied to the network.

If someone else made changes to the same network file that you updated offline, you can keep your version, the version on the network, or both. If you delete a network file on your computer while working offline but someone else on the network makes changes to that file, the file is deleted from your computer but not from the network. If you change a network file while working offline but someone else on the network deletes that file, you can save your version onto the network or delete it from your computer. If you are disconnected from the network when a new file is added to a shared network folder that you have made available offline, the new file is added to your computer when you reconnect and synchronize.

Setting Up Offline Files

If you use redirected folders of any type, it is recommended that you set up Offline Files. However, Offline Files does not depend on settings in the Folder Redirection node and is set up and configured on network shares separately from the Folder Redirection configuration. The tasks for implementing Offline Files are:

1. Configure the sharepoint.

2. Configure computers to use Offline Files.

3. Synchronize offline files and folders.

Configuring the Sharepoint   The first step in setting up Offline Files is to configure the sharepoint. You configure the sharepoint in the Sharing tab in the Properties dialog box for the shared folder.

To configure the sharepoint, complete the following steps:

1. Right-click the shared folder containing the offline files, and select Sharing And Security.

2. In the Sharing tab in the Properties dialog box for the shared folder, click Offline Settings.

3. In the Offline Settings dialog box, shown in Figure 6-4, select one of the following options:

   ❑ Only The Files And Programs That Users Specify Will Be Available Offline. Select this option if you want users to be able to determine which files will be available offline.

   ❑ All Files And Programs That Users Open From The Share Will Be Automatically Available Offline. Select this option if you want all files that users open from the shared resource to be automatically available offline. Select the Optimized For Performance check box if you want to automatically cache programs so that they can be run locally. This option is useful for file servers that host applications because it reduces network traffic and improves server scalability.

   ❑ Files Or Programs From The Share Will Not Be Available Offline. Select this option to prevent users from storing files offline.

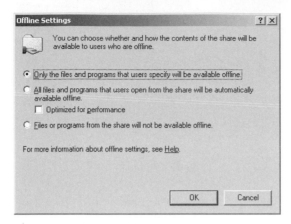

Figure 6-4   Offline Settings dialog box

4. Click OK.

5. In the Properties dialog box for the shared folder, click OK.

Configuring Computers and Servers to Use Offline Files   After you configure the sharepoint, you must configure clients to use Offline Files. Windows 2000, Windows XP, and Windows Server 2003 are able to use Offline Files. You can configure clients to use Offline Files manually in the Offline Files tab in the Folder Options dialog box for each client computer. Or, you can configure users' computers and servers to use Offline Files by setting policies in Administrative Templates/Network/Offline Files in both the Computer Configuration and User Configuration nodes. This section provides the procedure for manually configuring clients to use Offline Files.

> **Important**   In Windows Server 2003, Remote Desktop For Administration (formerly known as Terminal Services in Remote Administration mode in Windows 2000) provides remote access to the desktop of any computer running a member of the Windows Server 2003 family. Remote Desktop For Administration is installed by default on computers running Windows Server 2003, but it is not *enabled* by default.
>
> If Remote Desktop For Administration is enabled on a server, you cannot configure the server to use Offline Files because the Remote Desktop For Administration and Offline Files features are mutually exclusive. Therefore, before attempting to configure a server to use Offline Files (for the exercises in this lesson, or in a production setting), you must *disable* Remote Desktop For Administration. To do this on the server, right-click My Computer and select Properties. In the System Properties dialog box, select the Remote tab. In the Remote Desktop section, clear the Allow Users To Connect Remotely To This Computer check box and then click OK. Then configure the server to use Offline Files as described in the procedure "Configuring Computers and Servers to Use Offline Files" in this section.

To configure computers and servers to use Offline Files, complete the following steps:

1. Open My Computer.

2. On the Tools menu, click Folder Options.

3. In the Folder Options dialog box, click the Offline Files tab.

4. In the Offline Files tab, shown in Figure 6-5, select the Enable Offline Files check box. For computers running Windows 2000 Professional and Windows XP Professional, this box is selected by default.

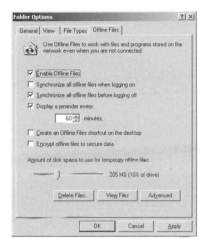

Figure 6-5   Folder Options dialog box, Offline Files tab

5. Select the Synchronize All Offline Files When Logging On check box if you want to fully synchronize offline files when a user logs on. Select the Synchronize All Offline Files Before Logging Off check box if you want to fully synchronize offline files before a user logs off. Full synchronization ensures that the network files reflect the latest changes. If you do not select these options, a quick synchronization occurs when a user logs on or off. A quick synchronization provides a complete version of online files, but it might not provide the most current version.

> **Note**   It is recommended that you always synchronize when you log on to your computer. This ensures that changes made on your computer are synchronized with changes that were made on the network while you were disconnected.

6. Select the Display A Reminder Every check box if you want to provide reminder balloons in the notification area of the desktop (lower right corner) when the computer goes offline. Specify in the Minutes box how often (in minutes) you want the reminders to appear.

7. Select the Create An Offline Files Shortcut On The Desktop check box if you want to place a shortcut to the Offline Files folder on the desktop.

8. Select the Encrypt Offline Files To Secure Data check box if you want to encrypt offline files to keep them safe from intruders who might gain unauthorized physical access to the client computer.

Note   This check box is disabled if you are not an administrator on the computer, the local drive is not NTFS or does not support encryption, or your system administrator has implemented an encryption policy for Offline Files.

9. Select the amount of disk space you want to use for temporary offline files on the slider bar in the lower portion of the Offline Files tab.

10. Click Advanced.

11. In the Offline Files–Advanced Settings dialog box, shown in Figure 6-6, select one of the following options to indicate how a computer behaves when the connection to another computer on the network is lost:

   ❑ Notify Me And Begin Working Offline. Select this option to specify that the user can work offline if the network connection is lost because network files will continue to be available.

   ❑ Never Allow My Computer To Go Offline. Select this option to specify that the user cannot work offline if the network connection is lost because network files will not be available.

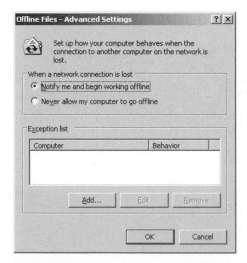

Figure 6-6   Offline Files–Advanced Settings dialog box

12. Click Add if you want a specific computer to receive a different treatment if the connection to another computer on the network is lost. If you click Add, the Offline Files–Add Custom Action dialog box appears. In the Computer box, type

the name of the computer that will receive different treatment. Then select the treatment you want the computer to receive in the When A Network Connection Is Lost section. Click OK.

13. In the Offline Files–Advanced Settings dialog box, click OK.

14. In the Folder Options dialog box, click OK.

Synchronizing Offline Files and Folders   You can determine the way you want your computer to synchronize your files when you log on and off the network. There are two ways to set up synchronization of offline files and folders. You can set up synchronization manually by using the Items To Synchronize dialog box, also referred to as the Synchronization Manager in documentation and Help. Or you can set up synchronization by setting policies in Administrative Templates/Network/Offline Files in both the Computer Configuration and User Configuration nodes. This section provides the procedure for manually setting up synchronization of offline files and folders.

To set up synchronization of offline files and folders, complete the following steps:

1. Click Start, point to All Programs, point to Accessories, and then click Synchronize.

> **Note**   You can also open the Items To Synchronize dialog box by typing **mobsync** on the command line.

2. In the Items To Synchronize dialog box, shown in Figure 6-7, click Setup.

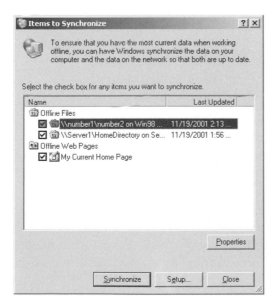

Figure 6-7   Items To Synchronize dialog box

3. In the Synchronization Settings dialog box, in the Logon/Logoff tab, shown in Figure 6-8, click the network connection that you want to use in the When I Am Using This Network Connection list.

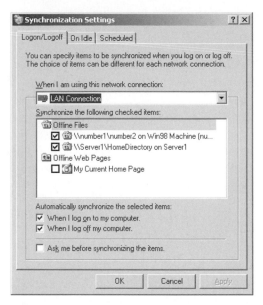

Figure 6-8   Synchronization Settings dialog box, Logon/Logoff tab

4. In the Synchronize The Following Checked Items list, select the check boxes next to the offline items that you want to synchronize, such as a folder on a mapped network drive or an Internet Explorer offline Web page.

5. Select the When I Log On To My Computer check box to synchronize the selected items when the user logs off. Select the When I Log Off My Computer check box to synchronize the selected items when the user logs off.

> **Note**   It is recommended that you always synchronize when you log on to your computer. This ensures that changes made on your computer are synchronized with changes that were made on the network while you were disconnected.

> **Note**   The When I Log On To My Computer and When I Log Off My Computer check boxes are selected by default if you selected the Synchronize All Offline Files When Logging On or Synchronize All Offline Files Before Logging Off options, respectively, in the Offline Files tab in the Folder Options dialog box. These options are part of the "Configure Computers to Use Offline Files" procedure.

6. Select the Ask Me Before Synchronizing The Items check box if you want Synchronization Manager to request permission before automatically synchronizing your offline items.

7. Click OK.

8. In the Items To Synchronize dialog box, click Close.

You can also specify items to be synchronized when a computer is idle by using the On Idle tab in the Synchronization Settings dialog box. By choosing when offline items are synchronized, you can better manage the work on your computer and on the network. Finally, you can schedule when synchronization occurs by using the Scheduled Synchronization Wizard, available from the Scheduled tab in the Synchronization Settings dialog box.

> **Note**   To manually synchronize offline files and folders immediately, right-click the file or folder you want to synchronize, and then click Synchronize.

Folder Redirection Best Practices

The following are the best practices for implementing folder redirection:

- **Allow the system to create the folders**   If you create the folders yourself, they might not have the correct permissions set.

- **Use fully qualified UNC paths, for example: \\servername\ sharename**   Although paths like C:*Foldername* can be used, it is not advisable because the path might not exist on the target computer.

> **Note**   If you use a UNC path with more than 260 characters, folder redirection fails because the path is truncated.

- **Accept defaults**   In general, accept the default folder redirection settings.

- **Place the My Pictures folder in the My Documents folder**   This is advisable unless there is a compelling reason not to, such as server scalability.

- **Consider what will happen if the policy is removed**   Keep in mind the behavior your folder redirection policies will have if the policy is removed, as described in the "Policy Removal Considerations" section earlier in the lesson.

- **Do not redirect My Documents to the home folder unless you have already deployed home directories in your organization**   Folder redirection to the home directory offers less security than standard folder redirection and is offered only for backward compatibility. If you redirect My Documents to the home directory, and if your users log on to the domain via Terminal Server clients, then don't specify a separate Terminal Services Home Directory.

■ **Enable Offline Files**   In the event of a network failure or for users who use portable computers, users must be able to access the information in redirected folders.

Troubleshooting Special Folders

Table 6-2 describes some troubleshooting scenarios when redirecting folders to network locations or using Offline Files.

Table 6-2   Folder Redirection and Offline Files Troubleshooting Scenarios

Problem: **Folders are not redirected.**

Causes	Solutions
The client computer is running Windows NT 4.0, Windows 98, or Windows 95.	Confirm that the client computer is running Windows 2000 Professional or Windows XP Professional.
Group Policy is not applied.	Verify that folder redirection Group Policy settings are applied by using Gpresult.exe.
The network share is unavailable and Offline Files is not enabled.	If the server that contains the redirected folders is offline and Offline Files is disabled, folders cannot be redirected.
The user does not have access permission to the share on which the folder is redirected.	Verify that the user has access to the folder where his or her data is redirected. Users should have Full Control permission for the redirected folder.
There is a disk quota on the target folder. A mapped drive has been used for the target path rather than a UNC path.	If a disk quota exists for the target folder, either enlarge it or have the user delete some files. A UNC path, rather than a mapped drive, is recommended for indicating the target path.

Problem: **Folder redirection is successful, but files and folders are unavailable.**

Causes	Solutions
Network connectivity problems.	Ping the server that stored the redirected folder to ensure network connectivity.
The network share is not available, and items are not available in the local cache.	Check user rights on the redirected folder. The user should have Full Control permission.
When using applications, open and save operations that do not use the redirected path.	Check the applications the user is using; some older applications might not recognize redirected folders.

Table 6-2   Folder Redirection and Offline Files Troubleshooting Scenarios

Problem: **Files available when online are not available when offline.**

Causes	Solutions
The files are located on a computer not running Windows 2000 Professional or Windows XP Professional.	Confirm that the files are located on a computer running Windows 2000 Professional or Windows XP Professional.
Offline Files is not enabled on the client computer.	Enable Offline Files on the client computer. Set Offline Files setting to automatic.
The Offline Files setting for the share is not set to automatic.	

Problem: **The user cannot make files and folders available offline.**

Causes	Solutions
Remote Desktop For Administration is enabled.	Check whether Remote Desktop For Administration is enabled by opening Properties for My Computer, selecting the Remote tab, and clearing the Allow Users To Connect Remotely To This Computer check box. Remote Desktop For Administration is not compatible with Offline Files.
The file or folder is a local file or folder and is not on a network share.	Verify that the file or folder is on a network share. Verify that Offline Files is configured.
Offline Files is not configured.	Verify that the Allow Or Disallow Use Of The Offline Files Feature setting in Computer Configuration\Administrative Templates\Network\Offline Files setting is not set to Enable.
A Group Policy setting was applied to disable Offline Files.	Verify that the folder is redirected successfully and is not local. Then verify that the user has the appropriate file security to read and write to the location where the folder is redirected.
The user does not have access to the file share.	

Table 6-2   Folder Redirection and Offline Files Troubleshooting Scenarios

Problem: **Files do not synchronize.**

Causes	Solutions
Files with extensions .mdb, .ldb, .mdw, .mde, and .db are not synchronized by default.	Verify extensions of files to be synchronized.
There are network connection problems when accessing the files to be synchronized.	Use Ping.exe to verify that the user can connect to the file share containing the files to be synchronized.
There is insufficient disk space on the client computer to synchronize files.	Check the amount of free disk space on the client.
There are insufficient user rights to read or write the files to be synchronized.	Verify that the Files Not Cached setting in Computer Configuration\Administrative Templates\Network\Offline Files setting is not set to Enable.
A Group Policy setting was applied specifying additional file name extensions that are not synchronized.	

Practice: Managing Special Folders

In this practice, you set up folder redirection. Normally, folder redirection is configured for users running Windows XP Professional clients. However, for training purposes, this practice configures folder redirection for a user on Server02.

Exercise 1: Setting Up Folder Redirection

In this exercise, you redirect Lorrin Smith-Bates's My Documents folder to a sharepoint on Server01.

To set up folder redirection, follow these steps:

1. Log on to Server01 as Administrator.

2. Create a shared folder named C:\Users on Server01, and share the folder with the sharename **Users**.

3. Modify the default share permissions so that Everyone is allowed Full Control. This is necessary for folder redirection to work properly. The access to the folder and its subfolders will be controlled by NTFS permissions set on the folder's access control list (ACL). The default ACL (seen on the Security tab of the folder's properties dialog box) provides best-practice security and functionality for folder redirection.

4. Create a GPO linked to the Seattle OU named **Special Folder Redirection**. Use the procedures provided earlier in this lesson to redirect the My Documents folder to \\Server01\Users. Set the Target Folder Location to Create A Folder For Each User Under The Root Path.

5. Log on to Server02, as Lorrin Smith-Bates. What happened in the Users folder on Server01?

   The folder for Lorrin Smith-Bates is created when he logs on. Inside the user's folder is another folder, My Documents. As an administrator, you cannot view the contents of Lorrin Smith-Bates's My Documents folder without permission from that user, or without taking ownership of the folder and granting yourself permissions.

6. Log off of Server02.

Lesson Review

The following questions are intended to reinforce key information presented in this lesson. If you are unable to answer a question, review the lesson materials and try the question again. You can find answers to the questions in the "Questions and Answers" section at the end of this chapter.

1. What is the purpose of folder redirection?

   _____

   _____

   _____

   _____

2. Which folders can be redirected?

   _____

   _____

3. Under what circumstances should you redirect My Documents to a home folder?

   _____

   _____

   _____

4. What is the purpose of the Offline Files feature?

   _____

   _____

5. Which of the following are true statements? (Choose all that apply.)

   a. Remote Desktop For Administration is installed by default on computers running Windows Server 2003.

   b. Remote Desktop For Administration is enabled by default on computers running Windows Server 2003.

  c. A server can be configured to use Offline Files and Remote Desktop For Administration at the same time.

  d. A server cannot be configured to use Offline Files and Remote Desktop For Administration at the same time.

  e. Before attempting to configure the computer to use Offline Files, you must disable Remote Desktop For Administration.

  f. Before attempting to configure the computer to use Offline Files, you must enable Remote Desktop For Administration.

  _____

  _____

  _____

  _____

  _____

  _____

6. Which of the following actions should you take if folder redirection is successful but files and folders are unavailable? (Choose all that apply.)

  a. Check the user's permissions for the redirected folder.

  b. Check network connectivity.

  c. Check that the redirected folder exists.

  d. Check to see whether Remote Desktop for Administration is enabled.

  e. Check to see whether the files have extensions that are not synchronized by default.

  _____

  _____

  _____

  _____

  _____

  _____

  _____

Lesson Summary

- The Folder Redirection node, located under User Configuration\Windows Settings in the Group Policy Object Editor console, enables you to redirect certain special folders to network locations. Windows Server 2003 operating systems allow the following special folders to be redirected: Application Data, Desktop, My Documents, My Pictures, and Start Menu.

- In Windows Server 2003 operating systems, a new feature enables you to redirect My Documents to a user's home folder. This option is intended only for organizations that have already deployed home folders and that want to maintain compatibility with an existing home folder environment. The ability to redirect My Documents to a user's home folder requires a Windows XP Professional client.

- There are two ways to set up folder redirection:

  1. Redirect special folders to one location for everyone in the site, domain, or OU.

  2. Redirect special folders to a location according to security group membership.

- The Offline Files feature provides users with access to redirected folders even when they are not connected to the network. If you use redirected folders of any type, it is recommended that you set up Offline Files.

- The tasks for implementing Offline Files are configure the sharepoint, configure computers to use Offline Files, and set up synchronization of offline files and folders.

Lesson 2: Managing Software Deployment with Group Policy

Software Installation And Maintenance is a feature of Microsoft IntelliMirror, which works in conjunction with Group Policy. Software Installation And Maintenance is the administrator's primary tool for managing software within an organization. Managing software with Software Installation And Maintenance provides users with immediate access to the software they need to perform their jobs and ensures that they have an easy and consistent experience when working with software throughout its life cycle. This lesson introduces you to software deployment with Group Policy.

After this lesson, you will be able to

- Identify the requirements for deploying software by using Group Policy
- Describe the tools provided for software development
- Differentiate between assigning applications and publishing applications
- Explain the purpose of Windows Installer packages
- Describe the three types of Windows Installer packages
- Explain the purpose of modifications
- Describe the two types of modifications
- Describe the steps in the software deployment process

Estimated lesson time: 15 minutes

Understanding Software Deployment with Group Policy

You use the Software Installation And Maintenance feature of IntelliMirror to create a managed software environment with the following characteristics:

- Users have access to the applications they need to do their jobs, no matter which computer they log on to.

- Computers have the required applications, without intervention from a technical support representative.

- Applications can be updated, maintained, or removed to meet the needs of the organization.

The Software Installation And Maintenance feature of IntelliMirror works in conjunction with Group Policy and Active Directory, establishing a Group Policy–based software management system. To deploy software by using Group Policy, an organization must be running an Active Directory domain, and client computers must be running Windows 2000 Professional or later.

The following tools are provided for software deployment with Group Policy:

- **Software Installation extension**   Located in the Group Policy Object Editor console on the server, this extension is used by administrators to manage software.

- **Add Or Remove Programs**   Located in Control Panel on the client machine, this option is used by users to manage software on their own computers.

Software Installation Extension

The *Software Installation* extension in the Group Policy Object Editor console, seen as the first node under the Computer Configuration and User Configuration nodes, is the key administrative tool for deploying software, allowing administrators to centrally manage

- Initial deployment of software

- Upgrades, patches, and quick fixes for software

- Removal of software

By using the Software Installation extension, you can centrally manage the installation of software on a client computer by assigning applications to users or computers or by publishing applications for users. You *assign* required or mandatory software to users or to computers. You *publish* software that users might find useful to perform their jobs. Both assigned and published software is stored in a *software distribution point (SDP)*, a network location from which users are able to get the software that they need. In Windows Server 2003, the network location can include SDPs located in other forests in which two-way forests trusts have been established.

> **Exam Tip**   Know the difference between assigning software and publishing software.

Assigning Applications

When you assign an application to a user, the application's local registry settings, including filename extensions, are updated and its shortcuts are created on the Start menu or desktop, thus advertising the availability of the application. The application advertisement follows the user regardless of which physical computer he or she logs on to. This application is installed the first time the user activates the application on the computer, either by selecting the application on the Start menu or by opening a document associated with the application.

When you assign an application to the computer, the application is advertised, and the installation is performed when it is safe to do so—the installation does not wait for a user to invoke the application. Typically, applications assigned to a computer are fully installed when the computer starts up so that there are no processes running on the computer that might interfere with installation.

Publishing Applications

When you publish an application to users, the application does not appear installed on the users' computers. No shortcuts are visible on the desktop or Start menu, and no updates are made to the local registry on the users' computers. Instead, published applications store their advertisement attributes in Active Directory. Then, information such as the application's name and file associations is exposed to the users in the Active Directory container. The application is available for the user to install by using Add Or Remove Programs in Control Panel or by clicking a file associated with the application (such as an .xls file for Microsoft Excel).

The Windows Installer Service

The Software Installation extension uses the *Windows Installer service* to systematically maintain software. The Windows Installer service runs in the background and allows the operating system to manage the installation process in accordance with the information in the Windows Installer package. The *Windows Installer package* is a file containing information that describes the installed state of the application.

Because the Windows Installer service manages the state of the installation, it always knows the state of the software. If there is a problem during software installation, Windows Installer can return the computer to its last known good state. If you need to modify features after software installation, Windows Installer allows you to do so. Because the Software Installation extension uses Windows Installer, users can take advantage of self-repairing applications. Windows Installer notes when a program file is missing and immediately reinstalls the damaged or missing files, thereby fixing the application. Finally, Windows Installer enables you to remove the software when it is no longer needed.

The Windows Installer service itself is affected by settings in Group Policy. You can find these settings in the Windows Installer node, which is located in the Windows Components node in the Administrative Templates node, for both the Computer Configuration and User Configuration nodes.

Windows Installer Packages   A Windows Installer package is a file that contains explicit instructions on the installation and removal of specific applications. You can deploy software using the Software Installation extension by using a Windows Installer package. There are two types of Windows Installer packages:

- **Native Windows Installer package (.msi) files**   These files have been developed as a part of the application and take full advantage of Windows Installer. The author or publisher of the software can supply a natively authored Windows Installer package.

- **Repackaged application (.msi) files**   These files are used to repackage applications that do not have a native Windows Installer package. Although repackaged Windows Installer packages work the same as native Windows Installer packages, a repackaged Windows Installer package contains a single product with all the components and applications associated with that product installed as a single feature. A native Windows Installer package contains a single product with many features that can be individually installed as separate features.

Customizing Windows Installer Packages   You can customize Windows Installer packages by using *modifications*, also called *transforms*. The Windows Installer package format provides for customization by allowing you to transform the original package by using authoring and repackaging tools. Some applications also provide wizards or templates that permit a user to create modifications.

For example, Microsoft Office XP supplies a Custom Installation Wizard that builds modifications. Using the Office XP Custom Installation Wizard, you can create a modification that allows you to manage the configuration of Office XP that is deployed to users. A modification might be designed to accommodate Microsoft Word as a key feature, installing it during the first installation. Less popular features, such as revision support or document translators, could install on first usage; other features, such as clip art, might not install at all. You might have another modification that provides all the features of Word and Excel but does not install Microsoft PowerPoint. In addition, you can make modifications to customize the installation of a Windows Installer package at the time of assignment or publication. The exact mix of which features to install and when to install them varies based on the audience for the application and how they use the software. You can use the following file types to modify an existing Windows Installer package:

- **Transform (.mst) files**   These files provide a means for customizing the installation of an application.

- **Patch (.msp) files**   These files are used to update an existing .msi file for software patches, service packs, and some software update files, including bug fixes. An .msp file provides instructions about applying the updated files and registry keys in the software patch, service pack, or software update.

Note   You cannot deploy .mst or .msp files alone. They must modify an existing Windows Installer package.

Application (.zap) Files

You can also deploy software using the Software Installation extension by using an *application file*. Application files are text files that contain instructions about how to publish an application, taken from an existing setup program (Setup.exe or Install.exe). Application files use the .zap extension.

Use .zap files when you can't justify developing a native Windows Installer package or repackaging the application to create a repackaged Windows Installer package. A .zap file does not support the features of Windows Installer. When you deploy an application by using a .zap file, the application is installed by using its original Setup.exe or Install.exe program. The software can only be published and users can only select it by using Add Or Remove Programs in Control Panel. It is recommended that you use .msi files to deploy software with Group Policy whenever possible.

Note   For more information on creating .zap files, see Microsoft Knowledge Base article 231747 titled "HOW TO: Publish non-MSI Programs with .zap Files."

Add Or Remove Programs in Control Panel

Add Or Remove Programs in Control Panel enables users to install, modify, or remove an existing published application or repair a damaged application. You can control which software is available to users within Add Or Remove Programs in Control Panel by using Group Policy settings. Users no longer need to look for a network share, use a CD-ROM, or install, fix, and upgrade software themselves. Publishing applications in Add Or Remove Programs is discussed more later in this lesson and in Lesson 3.

Software Deployment Approaches

Given that software can be either assigned or published, and targeted to users or computers, you can establish a workable combination to meet your software management goals. Table 6-3 details the different software deployment approaches.

Table 6-3   Software Deployment Approaches

	Publish (user only)	Assign (user)	Assign (computer)
After deployment, the software is available for installation:	The next time a user logs on.	The next time a user logs on.	The next time the computer starts.
Typically, the user installs the software from:	Add Or Remove Programs in Control Panel.	Start menu or desktop short-cut.	The software is already installed. (The software automatically installs when the computer reboots.)
If the software is not installed and the user opens a file associated with the software, does the software install?	Yes (if auto-install is turned on).	Yes.	Does not apply; the software is already installed.

Table 6-3   **Software Deployment Approaches**

	Publish (user only)	**Assign (user)**	**Assign (computer)**
Can the user remove the software by using Add Or Remove Programs in Control Panel?	Yes, and the user can choose to install it again from Add Or Remove Programs in Control Panel.	Yes, and the software is available for installation again from the typical install points.	No. Only the local administrator can remove the software; a user can run a repair on the software.
Supported installation files:	Windows Installer packages (.msi files), .zap files.	Windows Installer packages (.msi files).	Windows Installer packages (.msi files).

Modifications (.mst or .msp files) are customizations applied to Windows Installer packages. A modification must be applied at the time of assignment or publication, not at the time of installation.

Software Deployment Processes

The steps in software deployment vary, depending on whether the application is published or assigned and whether the application is automatically installed by activating a document associated with the application.

Software Deployment Process for Published Applications

The following sequence shows the installation process for published applications:

1. The user logs on to a client computer running Windows 2000 or later.

2. The user opens Add Or Remove Programs in Control Panel.

3. Add Or Remove Programs obtains the list of published software from Active Directory.

4. The user selects the desired application.

5. Add Or Remove Programs obtains the location of published software from Active Directory.

6. A request for the software is sent to the SDP.

7. The Windows Installer service is started, and it installs the requested Windows Installer package.

8. The user opens the newly-installed application.

Software Deployment Process for Assigned Applications

The following sequence shows the installation process for assigned applications:

1. The user logs on to a client computer running Windows 2000 or later.

2. The WinLogon process advertises applications on the user's desktop or on the Start menu.

3. The user selects the desired application from the desktop or the Start menu.

4. The Windows Installer service gets the Windows Installer package.

5. A request for the software is sent to the SDP.

6. The Windows Installer service is started, it installs the requested Windows Installer package, and it opens the application.

Software Deployment Process for Automatically Installed Applications

The following sequence shows the installation process for automatically installed applications, whether published or assigned:

1. The user logs on to a client computer running Windows 2000 or later.

2. The user double-clicks a document with an unknown filename extension.

3. Windows Server 2003 looks for information about the application in the local computer registry.

4. One of the following steps is taken:

   ❑ If information about the application is found in the local computer registry, the registry points to the location of the application on the SDP and the corresponding Windows Installer package is started. The Windows Installer service installs the package for the user and opens the application.

   ❑ If information about the application is not found in the local computer registry, Windows Server 2003 looks for information in Active Directory. If information about the application is found in Active Directory, it points to the location of the application on the SDP. The Windows Installer service installs the package for the user and opens the application.

Distributing Windows Installer Packages

Because the Windows Installer service is part of the operating system, it does not matter how Windows Installer packages get to the client computer. If you are deploying software to many users in a large organization that is using Windows 2000 Server or later and Active Directory, and all the workstations are using Windows 2000 Professional or later, you can deploy software with Group Policy. For large-scale deployments or deployments with computers running pre–Windows 2000 operating systems, you might also consider using the Microsoft Systems Management Server (SMS) along with Group Policy to handle software deployment.

Software deployment with Group Policy uses a *pull model*, which makes software available to users as it is needed. Applications are fully installed when a user chooses to use a user-assigned application for the first time or selects a file by choosing the file-name extension of an application. For a satisfactory end-user experience, software deployment with Group Policy requires a high-speed local area network (LAN) connection between the client computer and the distribution server containing the SDP.

SMS supports a robust distribution model that you can use when deploying software with Group Policy. You can use SMS to analyze your network infrastructure for software distribution and then use Group Policy to target users and computers and to install the software. SMS is a particularly useful tool if you are deploying software to many users in a large organization. It includes desktop management and software distribution features that significantly automate the task of upgrading software on client computers.

SMS uses a *push model* for software deployment, which you can use to coordinate and schedule software deployments—even arranging for off-hours distribution and installation—and to plan a single or multiple-phase rollout of software. It provides you with the ability to control and synchronize software deployments over multiple sites, helping to reduce compatibility issues that might otherwise occur.

The following are some areas where you might want to supplement software deployment with Group Policy by using SMS:

- **Non–Windows 2000–based clients**   SMS can distribute Windows Installer–based software to computers running Microsoft Windows 95 or later. Although you cannot centrally manage the non–Windows 2000–based computers with Group Policy settings, SMS allows these computers to benefit from the capabilities built into the Windows Installer service, such as self-repairing applications.

- **Deploying software over slow links**   By default, software deployment with Group Policy does not operate over slow network or dial-up connections. SMS provides options for deploying software to users who can connect only over slow network links, such as mobile users.

- **Software licensing and metering**   Software deployment with Group Policy does not have the ability to license or meter software.

- **Identification of computer configurations**   Before you distribute a managed application, you can use SMS to determine current computer configurations to make sure that the appropriate computers have the necessary system requirements to run the application.

Configuring SMS to handle software deployment is beyond the scope of this training kit. You can find detailed information about SMS in the *Microsoft Windows Server 2003 Resource Kit* from Microsoft Press.

Lesson Review

The following questions are intended to reinforce key information presented in this lesson. If you are unable to answer a question, review the lesson materials and try the question again. You can find answers to the questions in the "Questions and Answers" section at the end of this chapter.

1. What are the hardware requirements for deploying software by using Group Policy?

   _____

   _____

   _____

2. Describe the tools provided for software deployment.

   _____

   _____

   _____

3. What is the difference between assigning applications and publishing applications?

   _____

   _____

   _____

   _____

   _____

   _____

   _____

   _____

   _____

4. What is the purpose of Windows Installer packages?

   _____

   _____

5. Which of the following file extensions allows you to deploy software by using the Software Installation extension? (Choose all that apply.)

   a. .mst

   b. .msi

   c. .zap

   d. .zip

   e. .msp

   f. .aas

Lesson Summary

- The Software Installation extension in the Group Policy Object Editor console enables administrators to centrally manage the installation of software on a client computer by assigning applications to users or computers or by publishing applications for users.

- When you assign an application to a user, the application is advertised to the user on the Start menu the next time he or she logs on to a workstation, and local registry settings, including filename extensions, are updated. The application advertisement follows the user regardless of which physical computer he or she logs on to. Assign required or mandatory software to users or to computers.

- When you publish the application to users, the application does not appear installed on the users' computers. No shortcuts are visible on the desktop or Start menu, and no updates are made to the local registry on the users' computers. If users choose, they can install the software from Add Or Remove Programs in Control Panel. Publish software that users might find useful to perform their jobs.

■ A Windows Installer package is a file that contains explicit instructions on the installation and removal of specific applications. You can deploy software using the Software Installation extension by using a Windows Installer package. Windows Installer packages can be native or repackaged .msi files.

■ Modifications enable you to customize Windows Installer packages. Modifications can be transform (.mst) or patch (.msp) files. You cannot deploy .mst or .msp files alone. They must modify an existing Windows Installer package.

Lesson 3: Distributing Software with Group Policy

After you've familiarized yourself with the software deployment tools, the Windows Installer service, and the software deployment processes, you're ready to learn how to deploy software with Group Policy. This lesson walks you through the steps of deploying software with Group Policy.

After this lesson, you will be able to

- Plan and prepare a software deployment
- Set up an SDP
- Create a GPO for software deployment
- Specify software deployment properties for a GPO
- Add Windows Installer packages to a GPO
- Set Windows Installer package properties

Estimated lesson time: 45 minutes

Steps to Deploy Software with Group Policy

The tasks for deploying software with Group Policy are as follows:

1. Plan and prepare the software deployment.

2. Set up an SDP.

3. Create a GPO and a GPO console for software deployment.

4. Specify the software deployment properties for the GPO.

5. Add Windows Installer packages to the GPO, and select a package deployment method.

6. Set Windows Installer package properties.

Exam Tip   Know the tasks for deploying software with Group Policy.

Planning and Preparing a Software Deployment

Before you can begin deploying software with Group Policy, you must plan the deployment. When planning for software deployment, you should

- Review your organization's software requirements on the basis of your overall organizational structure within Active Directory and your available GPOs
- Determine how you want to deploy your applications

- Create a pilot to test how you want to assign or publish software to users or computers

- Prepare your software using a format that allows you to manage it based on what your organization requires, and test all Windows Installer packages or repackaged software

- Gather the Windows Installer packages (.msi files) for the software. Perform any necessary modifications to the packages and gather the transform (.mst) or patch (.msp) files

Table 6-4 describes strategies and considerations for deploying software. Some of these strategies might seem contradictory, but select the strategies that meet your business goals.

Table 6-4   Strategies and Considerations for Deploying Software

Strategy	Considerations
Create OUs based on software management needs.	Allows you to target applications to the appropriate set of users. Group Policy security settings are not required to target the appropriate set of users.
Deploy software close to the root in the Active Directory tree.	Makes it easy to provide all users in an organization with access to an application. This reduces administration because you can deploy a single GPO rather than having to re-create a GPO in multiple containers deep in the Active Directory tree.
Deploy multiple applications with a single GPO.	Reduces administration overhead by allowing you to create and manage a single GPO rather than multiple GPOs. The logon process is faster because a single GPO deploying 10 applications processes faster than 10 GPOs, each deploying one application. This strategy is appropriate in organizations where users share the same core set of applications.
Publish or assign an application only once in the same GPO or in a series of GPOs that might apply to a single user or computer.	Makes it easier to determine which instance of the application applies to the user or computer.

 Note   Software licenses are required for software written by independent software vendors and distributed using SDPs. It is your responsibility to match the number of users who can access software to the number of licenses you have on hand. It is also your responsibility to verify that you are working within the guidelines provided by each independent software vendor with the software.

Setting Up an SDP

After you have planned and prepared for software management, the next step is to copy the software to one or more SDPs, network locations from which users are able to get the software that they need.

To set up an SDP, complete the following steps:

1. Create the folders for the software on the file server that will be the SDP, and make the folders network shares—for example: \\servername\sharename\.

2. Copy the software, packages, modifications, all necessary files, and components to a folder on the SDP.

> **Note**   Some software supports special commands to facilitate the creation of an SDP. For example, Office XP should be prepared by running *setup /a* from a command prompt. This allows you to enter the software key once for all users, and to enter the network share (SDP) location to copy the files to. Other software might have other ways to expand any compressed files from the distribution media and transfer the files to the appropriate location.

3. Set the appropriate permissions on the folders. Administrators must be able to change the files (Full Control), and users must only view (Read) the files from the SDP folders and shares. Use Group Policy to manage the software within the appropriate GPO.

Using DFS to Manage SDPs

The Microsoft Distributed File System (DFS) provides users with convenient access to shared folders that are distributed throughout a network. With DFS, you can make files distributed across multiple servers appear to users as if they reside in one place on the network. For a software deployment with Group Policy, you can set up DFS to automatically direct users to the nearest SDP. Configuring DFS to manage SDPs is beyond the scope of this training kit. You can find detailed information about configuring DFS in the *Microsoft Windows Server 2003 Resource Kit* from Microsoft Press.

Creating a GPO and a GPO Console for Software Deployment

In this step, you create a GPO and a GPO console for the software deployment. The procedures for creating a GPO and a GPO console are covered in Chapter 5.

Specifying Software Deployment Properties for the GPO

In this step, you define the default settings for all Windows Installer packages in the GPO in the Software Installation Properties dialog box. The Software Installation Properties dialog box consists of the following tabs—General, Advanced, File Extensions, and Categories.

In the General and Advanced tabs, you specify how you want all Windows Installer packages in the GPO to be deployed and managed.

In the File Extensions tab, you specify which application users install when they select a file with an unknown extension. You can also configure a priority for installing applications when multiple applications are associated with an unknown file extension.

For example, if you use a GPO to deploy both Microsoft Office XP Professional and Microsoft FrontPage 2002, both applications can edit Spreadsheet Load Library files with the .sll extension. To configure the file extension priority so that users who are managed by this GPO always install FrontPage, set FrontPage as the application with the highest priority for the .sll extension. When a user managed by this GPO who has installed neither Microsoft Word 2002 nor FrontPage 2002 receives an .sll file (by e-mail or other means) and double-clicks the .sll file, Software Installation installs FrontPage 2000 and opens the .sll file for editing. Without Software Installation, the user would see the Open With dialog box and be asked to select the best alternative from the software already present on his or her computer. File extension associations are managed on a per-GPO basis. Changing the priority order in a GPO affects only users who have that GPO applied to them.

In the Categories tab, you can designate categories for organizing assigned and published applications to make it easier for users to locate the appropriate application from within Add Or Remove Programs in Control Panel.

 Note Some settings in the Software Installation Properties dialog box can be fine-tuned at the package level by editing the Properties dialog box for a specific Windows Installer package.

To specify software deployment properties for the GPO, complete the following steps:

1. Open the GPO console for the software deployment.

2. In the User Configuration or Computer Configuration node, right-click the Software Installation node and then click Properties.

3. In the General tab of the Software Installation Properties dialog box (shown in Figure 6-9), type the Uniform Naming Convention (UNC) path (\\servername\sharename) to the SDP for the Windows Installer packages (.msi files) in the GPO in the Default Package Location box.

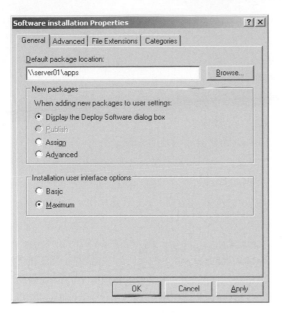

Figure 6-9   General tab of the Software Installation Properties dialog box

4. In the New Packages section, select one of the following options:

❑ Display The Deploy Software Dialog Box, which specifies that when you add new packages to the GPO, the Deploy Software dialog box will display, allowing you to choose whether to assign, publish, or configure package properties. This is the default setting.

❑ Publish, which specifies that when you add new packages to the GPO, they will be published by default with standard package properties. Packages can be published only to users, not computers. If this is an installation under the Computer Configuration node of the Group Policy Object Editor console, the Publish choice is unavailable.

❑ Assign, which specifies that when you add new packages to the GPO, they will be assigned by default with standard package properties. Packages can be assigned to users and computers.

❑ Advanced, which specifies that when you add new packages to the GPO, the Properties dialog box for the package will display, allowing you to configure all properties for the package.

5. In the Installation User Interface Options section, select one of the following options:

   ❑ Basic, which provides only a basic display for users during the installation of all packages in the GPO.

   ❑ Maximum, which provides all installation messages and screens for users during the installation of all packages in the GPO.

6. Click the Advanced tab. In the Advanced tab, shown in Figure 6-10, select any of the following options to be applied to all packages in the GPO:

   ❑ Uninstall The Applications When They Fall Out Of The Scope Of Management, which removes the application if it no longer applies to users or computers.

Off the Record   In rare instances, when applications installed with Software Installation cannot be uninstalled by using Group Policy or Add/Remove Programs, you can use the Msicuu.exe (Windows Installer Cleanup Utility) or the Msizap.exe (Windows Installer Zapper) programs. Msicuu and Msizap remove registry entries from a faulty installation. These utilities are part of the Windows Support Tools on the Windows Server 2003 CD in the Support\Tools folder. Msicuu is a graphical utility and Msizap is the command line version. MSICUU uses MSIZAP to remove applications. For detailed information about using these commands, refer to the Support Tools Help.

   ❑ Include OLE Information When Deploying Applications, which specifies whether to deploy information about Component Object Model (COM) components with the package.

   ❑ Make 32-Bit X86 Windows Installer Applications Available To Win64 Machines, which specifies whether 32-bit Windows Installer Applications (.msi files) can be assigned or published to 64-bit computers.

   ❑ Make 32-Bit X86 Down-Level (ZAP) Applications Available To Win64 Machines, which specifies whether 32-bit application files (.zap files) can be assigned or published to 64-bit computers.

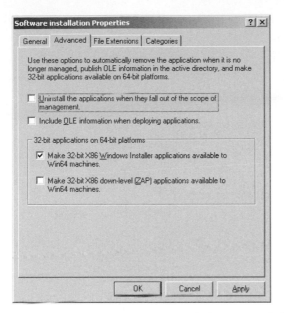

Figure 6-10   Advanced tab of the Software Installation Properties dialog box

7. Click the File Extensions tab. In the File Extensions tab, shown in Figure 6-11, select the file extension for which you want to specify an automatic software installation from the Select File Extension list.

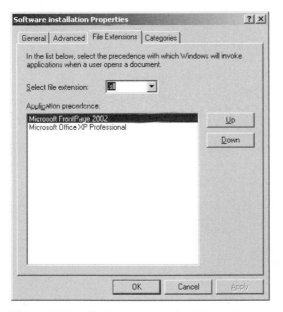

Figure 6-11   File Extensions tab of the Software Installation Properties dialog box

8. In the Application Precedence list box, move the application with the highest precedence to the top of the list by using the Up or Down button. The application at the top of the list is automatically installed if a document with the selected file-name extension is invoked before the application has been installed.

9. Click the Categories tab. In the Categories tab, shown in Figure 6-12, click Add.

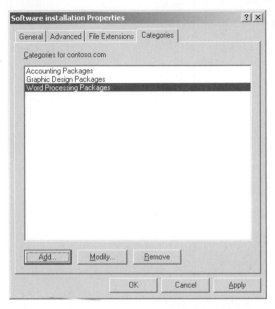

Figure 6-12   The Categories tab of the Software Installation Properties dialog box

10. In the Enter New Category dialog box, type the name of the application category to be used for the domain in the Category box and click OK.

> **Note**   The application categories that you establish are per domain, not per GPO. You need to define them only once for the whole domain.

11. Click OK.

Adding Windows Installer Packages to the GPO and Selecting Package Deployment Method

In this step, you specify the software applications you want to deploy by adding Windows Installer packages to the GPO. Then you specify how the package is deployed (either assigned or published).

Note   The procedures in this step assume that you have chosen the Display The Deploy Software Dialog Box option (the default option that allows you to choose whether to assign or publish the application) in the software deployment properties for the GPO.

To modify or update the software application, any modifications must be associated with the Windows Installer package at deployment time rather than when the Windows Installer is actually using the package. Transform (.mst) and patch (.msp) files are applied to Windows Installer packages (which have the .msi extension) in an order specified by the administrator. This order must be determined before the application is assigned or published.

To add Windows Installer packages to the GPO and select a package deployment method, complete the following steps:

1. Open the GPO console for the software deployment. In the Computer Configuration or User Configuration node, open Software Settings.

2. Right-click the Software Installation node, click New, and then click Package.

3. In the Open dialog box, in the File Name list, type the UNC path (\\servername \sharename) to the SDP for the Windows Installer packages (.msi files), and press ENTER. Select the .msi file, and then click Open.

Caution   Be sure to enter the UNC path to the SDP in the File Name list. If you merely browse and select the Windows Installer package to be added to the GPO, you have entered only the local path and clients will not be able to find the Windows Installer package.

4. In the Deploy Software dialog box (shown in Figure 6-13), click one of the following options:

   ❑ Published, which publishes the Windows Installer package to users without applying modifications to the package.

Note   If this is an application under the Computer Configuration node of the Group Policy Object Editor console, the Published option is unavailable, because packages can only be assigned to computers, not published.

   ❑ Assigned, which assigns the Windows Installer package to users or computers without applying modifications to the package.

   ❑ Advanced, which sets properties for the Windows Installer package, including published or assigned options and modifications.

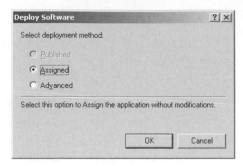

Figure 6-13   Deploy Software dialog box

5. Click OK. If you selected Published or Assigned, the Windows Installer package has been successfully added to the GPO and appears in the details pane. If you selected Advanced, the Properties dialog box for the Windows Installer package opens, where you can set properties for the Windows Installer package, such as deployment options and modifications. Setting Windows Installer package properties is covered in the next section.

Setting Windows Installer Package Properties

In this step, you can fine-tune the deployment of each application by setting Windows Installer package properties in the Properties dialog box for the package. The Properties dialog box for the Windows Installer package contains the following tabs:

- **General tab**   You can change the default name of the package and designate a support URL. Users can select a support URL from the Add Or Remove Programs window to be directed to a support Web page. A support URL can contain helpful information such as frequently asked questions (FAQs) and can assist in reducing calls to a help desk or support team.

- **Deployment tab**   You can designate the deployment type, deployment options, and installation user interface options. In the Upgrades tab, you can deploy a package that upgrades an existing package.

- **Upgrades tab**   This tab does not appear for packages created from application files (.zap files). Using the Upgrades tab is discussed in Lesson 4.

- **Categories tab**   You can select the categories under which the application is listed for users in Add Or Remove Programs in Control Panel, making it easier for users to find the application. Categories you set generally pertain to published applications only, as assigned applications do not appear in Add Or Remove Programs.

- **Modifications**   You can indicate the modifications (transforms or patches) you want to apply to the package and specify the order in which the modifications apply to the package.

■ **Security**   You can indicate permissions for the software installation. Permissions set for software installation pertain only to the package installation.

> **Note**   Some settings in the Properties dialog box for the Windows Installer package can be set at the GPO level by editing the Software Installation Properties dialog box.

To set Windows Installer package properties, complete the following steps:

1. Open the GPO console for the software deployment. In the Computer Configuration or User Configuration node, open Software Settings.

2. Click the Software Installation node.

3. In the details pane, right-click the package for which you want to set properties and then click Properties.

4. In the General tab of the Properties dialog box for the package, shown in Figure 6-14, you can type a new name for the package in the Name box, if desired. You can also type a URL that provides user support in the URL box.

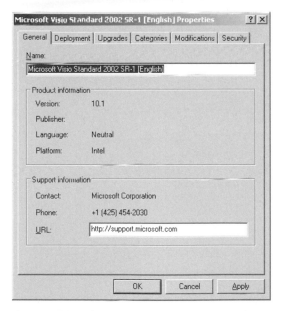

Figure 6-14   Properties dialog box for a package, General tab

5. Click the Deployment tab. In the Deployment tab of the Properties dialog box for the package, shown in Figure 6-15, select one of the following options in the Deployment Type area:

❑ Published, which allows users in the selected site, domain, or OU to install the application by using either Add Or Remove Programs in Control Panel or application installation by file activation. If this is an application under the Computer Configuration node of the Group Policy Object Editor console, the Published option is unavailable, because packages can only be assigned to computers, not published.

❑ Assigned, which allows users in the selected site, domain, or OU to receive this application the next time they log on (for assignment to users) or when the computer restarts (for assignment to computers).

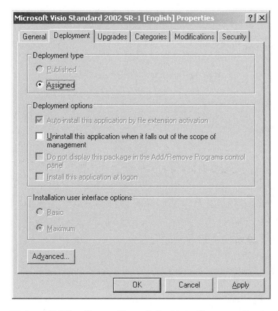

Figure 6-15 Properties dialog box for a package, Deployment tab

6. In the Deployment Options area, select one of the following options:

❑ **Auto-Install** This Application By File Extension Activation, which uses the application precedence for the filename extension as determined in the File Extensions tab of the Software Installation Properties dialog box. If this is an application under the Computer Configuration node of the Group Policy Object Editor console, the check box appears dimmed and selected, because by default the application is installed automatically.

❑ **Uninstall This Application**   When It Falls Out Of The Scope Of Management, which removes the application when users log on or computers start up in the event of relocation to a site, domain, or OU for which the application is not deployed.

❑ **Do Not Display**   This Package In The Add/Remove Programs Control Panel, which specifies that this package should not be displayed in Add Or Remove Programs in Control Panel.

❑ **Install**   This Application At Logon, which specifies that this package should be fully installed rather than just advertised by a shortcut. This option is available only for assigned applications. Avoid this option if the computer or user to which the application is assigned has a slow connection because the startup and logon procedures require a large amount of time when the application is first assigned.

7. In the Installation User Interface Options area, select one of the following options:

❑ Basic, which provides only a basic display to users during the install process.

❑ Maximum, which provides all installation messages and screens to users during the package installation.

8. Click Advanced to display the Advanced Deployment Options dialog box, shown in Figure 6-16. In the Advanced Deployment Options area, select any of the following check boxes:

❑ Ignore Language When Deploying This Package, which specifies whether to deploy the package even if it is in a different language.

❑ Make This 32-Bit X86 Application Available To Win64 Machines, which specifies whether the 32-bit program is assigned or published to 64-bit computers.

❑ Include OLE Class And Product Information, which specifics whether to deploy information about COM components with the package.

Figure 6-16   Advanced Deployment Options dialog box

9. Click OK.

10. Click the Categories tab. In the Categories tab of the Properties dialog box for the package, shown in Figure 6-17, click the category under which you want to display this application to users from the Available Categories list, and then click Select.

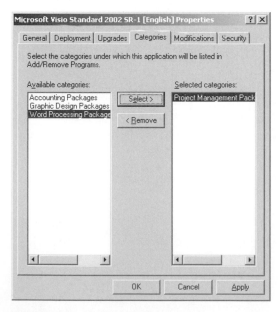

Figure 6-17   Properties dialog box for a package, Categories tab

11. Click the Modifications tab. In the Modifications tab, shown in Figure 6-18, do any of the following:

  ❑ To add modifications, click Add. In the Open dialog box, browse to find the transform file (.mst) or patch file (.msp), and then click Open. You can add multiple modifications.

  ❑ To remove modifications, select the modification you want to remove and then click Remove. Repeat until each unwanted modification has been removed.

  ❑ To set the order of modifications, select a modification and then click Move Up or Move Down. Modifications are applied according to the order specified in the list.

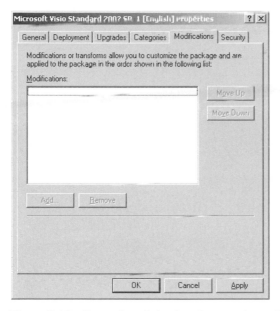

Figure 6-18   Properties dialog box for a package, Modifications tab

> **Important**   Do not click OK in the Modifications tab until you have finished configuring the modifications. When you click OK, the package is assigned or published immediately. If the modifications are not properly configured, you will have to uninstall the package or upgrade the package with a correctly configured version.

12. Click the Security tab. In the Security tab of the Properties dialog box for the package, shown in Figure 6-19, click the security group on which to set permissions. Administrators who manage the application installation should have the Full Control permission set to Allow. Users who use the software assigned or published by the application should have the Read permission set to Allow.

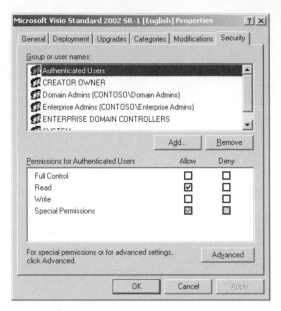

Figure 6-19   Properties dialog box for a package, Security tab

13. Click OK.

Software Deployment Best Practices

The following are the best practices for deploying software with Group Policy:

- **Assign or publish just once per GPO**   A Windows Installer package should be assigned or published no more than once in the same GPO. For example, if you assign Office to the computers affected by a GPO, do not assign or publish it to users affected by the GPO.

- **Assign or publish close to the root in the Active Directory hierarchy**   Because Group Policy settings apply by default to child Active Directory containers, it is efficient to assign or publish by linking a GPO to a parent OU or domain. Use security descriptors—access control entries (ACEs)—on the GPO for finer control over who receives the software.

- **Make sure Windows Installer packages include modifications before they are published or assigned**   Remember that modifications are applied to packages at the time of assignment or publication. Therefore, you should make sure the Modifications tab in the Properties dialog box for the package is set up as you intend before you click OK. If you neglect to do this and assign or publish a modified package before you have completely configured it, you must either remove the software and republish or reassign it or upgrade the software with a completely modified version.

- **Specify application categories for your organization**   It's easier for users to find an application in Add Or Remove Programs in Control Panel when you use categories.

- **Take advantage of authoring tools**   Developers familiar with the files, registry entries, and other requirements for an application to work properly can author native Windows Installer packages by using tools available from various software vendors.

- **Repackage existing software**   You can use commercially available tools to create Windows Installer packages for software that does not include natively authored .msi files. These work by comparing a computer's state before and after installation. For best results, install on a computer free of other application software.

- **Set properties for the GPO to provide widely scoped control**   Doing this saves administrative keystrokes when assigning or publishing a large number of packages with similar properties in a single GPO—for example, when all the software is published and it all comes from the same SDP.

- **Set properties for the Windows Installer package to provide fine control**   Use the package properties for assigning or publishing a single package.

- **Know when to use Group Policy Software Installation and Systems Management Server (SMS)**   Use Group Policy Software Installation for simple software installation and deployment scenarios. Use SMS when scheduling, performing inventory, reporting, checking status, and providing support for installation across a wide area network (WAN) is required.

Practice: Deploying Software with Group Policy

In this practice, you deploy (assign and publish) the Windows Server 2003 Administration Tools Pack with Group Policy. Installing the Administration Tools Pack on a computer that is not a domain controller allows you to administer Active Directory remotely. Windows Server 2003 ships with the Windows Installer package Adminpak.msi, which is used for installing the Windows Server 2003 Administration Tools Pack. Use the procedures provided earlier in this lesson to complete each exercise.

Exercise 1: Setting Up an SDP

In this exercise, you set up an SDP for the deployment of the Windows Server 2003 Administration Tools Pack.

To set up an SDP:

1. Log on to Server01 as Administrator.

2. Create a shared folder named **SDP** in C:\ (where *C* is the name of your system drive). Name the share **SDP**.

3. Set the appropriate permissions on the folder. Administrators must be able to change the files (Full Control), and Users must only view (Read) the files from the SDP folders and share. Then, on the Security tab of the SDP Properties dialog box, click Advanced and uncheck the box Allow Inheritable Permissions From The Parent To Propagate. In the Security dialog box that appears, click Copy. In the Permissions Entries list select the permission that grants Users Special permissions and click Remove. Click OK in the Advanced Security Settings For SDP dialog box, and click OK in the SDP Properties dialog box.

4. Search the Windows Server 2003 CD-ROM for Adminpak.msi. Copy the Adminpak.msi file to the shared SDP folder.

Exercise 2: Configuring a GPO for Software Deployment (Assign)

In this exercise, you create a GPO and a GPO console for the deployment of the Windows Server 2003 Administration Tools Pack.

1. Log on to Server02 as Lorrin Smith-Bates.

2. Click Start, click All Programs, click Administrative Tools, and make a note of what tools are available. There should be a limited number of tools used to administer the server—you should not see Active Directory administrative tools, such as Active Directory Users And Computers.

 Note   If the Administrative Tools folder does not appear in the All Programs menu, you will need to enables its display. Right-click the taskbar, and select Properties to display the Taskbar And Start Menu Properties dialog box. Click the Start Menu tab, click the Start Menu option, and then click Customize. In the Customize Start Menu dialog box, click the Advanced tab. In the Start Menu Items list under the System Administrative Tools node, select either Display On The All Programs Menu or Display On The All Programs Menu And The Start Menu.

3. Log off of Server02.

To configure a GPO for software deployment:

1. On Server01, create a GPO linked to the West OU. Name the GPO **West OU Applications**.

2. Create a console for the West OU Applications GPO. Name the console **West OU Applications GPO**.

3. In the West OU Applications GPO console, right-click the West OU Applications GPO and choose Properties. Click the Security tab, and add the Marketing group to the list of groups.

4. Ensure that the West OU Applications GPO applies to the Marketing group by setting the group's Apply Group Policy permission to Allow.

5. Deselect the Apply Group Policy permission (currently set to Allow) for the Authenticated Users group. Do not set this permission to Deny.

6. Close the Properties dialog box.

7. In the User Configuration node, Software Settings, right-click the Software Installation node, click New, and then click Package.

8. In the Open dialog box, in the File Name list, type the UNC path (**\\Server01\SDP**) to the SDP for the Windows Installer packages (.msi files), and press ENTER. Select the Adminpak.msi file, and then click Open.

9. When you're asked to select a deployment method, indicate that you want to assign the Adminpak.msi package to users.

10. Close and save the West OU Applications GPO console.

Exercise 3: Testing Software Deployment

In this exercise, you test the deployment of the Windows Server 2003 Administration Tools Pack that you assigned to users.

To test software deployment:

1. Log on to Server02 as Lorrin Smith-Bates in the contoso domain.

2. Click Start, click All Programs, and then click Administrative Tools. In addition to several other new administration tools, you should now be able to see Active Directory Users And Computers, Active Directory Sites And Services, and Active Directory Domains And Trusts in the Administrative Tools menu.

3. Open Active Directory Users And Computers. A Setup Wizard appears. By default, when an application is assigned to the user, it is installed the first time the user launches the application.

4. Log off Server02.

Exercise 4: Configuring a GPO for Software Deployment (Publish)

In this exercise, you create a GPO and a GPO console for the deployment of the Windows Server 2003 Administration Tools Pack.

To configure a GPO for software deployment:

1. Log on to Server02 as Pat Coleman.

2. Click Start, click All Programs, click Administrative Tools, and make a note of what tools are available. There should be a limited number of tools used to administer the server—you should not see Active Directory administrative tools. They were assigned to the OU in which Lorrin's account exists, but not to the OU in which Pat's account exists.

Note If the Administrative Tools folder does not appear in the All Programs menu, you will need to enable its display. Right-click the taskbar, and select Properties to display the Taskbar And Start Menu Properties dialog box. Click the Start Menu tab, click the Start Menu option, and then click Customize. In the Customize Start Menu dialog box, click the Advanced tab. In the Start Menu Items list under the System Administrative Tools node, select either Display On The All Programs Menu or Display On The All Programs Menu And The Start Menu.

3. Log off of Server02.

4. On Server01, create a GPO linked to the East OU. Name the GPO **East OU Applications**.

5. Create a console for the East OU Applications GPO. Name the console **East OU Applications GPO**.

6. In the East OU Applications GPO console, right-click the East OU Applications GPO and choose Properties. Click the Security tab, and add the Marketing group to the list of groups.

7. Ensure that the East OU Applications GPO applies to the Marketing group by setting the group's Apply Group Policy permission to Allow.

8. Deselect the Apply Group Policy permission (currently set to Allow) for the Authenticated Users group. Do not set this permission to Deny.

9. Close the properties dialog box.

10. In the User Configuration node, Software Settings, right-click the Software Installation node, click New, and then click Package.

11. In the Open dialog box, in the File Name list, type the UNC path (**Server01\SDP**) to the SDP for the Windows Installer packages (.msi files), and press ENTER. Select the Adminpak.msi file, and then click Open.

12. When you're asked to select a deployment method, indicate that you want to publish the Adminpak.msi package to users.

13. Right-click the Software Installations extension node, and select Properties. Click the Categories tab, click Add and type **Tools and Utilities** in the Enter New Category dialog box. Click OK to close the Software Installation Properties dialog box.

14. In the details pane of the console, right-click the package you just created and click Properties. Click the Categories tab. Select Tools And Utilities, and click Select. Click OK.

15. Close and save the East OU Applications GPO console.

Exercise 6: Testing Software Deployment

In this exercise, you test the deployment of the Windows Server 2003 Administration Tools Pack that you published to users.

To test software deployment:

1. Log on to Server02 as Pat Coleman.

2. Click Start, and then click Control Panel. In Control Panel, double-click the Add Or Remove Programs icon.

3. In the Add Or Remove Programs window, click the Add New Programs button on the left.

4. In the window provided by Add New Programs, shown in Figure 6-20, note that the Windows Server 2003 Administration Tools Pack is available for you to add to your network. Also note that from the Category list, you can select Tools And Utilities.

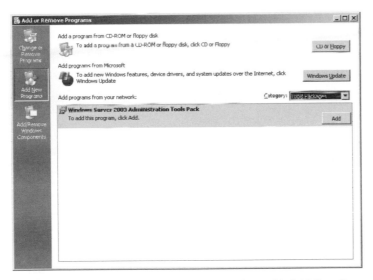

Figure 6-20   Add Or Remove Programs window, with Add New Programs selected

5. Log off Server02.

Lesson Review

The following questions are intended to reinforce key information presented in this lesson. If you are unable to answer a question, review the lesson materials and try the question again. You can find answers to the questions in the "Questions and Answers" section at the end of this chapter.

1. Why is it necessary to set up an SDP?

_____

_____

2. What feature is configured in the File Extensions tab in the Software Installation Properties dialog box?

_____

_____

_____

_____

3. What feature is configured in the Categories tab in the Software Installation Properties dialog box?

_____

_____

_____

_____

4. What feature is configured in the Modifications tab in the Properties dialog box for a Windows Installer package?

_____

_____

_____

_____

5. You want to ensure that all users of the KC23 workstation can run FrontPage 2000. What action should you take?

    a. Assign the application to the computer.

    b. Assign the application to users.

    c. Publish the application to the computer.

    d. Publish the application to users.

_____

_____

Lesson Summary

- The tasks for deploying software with Group Policy are the following: plan and prepare the software deployment, set up an SDP, create a GPO and a GPO console for software deployment, specify the software deployment properties for the GPO, add Windows Installer packages to the GPO and select a package deployment method, and set Windows Installer package properties.

- For a software deployment with Group Policy, you can set up DFS to automatically direct users to the nearest SDP.

- You can define software deployment properties that affect all Windows Installer packages in a GPO.

- You can also define software deployment properties that affect individual Windows Installer packages in a GPO.

Lesson 4: Maintaining Software Deployed with Group Policy

After the deployment of software applications, it might be necessary to redeploy, upgrade, or remove them at some point in the software life cycle. This lesson shows you how to redeploy, upgrade, and remove software deployed with Group Policy.

After this lesson, you will be able to

- Redeploy an application deployed with Group Policy
- Upgrade an application deployed with Group Policy
- Remove an application deployed with Group Policy

Estimated lesson time: 15 minutes

Redeploying Applications Deployed with Group Policy

You can redeploy an application previously deployed with Group Policy if there are small changes that need to be made to the original software deployment configuration. For example, you might have deployed only Word and Excel in your original Microsoft Office software deployment. You might now need to include PowerPoint in the Office deployment. As long as you make changes to the original Office package deployed with Group Policy, you can redeploy the application to the network.

To redeploy applications deployed with Group Policy, complete the following steps:

1. Open the GPO console for the deployed application. In the Computer Configuration or User Configuration node, open Software Settings.

2. Click the Software Installation node.

3. In the details pane, right-click the package you want to redeploy, click All Tasks, and then click Redeploy Application.

4. In the dialog box for the package, click Yes to redeploy the application to all computers on which it is already installed.

Upgrading Applications Deployed with Group Policy

Several events in the life cycle of the software can trigger an upgrade, including the following:

- The original developer of the software might release a new version with new and improved features.

- The organization might choose to use a different vendor's application.

Upgrades typically involve major changes to the software and normally have new version numbers. Usually a substantial number of files change for an upgrade. To establish the procedure to upgrade an existing application to the current release, you must first create a Windows Installer package that contains the upgrade and then configure the upgrade in the Upgrades tab in the Properties dialog box for the package.

> **Note**   The Upgrades tab is not available for packages created from application files (.zap files).

To upgrade applications deployed with Group Policy, complete the following steps:

1. Open the GPO console for the deployed application. In the Computer Configuration or User Configuration node, open Software Settings.

2. Click the Software Installation node.

3. Create a new Windows Installer package that contains the upgrade. Assign or publish this new package.

4. In the details pane, right-click the Windows Installer package that will function as the upgrade (not the package to be upgraded), and then click Properties.

5. In the Upgrades tab of the Properties dialog box for the upgrade package, shown in Figure 6-21, click Add.

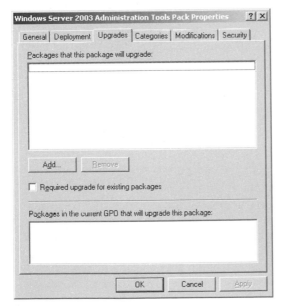

Figure 6-21   Properties dialog box for a package, Upgrades tab

6. In the Add Upgrade Package dialog box, shown in Figure 6-22, select one of the following options:

❑ Current Group Policy Object (GPO), if you want to upgrade a package in the current GPO.

❑ A Specific GPO, if you want to upgrade a package in another GPO. Then click Browse, select the GPO you want, and then in the Browse For A Group Policy Object dialog box, click OK.

Figure 6-22   Add Upgrade Package dialog box

A list of all the packages assigned or published within the selected GPO appears in the Package To Upgrade list. Depending on the GPO, this list can have zero or more entries.

7. Select the package you want to upgrade in the Package To Upgrade list.

8. Select one of the following options:

❑ Uninstall The Existing Package, Then Install The Upgrade Package, which removes the existing package before the upgrade is installed. This option is used if you want to replace an application with a completely different one (perhaps from a different vendor).

❑ Package Can Upgrade Over The Existing Package, which installs the upgrade without removing the previous version. This option is used if you want to install a newer version of the same product while retaining the user's application preferences, document type associations, and so on.

9. Click OK.

10. In the Upgrades tab in the Properties dialog box for the package, select the Required Upgrade For Existing Packages check box if you want the upgrade to be mandatory, and then click OK. If this is an upgrade under the Computer Configuration node of the Group Policy Object Editor console, the check box appears dimmed and selected, because packages can only be assigned to computers, not published.

> **Note**   If the Required Upgrade For Existing Packages check box is not selected, users have the option of applying the upgrade, which could cause application version variances within an organization.

11. Click OK.

Removing Applications Deployed with Group Policy

At some point, users might no longer require an application, so you might need to remove it. In Chapter 5, you learned to terminate the effects of a GPO by unlinking or deleting the GPO. However, if you delete a GPO that deploys a software application, the application cannot be uninstalled with Group Policy. If the application cannot be uninstalled with Group Policy, you (or the users) must manually uninstall the application from each client computer. To avoid this hazard, you must remove applications deployed with Group Policy in three steps:

1. Choose the software removal method you want to implement.

2. Allow the software removal to be processed.

3. Delete the GPO.

Because a great number of users and their computers can be affected by the removal of applications deployed with Group Policy, you should carefully consider the effects of removing these applications.

There are two options for removing software deployed with Group Policy. You can immediately uninstall the software from users and computers (known as a *forced removal*), or you can allow users to continue to use the software but prevent new installations (known as an *optional removal*).

You should choose a forced removal if a software application is no longer used. After the software is deleted, users will not be able to install or run the software. Although you specify that you want to "immediately" uninstall the software in this option, the software is actually deleted in the following fashion:

■ Software assigned to computers is automatically deleted from the computer the next time the computer is rebooted or turned on.

- Software assigned to computers that are not attached to the network is automatically deleted the next time the computer is connected to the network and rebooted or turned on when the computer account logs on to Active Directory.

- Software assigned or published to users is automatically deleted from the computer the next time the user logs on.

- Software assigned or published to users on computers that are not attached to the network is automatically deleted the next time the user logs on to Active Directory.

Caution   Because the software is not "immediately" deleted, do not delete the GPO until there has been sufficient time for the software removal to be processed.

You should choose an optional removal if a version of a software application is no longer supported. The software is removed from deployment without forcing the (physical) removal of the software from the computers of users who are still using the software. Users can continue to use the software until they remove it themselves. However, no user is able to install the software (from the Start menu, from Add Or Remove Programs in Control Panel, or by document invocation).

Note   When you originally deploy the software, if you want the application to be removed when a GPO no longer applies, select the Uninstall This Application When It Falls Out Of The Scope Of Management option in the Deployment tab in the Properties dialog box for the package.

To remove applications deployed with Group Policy, complete the following steps:

1. Open the GPO console for the deployed application. In the Computer Configuration or User Configuration node, open Software Settings.

2. Click the Software Installation node.

3. In the details pane, right-click the package you want to remove, click All Tasks, and then click Remove.

4. In the Remove Software dialog box, shown in Figure 6-23, select one of the following options:

   ❑ Immediately Uninstall The Software From Users And Computers. Select this option to specify that the application should be removed the next time a user logs on to or restarts the computer (forced removal).

   ❑ Allow Users To Continue To Use The Software, But Prevent New Installations. Select this option to specify that users can continue to use the application if they have already installed it (optional removal). If they remove the application or have never installed it, they will not be able to install it.

Note   If you select an optional removal, the package is removed from the GPO. If you determine later that you want a forced removal of the software, you must add the package to the GPO again and deploy it again, and then select a forced removal. Otherwise, you (or the users) must manually uninstall the application from each client computer.

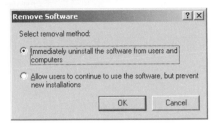

Figure 6-23   Remove Software dialog box

5. Click OK.

Lesson Review

The following questions are intended to reinforce key information presented in this lesson. If you are unable to answer a question, review the lesson materials and try the question again. You can find answers to the questions in the "Questions and Answers" section at the end of this chapter.

1. What is the difference between redeploying and upgrading an application deployed with Group Policy?

   _____

   _____

   _____

   _____

   _____

2. Why shouldn't you give users the option of applying an upgrade?

   _____

   _____

3. What happens if you delete a GPO that deploys a software application before you choose the software removal method you want to implement and allow the software removal to be processed?

_____

_____

_____

_____

_____

4. A software application deployed with Group Policy in your organization is no longer used. You no longer want users to be able to install or run the software. What action should you take?

   a. Execute a forced removal.

   b. Execute an optional removal.

   c. Redeploy the application.

   d. Upgrade the application.

_____

_____

Lesson Summary

- To maintain a software deployment, it might be necessary to redeploy, upgrade, or remove an application at some point in the software life cycle.

- You can redeploy an application previously deployed with Group Policy if there are small changes that need to be made to the original software deployment configuration. You can redeploy an application by using the Software Installation extension.

- To upgrade software deployed with Group Policy, you must first create a Windows Installer package that contains the upgrade and then configure the upgrade in the Upgrades tab in the Properties dialog box for the package.

- To remove software deployed with Group Policy, you must choose whether to uninstall the software from all users and computers or to merely prevent new installations of the software by using the Software Installation extension.

Lesson 5: Troubleshooting Software Deployed with Group Policy

To maintain software deployed with Group Policy, you must be able to troubleshoot the software deployment. Troubleshooting a software deployment involves using the Resultant Set Of Policy Wizard, the Gpresult.exe and Gpupdate.exe command-line tools, the Event Viewer, and log files to solve policy-related problems. This lesson shows you how to work with these tools to troubleshoot software deployed with Group Policy.

After this lesson, you will be able to

■ Troubleshoot software deployed with Group Policy

Estimated lesson time: 20 minutes

Tools to Troubleshoot Group Policy

As an administrator, you will likely have the task of finding solutions to problems with software deployed with Group Policy. If problems occur, you might need to perform some tests to verify that your Group Policy configuration is working properly, and diagnose and solve problems. Windows Server 2003 operating systems provide the following Group Policy troubleshooting tools to assist you in verifying your configuration and in diagnosing and solving problems:

■ Resultant Set Of Policy Wizard

■ Gpresult.exe

■ Gpupdate.exe

■ Event Viewer

■ Log files

The Group Policy troubleshooting tools were discussed in detail in Chapter 5. You must be proficient in the use of these tools to effectively troubleshoot software deployed with Group Policy.

Exam Tip   Know how to use Gpresult.exe to troubleshoot software deployed with Group Policy.

Advanced Diagnostic Information

If you turn on verbose logging as discussed in Chapter 5, you can use the advanced diagnostic information provided in the Advanced Deployment Options dialog box to troubleshoot software deployed with Group Policy. The Advanced Deployment Options dialog box, shown earlier in the chapter in Figure 6-16, lists the following:

- **Product Code**   A globally unique identifier (GUID) that identifies the application and its version.

- **Deployment Count**   Displays the number of times the package has been redeployed.

- **Script Name**   Displays the full path to the application assignment script (.aas file). An *application assignment script* contains instructions associated with the assignment or publication of a package and is generated for every published or assigned application in a GPO and stored in that domain's GPO.

To view advanced diagnostic information, complete the following steps:

1. Open the GPO console for the deployed application. In the Computer Configuration or User Configuration node, open Software Settings.

2. Click the Software Installation node.

3. In the details pane, right-click the package for which you want to view advanced diagnostic information and then click Properties.

4. Click the Deployment tab, and then click Advanced.

Software Deployment Troubleshooting Scenarios

Table 6-5 describes some troubleshooting scenarios related to software deployed with Group Policy.

Table 6-5   Software Deployment Troubleshooting Scenarios

Problem: **Published applications do not appear for the user in Add Or Remove Programs in Control Panel.**

Cause	Solution
The client is running Terminal Services on the desktop.	Use Addiag.exe to see whether Terminal Services is running on the user's desktop. Software deployed with Group Policy is not supported for Terminal Services clients. (Addiag.exe is a part of the Windows Support Tools on the Windows Server 2003 CD.)
Group Policy is not applied to this user.	Run Gpresult.exe for the user to ensure that the GPO is applied to the user.
The user has not logged on since the GPO was created.	Have the user log off and log back on. Ensure that the user is authenticated by the domain controller.
The GPO did not run.	Run Gpresult.exe to verify that the GPO runs.
The user cannot access Active Directory.	Check to see whether the user can access Active Directory.
The user cannot access the SDP.	Use Ping.exe to test connectivity. Check the user's permissions on the SDP.

Problem: **When a user activates a document with the extension used in a published application, the application does not install.**

Cause	Solution
Auto-install is not set. Additional causes and solutions are listed in the "Published applications do not appear for the user in Add Or Remove Programs in Control Panel" problem.	Ensure that Auto-Install This Application By File Extension Activation is checked in the Deployment tab in the Properties dialog box for the package.

Problem: **When a user activates a document with the extension used in a published application, an unexpected application automatically installs.**

Cause	Solution
The precedence of filename extensions has not been set properly.	Check to see that the File Extensions tab in the Software Installation Properties dialog box has the correct application precedence set.

Table 6-5   Software Deployment Troubleshooting Scenarios

Problem: **An application assigned to a computer does not install.**

Cause	Solution
The computer has not been restarted since the application was assigned and the GPO has not been applied.	Restart the computer.
The GPO does not apply to the computer.	Check the GPO console to make sure the GPO manages the computer.
Group Policy did not run.	Run Gpresult.exe for the computer to ensure that the GPO is applied to the computer.
The computer is not able to access Active Directory.	Use Ping.exe to test connectivity to the domain controller.
The computer is not able to access the SDP.	Use Ping.exe to test connectivity to the SDP.

Problem: **A user who has never installed a managed application selects the application to install. The installation begins, and one of many error messages appears.**

Cause	Solution
There are problems with the Windows Installer package.	Install the package on another computer, and make sure the package can be opened.
The user does not have the appropriate permissions to read the Windows Installer package from the SDP or to install the application to the installation target folder as defined in the package.	Verify that the user has Read permission on the SDP and Write access to the installation target directory.

Problem: **A previously installed, assigned application is unexpectedly removed.**

Cause	Solution
The Uninstall The Applications When They Fall Out Of The Scope Of Management check box in the Advanced tab of the Software Installation Properties dialog box is selected and the scope of management has changed.	Check to see whether the GPO containing the managed application still applies to the user or computer.
The software is managed by a GPO linked to a site or OU, and the computer moved to a new site or OU.	Check to see whether the computer has moved to a new site or OU.

Table 6-5   Software Deployment Troubleshooting Scenarios

Problem: **The user receives an error message such as "The feature you are trying to install cannot be found in the source directory."**

Cause	Solution
There are network or permissions problems.	Make sure the network is working correctly. Ensure that the user has Read and Apply Group Policy permissions for the GPO. Ensure that the folder containing the application on the SDP is shared. Ensure that the user has Read permission for the SDP. Ensure that the user has Read permission for the folder containing the application on the SDP.

Problem: **After removal of an application, the shortcuts for the application still appear on the user's desktop.**

Cause	Solution
The user has created shortcuts and the Windows Installer service has no knowledge of them.	The user must remove the shortcuts manually.
Automatic upgrade of the application has left shortcuts for the application being upgraded.	Check to see whether there is a new version of the application, and if so, delete the shortcuts.

Problem: **The user attempts to install a published or assigned application and receives an error message such as "Another installation is already in progress."**

Cause	Solution
The Windows Installer service is already running another installation.	The user should wait for the installation to complete and try again later.

Problem: **The user opens an already installed application, and the Windows Installer service starts.**

Cause	Solution
An application is undergoing automatic repair.	In both cases, the user must wait for the installation to complete.
A feature is being added.	

Table 6-5   Software Deployment Troubleshooting Scenarios

Problem: **The administrator receives error messages such as "Active Directory will not allow the package to be deployed" or "Cannot prepare package for deployment."**

Cause	Solution
The Windows Installer service cannot communicate with the computer on which the SDP is located.	Use Ping.exe to test connectivity with the SDP.
The package is corrupted.	Install the package on another computer, and make sure the package can be opened.

Real World   Troubleshooting Application Management Issues

If you are facing a difficult software distribution issue, and you've verified that the software deployment options are correct, you might want to enable Application Management debugging. To do this, you must go to the system experiencing the problem and log on as an administrator. You then enable Application Management debugging by editing the registry as described in the following steps:

1. Click Start, click Run, type **Regedit**, and then press ENTER. In the Registry Editor, expand the following path: HKEY_LOCAL_MACHINE\Software \Microsoft\Windows NT\CurrentVersion.

2. Right-click the CurrentVersion key, point to New, and then click Key. Type **Diagnostics** as the new key name, and then press ENTER.

3. Right-click the Diagnostics key, point to New, and then click DWORD Value. Type **AppMgmtDebugLevel** as the name of the new value, and then press ENTER. Double-click the AppMgmtDebugLevel value.

4. In the Edit DWORD Value dialog box, type **4b** in the Value Data box and then click OK. Close the Registry Editor.

Once you restart the computer (for applications assigned to the computer) or have logged on the user (for applications assigned or published to the user), you should be able to find the AppMgmt.log file in the *%systemroot%*\debug\usermode folder. Read the entries in this file to gain insight into the problems that are occurring with the application installation. If you don't see this log file, it could be that the application deployment policy is not even reaching the local client system. This could be the case if the policy is disabled or possibly being filtered through inheritance blocking or security filtering.

After you complete your debugging, be sure to remove the AppMgmtDebugLevel key so that you don't waste system resources logging information that you don't require.

Lesson Review

The following questions are intended to reinforce key information presented in this lesson. If you are unable to answer a question, review the lesson materials and try the question again. You can find answers to the questions in the "Questions and Answers" section at the end of this chapter.

1. Which of the following actions should you take if a user attempts to install an assigned application and receives the message "Another installation is already in progress?"

a. Check your permissions for the GPO.

b. Check network connectivity.

c. Check your permissions for the SDP.

d. Wait for the installation to complete.

_____

_____

_____

2. Which of the following actions should you take if a user attempts to install an assigned application and receives the message "The feature you are trying to install cannot be found in the source directory?" (Choose all that apply.)

a. Check your permissions for the GPO.

b. Check connectivity with the SDP.

c. Check your permissions for the SDP.

d. Wait for the installation to complete.

e. Set the auto-install property for the package.

_____

_____

_____

_____

3. You are preparing a package for deployment. Which of the following actions should you take if you receive the message "Cannot prepare package for deployment?"

    a. Check your permissions for the GPO.

    b. Check connectivity with the SDP.

    c. Check your permissions for the SDP.

    d. Set the appropriate category for the package.

    e. Set the auto-install property for the package.

    _____

    _____

    _____

4. Which of the following actions should you take if a user double-clicks a document associated with a published application and a different application than the expected one installs?

    a. Set the auto-install property for the package.

    b. Clear the auto-install property for the package.

    c. Adjust the precedence for the expected application in the Application Precedence list.

    d. Delete the unexpected application from the Application Precedence list.

    _____

    _____

    _____

Lesson Summary

- Windows Server 2003 operating systems assist you in verifying your configuration and in diagnosing and solving problems related to deploying software with Group Policy with the following Group Policy troubleshooting tools: Resultant Set Of Policy Wizard, Gpresult.exe and Gpupdate.exe command-line tools, Event Viewer, and log files.

Lesson 6: Implementing Software Restriction Policies

In the business-computing environment, a wide variety of software applications are available to users from many sources. Documents and Web pages can contain executable code in scripts, and e-mail messages can contain executable code in attachments. Merely accessing such documents, Web pages, and e-mail messages forces users to make decisions about running applications. Worse, viruses and Trojan horses that might be present in the executable code can cause security breaches and damage to network files. In Windows XP and Windows Server 2003 operating systems, software restriction policies have been developed to identify and control the running of software. This lesson shows you how to implement software restriction policies.

After this lesson, you will be able to

- Explain the purpose of software restriction policies
- Describe the default security levels
- Describe how software is identified by software restriction policies
- Explain the function of rules
- List rule precedence
- Set the default security level
- Create rules
- Designate file types

Estimated lesson time: 25 minutes

Understanding Software Restriction Policies

Software restriction policies, new in Windows XP and Windows Server 2003 operating systems, were created to address the problem of regulating unknown or untrusted code. Software restriction policies are security settings in a GPO provided to identify software and control its ability to run on a local computer, site, domain, or OU. Most organizations employ a set of known and trusted programs. However, if users install and run other programs, these programs might conflict with or change configuration data in the known and trusted programs. Or, the newly installed user programs could contain a virus or Trojan horse. Software restriction policies protect your computer environment from unknown code by enabling you to identify and specify the applications allowed to run. These policies can apply to computers or users, depending on whether you choose to modify settings in User Configuration or Computer Configuration. When software restriction policies are set, end users must adhere to the guidelines set up by administrators when executing programs.

With software restriction policies, you can:

- Control the ability of programs to run on your system. For example, you can apply a policy that does not allow certain file types to run in the e-mail attachment directory of your e-mail program if you are concerned about users receiving viruses through e-mail.

- Permit users to run only specific files on multiuser computers. For example, if you have multiple users on your computers, you can set up software restriction policies and access control settings in such a way that users do not have access to any software but specific files that are necessary for their work.

- Decide who can add trusted publishers to your computer.

- Control whether software restriction policies affect all users or just certain users on a computer.

- Prevent any files from running on your local computer, OU, site, or domain. For example, if you have a known virus, you can use software restriction policies to stop the computer from opening the file that contains the virus.

 Important   Software restriction policies should not be used as a replacement for antivirus software. Software restriction policies do not work on Windows NT 4.0 or Windows 2000 systems.

Default Security Levels

Software restriction policies run on one of two default security levels:

- Unrestricted, which allows software to run with the full rights of the user who is logged on to the computer

- Disallowed, which does not allow the software to run, regardless of the access rights of the user who is logged on to the computer

If the default security level is set to Unrestricted, you can identify and create rules for the set of programs that you want to prohibit from running. If the default security level is set to Disallowed, you can identify and create rule exceptions for the programs that you trust to run. Either option can be set as the default security level for a GPO, but when a GPO is created, the default security level is Unrestricted.

When you set the default security level to Disallowed, most software applications are restricted and you must apply a rule for nearly every application you want to run. Some applications must remain unrestricted for the operating system to function at all.

Four registry path rules are created automatically when you set the default security level to Disallowed:

- %HKEY_LOCAL_MACHINE\SOFTWARE\Microsoft\Windows NT\CurrentVersion \SystemRoot%

- %HKEY_LOCAL_MACHINE\SOFTWARE\Microsoft\Windows NT\CurrentVersion \SystemRoot%*.exe

- %HKEY_LOCAL_MACHINE\SOFTWARE\Microsoft\Windows NT\CurrentVersion \SystemRoot%\System32*.exe

- %HKEY_LOCAL_MACHINE\SOFTWARE\Microsoft\Windows\CurrentVersion \ProgramFilesDir%

These registry path rules are created as a safeguard against locking yourself and all users out of the system. Only advanced users should consider modifying or deleting these rules.

If you decide to use a default security level of Disallowed, consider the following issues:

- If a computer must run logon scripts, you must include a path rule that allows the scripts to run. For more information, refer to the "Path Rule" section in this lesson.

- Startup items are placed in HKEY_CURRENT_USER\Software\Microsoft\Windows \CurrentVersion\Run. If startup items must run, you must create a rule for them. For more information, refer to the "Path Rule" section in this lesson.

- Many applications start other programs to perform certain tasks, and you must create rules for these other programs. For example, Microsoft Word starts the Microsoft Clip Organizer to manage clip art.

How Software Restriction Policies Work

When a user encounters an application to be run, software restriction policies must first identify the software. Software can be identified by its

- Hash, a series of bytes with a fixed length that uniquely identify a program or file.

- Certificate, a digital document used for authentication and secure exchange of information on open networks, such as the Internet, extranets, and intranets.

- Path, a sequence of folder names that specifies the location of the software within the directory tree.

- Internet zone, a subtree specified through Internet Explorer. Zone options include Internet, Local Intranet, Restricted Sites, Trusted Sites, or Local Computer.

Rules

Software restriction policies identify and control the running of software by using rules. There are four types of rules, which correspond to the four ways of identifying software: a hash rule, a certificate rule, a path rule, and an Internet zone rule. These rules override the default security level. After software is identified by using a rule, you can decide whether or not to allow it to run by setting a security level (Disallowed or Unrestricted) for the program associated with the rule.

■ **Hash Rule**   A *hash* is a series of bytes with a fixed length that uniquely identify a program or file. The hash is computed by a *hash algorithm*. Software restriction policies can identify files by their hash, using both the SHA-1 (Secure Hash Algorithm) and the MD5 hash algorithm. For example, you can create a *hash rule* and set the security level to Disallowed to prevent users from running a certain file. A file can be renamed or moved to another folder and still result in the same hash. However, any change to the file changes its hash value and allows it to bypass restrictions. Software restriction policies recognize only hashes that have been calculated by using such policies.

■ **Certificate Rule**   A *certificate rule* identifies software by its signing certificate. For example, you can use certificate rules to automatically trust software from a trusted source in a domain without prompting the user. You can also use certificate rules to run files in disallowed areas of your operating system.

■ **Path Rule**   A *path rule* identifies software by its file path. For example, if you have a computer that has a disallowed default policy, you can still grant unrestricted access to a specific folder for each user. Simply create a path rule using the file path and set the security level of the path rule to Unrestricted. Some common paths for this type of rule are *%Userprofile%*, *%Windir%*, *%Appdata%*, *%Programfiles%*, and *%Temp%*. Because these rules are specified by path, if a program is moved, the path rule no longer applies. You can also create *registry path rules* that use the registry key of the software as the path.

■ **Internet Zone Rule**   *Internet zone rules* apply only to Windows Installer packages. A zone rule can identify software from a zone that is specified through Internet Explorer. These zones are Internet, Local Intranet, Restricted Sites, Trusted Sites, and Local Computer.

Rule Precedence

You can apply several rules to the same piece of software. The rules are applied in the following order of precedence, from highest to lowest:

1. Hash rule.

2. Certificate rule.

3. Path rule. When there are conflicting path rules, the most restrictive rule takes precedence. For example, if there is a path rule for C:\Windows, with a security level of Disallowed, and there is a path rule for C:\Windows\System32, with a security level of Unrestricted, the more restrictive path rule takes precedence. In this case, software programs in C:\Windows will not run, but programs in C:\Windows\System32 will run.

4. Internet zone rule.

Here is an example of rule precedence. If you have a file that has a hash rule applied to it with a security level of Unrestricted, but the file resides in a folder whose path rule is set to Disallowed, the file runs because the hash rule has precedence over the path rule.

Note   For software restriction policies to take effect, users must log off from and then log on to their computers.

Implementing Software Restriction Policies

To implement software restriction policies, you must complete the following tasks:

1. Set the default security level.

2. Create rules.

3. Designate file types.

Changing the default security level affects all files on the computers that have software restriction policies applied to them. In the details pane of a GPO console, the current default security level is indicated by a black circle with a check mark in it. Upon installation, the default security level of software restriction policies on all files on your system is set to Unrestricted.

To set the default security level of software restriction policies, complete the following steps:

1. Access the Group Policy Object Editor console for a GPO.

2. In the Group Policy Object Editor console, click Computer Configuration, double-click Windows Settings, double-click Security Settings, and then double-click Software Restriction Policies.

3. In the details pane, double-click Security Levels.

> **Note** If you don't see Security Levels and the details pane displays the message, "No Software Restriction Policies Defined," you will need to define new software restriction policies. Right-click the Software Restriction Policies node, and select New Software Restriction Policies.

4. Right-click one of the following:

   ❑ Disallowed, which does not allow the software to run, regardless of the access rights of the user who is logged on to the computer

   ❑ Unrestricted, which allows software to run with the full rights of the user who is logged on to the computer

5. Click Properties.

6. In the Disallowed or Unrestricted Properties dialog box (depending on your choice), click Set As Default.

Creating Rules

Rules identify and control the running of software and override the default security level. As mentioned previously, you can create four types of rules: hash rules, certificate rules, path rules, and Internet zone rules.

Creating a Hash Rule   Create a hash rule to prevent a virus, Trojan horse, or other file from running on your computer. If you want others in your organization to use a hash rule to prevent a virus from running, calculate the hash of the virus using software restriction policies and e-mail the hash value to others. Do not e-mail the virus. You can also prevent a virus from running on your computer by creating a path rule to prevent execution of e-mail attachments.

To create a hash rule, complete the following steps:

1. Access the Group Policy Object Editor console for a GPO.

2. In the Group Policy Object Editor console, click Computer Configuration, double-click Windows Settings, double-click Security Settings, and then double-click Software Restriction Policies.

3. Right-click Additional Rules, and then click New Hash Rule.

4. In the New Hash Rule dialog box, shown in Figure 6-24, browse to a file or paste a precalculated hash in the File Hash box.

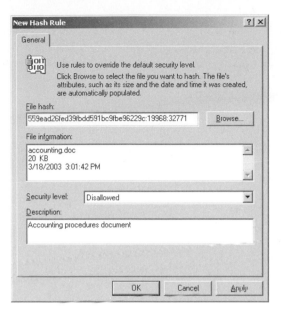

Figure 6-24 The New Hash Rule dialog box

5. In the Security Level list, select one of the following:

❑ Disallowed, which does not allow the software to run, regardless of the access rights of the user who is logged on to the computer

❑ Unrestricted, which allows software to run with the full rights of the user who is logged on to the computer

6. Type a description for this rule in the Description box, and then click OK.

Creating a Certificate Rule Create a certificate rule to automatically trust software from a trusted source in a domain without prompting the user or to run files in disallowed areas of your operating system. Certificate rules can be applied to scripts and Windows Installer packages. They do not apply to files with .exe or .dll filename extensions.

To create a certificate rule, complete the following steps:

1. Access the Group Policy Object Editor console for a GPO.

2. In the Group Policy Object Editor console, click Computer Configuration, double-click Windows Settings, double-click Security Settings, and then double-click Software Restriction Policies.

3. Right-click Additional Rules, and then click New Certificate Rule.

4. In the New Certificate Rule dialog box, shown in Figure 6-25, click Browse and then select a certificate.

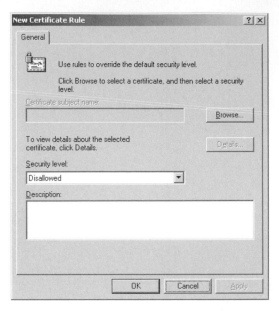

Figure 6-25 The New Certificate Rule dialog box

5. In the Security Level list, select one of the following:

❑ Disallowed, which does not allow the software to run, regardless of the access rights of the user who is logged on to the computer

❑ Unrestricted, which allows software to run with the full rights of the user who is logged on to the computer

6. Type a description for this rule, and then click OK.

Creating an Internet Zone Rule   Create an Internet zone rule to identify software from a zone that is specified through Internet Explorer. Zone rules apply only to Windows Installer packages.

To create an Internet zone rule, complete the following steps:

1. Access the Group Policy Object Editor console for a GPO.

2. In the Group Policy Object Editor console, click Computer Configuration, double-click Windows Settings, double-click Security Settings, and then double-click Software Restriction Policies.

3. Right-click Additional Rules, and then click New Internet Zone Rule.

4. In the New Internet Zone Rule dialog box, shown in Figure 6-26, select a zone from the Internet Zone list.

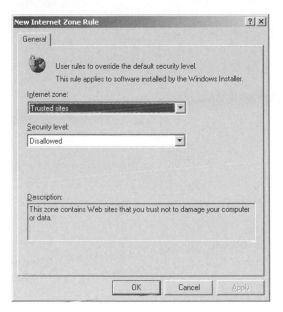

Figure 6-26   The New Internet Zone Rule dialog box

5. In the Security Level list, select one of the following:

❑ Disallowed, which does not allow the software to run, regardless of the access rights of the user who is logged on to the computer

❑ Unrestricted, which allows software to run with the full rights of the user who is logged on to the computer

Creating a Path Rule   Create a path rule to prevent users from executing applications in a path you specify. If you create a path rule for an application and intend to prevent the program from running by setting the security level to Disallowed, note that a user can still run the software by copying it to another location. Environment variables, such as *%Programfiles%* or *%Systemroot%*, can be used in your path rule. You can also create a registry path rule for files that are not always installed in specific file folders. The wildcard characters * and ? are supported in path rules. To prevent users from executing e-mail attachments, create a path rule for your e-mail program's attachment directory that prevents users from running e-mail attachments.

To create a path rule, complete the following steps:

1. Access the Group Policy Object Editor console for a GPO.

2. In the Group Policy Object Editor console, click Computer Configuration, double-click Windows Settings, double-click Security Settings, and then double-click Software Restriction Policies.

3. Right-click Additional Rules, and then click New Path Rule.

4. In the New Path Rule dialog box, shown in Figure 6-27, type a path in the Path box or browse to a file or folder.

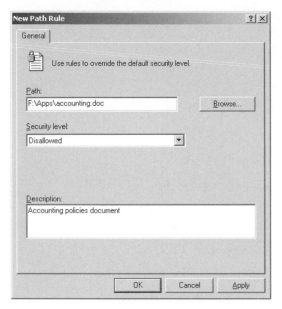

Figure 6-27   The New Path Rule dialog box

5. In the Security Level list, select one of the following:

❑ Disallowed, which does not allow the software to run, regardless of the access rights of the user who is logged on to the computer

❑ Unrestricted, which allows software to run with the full rights of the user who is logged on to the computer

6. Type a description for this rule, and then click OK.

Important   For certain folders, such as the Windows folder, setting the security level to Disallowed can adversely affect the operation of your operating system. Make sure that you do not disallow a crucial component of the operating system or one of its dependent programs.

To create a registry path rule, complete the following steps:

Note   You must be an administrator to create a registry path rule.

1. Click Start, point to Run, type **regedit**, and then click OK.

2. Right-click the registry key for which you want to create a rule, and click Copy Key Name. Make a note of the Value name located in the details pane.

3. Access the Group Policy Object Editor console for a GPO.

4. In the Group Policy Object Editor console, click Computer Configuration, double-click Windows Settings, double-click Security Settings, and then double-click Software Restriction Policies.

5. Right-click Additional rules, and then click New Path Rule.

6. In the New Path Rule dialog box, paste the registry path in the Path box. The registry path should be formatted as follows: %*[Registry Hive]\[Registry Key Name]\[Value Name]*%. Notice that the registry path is enclosed in percent (%) signs. The registry path rule can contain a suffix after the closing percent sign, for example, %HKEY_CURRENT_USER\Software\Microsoft\Windows\CurrentVersion\Explorer\Shell Folders\Cache%OLK* is valid. This registry path rule identifies the folder that Microsoft Outlook XP uses to store attachments before launching them.

> **Note**   The registry hive must not be abbreviated. For example, HKCU cannot be substituted for HKEY_CURRENT_USER.

7. In the Security Level list, select one of the following:

   ❑ Disallowed, which does not allow the software to run, regardless of the access rights of the user who is logged on to the computer

   ❑ Unrestricted, which allows software to run with the full rights of the user who is logged on to the computer

8. Type a description for this rule, and then click OK.

Designating File Types

File types that are affected by hash, certificate, path, and Internet zone rules must be listed in the Designated File Types setting in the Software Restriction Policies extension. The list of file types in the Designated File Types setting is shared by all rules. However, you can specify different designated files lists for computer policies and for user policies.

To designate or delete a file type, complete the following steps:

1. Access the Group Policy Object Editor console for a GPO.

2. In the Group Policy Object Editor console, click Computer Configuration, double-click Windows Settings, double-click Security Settings, and then double-click Software Restriction Policies.

3. In the details pane, double-click the Designated File Types setting.

4. In the Designated File Types Properties dialog box, shown in Figure 6-28, do one of the following:

   ❑ To add a file type, type the filename extension in the File Extension box and click Add. Click OK.

   ❑ To delete a file type, select the file type in the Designated File Types list and click Remove. Click OK.

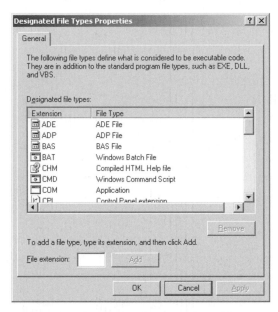

Figure 6-28   The Designated File Types Properties dialog box

Optional Tasks for Implementing Software Restriction Policies

When implementing software restriction policies, you can optionally complete the following tasks:

■ Prevent software restriction policies from applying to local administrators.

■ Set trusted publisher options.

To prevent software restriction policies from applying to local administrators, complete the following steps:

1. Access the Group Policy Object Editor console for a GPO.

2. In the Group Policy Object Editor console, click Computer Configuration, double-click Windows Settings, double-click Security Settings, and then double-click Software Restriction Policies.

3. In the details pane, double-click the Enforcement setting.

4. In the Enforcement Properties dialog box, shown in Figure 6-29, click All Users Except Local Administrators and then click OK.

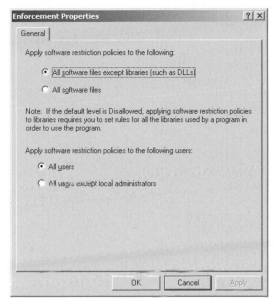

Figure 6-29   The Enforcement Properties dialog box

To set trusted publisher options, complete the following steps:

1. Access the Group Policy Object Editor console for a GPO.

2. In the Group Policy Object Editor console, click Computer Configuration, double-click Windows Settings, double-click Security Settings, and then double-click Software Restriction Policies.

3. In the details pane, double-click the Trusted Publishers setting.

4. In the Trusted Publishers Properties dialog box, shown in Figure 6-30, select the users that you want to have the right to decide what certificates will be trusted, and then click OK.

> **Note**   Local computer administrators have the right to specify trusted publishers on the local computer, while enterprise administrators have the right to specify trusted publishers on an OU level.

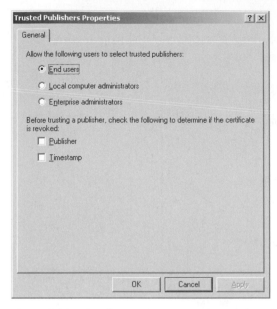

Figure 6-30   The Trusted Publishers Properties dialog box

Best Practices for Software Restriction Policies

The following are the best practices for applying software restriction policies:

- Create a separate GPO for software restriction policies so that you can disable them in an emergency without affecting the rest of your security settings.

- Test a software restriction policy before applying it to other computers. Do not disallow programs or files without the proper testing. Restrictions on certain files can seriously affect the operation of your computer or network.

- If you need to edit a software restriction policy, first disable it. If you apply the policy in parts and a user refreshes the policy before all of the parts are in effect, that user's computer might be adversely affected.

- If you experience problems with applied policies, reboot in safe mode. Software restriction policies do not apply in safe mode.

- If you accidentally lock down a workstation with software restriction policies, reboot in safe mode, log on as a local administrator, modify the policy, run Gpupdate.exe, reboot the computer, and log on normally.

- Use software restriction policies in conjunction with access control settings.

- Use caution when defining a default setting of Disallowed. When you set the default security level to Disallowed, every application is restricted. A policy must be applied for every application that you want to run.

Software Restriction Policies Troubleshooting

Table 6-6 describes some troubleshooting scenarios related to software restriction policies.

Table 6-6   Software Restriction Policies Troubleshooting Scenarios

Problem: **The user receives an error message such as "Windows cannot open this program because it has been prevented by a software restriction policy. For more information, open the Event Viewer console or contact your system administrator." Or, on the command line, the message "The system cannot execute the specified program" appears.**

Cause	Solution
The default security level (or a rule) was set to Disallowed, and the software will not start.	Check the event log to see whether the software program is set to Disallowed and what rule is applied.

Problem: **Modified software restriction policies are not taking effect.**

Cause	Solution
Software restriction policies that are specified in a domain through Group Policy override any policies that are configured locally. The problem might be occurring because there is a policy from the domain that is overriding your setting.	Use the Gpresult.exe command-line tool to determine which policies apply. Check domain-level policies for No Override settings.
Group Policy might not have refreshed its settings. Group Policy applies policy changes periodically; therefore, it is likely that the policy changes made in the directory have not yet been refreshed.	Refresh the policy with the command-line utility Gpupdate.exe.
The local computer on which you changed software restriction policies for the network cannot contact a domain controller.	The computer on which you modify software restriction policies must be able to contact a domain controller to update policy for a network. Ensure the computer can contact a domain controller.

Problem: **You have added a rule to software restriction policies, and you cannot log on to your computer.**

Cause	Solution
Your computer accesses many programs and files when it starts. You might have inadvertently set one of these programs or files to Disallowed. Because the computer cannot access the program or file, it cannot start properly.	Start your computer in safe mode, log on as a local administrator, and change software restriction policies to allow the program or file to run.

Table 6-6   Software Restriction Policies Troubleshooting Scenarios

Problem: **A new policy is not applying to a specific filename extension.**

Cause	Solution
The filename extension is not in the list of file types supported by the software restriction policies.	Add the filename extension to the list of supported file types in the Designated File Types setting.

Lesson Review

The following questions are intended to reinforce key information presented in this lesson. If you are unable to answer a question, review the lesson materials and try the question again. You can find answers to the questions in the "Questions and Answers" section at the end of this chapter.

1. What is the purpose of software restriction policies?

    _____

    _____

    _____

    _____

2. Explain the two default security levels.

    _____

    _____

    _____

    _____

    _____

    _____

    _____

    _____

    _____

3. Describe how software is identified by software restriction policies.

_____

_____

_____

_____

_____

_____

_____

_____

4. List the order of rule precedence.

_____

_____

_____

5. Which of the following rule types applies only to Windows Installer packages?

    a. Hash rules

    b. Certificate rules

    c. Internet zone rules

    d. Path rules

_____

Lesson Summary

- Software restriction policies address the problem of regulating unknown or untrusted code. Software restriction policies are security settings in a GPO provided to identify software and control its ability to run on a local computer, site, domain, or OU.

- There are two default security levels for software restriction policies: Disallowed, which does not allow the software to run, regardless of the access rights of the user who is logged on to the computer; and Unrestricted, which allows software to run with the full rights of the user who is logged on to the computer.

- Software restriction policies identify and control the running of software by using rules. There are four types of rules, which correspond to the four ways of identifying software: a hash rule, a certificate rule, a path rule, and an Internet zone rule. These rules override the default security level.

Case Scenario Exercise

You have been asked by Max Benson, CEO of Wide World Importers, to advise the company on some software deployment issues it is facing. Wide World Importers is an import/export company handling primarily clothing and textile products. They have offices in New York, New York; San Diego, California; and Fort Lauderdale, Florida. Wide World Importer's network is configured as a single Active Directory domain with sites and organizational units (OUs) for each location. Below each top-level OU is another layer of OUs representing the functional areas of Shipping, Finance, and Marketing. The users and client computers are distributed as shown in Table 6-7.

Table 6-7   Wide World Importers Network Structure

Office/OU	Users	Computers	Operating systems used
NY/Shipping	15	8	Windows 2000 Professional
NY/Finance	60	60	Windows 2000 Professional and Windows XP Professional
NY/Marketing	175	185	Windows 2000 Professional and Windows XP Professional
CA/Shipping	55	40	Windows 2000 Professional and Windows NT 4.0 Workstation
CA/Finance	110	110	Windows XP Professional
CA/Marketing	210	210	Windows 2000 Professional and Windows XP Professional
FL/Shipping	25	15	Windows NT 4.0 Workstation
FL/Finance	20	20	Windows 2000 Professional
FL/Marketing	140	150	Windows 2000 Professional and Windows XP Professional

The California and New York offices are connected by a dedicated T1 line. There are dedicated 256 Kbps Fractional T1 lines connecting the Florida office to both California and New York. Several Marketing users have mobile computers, and a portion of their time is spent traveling the world. Access to the main network is accomplished by dialing in to a local ISP, and then establishing a Layer Two Tunneling Protocol (L2TP) virtual private network (VPN) to the California office. There are three domain controllers and one file server at each location. The WAN links are used heavily during the day, but Wide World Importers does not plan to upgrade them any time soon. It is important that the software deployment strategy you suggest does not adversely affect the WAN links during business hours.

Max has indicated that he wants more control over software deployment and wants to leverage his investment in Windows Server 2003. The main software requirements of the company include Microsoft Office XP for all users, a third-party program used by the Marketing department, an application used by the Finance department for billing and accounting, and a proprietary shipping application developed for Wide World Importers. While all users work with Office XP, they don't all use the same applications. Many users work only with Outlook and Word, while others also make use of Access and PowerPoint. Still others use Excel on a daily basis.

Given the concerns of Wide World Importers as outlined here, answer the following questions.

Using GPO for software deployment, how can you configure things so as to not negatively affect the business by saturating the WAN links during deployment?

> On a single LAN, it is common to set up a single SDP to store the applications to be deployed using Group Policy. Bandwidth cannot be totally disregarded, but it is much less of an issue locally because high bandwidth is assumed. When WAN links are involved, the best way to prevent a deployment scenario where the client is installing the software over the WAN link is to provide an SDP at each office. Once that is accomplished, you could keep the GPOs separate for each office, with each GPO pointing to the local SDP. A more elegant solution is to configure the three SDPs as replica links in a DFS topology. This way, all software deployment can reference the same SDP, and client machines will automatically be referred to the SDP in their own site.

Max is concerned that it would be a huge burden for mobile users to deal with software installation when they are connected to the network from remote locations. What must you do to alleviate Max's concerns?

> Group Policy–based software deployment already includes the capability to detect slow links. When users are connected to the network over a slow link, software will not deploy. The users will get the software the next time they are in the office and they connect to the LAN. With Group Policy, we can control what constitutes a "slow" link. The default is 500 Kbps, which is often an acceptable setting. Most remote connections will fall below 500 Kbps, and certainly most LANs will be faster than 500 Kbps. However, perhaps you have some users that are able to use a VPN to connect to the office at 300 Kbps, and you would like that to be treated as a fast link. You could alter the Slow Link Detection setting such that any connection faster than 250 Kbps is not considered slow.

With respect to the marketing, finance, and shipping applications, what are some of the options and considerations when deciding how to deploy these applications?

> Although you could deploy all three applications at the domain level and use security filtering by adding ACEs to the GPO that limit the deployment to the appropriate users, the solution would require extra administrative work. For example, you would have to implement security groups that align with the deployment goals. The best option, because these applications map nicely to the OU structure of the company, is to deploy the applications at the appropriate OUs. For example, a single GPO to deploy the sales program could be linked to all three Marketing OUs.

The other consideration is whether to assign or publish this application. You must determine whether the applications are optional or mandatory. If these applications are optional, publishing to users would make the most sense. Users would have to take the initiative in choosing to go to Add/Remove Programs and install the application. Considering that these custom applications were developed specifically to be used by these departments, it is likely that the company would consider them mandatory. Assuming that is the case, you should assign them. If users move from computer to computer in the organization, you might decide that assigning them to the users is most appropriate. If each user has his or her own computer, assigning the applications to the appropriate computers is the best solution.

How do you recommend resolving the issue that many users work with different parts of the Office XP suite of applications?

Transforms are files that end with an extension of .mst. These files are deployed along with the .msi file to alter the configuration. Using transforms is an option for addressing this complication. It could be quite an administrative burden to develop .mst files for each of the different configurations used, and then deploy multiple GPOs with each of the different configurations.

It is important to understand transforms and when they are appropriate. In this case, for example, there was no indication that having extra software simply available would cause trouble. Therefore, you should consider assigning Office XP to users at the domain level. Doing this will make all file extension associations on the client systems, and it will advertise the applications by making all of the Start menu shortcuts available. Essentially, all the applications are set to install on first use. If some users never launch Excel, for example, the program files to run Excel will simply not be installed for that user. A complicated set of transforms in this case would seem to be a waste of administrative effort.

A small number of the client systems are running Windows NT 4.0 Workstation. How would you advise Wide World Importers regarding software installation for these systems?

Group Policy–based software installation will not apply to Windows 95, Windows 98, Windows Millennium Edition, or Windows NT systems. One option to remedy the issue is to purchase and use SMS. SMS is a powerful network management application that can be used to push software to pre–Windows 2000 operating systems. However, investing in SMS might not be the best option for the sole purpose of deploying software to a few Windows 9x and Windows NT systems. Instead, it might make more sense to upgrade these systems to Windows 2000, Windows Server 2003, or Windows XP (as appropriate). If for some reason these options don't work for the company, installing the software manually or using some other network management tool are the remaining options.

The shipping application is a proprietary application that does not have an .msi file associated with it. How would you recommend using Group Policy to deploy this application to the Shipping department?

There are two options for deploying an application that does not natively have an .msi file available. The simplest, but least flexible, is to create an application file, or .zap file. This allows an administrator to publish this application to users so that they can select to install that application from Add/Remove Programs. However, a .zap file will not take advantage of Windows Installer features such as installing with elevated privileges, automatic rollback, and automatic repair of damaged or missing program files. A .zap file also cannot be assigned to users or computers; it can only be published to users.

The other option is to use a third-party application to package the program into an .msi file. Veritas WinINSTALL is one such application that can create .msi files from executable files. A limited version of WinINSTALL is included on the Windows 2000 CD-ROM. However, this application is not available on the Windows Server 2003 CD-ROM.

Troubleshooting Lab

You are a domain administrator for Contoso Pharmaceuticals. Another administrator has assigned the Microsoft Baseline Security Analyzer application to all of the domain controllers in your organization. This administrator says that it has been two days and the policy has yet to appear on all the domain controllers. He asks you to look into the problem. You first check the deployment method and notice that the application is assigned to the Domain Controllers OU.

To set up the scenario, complete the following steps:

1. Log on to Server01.

2. Search for and download the Microsoft Baseline Security Analyzer (Mbsasetup.msi) from the Microsoft Web site. Place that .msi file in the shared SDP folder you created in Lesson 3.

3. Open the Active Directory Users And Computers console. Right-click the Domain Controllers OU, and click Properties.

4. In the Domain Controllers Properties dialog box, click the Group Policy tab, and then click New. Type **MBSA** as the name of the new policy, and then press ENTER.

5. Ensure that MBSA is selected, and then click Edit. In the Group Policy Object Editor, expand Computer Configuration and Software Settings, and then click Software Installation. Right-click Software Installation, point to New, and then click Package. In the Open dialog box, in the File Name box, type **server01\SDP\mbsasetup.msi** and then press ENTER.

6. In the Deploy Software dialog box, confirm that the software is to be Assigned and click OK. Press F5 and the new package appears in the details pane. Close the Group Policy Object Editor.

7. Ensure that MBSA is selected in the Domain Controllers Properties dialog box. Click Properties. Then select the Disable Computer Configuration Settings check box. In the Confirm Disable message box, click Yes. Click OK. Note that there is a warning icon for the MBSA policy in the Domain Controllers Properties dialog box.

8. Click OK in the Domain Controllers Properties dialog box.

Now you've configured the scenario described previously. The following steps take you through troubleshooting and resolving the issue:

1. Restart Server01 in an attempt to initiate application installation.

2. Log on to Server01 using the domain administrator user name and password.

3. Run the Gpresult.exe command. What do you see concerning the MBSA policy?

   The MBSA policy was not applied because the GPO is disabled.

4. Open the Active Directory Users And Computers console. Open the Domain Controllers Properties dialog box, and then open the MBSA policy properties dialog box. Clear the Disable Computer Configuration Settings check box. Click OK. Note that the warning icon has been removed from the MBSA policy on the Domain Controllers Properties dialog box.

5. Click OK in the Domain Controllers Properties dialog box.

6. Restart Server01. Log on to Server01 using the domain administrator user name and password.

7. You should see that the Microsoft Baseline Security Analyzer tool is now installed. Close all open MBSA windows.

Many different issues might cause an application not to be deployed. The most common reasons are policy inheritance blocking, security filtering, replication errors, network connectivity issues, or that the policy or part of the policy has been disabled. Gpresult.exe helps you identify these problems.

Note   You can remove the MBSA policy once you've completed this lab. The full benefit of software distribution is not realized in this lab because you have only two computers in your test environment and only one of those computers (Server01) is in an OU. The real benefits become obvious when there are many computers in one or more OUs to which you can automatically distribute software.

Chapter Summary

- The Software Installation extension in the Group Policy Object Editor console enables administrators to centrally manage the deployment of Windows Installer packages on a client computer by assigning applications to users or computers or by publishing applications for users.

- When you assign an application to a user, the application is advertised to the user on the Start menu the next time he or she logs on to a workstation, and local registry settings, including filename extensions, are updated.

- When you publish the application to users, the application does not appear installed on the users' computers. If users choose, they can install the software from Add Or Remove Programs in Control Panel. Publish software that users might find useful to perform their jobs.

- Modifications enable you to customize Windows Installer packages. Modifications can be transform (.mst) or patch (.msp) files. You cannot deploy .mst or .msp files alone. They must modify an existing Windows Installer package.

- You can redeploy an application previously deployed with Group Policy if there are small changes that need to be made to the original software deployment configuration.

- To upgrade software deployed with Group Policy, you must first create a Windows Installer package that contains the upgrade and then configure the upgrade in the Upgrades tab in the Properties dialog box for the package.

- Windows Server 2003 operating systems provide the following Group Policy troubleshooting tools to assist you in verifying your configuration and in diagnosing and solving problems related to deploying software with Group Policy: Resultant Set Of Policy Wizard, Gpresult.exe and Gpupdate.exe command-line tools, Event Viewer, and log files.

- Software restriction policies are security settings in a GPO provided to identify software and control its ability to run on a local computer, site, domain, or OU.

Exam Highlights

Before taking the exam, review the following key points and terms to help you identify topics you need to review. Return to the lessons for additional practice, and review the "Further Readings" sections in Part 2 for pointers to more information about topics covered by the exam objectives.

Key Points

- Folder Redirection enables you to redirect the following special folders: Application Data, Desktop, My Documents, My Pictures, and Start Menu.

- You can set up folder redirection in two ways:

    1. Redirect special folders to one location for everyone in the site, domain, or OU.

    2. Redirect special folders to a location according to security group membership.

- Redeploy an application previously deployed with Group Policy by using the Software Installation extension.

- Upgrade software deployed with Group Policy by creating a Windows Installer package that contains the upgrade, and then configure the upgrade in the Upgrades tab in the Properties dialog box for the package.

- Use the Resultant Set Of Policy Wizard, Gpresult.exe and Gpupdate.exe command-line tools, Event Viewer, and log files to troubleshoot Group Policy application deployment issues.

- Software restriction policies are a new feature in Windows Server 2003 operating systems, created to address the problem of regulating unknown or untrusted code.

Key Terms

Software Installation extension   An extension within Group Policy that is the administrator's primary tool for managing software within an organization. Software Installation works in conjunction with Group Policy and Active Directory, establishing a Group Policy–based software management system that allows you to centrally manage the initial deployment of software, mandatory and nonmandatory upgrades, patches, and quick fixes, and the removal of software.

Assign   To deploy a program to members of a group where acceptance of the program is mandatory.

Publish   To deploy a program to members of a group where acceptance of the program is at the discretion of the user.

Software distribution point (SDP)   In Software Installation, a network location from which users are able to get the software that they need.

Software restriction policies   Security settings in a GPO provided to identify software and control its ability to run on a local computer, site, domain, or OU.

Folder Redirection   An extension within Group Policy that allows you to redirect the following special folders: Application Data, Desktop, My Documents, My Pictures, and Start Menu.

Questions and Answers

Page
6-25

Lesson 1 Review

1. What is the purpose of folder redirection?

You redirect users' folders to provide a centralized location for storing important user folders. This centralized location, called a sharepoint, provides users with an access point for storing and finding information, and it provides administrators with an access point for managing information.

2. Which folders can be redirected?

Windows Server 2003 operating systems allow the following special folders to be redirected: Application Data, Desktop, My Documents, My Pictures, and Start Menu.

3. Under what circumstances should you redirect My Documents to a home folder?

Redirect My Documents to a user's home folder only if you have already deployed home directories in your organization. This option is intended only for organizations that want to maintain compatibility with their existing home directory environment.

4. What is the purpose of the Offline Files feature?

The Offline Files feature provides users with access to shared network folders even when they are not connected to the network.

5. Which of the following are true statements? (Choose all that apply.)

    a. Remote Desktop For Administration is installed by default on computers running Windows Server 2003.

    b. Remote Desktop For Administration is enabled by default on computers running Windows Server 2003.

    c. A server can be configured to use Offline Files and Remote Desktop For Administration at the same time.

    d. A server cannot be configured to use Offline Files and Remote Desktop For Administration at the same time.

    e. Before attempting to configure the computer to use Offline Files, you must disable Remote Desktop For Administration.

    f. Before attempting to configure the computer to use Offline Files, you must enable Remote Desktop For Administration.

The correct answers are a, d, and e. Remote Desktop For Administration is installed, but not enabled, by default on computers running Windows Server 2003. Because Remote Desktop For Administration and Offline Files are mutually exclusive, a server cannot be configured to use Offline Files and Remote Desktop For Administration at the same time. Therefore, before you can configure a computer to use Offline Files, you must disable Remote Desktop For Administration.

6. Which of the following actions should you take if folder redirection is successful but files and folders are unavailable? (Choose all that apply.)

   a. Check the user's permissions for the redirected folder.

   b. Check network connectivity.

   c. Check that the redirected folder exists.

   d. Check to see whether Remote Desktop for Administration is enabled.

   e. Check to see whether the files have extensions that are not synchronized by default.

   The correct answers are a and b. If folder redirection is successful but files and folders are unavailable, users might not have Full Control for the redirected folder or there might be a connectivity problem with the network. Because folder redirection is successful, the redirected folder does exist. You would check to see whether Remote Desktop For Administration is enabled or whether files have extensions that are not synchronized by default if you are troubleshooting Offline Files and file synchronization.

Page
6-36

Lesson 2 Review

1. What are the hardware requirements for deploying software by using Group Policy?

   To deploy software by using Group Policy, an organization must be running Windows 2000 Server or later, with Active Directory and Group Policy on the server, and Windows 2000 Professional or later on the client computers.

2. Describe the tools provided for software deployment.

   The Software Installation extension in the Group Policy Object Editor console on the server is used by administrators to manage software. Add Or Remove Programs in Control Panel is used by users to manage software on their own computers.

3. What is the difference between assigning applications and publishing applications?

   When you assign an application to a user, the application is advertised to the user the next time he or she logs on to a workstation, and local registry settings, including filename extensions, are updated. The application advertisement follows the user regardless of which physical computer he or she logs on to. When you publish the application to users, the application does not appear installed on the users' computers. No shortcuts are visible on the desktop or Start menu, and no updates are made to the local registry on the users' computers. The application is available for the user to install by using Add Or Remove Programs in Control Panel or by clicking a file associated with the application. You assign required or mandatory software to users or to computers. You publish software that users might find useful to perform their jobs.

4. What is the purpose of Windows Installer packages?

   A Windows Installer package is a file that contains explicit instructions on the installation and removal of specific applications.

5. Which of the following file extensions allows you to deploy software by using the Software Installation extension? (Choose all that apply.)

   a. .mst

   b. .msi

   c. .zap

   d. .zip

   e. .msp

   f. .aas

The correct answers are b and c. Files with the extension .msi are either native Windows Installer packages or repackaged Windows Installer packages, while files with the extension .zap are application files. Files with the extensions .mst and .msp are modifications and do not allow you to deploy software on their own. Files with the extension .aas are application assignment scripts, which contain instructions associated with the assignment or publication of a package.

Page
6-59

Lesson 3 Review

1. Why is it necessary to set up an SDP?

You must set up an SDP to provide a network location from which users can get the software that they need.

2. What feature is configured in the File Extensions tab in the Software Installation Properties dialog box?

In the File Extensions tab in the Software Installation Properties dialog box, you specify which application users install when they open a file with an unknown extension. You can also configure a priority for installing applications when multiple applications are associated with an unknown file extension.

3. What feature is configured in the Categories tab in the Software Installation Properties dialog box?

In the Categories tab in the Software Installation Properties dialog box, you can designate categories for organizing assigned and published applications to make it easier for users to locate the appropriate application from within Add Or Remove Programs in Control Panel.

4. What feature is configured in the Modifications tab in the Properties dialog box for a Windows Installer package?

In the Modifications tab in the Properties dialog box for a Windows Installer package, you can add modifications, remove modifications, and set the order of modifications. If the modifications are not properly configured, you will have to uninstall the package or upgrade the package with a correctly configured version.

5. You want to ensure that all users of the KC23 workstation can run FrontPage 2000. What action should you take?

   a. Assign the application to the computer.

   b. Assign the application to users.

   c. Publish the application to the computer.

   d. Publish the application to users.

The correct answer is a. Assigning the application to the KC23 workstation is the only way to ensure that all users of the workstation can run FrontPage 2000.

Page
6-67

Lesson 4 Review

1. What is the difference between redeploying and upgrading an application deployed with Group Policy?

You redeploy an application previously deployed with Group Policy if there are small changes that need to be made to the original software deployment configuration. You upgrade an application previously deployed with Group Policy if the original developer of the software releases a new version of the software or if your organization chooses to use a different vendor's application. Upgrades typically involve major changes to the software and normally have new version numbers. Usually a substantial number of files change for an upgrade.

2. Why shouldn't you give users the option of applying an upgrade?

If users have the option of applying the upgrade, they might or might not choose to apply it, which could cause application version variances within an organization.

3. What happens if you delete a GPO that deploys a software application before you choose the software removal method you want to implement and allow the software removal to be processed?

If you delete a GPO that deploys a software application before you choose the software removal method you want to implement and allow the software removal to be processed, the application cannot be uninstalled with Group Policy. If the application cannot be uninstalled with Group Policy, you (or the users) must manually uninstall the application from each client computer.

4. A software application deployed with Group Policy in your organization is no longer used. You no longer want users to be able to install or run the software. What action should you take?

   a. Execute a forced removal.

   b. Execute an optional removal.

   c. Redeploy the application.

   d. Upgrade the application.

The correct answer is a. If you no longer want users to be able to install or run the software, you should execute a forced removal.

Lesson 5 Review

1. Which of the following actions should you take if a user attempts to install an assigned application and receives the message "Another installation is already in progress?"

   a. Check your permissions for the GPO.

   b. Check network connectivity.

   c. Check your permissions for the SDP.

   d. Wait for the installation to complete.

   The correct answer is d. The message "Another installation is already in progress" indicates that Windows Installer is already running another installation. You must wait for the installation to complete and then try your installation again.

2. Which of the following actions should you take if a user attempts to install an assigned application and receives the message "The feature you are trying to install cannot be found in the source directory?" (Choose all that apply.)

   a. Check your permissions for the GPO.

   b. Check connectivity with the SDP.

   c. Check your permissions for the SDP.

   d. Wait for the installation to complete.

   e. Set the auto-install property for the package.

   The correct answers are b and c. The message "The feature you are trying to install cannot be found in the source directory" can be caused by a connectivity problem to the SDP or by insufficient user permission for the SDP. There are also other reasons for receiving this message.

3. You are preparing a package for deployment. Which of the following actions should you take if you receive the message "Cannot prepare package for deployment?"

   a. Check your permissions for the GPO.

   b. Check connectivity with the SDP.

   c. Check your permissions for the SDP.

   d. Set the appropriate category for the package.

   e. Set the auto-install property for the package.

   The correct answer is b. If you are preparing a package for deployment and you receive the message "Cannot prepare package for deployment", one of the actions you should take is to check connectivity with the SDP.

4. Which of the following actions should you take if a user double-clicks a document associated with a published application and a different application than the expected one installs?

    a. Set the auto-install property for the package.

    b. Clear the auto-install property for the package.

    c. Adjust the precedence for the expected application in the Application Precedence list.

    d. Delete the unexpected application from the Application Precedence list.

The correct answer is c. If a user double-clicks a document associated with a published application and a different application than the expected one installs, you should adjust the precedence for the expected application in the Application Precedence list.

Page
6-92

Lesson 6 Review

1. What is the purpose of software restriction policies?

Software restriction policies address the problem of regulating unknown or untrusted code. Software restriction policies are security settings in a GPO provided to identify software and control its ability to run on a local computer, site, domain, or OU.

2. Explain the two default security levels.

There are two default security levels for software restriction policies: Disallowed, which does not allow the software to run, regardless of the access rights of the user who is logged on to the computer; and Unrestricted, which allows software to run with the full rights of the user who is logged on to the computer. If the default security level is set to Disallowed, you can identify and create rule exceptions for the programs that you trust to run. If the default security level is set to Unrestricted, you can identify and create rules for the set of programs that you want to prohibit from running.

3. Describe how software is identified by software restriction policies.

Using software restriction policies, software can be identified by its

    ❑ Hash, a series of bytes with a fixed length that uniquely identify a program or file.

    ❑ Certificate, a digital document used for authentication and secure exchange of information on open networks, such as the Internet, extranets, and intranets.

    ❑ Path, a sequence of folder names that specifies the location of the software within the directory tree.

    ❑ Internet zone, a subtree specified through Internet Explorer. Zone options include Internet, Local Intranet, Restricted Sites, Trusted Sites, or Local Computer

4. List the order of rule precedence.

Rules are applied in the following order of precedence: hash rules, certificate rules, path rules (in a conflict, the most restrictive path rule takes precedence), and Internet zone rules.

5. Which of the following rule types applies only to Windows Installer packages?

    a. Hash rules

    b. Certificate rules

    c. Internet zone rules

    d. Path rules

The correct answer is c. Internet zone rules apply only to Windows Installer packages.

7 Planning a Host Name Resolution Strategy

Exam Objectives in this Chapter:

- Plan a strategy for placing global catalog servers. (Exam 70-296)
    - Plan a DNS namespace design.
    - Plan zone replication requirements.
    - Plan a forwarding configuration.
    - Plan for DNS security.
    - Examine the interoperability of DNS with third-party DNS solutions.

Why This Chapter Matters

Because Internet access and Active Directory itself rely so heavily on Domain Name System (DNS), the proper planning and configuration of a DNS name resolution infrastructure is a critical step in the architect and design phase of a Windows Server 2003 implementation. While installing and configuring services such as DNS and the Windows Internet Name Service (WINS) on computers running the Microsoft Windows Server 2003 family is relatively simple, deploying these services on a large enterprise network consists of more than installing software. This chapter is concerned not so much with the mechanics of installation as it is with planning a name resolution strategy. Implementing DNS on a large network requires the careful design of a namespace that insulates the internal network from the Internet and makes it possible to distribute the responsibility for the service among various administrators.

Lessons in this Chapter:

Before You Begin

This chapter requires basic understanding of Transmission Control Protocol/Internet Protocol (TCP/IP) communications, as well as familiarity with DNS server and client services, as implemented in the Microsoft Windows operating systems. To complete the hands-on exercises in this chapter, you need:

■ One Windows Server 2003 (Standard or Enterprise Edition) system installed as Server01. Server01 should currently be installed as domain controller in the contoso.com domain.

Lesson 1: **Understanding Name Resolution Requirements**

Name resolution is an essential function on all TCP/IP networks, and the network infrastructure design process includes a determination of what names your computers will use, and how those names will be resolved into Internet Protocol (IP) addresses. As with IP addressing itself, the names you choose for your computers are affected by your network's interaction with the Internet and by the applications the computers are running.

After this lesson, you will be able to

- Determine whether NetBIOS name resolution is required for an enterprise
- Explain the DNS name resolution process
- Identify the available options for providing DNS services to clients in your environment

Estimated lesson time: 40 minutes

What Types of Names Need To Be Resolved?

As you know, TCP/IP communications are based on IP addresses. Every IP datagram transmitted by a TCP/IP computer contains a source IP address, which identifies the computer sending the datagram, and a destination IP address, which identifies the computer that is to receive it. Routers use the network identifiers in the IP addresses to forward the datagrams to the appropriate locations, eventually getting them to their final destinations.

Friendly names are only for use by people; they do not change the way the TCP/IP computers communicate among themselves. Whenever you use a name instead of an address in an application, the computer must convert the name into the proper IP address before initiating communications with the target computer. This name-to-address conversion is called *name resolution*. When you type the name of an Internet server in your Web browser, for example, the first thing your computer does is resolve that name into an IP address. Once the computer has the address of the Internet server, it can send its first message, requesting access to the resource you specified in the browser.

To design a name resolution strategy for an enterprise network, you must know the types of names the computers will have to resolve. Networks running Microsoft Windows operating systems use two basic types of names for computers and other resources: Network Basic Input/Output System (NetBIOS) names and DNS names.

NetBIOS Names

Windows operating systems prior to Windows 2000 used NetBIOS names to identify the computers on the network. The NetBIOS name of a Windows system is the computer name that you assign it during the operating system installation. Windows includes several name resolution mechanisms for NetBIOS names, and chief among these is WINS.

While computers running Windows 2000 and later use a host name to identify themselves on the network, and use DNS as their primary name resolution mechanism, they can interoperate with earlier versions of Windows because they support a second NetBIOS name as well. If all the computers on your network are running Windows 2000 or later, Active Directory has been installed, and *no applications are using Net-BIOS*, it is possible to remove WINS servers and disable the NetBIOS Over TCP/IP (NetBT) protocol on your computers. You can do this by using the controls in the Net-BIOS Setting box, found in the WINS tab in the computer's Advanced TCP/IP Settings dialog box.

Until the time when each computer on your network meets all three of the requirements listed above, NetBIOS name resolution will be required in your environment. NetBIOS name resolution processes and services, such as WINS, have not changed fundamentally since Windows NT 4.0. Therefore, NetBIOS name resolution is not an objective of the MCSE Upgrade exams and are not discussed further in this training kit.

> **Note**   For more information on NetBIOS, refer to the *Microsoft Windows Server 2003 TCP/IP Protocols and Services Technical Reference* or the *Microsoft Windows Server 2003 Resource Kit*.

DNS Names

DNS is the name resolution mechanism that computers running Windows 2000 and later use to identify hosts and services on the network, and it is the mechanism used by all computers while running Internet-based applications and protocols.

Reviewing DNS Concepts, Components, and Processes

DNS consists of a hierarchical namespace, a collection of name servers, and DNS clients called *resolvers*. Each name server is the authoritative source for a small part of the namespace. When DNS servers receive name resolution requests from resolvers, they check their own records for the IP address associated with the requested name. If the server does not have the information needed, it passes the request to other DNS servers until it reaches the authoritative server for that name. That authoritative server is the ultimate source for information about that name, so the IP address it supplies is considered definitive. The authoritative server returns a reply containing the IP address to the requesting server, which in turn relays it back to the resolver, as shown in Figure 7-1.

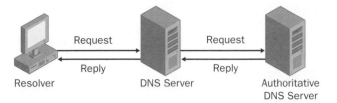

Figure 7-1   DNS servers relay requests and replies to other DNS servers

For DNS to function in this manner, it was necessary to divide the namespace in a way that would distribute it among many servers. It was also necessary to devise a methodology that would enable a server to systematically locate the authoritative source for a particular name. To accomplish these goals, the developers of DNS created the concept of the domain. A *domain* is an administrative entity that consists of a group of hosts (which are usually computers). When a DNS server is the authoritative source for a domain, it possesses information about the hosts in that domain, in the form of *resource records*. The most common resource record is the Host (A) resource record, which consists of the host name and its equivalent IP address.

Therefore, the full name for a computer in DNS consists of two basic parts: a host name and a domain name. Note the similarity between the DNS name and an IP address, which also consists of two parts: a network identifier and a host identifier. The host name identifies a specific computer and has to be unique in its domain.

Understanding Domains

The domain name part of a DNS name is hierarchical and consists of two or more words, separated by periods. The domain namespace takes the form of a tree that, much like a file system, has its root at the top. Just beneath the root is a series of top-level domains, and beneath each top-level domain is a series of second-level domains. At minimum, the complete DNS name for a computer on the Internet consists of a host name, a second-level domain name, and a top-level domain name, written in that order and separated by periods. The complete DNS name for a particular computer is called its *fully qualified domain name (FQDN)*.

Name Resolution and the Domain Hierarchy

The hierarchical nature of the DNS domain namespace is designed to make it possible for any DNS server on the Internet to use a minimum number of queries to locate the authoritative source for any domain name, as shown in Figure 7-2. This efficiency is possible because the domains at each level are responsible for maintaining information about the domains at the next lower level. For example, if a DNS server receives a name resolution request for www.adatum.com from a client resolver, and the server has no information about the adatum.com domain, it forwards the request to one of the root name servers on the Internet. This is called a *referral*.

Note The *root name servers* are the highest-level DNS servers in the namespace, and they maintain information about the top-level domains. Software developers preconfigure all DNS server implementations with the IP addresses of multiple root name servers, so they can send referrals to these servers at any time.

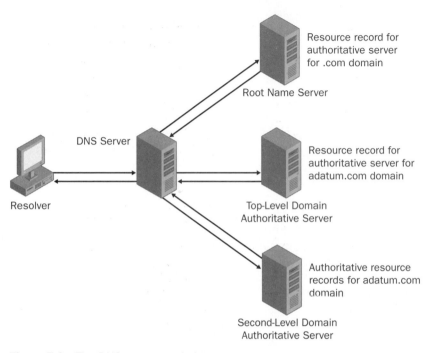

Figure 7-2 The DNS name resolution process

On receiving the request, the root name server reads the top-level domain in the requested name, in this case *com*, and returns a resource record that contains the IP addresses of the authoritative servers for the com domain to the requesting server. With this information, the requesting server can now send a duplicate of the client request to the authoritative server for the top-level, or com, domain. The top-level domain server reads the requested name and replies with a resource record that contains the IP addresses of the authoritative servers for the second-level domain—in this case, *adatum*.

The requesting server can now forward its request to the server that is ultimately responsible for the adatum.com domain. The adatum.com server reads the requested name and replies by sending the resource record for the host called *www* to the requesting server. The requesting server can now relay the resource record to the client that originally requested the resolution of the www.adatum.com FQDN. The client reads the IP address for www.adatum.com from the resource record and uses it to send packets to that server.

Reverse Name Resolution

The name resolution process described in the previous section is designed to convert DNS names into IP addresses. However, there are occasions when it is necessary for a computer to convert an IP address into a DNS name. This is called a *reverse name resolution*. Because the domain hierarchy is broken down by names, there is no apparent way to resolve an IP address into a name using iterative queries, except by forwarding the reverse name resolution request to every DNS server on the Internet, which is obviously impractical.

To address this problem, the developers of DNS created a special domain called *in-addr.arpa* (described in RFC 1035, "Domain Names - Implementation and Specification"), specifically designed for reverse name resolution. The in-addr.arpa second-level domain contains four additional levels of subdomains. Each of the four levels consists of subdomains that are named using the numerals 0 to 255. For example, beneath in-addr.arpa, there are 256 third-level domains, numbered from 0 to 255. Each of those 256 third-level domains has 256 fourth-level domains beneath it, also numbered from 0 to 255. Each fourth-level domain has 256 fifth-level domains and the fifth-level domains have 256 sixth-level domains, as shown in Figure 7-3.

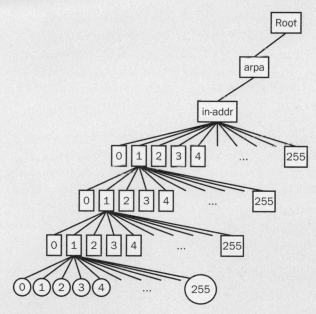

Figure 7-3   The DNS reverse lookup domain

Using this hierarchy, it is possible to express an IP address as a domain name, and to create a resource record in the domain that contains the name associated with the IP address. For example, to resolve the IP address 192.168.89.34 into a name, a DNS server would locate a domain called 34.89.168.192.in-addr.arpa in the usual manner and read the contents of a special type of resource record called a *Pointer (PTR)* resource record to determine the name associated with that IP address. The IP address is reversed in the domain name because in IP addresses, the host identifier is on the right and in FQDNs, the host name is on the left.

Caching to Improve DNS Query Performance

Although this might seem like a long and tedious process, the DNS name resolution procedure usually occurs in a few seconds or less. Several DNS elements speed up the process. The first reason for the quick responses is that the most commonly used top-level domains—such as *com*, *org*, and *net*—are actually hosted by the root name servers, eliminating one iteration from the request referral process.

The second reason is that most DNS server implementations maintain a cache of information they receive from other DNS servers. When a server possesses information about a requested FQDN in its cache, it responds directly using the cached information, rather than sending another referral to the authoritative server for the FQDN's domain. Therefore, if you have a DNS server on your network that has just successfully resolved the name www.adatum.com by contacting the authoritative adatum.com DNS server, a second user trying to access the same host a few minutes later would receive an immediate reply from the local DNS server, rather than having to wait for the entire referral process to repeat.

DNS Query Types

DNS servers recognize two types of name resolution requests: *recursive queries* and *iterative queries.* In a recursive query, the DNS server receiving the name resolution request takes full responsibility for resolving the name. If the server possesses information about the requested name, it replies immediately to the requestor. If the server has no information about the name, it sends referrals to other DNS servers until it obtains the information it needs. TCP/IP client computers send recursive queries to their designated DNS servers. In an iterative query, the servers that receive the name resolution request immediately respond with the best information they possess at the time, whether that information is a fully resolved name or a reference to another DNS server. DNS servers use iterative queries when communicating with each other. It is considered impolite to configure one DNS server to send a recursive query to another DNS server, except in the case of a special type of server called a forwarder, which is specifically configured to interact with other servers in this way.

Understanding the Domain Hierarchy Levels

The top two levels of the DNS hierarchy—the root and the top-level domains—exist primarily to respond to queries for information about other domains. The root name servers do nothing but respond to millions of iterative requests by sending out the addresses of the authoritative servers for the top-level domains.

> **Note**   There are seven primary top-level domains: *com*, *net*, *org*, *edu*, *mil*, *gov*, and *int*, plus two-letter international domain names representing most of the countries in the world, such as *fr* for France and *de* for Deutschland (Germany). There are also a number of newer top-level domains promoted by Internet entrepreneurs, such as *biz* and *info*, which have yet to be widely used commercially.

Each top-level domain has its own collection of second-level domains. Individuals and organizations can lease these domains for their own use. For example, the second-level domain adatum.com belongs to a company that purchased the name from one of the many Internet registrars now in the business of selling domain names to consumers. For the payment of an annual fee, you can purchase the rights to a second-level domain.

To use the domain name, you must supply the registrar with the IP addresses of the DNS servers that you want to be the authoritative sources for information about this domain. The administrators of the top-level domain servers then create resource records pointing to these authoritative sources so that any com server receiving a request to resolve a name in the adatum.com domain can reply with the addresses of the adatum.com servers.

> **Planning**   To create authoritative sources for your domain, you can deploy your own DNS servers, using Windows Server 2003 or another operating system, or you can pay to use your ISP's DNS servers.

> **Real World   Domain Naming**
>
> Once you purchase the rights to a second-level domain, you can create as many hosts as you want in that domain, simply by creating new resource records on the authoritative servers. You can also create as many additional domain levels as you want. For example, you can create the subdomains sales.adatum.com and marketing.adatum.com, and then populate each of these subdomains with hosts. The only limitations to the subdomains and hosts you can create in your second-level domain are that each domain name can be no more than 63 characters long, and that the total FQDN (including the trailing period) can be no more than 255 characters long. For the convenience of users and administrators, most domain names do not even approach these limitations.

Determining DNS Requirements

If you plan to give network users client access to the Internet, they must have direct access to one or more DNS servers. You can run your own DNS servers on your network for this purpose, or you can use your ISP's DNS servers. You do not need to register a domain name. The clients' DNS servers can be *caching-only servers*, meaning that they exist only to process name resolution requests sent by clients, and they can be located on your private network, with unregistered IP addresses.

Hosting an Internet Domain

If you plan to host an Internet domain, you must register a second-level domain name and give the IP addresses of your DNS servers to your domain registrar. These servers must have registered IP addresses and must be available on the Internet at all times. The servers do not have to be on your network, and do not have to be in the domain you have registered. You can use your ISP's DNS servers for this purpose (for a fee), but be aware that to create or modify the resource records stored there, you will occasionally have to change the server configuration. If you maintain your own DNS servers, you can manage the resource records yourself and retain full control over their security. If your ISP hosts your domain, you might have to have your ISP make the changes, and they might charge you an additional fee for each modification.

Hosting Internet Servers

If you plan on hosting Internet servers on your network, you must have access to a registered domain on the Internet, with authoritative DNS servers on which you can create resource records that assign host names to your servers. You can either register your own domain (in which case, you must meet the requirements described in the previous section, "Hosting an Internet Domain"), or you can use your ISP's DNS servers (in which case, the ISP must create the necessary resource records for you).

Using Active Directory

If you plan to run Active Directory directory service on your network, you must have at least one DNS server on the network that supports the *Service Location (SRV)* resource record, such as the DNS Server service in Windows Server 2003. Computers on the network running Windows 2000 and later versions use DNS to locate Active Directory domain controllers. To support Active Directory clients, the DNS server does not have to have a registered IP address or an Internet domain name.

Combining DNS Functions

In many cases, a network requires some or all of these DNS functions, and you must decide which ones you want to implement yourself and which you want to delegate to your ISP. It is possible to use a single DNS server to host both Internet and Active Directory domains, as well as to provide name resolution services for clients. However, when planning a DNS name resolution strategy for a medium or large network, you should run at least two DNS servers, to provide fault tolerance.

> **Note**   If you plan to use your ISP's DNS servers for any functions other than client name resolution, be sure that the DNS server implementation the ISP is using is compatible with the Windows Server 2003 DNS servers you are using, and that the ISP is able to provide the services you need.

You might also want to consider splitting up these functions by using several DNS servers. For example, you can use your ISP's DNS servers for client name resolution, even if you are running your own DNS servers for other purposes. The main advantage of using your ISP's servers is to conserve your network's Internet bandwidth. Remember that the Internet name resolution requests that DNS servers receive from client resolvers are recursive queries, giving the first server responsibility for sending iterative queries to other DNS servers on the Internet to resolve the name. When the DNS server receiving the recursive queries is on your private network, all the iterative queries the server generates and their responses go through your Internet access router, using your bandwidth. (See Figure 7-4.) If your clients use a DNS server on your ISP's network (which is nearly always a free service), only one query and one response go through your router. The ISP's DNS servers generate all the iterative queries, and these queries travel directly to the Internet.

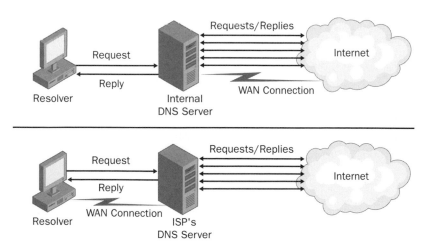

Figure 7-4   Using the ISP's DNS server saves Internet bandwidth

Practice: Specifying DNS Requirements

In this practice, you specify the DNS requirements for different network scenarios. Consider the following DNS functions:

1. Internet domain hosting

2. Internet client name resolution

3. Web server hosting

4. Active Directory domain hosting

For each of the DNS functions, specify whether you must have the following requirements. (Choose all that apply.)

    a. A DNS server with a registered IP address

    b. A registered domain name

    c. A DNS server with a connection to the Internet

    d. Administrative access to the DNS server

1. Internet domain hosting

   _____

2. Internet client name resolution

   _____

3. Web server hosting

   _____

4. Active Directory domain hosting

   _____

Lesson Review

The following questions are intended to reinforce key information presented in this lesson. If you are unable to answer a question, review the lesson materials and try the question again. You can find answers to the questions in the "Questions and Answers" section at the end of this chapter.

1. What is the technical term for a DNS client implementation?

   _____

2. In what domain would you find the PTR resource record for a computer with the IP address 10.11.86.4?

    a. 10.11.86.4.in-addr.arpa

    b. in-addr.arpa.4.86.11.10

    c. 4.86.11.10.in-addr.arpa

    d. in-addr.arpa.10.11.86.4

3. What is the maximum length of a single DNS domain name?

    a. 255 characters

    b. 15 characters

    c. 16 characters

    d. 63 characters

Lesson Summary

- Name resolution is the process of converting the friendly names you assign to computers into the IP addresses that TCP/IP systems need to communicate. The two types of names that Windows computers might have to resolve are DNS names and NetBIOS names.

- Individual users and organizations can register and lease second-level domain names, giving them the right to create any number of hosts and additional domain levels.

- Depending on the functions required by your network, a DNS server might require a registered IP address, a registered domain name, an Internet connection, or an Internet connection in combination with a registered IP address or registered domain name.

- Microsoft Windows versions prior to Windows 2000 use NetBIOS names to identify network computers. Windows supports a number of NetBIOS name resolution mechanisms, including WINS.

Lesson 2: Designing a DNS Namespace

Once you have determined how your network will use DNS, it is time to begin designing the DNS namespace for your network. The namespace design can include a host-naming pattern for all the computers on your network, as well as the more complex naming of the network's domains and subdomains, both on the Internet and in Active Directory.

After this lesson, you will be able to

- Create an effective DNS domain hierarchy
- Divide domain and host naming rules
- Create a namespace with internal and external domains

Estimated lesson time: 30 minutes

Using an Existing Namespace

If you are designing a new network from scratch, you are creating a new DNS namespace as well, which means that you don't have to work existing domains and hosts into your naming strategy. If the organization for which you are designing the network already has domain names in use, whether internal or external, or has a computer naming strategy already in place, it is probably best to retain those elements and build your new DNS namespace around them.

If the organization already has an Internet presence, they probably already have at least one registered domain name and the use of a DNS server to host the domain. You can continue using the existing domain name, even expanding it to include internal subdomains. You can also continue using the existing DNS server, or migrate the DNS services to a new server on the network you are designing. If you change the DNS server, you must inform the domain registrar so that they can alter the IP addresses of the authoritative servers in the top-level domain records. The changes can take a few days to propagate throughout the Internet, so it is a good idea to have an overlap period during which both the old and new DNS servers are operational.

Upgrading NetBIOS to DNS

If you are upgrading a NetBIOS network to Windows Server 2003 and Active Directory, you already have an internal NetBIOS namespace, which you can migrate to DNS, gradually or immediately. For example, if you are currently using WINS for NetBIOS name resolution, you can configure Windows Server 2003 DNS servers to resolve the NetBIOS names by sending queries to your WINS servers. You can also continue to use your existing NetBIOS names by integrating them into your DNS namespace design.

If you are deploying Active Directory on your network for the first time, and you have an existing namespace of any kind, be careful to design your Active Directory hierarchy in coordination with the names you already have.

Creating Internet Domains

Designing a DNS namespace for your organization's Internet presence is usually the easiest part of deploying DNS. Most organizations register a single second-level domain and use it to host all their Internet servers.

Registering a Domain

In most cases, the selection of a second-level domain name depends on what is available. A large portion of the most popular top-level domain, *com*, is already depleted, and you might find that the name you want to use is already taken. In this case, you have three alternatives: choose a different domain name, register the name in a different top-level domain, or attempt to purchase the domain name from its current owner.

If you are certain you want to use the second-level domain name you have chosen—for example, when the name is a recognizable brand of your organization—your best bet is usually to register the name in another top-level domain. Although the *org* and *net* domains are available to anyone, these domains are associated with nonprofit and network infrastructure organizations, respectively, and might not fit your business. As an alternative, a number of countries around the world with attractive top-level domain names have taken to registering second-level domains commercially.

Using Multiple Domains

Some organizations maintain multiple sites on the Internet, for various reasons. Your organization might be involved in several separate businesses that warrant individual treatment, or your company might have independent divisions with different sites. You might also want to create different sites for retail customers, wholesale customers, and providers. Whatever the reason, there are two basic ways to implement multiple sites on the Internet:

- **Register a single second-level domain name and then create multiple subdomains beneath it**   For the price of a single domain registration, you can create as many third-level domains as you need, and you can also maintain a single brand across all your sites. For example, a company called Contoso Pharmaceuticals might register the contoso.com domain, and then create separate Web sites for doctors and patients, in domains called doctors.contoso.com and patients.contoso.com.

- **Register multiple second-level domains**   If your organization consists of multiple completely unrelated brands or operations, this is often the best solution. You must pay a separate registration fee for each domain name you need, however, and you must maintain a separate DNS namespace for each domain. A problem might arise when you try to integrate your Internet domains with your internal network. You can select one of your second-level domains to integrate with your internal namespace, or you can leave your internal and external namespaces completely separate, as discussed later in this lesson.

Creating Internal Domains

Using DNS on an internal Windows Server 2003 network is similar to using DNS on the Internet in many ways. You can create domains and subdomains to support the organizational hierarchy of your network in any way you want. When you are designing a DNS namespace for a network that uses Active Directory, the DNS domain name hierarchy is directly related to the directory service hierarchy. For example, if your organization consists of a headquarters and a series of branch offices, you might choose to create a single Active Directory tree and assign the name adatum.com to the root domain in the tree. Then, for the branch offices, you create subdomains beneath adatum.com with names like miami.adatum.com and chicago.adatum.com. These names correspond directly to the domain hierarchy in your DNS namespace.

When selecting names for your internal domains, you should try to observe these rules:

- **Keep domain names short**   Internal DNS namespaces tend to run to more levels than Internet ones, and using long names for individual domains can result in excessively long FQDNs.

- **Avoid an excessive number of domain levels**   To keep FQDNs a manageable length and to keep administration costs down, limit your DNS namespace to no more than five levels from the root.

- **Create a naming convention and stick to it**   When creating subdomains, establish a rule that enables users to deduce what the name of a domain should be. For example, you can create subdomains based on political divisions (such as department names) or geographical divisions (such as names of cities), but do not mix the two at the same domain level.

- **Avoid obscure abbreviations**   Don't use abbreviations for domain names unless they are immediately recognizable by users. Domains using abbreviations such as NY for New York or HR for Human Resources are acceptable, but avoid creating your own abbreviations just to keep names short.

- **Avoid names that are difficult to spell**   Even though you might have established a domain naming rule that calls for city names, a domain called albuquerque.adatum.com will be all but impossible for most people (outside New Mexico) to spell correctly the first time.

When you are designing an internal DNS namespace for a network that connects to the Internet, consider the following rules:

- **Use registered domain names**   Although using a domain name on an internal network that you have not registered is technically not a violation of Internet protocol, this practice can interfere with the client name resolution process on your internal network.

- **Do not use top-level domain names or names of commonly known products or companies**   Naming your internal domains using names found on the Internet can interfere with the name resolution process on your client computers. For example, if you create an internal domain named microsoft.com, you cannot predict whether a query for a name in that domain will be directed to your DNS server or to the authoritative servers for microsoft.com on the Internet.

- **Use only characters that are compliant with the Internet standard**   The DNS server included with Microsoft Windows Server 2003 supports the use of Unicode characters in UTF-8 format, but the RFC 1123 standard, "Requirements For Internet Hosts—Applications and Support," limits DNS names to the uppercase characters (A–Z), the lowercase characters (a–z), the numerals (0–9), and the hyphen (-). You can configure the Windows Server 2003 DNS server to disallow the use of UTF-8 characters.

See Also   The two primary DNS standards are RFC 1034, "Domain Names - Concepts and Facilities," and RFC 1035, "Domain Names - Implementation and Specification." These and numerous other documents related to the development and operation of DNS are freely available at *http://www.ietf.org*.

Creating Subdomains

Owning a second-level domain that you have registered gives you the right to create any number of subdomains beneath that domain. The primary reason for creating subdomains is to delegate administrative authority for parts of the namespace. For example, if your organization has offices in different cities, you might want to maintain a single DNS namespace, but grant the administrators at each site autonomous control over the DNS records for their computers. The best way to do this is to create a separate subdomain for each site, locate it on a DNS server at that site, and delegate authority for the server to local network support personnel. This procedure also balances the DNS traffic load among servers at different locations, preventing a bottleneck that could affect name resolution performance.

Combining Internal and External Domains

When you are designing a DNS namespace that includes both internal and external (that is, Internet) domains, there are three possible strategies you can use, which are as follows:

- Use the same domain name internally and externally.
- Create separate and unrelated internal and external domains.
- Make the internal domain a subdomain of the external domain.

Using the Same Domain Name

Using the same domain name for your internal and external namespaces is a practice that Microsoft strongly discourages. When you create an internal domain and an external domain with the same name, you make it possible for a computer in the internal network to have the same DNS name as a computer on the external network. This duplication wreaks havoc with the name resolution process.

> **Note** It is possible to make this arrangement work by copying all the zone data from your external DNS servers to your internal DNS servers, but the extra administrative difficulties make this a less than ideal solution.

Using Separate Domain Names

When you use different domain names for your internal and external networks, you eliminate the potential name resolution conflicts that come with using the same domain name for both networks. However, using this solution requires you to register (and pay for) two domain names and to maintain two separate DNS namespaces. The different domain names can also be a potential source of confusion to users who have to distinguish between internal and external resources.

Using a Subdomain

The solution that Microsoft recommends for combining internal and external networks is to register a single Internet domain name and use it for external resources, and then create a subdomain beneath that domain name and use it for your internal network. For example, if you have registered the name adatum.com, you would use that domain for your external servers and create a subdomain, such as int.adatum.com for your internal network. If you have to create additional subdomains, you can create fourth-level domains beneath *int* for the internal network, and additional third-level domains beneath *adatum* for the external network.

The advantages of this solution are that it makes it impossible to create duplicate FQDNs, and it lets you delegate authority across the internal and external domains, which simplifies the DNS administration process. In addition, you have to register and pay for only one Internet domain name.

Creating an Internal Root

When you use the Windows Server 2003 DNS server with the namespace configurations described thus far, your network's namespace is technically part of the Internet DNS namespace, even if your private network computers are not accessible from the Internet. This is because all your DNS servers use the root of the Internet DNS as the ultimate source for information about any part of the namespace. When a client sends a name resolution request to one of your DNS servers and the server has no information about the name, it begins the referral process by sending an iterative query to one of the root name servers on the Internet.

If you have a large enterprise network with an extensive namespace, you can create your own internal root. You do this by creating a private root zone on one of your Windows Server 2003 DNS servers. This causes the DNS servers on your network to send their iterative queries to your internal root name server, rather than to the Internet root name server. Keeping DNS traffic inside the enterprise speeds up the name resolution process.

Planning   Creating an internal root is recommended when the majority of your clients do not need frequent access to resources outside your private namespace. If your clients access the Internet through a proxy server, you can configure the proxy to perform name resolutions by accessing the Internet DNS namespace instead of the private one. If your clients require access to the Internet but do not go through a proxy server, you should not create an internal root.

Creating Host Names

Once you have created the domain structure for your DNS namespace, it is time to populate these domains with hosts. You should create hosts the same way you create domains, by devising a naming rule and then sticking to it. In many cases, host-naming rules are based on users, geographical locations, or the function of the computer. When determining your naming rules, follow these principles:

- **Create easily remembered names**   Users and administrators should be able to figure out the host name assigned to a particular computer by using your naming rules alone.

■ **Use unique names throughout the organization**   Although it is possible to create identical host names as long as they are located in different domains, this practice is strongly discouraged. You might have to move a computer and put it in a new domain that already has a host by that name, causing duplication that interferes with name resolution.

■ **Do not use case to distinguish names**   Although you can use both uppercase and lowercase characters when creating a computer name on a computer running a Windows operating system, DNS itself is not case-sensitive. Therefore, you should not create host names that are identical except for the case of the letters, nor should you create host names that rely on case to be understandable.

■ **Use only characters supported by all of your DNS servers**   As with domain names, avoid using characters that are not compliant with the DNS standard unless all the DNS servers processing the names support these characters. The NetBIOS namespace supports a larger character set than DNS does. When you are upgrading a Windows network that uses NetBIOS names to one that uses DNS names, you might want to use the Unicode (UTF-8) character support in the Windows Server 2003 DNS server to avoid having to rename all your computers. However, you must not do this on computers that are visible from the Internet; these systems must use only the character set specified in RFC 1123.

Practice: Designing a DNS Namespace

Fabrikam, Inc., is constructing a new data network and has registered the Internet domain name fabrikam.com. You are to design a DNS namespace for the network and, in the diagram shown after the following list, write the fully qualified domain name for each computer in the space provided. Base your design on the following information:

■ Fabrikam.com is the only second-level domain name you can use.

■ The internal network should be in a different domain from the external network.

■ The company consists of three internal divisions: Sales, Human Resources, and Production. Each division is to be represented by a separate subdomain in the namespace.

■ Each division has departmental servers performing various roles and as many as 200 workstations, only some of which are shown in the diagram. Your host names should identify the function of each computer.

■ Three servers on an external perimeter network host the company's Internet services: Web, FTP, and e-mail. These servers must be in the domain fabrikam.com.

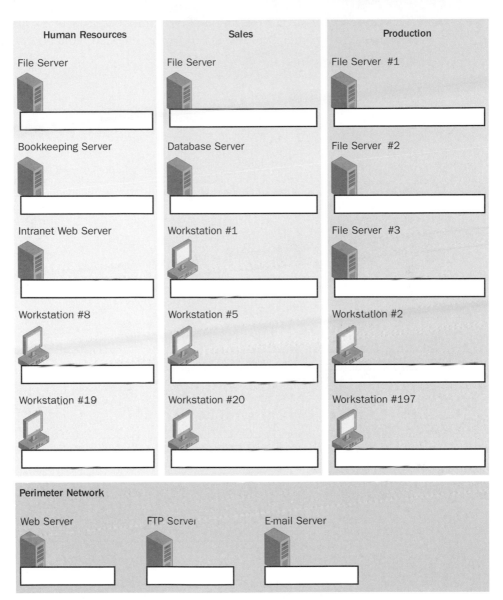

Correct answers for this practice can vary, but they should contain the following characteristics:

■ The servers in the perimeter network should have FQDNs consisting of host names in the second-level domain fabrikam.com.

■ All three internal divisions should be in a third-level domain beneath fabrikam.com.

■ Each of the three divisions should have a fourth-level domain name beneath the internal network's third-level domain.

■ Each computer should have a unique host name that reflects its function and differentiates it from other computers performing the same function.

The following diagram contains an example of a correctly designed namespace:

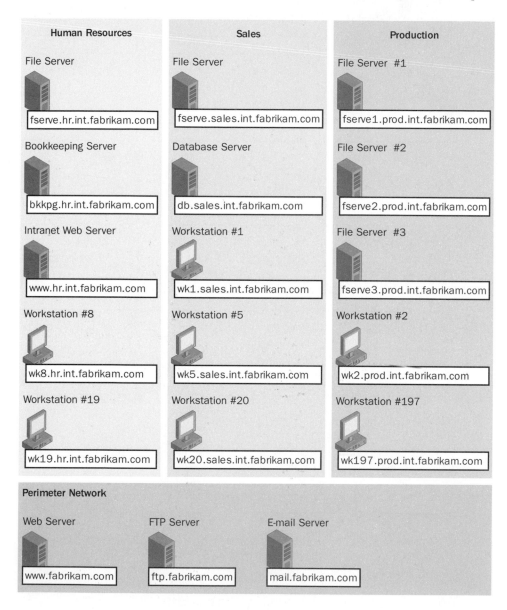

Lesson Review

The following questions are intended to reinforce key information presented in this lesson. If you are unable to answer a question, review the lesson materials and try the question again. You can find answers to the questions in the "Questions and Answers" section at the end of this chapter.

1. Which of the following is the best reason to create subdomains in a DNS namespace?

    a. To speed up the name resolution process

    b. To delegate administrative authority over parts of the namespace

    c. To create identical host names in different domains

    d. To duplicate an existing Internet namespace

    _____

2. Why should you never use the same domain name for your internal and external namespaces?

    _____

    _____

3. Which of the following domain naming examples, for an organization with the registered domain adatum.com, conforms to the practices recommended by Microsoft?

    a. An external domain named ext-adatum.com and an internal domain named int-adatum.com

    b. An external domain named ext.adatum.com and an internal domain named adatum.com

    c. An external domain named ext.adatum.com and an internal domain named int.adatum.com

    d. An external domain named adatum.com and an internal domain named int.adatum.com

    _____

Lesson Summary

- When creating a DNS namespace, devise naming rules for domains and hosts and stick to them.

- If you require multiple domains for your DNS infrastructure, you can either register several second-level domain names or register one domain name and create additional domain levels beneath it.

- Creating subdomains enables you to delegate authority over parts of the namespace and to balance the DNS traffic load among multiple servers.

- When combining internal and external domains, the recommended practice is to use a registered domain name for the external network and to create a subdomain beneath it for the internal network.

- Creating an internal root speeds up the name resolution process by keeping the process wholly inside the enterprise.

Lesson 3: Implementing a DNS Name Resolution Strategy

Once you have determined your network's name resolution requirements and designed your DNS namespace, it is time to actually implement the name resolution services by installing and configuring servers. Toward this end, you must first decide how many servers you need and where you are going to locate them, and then determine how you are going to configure the servers.

After this lesson, you will be able to

- Explain the functions of caching-only DNS servers and forwarders
- List the types of zones you can create on a Windows Server 2003 DNS server
- Understand the differences between file-based zones and Active Directory-integrated zones

Estimated lesson time: 30 minutes

How Many DNS Servers?

A Windows Server 2003 DNS server running on a computer with a 700 MHz Pentium III processor can handle up to 10,000 name resolution queries per second, so in most instances, private networks use multiple DNS servers for reasons other than a heavy client load. Some other reasons for deploying multiple DNS servers on your network are as follows:

- **Providing redundancy** For a network that relies heavily on DNS name resolution, having a single DNS server means having a single point of failure. You should plan to deploy a sufficient number of DNS servers so that at least two copies of every zone are always online.

- **Improving performance** For a DNS client, the combination of a nearby DNS server and a reduced traffic load on that server means improved name resolution performance.

- **Balancing traffic load** Even when a single server is capable of handling the name resolution requests for your entire network, the network might not be up to the task. Having all the network's DNS traffic converge on a single subnet can overload the LAN and slow down the name resolution process, as well as interfere with the other computers sharing the network. Deploying multiple servers on different subnets enables you to balance the DNS traffic between them and avoid creating bottlenecks.

- **Reducing WAN traffic** When your network consists of LANs at multiple sites, connected by multiple wide area network (WAN) links, it is usually best to have a DNS server at each site. WAN links are relatively slow compared to LAN connections, and their bandwidth can be quite expensive. Having a DNS server at each site prevents name resolution traffic from monopolizing the WAN connections. This practice also prevents router or WAN connection failures from interrupting name resolution services.

■ **Delegating authority**   In a large organization, it might be impractical for a single administrative team to maintain the DNS namespace for the entire enterprise. It is often more efficient to split the namespace into several domains and have the administrative staff in each department, division, or office location maintain their own DNS resource records. While it is not essential that you allocate a separate DNS server to each domain, circumstances usually dictate this setup.

■ **Supporting Active Directory**   The Active Directory directory service relies heavily on DNS. Active Directory clients use DNS to locate domain controllers and browse the network. You should deploy enough DNS servers to support the needs of Active Directory and its clients.

You should consider all these factors when deciding how many DNS servers you need, and when balancing them against factors such as hardware and software costs and the administrative burden of running multiple servers.

Understanding DNS Server Types

You can deploy Windows Server 2003 DNS servers in a number of different configurations, depending on your infrastructure design and your users' needs.

Using Caching-Only Servers

It is not essential for a DNS server to be the authoritative source for a domain. In its default configuration, a Windows Server 2003 DNS server can resolve Internet DNS names for clients immediately after its installation. A DNS server that contains no zones and is hosting no domains is called a *caching-only server*. If you have Internet clients on your network but you do not have a registered domain name and are not using Active Directory, you can deploy caching-only servers that simply provide Internet name resolution services for your clients.

Off the Record   The Windows Server 2003 DNS server comes configured with the names and IP addresses of the root name servers on the Internet, so it can resolve any Internet DNS name, using the name resolution processes described in Lesson 1 of this chapter. As the server performs client name resolutions, it builds up a cache of DNS information, just like any other DNS server, and begins to satisfy some name resolution requests using information in the cache.

In some instances, you might want to use some caching-only servers on your network, even if you are hosting domains. For example, if you want to install a DNS server at a branch office for the purpose of Internet name resolution, you are not required to host a part of your namespace there. You can simply install a caching-only server in the remote location and configure it to forward all name resolution requests for your company domains to a DNS server at the home office, while the caching-only server resolves all Internet DNS names itself.

> **Exam Tip**   Be sure you understand the difference between a caching-only DNS server and one that hosts domains.

Using Forwarders

A *forwarder* is a DNS server that receives queries from other DNS servers that are explicitly configured to send them. With Windows Server 2003 DNS servers, the forwarder requires no special configuration. However, you must configure the other DNS servers to send queries to the forwarder. To do this, from the Action menu in the DNS console, click Properties to display the server's Properties dialog box, click the Forwarders tab, and then supply the IP address of the DNS server that will act as a forwarder. (See Figure 7-5.) You can also specify multiple forwarder IP addresses to provide fault tolerance.

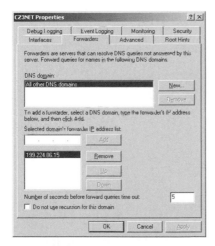

Figure 7-5   The Forwarders tab in a DNS server's Properties dialog box

You can use forwarders in a variety of ways to regulate the flow of DNS traffic on your network. As explained earlier, a DNS server that receives recursive queries from clients frequently has to issue numerous iterative queries to other DNS servers on the Internet to resolve names, generating a significant amount of traffic on the network's Internet connection.

There are several scenarios in which you can use forwarders to redirect this Internet traffic. For example, if a branch office is connected to your corporate headquarters using a T-1 leased line and the branch office's Internet connection is a much slower shared dial-up modem, you can configure the DNS server at the branch office to use the DNS server at headquarters as a forwarder, as shown in Figure 7-6. The recursive queries generated by the clients at the branch office then travel over the T-1 to the forwarder at the headquarters, which resolves the names in the usual manner and returns the results to the branch office DNS server. The clients at the branch office can then use the resolved names to connect to Internet servers directly, over the dial-up connection. No DNS traffic passes over the branch office's Internet connection.

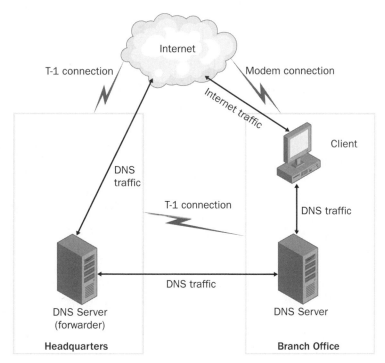

Figure 7-6   Using a forwarder to reroute DNS traffic

You can also use forwarders to limit the number of servers that transmit name resolution queries through the firewall to the Internet. If you have five DNS servers on your network, all of which provide both internal and Internet name resolution services, you have five points where your network is vulnerable to attacks from the Internet. By configuring four of the DNS servers to send all their Internet queries to the fifth server, you create only one point of vulnerability.

Chaining Forwarders

One DNS server that is functioning as a forwarder can also forward its queries to another forwarder. To combine the two scenarios described in the previous section, you can configure your branch office servers to forward name resolution requests to various DNS servers at headquarters, and then have the headquarters servers forward all Internet queries to the one server that transmits through the firewall.

Using Conditional Forwarding

One of the new features in Windows Server 2003 is the ability to configure the DNS server to forward queries conditionally, based on the domain specified in the name resolution request. By default, the forwarder addresses you specify in the Forwarders tab in a DNS server's Properties dialog box apply to all other DNS domains. However, when you click New and specify a different domain, you can supply different forwarder addresses so that requests for names in that domain are sent to different servers.

As an example of conditional forwarding, consider a network that uses a variety of registered domain names, including contoso.com. When a client tries to resolve a name in the contoso.com domain and sends a query to a DNS server that is not an authoritative source for that domain, the server normally must resolve the name in the usual manner, by first querying one of the root name servers on the Internet. However, using conditional forwarding, you can config-ure the client's DNS server to forward all queries for the contoso.com domain directly to the authoritative server for that domain, which is on the company net-work. This configuration keeps all the DNS traffic on the private network, speed-ing up name resolution and conserving the company's Internet bandwidth.

You can also use conditional forwarding to minimize the network traffic that internal name resolution generates by configuring each of your DNS servers to forward queries directly to the authoritative servers for their respective domains. This practice is an improvement even over creating an internal root, because there is no need for the servers to query the root name server to determine the addresses of the authoritative servers for a particular domain.

Using conditional forwarding extensively on a large enterprise network has two main drawbacks: the amount of administrative effort needed to configure all the DNS servers with forwarder addresses for all the domains in the namespace, and the static nature of the forwarding configuration. If your network is expanding rapidly and you are frequently adding or moving DNS servers, the need to con-tinually reconfigure the forwarder addresses might be more trouble than the sav-ings in network traffic are worth.

Creating Zones

A *zone* is an administrative entity you create on a DNS server to represent a discrete portion of the namespace. Administrators typically divide the DNS namespace into zones to store them on different servers and to delegate their administration to different people. Zones always consist of entire domains or subdomains. You can create a zone that contains multiple domains, as long as those domains are contiguous in the DNS namespace. For example, you can create a zone containing a parent domain and its child because they are directly connected, but you cannot create a zone containing two child domains without their common parent because the two children are not directly connected. (See Figure 7-7.)

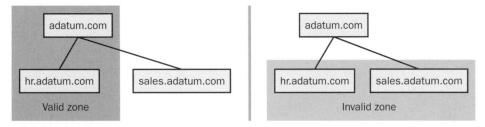

Figure 7-7   Valid zones must consist of contiguous domains

You can divide the DNS namespace into multiple zones and host them on a single DNS server if you want to, although there is usually no persuasive reason to do so. The DNS server in Windows Server 2003 can support as many as 200,000 zones on a single server, although it is hard to imagine what scenario would require this many. In most cases, an administrator creates multiple zones on a server and then delegates most of them to other servers, which then become responsible for hosting them.

Every zone consists of a zone database, which contains the resource records for the domains in that zone. The DNS server in Windows Server 2003 supports three zone types (as shown in Figure 7-8), which specify where the server stores the zone database and what kind of information it contains.

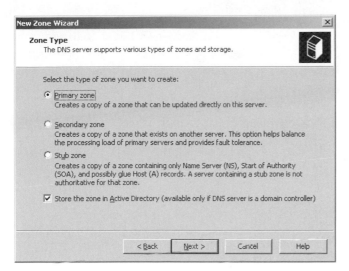

Figure 7-8   The Zone Type page of the New Zone Wizard

The three zone types are as follows:

- **Primary zone**   A primary zone contains the master copy of the zone database, where administrators make all changes to the zone's resource records. If the Store The Zone In Active Directory (Available Only If DNS Server Is A Domain Controller) check box is cleared, the server creates a primary master zone database file on the local drive. This is a simple text file that is compliant with most non-Windows DNS server implementations.

- **Secondary zone**   A duplicate of a primary zone on another server, the secondary zone contains a backup copy of the primary master zone database file, stored as an identical text file on the server's local drive. You cannot modify the resource records in a secondary zone manually; you can only update them by replicating the primary master zone database file, using a process called a zone transfer. You should always create at least one secondary zone for each primary zone in your namespace, both to provide fault tolerance and to balance the DNS traffic load.

- **Stub zone**   A copy of a primary zone that contains Start Of Authority (SOA) and Name Server (NS) resource records, plus the Host (A) resource records that identify the authoritative servers for the zone. The stub zone forwards or refers requests. When you create a stub zone, you configure it with the IP address of the server that hosts the zone from which you created the stub. When the server hosting the stub zone receives a query for a name in that zone, it either forwards the request to the host of the zone or replies with a referral to that host, depending on whether the query is recursive or iterative.

You can use each of these zone types to create forward lookup zones or reverse lookup zones. Forward lookup zones contain name-to-address mappings and reverse lookup zones contain address-to-name mappings. If you want a DNS server to perform name and address resolutions for a particular domain, you must create both forward and reverse lookup zones containing that domain.

Practice: Understanding DNS Server Functions

Review the following descriptions of DNS servers, and specify whether the DNS server is an example of a caching-only server, a forwarder, conditional forwarding, or a server with a stub zone.

1. A DNS server that contains only SOA, NS, and A resource records

   _____

2. A DNS server that receives all the unresolvable queries from another server, which has been specifically configured to send them

   _____

3. A DNS server with no zones that services client name resolution requests

   _____

4. A DNS server that sends all name resolution requests for a specific domain to another server

   _____

Using File-Based Zones

When you create primary and secondary zones, you must configure zone transfers from the primary to the secondaries to keep them updated. In a *zone transfer*, the server hosting the primary zone copies the primary master zone database file to the secondary zone, so that their resource records are identical. This enables the secondary zone to perform authoritative name resolutions for the domains in the zone, just as the primary can. You can configure zone transfers to occur when you modify the contents of the primary master zone database file, or at regular intervals.

Originally, the DNS standards defined the zone transfer process as a complete replication of the entire zone database file. At specified times, the DNS server hosting the primary zone transmits the file to all the servers hosting secondary copies of that zone. File-based zone transfers use a relatively simple technique in which the servers transmit the zone database file in its native form, or sometimes with compression. You must manually create secondary zones and configure the servers to perform the zone transfers. A later DNS standard document (RFC 1995, "Incremental Zone Transfer in DNS") defines a new replication method called *incremental zone transfers.* An incremental zone transfer consists of only the data that has changed since the last zone transfer. The Windows Server 2003 DNS server supports incremental zone transfers, but reverts to full transfers when one of the servers does not support the new standard.

> **Planning**   A Windows Server 2003 DNS server can host both primary and secondary zones on the same server, so you don't have to install additional servers just to create secondary zones. You can configure each of your DNS servers to host a primary zone, and then create secondary zones on each server for one or more of the primaries on other servers. Each primary can have multiple secondaries located on servers throughout the network. This configuration provides not only fault tolerance, but also prevents all the traffic for a single zone from flooding a single LAN.

Using Active Directory–Integrated Zones

When you are running the DNS server service on a computer that is an Active Directory domain controller and you select the Store The Zone In Active Directory (Available Only If DNS Server Is A Domain Controller) check box while creating a zone in the New Zone Wizard, the server does not create a zone database file. Instead, the server stores the DNS resource records for the zone in the Active Directory database. Storing the DNS database in Active Directory provides a number of advantages, including ease of administration, conservation of network bandwidth, and increased security.

In Active Directory–integrated zones, the zone database is replicated automatically, along with all other Active Directory data. Active Directory uses a multiple master replication system so that copies of the database are updated on all domain controllers in the domain. You don't have to create secondary zones or manually configure zone transfers because Active Directory performs the database replication automatically.

By default, Windows Server 2003 replicates the database for a primary zone stored in Active Directory to all the other domain controllers running the DNS server in the Active Directory domain where the primary is located. You can also modify the scope of zone database replication to keep copies on all domain controllers throughout the enterprise, or on all domain controllers in the Active directory domain, whether or not they are running the DNS server.

If all your domain controllers are running Windows Server 2003, you can also create a custom replication scope that copies the zone database to the domain controllers you specify. To modify the replication scope for an Active Directory–integrated zone, open the zone's Properties dialog box in the DNS console, and in the General tab, click the Change button with the label Replication: All DNS Servers In the Active Directory Domain to display the Change Zone Replication Scope dialog box.

Caution   Both DNS and Active Directory use administrative entities called domains, but the two are not necessarily congruent. For the sake of clarity, you might want to consider creating an Active Directory domain hierarchy that corresponds to your DNS domain hierarchy, but if you don't, be sure that everyone responsible for these two services remembers the distinction between DNS domains and Active Directory domains.

Active Directory conserves network bandwidth by replicating only the DNS data that has changed since the last replication, and by encrypting the data before transmitting it between servers. The zone replications also use the full security capabilities of Active Directory, which are considerably more robust than those of file-based zone transfers.

Because Windows Server 2003 automatically replicates the Active Directory database to other domain controllers, creating secondary zones is not a prerequisite for replication. Indeed, you cannot create an Active Directory–integrated secondary zone. However, you can create a file-based secondary zone from an Active Directory–integrated primary zone, and there are occasions when you might want to do this. For example, if no other domain controllers are running DNS in the Active Directory domain, there are no other domain controllers in the domain, or your other DNS servers are not running Windows Server 2003, you might have to create a standard secondary zone instead of relying on Active Directory replication. If you do this, you must manually configure the DNS servers to perform zone transfers in the normal manner.

Practice: Creating a Zone

In this practice, you implement the namespace design you created in the practice for Lesson 2 of this chapter by creating a new DNS zone on your Server01 computer, and then populating that zone with subdomains and resource records corresponding to your Fabrikam, Inc., namespace.

Exercise 1: Creating a Zone

In this exercise, you create a new DNS zone on Server01. This zone is for practice purposes only and will not interact or interfere with the existing zones.

1. Log on to Server01 as Administrator.
2. Click Start, point to All Programs, point to Administrative Tools, and then click DNS. The DNS console appears, with SERVER01 (local) listed in the console tree.
3. Expand the Forward Lookup Zones folder.
4. Click the Forward Lookup Zones folder, and then, on the Action menu, click New Zone. The New Zone Wizard appears.
5. Click Next. The Zone Type page appears.

6. Leave the (default) Primary Zone option selected, and then clear the Store The Zone In Active Directory (Available Only If DNS Server Is A Domain Controller) check box. Click Next. The Zone Name page appears.

7. Type **fabrikam.com** in the Zone Name text box, and then click Next. The Zone File page appears.

8. Accept the default Create A New File With This File Name option selected and the default file name supplied (fabrikam.com.dns). Click Next. The Dynamic Update page appears.

9. Accept the default Do Not Allow Dynamic Updates option selected. Click Next. The Completing The New Zone Wizard page appears.

10. Click Finish. A new fabrikam.com zone icon appears in the Forward Lookup Zones folder.

Exercise 2: Creating Subdomains

In this exercise, you create subdomains corresponding to your namespace design in the fabrikam.com zone. The subdomains enable you to create the resource records for the computers in the subdomains.

1. In the DNS console, select the fabrikam.com zone in the console tree and, from the Action menu, select New Domain A New DNS Domain dialog box appears.

2. Type the name you selected as the internal third-level domain name for fabrikam.com during your Lesson 2 practice, and then click OK. The new subdomain appears in the detail pane.

> **Note** When typing the subdomain name in the New DNS Domain dialog box, type only the third-level domain name. For example, if you chose int.fabrikam.com as the internal domain for your namespace, you would type **int** in the dialog box, not **int.fabrikam.com**. Each domain you create is added to the existing domain structure in the zone.

3. Repeat steps 1 and 2 to create all the other subdomains in your namespace design.

4. For example, to create a subdomain called hr.int.fabrikam.com, you would expand the fabrikam.com zone, select the int domain, and create a new domain within it, giving the new domain the name hr.

Exercise 3: Creating Resource Records

In this exercise, you populate the zone and subdomains with resource records corresponding to the computers in your Fabrikam, Inc., namespace design.

1. Click the fabrikam.com zone in the console tree.

2. From the Action menu, select New Host (A). The New Host dialog box appears.

3. In the Name (Use Parent Domain Name If Blank) text box, type the host name you selected for the Web server in the perimeter network.

> **Note**   Type only the host name, not the FQDN, in the text box. Notice that in the Fully Quali-fied Domain Name (FQDN) box, the console automatically appends the domain name to the host name you supply and displays the FQDN for the resource record.

4. Type **10.10.10.1** in the IP Address text box, and then click Add Host. A DNS mes-sage box appears, stating that the server successfully created the host resource record.

5. Click OK. The New Host dialog box reappears with the Name text box blanked out, ready to create another Host (A) resource record.

6. Repeat steps 3 to 5 to create Host (A) resource records for the FTP and e-mail serv-ers in the perimeter network using other addresses on the same subnet.

7. Select each of the subdomains you created in the fabrikam.com zone in Procedure 2, and create Host (A) resource records for the computers in the subdomains using the process outlined in steps 2 to 5.

   When you are finished, all the computers in your namespace design should have Host (A) resource records in the fabrikam.com domain with FQDNs correspond-ing to those in the diagram you created in your Lesson 2 practice.

8. Close the DNS console.

Lesson Review

The following questions are intended to reinforce key information presented in this lesson. If you are unable to answer a question, review the lesson materials and try the question again. You can find answers to the questions in the "Questions and Answers" section at the end of this chapter.

1. Which of the following DNS zone types cannot be stored in the Active Directory database?

   a. Primary

   b. Secondary

   c. Stub

   d. None of the above

2. Storing DNS resource records in the Active Directory database eliminates the need for which of the following? (Choose all that apply.)

   a. Stub zones

   b. Secondary zones

   c. Zone transfers

   d. Primary zones

Lesson Summary

- In addition to supporting clients, administrators deploy multiple DNS servers to provide fault tolerance, balance the client load and the network traffic, delegate authority over specific domains, and support Active Directory.

- A caching-only server is a DNS server that is not the authority for any domains, but simply provides name resolution services for clients.

- You can configure a DNS server to forward all name resolution requests it cannot resolve itself to a server called a forwarder.

- A zone is an administrative entity on a DNS server that represents a specific portion of the DNS namespace. There are three types of zones: primary, secondary, and stub.

- You can configure a Windows Server 2003 DNS server to store zone databases either in files, requiring a replication process called a zone transfer, or in Active Directory, which replicates them automatically.

Lesson 4: Planning DNS Security

Although DNS servers perform functions that are intrinsically benign, the possibility of their compromise does pose a significant threat to your network security. Part of the design process for your name resolution strategy is keeping your DNS servers, and the information they contain, safe from intrusion by potential predators.

After this lesson, you will be able to

- List the potential threats to a DNS server
- Describe the techniques you can use to protect a DNS server from unauthorized access

Estimated lesson time: 20 minutes

Determining DNS Security Threats

DNS name resolution is an essential part of TCP/IP networking. Both Internet and Active Directory communications rely on the ability of DNS servers to supply clients with the IP addresses they need. There are two primary security threats associated with DNS: interruption of service and compromise of DNS data. As part of your name resolution strategy, you must evaluate the threats to your DNS servers and the possible consequences, and then take steps to protect the servers without compromising their functionality.

Some potential threats to your DNS servers are as follows:

- **Denial-of-service (DoS) attacks**   Flooding a DNS server with huge numbers of recursive queries can eventually force the processor to 100 percent usage, preventing the server from processing name resolution requests from actual clients. This type of attack does not require a great deal of skill from the attacker and can be extremely effective in shutting down a network. The inability to resolve DNS names can prevent users from accessing Internet resources and even from logging on to Active Directory servers.

- **Footprinting**   Intruders gather information about a network's infrastructure by intercepting DNS data, usually to identify targets. By capturing DNS traffic, intruders can learn the domain names, host names, and IP addresses you are using on your network. This information frequently discloses the functions of specific computers on the network, enabling the intruder to decide which ones are worth attacking in other ways.

- **IP spoofing**   Intruders can use a legitimate IP address (often obtained through footprinting) to gain access to network services or to send damaging packets to network computers. Spoofing can enable packets to get through filters that are designed to block traffic from unauthorized IP addresses. Once granted access to computers and services by using this technique, the attacker can cause a great deal of damage.

- **Redirection**   In this type of attack, an intruder causes a DNS server to forward name resolution request messages to an incorrect server that is under the attacker's control. The attacker usually accomplishes this by corrupting the DNS cache in a server that is using unsecured dynamic updates.

Securing DNS

A number of techniques can protect your DNS servers and your namespace data from attack, and it is up to you to locate the threats to your servers and to determine what steps to take to protect against them. As with most security problems, it is just as possible to err on the side of caution as it is to be negligent. As an example of negligence, not implementing security measures can leave your DNS servers open to access from the Internet and can allow them to exchange zone data and dynamic updates with any other computer. This leaves the servers vulnerable to any of the attacks described in the previous section.

At the opposite extreme, you can close off your network from the outside world by denying all Internet access, creating an internal root, using Active Directory domain controllers for your DNS servers, limiting administrative access to the DNS servers, and encrypting all DNS communications. These measures secure the DNS servers from most forms of attack, but they also compromise the functionality of the network by preventing users from accessing the Internet. There certainly are times when extreme measures like these are warranted, but it is up to you to decide what level of security your network requires.

Some of the security measures you can use to protect your DNS servers from external (and even internal) intrusion are described in the following sections.

Providing Redundant DNS Services

When you use registered domain names on your network, your DNS servers must be accessible from the Internet, and they are therefore vulnerable to DoS attacks and other forms of intrusion. To prevent intruders from crippling your network by these attacks, it is a good idea to use multiple DNS servers to provide redundant services to your users. This type of protection can be as simple as configuring your DNS clients to use your ISP's DNS server when yours is unavailable or unresponsive. This way, your users can continue to access Internet services even when someone disables your own DNS server by a DoS attack. Unless the intruder attacks both your DNS server and the ISP's DNS server, name resolution services continue to function properly.

> **Planning**   You can also deploy your own redundant DNS servers to provide even more pro-
> tection. Placing a second server on another subnet, or at another site, can give your users a
> fallback in case an attack takes place on one of the servers. In addition, running your own
> servers enables you to provide redundant name resolution services for Active Directory, which
> your ISP's DNS servers probably cannot do.

Deploying multiple DNS servers is also a way to protect your namespace from footprinting. Install one server on your perimeter network, for Internet name resolution,
and another on your internal network, to host your private namespace and provide
internal name resolution services. Then configure the internal DNS server to forward all
Internet name resolution requests to the external DNS server. This way, no computers
on the Internet communicate directly with your internal DNS server, making it less vulnerable to all kinds of attacks.

Limiting DNS Interface Access

Another way of securing DNS servers against unauthorized access from the Internet is to
limit the network interfaces over which the server can receive name resolution requests.
If you have configured your DNS server computer with multiple IP addresses, you can
click the Interfaces tab in the server's Properties dialog box in the DNS console and
specify the IP addresses that DNS clients can use to contact the server. (See Figure 7-9.)
For example, if a server is connected to both an internal network and to the Internet,
you can prevent the server from receiving name resolution requests that originate on
the Internet.

Figure 7-9   The Interfaces tab in a DNS server's Properties dialog box

Securing Zone Replication

Although it is possible to footprint a namespace by capturing name resolution traffic, a more efficient method (for the attacker) is to intercept zone replication traffic. By capturing zone transfer packets, for example, an intruder can get a complete picture of a zone and all its domains and hosts at once.

The best and simplest way to secure zone replication traffic is to deploy all your DNS servers on your domain controllers and store all your zones in Active Directory. Active Directory is then responsible for performing all zone replication. All Active Directory domain controllers perform a mutual authentication procedure before they exchange data, so a potential intruder cannot use IP spoofing to impersonate a domain controller. In addition, Active Directory encrypts all traffic, which prevents anyone capturing the packets from reading the data they contain. Finally, access to the domain controllers themselves is restricted by the policies you already have in place to protect your other Active Directory data.

> **Planning**   If you cannot use Active Directory–integrated zones on your network, you must create standard file-based zones and use zone transfers to replicate the DNS namespace data. Although zone transfers are inherently less secure than Active Directory replication, there are still techniques you can use to prevent intruders from intercepting your DNS data.

One way to protect zone transfer data is to specify the IP addresses of the DNS servers that you allow to participate in zone transfers. If you do not do this, a potential intruder can simply install a DNS server, create a secondary zone, and request a zone transfer from your primary zone. The intruder then has a complete copy of your zone and all the information in it.

To limit zone transfers on a Windows Server 2003 DNS server, open the DNS console, display the Properties dialog box for a primary zone, and then click the Zone Transfers tab to display the dialog box shown in Figure 7-10. Select the Allow Zone Transfers check box, and then choose either the Only To Servers Listed On The Name Servers Tab or Only To The Following Servers option. You can then specify, in either the IP Address text box or the Name Servers tab, the IP addresses of the DNS servers that contain your secondary zones.

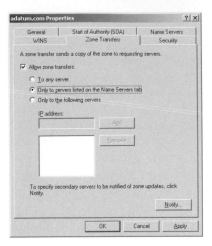

Figure 7-10   The Zone Transfers tab in a DNS zone's Properties dialog box

Although the preceding technique can prevent unauthorized DNS servers from receiving zone transfers, it does not protect the packets containing the zone transfer data themselves. An intruder with a protocol analyzer, such as the Microsoft Network Monitor application, can capture the zone transfer traffic and read the data inside the packets. To prevent this, you can configure your DNS servers to encrypt their traffic using the Internet Protocol Security extensions (IPSec) or virtual private networking.

See Also   For more information on securing network traffic using encryption, see Chapter 11.

Preventing Cache Corruption

Potential attackers might try to load a DNS server's name cache with incorrect information in an effort to redirect client connections to other servers and gather information from the clients. The Windows Server 2003 DNS server includes a feature that helps to prevent corruption of the cache. In a DNS server's Properties dialog box, click the Advanced tab (shown in Figure 7-11) and then select the Secure Cache Against Pollution check box under Server Options.

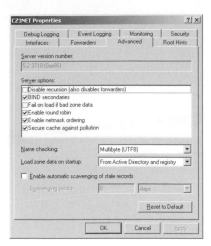

Figure 7-11   The Advanced tab in a DNS server's Properties dialog box

Activating this feature prevents the server from caching unrelated resource records included in reply messages. For example, if a DNS server sends a query to an Internet server requesting the resolution of a name in the adatum.com domain, it would normally cache all the resource records supplied by the Internet server, no matter what information they contained. If you activate the Secure Cache Against Pollution option, however, the DNS server caches only resource records for names in the adatum.com domain. The server ignores all records for names in other domains.

Using Secure Dynamic Update

As DNS was originally designed, administrators had to create all resource records by hand, typing the host name of each computer and its IP address or other information. This eventually became a problem as the use of automatic IP addressing solutions such as the Dynamic Host Configuration Protocol (DHCP) became more prevalent. DHCP is designed to automatically supply IP addresses and other TCP/IP configuration parameters to computers, which means that it is possible for a computer's IP address to change periodically. Because it would be impractical for network administrators to keep track of these changes and modify the appropriate resource records manually, the developers of DNS created a new standard, referred to as *dynamic update.*

> **See Also**   Dynamic updates are defined in a standard published by the Internet Engineering Task Force (IETF) as RFC 2136, "Dynamic Updates in the Domain Name System (DNS Update)."

Dynamic update enables DNS clients on the network to send messages to their DNS servers during system startup. These messages contain the IP addresses the DHCP server has assigned to the clients, and this information is used by the DNS server to update its resource records with the new information.

Although dynamic update saves DNS administrators a lot of work, it also leaves the DNS servers vulnerable to serious forms of attack. An intruder could create a false dynamic update message and send it to your network's DNS server. The message could state that your company's Internet Web server has changed its IP address, forcing your DNS server to add a counterfeit address to the resource record for the Web server's host name. From then on, Internet traffic intended for your company Web server would be redirected to a server under the attacker's control.

To prevent this from occurring, you should create Active Directory–integrated zones whenever possible and configure them to accept only secure dynamic updates. The procedure is to display the zone's Properties dialog box, click the General tab, and from the Dynamic Updates drop-down list, select Secure Only. (See Figure 7-12.)

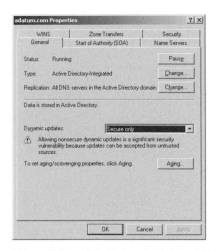

Figure 7-12   The General tab in a DNS zone's Properties dialog box

Using Standard Security Measures

In addition to these specialized DNS security measures, you can also protect your Windows Server 2003 DNS servers from attack using the same techniques you use for any computer on your network. Limiting physical access to the server and using permissions to control administrative access are basics that you should include in the case of a DNS server, because intruders can come from inside the organization as well as from outside. You can also use the packet filtering capabilities of your firewall to control access to the computer itself and to Transmission Control Protocol (TCP) and User Datagram Protocol (UDP) port number 53, which is the well-known port number for DNS.

Practice: Understanding DNS Security Techniques

For each of the following DNS security techniques, specify which types of attack they help to prevent: DoS, IP spoofing, redirection, or footprinting. (Choose all that apply.)

1. Using only secure dynamic updates

   _____

2. Installing redundant DNS servers on different networks

   _____

3. Encrypting zone transfer traffic

   _____

4. Using Active Directory–integrated zones

   _____

5. Preventing cache pollution

   _____

6. Restricting zone transfers to specific IP addresses

   _____

Lesson Review

The following questions are intended to reinforce key information presented in this lesson. If you are unable to answer a question, review the lesson materials and try the question again. You can find answers to the questions in the "Questions and Answers" section at the end of this chapter.

1. Which of the following forms of protection does Active Directory provide when you create Active Directory–integrated zones instead of file-based zones? (Choose all that apply.)

   a. Cache pollution prevention

   b. Encrypted zone replication

   c. Authenticated zone replication

   d. Secure dynamic updates

   _____

2. The DNS Update standard was developed as a response to the widespread use of which of the following?

   a. Active Directory

   b. DHCP

   c. Zone transfers

   d. Protocol analyzers

   _____

3. Using your ISP's DNS servers as a redundant name resolution mechanism helps to combat which type of attack?

   _____

Lesson Summary

■ DNS servers are subject to several forms of attack, including DoS, footprinting, IP spoofing, and redirection.

■ Using redundant DNS servers on different networks provides protection from DoS attacks.

■ Securing zone replication prevents attackers from footprinting the network. The best form of protection is to create Active Directory–integrated zones, but you can also protect zone transfers by limiting them to specific IP addresses and by encrypting network traffic.

■ Securing dynamic updates and using cache pollution protection prevents intruders from loading a DNS server with false data.

■ Use standard network security measures, such as physical access control and permissions, to protect DNS servers from internal attacks.

Lesson 5: Troubleshooting Name Resolution

DNS name resolution failure is one of the common causes of Internet access problems. On a network running Windows Server 2003 servers, the inability to resolve DNS names can bring client activities to a standstill because Active Directory relies on DNS and is responsible for controlling all client access to Windows server resources. When a client's attempts to resolve DNS names fail, there are usually two possible causes: either the client is incorrectly configured, or the DNS server itself is inaccessible or not functioning properly. These problems are discussed in the following sections.

After this lesson, you will be able to

- List the reasons that a DNS client might experience name resolution failures
- List the reasons that a DNS server might supply incorrect information
- List the reasons that a DNS server might be unable to resolve names for which it is not the authority

Estimated lesson time: 20 minutes

Troubleshooting Client Configuration Problems

When a client reports a failure to access a TCP/IP resource, such as a "Name Not Found" error message, the first order of business is to determine whether the computer has any TCP/IP connectivity at all. Once you have determined that the computer is connected to the network and that it can access TCP/IP resources, the usual method for isolating a name resolution problem is to try accessing a server using its IP address instead of its DNS name. If the computer can access the server using the IP address, you know that the problem is related to the name resolution process.

The next order of business is to check the client computer's TCP/IP configuration parameters. Assuming that the client is running Windows 2000 or Windows XP, display a Command Prompt window, type **ipconfig /all** at the prompt, and press ENTER. The resulting display contains all the computer's TCP/IP settings, including the IP addresses of the DNS servers it is configured to use.

Check to see that the IP addresses listed under DNS Servers in the Ipconfig.exe display are correct for a computer on the client's network. If they are not correct, you can modify them using Network Connections in Control Panel. If the IP addresses of the DNS servers are correct, use the Ping.exe tool at the command prompt to determine whether the client computer can contact them. You do this by using the following syntax, where *ipaddress* is the address of the DNS server:

```
ping ipaddress
```

If the ping test fails, you know that either the DNS server is not running at all or a network connectivity problem is preventing the client from accessing the DNS server. If you have already checked the client computer's general network connectivity, there might be a problem with the router or other connection device that provides access to the network on which the DNS server is located. If this is the case, follow the protocol established at your organization for troubleshooting a network connectivity problem. This protocol might require you to escalate the incident to another technician or to begin the troubleshooting process yourself. In either case, if the client's computer can access the network and is configured with the correct DNS server addresses, you can be sure the problem lies elsewhere in the network.

Troubleshooting DNS Server Problems

If a client computer is able to access the network and you have ruled out other network connectivity problems, the cause of the name resolution failures lies in the DNS server itself. A variety of conditions can prevent DNS servers from fulfilling their functions, as described in the following sections.

Nonfunctioning DNS Servers

If a client is unable to ping a DNS server and there is no client configuration or network connectivity problem, the DNS server itself might not be functioning or might be suffering from its own configuration or connectivity problem. Assuming the server is turned on and the operating system is running as it should, you should begin by checking the server's own TCP/IP client configuration parameters.

DNS and TCP/IP Configuration

Windows Server 2003 DNS servers should have static IP addresses. If the server is configured to obtain its IP address from DHCP, make sure that the DHCP server is manually allocating the address so that it never changes, and that the DNS server is actually using the IP address the DNS clients are configured to use. You can use the same **ipconfig /all** command to view the DNS server's IP address and other TCP/IP settings, whether or not they are assigned by DHCP.

If clients are able to ping the DNS server but are not receiving replies to name resolution requests, the problem could be that the DNS Server service is not running. Display the Services console, and check to see that its status is Started. In nearly all cases, the Startup Type selector for the DNS Server service should be set to Automatic. If the Startup Type selector is set to Manual, it is likely that the server restarted and no one manually started the DNS Server service. If the Startup Type selector for the DNS Server service is Automatic and the service is not running, either someone stopped it deliberately or a problem caused it to stop. Check the logs in the Event Viewer console for any indication of a problem, and check with your colleagues to see whether someone is working on the server and has stopped it for a reason.

If you can find no reason for the DNS Server service to have stopped, you can try to start it again. Then test it carefully to see whether it is functioning properly.

> **Tip**   To test the functionality of a Windows Server 2003 DNS server, display the server's Properties dialog box in the DNS console and then click the Monitoring tab. Choose whether you want to perform a simple (iterative) query or a recursive query test, and then click Test Now. Windows Server 2003 also includes a tool called Nslookup.exe, which you can use to test the functionality of a specific DNS server from any location on the network.

Troubleshooting Incorrect Name Resolutions

In some cases, client computers are able to complete the DNS name resolution process, but the DNS server supplies them with outdated or incorrect information. If the clients are attempting to resolve names for which the DNS server is the authoritative source, it is possible that the DNS server has bad information in its resource records. This could be attributable to any of the following causes:

- **Incorrect resource records**   If your DNS servers rely on administrators to manually create and modify resource records, the possibility of typographical errors always exists. If this is the case, the only solution is to manually check and correct the resource records on the server.

- **Dynamic updates failed to occur**   If you have configured your DNS servers to use dynamic updates and those updates have not occurred for any reason, the server's resource records could contain incorrect or outdated IP addresses. In this event, you can correct the resource records manually, or you can trigger a new dynamic update by traveling to the computer whose resource record is wrong and typing ipconfig /registerdns at a command prompt. This causes the DNS client on the computer to re-register its IP address with the DNS server. If dynamic updates still fail to occur, check to see whether the server supports them and is configured to accept them.

- **Zone transfers failed to occur**   If the DNS server is incorrectly resolving names from a secondary zone, it is possible that a zone transfer has failed to occur, leaving outdated information in the secondary zone database file. Try to manually trigger a zone transfer by right-clicking the secondary zone and choosing Transfer From Master. If the zone transfer still does not occur, the problem might be due to incompatible DNS server implementations, such as different compression formats or unsupported resource record types. If this is the case, you might have to update the secondary zone's resource records manually, until you can update one or both servers to compatible DNS software implementations.

If the DNS server supplying incorrect information is not the authority for the names it is resolving, it is possible that the server's cache contains incorrect or outdated information. The best solution for this problem is to clear the cache, which you do in Windows Server 2003 by clicking the server's icon in the DNS console and, from the Action menu, selecting Clear Cache.

> **Caution**   DNS servers supplying incorrect information, whether from their own zones or from the cache, might be doing so because an unauthorized user has planted the incorrect information or polluted the cache. See Lesson 4 of this chapter for more information on DNS-related security hazards and techniques for protecting your servers from them.

Troubleshooting Outside Name Resolution Failures

In some cases, you might discover that a DNS server can successfully resolve names for which it is the authority but fails to resolve names in other domains. This problem is typically due to a recursion failure, meaning that the server either is not forwarding queries for other domains to the appropriate place or is not forwarding queries at all.

One possible cause of recursion failures is that the server is configured with incorrect root hints. *Root hints* are a DNS server's list of root name server addresses, which it uses to resolve names outside its domain. If the server cannot contact one of the root name servers, it cannot discover the IP addresses of the authoritative servers for the domain that contains the name it is trying to resolve. The DNS server in Windows Server 2003 comes preconfigured with root hints for the Internet root name servers, as shown in Figure 7-13.

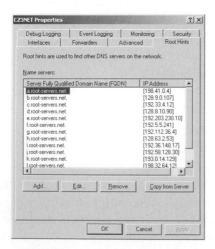

Figure 7-13   The Root Hints tab in a DNS server's Properties dialog box

Off the Record   The addresses of the Internet root name servers rarely change, and it is not likely that a Windows DNS server would be unable to contact even one of these servers, unless someone modifies the root hints. It is more common for a network connectivity problem to be affecting the server's communication with the root name servers.

Incorrect root hints are more likely to cause problems in a DNS namespace that is isolated from the Internet and contains its own internal root. If this is the case, the person who initially configured the DNS server probably either forgot to add the internal root name server to the list of root hints or typed the root name server's address incorrectly. Correcting the root hints in the DNS console should resolve the problem.

It is also possible that the server is configured not to use recursion at all. Windows Server 2003 DNS servers use recursion by default, but it is possible to prevent the server from using recursion by selecting the Disable Recursion (Also Disables Forwarders) check box under Server Options in the Advanced tab in the server's Properties dialog box. You can also prevent recursion when configuring a Windows DNS server to use forwarders. When you display a DNS server's Properties dialog box, you can select the Do Not Use Recursion For This Domain check box in the Forwarders tab. This prevents the server from using any recursion should the forwarder be unable to resolve a name. If you require the server to use recursion, be sure that these options are not selected.

Lesson Review

The following questions are intended to reinforce key information presented in this lesson. If you are unable to answer a question, review the lesson materials and try the question again. You can find answers to the questions in the "Questions and Answers" section at the end of this chapter.

1. A DNS server that can resolve names for which it is the authority, but not other names, is experiencing a failure in which of the following processes?

   a. Zone transfer

   b. Dynamic update

   c. Authentication

   d. Recursion

2. Which of the following is *not* a reason for a DNS server to supply an incorrect IP address for a name for which it is authoritative?

   a. An incorrect IP address in the root hints list.

   b. A zone transfer failed to occur.

   c. A dynamic update failed to occur.

   d. A typographic error in a resource record.

---

3. When a client can successfully ping a DNS server but fails to receive any response to a name resolution query from that server, which of the following might be the cause of the problem?

   a. The server is not the authority for the requested name.

   b. The server's cache is polluted.

   c. The DNS Server service is not started.

   d. The server has an incorrect IP address.

Lesson Summary

■ When a client computer is unable to resolve a DNS name and the DNS server is functioning properly, the problem is usually due to a client configuration or network connectivity problem.

■ Use Ipconfig.exe to display a computer's TCP/IP configuration settings, Ping.exe to test TCP/IP connectivity, and Nslookup.exe to test a DNS server's name resolution capabilities.

■ If a Windows Server 2003 DNS server computer is accessible from the network but is not resolving names, the DNS Server service might not be running.

■ A DNS server might supply outdated or incorrect name resolution information because of an error in a resource record, a dynamic update failure, or a zone transfer failure.

■ A DNS server that can resolve names for which it is authoritative, but not other names, might have incorrect root hints, or its recursion capabilities might be disabled.

Case Scenario Exercise

You are the network infrastructure design specialist for Litware Inc., a manufacturer of specialized scientific software products. You are in charge of information technology for a new branch office. The office building is a three-story brick structure built in the late 1940s, which has since been retrofitted by various tenants with several different types of network cabling. Your network design for the building calls for the installation of four LANs, each of which is connected to a fifth, backbone network. The backbone is connected to the company's home office using a T-1 leased line, and a second T-1 connects the backbone to an ISP's network, for Internet access.

The network in the new building uses the Active Directory directory service, with four computers that run Windows Server 2003 functioning as domain controllers. Each of the four domain controllers has the Microsoft DNS Server service installed. Although the other Litware offices do not use Active Directory, corporate management is considering deploying the directory service throughout the enterprise. This installation is considered the pilot program.

The company owns the litware.com domain name, which it uses for its Internet servers. Because the company Web servers have been moved to your network, you are also responsible for hosting this domain name on the Internet. In addition, the home office wants you to design a DNS namespace that would be scalable enough to eventually include the entire enterprise.

Given this information, answer the following questions:

1. Which of the following domain naming solutions is most suitable for the company network?

   a. Use the litware.com domain for the company's Internet servers and for the enterprise network's internal Active Directory domain.

   b. Use the litware.com domain for the company's Internet servers, and create an internal.litware.com domain for the enterprise network's Active Directory servers.

   c. Create an external.litware.com domain for the company's Internet servers and an internal.litware.com domain for the enterprise network's Active Directory servers.

   d. Use the litware.com domain for the company's Internet servers, and register a new domain called litware-int.com for the enterprise network's Active Directory servers.

2. Which of the following zoning solutions provides the most security for the internal network and Web servers?

    a. Connect one of the Active Directory domain controllers to the same network as the Web servers, and create an Active Directory–integrated primary zone for the litware.com domain.

    b. Connect one of the Active Directory domain controllers to the same network as the Web servers, and create a file-based primary zone for the litware.com domain.

    c. Install the DNS Server service on one of the Web servers, and create a file-based primary zone for the litware.com domain.

    d. Connect a new computer running Windows Server 2003 to the same network as the Web servers, install the DNS Server service, and create a file-based primary zone for the litware.com domain.

3. In the company's Active Directory deployment plan, each of the other Litware Inc. offices is to be responsible for maintaining its own DNS records once they deploy their own Active Directory domain controllers. Which of the following DNS namespace designs would best facilitate this intention?

    a. Create a separate third-level domain beneath litware.com for each of the Litware Inc. offices. Create a separate file-based primary zone for each third-level domain at the home office, and a file-based secondary zone at each branch office for that office's domain only. Then give the administrators at each office permission to modify the zone on their local domain controller.

    b. Use the litware.com domain for the entire enterprise. Create a file-based primary zone containing that domain at the home office and a file-based secondary zone at each of the branch offices. Then give the administrators at each office the permissions needed to modify their local zone.

    c. Create a separate third-level domain beneath litware.com for each of the Litware Inc. offices. Create a separate Active Directory–integrated primary zone at each office for that office's domain only, and replicate it on the domain controllers at the other offices. Then give the administrators at each office permission to modify the zone for their domain only on their local domain controller.

    d. Use the litware.com domain for the entire enterprise. Create an Active Directory-integrated primary zone containing that domain at the home office, and replicate it to the Active Directory domain controllers at each of the branch offices. Then give the administrators at each office permission to modify the zone on their local domain controller.

Troubleshooting Lab

You want to create a troubleshooting flowchart that proceeds logically from items 1 through 10. The first item is:

1. A client computer fails to access an intranet Web server.

The last item is:

10. The resource record for the intranet Web site has not been modified because of a dynamic update failure. The client can now access the Web server using its DNS name.

Reorder the following items to complete items 2 through 9 on your flow chart.

a. Use Ipconfig.exe to check the source of the Web server's IP address. The Web server uses DHCP to obtain its address.

b. On the Web server, type **ipconfig /registerdns** at a command prompt and then press ENTER.

c. Use Ping.exe to test the client computer's TCP/IP connection to the DNS server. The test succeeds.

d. Use Ipconfig.exe to check the Web server's DNS server addresses. The addresses are correct.

e. Use Ipconfig.exe to check the client computer's DNS server addresses. The addresses are correct.

f. Check the resource record for the Web server on the DNS server. The IP address in the resource record does not match the Web server's current IP address.

g. Check the DNS server to see whether the DNS service is running. The service is running normally.

h. Try to connect to the Web server using its IP address instead of its DNS name. The connection succeeds.

Chapter Summary

■ When creating a DNS namespace, devise naming rules for domains and hosts and stick to them.

■ Creating subdomains enables you to delegate authority over parts of the namespace and balance the DNS traffic load among multiple servers.

■ When combining internal and external domains, recommended practice is to use a registered domain name for the external network and to create a subdomain beneath it for the internal network.

■ Securing zone replication prevents attackers from footprinting the network. The best form of protection is to create Active Directory–integrated zones, but you can also protect zone transfers by limiting them to specific IP addresses and encrypting network traffic.

■ Securing dynamic updates and using cache pollution protection prevents intruders from loading a DNS server with false data.

■ When a client computer is unable to resolve a DNS name and the DNS server is functioning properly, the problem is usually due to a client configuration or network connectivity problem.

Exam Highlights

Before taking the exam, review the following key points and terms to help you identify topics you need to review. Return to the lessons for additional practice, and review the "Further Reading" sections in Part 2 for pointers to more information about topics covering the exam objectives.

Key Points

■ When designing a DNS name resolution strategy, you decide how many domains you need and what to name them. Then you populate those domains with hosts.

■ To implement a DNS name resolution strategy, you create zones on your DNS servers and populate them with resource records. A zone represents a part of the DNS namespace that can consist of one or more domains.

■ Name resolution problems are caused primarily by incorrect configuration of the TCP/IP client. However, the DNS server can also be at fault due to outdated cache information or a nonfunctioning service.

Key Terms

Resolver The DNS client component included in all operating systems supporting TCP/IP. The resolver queries the name server for a host name or address and then returns that information to the requesting client.

Fully qualified domain name (FQDN) The combination of a computer's host name and all its domain names, tracing all the way to the root of the DNS namespace.

Iterative query A DNS name resolution request that instructs the receiving server to respond immediately with the best information in its possession, whether that information is a resolved name or a referral to another server. DNS servers typically send iterative queries to other servers.

Recursive query A DNS name resolution request that instructs the receiving server to take full responsibility for resolving the name, including sending the query to other servers. The only acceptable replies to a recursive query are a successfully resolved name or name resolution failure. Client resolvers typically send recursive queries to their DNS servers.

Questions and Answers

Page
7-12
Lesson 1 Practice

In this practice, you specify the DNS requirements for different network scenarios. Consider the following DNS functions:

1. Internet domain hosting

2. Internet client name resolution

3. Web server hosting

4. Active Directory domain hosting

For each of the DNS functions, specify whether you must have the following requirements. (Choose all that apply.)

    a. A DNS server with a registered IP address

    b. A registered domain name

    c. A DNS server with a connection to the Internet

    d. Administrative access to the DNS server

1. Internet domain hosting

    a, b, c, and d

2. Internet client name resolution

    c

3. Web server hosting

    a, c, and d

4. Active Directory domain hosting

    d

Page
7-12
Lesson 1 Review

1. What is the technical term for a DNS client implementation?

    Resolver

2. In what domain would you find the PTR resource record for a computer with the IP address 10.11.86.4?

    a. 10.11.86.4.in-addr.arpa

    b. in-addr.arpa.4.86.11.10

    c. 4.86.11.10.in-addr.arpa

    d. in-addr.arpa.10.11.86.4

  c

3. What is the maximum length of a single DNS domain name?

    a. 255 characters

    b. 15 characters

    c. 16 characters

    d. 63 characters

  d

Page
7-23

Lesson 2 Review

1. Which of the following is the best reason to create subdomains in a DNS namespace?

    a. To speed up the name resolution process

    b. To delegate administrative authority over parts of the namespace

    c. To create identical host names in different domains

    d. To duplicate an existing Internet namespace

     b

2. Why should you never use the same domain name for your internal and external namespaces?

  Because this practice makes it possible to assign computers duplicate FQDNs that would interfere with the name resolution process

3. Which of the following domain naming examples, for an organization with the registered domain adatum.com, conforms to the practices recommended by Microsoft?

    a. An external domain named ext-adatum.com and an internal domain named int-adatum.com

    b. An external domain named ext.adatum.com and an internal domain named adatum.com

    c. An external domain named ext.adatum.com and an internal domain named int.adatum.com

    d. An external domain named adatum.com and an internal domain named int.adatum.com

d

Page
7-32

Lesson 3 Practice

1. A DNS server that contains only SOA, NS, and A resource records

   A server with a stub zone

2. A DNS server that receives all the unresolvable queries from another server, which has been specifically configured to send them

   A forwarder

3. A DNS server with no zones that services client name resolution requests

   A caching-only server

4. A DNS server that sends all name resolution requests for a specific domain to another server

   Conditional forwarding

Page
7-36

Lesson 3 Review

1. Which of the following DNS zone types cannot be stored in the Active Directory database?

   a. Primary

   b. Secondary

   c. Stub

   d. None of the above

   b

2. Storing DNS resource records in the Active Directory database eliminates the need for which of the following? (Choose all that apply.)

   a. Stub zones

   b. Secondary zones

c. Zone transfers

d. Primary zones

b and c

Page
7-45
Lesson 4 Practice

For each of the following DNS security techniques, specify which types of attack they help to prevent: DoS, IP spoofing, redirection, or footprinting. (Choose all that apply.)

1. Using only secure dynamic updates

Redirection

2. Installing redundant DNS servers on different networks

DoS

3. Encrypting zone transfer traffic

Footprinting

4. Using Active Directory–integrated zones

IP spoofing, footprinting

5. Preventing cache pollution

Redirection

6. Restricting zone transfers to specific IP addresses

Footprinting

Page
7-45
Lesson 4 Review

1. Which of the following forms of protection does Active Directory provide when you create Active Directory–integrated zones instead of file-based zones? (Choose all that apply.)

a. Cache pollution prevention

b. Encrypted zone replication

c. Authenticated zone replication

d. Secure dynamic updates

b and c

2. The DNS Update standard was developed as a response to the widespread use of which of the following?

a. Active Directory

b. DHCP

   c. Zone transfers

   d. Protocol analyzers

    b

3. Using your ISP's DNS servers as a redundant name resolution mechanism helps to combat which type of attack?

   Denial-of-service (DoS)

Page
7-51

Lesson 5 Review

1. A DNS server that can resolve names for which it is the authority, but not other names, is experiencing a failure in which of the following processes?

   a. Zone transfer

   b. Dynamic update

   c. Authentication

   d. Recursion

    d

2. Which of the following is *not* a reason for a DNS server to supply an incorrect IP address for a name for which it is authoritative?

   a. An incorrect IP address in the root hints list.

   b. A zone transfer failed to occur.

   c. A dynamic update failed to occur.

   d. A typographic error in a resource record.

    a

3. When a client can successfully ping a DNS server but fails to receive any response to a name resolution query from that server, which of the following might be the cause of the problem?

   a. The server is not the authority for the requested name.

   b. The server's cache is polluted.

   c. The DNS Server service is not started.

   d. The server has an incorrect IP address.

    c

Case Scenario Exercise

1. Which of the following domain naming solutions is most suitable for the company network?

   a. Use the litware.com domain for the company's Internet servers and for the enterprise network's internal Active Directory domain.

   b. Use the litware.com domain for the company's Internet servers, and create an internal.litware.com domain for the enterprise network's Active Directory servers.

   c. Create an external.litware.com domain for the company's Internet servers and an internal.litware.com domain for the enterprise network's Active Directory servers.

   d. Use the litware.com domain for the company's Internet servers, and register a new domain called litware-int.com for the enterprise network's Active Directory servers.

   b

2. Which of the following zoning solutions provides the most security for the internal network and Web servers?

   a. Connect one of the Active Directory domain controllers to the same network as the Web servers, and create an Active Directory–integrated primary zone for the litware.com domain.

   b. Connect one of the Active Directory domain controllers to the same network as the Web servers, and create a file-based primary zone for the litware.com domain.

   c. Install the DNS Server service on one of the Web servers, and create a file-based primary zone for the litware.com domain.

   d. Connect a new computer running Windows Server 2003 to the same network as the Web servers, install the DNS Server service, and create a file-based primary zone for the litware.com domain.

   d

3. In the company's Active Directory deployment plan, each of the other Litware Inc. offices is to be responsible for maintaining its own DNS records once they deploy their own Active Directory domain controllers. Which of the following DNS namespace designs would best facilitate this intention?

   a. Create a separate third-level domain beneath litware.com for each of the Litware Inc. offices. Create a separate file-based primary zone for each third-level domain at the home office, and a file-based secondary zone at each branch office for that office's domain only. Then give the administrators at each office permission to modify the zone on their local domain controller.

   b. Use the litware.com domain for the entire enterprise. Create a file-based primary zone containing that domain at the home office and a file-based secondary zone at each of the branch offices. Then give the administrators at each office the permissions needed to modify their local zone.

   c. Create a separate third-level domain beneath litware.com for each of the Litware Inc. offices. Create a separate Active Directory–integrated primary zone at each office for that office's domain only, and replicate it on the domain controllers at the other offices. Then give the administrators at each office permission to modify the zone for their domain only on their local domain controller.

   d. Use the litware.com domain for the entire enterprise. Create an Active Directory-integrated primary zone containing that domain at the home office, and replicate it to the Active Directory domain controllers at each of the branch offices. Then give the administrators at each office permission to modify the zone on their local domain controller.

   c

Troubleshooting Lab

Page
7-55

You want to create a troubleshooting flowchart that proceeds logically from items 1 through 10. The first item is:

   1. A client computer fails to access an intranet Web server.

The last item is:

   10. The resource record for the intranet Web site has not been modified because of a dynamic update failure. The client can now access the Web server using its DNS name.

Reorder the following items to complete items 2 through 9 on your flow chart.

   2. h, 3. e, 4. c, 5. g, 6. d, 7. a, 8. f, 9. b

8 Implementing, Managing, and Maintaining Name Resolution

Exam Objectives in this Chapter:

- Install and configure the DNS Server service (Exam 70-292).

  - ❑ Configure DNS server options.

  - ❑ Configure DNS zone options.

  - ❑ Configure DNS forwarding.

- Manage DNS (Exam 70-292).

  - ❑ Manage DNS zone settings.

  - ❑ Manage DNS record settings.

  - ❑ Manage DNS server options.

Why This Chapter Matters

Domain Name System (DNS) is a vital element in a network infrastructure—critical to the functioning of Active Directory directory service and computers running Microsoft Windows 2000 or later. In small organizations, DNS should be deployed on at least two servers for fault tolerance. In medium and large organizations, DNS must be distributed throughout the network and kept up to date. Network administrators are tasked with the responsibility of maintaining this infrastructure, which requires understanding the nuances of features such as zone transfers, delegations, stub zones, round robin, and netmask ordering.

This chapter introduces you to the main configuration options available for DNS servers and zones, many of which are available in the server properties and zone properties dialog boxes. In addition, this chapter teaches you how and why to implement delegations and stub zones in your networks running a member of the Microsoft Windows Server 2003 family.

Lessons in this Chapter:

Before You Begin

To complete this chapter, you must have

- Networked two computers, named Server01 and Server02.

- Server01 should be a domain controller in the contoso.com domain. It should be assigned a static IP address. In this chapter, the address 192.168.0.1/24 will be used for Server01. It should be running DNS Server and hosting the primary zone for contoso.com. Its DNS server configuration should point to its own IP address of 192.168.0.1.

- Server02 should be a member server in the contoso.com domain. It should be assigned a static IP address. In this chapter, the address 192.168.0.2/24 will be used for Server02. Its DNS server configuration should point to Server01 at 192.168.0.1.

- Ideally, Server01 should have Internet connectivity. If it does not, several steps in the exercises in this chapter will produce errors. Those errors are highlighted in the exercises, and will not interfere with the successful completion of the exercises.

Lesson 1: Installing and Configuring DNS Servers

A default installation of DNS during the promotion of an Active Directory domain controller provides a DNS configuration that enables clients to locate computers and services within the domain. Properly configured and connected to the Internet, Windows Server 2003 DNS servers can also resolve clients' queries for Internet-based hosts as well.

After this lesson, you will be able to

- Install and configure a DNS server
- Create DNS zones and resource records
- Describe the difference between primary, secondary, caching-only, and stub servers
- Create a caching-only server
- Describe several of the most common types of resource records
- Configure a DNS server to listen for queries on selected network adapters
- Configure a DNS server to forward all or select DNS queries to an upstream DNS server
- Determine when it is necessary to modify root hints
- View and clear the DNS server cache

Estimated lesson time: 30 minutes

Installing the DNS Server Service

By default, all computers running Windows Server 2003 and Windows XP have the DNS Client service installed and running. However, the DNS Server service is not installed by default in any Windows operating system. To install the DNS Server service on a computer running Windows Server 2003, you first need to add the DNS server role through the Manage Your Server page.

Once you have added this role, the DNS console appears in the Administrative Tools program group. The DNS console is the main tool for configuring and monitoring DNS servers, zones, domains, and resource records.

Note   Alternatively, you can install the DNS Server service through Add Or Remove Programs in Control Panel. Select Add/Remove Windows Components, and use the Windows Components Wizard to install the Domain Name System (DNS) subcomponent within the Networking Services Windows component. Exercise 1 includes the detailed steps for installing the DNS Server service using the Windows Components Wizard.

To install a DNS server, complete the following steps:

1. Verify that you have assigned the computer a static address.

2. Click Start and then click Manage Your Server to open the Manage Your Server page.

3. Click Add Or Remove A Role.

4. On the Preliminary Steps page of the Configure Your Server Wizard, follow the instructions and then click Next.

5. On the Server Role page, select DNS Server in the Server Role list and then click Next.

6. In the Summary Of Selections page, click Next. You will be prompted to insert the Windows Server 2003 CD-ROM.

   When the DNS server component has finished installing, the Configure A DNS Server Wizard appears.

7. To configure the DNS server you have just installed, follow the prompts and accept all default settings to complete the Configure A DNS Server Wizard. (The Configure A DNS Server Wizard is discussed in more detail in Exercise 3.)

Configuring a DNS Server

To simplify the customization of DNS server settings and the creation of new zones, you can run the Configure A DNS Server Wizard. This wizard is invoked automatically when you add the DNS server role. After the wizard is run, you can refine your DNS server configuration later through the DNS administrative console. You can also configure your DNS server completely through the server properties dialog box in the DNS console without ever running the Configure A DNS Server Wizard.

To run or rerun the Configure A DNS Server Wizard after the DNS Server service is installed, right-click the server you want to configure in the DNS console tree and then select Configure A DNS Server.

Creating Zones

DNS servers support two types of zones: *forward lookup* and *reverse lookup*. In forward lookup zones, DNS servers map fully qualified domain names (FQDNs) to Internet Protocol (IP) addresses. In reverse lookup zones, DNS servers map IP addresses to FQDNs.

Note   You can create a root server in a DNS namespace by naming a zone with a single dot (.). When you perform this task, you cannot configure the server to forward queries to another name server.

To create forward and reverse lookup zones, you can use the Configure A DNS Server Wizard. You can also create new zones at any time by using the DNS console. To do so, right-click either the Forward Lookup Zones folder or the Reverse Lookup Zones folder, and then select New Zone. This process launches the New Zone Wizard.

Zone Types

The New Zone Wizard allows you to configure the server's role in each of its zones. These roles include the following:

- Primary Zone data provides the original source records for all domains in the zone. Zone data can be transferred to a secondary zone for fault tolerance and load balancing.

- Secondary Zone data is an authoritative backup for the primary zone or for other secondary zones.

- Stub Zone data contains only those resource records necessary to identify the authoritative DNS servers for the master zone.

> **Note**   See Chapter 7 for more information about zone types and the scenarios in which each is utilized.

Understanding Server Types

The DNS *server type* refers to the type of zone the server is hosting—or, in the case of caching-only servers, whether it is hosting a zone at all. The following sections describe some essential features of the various server types.

Primary Servers

A primary server is created when a primary zone is added, either through the New Zone Wizard, the Configure A DNS Server Wizard, or command-line tools.

The primary server for a zone acts as the zone's central point of update. Newly created zones are always this type. With Windows Server 2003, you can deploy primary zones in one of two ways: as standard primary zones or primary zones integrated with Active Directory.

Standard Primary Zones   For standard primary zones, only a single server can host and load the master copy of the zone. If you create a zone and keep it as a standard primary zone, no additional primary servers for the zone are permitted.

The standard primary model implies a single point of failure. For example, if the primary server for a zone is unavailable to the network, no changes to the zone can be made.

Note that queries for names in the zone are not affected and can continue uninterrupted, as long as secondary servers for the zone are available to answer those queries.

Active Directory–Integrated Zones   When you deploy an Active Directory–integrated zone, zone data is stored and replicated in Active Directory. Using an Active Directory–integrated zone increases fault tolerance and (by default) turns every domain controller in the domain running the DNS Server service into a primary server. To configure a primary zone as an Active Directory–integrated zone, the original DNS server on which the zone is created must be an Active Directory domain controller. The process of deploying Active Directory–integrated zones is discussed in Chapter 7.

There are several advantages to integrating your DNS zone with Active Directory. First, because Active Directory performs zone replication, an implementation of Active Directory–integrated zones that uses domain controllers as DNS servers eliminates the need to configure zone transfers to secondary DNS servers. Fault tolerance, along with improved performance from the availability of multiple read/write primary servers, is provided by the presence of multimaster replication on your network. Second, Active Directory allows for single properties of resource records to be updated and replicated among DNS servers. Avoiding the transfer of many and complete resource records decreases the load on network resources during zone transfers. Finally, Active Directory integration allows you to configure access security for stored records, which prevents unauthorized updates.

Planning   If you can deploy an Active Directory–integrated zone, do. It reduces administrative headaches, improves security, and minimizes zone transfer traffic. Because of these advantages, you should plan to use a standard primary or secondary zone only when you want to deploy a DNS server on a computer that is not an Active Directory domain controller.

Secondary Servers

DNS design specifications recommend that at least two DNS servers be used to host each zone. For standard primary zones, secondary servers provide a means to offload DNS query traffic in areas of the network where a zone is heavily queried and used. Additionally, if a primary server is down, a secondary server provides name resolution in the zone until the primary server is available.

The servers from which secondary servers acquire zone information are called *masters*. A master can be the primary server or another secondary server. You specify the secondary server's master servers when the server's secondary zone is created, through either the New Zone Wizard, the Configure A DNS Server Wizard, or command-line tools.

Off the Record   Secondary servers are best placed as close as possible to clients that have a high demand for names used in the zone. Also, you should consider placing secondary servers across a router, either on other subnets or across wide area network (WAN) links. This setup provides efficient use of a secondary server as a backup in cases where an intermediate network link becomes the point of failure between DNS servers and clients that use the zone.

Stub Servers

Stub DNS servers host *stub zones*, which are abbreviated copies of a zone that contain only a list of the authoritative name servers for its master zone. A DNS server hosting a stub zone attempts to resolve queries for computer names in the master zone by querying the name servers listed. Stub zones are most frequently used to enable a parent zone to keep an updated list of the name servers available in a child zone.

Caching-Only Servers

Caching-only servers do not host any zones and are not authoritative for any particular domain. The information they contain is limited to what has been cached while resolving queries.

In determining when to use this kind of server, note that when it is initially started, it has no cached information. The information is obtained over time as client requests are serviced. However, if you are dealing with a slow WAN link between sites, this option might be ideal because once the cache is built, traffic across the WAN link decreases. DNS queries are also resolved faster, improving the performance of network applications. In addition, the caching-only server does not perform zone transfers, which can also be network-intensive in WAN environments. Finally, a caching-only DNS server can be valuable at a site where DNS functionality is needed locally, but administering domains or zones is not desirable for that location.

Exam Tip   When you need to minimize name resolution traffic across WAN links without increasing zone transfer traffic, install a caching-only server.

By default, the DNS Server service acts as a caching-only server. Caching-only servers thus require little or no configuration.

To install a caching-only DNS server, complete the following steps:

1. Install the DNS server role on the server computer.

2. Verify that server root hints are configured or updated correctly.

3. Do not configure the DNS server with any zones.

Creating Resource Records

New zones contain only two resource records: the Start Of Authority (SOA) record corresponding to the zone, and a Name Server (NS) record corresponding to the local DNS server created for the zone. After you create a zone, you must add resource records to it. Although some records might be added automatically, others might need to be added manually.

To add common resource records for a zone, right-click the zone icon in the DNS console and from the shortcut menu, select the appropriate resource record you want to create, as shown in Figure 8-1.

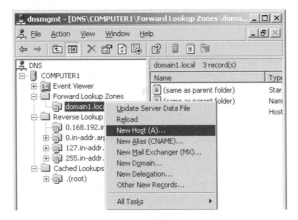

Figure 8-1 Creating resource records

To select from a long list of resource record types to add to a zone, complete the following steps:

1. Open the DNS console.

2. In the console tree, right-click the applicable zone and select Other New Records. The Resource Record Type dialog box appears.

3. In the Select A Resource Record Type list box, select the type of resource record you want to add.

4. Click Create Record.

5. In the New Resource Record dialog box, enter the information needed to complete the resource record.

6. After you specify all the necessary information for the resource record, click OK to add the new record to the zone.

7. Click Done to return to the DNS console.

Resource Record Format

Resource records appear in varying formats, depending on the context in which they are used. For example, when lookups and responses are made using DNS, resource records are represented in binary form in packets. In the DNS console, resource records are represented graphically so that they can be viewed and modified easily. However, at the source—in the zone database files—resource records are represented as text entries. In fact, by creating resource records in the DNS console, you are automatically adding text entries to the corresponding zone's database file.

In these zone files, resource records have the following syntax:

```
Owner TTL Class Type RDATA
```

Table 8-1 describes each of these fields.

Table 8-1   Typical Resource Record Fields

Name	Description
Owner	The name of the host or the DNS domain to which this resource record belongs.
Time To Live (TTL)	A 32-bit integer that represents, in seconds, the length of time that a DNS server or client should cache this entry before it is discarded. This field is optional, and if it is not specified, the client uses the minimum TTL in the SOA record.
Class	The field that defines the protocol family in use. For Windows DNS servers, the resource record is always of the class Internet, abbreviated IN. This field is optional and is not automatically generated.
Type	The field that identifies the type of resource record, such as A or SRV.
RDATA	The resource record data. It is a variable-length field that represents the information being described by the resource record type. For example, in an A resource record, this is the 32-bit IP address that represents the host identified by the owner.

Most resource records are represented as single-line text entries. If an entry is going to span more than one line, parentheses can encapsulate the information. In many implementations of DNS, only the SOA resource record can contain multiple lines. For readability, blank lines and comments ignored by the DNS server are often inserted in the zone files. Comments always start with a semicolon (;) and end with a carriage return.

Record Types

The most common resource records you need to create manually include the following:

- Host (A)
- Alias (CNAME)

- Mail exchanger (MX)

- Pointer (PTR)

- Service location (SRV)

Host (A) Resource Records   Host (A) resource records make up the majority of resource records in a zone database. These records are used in a zone to associate DNS domain names of computers (or hosts) to their IP addresses. They can be added to a zone in different ways:

- You can manually create an A resource record for a static Transmission Control Protocol/Internet Protocol (TCP/IP) client computer using the DNS console or the Dnscmd.exe support tool at the command line.

- Computers running Windows Server 2003 use the DHCP Client service to dynamically register and update their own A resource records in DNS when an IP configuration change occurs.

- Dynamic Host Configuration Protocol (DHCP)–enabled client computers running earlier versions of Microsoft operating systems can have their A resource records registered and updated by proxy if they obtain their IP lease from a qualified DHCP server. (The DHCP service provided with Windows 2000 and Windows Server 2003 support this feature.)

Once created in the DNS console, an A resource record that maps the host name server1.lucernepublishing.com to the IP address 172.16.48.1 is represented textually within the lucernepublishing.com.dns zone file as follows:

```
server1              A      172.16.48.1
```

> **Exam Tip**   If you can ping a computer by IP address but not by name, the computer is missing an A resource record in DNS. You can attempt to remedy this situation by executing the Ipconfig /registerdns command at the computer that is missing its A record—but only if the client computer is running a version of Windows 2000, Windows XP, or Windows Server 2003. For non-Windows clients, such as Linux, UNIX, and Macintosh computers, you must create the A resource record manually in DNS.

Alias (CNAME) Resource Records   Alias (CNAME) resource records are also sometimes called *canonical names*. These records allow you to use more than one name to point to a single host. For example, the well-known server names (ftp, www) are registered using CNAME resource records. These records map the host name specific to a given service (such as ftp.lucernepublishing.com) to the actual A resource record of the computer hosting the service (such as server-boston.lucernepublishing.com).

CNAME resource records are also recommended for use in the following scenarios:

- When a host specified in an A resource record in the same zone needs to be renamed

- When a generic name for a well-known server such as www needs to resolve to a group of individual computers (each with individual A resource records) that provide the same service (for example, a group of redundant Web servers)

Once created in the DNS console, a CNAME resource record that maps the alias ftp.lucernepublishing.com to the host name ftp1.lucernepublishing.com would be represented textually within the lucernepublishing.com.dns zone file as follows:

```
ftp             CNAME      ftp1.lucernepublishing.com.
```

Mail Exchanger (MX) Resource Records   The mail exchanger (MX) resource record is used by e-mail applications to locate a mail server within a zone. It allows a domain name such as lucernepublishing.com, specified in an e-mail address such as joe@lucernepublishing.com, to be mapped to the A resource record of a computer hosting the mail server for the domain. This type of record thus allows a DNS server to handle e-mail addresses in which no particular mail server is specified.

Often, multiple MX records are created to provide fault tolerance and failover to another mail server when the preferred server listed is not available. Multiple servers are given a server preference value, with the lower values representing higher preference. Once created in the DNS console, such MX resource records would be represented textually within the lucernepublishing.com.dns zone file as follows:

```
@       MX     1     mailserver1.lucernepublishing.com.
@       MX     10    mailserver2.lucernepublishing.com.
@       MX     20    mailserver3.lucernepublishing.com.
```

> **Note**   In this example, the @ symbol represents the local domain name contained in an e-mail address.

Pointer (PTR) Resource Records   The pointer (PTR) resource record is used only in reverse lookup zones to support reverse lookups, which perform queries for host names based on IP addresses. Reverse lookups are performed in zones rooted in the in-addr.arpa domain. PTR resource records are added to zones by the same manual and automatic methods used to add A resource records.

Once created in the DNS console, a PTR resource record that maps the IP address 172.16.48.1 to the host name server1.lucernepublishing.com would be represented textually within a zone file as follows:

```
1               PTR     server1.lucernepublishing.com.
```

> **Note**   In this example, the 1 represents the Network ID assigned to the host within the 48.16.172.in-addr.arpa domain. This domain, which is also the name of the hosting zone, corresponds to the 172.16.48.0 subnet.

Service Location (SRV) Resource Records   Service location (SRV) resource records enable you to specify the location of specific services in a domain. Client applications that are SRV-aware can use DNS to retrieve the SRV resource records for the application servers.

Windows Server 2003 Active Directory is an example of an SRV-aware application. The Netlogon service uses SRV records to locate domain controllers in a domain by searching the domain for the Lightweight Directory Access Protocol (LDAP) service.

> **Tip**   All the SRV records required for an Active Directory domain controller can be found in a file named Netlogon.dns, located in the WINDOWS\System32\Config folder. If SRV records are missing in your DNS zone, you can reload them automatically by running the Netdiag /fix command at a command prompt. (The Netdiag.exe command is available after you install Windows Server 2003 Support Tools from the Windows Server 2003 CD-ROM.)

If a computer needs to locate an LDAP server in the lucernepublishing.com domain, the DNS client sends an SRV query for the name:

`_ldap._tcp.lucernepublishing.com.`

The DNS server then responds to the client with all records matching the query.

Although most SRV resource records are created automatically, you might need to create them through the DNS console to add fault tolerance or troubleshoot network services. The following example shows the textual representation of two SRV records that have been configured manually in the DNS console:

```
_ldap._tcp     SRV     0  0 389     dc1.lucernepublishing.com.
               SRV     10 0 389     dc2.lucernepublishing.com.
```

In the example, an LDAP server (domain controller) with a priority of 0 (highest) is mapped to port 389 at the host dc1.lucernepublishing.com. A second domain controller with a lower priority of 10 is mapped to port 389 at the host dc2.lucernepublishing.com. Both entries have a 0 value in the weight field, which means no load balancing has been configured among servers with equal priority.

Exam Tip   You can deploy Active Directory with the "least amount of administrative effort" by installing your network's first DNS domains, along with its first Active Directory domains, on computers running Windows Server 2003. This news is hardly surprising because only in Windows environments are the many SRV records required for Active Directory created automatically. If you want to deploy DNS on a UNIX server and integrate the UNIX server into an Active Directory infrastructure, configure the UNIX server as a secondary DNS server.

Viewing and Clearing the DNS Server Cache

The contents of the DNS server cache can be viewed only in the DNS console. To view the cache contents, from the View menu select Advanced. Once the DNS console View mode is set to Advanced, a new folder appears in the DNS console tree, Cached Lookups. This folder hierarchically organizes the cached lookups for queries that the DNS server has performed. In other words, this folder displays the DNS server cache in a hierarchical format. Figure 8-2 shows sample contents of the Cached Lookups folder.

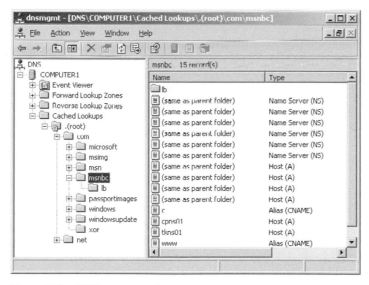

Figure 8-2   DNS server cache

To clear the DNS server cache, you can right-click the DNS server icon in the DNS console and select Clear Cache. Alternatively, you can restart the DNS Server service or use the Dnscmd /clearcache command.

Exploring DNS Server Properties Tabs

The DNS server properties dialog box allows you to configure settings that apply to the DNS server and all its hosted zones. You can access this dialog box in the DNS console tree by right-clicking the DNS server you want to configure and then selecting Properties. The DNS server properties dialog box contains eight tabs, which are introduced next.

Interfaces Tab

The Interfaces tab allows you to specify which of the local computer's IP addresses should listen for DNS requests. For example, if your server is multihomed and has one IP address for the local network and another IP address connected to the Internet, you can prevent the DNS server from servicing DNS queries from outside the local network. To perform this task, specify that the DNS server listen only on the computer's internal IP address.

By default, the setting on this tab specifies that the DNS server listens on all IP addresses associated with the local computer.

Forwarders Tab

The Forwarders tab allows you to forward DNS queries received by the local DNS server to upstream DNS servers, called *forwarders*. Using this tab, you can specify the IP addresses of the upstream forwarders, and you can specify the domain names of queries that should be forwarded. For example, in Figure 8-3, all queries received for the domain lucernepublishing.com will be forwarded to the DNS server 207.46.132.23. When, after receiving and forwarding a query from an internal client, the local forwarding server receives a query response back from 207.46.132.23, the local forwarding server then passes this query response back to the original querying client. The process of forwarding selected queries in this way is known as *conditional forwarding*.

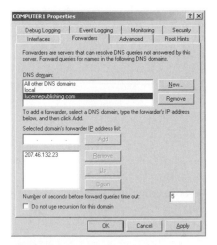

Figure 8-3   Forwarders tab

In all cases, a DNS server configured for forwarding uses forwarders only after it has determined that it cannot resolve a query using its authoritative data (primary or secondary zone data) or cached data.

> **Tip**   To specify how long the forwarding server should wait for a response from a forwarder before timing out, on the Forwarders tab, enter a value in the Number Of Seconds Before Forward Queries Time Out text box. The default setting is 5.

When to Use Forwarders   In some cases, network administrators might not want DNS servers to communicate directly with external servers. For example, if your organization is connected to the Internet by means of a slow wide area link, you can optimize name resolution performance by channeling all DNS queries through one forwarder, as shown in Figure 8-4. Through this method, the server cache of the DNS forwarder has the maximum potential to grow and reduce the need for external queries.

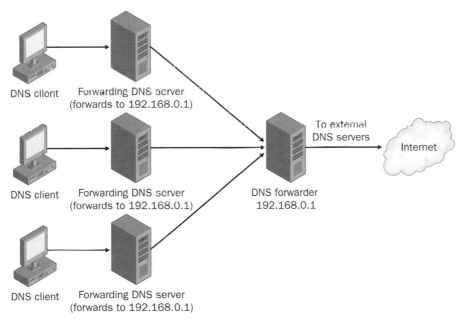

Figure 8-4   Using forwarding to consolidate caching

Another common use of forwarding is to allow DNS clients and servers inside a firewall to resolve external names securely. When an internal DNS server or client communicates with external DNS servers by making iterative queries, normally the ports used for DNS communication with all external servers must be left open to the outside world through the firewall. However, by configuring a DNS server inside a firewall to forward external queries to a single DNS forwarder outside your firewall, and by then opening ports only to this one forwarder, you can resolve names without exposing your network to outside servers. Figure 8-5 illustrates this arrangement.

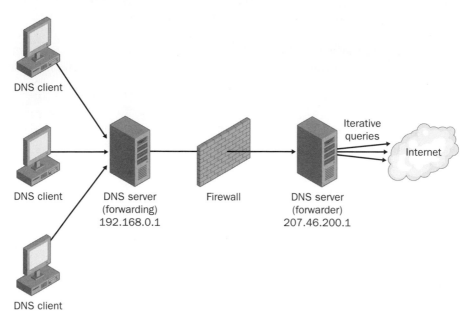

Figure 8-5 Secure iteration with forwarders

Disabling Recursion The Forwarders tab allows you to disable recursion on any queries, specified by domain, that have been configured to be forwarded to an upstream server. When recursion is not disabled (the default), the local DNS server attempts to resolve a fully qualified domain name (FQDN) after a forwarder has failed to do so. This condition is preferable if you want to optimize settings for fault tolerance: if the upstream forwarder is down, name resolution can fall back to the local DNS server.

However, when under this default setting the forwarder receives the forwarded query and still fails to resolve it, the subsequent fallback recursion that occurs at the local DNS server is usually redundant and delays an inevitable query failure message response. Disabling recursion on queries for which forwarding has been configured thus optimizes the speed of negative query responses at the expense of fault tolerance.

When forwarders are configured this way in combination with disabling recursion, the local DNS server is known as a *slave server* because in these cases, it is completely dependent on the forwarder for queries that it cannot resolve locally.

Note Do not confuse the use of the term *slave server* with the term *slave zone*, which is used in some implementations of DNS. In some non-Microsoft DNS servers, such as Berkeley Internet Name Domain (BIND), primary zones are called *master zones* and secondary zones are called *slave zones*.

Advanced Tab

The Advanced tab allows you to enable, disable, and configure certain DNS server options and features such as recursion, round robin, automatic scavenging, and netmask ordering. To learn more about the features configurable on this tab, see Lesson 3 in this chapter.

Note   Whereas the Forwarders tab allows you to disable recursion on selected queries for domains used with forwarders, the Advanced tab allows you to disable recursion for all queries received by the local DNS server.

Note   If you disable recursion on a DNS server using the Advanced tab, you cannot use forwarders on the same server, and the Forwarders tab becomes inactive.

Root Hints Tab

The Root Hints tab contains a copy of the information found in the WINDOWS\System32\Dns\Cache.dns file. For DNS servers answering queries for Internet names, this information does not need to be modified. However, when you are configuring a root DNS server (named ".") for a private network, you should delete the entire Cache.dns file. (When your DNS server is hosting a root server, the Root Hints tab itself is unavailable.)

In addition, if you are configuring a DNS server within a large private namespace, you can use this tab to delete the Internet root servers and specify the root servers in your network instead.

Note   Every few years, the list of root servers on the Internet is slightly modified. Because the Cache.dns file already contains so many possible root servers to contact, it is not necessary to modify the root hints file as soon as these changes occur. However, if you do learn of the availability of new root servers, you can choose to modify your root hints accordingly. As of this writing, the last update to the root servers list was made on November 5, 2002. You can download the latest version of the named cache file from InterNIC at *ftp://rs.internic.net /domain/named.cache*.

Figure 8-6 shows the Root Hints tab.

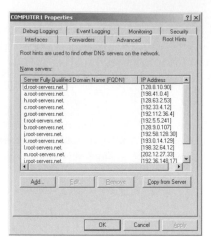

Figure 8-6   Root Hints tab

Debug Logging Tab

The Debug Logging tab allows you to troubleshoot the DNS server by logging the packets it sends and receives. Because logging all packets is resource-intensive, this tab allows you to determine which packets to log, as specified by transport protocol, source IP address, packet direction, packet type, and packet contents.

Event Logging Tab

You can access the DNS Events log in the DNS console tree in the Event Viewer node. This log maintains a record of errors, warnings, and other events that allow you to troubleshoot or monitor DNS performance.

The Event Logging tab allows you to restrict the events written to the DNS Events log file to only errors or to only errors and warnings. It also allows you to disable DNS logging. For more powerful features related to the filtering of DNS events, use the Filter tab of the DNS Events Properties dialog box. You can open this dialog box by selecting Event Viewer in the left pane of the DNS console, right-clicking DNS Events in the right pane, and selecting Properties.

Monitoring Tab

The Monitoring tab allows you to test basic DNS functionality with two simple tests. The first test is a simple query against the local DNS server. To perform the first test successfully, the server must be able to answer forward and reverse queries targeted at itself.

The second test is a recursive query to the root DNS servers. To perform this second test successfully, the DNS server computer must be able to connect to the root servers specified on the Root Hints tab.

The Monitoring tab, shown in Figure 8-7, also allows you to schedule these tests to be conducted at regularly specified intervals. The results of the tests, whether performed manually or automatically, are shown in the Test Results area of the tab.

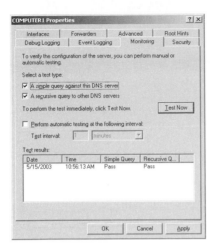

Figure 8-7   Monitoring tab

Security Tab

The Security tab is available only when the DNS server is also a domain controller. This tab allows you to control which users are granted permissions to view, configure, and modify the DNS server and its zones. By clicking the Advanced button, you can further refine settings related to DNS server permissions.

Practice: Installing and Configuring a DNS Server

In this practice, you install and configure a DNS server on Server02, configure a primary zone, and test the DNS server.

Exercise 1: Installing the DNS Windows Component

To complete this exercise, you must have the Windows Server 2003 installation CD-ROM loaded in Server02.

1. Log on to Server02.

2. Open a command prompt and ping server01.contoso.com, and then ping server02.contoso.com.

    These two ping tests should succeed. If not, review the configuration of the servers against the guidelines in the "Before You Begin" section at the beginning of the chapter.

3. Open Control Panel, and then click Add Or Remove Programs.

    The Add Or Remove Programs window opens.

4. Click Add/Remove Windows Components.

   The Windows Components page of the Windows Components Wizard opens.

5. In the Components area, highlight the Networking Services component. Be sure not to select the Networking Services check box.

6. Click Details.

   The Networking Services window opens.

7. In the Subcomponents Of Networking Services area, select the Domain Name System (DNS) check box.

8. Click OK.

   In the Windows Components Wizard, the Networking Services check box should now be unavailable.

9. Click Next.

   The Configuring Components page appears while the new component is being installed. After installation is complete, the Completing The Windows Components Wizard page appears.

10. Click Finish.

11. Click Close to close the Add Or Remove Programs window.

12. Open Network Connections in Control Panel, and open the properties windows for your network connection.

13. In the This Connection Uses The Following Items area, select Internet Protocol (TCP/IP) and click the Properties button.

14. Set the Preferred DNS Server address to Server02's IP address, 192.168.0.2. This ensures that Server02 is a client to the DNS service running on Server02.

15. Click OK, and close the network connection properties window.

16. In the command prompt window, type the command **ipconfig /flushdns**. This command resets the computer's cache of host name resolutions.

17. Ping server01.contoso.com and server02.contoso.com. Do the ping tests succeed? Why or why not?

   _____

   _____

   _____

   _____

   _____

Exercise 2: Configuring Forwarding

1. Log on to Server02.

2. Open the DNS console.

3. Right-click Server02 in the console tree and select Properties.

4. Click the Forwarders tab.

5. Highlight All Other DNS Domains.

6. In the Selected Domain's Forwarder IP Address List box, type **192.168.0.1**.

7. Click Add.

8. Click OK.

9. From the command prompt, ping server01.contoso.com and server02.contoso.com. Do the ping tests succeed? Why or why not?

   _____

   _____

   _____

10. In the DNS console, select the View menu and choose Advanced.

11. Expand the Cached Lookups node.

12. Drill down to find the cached resource record or records for contoso.com.

13. What records do you see? Why is server02.contoso.com not listed?

    _____

    _____

Exercise 3: Configuring a Primary Zone

1. Log on to Server02.

2. Open the DNS console.

3. Right-click Server02 in the console tree, and select Configure A DNS Server from the shortcut menu.

   The Configure A DNS Server Wizard launches.

4. Click Next.

   The Select Configuration Action page appears.

5. Select the Create Forward And Reverse Lookup Zones option, and then click Next.

   The Forward Lookup Zone page appears.

6. Click Next to accept the default selection, Yes, Create A Forward Lookup Zone Now.

   The Zone Type page appears.

7. Click Next to accept the default selection, Primary Zone.

   The Zone Name page appears.

8. In the Zone Name text box, type **nwtraders.com**, and then click Next.

   The Zone File page appears.

9. Click Next to accept the default selection, Create A New File With This File Name.

   The Dynamic Update page appears.

10. Click Next to accept the default selection, Do Not Allow Dynamic Updates.

    The Reverse Lookup Zone page appears.

11. Click Next to accept the default selection, Yes, Create A Reverse Lookup Zone Now.

    The Zone Type page appears.

12. Click Next to accept the default selection, Primary Zone.

    The Reverse Lookup Zone page appears.

13. In the Network ID text box, type **192.168.0**.

    The reverse lookup zone name is automatically configured in the Reverse Lookup Zone Name text box.

14. Click Next.

    The Zone File page appears.

15. Click Next to accept the default selection, Create A New File With This File Name.

    The Dynamic Update page appears.

16. Click Next to accept the default selection, Do Not Allow Dynamic Updates.

    The Forwarders page appears.

17. Click Yes, It Should Forward Queries To DNS Servers With The Following IP Addresses, and type Server01's address, **192.168.0.1**. Then click Next.

    If Server01 does not have Internet connectivity, the Searching For Root Hints dialog box will be visible for some time and, after the last step in this exercise, you will receive an error regarding Root Hints.

    The Completing The Configure A DNS Server Wizard page appears.

18. Click Finish.

19. In the DNS console, expand the console tree in the left pane so that you can see the new zone nwtraders.com listed in the Forward Lookup Zones folder. You can also see the new zone 192.168.0.x Subnet listed in the Reverse Lookup Zones folder. (If the DNS console is displayed in Advanced view, the zone will appear as 0.168.192.in-addr.arpa.)

Exercise 4: Testing the DNS Server

Windows Server 2003 allows you to verify your DNS server configuration with two tests locally on the DNS server computer. These two tests are included on the Monitoring tab of the server properties dialog box, available through the DNS console.

1. While you are logged on to Server02 as Administrator, make sure you are connected to the Internet.

2. In the console tree within the DNS console, right-click Server02 and select Properties.

   The SERVER02 Properties dialog box opens.

3. Click the Monitoring tab.

4. Select the A Simple Query Against This DNS Server check box and the A Recursive Query To Other DNS Servers check box.

5. Click Test Now.

   The Test Results area shows the successful results of the tests you have just performed. If Server01 does not have Internet connectivity, the Recursive Query test will fail.

6. Click OK to close the Server02 Properties dialog box.

> **Exam Tip**   You need to understand the DNS server tests for the exam. First, know that the simple test is based on a reverse lookup of the loopback address 127.0.0.1. Therefore, if the simple test fails, you should verify that a record named 1 is found in the reverse lookup zone named 0.0.127.in-addr.arpa (visible only in the DNS console Advanced view). Next, the recursive test verifies that the DNS server can communicate with other DNS servers and that the root hints are correctly configured.

Lesson Review

The following questions are intended to reinforce key information presented in this lesson. If you are unable to answer a question, review the lesson materials and try the question again. You can find answers to the questions in the "Questions and Answers" section at the end of this chapter.

1. You have just updated a host resource record. What other associated resource record might now need to be updated?

   _____

2. You administer a network that consists of a single domain. On this network, you have configured a new DNS server named DNS1 to answer queries for Internet names from the local domain. However, although DNS1 is connected to the Internet, it continues to fail its recursive test on the Monitoring tab of the server properties dialog box. Which of the following could be the potential cause for the failure?

   a. You have configured DNS1 in front of a firewall.

   b. DNS1 hosts a zone named ".".

   c. Your root hints have not been modified from the defaults.

   d. You have not configured DNS1 to forward any queries to upstream servers.

   _____

3. Which resource record is used to resolve domain names specified in e-mail addresses to the IP address of the mail server associated with the domain?

   a. PTR

   b. MX

   c. A

   d. CNAME

   _____

4. On a new DNS server, you create a zone "." and then create subdomains from that root domain. Which function will the new server be able or unable to perform?

   a. The server will be unable to cache names.

   b. The server will be able to function only as a forwarding server.

   c. The server will be unable to resolve Internet names.

   d. The server will be unable to connect to the Internet.

   _____

5. How can you use forwarding to increase security of DNS queries?

_____

_____

_____

_____

_____

_____

_____

6. Which of the following events could serve as a legitimate reason to modify (but not delete) the default root hints on the Root Hints tab of a DNS server properties dialog box? (Choose all that apply.)

a. The Internet root servers have changed.

b. The server will not be used as a root server.

c. You have disabled recursion on the server.

d. Your server is not used to resolve Internet names.

Lesson Summary

- DNS servers are authoritative for the zones they host. Forward lookup zones answer queries for IP addresses, and reverse lookup zones answer queries for FQDNs.

- A DNS server that hosts a primary DNS zone is said to act as a primary DNS server. Primary DNS servers store original source data for zones. With Windows Server 2003, you can implement primary zones in one of two ways: as standard primary zones, in which zone data is stored in a text file, or as an Active Directory–integrated zone, in which zone data is stored in the Active Directory database.

- A DNS server that hosts a secondary DNS server is said to act as a secondary DNS server. Secondary DNS servers are authoritative backup servers for the primary server. The servers from which secondary servers acquire zone information are called masters. A master can be the primary server or another secondary server.

- A caching-only server forwards all requests to other DNS servers and hosts no zones. However, caching-only servers cache responses received from other DNS servers and can therefore improve name resolution for a network that does not host a zone.

■ New zones contain only two resource records: the SOA record corresponding to the zone, and an NS record corresponding to the local DNS server created for the zone. After you create a zone, additional resource records need to be added to it. The most common resource records to be added are host (A), alias (CNAME), MX, and PTR.

■ The Forwarders tab of the DNS server properties dialog box allows you to forward DNS queries received by the local DNS server to upstream DNS servers, called forwarders. This tab also allows you to disable recursion for select queries (as specified by domain).

■ By configuring a DNS server inside a firewall to forward external queries to a single DNS forwarder outside your firewall, and by then opening ports through the firewall only to this one forwarder, you can resolve DNS names without exposing your network to outside servers.

■ The Root Hints tab provides a simple way to modify the contents in the Cache.dns file. If you are using your DNS server to resolve Internet names, you do not normally need to modify these entries. However, if you are using your DNS server only to answer queries for hosts in a separate and private DNS namespace, you should alter these root hints to point to the root servers in your network. Finally, if your DNS server computer is itself the root server (named ".") of your private namespace, you should delete the Cache.dns file.

■ The Monitoring tab of the DNS server properties dialog box allows you to check basic DNS functionality with two simple tests: a simple query against the local DNS server, and a recursive query to the root DNS servers.

Lesson 2: Configuring Zone Properties and Transfers

You can perform many essential tasks related to administering and managing a DNS infrastructure through the properties dialog boxes of your network's hosted zones. These tasks include configuring and managing zone transfers, enabling dynamic updates, and modifying zone types.

After this lesson, you will be able to

- Configure a DNS zone for dynamic updates
- Change the DNS zone type
- Store zone data in the Active Directory database
- Add Name Server (NS) resource records to a zone
- Configure zone transfers from secondary zones
- Describe the events that can trigger a zone transfer
- Describe the process of a zone transfer

Estimated lesson time: 20 minutes

Exploring DNS Zone Properties

The primary means to configure zone settings is through the zone properties dialog box, which is accessible through the DNS console. Each properties dialog box for a standard zone has five tabs: General, Start Of Authority (SOA), Name Servers, WINS, and Zone Transfers. Properties dialog boxes for Active Directory–integrated zones include a sixth tab, Security, that allows you to configure access permissions for the zone.

General Tab

The General tab, shown in Figure 8-8, allows you to temporarily suspend name resolution and to configure four basic features: zone type (including Active Directory integration), zone file name, dynamic updates, and aging.

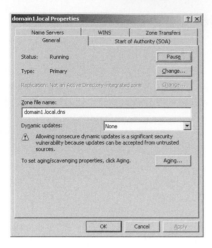

Figure 8-8   General tab

Zone Status   The Pause button allows you to pause and resume name resolution for the zone. Note that this feature does not allow you to pause or resume the DNS Server service.

Zone Type   Clicking Change opens the Change Zone Type dialog box, which allows you to reconfigure the zone as a primary, secondary, or stub zone. Selecting the Store The Zone In Active Directory check box in the Change Zone Type dialog box allows you to store the primary zone information in the Active Directory database instead of in the *WINDOWS*\System32\Dns folder. In Active Directory–integrated zones, zone data is replicated through Active Directory.

Zone Replication   When you opt to store zone information in the Active Directory database, the Change button for Replication becomes enabled. This button allows you to configure replication parameters for the Active Directory–integrated zone.

Clicking the Change button opens the Change Zone Replication Scope dialog box, shown in Figure 8-9. This dialog box allows you to determine among which servers in the Active Directory forest the zone data should be replicated.

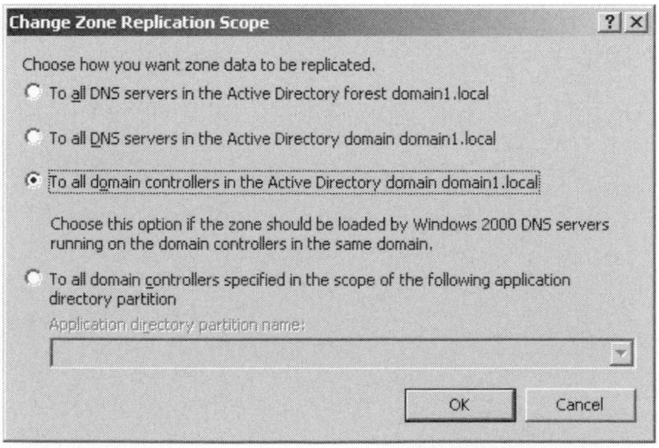

Figure 8-9   Setting the zone replication scope

Table 8-2 describes the four options available in this dialog box.

Table 8-2   Zone Replication Options

Options	Description
To All DNS Servers In The Active Directory Forest	Replicates zone data to all DNS servers running on domain controllers in the Active Directory forest. Usually, this option provides the broadest scope of replication.
To All DNS Servers In The Active Directory Domain	Replicates zone data to all DNS servers running on domain controllers in the Active Directory domain.
To All Domain Controllers In The Active Directory Domain	Replicates zone data to all domain controllers in the Active Directory domain. If you want Microsoft Windows 2000 DNS servers to load an Active Directory zone, you must select this setting for that zone.
To All Domain Controllers Specified In The Scope Of The Following Application Directory Partition	Replicates zone data according to the replication scope of the specified application directory partition. For a zone to be stored in the specified application directory partition, the DNS server hosting the zone must be enlisted in the specified application directory partition.

When deciding which replication option to choose, consider that the broader the replication scope, the greater the network traffic caused by replication. For example, if you choose to have Active Directory–integrated DNS zone data replicated to all DNS servers in the forest, this setting produces greater network traffic than does replicating the DNS zone data to all DNS servers in a single Active Directory domain in that forest. On the other hand, replicating zone data to all DNS servers in a forest can improve forestwide name resolution performance and increase fault tolerance.

Application Directory Partitions and DNS Replication   An *application directory partition* is a directory partition that is replicated among a specified subset of domain controllers running Windows Server 2003.

■ Built-in application directory partitions

For DNS, two built-in application directory partitions exist for each Active Directory domain: DomainDnsZones and ForestDnsZones. The DomainDnsZones application directory partition is replicated among all DNS servers that are also domain controllers in an Active Directory domain. The ForestDnsZones application directory partition is replicated among all DNS servers that are also domain controllers in an Active Directory forest. Each of these application directory partitions is designated by a DNS subdomain and an FQDN. For example, in an Active Directory domain named bern.lucernepublishing.com whose root domain in the Active Directory forest is lucernepublishing.com, the built-in DNS application partition directories are specified by these FQDNs: DomainDnsZones.bern.lucernepublishing.com and ForestDnsZones.lucernepublishing.com.

When you select the To All DNS Servers In The Active Directory Forest option in the Change Zone Replication Scope dialog box, you are in fact choosing to store DNS zone data in the ForestDnsZones application directory partition. When you select the To All DNS Servers In The Active Directory Domain option, you are choosing to store DNS zone data in the DomainDnsZones application directory partition.

Note If either of these application directory partitions is deleted or damaged, you can re-create them in the DNS console by right-clicking the server node and selecting Create Default Application Directory Partitions. If the default DNS application directory partitions are currently available, the Create Default Application Directory Partitions option will not be available.

■ Creating custom application directory partitions

You can also create your own custom application directory partitions for use with DNS and enlist chosen domain controllers in your network to host replicas of this partition.

To accomplish this task, first create the partition by typing the following command:

```
dnscmd servername /createdirectorypartition FQDN
```

Then enlist other DNS servers in the partition by typing the following command:

```
dnscmd servername /enlistdirectorypartition FQDN
```

For example, to create an application directory partition named SpecialDns on a computer named Server01 in the Active Directory domain contoso.com, type the following command:

```
dnscmd server01 /createdirectorypartition SpecialDns.contoso.com
```

To enlist a computer named Server02 in the application directory partition, type the following command:

```
dnscmd server02 /enlistdirectorypartition SpecialDns.contoso.com
```

Note You must be a member of the Enterprise Admins group to create an application directory partition.

To store DNS data in a custom application directory partition, select the fourth (bottom) option in the Change Zone Replication Scope dialog box, and specify the custom application directory partition in the drop-down list box. This option—To All Domain Controllers Specified In The Scope Of The Following Application Directory Partition—is available only if custom application directory partitions are available for DNS on your network.

■ Replication with Windows 2000 servers

Because application directory partitions are not available on Windows 2000 domain controllers, you must select the third option in the Change Zone Replication Scope dialog box if you want the zone data to be read by Windows 2000 DNS servers. With this option—To All Domain Controllers In the Active Directory Domain—data is not replicated merely among all DNS server domain controllers, but among all domain controllers regardless of whether they are also DNS servers.

> **Exam Tip**   Expect to be tested on application directory partition concepts and commands, as well as the options in the Change Zone Replication Scope dialog box.

Zone File Name   For standard zones not stored in Active Directory, the default zone filename is created by adding a .dns extension to the zone name. The Zone File Name text box on the General tab allows you to change the default name of this file.

Dynamic Updates   The General tab also allows you to configure the dynamic updates settings for a zone. Three dynamic update settings are available for Active Directory–integrated DNS zones: None, Nonsecure And Secure, and Secure Only. For standard zones, only two settings are available: None and Nonsecure And Secure.

When you select the None setting in the properties for a zone, you must manually perform registrations and updates to zone records. However, when you enable either the Nonsecure And Secure setting or the Secure Only setting, client computers can automatically create or update their own resource records. This functionality greatly reduces the need for manual administration of zone records, especially for DHCP clients and roaming clients.

Figure 8-10 illustrates a typical dynamic update process.

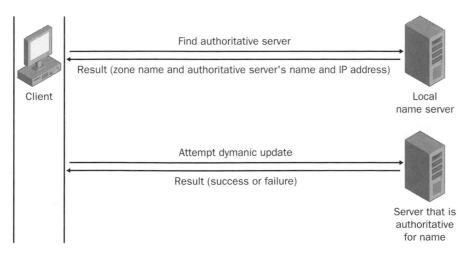

Figure 8-10   Dynamic update process

Whenever a triggering event occurs on a DNS client computer, the DHCP Client service, not the DNS Client service, attempts to perform a dynamic update of the A resource record with the DNS server. This update process is designed so that if a change to the IP address information occurs because of DHCP, this update is immediately sent to the DNS server. The DHCP Client service attempts to perform this dynamic update function for all network connections used on the system, including those not configured to use DHCP. Whether this attempt at a dynamic update is successful depends first and foremost on whether the zone has been configured to allow dynamic updates.

Dynamic Update Triggers   The following events trigger the DHCP Client service to send a dynamic update to the DNS server:

- The DNS client computer is turned on.

- An IP address lease changes or renews with the DHCP server for any one of the local computer's installed network connections—for example, when the computer is started or if the Ipconfig /renew command is used.

- An IP address is added, removed, or modified in the Transmission Control Protocol/Internet Protocol (TCP/IP) properties configuration for any one of the local computer's installed network connections.

- A member server within the zone is promoted to a domain controller.

- The Ipconfig /registerdns command is used on a DNS client computer to manually force a refresh of the client name registration in DNS.

Secure Dynamic Updates   Secure dynamic updates can be performed only in Active Directory–integrated zones. For standard zones, the Secure Only option does not appear in the Dynamic Updates drop-down list box. These updates use the secure Kerberos authentication protocol to create a secure context and ensure that the client updating the resource record is the owner of that record.

> **Note**   Only clients running a version of Windows 2000, Microsoft Windows XP, or Windows Server 2003 can attempt to send dynamic updates to a DNS server. Dynamic updates are not available for any version of Windows NT, Windows 95, Microsoft Windows 98, or Microsoft Windows Millenium Edition (Me). However, a DNS client computer (such as a DHCP server) can perform dynamic updates on behalf of other clients if the server is configured to do so.

- Secure Dynamic Updates and the DnsUpdateProxy group

    When only secure dynamic updates are allowed in a zone, only the owner of a record can update that record. (The owner of a record is the computer that originally registers the record.) This restriction can cause problems in situations where a DHCP server is being used to register host (A) resource records on behalf of client computers that cannot perform dynamic updates. In such cases, the DHCP server becomes the owner of the record, not the computers themselves. If the down-level client computer is later upgraded to Windows 2000 or some other operating system that is capable of performing dynamic updates, the computer will not be recognized as the owner and will consequently be unable to update its own records. A similar problem might arise if a DHCP server fails that has registered records on behalf of down-level clients: none of the clients will be able to have their records updated by a backup DHCP server.

To avoid such problems, add to the DnsUpdateProxy security group DHCP servers that register records on behalf of other computers. Members of this group are prevented from recording ownership on the resource records they update in DNS. This caveat consequently loosens security for these records until they can be registered by the real owner.

Exam Tip   Expect to be tested on DnsUpdateProxy on the exam.

Aging   By clicking Aging on the General tab, you can open the Zone Aging/Scavenging Properties dialog box, as shown in Figure 8-11. These properties provide a means of finding and clearing outdated records from the zone database.

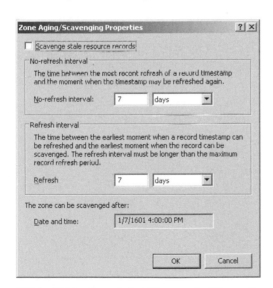

Figure 8-11   Zone Aging/Scavenging Properties dialog box

Enabling Aging   *Aging* in DNS refers to the process of placing a timestamp on a dynamically registered resource record and then tracking the age of this record. *Scavenging* refers to the process of deleting outdated resource records on which timestamps have been placed. Scavenging can occur only when aging is enabled. Both aging and scavenging are disabled by default.

To enable aging for a particular zone, you have to enable this feature both at the zone level and at the server level. To enable aging at the zone level, in the Zone Aging/Scavenging Properties dialog box, select the Scavenge Stale Resource Records check box. To enable aging at the server level, first open the Server Aging/Scavenging Properties dialog box by right-clicking the server icon in the DNS console and then clicking Set Aging/Scavenging For All Zones. Then, in the Server Aging/Scavenging Properties dialog box, select the Scavenge Stale Resource Records check box.

After aging is enabled, a timestamp based on the current server time is placed on all dynamically registered records in the zone. When the DHCP Client service or DHCP server later performs a dynamic update of the records, a timestamp refresh is attempted. Manually created resource records are assigned a timestamp of 0; this value indicates that they will not be aged.

Note When aging and scavenging are enabled for a zone, zone files cannot be read by pre-Windows 2000 DNS servers.

Modifying No-Refresh Intervals The *no-refresh interval* is the period after a timestamp during which a zone or server rejects a timestamp refresh. The no-refresh feature prevents unnecessary refreshes from being processed by the server and reduces unnecessary zone transfer traffic. The default no-refresh interval is seven days.

Modifying Refresh Intervals The *refresh interval* is the time after the no-refresh interval during which timestamp refreshes are accepted and resource records are not scavenged. After the no-refresh and refresh intervals expire, records can be scavenged from the zone. The default refresh interval is seven days. Consequently, when aging is enabled, dynamically registered resource records can be scavenged after 14 days by default.

Tip If you modify the no-refresh or refresh interval, be sure to follow the guideline that the refresh interval should be equal to or greater than the no-refresh interval.

Performing Scavenging Scavenging in a zone is performed either automatically or manually. For scavenging to be performed automatically, you must enable automatic scavenging of stale resource records on the Advanced tab of DNS server properties. When this feature is not enabled, you can perform manual scavenging in a zone by right-clicking the server icon in the DNS console tree and then selecting Scavenge Stale Resource Records from the shortcut menu.

Start Of Authority (SOA) Tab

The Start Of Authority (SOA) tab, shown in Figure 8-12, allows you to configure the SOA resource record for the zone. When a DNS server loads a zone, it uses the SOA resource record to determine basic, authoritative information about the zone. These settings also determine how often zone transfers are performed between primary and secondary servers.

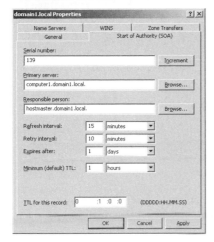

Figure 8-12   Start Of Authority (SOA) tab

Serial Number   The Serial Number text box on the Start Of Authority (SOA) tab contains the revision number of the zone file. This number increases each time a resource record changes in the zone or when the value is manually incremented on this tab by clicking Increment.

When zones are configured to perform zone transfers, the master server is intermittently queried for the serial number of the zone. This query is called the *SOA query*. If, through the SOA query, the serial number of the master zone is determined to be equivalent to the local serial number, no transfer is made. However, if the serial number for the zone at the master server is greater than that at the requesting secondary server, the secondary server initiates a transfer.

Primary Server   The Primary Server text box on the Start Of Authority (SOA) tab contains the full computer name for the primary DNS server of the zone. This name must end with a period.

Responsible Person   When this text box is configured, it contains a Responsible Person (RP) resource record of the person responsible for administering the zone. An RP resource record specifies a domain mailbox name for the responsible person. The name of the record entered into this field should always end with a period.

Refresh Interval   The value you configure in the Refresh Interval field determines how long a secondary DNS server waits before querying the master server for a zone renewal. When the refresh interval expires, the secondary DNS server requests a copy of the current SOA resource record for the zone from its master server source, which then answers this SOA query. The secondary DNS server then compares the serial number of the source server's current SOA resource record (as indicated in the master's response) with the serial number of its own local SOA resource record. If they are different, the secondary DNS server requests a zone transfer from the primary DNS server. The default value for this setting is 15 minutes.

> **Exam Tip**   Increasing the refresh interval decreases zone transfer traffic.

Retry Interval   The value you configure in the Retry Interval box determines how long a secondary server waits before retrying a failed zone transfer. Normally, this time is less than the refresh interval. The default value is 10 minutes.

Expires After   The value you configure in the Expires After box determines the length of time that a secondary server, without any contact with its master server, continues to answer queries from DNS clients. After this time elapses, the data is considered unreliable. The default value is 1 day.

Minimum (Default) TTL   The value you configure in the Minimum (Default) TTL box determines the default Time to Live (TTL) that is applied to all resource records in the zone. The default value is 1 hour.

TTL values are not relevant for resource records within their authoritative zones. Instead, the TTL refers to the cache life of a resource record in nonauthoritative servers. A DNS server that has cached a resource record from a previous query discards the record when that record's TTL has expired.

> **Exam Tip**   If you have deployed caching-only servers in your network in addition to a primary server, increasing the minimum TTL can decrease name resolution traffic between the caching-only servers and the primary server.

TTL For This Record   The value you configure in the TTL For This Record text box determines the TTL of the present SOA resource record. This value overrides the default value setting in the preceding field.

Once configured in the DNS console, an SOA resource record is represented textually in the zone file, as shown in this example:

```
@IN SOA Server01.contoso.com. hostmaster.contoso.com. (
  5099    ; serial number
  3600    ; refresh (1 hour)
  600    ; retry (10 mins)
  86400    ; expire (1 day)
  60  )  ; minimum TTL (1 min)
```

Name Servers Tab

The Name Servers tab allows you to configure NS resource records for a zone. These records cannot be created elsewhere in the DNS console. You use NS resource records to specify the authoritative name servers for a given zone. The NS resource record of the first primary server of a zone is configured automatically.

> **Note** Every zone must contain at least one NS resource record at the zone root.

The following line is an example NS record taken from the database file for the lucernepublishing.com zone:

```
@ NS  dns1.lucernepublishing.com.
```

In this record, the "@" symbol represents the zone defined by the SOA record in the same zone file. The complete entry, then, effectively maps the lucernepublishing.com domain to a DNS server hosted on a computer named dns1.lucernepublishing.com.

> **Exam Tip** In primary zones, zone transfers by default are allowed only to servers specified on the Name Servers tab. This restriction is new to Windows Server 2003.

WINS Tab

You use the WINS tab—or the WINS-R tab in reverse lookup zones—to configure Windows Internet Name Service (WINS) servers to aid in name resolution for a given zone after DNS servers have failed to resolve a queried name.

Zone Transfers Tab

The Zone Transfers tab, shown in Figure 8-13, allows you to restrict zone transfers from the local master server. For primary zones, zone transfers to secondary servers by default are restricted only to name servers configured on the Name Servers tab. Alternatively, you can customize zone transfer restrictions by selecting the Only To The Following Servers option and then specifying the IP addresses of allowed secondary servers in the list below this option.

Secondary zones by default do not allow zone transfers to other secondary zones, but you can enable this feature simply by selecting the Allow Zone Transfers check box.

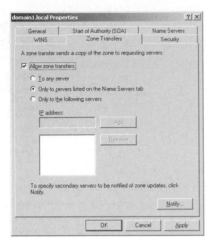

Figure 8-13   Zone Transfers tab

Off the Record   In Windows 2000, the default setting on the Zone Transfers tab for primary zones was to allow transfers to any server, but this feature created an unnecessary security hole. Think about it: why would you want to enable anyone who can access your DNS server to set up a secondary server and peruse your network's resource records? Restricting zone transfers by default to known name servers is a lot smarter—it allows you to prevent unauthorized copying of zone data.

Notification   The Zone Transfers tab also allows you to configure notification to secondary servers. To perform this task, click Notify on the Zone Transfers tab when zone transfers are enabled. This action opens the Notify dialog box, in which you can specify secondary servers that should be notified whenever a zone update occurs at the local master server. By default, all servers listed on the Name Servers tab are automatically notified of zone changes.

Notification and Zone Transfer Initiation   Zone transfers in standard zones can be triggered by any of three events:

- They can be triggered when the refresh interval of the primary zone's SOA resource record expires.

- They can be triggered when a secondary server boots up.

  In both cases, the secondary server initiates an SOA query to find out whether any updates in the zone have occurred. Transfers occur only if the zone database has been revised.

■ Zone transfers are automatically triggered when a change occurs in the configuration of the primary server and this server has specified particular secondary DNS servers to be notified of zone updates.

When a zone transfer initiates, the secondary server performs either an incremental zone transfer (IXFR) query or an all zone transfer (AXFR) query to the master server. Computers running Windows 2000 Server and Windows Server 2003 perform IXFR queries by default. Through IXFR queries, only the newly modified data is transferred across the network. Computers running Windows NT Server do not support IXFR queries and can perform only AXFR queries. Through AXFR queries, the entire zone database is transferred to the secondary server.

Primary DNS servers running Windows Server 2003 support both IXFR and AXFR zone transfers.

Note   You do not need to configure zone transfers or notification among domain controllers or DNS servers in Active Directory–integrated zones. For the servers within these zones, transfers are conducted automatically.

Practice: Deploying a Secondary DNS Server

In this practice, you create a secondary zone and then configure zone transfers between the two zones. You also review notification settings between the master and secondary zones.

Exercise 1: Configuring a Secondary Zone

1. Log on to Server02.

2. Open the DNS console, and add Server01 to the console so that you can administer both Server01 and Server02. To add Server01, click the DNS node, select Connect To DNS Server from the Action menu, and specify Server01 in the Connect To DNS Server dialog box.

3. Expand Server01's node in the tree pane. Expand Forward Lookup Zones, and select the zone contoso.com.

4. Right-click contoso.com in the tree pane, and choose Properties.

5. Click the Name Servers tab.

6. Click Add. The New Resource Record dialog box appears.

7. Type **server02.contoso.com** in the Server Fully Qualified Domain Name box.

8. Click Resolve. Confirm that Server02's IP address, 192.168.0.2 appears in the IP Address box.

9. Click OK to close the New Resource Record dialog box.

10. Click OK to close the contoso.com zone properties dialog box.

11. Expand the Server02 node in the console's tree pane.

12. In the DNS console tree, right-click Forward Lookup Zones and select New Zone. The New Zone Wizard launches.

13. In the New Zone Wizard, click Next. The Zone Type page appears.

14. On the Zone Type page, select the Secondary Zone option and then click Next. The Zone Name page appears.

15. On the Zone Name page, in the Zone Name text box, type **contoso.com** and then click Next. The Master DNS Servers page appears.

16. In the Master DNS Server page, in the IP Address text box, type **192.168.0.1**, click Add, and then click Next. The Completing The New Zone Wizard page appears.

17. Click Finish.

18. In the DNS console tree, expand Forward Lookup Zones and select the contoso.com node.

19. Right-click the contoso.com node, and then select Transfer From Master.

20. If the zone fails to load, wait 1 minute and then try again. Repeat this step until the zone loads successfully.

21. When a copy of the contoso.com zone appears in the DNS console on Server02, take a few moments to browse the zone properties dialog box and the items on the zone's Action (shortcut) menu.

22. Use both server nodes in the DNS console on Server02 to answer the following questions in the spaces provided.

    Which functions on the Action menu are available for the contoso.com zone through the SERVER02 node that are not available on the Action menu for the same zone through the SERVER01 node?

    New functions are Transfer From Master and Reload From Master.

    Can you create or configure resource records for contoso.com through the SERVER02 node in the DNS console?

    No, you cannot create or configure resource records for contoso.com through the SERVER02 node.

Exercise 2: Reviewing Notification Settings

1. Log on to Server02.

2. Open the DNS console, and add Server01 to the console as described in Exercise 1 so that you can administer both Server01 and Server02.

3. Expand the Server01 icon, expand the Forward Lookup Zones icon, and then open the contoso.com properties dialog box associated with this primary zone.

4. On the Zone Transfers tab, click Notify. The Notify dialog box opens.

   By default, the primary zone automatically notifies the servers listed on the Name Servers tab of zone changes.

   Because Server02 is now configured on the Name Servers tab, the secondary server is notified of any zone changes. When Server02 receives notification from the primary server, this secondary DNS server normally initiates an IXFR query for an incremental zone transfer.

5. Click Cancel.

6. In the contoso.com Properties dialog box, click the Start Of Authority (SOA) tab. Using the settings configured on this tab, answer the following questions in the spaces provided.

   According to the settings on the Start Of Authority (SOA) tab, if Server02 loses contact with Server01, how long will the DNS server on Server02 continue to answer queries from DNS clients?

   One day

   How often is Server02 configured to query Server01 to find out whether any changes have been made to the zone?

   Every 15 minutes

   If Server02 discovers it cannot contact Server01 when it initiates an SOA query, how long does it wait before trying again?

   10 minutes

   If another primary DNS server named dns.nwtraders.com successfully queries Server01 for the IP address of Server02, how long does Server02's A resource record stay alive in the cache of dns.nwtraders.com?

   1 hour

7. Click OK to close the contoso.com Properties dialog box.

Lesson Review

The following questions are intended to reinforce key information presented in this lesson. If you are unable to answer a question, review the lesson materials and try the question again. You can find answers to the questions in the "Questions and Answers" section at the end of this chapter.

1. Describe the process by which secondary servers determine whether a zone transfer should be initiated.

   _____

   _____

   _____

   _____

2. What is the difference between IXFR and AXFR queries?

   _____

   _____

   _____

3. You have multiple DHCP servers on your network, some of which are configured to register DNS records on behalf of pre-Windows 2000 clients. You have configured DNS to allow only secure updates. However, you find that some DNS records are not being updated properly. How can you solve this problem?

   _____

   _____

4. You oversee administration for a wide area network (WAN) belonging to the Proseware company, which has one central office in Rochester and two branch offices in Buffalo and Syracuse. The network, which consists of one domain, has one primary DNS zone running on a Windows Server 2003 computer at the central office, and one secondary DNS zone at each branch. Network users are complaining that they often cannot connect to sites at remote branches. Administrators have determined that network bandwidth between the central office and branches has become saturated with zone transfers, and that zone transfers are being initiated before they can complete. Which of the following steps would help resolve the problem with the least effort?

   a. Install Active Directory on the network, and promote the servers hosting the secondary DNS zones to domain controllers.

   b. Increase the network bandwidth by establishing a fiber-optic connection between the two sites.

   c. Increase the refresh interval on the primary DNS server.

   d. Increase the refresh interval on the secondary DNS servers.

---

5. You discover that an administrator has adjusted the default TTL value for your company's primary DNS zone to 5 minutes. Which of the following is the most likely effect of this change?

   a. Resource records cached on the primary DNS server expire after 5 minutes.

   b. DNS clients have to query the server more frequently to resolve names for which the server is authoritative.

   c. Secondary servers initiate a zone transfer every 5 minutes.

   d. DNS hosts reregister their records more frequently.

Lesson Summary

- When you deploy a DNS server on a domain controller, you can choose to store the zone data in the Active Directory database. Active Directory–integrated zones minimize zone transfer traffic, improve security, decrease administrative overhead, and improve fault tolerance. Zone data can be configured to be replicated among all DNS servers in the Active Directory forest, among all DNS servers in the Active Directory domain, among all domain controllers in the Active Directory domain, or among all servers enlisted in a custom application directory partition.

- When a DNS zone allows dynamic updates, certain DNS client computers can register and update their resource records with a DNS server. When secure dynamic updates are required in the zone, only the owner of the record can update the record. Secure dynamic updates can be required only on Active Directory–integrated zones. Client computers running Windows 2000, Windows XP, and Windows Server 2003 can perform dynamic updates.

- The DnsUpdateProxy group is typically used for DHCP servers performing dynamic DNS updates on behalf of other computers. Members of this group do not record ownership on the resource records they register in DNS. This caveat prevents problems from arising in zones that allow only secure dynamic updates.

- The Start Of Authority (SOA) tab allows you to configure the zone's SOA resource record and several parameters that affect zone transfers, such as Refresh Interval, Retry Interval, Expires After, and Minimum (Default) TTL.

- The Zone Transfers tab allows you to control transfers from the current zone. By default, zone transfers are not allowed, and they must be explicitly enabled when adding a secondary zone.

Lesson 3: Configuring Advanced DNS Server Properties

Advanced DNS server properties refer to the nine settings that can be configured on the Advanced tab of the DNS server properties dialog box. These properties relate to server-specific features such as disabling recursion, handling resolution of multihomed hosts, and achieving compatibility with non-Microsoft DNS servers.

After this lesson, you will be able to

- Describe the function and purpose of all of the options available for configuration on the Advanced tab of the DNS server properties dialog box
- Reset all advanced server settings to defaults

Estimated lesson time: 20 minutes

Tuning Advanced Server Options

When initialized for service, DNS servers running on Windows Server 2003 apply installation settings taken either from the boot information file, the Registry, or the Active Directory database. You can modify these settings on the Advanced tab of the server properties dialog box in the DNS console, as shown in Figure 8-14.

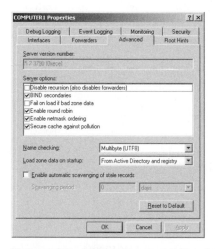

Figure 8-14   DNS server properties Advanced tab

The server installation settings include six server options, which are either on or off, and three other server features with various selections for configuration. Table 8-3 shows the defaults settings for all nine features.

Table 8-3   Default DNS Installation Settings

Property	Setting
Disable Recursion	Off
BIND Secondaries	On
Fail On Load If Bad Zone Data	Off
Enable Round Robin	On
Enable Netmask Ordering	On
Secure Cache Against Pollution	On
Name Checking	Multibyte (UTF8)
Load Zone Data On Startup	From Active Directory And Registry
Enable Automatic Scavenging Of Stale Records	Off (requires configuration when enabled)

In most situations, these installation defaults are acceptable and do not require modification. However, when needed, you can use the DNS console to tune these advanced parameters and accommodate special deployment needs and situations.

> **Exam Tip**   Be familiar with Disable Recursion, BIND Secondaries, Enable Round Robin, and Enable Netmask Ordering.

You can restore these default settings at any time using the Advanced tab by clicking Reset To Default.

The following sections describe the available installation options in more detail.

Disable Recursion

The Disable Recursion server option is disabled by default. Consequently, the DNS server performs recursion to resolve client queries unless a special client configuration overrides this default behavior. Through recursion, the DNS server queries other servers on behalf of the requesting client and attempts to fully resolve an FQDN. Queries continue through iteration until the server receives an authoritative answer for the queried name. The server then forwards this answer back to the original requesting client.

When the Disable Recursion option is enabled, however, the DNS Server service does not answer the query for the client but instead provides the client with *referrals*, which are resource records that allow a DNS client to perform iterative queries to resolve an FQDN. This option might be appropriate, for example, when clients need to resolve Internet names but the local DNS server contains resource records only for the private namespace. Another case in which recursion might be disabled is when, because of its configuration or placement within a local network, a DNS server is incapable of resolving DNS names external to the local network.

> **Warning**   If you disable recursion on a DNS server using the Advanced tab, you will not be able to use forwarders on the same server, and the Forwarders tab becomes inactive.

BIND Secondaries

The BIND Secondaries option is enabled by default. As a result, DNS servers running on Windows Server 2003 do not use fast transfer format when performing a zone transfer to secondary DNS servers based on BIND. This restriction allows for zone transfer compatibility with older versions of BIND.

> **Note**   BIND is a common implementation of DNS written and ported to most available versions of the UNIX operating system.

Fast transfer format is an efficient means of transferring zone data that provides data compression and allows multiple records to be transferred per individual Transmission Control Protocol (TCP) message. Fast zone transfer is always used among Windows-based DNS servers, so the BIND Secondaries option does not affect communications among Windows servers. However, only BIND versions 4.9.4 and later can handle these fast zone transfers.

If you know your DNS server will be performing zone transfers with DNS servers using BIND version 4.9.4 or later, you should disable this option to allow fast zone transfers to occur.

> **Note**   As of this writing, the most current version of BIND is 9.2.2.

Fail On Load If Bad Zone Data

By default, the Fail On Load If Bad Zone Data option is disabled. As a result, a DNS server running on Windows Server 2003 loads a zone even when it determines that errors exist in the zone's database file. Errors are logged, but the zone load still proceeds. After the zone loads, the DNS server can attempt to answer queries for the zone in question.

When you enable this option, however, the DNS server does not load a zone when the server determines that errors exist in the zone's database file.

Enable Netmask Ordering

The Enable Netmask Ordering option is selected by default. This default setting ensures that, in response to a request to resolve a single computer name matching multiple host (A) resource records, DNS servers in Windows Server 2003 first return to the client any IP address that is in the same subnet as the client.

> **Note**   Multihomed computers typically have registered multiple host (A) resource records for the same host name. When a client attempts to resolve the host name of a multihomed computer by contacting a DNS server, the DNS server returns to the client a *response list* or *answer list* containing all the resource records matching the client query. Upon receiving the response list from the DNS server, a DNS client attempts to contact the target host with the first IP address in the response list. If this attempt fails, the client then attempts to contact the second IP address, and so on. The Enable Netmask Ordering option and the Enable Round Robin option are both used to change the order of resource records returned in this response list.

Simple Example: Local Network Priority   A multihomed computer, server1.lucernepublishing.com, has three A resource records for each of its three IP addresses in the lucernepublishing.com zone. These three records appear in the following order in the zone, either in the zone file or in Active Directory:

```
server1   IN   A   192.168.1.27
server1   IN   A   10.0.0.14
server1   IN   A   172.16.20.4
```

When a DNS client resolver at IP address 10.4.3.2 queries the server for the IP addresses of the host server1.lucernepublishing.com, the DNS Server service notes that the originating IP network address (10.0.0.0) of the client matches the network (class A) ID of the 10.0.0.14 address in the answer list of resource records. The DNS Server service then reorders the addresses in the response list, as follows:

```
server1   IN   A   10.0.0.14
server1   IN   A   192.168.1.27
server1   IN   A   172.16.20.4
```

If the IP address of the requesting client has no local network match with any of the resource records in the answer list, the list is not prioritized in this manner.

Complex Example: Local Subnet Priority   In a network that uses IP subnetting (nondefault subnet masks), a DNS server first returns any IP addresses that match both the client's network ID and subnet ID before returning any IP addresses that match only the client's network ID.

For example, a multihomed computer, server1.lucernepublishing.com, has four A resource records corresponding to each of its four IP addresses in the lucernepublishing.com zone. Two of these IP addresses are for distinct and separate networks. The other two IP addresses share a common IP network address, but because custom netmasks of 255.255.248.0 are used, the IP addresses are located in different subnets. These example resource records appear in the following order in the zone, either in the zone file or in Active Directory:

```
server1   IN  A  192.168.1.27
server1   IN  A  172.16.22.4
server1   IN  A  10.0.0.14
server1   IN  A  172.16.31.5
```

If the IP address of the requesting client is 172.16.22.8, both IP addresses that match the same IP network as the client, the 172.16.0.0 network, are returned at the top of the response list to the client. However, in this example, the 172.16.22.4 address is placed ahead of the 172.16.31.5 address because it matches the client IP address down through the 172.16.20.0 subnet address.

The reordered answer list returned by the DNS service follows:

```
server1   IN  A  172.16.22.4
server1   IN  A  172.16.31.5
server1   IN  A  192.168.1.27
server1   IN  A  10.0.0.14
```

Exam Tip   Netmask ordering is often referred to as the LocalNetPriority setting on MCSE exams. This name originates from the corresponding LocalNetPriority option used with the Dnscmd.exe command-line utility.

Enable Round Robin

The Enable Round Robin option is selected by default. This setting ensures that, in response to a request to resolve the name of a multihomed computer, DNS servers in Windows Server 2003 rotate the order of matching A resource records in the response list returned to subsequent clients. This feature provides a simple way to balance the network load for frequently queried multihomed computers among all the computer's network adapters. This feature is also commonly used to balance requests between multiple servers that offer identical network services, such as an array of Web servers providing content for a single Web site.

Note   Local subnet priority supersedes the use of round robin rotation for multihomed computers. When enabled, however, round robin is used as a secondary method to sort multiple records returned in a response list.

Round Robin Example   The Web server named server1.lucernepublishing.com has three network adapters and three distinct IP addresses. In the stored zone (either in a database file or in Active Directory), the three A resource records mapping the host name to each of its IP addresses appear in this fixed order:

```
server1   IN   A   10.0.0.1
server1   IN   A   10.0.0.2
server1   IN   A   10.0.0.3
```

The first DNS client—Client1—that queries the server to resolve this host's name receives the list in this default order. However, when a second client—Client2—sends a subsequent query to resolve this name, the list is rotated as follows:

```
server1   IN   A   10.0.0.2
server1   IN   A   10.0.0.3
server1   IN   A   10.0.0.1
```

Disabling Round Robin   When you clear the Enable Round Robin check box, round robin is disabled for the DNS server. In this case, when clients query the DNS server to resolve the host name of a multihomed computer, the server always returns the matching A resource records in the order in which those records appear in the zone.

Secure Cache Against Pollution

By default, the Secure Cache Against Pollution option is enabled. This setting allows the DNS server to protect its cache against referrals that are potentially polluting or nonsecure. When the setting is enabled, the server caches only those records with a name that corresponds to the domain for which the original queried name was made. Any referrals received from another DNS server along with a query response are simply discarded.

For example, if a query is originally made for example.microsoft.com, and a referral answer provides a record for a name outside the microsoft.com domain name tree (such as msn.com), that name is discarded if the Secure Cache Against Pollution option is enabled. This setting helps prevent unauthorized computers from impersonating another network server.

When this option is disabled, however, the server caches all the records received in response to DNS queries—even when the records do not correspond to the queried-for domain name.

Name Checking

By default, the Name Checking drop-down list box on the Advanced tab of the DNS server properties dialog box is set to Multibyte (UTF8). Thus, the DNS service by default verifies that all domain names handled by the DNS service conform to the Unicode Transformation Format (UTF). *Unicode* is a 2-byte encoding scheme, compatible with the traditional 1-byte US-ASCII format, that allows for binary representation of most languages. Each name-checking method is described in Table 8-4.

Table 8-4   Name-Checking Methods

Method	Description
Strict RFC (ANSI)	Uses strict checking of names. These restrictions, set in Request for Comments (RFC) 1123, include limiting names to uppercase and lower-case letters (A–Z, a–z), numbers (0–9), and hyphens (-). The first character of the DNS name can be a number.
Non RFC (ANSI)	Permits names that are nonstandard and that do not follow RFC 1123 Internet host naming specifications.
Multibyte (UTF8)	Permits recognition of characters other than ASCII, including Unicode, which is normally encoded as more than one octet (8 bits) in length.
	With this option, multibyte characters can be transformed and represented using UTF-8 support, which is provided with Windows Server 2003.
	Names encoded in UTF-8 format must not exceed the size limits clarified in RFC 2181, which specifies a maximum of 63 octets per label and 255 octets per name. Character count is insufficient to determine size because some UTF-8 characters exceed one octet in length. This option allows for domain names using non-English alphabets.
All Names	Permits any naming conventions.

Despite the flexibility of the UTF-8 name-checking method, you should consider changing the Name Checking option to Strict RFC when your DNS servers perform zone transfers to non-Windows servers that are not UTF-8–aware. Although DNS server implementations that are not UTF-8–aware might be able to accept the transfer of a zone containing UTF-8 encoded names, these servers might not be able to write back those names to a zone file or reload those names from a zone file.

You should use the other two Name Checking options, Non RFC and All Names, only when a specific application requires them.

Load Zone Data On Startup

By default, the Load Zone Data On Startup drop-down list box is set to the From Active Directory And Registry option. Thus, by default DNS servers in Windows Server 2003 initialize with the settings specified in the Active Directory database and the server Registry. However, this setting includes two other options, From Registry and From File.

When you configure the Load Zone Data On Startup setting to the From Registry option, the DNS server is initialized by reading parameters stored in the Windows Registry. When you configure this setting to the From File option, the DNS server is initialized by reading parameters stored in a boot file, such as those used by BIND servers.

To use such a file, you should supply a copy of a boot file from a BIND-based DNS server. On BIND-based DNS servers, this file is typically called the Named.boot file. The format of this file must be the older BIND 4 format, not the more recent BIND 8 boot file format. When a boot file is used, settings in the file are applied to the server, overriding the settings stored in the Registry on the DNS server. However, for any parameters not configurable using boot file directives, Registry defaults (or stored reconfigured server settings) are applied by the DNS Server service.

Enable Automatic Scavenging Of Stale Records

By default, the Enable Automatic Scavenging Of Stale Records option is cleared on the Advanced tab. According to this setting, DNS servers in Windows Server 2003 by default do not automatically delete stale or outdated resource records from a zone for which Aging has been enabled.

When this setting is enabled, scavenging of stale resource records is performed automatically at the interval configured in the Scavenging Period.

Lesson Review

The following questions are intended to reinforce key information presented in this lesson. If you are unable to answer a question, review the lesson materials and try the question again. You can find answers to the questions in the "Questions and Answers" section at the end of this chapter.

1. You are the network administrator for Lucerne Publishing. The Lucerne Publishing network consists of a single domain, lucernepublishing.com, that is protected from the Internet by a firewall. The firewall runs on a computer named NS1 that is directly connected to the Internet. NS1 also runs the DNS Server service, and its firewall allows DNS traffic to pass between the Internet and the DNS Server service on NS1 but not between the Internet and the internal network. The DNS Server service on NS1 is configured to use round robin. Behind the firewall, two computers are running Windows Server 2003—NS2 and NS3—which host a primary and secondary DNS server, respectively, for the lucernepublishing.com zone.

   Users on the company network report that, although they use host names to connect to computers on the local private network, they cannot use host names to connect to Internet destinations such as www.microsoft.com.

Which of the following actions requires the least amount of administrative effort to enable network users to connect to Internet host names?

a. Disable recursion on NS2 and NS3.

b. Enable netmask ordering on NS1.

c. Configure NS2 and NS3 to use NS1 as a forwarder.

d. Disable round robin on NS1.

---

2. You are the administrator for a large network consisting of 10 domains. You have configured a standard primary zone for the mfg.lucernepublishing.com domain on a DNS server computer named Server1. You have also configured a UNIX server, named Server2, to host a secondary zone for the same domain. The UNIX server is running BIND 8.2.1.

You notice that zone transfers between the primary and secondary servers seem to generate more traffic than expected, putting a strain on network resources.

What can you do to decrease the network burden of zone transfers between the primary and secondary servers?

a. Clear the BIND Secondaries check box on Server1.

b. Configure a boot file on Server1 to initialize BIND-compatible settings.

c. Select the BIND Secondaries check box on Server1.

d. Configure a boot file on Server2 to enable fast zone transfers.

---

3. What is the function of round robin? Which feature takes priority, round robin or netmask ordering?

---

4. You are the chief network administrator for the Proseware company network, which has four branch offices. Each branch office has its own LAN, which is connected to the Internet using a T1 line. Through virtual private network (VPN) connectivity over the Internet, a single intranet is maintained and replicated over Web servers at each branch office. The four Web servers have unique IP addresses but share a single FQDN, intranet.proseware.com, as shown in Figure 8-15.

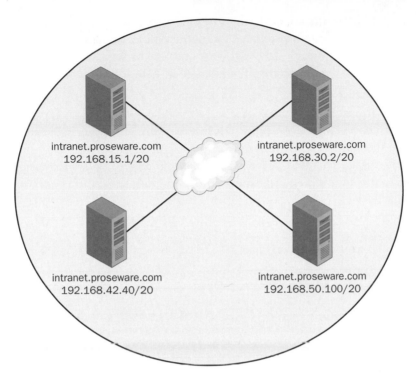

Figure 8-15   Proseware intranet servers

Within the Proseware network, a DNS client computer with the IP address 192.168.33.5 submits a query to a DNS server for the name intranet.proseware.com. Assuming that the Netmask Ordering option is enabled on the DNS server, which IP address is returned to the DNS client? (Hint: Determine which of the four Web servers shares the same subnet ID as that of the querying client computer.)

Lesson Summary

■ The Advanced tab of the DNS server properties dialog box allows you to configure nine installation settings.

■ The Disable Recursion server option is disabled by default, so recursion is enabled for the DNS server, and the server performs queries for its clients unless a special client configuration overrides this behavior.

■ The BIND Secondaries option is enabled by default. Thus, DNS servers in Windows Server 2003 do not use fast transfer format when performing a zone transfer to BIND-based DNS servers. This feature allows for zone transfer compatibility with older versions of BIND.

■ The Enable Netmask Ordering option is selected by default. As a result, in response to a request to resolve the name of a multihomed computer (a computer with more than one IP address), DNS servers in Windows Server 2003 by default first return to the client any IP address that is in the same subnet as the client's.

■ The Enable Round Robin option is selected by default. Thus, in response to a request to resolve the name of a multihomed computer, and in cases where subnet prioritization does not apply, DNS servers in Windows Server 2003 by default rotate the order of matching A resource records in the response list returned to different clients. This feature provides a simple way to balance the network load for frequently queried multihomed computers among all the computer's network adapters.

Lesson 4: Creating Zone Delegations

Managing a large namespace such as that of the Internet would be impossible were it not for the potential to delegate the administration of domains. Through the delegation process, a new zone is created when the responsibility for a subdomain within a DNS namespace is assigned to a separate entity, which can be an autonomous organization or a branch within your company.

You can create a zone delegation in the DNS console by running the New Delegation Wizard.

After this lesson, you will be able to

- Create a delegated zone within a DNS namespace
- Explain the benefits of zone delegations

Estimated lesson time: 15 minutes

Delegating Zones

To delegate a zone means to assign authority over portions of your DNS namespace to subdomains within this namespace. A zone delegation occurs when the responsibility for the resource records of a subdomain is passed from the owner of the parent domain to the owner of the subdomain. For example, in Figure 8-16, the management of the microsoft.com domain is delegated across two zones: microsoft.com and mydomain.microsoft.com. In the example, the administrator of the mydomain.microsoft.com zone controls the resource records for that subdomain.

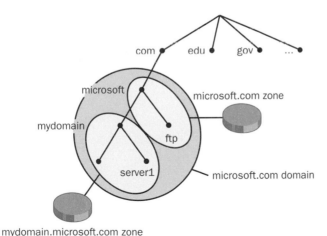

Figure 8-16   Zone delegation example

When To Delegate Zones

You should consider delegating a zone within your network whenever any of the following conditions are present:

- You need to delegate management of a DNS domain to a branch or department within your organization.

- You need to distribute the load of maintaining one large DNS database among multiple name servers to improve name resolution performance and fault tolerance.

- You need hosts and host names to be structured according to branch or departmental affiliation within your organization.

When choosing how to structure zones, you should use a plan that reflects the structure of your organization.

How Delegations Work

For a delegation to be implemented, the parent zone must contain both an A resource record and an NS resource record pointing to the authoritative server of the newly delegated domain. These records are necessary both to transfer authority to the new name servers and to provide referrals to clients performing iterative queries. In this section, you walk through an example of delegating a subdomain to a new zone.

Note   A and NS resource records are automatically created by the DNS console when you create a new delegation.

In Figure 8-17, an authoritative DNS server computer for the newly delegated example.microsoft.com subdomain is given a name based on a derivative subdomain included in the new zone (ns1.us.example.microsoft.com). To make this server known to others outside the newly delegated zone, two resource records are needed in the microsoft.com zone to complete delegation to the new zone. These records are automatically created when you run the New Delegation Wizard in the DNS console.

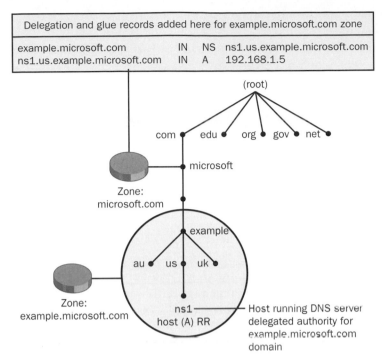

Figure 8-17   Resource records for delegation

These records include the following:

- An NS record (also known as a *delegation record*) to create the actual delegation. This record is used to advertise to querying clients that the computer named ns1.us.example.microsoft.com is an authoritative server for the delegated subdomain.

- An A resource record (also known as a *glue record*) to resolve the name of the server specified in the NS record to its IP address. Glue records are necessary when the name server that is authoritative for the delegated zone is also a member of the delegated domain. The process of resolving the host name in this record to the delegated DNS server in the NS record is sometimes referred to as *glue chasing*.

Note   After you have created a delegation through the DNS console, a glue record appears automatically in the zone data. However, this record is hidden from view in the DNS console.

Suppose an external DNS server (acting as a client) wants to resolve the FQDN box.example.microsoft.com. When this computer queries a name server that is authoritative for the microsoft.com domain, this name server responds with the glue record, informing the querying client that a name server that is authoritative for the example.microsoft.com domain is ns1.us.example.microsoft.com, with an IP address of

192.168.1.5. The querying computer then performs another iterative query to the name server ns1.us.example.microsoft.com. This latter name server finally responds to the querying computer with the IP address of the host box.example.microsoft.com, for which the name server is authoritative.

> **Note**   Delegations take precedence over forwarding. If, in the preceding example, the server that is authoritative for the microsoft.com domain were configured to forward to all queries that it could not answer, the server would still answer a query for the name box.example.microsoft.com by contacting ns1.us.example.microsoft.com, not by contacting the forwarder specified on the Forwarders tab.

Creating a Zone Delegation

To create a zone delegation, first create the primary zone for the domain to be delegated on the server that will be hosting the delegated zone. Then run the New Delegation Wizard on the server hosting the parent zone by right-clicking the parent zone node in the DNS console and selecting New Delegation.

To complete the New Delegation Wizard, you need to specify the name of the delegated subdomain and the name of at least one name server that will be authoritative for the new zone. After you run the wizard, a node appears in the DNS console tree representing the newly delegated subdomain, and this node contains the delegation (NS) resource record of the authoritative server you have just specified. The glue record appears in the zone data but not in the DNS console.

Practice: Creating a Zone Delegation

In this practice, you create a new zone on Server02 that becomes a delegated subdomain of the contoso.com domain. You then create a delegation on Server01 that is linked to this new zone on Server02. Finally, you verify the new configuration.

Exercise 1: Creating a Zone To Be Delegated

1. Log on to Server02.
2. Open the DNS console.
3. In the DNS console tree, expand Server02, right-click the Forward Lookup Zones node, and select New Zone.

   The New Zone Wizard launches.
4. Click Next.

   The Zone Type page appears.

5. Click Next to accept the default selection, Primary Zone.

   The Zone Name page appears.

6. In the Name text box, type **sub.contoso.com** and click Next.

   The Zone File page appears.

7. Click Next to accept the default selection, Create A New File With This File Name.

   The Dynamic Update page appears.

8. Click Next to accept the default selection, Do Not Allow Dynamic Updates.

   The Completing The New Zone Wizard page appears.

9. Click Finish.

Exercise 2: Adding Host (A) Resource Records to the Zone

1. Log on to Server02.

2. Open the DNS console.

3. Expand Server02, Forward Lookup Zones, and select the sub.contoso.com node.

4. Right-click the sub.contoso.com node, and select New Host (A). The New Host dialog box appears.

5. In the Name text box, type **Server01**.

6. In the IP Address text box, type **192.168.0.1** (the IP address currently assigned to Server01) and then click Add Host.

   A message box indicates that the host record was successfully created.

7. Click OK. The New Host dialog box remains open, with the Name text box and IP Address text box now empty.

8. In the Name text box, type **Server02**.

9. In the IP Address text box, type **192.168.0.2** (or the IP address currently assigned to Server02).

10. Click Add Host.

    A message box indicates that the host record was successfully created.

11. Click OK, and then click Done.

Exercise 3: Creating a Delegation

1. Log on to Server02.

2. Open the DNS console, and add Server01 to the console so that you can administer both Server01 and Server02.

3. Expand the Server01 node, expand Forward Lookup Zones, and select the contoso.com node.

4. Right-click the contoso.com node, and select New Delegation

   The New Delegation Wizard launches.

5. Click Next.

   The Delegated Domain Name page appears.

6. In the Delegated Domain text box, type **sub**, and then click Next.

   The Name Servers page appears.

7. Click Add.

   The New Resource Record dialog box appears.

8. In the Server Fully Qualified Domain Name (FQDN) text box, type **Server02.sub.contoso.com**.

9. In the IP Address text box, type **192.168.0.2** (or the IP address currently assigned to Server02).

10. Click Add, and then click OK.

11. On the Name Servers page of the New Delegation Wizard, click Next.

    The Completing The New Delegation Wizard page appears.

12. Click Finish.

    In the DNS console tree, you will now see the sub delegation node under the contoso.com zone.

13. Use the DNS console to answer the following question: how many host (A) resource records does Server01 hold for the sub.contoso.com domain?

    _____

Exercise 4: Testing the Configuration

1. Log on to Server01, which uses the local DNS server for name resolution.

2. Open a command prompt and type **ping Server01.sub.contoso.com**. Then press ENTER.

   An output indicates that the host Server01.sub.contoso.com is responding from the IP address 192.168.0.1. If the ping is unsuccessful, at the command prompt type **ipconfig /flushdns**, wait 2 minutes, and then press ENTER.

3. After the Ping output has completed, at the command prompt type **ping Server02.sub.contoso.com**, and then press ENTER.

An output indicates that Server02.sub.contoso.com is responding from the IP address 192.168.0.2. If the ping is unsuccessful, at the command prompt type **ipconfig /flushdns**, wait 2 minutes, and then press ENTER.

The new computer names are being resolved to IP addresses even though the local computer, Server01, conducts name resolution through the local DNS server, which contains no host records for the sub.contoso.com domain. The local DNS server is correctly forwarding queries for hosts within the sub.contoso.com subdomain to the name server authoritative for that domain, which is Server02.

Lesson Review

The following questions are intended to reinforce key information presented in this lesson. If you are unable to answer a question, review the lesson materials and try the question again. You can find answers to the questions in the "Questions and Answers" section at the end of this chapter.

1. You are designing the DNS namespace for a company named Proseware, which has a registered domain name of proseware.com. Proseware has a central office in Rochester and one branch office each in Buffalo and Syracuse. Each office has a separate LAN and network administrator. You want to configure a single DNS server at each location, and you want the central office to host the proseware.com domain. In addition, you want the administrators in Buffalo and Syracuse to maintain responsibility for DNS names and name resolution within their networks.

   Which of the following steps should you take?

   a. Configure a standard primary server in Rochester to host the proseware.com zone. Delegate a subdomain to each of the branch offices. Configure a secondary server in both Buffalo and Syracuse to host each of the delegated subdomains.

   b. Configure a standard primary server in Rochester to host the proseware.com zone. Configure a secondary server in both Buffalo and Syracuse to improve performance and fault tolerance to the zone.

   c. Configure the DNS server in Rochester to host a standard primary zone for the proseware.com domain. Configure the DNS servers in both Buffalo and Syracuse to each host a standard primary zone for a subdomain of proseware.com. Create a delegation from the DNS server in Rochester to each of these subdomains.

   d. Configure the DNS server in Rochester to host a standard primary zone for the proseware.com domain. Configure the DNS servers in both Buffalo and Syracuse to host a standard primary zone for a subdomain of proseware.com. Add secondary zones on each DNS server to pull transfers from the primary zones hosted on the other two DNS servers.

2. You are the administrator for your company's network, which consists of a central office LAN and three branch office LANs, each located in different cities. You have decided to design a new DNS infrastructure while deploying Active Directory on your network. Your goals for the network are first to implement a single Active Directory forest across all four locations and second to minimize response times for users connecting to resources anywhere on the network. Assume that all branch offices have domain controllers running DNS servers.

   Which of the following actions best meets these goals?

   a. Configure a single Active Directory domain for all four locations and configure a single Active Directory–integrated DNS zone that replicates through the entire domain.

   b. Configure a single Active Directory domain for all four locations, and configure a standard primary zone at the central office with zone transfers to secondary zones at each branch office.

   c. Configure an Active Directory domain and a DNS domain for the central office, delegate a DNS subdomain to each branch office, and configure an Active Directory–integrated zone in each location that replicates through the entire forest.

   d. Configure an Active Directory domain and a DNS domain for the central office, delegate a DNS subdomain to each branch office, and configure an Active Directory–integrated zone in each location that replicates through the entire domain.

   _____

3. Which resource records are added to a parent zone to delegate a given subdomain? What are the specific functions of these records?

   _____

   _____

   _____

   _____

4. The DNS server NS1 hosts the zone lucernepublishing.com and is configured to forward all queries for which the server is not authoritative. NS1 receives a query for sub.lucernepublishing.com, a delegated subdomain. Where will the query be directed?

   _____

   _____

Lesson Summary

- To delegate a zone means to assign authority over portions of your DNS namespace to subdomains within this namespace. A zone delegation occurs when the responsibility for the resource records of a subdomain is passed from the owner of the parent domain to the owner of the subdomain.

- You should consider delegating a zone within your network when you need to delegate management of a DNS domain to a branch or department within your organization, when you need to distribute the load of maintaining one large DNS database among multiple name servers to improve name resolution performance and fault tolerance, or when you need hosts and host names to be structured according to branch or departmental affiliation within your organization.

- For a delegation to be implemented, the parent zone must contain both an A resource record and an NS resource record pointing to the authoritative server of the newly delegated domain. These records are necessary to both transfer authority to the new name servers and provide referrals to clients performing iterative queries. These records are automatically created by the DNS console when you create a new delegation.

- To create a zone delegation, first create the domain to be delegated on the server that will be hosting the delegated zone. Then run the New Delegation Wizard on the server hosting the parent zone by right-clicking the parent zone node in the DNS console and selecting New Delegation.

Lesson 5: Deploying Stub Zones

A *stub zone* is an abbreviated copy of a zone, updated regularly, that contains only the NS records belonging to a master zone. A server hosting a stub zone does not answer a query directly for the zone, but instead directs these queries to any of the name servers specified in the stub zone's NS resource records.

After this lesson, you will be able to

- Create a stub zone
- Describe the benefits and limitations of stub zones

Estimated lesson time: 30 minutes

Understanding Stub Zones

When you configure a new zone using the New Zone Wizard, you have the option of creating the new zone as a primary, secondary, or stub zone. When you create a stub zone, a zone is configured that maintains only those records—NS resource records—needed to locate the name servers of the master zone specified by the name of the stub zone.

Stub zones are used to keep all the NS resource records from a master zone current. To configure a stub zone, you need to specify at least one name server, the master, with an IP address that doesn't change. Any new name servers you add to the master zone later are updated to the stub zone automatically through zone transfers.

You cannot modify a stub zone's resource records. Any changes you want to make to these records in a stub zone must be made in the original primary zone from which the stub zone is derived.

Benefits of Stub Zones

Stub zones allow you to achieve the following benefits:

- **Improve name resolution**   Stub zones enable a DNS server to perform recursion by using the stub zone's list of name servers without querying the root server.

- **Keep foreign zone information current**   By updating the stub zone regularly, the DNS server hosting the stub zone maintains a current list of name servers for a different zone, such as a delegated zone on a different DNS server.

- **Simplify DNS administration**   By using stub zones throughout your DNS infrastructure, you can distribute zone information without using secondary zones.

Important   Stub zones do not serve the same purpose as secondary zones and are not an alternative when planning for fault tolerance, redundancy, or load sharing.

When To Use Stub Zones

Stub zones are most frequently used to keep track of the name servers that are authoritative for delegated zones. Most often, stub zones are hosted on the parent DNS servers of those delegated zones.

A DNS server that has delegated a child zone to a different DNS server is usually informed of new authoritative DNS servers added to the child zone only when the resource records for these new DNS servers are manually added to the parent zone. With stub zones, a DNS server can host a stub zone for one of its delegated (child) zones and obtain updates of that zone's authoritative servers whenever additional name servers are added to the master zone. This functionality is explained in the following example, illustrated in Figure 8-18.

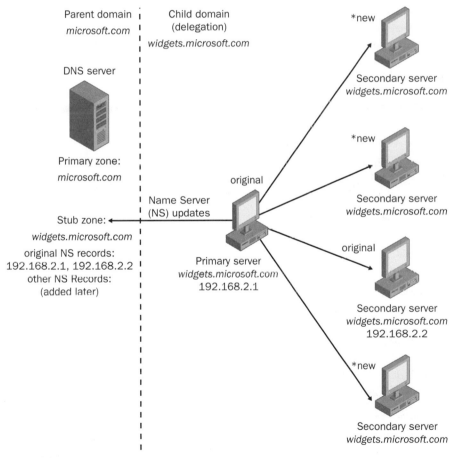

Figure 8-18   Stub zones and delegations

Stub Zone Example

A DNS server that is authoritative for the parent zone microsoft.com delegated a child zone, widgets.microsoft.com, to separate DNS servers. When the delegation for the child zone widgets.microsoft.com was originally performed, it contained only two NS resource records for the widgets.microsoft.com zone's authoritative DNS servers. Later, administrators of this zone configured additional DNS servers as authoritative for the zone but did not notify the administrators of the parent zone, microsoft.com. As a result, the DNS server hosting the parent zone is not informed of the new DNS servers that are authoritative for its child zone, widgets.microsoft.com, and continues to query the only two authoritative DNS servers that exist in the stub zone.

You can remedy this situation by configuring the DNS server that is authoritative for the parent zone, microsoft.com, to host a stub zone for its child zone, widgets.microsoft.com. When the administrator of the authoritative DNS server for microsoft.com updates the resource records for its stub zone, it queries the master server for widgets.microsoft.com to obtain that zone's authoritative DNS server records. Consequently, the DNS server that is authoritative for the parent zone learns about the new name servers that are authoritative for the widgets.microsoft.com child zone and is able to perform recursion to all the child zone's authoritative DNS servers.

> **Important**   A stub zone cannot be hosted on a DNS server that is authoritative for the same zone. For example, the stub zone for widgets.microsoft.com cannot be hosted on a DNS server that is authoritative for widgets.microsoft.com. The stub zone for this domain can bc hosted on a DNS server that is authoritative for a different zone, such as a parent zone containing a delegation for widgets.microsoft.com. If the microsoft.com zone contained a delegation to widgets.microsoft.com, the DNS server hosting microsoft.com could also host a stub zone for widgets.microsoft.com.

Other Uses for Stub Zones

You can also use stub zones to facilitate name resolution across domains in a manner that avoids searching the DNS namespace for a common parent server. Stub zones can thus replace secondary zones in cases where achieving DNS connectivity across domains is important but providing data redundancy for the master zone is not. Also note that stub zones improve name resolution and eliminate the burden to network resources that would otherwise result from large zone transfers.

Figure 8-19 illustrates using stub zones to facilitate name resolution in this way. In the example, a query for the host name ns.mgmt.ldn.microsoft.com is submitted to two different name servers. In the first case, the server authoritative for the mfg.wa.microsoft.com domain accepts the query. Many other name servers must then be contacted before the destination name server that is authoritative for the appropriate domain (mgmt.ldn.microsoft.com) receives the query. In the second case, the DNS server that is authoritative for the actg.wa.microsoft.com domain receives a query for the same name, ns.mgmt.ldn.microsoft.com. Because this second server also hosts a stub zone for the destination mgmt.ldn.microsoft.com, the server already knows the address of the server that is authoritative for the record for the host ns.mgmt.ldn.microsoft.com, and it sends a recursive query directly to the authoritative server.

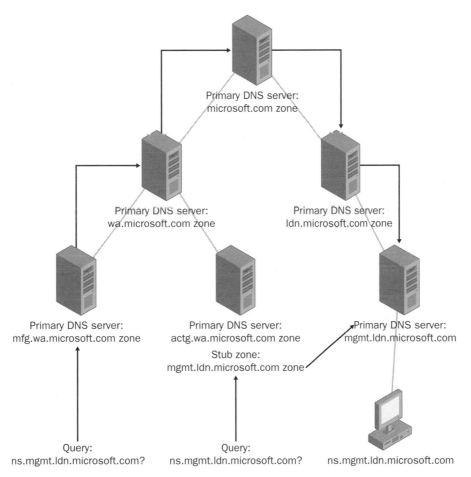

Figure 8-19   Using stub zones across domains

Stub Zone Resource Records

A stub zone contains SOA, NS, and A glue resource records for authoritative DNS servers in a zone. The SOA type identifies the primary DNS server for the actual zone (master server) and other zone property information. The NS resource record type contains a list of authoritative DNS servers for a zone (primary and secondary servers). The A glue resource records hold the IP addresses of the DNS servers authoritative for the zone.

> **Note**   As with delegations, stub zones contain glue records in the zone data, but these glue records are not visible in the DNS console.

Stub Zone Resolution

When a DNS client performs a recursive query operation on a DNS server hosting a stub zone, the DNS server uses the stub zone's resource records to resolve the query. The DNS server then queries the authoritative servers specified in the stub zone's NS resource records. If the DNS server cannot find any of the authoritative name servers listed in its stub zone, it attempts standard recursion.

The DNS server stores the resource records it receives from a stub zone's authoritative servers in its cache and not in the stub zone itself; only the SOA, NS, and A resource records returned in response to the query are stored in the stub zone. The resource records stored in the cache are cached according to the Time to Live (TTL) value in each resource record. The SOA, NS, and A resource records, which are not written to the cache, expire according to the interval specified in the stub zone's SOA resource record, which is created during the creation of the stub zone and updated during transfers to the stub zone from the original primary zone.

When a DNS server receives a query for which recursion has been disabled, the DNS server returns a referral pointing to the servers specified in the stub zone.

Stub Zone Updates

When a DNS server loads a stub zone, it queries the zone's master server for the SOA resource record, NS resource records at the zone's root, and A resource records. During updates to the stub zone, the master server is queried by the DNS server hosting the stub zone for the same resource record types requested during the loading of the stub zone. The SOA resource record's refresh interval determines when the DNS server hosting the stub zone attempts a zone transfer (update). Should an update fail, the SOA resource record's retry interval determines when the update is retried. Once the retry interval has expired without a successful update, the expiration time as specified in the SOA resource record's Expires field determines when the DNS server stops using the stub zone data.

You can use the DNS console to perform the following stub zone update operations:

- **Reload**   This operation reloads the stub zone from the local storage of the DNS server hosting it.

- **Transfer From Master**   The DNS server hosting the stub zone determines whether the serial number in the stub zone's SOA resource record has expired and then performs a zone transfer from the stub zone's master server.

■ **Reload From Master**   This operation performs a zone transfer from the stub zone's master server regardless of the serial number in the stub zone's SOA resource record.

Practice: Deploying a Stub Zone

In this practice, you create a stub zone on Server01 that pulls transfers from the delegated subdomain sub.contoso.com.

Exercise 1: Creating a Stub Zone

1. Log on to Server02.

2. Open the DNS console, and add Server01 to the console so that you can administer both Server01 and Server02.

3. Expand the Server02 node, expand Forward Lookup Zones, and select sub.contoso.com.

4. Right-click sub.contoso.com in the tree pane, and click Properties.

5. Click the Name Servers tab.

6. Click Add. The New Resource Record dialog box appears.

7. Type **scrvcr01.contoso.com** in the Server Fully Qualified Domain Name (FQDN) box.

8. Click Resolve. Confirm that Server01's IP address, 192.168.0.1 appears in the IP Address box.

9. Click OK to close the New Resource Record dialog box.

10. Click OK to close the sub.contoso.com zone properties dialog box.

11. Expand the Server01 node, right-click the Forward Lookup Zones node, and select New Zone.

    The New Zone Wizard launches.

12. Click Next.

    The Zone Type page appears.

13. Select Stub Zone, clear the Store The Zone In Active Directory check box, and click Next.

    The Zone Name page appears.

14. In the Zone Name text box, type **sub.contoso.com**, and then click Next.

    The Zone File page appears.

15. Click Next to accept the default selection, Create A New File With This File Name.

    The Master DNS Servers page appears.

16. In the IP Address text box, type **192.168.0.2** (or the IP address currently assigned to Server02), click Add, and then click Next.

    The Completing The New Zone Wizard page appears.

17. Click Finish.

    The sub.contoso.com zone now appears in the DNS console tree under the Forward Lookup Zones node.

18. Right-click the sub.contoso.com node in the console tree (not the details pane), and then select Transfer From Master.

> **Tip** If you receive an error message, wait 10 seconds and try step 15 again.

19. When the zone loads successfully, the node shows only three resource records: the SOA resource record for the zone and the NS resource records pointing to Server02 and Server01.

Lesson Review

The following questions are intended to reinforce key information presented in this lesson. If you are unable to answer a question, review the lesson materials and try the question again. You can find answers to the questions in the "Questions and Answers" section at the end of this chapter.

1. What is the most common use of a stub zone?

    _____

    _____

2. Which of the following is not a benefit of using a stub zone?

    a. Improving name resolution performance

    b. Keeping foreign zone information current

    c. Simplifying DNS administration

    d. Increasing fault tolerance for DNS servers

    _____

3. When would you choose to implement a stub zone over a secondary zone? When would you choose to implement a secondary zone over a stub zone?

_____

_____

_____

_____

_____

_____

_____

_____

Lesson Summary

- A stub zone is an abbreviated copy of a zone, updated regularly, that contains only the NS records belonging to a master zone. Stub zones are most frequently used to keep track of the name servers that are authoritative for delegated zones and are most frequently hosted on the parent DNS servers of those delegated zones.

- Stub zones can also be used to facilitate name resolution across domains in a manner that avoids searching the DNS namespace for a common parent server.

- To create a stub zone, you open the New Zone Wizard by right-clicking the DNS server icon in the DNS console and selecting New Zone. In the New Zone Wizard, you select the stub zone type and then follow the wizard's instructions.

- To configure a stub zone, you need to specify at least one name server, the master, with an IP address that doesn't change. Any new name servers that you add to the master zone are later updated to the stub zone automatically through zone transfers.

- Stub zones do not serve the same purpose as secondary zones and are not an alternative when planning for fault tolerance, redundancy, or load sharing.

Case Scenario Exercise

You have been hired as a consultant by Lucerne Publishing, which is in the process of redeploying its DNS server infrastructure on Windows Server 2003. Lucerne Publishing's in-house network designer, Klaus, has requested your services for your expertise in Windows Server 2003.

Lucerne Publishing has its headquarters in Lucerne and has two branch offices in Bern and Geneva. The Lucerne branch hosts the parent domain, lucernepublishing.com. The Bern and Geneva offices each host subdomains and contain their own domain controllers.

Figure 8-20 presents the relevant portion of the network.

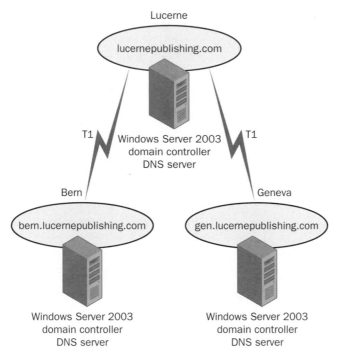

Figure 8-20 Lucerne Publishing's network

Klaus wants to achieve four goals in his network:

- Minimize name resolution traffic across WAN links
- Minimize DNS replication traffic across WAN links
- Secure DNS replication traffic across WAN links
- Optimize name resolution traffic for client computers

1. Which of these goals are met by deploying an Active Directory–integrated zone on domain controllers in all three locations throughout the network?

2. If an Active Directory–integrated zone is deployed for the lucernepublishing.com domain, which option should you recommend be configured in the Change Zone Replication Scope dialog box shown in Figure 8-21? Assume that improving name resolution response time is more important than minimizing network traffic.

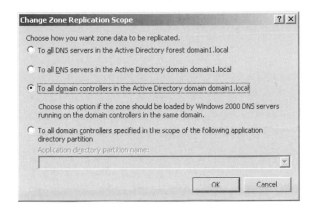

Figure 8-21   Zone replication scope settings for the lucernepublishing.com domain

3. The Bern branch office has 200 employees, and you want to deploy DNS in a way that minimizes the administrative load for network managers at the Lucerne office. However, you also want DNS servers in headquarters to be updated on any new authoritative servers deployed in the Bern office. How can you achieve these goals?

4. Klaus has informed you that his network administrators have unsuccessfully attempted to deploy a test secondary DNS server in one of the branch offices. He says the administrators specified the correct IP address of a primary DNS server running Windows Server 2003 in the Lucerne office, yet the secondary server was unable to transfer data from the primary zone. Given that this test network was successfully deployed on Windows 2000 a few years ago, what is the most likely cause of the problem?

Troubleshooting Lab

You are the administrator of Contoso, Ltd.'s network. Recently, users have been complaining of problems when they attempt to log on. You discover that critical SRV records are missing from the DNS zones for contoso.com and apply the Netdiag.exe utility to correct the problem.

To create the faulty DNS zone:

1. Log on to Server01.

2. Open the DNS console.

3. Expand the Server01 node, and expand Forward Loop Zones_msdcs.contoso.com\dc_tcp.

4. Delete the following two SRV resource records: _kerberos._tcp.dc._msdcs.contoso.com, and _ldap._tcp.dc._msdcs.contoso.com.

5. Close the DNS console.

To troubleshoot and correct the problem:

1. Install the Support Tools on Server01 by launching Suptools.msi. Suptools.msi is located on the Windows Server 2003 CD-ROM in the Support\Tools folder.

   Make sure Server01 is not connected to the Internet when you perform the following step.

2. At a command prompt, type **netdiag /fix**.

3. The utility runs for a few moments. After it has completed, browse the output. You will see that some tests have failed and some fixes have been applied.

4. Open the DNS console and browse to the _tcp.dc._msdcs.contoso.com domain.

   In the details pane, you can see that the two records you deleted have been re-created.

Chapter Summary

- The Forwarders tab of the DNS server properties dialog box allows you to forward DNS queries received by the local DNS server to upstream DNS servers, called forwarders. This tab also allows you to disable recursion for select queries (as specified by domain).

- The Root Hints tab of the DNS server properties dialog box provides a simple way to modify the contents in the Cache.dns file. If you are using your DNS server to resolve Internet names, you do not normally need to modify these entries. However, if you are using your DNS server only to answer queries for hosts in a separate and private DNS namespace, you should alter these root hints to point to the root servers in your network. Finally, if your DNS server computer is itself the root server (named ".") of your private namespace, you should delete the Cache.dns file.

- When you deploy a DNS server on a domain controller, you can choose to store the zone data in the Active Directory database. Active Directory–integrated zones minimize zone transfer traffic, improve security, decrease administrative overhead, and improve fault tolerance. You can configure zone data to be replicated among all DNS servers in the Active Directory forest, among all DNS servers in the Active Directory domain, among all domain controllers in the Active Directory domain, or among all servers enlisted in a custom application directory partition.

- The SOA resource record includes several parameters that affect zone transfers, such as Refresh Interval, Retry Interval, Expires After, and Minimum (Default) TTL.

- When nonsecure dynamic updates are allowed in a zone, any computer can update a resource record in a DNS zone. When only secure dynamic updates are allowed, only the owner of a record can update it. Secure dynamic updates can be required only on Active Directory–integrated zones.

- The DnsUpdateProxy group is typically used for DHCP servers performing dynamic DNS updates on behalf of other computers. Members of this group do not record ownership on the resource records they register in DNS. This caveat prevents problems from arising in zones that allow only secure dynamic updates.

- The Zone Transfers tab allows you to restrict transfers from the current zone. By default, zone transfers to secondary servers are allowed only to servers specified on the Name Server tab in the zone properties.

- Through netmask ordering, an IP address whose subnet matches that of the querying DNS client is placed at the top of the response list.

- Through round robin, the order of all matching A resource records is rotated in the response list returned to successive querying clients. This feature provides a simple way to balance the network load for frequently accessed network services among all the servers hosting that service.

- To delegate a zone means to assign authority over portions of your DNS namespace to subdomains within this namespace. A zone delegation occurs when the responsibility for the resource records of a subdomain is passed from the owner of the parent domain to the owner of the subdomain.

- A stub zone is an abbreviated copy of a zone, updated regularly, that contains only the SOA and NS resource records belonging to the master zone. Stub zones are most frequently used to keep track of the name servers that are authoritative for delegated zones and are most frequently hosted on the parent DNS servers of those delegated zones.

Exam Highlights

Before taking the exam, review the following key points and terms to help you identify topics you need to review. Return to the lessons for additional practice and review the "Further Readings" sections in Part 2 for pointers to more information about topics covered by the exam objectives.

Key Points

■ Understand the various zone replication scope options available for Active Directory–integrated zones.

■ Understand the scenarios in which forwarding is likely to be deployed.

■ Understand the implications of enabling or disabling round robin, netmask ordering, BIND secondaries, and recursion.

■ Understand the difference between secure and nonsecure dynamic updates.

■ Understand the function of the DnsUpdateProxy group.

■ Understand the implications of increasing or decreasing the Refresh Interval, Retry Interval, Expires After, and Minimum (Default) TTL parameters in the SOA resource record.

■ Understand the scenarios in which primaries, secondaries, stub zones, and Active Directory–integrated zones are likely to be deployed.

■ Understand the scenarios in which delegations are likely to be configured.

Key Terms

application directory partition   A partition of data replicated in the Active Directory database on a subset of domain controllers. Application directory partitions contain information for use by a particular application or service, such as DNS.

iteration (iterative queries)   The process of querying different DNS servers in succession to resolve a computer name to an IP address.

Questions and Answers

Page
8-19

Lesson 1, Practice, Exercise 1

17. Ping server01.contoso.com and server02.contoso.com. Do the ping tests succeed? Why or why not?

The ping test for server01.contoso.com should fail, because when Server02 attempts to resolve the name to an address, it queries the DNS service running on Server02, and that DNS service does not have a zone for contoso.com or a host (A) record for server01.contoso.com. The ping test for server02.contoso.com succeeds because the system can resolve its own name. DNS is not involved in that resolution.

Page
8-21

Lesson 1, Practice, Exercise 2

1. From the command prompt, ping server01.contoso.com and server02.contoso.com. Do the ping tests succeed? Why or why not?

The ping tests succeed. When pinging server01.contoso.com, the computer queries the DNS Server on Server02, which forwards the query to Server01. Server01 is authoritative for the contoso.com domain and returns the host record for server01.contoso.com.

13. What records do you see? Why is server02.contoso.com not listed?

Server01's resource record is cached. Server02's is not cached because when Server02 pings server02.contoso.com, it resolves its own name without querying DNS.

Page
8-24

Lesson 1 Review

1. You have just updated a host resource record. What other associated resource record might now need to be updated?

The PTR record associated with the same host

2. You administer a network that consists of a single domain. On this network, you have configured a new DNS server named DNS1 to answer queries for Internet names from the local domain. However, although DNS1 is connected to the Internet, it continues to fail its recursive test on the Monitoring tab of the server properties dialog box. Which of the following could be the potential cause for the failure?

   a. You have configured DNS1 in front of a firewall.

   b. DNS1 hosts a zone named ".".

   c. Your root hints have not been modified from the defaults.

   d. You have not configured DNS1 to forward any queries to upstream servers.

b

3. Which resource record is used to resolve domain names specified in e-mail addresses to the IP address of the mail server associated with the domain?

   a. PTR

   b. MX

   c. A

   d. CNAME

   b

4. On a new DNS server, you create a zone "." and then create subdomains from that root domain. Which function will the new server be able or unable to perform?

   a. The server will be unable to cache names.

   b. The server will be able to function only as a forwarding server.

   c. The server will be unable to resolve Internet names.

   d. The server will be unable to connect to the Internet.

   c

5. How can you use forwarding to increase security of DNS queries?

   When an internal DNS server performs iterative queries on the Internet to resolve names, this process requires your internal network to be exposed to outside servers. Through forwarding, you can restrict cross-firewall DNS traffic to only two computers—the internal forwarding DNS server and the DNS forwarder outside a firewall. With this arrangement, the external forwarder can perform iterative queries on behalf of internal servers without exposing the network.

6. Which of the following events could serve as a legitimate reason to modify (but not delete) the default root hints on the Root Hints tab of a DNS server properties dialog box? (Choose all that apply.)

   a. The Internet root servers have changed.

   b. The server will not be used as a root server.

   c. You have disabled recursion on the server.

   d. Your server is not used to resolve Internet names.

   a, d

Page
8-42
Lesson 2 Review

1. Describe the process by which secondary servers determine whether a zone transfer should be initiated.

   The secondary server conducts an SOA query, in which the serial number value in the primary zone's SOA resource record is compared to the serial number value in the secondary server's own version of the zone database. If the secondary server determines that the master zone has a higher serial number, a transfer is initiated.

2. What is the difference between IXFR and AXFR queries?

IXFR queries initiate an incremental zone transfer. In these transfers, only the updated information is transferred across the network. AXFR queries initiate an all zone transfer. In these transfers, the complete zone database is transferred across the network.

3. You have multiple DHCP servers on your network, some of which are configured to register DNS records on behalf of pre-Windows 2000 clients. You have configured DNS to allow only secure updates. However, you find that some DNS records are not being updated properly. How can you solve this problem?

Add the DHCP servers to the DnsUpdateProxy built-in security group.

4. You oversee administration for a wide area network (WAN) belonging to the Proseware company, which has one central office in Rochester and two branch offices in Buffalo and Syracuse. The network, which consists of one domain, has one primary DNS zone running on a Windows Server 2003 computer at the central office, and one secondary DNS zone at each branch. Network users are complaining that they often cannot connect to sites at remote branches. Administrators have determined that network bandwidth between the central office and branches has become saturated with zone transfers, and that zone transfers are being initiated before they can complete. Which of the following steps would help resolve the problem with the least effort?

   a. Install Active Directory on the network, and promote the servers hosting the secondary DNS zones to domain controllers.

   b. Increase the network bandwidth by establishing a fiber-optic connection between the two sites.

   c. Increase the refresh interval on the primary DNS server.

   d. Increase the refresh interval on the secondary DNS servers.

   c

5. You discover that an administrator has adjusted the default TTL value for your company's primary DNS zone to 5 minutes. Which of the following is the most likely effect of this change?

   a. Resource records cached on the primary DNS server expire after 5 minutes.

   b. DNS clients have to query the server more frequently to resolve names for which the server is authoritative.

   c. Secondary servers initiate a zone transfer every 5 minutes.

   d. DNS hosts reregister their records more frequently.

   b

Lesson 3 Review

1. You are the network administrator for Lucerne Publishing. The Lucerne Publishing network consists of a single domain, lucernepublishing.com, that is protected from the Internet by a firewall. The firewall runs on a computer named NS1 that is directly connected to the Internet. NS1 also runs the DNS Server service, and its firewall allows DNS traffic to pass between the Internet and the DNS Server service on NS1 but not between the Internet and the internal network. The DNS Server service on NS1 is configured to use round robin. Behind the firewall, two computers are running Windows Server 2003—NS2 and NS3—which host a primary and secondary DNS server, respectively, for the lucernepublishing.com zone.

   Users on the company network report that, although they use host names to connect to computers on the local private network, they cannot use host names to connect to Internet destinations such as www.microsoft.com.

   Which of the following actions requires the least amount of administrative effort to enable network users to connect to Internet host names?

   a. Disable recursion on NS2 and NS3.

   b. Enable netmask ordering on NS1.

   c. Configure NS2 and NS3 to use NS1 as a forwarder.

   d. Disable round robin on NS1.

   c

2. You are the administrator for a large network consisting of 10 domains. You have configured a standard primary zone for the mfg.lucernepublishing.com domain on a DNS server computer named Server1. You have also configured a UNIX server, named Server2, to host a secondary zone for the same domain. The UNIX server is running BIND 8.2.1.

   You notice that zone transfers between the primary and secondary servers seem to generate more traffic than expected, putting a strain on network resources.

   What can you do to decrease the network burden of zone transfers between the primary and secondary servers?

   a. Clear the BIND Secondaries check box on Server1.

   b. Configure a boot file on Server1 to initialize BIND-compatible settings.

   c. Select the BIND Secondaries check box on Server1.

   d. Configure a boot file on Server2 to enable fast zone transfers.

   a

3. What is the function of round robin? Which feature takes priority, round robin or netmask ordering?

Round robin rotates the order of matching resource records in the response list returned to DNS clients. Each successive DNS client that queries for a multihomed name gets a different resource record at the top of the list. Round robin is secondary to subnet prioritization. When the Enable Netmask Ordering check box is also selected, round robin is used as a secondary means to order returned resource records for multihomed computers.

4. You are the chief network administrator for the Proseware company network, which has four branch offices. Each branch office has its own LAN, which is connected to the Internet using a T1 line. Through virtual private network (VPN) connectivity over the Internet, a single intranet is maintained and replicated over Web servers at each branch office. The four Web servers have unique IP addresses but share a single FQDN, intranet.proseware.com, as shown in Figure 8-15.

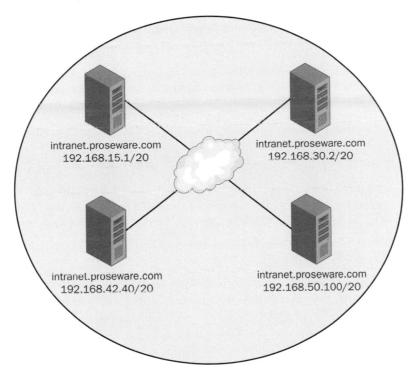

Figure 8-15   Proseware intranet servers

Within the Proseware network, a DNS client computer with the IP address 192.168.33.5 submits a query to a DNS server for the name intranet.proseware.com. Assuming that the Netmask Ordering option is enabled on the DNS server, which IP address is returned to the DNS client? (Hint: Determine which of the four Web servers shares the same subnet ID as that of the querying client computer.)

192.168.42.40

Page
8-59

Lesson 4, Practice, Exercise 3

13. Use the DNS console to answer the following question: how many host (A) resource records does Server01 hold for the sub.contoso.com domain?

> None

Page
8-61

Lesson 4 Review

1. You are designing the DNS namespace for a company named Proseware, which has a registered domain name of proseware.com. Proseware has a central office in Rochester and one branch office each in Buffalo and Syracuse. Each office has a separate LAN and network administrator. You want to configure a single DNS server at each location, and you want the central office to host the proseware.com domain. In addition, you want the administrators in Buffalo and Syracuse to maintain responsibility for DNS names and name resolution within their networks.

Which of the following steps should you take?

a. Configure a standard primary server in Rochester to host the proseware.com zone. Delegate a subdomain to each of the branch offices. Configure a secondary server in both Buffalo and Syracuse to host each of the delegated subdomains.

b. Configure a standard primary server in Rochester to host the proseware.com zone. Configure a secondary server in both Buffalo and Syracuse to improve performance and fault tolerance to the zone.

c. Configure the DNS server in Rochester to host a standard primary zone for the proseware.com domain. Configure the DNS servers in both Buffalo and Syracuse to each host a standard primary zone for a subdomain of proseware.com. Create a delegation from the DNS server in Rochester to each of these subdomains.

d. Configure the DNS server in Rochester to host a standard primary zone for the proseware.com domain. Configure the DNS servers in both Buffalo and Syracuse to host a standard primary zone for a subdomain of proseware.com. Add secondary zones on each DNS server to pull transfers from the primary zones hosted on the other two DNS servers.

> c

2. You are the administrator for your company's network, which consists of a central office LAN and three branch office LANs, each located in different cities. You have decided to design a new DNS infrastructure while deploying Active Directory on your network. Your goals for the network are first to implement a single Active Directory forest across all four locations and second to minimize response times for users connecting to resources anywhere on the network. Assume that all branch offices have domain controllers running DNS servers.

Which of the following actions best meets these goals?

a. Configure a single Active Directory domain for all four locations and configure a single Active Directory–integrated DNS zone that replicates through the entire domain.

b. Configure a single Active Directory domain for all four locations, and configure a standard primary zone at the central office with zone transfers to secondary zones at each branch office.

c. Configure an Active Directory domain and a DNS domain for the central office, delegate a DNS subdomain to each branch office, and configure an Active Directory–integrated zone in each location that replicates through the entire forest.

d. Configure an Active Directory domain and a DNS domain for the central office, delegate a DNS subdomain to each branch office, and configure an Active Directory–integrated zone in each location that replicates through the entire domain.

a

3. Which resource records are added to a parent zone to delegate a given subdomain? What are the specific functions of these records?

An NS resource record and an A resource record are created in the delegated subdomain on the parent zone. The NS resource record directs queries to the DNS server, specified by name, that is authoritative for the delegated zone. The A resource record, called a glue record, allows the computer name specified in the NS resource record to be mapped to an IP address.

4. The DNS server NS1 hosts the zone lucernepublishing.com and is configured to forward all queries for which the server is not authoritative. NS1 receives a query for sub.lucernepublishing.com, a delegated subdomain. Where will the query be directed?

The query will be directed to the server that is authoritative for the sub.lucernepublishing.com zone, not to the configured forwarder.

Page
8-70
Lesson 5 Review

1. What is the most common use of a stub zone?

Stub zones are most frequently used by a parent zone to keep an updated list of NS resource records for delegated subdomains.

2. Which of the following is not a benefit of using a stub zone?

   a. Improving name resolution performance

   b. Keeping foreign zone information current

   c. Simplifying DNS administration

   d. Increasing fault tolerance for DNS servers

d

3. When would you choose to implement a stub zone over a secondary zone? When would you choose to implement a secondary zone over a stub zone?

A stub zone is useful when you have delegated a subdomain and want to keep your records of the NS resource records for that delegation updated. Stub zones are also useful when you need to improve name resolution by providing links to authoritative DNS servers across domains. In both cases, a stub zone is preferable to a secondary server when you want to avoid the storage demands of a full secondary zone or the network resource demands associated with zone transfers. You should implement a secondary zone instead of a stub zone when you need to provide data redundancy for your master zone and when improving query response times is more important than minimizing the use of network resources.

Page
8-73
Case Scenario Exercise

1. Which of these goals are met by deploying an Active Directory–integrated zone on domain controllers in all three locations throughout the network?

All four goals are met by this solution.

2. If an Active Directory–integrated zone is deployed for the lucernepublishing.com domain, which option should you recommend be configured in the Change Zone Replication Scope dialog box shown in Figure 8-21? Assume that improving name resolution response time is more important than minimizing network traffic.

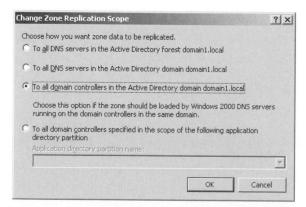

Figure 8-16   Zone replication scope settings for the lucernepublishing.com domain

To All DNS Servers In The Active Directory Forest Lucernepublishing.com

3. The Bern branch office has 200 employees, and you want to deploy DNS in a way that minimizes the administrative load for network managers at the Lucerne office. However, you also want DNS servers in headquarters to be updated on any new authoritative servers deployed in the Bern office. How can you achieve these goals?

Create a delegation for the bern.lucernepublishing.com domain, and then deploy a stub zone at headquarters that transfers NS records from the primary server of the bern.lucernepublishing.com.

4. Klaus has informed you that his network administrators have unsuccessfully attempted to deploy a test secondary DNS server in one of the branch offices. He says the administrators specified the correct IP address of a primary DNS server running Windows Server 2003 in the Lucerne office, yet the secondary server was unable to transfer data from the primary zone. Given that this test network was successfully deployed on Windows 2000 a few years ago, what is the most likely cause of the problem?

In Windows Server 2003, zone transfers are not permitted by default. By selecting the Allow Zone Transfers check box in the zone properties dialog box, selecting Only To Servers Listed On The Name Servers Tab, and then specifying the secondary server on the Name Servers tab in zone properties, you create the necessary NS resource record and allow zone transfers.

9 Planning and Implementing Server Roles and Security

Exam Objectives in this Chapter:

- Configure security for servers that are assigned specific roles (Exam 70-296).

- Plan security for servers that are assigned specific roles. Roles might include domain controllers, Web servers, database servers and mail servers (Exam 70-296).

    - Deploy the security configuration for servers that are assigned specific roles.

    - Create custom security templates based on server roles.

- Implement secure network administration procedures (Exam 70-292).

    - Implement security baseline settings, and audit security settings by using security templates.

    - Implement the principle of least privilege.

- Plan a framework for planning and implementing security (Exam 70-296).

    - Plan for security monitoring.

    - Plan a change and configuration management framework for security.

Why This Chapter Matters

Security is "job number one" at enterprises these days, and your ability to harden servers against attack or unintentional damage is critical for you and your network. This chapter presents the variety of security parameters that can be configured for a baseline security setting, and the settings that can be further modified and hardened based on servers' roles. You will learn how to create a role-based security configuration using Active Directory directory service organizational units, Group Policy objects, and security templates. Understanding how to use these tools effectively can help you deploy and harden large numbers of computers on a network without having to configure each one manually. You will also learn how to test and deploy security configurations effectively to ensure a smooth process of security change management.

Lessons in this Chapter:

Before You Begin

To complete the hands-on exercises in this chapter, you need:

- One Windows Server 2003 (Standard or Enterprise Edition) system installed as Server01. Server01 should currently be installed as a domain controller in the contoso.com domain.

Lesson 1: Windows Server 2003 Security Configuration

Windows Server 2003 is configured, by default, to perform a variety of roles for any given enterprise. Chances are, however, that you will be applying a server to one specific role or a small number of roles. It is therefore possible to hone the default security settings so that each server is hardened appropriately for its role. In this lesson, you will explore the variety of security settings that are available for configuration, and you will examine the recommended settings for specific server roles.

After this lesson, you will be able to

- Identify the tools and options you can use to manage security configuration
- Identify audit, event log, system services, and security options settings
- Create a baseline security configuration
- Create role-based security configurations for domain controllers, infrastructure servers, file and print servers, and application servers
- Implement baseline security for multiple security roles
- Implement the principle of least privilege using a security template

Estimated lesson time: 45 minutes

Security Configuration Overview

Windows Server 2003 provides numerous settings to secure hardware devices, operating system components, and features. To plan a security configuration for your enterprise, you must understand and evaluate the configuration settings available to you and determine what constitutes good security. Then, you must design a security implementation that applies a standard, baseline security policy for all systems, and then modifies that baseline for particular systems based on their roles.

Once you have designed the security configuration, you must be able to implement that configuration. In the past, many tools and low-level Registry adjustments were necessary to fulfill a security policy. Settings can be configured using a variety of tools on an individual server, but of course a manual approach to security configuration is both inefficient—particularly in environments with several servers—and difficult to maintain.

Group Policy

To increase the efficiency of applying a security configuration, Windows Server 2003 supports the implementation and maintenance of security configuration through Group Policy Objects (GPOs). As you learned in Chapter 5, GPOs can be linked to sites, domains, and organizational (OUs) in Active Directory and can drive the configuration of users and computers within the scope of the GPO link. For example, a GPO could be configured with the security settings for Web servers in your environment, and then linked to an OU in which the servers' computer accounts exist. Those Web servers would then be secured based on the policies in the GPO. If administrators were to change the settings on an individual server, Group Policy refresh would reset the settings to adhere to the security policies of the GPO. GPOs thus allow you to deploy security settings more efficiently and to be confident that the settings are being maintained over time.

Security Templates

Windows Server 2003 also supports deploying security settings by using *security templates*, which are text files that, when applied to a server, determine the server's security configuration. Security templates are useful in several scenarios, including situations in which a server is not subject to Group Policy. Security templates can also be used to export the security configuration from one server and apply that configuration to another server. It is even possible to deploy a security template via Group Policy.

Security Configuration Tools

The primary tools used to centrally plan, implement, maintain, and troubleshoot security configuration include: Group Policy Object Editor, Active Directory Users And Computers or the Group Policy Management Console to administer GPO properties and links, the Security Configuration And Analysis and Security Templates snap-ins that support the management and deployment of security templates, and the Secedit.exe command.

Windows Server 2003 Security Settings

In this section, you will learn about many of the security settings that can be configured for a server. Keep in mind that each of these settings can be managed on an individual server by using administrative snap-ins, or they can be deployed and maintained on one or more servers through security templates or Group Policy. Later in this chapter, you will learn how to use each tool as you explore the planning and implementation of server security.

Audit Policies

Auditing is an important part of a secure baseline installation because it enables you to gather information about the computer's activities as they happen. If a security incident occurs, you want to have as much information about the event as possible, and auditing specific system components makes the information available. The problem with auditing is that it can easily give you an embarrassment of riches. You can't have too much information when a security breach occurs, but most of the time your servers will be operating normally. If you configure the system to audit too many events, you can end up with enormous log files consuming large amounts of disk space and making it difficult to find the information that is most pertinent. The object of an audit configuration is to achieve a balance between enough auditing information and too much.

When you configure Windows Server 2003 to audit events, the system creates entries in the Security log that you can see in the Event Viewer console. (See Figure 9-1.) Each audit entry contains the action that triggered the event, the user and computer objects involved, and the event's date and time.

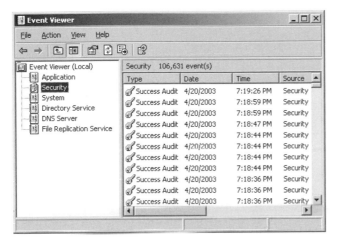

Figure 9-1   The Event Viewer console

The following audit policies are available:

- **Audit Account Logon Events**   Each instance of a user logging on to a computer. This policy is intended primarily for domain controllers, which authenticate users as they log on to other computers. There is typically no need to activate this policy on a member server.

> **Note**   Chapter 4 provides additional detail regarding account logon and logon event auditing.

- **Audit Account Management**   Each account management event that occurs on the computer, such as creating, modifying, or deleting a user object, or changing a password. On a member server, this policy applies only to local account management events. If your network relies on Active Directory for its accounts, administrators seldom have to work with local accounts. However, activating this policy can detect unauthorized changes to accounts in the local directory—the Security Accounts Manager (SAM)—of the local computer.

- **Audit Directory Service Access**   A user accessing an Active Directory object that has its own system access control list (SACL). This policy applies only to domain controllers, so there is no need for you to enable it on your member servers.

■ **Audit Logon Events**   Users logging on to or off the local computer when the local computer or a domain controller authenticates them. You use this policy to track user logons and logoffs, enabling you to determine which user was accessing the computer when a specific event occurred.

> **Exam Tip**   Be certain to understand the difference between logon events and account logon events.

■ **Audit Object Access**   A user accesses an operating system element such as a file, folder, or registry key. To audit elements like these, you must enable this policy and you must enable auditing on the resource you want to monitor. For example, to audit user accesses of a particular file or folder, you display its Properties dialog box with the Security tab active, navigate to the Auditing tab in the Advanced Security Settings dialog box for that file or folder (as shown in Figure 9-2), and then add the users or groups whose access to that file or folder you want to audit.

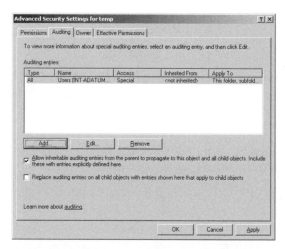

Figure 9-2   The Advanced Security Settings dialog box

■ **Audit Policy Change**   Someone changes one of the computer's audit policies, user rights assignments, or trust policies. This policy is a useful tool for tracking changes administrators make to the computer's security configuration. For example, an administrator might disable a policy temporarily to perform a specific task and then forget to re-enable it. Auditing enables you to track the administrator's activities and notice the oversight.

■ **Audit Privilege Use**   A user exercises a user right. By default, Windows Server 2003 excludes the following user rights from auditing because they tend to generate large numbers of log entries: Bypass Traverse Checking, Debug Programs, Create A Token Object, Replace Process Level Token, Generate Security Audits, Back Up Files And Directories, and Restore Files And Directories.

Tip   It is possible to enable auditing of the user rights listed here by adding the following key to the registry in the Microsoft Windows operating system: HKEY_LOCAL_MACHINE\SYSTEM \CurrentControlSet\Control\Lsa\FullPrivilegeAuditing=3,1. However, if you do this, you should be prepared to deal with the large number of log entries that auditing these user rights generates by increasing the maximum size of the logs and having a policy for frequent evaluation and clearance of the logs.

- **Audit Process Tracking**   The computer experiences an event such as a program activation or a process exit. While this policy gathers information that is valuable when analyzing a security incident, it also generates a large number of log entries.

- **Audit System Events**   Someone shuts down or restarts the computer or an event occurs that affects system security or the security log.

When you enable one of these audit policies, you can select three possible values, which determine the conditions for creating an audit entry, as follows:

- **Successes only (select the Success check box)**   Only when the specified action completes successfully

- **Failure only (select the Failure check box)**   Only when the specified action fails

- **Successes and Failures (select both the Success and Failure check boxes)**   Whether the specified action succeeds or fails

- **No auditing (clear both the Success and Failure check boxes)**   No audit entries for the specified actions under any circumstances

For security purposes, auditing failures can often be more valuable than auditing successes. For example, the default Audit Account Logon Events policy value for domain controllers is to audit successful logons only. This enables you to determine who was logged on to the network at any time. However, if an unauthorized user attempts to penetrate an administrative account by guessing passwords, the audit log would not contain any evidence of these attempts. Selecting the Failure check box for the Audit Account Logon Events policy gives you information about the failed logon attempts as well as the successful ones.

Event Log Policies

The Event Log is an essential tool for Windows Server 2003 administrators, and the Event Log policies control various aspects of the log's performance, including the maximum size of the logs, who has access to them, and how the logs behave when they reach their maximum size.

Each log—application, security, and system—has four policies:

- **Maximum log size** Specifies the maximum size the system permits, in kilobytes. Values must be in 64 KB increments, and the maximum value is 4,194,240 (4 gigabytes).

- **Prevent local guests group from accessing log** Specifies whether members of the local Guests group on the computer are permitted to view the log file.

- **Retain log** Specifies the number of days for which the log should retain information.

- **Retention method for log** Specifies the behavior of the log when it reaches its maximum size, using the following options:

  - ❑ Overwrite Events By Days—The log retains the number of days of entries specified by the retain log policy. Once the log grows to the specified number of days, the system erases the oldest day's entries each day.

  - ❑ Overwrite Events As Needed—The log erases the oldest individual entries as needed once the log file has reached the size specified in the maximum log size policy.

  - ❑ Do Not Overwrite Events (Clear Log Manually)—The system stops creating new entries when the log reaches the size specified in the maximum log size policy.

Creating an event logging configuration usually requires some experimentation. The best way to proceed is to configure the events and resources you want to audit, and then let the logs accrue for several days. Calculate the average number of entries for each log per day and then decide how many days of history you want to retain. This enables you to determine a suitable maximum size for your logs.

Before setting the retain log and retention method for log policies, you should decide how often someone is going to review the logs and clear or archive them when necessary. If it is essential to retain all log information, you can specify a maximum size for the log and then enable the Security Options policy, Audit: Shut Down System Immediately If Unable To Log Security Audits, which forces you to manage the logs regularly.

System Services Policies

Services are programs that run continuously in the background, waiting for other applications to call on them. For this reason, services present potential surfaces for attack, which intruders might be able to exploit. Windows Server 2003 installs a number of services with the operating system, and configures quite a few with the Automatic startup type, so that these services load automatically when the system starts. Because servers often serve designated roles, it is possible using System Services policies to disable services that a server does not need to perform its specific function.

Table 9-1 describes the services that Windows Server 2003 typically installs on a member server. The Automatic column contains the services that Windows Server 2003 requires for basic system management and communications. The Manual column contains services that do not have to be running all the time, but which must be available so that other processes can activate them. The Disabled column contains services that the typical member server does not need, and which you can deactivate by setting its startup parameter to Disabled, unless the computer has a specific need for them.

> **Note**   Member servers are computers running Windows Server 2003 that are joined to a domain but are not domain controllers.

Table 9-1   Typical Member Server Service Assignments

Automatic	Manual	Disabled
Automatic Updates	Background Intelligent Transfer Service	Alerter
Computer Browser	COM+ Event System	Application Management
DHCP Client	Logical Disk Manager Administrative Service	ClipBook
Distributed Link Tracking Client	Network Connections	Distributed File System
DNS Client	NT LM Security Support Provider	Distributed Transaction Coordinator
Event Log	Performance Logs And Alerts	Fax Service (only present when a modem is installed)
IPSEC Services	Terminal Services	Indexing Service
Logical Disk Manager	Windows Installer	Internet Connection Firewall (ICF)/Internet Connection Sharing (ICS)
Net Logon	Windows Management Instrumentation Driver Extensions	License Logging
Plug And Play		Messenger
Protected Storage		NetMeeting Remote Desktop Sharing
Remote Procedure Call (RPC)		Network DDE
Remote Registry		Network DDE DSDM
Security Accounts Manager		Print Spooler
Server		Remote Access Auto Connection Manager
System Event Notification		Remote Access Connection Manager

Table 9-1 Typical Member Server Service Assignments

Automatic	Manual	Disabled
TCP/IP NetBIOS Helper		Removable Storage
Windows Management Instrumentation		Routing And Remote Access
Windows Time		Secondary Logon
Workstation		Smart Card
		Task Scheduler
		Telephony
		Telnet
		Uninterruptible Power Supply

Security Options Policies

Security Options policies allow you to secure specific server components and features. Almost all these policies are undefined in a default member server installation, but you can activate them and use them to secure servers against a wide variety of accidents and threats.

Some of the most useful Security Options policies are as follows:

- **Accounts: Administrator Account Status**   Enables or disables the computer's local Administrator account.

- **Accounts: Guest Account Status**   Enables or disables the computer's local Guest account.

- **Accounts: Rename Administrator Account**   Specifies an alternative name for the security identifier (SID) associated with the local Administrator account.

- **Accounts: Rename Guest Account**   Specifies an alternative name for the SID associated with the local Guest account.

- **Audit: Audit The Use Of Backup And Restore Privilege**   Causes the computer to audit all user privileges when the Audit Privilege Use policy is enabled, including all file system backups and restores.

- **Audit: Shut Down System Immediately If Unable To Log Security Audits**   Causes the computer to shut down if the system is unable to add auditing entries to the security log because the log has reached its maximum size.

- **Devices: Allowed To Format And Eject Removable Media**   Specifies which local groups are permitted to format and eject removable NTFS file system media.

- **Devices: Restrict CD-ROM Access To Locally Logged-on User Only**   Prevents network users from accessing the computer's CD-ROM drives.

- **Devices: Restrict Floppy Access To Locally Logged-on User Only** Prevents network users from accessing the computer's floppy disk drive.

- **Domain Member: Maximum Machine Account Password Age** Specifies how often the system changes its computer account password.

- **Interactive Logon: Do Not Require CTRL+ALT+DEL** Select the Disable option to protect users against Trojan horse attacks that attempt to intercept users' passwords.

- **Interactive Logon: Require Domain Controller Authentication To Unlock Workstation** Prevents unlocking the computer using cached credentials. The computer must be able to use a domain controller to authenticate the user attempting to unlock the system for the process to succeed.

- **Microsoft Network Client: Digitally Sign Communications (Always)** The computer requires packet signatures for all Server Message Block (SMB) client communications.

- **Microsoft Network Server: Digitally Sign Communications (Always)** The computer requires packet signatures for all Server Message Block (SMB) server communications.

- **Network Access: Do Not Allow Anonymous Enumeration Of SAM Accounts And Shares** Prevents anonymous users from determining the names of local user accounts and shares. This prevents potential intruders from gathering information about the computer without being authenticated.

- **Network Access: Remotely Accessible Registry Paths And Subpaths** Specifies which registry paths and subpaths qualified users can access over the network.

- **Network Access: Shares That Can Be Accessed Anonymously** Specifies which shares anonymous users are permitted to access.

- **Network Security: Force Logoff When Logon Hours Expire** Causes the computer to terminate existing local user connections when they reach the end of their specified logon time.

- **Shutdown: Allow System To Be Shut Down Without Having To Log On** Activates the Shut Down button in the Log On To Windows dialog box.

Restricted Groups Policies

In baseline and server role security configurations, it is important to manage the membership of local groups on domain computers, particularly built-in and local groups that have built-in and default user rights, such as the Administrators, Power Users, Backup Operators, Print Operators, Server Operators, and Account Operators groups.

To use *restricted group policies*, simply add a policy with the name of a group, and then configure its members. You can also configure the Members Of property of the group—ensuring that it is nested in appropriate groups. When security policies are applied or refreshed, the restricted group policy will ensure that the Members and Members Of properties remain consistent with organizational security policy.

Registry Policies

Registry policies allow you to set the ACL of registry keys. Rather than set ACLs of registry keys manually, registry policies provide centralized administration and maintenance of a secured registry and make it easy to reset registry key ACLs should they need to be changed.

> **Note** You cannot use registry policies to add new registry keys or values, or change the data in registry values. Registry policies allow you to manage the security of existing keys.

File System

File system policies, like registry policies, provide centralized management of ACLs on files and folders. When you add a policy for a file or folder and configure its ACL, any system that contains a file or folder that matches the policy will enforce the ACL specified by the policy.

User Rights

User rights policies determine user logon rights and privileges. Logon rights include the right to log on locally or through Terminal Services or over the network. Privileges include the ability to back up or restore files, shut down the system, or run as a service. User rights policies are described in the section regarding domain controller security, later in this lesson.

Account Policies

Account policies include policies that determine password requirements, account lockout, and Kerberos settings. Password policies include minimum length, history, complexity, and how frequently passwords must be changed. Account lockout policies determine the number of failed logon attempts within a specified time frame that trigger account lockout, as well as the policy to reset locked out accounts. Kerberos policies configure Kerberos ticket lifetime and renewal time, whether user logon restrictions are honored, and clock skew time. Chapter 4 discusses account policies in detail.

Creating Role-Specific Server Configurations

The Windows Server 2003 default configuration is far more secure than those of previous versions of the Microsoft Windows operating system, but there are still security settings you should consider modifying from their defaults. By creating a baseline, or standard, security configuration, you can then apply additional modifications based on server roles.

Baseline Security Configuration

The security requirements for the various servers on your network might differ, but a good place to start is creating a security configuration for a standard member server.

By considering the audit, event log, services, and security options policies discussed in the previous section, and comparing the default settings to the needs of your environment, you can create a baseline security configuration for member servers. Once a baseline security configuration for your servers is in place, you can consider the special needs of the servers performing particular roles in your enterprise. Domain controllers, infrastructure servers, file and print servers, and application servers all are vulnerable to unique threats, and their security requirements can be quite different.

By combining the policy settings in a role-specific GPO with those in your baseline configuration, you can create a secure environment for each server role without much duplication of effort.

> **Exam Tip**   This approach to security configuration—creating a baseline for all servers and then applying role-specific configurations to specify settings that are unique for a server role—is a critical approach to understand for the 70-292 and 70-296 exams.

Securing Domain Controllers

On a Windows Server 2003 network that uses Active Directory, no servers are more vital than the domain controllers. Because domain controllers provide authentication services for most network operations and store and distribute group policies, their failure or compromise can be a catastrophe for network productivity. The domain controller role requires special security considerations that go beyond those of a baseline configuration.

Isolating Domain Controllers   Because of the importance of domain controllers, your security measures should minimize the threats to the computers in every possible way. Physically, domain controllers should always be in a secured location, such as a server closet or a data center that is accessible only to administrative personnel who have reason to be there. Secure the console with a complex password so that even people who are in the room for other reasons are not able to access the server.

In addition to limiting physical access to your domain controller, you should limit the access provided by the network connection. This means reducing the number of open ports on the computer by minimizing the number of applications and services it runs. Many domain controllers running Windows Server 2003 also run the DNS Server service because DNS is intimately associated with Active Directory, but you should avoid running services and applications that are unnecessary to the domain controller role.

Setting Audit and Event Log Policies   When you install Active Directory on a computer running Windows Server 2003 and create a new domain, the system puts the domain controller's computer object in an organizational unit named Domain Controllers. The Default Domain Controllers Policy, one of two GPOs that are created by default when you install the first domain controller in a domain, is linked to the Domain Controllers OU. The Default Domain Controllers Policy provides some additional security settings beyond the default settings in the Default Domain Policy linked to the domain, but you might want to augment or modify them. Domain controllers are thus automatically configured for their role by the Default Domain Controllers Policy

For example, the Default Domain Controllers Policy enables the following audit policies, but configures them to audit only successes:

■ Audit Account Logon Events

■ Audit Account Management

■ Audit Directory Service Access

■ Audit Logon Events

■ Audit Policy Change

■ Audit System Events

Depending on the policy settings you use in your baseline security configuration, you might want to modify these settings to audit failures as well as successes, or to define additional policies such as Audit Object Access and Audit Process Tracking. If you decide to implement additional audit policies, be sure to consider the Event Log policies as well, because you might have to specify a larger maximum size for the security log to hold all the entries that these policies create.

Assigning User Rights   The Default Domain Policy contains no user rights assignments, but the Default Domain Controllers Policy does. Most user rights assigned by policies in the Default Domain Controllers Policy are intended to give administrators the privileges and logon rights they need to manage the domain controller, while granting users only the minimum rights they need to access the domain controller's services. For the most part, the settings for the User Rights Assignment policy in the Default Domain Controllers Policy are acceptable, and you should use them on your domain controllers. However, there are a few changes you might want to make.

- **Debug Programs**   The Debug Programs user right enables you to use a debugging tool to access any process running on the computer or even the operating system kernel itself. Software developers use these tools to debug applications they are in the process of creating. This user right provides access to sensitive areas of the operating system that a potential intruder might be able to abuse. By default, the GPO linked to the Domain Controllers organizational unit grants this right to the Administrators group. However, if no one in your organization is developing or debugging software, you can revoke the Debug Programs user right from the Administrators group and close what could be a serious security breach.

- **Add Workstations To Domain**   By default, all authenticated users have the right to add up to 10 computer accounts to an Active Directory domain. Adding an account creates a new computer object in the Computers container. Computer accounts are full security principals in Windows Server 2003, able to authenticate and access domain resources. This right can allow any authenticated user to create unauthorized domain workstations that an intruder could use when the computer account is idle.

   Many large network installations rely on IT support personnel to install new workstations and manually create new computer objects. In this case, you can revoke the Authenticated Users group's Add Workstations To Domain right without causing problems.

- **Allow Log On Locally**   The Allow Log On Locally user right enables specified users and groups to log on to the computer interactively from the console. Obviously, users with this right have access to many important operating system elements and could cause a great deal of damage, either accidentally or deliberately. It is therefore important to grant this right only to users and groups that absolutely need it.

   The Default Domain Controllers Policy grants the Allow Log On Locally user right to the following built-in groups:

   ❑ Account Operators

   ❑ Administrators

   ❑ Backup Operators

❑ Print Operators

❑ Server Operators

How (or whether) you use the built-in groups is your decision, but based on their intended use, the Account Operators and Print Operators groups typically do not need to perform their tasks from a domain controller console, so you can usually revoke these two groups' Allow Log On Locally right.

■ **Shut Down The System**   You should control the ability to shut down a domain controller very carefully, because shutting down a domain controller can affect systems all over the network. The Default Domain Controllers Policy grants this user right to the following groups:

❑ Administrators

❑ Backup Operators

❑ Print Operators

❑ Server Operators

In most environments, members of the Backup Operators and Print Operators groups should not need to shut down a domain controller, so you can revoke their right to do this.

> **Important**   For the restrictions imposed by your assignments of Shut Down The System user right to be meaningful, you must also revoke the Security Options policy, Shutdown: Allow System To Be Shut Down Without Having To Log On. If you enable this option, any user can shut down the computer without authentication, which means that they are not subject to user rights restrictions.

Configuring Services   In addition to the services required by member servers, as listed earlier in Table 9-1, domain controllers require the following additional services, which you should enable with the startup type set to Automatic:

■ Distributed File System

■ File Replication Service

■ Intersite Messaging

■ Kerberos Key Distribution Center

■ Remote Procedure Call (RPC)

Securing Infrastructure Servers

Infrastructure servers are computers that run network support services such as DNS, DHCP, and Windows Internet Name Service (WINS). An infrastructure server can run any or all these services and might also fill other roles, such as an application or file and print server.

For an infrastructure server that provides all these services, you should enable the following services with the startup type set to Automatic:

- DHCP Server
- DNS Server
- NT LM Security Support Provider
- Windows Internet Name Service (WINS)

Configuring DNS Security   It is common for administrators to run the DNS Server service on Windows Server 2003 domain controllers, particularly when they use Active Directory–integrated zones. One benefit of storing the zone database in Active Directory is that the directory service takes over securing and replicating the DNS data. However, even if you do use Active Directory–integrated zones, there are additional security measures you might consider.

> **See Also**   The Microsoft DNS Server service has its own security features, such as secured dynamic update and authorized zone transfers. For more information on implementing these features, see Chapter 8.

- **Protecting Active Directory–Integrated DNS**   When you create Active Directory–integrated zones on your DNS server, the zone database is stored as part of the Active Directory database, which protects it from direct access by unauthorized users. However, you should still take steps to ensure that the MicrosoftDNS container object in Active Directory (shown in Figure 9-3) is secure.

Figure 9-3   The MicrosoftDNS container in the Active Directory Users And Computers console

Tip   To access the MicrosoftDNS container object in the Active Directory Users And Computers console, you must first select the Advanced Features option from the console's View menu. The console then displays additional containers, including the System container, which contains MicrosoftDNS.

By default, the DnsAdmins, Domain Admins, and Enterprise Admins groups all have the Full Control permission for the MicrosoftDNS container. The local Administrators group lacks the Full Control permission, but it does have the permissions needed to create new objects and modify existing ones. You might modify these defaults to limit the number of users with permission to modify this container.

■ **Protecting DNS Database Files**   For DNS zones that are not integrated into Active Directory, the zone databases are simple text files stored in the C:\Windows\System32\Dns folder by default. Windows Server 2003 creates DNS debug logs in the same folder. The permissions for this folder grant the Administrators group Full Control, while the Server Operators group receives all permissions except Full Control. The Authenticated Users group receives the permissions needed to read and execute files in this folder.

You don't need file system permissions to maintain the DNS zone databases using the DNS console or to access DNS server information using a client. Therefore, there is no reason for the Authenticated Users group to have file system permissions. By enabling users to view the DNS data files, you give them an opportunity to gather information about your domain that they could use to stage an attack against the network. You can safely revoke the Authenticated Users group's permissions for this folder, and even limit the Server Operators group to read-only access, if desired.

Configuring DHCP Security   The interruption of a DHCP server's functions might not have an immediate effect on your network, but eventually your DHCP clients' leases will expire and they will be unable to obtain new ones. Apart from enabling the DHCP Server service itself, there is little you can do to configure DHCP using a GPO. However, there are security measures that can help to ensure uninterrupted performance.

Denial of service attacks (DoS) constitute one of the biggest threats to DHCP servers. It is relatively simple for an unscrupulous individual to create a script that sends repeated requests for IP address assignments to the server until all the addresses in the scope are depleted. Legitimate clients are then unable to obtain addresses until the bogus leases expire. Several techniques can defend against denial of service attacks, including the following:

- **Use the 80/20 address allocation method**   Use two DHCP servers to provide addresses for each subnet, with 80 percent of the available addresses in one server's scope and 20 percent in the other. This ensures that there are addresses available to clients, even if one of the servers is under attack.

- **Create a DHCP server cluster**   Clustering enables you to use multiple servers to create a single network entity. If one server fails, the other servers in the cluster take up the slack.

- **Monitor DHCP activity**   You can monitor the activity of a DHCP server by using tools such as the Performance console and Network Monitor or by enabling audit logging on the DHCP server.

DHCP audit logging is not integrated into the main Windows Server 2003 auditing facility. You can enable DHCP audit logging by using group policies, but you cannot access the logs using the Event Viewer console. To enable DHCP audit logging, you must open the DHCP console, display the Properties dialog box for the DHCP server, and then select the Enable DHCP Audit Logging check box in the General tab. The server stores the log files in the C:\Windows\System32\Dhcp folder, by default.

Securing File and Print Servers

Security for a file and print server will most closely reflect the settings of your baseline configuration. The two main changes you must make for the file and print server role are as follows:

- **Enable the Print Spooler service**   Use the appropriate policy in the System Services container of your GPO to enable the Print Spooler service with the Automatic startup type. The server needs this service to receive print jobs from other computers on the network.

- **Disable the Microsoft Network Server: Digitally Sign Communications (Always) security policy**   When this security option is enabled, users are unable to view the print queue on the server, even though they are able to submit print jobs. Defining this policy with a value of Disabled in the Security Options container of your GPO ensures that your clients can access the print queue on the server.

> **Note**   To view print queues on file and print servers, client computers must have also disabled the Security Options policy, Microsoft Network Client: Digitally Sign Communications (Always) (or its equivalent).

Configuring Permissions Using a GPO

One of the most important security measures for a file and print server is protection for the user data stored on the server drives. You create this protection by using the NTFS file system on your drives and by using NTFS permissions to control access to the server drives. You can specify the permissions for your NTFS drives in a GPO by browsing to the File System container in the Group Policy Object Editor console and, from the Action menu, selecting Add File. In the series of dialog boxes that appear, you perform the following tasks:

1. Specify the files or folders for which you want to configure file system permissions.

2. Specify the permissions you want to assign to the selected files or folders.

3. Specify whether you want the permissions to be inherited by subfolders.

> **Tip**   In addition to file system permissions, you can also use a GPO to configure registry permissions on a computer running Windows Server 2003. Browse to the Registry container and, from the Action menu, choose Add Key. The process resembles configuring file system permissions, except that you select a registry key instead of a file or folder.

Securing Application Servers

It is difficult, if not impossible, to create a generic security configuration for application servers, because the requirements of the individual applications are usually unique. Windows Server 2003 includes some software that enables the computer to function as an application server—most notably Internet Information Services (IIS), which provides World Wide Web, File Transfer Protocol (FTP), and other Internet server services—but in most cases, application servers run external software products, such as database or e-mail servers. To secure these applications, you must compare the security requirements of your network and your users with the security features provided by the application itself.

> **Tip**   The "Windows Server 2003 Security Guide" is an excellent source of information about security configuration and strategy. You can locate the guide at *http://go.microsoft.com /fwlink/?LinkId=14846.*

Applying the Principle of Least Privilege

One of the most important concepts that should guide your development and implementation of security policy is *the principle of least privilege.* Using this principle means that no employee and no user of information systems has more privileges or access to information and resources than they need to do their job. This principle includes removing privileges and access when employees change jobs within the organization or when they leave the company. The principle of least privilege also means that visitors to the organization or to any information resources—such as the public, contractors, temporary workers, partner representatives, and so on—should be treated in the same manner. No one, and that includes system administrators and IT workers, should have any more access or rights than they need to do their job.

> **Exam Tip**   As in Windows 2000, it is a best practice to log on with a user account and to use secondary logon—the Run As command—to launch administrative tools with appropriate levels of elevated credentials.

There are many ways to implement and follow this maxim. The ways can be categorized according to those that are possible using security templates and those that require other mechanisms to implement. This subject is broad, and the following lists are by no means comprehensive. Instead, they are meant to teach the paradigm.

Least Privilege Opportunities in Security Templates

The following opportunities can be addressed in GPOs or in security templates that can be applied to computers or deployed using GPOs:

- Develop a strong password policy to keep unauthorized individuals off systems.
- Assign user rights sparingly. Reduce rights, especially access and logon rights, as much as possible. Set different rights on computers with different roles.
- Use security options to block access and restrict activity.
- Use file and Registry ACLs.
- Use the Restricted Groups section to force and limit membership in sensitive groups.

- Use the System Services section to disable services and restrict who can manage them.

- Develop a baseline plan for every computer role and implement using templates that are imported into GPOs on representative OUs.

- Apply a comprehensive auditing strategy.

Other Least Privilege Opportunities

These opportunities can be addressed using tools other than security templates and GPOs:

- Group users by role so that privileges and permissions can be granted by role.

- Configure ACLs for files, folders, Registry keys, directory objects, and printers to allow only the exact access any group of users needs.

- Physically protect servers. Allow access only to authorized personnel and screen this authorization.

- Review audit logs and other logs in a search for needs to restrict further access.

- Use Web proxies to limit user access to external resources.

- Use firewalls to limit access to internal networks.

Lesson Review

The following questions are intended to reinforce key information presented in this lesson. If you are unable to answer a question, review the lesson materials and try the question again. You can find answers to the questions in the "Questions and Answers" section at the end of this chapter.

1. Which of the following audit policies enables you to tell what applications were running when a security event occurred?

    a. Audit Object Access

    b. Audit Privilege Use

    c. Audit Process Tracking

    d. Audit System Events

2. Under what conditions can you not revoke the Debug Programs right from all users and groups?

_____

3. Which of the following tasks can users not perform when you enable the Security Options policy, Microsoft Network Server: Digitally Sign Communications (Always) on a computer running Windows Server 2003?

    a. Submit jobs to a print queue on the server

    b. View the print queues on the server

    c. Install printer drivers stored on the server

    d. Create printer shares on the server

4. Enabling which of the following audit policies is likely to require changing the Maximum Security Log Size value as well?

    a. Audit Process Tracking

    b. Audit Policy Change

    c. Audit Account Logon Events

    d. Audit Directory Service Access

Lesson Summary

- Audit and Event Log policies enable you to specify what information a computer logs, how much information the computer retains in logs, and how the computer behaves when logs are full.

- Windows Server 2003 loads many services by default that a member server usually doesn't need. You can use System Services settings to specify the startup type for each service on a computer.

- The domain controller role is the only role assigned its own GPO by default. To create your own policy settings for domain controllers, you can modify the existing Default Domain Controllers Policy or create a new one.

- Domain controllers require more security than any other server role. You should secure the server physically, and then use Group Policy to specify auditing and Event Log settings, user rights assignments, and the services the computer should run.

- Infrastructure servers run network support services such as DNS, DHCP, and WINS.

- DNS servers using Active Directory–integrated zones use the directory service to secure their data, but for servers that use file-based zones, you must take steps to secure the DNS database and log files.

- You can use a GPO to protect the files on your server drives by assigning file system permissions.

Lesson 2: Deploying Security Configuration with Group Policy Objects

Administering dozens of security settings on a server-by-server basis is obviously not an efficient way to approach security configuration in an enterprise. Fortunately, each of the settings discussed in Lesson 1 can be configured using Group Policy Objects (GPOs). As you learned in Chapter 5, GPOs can be linked to sites, domains, and OUs, and can be used to configure settings for users and computers underneath those containers. In this lesson, you will learn how to use GPOs and Active Directory OUs to deploy a centrally managed baseline security configuration and role-based security settings.

After this lesson, you will be able to

- Assign multiple GPOs to one object
- Understand group policy inheritance rules

Estimated lesson time: 20 minutes

Applying a Baseline Security Configuration

The security settings discussed in Lesson 1 can be configured using a *Group Policy Object (GPO)*. Once a GPO has been linked to an Active Directory site, domain, or organizational unit (OU), the user and computer objects under that link will inherit the configuration specified by the GPO. For example, when you link a GPO to a domain, all the users and computers in that domain inherit the settings specified in the GPO.

By default, Windows Server 2003 places all domain members' computer objects in the Computers container. Because the Computers container is not a domain, site, or organizational unit object, you cannot link a GPO to it. Furthermore, because this container also contains the computer objects for all your workstations as well as your servers, you would not want to apply a baseline security configuration designed for servers to the container.

Understanding Container Objects

The Computers container object is a special Active Directory object called a *container*, which Windows Server 2003 creates by default when you create the first domain controller for a new domain. The system also creates other container objects named Users, Builtin, and ForeignSecurityPrincipals. The term container can be misleading in the case of these four container objects because many directory services, including Active Directory, refer to any object that can have other objects beneath it as a container. Objects that cannot contain other objects are called *leaves*.

The Computers, Users, Builtin, and ForeignSecurityPrincipals container objects are different, however, because their object type is literally called a container. These container objects do not have the same properties as Active Directory objects—such as domains, sites, and organizational units—which function as generic containers. You cannot delete the Computers, Users, Builtin, and ForeignSecurityPrincipals container objects, nor can you create new objects using the container object type. You also cannot link GPOs to these objects. You can, however, create new generic containers, such as organizational units, and link GPOs to them.

To create a baseline installation for your member servers only, the best practice is to create a new organizational unit in your domain, and then move the computer objects representing the member servers into it. This way, you can link a GPO containing your security baseline to the member servers' organizational unit and all computer objects in that container will inherit the security settings from that GPO.

Tip   Do not put the computer objects for other types of systems, such as domain controllers or workstations, in your member servers organizational unit unless you want them to have the same baseline configuration as your member servers. Workstations do not need most of the configuration settings discussed in this lesson, and domain controllers have their own requirements. As a rule, you should place each type of computer that requires a different configuration in its own organizational unit.

Applying Role-Based Security Configurations

To deploy role-based security configurations, you can use a separate GPO for each role that contains the unique settings required for that role. You can use the role-specific GPO to do any of the following:

- Modify settings you configured in the baseline
- Configure settings that are not defined in the baseline
- Leave the baseline settings for specific parameters unchanged

As you learned in Chapter 5, you can determine the scope of a GPO two ways: by linking the GPO to a container in which one type of computer or user object exists, or by linking the GPO to a more generic container and using GPO filtering to limit the scope of its application.

It is best practice, when managing security configurations with GPOs, to create separate OUs for each server role, and to link appropriate GPOs to each OU, rather than to use GPO filtering. You can deploy your server GPOs using one of two approaches:

- Create role-specific organizational units anywhere in Active Directory. Assign multiple GPOs to each organizational unit. For example, you might have a Web Servers OU somewhere in your Active Directory. You would link the GPO containing your baseline settings and the GPO containing security configuration settings for Web servers to the Web Servers OU. Computers in that OU would inherit settings from both GPOs.

- Create a hierarchy of organizational units in which the baseline GPO is linked to a parent OU that contains role-specific OUs. Role-specific GPOs would be linked to each role-specific OU. Group Policy inheritance ensures that servers in a role-specific OU inherit settings from both the baseline GPO and the role-specific OU.

Both of these options will be explored in this section.

Applying Multiple GPOs

A GPO can be linked to a domain and/or to as many sites and OUs as you want. Therefore, if servers running Windows Server 2003 on your network are performing different roles, you can create separate organizational units for them anywhere in Active Directory. Figure 9-4 shows role-specific OUs created at the top-level of the OU structure.

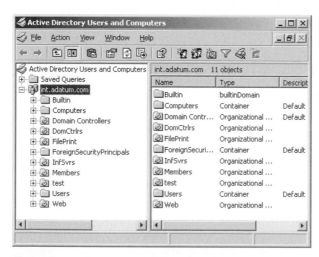

Figure 9-4   Organizational units for server roles

In the figure, you see the Domain Controllers organizational unit that the Windows Server 2003 creates by default when you create the domain, as well as new organizational units for member servers (named Members), infrastructure servers (named InfSvrs), file and print servers (named FilePrint), and application servers (named Web). To create a separate security configuration for each server role, you would use a procedure like the following one:

1. Create a new GPO linked to the Members container, and use it to create your baseline security configuration.

2. Create a new GPO linked to each of the role-specific OUs, and use it to create a role-specific security configuration.

3. Link the baseline GPO currently linked to the Members container to each of the role-specific OUs.

> **Important** When you link a GPO to multiple container objects, you are only creating links between the object pairs; you are not creating copies of the GPO. Therefore, when you modify the policy settings for the GPO from one of the linked containers, the changes you make affect all the containers to which you have linked the GPO.

4. Move the baseline GPO to the bottom of the Group Policy Object Links list in each of the role-specific OUs.

The order in which the GPOs appear in the Group Policy Object Links list is critical. GPOs that are higher in the list have higher priority so that a setting in the first policy listed will overwrite a setting in the second. Because you want the policies in the role-specific GPO to override any conflicting policies in the baseline GPO, the role-specific GPO should be the first policy listed.

Creating a Container Hierarchy

Instead of manually linking several GPOs to each of the role-specific OUs in Active Directory, you can also create a hierarchy of OUs, as shown in Figure 9-5. In this figure, you see the Members OU, with the role-specific OUs beneath it.

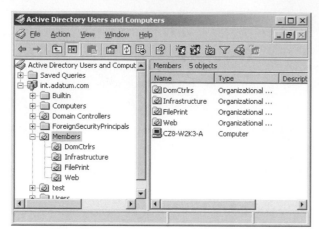

Figure 9-5   An organizational unit hierarchy

Tip   If you plan to create a hierarchy of organizational units that includes domain controllers in one of the role-specific containers, you will not be able to move the Domain Controllers organizational unit object that Windows Server 2003 creates automatically at domain creation to another location in the tree. However, you can create a new organizational unit object in the hierarchy and move the computer objects there from the Domain Controllers container.

As with most tree hierarchies in Windows operating systems, the settings from GPO links to a domain or OU are inherited by users and computers in OUs beneath the parent. Therefore, when you create a GPO and link it to the Members container, not only do the computer objects in Members receive the policy settings from the GPO, all the computers in the role-specific organizational units receive these settings.

To create security configurations for the servers in the role-specific organizational units, you create a new GPO for each container. When you do this, the policy settings in the GPOs linked to the role-specific containers take precedence over the settings for the same policies in the parent container's GPO. The rules governing the combination of inherited and direct policy settings are as follows:

- If the parent container's GPO contains a policy setting and the same policy is undefined in the child container's GPO, computers in the child container apply the setting from the parent GPO.

- If the child container's GPO contains a policy setting and the same policy is undefined in the parent container's GPO, computers in the child container apply the setting from the child GPO.

■ If the parent container's GPO contains a policy setting and the same policy has a different setting in the child container's GPO, computers in the child container apply the setting from the child GPO.

Although Active Directory objects inherit Group Policy settings from their parent objects by default, it is possible to block Group Policy inheritance. Display the Properties dialog box for a site, domain, or OU, click the Group Policy tab, and then select the Block Policy Inheritance check box. The properties of a GPO link will allow you to configure No Override, which ensures that the settings configured in the GPO will apply even if subcontainers are blocking inheritance, or if other GPOs contain conflicting settings. See Chapter 5 for more details regarding Group Policy inheritance and exceptions.

GPO Application

When a policy is left undefined by all the GPOs that apply to a computer, Windows Server 2003 uses its default, out-of-box setting or the setting that has been manually configured on the system. For example, if you do not configure a particular service with the Automatic startup type, Windows Server 2003 itself might configure that service to load automatically. If you want to be certain that a service is disabled, you must activate the System Services policy for that service and select the Disabled option.

When you apply multiple GPOs to a container, whether with multiple links to a single OU or with a hierarchical OU and GPO-link structure, it is important to understand the difference between an undefined policy and an explicit policy setting. An undefined policy is not necessarily the same as a Disabled setting. When you leave a policy undefined in the GPO, the computers to which that GPO applies use the operating system's default setting, which might be Enabled, Disabled, or something else, depending on the policy. If you define a policy with an Enabled value in the parent container's GPO, you must explicitly define the same policy in the child container's GPO to assign it a different value, even if that value is the same as the Windows Server 2003 default setting. An undefined policy does not reset the setting to the system's default—it allows parent GPO settings to pass through to the system.

 Exam Tip   Because security and Group Policy are heavily emphasized objectives, and because security configuration can be deployed through GPOs, you should be very familiar with Group Policy concepts discussed in Chapter 5 and the use of GPOs to configure role-based security, discussed in this lesson.

Practice: Deploying Role-Based Security Using Group Policy

In this practice, you will use a GPO to create a secure baseline installation for the member servers on your network, and then modify that baseline with GPOs that create role-based security configurations.

Exercise 1: Creating a Baseline Security Group Policy Object

In this exercise, you create a new GPO for the Member Servers OU and use it to create a secure baseline configuration for member servers in contoso.com.

1. Log on to Server01 as an administrator.

2. Open Active Directory Users And Computers, and create a top-level OU in the contoso.com domain named **Member Servers**.

3. Right-click the Member Servers OU, and click Properties. The Member Servers Properties dialog box appears.

4. Click the Group Policy tab, and then click New. A New Group Policy Object entry appears in the Group Policy Object Links list, with the name of the entry highlighted for renaming.

5. Type **Member Server Baseline**, and then press ENTER.

6. Click Edit. The Group Policy Object Editor console appears, with the Member Server Baseline GPO at the root of the console tree.

7. In the Computer Configuration container, expand the Windows Settings, Security Settings, and Local Policies containers.

8. Click the Audit Policy container. A list of audit policies appears in the console's details pane.

9. Double-click the Audit Account Logon Events policy. The Audit Account Logon Events Properties dialog box appears.

10. Select the Define These Policy Settings check box. The two Audit These Attempts check boxes are activated, with the Success check box selected by default.

11. Select the Failure check box, and click OK.

12. Configure the remaining audit policies using the following settings:

   ❑ Audit Account Management—Success and Failure

   ❑ Audit Directory Service Access—Success and Failure

   ❑ Audit Logon Events—Success and Failure

   ❑ Audit Object Access—Success and Failure

   ❑ Audit Policy Change—Success and Failure

❑ Audit Privilege Use—Failure only

❑ Audit Process Tracking—No auditing

❑ Audit System Events—Success and Failure

You are configuring the Audit Process Tracking policy to audit neither successes nor failures because of the large number of log entries this policy creates. However, you should still select the Define These Policy Settings check box in the Audit Process Tracking Properties dialog box, leaving the Success and Failure check boxes cleared, to ensure that the configuration you want (no auditing) overrides settings from any other GPO linked to a parent container.

13. In the console's scope pane, click the Event Log container. A list of Event Log policies appears in the details pane.

14. Configure the Event Log policies using the following settings:

❑ Maximum Application Log Size—10240 KB

❑ Maximum Security Log Size—184320 KB

❑ Maximum System Log Size 10240 KB

❑ Prevent Local Guests Group From Accessing Application Log—Enabled

❑ Prevent Local Guests Group From Accessing Security Log   Enabled

❑ Prevent Local Guests Group From Accessing System Log—Enabled

❑ Retention Method For Application Log—Overwrite Events As Needed

❑ Retention Method For Security Log—Overwrite Events As Needed

❑ Retention Method For System Log—Overwrite Events As Needed

The remaining Event Policies can remain Not Defined.

15. Click the System Services container in the scope pane. A list of services appears in the details pane.

16. Double-click the Alerter service entry. The Alerter Properties dialog box appears.

17. Select the Define This Policy Setting check box. The Disabled service startup mode is selected by default.

18. Leave the default service startup mode unchanged, and then click OK.

19. Activate each of the other service policies listed in Table 9-1, and configure their service startup modes using the table's values.

20. Close the Group Policy Object Editor console.

21. Close the Member Servers Properties dialog box.

Exercise 2: Modifying the Domain Controllers Container's GPO

1. In Active Directory Users and Computers, right-click the Domain Controllers OU and click Properties. The Domain Controllers Properties dialog box appears.

2. Click the Group Policy tab.

3. Ensure that the Default Domain Controllers Policy is selected, and click Edit. The Group Policy Object Editor console appears, with the Default Domain Controllers Policy object at the root of the scope pane.

4. Expand the Windows Settings, Security Settings, and Local Policies containers, and then select the Audit Policy container. The list of audit policies appears in the details pane.

5. Double-click the Audit Account Logon Events policy. The Audit Account Logon Events Properties dialog box appears.

   Windows Server 2003 defines this policy for domain controllers by default, with only the Success option selected.

6. Select the Failure check box, and then click OK.

7. Modify the following audit policies in the same way, by selecting the Failure check box.

   ❑ Audit Account Management

   ❑ Audit Directory Service Access

   ❑ Audit Logon Events

   ❑ Audit Policy Change

   ❑ Audit System Events

8. In the scope pane, select the User Rights Assignment container. The list of user rights appears in the details pane.

9. Double-click the Debug Programs user right. The Debug Programs Properties dialog box appears.

10. Select the Administrators group, and then click Remove. Click OK.

11. Double-click the Add Workstations To Domain user right. The Add Workstations To Domain Properties dialog box appears.

12. Select the Authenticated Users group, and then click Remove. Click OK.

13. Double-click the Allow Log On Locally user right. The Allow Log On Locally Properties dialog box appears.

14. Select the Account Operators and Print Operators groups, and then click Remove. Click OK.

15. Select the System Services container. The list of services appears in the details pane.

16. Double-click the Distributed File System service policy. The Distributed File System Properties dialog box appears.

17. Select the Define This Policy Setting check box, and then click the Automatic option button. Click OK.

18. Modify the following System Services policies in the same way, assigning them the Automatic startup type.

    ❑ File Replication Service

    ❑ Intersite Messaging

    ❑ Kerberos Key Distribution Center

    ❑ Remote Procedure Call (RPC) Locator

19. Close the Group Policy Object Editor console.

20. Close the Domain Controllers Properties dialog box.

Exercise 3: Linking the Member Server Baseline GPO to the Domain Controllers OU

1. In Active Directory Users And Computers, right-click the Domain Controllers OU and click Properties. The Domain Controllers Properties dialog box appears.

2. Click the Group Policy tab, and then click Add. The Add A Group Policy Object Link dialog box appears.

3. In the Look In drop-down list, select contoso.com.

4. In the Domains, OUs, And Linked Group Policy Objects list, double-click the Member Servers.contoso.com entry.

5. Select the Member Server Baseline GPO, and then click OK. A link to the Member Server Baseline GPO appears in the Group Policy Object Links list.

6. Ensure that the Member Server Baseline GPO is at the bottom of the Group Policy Object Links list. If it is not, select the Member Server Baseline entry in the list, and then click Down. The Member Server Baseline entry moves to the bottom of the list.

   Remember that GPOs that are higher in the list have higher priority. Because the Default Domain Controllers Policy hardens security for domain controllers beyond the settings of the baseline configuration, you want the Default Domain Controllers Policy at the top of the list. Then, if any policy setting in the Default Domain Controllers Policy is in conflict with a setting in the baseline GPO, the setting in the Default Domain Controllers Policy will be applied.

7. Click OK to close the Domain Controllers Properties dialog box.

Exercise 4: Applying Role-Based Security Configurations

1. Open Active Directory Users And Computers, and create the following OUs under the Member Servers OU:

   ❑ **Infrastructure Servers**

   ❑ **File and Print Servers**

2. Right-click the File and Print Servers OU, and click Properties.

3. Click the Group Policy tab, and then click New. A New Group Policy Object entry appears in the Group Policy Object Links list, with the name of the entry highlighted for renaming.

4. Type **File and Print Servers Security**, and then press ENTER.

5. Click Edit. The Group Policy Object Editor console appears, with the File And Print Servers Security GPO at the root of the console tree.

6. Using the recommendations in Lesson 1, configure security settings that are unique to file and print servers when compared to the baseline. When you are finished, close the Group Policy Object Editor and the File And Print Servers Properties boxes.

7. Repeat steps 2 through 6 for the Infrastructure Servers OU, creating a GPO that includes settings that are unique to infrastructure servers when compared to the baseline.

   Computers in the role-specific OUs will inherit policy settings in the Member Server Baseline GPO linked to the Member Servers OU. They will then apply settings configured in the GPO linked to their role-specific OU.

Lesson Review

The following questions are intended to reinforce key information presented in this lesson. If you are unable to answer a question, review the lesson materials and try the question again. You can find answers to the questions in the "Questions and Answers" section at the end of this chapter.

1. After installing several member servers running Windows Server 2003 on your Active Directory network, you want to deploy a baseline security configuration that you have designed for the member servers only, using group policies. Which of the following tasks must you perform to accomplish this objective? (Choose all that apply.)

   a. Create a new domain.

   b. Create a new organizational unit.

   c. Move the computer objects representing the member servers.

    d. Create a new GPO.

    e. Modify the domain GPO.

    f. Link a GPO to the Computers container.

    g. Link a GPO to an organizational unit.

2. In the GPO for the contoso.com domain, you define the Audit Account Logon Events policy by specifying that both successes and failures be audited. In the GPO for the Sales OU, you leave the Audit Account Logon Events policy undefined. What will be the effective setting for this policy for a computer in the Sales OU?

_____

3. Although Windows Server 2003 creates a GPO for the Domain Controllers container with default role-specific policy settings in it, you have other policy settings you want to apply to your domain controllers. Which of the following methods can you use to apply these settings? (Choose all that apply.)

    a. Modify the policy settings in the Domain Controllers container's existing GPO.

    b. Create a new organizational unit object and create a GPO for it containing the desired policy settings. Then move the Domain Controllers container to make it a child of the new object.

    c. Create a second GPO for the Domain Controllers container.

    d. Create a new child organizational unit object beneath the Domain Controllers container object, and then create a GPO for the new object containing the desired policy settings.

4. When creating a GPO for an organizational unit named Servers, you define a particular audit policy and configure it to audit successes only. When creating a GPO for an organizational unit named Infrastructure, which is a child of the Servers organizational unit, you configure the same policy to audit failures only. What is the effective value of that policy for a computer object in the Infrastructure container?

    a. Undefined

    b. Success only

    c. Failure only

    d. Success and Failure

Lesson Summary

- GPOs include a great many security options you can use to configure specific behaviors of a computer running Windows Server 2003.

- Active Directory objects do not contain GPOs; they are only linked to them. You can link a single GPO to multiple objects and make global changes by modifying that single GPO.

- Organizational unit objects inherit policy settings from the GPOs applied to their parent objects.

- Policy settings from a GPO linked directly to an object take precedence over settings inherited from a parent object's GPO.

- When creating security configurations for servers that perform specific roles, you can build on your secure baseline configuration.

- To configure baseline and role-based security using GPOs, you can choose to link two GPOs (the baseline and the role-based GPO) to an OU, or create an OU hierarchy in which the baseline GPO is linked to a parent OU and the role-based GPOs are linked to child OUs.

Lesson 3: **Managing Security Configuration with Security Templates**

Windows Server 2003 includes another mechanism for deploying security configuration settings called security templates. A *security template* is a collection of configuration settings stored as a text file with the .inf extension. A security template contains many of the same security parameters discussed in the previous lessons, and it presents them in a unified interface that enables you to save your configurations as files and deploy them when and where they are needed. In this lesson, you will learn about security templates and the methods you can use to apply them, including deployment to multiple computers through Group Policy, scripted deployments, and analysis of a computer's existing security configuration.

After this lesson, you will be able to

■ Use the Security Templates snap-in for Microsoft Management Console (MMC)

■ Describe the functions of the Windows Server 2003 predefined security templates

■ Create and modify templates to define baseline and role-specific security configurations

■ Use group policies to deploy security templates

■ Use the Security Configuration And Analysis snap-in to compare a computer's security settings with a security template and apply a template to the computer

■ Understand the functions of the Secedit.exe command-line utility

Estimated lesson time: 30 minutes

Understanding Security Templates

Security templates consist of policies and settings you can use to control a computer's security configuration using local policies or group policies. You can use security templates to configure any of the following types of policies and parameters:

■ **Account Policies**   Enables you to specify password restrictions, account lockout policies, and Kerberos policies

■ **Local Policies**   Enables you to configure audit policies, user rights assignments, and security options policies

■ **Event Log policies**   Enables you to configure maximum event log sizes and roll-over policies

■ **Restricted Groups**   Enables you to specify the users who are permitted to be members of specific groups

■ **System Services**   Enables you to specify the startup types and permissions for system services

- **Registry permissions** Enables you to set access control permissions for specific registry keys

- **File System permissions** Enables you to specify access control permissions for NTFS files and folders

You can deploy security templates in a variety of ways, using Active Directory directory service Group Policy Objects, the Windows Server 2003 Security Configuration And Analysis snap-in, or the Secedit.exe command-line utility. When you associate a security template with an Active Directory object, the settings in the template become part of the GPO associated with the object. You can also apply a security template directly to a computer, in which case the settings in the template become part of the computer's local policies.

There are several advantages to storing your security configuration parameters in security templates. Because the templates are plain text files, you can work with them manually as with any text file, cutting and pasting sections as needed. Second, templates make it easy to store security configurations of various types so that you can easily apply different levels of security to computers performing different roles.

Tip Storing your security settings in templates also provides an adequate backup of a computer's security configuration that you can use to quickly and easily restore the system to its original configuration. For example, when working with GPOs, it is easy to forget what changes you have made, and manually restoring the GPO to its original configuration can be difficult. If you have a security template containing your original settings, you can simply apply it to the GPO to return to your default settings.

Using the Security Templates Snap-in

To work with security templates, you use the Security Templates snap-in. By default, the Windows Server 2003 Administrative Tools folder does not include an MMC console with the Security Templates snap-in, so you have to create one yourself using the MMC Add/Remove Snap-in function. When you do this, the console provides an interface like the one shown in Figure 9-6.

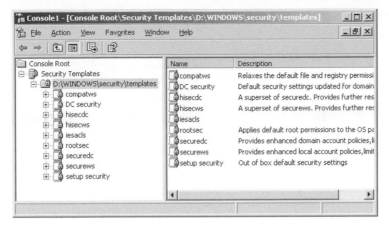

Figure 9-6   The Security Templates snap-in

The scope pane of the Security Templates snap-in contains a list of all the template files the program finds in the Windows\Security\Templates folder on the system drive. The snap-in interprets any file in this folder that has an .inf extension as a security template, even though the extensions do not appear in the console.

> **Tip**   You can add security templates in other folders to the console by selecting New Template Search Path from the Action menu and then browsing to the folder containing your templates. Please note, however, that not all the files with .inf extensions on a computer running Windows Server 2003 are security templates. The operating system uses files with .inf extensions for other purposes as well.

When you expand one of the templates in the scope pane, you see a hierarchical display of the policies in the template (as shown in Figure 9-7), as well as their current settings. You can modify the policies in each template just as you would using the Group Policy Object Editor console.

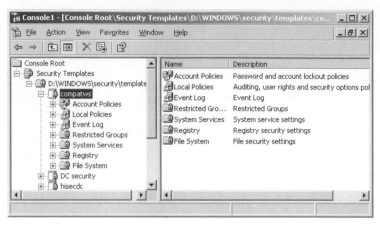

Figure 9-7   The contents of a security template

Default Security Templates

Windows Server 2003 includes a selection of predefined security templates you can use as is or modify to your needs. These templates provide different levels of security for servers performing specific roles. The predefined templates are located in the Windows\Security\Templates folder unless otherwise noted:

- **Setup Security.inf**   Contains the default security settings created by the Windows Server 2003 Setup program. The settings in the template depend on the nature of the installation, such as whether it was an upgrade or a clean install. You can use this template to restore the original security configuration to a computer you have modified.

> **Important**   When you use a security template to restore a computer's default settings, remember that the template might overwrite existing permissions modified by the installation of other applications. After you restore the default settings, you might have to reinstall your applications or modify certain file system or registry permissions manually.

- **DC Security.inf**   A computer running Windows Server 2003 creates this template only when you promote the computer to a domain controller. The template contains the default file system and registry permissions for domain controllers, as well as system service modifications.

Caution   The Setup Security.inf and DC Security.inf templates contain a large number of settings, and in particular a long list of file-system permission assignments. For this reason, you should not apply these templates to a computer by using group policies. Computers running Microsoft Windows operating systems periodically refresh group policy settings by accessing the GPOs on the network's domain controllers, and a template of this size can generate a great deal of Active Directory traffic on the network. Instead of using group policies, you should apply the template using the Security Configuration And Analysis snap-in or the Secedit.exe utility.

- **Securedc.inf**   This template contains policy settings that increase the security on a domain controller to a level that remains compatible with most functions and applications. The template includes more stringent account policies, enhanced auditing policies and security options, and increased restrictions for anonymous users and LAN Manager systems.

- **Hisecdc.inf**   This template contains policy settings that provide an even greater degree of security for domain controllers than the Securedc.inf template. Applying this template causes the computer to require digitally signed communications and encrypted secure channel communications instead of just requesting it, as Securedc.inf does. This template also adds registry and file security, removes all members from the Power Users group, and disables additional services.

- **Compatws.inf**   By default, the members of the local Users group on a computer running a Windows operating system can run only applications that meet requirements of the Designed For Windows Logo Program For Software. To run applications that are not compliant with the program, a user must be a member of the Power Users group. Some administrators want to grant users the ability to run these applications without giving them all the privileges of the Power Users group. The Compatws.inf template modifies the default file system and registry permissions for the Users group, enabling the members to run most applications, and also removes all members from the Power Users group.

Caution   The Compatws.inf template is not intended for domain controllers, so you should not link it to a site, to the domain, or to the Domain Controllers OU.

- **Securews.inf**   This template contains policy settings that increase the security on a workstation or member server to a level that remains compatible with most functions and applications. The template includes many of the same account and local policy settings as Securedc.inf, and it implements restrictions on LAN Manager, digitally signed communications and greater anonymous user restrictions.

■ **Hisecws.inf**   This template contains policy settings that provide higher security than Securews.inf on a workstation or member server. In addition to having many of the same settings as Hisecdc.inf, this template increases security for NTLM, removes all members from the Power Users group, and makes the Domain Admins group and the local Administrator account the only members of the local Administrators group.

> **Tip**   The Securedc.inf, Securews.inf, Hisecdc.inf, and Hisecws.inf templates are all designed to build on the default Windows security settings, and they do not themselves contain those default settings. If you have modified the security configuration of a computer substantially, you should first apply the Setup Security.inf template (and the DC Security.inf template as well, for domain controllers) before applying one of the secure or highly secure templates.

■ **Rootsec.inf**   This template contains only the default file system permissions for the system drive on a computer running Windows Server 2003. You can use this template to restore the default permissions to a system drive that you have changed, or to apply the system drive permissions to the computer's other drives.

■ **Iesacls.inf**   This template applies registry permissions on keys integral to Microsoft Internet Explorer.

Modifying Security Templates

To create a baseline security policy, you might want to modify the predefined templates.

> **Tip**   If you want to make changes to any of the policies in the predefined templates, you should make a backup copy of the template file first to preserve its original configuration. You can copy a template by simply copying and pasting the file in the normal manner using Microsoft Windows Explorer, or you can use the Security Templates snap-in by selecting a template and, from the Action menu, choosing Save As and supplying a new file name.

Use the Security Templates snap-in to modify security templates by following these steps:

1. Using Windows Explorer, create a new folder for custom templates.

2. Copy a predefined template into the new folder to create a custom baseline template.

3. Create a console with the Security Templates snap-in.

4. Add the new folder location to the template search path.

5. Modify the custom template.

6. Save the template.

7. If necessary, modify a template by editing its .inf file.

Tip   You should add most template settings using the Security Templates snap-in. The template file is a text file, but the required syntax might be confusing, and using the snap-in ensures that settings are changed using the proper syntax. However, the exception to this rule is adding Registry settings that are not already listed in the Security Option portion of the template. As new security settings become known, if they can be configured using a Registry key, you can add them to a security template. To do so, you add them to the [Registry Values] section of the template. The article "How to Add Custom Registry Settings to Security Configuration Editor" helps you understand how to perform this task. You can find it at *http://support.microsoft.com/?kbid=214752.*

Deploying Security Templates Using Group Policy Objects

Creating and modifying security templates does not improve security unless you apply those templates. To configure a large group of computers in a single operation, you can import a security template into the Group Policy Object for a domain, site, or organizational unit object in Active Directory. However, there are a few cautions that you must observe when using group policies to deploy security templates.

Group Policy Deployment Cautions

As with other security settings, the configuration parameters you import into the Group Policy Object for a specific container are inherited by all the objects in that container, including other containers. Most networks use different levels of security for computers performing various roles, so it is relatively rare for administrators to apply a security template to a domain or site object—because then all the computers in that domain or site receive the same settings. At the very least, your domain controllers should have a higher level of security than the other computers on your network.

Tip   When creating security templates for deployment via GPOs, the best practice is to place your computers into organizational units according to their roles and create individual security templates for each OU. This way you can customize the security configuration for each role and modify the template for each role as needed, without affecting the others.

Another consideration when importing security templates into Group Policy Objects is the amount of data in the template itself. Every computer running a Windows operating system in an Active Directory container refreshes its Group Policy settings at a regular interval, by default every 16 hours, even if the GPOs have not been modified. A security template can contain a large number of settings, and the continual refreshing of large templates to a large fleet of computers could generate a great deal of Active Directory traffic and place a heavy burden on the network's domain controllers.

> **Note**   When you look at the sizes of the predefined security templates included with Windows Server 2003, you can easily see which ones you should not deploy using group policies. Most of the templates are less than 10 kilobytes, with the notable exceptions of the DC Security.inf and Setup Security.inf templates, which are 127 and 784 kilobytes, respectively.

Importing Security Templates into GPOs

To deploy a security template using group policies, you select an Active Directory object that has a GPO and import the template into the GPO. The template's settings then become part of the GPO, overwriting any existing values. The importation process proceeds as follows:

1. Open the Active Directory Users And Computers console.

2. Select the domain or organizational unit object to which you want to apply the template and, from the Action menu, choose Properties. The Properties dialog box for that object appears.

3. Click the Group Policy tab, select a Group Policy Object from the Group Policy Object Links list, and then click Edit. The Group Policy Object Editor console appears.

> **Tip**   Instead of using an existing Group Policy Object, you can also create a new one by clicking New and then supplying a name for the GPO.

4. Under Computer Configuration, expand the Windows Settings subheading, and then click Security Settings.

5. From the Action menu, select Import Policy. The Import Policy From dialog box appear.

6. Select the security template file you want to import, and then click Open. The settings in the template are imported into the Group Policy Object.

7. Close the Group Policy Object Editor console, and then click OK in the Properties dialog box for the object you selected.

8. Close the Active Directory Users And Computers console.

The Security Configuration And Analysis Tool

Security Configuration And Analysis is an MMC snap-in you can use to interactively apply a security template to the local computer. However, in addition to configuring the security settings for the computer, the snap-in also provides the ability to analyze the current system security configuration and compare it to a baseline saved as a security template. This enables you to quickly determine whether someone has changed a computer's security settings and whether the system conforms to your organization's security policies.

As with the Security Templates snap-in, Windows Server 2003 does not include a shortcut to a Security Configuration And Analysis console, so you must add the snap-in to a console yourself. When you do this for the first time, the console contains nothing but the Security Configuration And Analysis heading, as shown in Figure 9-8.

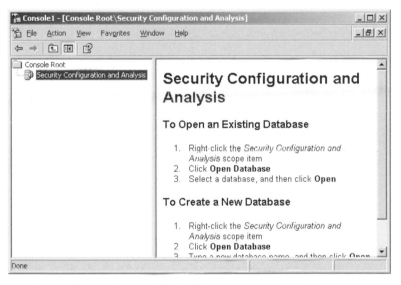

Figure 9-8   The Security Configuration And Analysis snap-in

Analyzing a System

To use the Security Configuration And Analysis snap-in, you must first create a database that will contain a collection of security settings. The database is the interface between the actual security settings on the computer and the settings stored in your security templates. After you create a database (or open an existing one), you then import one or more security templates of your choice. If you import more than one template, you must decide whether to clear the database. If the database is cleared, only the settings in the new template will be part of the database. If the database is not cleared, additional template settings that are defined will override settings from previously imported templates. If settings in additional templates are not defined, the settings in the database from previously imported templates will remain.

Once you have imported one or more templates to create the database, you can proceed to applying the settings in that database to the computer or analyzing the computer's current settings.

> **Important**   Remember that settings in a database do not modify the computer's settings or the settings in a template until that database is either used to configure the computer or exported to a template.

When you begin the analysis by selecting Analyze Computer Now from the Action menu, the system prompts you for the location of its error log file, and then proceeds to compare the settings in the template to the computer's current settings. Once the analysis is complete, the console produces a display similar to that of the Security Templates snap-in (as shown in Figure 9-9), containing all the standard security settings found in a template.

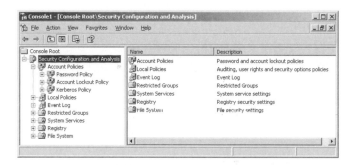

Figure 9-9   The contents of a security database

The big difference between the Security Templates console and this display, however, is that the policies listed in the details pane have columns containing the database settings and the computer settings. The Database Settings column contains the values imported from the template you selected, while the Computer Settings column contains the system's current settings. The comparison of the two values for each policy is reflected in the flag on each policy name, as shown in Figure 9-10. The meanings of the flags are as follows;

- **X in a red circle**   Indicates that the policy is defined in both the database and on the computer, but that the configured values do not match

- **Green check mark in a white circle**   Indicates that the policy is defined in both the database and on the computer, and that the configured values do match

- **Question mark in a white circle**   Indicates that the policy is not defined in the database and therefore was not analyzed, or that the user running the analysis did not have the permissions needed to access the policy on the computer

- **Exclamation point in a white circle**   Indicates that the policy is defined in the database, but does not exist on the computer

- **No flag**   Indicates that the policy is not defined in the database or on the computer

Figure 9-10   Results of a security analysis

Changing Security Settings

As you examine the elements of the database and compare the template values with those of the computer, you might find discrepancies and want to make changes to the computer's configuration. There are several ways in which you can do this, as follows:

- **Apply the database settings to the computer**   If you want to use the exact settings from the template you imported into the database, you can simply select Configure Computer Now from the Action menu to apply them to the computer.

- **Modify the database settings**   You can double-click any policy in the console tree to display its Properties dialog box and modify its value in the database.

> **Caution**   Modifying a policy value in the Security Configuration And Analysis snap-in changes the database value only, not the actual computer setting. For the changes you make to take effect on the computer, you must either apply the database settings to the computer using the Configure Computer Now command or export the database to a new template and apply it to the computer using any of the standard methods.

- **Create a new template**   You can select Export Template from the Action menu to create an entirely new template from the settings currently in the database, and then apply the template to the computer using any of the standard methods.

> **Important**   The Export Template feature creates a new template from the current database settings at the time you execute the command, not from the computer's current settings.

- **Modify the computer's settings manually**   You can always modify the computer's security settings directly by using a member server's Local Security Settings console (open the console by selecting Local Security Policy from the Administrative Tools menu), by modifying the appropriate Group Policy Object, or by manually manipulating file system or registry permissions.

Secedit.exe

Secedit.exe is a command-line utility that can perform the same functions as the Security Configuration And Analysis snap-in. The advantage of Secedit.exe is that you can call it from scripts and batch files, enabling you to automate your security template deployments. Another big advantage of Secedit.exe is that you can use it to apply only part of a security template to a computer, something you cannot do with the Security Configuration And Analysis snap-in or with Group Policy Objects. For example, if you want to apply the file system's permissions from a template, but leave all the other settings alone, Secedit.exe is the only way to do it.

To use Secedit.exe, you run the program from the command prompt with one of the following six main parameters, plus additional parameters for each function:

- **Configure**   Applies all or part of a security database to the local computer. You can also configure the program to import a security template into the specified database before applying the database settings to the computer.

- **Analyze**   Compares the computer's current security settings with those in a security database. You can configure the program to import a security template into the database before performing the analysis. The program stores the results of the analysis in the database itself, which you can view later using the Security Configuration And Analysis snap-in.

- **Import**   Imports all or part of a security template into a specific security database.

- **Export**   Exports all or part of the settings from a security database to a new security template.

- **Validate**   Verifies that a security template is using the correct internal syntax.

- **Generaterollback**   Creates a security template you can use to restore a system to its original configuration after applying another template.

> ### Example Secedit.exe Commands
>
> To configure the machine using the XYZ template:
>
> *secedit /configure /db xyz.sdb /cfg xyz.inf /log xyz.log*
>
> To create a rollback template for the XYZ template:
>
> *secedit /generaterollback /cfg xyz.inf /rbk xyzrollback.inf*
>
> */log xyzrollback.log*
>
> For full details regarding Secedit.exe and its switches, refer to the Windows Server 2003 Help and Support Center.

Practice: Security Templates

In this practice, you create a customized MMC console with the Security Templates and the Security Configuration And Analysis snap-ins. You then analyze the computer against one of the predefined security templates included with Windows Server 2003. You will also use the console to create a new security template based on one of the predefined templates and modify the template to provide a customized security level.

Exercise 1: Creating a Custom MMC Console

In this procedure, you create a comprehensive security template management tool by adding the Security Templates and Security Configuration And Analysis snap-ins to a custom console.

1. Log on to Server01 as an administrator.

2. Click Start, and then click Run. The Run dialog box appears.

3. In the Open text box, type **mmc** and then click OK. The Console1 window appears.

4. From the File menu, select Add/Remove Snap-in. The Add/Remove Snap-in dialog box appears with the Standalone tab selected.

5. Click Add. The Add Standalone Snap-in dialog box appears.

6. Scroll down in the Available Standalone Snap-ins list, and select Security Templates.

7. Click Add. Security Templates appears in the Add/Remove Snap-in dialog box.

8. In the Available Standalone Snap-ins list, select Security Configuration And Analysis.

9. Click Add, and then click Close. Security Configuration And Analysis appears in the Add/Remove Snap-in dialog box, along with the Security Templates snap-in.

10. Click OK. The two snap-ins appear in the Console Root window.

11. From the File menu, select Save As. The Save As dialog box appears.

12. In the File Name text box, type **Security Console.msc** and then click Save. The name of the console shown in the title bar changes to Security Console.

13. Leave the console open for the next exercise.

Exercise 2: Analyzing a Computer

1. In the Security Console you created, click the Security Configuration And Analysis snap-in in the scope pane.

2. From the Action menu, select Open Database. The Open Database dialog box appears.

3. In the File Name text box, type **Windb.sdb** and then click Open. The Import Template dialog box appears.

4. Click the Hisecdc.inf template, and then click Open.

5. From the Action menu, select Analyze Computer Now. The Perform Analysis dialog box appears.

6. Click OK to accept the default log file name. An Analyzing System Security message box appears to show a progress indicator as the snap-in performs the analysis.

7. When the analysis is complete, expand the Security Configuration And Analysis node and the Account Policies node in the console's scope pane.

8. Click the Password Policy node in the scope pane.

   Notice that the console has flagged some of the six password policies with a red X, indicating that the database settings for those policies do not match the template settings.

9. Double-click the Minimum Password Age policy in the details pane. The Minimum Password Age Properties dialog box appears.

10. Modify the Password Can Be Changed After selector value from 2 to 1, and then click OK.

    Notice that the red X next to the Minimum Password Age policy has changed to a green check mark. This is because you have changed the setting in the database to match that of the computer.

11. Click the Security Configuration And Analysis node in the scope pane.

12. From the Action menu, select Configure Computer Now. The Configure System dialog box appears.

13. Click OK to accept the default log file path. A Configuring Computer Security message box displays to show a progress indicator as the snap-in configures the computer using the settings in the database.

14. From the Action menu, select Analyze Computer Now a second time. The Perform Analysis dialog box appears.

15. Click OK to accept the default log file path. An Analyzing System Security message box appears to show a progress indicator as the snap-in performs the analysis.

16. When the analysis is complete, expand the Security Configuration And Analysis node and the Account Policies node in the console's scope pane.

17. Click the Password Policy node in the scope pane.

    Notice that all the password policies are now flagged with green check marks, indicating that the computer settings match the database settings. This is because you have just applied the database settings to the computer. Notice also that the Minimum Password Age value is 1 day, instead of the 2 days specified in the Hisecdc.inf template. This is because you changed the value of this policy in the database prior to applying the database to the computer.

18. Leave the Security Console open for the following exercise.

Exercise 3: Modifying an Existing Template

> **Tip**   Best practices recommend never modifying default templates. Instead, new templates or copies of predefined templates are placed in a separate location and then modified to create custom templates.

1. Using Windows Explorer, create a folder in your My Documents folder named Custom Templates.

2. In the Security Console you created, right-click Security Templates and choose New Template Search Path.

3. Select the Custom Templates folder, and click OK.

4. Expand the Security Templates node and the C:\Windows\Security\Templates node.

5. Click the Securews template in the scope pane and, from the Action menu, select Save As. The Save As dialog box appears.

6. Browse to the Custom Templates folder you created, and save the template as **Custom.inf**.

7. Click the C:\Documents and Settings\<*username*>\My Documents\Custom Templates node in the scope pane. From the Action menu, select Refresh. The Custom template appears in the console.

8. Expand Custom template and the Local Policies container, and then click the Security Options node.

9. Modify the values of the following security options as shown:

   ❑ Devices: Restrict CD-ROM Access To Locally Logged-on User Only—Enabled

   ❑ Interactive Logon: Prompt User To Change Password Before Expiration—1 Day

   ❑ Shutdown: Allow System To Be Shut Down Without Having To Log On—Disabled

10. Click the File System node and, from the Action menu, click Add File. The Add A File Or Folder dialog box appears.

11. In the Folder text box, type **D:** and then click OK. The Database Security For D:\ dialog box appears.

12. Click the Users group and, in the Permissions For Users box, select the Modify and Write check boxes in the Allow column. Then click OK. The Add Object dialog box appears.

13. Accept the default option button by clicking OK. The D:\ drive appears in the File System list.

14. Right-click the Custom template name, and choose Save.

15. Open the Custom.inf template using Notepad.

16. Examine the [Registry Values] section. In this section, you can edit or add registry values that will be configured when the template is applied.

17. Close Notepad.

Exercise 4: Applying a Template

1. Open a command prompt window, and change the directory to your Custom Templates folder by typing the command:

   ```
   cd "%userprofile%\My Documents\Custom Templates"
   ```

2. Create a rollback template by using this command:

   ```
   secedit /generaterollback /cfg custom.inf /rbk customrollback.inf /log
   customrollback.log
   ```

   The command indicates that rollback does not support File Security and Registry Security.

3. Type **Y**, when asked if you want to continue the operation.

    Customrollback.inf and Customrollback.log files are created in the Custom Templates folder.

    Using the Rollback command creates a template that can be used to roll back the security settings to the way they were before the Custom.inf template was applied. The Customrollback.inf template is made first, and then the Custom.inf template is applied. Rollback is not supported for file and Registry security. That is, any permissions edited in these sections of the template file will not be reversible by applying the rollback template.

4. In the Security Console you created, right-click the Security Configuration And Analysis node in the console and select Open Database.

    A database is not created automatically, so the first step is to create one.

5. In the File Name text box, type the name for the new database: **Customdb.sdb**.

6. Click Open.

    The Import Templates dialog box appears. You can now import one or more templates into the database.

7. In the Import Template dialog box, browse to the Custom Templates folder, select the Custom.inf template, and click Open.

    In Exercise 2, you used a database to analyze a computer. In this exercise, you use a database to configure a computer and thereby to apply the settings in the database.

8. Right-click Security Configuration And Analysis, and select Configure Computer Now.

9. Click OK when asked to confirm the location of the error log.

    The error log is also a good source of information about which templates were applied and when.

10. Wait for the configuration to complete, and close the Security Console without saving it.

Exercise 5: Recovering from the Application of a Bad Template

You could change the security settings and find that the computer has been rendered inaccessible on the network, or that security has been changed to make the computer less secure than is required. If a rollback template was made before the template was applied, you can roll the system back to a previous security state. Remember that rollback does not support reversing changes to registry and file system ACLs. If you need to recover Registry and file system permissions to an installation state, you can do so by applying one of the default installation templates.

In this exercise, you restore security configuration settings by applying a rollback template.

1. Open the Security Console.

2. Right-click Security Configuration And Analysis, and select Open Database.

3. In the Open Database dialog box, select the Customdb.sdb database and click Open.

4. Right-click Security Configuration And Analysis, and select Import Template.

5. In the Import Template dialog box, browse to the Custom Templates folder and select the Customrollback.inf template.

6. Select the Clear This Database Before Importing check box, and click Open.

   If the check box is not selected, and if you import multiple templates, the settings in both templates are applied. The settings in a template that is imported will override defined settings in previously imported templates.

7. Right-click Security Configuration And Analysis, and select Configure Computer Now.

8. Click OK to approve the error log file.

9. Close the Security Console.

Lesson Review

The following questions are intended to reinforce key information presented in this lesson. If you are unable to answer a question, review the lesson materials and try the question again. You can find answers to the questions in the "Questions and Answers" section at the end of this chapter.

1. You are the new administrator for an Active Directory network, and while it is clear that someone has changed the security configuration of the network's domain controllers, your predecessor left no records of the exact changes he made. Which of the following security templates should you apply to the domain controllers to restore their default security settings and then implement the highest possible level of security?

   a. Compatws.inf and then Securedc.inf

   b. Securedc.inf and then Hisecdc.inf

   c. Hisecdc.inf and then Setup Security.inf

   d. DC Security.inf and then Hisecdc.inf

   e. Setup Security.inf and then Securedc.inf

2. Why should you not use group policies to apply the Setup Security.inf template to a computer?

_____

_____

_____

3. What are the three ways to apply a security template to a computer running a Windows operating system?

_____

_____

4. Why is it not common practice to apply security templates to Active Directory domain objects?

_____

_____

_____

5. Name two security template deployment tasks that the Scccdit.exe utility can perform which group policies and the Security Configuration And Analysis snap-in cannot.

_____

_____

6. When you use the Security Configuration And Analysis snap-in to export a template, where do the settings in the new template come from?

   a. From the computer's current security settings

   b. From the snap-in's currently loaded database

   c. From the security template you imported into the database

   d. From a Group Policy Object you specify

7. You would like to apply a new Registry setting to all the servers on your network. What is an efficient way to perform that task?

_____

_____

_____

_____

8. Which of the following settings can be applied using Security Configuration And Analysis and a security template? (Choose all that apply.)

   a. The password must be 15 characters long.

   b. The Accountants group is not allowed to access this computer over the network.

   c. IPSec must be used for all communications between Computer1 and Computer2.

   d. The root file permissions should be Everyone Full Control.

9. Which steps might be necessary to recover from the application of a security template to a file server that prevented all users from accessing the server over the network? Choose the most efficient way.

   a. Log on locally to the file server as Administrator, and apply the root security template.

   b. Log on locally to the file server as Administrator, and apply the rollback template produced from the bad security template.

   c. Log on remotely to the file server as Enterprise Admin, and use the Local Security Policy console to change the user rights policies that might be incorrect.

   d. Log on remotely to the file server as Administrator, and apply the rollback template produced from the security template.

Lesson Summary

- A security template is a collection of configuration settings stored as a text file with an .inf extension.

- Security templates contain basically the same security parameters as Group Policy Objects, including account, local, and event log policies, file system and registry permissions, system service parameters, and restricted groups.

- Windows Server 2003 includes a number of predefined templates that enable you to restore the default security parameters created by the Windows Setup program and to implement secure and highly secure configurations for workstations, member servers, and domain controllers.

- To create and modify security templates, you use the Security Templates snap-in for Microsoft Management Console.

- To apply a security template to a computer, you can use GPOs, the Security Configuration And Analysis snap-in, or the Secedit.exe utility.

- You should not use group policies to deploy large security templates because of the burden they create on the network and on the domain controllers.

- You can use the Security Configuration And Analysis snap-in to deploy security templates on the local computer.

- The Security Configuration And Analysis snap-in can also analyze the computer's security configuration by comparing its current security settings to those of a security template and flagging the discrepancies.

- Secedit.exe is a command-line tool that performs the same functions as the Security Configuration And Analysis snap-in, and can also apply specific parts of templates to the computer. You can use Secedit.exe in scripts and batch files to automate security template deployments.

- You can use Secedit.exe to produce a rollback template, a template that can undo the harmful effects applied by a bad template.

Lesson 4: Planning a Security Framework

In recent years, security has become an increasingly important part of the network designer's and administrator's jobs. Security is no longer an afterthought; you must include security considerations in all your network planning from the outset, and at every level. Many of the lessons in this book are concerned with security issues, but before you deploy the security features in Windows Server 2003, your organization should have a framework for designing and implementing security policies.

After this lesson, you will be able to

- Understand the process of designing, implementing, and managing a security strategy
- Create a security design team
- Map a security life cycle

Estimated lesson time: 15 minutes

High-Level Security Planning

Windows Server 2003 includes a great many features, tools, and capabilities to support the implementation of a secure enterprise. However, before you deploy specific security features, someone must decide which features are appropriate for your organization. A security framework is a logical, structured process by which your organization performs tasks like the following:

- Estimating security risks
- Specifying security requirements
- Selecting security features
- Implementing security policies
- Designing security deployments
- Specifying security management policies

This lesson, therefore, is concerned not so much with developing a security solution for your organization, but with the process your organization uses to develop a security solution.

Creating a Security Design Team

Security is not strictly an IT issue anymore, so the first step in creating a security framework is to determine which people in your organization are going to be responsible for designing, implementing, and maintaining the security policies. Technical people, such as network administrators, might be familiar with the capabilities of specific security mechanisms and how to implement them, but they are not necessarily the best people to identify the resources that are most at risk or the forces that threaten them. Management might be more familiar with the resources that need to be protected and the potential ramifications of their being compromised, but is probably not familiar with the tools that can be used to protect those resources. There are also economic issues to consider, and the effect of new security policies on employee productivity and morale.

All these arguments lead to the conclusion that most organizations need to assemble a team or committee responsible for providing a balanced picture of the organization's security status and capable of deciding how to implement security policies. The number of people on the team and their positions in the company depend on the organization's size and political structure. A well-balanced team should consist of people who can answer questions such as the following:

- What are your organization's most valuable resources?

- What are the potential threats to your organization's resources?

- Which resources are most at risk?

- What are the consequences if specific resources are compromised?

- What security features are available?

- Which security features are best for protecting specific resources?

- How secure is secure enough?

- What is involved in implementing specific security features?

- How do particular security features affect users, administrators, and managers?

Mapping Out a Security Life Cycle

Creating a security framework is not a one-time project that ends when you have finished designing the initial security plan for your network. Security is an ongoing concern, and the responsibilities of the security design team are ongoing as well. A security life cycle typically consists of three basic phases:

- Designing a security infrastructure

- Implementing security features

- Ongoing security management

These phases are discussed in the following sections.

Designing a Security Infrastructure

The initial design phase of a security infrastructure should run concurrently with the network design. Security issues can have a major effect on many elements of your network design, including the hardware components you purchase, the locations you select for the hardware, and how you configure individual devices. The design phase begins with identifying the resources that need protection and evaluating the threats to those resources.

Even the smallest organization has information it should protect, such as financial data and customer lists. Other valuable commodities might include order entry data, research and development information, and confidential correspondence. In more extreme cases, your organization might possess secret government or military information. The threats to your data can range from the casual to the felonious. In many cases, a modicum of security can protect your confidential data from curious employees and casual Internet predators. However, targeted threats, such as those mounted by business competitors and even rival governments, require more serious security measures.

> **Tip**   In addition to deliberate attempts to penetrate security, your confidential data is in danger from accidents, thefts of equipment, and natural disasters. When planning the protection of your data, don't forget to include fault tolerance solutions that can prevent data loss due to drive failures, fires, and other accidents.

Once your team has identified the resources that need protection and has determined how severe the threats are, you can plan how to secure the resources. This is where the technically oriented members of the team come into play, because they are familiar with the security measures that are available and what is involved in deploying them. Depending on the requirements of the organization, the security plan might consist of merely taking advantage of the features already included in the network's operating systems and other hardware and software components, or you might have to purchase additional security products, such as firewalls, smart card readers, or biometric devices.

A typical security plan for a network includes implementations of the following security principles:

- **Authentication**   The verification of a user's identity before providing access to secured resources. Authentication mechanisms can use encrypted passwords, certificates, and hardware devices such as smart cards and biometric sensors, depending on the degree of security required.

- **Access control**   The granting of specific levels of access based on a user's identity. Access control capabilities are built into most network operating systems and applications.

- **Encryption**   The process of protecting data through the application of a cryptographic algorithm that uses keys to encrypt and decrypt data. The strength of an encryption mechanism is based on the capabilities of the algorithm itself, the number and types of keys the system uses, and the method of distributing the keys.

- **Firewalls**   A system designed to prevent unauthorized access to a private network from outside. Firewalls can use a variety of mechanisms to secure a network, including packet filtering, network address translation, application gateways, and proxy servers.

- **Auditing**   A process by which administrators monitor system and network activities over extended periods. Most network operating systems and applications include some form of auditing that administrators can configure to their needs.

The security plan is not just a matter of technology. Your security team is also responsible for creating security policies for the organization. For example, you might agree to use encrypted passwords for user authentication, but you must also decide who is going to supply the passwords, how long the passwords should be, how often they should change, and so forth.

Implementing Security Features

After deciding what security mechanisms you are going to use and designing your security policies, the next step is to devise an implementation plan for these mechanisms and policies. In some cases, the implementation plan might consist of a procedure and timetable for the process of evaluating, purchasing, installing, and configuring security hardware and software products. For security mechanisms included with operating systems and applications, the implementation plan might consist of modifications to an existing installation or configuration routine.

Implementing security policies can be more problematic than implementing security technologies because you must devise a way to disseminate the policies to everyone who needs them and to ensure compliance. In some cases, your software will contain mechanisms that enable you to enforce your policies; in other cases, you might have to compel your users to comply.

Enforcing Security Policies

For a simple example of enforcing security policies, your team might decide that the network users must use passwords at least eight characters long, containing numeric characters and symbols as well as letters, and that users must change their passwords once a month. You can advise the users of these new requirements by sending a general e-mail, but the most important part of the implementation plan would be using a tool such as Windows Server 2003 Group Policy to enforce your requirements. In this case, Windows Server 2003 has preconfigured password policies that enable you to require the use of eight-character, complex passwords, modified every 30 days. In other cases, however, enforcing compliance might be more complicated—for example, asking users not to store their password information in their unlocked desks.

Ongoing Security Management

With your security mechanisms and policies in place, you might be tempted to think that the work of your team is finished, but this is definitely not the case. Security is an ongoing concern that requires the continued attention of the entire team.

For the technical staff, security management means regular checking of audit logs and other resources, as well as monitoring individual systems and network traffic for signs of intrusion. Administrators must also update the security software products as needed. Beyond these regular tasks, however, the entire team must be aware that the organization's security situation changes constantly. Every day can bring new resources to protect or new threats to existing resources. Security is often an arms race between the intruders and the protectors, and whichever side becomes lax or complacent ends up losing the race.

Lesson Review

The following questions are intended to reinforce key information presented in this lesson. If you are unable to answer a question, review the lesson materials and try the question again. You can find answers to the questions in the "Questions and Answers" section at the end of this chapter.

1. List the three phases of a security life cycle.

   _____

2. Which of the following Windows Server 2003 features can you use to ensure that users supply passwords of a specified length?

   a. Audit policies

   b. Group policies

   c. Authentication protocols

   d. Access control lists

3. List three tasks that a security design team typically performs.

   _____

   _____

Lesson Summary

- Security is a concern through the entire process of network design and implementation.

- For most organizations, the best strategy is to create a security design team responsible for all aspects of the organization's security strategy.

- The typical functions of a security design team are to determine what resources need protection, to identify the threats to those resources, and to specify what mechanisms the organization will use to protect the resources.

- Security mechanisms can include authentication, access control, encryption, firewalls, and auditing. The team should also create security policies for the organization and a way to enforce them.

- After the design and implementation of the security strategy is completed, the team is still responsible for the ongoing management of the security mechanisms, as well as for the constantly reevaluating the threats to the organization's resources.

Lesson 5: Creating a Testing and Deployment Plan

Before you actually implement security policies on your production network, you must be sure the settings you choose are suitable for your computer, function properly, and satisfy your organization's security requirements. To verify the functionality of your security configuration, the best practice is to first test it in a lab environment and then create a limited pilot deployment on your live network. Then, if the configuration exhibits no major problems, you can proceed to deploy it throughout your network.

After this lesson, you will be able to

- Create a plan for testing security configuration settings in a lab environment
- Plan a pilot deployment of new configuration settings on a live network

Estimated lesson time: 20 minutes

Creating a Testing Environment

For the initial testing phase of deploying a configuration, you want to implement your security parameter settings in a lab environment. The lab network environment should closely resemble the actual environment in which you will deploy your configurations, but it should be isolated from your live production environment. The testing process consists of the following five basic steps:

- Creating a test plan
- Creating test cases
- Building a lab
- Conducting the tests
- Evaluating the results

Creating a Test Plan

For the first phase of the testing process, you should create a test plan that specifies what you want to accomplish and how the testing process will proceed. The specific goals for your test plan will vary depending on the nature of your organization and how it uses the network, but some of the most typical testing objectives are as follows:

- Hardware compatibility testing
- Application and operating system compatibility testing
- Hardware and software product evaluation

- Performance baseline determination
- Security testing
- Documentation of installation and configuration procedures
- Documentation of administrative procedures

Tip   While the focus of this lesson, and of the related exam objectives, is on the configuration and deployment of security parameters, your test plan can and should encompass all aspects of network compatibility and performance.

In addition to general testing objectives such as these, you will probably also have goals that are specific to your organization and its security requirements. To achieve your testing objectives, your plan should specify elements such as the following:

- The structure of the test lab
- A list of all hardware, software, and personnel required for the testing process
- What tools and techniques the testers will use
- The methodology and duration for each phase of the testing
- How the testers will document the testing process and the results

Creating Test Cases

To test specific elements of your network installation, you create test cases. A *test case* is a procedure that fully tests a particular feature or setting. For example, if you have decided to use a particular set of account policy values to control your users' passwords, the test case for those policies might consist of implementing them on the lab network and then having people log on and off those computers, deliberately duplicating common user logon errors and attempting to guess passwords using the brute force method. The results for that test case might lead you to use the account policy parameters as is or it might lead you to modify them to enhance or reduce the security they provide.

As documented in the test plan, each test case should include the following information:

- The purpose of the test case
- The hardware and software required to perform the test
- The installation and configuration procedures required before the test can proceed
- The procedure for performing the test

Creating detailed and complete test cases is one of the most critical elements of the test plan. For the example given, it might be tempting to create a brief test case that specifies what account policy settings to use and, in general terms, how the testing should proceed. However, this practice introduces an element of chance that can jeopardize the validity of the test. If you create detailed, step-by-step testing procedures for your test cases, not only can you repeat the test using the exact same methodology, it is also possible for different people to perform the same test in the same way.

Building a Lab

The nature of the testing lab itself depends on a variety of factors, including the size and nature of the organization, the amount of testing to be done, the complexity of the network, and the duration of the testing process. Security configuration testing is not the only part of designing and constructing a network in which a lab environment is useful. You can use a lab for any or all the following purposes:

- Developing the overall design of the network

- Evaluating hardware and software products

- Planning performance and capacity

- Determining bandwidth requirements

- Establishing administrative policies

- Training users and support staff

- Documenting deployment and administration procedures

For a large organization, a permanent lab installation can be a worthwhile investment that enables network administrators to continually evaluate upgrades and new technologies, in preparation for their deployment on the live network. For organizations that are not quite so large or that have limited budgets, the lab can be an ad hoc arrangement that consists of computers and other equipment that administrators will later deploy in a production environment.

The object of creating a lab is to duplicate the organization's live computing environment as closely as possible, within practical limits. For some organizations, a simple isolated local area network (LAN), consisting of a handful of computers connected to a hub, is sufficient. For larger organizations, a more elaborate lab setup might be necessary. For example, if your network consists of offices at remote locations connected by wide area network (WAN) links, you might want to integrate the WAN links into your lab environment as well.

> **Real World   WAN Testing**
>
> While it would be impractical for most organizations to install expensive WAN connections solely for testing purposes, there are other ways to incorporate WAN links into your lab network. For a new network rollout, you might be able to use the WAN connections for the production network during a preliminary testing phase, and then use the same connections for the live deployment when you have completed the testing. You can also substitute lower cost WAN technologies in the lab for the real ones on the production network.
>
> For example, if your network design calls for T-1 leased lines to connect your offices, you can create a reasonable facsimile of the live network in the lab using modems and dial-up connections. Obviously, this type of arrangement does not enable you to test technology-dependent elements such as WAN bandwidth utilization, but it can provide a more accurate representation of your live production network than you could achieve with LAN technology alone.
>
> Creating a WAN testing environment using actual WAN links obviously requires that you disperse the testing facilities among your network locations. Depending on the needs of your organization, you might want to build a lab network at each site so that the staff at each location can use its own lab network for its own testing and training operations, or you can create a satellite installation at each site, accessible through remote control and intended only to provide a terminus for the WAN connection.

Conducting the Tests

The ease or difficulty of the actual testing process depends largely on the amount of detail in your test plan. If you create highly specific test cases with step-by-step instructions for the testing procedure, virtually anyone can do the testing, as many times as needed. If your test cases are more general, you might have to count on the insight of the particular individuals who perform the tests to determine the results.

The first step of the testing process is to configure the computers and other components required for the test according to the specifications in your test case. Once you have created the environment you need, you can begin the actual testing.

> **Tip**   In many cases, you can use this configuration process as an opportunity to test your deployment plans for hardware, software, or configuration settings. This is just one way you can integrate testing your security configuration into a comprehensive program of testing network administration and rollout.

When testing security configurations, your two main objectives are to determine whether the parameter settings you have chosen provide the security you need and whether the settings interfere with normal operation of the network. Your test cases should include procedures that duplicate all the network's standard functions with the security parameters in place. For example, you should have testers run all the applications and access all the network shares your users need to ensure that the security parameters don't inhibit access to these resources. Then, the testers should attempt to bypass the security measures you have implemented to see whether they are secure enough, and duplicate typical user errors, such as incorrect logon passwords to document the system's reaction.

Evaluating the Results

One of the most important elements of the testing process is careful documentation of every action and its results. Once the testing process is finished, you should have a complete record of everything that occurred to be used in evaluation. With detailed test cases and well-documented test results, it is even possible for individuals not involved in making the decisions to do the testing, leaving the evaluation to the organization's policy makers.

As a result of the testing, you might decide that your security configuration parameters are acceptable as is or you might have to modify them, in which case you should repeat the tests using the new settings. It is when you have to repeat the tests that you realize the benefits of creating detailed test cases. When you document the testing procedures completely, you can repeat them exactly and compare the results with the original tests.

Creating a Pilot Deployment

The one element that is extremely difficult to duplicate adequately in a lab environment, no matter what your budget, is network activity. While there are ways to generate traffic on a lab network, it is hard to duplicate actual working conditions. For this reason, you should follow up your lab testing with a pilot deployment. A *pilot deployment* is an implementation of your actual configuration on the production network in a limited and controlled fashion.

The object of a pilot deployment is to select a small sampling of network users, deploy your tested hardware and software configurations on their computers, and have them work under normal operating conditions. A limited deployment like this enables you to monitor the performance of the network more closely and react quickly to any problems that arise. In addition, the pilot program enables you to refine and practice the deployment process you will use on the entire network; it is also an opportunity to train the help desk and other support personnel who will troubleshoot problems when the configuration goes live.

> **Important**   It is extremely important that your pilot deployment not include technologies or configuration settings you haven't previously tested in a lab setting. Modifying the deployment between the lab phase and the pilot phase contaminates the results of the pilot project. If problems occur, you might not be able to determine whether they result from a fault in your original configuration or from the changes you made after testing.

Creating a Pilot Deployment Plan

As with the testing phase, planning and preparation are crucial to a successful pilot deployment. The users in the pilot program are not as rigidly controlled in their activities as the lab testers are, so there is no need to create specific user procedures. After all, the object of the pilot deployment is to have users work as they normally do. What does require careful planning, however, is the selection of the pilot users and creating a support system for them.

Selecting Users for a Pilot Deployment

There are three factors to consider when selecting the users who will participate in your pilot deployment: the nature of the configuration parameters you are rolling out, the users' roles in the organization, and the users' own capabilities. Depending on what parameters you are testing, you might want to select a single workgroup or department for the pilot plan or a cross-section of users throughout the organization. A single group or department is easier to monitor and troubleshoot, but a cross-section provides a better picture of the new configuration's effect on the entire network.

The users participating in a pilot plan should not be performing critical roles. The users must be able to tolerate some down time, should problems occur, without unduly affecting the company's business or reputation. In addition, the users you select should have temperaments that enable them to deal with problems without panic or hysterics.

Training Users and Support Staff

Your pilot plan should specify the training your selected users need to work with the new configuration. For a pilot deployment of new security parameters, the user training might consist of nothing more than a new logon procedure, but if you are deploying new applications or operating systems, more extensive training might be necessary. You can treat the user training as a dry run for the enterprise-wide deployment that is to follow, so the pilot program should include a complete training plan, including a curriculum, and identifying who will be performing the training and when.

Providing Technical Support

Because problems are likely to occur during a pilot deployment, your plan should also specify what technical support the users will receive and who will provide it. Depending on the nature of the deployment, you might want to have your regular help desk staff handle the pilot users' problems, or you might want to assemble a support staff specifically for the pilot project. If you choose the latter, you must create an entirely separate support network and inform the users how to report problems and to whom. As with the users, you might have to provide additional training for your support personnel if you are introducing new technologies in the pilot deployment.

The support staff for the pilot deployment must have protocols in place for rapidly escalating problems, particularly those that point to problems with the new technologies you are deploying. If serious problems occur, it might become necessary to abort the pilot deployment and return the network to its original configuration.

Creating a Rollback Procedure

Because of the limited scope of the pilot deployment, any problems that occur as a result of undiscovered incompatibilities or misconfigurations will not be widespread and should not have a serious effect on network productivity. However, you should always have a rollback procedure as part of your pilot deployment plan so that you can return to your original network configuration if serious problems arise that demand further development and testing. Your plan should include detailed procedures for the rollback, plus specific conditions under which the rollback should occur.

See Also One of the best ways to implement a rollback strategy is to create a rollback security template using the Secedit.exe utility. For more information on using this tool, see Lesson 3 of this chapter.

Lesson Review

The following questions are intended to reinforce key information presented in this lesson. If you are unable to answer a question, review the lesson materials and try the question again. You can find answers to the questions in the "Questions and Answers" section at the end of this chapter.

1. What are the two main reasons for creating test cases with specific step-by-step testing procedures?

_____

_____

2. How does a pilot deployment differ from a lab testing program?

_____

_____

3. What is the function of a rollback procedure in a pilot deployment?

_____

_____

Lesson Summary

- Testing is an essential part of any security configuration deployment. A proper testing program consists of two main phases: lab testing and a pilot deployment.

- A testing lab is defined as a network that is isolated from the organization's production network and is used to test specific network elements.

- A testing plan consists of individual test cases. A test case is a detailed procedure that fully tests a particular feature or setting.

- A pilot deployment is the introduction of technologies or configuration parameters that have already been tested in a lab onto a live production network on a limited basis.

- A pilot deployment plan specifies which users will participate in the deployment and how the users will be supported, and it should include a rollback plan in the event that serious problems occur.

Case Scenario Exercise

You are the network infrastructure design specialist for Litware Inc., a manufacturer of specialized scientific software products, and you have already created a basic network design for the company's new office building. You are currently in the process of designing a security infrastructure for the company's computers that run Windows Server 2003.

Unbeknownst to you, the IT director at the home office has engaged a consulting firm to create a security configuration for all the company's Windows Server 2003 servers. Based on the requirements supplied by the home office, the consultants have supplied you with a series of security templates to implement their configurations for various server roles. Based on this information, answer the following questions.

1. After receiving the security templates from the consultant, you examine one of them by creating a new database in the Security Configuration And Analysis snap-in on one of your Web servers, importing the new security template into the database, and performing an analysis. While examining the results of the analysis, you notice there are quite a few discrepancies between the security settings you have configured on the computer and the settings in the template. You decide that you want to use a combination of the settings in the template and the settings you have already configured on the computer. Which of the following procedures should you use to create a composite security configuration and implement it on all your Web servers?

   a. In the new database you created, modify the values of the policies corresponding to the template settings you want to use. Then export the database to a new template and apply it to the Web servers' organizational unit.

   b. In the new database you created, modify the values of the policies corresponding to the current computer settings you want to use. Then export the database to a new template and apply it to the Web servers' organizational unit.

   c. Export the database to a new template without making any changes, and apply it to the Web servers' organizational unit.

   d. Use the Secedit.exe program to apply only the individual policy settings from the template you want to use on the Web servers.

2. Which of the following tools can you use to compare the templates supplied by the consultant with the security configurations you have already created on your servers? (Choose all that apply.)

   a. The Security Templates snap-in

   b. Secedit.exe

   c. The Security Configuration And Analysis snap-in

   d. The Group Policy Object Editor console

3. To deploy the security templates, you begin by creating an organizational unit object for each server role in your Active Directory tree. Which of the following procedures can you use to apply the security templates to the organizational units?

   a. Use the Security Templates snap-in to create Group Policy Objects for each organizational unit using the supplied templates.

   b. Apply the templates to the correct organizational units using the Security Configuration And Analysis snap-in.

   c. Use Secedit.exe to apply the security templates to the appropriate Group Policy Objects.

   d. Create a Group Policy Object for each organizational unit, and apply the appropriate template to it using the Group Policy Object Editor console.

Troubleshooting Lab

1. A user calls your company's network help desk to report that she has just sent a large print job to her departmental print server by mistake and wants to delete it from the print queue. However, when she tries to access the queue, she receives the error message "Unable to connect. Access denied." You log on from your workstation with the user's account and are able to access the print queue in the normal manner. Which of the following could be the problem?

   a. The Microsoft Network Server: Digitally Sign Communications (Always) security option is enabled on the print server.

   b. The Microsoft Network Server: Digitally Sign Communications (Always) security option is enabled on the user's workstation.

   c. The Microsoft Network Client: Digitally Sign Communications (Always) security option is enabled on the print server.

   d. The Microsoft Network Client: Digitally Sign Communications (Always) security option is enabled on the user's workstation.

2. In an effort to cooperate with your company's new emphasis on security, you have used GPOs to enable all the available audit policies on the computers that are running Windows Server 2003. A few days after making these changes, you unlock the data center one morning to find that your domain controller shut down during the night. Which of the following modifications might prevent this from happening again? (Choose all that apply.)

   a. Revoke the Administrators group's Debug Programs user right.

   b. Increase the default value specified in the Maximum Security Log Size policy.

   c. Disable the Shutdown: Allow System To Be Shut Down Without Having To Log In security option.

   d. Disable the Audit: Shut Down System Immediately If Unable To Log Security Audits security option.

3. The director of IT for a growing company plans to install three new Windows Server 2003 domain controllers on the network, so she assigns each of the three new network administrators who have recently joined the firm the task of installing one of the new servers. She gives each of the administrators a worksheet containing the information they need to perform the installation, including the proper domain names and IP addresses. She also informs them that all the domain controllers on the company network must use the Hisecdc.inf security template included with Windows Server 2003, but with several key changes to certain security policies, which she supplies to them as a printed list of policies and their new values.

The three administrators, Tom, Dick, and Harry, each go off to perform their tasks separately. They proceed as follows:

❑ Tom opens the Security Configuration And Analysis snap-in on his domain controller, creates a new database, and imports the Hisecdc.inf security template into it. After performing an analysis using the snap-in, Tom opens each policy on the list of changes the director has given him and modifies it to the value on the list.

❑ Dick uses the Security Templates snap-in to create a new template containing the settings on the list of changes the director has given him. Then he creates two Group Policy Objects, links them both to the Domain Controllers organizational unit in Active Directory, and applies the templates to the Group Policy Objects, Hisecdc.inf to the first one and the new template he created to the second.

❑ Harry uses the Security Templates snap-in to modify the Hisecdc.inf template by changing the policies on the list of changes to the values specified on the list. Then he uses the Secedit.exe utility to apply the modified template to the domain controller.

Based on this information, which of the following statements is true?

a. None of the three administrators has correctly configured the new domain controllers with the appropriate security settings.

b. One of the three domain controllers is correctly configured with the appropriate security settings; the other two are not.

c. Two of the three domain controllers are correctly configured with the appropriate security settings; the other one is not.

d. All three of the new domain controllers are correctly configured with the appropriate security settings.

Chapter Summary

■ Windows Server 2003 provides administrators the ability to configure server security settings using Group Policy and security templates.

■ The Default Domain Policy determines password, account lockout, and Kerberos policies for all accounts in the Active Directory domain.

■ The domain controller role is the only one that has its own default GPO assigned by Windows Server 2003. To create your own policy settings for domain controllers, you can modify the Default Domain Controllers Policy or create a new GPO linked to the Domain Controllers OU.

- You can create a baseline security configuration in a GPO directly, or import a security template into a GPO. Link the baseline security GPO to OUs in which member servers' computer objects exist.

- You can apply role-specific security configurations using separate GPOs for each role. The settings in those GPOs can be configured using the Group Policy Object Editor or by importing a security template.

- Security templates are .inf files that contain security configuration settings. They can be applied to a computer using group policies, the Security Configuration And Analysis snap-in, or the Secedit.exe utility. The Security Templates snap-in allows you to create and modify security templates.

- Windows Server 2003 includes a number of predefined templates that enable you to restore the default security parameters created by the Windows installation program and to implement secure and highly secure configurations for workstations, member servers, and domain controllers.

- A security design team typically determines what resources need protection, identifies the threats to those resources, and specifies what mechanisms the organization will use to protect the resources. Security mechanisms can include authentication, access control, encryption, firewalls, and auditing.

- A proper testing program for a security configuration consists of two main phases: lab testing and a pilot deployment.

Exam Highlights

Before taking the exam, review the following key points and terms to help you identify topics you need to review. Return to the lessons for additional practice, and review the "Further Reading" sections in Part 2 for pointers to more information about topics covering the exam objectives.

Key Points

- To create a secure baseline installation for computers that are running Windows Server 2003, you can use Group Policy Objects (GPOs) to deploy a wide variety of configuration settings.

- Servers on a network usually perform specific roles that have their own security requirements. You can accommodate these roles by creating GPOs that build on your secure baseline.

- Different server roles can require modifications to the baseline policy settings, new policy settings, or protection provided by other security features in the operating system or application.

- You can apply multiple GPOs to a single Active Directory object, with the policy settings that the system applies last taking precedence.

- Using the Security Configuration And Analysis snap-in and a security template, you can analyze a computer to determine whether any of its security settings have been changed, and then, if necessary, apply the template to the computer to restore the modified parameters to their correct settings.

- Secedit.exe enables you to apply all or part of a template to a computer from the command line. You can therefore integrate Secedit commands into scripts to perform unattended system configurations.

Key Terms

Infrastructure server   A server that provides network support services, such as DNS, DHCP, and WINS.

Pilot deployment   The implementation of a tested configuration on a representative portion of a live production network. A pilot deployment enables you to test a configuration under real-world conditions with actual users, before you perform a general deployment on the entire network.

Rollback procedure   In the event that severe problems occur during a pilot deployment, you should always be prepared to roll your systems back to their original configuration. Before you begin the deployment, you should have a rollback procedure in place to make this possible.

Security template   A security template is a collection of configuration settings stored as a text file with an .inf extension. You can deploy templates in a variety of ways on multiple computers.

Questions and Answers

Page
9-22

Lesson 1 Review

1. Which of the following audit policies enables you to tell what applications were running when a security event occurred?

    a. Audit Object Access

    b. Audit Privilege Use

    c. Audit Process Tracking

    d. Audit System Events

    c

2. Under what conditions can you not revoke the Debug Programs right from all users and groups?

    When software developers are working with debugging tools on your network.

3. Which of the following tasks can users not perform when you enable the Security Options policy, Microsoft Network Server: Digitally Sign Communications (Always) on a computer running Windows Server 2003?

    a. Submit jobs to a print queue on the server

    b. View the print queues on the server

    c. Install printer drivers stored on the server

    d. Create printer shares on the server

    b

4. Enabling which of the following audit policies is likely to require changing the Maximum Security Log Size value as well?

    a. Audit Process Tracking

    b. Audit Policy Change

    c. Audit Account Logon Events

    d. Audit Directory Service Access

    a

Lesson 2 Review

1. After installing several member servers running Windows Server 2003 on your Active Directory network, you want to deploy a baseline security configuration that you have designed for the member servers only, using group policies. Which of the following tasks must you perform to accomplish this objective? (Choose all that apply.)

   a. Create a new domain.

   b. Create a new organizational unit.

   c. Move the computer objects representing the member servers.

   d. Create a new GPO.

   e. Modify the domain GPO.

   f. Link a GPO to the Computers container.

   g. Link a GPO to an organizational unit.

   b, c, d, and g

2. In the GPO for the contoso.com domain, you define the Audit Account Logon Events policy by specifying that both successes and failures be audited. In the GPO for the Sales OU, you leave the Audit Account Logon Events policy undefined. What will be the effective setting for this policy for a computer in the Sales OU?

   The policy will be defined specifying that both successes and failures are audited.

3. Although Windows Server 2003 creates a GPO for the Domain Controllers container with default role-specific policy settings in it, you have other policy settings you want to apply to your domain controllers. Which of the following methods can you use to apply these settings? (Choose all that apply.)

   a. Modify the policy settings in the Domain Controllers container's existing GPO.

   b. Create a new organizational unit object and create a GPO for it containing the desired policy settings. Then move the Domain Controllers container to make it a child of the new object.

   c. Create a second GPO for the Domain Controllers container.

   d. Create a new child organizational unit object beneath the Domain Controllers container object, and then create a GPO for the new object containing the desired policy settings.

   a and c

4. When creating a GPO for an organizational unit named Servers, you define a particular audit policy and configure it to audit successes only. When creating a GPO for an organizational unit named Infrastructure, which is a child of the Servers organizational unit, you configure the same policy to audit failures only. What is the effective value of that policy for a computer object in the Infrastructure container?

    a. Undefined

    b. Success only

    c. Failure only

    d. Success and Failure

c

Page
9-54

Lesson 3 Review

1. You are the new administrator for an Active Directory network, and while it is clear that someone has changed the security configuration of the network's domain controllers, your predecessor left no records of the exact changes he made. Which of the following security templates should you apply to the domain controllers to restore their default security settings and then implement the highest possible level of security?

    a. Compatws.inf and then Securedc.inf

    b. Securedc.inf and then Hisecdc.inf

    c. Hisecdc.inf and then Setup Security.inf

    d. DC Security.inf and then Hisecdc.inf

    e. Setup Security.inf and then Securedc.inf

d

2. Why should you not use group policies to apply the Setup Security.inf template to a computer?

Because the template contains a large number of file-system and registry permissions, and the repeated refreshing of the group policy would generate a large amount of Active Directory traffic.

3. What are the three ways to apply a security template to a computer running a Windows operating system?

Group policies, the Security Configuration And Analysis snap-in, and the Secedit.exe command-line utility.

4. Why is it not common practice to apply security templates to Active Directory domain objects?

   Because a security template applied to a domain object confers its settings on all the computers in the domain, and it is rare for computers performing different roles to use exactly the same security settings.

5. Name two security template deployment tasks that the Secedit.exe utility can perform which group policies and the Security Configuration And Analysis snap-in cannot.

   Apply just a part of a security template to a computer and perform unattended template deployments by using scripts or batch files.

6. When you use the Security Configuration And Analysis snap-in to export a template, where do the settings in the new template come from?

   a. From the computer's current security settings

   b. From the snap-in's currently loaded database

   c. From the security template you imported into the database

   d. From a Group Policy Object you specify

   b

7. You would like to apply a new Registry setting to all the servers on your network. What is an efficient way to perform that task?

   Any Registry value can be added to a security template Inf file using Notepad. It should be added to the [Registry Values] section. The next time the template is applied, the Registry setting will be changed. You can write batch scripts to apply the template to multiple machines, or you can import the template into Group Policy.

8. Which of the following settings can be applied using Security Configuration And Analysis and a security template? (Choose all that apply.)

   a. The password must be 15 characters long.

   b. The Accountants group is not allowed to access this computer over the network.

   c. IPSec must be used for all communications between Computer1 and Computer2.

   d. The root file permissions should be Everyone Full Control.

   a, b, d

9. Which steps might be necessary to recover from the application of a security template to a file server that prevented all users from accessing the server over the network? Choose the most efficient way.

    a. Log on locally to the file server as Administrator, and apply the root security template.

    b. Log on locally to the file server as Administrator, and apply the rollback template produced from the bad security template.

    c. Log on remotely to the file server as Enterprise Admin, and use the Local Security Policy console to change the user rights policies that might be incorrect.

    d. Log on remotely to the file server as Administrator, and apply the rollback template produced from the security template.

b

Page 9-62

Lesson 4 Review

1. List the three phases of a security life cycle.

Design, implementation, and management

2. Which of the following Windows Server 2003 features can you use to ensure that users supply passwords of a specified length?

    a. Audit policies

    b. Group policies

    c. Authentication protocols

    d. Access control lists

b

3. List three tasks that a security design team typically performs.

Determine the resources to protect, identify threats to those resources, and specify how to protect the resources.

Page 9-70

Lesson 5 Review

1. What are the two main reasons for creating test cases with specific step-by-step testing procedures?

    ❑ To make it possible to repeat the tests exactly the same way

    ❑ To enable any user to perform the tests

2. How does a pilot deployment differ from a lab testing program?

A pilot deployment is conducted on a live network using actual users performing their daily tasks in the usual manner.

3. What is the function of a rollback procedure in a pilot deployment?

A rollback procedure enables you to abort the pilot deployment and return the network to its original configuration.

Page
9-71

Case Scenario Exercise

1. After receiving the security templates from the consultant, you examine one of them by creating a new database in the Security Configuration And Analysis snap-in on one of your Web servers, importing the new security template into the database, and performing an analysis. While examining the results of the analysis, you notice there are quite a few discrepancies between the security settings you have configured on the computer and the settings in the template. You decide that you want to use a combination of the settings in the template and the settings you have already configured on the computer. Which of the following procedures should you use to create a composite security configuration and implement it on all your Web servers?

a. In the new database you created, modify the values of the policies corresponding to the template settings you want to use. Then export the database to a new template and apply it to the Web servers' organizational unit.

b. In the new database you created, modify the values of the policies corresponding to the current computer settings you want to use. Then export the database to a new template and apply it to the Web servers' organizational unit.

c. Export the database to a new template without making any changes, and apply it to the Web servers' organizational unit.

d. Use the Secedit.exe program to apply only the individual policy settings from the template you want to use on the Web servers.

b

2. Which of the following tools can you use to compare the templates supplied by the consultant with the security configurations you have already created on your servers? (Choose all that apply.)

a. The Security Templates snap-in

b. Secedit.exe

c. The Security Configuration And Analysis snap-in

d. The Group Policy Object Editor console

b and c

3. To deploy the security templates, you begin by creating an organizational unit object for each server role in your Active Directory tree. Which of the following procedures can you use to apply the security templates to the organizational units?

   a. Use the Security Templates snap-in to create Group Policy Objects for each organizational unit using the supplied templates.

   b. Apply the templates to the correct organizational units using the Security Configuration And Analysis snap-in.

   c. Use Secedit.exe to apply the security templates to the appropriate Group Policy Objects.

   d. Create a Group Policy Object for each organizational unit, and apply the appropriate template to it using the Group Policy Object Editor console.

   d

Page
9-72

Troubleshooting Lab

1. A user calls your company's network help desk to report that she has just sent a large print job to her departmental print server by mistake and wants to delete it from the print queue. However, when she tries to access the queue, she receives the error message "Unable to connect. Access denied." You log on from your workstation with the user's account and are able to access the print queue in the normal manner. Which of the following could be the problem?

   a. The Microsoft Network Server: Digitally Sign Communications (Always) security option is enabled on the print server.

   b. The Microsoft Network Server: Digitally Sign Communications (Always) security option is enabled on the user's workstation.

   c. The Microsoft Network Client: Digitally Sign Communications (Always) security option is enabled on the print server.

   d. The Microsoft Network Client: Digitally Sign Communications (Always) security option is enabled on the user's workstation.

   d

2. In an effort to cooperate with your company's new emphasis on security, you have used GPOs to enable all the available audit policies on the computers that are running Windows Server 2003. A few days after making these changes, you unlock the data center one morning to find that your domain controller shut down during the night. Which of the following modifications might prevent this from happening again? (Choose all that apply.)

    a. Revoke the Administrators group's Debug Programs user right.

    b. Increase the default value specified in the Maximum Security Log Size policy.

    c. Disable the Shutdown: Allow System To Be Shut Down Without Having To Log In security option.

    d. Disable the Audit: Shut Down System Immediately If Unable To Log Security Audits security option.

b and d

3. The director of IT for a growing company plans to install three new Windows Server 2003 domain controllers on the network, so she assigns each of the three new network administrators who have recently joined the firm the task of installing one of the new servers. She gives each of the administrators a worksheet containing the information they need to perform the installation, including the proper domain names and IP addresses. She also informs them that all the domain controllers on the company network must use the Hisecdc.inf security template included with Windows Server 2003, but with several key changes to certain security policies, which she supplies to them as a printed list of policies and their new values.

The three administrators, Tom, Dick, and Harry, each go off to perform their tasks separately. They proceed as follows:

    ❑ Tom opens the Security Configuration And Analysis snap-in on his domain controller, creates a new database, and imports the Hisecdc.inf security template into it. After performing an analysis using the snap-in, Tom opens each policy on the list of changes the director has given him and modifies it to the value on the list.

    ❑ Dick uses the Security Templates snap-in to create a new template containing the settings on the list of changes the director has given him. Then he creates two Group Policy Objects, links them both to the Domain Controllers organizational unit in Active Directory, and applies the templates to the Group Policy Objects, Hisecdc.inf to the first one and the new template he created to the second.

❑ Harry uses the Security Templates snap-in to modify the Hisecdc.inf template by changing the policies on the list of changes to the values specified on the list. Then he uses the Secedit.exe utility to apply the modified template to the domain controller.

Based on this information, which of the following statements is true?

a. None of the three administrators has correctly configured the new domain controllers with the appropriate security settings.

b. One of the three domain controllers is correctly configured with the appropriate security settings; the other two are not.

c. Two of the three domain controllers are correctly configured with the appropriate security settings; the other one is not.

d. All three of the new domain controllers are correctly configured with the appropriate security settings.

c

10 Managing and Maintaining a Server Environment

Exam Objectives in this Chapter:

- Troubleshoot Terminal Services (Exam 70-292).
  - Diagnose and resolve issues related to Terminal Services security.
  - Diagnose and resolve issues related to client access to Terminal Services.
- Manage software update infrastructure (Exam 70-292).
- Manage servers remotely (Exam 70-292).
  - Manage a server by using Remote Assistance.
  - Manage a server by using Terminal Services remote administration mode.
  - Manage a server by using available support tools.
- Manage a Web server (Exam 70-292).
  - Manage Internet Information Services (IIS).
  - Manage security for IIS.
- Plan secure network administration methods (Exam 70-296).
  - Create a plan to offer Remote Assistance to client computers.
  - Plan for remote administration using Terminal Services.
- Install and configure a software update infrastructure (Exam 70-292).
  - Install and configure software update services.
  - Install and configure automatic client update settings.
  - Configure software updates on earlier operating systems.

Why This Chapter Matters

Microsoft Windows Server 2003 provides enormous functionality, both for the enterprise and for the administrator. In this chapter, you will explore some technologies that will enable you to manage and maintain servers more effectively, including remote administration using Microsoft Management Console (MMC) snap-ins, Web Interface For Remote Administration, Remote Desktop For Administration, and Remote Assistance. You will also learn about three of the most valuable roles that Windows Server 2003 can play: Terminal Server, which provides applications in a multiuser environment; Internet Information Services (IIS), to support Web-based deployment of data and applications; and Software Update Services, a new technology that enables you to centralize the application of security updates and critical patches to the computers in your environment.

Lessons in this Chapter:

Before You Begin

To perform the practices related to the objectives in this chapter, you must have

- Two Windows Server 2003 (Standard or Enterprise Edition) systems installed as Server01 and Server02, respectively. Server01 should be a domain controller in the contoso.com domain. Server02 should be a member server in contoso.com.

- Access to both servers with administrative credentials.

Lesson 1: Remote Administration of Windows Server 2003

In a medium- to large-scale enterprise or in a secure environment, you won't likely be administering servers by logging on at the local console. Instead, you will be managing servers—and desktops for that matter—remotely. Windows Server 2003 provides a number of powerful options for remote administration, including Microsoft Management Console snap-ins (which can connect to remote systems), Web Interface for Remote Administration, Remote Desktop For Administration, and Remote Assistance. In this lesson, you will learn about each of these methods for remote administration.

After this lesson, you will be able to

- Construct an MMC to manage a computer remotely
- Configure a server to enable Remote Desktop For Administration
- Assign users to the appropriate group to allow them to administer servers remotely
- Connect to a server using Remote Desktop Connection
- Enable a computer to accept requests for Remote Assistance
- Use one of the available methods to request and establish a Remote Assistance session

Estimated lesson time: 30 minutes

The Microsoft Management Console

The administrative framework of Windows Server 2003 is the MMC. The MMC provides a standardized, common interface for one or more tools, called *snap-ins*, that are specialized for individual tasks. The default administrative tools in Windows Server 2003 are MMC consoles with one or more snap-ins suited to a specific purpose. The Active Directory Users And Computers administrative tool, for example, is an MMC console with the Active Directory Users And Computers snap-in.

The MMC provides a two-paned framework consisting of a tree pane, also called a *scope pane*, and a details pane. The MMC menus and a toolbar provide commands for manipulating the parent and child windows, snap-ins, and the console itself.

Navigating the MMC

An empty MMC is shown in Figure 10-1. Note that the console has a name and that there is a Console Root. This Console Root will contain any snap-ins you choose to include.

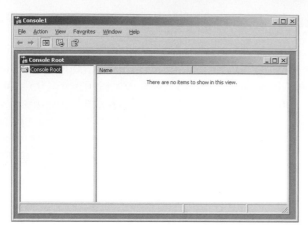

Figure 10-1 An empty MMC

Each console includes a console tree, a console menu and toolbars, and the details pane. The contents of these will vary, depending on the design and features of the snap-in use. Figure 10-2 shows a populated MMC with two snap-ins loaded, and a child window of the Device Manager snap-in.

Figure 10-2 A populated MMC

Using the MMC Menus and Toolbar

Although each snap-in will add its unique menu and toolbar items, in many situations you will use several key menus and commands that are common to most snap-ins, as shown in Table 10-1.

Table 10-1   Common MMC Menus and Commands

Menu	Commands
File	Create a new console, open an existing console, add or remove snap-ins from a console, set options for saving a console, open recently used consoles, and an exit command
Action	Varies by snap-in, but generally includes export, output, configuration, and help features specific to the snap-in
View	Varies by snap-in, but includes an option to customize general console characteristics
Favorites	Allows for adding and organizing saved consoles
Window	Open a new window, cascade, tile, and switch between open child windows in this console
Help	General help menu for the MMC as well as loaded snap-in help modules

Extending the MMC with Snap-Ins

A snap-in extends the MMC by adding specific management capability and functionality. There are two types of snap-ins: stand-alone and extension.

- **Stand-Alone Snap-Ins**   Stand-alone snap-ins are provided by the developer of an application. All Administrative Tools for Windows Server 2003, for example, are either single snap-in consoles or preconfigured combinations of snap-ins useful to a particular category of tasks. The Computer Management snap-in, for example, is a collection of individual snap-ins useful to a unit.

- **Extension Snap-Ins**   Extension snap-ins, or extensions, are designed to work with one or more stand-alone snap-ins, based on the functionality of the stand-alone. When you add an extension, Windows Server 2003 places the extension into the appropriate location within the stand-alone snap-in.

Many snap-ins offer stand-alone functionality and extend the functionality of other snap-ins. For example, the Event Viewer snap-in reads the event logs of computers. If the Computer Management object exists in the console, Event Viewer automatically extends each instance of a Computer Management object and provides the event logs for the computer. Alternatively, the Event Viewer can also operate in stand-alone mode, in which case, it does not appear as a node below the Computer Management node.

Off the Record   Spend a few minutes analyzing your daily tasks, and group them by type of function and frequency of use. Build two or three customized consoles that contain the tools you use most often. You will save quite a bit of time not needing to open, switch among, and close tools as often.

Building a Customized MMC

You can combine one or more snap-ins or parts of snap-ins to create customized MMCs, which can then be used to centralize and combine administrative tasks. Although you can use many of the preconfigured consoles for administrative tasks, customized consoles allow for individualization to your needs and standardization within your environment.

Tip   By creating a custom MMC, you do not have to switch between different programs or individual consoles.

To create a customized MMC console:

1. Click Start, and then click Run.

2. In the Open text box, type **mmc** and then click OK.

3. From the File menu, click Add/Remove Snap-In.

   The Add/Remove Snap-In dialog box appears with the Standalone tab active. Notice that there are no snap-ins loaded.

4. In the Add/Remove Snap-In dialog box, click Add to display the Add Standalone Snap-In dialog box.

5. Locate the snap-in you want to add, and then click Add

6. Many snap-ins present a dialog box such as that shown in Figure 10-3. You can choose to focus the snap-in on the Local Computer or on Another Computer on the network. After selecting the computer, click Finish.

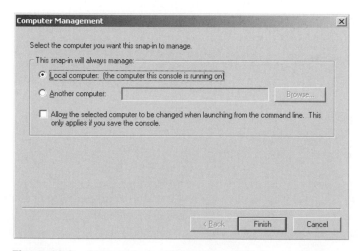

Figure 10-3   Setting the local/remote context for a snap-in

Exam Tip   By building a customized MMC and adding snap-ins focused on other computers, you can create administrative tools with the inherent ability to administer remote systems.

7. In the Add Standalone Snap-In dialog box, click Close, and then in the Add/ Remove Snap-Ins dialog box, click OK.

8. The snap-in now appears in the console tree.

9. To save the customized MMC, from the File menu, choose Save.

Console Options

Console options determine how an MMC operates in terms of what nodes in the console tree can be opened, what snap-ins can be added, and what windows can be created. Console options are specified in the Options dialog box, which can be opened by clicking Options on the File menu.

Author Mode   When you save a console in Author mode, which is the default, you enable full access to all of the MMC functionality, including:

■ Adding or removing snap-ins

■ Creating windows

■ Creating taskpad views and tasks

■ Viewing portions of the console tree

■ Changing the options on the console

■ Saving the console

User Modes   If you plan to distribute an MMC with specific functions, you can set the desired user mode and then save the console. By default, consoles will be saved in the Administrative Tools folder in the users' profile. Table 10-2 describes the user modes that are available for saving the MMC.

Table 10-2   MMC User Modes

Type of user mode	Description
Full Access	Allows users to navigate between snap-ins and open windows, and to access all portions of the console tree
Limited Access, Multiple Windows	Prevents users from opening new windows or accessing a portion of the console tree, but allows them to view multiple windows in the console
Limited Access, Single Window	Prevents users from opening new windows or accessing a portion of the console tree, and allows them to view only one window in the console

> **Note** MMCs, when saved, have an *.msc extension. Active Directory Users And Comput-
> ers, for example, is named Dsa.msc (Directory Services Administrator).

Remote Administration with the MMC

Earlier in this lesson, you learned that you can build a customized MMC console with snap-ins that are focused on remote computers. In addition, many snap-ins allow you to change the focus of the snap-in by right-clicking the snap-in in the scope pane and choosing a command such as Connect To Another Computer, Connect To Domain, Connect To Domain Controller, and so forth. When you do so, you connect using Remote Procedure Call (RPC).

To connect to and manage another system using MMC snap-ins, you must launch the console with an account that has sufficient credentials on the remote computer. If your credentials do not have sufficient privileges on the target computer, snap-ins will load, but they either will function in read-only mode or will not display any information.

> **Tip** You can use Run As, or secondary logon, to launch a console with credentials other
> than those with which you are currently logged on.

The Computer Management console, for example, allows you to connect to a remote computer. After doing so, all the extensions and snap-ins that are part of the Computer Management console are available as you remotely administer the computer.

To remotely administer a computer with the Computer Management console:

1. Open the Computer Management console by clicking Start, right-clicking My Computer, and choosing Manage from the shortcut menu.

2. Right-click Computer Management in the tree pane, and choose Connect To Another Computer.

3. In the following dialog box, type the name or IP address of the computer or browse the network for it and then click OK to connect.

Once connected, you can perform administrative tasks on the remote computer.

Web Interface for Remote Administration

The Web Interface for Remote Administration enables you to manage a server using a Web browser on a remote computer, as shown in Figure 10-4. It is installed by default on Windows Server 2003, Web Edition, and cannot be installed on a domain controller.

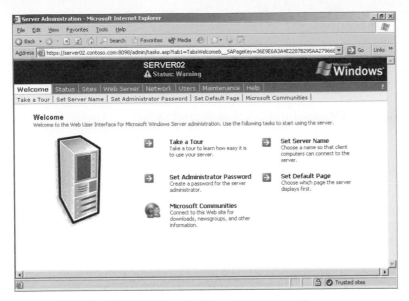

Figure 10-4   The Web Interface for Remote Administration

To install Web Interface for Remote Administration on all other servers:

1. Open Add Or Remove Programs from Control Panel.

2. Click Add/Remove Windows Components.

3. In the Windows Components Wizard, select Application Server. (Do not click the check box.)

4. Click Details.

5. Select Internet Information Services (IIS). (Do not click the check box.)

6. Click Details.

7. Select World Wide Web Service. (Do not click the check box.)

8. Click Details.

9. Select the Remote Administration (HTML) check box.

10. Click OK in the three open dialog boxes, and then click Next in the Windows Components Wizard. During installation, you'll be asked to insert your Windows Server 2003 CD.

To administer a server using Web Interface for Remote Administration, open Internet Explorer (version 6.0 or greater is recommended) and navigate to https://*Computer-Name*:8098.

Managing Servers with Remote Desktop For Administration

The Windows 2000 Server family introduced a tightly integrated suite of tools and technologies that enabled Terminal Services for both remote administration and application sharing. The evolution has continued: Terminal Services is now an integral, default component of the Windows Server 2003 family, and Remote Desktop For Administration has been improved and positioned as an out-of-the-box capability so that, with one click, a Windows Server 2003 computer will allow two concurrent connections for remote administration. By adding the Terminal Server component and configuring appropriate licensing, an administrator can further extend the technologies to allow multiple users to run applications on the server.

Enabling and Configuring Remote Desktop For Administration

The Terminal Services service enables Remote Desktop For Administration, Remote Assistance, and Terminal Server for application sharing. The service is installed by default on Windows Server 2003 and configured to support Remote Desktop For Administration. Remote Desktop For Administration allows only two concurrent remote connections and does not include the application-sharing components of Terminal Server. Therefore, Remote Desktop For Administration operates with very little overhead on the system and with no additional licensing requirements.

> **Note**   Because Terminal Services and its dependent Remote Desktop For Administration are default components of Windows Server 2003, every server has the capability to provide remote connections to its console. The term *terminal server*, therefore, now refers specifically to a Windows Server 2003 computer that provides application sharing to multiple users through the addition of the Terminal Server component. Terminal Server is discussed in Lesson 2.

Other components—Terminal Server and the Terminal Server Licensing service—must be added using Add Or Remove Programs. However, all administrative tools required to configure and support client connections and to manage Terminal Server are installed by default on every Windows Server 2003 computer. All of the tools and their functions are described in Table 10-3.

To enable Remote Desktop connections on a Windows Server 2003 computer, open the System properties from Control Panel. On the Remote tab, select Allow Users To Connect Remotely To This Computer.

Table 10-3   Default Components of Terminal Server and Remote Desktop For Administration

Installed software	Purpose
Terminal Services Configuration	Setting properties on the Terminal Server, including session, network, client desktop, and client remote control settings.
Terminal Services Manager	Sending messages to connected Terminal Server clients, disconnecting or logging off sessions, and establishing remote control or shadowing of sessions.
Remote Desktop Connection Installation Files	Installation of the Windows Server 2003 or Windows XP Remote Desktop Connection application. The 32-bit Remote Desktop Connection client software is installed in *%Systemroot%*\System32\Clients\Tsclient\Win32 of the Terminal Server.
Terminal Services Licensing	Configuration of licenses for client connections to a terminal server. This tool is not applicable for environments that utilize only Remote Desktop For Administration.

> **Note**   If the Terminal Server is a domain controller, you must also configure the Group Policy on the domain controller to Allow Logon Through Terminal Services to the Remote Desktop Users group. By default, Non-Domain Controller servers will allow Terminal Services connections by this group.

Remote Desktop Connection

Remote Desktop Connection is the client-side software used to connect to a server in the context of either Remote Desktop For Administration or Terminal Server modes. There is no functional difference from the client perspective between Remote Desktop For Administration and Terminal Server.

On Microsoft Windows XP and Windows Server 2003 computers, Remote Desktop Connection is installed by default, although it is not easy to find in its default location in the All Programs\Accessories\Communications program group on the Start menu.

For other platforms, Remote Desktop Connection can be installed from the Windows Server 2003 CD or from the client installation folder (*%Systemroot%*\System32\Clients\Tsclient\Win32) on any Windows Server 2003 computer. The .msi-based Remote Desktop Connection installation package can be distributed to Windows 2000 systems using Group Policy or SMS.

> **Tip**   It is recommended that you update previous versions of the Terminal Services Client to the latest version of Remote Desktop Connection. Doing so will provide the most efficient, secure, and stable environment possible, through improvements such as a revised user interface, 128-bit encryption, and alternate-port selection.

Figure 10-5 shows the expanded Remote Desktop Connection configured to connect to Server01 in the contoso.com domain.

Figure 10-5   Remote Desktop Connection

Configuring Remote Desktop

You can control many aspects of Remote Desktop from both the client and server sides. Table 10-4 lists client-side settings and their use for each tab of Remote Desktop Connection shown in Figure 10-5.

Table 10-4   Remote Desktop Client-Side Settings

Setting	Function
General	Options for the selection of the computer to which connection should be made, the setting of static log on credentials, and the saving of settings for this connection.
Display	Controls the size of the Remote Desktop Connection window, color depth, and whether control-bar functions are available in full-screen mode.
Local Resources	Options to bring sound events to your local computer, in addition to standard mouse, keyboard, and screen output. Controls how the Windows key combinations are to be interpreted by the remote computer (for example, ALT+TAB), and whether local disk, printer, and serial port connections should be available to the remote session.

Table 10-4   Remote Desktop Client-Side Settings

Setting	Function
Programs	Sets the path and target folder for any program you want to start once the connection is made.
Experience	Categories of display functions can be enabled or disabled based on available bandwidth between the remote and local computers. Items include showing desktop background, showing the contents of the window while dragging, menu and window animation, themes, and whether bitmap caching should be enabled. (This transmits only the changes in the screen rather than repainting the entire screen with each refresh period.)

The Terminal Services Configuration console in the Administrative Tools folder allows you to configure the server-side settings of Remote Desktop. Figure 10-6 shows the RDP-Tcp Properties dialog box in the Terminal Services Configuration console.

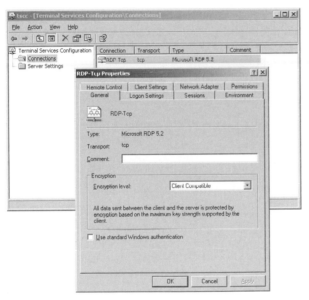

Figure 10-6   RDP-Tcp Properties dialog box to configure server-side settings of Remote Desktop

Table 10-5 lists server-side settings and their use for each tab of the RDP-Tcp Properties dialog box shown in Figure 10-6.

Table 10-5   Remote Desktop Server-Side Settings

Setting	Function
General	Sets the encryption level and authentication mechanism for connections to the server.
Logon Settings	Allows static credentials to be set for the connection rather than using those provided by the client.
Sessions	Includes options to override client settings, including settings for ending a disconnected session, session limits and idle timeout, and reconnection allowance.
Environment	Overrides the settings from the user's profile for this connection for starting a program upon connection. Path and target settings set here override those set by the Remote Desktop Connection.
Remote Control	Specifies whether remote control of a Remote Desktop Connection session is possible, and if it is, whether the user must grant permission at the initiation of the remote control session. Additional settings can restrict the remote control session to viewing only or allow full interactivity with the Remote Desktop Connection client session.
Client Settings	Overrides settings from the client configuration, controls color depth, and disables various mappings.
Network Adapters	Specifies which network cards on the server will accept Remote Desktop For Administration connections.
Permissions	Allows additional permissions to be set on this connection.

Terminal Services Troubleshooting

When using Remote Desktop For Administration, you are creating a connection to a server's console. There are several potential causes of failed connections or problematic sessions:

- **Network failures**   Errors in standard Transmission Control Protocol/Internet Protocol (TCP/IP) networking can cause a Remote Desktop connection to fail or be interrupted. If Domain Name System (DNS) is not functioning, a client might not be able to locate the server by name. If routing is not functioning, or the Terminal Services port (by default, port 3389) is misconfigured on either the client or the server, the connection will not be established.

- **Credentials**   Users must belong to the Administrators or Remote Desktop Users group to successfully connect to the server using Remote Desktop For Administration.

Exam Tip   Watch for group membership if access is denied when establishing a Remote Desktop For Administration connection. In earlier versions of Terminal Server, you had to be a member of the Administrators group to connect to the server, although special permissions could be established manually.

- **Policy**   Domain controllers will allow connections via Remote Desktop only to administrators. You must configure the domain controller security policy to allow connections for all other remote user connections.

- **Too many concurrent connections**   If sessions have been disconnected without being logged off, the server might consider its concurrent connection limit to have been reached even though there are not two human users connected at the time. An administrator might, for example, close a remote session without logging off. If two more administrators attempt to connect to the server, only one will be allowed to connect before the limit of two concurrent connections is reached.

Exam Tip   Remote Desktop For Administration supports only two remote connections to the Terminal Server. This limit is fixed and cannot be increased.

See Also   For more information about Remote Desktop For Administration, see Help and Support Center. For the latest developments, search *http://www.microsoft.com* for "Remote Desktop."

Using Remote Assistance

Computer users, particularly users without much technical expertise, often have configuration problems or usage questions that are difficult for a friend, family member, or even a support professional to diagnose and fix over the telephone. Remote Assistance provides a way for users to get the help they need and makes it easier and less costly for corporate help desks to assist their users.

Remote Assistance is a feature of Windows XP and Windows Server 2003 that enables a user (an administrator, trainer, or technical support representative) at one location to connect to a distant user's computer, chat with the user, and either view all the user's activities or take complete control of the system.

Off the Record   In Microsoft interfaces and documentation, the person connecting to a client using Remote Assistance is referred to as an expert or a helper.

Remote Assistance can eliminate the need for administrative personnel to travel to a user's location for any of the following reasons:

- **Technical support** A system administrator or help desk operator can use Remote Assistance to connect to a remote computer to modify configuration parameters, install new software, or troubleshoot user problems.

- **Troubleshooting** By connecting in read-only mode, an expert can observe a remote user's activities and determine whether improper procedures are the source of problems the user is experiencing. The expert can also connect in interactive mode to try to re-create the problem or to modify system settings to resolve it. This is far more efficient than trying to give instructions to inexperienced users over the telephone.

- **Training** Trainers and help desk personnel can demonstrate procedures to users right on their systems, without having to travel to their locations.

Configuring Remote Assistance

To receive remote assistance, the computer running Windows Server 2003 or Windows XP must be configured to use the Remote Assistance feature in one of the following ways:

- **Using Control Panel** Display the System Properties dialog box from Control Panel, and click the Remote tab. Then select the Turn On Remote Assistance And Allow Invitations To Be Sent From This Computer check box.

> **Tip**   By clicking the Advanced button in the Remote tab in the System Properties dialog box, the user can specify whether to let the expert take control of the computer or simply view activities on the computer. The user can also specify the amount of time that the invitation for remote assistance remains valid.

- **Using Group Policies** Use the Group Policy Object Editor console to open a GPO for an Active Directory domain, site, or organizational unit object containing the client computer. Browse to the Computer Configuration\Administrative Templates\System\Remote Assistance container, and enable the Solicited Remote Assistance policy. The policy's dialog box is shown in Figure 10-7.

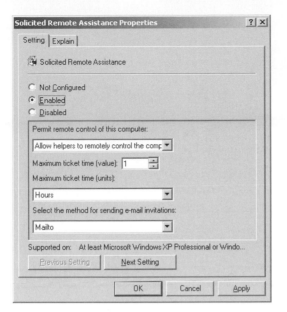

Figure 10-7   The Solicited Remote Assistance Properties dialog box

Tip   The Solicited Remote Assistance policy also enables you to specify the degree of control the expert receives over the client computer, the duration of the invitation, and the method for sending e-mail invitations.

Creating an Invitation

To receive remote assistance, a client must issue an invitation and send it to a particular expert. The client can send the invitation to the expert using Microsoft Windows Messenger or e-mail, or send it as a file. Figure 10-8 shows the screen in Help and Support Center used to invite someone for assistance.

To successfully send and use a Remote Assistance invitation through e-mail, both computers must be using a Messaging Application Programming Interface (MAPI)–compliant e-mail client.

To use the Windows Messenger service for your Remote Assistance connection, you must have the assistant's Windows Messenger user name in your contact list and the expert must be online. At that point, you can make the request from a Windows Messenger client or the Help And Support Center.

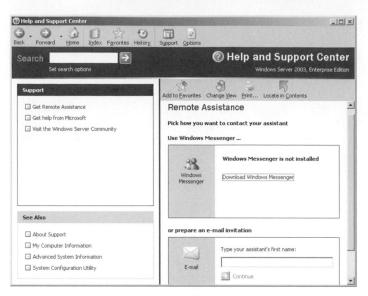

Figure 10-8   The Remote Assistance invitation screen in the Help and Support Center

Tip   When users create invitations, they can specify a password that the expert has to supply to connect to their computers. You should urge your users to always require passwords for Remote Assistance connections, and instruct them to supply the expert with the correct password using a different medium from the one they are using to send the invitation.

Accepting an Invitation

When a user initiates an invitation for Remote Assistance, the client sends an encrypted ticket based on Extensible Markup Language (XML) to the expert, who is prompted to accept the invitation. When the expert accepts the invitation, the user is prompted to confirm the Remote Assistance connection.

The Remote Assistance application, which enables the expert to connect to the remote computer, is shown in Figure 10-9. Using this interface, the user and the expert can talk or type messages to each other and, by default, the expert can see everything that the user is doing on the computer. If the client computer is configured to allow remote control, the expert can also click the Take Control button and operate the client computer interactively.

Figure 10-9   The expert's Remote Assistance interface

Offering Remote Assistance to a User

You can also configure Remote Assistance so that you can initiate troubleshooting without receiving an invitation from the user. To do this, you must enable the Offer Remote Assistance Local Group Policy setting on the target (user's) computer:

1. Open Group Policy Object Editor, and modify the target computer's local policy or a GPO that applies to the target computer.

2. Expand the Computer Configuration node, Administrative Templates, and System, and then click Remote Assistance.

3. Double-click Offer Remote Assistance, and then select Enabled.

4. Next, click Show, and then specify the individual users who will be allowed to offer assistance by assigning helpers within the context of this policy. These "helper" additions to the list should be in the form of domain\username, and must be a member of the local administrators group on the local computer.

Tip   The Offer Remote Assistance policy enables you to specify the names of users or groups that can function as experts, and whether those experts can perform tasks or just observe.

You can now initiate Remote Assistance from your computer, to a user's computer, providing that the credentials you supply match those of an expert defined in the Offer Remote Assistance policy:

1. Open the Help And Support Center, click Tools, and then click Help And Support Center Tools. Next click Offer Remote Assistance.

2. In the right pane, type the name or IP address of the target computer and then click Connect. (If prompted that several users are logged on, choose a user session.) Then click Start Remote Assistance.

    The user receives a pop-up box showing that the help-desk person is initiating a Remote Assistance session.

3. The user accepts, and Remote Assistance can proceed.

Securing Remote Assistance

Because an expert offering remote assistance to another user can perform virtually any activity on the remote computer that the local user can, this feature can be a significant security hazard. An unauthorized user who takes control of a computer using Remote Assistance can cause almost unlimited damage. However, Remote Assistance is designed to minimize the dangers. Some protective features of Remote Assistance are as follows:

Invitations No person can connect to another computer using Remote Assistance unless that person has received an invitation from the client. Clients can configure the effective lifespan of their invitations in minutes, hours, or days to prevent experts from attempting to connect to the computer later.

Interactive connectivity When an expert accepts an invitation from a client and attempts to connect to the computer, a user must be present at the client console to grant the expert access. You cannot use Remote Assistance to connect to an unattended computer.

Client-side control The client always has ultimate control over a Remote Assistance connection. The client can terminate the connection at any time by pressing the Esc key or clicking Stop Control (ESC) in the client-side Remote Assistance page.

Remote control configuration Using the System Properties dialog box or Remote Assistance group policies, users and administrators can specify whether experts are permitted to take control of client computers. An expert who has read-only access cannot modify the computer's configuration in any way using Remote Assistance. The group policies also enable administrators to grant specific users expert status so that no one else can use Remote Assistance to connect to a client computer, even with the client's permission.

Firewalls   Remote Assistance runs on top of Terminal Services technology, which means it must use the same port used by Terminal Services: port 3389. Remote Assistance will not work when outbound traffic from port 3389 is blocked. Additionally, there are several other firewall-related concerns, particularly in relation to Network Address Translation (NAT):

■ Remote Assistance supports Universal Plug and Play (UPnP) to Traverse Network Address Translation devices. This is helpful on smaller, home office networks, as Windows XP Internet Connection Sharing (ICS) supports UPnP. However, Windows 2000 ICS does *not* support UPnP.

> **Exam Tip**   Watch for questions that use Windows 2000 ICS for remote assistance from a big, corporate help desk to a small satellite office. Because Windows 2000 ICS does not support UPnP, Remote Assistance problems will abound.

■ Remote Assistance will detect the Internet IP address and TCP port number on the UPnP NAT device and insert the address into the Remote Assistance encrypted ticket. The Internet IP address and TCP port number will be used to connect through the NAT device by the helper or requester workstation to establish a Remote Assistance session. The Remote Assistance connection request will then be forwarded to the client by the NAT device.

■ Remote Assistance will not connect when the requester is behind a non-UPnP NAT device when e-mail is used to send the invitation file. When sending an invitation using Windows Messenger, a non-UPnP NAT device will work if one client is behind a NAT device. If both the helper and requester computers are behind non-UPnP NAT devices, the Remote Assistance connection will fail.

If you are using a software-based personal firewall or NAT in a home environment, you can use Remote Assistance with no special configurations. However, if you are using a hardware-based firewall in a home environment, the same restrictions apply: you must open port 3389 to use Remote Assistance.

> **Security Alert**   There are several issues to consider when managing and administering Remote Assistance in the corporate environment or large organization. You can specify an open environment in which employees can receive Remote Assistance from outside the corporate firewall, or you can restrict Remote Assistance by means of Group Policy and specify various levels of permissions, such as allowing Remote Assistance only from within the corporate firewall. Connections from outside the firewall require port 3389 to be open.

> **Note**   The Instant Messenger Service itself relies on port 1863 being open.

Practice: Remote Desktop For Administration

In this practice, you will configure Server01 to enable Remote Desktop For Administration connections. You will then optimize Server01 to ensure availability of the connection when the connection is not in use, and you will limit the number of simultaneous connections to one. You then run a remote administration session from Server02.

Exercise 1: Configuring the Server for Remote Desktop

In this exercise, you will enable Remote Desktop connections, change the number of simultaneous connections allowed to the server, and configure the disconnection settings for the connection.

1. Logon to Server01 as Administrator.

2. Open the System Properties from Control Panel.

3. On the Remote tab, enable Remote Desktop. Close System Properties.

4. Open the Terminal Services Configuration console from the Administrative Tools folder.

5. In the Terminal Services Configuration MMC, right-click the RDP-Tcp connection in the details pane, and then click Properties.

6. On the Network Adapter tab, change the Maximum Connections to 1.

7. On the Sessions tab, select both of the Override User Settings check boxes, and specify the following settings:

   ❑ End a disconnected session: 5 minutes

   ❑ Active session limit: Never

   ❑ Idle session limit: 5 minutes

   ❑ When session limit is reached or connection is broken: Disconnect from session

   This configuration will ensure that only one person at a time can be connected to the Terminal Server, that any disconnected session will be closed in 5 minutes, and that an idle session will be disconnected in 5 minutes. These settings are useful because a session that is disconnected or idle will not immediately terminate the Remote Desktop For Administration connection.

8. Click OK to close the RDP-Tcp Properties dialog box.

Exercise 2: Connecting to the Server with Remote Desktop Connection

1. On Server02, open Remote Desktop Connection (from All Programs Accessories, Communications program group) and connect to and log on to Server01.

2. On Server01, open the Terminal Services Manager MMC. You should see the remote session connected to Server01.

3. Leave the session idle for 5 minutes, or close the Remote Desktop Connection without logging off the Terminal Server session, and the session should be disconnected automatically in 5 minutes.

You have now learned how to log on to Server01 remotely. Using Remote Desktop For Administration you can perform any tasks on the Server01 computer that you could accomplish while logged on interactively at the console.

Lesson Review

The following questions are intended to reinforce key information presented in this lesson. If you are unable to answer a question, review the lesson materials and try the question again. You can find answers to the questions in the "Questions and Answers" section at the end of this chapter.

1. Can a snap-in have focus on both the local computer and a remote computer simultaneously?

   _____

   _____

2. What credentials are required for administration of a remote computer using the MMC?

   _____

   _____

3. Can an existing MMC snap-in be changed from local to remote context, or must a snap-in of the same type be loaded into the MMC for remote connection?

   _____

   _____

4. Are all functions within a snap-in used on a local computer usable when connected remotely?

   _____

   _____

   _____

5. How many simultaneous connections are possible to a server using Remote Desktop For Administration? Why?

_____

_____

_____

_____

6. What would be the best way to give administrators the ability to administer a server remotely through Terminal Services?

    a. Don't do anything; they already have access because they are administrators.

    b. Remove the Administrators group from the permission list on the Terminal Server connection, and put the Administrator account in the Remote Desktop Users group.

    c. Create a separate, lower-authorization user account for Administrators to use daily, and place that account in the Remote Desktop Users group.

_____

_____

_____

7. What tool is used to enable Remote Desktop on a server?

    a. Terminal Services Manager

    b. Terminal Services Configuration

    c. System properties in Control Panel

    d. Terminal Services Licensing

_____

8. How is Remote Assistance like Remote Desktop For Administration? How is it different?

_____

_____

_____

_____

_____

_____

_____

9. Which of the following are firewall-related constraints relating to Remote Assistance?

    a. Port 3389 must be open.

    b. NAT cannot be used.

    c. Internet Connection Sharing is not possible.

    d. You cannot use Remote Assistance across a Virtual Private Network (VPN).

Lesson Summary

- Some snap-ins can be used to configure remote computers; others are limited to local computer access.

- Remote Desktop For Administration allows for the same administration of a server from a remote location as if logged on to the local console interactively.

- Remote Desktop For Administration requires permissions to attach with Remote Desktop Connection. By default, this permission is granted only to the Remote Desktop Users group.

- Remote Assistance is available only with Windows XP and Windows Server 2003

- Remote Assistance is like Remote Desktop For Administration for the desktop, allowing remote viewing and control of remote computers.

- Two users are required for Remote Assistance to be viable: one user at the target desktop, and the expert helper at another computer. Both must agree on the control actions taken during the session, and the session can be ended by either party at any time. At no time can an expert take unauthorized control of a user's computer.

- Port 3389, the same port used by Remote Desktop For Administration, must be open at the firewall for Remote Assistance sessions to be established.

Lesson 2: Supporting and Troubleshooting Terminal Server

In Lesson 1, you learned how to use terminal services, specifically Remote Desktop For Administration, to connect to a server session from a remote client. You learned that Remote Desktop For Administration is installed on every Windows 2003 Server by default, and that once it is enabled using the System application in Control Panel, a server will support two concurrent connections from users who belong to the Remote Desktop Users group.

Windows Server 2003 terminal services also supports providing applications to multiple users running concurrent sessions. This feature, similar to the Terminal Services Application Server mode of Windows 2000 Server, is now called Terminal Server. In this lesson, you will learn about Terminal Server and the unique issues related to supporting and troubleshooting a Terminal Server environment.

After this lesson, you will be able to

- Configure Terminal Server
- Manage Terminal Server licensing
- Administer and support user connections to Terminal Server

Estimated lesson time: 30 minutes

Installing and Configuring a Terminal Server Environment

There are several key considerations related to the deployment of a Terminal Server environment.

The Terminal Server Component

Terminal Server can be installed using the Add/Remove Windows Components Wizard, which itself is found in Add Or Remove Programs, or by using the Configure Your Server Wizard, which can be launched from the Manage Your Server page. It is best practice to configure stand-alone member servers as terminal servers, not domain controllers. Hardware recommendations can be found in the Help And Support Center.

Applications

Because applications on a terminal server will be provided to multiple users, perhaps concurrently, certain registry keys, files, and folders must be installed differently on a terminal server than on a non–terminal server. You should always use the Add Or Remove Programs tool in Control Panel to install an application on a terminal server. Add Or Remove Programs will automatically switch the terminal server into installation mode prior to launching the application's setup routine. While in installation mode, the terminal server manages the configuration of the application appropriately so that the application can run in multiuser mode.

Occasionally, an application, patch, or other installation-related process cannot be initiated via Add Or Remove Programs. For example, a vendor might provide an online update feature for its application and this capability cannot be launched from Add Or Remove Programs. In such cases, open a command prompt and issue the **change user /install** command prior to invoking the installation or patch process. Once the process has completed, issue the **change user /execute** command. Also note that some applications require compatibility scripts to modify their installation behavior on a terminal server.

It is best practice to install Terminal Server prior to installing any applications that will be run in multiuser mode. Similarly, prior to removing Terminal Server from a server, you should uninstall all applications that were installed in multiuser mode. If you must install additional applications on an existing Terminal Server, be sure to reset (log off) any current user sessions using Terminal Server Connections and to disable new connections using the **change logon /disable** command. Once applications have been installed, use the **change logon /enable** command to allow new connections once again. The Remote tab of System Properties, shown in Figure 10-10 will also allow you to enable and disable terminal services connections.

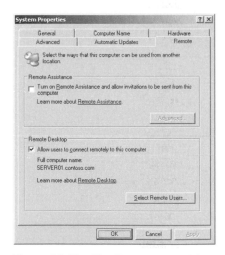

Figure 10-10   The Remote tab of System Properties

When installing Terminal Server, you will be given the choice of Full Security and Relaxed Security. Full Security, the default, protects certain operating system files, registry keys, and shared program files. Older applications might not function in this more secure configuration, at which point you might opt for Relaxed Security. The setting can be changed at any time using the Server Settings in the Terminal Services Configuration console, shown in Figure 10-11.

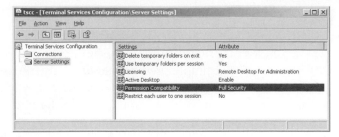

Figure 10-11   Server Settings in the Terminal Services Configuration console

Many administrators misunderstand the use of the Terminal Services Home Folder. This setting, which can be configured as part of the user account, as shown in Figure 10-12, or through Group Policy, determines the location of a folder that is used by Terminal Services to store user-specific files for multiuser applications. It does not affect the storage location for user data files. By default, the Terminal Services Home Folder is created as a folder named Windows in the user's profile. To manage where user data is stored, configure a user's standard Home Folder setting on the Profile tab of the user account, or use the best practice of redirecting the My Documents folder.

Figure 10-12   The Terminal Services Home Folder setting of a user account

Installation of Remote Desktop Connection

The Remote Desktop Connection (Mstsc.exe) is installed by default on all Windows Server 2003 and Windows XP computers. The Remote Desktop Connection client supports all 32-bit Windows platforms and can be installed with Group Policy on Windows 2000 systems, or with other software deployment methods on earlier platforms. Once installed, the client can be tricky to locate in the Start menu: look in the All Programs\Accessories\Communications program group, and then do yourself a favor and create a shortcut to the client in a more accessible location.

Licensing

After a 120-day evaluation period, connections to a computer running Terminal Server will not be successful unless the terminal server can obtain a client license from a Terminal Server License Server. Therefore, as part of your terminal server deployment, you must install a Terminal Server License Server, preferably on a server that is not itself a terminal server.

Use Add Or Remove Programs to install Terminal Server Licensing. You will be asked whether the server should be an Enterprise License Server or a Domain License Server. An Enterprise License Server is the most common configuration—the server can provide licenses to terminal servers in any Windows 2000 or Windows Server 2003 domain in the forest. Use a Domain License Server when you want to maintain a separate license database for each domain, or when terminal servers are running in a workgroup or a Windows NT 4.0 domain.

Once installed, Terminal Server Licensing is managed with the Terminal Server Licensing console in Administrative Tools. The first task you will perform is activating the Terminal Server License Server by right-clicking the Terminal Server License Server and choosing Activate Server. Once the server has been activated, client license packs must be installed. The Help And Support Center includes detailed instructions for this process. Terminal Server Licensing supports two types of client access licenses (CALs): Per Device and Per Session. Both types of CALs can be managed by the same Terminal Server License Server.

> **Exam Tip**   Terminal Server Licensing is maintained separately from server and client access licenses (CALs) for Windows Server 2003. Terminal Server CALs are licenses for the connection to a user session on a terminal server—you must still consider licensing requirements for the applications that users access within their session. Consult the applications' End User License Agreements (EULAs) to determine appropriate licensing for applications hosted on a terminal server.

Managing and Troubleshooting Terminal Server

Several tools exist that can configure terminal servers, terminal services user settings, connections, and sessions. These include Group Policy Object Editor, Terminal Services Configuration, Active Directory Users And Computers, and the Remote Desktop Connection client itself. This section will help you understand the use of each tool and the most important configuration settings by examining the creation, use, and deletion of a user session.

Points of Administration

Several processes occur as a user connects to a terminal server; and at each step, there are opportunities to configure the behavior of the connection.

The Remote Desktop Connection client allows 32-bit Windows platforms to connect to a Terminal Server using the Remote Desktop Protocol (RDP). The client has been greatly improved over earlier versions of the Terminal Services client, and it now includes a wider variety of data redirection types (including file system, serial port, printer, audio, and time zone) and supports connections in up to 24-bit color. The client includes numerous settings that configure the connection and the user's experience. Some of those settings are seen in Figure 10-13. Settings are saved in Remote Desktop Connection (.rdp) files that can easily be opened for future connections or distributed to other users as a connection profile. Settings in the .rdp file or the Remote Desktop Connection client affect the current user's connection to the specified terminal server.

Figure 10-13   The Remote Desktop Connection client

When a user connects to a terminal server, the server will examine the terminal services properties of the user's account to determine certain settings. If terminal services user accounts are stored on the terminal server, the Local Users And Groups snap-in will expose terminal services settings in the properties of user accounts. More commonly, user accounts are in Active Directory, in which case Active Directory Users And Computers exposes terminal services settings on the Environment, Remote Control, and Terminal Services Profile tabs within the user properties dialog box, as shown in Figure 10-12. Settings in the user account will override settings in the Remote Desktop client.

A client connects to the terminal server by specifying the server's name or IP address. The terminal server receives the connection request via the specified network adapter. This connection is represented by a connection object, visible in the Terminal Services

Configuration console shown in Figure 10-14. The connection object's properties configure settings that affect all user connections through the network adapter. Settings in the connection will override client-requested settings and settings in the user account.

> **Exam Tip**   A terminal server's RDP-Tcp connection properties, accessible through Terminal Services Configuration, will override client and user account settings for all user sessions through the connection on that individual terminal server.

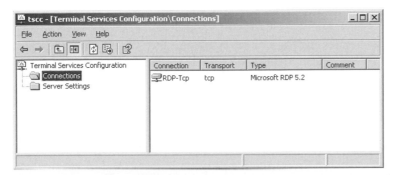

Figure 10-14   Terminal Services Configuration

Windows Server 2003 Group Policy includes numerous computer-based and user-based policies to control terminal services. Configurations specified by group policy objects (GPOs) will override settings in Remote Desktop Connection, in the user account, or on the RDP-Tcp connections of terminal servers. Of course, those settings will apply only to the users or computers within the scope of the organizational unit (OU) to which the GPO is linked. In an environment consisting only of terminal servers running one of the Windows Server 2003 family operating systems, Group Policy will enable terminal services configuration with the least administrative effort. Terminal services group policies do not apply to terminal servers running earlier versions of Windows.

Once a user session has been enabled, the Terminal Services Manager administrative tool can be used to monitor users, sessions, and applications on each terminal server. Terminal Services Manager can also be used to manage the server and to connect to, disconnect from, or reset user sessions or processes.

Before continuing the examination of Terminal Server configuration options and tools, take a moment to memorize the order of precedence for configuration settings:

1. Computer-level group policies. Most Terminal Services configuration can be set by group policy objects (GPOs) linked to an OU in which terminal server computer objects are created. These policies override settings made with any other tool.

2. User-level group policies.

3. Configuration of the terminal server or the RDP-Tcp connection using the Terminal Services Configuration tool. While this tool is server and connection specific, and therefore cannot specify a single configuration as Group Policy can, this tool is able to configure Windows 2000 terminal servers. In addition, there are times when a configuration should be different between terminal servers or between connections. Terminal Services Configuration is the tool to manage such a scenario.

4. User account properties configured with Active Directory Users And Computers.

5. Remote Desktop Connection client configuration.

Connection Configuration

A user's ability to connect and log on to a terminal server is determined by a number of factors, each of which, if not functioning properly, produces a unique error message:

■ The connection on the terminal server must be accessible. If the client cannot reach the server using TCP/IP or if the terminal server's RDP-Tcp connection is disabled, a particularly uninformative error message appears that indicates the client cannot connect to the server.

■ Remote Desktop must be enabled. The ability of a terminal server to accept new connections can be controlled on the Remote tab of the System properties dialog box or by using the **change logon /disable** and **change logon /enable** commands. If logon has been disabled, an error message appears indicating that terminal server sessions are disabled or that remote logons are disabled.

■ The server must have available connections. The properties of the connection—the default RDP-Tcp connection, for example—determine the number of available connections on the Network Adapter tab shown in Figure 10-15. If sufficient connections are not available, an error message appears that indicates a network error is preventing connection.

Figure 10-15   The Network Adapter tab of the RDP-Tcp Properties dialog box

■ Encryption must be compatible. The default allows any client to connect to a terminal server without regard to its encryption capability. If you modify the encryption requirements for a connection using the Encryption Level list on the General tab of the connection properties, shown in Figure 10-16, clients that are not capable of that encryption mode will not be allowed to connect.

Figure 10-16   The General tab of the RDP-Tcp Properties dialog box

■ The user must have sufficient connection permissions. As shown in Figure 10-17, the Remote Desktop Users group has User Access permissions, which gives the group sufficient permissions to log on to the server. The access control list (ACL) of the connection can be modified to control access in configurations that differ from the default. Refer to the Help And Support Center for more information. If a user does not have sufficient permission to the connection, an error message will appear that indicates the user does not have access to the session.

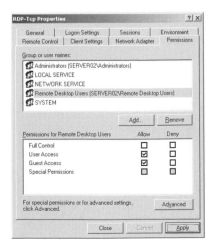

Figure 10-17   The Permissions tab of the RDP-Tcp Properties dialog box

- The user must have the user logon right to log on to the terminal server. Windows Server 2003 separates the right required to log on *locally* to a server from the right required to log on to a server using a remote desktop connection. The user rights Allow Log On Through Terminal Services, seen in Figure 10-18, and Deny Log On Through Terminal Services can be used to manage this right, using either local policy or Group Policy. On member servers, the local Administrators and Remote Desktop Users groups have the right to log on through terminal services. On domain controllers, only Administrators have the right by default. If a user does not have sufficient logon rights, an error message will appear that clearly indicates the policy of the terminal server does not allow logon.

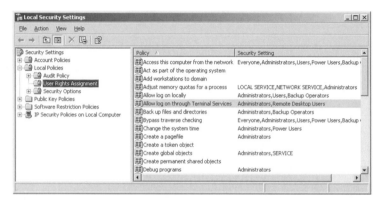

Figure 10-18   The Allow Logon Through Terminal Services user right

- The user must belong to the right group or groups. Assuming you have managed connection permissions and the right to log on through terminal services by assigning rights and permissions to a group, the user attempting to connect to the terminal server must be in that group. With the default configuration of Terminal Server on a member server, users must be members of the Remote Desktop Users group to successfully connect to a terminal server.

- Allow Logon To Terminal Server must be enabled. The user account's Terminal Services Profile tab, seen in Figure 10-12, indicates the user is allowed to log on to a terminal server. If this setting is disabled, the user will receive an error message indicating the interactive logon privilege has been disabled. This error message is easy to confuse with insufficient user logon rights; however, in that case, the error message indicates the local policy of the server is not allowing logon.

Note   A terminal server has one RDP-Tcp connection by default and can have only one connection object per network adapter, but if a terminal server has multiple adapters you can create connections for those adapters. Each connection maintains properties that affect all user sessions connected to the connection on that server.

Device Redirection

Once a user has successfully connected, Windows Server 2003 and the Remote Desktop Connection client provide a wide array of device redirection options, including:

- Audio redirection, which allows audio files played within the terminal server session to be played by the user's PC. This feature is specified on the Local Resources tab of the Remote Desktop Connection client, shown in Figure 10-13. However, audio redirection (or audio mapping) is disabled by default on the Client Settings tab of the RDP-Tcp Properties dialog box, as seen in Figure 10-19. Audio redirection can be specified by a GPO.

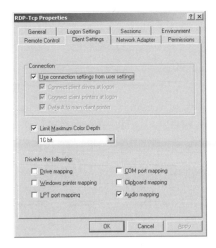

Figure 10-19   The RDP-Tcp Properties dialog box Client Settings tab

- Drive redirection (or drive mapping), which allows the user to access drives that are local to the user's PC from within the terminal server session. Local drives are visible in My Computer under the Other group, as seen in Figure 10-20. This option is disabled by default and can be enabled on the Local Resources tab of the Remote Desktop Connection client. Terminal Server Configuration can override the client setting and disable drive redirection from the properties of the connection. These settings can also be specified by group policy. The user account's Connect Client Drives At Logon setting does *not* affect drive redirection using the Remote Desktop Connection client—it is meant to manage drive redirection for Citrix Integrated Computing Architecture (ICA) clients.

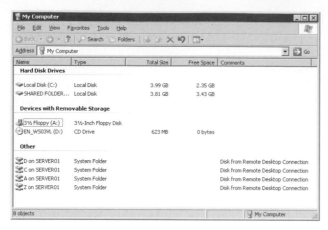

Figure 10-20   My Computer in a terminal server session showing redirected client drives

- Printer redirection (or Windows printer mapping), which allows the user to access printers that are local to the user's PC, as well as network printers that are installed on the user's PC, from within the terminal server session. The Printers And Faxes folder will display printers that are installed on the terminal server as well as the client's redirected printers, as shown in Figure 10-21.

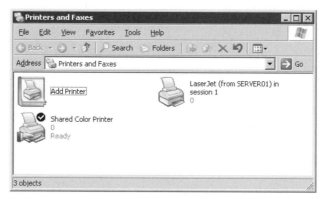

Figure 10-21   The Printers And Faxes folder, which shows a client's redirected printer

Like drive redirection, printer redirection is specified on the Local Resources tab of the Remote Desktop Connection client. Printer redirection can be disabled by properties of the RDP-Tcp connection. Printer redirection will also be disabled if the Connect Client Printers At Logon setting is not enabled in the user account properties, shown in Figure 10-22. Interestingly, checking this option in the user account does *not* cause printer redirection to occur—the client must specify redirection on the Local Resources tab—but if this option is disabled, the user account setting will override the client setting. The user account properties also provide a Default To Main Client Printer setting which, if enabled while printer redirection is in effect, will set the default printer in the terminal server session to the same printer set as default on the user's PC. If the Default To Main Client Printer setting is disabled, the terminal server session will use the default printer of the terminal server computer. Printer redirection settings can be specified by a GPO.

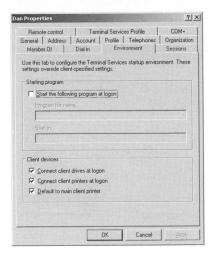

Figure 10-22   The Environment tab of a user's properties dialog box

- Serial Port redirection, which allows a user to launch an application within a terminal server session that uses a device, such as a bar-code reader, attached to the serial port of the user's PC. This feature is on the Local Resources tab of the client and can be disabled in the properties of the RDP-Tcp connection. Serial port redirection can be specified by a GPO.

- LPT and COM port mapping, which allow a user to install a printer within the terminal server session that maps to a printer attached to an LPT or COM port on the user's PC. This method of printer redirection is not necessary with Windows Server 2003 and the Remote Desktop Connection client, which support printer redirection in a much simpler way, as described previously. LPT and COM port mapping are, however, still done by default. The RDP-Tcp connection properties can disable port mapping, as can a GPO.

- Clipboard mapping, which allows the user to copy and paste information between a terminal server session and the desktop. This feature is enabled by default in the Remote Desktop Connection client and cannot be changed within the client's user interface (UI). The RDP-Tcp connection properties can disable clipboard mapping, as can a GPO.

Managing User Sessions

Windows Server 2003 provides flexible and powerful ways to manage, troubleshoot, and optimize user sessions on terminal servers.

Managing Sessions and Processes

The Terminal Services Manager console provides the capability to monitor and control sessions and processes on a terminal server. You can disconnect, log off, or reset a user or session; send a message to a user; or end a process launched by any user. Task Manager can also be used to monitor and end processes—just be certain to select the Show Processes From All Users check box. If a terminal server is acting lethargic, use Terminal Server Manager or Task Manager to look at the processes being run by all users to determine whether one process has stopped responding and is consuming more than its fair share of processor time.

A variety of settings determines the behavior of a user session that has been active, idle, or disconnected for a period of time. These settings can be configured on the Sessions tab of the RDP-Tcp Properties dialog box in the Terminal Services Configuration console, shown in Figure 10-23. The settings can also be configured with Group Policy.

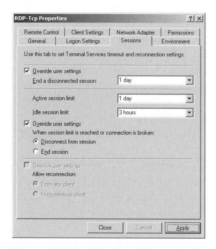

Figure 10-23   The Sessions tab of the RDP-Tcp Properties dialog box

Load-Balancing Terminal Servers

In previous implementations of terminal services, it was difficult to load-balance terminal servers. Windows Server 2003 Enterprise and Datacenter Editions introduce the ability to create server clusters, which are logical groupings of terminal servers. When a user connects to the cluster, he or she is directed to one server. If the session is disconnected and the user attempts to reconnect, the terminal server receiving the connection will check with the Session Directory to identify which terminal server is hosting the disconnected session, and it will redirect the client to the appropriate server.

To configure a terminal server cluster, you need:

■ A load-balancing technology, such as Network Load Balancing (NLB) or DNS round-robin. The load-balancing solution will distribute client connections to each of the terminal servers.

■ A Terminal Services Session Directory. You must enable the Terminal Services Session Directory, which is installed by default on Windows Server 2003 Enterprise and Datacenter Editions, using the Services console in Administrative Tools. It is best practice to enable the session directory on a server that is not itself running Terminal Server. The Terminal Services Session Directory maintains a database that tracks each user session on servers in the cluster. The computer running the session directory creates a Session Directory Computers local group, to which you must add the computer accounts of all the servers in the cluster.

■ Terminal server connection configuration. Finally, you must direct the cluster's servers to the session directory, which involves specifying that the server is part of a directory, the name of the session directory server, and the name for the cluster (which can be any name you want, as long as the same name is specified for each server in the cluster). These settings can be specified in the Server Settings node of Terminal Server Configuration, or they can be set using a GPO applied to an OU that contains the computer objects for the cluster's terminal servers.

When a user connects to the cluster, the following process occurs:

1. When the user logs on to the terminal server cluster, the terminal server receiving the initial client logon request sends a query to the session directory server.

2. The session directory server checks the username against its database and sends the result to the requesting server.

   ❑ If the user has no disconnected sessions, logon continues at the server hosting the initial connection.

   ❑ If the user has a disconnected session on another server, the client session is passed to that server and logon continues.

3. When the user logs on to a new or disconnected session, the session directory is updated.

Exam Tip   Be sure to know the pieces that are required to establish a terminal server cluster. Should you decide to implement a terminal server cluster in your enterprise, you can refer to the Help And Support Center for detailed instructions for doing so.

Remote Control

Terminal Server allows an administrator to view or take control of a user's session. This feature not only allows administrators to monitor user actions on a terminal server, but it also acts like Remote Assistance, allowing a help desk employee to control a user's session and perform actions that the user is able to see as well.

To establish remote control, both the user and the administrator must be connected to terminal server sessions. The administrator must open the Terminal Server Manager console from the Administrative tools group, right-click the user's session, and choose Remote Control. By default, the user will be notified that the administrator wants to connect to the session, and then the user can accept or deny the request.

> **Important**   Remote Control is available only by using Terminal Server Manager *within* a terminal server session. You cannot establish remote control by opening Terminal Server Manager on your PC.

Remote control settings include the ability to remotely view and control a session, as well as control whether the user should be prompted to accept or deny the administrator's access. These settings can be configured in the user account properties, on the Remote Control tab shown in Figure 10-24, and they can be configured by the properties of the RDP-Tcp connection, which will override user account settings. Group policy can also be used to specify remote control configuration.

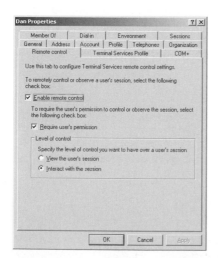

Figure 10-24   The Remote Control tab of a user's properties dialog box

In addition to enabling remote control settings, an administrator must have permissions to establish remote control over the terminal server connection. Using the Permissions

Exam 70-292: Managing and Maintaining a Microsoft Windows Server 2003 Environment for an MCSA Certified on Windows 2000

Objective	Pages
Managing Users, Computers, and Groups (1.0)	
Create and manage groups	4-25 to 4-47, 15-3 to 15-7
■ Identify and modify the scope of a group	
■ Find domain groups in which a user is a member	
■ Manage group membership	
■ Create and modify groups by using the Active Directory Users and Computers Microsoft Management Console (MMC) snap-in	
■ Create and modify groups by using automation	
Create and manage user accounts	4-3 to 4-24, 15-8 to 15-12
■ Create and modify user accounts by using the Active Directory Users and Computers MMC snap-in	
■ Create and modify user accounts by using automation	
■ Import user accounts	
Troubleshoot user authentication issues.	4-48 to 4-66, 15-13 to 15-17
Managing and Maintaining Access to Resources (2.0)	
Troubleshoot Terminal Services	10-26 to 10-45, 16-3 to 16-14
■ Diagnose and resolve issues related to Terminal Services security	
■ Diagnose and resolve issues related to client access to Terminal Services	
Managing and Maintaining a Server Environment (3.0)	
Manage software update infrastructure	10-57 to 10-77, 17-5 to 17-12
Manage servers remotely	10-3 to 10-25, 17-13 to 17-18
■ Manage a server by using Remote Assistance	
■ Manage a server by using Terminal Services remote administration mode	
■ Manage a server by using available support tools	
Manage a Web server	10-46 to 10-56, 17-19 to 17-24
■ Manage Internet Information Services (IIS)	
■ Manage security for IIS	
Managing and Implementing Disaster Recovery (4.0)	
Perform system recovery for a server	13-3 to 13-52, 18-3 to 18-16
■ Implement Automated System Recovery (ASR)	
■ Restore data from shadow copy volumes	
■ Back up files and System State data to media	
■ Configure security for backup operations	
Implementing, Managing, and Maintaining Name Resolution (5.0)	
Install and configure the DNS Server service	8-3 to 8-71, 19-5 to 19-28
■ Configure DNS server options	
■ Configure DNS zone options	
■ Configure DNS forwarding	
Manage DNS	8-3 to 8-71, 19-5 to 19-28
■ Manage DNS zone settings	
■ Manage DNS record settings	
■ Manage DNS server options	
Implementing, Managing, and Maintaining Network Security (6.0)	
Implement secure network administration procedures	9-3 to 9-23, 9-37 to 9-57, 20-4 to 20-14
■ Implement security baseline settings and audit security settings by using security templates	
■ Implement the principle of least privilege	
Install and configure software update infrastructure	10-57 to 10-77, 20-15 to 20-25
■ Install and configure software update services	
■ Install and configure automatic client update settings	
■ Configure software updates on earlier operating systems	

> **Note** Exam objectives are subject to change at anytime without prior notice and at Microsoft's sole discretion. Please visit Microsoft's Training & Certification Web site (*www.microsoft.com/traincert*) for the most current listing of exam objectives.

Exam 70-296: Planning, Implementing, and Maintaining a Microsoft Windows Server 2003 Environment for an MCSE Certified on Windows 2000

Objective	Pages

Planning and Implementing Server Roles and Server Security (1.0)

Configure security for servers that are assigned specific roles.	9-3 to 9-57, 21-3 to 21-5
Plan security for servers that are assigned specific roles. Roles might include domain controllers, Web servers, database servers, and mail servers.	9-3 to 9-71, 21-6 to 21-11
■ Deploy the security configuration for servers that are assigned specific roles.	
■ Create custom security templates based on server roles.	

Planning, Implementing, and Maintaining a Network Infrastructure (2.0)

Plan a host name resolution strategy.	7-3 to 7-46, 22-3 to 22-16
■ Plan a DNS namespace design.	
■ Plan zone replication requirements.	
■ Plan a forwarding configuration.	
■ Plan for DNS security.	
■ Examine the interoperability of DNS with third-party DNS solutions.	

Planning, Implementing, and Maintaining Server Availability (3.0)

Plan services for high availability.	14-2 to 14-49, 23-3 to 23-7
■ Plan a high availability solution that uses clustering services.	
■ Plan a high availability solution that uses Network Load Balancing.	
Plan a backup and recovery strategy.	13-3 to 13-52, 23-8 to 23-13
■ Identify appropriate backup types. Methods include full, incremental, and differential.	
■ Plan a backup strategy that uses volume shadow copy.	
■ Plan system recovery that uses Automated System Recovery (ASR).	

Planning and Maintaining Network Security (4.0)

Plan secure network administration methods.	10-3 to 10-25, 24-4 to 24-9
■ Create a plan to offer Remote Assistance to client computers.	
■ Plan for remote administration by using Terminal Services.	
Plan security for wireless networks.	11-26 to 11-35, 24-10 to 24-15
Plan security for data transmission.	11-3 to 11-25, 24-16 to 24-20
■ Secure data transmission between client computers to meet security requirements.	
■ Secure data transmission by using IPSec.	

Planning, Implementing, and Maintaining Security Infrastructure (5.0)

Configure Active Directory directory service for certificate publication.	12-3 to 12-31, 25-4 to 25-8
Plan a public key infrastructure (PKI) that uses Certificate Services.	12-3 to 12-31, 4-48 to 4-66, 25-9 to 25-14
■ Identify the appropriate type of certificate authority to support certificate issuance requirements.	
■ Plan the enrollment and distribution of certificates.	
■ Plan for the use of smart cards for authentication.	
Plan a framework for planning and implementing security.	9-3 to 9-71, 24-15 to 25-19
■ Plan for security monitoring.	
■ Plan a change and configuration management framework for security.	
Plan a security update infrastructure. Tools might include Microsoft Baseline Security Analyzer and Microsoft Software Update Services.	10-57 to 10-77, 25-20 to 25-24

Objective	Pages

Planning and Implementing an Active Directory Infrastructure (6.0)

Plan a strategy for placing global catalog servers.	1-35 to 1-48, 26-5 to 26-8
■ Evaluate network traffic considerations when placing global catalog servers.	
■ Evaluate the need to enable universal group caching.	
Implement an Active Directory directory service forest and domain structure.	2-3 to 2-47, 3-3 to 3-37, 26-9 to 26-19
■ Create the forest root domain.	
■ Create a child domain.	
■ Create and configure Application Data Partitions.	
■ Install and configure an Active Directory domain controller.	
■ Set an Active Directory forest and domain functional level based on requirements.	
■ Establish trust relationships. Types of trust relationships might include external trusts, shortcut trusts, and cross-forest trusts.	

Managing and Maintaining an Active Directory Infrastructure (7.0)

Manage an Active Directory forest and domain structure.	3-3 to 3-52, 27-4 to 27-11
■ Manage trust relationships.	
■ Manage schema modifications.	
■ Add or remove a UPN suffix.	
Restore Active Directory directory services.	3-53 to 3-73, 27-12 to 27-16
■ Perform an authoritative restore operation.	
■ Perform a nonauthoritative restore operation.	

Planning and Implementing User, Computer, and Group Strategies (8.0)

Plan a user authentication strategy.	4-48 to 4-66, 28-3 to 28-15
■ Plan a smart card authentication strategy.	
■ Create a password policy for domain users.	

Planning and Implementing Group Policy (9.0)

Plan Group Policy strategy.	5-3 to 5-91, 29-4 to 29-13
■ Plan a Group Policy strategy by using Resultant Set of Policy (RSoP) Planning mode.	
■ Plan a strategy for configuring the user environment by using Group Policy.	
■ Plan a strategy for configuring the computer environment by using Group Policy.	
Configure the user environment by using Group Policy.	6-4 to 6-93, 12-21 to 12-31, 29-14 to 29-22
■ Distribute software by using Group Policy.	
■ Automatically enroll user certificates by using Group Policy.	
■ Redirect folders by using Group Policy.	
■ Configure user security settings by using Group Policy.	

Managing and Maintaining Group Policy (10.0)

Troubleshoot issues related to Group Policy application deployment. Tools might include RSoP and the gpresult command.	6-29 to 6-76, 30-4 to 30-12
Troubleshoot the application of Group Policy security settings. Tools might include RSoP and the gpresult command.	5-83 to 5-91, 30-13 to 30-20

Microsoft

tab of the RDP-Tcp Properties dialog box, you can assign the Full Control permission or, by clicking Advanced, selecting a permission entry, clicking Edit, and assigning the Remote Control permission to a group, as shown in Figure 10-25.

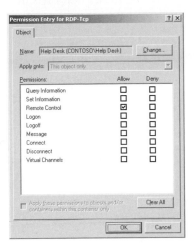

Figure 10-25   The Remote Control permission

> **Note**   For more information about implementing Terminal Server in a production environment, be sure to read the Microsoft Press book: *Microsoft Windows Server 2003 Terminal Services*.

Practice: Preparing Terminal Server

In this practice, you will install Terminal Server on Server02, configure a user account to enable Terminal Server logon, and configure device redirection.

Exercise 1: Installing Terminal Server

1. Log on to Server 02.

2. Open Add Or Remove Programs from Control Panel.

3. Click Add/Remove Windows Components.

   The Windows Components Wizard appears.

4. Select Terminal Server.

   A Configuration Warning appears reminding you that the Internet Explorer Enhanced Security Configuration will restrict users' Web access.

5. Click Yes.

6. Click Next.

   A message appears discussing the installation of applications on a terminal server.

7. Click Next.

8. Ensure that Full Security is selected, and click Next.

   The Configuring Components page appears while Terminal Server is installed.

9. Click Finish.

10. Restart Server02.

Exercise 2: Configuring Terminal Server Users

1. Log on to Server01 as Administrator.

2. Open Active Directory Users And Computers.

3. Create a user account in the Users container named Lorrin Smith-Bates.

   You might already have an account for Lorrin Smith-Bates if you have worked through lessons in other chapters. Write down the username and password assigned to this account, as you will be logging on as Lorrin Smith-Bates in the next exercise.

4. Create a global security group account in the Users container named Contoso Terminal Server Users.

5. Add Lorrin Smith-Bates to the Contoso Terminal Server Users group.

6. Add the Contoso Terminal Server Users group to the Print Operators group.

   Because Lorrin is a user, he would not be able to log on to Server01, a domain controller. For the purposes of this practice, Lorrin needs the right to log on locally to Server01, and nesting his account in the Print Operators group is an easy way to achieve that goal.

7. Log off of Server01.

8. Log on to Server02 as Administrator.

9. Click Start and right-click My Computer. Choose Manage.

10. Expand the Local Users And Groups snap-in in the scope pane.

11. Select the Groups node.

12. Double-click Remote Desktop Users in the details pane.

13. Add the Contoso Terminal Server Users group as a member.

Exercise 3: Logging On to Terminal Server with Device Redirection

1. Log on to Server01 as Lorrin Smith-Bates.

2. Open Remote Desktop Connection from the All Programs\Accessories\Communications program group.

3. In the Computer box, type **server02.contoso.com** and click Connect.

4. In the remote desktop session, log on to Server02 as Lorrin Smith-Bates.

5. Open My Computer, and notice that the drives shown are the drives on Server02.

6. In the remote desktop session, log off of Server02.

7. Open Remote Desktop Connection again.

8. Click the Options button.

9. Click the Local Resources tab.

10. Select the Disk Drives check box.

11. Click Connect.

12. A Security Warning appears. Click OK.

13. In the remote desktop session, log on to Server02 as Lorrin Smith-Bates.

14. Open My Computer, and note that the drives on Server01 are shown as being in the group called Other.

15. In the remote desktop session, log off of Server02.

16. Do not log off of Server01. Log directly on to Server02 as Administrator.

17. On Server02, open the Terminal Services Configuration console from the Administrative Tools folder.

18. Click Connections in the scope pane.

19. Double-click RDP-Tcp in the details pane.

20. Click the Client Settings tab.

21. Select the Drive Mapping check box.

22. Click OK to close the RDP-Tcp Properties dialog box.

23. On Server01, still logged on as Lorrin, open Remote Desktop Connection.

24. Ensure that **server02.contoso.com** is entered as the computer and, on the Local Resources tab, that the Disk Drives check box is still selected.

25. Click Connect, and log on to Server02 as Lorrin Smith-Bates.

26. Open My Computer.

   Local drives are no longer redirected. The setting in the properties of the RDP-Tcp connection overrides client settings.

Lesson Review

The following questions are intended to reinforce key information presented in this lesson. If you are unable to answer a question, review the lesson materials and try the question again. You can find answers to the questions in the "Questions and Answers" section at the end of this chapter.

1. You have enabled Remote Desktop connections on Server02, a member server in the contoso.com domain. Terminal Server is installed on Server02. You want Danielle Tiedt to be able to connect using the Remote Desktop Connection client. What additional configuration must first be performed on Server02?

   _____

2. You have enabled Remote Desktop connections on Server01, a domain controller in the contoso.com domain. Terminal Server is installed on Server01. You want Jay Adams to be able to connect using the Remote Desktop Connection client. Jay is a member of the Remote Desktop Users group on Server01. What additional configuration must first be performed for Jay to successfully connect?

   _____

   _____

   _____

3. Name three locations where you can configure Terminal Server settings that will override settings on the Remote Desktop Connection client.

   _____

   _____

   _____

Lesson Summary

- Terminal Server provides applications in a multiuser environment. Those applications must be installed using Add Or Remove Programs or the Change User command.

- For a user to successfully connect, Remote Desktop connections must be enabled on the server, the server's connection (for example, the RDP-Tcp connection) must allow connections for a group to which the user belongs, the user must be in a group that is granted the right Allow Logon Through Terminal Services, and the user account must Allow Logon To Terminal Server. On a member server, all the appropriate permissions are configured by default for the Remote Desktop Users group, so you must simply enable Remote Desktop connections and add the user to that group.

■ A domain controller's security policy does not, by default, grant the Allow Logon Through Terminal Services user right.

■ Various Terminal Server settings can be configured on the client, in the user account, on the connection, or on the server. Most of these settings can additionally be configured through Group Policy for terminal servers running Windows Server 2003.

■ Windows Server 2003 and the Remote Desktop Connection client support device redirection including audio devices, printers, and disks.

■ To load-balance terminal servers, you must configure a load-balancing technology, such as NLB or DNS round-robin; enable the Terminal Services Session Directory on a server; add computer accounts for the servers to the directory server's Session Directory Computers local group; and configure the servers to belong to the cluster via Terminal Server Configuration or Group Policy.

■ You can monitor and remotely control a user's terminal services session by connecting to the terminal server with the Remote Desktop Connection client, opening Terminal Server Manager, right-clicking the user session, and choosing Remote Control.

Lesson 3: Configuring and Managing Web Servers Using IIS

As more applications and collaboration activities become focused on the Web for delivery, it becomes increasingly important to be able to maintain and secure a Web server. Windows Server 2003 provides re-architected and significantly improved Internet Information Services (IIS). In this lesson, you will learn how to configure and manage IIS. You will discover how to configure Web and File Transfer Protocol (FTP) sites, virtual directories, and IIS security.

After this lesson, you will be able to

- Install IIS
- Set up a Web and FTP site
- Configure a Web default content page
- Create a Web virtual directory
- Modify IIS authentication and security settings
- Back up the IIS metabase

Estimated lesson time: 20 minutes

Installing IIS 6.0

To decrease the attack surface of a Windows Server 2003 system, IIS is not installed by default. It must be added using the Add/Remove Windows Components Wizard from Add Or Remove Programs, located in Control Panel. Select Application Server, click Details, and then select Internet Information Services (IIS). You can control the sub-components of IIS that are installed, but unless you are very familiar with the role of subcomponents, do not remove any default components. However, you might want to add components, such as ASP.NET, FTP, or Microsoft FrontPage Server Extensions.

Administering the Web Environment

When IIS is installed, a default Web site is created, allowing you to implement a Web environment quickly and easily. However, you can modify that Web environment to meet your needs. Windows Server 2003 provides the tools necessary to administer IIS and its sites.

After installation has completed, you can open the Internet Information Services (IIS) Manager console from the Administrative Tools group. By default, IIS is configured to serve only static content. To enable dynamic content, select the Web Service Extensions node. As shown in Figure 10-26, all the extensions are prohibited by default. Select the appropriate extension, and click Allow.

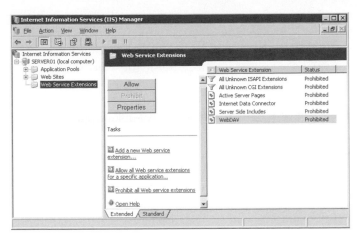

Figure 10-26   The Internet Information Services (IIS) Manager snap-in

The fundamental processes that take place as a client accesses a resource from IIS are:

- The client enters a URL (Universal Resource Locator) in the form *http://dns.domain .name/virtualdirectory/page.htm* or *ftp://dns.domain.name/virtualdirectory.*

- Domain Name Service (DNS) resolves the name to an IP address and returns the address to the client.

- The client connects to the server's IP address, using a port that is specific to the service (typically, port 80 for HTTP and port 21 for FTP).

- The URL does not represent the physical path to the resource on the server, but a virtualization of the path. The server translates the incoming request into the physical path and produces appropriate resources to the client. For example, the server might list files in the folder to an FTP client, or might deliver the home page to an HTTP client.

- The process can be secured with authentication (credentials, including a user name and password) and authorization (access control through permissions).

You can see this process in action by opening a browser and typing **http://server01**. The server produces the Under Construction page to the client browser.

Configuring and Managing Web and FTP Sites

IIS installation configures a single Web site, the Default Web Site. Although IIS, depending on your server's hardware configuration, can host thousands or tens of thousands of sites, the Default Web Site is a fine place to explore the functionality and administration of Web sites on IIS. This default Web site is accessible if you open a browser and type the URL: **http://server01.contoso.com**. The page that is fetched is the Under Construction page.

Remember that a browser's request to a Web server is directed at the server's IP address, which was resolved from the URL by DNS. The request includes the URL, and the URL often includes only the site name (*www.microsoft.com*, for example). How does the server produce the home page? If you examine the Web Site tab of the Default Web Site Properties, as shown in Figure 10-27, you see that the site is assigned to All Unassigned IP addresses on port 80. So the request from the browser hits port 80 on the server, which then identifies that it is the Default Web Site that should be served.

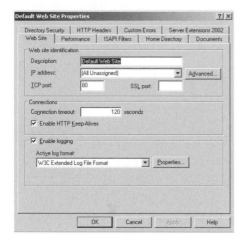

Figure 10-27   The Web Site tab of the Default Web Site Properties dialog box

The next question, then, is what information should be served. If the URL includes only the site name (for example, *www.microsoft.com* or *server01.contoso.com*), the page that will be returned is fetched from the home directory. The Home Directory tab, as shown in Figure 10-28, displays the physical path to the home directory, typically *c:\inetpub\wwwroot*.

Figure 10-28   The Home Directory tab of the Default Web Site Properties dialog box

Which file, exactly, should be returned to the client? That is defined on the Documents tab, as shown in Figure 10-29. IIS searches for files in the order they are listed. As soon as it finds a file of that name in the local path of the home directory, that page is returned to the client and the server stops looking for other matches. If no match is found, the IIS returns an error (404 – File Not Found) to the client indicating the page could not be found.

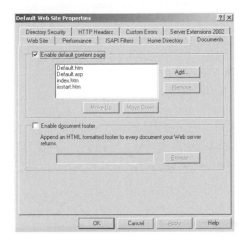

Figure 10-29   The Documents tab of the Default Web Site Properties dialog box

A browser could, of course, refer to a specific page in the URL, for example *http://server01.contoso.com/contactinfo.htm*. In that event, the specific page is fetched from the home directory. If it is not found, a File Not Found error (404) is returned.

To create a Web site, right-click the Web Sites node or an existing Web site in IIS Manager and choose New Web Site. To configure a Web site, open its Properties. You can configure the IP address of the site. If a server has multiple IP addresses, each IP address can represent a separate Web site. Multiple sites can also be hosted using different ports for each site or using host headers. The specifics of these options are beyond the scope of this book. You can also configure the path to the directory that is used as the home directory. And you can modify the list or order of documents that can be fetched as the default content page.

A URL can also include more complex path information, such as *http://www.microsoft.com/windowsserver2003*. This URL is not requesting a specific page; there is no extension such as .htm or .asp on the end of the URL. Instead, it is requesting information from the windowsserver2003 directory. The server evaluates this additional component of the URL as a virtual directory. The folder that contains the files referred to as windowsserver2003 can reside anywhere; they do not have to be located on the IIS server.

To create a virtual directory, right-click a Web site and choose New Virtual Directory. The wizard will prompt you for the alias, which becomes the folder name used in the URL, and the physical path to the resource, which can be on a local volume or remote server.

> **Exam Tip**   You can also create a Web virtual directory on an NTFS drive by right-clicking a folder in Windows Explorer, choosing Properties, and then clicking the Web Sharing tab.

FTP sites work, and are administered, similarly to Web sites. IIS installs one FTP site, the Default FTP Site, and configures it to respond to all incoming FTP requests (all unassigned addresses, port 21). The FTP site returns to the client a list of files from the folder specified in the Home Directory tab. FTP sites can also include virtual directories so that, for example, *ftp://server01.contoso.com/pub* can return resources from a different server than *ftp://server01.contoso.com/vendor-uploads*. FTP URLs and sites do not use default documents.

Backing Up IIS Configuration

Complex IIS servers might host tens of thousands of sites, each with customized settings to make them tick. Losing all that configuration information could be painful, so although a normal file system backup might allow you to restore the data files after a failure, the configuration would be lost. To back up or restore the IIS configuration, you must back up or restore the metabase and the schema, Extensible Markup Language (XML) documents that arc used to store settings.

To back up the IIS configuration:

1. Right-click the server node in IIS Manager and, from the All Tasks menu, choose Backup/Restore Configuration.

   The metabase and schema are backed up to the directory *%Windir%*\System32 \Inetsrv\Metaback.

2. Use any backup procedure to back up the contents of the Metaback directory.

> **Important**   Backing up IIS configuration does not back up Web site content. Use any backup procedure to back up content.

Securing Files on IIS

Security for files accessed by way of IIS falls into several categories: authentication, authorization through NTFS permissions, and IIS permissions. Authentication is, of course, the process of evaluating credentials in the form of a user name and password. By default, all requests to IIS are serviced by impersonating the user with the IUSR_*computername* account. Before you begin restricting access of resources to specific users, you must create domain or local user accounts and require something more than this default, Anonymous authentication.

Configuring Authentication Methods

You can configure the following authentication methods on the Directory Security tab of the server, a Web (or FTP) site, a virtual directory, or a file.

Web Authentication Options   The seven Web authentication options are as follows:

- **Anonymous authentication**   Users can access the public areas of your Web site without a user name or password.

- **Basic authentication**   This option requires that a user have a local or domain user account. Credentials are transmitted in clear text.

- **Digest authentication**   This option offers the same functionality as Basic authentication, while providing enhanced security in the way that a user's credentials are sent across the network. Digest authentication relies on the HTTP 1.1 protocol.

- **Advanced Digest authentication**   This option works only when the user account is part of an Active Directory. User credentials are collected and stored on the domain controller as an MD5 hash or message digest. Advanced Digest authentication requires the user to be using Internet Explorer 5 or later and the HTTP 1.1 protocol.

- **Integrated Windows authentication**   With this option, information is collected through a secure form of authentication (sometimes referred to as Windows NT Challenge/Response authentication), where the user name and password are hashed *before* being sent across the network.

- **Certificate authentication**   This option adds Secure Sockets Layer (SSL) security through client or server certificates, or both. This option is available only if you have Certificate Services installed and configured.

- **.NET Passport authentication**   This option provides a single sign-in service through SSL, HTTP redirects, cookies, Microsoft JScript, and strong symmetric key encryption.

FTP Authentication Options   The two FTP authentication options are as follows:

- **Anonymous FTP authentication**   This option gives users access to the public areas of your FTP site without prompting them for a user name or password.

- **Basic FTP authentication**   This option requires users to log on with a user name and password corresponding to a valid Windows user account.

Defining Resource Access with Permissions

Once authentication has been configured, permissions are assigned to files and folders. A common way to define resource access with IIS is through NTFS permissions. NTFS permissions, because they are attached to a file or folder, act to define access to that resource regardless of how the resource is accessed.

IIS also defines permissions on sites and virtual directories. Although NTFS permissions define a specific level of access to existing Windows user and group accounts, the directory security permissions configured for a site or virtual directory apply to *all* users and groups.

Table 10-6 details Web permission levels. These permissions can be set on the Virtual Directory or Home Directory tabs of the properties dialog box for a virtual directory or a Web site.

Table 10-6   IIS Directory Permissions

Permission	Explanation
Read (default)	Users can view file content and properties.
Write	Users can change file content and properties.
Script Source Access	Users can access the source code for files, such as the scripts in an Active Server Pages (ASP) application. This option is available only if either Read or Write permissions are assigned. Users can access source files. If Read permission is assigned, source code can be read. If Write permission is assigned, source code can be written to as well. Be aware that allowing users to have read and write access to source code can compromise the security of your server.
Directory Browsing	Users can view file lists and collections.

The Execute permissions control the security level of script execution and are described in Table 10-7. These permissions can be set on the Virtual Directory or Home Directory tabs of the properties dialog box for a virtual directory or a Web site.

Table 10-7   IIS Application Execute Permissions

Permission	Explanation
None	Set permissions for an application to None to prevent any programs or scripts from running.
Scripts Only	Set permissions for an application to Scripts Only to enable applications mapped to a script engine to run in this directory without having permissions set for executables. Setting permissions to Scripts only is more secure than setting them to Scripts and Executables because you can limit the applications that can be run in the directory.

Table 10-7   IIS Application Execute Permissions

Permission	Explanation
Scripts and Executables	Set permissions for an application to Scripts and Executables to allow any application to run in this directory, including applications mapped to script engines and Windows binaries (.dll and .exe files).

Exam Tip   If IIS permissions and NTFS permissions are both in place, the effective permissions will be the more restrictive of the two.

See Also   For more information about IIS, see the *Microsoft IIS 6.0 Administrator's Pocket Consultant* (Microsoft Press, 2003).

Practice: Administering IIS

In this practice, you will install IIS on Server01 and configure a new Web site and virtual directory.

Exercise 1: Installing IIS

1. Log on to Server01 with administrative credentials.
2. Open Add Or Remove Programs from the Control Panel, and click Add/Remove Windows Components.
3. Select Application Server, and click Details.
4. Select Internet Information Services (IIS), and click Details.
5. Ensure that, at a minimum, Common Files, File Transfer Protocol (FTP) Service, Internet Information Services Manager, and World Wide Web Service are selected.
6. Complete the installation.

Exercise 2: Preparing Simulated Web Content

1. Create a folder on the C:\ drive named ContosoCorp.
2. Create a folder on the C:\ drive named Docs.
3. Inside the Docs folder, create a folder named Project 101.
4. Open Notepad, and create a file with the text "Welcome to Contoso." Save the file as: **"C:\ContosoCorp\Default.htm"**, being certain to surround the name with quotation marks.

5. Create a second file with the text "This is the site for Project 101." Save the file as: **"C:\Docs\Project 101\Default.htm"**, being certain to surround the name with quotation marks.

Exercise 3: Creating a Web Site

1. Open the Internet Information Services (IIS) Manager snap-in from the Administrative Tools group.

2. Right-click the Default Web Site and choose Stop.

3. Right-click the Web Sites node and choose New Web Site.

4. Give the site the description Contoso and the path C:\ContosoCorp. All other default settings are acceptable.

Exercise 4: Creating a Secure Virtual Directory

1. Right-click the Contoso site, and choose New Virtual Directory.

2. Enter the alias Project101 and the path C:\Docs\Project 101 in the Virtual Directory Creation Wizard. Accept the other defaults.

3. Open the properties of the Project101 virtual directory.

4. Click Directory Security.

5. In the Authentication And Access Control area, click Edit.

6. Deselect the option to enable anonymous access. Permission to the files in the site will now require valid user accounts. Click OK twice.

7. Open Internet Explorer, and type **http://server01.contoso.com**. The Welcome To Contoso page should appear.

8. Type the URL **http://server01.contoso.com/Project101**. You will be prompted for credentials. Log on as Lorrin Smith-Bates (specify the domain with the user name, such as contoso\lsmithbates), and the Project101 home page appears.

9. Change the permissions on the C:\Docs\Project 101\Default.htm document so that only Administrators can read the document.

10. Close and reopen Internet Explorer. Connect to *http://server01.contoso.com /Project101*, and authenticate as Administrator. The page should appear.

11. Close and reopen Internet Explorer again. Now, connect to the same URL as Lorrin Smith-Bates. You should receive an Access Denied error (401 - Unauthorized).

Lesson Review

The following questions are intended to reinforce key information presented in this lesson. If you are unable to answer a question, review the lesson materials and try the question again. You can find answers to the questions in the "Questions and Answers" section at the end of this chapter.

1. You're setting up a Web site in IIS on Server01. The site's Internet domain name is *adatum.com*, and the site's home directory is C:\Web\Adatum. Which URL should Internet users use to access files in the home directory of the site?

   a. *http://server01.web.adatum*

   b. *http://web.adatum.com/server01*

   c. *http://server01.adatum/home*

   d. *http://server01.adatum.com*

2. Data for your corporate intranet is currently stored on the D drive of your IIS server. It is decided that the HR department will serve information about the company benefits and policies from its server, and that the URL to access the HR information should be *http://intranet.contoso.com/hr*. What do you need to configure?

   a. A new Web site

   b. A new FTP site

   c. A virtual directory from file

   d. A virtual directory

3. You want to ensure the highest level of security for your corporate intranet without the infrastructure of certificate services. The goal is to provide authentication that is transparent to users and to allow you to secure intranet resources with the group accounts existing in Active Directory. All users are within the corporate firewall. What authentication method should you choose?

   a. Anonymous Access

   b. Basic Authentication

   c. Digest Authentication

   d. Integrated Windows Authentication

Lesson Summary

- IIS is not installed by default. You can install it using the Windows Components Wizard through Add Or Remove Programs.

- A Web or FTP site's home directory is the physical location of resources to be served by that site.

- A virtual directory is an alias and a path that points the IIS server to the location of resources. The URL takes the form *http://server.dns.name/virtualdirectory*. The resources can be located on a local volume or remote server.

- IIS supports multiple levels of authentication. By default, Anonymous Authentication allows any connecting user to access public areas of the site, and Integrated Windows Authentication allows you to assign NTFS permissions to resources that you want to secure further.

- Access to IIS resources on NTFS volumes is controlled by ACLs, exactly as if the resource were being accessed by Windows Explorer.

- IIS has directory and application permissions. If both IIS permissions and NTFS permissions are applied, the more restrictive permissions are effective.

- The IIS configuration can be backed up using IIS Manager. It is backed up to the *%Windir%*\System32\Inetsrv\Metaback directory. From there, any backup procedure can transfer the metabase and schema files to backup media.

Lesson 4: Administering Software Update Services

To maintain a secure computing environment, it is critical to keep systems up to date with security patches. Since 1998, Microsoft has provided Windows Update as a Web-based source of information and downloads. With Windows XP and Windows 2000 Service Pack 3, Microsoft added Automatic Updates, whereby a system automatically connects to Windows Update and downloads any new, applicable patches or "hot-fixes." Although the Windows Update servers and Automatic Updates client achieve the goal of keeping systems current, many administrators are uncomfortable with either computers or users deciding which patches should be installed, because a patch might interfere with the normal functioning of a business-critical application.

The latest improvements to these technologies deliver Software Update Services (SUS). SUS is a client-server application that enables a server on your intranet to act as a point of administration for updates. You can approve updates for SUS clients, which then download and install the approved updates automatically without requiring local administrator account interaction.

After this lesson, you will be able to

- Install SUS on a Windows Server 2003 computer
- Configure SUS
- Install or deploy Automatic Updates for SUS clients
- Administer SUS and Automatic Updates
- Monitor, troubleshoot, back up, and restore SUS

Estimated lesson time: 30 minutes

Understanding SUS

Since 1998, Microsoft Windows operating systems have supported Windows Update, a globally distributed source of updates. Windows Update servers interact with client-side software to identify critical updates, security rollups, and enhancements that are appropriate to the client platform, and then to download approved patches.

Administrators wanted a more centralized solution that would assure more direct control over updates that are installed on their clients. Software Update Services is a response to that need. SUS includes several major components:

- **Software Update Services, running on an Internet Information Services (IIS) server**   The server-side component is responsible for synchronizing information about available updates and, typically, for downloading updates from the Microsoft Internet-based Windows Update servers or from other intranet servers running SUS.

- **The SUS administration Web site**   All SUS administration is Web-based. After installing and configuring SUS, administration typically consists of ensuring that the SUS server is synchronizing successfully, and approving updates for distribution to network clients.

- **Automatic Updates**   The Automatic Updates client is responsible for downloading updates from either Windows Update or an SUS server, and installing those updates based on a schedule or an administrator's initiation.

- **Group Policy settings**   Automatic Updates clients can be configured to synchronize from an SUS server rather than the Windows Update servers by modifying the clients' registries or, more efficiently, by configuring Windows Update policies in a Group Policy Object (GPO).

Installing SUS on a Windows Server 2003 Computer

SUS has both client and server components. The server component runs on a Windows 2000 Server (Service Pack 2 or later) or a Windows Server 2003 computer. Internet Information Services (IIS) must be installed before setting up SUS and, as you learned in Lesson 3, IIS is not installed by default on Windows Server 2003. For information about how to install IIS, see Lesson 3.

SUS is not included with the Windows Server 2003 media, but it is a free download from the Microsoft SUS Web site at *http://go.microsoft.com/fwlink/?LinkID=6930*. The client and server components are available in separate downloads.

> **Note**   The SUS download is not available in every localized language. However, this download determines the installation and administrative interface for the server component only. Patches for *all* locales can be made available through SUS.

After downloading the latest version of SUS, double-click the installation file for the server component and the installation routine will start. After you agree to the license agreement, choose Custom setup and the Setup Wizard will prompt you for the following information:

- **Choose File Locations**   Each Windows Update patch consists of two components: the patch file itself and metadata that specifies the platforms and languages to which the patch applies. SUS always downloads metadata, which you will use to approve updates and which clients on your intranet will retrieve from SUS. You can choose whether to download the files themselves and, if so, where to save the updates.

Tip   If you elect to maintain the update files on Microsoft Windows Update servers, Automatic Updates clients will connect to your SUS server to obtain the list of approved updates and will then connect to Microsoft Windows Update servers to download the files. You can thereby maintain control of client updating and take advantage of the globally dispersed hosting provided by Microsoft.

If you choose the Save The Updates To This Local Folder option, the Setup Wizard defaults to the drive with the most free space and will create a folder called SUS on that drive. You can save the files to any NTFS partition; Microsoft recommends a minimum of 6 gigabytes (GB) of free space.

Note   The SUS partition and the system partition must be formatted as NTFS.

- **Language Settings**   Although the SUS administrative interface is provided in English and a few additional languages, patches are released for all supported locales. This option specifies the localized versions of Windows servers or clients that you support in your environment.

- **Handling New Versions Of Previously Approved Updates**   Occasionally, an update itself is updated. You can direct SUS to automatically approve updates that are new versions of patches that you have already approved, or you can continue to approve each update manually.

- **Ready To Install**   Before installation begins, the Setup Wizard will remind you of the URL clients should point to, http://*SUS_servername*. Note this path because you will use it to configure network clients.

- **Installing Microsoft Software Update Services**   The Setup Wizard installs SUS.

- **Completing the Microsoft Software Update Services Setup Wizard**   The final page of the Setup Wizard indicates the URL for the SUS administration site, http://*SUS_servername*/SUSAdmin. Note this path as well, because you will administer SUS from that Web location. When you click Finish, your Web browser will start and you will be taken automatically to the SUS administration page.

Software Update Services installs the following three components on the server:

- The Software Update Synchronization Service, which downloads content to the SUS server

- An IIS Web site that services update requests from Automatic Updates clients

- An SUS administration Web page, from which you can synchronize the SUS server and approve updates

---

IIS Lockdown

When you run the SUS installation on Windows 2000, the SUS Setup Wizard launches the IIS Lockdown Wizard to secure IIS 5.0. Windows Server 2003 is locked down by default, so IIS Lockdown is not necessary.

If you have Web applications running on an IIS server, those applications might not function properly after SUS has been installed. You can re-enable Internet Server Application Programming Interface (ISAPI) filters and open other components that are secured by IIS Lockdown. However, because of the sensitive nature of operating system updates, you should consider running SUS on a dedicated server without other IIS applications.

Configuring and Administering SUS

You will perform three administrative tasks related to SUS: configuring SUS settings, synchronizing content, and approving content. These tasks are performed using the SUS Administration Web site, shown in Figure 10-30, which can be accessed by navigating to http://*SUS_servername*/SUSAdmin with Internet Explorer 5.5 or later, or by opening Microsoft Software Update Services from the Administrative Tools programs group. The administration of SUS is entirely Web-based.

Tip You might need to add Server01 to the Local Intranet trusted site list to access the site. Open Internet Explorer, and choose Internet Options from the Tools menu. Click the Security tab. Select Trusted Sites, and click Sites. Add Server01 and Server01.contoso.com to the trusted site list.

Note You must be a local administrator on the SUS server to administer and configure Software Update Services. This is another consideration as you review dedicating the SUS server. With a dedicated SUS server, you can delegate administration of SUS without inadvertently delegating authority over other server roles or applications.

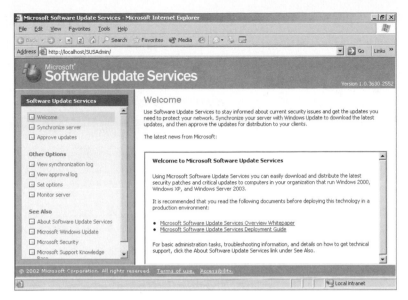

Figure 10-30   The SUS Administration Web site

Configuring Software Update Services

Although some of the configuration of SUS can be specified during a custom installation, all SUS settings are accessible from the SUS Administration Web page. From the Software Update Services administration page, click Set Options in the left navigation bar. The Set Options page is shown in Figure 10-31.

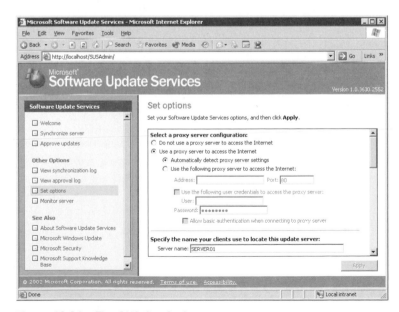

Figure 10-31   The SUS Set Options page

The configuration settings are as follows:

- **Proxy server configuration**   If the server running SUS connects to Windows Update using a proxy server, you must configure proxy settings.

> **Tip**   Although the SUS server can be configured to access Windows Update through a proxy server that requires authentication, the Automatic Updates client cannot access Windows Update if the proxy server requires authentication. If your proxy server requires authentication, you can configure SUS to authenticate and you must store all update content—files as well as metadata—locally.

- **DNS name of the SUS server**   In the Server Name box, type the fully qualified domain name (FQDN) of the SUS server—for example, **sus1.contoso.com**.

- **Content source**   The first SUS server you install will synchronize its content from Microsoft Windows Update. Additional SUS servers can synchronize from Windows Update, from a "parent" SUS server, or from a manually created content distribution point. See the "SUS Topology" sidebar for more information.

- **New versions of approved updates**   The Set Options page allows you to modify how SUS handles new versions of previously approved updates. This option is discussed earlier in the lesson.

- **File storage**   You can modify the storage of metadata and update files. This option is also discussed earlier in the lesson.

> **Tip**   If you change the storage location from a Windows Update server to a local server folder, you should immediately perform a synchronization to download the necessary packages to the selected location.

- **Languages**   This setting determines the locale-specific updates that are synchronized. Select only languages for locales that you support in your environment.

> **Tip**   If you remove a locale, the packages that have been downloaded are not deleted; however, clients will no longer receive those packages. If you *add* a locale, perform a manual synchronization to download appropriate packages for the new locale

SUS Topology

Software Update Services is all about enabling you to control the approval and distribution of updates from Microsoft Windows Update. In a small organization, SUS can be as simple as one server, synchronizing from Windows Update and providing a list of approved updates to clients.

In a larger organization, SUS topologies can be developed to make SUS more scalable and efficient.

■ **Multiple server topology**   Each SUS server synchronizes content from Windows Update and manages its own list of approved updates. This is a variation of a single-server model, and each SUS server administrator has control over that server's list of approved updates. Such a configuration also allows an organization to maintain a variety of patch and update configurations (one per SUS server). Clients can be directed to obtain updates from an SUS server with the appropriate list of approved updates.

■ **Strict parent/child topology**   A "parent" SUS server synchronizes content from Windows Update and stores updates in a local folder. The SUS administrator then approves updates. Other SUS servers in the enterprise synchronize from the parent and are configured, on the Set Options page, to Synchronize List Of Approved Items Updated From This Location (Replace Mode). This setting causes the child SUS servers to synchronize both the update files and the list of approved updates. Network clients can then be configured to retrieve updates from the SUS server in or closest to their site. In this configuration (Synchronize List Of Approved Items), administrators of child SUS servers *cannot* approve or disapprove updates; that task is managed on the parent SUS server only.

■ **Loose parent/child topology**   A "parent" SUS server synchronizes content from Windows Update and stores updates in a local folder. Other SUS servers in the enterprise synchronize from the parent. Unlike the strict configuration, these additional SUS servers do not synchronize the list of approved updates, so administrators of those servers can approve or disapprove updates independently. Although this topology increases administrative overhead, it is helpful when an organization wants to minimize Internet exposure (because only the parent SUS server needs to connect to the Internet), and it requires (as in the multiple-server model) distributed power of update approval or a variety of client patch and update configurations.

■ **Test/production topology** This model allows an organization to create a testing or staging of updates. The parent SUS server downloads updates from Windows Update, and an administrator approves updates to be tested. One or more clients retrieve updates from the parent SUS server and act as test platforms. Once updates have been approved, tested, and verified, the contents of the parent SUS server are copied to a manually created content distribution point on a second IIS server. Production SUS servers synchronize both the updates and the list of approved updates from the manual content distribution point. The steps for configuring such a manual distribution point are detailed in the Software Update Service Deployment White Paper, available from the Microsoft SUS Web site.

Synchronizing SUS

On the SUS Administration Web page, click Synchronize Server. On the Synchronize Server page (shown in Figure 10-32), you can start a manual synchronization or configure automatic, scheduled synchronization. Click Synchronize Now and, when synchronization is complete, you will be informed of its success or failure. In addition, if the synchronization was successful, you will be taken to the Approve Updates page.

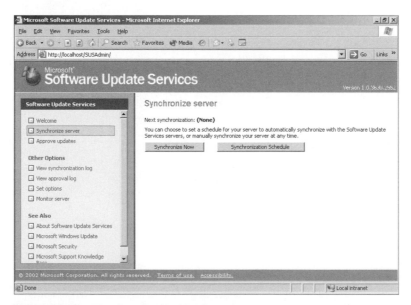

Figure 10-32 The Synchronize Server page

To schedule synchronization, click Synchronization Schedule. You can configure the time of day for synchronization, as shown in Figure 10-33, and whether synchronization occurs daily or weekly on a specified day. When a scheduled synchronization fails, SUS will try again for the Number Of Synchronization Retries To Attempt setting. Retries occur at 30-minute intervals.

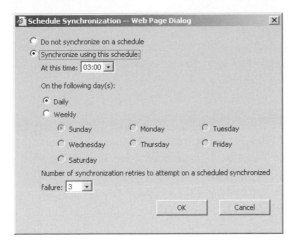

Figure 10-33   The Schedule Synchronization Web Page Dialog page

Approving Updates

To approve updates for distribution to client computers, click Approve Updates in the left navigation bar. The Approve Updates page, as shown in Figure 10-34, appears. Select the updates you want to approve, and then click Approve. If you are unsure about the applicability of a particular update, click the Details link in the update summary. The Details page that opens will include a link to the actual *.cab file that is used to install the package and a link to the Read More page about the update, which will open the Microsoft Knowledge Base article related to the update.

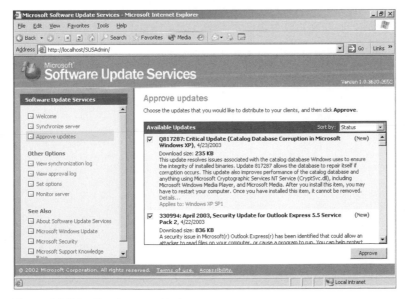

Figure 10-34   The Approve Updates page

Tip The first synchronization will download dozens of updates. It might be tedious to scroll and click each check box for approval. Instead, after clicking the first check box, press TAB twice to navigate to the next check box, and press the spacebar to select (or clear) the item.

The Automatic Updates Client

The client component of SUS is Windows Automatic Updates, which is supported on Windows 2000, Windows XP, and Windows Server 2003. The Automatic Updates client is included with Windows Server 2003, Windows 2000 Service Pack 3, and Windows XP Service Pack 1.

For clients running earlier releases of the supported platforms, you can download Automatic Updates as a stand-alone client from the Microsoft SUS Web site, at *http://go.microsoft.com/fwlink/?LinkID=6930*. The client, provided as an .msi file, can be installed on a stand-alone computer or by means of Group Policy (by assigning the package in the Computer Configuration\Software Settings policy), SMS, or even a logon script. If a localized version of the client is not available, install the English version on any locale.

The Automatic Updates client of Windows Server 2003 is configured to connect automatically to the Microsoft Windows Update server, download updates, and then prompt the user to install them. This behavior can be modified by accessing the Automatic Updates tab in the System Properties dialog box, accessible by clicking System in Control Panel in Windows XP and Windows Server 2003. In Windows 2000, click Automatic Updates in Control Panel. The Automatic Updates tab is shown in Figure 10-35. Automatic Updates can also be configured using GPOs or registry values.

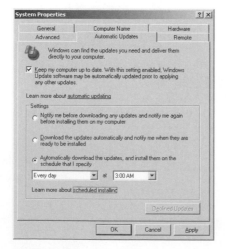

Figure 10-35 The Automatic Updates tab of the System Properties dialog box

Download Behavior

Automatic Updates supports two download behaviors:

■ **Automatic**   Updates are downloaded without notification to the user.

■ **Notification**   If Automatic Updates is configured to notify the user before down-loading updates, it registers the notification of an available update in the system event log and to a logged-on administrator of the computer. If an administrator is not logged on, Automatic Updates waits for a user with administrator credentials before offering notification by means of a balloon in the notification area of the system tray.

Once update downloading has begun, Automatic Updates uses the Background Intelligent Transfer Service (BITS) to perform the file transfer using idle network bandwidth. BITS ensures that network performance is not hindered because of file transfer. All patches are checked by the SUS server to determine whether they have been correctly signed by Microsoft. Similarly, the Automatic Updates client confirms the Microsoft signature and also examines the cyclical redundancy check (CRC) on each package before installing it.

Installation Behavior

Automatic Updates provides two options for installation:

■ **Notification**   Automatic Updates registers an event in the system log indicating that updates are ready for installation. Notification will wait until a local administrator is logged on before taking further action. When an administrative user is logged on, a balloon notification appears in the system tray. The administrator clicks the balloon or the notification icon, and then can select from available updates before clicking Install. If an update requires restarting the computer, Automatic Updates cannot detect additional updates that might be applicable until after the restart.

■ **Automatic (Scheduled)**   When updates have been downloaded successfully, an event is logged to the system event log. If an administrator is logged on, a notification icon appears, and the administrator can manually launch installation at any time until the scheduled installation time.

At the scheduled installation time, an administrator who is logged on will be notified with a countdown message prior to installation and will have the option to cancel installation, in which case the installation is delayed until the next scheduled time. If a nonadministrator is logged on, a warning dialog appears, but the user cannot delay installation. If no user is logged on, installation occurs automatically. If an update requires restart, a five-minute countdown notification appears informing users of the impending restart. Only an administrative user can cancel the restart.

Tip If the computer is not turned on at the scheduled Automatic Updates installation time, installation will wait to the next scheduled time. If the computer is never on at the scheduled time, installation will not occur. Ensure that systems remain turned on to be certain that Automatic Updates install successfully.

Configuring Automatic Updates Through Group Policy

Exam Tip Be sure to understand the policies and their impact on the behavior of update download and installation for an SUS client.

The Automatic Updates client will, by default, connect to the Microsoft Windows Update server. Once you have installed SUS in your organization, you can direct Automatic Updates to connect to specific intranet servers by configuring the registry of clients manually or by using Windows Update group policies.

To configure Automatic Updates using GPOs, open a GPO and navigate to the Computer Configuration\Administrative Templates\Windows Components\Windows Update node. The Windows Update policies are shown in Figure 10-36.

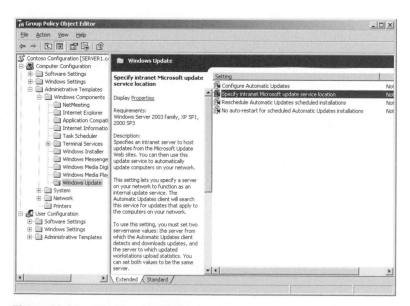

Figure 10-36 Windows Update policies

Note   If you edit policy on a Windows 2000 Active Directory server, the policies might not appear. Automatic Updates policies are described by the *%Windir%*\Inf\Wuau.inf administrative template, which is installed by default when Automatic Updates is installed. If Automatic Updates has not been installed on the domain controller to which you are connected (typically, the PDC Emulator), you must right-click the Administrative Templates node and choose Add/Remove Templates, click Add, and then locate the Wuau.inf template, perhaps by copying it from a system that does have Automatic Updates installed.

The following policies are available, each playing an important role in configuring effective update distribution in your enterprise:

- **Configure Automatic Updates**   The Configure Automatic Updates Behavior determines the behavior of the Automatic Updates client. There are three options: Notify For Download And Notify For Install, Auto Download And Notify For Install, and Auto Download And Schedule The Install. These options are combinations of the installation and download behaviors discussed earlier in the lesson.

- **Specify Intranet Microsoft Update Service Location**   This policy allows you to redirect Automatic Updates to a server running SUS. By default, the client will log its interactions on the SUS server to which it connects. However, this policy allows you to point clients to another server running IIS for statistics logging. This dual policy provides the opportunity for clients to obtain updates from a local SUS server, but for all clients to log SUS statistics in a single location for easier retrieval and analysis of the log data, which is stored as part of the IIS log, IIS logs typically reside in *%Windir%*\System32\Logfiles\W3svc1.

- **Reschedule Automatic Updates Scheduled Installations**   If installations are scheduled and the client computer is turned off at the scheduled time, the default behavior is to wait for the next scheduled time. The Reschedule Automatic Updates Scheduled Installations policy, if set to a value between 1 and 60, causes Automatic Updates to reschedule installation for the specified number of minutes after system startup.

- **No Auto-Restart For Scheduled Automatic Updates Installations**   This policy causes Automatic Updates to forego a restart required by an installed update when a user is logged on to the system. Instead, the user is notified that a restart is required for installation to complete, and can restart the computer at his or her discretion. Remember that Automatic Updates cannot detect new updates until restart has occurred.

Automatic Updates clients poll their SUS server every 22 hours, minus a random offset.

Any delay in patching should be treated as unacceptable when security vulnerabilities are being actively exploited. In such situations, install the patch manually so that systems do not have to wait to poll, download, and install patches.

After approved updates have been downloaded from the SUS server, they will be installed as configured—manually or automatically—at the scheduled time. If an approved update is later unapproved, that update is not uninstalled; but it will not be installed by additional clients. An installed update *can* be uninstalled manually, using the Add Or Remove Programs application in Control Panel.

SUS Troubleshooting

Although SUS works well, there are occasions that warrant monitoring and troubleshooting.

Monitoring SUS

The Monitor Server page of the SUS Administration Web site displays statistics that reflect the number of updates available for each platform, and the date and time of the most recent update. The information is summarized from the Windows Update metadata that is downloaded during each synchronization. Metadata information is written to disk and stored in memory to improve performance as systems request platform-appropriate updates.

You can also monitor SUS and Automatic Updates using the following logs:

- **Synchronization Log**   You can retrieve information about current or past synchronizations, and the specific packages that were downloaded by clicking View Synchronization Log in the left navigation bar. You can also use any text editor to open the (Extensible Markup Language) XML–based database (History-Sync.xml) directly from the SUS Web site's \AutoUpdate\Administration directory in IIS.

- **Approval Log**   For information about packages that have been approved, click View Approval Log in the left navigation bar. Alternatively, you can open History-Approve.xml from the SUS Web site's \AutoUpdate\Administration directory in IIS.

- **Windows Update Log**   The Automatic Updates client logs activity in the *%Windir%*\Windows Update.log file on the client's local hard disk.

- **Wutrack.bin**   The client's interaction with SUS is logged to the specified statistics server's IIS logs, typically stored in the folder *%Windir%*\System32\Logfiles\W3svc1. These logs, which are verbose and cryptic, are designed to be analyzed by programs, not by humans.

Exam Tip   Although you should know what logs are available and where they are located, you are not required in the exams to be able to interpret cryptic messages or log entries. The Software Update Services Deployment White Paper includes appendices with detailed information about event descriptions and log syntax.

SUS System Events

The synchronization service generates event log messages for each synchronization performed by the server, and when updates are approved. These messages can be viewed in the System log using Event Viewer. The events relate to the following scenarios:

- **Unable to connect**   Automatic Updates could not connect to the update service (Windows Update or the computer's assigned SUS server).

- **Install ready–no recurring schedule**   Updates listed in the event were downloaded and are pending installation. An administrator must click the notification icon and click Install.

- **Install ready–recurring schedule**   Updates listed in the event are downloaded and will be installed at the date and time specified in the event.

- **Installation success**   Updates listed in the event were installed successfully.

- **Installation failure**   Updates listed in the event failed to install properly.

- **Restart required–no recurring schedule**   An update requires a restart. If installation behavior is set for notification, restart must be performed manually. Windows cannot search for new updates until the restart has occurred.

- **Restart required–recurring schedule**   When Automatic Updates is configured to automatically install updates, an event is registered if an update requires restart. Restart will occur within five minutes. Windows cannot search for new updates until after the restart has occurred.

Troubleshooting SUS

Software Update Services on a Windows Server 2003 computer might require the following troubleshooting steps:

- **Reloading the memory cache**   If no new updates appear since the last time you synchronized the server, it is possible that no new updates are available. However, it is also possible that memory caches are not loading new updates properly. From the SUS administration site, click Monitor Server and then click Refresh.

- **Restarting the synchronization service**   If you receive a message that the synchronization service is not running properly, or if you cannot modify settings in the Set Options page of the administration Web site, open the Services console, right-click Software Update Services Synchronization Service, and choose Restart.

- **Restarting IIS**   If you cannot connect to the administration site, or if clients cannot connect to the SUS serve, restart the World Wide Web Publishing Service in the same manner.

If Automatic Updates clients do not appear to be receiving updates properly, open the registry of a client and ensure that the following values appear in HKEY_LOCAL_MACHINE\Software\Policies\Microsoft\Windows\WindowsUpdate:

- **WUSever**   Should have the URL of the SUS server—for example, http://*SUS_server name*.

- **WUStatusServer**   Should have the URL of the same SUS server or another IIS server on which synchronization statistics are logged.

And ensure the following value appears in the AU subkey:

- **UseWUServer**   Should be set to dword:00000001.

SUS Backup and Recovery

As with any other server role or application, you must plan for recovery in the event of a server failure.

Backing Up SUS

To back up SUS, you must back up the folder that contains SUS content, the SUS Administration Web site, and the IIS metabase.

> **Exam Tip**   The process described to back up the IIS metabase is useful not only for backing up SUS, but for any other Web site or application running on Windows Server 2003 and IIS 6.0.

First, back up the metabase—an XML database containing the configuration of IIS. Using the Internet Information Services (IIS) Manager console, select the server to back up and, from the Action menu, select All Tasks, and then Backup/Restore Configuration. Click Create Backup, and enter a name for the backup. When you click OK, the metabase is backed up.

Then back up the following using Backup (Ntbackup.exe) or another backup utility:

- The default Web site, which is located (unless otherwise configured) in C:\Inetpub\Wwwroot.

- The SUS Administration Web site. SUSAdmin is, by default, a subfolder of C:\Inet-pub\Wwwroot. In that event, it will be backed up when you back up the default Web site.

- The AutoUpdate virtual directory, also by default a subfolder of C:\Inet-pub\Wwwroot.

- The SUS content location you specified in SUS setup or the SUS options. You can confirm the SUS content location in IIS Manager by clicking Default Web Site and examining the path to the Content virtual root in the details pane.

- The metabase backup directory, *%Windir%*\System32\Inetsrv\Metaback, which contains the copy of the metabase made earlier.

> **See Also**   For more information about the Backup Utility, see Chapter 13.

This process of backing up the metabase, and then backing up the components of SUS, should be repeated regularly because updates will be added and approved with some frequency.

SUS Server Recovery

To restore a failed SUS server, perform the following steps. If a certain step is unnecessary, you can skip it, but perform the remaining steps in sequence.

1. Disconnect the server from the network to prevent it from being infected with viruses.

2. Install Windows Server 2003, being sure to give the server the same name it had previously.

3. Install IIS with the same components it had previously.

4. Install the latest service pack and security fixes. If the server must be connected to the network to achieve this step, take all possible precautions to prevent unnecessary exposure.

5. Install SUS into the same folder it was previously installed.

6. Run Backup to restore the most recent backup of SUS. This will include the SUS content folder, the Default Web Site, including the SUSAdmin and AutoUpdate virtual directories, and the IIS metabase backup.

7. Open the IIS Manager, and select the server to restore. From the Action menu, select All Tasks and then Backup/Restore Configuration, and select the backup that was just restored. Click Restore.

8. Confirm the success of your recovery by opening the SUS Administration Web site and clicking Set Options. Check that the previous settings are in place and that the previously approved updates are still approved.

> **Note**   The preceding steps apply to Windows Server 2003 only. If you are recovering a Windows 2000–based SUS server, refer to SUS documentation for appropriate steps.

Designing a Network Security Update Infrastructure

A network *security update infrastructure* is a series of policies that are designed to help the network administrator perform the following tasks:

- **Determine which computers need to be updated**   In some cases, a new security update might apply only to computers performing a specific function or using a specific application or feature. Network administrators must understand each release's specific function and determine which computers require the update.

- **Test update releases on multiple system configurations**   A security update that causes a malfunction might be just an annoyance on a single computer, but on a large network, it could be a catastrophe. Network administrators must perform their own tests of all security updates before deploying them on the entire network.

- **Determine when updates are released**   Microsoft frequently releases security updates that might or might not be applicable to the systems on your network. Network administrators must be aware of new releases when they occur and must understand the specific issues each release addresses.

- **Deploy update releases on large fleets**   Manually installing security updates on hundreds or thousands of computers requires enormous amounts of time, effort, and expense. To deploy updates on a large network efficiently, the process must be automated.

Using Microsoft Baseline Security Analyzer

You have learned in this lesson that SUS plays a major role in the creation of a network security update infrastructure. SUS does not, however, provide an easy way to confirm the update status of a specific computer. The Microsoft Baseline Security Analyzer (MBSA) is a graphical tool (shown in Figure 10-37) that can check for common security lapses on a single computer or multiple computers running various versions of the Windows operating system. These lapses are typically due to incorrect or incomplete configuration of security features and failure to install security updates. The security faults that MBSA can detect are as follows:

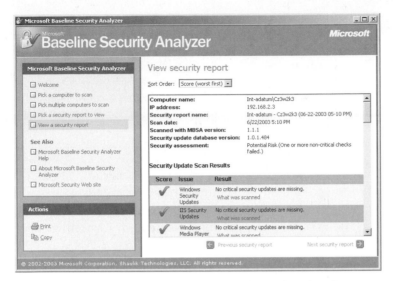

Figure 10-37   The Microsoft Baseline Security Analyzer interface

- **Missing security updates**   Using a list of current update releases obtained from a Microsoft Internet server or from a local Microsoft Software Update Services (SUS) server, MBSA determines whether all the required service packs and security updates have been installed on the computer, and if not, it compiles a list of the updates that need to be installed.

Tip   MBSA replaces an earlier security checking utility named Microsoft Network Security Hotfix Checker (Hfnetchk.exe), which operates from the command line and checks computers only for missing updates. MBSA includes all the functionality of Hfnetchk.exe, including the command-line interface, which you can activate by running Mbsacli.exe with the /hf parameter.

- **Account vulnerabilities**   MBSA checks to see whether the Guest account is activated on the computer; whether there are more than two accounts with Administrator privileges; whether anonymous users have too much access to the computer; and whether the computer is configured to use the Autologon feature.

- **Improper passwords**   MBSA checks the passwords on all the computer's accounts to see whether they are configured to expire, are blank, or are too simple.

- **File system vulnerabilities**   MBSA checks to see whether all the disk drives on the computer are using the NTFS file system.

- **IIS and SQL vulnerabilities**   If the computer is running IIS or Microsoft SQL Server, MBSA examines these applications for a variety of security weaknesses.

In addition, MBSA displays other information about security on the computer, such as a list of shares, the Windows operating system version number, and whether auditing is enabled.

> **See Also**   MBSA is not included with Windows Server 2003, but it is available without charge from the Microsoft Web site at *http://download.microsoft.com/download/8/e/e /8ee73487-4d36-4f7f-92f2-2bdc5c5385b3/mbsasetup.msi*.

MBSA is an informational tool that can display security information about a computer, but it cannot do anything to remedy the vulnerabilities that it finds. You can use MBSA to determine which security updates to install on specific computers, but to develop an effective security update infrastructure, you must implement a system to keep track of which security updates have been installed on every computer in the enterprise.

Lesson Review

The following questions are intended to reinforce key information presented in this lesson. If you are unable to answer a question, review the lesson materials and try the question again. You can find answers to the questions in the "Questions and Answers" section at the end of this chapter.

1. You are configuring a Software Update Services infrastructure. One server is synchronizing metadata and content from Windows Update. Other servers (one in each site) are synchronizing content from the parent SUS server. Which of the following steps are required to complete the SUS infrastructure? (Choose all that apply.)

   a. Configure Automatic Updates clients using Control Panel on each system.

   b. Configure GPOs to direct clients to the SUS server in their sites.

   c. Configure a manual content distribution point.

   d. Approve updates using the SUS administration page.

2. You are configuring SUS for a group of Web servers. You want the Web servers to update themselves nightly based on a list of approved updates on your SUS server. However, once in a while an administrator is logged on, performing late-night maintenance on a Web server, and you do not want update installation and potential restart to interfere with those tasks. What Windows Update policy configuration should you use in this scenario?

   a. Notify For Download And Notify For Install

   b. Auto Download And Notify For Install

   c. Auto Download And Schedule The Install.

   _____

   _____

   _____

3. You want all network clients to download and install updates automatically during night hours, and you have configured scheduled installation behavior for Automatic Updates. However, you discover that some users are turning off their machines at night and updates are not being applied. Which policy allows you to correct this situation without changing the installation schedule?

   a. Specify Intranet Microsoft Update Service Location

   b. No Auto-Restart For Scheduled Automatic Updates Installations

   c. Reschedule Automatic Updates Scheduled Installations

   d. Configure Automatic Update

   _____

   _____

   _____

   _____

   _____

Lesson Summary

- SUS is an intranet application that runs on IIS 6.0 (or on IIS 5.0 on a Windows 2000 Server) and is administered through a Web-based administration site: http://SUS_Servername/SUSAdmin.

- The SUS server synchronizes information about critical updates and security rollups and allows an administrator to configure approval centrally for each update. Typically, an enterprise configures SUS to download the actual update files as well.

- Automatic Updates, which runs on Windows 2000, Windows XP, and Windows Server 2003, is responsible for downloading and installing updates on the client.

- Group Policy can be used to configure Automatic Updates to retrieve patches from an SUS server rather than from the Windows Update servers. GPOs can also drive the download, installation, and restart behavior of the client computers.

- Microsoft Baseline Security Analyzer is a tool that scans computers on a network and examines them for security vulnerabilities, such as missing security updates, improper passwords, and account vulnerabilities.

Case Scenario Exercise

You are configuring an update strategy for a network consisting of 1,000 clients running a mix of Windows XP and Windows 2000. Developers use Windows Server 2003 as their desktop operating system. Your goal is to prevent users from downloading updates directly from Windows Update, and to create a structure in which you can approve critical patches and security rollups for distribution.

Exercise 1: Installing SUS

1. Log on to Server01 with administrative credentials.

2. Navigate to *http://go.microsoft.com/fwlink/?LinkId=6930*. You will be prompted to add the site to your trusted sites list, which you should do.

3. Download the SUS server component.

4. Start the SUS installation by double-clicking the downloaded file.

5. On the Welcome screen, click Next.

6. Read and accept the End User License Agreement, and then click Next.

7. Choose a Custom installation, and then click Next.

8. On the Choose File Locations page, choose Save The Updates To This Local Folder. The default, C:\SUS\Content, is fine. Click Next.

> **Note**   The updates might consist of several hundred megabytes of files. If you have a slow Internet connection, or if you want to save time during this exercise, choose the second option, Keep The Updates On A Microsoft Windows Update Server instead.

9. For Language Settings, choose English Only and then click Next.

10. On the following page, choose I Will Manually Approve New Versions Of Approved Updates and then click Next.

11. The following page should indicate that the client download location is *http://SERVER01*. Click Install.

12. When installation is complete, click Finish. Internet Explorer will be opened, and it will take you to the SUS administration page. Continue with Exercise 2.

Exercise 2: Synchronizing SUS

1. If you are not already viewing the SUS administration page, open Internet Explorer and navigate to *http://SERVER01/SUSAdmin*.

> **Note**   To view the SUS administration site, you might need to add Server01 to the Local Intranet trusted site list to access the site. Open Internet Explorer, and choose Internet Options from the Tools menu. Click the Security Tab. Select Trusted Sites, and click Sites. Add **Server01** and **Server01.contoso.com** to the trusted site list.

2. Click Synchronize Server on the left navigation bar.

3. Click Synchronization Schedule.

   You will manually synchronize for this exercise. However, you can examine synchronization options by clicking Synchronize Using This Schedule. When you are finished exploring settings, click Cancel.

4. On the Synchronize Server page, click Synchronize Now. If you have elected to download updates to the server, synchronization might take some time.

5. After synchronization has occurred, you will be redirected automatically to the Approve Updates page. You can also click Approve Updates on the left navigation bar.

6. Approve a small number of updates so that you can return later to experiment further with approval and automatic updates.

7. Examine other pages of the SUS administration site. After you have familiarized yourself with the site, close Internet Explorer.

Exercise 3: Configuring Automatic Updates

1. Open Active Directory Sites And Services.

> **Note**   Most enterprises have found little reason to link GPOs to sites, rather than to OUs or the domain. However, SUS-related policies lend themselves well to site application because you are directing clients to the most site-appropriate SUS server.

2. Right-click the Default-First-Site-Name site, and choose Properties.

3. Click the Group Policy tab.

4. Click New, and name the new GPO **SUS-Site1**.

5. Click Edit. The Group Policy Object Editor opens.

6. Navigate to Computer Configuration\Administrative Templates\Windows Components\Windows Update.

7. Double-click the policy Specify Intranet Microsoft Update Service Location.

8. Click Enabled.

9. In *both* text boxes, type **http://server01.contoso.com**.

10. Click OK.

11. Double-click the policy Configure Automatic Updates.

12. Click Enabled.

13. In the Configure Automatic Updating drop-down list, choose 4-Auto Download And Schedule The Install.

14. Confirm the installation schedule as daily at 3:00 A.M.

15. Click OK.

16. Double-click the policy Reschedule Automatic Updates Scheduled Installations.

17. Click Enabled.

18. In the Wait After System Startup (Minutes) box, type **1**.

> **Exam Tip**   The Wait After System Startup policy is used to reschedule a scheduled installation that was missed, typically when a machine was turned off at the scheduled date and time.

19. Click OK.

20. Close the Group Policy Object Editor and the Properties dialog box for Default-First-Site-Name.

21. To confirm the configuration, you can restart Server02, which is also within the scope of the new policy. Open System from Control Panel, and click the Automatic Updates tab. You will see that configuration options are disabled, as they are now being determined by policy.

Troubleshooting Lab

Contoso, Ltd. wants to configure an intranet site for company and departmental news. The specifications call for the site to be easy to use by employees, who will use the latest version of Internet Explorer.

Before you begin this lab:

- You must have installed IIS on Server02 as described in Lesson 3, Exercise 1.

- On Server01, create a global security group named **Project Contractors**.

- Create a user account for **Jay Adams**. Make note of his username and password—you will be logging on as Jay Adams during the exercise.

- Confirm the existence of, or create, a user account for **Lorrin Smith-Bates**. Make note of his username and password—you will be logging on as Lorrin Smith-Bates during the exercise.

- Add Jay Adams to the Project Contractors and Print Operators groups.

- Add Lorrin Smith-Bates to the Print Operators group.

Exercise 1: Creating Sample Web Content

> **Note** There are several ways to create a virtual directory. In this situation, please use the methods described.

1. Log on to Server02 with administrative credentials.

2. Create a folder named **C:\ContosoIntranetNews**.

3. Open Notepad, and create a file with the text "Contoso Company News." Save the file as **"C:\ ContosoIntranetNews\Default.htm"**, being certain to surround the name with quotation marks.

4. In the C:\ContosoIntranetNews folder's Properties dialog box, click the Web Sharing tab.

5. From the Share On drop-down list, choose Contoso. If you did not complete the exercises in Lesson 3, you will not have the Contoso Web site; choose the Default Web Site instead. Click Share This Folder, and type the alias **News**. The default permissions are adequate. Click OK.

Exercise 2: Testing Intranet Access

In this exercise, you will confirm the functionality of the intranet and optimize its ease of use.

1. Log on to Server01 as Lorrin Smith-Bates.

2. Open Internet Explorer and type the URL **http://server02.contoso.com/News**.

3. You will be prompted for credentials. Authenticate as **Contoso\Lorrin** (or the user name you specified for Lorrin Smith-Bates). The Contoso Company News page should appear.

4. Close Internet Explorer.

5. Log off of Server01.

6. Log on to Server01 as Jay Adams

7. Open Internet Explorer, and type the URL: **http://server02.contoso.com/News**.

8. You will be prompted for credentials. Authenticate as **Contoso\Jay** (or the user name you specified for Jay Adams). The Contoso Company News page should appear.

The Problems

Users at Contoso are complaining that they are constantly being prompted for credentials when accessing the Company News site. In addition, contractors are able to access the news site, and management wants to restrict them from accessing the intranet news.

The Solutions

1. Why are users being prompted for credentials? How can you solve the problem? If you believe you know the answer, make appropriate changes and repeat steps 1 to 4 of Exercise 2 to confirm the success of your solution. If you need direction, turn to the "Question and Answers" section at the end of the chapter.

_____

_____

_____

_____

_____

_____

_____

_____

2. How can you restrict users in the Project Contractors group from accessing the company news? If you believe you know the answer, make appropriate changes and repeat steps 5 to 8 of Exercise 2 to confirm the success of your solution. If you need direction, turn to the "Question and Answers" section at the end of the chapter.

_____

_____

_____

_____

Chapter Summary

- Remote Desktop For Administration and Terminal Server require permissions and user rights for users that attempt to connect with the Remote Desktop Connection client. By default, permission to connect and the right to log on through terminal services are granted only to the Remote Desktop Users group, and that group contains, by default, only the Administrator account.

- IIS supports multiple levels of authentication. Anonymous Authentication allows any connecting user to access public areas of the site, and Integrated Windows Authentication allows you to assign NTFS permissions to resources that you want to secure further.

- The IIS configuration can be backed up using IIS Manager. It is backed up to the *%Windir%*\System32\Inetsrv\Metaback directory. From there, any backup procedure can transfer the metabase and schema files to backup media.

- SUS is an intranet application that runs on IIS 6.0 (or on IIS 5.0 on a Windows 2000 Server) and is administered through a Web-based administration site, http: //*SUS_Servername*/SUSAdmin.

- Group Policy can be used to configure Automatic Updates to retrieve patches from an SUS server rather than from the Windows Update servers. GPOs can also drive the download, installation, and restart behavior of the client computers.

Exam Highlights

Before taking the exam, review the following key points and terms to help you identify topics you need to review. Return to the lessons for additional practice and review the "Further Readings" sections in Part 2 for pointers to more information about topics covered by the exam objectives.

Key Points

- A domain controller's security policy does not, by default, grant the Allow Logon Through Terminal Services user right.

- Port 3389, the same port used by Remote Desktop For Administration and Terminal Server, must be open at the firewall for Remote Assistance sessions to be established.

- IIS is not installed by default for Windows Server 2003. You can install it using the Windows Components Wizard through Add Or Remove Programs.

- Experience and understand the configuration of a Web site and virtual directory. If you are not experienced with IIS, be certain to implement the Practice in Lesson 3 as well as the Troubleshooting Lab.

■ Software Update Services does not distribute service packs or update applications.

■ Have an understanding of SUS installation and configuration. Although the exam objectives will not address SUS setup directly, the way you configure SUS impacts the tasks you will perform to maintain the SUS infrastructure, so it is important to be comfortable with the big picture of SUS.

■ Focus on SUS administrative tasks, such as synchronizing, approving updates, viewing logs and events, and configuring Automatic Updates through System in Control Panel (on a stand-alone computer) or using Group Policy in a larger environment. Remember that you cannot direct a computer to an SUS server using the Automatic Updates properties on a client. You must use Group Policy or a registry entry to redirect the client to an intranet server rather than Microsoft Windows Update.

Key Terms

Remote Desktop For Administration   Remote Desktop For Administration is installed by default on Windows Server 2003 and allows for the same administration of a server from a remote location as if logged on to the local console interactively. This was called Terminal Services, Administration Mode in Windows 2000.

Terminal Server   Terminal Server provides applications in a multiuser environment. Those applications must be installed using Add Or Remove Programs or the Change User command. This was called Terminal Services, Application Mode in Windows 2000.

Virtual directory   A virtual directory is an IIS object that allows a folder on any local or remote volume to appear as a subfolder of a Web site.

Questions and Answers

Page
10-23

Lesson 1 Review

1. Can a snap-in have focus on both the local computer and a remote computer simultaneously?

   No. Snap-ins can be configured to connect to the local computer or a remote computer, but not to both simultaneously.

2. What credentials are required for administration of a remote computer using the MMC?

   You must have administrative credentials on the remote computer to perform remote administration.

3. Can an existing MMC snap-in be changed from local to remote context, or must a snap-in of the same type be loaded into the MMC for remote connection?

   A snap-in's context might be changed by accessing the properties of the snap-in. A snap-in does not have to be reloaded to change its configuration.

4. Are all functions within a snap-in used on a local computer usable when connected remotely?

   No, not all functionality is available. The Device Manager component in the Computer Management snap-in, for example, can be used only to view remote computer configurations: no changes can be made to the remote computer's device configuration.

5. How many simultaneous connections are possible to a server using Remote Desktop For Administration? Why?

   Three; two remote connections and one at the console (but that's not fair, is it?). Technically, then, two is the limit because the application-sharing components are not installed with terminal services when configured for Remote Desktop For Administration.

6. What would be the best way to give administrators the ability to administer a server remotely through Terminal Services?

   a. Don't do anything; they already have access because they are administrators.

   b. Remove the Administrators group from the permission list on the Terminal Server connection, and put the Administrator account in the Remote Desktop Users group.

   c. Create a separate, lower-authorization user account for Administrators to use daily, and place that account in the Remote Desktop Users group.

   The correct answer is c. It is a best practice to log on using an account with minimal credentials, and then to launch administrative tools with higher-level credentials using Run As.

7. What tool is used to enable Remote Desktop on a server?

   a. Terminal Services Manager

   b. Terminal Services Configuration

   c. System properties in Control Panel

   d. Terminal Services Licensing

   c

8. How is Remote Assistance like Remote Desktop For Administration? How is it different?

   Remote Assistance allows for remote control of a computer as if the user were physically at the console, as does a connection to a Terminal Server via Remote Desktop For Administration.

   Remote Desktop For Administration is controlled solely by the directory of accounts, either local or domain, that is configured for the Terminal Server connections on that computer. Remote Assistance requires a "handshake" of sorts between the user and the expert helper.

9. Which of the following are firewall-related constraints relating to Remote Assistance?

   a. Port 3389 must be open.

   b. NAT cannot be used.

   c. Internet Connection Sharing is not possible.

   d. You cannot use Remote Assistance across a Virtual Private Network (VPN).

   a

Page
10-44

Lesson 2 Review

1. You have enabled Remote Desktop connections on Server02, a member server in the contoso.com domain. Terminal Server is installed on Server02. You want Danielle Tiedt to be able to connect using the Remote Desktop Connection client. What additional configuration must first be performed on Server02?

   Add Danielle Tiedt to the local Remote Desktop Users group on Server02.

2. You have enabled Remote Desktop connections on Server01, a domain controller in the contoso.com domain. Terminal Server is installed on Server01. You want Jay Adams to be able to connect using the Remote Desktop Connection client. Jay is a member of the Remote Desktop Users group on Server01. What additional configuration must first be performed for Jay to successfully connect?

   Configure a GPO, such as the Default Domain Controllers GPO, so that the user right Allow Logon Through Terminal Services is configured and assigned to the Remote Desktop Users group.

3. Name three locations where you can configure Terminal Server settings that will override settings on the Remote Desktop Connection client.

   The properties of user objects in Active Directory, the properties of the terminal server connection (for example, RDP-Tcp connection), and terminal services group policies.

Page
10-55
Lesson 3 Review

1. You're setting up a Web site in IIS on Server01. The site's Internet domain name is *adatum.com*, and the site's home directory is C:\Web\Adatum. Which URL should Internet users use to access files in the home directory of the site?

   a. *http://server01.web.adatum*

   b. *http://web.adatum.com/server01*

   c. *http://server01.adatum/home*

   d. *http://server01.adatum.com*

   d

2. Data for your corporate intranet is currently stored on the D drive of your IIS server. It is decided that the HR department will serve information about the company benefits and policies from its server, and that the URL to access the HR information should be *http://intranet.contoso.com/hr*. What do you need to configure?

   a. A new Web site

   b. A new FTP site

   c. A virtual directory from file

   d. A virtual directory

   d

3. You want to ensure the highest level of security for your corporate intranet without the infrastructure of certificate services. The goal is to provide authentication that is transparent to users and to allow you to secure intranet resources with the group accounts existing in Active Directory. All users are within the corporate firewall. What authentication method should you choose?

   a. Anonymous Access

   b. Basic Authentication

   c. Digest Authentication

   d. Integrated Windows Authentication

   d

Lesson 4 Review

1. You are configuring a Software Update Services infrastructure. One server is synchronizing metadata and content from Windows Update. Other servers (one in each site) are synchronizing content from the parent SUS server. Which of the following steps are required to complete the SUS infrastructure? (Choose all that apply.)

    a. Configure Automatic Updates clients using Control Panel on each system.

    b. Configure GPOs to direct clients to the SUS server in their sites.

    c. Configure a manual content distribution point.

    d. Approve updates using the SUS administration page.

    The correct answers are b and d.

2. You are configuring SUS for a group of Web servers. You want the Web servers to update themselves nightly based on a list of approved updates on your SUS server. However, once in a while an administrator is logged on, performing late-night maintenance on a Web server, and you do not want update installation and potential restart to interfere with those tasks. What Windows Update policy configuration should you use in this scenario?

    a. Notify For Download And Notify For Install

    b. Auto Download And Notify For Install

    c. Auto Download And Schedule The Install.

    The correct answer is c. You want the Web servers to update themselves, so you must schedule the installation of updates. However, an administrator always has the option to cancel the installation.

3. You want all network clients to download and install updates automatically during night hours, and you have configured scheduled installation behavior for Automatic Updates. However, you discover that some users are turning off their machines at night and updates are not being applied. Which policy allows you to correct this situation without changing the installation schedule?

    a. Specify Intranet Microsoft Update Service Location

    b. No Auto-Restart For Scheduled Automatic Updates Installations

    c. Reschedule Automatic Updates Scheduled Installations

    d. Configure Automatic Update

    The correct answer is c. Updates are automatically downloaded using background processes and idle bandwidth, but the installation is triggered by the specified schedule. If a computer is turned off at the installation time, it waits until the next scheduled date and time. The Reschedule Wait Time policy, if set between 1 and 60, causes Automatic Updates to start the update installation 1 to 60 minutes after system startup.

Troubleshooting Lab Solutions

1. Why are users being prompted for credentials? How can you solve the problem? If you believe you know the answer, make appropriate changes and repeat steps 1 to 4 of Exercise 2 to confirm the success of your solution.

You are being prompted for credentials because Company News is not allowing anonymous access. When you create a virtual directory by using the Web Sharing tab, anonymous access is disabled by default. You can enable anonymous access by performing the following steps.

1. Using IIS Manager, open the properties of the News virtual directory.

2. Click the Directory Security tab, and click Edit in the Authentication And Access Control area.

3. Enable anonymous access.

2. How can you restrict users in the Project Contractors group from accessing the company news? If you believe you know the answer, make appropriate changes and repeat steps 5 to 8 of Exercise 2 to confirm the success of your solution.

You can restrict access using NTFS permissions. On Server02, open Windows Explorer and open the properties dialog box for C:\ContosoIntranetNews. Click the Security tab, and add the Project Contractors group. Select the check box to Deny Full Control.

11 Securing Network Communication

Exam Objectives in this Chapter:

- Plan security for data transmission (Exam 70-296).

  - Secure data transmission between client computers to meet security requirements.

  - Secure data transmission using IPSec.

- Plan security for wireless networks (Exam 70-296).

Why This Chapter Matters

The Microsoft Windows Server 2003 family of operating systems includes a variety of security mechanisms, some of which you have studied in previous chapters. Until now, however, you have not learned how to protect data as it is transmitted across a network. In Windows Server 2003, Internet Protocol Security (IPSec) is the primary mechanism for securing network transmissions, by both digitally signing and encrypting them. Although IPSec is easy to deploy in its default configuration, it is important for you, as a network administrator, to understand what is going on behind the scenes in IPSec communications so that you can plan for a level of security appropriate to your needs.

The recent growth in the popularity of wireless networks has exposed to a greater degree data being transmitted, without even the bounds of a physical cable, and this growth has provided a new, vulnerable point of access for threats to your network. Therefore, it is critical to understand the methods used to secure wireless communication so that you can, again, plan for appropriate levels of security prior to deploying your first wireless device.

Lessons in this Chapter:

Before You Begin

To perform the practices related to the objectives in this chapter, you must have

- One Windows Server 2003 (Standard or Enterprise Edition) system
- Access to the server with administrative credentials

Lesson 1: Planning an IPSec Implementation

Many of the Windows Server 2003 security mechanisms you have studied so far in this book are designed to protect valuable data, but few of them are capable of protecting data while it is in transit over the network. You can store your files in encrypted form using the Encrypting File System (EFS), for example, or an individual application might be able to protect files with a password, but when you access the file over the network or send it to someone else, your computer always decrypts it first. The *IP Security (IPSec) extensions* are a means of securing the actual network communications themselves so that intruders cannot compromise your data by intercepting it as it travels over the network.

After this lesson, you will be able to

- List the major threats to network communications
- Describe the functions of IPSec
- Understand the functions and architecture of the IPSec protocols

Estimated lesson time: 30 minutes

Evaluating Threats

When you log on to a file transfer protocol (FTP) server on your network, you have to supply a user name and a password to be granted access. The FTP client program you use probably does not display the password on the screen as you type it, but of course the password must be included in the data packets the client sends over the network to the FTP server.

Figure 11-1 shows a screen capture from Microsoft Network Monitor, which is displaying the contents of an FTP packet that the program captured from the network. In this packet, you can clearly see the password (which is "password") associated with the user account that the client is supplying to the server. If you are a network administrator and you use the Administrator account to access the FTP server, someone capturing the packets in this way could learn the Administrator password and possibly wreak havoc on the network.

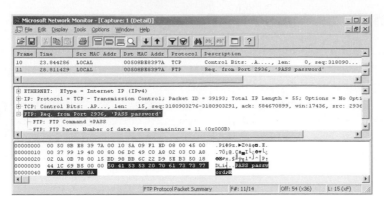

Figure 11-1   Network Monitor, displaying an FTP password

This is just an example of how easy it is for unauthorized people to capture and access your data as it is being transmitted. A user running a protocol analyzer such as Network Monitor can capture the packets containing your data files, your e-mail messages, or other confidential communications, and reconstruct the data for his or her own use.

Unauthorized personnel can use this captured data against you in many ways, including the following:

- **Compromising keys**   In the same way that captured packets can contain passwords, they can also contain encryption keys. An intruder capturing a key can then decrypt any data using that key. The public key infrastructure (PKI) used on networks running Microsoft Windows is not threatened by this practice because it uses separate public and private keys for encryption and decryption, and the private keys are never transmitted over the network. However, other encryption systems use a single key to encrypt and decrypt data, and if an intruder captures that key, the entire security system is compromised.

- **Spoofing**   Spoofing is digitally masquerading as another person or system by using captured Internet Protocol (IP) addresses and other information. By capturing network packets, an intruder can discover valid IP addresses, packet sequence numbers, and the other personal information needed to create new packets that appear to have originated from the actual user's computer. Using this method, the intruder can send messages in the victim's name, receive data that was meant for the victim, and even engage in financial or other transactions using the victim's accounts. Sometimes an attacker will simultaneously initiate a denial-of-service (DoS) attack on the victim's computer to prevent the victim from sending any further messages while the attacker assumes the victim's identity.

Security Alert   Even when you use applications that encrypt your passwords for transmission, intruders can still sometimes use those passwords by simply pasting the encrypted string into a spoofed message. Even though the intruder doesn't actually know what the password is, the authenticating system could decrypt it and accept it as genuine.

- **Modifying data**   When intruders capture data packets from the network, they can not only read the information inside, they can also modify it, and then send the packets to the recipient. The packets arriving at the destination, therefore, might contain information the true sender did not create, even though the packets appear to be genuine.

- **Attacking applications**   In addition to modifying the data in captured packets, intruders might add their own software to the packets and use the packets to introduce the software into the destination computer. Viruses, worms, and Trojan horses are just some of the dangerous types of code that can infiltrate your network in this way.

Introducing Network Security Protocols

Network security protocols are used to manage and secure authentication, authorization, confidentiality, integrity, and nonrepudiation. In a Microsoft Windows Server 2003 network, the major protocols used are Kerberos, NTLM, IPSec, and their various subprotocols. Other network communication protocols support these protocols, and other security settings support and protect the use of these security protocols. Table 11-1 lists the security paradigms and the protocols that support them.

Table 11-1   Network Security Protocols

Paradigm	Purpose	Protocols
Authentication	To prove you are who you say you are	Kerberos and NTLM (The NTLM authentication protocol is not available by default, but it can be configured.)
Authorization	To determine what you can do on the network after you have authenticated	Kerberos and NTLM
Confidentiality	To keep data secret	Encryption components of Kerberos, NTLM, and IPSec (to secure communications other than authentication)
Integrity	To ensure that the data received is the same data that is sent	Components of Kerberos, NTLM, and IPSec

Table 11-1 Network Security Protocols

Paradigm	Purpose	Protocols
Nonrepudia-tion	To determine exactly who sent and received the message	Kerberos and IPSec

This lesson and the next will focus specifically on IPSec. The functionality and technical details of Kerberos and NTLM are beyond the scope of this training kit.

Protecting Data with IPSec

IPSec is designed to protect data by digitally signing and encrypting it before transmission. IPSec encrypts the information in IP datagrams by encapsulating it so that even if the packets are captured, none of the data inside can be read. Using IPSec protects your network against all the threats listed in the previous section.

Because IPSec operates at the network layer as an extension to the IP protocol, it provides end-to-end encryption—meaning that the source computer encrypts the data, and it is not decrypted until it reaches its final destination. Intermediate systems, such as routers, treat the encrypted part of the packets purely as payload, so they do not have to perform any decryption; they just forward the encrypted payload as is. The routers do not have to possess the keys needed to decrypt the packets, nor do they have to support the IPSec extensions in any way.

Off the Record By contrast, encrypting network traffic at the data-link layer would require each router that forwards packets to decrypt the incoming data and then re-encrypt it again before transmitting it. This would add a tremendous amount of processing overhead to each router and slow down the entire network.

Other protocols besides IPSec, such as Secure Sockets Layer (SSL), provide network traffic encryption but they are application-layer protocols that can encrypt only specific types of traffic. For example, SSL encrypts only communications between Web clients and servers. IPSec can encrypt any traffic that takes the form of IP datagrams, no matter what kind of information is inside them.

IPSec Functions

In addition to encrypting IP datagrams, the IPSec implementation in Windows Server 2003 provides a variety of security functions, including the following:

- **Key generation**   For two computers to communicate over the network using encrypted IP datagrams, both must have access to a shared encryption key. This key enables each computer to encrypt its data and the other computer to decrypt it. However, the key cannot be transmitted over the network without compromising the security of the system. Therefore, computers preparing to communicate with each other using IPSec both use a technique called the *Diffie–Hellman algorithm* to compute identical encryption keys. The computers publicly exchange information about the calculations that enable them to arrive at the same result, but they do not exchange the keys themselves or information that would enable a third party to calculate the key.

- **Cryptographic checksums**   In addition to encrypting the data transmitted over the network, IPSec uses its cryptographic keys to calculate a checksum for the data in each packet, called a *hash message authentication code (HMAC)*, and then transmits it with the data. If anyone modifies the packet while it is in transit, the HMAC calculated by the receiving computer will be different from the one in the packet. This prevents attackers from modifying the information in a packet or adding information to it (such as a virus).

   IPSec supports two hash functions: HMAC in combination with Message Digest 5 (MD5) and HMAC in combination with Secure Hash Algorithm-1 (SHA1.) HMAC-SHA1 is the more secure function, partly because of SHA1's longer key length. (SHA1 uses a 160-bit key as opposed to the 128-bit key used by MD5.) HMAC-MD5 is strong enough for a normal security environment, but HMAC-SHA1 is the better choice for a high-level security environment and it meets the United States government's security requirements for high-level security.

- **Mutual authentication**   Before two computers can communicate using IPSec, they must authenticate each other to establish a trust relationship. Windows Server 2003 IPSec can use Kerberos, digital certificates, or a preshared key for authentication. Once the computers have authenticated each other, the cryptographic checksum in each packet functions as a digital signature, preventing anyone from spoofing or impersonating one of the computers.

- **Replay prevention**   In some cases, attackers might be able to use data from captured packets against you, even when the data in the packets is encrypted. Using traffic analysis, it is possible to determine the function of some encrypted packets. For example, the first few packets that two computers exchange during a secured transaction are likely to be authentication messages. Sometimes, by retransmitting these same packets, still in their encrypted form, attackers can use them to gain access to secured resources. IPSec prevents packet replays from being effective by assigning a sequence number to each packet. An IPSec system will not accept a packet that has an incorrect sequence number. This is also referred to as *antireplay services*.

- **IP packet filtering**   IPSec includes its own independent packet filtering mechanism that enables you to prevent denial-of-service attacks by blocking specific types of traffic through the use of IP addresses, protocols, ports, or any combination of the three.

IPSec Protocols

The IPSec standards define two protocols that provide different types of security for network communications: IP Authentication Header (AH) and IP Encapsulating Security Payload (ESP). These protocols are discussed in the following sections.

IP Authentication Header

The IP Authentication Header protocol does not encrypt the data in IP packets, but it does provide authentication, antireplay, and integrity services. You can use AH by itself or in combination with ESP. Using AH alone provides basic security services, with relatively low overhead. AH by itself does not prevent unauthorized users from reading the contents of captured data packets. However, using AH does guarantee that no one has modified the packets en route, and that the packets did actually originate at the system identified by the packet's source IP address.

See Also   IPSec is capable of operating in two modes: transport mode and tunnel mode. These descriptions of the AH and ESP protocols refer to transport mode operations. For more information on tunnel mode, see "Transport Mode and Tunnel Mode" later in this lesson.

When a computer uses AH to protect its transmissions, the system inserts an AH header into the IP datagram, immediately after the IP header and before the datagram's payload, as shown in Figure 11-2.

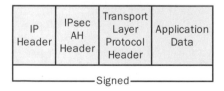

Figure 11-2   The AH header location

The contents of the AH header are shown in Figure 11-3.

Next Header	Payload Length	Reserved
Security Parameters Index		
Sequence Number		
Authentication Data		

Figure 11-3   The AH header format

The functions of the header fields are as follows:

■ **Next Header**   Contains a code specifying the protocol that generated the header immediately following the AH header, using the protocol codes specified by the Internet Assigned Numbers Authority (IANA). If IPSec is using AH alone, this field contains the code for the protocol that generated the datagram's payload, which is usually Transmission Control Protocol (TCP), User Datagram Protocol (UDP), or Internet Control Message Protocol (ICMP).

> **See Also**   The IP header has a Protocol field that contains a code identifying the protocol that generated the datagram's payload. Normally, this code has a value of 6 for TCP, 17 for UDP, or 1 for ICMP. However, in a packet using AH, the Protocol field has a value of 51 because the AH header immediately follows the IP header. The Next Header field in the AH header contains the code representing the TCP, UDP, or ICMP that generated the payload.

■ **Payload Length**   Specifies the length of the AH header.

■ **Reserved**   Unused.

■ **Security Parameters Index**   Contains a value that, in combination with the packet's destination IP address and its security protocol (AH), defines the datagram's *security association*. A security association is a list of the security measures, negotiated by the communicating computers, that the systems will use to protect the transmitted data.

■ **Sequence Number**   Contains a value that starts at 1 in the first packet using a particular security association, and is incremented by 1 in every subsequent packet using the same security association. This field provides the IPSec antireplay service. If an IPSec system receives packets with the same sequence numbers and the same security association, it discards the duplicates.

■ **Authentication Data**   Contains an *integrity check value (ICV)* that the sending computer calculates, based on selected IP header fields, the AH header, and the datagram's IP payload. The receiving system performs the same calculation and compares its results to this value.

> **Note** The ICV is the message authentication code. Its main purpose is to authenticate a message and verify its integrity.

IP Encapsulating Security Payload

The IP Encapsulating Security Payload (ESP) protocol is the one that actually encrypts the data in an IP datagram, preventing intruders from reading the information in packets they capture from the network. ESP also provides authentication, integrity, and anti-replay services. Unlike AH, which inserts only a header into the IP datagram, ESP inserts a header and a trailer, which surround the datagram's payload, as shown in Figure 11-4. The protocol encrypts all the data following the ESP header, up to and including the ESP trailer. Therefore, someone who captures a packet encrypted using ESP, could read the contents of the IP header, but could not read any part of the datagram's payload, including the TCP, UDP, or ICMP header.

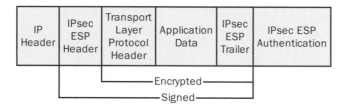

Figure 11-4   The ESP header and trailer locations

An IPSec packet can use ESP by itself or in combination with AH. When a packet uses both protocols, the ESP header follows the AH header, as shown in Figure 11-5. Although AH and ESP perform some of the same functions, using both protocols provides the maximum possible security for a data transmission. When ESP computes its ICV, it calculates the value only on the information between the ESP header and trailer; no IP header fields are included in an ESP ICV. Therefore, it is possible for an attacker to modify the contents of the IP header in an ESP-only packet and have those changes go undetected by the recipient. AH includes most of the IP header in its ICV calculation, so combining AH with ESP provides more protection than using ESP alone.

IP Header	IPsec AH Header	IPsec ESP Header	Transport Layer Protocol Header	Application Data	IPsec ESP Trailer	IPsec ESP Authentication

————————— Encrypted —————————

Figure 11-5   An IP datagram using AH and ESP

The contents of the ESP header are shown in Figure 11-6.

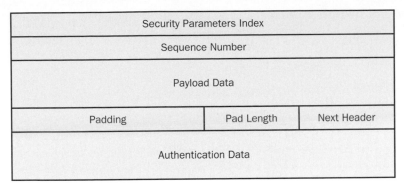

Security Parameters Index		
Sequence Number		
Payload Data		
Padding	Pad Length	Next Header
Authentication Data		

Figure 11-6   The ESP message format

The functions of the header fields are as follows:

- **Security Parameters Index**   Contains a value that, in combination with the packet's destination IP address and its security protocol (AH or ESP), defines the datagram's security association.

- **Sequence Number**   Contains a value that starts at 1 in the first packet using a particular security association, and is incremented by 1 in every subsequent packet using the same security association. This field provides IPSec's antireplay service. If an IPSec system receives packets with the same sequence numbers and the same security association, it discards the duplicates.

- **Payload Data**   Contains the TCP, UDP, or ICMP information carried inside the original IP datagram.

- **Padding**   Consists of padding added to the Payload Data field to ensure the Payload Data has a boundary required by the encryption algorithm.

- **Pad Length**   Specifies the number of bytes of padding the system added to the Payload Data field to fill out a 32-bit word.

- **Next Header**   Contains a code specifying the protocol that generated the header immediately following the ESP header, using the protocol codes specified by the IANA. In virtually all cases, this field contains the code for the protocol that generated the datagram's payload, which is usually TCP, UDP, or ICMP.

See Also   When an IPSec system is using AH and ESP together, the Protocol field in the IP header contains the value 51 because the AH header immediately follows the IP header. The Next Header field in the AH header has the value 50 because the ESP header immediately follows the AH header. Finally, the Next Header field in the ESP header contains the code for the protocol that generated the payload, which is usually TCP, UDP, or ICMP.

■ **Authentication Data**   Contains an ICV based on the information after the ESP header, up to and including the ESP trailer. The receiving system uses the ICV to verify the packet's integrity by performing the same calculation and comparing the results with this value.

Transport Mode and Tunnel Mode

IPSec can operate in two modes: *transport mode* and *tunnel mode.* To protect communications between computers on a network, you use transport mode, in which the two end systems must support IPSec but intermediate systems (such as routers) need not. All the discussion of the AH and ESP protocols so far in this lesson applies to transport mode.

Tunnel mode is designed to provide security for wide area network (WAN) connections, and particularly virtual private network (VPN) connections, which use the Internet as a communications medium. In a tunnel mode connection, the end systems do not support and implement the IPSec protocols; the routers at both ends of the WAN connection do this.

The tunnel mode communications process proceeds as follows:

1. Computers on one of the private networks transmit their data using standard, unprotected IP datagrams.

2. The packets reach the router that provides access to the WAN, which encapsulates them using IPSec, encrypting and hashing data as needed.

3. The router transmits the protected packets to a second router at the other end of the WAN connection.

4. The second router verifies the packets by calculating and comparing ICVs, and decrypts them if necessary.

5. The second router repackages the information in the packets into standard, unprotected IP datagrams and transmits them to their destinations on the private network.

IPSec also uses a different packet structure in tunnel mode. Unlike transport mode, in which IPSec modifies the existing IP datagram by adding its own headers, tunnel mode implementations create an entirely new datagram and use it to encapsulate the existing datagram, as shown in Figure 11-7. The original datagram, inside the new datagram, remains unchanged. The IPSec headers are part of the outer datagram, which exists only to get the inner datagram from one router to the other.

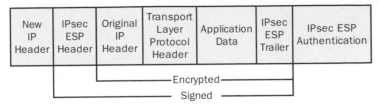

Figure 11-7   An IPSec tunnel mode packet

Lesson Review

The following questions are intended to reinforce key information presented in this lesson. If you are unable to answer a question, review the lesson materials and try the question again. You can find answers to the questions in the "Questions and Answers" section at the end of this chapter.

1. Which of the following ESP header fields provides the protocol's antireplay capability?

   a. Sequence Number

   b. Security Parameters Index

   c. Pad Length

   d. Next Header

2. Specify the proper order for the following components in an IPSec transport mode packet using both AH and ESP and containing TCP data.

   a. ESP trailer

   b. IP header

   c. ESP header

   d. TCP header

   e. AH header

   f. TCP data

3. Which of the following IPSec characteristics is different when a connection is operating in tunnel mode instead of transport mode? (Choose all that apply.)

   a. The order of the fields in the ESP header

   b. The location of the ESP header in the datagram

   c. The location of the ESP trailer in the datagram

   d. The value of the Next Header field in the ESP header

Lesson Summary

■ IPSec is a set of extensions to the IP protocol that provide protection for data as it is transmitted over the network. IPSec includes two protocols, IP Authentication Header and IP Encapsulating Security Payload, which can be used separately or together.

■ IPSec features include Diffie–Hellman key generation, cryptographic checksums, mutual authentication, replay prevention, and IP packet filtering.

■ The IP Authentication Header protocol provides authentication, antireplay, and data integrity services, but it does not encrypt data.

■ The IP Encapsulating Security Payload protocol encrypts the information in IP datagrams, and it provides authentication, antireplay, and data integrity services.

■ IPSec can operate in transport mode or tunnel mode. Transport mode is for securing communications between end users on a network, and tunnel mode is for securing WAN communications between routers.

Lesson 2: Deploying IPSec

All versions of Microsoft Windows beginning with Windows 2000 include support for IPSec, as do several non-Microsoft operating systems. IPSec is based on standards published by the Internet Engineering Task Force (IETF), so all IPSec implementations conforming to those standards should be compatible. In Windows operating systems, the administration of IPSec is based on *IPSec policies*, which specify when and how IPSec should be used to secure network communications.

After this lesson, you will be able to

- List the components of a Windows Server 2003 IPSec implementation
- List the default IPSec policies included with Windows Server 2003 and their applications
- Understand the functions of an IPSec policy's components
- Use the IP Security Policies snap-in to manage IPSec policies

Estimated lesson time: 20 minutes

IPSec Components

The IPSec implementation in Windows Server 2003 consists of the following components:

- **IPSec Policy Agent** A service (appearing as IPSEC Services on every computer running Windows Server 2003) that accesses IPSec policy information stored in the Active Directory database or the Windows registry.

- **Internet Key Exchange (IKE)** IKE is the protocol that IPSec computers use to exchange information about generating Diffie–Hellman keys and to create a security association (SA). The IKE communication process proceeds in two stages. The first stage, called the Phase 1 SA, includes the negotiation of which encryption algorithm, hashing algorithm, and authentication method the systems will use. The second stage consists of the establishment of two Phase 2 SAs, one in each direction. This stage includes the negotiation of which IPSec protocols, hashing algorithm, and encryption algorithm the systems will use, as well as the exchange of information about authentication and key generation.

- **IPSec Driver** Performs the actual preparations that enable secure network communication to take place, including the generation of checksums, the construction of IPSec packets, and the encryption of the data to be transmitted. The driver receives a filter list from the IPSec policy the system is using and compares each outgoing packet to that list. When a packet meets the criteria of the filter list, the IPSec driver initiates the IKE communications process with the destination system, adds the AH and ESP headers to the outgoing packet, and encrypts the data inside, if necessary. For incoming packets, the IPSec driver calculates hashes and checksums as needed and compares them to those in the packet that just arrived.

Planning an IPSec Deployment

Configuring computers running Windows Server 2003 to use IPSec is relatively simple. However, before the actual deployment, you must consider just what network traffic you need to protect and how much protection you want to provide. IPSec is resource intensive in two different ways. First, the addition of AH and ESP headers to each packet increases the amount of traffic on your network. Second, calculating hashes and encrypting data both require large amounts of processor time. Unless you have planned your network design to account for the resources that IPSec needs, using IPSec for all your network traffic simply because you can is usually not a good idea.

Windows Server 2003 IPSec enables you to specify exactly what traffic to protect using IPSec, and what degree of protection to apply. IPSec does this using packet filters. You can specify IP addresses, protocols, and ports when creating a filter, and the system secures all traffic that meets the filter criteria using IPSec.

Another factor to consider when planning an IPSec deployment is support for the protocols on your network's various computers. Systems running versions of the Windows operating system earlier than Windows 2000 cannot use IPSec. In the case of operating systems other than the Windows operating system, you must determine whether they support IPSec and do your own testing to be sure that the implementations are compatible.

Working with IPSec Policies

The IP Security Policies snap-in for Microsoft Management Console (MMC) is the tool you use to view and manage IPSec policies on a computer running Windows Server 2003. By default, the snap-in is incorporated into the Group Policy Object Editor console, and on member servers, into the Local Security Policy console. You can also add the snap-in to a new MMC console and configure it to manage the policies on any individual computer or Active Directory domain.

You deploy IPSec policies in much the same way as other types of Windows Server 2003 policy settings; you can apply them to individual computers, but for network installations, it is more common to deploy IPSec policies by assigning them to Active Directory sites, domains, or organizational units (OUs). IPSec policies flow down through the Active Directory hierarchy just like other group policy settings. When you apply an IPSec policy to an OU, for example, all the computers in the domain inherit that policy.

Once you have created IPSec policies in the appropriate places, you must then activate them by selecting Assign from the Action menu in the IP Security Policies snap-in. You can view the policy that is currently in effect for any computer on the network, as well as detailed information about IPSec activities, using the IP Security Monitor snap-in.

Using the Default IPSec Policies

When you open the IP Security Policies snap-in (shown Figure 11-8), you see the three policies that Windows Server 2003 always creates by default. These three policies are as follows, listed in order of increasing security:

- **Client (Respond Only)** Configures the computer to use IPSec only when another computer requests IPSec. The computer using this policy never initiates an IPSec negotiation; it only responds to requests from other computers for secured communications.

- **Server (Request Security)** Configures the computer to request the use of IPSec when communicating with another computer. If the other computer supports IPSec, the IPSec negotiation begins. If the other computer does not support IPSec, the systems establish a standard, unsecured IP connection.

- **Secure Server (Require Security)** Configures the computer to require IPSec security for all communications. If the computer attempts to communicate with a computer that does not support IPSec, the initiating computer terminates the connection.

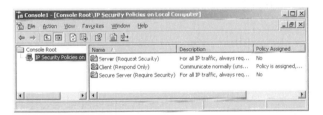

Figure 11-8   The IP Security Policies snap-in

These default policies are intended for computers performing different roles. The Client (Respond Only) policy is intended for computers that connect sometimes to secured servers, and sometimes to systems that do not require the security of IPSec. Using the Client (Respond Only) policy, the system incurs the additional overhead generated by IPSec only when necessary. The Server (Request Security) policy is intended for computers that do not require the highest levels of security and might communicate with systems not supporting IPSec. The Secure Server (Require Security) policy is intended for computers working with sensitive data that must be secured at all times. Before implementing this policy, you must make sure all the computers that need to access the secured server support IPSec.

Modifying IPSec Policies

In addition to using the default IPSec policies as they are, you can modify them or create new policies of your own.

> **Tip**   Although you can modify the properties of the default IPSec policies, the best practice is to leave them intact and create new policies of your own using the default policies as models.

IPSec policies consist of three elements, which are as follows:

■ **Rules**   A rule is a combination of an IP filter list and a filter action that specifies when and how the computer should use IPSec. An IPSec policy can consist of multiple rules, as shown in Figure 11-9.

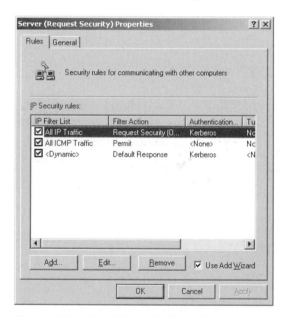

Figure 11-9   The IP Security Rules list

■ **IP filter lists**   A collection of filters that specify what traffic the system should secure with IPSec, based on IP addresses, protocols, or port numbers. You can also create filters using a combination of these criteria, as shown in Figure 11-10.

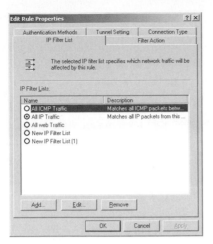

Figure 11-10   The IP Filter Lists list

■ **Filter actions**   Configuration parameters that specify exactly how IPSec should secure the filtered packets. Filter actions specify whether IPSec should use AH, ESP, or both, as well as what data integrity and encryption algorithms the system should use. (See Figure 11-11.)

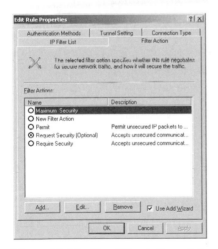

Figure 11-11   The Filter Actions list

To help create a new policy, the IP Security Policies snap-in provides wizards for creating rules, filter lists, and filter actions. However, you can elect not to use the wizards and create the policy elements using standard dialog boxes.

Exam Tip   When preparing for the upgrade exams, be sure you are familiar with the components of an IPSec policy and with the functions of each component.

Command-Line Tools

Netsh.exe is a native Windows Server 2003 command-line scripting tool that you can use to display or modify the local or remote network configuration of a computer running Windows Server 2003. You can run Netsh from a batch file or from the command prompt. The Netsh IPSec commands cannot be used on other versions of Windows.

> **See Also**   You can find a complete list of Netsh IPSec commands in the Windows Server 2003 Help And Support Center. You can locate them by clicking Tools on the Help And Support Center home page and then clicking Command Line Reference A-Z. Note that many of the commands look complex, but they can be simplified. If you use the same choices as the command uses for its defaults, the commands you must type in can be reduced. For example, you don't need to use the word "Kerberos" if that is the form of authentication you want to use. Enter nothing, and the command defaults to using Kerberos authentication.

Netdiag.exe is a command-line tool that you can use to display IPSec information as well as to test and view network configuration. Netdiag is available for Windows Server 2003, Windows 200, and Windows XP. However, it must be installed in a different way for each operating system. For Windows Server 2003, Netdiag is installed with the Windows Server 2003 Support Tools. For Windows 2000, Netdiag is included with the Windows 2000 Resource Kit tools that you can also download from the Microsoft Web site. It is also available on the Windows XP Installation CD-ROM, and is installed by running Setup.exe from the Support\Tools folder.

You can obtain general network diagnostic information (not IPSec-specific) by using the Netdiag command. For example, the Netdiag /v /l command provides the IP configuration and routing configuration for a computer, tests WINS and DSN name resolution, reports the build version of the computer and the hotfixes that are installed, tests the validity of domain membership, verifies that clients can contact domain controllers, and checks trust relationships. All this information can be useful in eliminating general networking problems before attempting to diagnose IPSec issues.

However, although the Netdiag.exe tool is available for Windows Server 2003, the Netdiag /test:ipsec option is removed. Use the Netsh command instead. Because Netsh IPSec context commands will not work with down-level Windows computers, use Netdiag for them. You might want to remotely examine the IPSec policy of a computer running Windows XP or Windows 2000 that is communicating, or attempting to communicate, with Windows Server 2003. In this case, use a Remote Desktop session and the Netdiag tool.

Practice: Creating an IPSec Policy

In this practice, you use the IP Security Policies snap-in to view the properties of the default IPSec policies and create a new policy of your own.

Exercise 1: Creating an MMC Console and Viewing the Default Policies

In this exercise, you create an MMC console containing the IP Security Policies snap-in and use it to view the default IPSec policies on your server.

1. Log on to Windows Server 2003 as Administrator.

2. Click Start, and then click Run. The Run dialog box appears.

3. In the Open text box, type **mmc** and then click OK. The Console1 window appears.

4. From the File menu, select Add/Remove Snap-in. The Add/Remove Snap-in dialog box appears.

5. Click Add. The Add Standalone Snap-in dialog box appears.

6. Scroll down the Available Standalone Snap-ins list, select IP Security Policy Management, and then click Add. The Select Computer Or Domain dialog box appears.

7. With the default Local Computer option selected, click Finish.

8. Click Close to close the Add Standalone Snap-in dialog box. The IP Security Policies On Local Computer snap-in now appears in the Add/Remove Snap-in dialog box.

9. Click OK to close the Add/Remove Snap-in dialog box. The snap-in you selected now appears in the scope pane of the MMC console.

10. Click the IP Security Policies on Local Computer heading in the scope pane. The three default IPSec policies described earlier in this lesson appear in the details pane.

11. Select the Secure Server (Require Security) policy in the details pane and, from the Action menu, select Properties. The Secure Server (Require Security) Properties dialog box appears.

    Notice that the Rules tab in the Secure Server (Require Security) Properties dialog box contains three rules, one applying to all IP traffic, one for all ICMP traffic, and one that is dynamic.

12. Select All IP Traffic from the IP Security Rules list, and then click Edit. The Edit Rule Properties dialog box appears.

    Notice that the All IP Traffic option is selected in the IP Filter List tab.

13. Click the Filter Action tab.

   Notice that the Require Security option is selected in the Filter Actions list.

14. Click the Authentication Methods tab.

   Notice that the policy is configured to use Kerberos for authentication.

15. Click OK to close the Edit Rule Properties dialog box.

16. Click OK to close the Secure Server (Require Security) Properties dialog box.

Exercise 2: Creating a New IPSec Policy

In this exercise, you use the IP Security Policies snap-in to create a new IPSec policy on the computer.

1. In the console you created in Exercise 1, select the IP Security Policies On Local Computer heading in the scope pane and, from the Action menu, select Create IP Security Policy. The IP Security Policy Wizard appears.

2. Click Next. The IP Security Policy Name page appears.

3. In the Name text box, type **Web Server Security** and then click Next. The Requests For Secure Communication page appears.

4. Click Next to accept the default Activate The Default Response Rule setting. The Default Response Rule Authentication Method page appears.

   The default authentication method for Active Directory systems is Kerberos V5 protocol, but on this page, you could elect to use a digital certificate or a pre-shared key in the form of a character string that you supply to all the computers involved in secured communications.

5. Click Next to accept the default Active Directory Default (Kerberos V5 Protocol) option. The Completing The IP Security Policy Wizard page appears.

6. Make sure the Edit Properties check box is selected, and then click Finish. The Web Server Security Properties dialog box appears.

7. In the Rules tab, make sure that the Use Add Wizard check box is selected and then click Add. The Security Rule Wizard appears.

8. Click Next. The Tunnel Endpoint page appears.

   On this page, you specify whether you want IPSec to run in transport mode or tunnel mode. To use tunnel mode, you must specify the IP address of the system functioning as the tunnel endpoint. This is usually a router that provides a WAN connection to a remote site.

9. Click Next to accept the default This Rule Does Not Specify A Tunnel option. The Network Type page appears.

   This page enables you to specify whether you want the rule to apply to local area network (LAN) traffic only, remote access traffic only, or both.

10. Click Next to accept the default All Network Connections option. The IP Filter List page appears.

11. Click Add. The IP Filter List dialog box appears.

12. In the Name text box, type **All Web Traffic** and then click Add. The IP Filter Wizard appears.

13. Click Next. The IP Filter Description And Mirrored Property page appears.

14. Click Next to accept the default Mirrored. Match Packets With The Exact Opposite Source And Destination Addresses check box. The IP Traffic Source page appears.

15. In the Source Address list, select Any IP Address and then click Next. The IP Traffic Destination page appears.

16. In the Destination Address list, select My IP Address and then click Next. The IP Protocol Type page appears.

17. In the Select A Protocol Type list, select TCP and then click Next. The IP Protocol Port page appears.

18. Click the To This Port option, type **80** in the text box provided, and then click Next. The Completing The IP Filter Wizard page appears.

19. Click Finish. The new IP filter you created appears in the IP Filters list. Click OK to close the IP Filter List dialog box.

20. In the IP Filter List page of the Security Rule Wizard, select the All Web Traffic filter option you just created, and then click Next. The Filter Action page appears.

21. Make sure the Use Add Wizard check box is selected, and then click Add. The Filter Action Wizard appears.

22. Click Next. The Filter Action Name page appears.

23. In the Name text box, type **Maximum Security** and then click Next. The Filter Action General Options page appears.

24. Click the Negotiate Security option, and then click Next. The Communicating With Computers That Do Not Support IPSec page appears.

25. Click Next to accept the default Do Not Communicate With Computers That Do Not Support IPSec option. The IP Traffic Security page appears.

26. Click the Custom option, and then click Settings. The Custom Security Method Settings dialog box appears.

27. Select the Data And Address Integrity Without Encryption (AH) check box to activate the IP Authentication Header protocol, and then click OK to return to the IP Traffic Security page.

28. Click Next. The Completing The IP Security Filter Action Wizard page appears.

29. Click Finish to return to the Filter Action page in the Security Rule Wizard.

30. Select the Maximum Security filter action option you just created, and then click Next. The Authentication Method page appears.

31. Click Next to accept the default Active Directory Default (Kerberos V5 Protocol) option. The Completing The Security Rule Wizard page appears.

32. Clear the Edit Properties check box, and then click Finish.

33. Click OK to close the Web Server Security Properties dialog box.

34. The new Web Server Security policy you created now appears in the IP Security Policies On Local Computer snap-in.

35. Click the Web Server Security policy in the details pane and, from the Action menu, select Assign.

36. Close the IP Securities Policies On Local Computer snap-in.

Lesson Review

The following questions are intended to reinforce key information presented in this lesson. If you are unable to answer a question, review the lesson materials and try the question again. You can find answers to the questions in the "Questions and Answers" section at the end of this chapter.

1. Which IPSec policy can you use to encrypt all traffic to and from a particular database application on a server running Windows Server 2003?

    a. Client (Respond Only).

    b. Secure Server (Require Security).

    c. Server (Request Security).

    d. You must create a new custom policy.

2. Which of the following pieces of information must you supply when creating a policy that configures IPSec to use tunnel mode?

    a. The IP address of the router's WAN interface

    b. The port number associated with the WAN technology used for the tunnel

    c. The IP address of the router at the far end of the tunnel

    d. The network layer protocol used for the WAN connection

3. Which IPSec component is responsible for actually encrypting the information in IP datagrams?

   a. Internet Key Exchange

   b. IPSEC Services

   c. IPSec driver

   d. The IP Security Policies snap-in

Lesson Summary

- The IPSec implementation in Windows Server 2003 consists of IPSEC Services, Internet Key Exchange (IKE), and the IPSec driver.

- When planning an IPSec deployment, you must consider the impact of using IPSec on your computers and on your network. IPSec hashing and encryption calculations can be extremely processor intensive, and the added overhead of the AH and ESP headers can increase the level of network traffic. You must also consider whether all the computers on your network support IPSec.

- The Windows Server 2003 IPSec implementation is based on IPSec policies. You can manage IPSec policies by using the IP Security Policies snap-in for Microsoft Management Console.

- Windows Server 2003 IPSec has three default policies: Client (Respond Only), Secure Server (Require Security), and Server (Request Security). You can use these policies or create your own.

- IPSec policies consist of rules, IP filter lists, and filter actions. A rule is a combination of an IP filter list and a filter action. IP filter lists specify what traffic IPSec should protect, and filter actions specify what type of protection IPSec should apply.

Lesson 3: Securing a Wireless Network

Wireless networking has existed for many years, but it is only recently, with the publication of the 802.11 series of standards by the Institute of Electrical and Electronics Engineers (IEEE), that *wireless local area networking (WLAN)* technologies have become mainstream products. WLANs enable home and business users to set up computer networks between places that were previously inaccessible, and they enable portable computer users to roam freely while connected to the network. However, wireless networking creates unique security challenges that administrators must address.

After this lesson, you will be able to

- List the standards that define common WLAN technologies
- Describe the security problems inherent in wireless networking
- List the mechanisms that WLANs running IEEE 802.11 based on the Windows operating system can use to authenticate clients and encrypt transmitted data

Estimated lesson time: 30 minutes

Understanding Wireless Networking Standards

Until recently, wireless networking was based on standards defining physical layer technologies that, while reasonably effective, were much slower than the average network and not altogether reliable. These technologies were also expensive and difficult to implement. However, in 1999, the IEEE released the first standard in the 802.11 working group, called "Wireless LAN Medium Access Control (MAC) and Physical Layer (PHY) Specifications," defining a new series of technologies for the WLAN physical layer. For the wireless networking industry, the key document in this series of standards was *IEEE 802.11b*, "Wireless LAN Medium Access Control (MAC) and Physical Layer (PHY) specifications—Amendment 2: Higher-Speed Physical Layer (PHY) Extension in the 2.4 GHz Band."

The 802.11b standard defines a physical layer specification that enables WLANs to run at speeds up to 11 megabits per second (Mbps), slightly faster than a standard Ethernet network. When products conforming to this standard arrived on the market, they quickly became a popular solution, both for home and business use. Prices dropped accordingly and, for the first time, wireless networking became a major force in the industry.

Development continues on standards that are designed to provide even higher WLAN transmission speeds. The 802.11a standard, "Wireless LAN Medium Access Control (MAC) and Physical Layer (PHY) specifications: Amendment 1: High-speed Physical Layer in the 5 GHz band" defines a medium with speeds running up to 54 Mbps, while 802.11g, "Wireless LAN Medium Access Control (MAC) and Physical Layer (PHY) specifications—Amendment 4: Further Higher Data Rate Extension in the 2.4 GHz Band," calls for higher transmission speeds using the same 2.4 GHz frequencies as 802.11b.

See Also   For more information on IEEE standards, and to obtain the standards themselves, see the IEEE Web site at *http://www.ieee.org*.

Wireless Networking Topologies

In computer networking, the term *topology* typically refers to the pattern of the cables used to connect the computers. Wireless networks do not use cables, but they still have a topology, which defines how the wireless devices interact at the physical layer. At the physical layer, IEEE 802.11b WLANs use direct sequence spread spectrum communications at a frequency of 2.4 GHz, and the devices can communicate with each other using two basic topologies: ad hoc and infrastructure.

Off the Record   Cabled networks are sometimes referred to as *bounded* media because their signals are confined to a given space—that is, the interior of the cable. Wireless networks are therefore called *unbounded* media because their signals are not physically restricted in this way.

An *ad hoc network* consists of two or more wireless devices communicating directly with each other. The signals generated by WLAN network interface adapters are omnidirectional out to a range that is governed by environmental factors, as well as the nature of the equipment involved. This range is called a *basic service area (BSA)*. When two wireless devices come within range of each other, as shown in Figure 11-12, they are able to connect and communicate, immediately forming a two-node network. Wireless devices within the same basic service area are called a *basic service set (BSS)*.

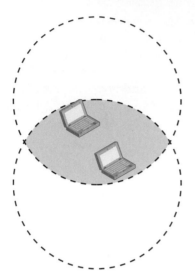

Figure 11-12   An ad hoc network

Other wireless devices coming within the transmission range of the first two wireless devices can also participate in the network. Ad hoc networking is not transitive, however. A wireless device that comes within range of another device, but still lies outside the range of a third, can communicate only with the device in its range.

> **Note**   The ad hoc topology is most often used on home networks or for very small businesses that have no cabled network components at all.

An *infrastructure network* uses a wireless device called an access point as a bridge between wireless devices and a standard cabled network. An *access point* is a small unit that connects to an Ethernet network (or other cabled network) by cable, but that also contains an 802.11b-compliant wireless transceiver. Other wireless devices coming within range of the access point are able to communicate with the cabled network, just as though they were connected by a cable themselves. (See Figure 11-13.) The access point functions as a transparent bridge, effectively extending the cabled local area network (LAN) to include the wireless devices.

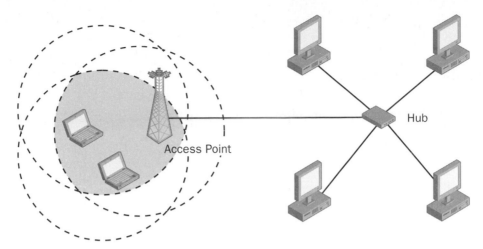

Figure 11-13   An infrastructure network

> **Note**   On an infrastructure network, wireless devices communicate only with the access point; they do not communicate with each other directly. Therefore, even if two wireless computers are within range of each other, they must still use the access point to communicate.

Most business networks use the infrastructure topology because it provides complete connectivity between wireless devices and the cabled network.

Understanding Wireless Network Security

Unlike bounded media, in which every device on the network must be physically connected to a cable for communication to occur, wireless networks transmit signals in all directions, and any compatible device coming within transmission range might be able to connect to the network. Depending on how many access points you have and where they are located, the boundary of your equipment's effective range can easily fall outside a controllable area. For example, placing an access point near a building's outer wall can enable an unauthorized user with a wireless-equipped laptop to access your network from a car parked outside the building.

For this reason, security should be a major concern for all wireless network installations. The two primary threats when it comes to wireless networking are as follows:

■ **Unauthorized access**   An unauthorized user with a wireless workstation connects to the network and accesses network resources. This is the functional equivalent of a user connecting to a cabled network by plugging into an available jack or splicing into the cable, but on a wireless network, the process of making the network connection is much easier. On an infrastructure network, this type of attack compromises the entire network because the user might be able to access bounded as well as unbounded resources. To prevent unauthorized users from connecting to a wireless network, you must implement a system that authenticates and authorizes users before they receive significant access.

■ **Data interception**   A user running a protocol analyzer with a wireless network interface adapter might be able to capture all the packets transmitted between the other wireless devices and the access point. In this case, the device can be as simple as a laptop running Microsoft Network Monitor with a network interface adapter that supports promiscuous mode operation. This type of attack endangers only the data transmitted over the air, but it also leaves no traces, so it is virtually undetectable. The only way to protect against this type of attack is to encrypt all packets transmitted over wireless connections. This does not prevent intruders from capturing the packets, but it does prevent them from reading the data inside.

Controlling Wireless Access Using Group Policies

Windows Server 2003 provides security capabilities for wireless networking in the form of group policies you can use to restrict users' wireless access to the network. In the Group Policy Object Editor console, you can create a policy in the Computer Configuration\Windows Settings\Security Settings\Wireless Network (IEEE 802.11) Policies subheading that enables you to specify whether wireless-equipped computers can connect to ad hoc networks only, infrastructure networks only, or both. (See Figure 11-14.)

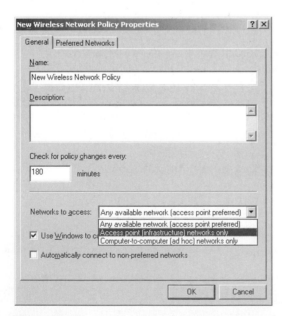

Figure 11-14   The New Wireless Network Policy Properties dialog box

In the Preferred Networks tab, you can specify the networks to which users can connect and set properties for the IEEE 802.1X security protocol, such as which authentication protocol to use (see Figure 11-15). Using these group policy settings, you can configure the wireless networking properties for all the computers on your WLAN.

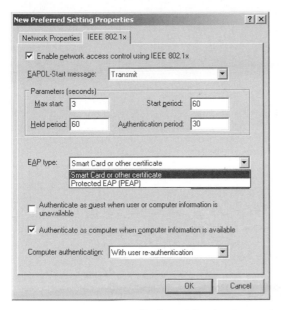

Figure 11-15   The New Preferred Setting Properties dialog box

Authenticating Users

You can use several methods to authenticate users attempting to connect to your WLAN and to prevent unauthorized access by outsiders. The IEEE 802.11 standard itself defines two methods: Open System authentication and Shared Key authentication. Windows Server 2003 supports a third method, based on another standard called IEEE 802.1X.

Open System Authentication

Open System authentication is the default authentication method used by IEEE 802.11 devices, and it actually provides no authentication at all. Open System authentication is simply an exchange of messages in which one system identifies itself to another and the other system replies. There is no exchange of passwords, keys, or any other type of credential, and there is no way for a device configured to use Open System authentication to refuse authentication to another.

Shared Key Authentication

Shared Key authentication is a system by which wireless devices authenticate each other using a secret key that both possess. The key is assumed to have been shared before authentication using a secure channel independent of 802.11 communications to prevent it from being compromised during transmission. Shared Key authentication is not a particularly secure method because all the computers in the same BSS must possess the same key. Compromising the key on one system nullifies the authentication security for the entire BSS.

> **Important**   Shared Key authentication requires the use of the Wired Equivalent Privacy (WEP) algorithm. If WEP is not implemented, Shared Key authentication is not available.

During a Shared Key authentication, messages are exchanged between the requester and the responder as follows:

1. The system requesting authentication asserts its identity to the other system, using a message that contains a value that identifies the shared key (not the shared key itself) the system is using.

2. The system receiving the authentication request responds with a message containing the authentication result. If the authentication is successful, the response message includes a 128-byte block of challenge text generated by the WEP pseudo-random number generator.

3. The requester copies the challenge text from the response message to a new message and encrypts it with WEP, using the shared key as an encryption key.

4. The responder decrypts the message and compares the decrypted challenge text with the text the system transmitted in step 2. If the values match, the responder grants the authentication.

IEEE 802.1X Authentication

The *IEEE 802.1X* standard, "Port Based Network Access Control," defines a method of authenticating and authorizing users connecting to an IEEE 802 LAN, and blocking those users' access to the LAN should the authentication fail. IEEE 802.1X can authenticate users connecting to any type of LAN, such as Ethernet or Token Ring, but in this case, it is particularly valuable for IEEE 802.11 wireless LANs.

Most IEEE 802.1X implementations function as clients of a server running a *Remote Authentication Dial-In User Service (RADIUS)*, such as the Internet Authentication Service (IAS) included with Windows Server 2003. The RADIUS server provides centralized authentication and authorization services for the entire network. For WLAN authentication, RADIUS typically uses one of the following two authentication protocols:

■ *Extensible Authentication Protocol-Transport Level Security (EAP-TLS)*—EAP is an authentication protocol that is designed to be adaptable so that it can carry a variety of *authentication mechanisms* within a given packet framework. TLS is an authentication mechanism that transports its messages within EAP packets and provides mutual authentication, integrity-protected negotiation of cryptographic service providers, and secret key exchange between two systems that use public key cryptography. The networks that use EAP-TLS typically have a public key infrastructure (PKI) in place and use certificates for authentication that are stored on the computer or on smart cards.

■ *Protected EAP-Microsoft Challenge-Handshake Authentication Protocol, version 2 (PEAP-MS-CHAP v2)*—PEAP is a variation on EAP that is designed for use on wireless networks that do not have a PKI in place. With PEAP, you can use a password-based authentication method, such as MS-CHAP, to securely authenticate wireless connections. PEAP creates an encrypted channel before the password-based authentication occurs. Therefore, password-based authentication exchanges such as those that occur in MS-CHAP v2 are not subject to offline dictionary attacks. (Put simply, an offline dictionary attack uses a brute-force dictionary attack to make repeated attempts to decrypt captured packets that use an encryption key derived from a user's password. This process is made easier for the intruder when the encryption key is derived from a weak password.)

Important   To use PEAP-MS-CHAP v2 for wireless network authentication, the wireless client must be running either Windows Server 2003 or Windows XP with SP1 installed.

With this system in place, an access point receiving a connection request from a wireless client forwards the request to the RADIUS server, which uses information in a data store, such as the Active Directory database, to determine whether the client should be granted access to the network.

Encrypting Wireless Traffic

To prevent data transmitted over a wireless network from being compromised through unauthorized packet captures, the IEEE 802.11 standard defines an encryption mechanism called *Wired Equivalent Privacy (WEP)*. WEP is an encryption system that uses the RC4 cryptographic algorithm developed by RSA Security Inc. WEP depends on encryption keys that are generated by a mechanism external to WEP itself. In cases where WEP is used with IEEE 802.1X to create a comprehensive wireless security solution for the Windows operating system, WEP uses the keys generated by the EAP-TLS or PEAP-MS-CHAP v2 authentication protocol to encrypt the data in the packets.

Off the Record   Microsoft recommends using the WEP and IEEE 802.1X combination as a suitable security configuration for wireless clients running the Windows operating system.

The degree of protection that WEP provides is governed by configurable parameters that control the length of the keys used to encrypt the data and the frequency with which the systems generate new keys. Longer and more frequently changed keys produce better security.

> **Exam Tip**   When preparing for the exam, be sure you are familiar with the security hazards inherent in wireless networking, and with the mechanisms that Windows operating systems can use to authenticate wireless clients and encrypt their traffic.

Lesson Review

The following questions are intended to reinforce key information presented in this lesson. If you are unable to answer a question, review the lesson materials and try the question again. You can find answers to the questions in the "Questions and Answers" section at the end of this chapter.

1. Which of the following authentication mechanisms enables clients to connect to a wireless network using smart cards?

   a. Open System authentication

   b. Shared Key authentication

   c. IEEE 802.1X authentication using EAP-TLS

   d. IEEE 802.1X authentication using PEAP-MS-CHAP v2

2. You are installing an IEEE 802.11b wireless network in a private home using computers running Windows XP, and you decide that data encryption is not necessary, but you want to use Shared Key authentication. However, when you try to configure the network interface adapter on the clients to use Shared Key authentication, the option is not available. Which of the following explanations could be the cause of the problem?

   a. WEP is not enabled.

   b. Windows XP SP1 is not installed on the computers.

   c. Windows XP does not support Shared Key authentication.

   d. A PKI is required for Shared Key authentications.

3. Which of the following terms describe a wireless network that consists of two laptop computers with wireless network interface adapters communicating directly with each other? (Choose all that apply.)

   a. Basic service set

   b. Infrastructure network

   c. Ad hoc network

   d. Access point

Lesson Summary

- Most wireless LANs today are based on the 802.11 standards published by the IEEE.

- WLANs have two primary security hazards: unauthorized access to the network and eavesdropping on transmitted packets.

- To secure a wireless network, you must authenticate the clients before they are granted network access and encrypt all packets transmitted over the wireless link.

- To authenticate IEEE 802.11 wireless network clients, you can use Open System authentication, Shared Key authentication, or IEEE 802.1X.

- To encrypt transmitted packets, the IEEE 802.11 standard defines the Wired Equivalent Privacy (WEP) mechanism.

Case Scenario Exercise

You are the network infrastructure design specialist for Litware Inc., a manufacturer of specialized scientific software products, and you have already created a network design for its new office building. You are in the process of designing an IPSec deployment for the network to protect the network transmissions of certain network users.

The primary goal of this project is to protect the network transmissions of the Research and Development department, which regularly works on government contracts using confidential company information and secret documents. The confidential material is stored on several database servers in the building's data center. Because these database servers perform no other company functions, you want to require the use of IPSec to encrypt all traffic accessing them. However, the users in the Research and Development department also have to access other company services that do not need such high security, such as e-mail and the company's customer database.

In addition to being accessible by the Research and Development users in the building, the information in the Research and Development databases must also be available to specific people in the company's headquarters in another city. The building is connected to the headquarters by a T-1 WAN link, but you must secure this access with IPSec as well.

Based on this information, answer the following questions.

1. Which of the following IPSec policies should you assign to the organizational unit object containing the Research and Development users' workstations?

    a. The default Secure Server (Require Security) policy

    b. The default Client (Respond Only) policy

    c. A policy that secures all TCP traffic, using both the AH and ESP protocols

    d. A policy that secures all traffic to the port number of the database application, using the AH protocol

2. Which of the following procedures should you use to secure the WAN traffic between the users in the company headquarters and the Research and Development database servers? (Choose all that apply.)

    a. Configure the routers at both ends of the WAN connection to use IPSec in tunnel mode

    b. Configure the database servers with the Secure Server (Require Security) policy

    c. Configure the workstations of the users at the headquarters with the Client (Respond Only) policy

    d. Configure the database servers and the workstations at the headquarters to use IPSec in tunnel mode

After implementing your IPSec plan, you prepare to deploy a wireless LAN, which will enable users with laptop computers running Windows XP to roam anywhere in the building and remain connected to the network.

The wireless equipment you have selected conforms to the IEEE 802.11b standard and consists of network interface cards for all the laptops and an access point for each floor of the building. Because the laptop users might be working with sensitive data, you want to make sure the wireless network is secure. You have been considering a number of security strategies for the WLAN, but you have not made a final decision. Based on the information provided, answer the following questions.

1. Which of the following tasks would wireless users not be able to do if you decided to use Shared Key authentication?

    a. Use WEP encryption for all wireless transmissions

    b. Roam from one access point to another

    c. Access resources on other wireless computers

    d. Participate in an infrastructure network

2. Which of the following tasks would you need to perform to use IEEE 802.1X and WEP to secure the WLAN? (Choose all that apply.)

    a. Install IAS on a computer running Windows Server 2003.

    b. Deploy a public key infrastructure on the network by installing Certificate Services.

    c. Install smart card readers in all the laptop computers.

    d. Install SP1 on all the laptops running Windows XP.

3. If you elect to use Open System authentication with WEP encryption, to which of the following vulnerabilities would the WLAN be subject?

   a. Unauthorized users connecting to the network

   b. Compromised passwords from unencrypted WLAN authentication messages

   c. Interception of transmitted data by someone using a wireless protocol analyzer

   d. Inability of wireless computers to access resources on the cabled network

Troubleshooting Lab

You are a network administrator for a company whose president has recently become extremely security-conscious as the result of an incident in which confidential documents found their way into the hands of a competing company. You have been ordered to encrypt all sensitive network communications, and you just finished deploying IPSec on all the network's computers. To ensure the security of the network, you assigned the Secure Server (Require Security) policy to the Group Policy Object for your Active Directory domain. Now, the day after the deployment, you are getting numerous complaints from users about slow performance from their computers. Which of the following procedures might lessen the impact of IPSec on network performance, while keeping the network sufficiently secure? (Choose all that apply.)

   a. Switch the IPSec policy assigned to the domain from Secure Server (Require Security) policy to Server (Request Security).

   b. Using organizational unit objects instead of the domain, assign the Secure Server (Require Security) policy to the company servers and the Client (Respond Only) policy to the workstations.

   c. Modify the Secure Server (Require Security) policy to use only the AH protocol.

   d. Create a new IPSec policy that encrypts only the traffic to and from the computers containing confidential documents.

   e. Install additional memory in all the network computers.

   f. Upgrade the network from 10Base-T to 100Base-TX.

Chapter Summary

- IPSec is a set of extensions to the IP protocol that provide protection for data as it is transmitted over the network. IPSec includes two protocols, IP Authentication Header and IP Encapsulating Security Payload, which can be used separately or together.

- IPSec can operate in transport mode or tunnel mode. Transport mode secures communications between end users on a network, and tunnel mode secures WAN communications between routers.

- The IPSec implementation in Windows Server 2003 consists of IPSEC Services, Internet Key Exchange (IKE), and the IPSec driver.

- Windows Server 2003 IPSec has three default policies: Client (Respond Only), Secure Server (Require Security), and Server (Request Security). You can use these policies or create your own.

- IPSec policies consist of rules, IP filter lists, and filter actions. A rule is a combination of an IP filter list and a filter action. IP filter lists specify what traffic IPSec should protect, and filter actions specify what type of protection IPSec should apply.

- Incompatible configuration settings are a common cause of IPSec communication problems.

- Most wireless LANs in use today are based on the 802.11 standards published by the IEEE.

- To secure a wireless network, you must authenticate clients before they are granted network access and also encrypt all packets transmitted over the wireless link.

- To authenticate IEEE 802.11 wireless network clients, you can use Open System authentication, Shared Key authentication, or IEEE 802.1X.

- To encrypt transmitted packets, the IEEE 802.11 standard defines the Wired Equivalent Privacy (WEP) mechanism.

Exam Highlights

Before taking the exam, review the following key points and terms to help you identify topics you need to review. Return to the lessons for additional practice, and review the "Further Reading" sections in Part 2 for pointers to more information about topics covering the exam objectives.

Key Points

- In Windows Server 2003, IPSec policies control when and how IPSec is used to protect network traffic from being compromised.

- IPSec policies consist of rules, IP filter lists, and filter actions. A rule is a combination of IP filter actions and filter lists. IP filter lists are combinations of IP addresses, protocols, and ports that specify what traffic IPSec should protect. Filter actions specify which IPSec features the system should use to protect the traffic conforming to the IP filter list settings.

- To deploy IPSec on a network, you assign an IPSec policy to a Group Policy Object or to a particular computer.

- Because wireless network transmissions are omnidirectional, signals might be accessed by unauthorized users. The two primary dangers are that unauthorized computers can connect to the WLAN and that they can intercept transmitted packets and read the data inside. To prevent these occurrences, you must authenticate users when they connect to the WLAN and encrypt all traffic transmitted over the WLAN.

- To authenticate IEEE 802.11 wireless network clients, you can use Open System authentication, Shared Key authentication, or IEEE 802.1X. To encrypt transmitted packets, the IEEE 802.11 standard defines the Wired Equivalent Privacy (WEP) mechanism. Microsoft recommends the use of IEEE 802.1X authentication in combination with WEP encryption.

Key Terms

Spoofing   The impersonation of another user or computer, usually for illicit purposes.

Ad hoc network   A network in which wireless computers communicate directly with each other.

Infrastructure network   A network in which wireless computers communicate with an access point that is connected to a cabled network, providing access to both bounded and unbounded network resources.

Basic service area (BSA)   The effective transmission range in which wireless devices can communicate. A new wireless device cannot connect to an existing wireless network until it enters its BSA.

Basic service set (BSS)   A group of wireless devices communicating with a basic service area.

Page
11-13

Lesson 1 Review

1. Which of the following ESP header fields provides the protocol's antireplay capability?

   a. Sequence Number

   b. Security Parameters Index

   c. Pad Length

   d. Next Header

   a

2. Specify the proper order for the following components in an IPSec transport mode packet using both AH and ESP and containing TCP data.

   a. ESP trailer

   b. IP header

   c. ESP header

   d. TCP header

   e. AH header

   f. TCP data

   b, e, c, d, f, a

3. Which of the following IPSec characteristics is different when a connection is operating in tunnel mode instead of transport mode? (Choose all that apply.)

   a. The order of the fields in the ESP header

   b. The location of the ESP header in the datagram

   c. The location of the ESP trailer in the datagram

   d. The value of the Next Header field in the ESP header

   b and d

Lesson 2 Review

1. Which IPSec policy can you use to encrypt all traffic to and from a particular database application on a server running Windows Server 2003?

    a. Client (Respond Only).

    b. Secure Server (Require Security).

    c. Server (Request Security).

    d. You must create a new custom policy.

    d

2. Which of the following pieces of information must you supply when creating a policy that configures IPSec to use tunnel mode?

    a. The IP address of the router's WAN interface

    b. The port number associated with the WAN technology used for the tunnel

    c. The IP address of the router at the far end of the tunnel

    d. The network layer protocol used for the WAN connection

    a

3. Which IPSec component is responsible for actually encrypting the information in IP datagrams?

    a. Internet Key Exchange

    b. IPSEC Services

    c. IPSec driver

    d. The IP Security Policies snap-in

    c

Lesson 3 Review

1. Which of the following authentication mechanisms enables clients to connect to a wireless network using smart cards?

    a. Open System authentication

    b. Shared Key authentication

    c. IEEE 802.1X authentication using EAP-TLS

    d. IEEE 802.1X authentication using PEAP-MS-CHAP v2

    c

2. You are installing an IEEE 802.11b wireless network in a private home using computers running Windows XP, and you decide that data encryption is not necessary, but you want to use Shared Key authentication. However, when you try to configure the network interface adapter on the clients to use Shared Key authentication, the option is not available. Which of the following explanations could be the cause of the problem?

   a. WEP is not enabled.

   b. Windows XP SP1 is not installed on the computers.

   c. Windows XP does not support Shared Key authentication.

   d. A PKI is required for Shared Key authentications.

   a

3. Which of the following terms describe a wireless network that consists of two laptop computers with wireless network interface adapters communicating directly with each other? (Choose all that apply.)

   a. Basic service set

   b. Infrastructure network

   c. Ad hoc network

   d. Access point

   a and c

Page
11-35

Case Scenario Exercise

1. Which of the following IPSec policies should you assign to the organizational unit object containing the Research and Development users' workstations?

   a. The default Secure Server (Require Security) policy

   b. The default Client (Respond Only) policy

   c. A policy that secures all TCP traffic, using both the AH and ESP protocols

   d. A policy that secures all traffic to the port number of the database application, using the AH protocol

   b

2. Which of the following procedures should you use to secure the WAN traffic between the users in the company headquarters and the Research and Development database servers? (Choose all that apply.)

    a. Configure the routers at both ends of the WAN connection to use IPSec in tunnel mode

    b. Configure the database servers with the Secure Server (Require Security) policy

    c. Configure the workstations of the users at the headquarters with the Client (Respond Only) policy

    d. Configure the database servers and the workstations at the headquarters to use IPSec in tunnel mode

b and c

1. Which of the following tasks would wireless users not be able to do if you decided to use Shared Key authentication?

    a. Use WEP encryption for all wireless transmissions

    b. Roam from one access point to another

    c. Access resources on other wireless computers

    d. Participate in an infrastructure network

b

2. Which of the following tasks would you need to perform to use IEEE 802.1X and WEP to secure the WLAN? (Choose all that apply.)

    a. Install IAS on a computer running Windows Server 2003.

    b. Deploy a public key infrastructure on the network by installing Certificate Services.

    c. Install smart card readers in all the laptop computers.

    d. Install SP1 on all the laptops running Windows XP.

a and d

3. If you elect to use Open System authentication with WEP encryption, to which of the following vulnerabilities would the WLAN be subject?

    a. Unauthorized users connecting to the network

    b. Compromised passwords from unencrypted WLAN authentication messages

    c. Interception of transmitted data by someone using a wireless protocol analyzer

    d. Inability of wireless computers to access resources on the cabled network

a

Troubleshooting Lab

You are a network administrator for a company whose president has recently become extremely security-conscious as the result of an incident in which confidential documents found their way into the hands of a competing company. You have been ordered to encrypt all sensitive network communications, and you just finished deploying IPSec on all the network's computers. To ensure the security of the network, you assigned the Secure Server (Require Security) policy to the Group Policy Object for your Active Directory domain. Now, the day after the deployment, you are getting numerous complaints from users about slow performance from their computers. Which of the following procedures might lessen the impact of IPSec on network performance, while keeping the network sufficiently secure? (Choose all that apply.)

    a. Switch the IPSec policy assigned to the domain from Secure Server (Require Security) policy to Server (Request Security).

    b. Using organizational unit objects instead of the domain, assign the Secure Server (Require Security) policy to the company servers and the Client (Respond Only) policy to the workstations.

    c. Modify the Secure Server (Require Security) policy to use only the AH protocol.

    d. Create a new IPSec policy that encrypts only the traffic to and from the computers containing confidential documents.

    e. Install additional memory in all the network computers.

    f. Upgrade the network from 10Base-T to 100Base-TX.

    d and f

12 Creating and Managing Digital Certificates

Exam Objectives in this Chapter:

- Configure Active Directory directory service for certificate publication (Exam 70-296).
- Plan a public key infrastructure (PKI) using Certificate Services (Exam 70-296).
    - ❏ Identify the appropriate type of certification authority to support certificate issuance requirements.
    - ❏ Plan the enrollment and distribution of certificates.
    - ❏ Plan for the use of smart cards for authentication.
- Configure the user environment by using Group Policy (Exam 70-296).
    - ❏ Automatically enroll user certificates by using Group Policy.

Why This Chapter Matters

The public key infrastructure (PKI) is an important element of the security philosophy of the Microsoft Windows Server 2003 family, and digital certificates provide the cornerstone of the PKI. With certificates, you can protect network data and secure communications using a variety of cryptographic algorithms and key lengths that enable you to implement as much security as you need for your organization. Before you actually use certificates on your network, you must understand the architecture of the PKI and create a plan that is suitable for your network.

Lessons in this Chapter:

Before You Begin

This chapter requires that you have a basic understanding of Windows Server 2003 security, Active Directory directory service, and group policies.

To perform the practices related to the objectives in this chapter, you must have

- One Windows Server 2003 (Standard or Enterprise Edition) system with Internet Information Services (IIS) installed

- Access to the server with administrative credentials

Lesson 1: Introducing Certificates

As an increasing number of important business transactions are performed digitally, the issue of security for network communications has become vitally important. Digital transactions both within an organization and between organizations require protection from a variety of threats, including message interception, identity spoofing, and message repudiation. To provide this protection, Windows Server 2003 includes the components needed to create a PKI.

After this lesson, you will be able to

- List the capabilities of secret key encryption
- Describe the contents of a certificate
- Describe the function of a certification authority

Estimated lesson time: 20 minutes

Introducing the Public Key Infrastructure

A *public key infrastructure* is a collection of software components and operational policies that govern the distribution and use of public and private keys through the use of digital certificates. To protect data transmitted over a network, computers use various types of encryption to encode messages and create digital signatures that verify their authenticity. For one computer to encrypt a message and another computer to decrypt it, both must possess a key.

Understanding Secret Key Encryption

Encryption is essentially a system in which one character is substituted for another. If you create a key specifying that the letter A should be replaced by Q, the letter B by O, the letter C by T, and so forth, any message you encode using that key can be decoded by anyone else who has that key. This is called *secret key encryption* because you must protect the key from compromise. For computer transactions, this simple type of encryption is all but useless because there is usually no practical way to distribute the secret key to all recipients. After all, if the object is to send an encrypted message to a recipient over the network, it would hardly be appropriate to first send the secret encryption key in an unsecured message.

For encryption on a data network to be both possible and practical, computers typically use a form of public key encryption. In *public key encryption*, every user has two keys, a public key and a private key. As the names imply, the public key is freely available to anyone, while the private key is carefully secured and never transmitted over the network. The way the system works is that data encrypted with the public key can be decrypted only with the private key, and conversely, data encrypted with the private key can be decrypted only by using the public key. The protection of the private key is what guarantees the security of messages encrypted using this system.

Encrypting Data   If someone wants to send you a message and make sure no one but you can read it, that person must obtain your public key and use it to encrypt the message. The person can then transmit the message to you over the network, secure in the knowledge that only you possess the private key needed to decrypt it. Even if an intruder were to intercept the message during transmission, it would still be in its encrypted form and therefore impenetrable. Once you receive the message and decrypt it using your private key, you could reply to it by using the other party's own public key to encrypt your response, which only that person can decrypt using the private key.

Digitally Signing Data   If you want to send someone a message and have them be absolutely sure it came from you, you can digitally sign it by using your private key to encrypt all or part of the data. Anyone receiving the message can then decrypt the encoded data using your public key. The fact that your public key successfully decrypted the message proves that you sent it, because only your private key could have encrypted it. This process not only prevents other users from impersonating you by sending messages in your name, it also provides the recipient with proof that you sent the message so that you cannot repudiate it later.

> **Note**   It is usually not practical to encrypt an entire message for the purpose of digitally signing it. Instead, most PKI systems create a hash from the message and then encrypt the hash using the private key. A *hash* is a digital summary of the message created by removing redundant bits according to a specialized hashing algorithm.

Verifying Data   When you want to be certain the message you are sending to a recipient is not modified en route, you can use a hashing algorithm to create a hash from the message, and then encrypt both the message and the hash using your private key. When the message arrives at its destination, the recipient's computer decrypts the message using your public key, and then uses the same hashing algorithm to create a hash from the incoming message. If the hash included with the message matches the hash calculated by the receiving system, the message is verified as being unchanged since its transmission.

Using Certificates

For public key encryption to be a reliable form of communication, there has to be a verifiable mechanism for the distribution of public keys. Otherwise, an imposter could distribute a public key using another person's name and receive encrypted messages intended for that person, which the imposter could decrypt using the corresponding private key. To distribute public keys, Windows Server 2003 and most other systems supporting a PKI use digital certificates. A *digital certificate* is a document that verifiably associates a public key with a particular person or organization.

Understanding Certificate Contents

A digital certificate contains the public key for a particular entity, such as a user or an organization, plus information about the entity and about the certification authority (CA) that issued the certificate. The Telecommunication Standardization Sector of the International Telecommunication Union (ITU-T) has published a standard called X.509 (03/00), "The Directory: Public-key and Attribute Certificate Frameworks," which defines the format of the certificates used by most PKI systems, including Windows Server 2003. In addition to the public key, every digital certificate contains these attributes:

- **Version** Identifies the version of the X.509 standard used to format the certificate

- **Serial number** A value assigned by the CA that uniquely identifies the certificate

- **Signature algorithm identifier** Specifies the algorithm the CA used to calculate the certificate's digital signature

- **Issuer name** Specifies the name of the entity that issued the certificate

- **Validity period** Specifies the period during which the certificate is valid

- **Subject name** Specifies the name of the entity for which the certificate is issued

Most certificates also contain other attributes, which are specific to the intended functions of the certificates.

To use public key encryption, you must obtain a certificate from an administrative entity called a *certification authority (CA)*. A CA can be a third-party company that is trusted to verify the identities of all parties involved in a digital transaction, or it can be a piece of software on a computer running Windows Server 2003 or another operating system. The type of CA you use for your organization depends on who is involved in the secure transactions.

Obtaining a certificate from a CA can be a manual process, with the user explicitly requesting that a CA issue a certificate, or an automatic one, with an application requesting and obtaining a certificate in the background as part of its normal function. No matter how the process occurs, the CA issues a public key and a private key as a matched pair. The private key is stored on the user's computer in encrypted form, and the public key is issued as part of a certificate. The certificate is essentially a carrier for the public key and related information and, as such, facilitates the distribution of the key to the people who need it.

Using Internal and External CAs

For a certificate to be useful in securing a digital transaction, it must be issued by an authority that both parties to the transaction trust to verify each other's identity. When you are designing your own PKI for your network, you can deploy your own certification authorities, use a third-party CA, or use both. Your choice typically depends on whether the parties involved in the transaction work for the same company or different ones.

If you want to ensure that internal communications in your organization are secure, you would be best served by installing your own CAs. Windows Server 2003 includes Certificate Services, a service that functions as a CA. All the users in your organization can usually trust a CA run by the company to verify other users' identities. However, if your organization engages in digital transactions with other companies, an internal CA is typically not useful because the other companies are not going to trust your own CA to verify your identity.

For securing external transactions, the best practice is to obtain certificates from a neutral third-party organization that functions as a commercial certification authority. Companies such as Thawte and VeriSign, Inc., are examples of commercial CAs that are trusted throughout the IT industry.

Real World   Using Certificates

For a Windows operating system user, one of the most common occasions for encountering certificates occurs when you download software from the Internet and Microsoft Internet Explorer displays a dialog box, like the one in the following illustration, that prompts you to confirm that you want to install the software. This dialog box specifies the manufacturer of the software and indicates whether the download includes a certificate that verifies the source of the download.

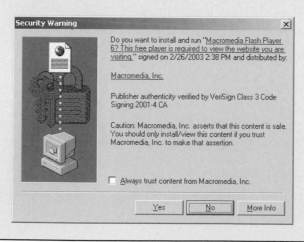

If a certificate is included, it contains the software manufacturer's public key, which your computer uses to decrypt the download's digital signature. If decryption is successful, you know that the software you downloaded was digitally signed using the private key corresponding to the public key in the certificate. As long as you trust the authority that issued the certificate to verify the software manufacturer's identity, you know that the download came from the manufacturer and was not tampered with en route.

Understanding PKI Functions

With a Windows Server 2003 PKI in place, network administrators can perform the following tasks:

- **Publish certificates** Certificate Services can create certificates and publish them on a Web site or in Active Directory, where clients—such as users, computers, and applications—can retrieve them.

- **Enroll clients** *Enrollment* is the term used to describe the process by which a client requests and receives a certificate from a certification authority. When a client requests a certificate, the CA (or the CA administrator) verifies the client's identity and then issues a certificate in the client's name.

- **Use certificates** Once a client requests and receives a certificate, the client can use it to secure its communications in various ways, depending on the capabilities of the certificate and the functions for which it was issued.

- **Renew certificates** Certificates are typically valid for a finite period. At the end of that period, the client must either renew the certificate with the CA or stop using it.

- **Revoke certificates** When a CA administrator explicitly revokes a certificate, the CA adds it to a certificate revocation list (CRL). The CA publishes this list at regular intervals to inform the other systems on the network of certificates that they should no longer honor.

Practice: Viewing a Certificate

In this practice, you install the Macromedia Shockwave Player software on a computer running Windows Server 2003. During the installation procedure, you can display the certificate that verifies the identity of the software's publisher.

1. Log on to Windows Server 2003 as Administrator.

2. Click Start, point to All Programs, and then click Internet Explorer. A Microsoft Internet Explorer window appears.

3. From the Tools menu, select Internet Options and then click the Security tab.

4. For the Internet zone, move the Security Level For This Zone slider to Medium, and then click OK.

   Changing the Security Level prevents the Internet Explorer Enhanced Security Configuration feature from blocking access to the Certificate Services Web page.

5. In the Address text box, type **http://sdc.shockwave.com/shockwave/download** and then press ENTER. The Macromedia Shockwave Player Download Center page appears.

6. Click the Install Now button. The Security Warning dialog box appears.

   This dialog box specifies that you are about to install the Shockwave Player software and states that the computer has confirmed the authenticity of the publisher.

7. Click the Macromedia, Inc., hyperlink. The Certificate dialog box appears with the General tab active.

   Notice that the software uses a certificate supplied by VeriSign, which provides assurance that the software comes from the specified publisher and has not been modified.

8. Click the Details tab.

   This tab displays a list of all the certificate's attributes.

9. Click OK to close the Certificate dialog box, and then click Yes in the Security Warning dialog box. The software installation proceeds.

10. Close Internet Explorer after the installation completes.

Lesson Review

The following questions are intended to reinforce key information presented in this lesson. If you are unable to answer a question, review the lesson materials and try the question again. You can find answers to the questions in the "Questions and Answers" section at the end of this chapter.

1. Which of the following pieces of information is not included as part of a digital certificate?

   a. Validity period

   b. Private key

   c. Signature algorithm identifier

   d. Public key

2. For each of the following messaging scenarios, specify which key you should use to encrypt the message: the sender's public key, the sender's private key, the recipient's public key, or the recipient's private key.

    a. To send a message that can't be read by anyone but the recipient

_____

    b. To assure the recipient that the message you are sending actually came from you

_____

Lesson Summary

- Public key encryption uses two keys, a public key and a private key.

- Data encrypted with the public key can be decrypted only by using the private key, and data encrypted using the private key can be decrypted only with the public key.

- A PKI is a collection of software components and operational policies that govern the distribution and use of public and private keys.

- Private keys must never be transmitted over a network. Public keys are distributed in digital certificates.

- Certificates are issued by a certification authority (CA). You can run your own CA using Windows Server 2003, or you can obtain your certificates from a third-party commercial CA.

Lesson 2: Designing a Public Key Infrastructure

As with most elements of a network, implementing a public key infrastructure requires careful planning before you begin deployment. Planning a PKI typically consists of the following basic steps:

■ Defining certificate requirements

■ Creating a certification authority infrastructure

■ Configuring certificates

After this lesson, you will be able to

■ List the types of certificates a Windows Server 2003 CA can issue

■ Describe the structure of a CA hierarchy

■ List the differences between enterprise and stand-alone CAs

■ Configure certificate parameters

Estimated lesson time: 30 minutes

Defining Certificate Requirements

As in most phases of designing a network, the first step of the planning phase is to determine the requirements of the users. In the case of a PKI design, you must determine what your client's security needs are; how certificates can help provide that security; which users, computers, services, and applications will use certificates; and what kinds of certificates your clients need. In many cases, you will have already answered some or all of these questions as you develop an overall security strategy.

A PKI using computers running Windows Server 2003 can create certificates that support any or all of the following applications:

■ **Digital signatures**   Digital signatures are used to confirm that the person sending a message, file, or other data is actually who he or she purports to be. Digital signatures do not protect the data itself from compromise; they only verify the identity of the sender.

■ **Encrypting File System user and recovery certificates**   The Windows Server 2003 Encrypting File System (EFS) enables users to store data on disk in encrypted form to prevent other users from accessing it. To prevent loss of data resulting from users leaving the organization or losing their encryption keys, EFS allows designated recovery agents to create public keys that can decode the encrypted information. As with IPSec, EFS does not have to use the PKI for its encryption keys, but the use of a PKI simplifies managing EFS.

- **Internet authentication**   You can use the PKI to authenticate clients and servers as they establish connections over the Internet so that servers can identify the clients connecting to them and clients can confirm that they are connecting to the correct servers.

- **IP Security**   The IP Security extensions (IPSec) enable you to encrypt and digitally sign communications to prevent them from being compromised as they are transmitted over a network. The Windows Server 2003 IPSec implementation does not have to use a PKI to obtain its encryption keys, but you can use the PKI for this purpose.

- **Secure e-mail**   Internet e-mail protocols transmit mail messages in plain text, making it relatively easy to intercept them and read their contents. With the PKI, you can secure e-mail communications by encrypting the actual message text using the recipient's public key, and you can digitally sign the messages using your private key.

- **Smart card logon**   A smart card is a credit card–size device that contains memory and possibly an integrated circuit. Windows Server 2003 can use a smart card as an authentication device that verifies the identity of a user during logon. The smart card contains the user's certificate and private key, enabling the user to log on to any workstation in the enterprise with full security.

- **Software code signing**   The Microsoft Authenticode technology uses certificates to confirm that the software users download and install actually comes from the publisher and has not been modified.

- **Wireless network authentication**   The increasing popularity of wireless local area networking (LAN) technologies, such as those based on the 802.11 standard, raises an important security issue. When you install a wireless LAN, you must make sure that only authorized users can connect to the network and that no one can eavesdrop on the wireless communications. You can use the Windows Server 2003 PKI to protect a wireless network by identifying and authenticating users before they are granted access to the network.

Once you have decided what applications you want to secure with certificates, you can create a plan indicating the level of security for each user. For example, you might decide that you want everyone on your network to use secured e-mail, while only the Research and Development and Accounting departments need IPSec for all their network communications. Users' locations can also be significant. You might want to use software code signing and Internet authentication for clients who connect to your network over the Internet, but you might prefer to omit these requirements for internal users.

When defining the certificate security requirements for your network, the best practice is to create a small set of security definitions and apply them to your users and computers as needed. For example, Table 12-1 shows a certificate plan for an organization that includes four levels of security: basic, medium, high, and external. The basic security level, applied to most users in the organization, uses certificates to provide encrypted e-mail and EFS services. Medium-level security, which is used for general users in departments with more sensitive information, adds IPSec to secure their LAN communications. Top-level executives and people working with highly sensitive information use high security and must use a smart card to log on to the network. Because the organization runs a Web site where registered customers can download software products, a special classification for external users calls for certificates that provide software code signing and Internet authentication.

Table 12-1   Sample Certificate Plan

Basic security	Medium security	High security	External security
Secure e-mail	Secure e-mail	Secure e-mail	Software code signing
Encrypting File System	Encrypting File System	Encrypting File System	Internet authentication
	IPSec	IPSec	
		Smart card logon	

Creating a CA Infrastructure

Once you have decided what you are going to use certificates for and who is going to need them, you can plan the infrastructure of certification authorities that will provide the certificates you need. Certification authorities function using a hierarchy in which each CA is validated by a CA at a higher level until you reach the root CA, the ultimate authority for the organization. CAs issue certificates not only to applications and users, but also to other CAs. If you trust a particular root CA, you should also trust any lower-level CAs that are authenticated and validated by that root CA. Trusts between CAs flow downward through the hierarchy, just as file system permissions do. (See Figure 12-1.)

When creating a CA infrastructure for your organization, you must decide how many CAs you need, who is going to provide them, where to locate them, and what the trust relationships between them should be.

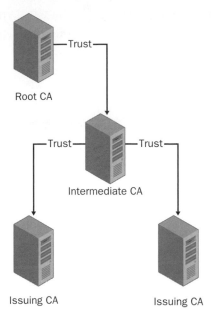

Figure 12-1   Certification authority trusts flow downward

Using Internal or External CAs

You can use either internal CAs running on your own computers or external CAs provided by a commercial service for all your certificate needs. Some applications (such as software code signing) clearly call for one or the other, but in many cases, the choice depends on the needs and capabilities of your organization. The advantages and disadvantages of using internal and external CAs are summarized in Table 12-2.

Table 12-2   Advantages and Disadvantages of Internal and External CAs

Advantages of an internal CA	Disadvantages of an internal CA	Advantages of an external CA	Disadvantages of an external CA
Direct control over certificates	Increased certificate management overhead	Instills customers with greater confidence in the organization	High cost per certificate
No per-certificate fees	Longer, more complex deployment	Provider liable for PKI failures	No autoenrollment possible
Can be integrated into Active Directory	Organization must accept liability for PKI failures	Expertise in the technical and legal ramifications of certificate use	Less flexibility in configuring and managing certificates
Allows configuring and expanding PKI for minimal cost	Limited trust by external customers	Reduced management overhead	Limited integration with the organization's infrastructure

In many cases, organizations use a combination of internal and external CAs. They use their own CAs to secure their internal communications and use external CAs when they must secure communications with outside parties, such as customers.

How Many CAs?

If you decide to use internal CAs for your network, the next step is to determine how many CAs you need and where to locate them. A single CA running on Windows Server 2003 can support as many as 35 million certificates, issuing two million or more a day. As a result, most organizations use multiple CAs due to logistical factors other than the number of certificates required.

A variety of factors affect the performance of a CA and can influence your decision as to how many CAs you need. Some of these factors are as follows:

- **Number and speed of processors**   The CPU performance of a server is the single most influential factor in that server's performance as a CA. A server with multiple processors or faster processors will perform better as a CA, particularly when issuing certificates with long encryption keys.

- **Key length**   The length of the encryption keys in your certificates is a major factor in determining the impact of CA service on the computer's CPU. Longer keys require more processing time and can slow down the certificate enrollment process.

- **Disk performance**   A high-performance disk subsystem in a CA can influence the certificate enrollment rate; however, the degree of influence depends on other factors, such as the CPU performance and key length. If the CA issues certificates with unusually long keys, processing time for each certificate increases, slowing down the enrollment rate and lessening the impact on the disk subsystem. With shorter keys, disk performance is more critical because the disk subsystem can more easily become the bottleneck slowing down the enrollment rate.

Based on these criteria, many organizations would be adequately served by a single CA, but there are several reasons for implementing multiple CAs anyway. One reason is fault tolerance. Having two or more CAs enables the PKI to service clients even if one of the servers fails. Another reason is load distribution when servicing an organization spread out over multiple locations. A corporation with several offices might want a CA in each office to reduce wide area network (WAN) traffic and to keep the certificate enrollment process local. It might also be necessary to deploy multiple CAs so that different servers can issue certificates for different purposes.

Creating a CA Hierarchy

When you deploy multiple CAs in a single organization, the relationships between them are hierarchical, based on a network of parent/child relationships. Every CA in a PKI is either a *root CA* or a *subordinate CA*. A root CA is the parent that issues certificates to the subordinate CAs beneath it. If a client trusts the root CA, it must also trust all the subordinate CAs that have been issued certificates by the root CA.

> **Note**   Root CAs are the only CAs that do not have a certificate issued by a higher authority. A root CA issues its own *self-signed certificate*, which functions as the top of the certificate chain for all the certificates issued by all the CAs subordinate to the root.

Subordinate CAs can also issue certificates to other subordinate CAs. In this case, the CA in the middle is called an *intermediate CA*. An intermediate CA is subordinate to the root CA but higher than the other subordinate CAs to which it issues certificates.

Every certificate issued by every CA in the hierarchy can trace its trust relationships back to a root CA. The CA that issues your certificate might possess a certificate issued by another CA, which, in turn, might possess a certificate issued by a root CA. This hierarchy of relationships is called a *certificate chain*. In Windows Server 2003, you can display the certificate chain for any certificate by clicking the Certification Path tab in the Certificate dialog box, as shown in Figure 12-2.

Figure 12-2   The Certification Path tab in the Certificate dialog box

In a large PKI implementation, a three-layer CA hierarchy like the one in Figure 12-1 is typical. The root CA exists only to issue certificates to the intermediate CAs, thereby functioning as the ultimate authority for the PKI. Beneath the CA are one or more intermediate CAs, which issue certificates to the subordinate CAs at the next level. Generally speaking, you create multiple intermediate CAs to separate different classes of certificates—for example, one intermediate CA for internal user certificates and one for external certificates. At the bottom layer of the hierarchy are the subordinate CAs, also known as *issuing CAs* because these servers actually enroll client users and applications. Intermediate and root CAs usually do not issue certificates directly to clients, only to subordinate CAs.

> **Tip**   The security of the higher-level CAs in a PKI hierarchy is critical because, if an intruder penetrates the security of one high-level CA, all its subordinates are compromised as well. For this reason, it is common practice to leave root and intermediate CAs offline after they issue certificates to their subordinates. You can take a CA offline by shutting down Certificate Services, by disconnecting the Windows Server 2003 CA server from the network, or by shutting the server down completely.

Understanding Windows Server 2003 CA Types

When you configure a server running Windows Server 2003 to function as a CA, you can configure it to be either a root CA or a subordinate CA. In addition, you select one of the following two types for the CA:

- **Enterprise**   *Enterprise CAs* are integrated into the Active Directory directory service. They use certificate templates, publish their certificates and CRLs to Active Directory, and use the information in the Active Directory database to approve or deny certificate enrollment requests automatically. Because the clients of an enterprise CA must have access to Active Directory to receive certificates, enterprise CAs are not suitable for issuing certificates to clients outside the enterprise.

- **Stand-alone**   *Stand-alone CAs* do not use certificate templates or Active Directory; they store their information locally. In addition, by default, stand-alone CAs do not automatically respond to certificate enrollment requests, as enterprise CAs do. Requests wait in a queue for an administrator to manually approve or deny them. Stand-alone CAs are intended for situations in which users outside the enterprise submit requests for certificates.

Whether you choose to create an enterprise CA or a stand-alone CA, you can also specify that the CA be a root or a subordinate. An enterprise root CA is the top of the hierarchy. There can be only one enterprise root in any CA hierarchy. All other CAs in the hierarchy must be enterprise subordinate CAs.

Stand-alone CAs can function in the same type of hierarchy as enterprise CAs; you can create a stand-alone root CA with stand-alone subordinate CAs beneath it. If you want to create only one stand-alone CA for your PKI, it must be a root CA because every CA hierarchy must be traceable back to a root.

> **Tip**   If you plan to use smart cards to authenticate users on your network, you must create enterprise CAs because smart card certificates must be associated with Active Directory user accounts to be functional.

> **Exam Tip**   Be sure to understand the differences between enterprise root CAs, enterprise subordinate CAs, stand-alone root CAs, and stand-alone subordinate CAs.

Configuring Certificates

With your security requirements and your CA hierarchy design in place, you can decide on a configuration for the certificates that the CA will issue to your clients. Criteria to consider when planning certificate configurations are as follows:

- **Certificate type**   Specifies the function of the certificate. Windows Server 2003 includes a collection of certificate templates that enable you to easily configure a CA to issue specific types of certificates.

- **Encryption key length and algorithm**   The length of the encryption keys included in your certificates and the encryption algorithm the certificates use dictate how difficult certificates are to penetrate and how secure the information they protect is. Longer keys provide greater security, but they also require more processor time when creating and processing certificates. Different algorithms provide various degrees of security, also at the expense of processor time.

- **Certificate lifetime**   The lifetime of a certificate specifies how long the client can use it before it must be renewed. Longer lifetimes increase the chances that a certificate can be compromised. For certificates with longer encryption keys and stronger algorithms, however, longer lifetimes are often justified. Shorter lifetimes increase the number of certificates your CAs must issue, affecting network traffic and the server processing load. The default certificate lifetime for enterprise and stand-alone root CAs is two years.

- **Renewal policies**   You can configure a CA to issue new public and private keys when renewing a certificate or to reuse the existing keys. Issuing new keys increases the security the certificate provides, but it also increases the processing load on the CA.

Practice: Installing a Windows Server 2003 Certification Authority

In this practice, you install Certificate Services on a computer running Windows Server 2003 and configure it to function as a stand-alone root CA.

> **Important**   Make sure you have Internet Information Services (IIS) installed on the computer before you install Certificate Services.

1. Log on to Server02 as Administrator.

2. Click Start, point to Control Panel, and then click Add Or Remove Programs. The Add Or Remove Programs dialog box appears.

3. Click Add/Remove Windows Components. The Windows Components Wizard appears.

4. Click Certificate Services (without selecting the check box), and then click Details. The Certificate Services dialog box appears.

5. Select the Certificate Services CA and the Certificate Services Web Enrollment Support check boxes.

   A Microsoft Certificate Services message box appears, warning you that once you install Certificate Services, you cannot change the computer's machine name or domain membership without affecting the function of the CA. Click Yes to continue.

6. Click OK in the Certificate Services dialog box.

7. In the Windows Components Wizard, click Next. The CA Type page appears.

8. Click the Stand-alone Root CA option, and then click Next. The CA Identifying Information page appears.

9. In the Common Name For This CA text box, type **Issuing** and then click Next. The Certificate Database Settings page appears.

10. Click Next to accept the default database settings.

11. A Microsoft Certificate Services message box appears, stating that the system must temporarily stop the IIS service to complete the installation. Click Yes to proceed. The Configuring Components page appears, displaying a progress indicator as the wizard installs Certificate Services.

12. Depending on your configuration, another Microsoft Certificate Services message box might appear, stating that the system must activate Active Server Pages (ASP) in IIS. Click Yes to proceed. The Configuring Components page finishes showing the progress of the installation.

13. When the Completing The Windows Components Wizard page appears, click Finish. Close the Add Or Remove Programs dialog box.

Lesson Review

The following questions are intended to reinforce key information presented in this lesson. If you are unable to answer a question, review the lesson materials and try the question again. You can find answers to the questions in the "Questions and Answers" section at the end of this chapter.

1. Which of the following types of certificates can be issued only by an enterprise certification authority?

   a. IPSec

   b. Smart card logon

   c. Software code signing

   d. Wireless network authentication

2. Which of the following modifications to a certificate configuration does not increase the burden on the CA's processor?

   a. Increasing the key length

   b. Increasing the certificate's lifetime

   c. Issuing new keys with each certificate renewal

   d. Changing the certificate type

3. Where does a root CA obtain its own certificate?

   a. From a third-party certification authority

   b. From a subordinate CA

   c. From another root CA

   d. From itself

Lesson Summary

- The first step in planning a PKI is to study the security enhancements certificates can provide and determine which of your organization's security requirements you can satisfy with certificates.

- Certificates are issued by certification authorities, which you can run on your own computers or obtain from third-party providers.

- When running multiple CAs in an enterprise, you configure them in a hierarchy, with a root CA at the top, intermediate CAs at the second level, and subordinate (or issuing) CAs at the bottom.

- Every certificate has a chain of trust relationships running from the CA that issued it all the way up to a root CA.

- The configuration parameters of certificates themselves include the certificate type, the encryption algorithm and key length the certificates use, each certificate's lifetime, and the renewal policies that dictate how the CA behaves when processing certificate renewal requests.

Lesson 3: Managing Certificates

Once you have completed your PKI design and installed your CAs, the next step in deploying PKI to consider is the ongoing management of your CAs and their certificates. This includes administering certificate enrollment, managing the certificates themselves, and publishing certificate revocation lists.

After this lesson, you will be able to

- Control autoenrollment in enterprise CAs
- Submit certificate requests to a CA using the Certificates console or the pages created by the Certificate Services Web Enrollment Support interface
- Publish certificate revocation lists

Estimated lesson time: 30 minutes

Understanding Certificate Enrollment and Renewal

The actual process by which CAs issue certificates to clients varies depending on the types of CAs you have installed. If you have installed enterprise CAs, you can use *autoenrollment*, in which the CA receives certificate requests from clients, evaluates them, and automatically determines whether to issue the certificate or deny the request. If you have installed stand-alone CAs, you cannot use autoenrollment, so you must arrange for an administrator to monitor the CA (using the Certification Authority console) for incoming requests and to make decisions about whether to issue or deny the requests.

Exam Tip When preparing for the 70-296 exam, be sure to understand the circumstances in which clients use autoenrollment and manual enrollment, and to be familiar with the Microsoft Management Console (MMC) snap-ins used to manage certificates and certification authorities.

Using Autoenrollment

Autoenrollment enables clients to automatically request and receive certificates from a CA, with no manual intervention from administrators. To use autoenrollment, you must have domain controllers running Windows Server 2003, an enterprise CA running on Windows Server 2003, and clients running Microsoft Windows XP Professional. You control the autoenrollment process by using a combination of Group Policy settings and certificate templates.

By default, Group Policy Objects (GPOs) contain settings that enable autoenrollment for all user and computer objects in a domain. You configure these settings by opening the Autoenrollment Settings policy, located in the Windows Settings\Security Settings\Public Key Policies folder in both the Computer Configuration and User Configuration nodes in the Group Policy Object Editor. In the Autoenrollment Settings Properties dialog box (shown in Figure 12-3), you can disable autoenrollment entirely for the objects receiving these GPO settings. You can also enable the objects to renew and update their certificates automatically.

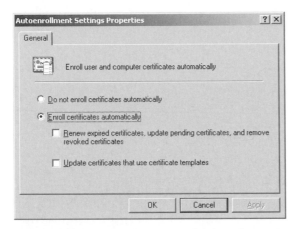

Figure 12-3   The Autoenrollment Settings Properties dialog box

The other mechanism you can use to control autoenrollment is built into the certificate templates that define the properties of specific certificate types. To manage certificate templates, you use the Certificate Templates snap-in, as shown in Figure 12-4. Using this tool, you can specify the validity and renewal periods of specific certificate types and choose cryptographic service providers for them. Using the Security tab for a particular template, you can also specify which users and groups are allowed to request certificates using that template.

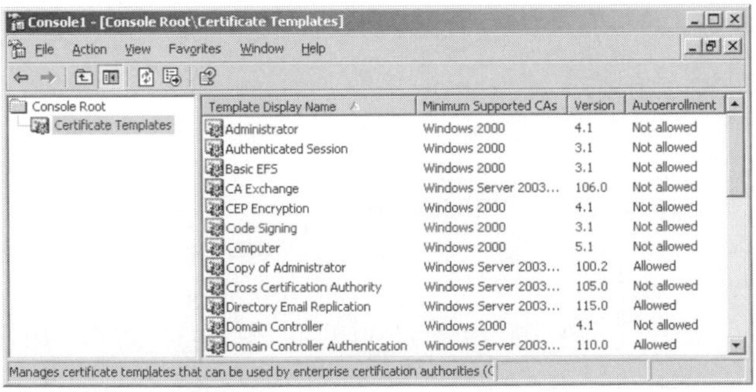

Figure 12-4   The Certificate Templates snap-in

When a client requests a particular type of certificate, the CA checks the properties of the client's Active Directory object to determine whether the client has the permissions needed to receive the certificate. If the client has the appropriate permissions, the CA issues the certificate automatically.

Using Manual Enrollment

Stand-alone CAs cannot use autoenrollment, so when a stand-alone CA receives a certificate request from a client, it stores the request in a queue until an administrator decides whether to issue the certificate. To monitor and process incoming requests, administrators use the Certification Authority console, as shown in Figure 12-5.

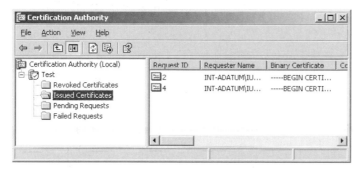

Figure 12-5   The Certification Authority console

In the Certification Authority console, incoming certificate enrollment requests appear in the Pending Requests folder. After evaluating the information in each request, an administrator can choose to issue or deny each request. Administrators can also view the properties of issued certificates and revoke certificates as needed.

Manually Requesting Certificates

In some cases, the process of requesting a certificate and receiving it from a CA is invisible to both the client and the administrator. Certain applications might request certificates and receive them in the background, and then proceed to function in the normal manner. In other cases, however, users must explicitly request certificates, using one of the tools that Windows Server 2003 provides.

Using the Certificates Snap-in

The Certificates snap-in (shown in Figure 12-6) is a tool you can use to view and manage the certificates of a specific user or computer. The snap-in's main display consists of folders that contain categories for all the certificates accessible to the designated user or computer. If your organization uses enterprise CAs, the Certificates snap-in also enables you to request and renew certificates using the Certificate Request Wizard and Certificate Renewal Wizard

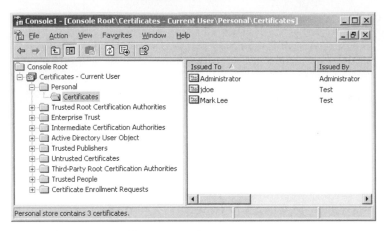

Figure 12-6   The Certificates snap-in

Off the Record   The Certificates snap-in is limited to use with enterprise CAs because the snap-in reads certificate information for the user or computer from Active Directory, and clients of stand-alone CAs are not expected to have access to Active Directory resources.

Using Web Enrollment

When you install Certificate Services on a computer running Windows Server 2003, you have the option of installing the Certificate Services Web Enrollment Support module as well. To function properly, this module requires you to have IIS installed on the computer first, along with support for ASP. Selecting this module during the Certificate Services installation creates a series of Web pages on the computer running the CA (shown in Figure 12-7); these pages enable users to submit requests for particular types of certificates.

Tip   You can also install the Certificate Services Web Enrollment Support module on a server running Windows Server 2003 that is not a CA, enabling you to integrate this module into existing Web servers.

The Web Enrollment Support interface is intended to give internal or external network users access to stand-alone CAs. Because stand-alone servers do not use certificate templates, the requests submitted by clients must include all the necessary information about the certificates being requested and about the users of the certificates. When clients request certificates using the Web Enrollment Support interface, they can select from a list of predefined certificate types or create an advanced certificate request in which they specify all the required information in a Web-based form. (See Figure 12-8.)

Figure 12-7   The Microsoft Certificate Services Web Enrollment Support interface

Figure 12-8   The Web Enrollment Support interface's Advanced Certificate Request page

Off the Record   The Web Enrollment Support interface can generate requests for most certificate types, but it cannot generate requests for certificates that are exclusive to enterprise CAs, such as smart card logon certificates.

Revoking Certificates

Several conditions can prompt an administrator to revoke a certificate. If a private key is compromised, an unauthorized user has gained access to the CA, or the administrator wants to issue a certificate using different parameters (such as longer keys), she or he must revoke the certificates that are no longer usable. A CA maintains a CRL, which it publishes to clients on a regular basis. Enterprise CAs publish their CRLs in the Active Directory database, so clients can access them using the standard Active Directory communication protocol, called Lightweight Directory Access Protocol (LDAP). A stand-alone CA stores its CRL as a file on the server's local drive, so clients must access it using an Internet communications protocol, such as Hypertext Transfer Protocol (HTTP) or File Transfer Protocol File Transfer Protocol (FTP).

Every certificate contains the path to the CA's distribution point for CRLs. You can modify this path in the Certification Authority console by displaying the Properties dialog box for the CA, and then clicking the Extensions tab. (See Figure 12-9.) However, if you plan to modify a CA's CRL distribution point, you must do so before it issues certificates. When an application authenticates a client using a certificate, it checks the CRL distribution point specified in the certificate to make sure the certificate has not been revoked. If the CRL is not at its specified distribution point, the application rejects the certificate.

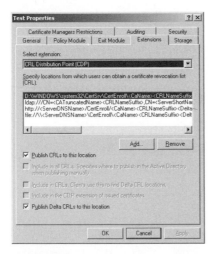

Figure 12-9   The Extensions tab in a CA's Properties dialog box

By selecting the Revoked Certificates folder in the Certification Authority console and then displaying its Properties dialog box (shown in Figure 12-10), you can specify how often the CA should publish a new CRL, and also configure the CA to publish delta CRLs. A *delta CRL* is a list of all certificates revoked since the last CRL publication. In organizations with large numbers of certificates, using delta CRLs instead of base CRLs can save a great deal of network bandwidth. For example, rather than publishing a base CRL every week, you can choose to publish delta CRLs weekly and publish the base CRLs monthly.

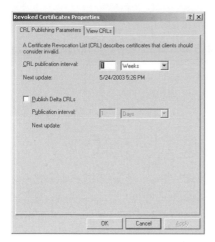

Figure 12-10   The Revoked Certificates Properties dialog box

Exam Tip   Chapter 4 discussed the use of smart cards for user authentication, and Chapter 11 discussed IPSec. Those technologies are easier to support with a well-implemented PKI. Be sure to review those topics as you prepare for the exam.

Practice: Requesting a Certificate

In this practice, you use the Web Enrollment Support interface to request a certificate from the CA you installed in the Lesson 2 practice. Then you instruct the CA to issue the certificate and use the Web Enrollment Support interface to retrieve it. Finally, you view the contents of the certificate using the Certificates snap-in.

Important   These practice exercises require you to have installed Certificate Services, as described in the Lesson 2 practice. In addition, you must have installed IIS on the computer before you installed Certificate Services, and you must have adjusted the security setting in Microsoft Internet Explorer as described in the Lesson 1 practice.

Exercise 1: Requesting a Certificate

In this exercise, you access the CA by using the Web Enrollment Support interface and request a certificate from the CA.

1. Log on to Server02 as Administrator.

2. Click Start, and then click Internet Explorer. A Microsoft Internet Explorer window appears.

3. In the Address text box, type **http://localhost/certsrv** and press ENTER. The Microsoft Certificate Services Web page appears.

4. Click Request A Certificate. The Request A Certificate page appears.

5. Click Advanced Certificate Request. The Advanced Certificate Request page appears.

6. Click Create And Submit A Request To This CA. The Advanced Certificate Request form appears.

7. In the Name text box, type **Lorrin Smith-Bates**.

8. In the Type Of Certificate Needed drop-down list, select IPSec Certificate.

9. In the CSP drop-down list, select Microsoft Strong Cryptographic Provider.

10. In the Key Size text box, type **2048**, and then click Submit at the bottom of the form.

11. A Potential Scripting Violation message box appears, prompting you to confirm your request. Click Yes.

12. An Internet Explorer message box might appear to inform you that others might intercept information sent over the Internet. Click Yes to continue.

13. The Certificate Pending page appears, informing you that your request has been submitted to the CA.

14. Leave Internet Explorer running.

Exercise 2: Issuing a Certificate

In this exercise, you use the Certification Authority console to issue the certificate you requested in the first exercise.

1. Click Start, point to Administrative Tools, and then click Certification Authority. The Certification Authority console appears.

2. Expand the Issuing icon in the scope pane, and then click the Pending Requests folder.

3. The request you generated in the first exercise appears in the details pane.

4. Right-click the request and, from the shortcut menu, point to All Tasks, and then select Issue. The request disappears from the folder.

5. Click the Issued Certificates folder. Notice that the request you just approved now appears in the Issued Certificates list.

6. Close the Certification Authority console.

Exercise 3: Retrieving a Certificate

In this exercise, you use the Web Enrollment Support interface to retrieve the certificate you just issued.

1. Return to the Internet Explorer window.

2. In the Address text box, type **http://localhost/certsrv** and then press ENTER. The Microsoft Certificate Services Web page appears.

3. Click View The Status Of A Pending Certificate Request. The View The Status Of A Pending Certificate Request page appears.

4. Click IPSec Certificate. The Certificate Issued page appears, stating that the certificate you requested was issued to you.

5. Click Install This Certificate. A Potential Scripting Violation message box appears, prompting you to confirm the installation of the certificate.

6. Click Yes. The Certificate Installed page appears.

7. Close Internet Explorer.

Exercise 4: Viewing a Certificate

In this exercise, you use the Certificates snap-in to view the certificate you just installed.

1. Click Start, and then click Run. The Run dialog box appears.

2. In the Open text box, type **mmc** and then click OK. The Console1 window appears.

3. From the File menu, select Add/Remove Snap-in. The Add/Remove Snap-in dialog box appears.

4. Click Add. The Add Standalone Snap-in dialog box appears.

5. In the Available Standalone Snap-ins list, select Certificates.

6. Click Add. The Certificates Snap-in dialog box appears.

7. Click Finish to accept the default My User Account option, and then click Close. The Certificates—Current User snap-in appears in the Add/Remove Snap-in dialog box.

8. Click OK. A Certificates—Current User entry appears in the Console Root window.

9. Expand the Certificates—Current User icon, expand the Personal folder, and then click the Certificates subfolder. The certificate issued to Lorrin Smith-Bates appears in the details pane.

10. Double-click the Lorrin Smith-Bates certificate. A Certificate dialog box appears.

11. Click the Details tab.

   Notice that the Public Key entry detail shows the 2048-bit key length you specified in your request and the Enhanced Key Usage detail indicates that the certificate is to be used for IP Security.

12. Click OK to close the Certificate dialog box.

13. Close the Console1 window.

14. If a Microsoft Management Console message box appears, click No to save the console settings.

Lesson Review

The following questions are intended to reinforce key information presented in this lesson. If you are unable to answer a question, review the lesson materials and try the question again. You can find answers to the questions in the "Questions and Answers" section at the end of this chapter.

1. Which of the following tools does an administrator use to manually issue certificates to clients of a stand-alone CA?

   a. The Certificates snap-in

   b. The Certification Authority console

   c. The Web Enrollment Support interface

   d. The Certificate Templates snap-in

   _____

2. What is the advantage of using delta CRLs instead of base CRLs?

   _____

   _____

   _____

3. Which of the following must a user have to receive certificates from an enterprise CA using autoenrollment? (Choose all that apply.)

   a. Permission to use certificate templates

   b. Membership in an organizational unit to which administrators have applied a Group Policy Object

   c. Access to Active Directory

   d. Access to the Certificates snap-in

   _____

Lesson Summary

- Only enterprise CAs can use autoenrollment, in which clients send certificate requests to a CA and the CA automatically issues or denies the certificate.

- For a client to receive certificates using autoenrollment, it must have permission to use the certificate template for the type of certificate it is requesting.

- Stand-alone CAs do not use certificates or autoenrollment. Certificate requests are stored in a queue on the CA until an administrator approves or denies them.

- Clients can request certificates by using the Certificates console (for enterprise CAs only) or Web Enrollment Support pages (for stand-alone CAs).

- CAs publish certificate revocation lists (CRLs) at regular intervals to inform authenticating computers of certificates they should no longer honor.

Case Scenario Exercise

You are the network infrastructure design specialist for Litware Inc., a manufacturer of specialized scientific software products, and you have already created a network design for its new office building, as described in the Case Scenario Exercise in Chapter 7. You are designing a PKI solution for the entire corporate network, which will enable all network users to encrypt and digitally sign their e-mail. In addition, you want the employees of the Research and Development department, who work with highly sensitive data, to be authenticated using smart card logons, to store their data files using EFS, and to transmit their files in encrypted form using IPSec. You also want to enable registered users of the company's products to be able to download software updates from your company's Web servers without fear of viruses or other forms of tampering.

To achieve these goals, you have designed a hierarchy of certification authorities using three levels. The design calls for a single enterprise root CA at the company's headquarters and one or more enterprise subordinate CAs at each of the company's branch offices. Depending on the number of users, an office might have a single issuing CA or an intermediate CA and two subordinate issuing CAs.

1. After the initial deployment of the PKI, which of the CAs can safely be taken offline? (Choose all that apply.)

    a. The root CA

    b. The intermediate CAs

    c. One of the issuing CAs at each office with an intermediate CA

    d. All the issuing CAs

2. Does the PKI design described here satisfy all the specified goals?

   a. Yes, the design satisfies all the specified goals.

   b. No, the design satisfies the goals for the network's internal users, but not for the external users.

   c. No, the design satisfies all the stated goals except for the goal of smart card logons.

   d. No, the design does not satisfy any of the stated goals.

---

3. Which of the following procedures can you use to ensure that only the employees in the Research and Development department receive certificates for smart card logons, EFS, and IPSec?

   a. Grant the Research and Development users the permissions they need to access the Certificates console, which they can use to request the appropriate certificates.

   b. Using Group Policy Objects, turn off autoenrollment for the domain and enable autoenrollment for an organizational unit containing the Research and Development users.

   c. Grant the Research and Development users permission to use the Smartcard Logon, Basic EFS, and IPSec certificate templates.

   d. Install the Certificate Services Web Enrollment Support module, and restrict access to the certificate enrollment Web pages so that only the Research and Development users can access them.

Troubleshooting Lab

You are a user on a large corporate network, and you are trying to secure your network communications using IPSec. After capturing a traffic sample, you discover that your transmissions are not being encrypted. The network uses certificates to provide IPSec encryption keys, and the certificates are issued by a hierarchy of stand-alone CAs that service the entire enterprise. You think that your transmissions are not being encrypted because you don't possess the correct certificate, so you open Microsoft Management Console, load the Certificates snap-in, and attempt to request an IPSec certificate. However, the snap-in displays an error message stating that the Certificate Request Wizard cannot start because no trusted CAs are available.

Which of the following procedures would enable you to request the certificate you need?

a. Log on to the workstation as Administrator, and try requesting the certificate again.

b. Use the Web Enrollment Support pages for your CA instead of the Certificates snap-in.

c. Call the network help desk, and have someone give you the permissions you need to request the certificate.

d. Activate the Secure Server (Require Security) policy in your workstation's Local Security Settings console.

Chapter Summary

- Public key encryption uses two keys, a public key and a private key. Data encrypted with the public key can be decrypted only by using the private key, and data encrypted using the private key can be decrypted only with the public key.

- A public key infrastructure is a collection of software components and operational policies that govern the distribution and use of public and private keys.

- Certificates are issued by a certification authority (CA). You can run your own CA using Windows Server 2003, or you can obtain your certificates from a third-party commercial CA.

- The first step in planning a PKI is to study the security enhancements certificates can provide and determine which of your organization's security requirements you can satisfy with certificates.

- When running multiple CAs in an enterprise, you configure them in a hierarchy, with a root CA at the top, intermediate CAs at the second level, and subordinate (or issuing) CAs at the bottom.

- The configuration parameters of certificates themselves include the certificate type, the encryption algorithm and key length the certificates use, the certificate's lifetime, and the renewal policies that dictate how the CA behaves when processing certificate renewal requests.

- Only enterprise CAs can use autoenrollment, in which clients send certificate requests to a CA and the CA automatically issues or denies the certificate.

- For a client to receive certificates using autoenrollment, it must have permission to use the certificate template for the type of certificate it is requesting.

- Stand-alone CAs do not use certificates or autoenrollment. Certificate requests are stored in a queue on the CA until an administrator approves or denies them.

- CAs publish certificate revocation lists (CRLs) at regular intervals to inform authenticating computers of certificates they should no longer honor.

Exam Highlights

Before taking the exam, review the following key points and terms to help you identify topics you need to review. Return to the lessons for additional practice, and review the "Further Reading" sections in Part 2 for pointers to more information about topics covering the exam objectives.

Key Points

- In an Active Directory environment, you should create enterprise (as opposed to stand-alone) CAs. Enterprise CAs support autoenrollment and use certificate templates and Active Directory object information to automatically issue certificates to clients.

- Certificate Services is a Windows Server 2003 service that enables administrators to configure, issue, and revoke digital certificates for specific security functions, such as secure e-mail, EFS, IPSec, Internet server authentication, and smart card logons.

- Windows Server 2003 Certificate Services supports two basic types of certification authorities: enterprise and stand-alone. Enterprise CAs are intended for internal clients and store their information in Active Directory. Stand-alone CAs are intended for external clients, and store their information in a database file.

- Clients can obtain certificates in three ways: through autoenrollment, by using the Certificates snap-in, and by using the Web Enrollment Support interface.

- A smart card is a portable device that contains a user's certificate and private key, enabling the user to log on to the network from any workstation equipped with the appropriate hardware. Support for smart card logons is provided only by enterprise CAs, in conjunction with Active Directory.

Key Terms

Public key encryption A security system in which each user has two encryption keys, a public key and a private key. Data encrypted using the public key can be decrypted only by the private key, and data encrypted using the private key can be decrypted only by using the public key.

Hash A digital summary of a message created by removing redundant bits according to a specialized hashing algorithm. Hashes are used to digitally sign messages and to confirm that messages have not been tampered with in transmission.

Delta CRL A list containing only the certificates that have been revoked since the last certificate revocation list was published. Using delta CRLs instead of base CRLs (which contain the entire list of all revoked certificates) can save network bandwidth.

Questions and Answers

Page
12-8
Lesson 1 Review

1. Which of the following pieces of information is not included as part of a digital certificate?

    a. Validity period

    b. Private key

    c. Signature algorithm identifier

    d. Public key

    b

2. For each of the following messaging scenarios, specify which key you should use to encrypt the message: the sender's public key, the sender's private key, the recipient's public key, or the recipient's private key.

    a. To send a message that can't be read by anyone but the recipient

    The recipient's public key

    b. To assure the recipient that the message you are sending actually came from you

    The sender's private key

Page
12-19
Lesson 2 Review

1. Which of the following types of certificates can be issued only by an enterprise certification authority?

    a. IPSec

    b. Smart card logon

    c. Software code signing

    d. Wireless network authentication

    b

2. Which of the following modifications to a certificate configuration does not increase the burden on the CA's processor?

    a. Increasing the key length

    b. Increasing the certificate's lifetime

    c. Issuing new keys with each certificate renewal

    d. Changing the certificate type

    d

3. Where does a root CA obtain its own certificate?

    a. From a third-party certification authority

    b. From a subordinate CA

    c. From another root CA

    d. From itself

    d

Page
12-30

Lesson 3 Review

1. Which of the following tools does an administrator use to manually issue certificates to clients of a stand-alone CA?

    a. The Certificates snap-in

    b. The Certification Authority console

    c. The Web Enrollment Support interface

    d. The Certificate Templates snap-in

    b

2. What is the advantage of using delta CRLs instead of base CRLs?

Delta CRLs contain only a list of the certificates revoked since the last CRL publication. They therefore save network bandwidth by reducing the size of the published list.

3. Which of the following must a user have to receive certificates from an enterprise CA using autoenrollment? (Choose all that apply.)

    a. Permission to use certificate templates

    b. Membership in an organizational unit to which administrators have applied a Group Policy Object

    c. Access to Active Directory

    d. Access to the Certificates snap-in

    a and c

Page
12-31

Case Scenario Exercise

1. After the initial deployment of the PKI, which of the CAs can safely be taken offline? (Choose all that apply.)

   a. The root CA

   b. The intermediate CAs

   c. One of the issuing CAs at each office with an intermediate CA

   d. All the issuing CAs

   a and b

2. Does the PKI design described here satisfy all the specified goals?

   a. Yes, the design satisfies all the specified goals.

   b. No, the design satisfies the goals for the network's internal users, but not for the external users.

   c. No, the design satisfies all the stated goals except for the goal of smart card logons.

   d. No, the design does not satisfy any of the stated goals.

   b

3. Which of the following procedures can you use to ensure that only the employees in the Research and Development department receive certificates for smart card logons, EFS, and IPSec?

   a. Grant the Research and Development users the permissions they need to access the Certificates console, which they can use to request the appropriate certificates.

   b. Using Group Policy Objects, turn off autoenrollment for the domain and enable autoenrollment for an organizational unit containing the Research and Development users.

   c. Grant the Research and Development users permission to use the Smartcard Logon, Basic EFS, and IPSec certificate templates.

   d. Install the Certificate Services Web Enrollment Support module, and restrict access to the certificate enrollment Web pages so that only the Research and Development users can access them.

   c

Page
12-33

Troubleshooting Lab

Which of the following procedures would enable you to request the certificate you need?

a. Log on to the workstation as Administrator, and try requesting the certificate again.

b. Use the Web Enrollment Support pages for your CA instead of the Certificates snap-in.

c. Call the network help desk, and have someone give you the permissions you need to request the certificate.

d. Activate the Secure Server (Require Security) policy in your workstation's Local Security Settings console.

b

13 Managing and Implementing Disaster Recovery

Exam Objectives in this Chapter:

- Perform system recovery for a server (Exam 70-292).

    - ❑ Implement Automated System Recovery (ASR).

    - ❑ Restore data from shadow copy volumes.

    - ❑ Back up files and System State data to media.

    - ❑ Configure security for backup operations.

- Plan a backup and recovery strategy (Exam 70-296).

    - ❑ Identify appropriate backup types. Methods include full, incremental, and differential.

    - ❑ Plan a backup strategy that uses Volume Shadow Copy.

    - ❑ Plan system recovery that uses Automated System Restore (ASR).

Why This Chapter Matters

You've worked hard to configure and maintain a best practice server environment. You have outfitted the server with a sophisticated RAID subsystem, carefully managed file and share permissions, locked down the server with policy, and physically secured the server to prevent unauthorized interactive log on. But today, none of that matters because the building's fire sprinklers went off last night, and today your servers are full of water. All that matters today is that you are able to restore your data from backup.

Among the many high-priority tasks for any network administrator is the creation and management of a solid backup and restore procedure. The Microsoft Windows Server 2003 family offers powerful and flexible tools that will enable you to perform backups of local and remote data, including open and locked files, and to schedule those backups for periods of low utilization, such as during the night.

This chapter examines the Backup Utility's graphical user interface (GUI) and command-line functionality in the protection of data files. You will learn how to plan an effective backup and media management strategy, how to execute backups, and how to restore data correctly in a variety of scenarios. You will also leverage the new Volume Shadow Copy Service (VSS) to allow faster recovery of data lost by administrators and users alike. Then, you will learn how to use the Backup Utility to recover the operating system by using Automated System Restore (ASR).

Lessons in this Chapter:

Before You Begin

To complete the hands-on exercises in this chapter, you need:

- A Windows Server 2003 (Standard or Enterprise) installed as Server01 and configured as a domain controller in the domain contoso.com. A second computer running Windows Server 2003 installed as Server02 and configured as a member server in the domain contoso.com.

- To perform the optional Automated System Recovery exercise in Lesson 4, you will need about 1.7 GB of free disk space on Server02 and a second hard disk in Server02.

- If you complete the Automated System Recovery exercise, all data on the disk containing the system volume will be erased. Do not perform the Automated System Recovery if you want to maintain any data on that disk.

Lesson 1: Fundamentals of Backup

At the core of every backup procedure is a backup tool and a backup plan. Windows Server 2003 provides a robust, flexible program called the Backup Utility. The Backup Utility supports much of the functionality found in third-party tools, including the ability to schedule backups, and it interacts closely with VSS and the Removable Storage Management (RSM) system. In this lesson, you will examine the conceptual and procedural issues pivotal to the backing up of data so that you understand the fundamentals of planning for and creating backup jobs with the Backup Utility.

After this lesson, you will be able to

- Back up data on local and remote computers
- Understand backup job types
- Create a backup strategy combining normal and incremental or differential backups

Estimated lesson time: 20 minutes

Introducing the Backup Utility

The Backup Utility in Windows Server 2003, sometimes referred to by its executable name, Ntbackup, can be opened by clicking Backup in the All Programs\Accessories\System Tools program group in the Start menu. Alternatively, it can be launched by typing **ntbackup.exe** in the Run dialog box.

The first time you launch the Backup Utility, it runs in Wizard mode, as shown in Figure 13-1. This chapter focuses on the more commonly used Backup Utility interface. If you agree with most administrators that it is easier to use the standard utility than the wizard, clear the Always Start In Wizard Mode check box and then click Advanced Mode.

Figure 13-1   The Backup Or Restore Wizard

As you can see on the utility's Welcome tab in Figure 13-2, you can back up data manually (the Backup tab) or using the Backup Wizard. You can also schedule unattended backup jobs. The Backup Utility is also used to restore data manually (the Restore And Manage Media tab) or using the Restore Wizard. The Automated System Recovery Wizard, which backs up critical operating system files, will be discussed later in Lesson 4.

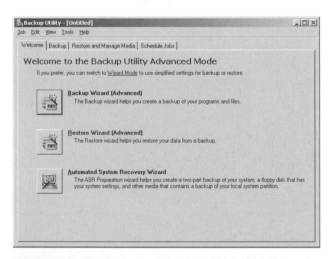

Figure 13-2   The Welcome tab of the Backup Utility

This lesson focuses on data backup planning and execution, and to explore the capability of the Backup Utility we will use the Backup tab, as shown in Figure 13-3, rather than the Backup Wizard.

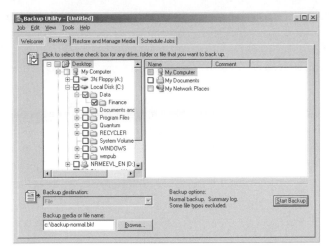

Figure 13-3   The Backup tab of the Backup Utility

Selecting Files to Back Up

You can use the Backup tab to select the files and folders to be backed up. Items might be on local volumes or in network folders. When you select an entire folder for backup, a blue check mark appears. If you select only certain items in a folder, the folder displays a dimmed check mark to indicate a partial backup.

To back up files or folders from remote machines, either select the items from a mapped drive or expand My Network Places. The latter method is the equivalent of using a Universal Naming Convention (UNC), such as *Server01**Sharename**Path-to-resource*. Although selecting files and folders through My Network Places is more cumbersome (because you must navigate more levels of the interface to locate the files), it has an advantage because drive mappings are more likely to change over time than UNCs.

> **Tip**   You can save the set of selected files and folders by using the Save Selections command in the Job menu. You can later load the selections by using Load Selections from the Job menu, saving the time required to re-create your selection.

Selecting the Backup Destination

The Backup Utility allows you to create a backup job on a variety of media types (a tape drive or a removable drive such as the Iomega Jaz drive) and, most importantly, directly to file on a disk volume. If the destination is a tape, the name specified must match the name of a tape that is mounted in the tape device.

If backing up to a file, the Backup Utility creates a .bkf file in the specified location, which can be a local volume or remote folder. It is not uncommon for administrators using the Backup Utility to back up a file on each server and consolidate the resulting files on a central server, which then transfers the backups to removable media. To achieve such a consolidation, the backup destination is configured as either a UNC to a single location on a central server or a local file on each server, which is later copied to a central location.

The Backup Utility has two important limitations. First, it does not support writable DVD and CD formats. To work around this limitation, you can back up to a file and then transfer the file to CD or DVD. Second, backing up to any destination *except* a file requires that the target media be in a device physically attached to the system. This means, for example, that you cannot back up data to a tape drive attached to a remote server.

Determining a Backup Strategy

After selecting the files to back up and specifying the backup destination, you need to make at least one more critical choice. You must specify the backup type. The backup type determines which of your selected files is in fact transferred to the destination media. To set the backup type, click Start Backup and then click Advanced. The Advanced Backup Options dialog box appears, allowing you to specify the backup type.

Each backup type relates in one way or another to an attribute maintained by every file: archive. The archive (A) attribute is a flag that is set when a file has been created or changed. To reduce the size and duration of backup jobs, most backup types will transfer to media only the files that have their archive attribute set. The most common source of confusion regarding the archive attribute arises from terminology. You will frequently hear, "The file is marked as backed up," which really means that the archive attribute is *cleared* after a particular backup job. The next job will not transfer that file to media. If the file is modified, however, the archive attribute will again be set, and the file will be transferred at the next backup.

> **Exam Tip**   As you explore each backup type, keep track of how the archive attribute is used and treated by the backup type. You will need to know the advantages and disadvantages of each backup type and how to fully restore a data structure based on the backup procedures that have been implemented.

Normal Backups

With normal backups, all selected files and folders are backed up. Normal backups clear the archive attribute for all selected files. A normal backup does not use the archive attribute to determine which files to back up; all selected items are transferred to the destination media. Every backup strategy begins with a normal backup that essentially creates a baseline, capturing all files in the backup job.

Normal backups are the most time-consuming and require the most storage capacity of any backup type. However, because they generate a complete backup, normal backups are the most efficient type from which to restore a system. You do not need to restore multiple jobs.

Incremental Backups

With incremental backups, selected files with the archive attribute set are backed up to the destination media and the archive attribute is cleared. If you perform an incremental backup one day after a normal backup has been performed, the job will contain only the files that were created or changed during that day. Similarly, if you perform an incremental backup one day after another incremental backup, the job will contain only the files that were created or changed during that day.

Incremental backups are the fastest and smallest type of backup. However they are less efficient as a restore set, because you must restore the normal backup and then restore, in order of creation, each subsequent incremental backup.

Differential Backups

With differential backups, selected files with the archive attribute set are backed up, but the archive attribute is not cleared. Because a differential backup uses the archive attribute, the job includes only files that have been created or changed since the last normal or incremental backup. A differential backup does not clear the archive attribute; therefore, if you perform differential backups two days in a row, the second job will include all the files in the first backup, as well as any files that were created or changed during the second day. As a result, differential backups tend to be larger and more time-consuming than incremental backups, but less so than normal backups.

Differential backups are significantly more efficient than incremental backups as a restore set, however. To fully restore a system, you would restore the normal backup and the most recent differential backup.

Copy Backups

With copy backups, all selected files and folders are backed up. Copy neither uses nor clears the archive attribute. Copy backups are not used for typical or scheduled backups. Instead, copy backups are useful to move data between systems or to create an archival copy of data at a point in time without disrupting standard backup procedures.

Daily Backups

With daily backups, all selected files and folders that have changed during the day are backed up, based on the modify date of the files. The archive attribute is neither used nor cleared. If you want to back up all files and folders that change during the day without affecting a backup schedule, use a daily backup.

Combining Backup Types

Although creating a normal backup every night ensures that a server can be restored from a single job the next day, a normal backup might take too much time to create, perhaps causing the overnight job to last well into the morning and thus disrupting performance during working hours. To create an optimal backup strategy, you must take into account the time and size of the backup job, as well as the time required to restore a system in the event of failure. Two common solutions are as follows:

- **Normal and differential backups**   On Sunday a normal backup is performed, and on Monday through Friday nights, differential backups are performed. Differential backups do not clear the archive attribute, which means that each backup includes all changes since Sunday. If data becomes corrupt on Friday, you need to restore only the normal backup from Sunday and the differential backup from Thursday. This strategy takes more time to back up, particularly if data changes frequently, but it is easier and faster to restore because the backup set is on fewer disks or tapes.

- **Normal and incremental backups**   On Sunday a normal backup is performed, and on Monday through Friday incremental backups are performed. Incremental backups clear the archive attribute, which means that each backup includes only the files that changed since the previous backup. If data becomes corrupt on Friday, you need to restore the normal backup from Sunday and each of the incremental backups, from Monday through Thursday. This strategy takes less time to back up but more time to restore.

Practice: Performing Different Backup Types

In this practice, you will create several backup jobs, examining the role of the archive attribute.

Exercise 1: Creating Sample Data

1. Log on to Server01 as Administrator.

2. Open Notepad, and create a text file with the following lines. Type each line carefully.

```
md c:\Data
net share data=C:\Data
md c:\Data\Finance
cd c:\data\Finance
echo Historical Financial Data > Historical.txt
echo Current Financials > Current.txt
echo Budget > Budget.txt
echo Financial Projections > Projections.txt
```

3. Save the file as "c:\createfiles.bat", including the quotation marks.

4. Open a command prompt window, and type **cd c:**.

5. Type the command **createfiles.bat**.

6. Open Windows Explorer, and navigate to the c:\data\finance directory. You should see the following display:

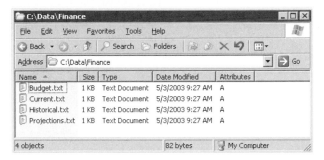

7. If the Attributes column is not visible, right-click the column header Date Modified and select Attributes. The archive attribute is displayed.

> **Note**   Leave Windows Explorer open on C:\Data\Finance. You will refer to it throughout this practice.

Exercise 2: Performing a Normal Backup

1. Open the Backup Utility by running Ntbackup.exe from the command line or by selecting Backup from the All Programs\Accessories\System Tools group on the Start menu.

2. Clear the Always Start In Wizard Mode check box.

3. Click Advanced Mode.

4. Select the Backup tab.

5. Expand My Computer, the C drive, and then the Data folder so that you can see the Finance folder.

6. Add a check mark next to the Finance folder.

   The Finance folder has a blue check mark, meaning a complete backup, whereas its parent folder has a dimmed check mark, indicating a partial backup. Any files *added* to the Finance folder will be included in the backup, but any files added to the Data folder will not.

7. On the Job menu, choose Save Selections.

8. In the Save As dialog box, save the selections as **Finance Backup.bks**.

9. On the Backup tab, in the Backup Media Or Filename box, type: **c:\backup-normal.bkf**.

> **Note**   In production environments, you will be likely to use removable media for backups, but to keep hardware requirements to a minimum, practices in this lesson will back up and restore using local files. If you have access to a tape drive, feel free to use it during these practices.

10. Click Start Backup, and then click Advanced.

11. Confirm that Normal is selected in the Backup Type drop-down box, and then click OK.

12. Select Replace The Data On The Media With This Backup, and click Start Backup.

13. Observe the Backup Progress dialog box. When the backup is complete, click Report.

14. Examine the report. No errors should be reported.

15. Close the report and the Backup Utility.

    Note that in Windows Explorer, the Attributes column no longer shows the archive attribute.

Exercise 3: Performing Differential Backups

1. Open C:\Data\Finance\Current.txt, and add some text. Save and close the file.

2. Examine C:\Data\Finance in Windows Explorer. What files are showing the archive attribute? Only the one you just changed.

3. Open the Backup Utility, and click the Backup tab.

4. From the Job menu, choose Load Selections to load the Finance Backup.bks selections.

5. In the Backup Media Or Filename box, type **c:\backup-diff-day1.bkf**.

6. Click Start Backup.

7. Click Advanced, and select Differential as the backup type.

8. Start the backup and, when complete, confirm that no errors occurred.

9. Close the Backup Utility.

10. Examine the folder in Windows Explorer. Which files have their archive attribute set? The file Current.txt is still flagged for archiving.

11. Open the Budget file, and make some changes. Save and close the file. Confirm that its archive attribute is now set.

12. Repeat steps 3 through 9, creating a differential backup job in the location **c:\backup-diff-day2.bkf**. Be sure to look at the resulting backup report. How many files were copied for the backup?

    Two.

Exercise 4: Performing Incremental Backups

1. Open the Backup Utility, and click the Backup tab.

2. From the Job menu, choose Load Selections to load the Finance Backup.bks selections.

3. In the Backup Media Or Filename box, type **c:\backup-inc-day2.bkf**.

4. Click Start Backup.

5. Click Advanced, and select Incremental as the backup type.

6. Start the backup and, when complete, confirm that no errors occurred.

7. Close the Backup Utility.

8. Examine the folder in Windows Explorer. Which files have their archive attribute set?

    None.

9. Open the Projections file, and make some changes. Save and close the file. It should show the archive attribute in Windows Explorer.

10. Repeat steps 1 through 8, creating an incremental backup job in the location **c:\backup-inc-day3.bkf**.

Lesson Review

The following questions are intended to reinforce key information presented in this lesson. If you are unable to answer a question, review the lesson materials and try the question again. You can find answers to the questions in the "Questions and Answers" section at the end of this chapter.

1. Which of the following locations are *not* allowed to be used for a backup of a Windows Server 2003 system? (Choose all that apply.)

    a. Local tape drive

    b. Local CD-RW

    c. Local hard drive

    d. Shared folder on a remote server

    e. Local DVD+R

    f. Local removable drive

    g. Tape drive on a remote server

2. You are to back up a Windows Server 2003 file server every evening. You perform a manual, normal backup. You will then schedule a backup job to run every evening for the next two weeks. Which backup type will complete the fastest?

    a. Normal

    b. Differential

    c. Incremental

    d. Copy

3. You are to back up a Windows Server 2003 file server every evening. You perform a manual, normal backup. You will then schedule a backup job to run every evening for the next two weeks. Which backup type will provide the simplest recovery of lost data?

    a. Normal

    b. Differential

    c. Incremental

    d. Daily

4. You are to back up a Windows Server 2003 file server every evening. You perform a normal backup. On the second evening, you consider whether to use incremental or differential backup. Will there be any difference in the speed or size of those two backup jobs? If the server were to fail the following day, would there be any difference in the efficiency of recovery?

_____

_____

_____

_____

_____

_____

_____

_____

_____

_____

_____

5. Review the steps taken during the practice. Predict the contents of the following backup jobs:

- ❑ backup-normal.bkf
- ❑ backup-diff-day1.bkf
- ❑ backup-diff-day2.bkf
- ❑ backup-inc-day2.bkf
- ❑ backup-inc-day3.bkf

Are there any differences between the contents of backup-diff-day2 and backup-inc-day2?

- ❑ backup-normal.bkf: Historical, Current, Budget and Projections
- ❑ backup-diff-day1.bkf: Current
- ❑ backup-diff-day2.bkf: Current and Budget
- ❑ backup-inc-day2.bkf: Current and Budget
- ❑ backup-inc-day3.bkf: Projections

> **Note**   You can find the answers in the "Questions and Answers" section at the end of the lesson. However, you should test your predictions by performing the practice in Lesson 2.

_____

_____

_____

_____

Lesson Summary

- The Backup Utility (Ntbackup.exe) allows you to back up and restore data from local and remote folders.

- You can back up to local files, tape drives, and removable media or to shared folders on remote servers. You cannot back up to writable CD or DVD formats.

- A normal backup is a complete backup of all selected files and folders. It is always the starting point of any backup strategy.

- An incremental backup copies selected files that have changed since the most recent normal or incremental backup. Both normal and incremental backups clear the archive attribute.

■ A differential backup copies all selected files that have changed since the last normal or incremental backup. Differential backups do *not* clear the archive attribute.

■ Copy backups and daily backups are less frequently used. They back up all selected files, in the case of copy backup, or files modified on a specific date, in the case of daily backup. They do not reset the archive attribute, so they can be used to capture data for backup or transfer without interfering with the normal backup schedule.

Lesson 2: Restoring Data

In conjunction with the design of a backup strategy, you must create and verify restore procedures to ensure that appropriate personnel are knowledgeable in the concepts and skills that are critical to data recovery. This lesson will share the processes and options available for restoring data using the Backup Utility.

After this lesson, you will be able to

- Restore data to its original location or an alternate folder
- Configure restore options

Estimated lesson time: 10 minutes

Restoring with the Backup Utility

Restoring data is a straightforward procedure. After opening the Backup Utility and click-ing the Restore And Manage Media tab as shown in Figure 13-4, you will be able to select the backup set from which to restore. The Backup Utility will then display the files and folders that the backup set contains by examining the backup set's catalog. You can then select the specific files or folders you want to restore. As with the backup selection, a blue check mark indicates that a file or folder will be fully restored. A dimmed check mark on a folder means that some, but not all, of its contents will be restored.

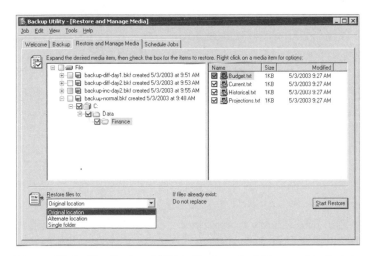

Figure 13-4   The Backup Utility's Restore And Manage Media tab

You are also asked to specify the restore location. For this option, you have three choices:

- **Original location**   Files and folders will be restored to the location from which they were backed up. The original folder structure will be maintained or, if folders were deleted, re-created.

- **Alternate location**   Files and folders will be restored to a folder you designate in the Alternate Location box. The original folder structure is preserved and created beneath that folder, where the designated alternate location is equivalent to the root (volume) of the backed up data. So, for example, if you backed up a folder C:\Data\Finance and you restored the folder to C:\Restore, you would find the Finance folder in C:\Restore\Data\Finance.

- **Single folder**   Files are restored to the folder you designate, but the folder structure is not maintained. All files are restored to a single folder.

After selecting the files to restore and the restore location, click Start Restore. Click OK and the restore process will begin. Confirm that no errors occurred.

Restore Options

The Backup Utility supports several options for how files in the restore location are handled during a restore. Options are specified in the Options dialog box, which is opened by clicking Options on the Tools menu. The following options are found on the Restore tab of the Options dialog box shown in Figure 13-5:

- **Do Not Replace The File On My Computer.**   This option, the default, causes the restore process to skip files that are already in the target location. A common scenario leading to this choice is one in which some, but not all, files have been deleted from the restore location. This option will restore such missing files with the backed-up files.

- **Replace The File On Disk Only If The File On Disk Is Older.**   This option directs the restore process to overwrite existing files unless those files are more recent than the files in the backup set. The theory is that if a file in the target location is more recent than the backed-up copy, it is possible that the newer file contains information you do not want to overwrite.

- **Always Replace The File On My Computer.**   Under this restore option, all files are overwritten by their backed-up versions, regardless of whether the file is more recent than the backup. You will lose data in files that were modified since the backup date. Any files in the target location that are *not* in the backup set will remain, however.

Figure 13-5   Restore tab options

After selecting files to restore, restore options, and a restore destination, click Start Restore and then confirm the restore. The Start Restore dialog box appears.

Before confirming the restore, you can configure how the restore operation will treat security settings on the backed-up files by clicking Advanced in the Confirm Restore dialog box and selecting the Restore Security option. If data was backed up from, and is being restored to, an NTFS volume, the default setting will restore permissions, audit settings, and ownership information. Deselecting this option will restore the data without its security descriptors, and all restored files will inherit the permissions of the target restore volume or folder.

Practice: Restoring Data

In this practice, you will verify your backup and restore procedures by using a common method: restoring to a test location.

Exercise 1: Verifying Backup and Restore Procedures

To verify backup and restore procedures, many administrators will perform a test restore of a backup set. So as not to damage production data, that test restore is targeted not at the original location of the data, but at another folder, which can then be discarded following the test. In a production environment, your verification should include restoring the backup to a "standby" server, which would entail making sure that the backup device (that is, the tape drive) is correctly installed on a server that can host data in the event that the primary server fails. To do this, perform the following steps:

1. Log on to Server01 as Administrator.

2. Open the Backup Utility.

3. Click the Restore And Manage Media tab.

4. Click the plus sign to expand the File node.

5. Click the plus sign to expand Backup-normal.bkf.

6. Click the check box to select C:.

7. Select the C: node.

8. Expand the C: and Data nodes. You will notice that your selection of the C: folder has selected its child folders and files.

9. In the Restore Files To drop-down box, select Alternate Location.

10. In the Alternate Location field, type **C:\TestRestore**.

11. Click Start Restore.

12. In the Confirm Restore dialog box, click OK.

> **Note**   If a Check Backup File Location dialog box appears asking you to verify the backup file location, verify that the path is correct and then click OK.

13. When the restore job is complete, click Report and examine the log of the restore operation.

14. In Windows Explorer, open the C:\TestRestore folder, and verify that the folder structure and files restored correctly.

15. Repeat steps 2 through 12, this time restoring the file backup-diff-day2.bkf. When the restore job is finished, continue to step 16 to examine its report.

16. When the restore job finishes, click Report to view the restore job log. If you accidentally close the job status window, choose the Report command from the Tools menu, select the most recent report, and click View.

17. Examine the report for the job you just restored. How many files were restored?

    None.

    Why?

    The answer lies in the restore options.

18. Choose the Options command from the Tools menu, and click the Restore tab. Now you can identify the problem. The default configuration of the Backup Utility is that it does not replace files on the computer. Therefore, the differential job, which contains files that were updated after the normal backup, was not successfully restored.

19. Choose Always Replace The File On My Computer.

20. Repeat the restore operation of backup-diff-day2.bkf. The report should confirm that two files were restored.

21. You have now verified your backup and restore procedures, including the need to modify restore options. Delete the C:\TestRestore folder.

Lesson Review

The following questions are intended to reinforce key information presented in this lesson. If you are unable to answer a question, review the lesson materials and try the question again. You can find answers to the questions in the "Questions and Answers" section at the end of this chapter.

1. A user has accidentally deleted the data in a Microsoft Word document and saved the document, thereby permanently altering the original file. A normal backup operation was performed on the server the previous evening. Which restore option should you select?

    a. Do not replace the file on my computer.

    b. Replace the file on disk only if the file on disk is older.

    c. Always replace the file on my computer.

_____

_____

2. An executive has returned from a business trip. Before the trip, she copied files from a network folder to her hard drive. The folder is shared with other executives, who modified their files in the folder while she was away. When she returned, she moved her copy of the files to the network share, thereby updating her files with the changes she made while away, but also overwriting all the files that had been changed by other executives. The other executives are unhappy that their files have been replaced with the versions that were active when she left for her trip. Luckily, you performed a normal backup operation on the folder the previous evening. What restore option should you choose?

    a. Do not replace the file on my computer.

    b. Replace the file on disk only if the file on disk is older.

    c. Always replace the file on my computer.

_____

_____

_____

_____

> **Tip** Users should be trained to use the Offline Files feature so that this kind of disaster, which is not uncommon, can be avoided. Offline Files synchronizes changed files only, so only the updates the executive in our example made would have been uploaded to the network, leaving the other executives' changes intact. The Offline Files feature is discussed in Chapter 6.

3. You would like to test the restore procedures on your server, but would also like to avoid affecting the production copies of the backed-up data. What is the best restore location to use?

   a. Original location

   b. Alternate location

   c. Single folder

   _____

   _____

   _____

Lesson Summary

- The Backup Utility will also allow you to restore backed-up data.

- When restoring a lost file or folder, it is common to select Original Location as the restore location.

- When testing restore procedures, it is common to select Alternate Location as the restore location so that you do not affect the original copies of the backed-up files and folders.

- When restoring a differential or incremental backup set after restoring the normal backup set, you will need to select the restore option Always Replace The File On My Computer.

- When restoring a folder in which files have been lost, but some files are intact, you should select the restore option Do Not Replace The File On My Computer or Replace The File On Disk Only If The File On Disk Is Older.

Lesson 3: Advanced Backup and Restore

Now that you have created a backup plan and verified your procedures for backup and restore, you will want to understand the process in more depth so that you can configure backup operations to be more flexible, more automated, or perhaps even easier. This lesson will explore the technologies underlying data backup, such as VSS and RSM, and will lay out options for scripting and scheduling backup operations. You will then leverage the new Shadow Copies Of Shared Folders feature to enable users to recover from simple data loss scenarios without administrative intervention.

After this lesson, you will be able to

- Configure group membership to enable a user to perform backup and restore operations
- Manage tape backup media
- Catalog backup sets
- Configure backup options
- Execute a backup from a command prompt
- Schedule backup jobs
- Configure and utilize Shadow Copies Of Shared Folders

Estimated lesson time: 30 minutes

Understanding the Volume Shadow Copy Service

Windows Server 2003 offers the Volume Shadow Copy Service (VSS), also referred to as *snap backup*. VSS allows the backing up of databases and other files that are held open or locked because of operator or system activity. Shadow copy backups allow applications to continue to write data to a volume during backup, and they allow administrators to perform backups at any time without locking out users or risking skipped files.

Although VSS is an important enhancement to the backup functionality of Windows Server 2003, it is nevertheless best practice to perform backups when utilization is low. If you have applications that manage storage consistency differently while files are open, that can affect the consistency of the files in the backup of those open files. For critical applications, or for applications such as Microsoft SQL Server that offer native backup capabilities, consult the documentation for the application to determine the recommended backup procedure.

Backup Security

You must have the Backup Files And Directories user right, or NTFS Read permission, to back up a file. Similarly, you must have the Restore Files And Directories user right, or NTFS Write permission to the target destination, to restore a file. Privileges are assigned to both the Administrators and Backup Operators groups, so the minimum required privileges can be given to a user, a group, or a service account by nesting the account in the Backup Operators group on the server.

Users with the Restore Files And Directories user right can remove NTFS permissions from files during restore. In Windows Server 2003, they can additionally transfer ownership of files between users.

Therefore, it is important to control the membership of the Backup Operators group and to physically secure backup tapes. A "loose" backup tape makes it easy for any intelligent individual to restore and access sensitive data.

Managing Media

The Backup Utility of Windows Server 2003 works closely with the RSM service. RSM, which is designed to manage robotic tape libraries and CD-ROM libraries, accepts requests for media from other services or, in this case, applications, and ensures that the media is correctly mounted or loaded.

RSM is also used with single-media devices, such as a manually loaded backup tape drive, CD-ROM, or Iomega Jaz drive. In the case of single-media drives, RSM keeps track of media through their labels or serial numbers. The impact of RSM is that, even in a single-media drive backup system, each tape must have a unique label.

Media Pools

The Backup Utility of Windows Server 2003 manages tapes with RSM using *media pools*, as seen in Figure 13-6.

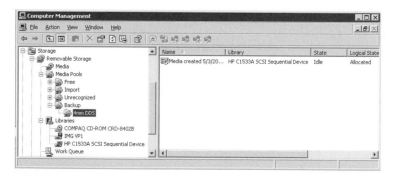

Figure 13-6   Media pools

There are four media pools related to backup:

- **Unrecognized**   Tape media that are completely blank or in a foreign format are contained in the Unrecognized pool until they are formatted.

- **Free**   This pool contains newly formatted tape media, as well as tapes that have been specifically marked as free by an administrator. Free media can be moved into the backup media pool by writing a backup set to them.

- **Backup**   This pool contains media that have been written to by the Backup Utility. The Backup Utility will only write to media in the Free media pool (and it will label the tape with the name you enter just before starting the backup) and to media, specified by name, in the Backup media pool.

- **Import**   This pool contains tape media that are not cataloged on the local disk drive. Cataloging such a tape will move the tape into the backup media pool.

Managing Tapes and Media Pools

In conjunction with backup procedures and tape rotation, you will need to manage your tapes in and out of these media pools. To that end, the following actions are available from the Restore And Manage Media tab of the Backup Utility:

- **Format a tape.**   Right-click a tape, and choose Format. Formatting is not a secure way to erase tapes. If you need to erase tapes for legal or security reasons, use an appropriate third-party utility. Formatting does, however, prepare a tape and move it into the free media pool. Not all drives support formatting.

- **Retension a tape.**   Right-click a tape, and choose Retension. Not all drives support retensioning.

- **Mark a tape as free.**   Right-click a tape, and choose Mark As Free. This moves the tape into the free media pool. It does *not* erase the tape. If you need to erase tapes for legal reasons, use an appropriate third-party utility.

Catalogs

When the Backup Utility creates a backup set, it also creates a catalog listing files and folders included in the backup set. That catalog is stored on the disk of the server (the local or on-disk catalog) and in the backup set itself (the on-media catalog). The local catalog facilitates quick location of files and folders to restore. The Backup Utility can display the catalog immediately, rather than having to load the catalog from the typically slower backup media. The on-media catalog is critical if the drive containing the local catalog has failed or if you transfer the files to another system. In those cases, Windows can re-create the local catalog from the on-media catalog.

The Restore And Manage Media tab of the Backup Utility allows you to manage catalogs, as follows:

- **Delete Catalog**   Right-click a backup set, and choose Delete Catalog if you have lost or damaged the backup media or if you are transferring files to another system and no longer require its local catalog. The on-media catalog is not affected by this command.

- **Catalog**   A tape from a foreign system that is not cataloged on the local machine will appear in the import media pool. Right-click the media, and choose the Catalog command. Windows will generate a local catalog from the tape or file. This does not create or modify the on-media catalog.

> **Tip**   If you have all the tapes in the backup set and the tapes are not damaged or corrupted, open the backup Options dialog box and, on the General tab, select Use The Catalogs On The Media To Speed Up Building Restore Catalogs On Disk. If you are missing a tape in the backup set or a tape is damaged or corrupted, clear that option. This will ensure that the catalog is complete and accurate; however, it might take a long time to create the catalog.

Backup Options

Backup options are configured by choosing the Options command from the Tools menu. Many of these options configure defaults that are used by the Backup Utility and the Ntbackup command. Those settings can be overridden by options of a specific job.

General Options

The General tab of the Options dialog box includes the following settings:

- **Compute Selection Information Before Backup And Restore Operations**   This backup option estimates the number of files and bytes that will be backed up or restored before beginning the operation.

- **Use The Catalogs On The Media To Speed Up Building Restore Catalogs On Disk**   If a system does not have an on-disk catalog for a tape, this option allows the system to create an on-disk catalog from the on-media catalog. However, if the tape with the on-media catalog is missing or if media in the set is damaged, you can deselect this option and the system will scan the entire backup set (or as much of it as you have) to build the on-disk catalog. Such an operation can take several hours if the backup set is large.

- **Verify Data After The Backup Completes**   The system compares the contents of the backup media to the original files and logs any discrepancies. This option obviously adds a significant amount of time for completing the backup job. Discrepancies are likely if data changes frequently during backup or verification, and it is not recommended to verify system backups because of the number of changes that happen to system files on a continual basis. So long as you rotate tapes and discard tapes before they are worn, it should not be necessary to verify data.

■ **Backup The Contents Of Mounted Drives**   A mounted drive is a drive volume that is mapped to a folder on another volume's namespace, rather than, or in addition to, having a drive letter. If this option is deselected, only the path of the folder that is mounted to a volume is backed up and the contents are not. By selecting this option, the contents of the mounted volume is also backed up. There is no disadvantage in backing up a mount point; however, if you back up the mount point and the mounted drive as well, your backup set will have duplication.

If you primarily back up to file and then save that file to another media, *clear* the following options. If you primarily back up to a tape or another media managed by Removable Storage, *select* the following options:

■ Show Alert Message When I Start The Backup Utility And Removable Storage Is Not Running.

■ Show Alert Message When I Start The Backup Utility And There Is Recognizable Media Available.

■ Show Alert Message When New Media Is Inserted.

■ Always Allow Use Of Recognizable Media Without Prompting.

> **Tip**   The Always Allow Use Of Recognizable Media Without Prompting option can be selected if you are using local tape drives for backup only, not for Remote Storage or other functions. The option eliminates the need to allocate free media using the Removable Storage node in the Computer Management console.

Backup Logging

The Options dialog box has a tab named Backup Log. Logging alerts you to problems that might threaten the viability of your backup, so consider your logging strategy as well as your overall backup plan. Although detailed logging will list every file and path that was backed up, the log is so verbose you are likely to overlook problems. Therefore, summary logging is recommended and is the default. Summary logs report skipped files and errors.

The system will save 10 backup logs to the path *%UserProfile%*\Local Settings\Application Data\Microsoft\Windows NT\Ntbackup\Data. There is no way to change the path or the number of logs that are saved before the oldest log is replaced. You can, of course, include that path in your backup and thereby back up old logs.

File Exclusions

The Exclude Files tab of the Options dialog box also allows you to specify extensions and individual files that should be skipped during backup. Default settings result in the Backup Utility skipping the page file, temporary files, client-side cache, debug folder, and the file replication service (FRS) database and folders, as well as other local logs and databases.

Files can be excluded based on ownership of the files. Click Add New under Files Excluded For All Users to exclude files owned by any user. Click Add New under Files Excluded For User *<username>* if you want to exclude only files that you own. You can specify files based on Registered File Type or based on an extension using the Custom File Mask. Finally, you can restrict excluded files to a specific folder or hard drive using the Applies To Path and the Applies To All Subfolders options.

Advanced Backup Options

After selecting files to back up and clicking Start Backup, you can configure additional, job-specific options by clicking Advanced. Among the more important settings in the Advanced Backup Options dialog box are the following:

- **Verify Data After Backup** This setting overrides the default setting in the Options dialog box.

- **If Possible, Compress The Backup Data To Save Space** This setting compresses data to save space on the backup media, an option not available unless the tape drive supports compression.

- **Disable Volume Shadow Copy** VSS allows the backup of locked and open files. If this option is selected, some files that are open or in use might be skipped.

The Ntbackup Command

The Ntbackup command provides the opportunity to script backup jobs on Windows Server 2003. Its syntax is

```
Ntbackup backup {"path to backup" or "@selectionfile.bks"} /j "Job Name" options
```

The command's first switch is *backup*, which sets its mode—you cannot restore from the command line. That switch is followed by a parameter that specifies what to back up. You can specify the actual path to the local folder, network share, or file that you want to back up. Alternatively, you can indicate the path to a backup selection file (.bks file) to be used with the syntax *@selectionfile*.bks. The at (@) symbol must precede the name of the backup selection file. A backup selection file contains information on the files and folders you have selected for backup. You have to create the selection file using the graphical user interface (GUI) version of the Backup Utility.

The third switch, /J *"JobName"*, specifies the descriptive job name, which is used in the backup report.

You can then select from a staggering list of switches, which are grouped below based on the type of backup job you want to perform.

Backing Up to a File

Use the switch

/F "FileName"

where *FileName* is the logical disk path and file name. You must not use the following switches with this switch: /T, /P, or /G.

The following example backs up the remote Data share on Server01 to a local file on the E drive:

```
ntbackup backup "\\server01\Data" /J "Backup of Server 01 Data folder"
/F "E:\Backup.bkf"
```

Appending to a File or Tape

Use the switch

/A

to perform an append operation. If appending to a tape rather than a file, you must use either /G or /T in conjunction with this switch. It cannot be used with /N or /P.

The following example backs up the remote Profiles share on Server02 and appends the set to the job created in the first example:

```
ntbackup backup "\\server02\Profiles"
/J "Backup of Server 02 Profiles folder" /F "E:\Backup.bkf" /A
```

Backing Up to a New Tape or File, or Overwriting an Existing Tape

Use the switch

/N "MediaName"

where *MediaName* specifies the new tape name. You must not use /A with this switch.

Backing Up to a New Tape

Use the switch

/P "PoolName"

where *PoolName* specifies the media pool that contains the backup media. This is usually a subpool of the backup media pool, such as 4mm DDS. You cannot use the /A, /G, /F, or /T switches if you are using /P.

The following example backs up files and folders listed in the backup selection file c:\backup.bks to a tape drive:

```
ntbackup backup @c:\backup.bks /j "Backup Job 101"
/n "Command Line Backup Job" /p "4mm DDS"
```

Backing Up to an Existing Tape

To specify a tape for an append or overwrite operation, you must use either the /T or /G switch along with either /A (append) or /N (overwrite). Do not use the /P switch with either /T or /G.

To specify a tape by name, use the /T switch with the following syntax:

/T "TapeName"

where *TapeName* specifies a valid tape in the media pool.

To back up the selection file and append it to the tape created in the previous example, you would use this command line:

```
ntbackup backup @c:\backup.bks /j "Backup Job 102"
/a /t "Command Line Backup Job"
```

To specify a tape by its GUID, rather than its name, use the /G switch with the following syntax:

/G "GUIDName"

where *GUIDName* specifies a valid tape in the media pool.

Job Options

For each of the job types just described, you can specify additional job options using the following switches:

- **/M {*BackupType*}**   Specifies the backup type, which must be one of the following: normal, copy, differential, incremental, or daily.

- **/D {"*SetDescription*"}**   Specifies a label for the backup set.

- **/V:{yes | no}**   Verifies the data after the backup is complete.

- **/R:{yes | no}**   Restricts access to this tape to the owner or members of the Administrators group.

- **/L:{f | s | n}**   Specifies the type of log file: f=full, s=summary, n=none (no log file is created).

- **/RS:{yes | no}**   Backs up the migrated data files located in Remote Storage.

> **Tip**   The /RS switch is not required to back up the local Removable Storage database, which contains the Remote Storage placeholder files. When you backup the %*Systemroot*% folder, the Backup Utility automatically backs up the Removable Storage database as well.

- **/HC:{on | off}**   Uses hardware compression, if available, on the tape drive.

- **/SNAP:{on | off}**   Specifies whether the backup should use a Volume Shadow Copy.

Scheduling Backup Jobs

To schedule a backup job, create the job in the Backup Utility and then click Start Backup and configure advanced backup options. After all options have been configured, click Schedule and, in the Set Account Information dialog box, type the user name and password of the account to be used by the backup job.

> **Tip**   Security best practices suggest that you create an account for each service rather than run services under the System account. Do not configure a service to run using a User account, such as your User account or the Administrator account. When the password changes on a User account, you must modify the password setting on all services that run under the context of that account. The account for the backup job should belong to the Backup Operators group.

In the Scheduled Job Options dialog box, enter a job name and click Properties. The Schedule Job dialog box appears, as shown in Figure 13-7. Configure the job date, time, and frequency. The Advanced button will let you configure additional schedule settings, including a date range for the job. The Settings tab of the Schedule Job dialog box allows you to refine the job—for example by specifying that the job should take place only if the machine has been idle for a period of time.

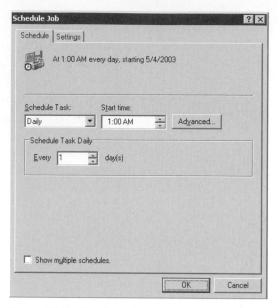

Figure 13-7   The Schedule Job dialog box

Once a job has been scheduled, you can edit the schedule by clicking the Schedule Jobs tab of the Backup Utility. Jobs are listed on a calendar. Click a job to open its schedule. Although you can also add a backup job by clicking Add Job on the Schedule Jobs tab, clicking Add Job will launch the backup wizard so that you can select the files to back up and some properties of the backup job. Most administrators find it more convenient to create a backup job on the Backup tab directly and then click Start Backup and Schedule, as described previously.

Shadow Copies of Shared Folders

Windows Server 2003 supports another way for administrators and users alike to recover quickly from damage to files and folders. Using VSS, Windows Server 2003 automatically caches copies of files as they are modified. If a user deletes, overwrites, or makes unwanted changes to a file, you can simply restore a previous version of the file. This is a valuable feature, but it is not intended to replace backups. Instead, it is designed to facilitate quick recovery from simple, day-to-day problems—not recovery from significant data loss.

Note   Shadow Copies feature is supported only on NTFS volumes, not FAT volumes.

Enabling and Configuring Shadow Copies

The Shadow Copies feature for shared folders is not enabled by default. To enable the feature, open the Properties dialog box of a drive volume from Windows Explorer or the Disk Management snap-in. On the Shadow Copies tab, as shown in Figure 13-8, select the volume and click Enable. Once Shadow Copies is enabled, all shared folders on the volume will be shadowed; specific shares on a volume cannot be selected. You can, however, manually initiate a shadow copy by clicking Create Now.

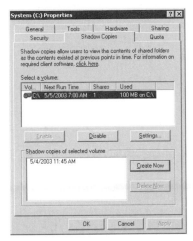

Figure 13-8   The Shadow Copies tab of a volume's Properties dialog box

Caution   If you click Disable, you delete all copies that were created by VSS. Consider carefully whether you want to disable VSS for a volume or whether you might be better served by modifying the schedule to prevent new shadow copies from being made.

The default settings configure the server to make copies of shared folders at 7:00 A.M. and noon, Monday through Friday; and 10 percent of the drive space, on the same drive as the shared folder, is used to cache shadow copies.

Each of the following settings can be modified by clicking Settings on the Shadow Copies tab:

- **Storage volume**   To enhance performance (not redundancy), you can move the shadow storage to another volume. This must be done when no shadow copies are present. If shadow copies exist and you want to change the storage volume, you must delete all shadow copies on the volume and then change the storage volume.

- **Details**   The Details dialog box lists shadow copies that are stored and space utilization statistics.

- **Storage limits**   This can be as low as 100 MB. When the shadow copy runs out of storage, it deletes older versions of files to make room for newer versions. The proper configuration of this setting depends on the total size of shared folders on a volume with shadowing enabled; the frequency with which files change, and the size of those files; and the number of previous versions you want to retain. In any event, a maximum of 63 previous versions will be stored for any one file before the earliest version is removed from the shadow storage.

- **Schedule**   You can configure a schedule that reflects the work patterns of your users, ensuring that enough previous versions are available without prematurely filling the storage area and thereby forcing the removal of old versions. Remember that when a shadow copy is made, any files that have changed since the previous shadow copy are copied. If a file has been updated several times between shadow copies, those interim versions will not be available.

Using Shadow Copy

Shadow copies of shared folders allow you to access previous versions of files that the server has cached on the configured schedule. This will allow you to do the following:

- Recover files that were accidentally deleted
- Recover from accidentally overwriting a file
- Compare versions of files while working

To access previous versions, click the properties of a folder or file and click the Previous Versions tab, as shown in Figure 13-9.

Figure 13-9   The Previous Versions tab of a shared resource

The Previous Versions tab will not be available if Shadow Copies is not enabled on the server or if there are no previous versions stored on the server. It will also be unavailable if the Shadow Copy Client has not been installed on the client system. Windows Server 2003 has the Shadow Copy Client functionality installed by default. For Windows XP clients, the Shadow Copy Client software (named the Previous Versions Client) is located in the *%Systemroot%*\System32\Clients\Twclient\x86 folder of a Windows Server 2003 system. The Shadow Copy Client (.msi) file can be deployed using Group Policy, SMS, or an e-mail message. Finally, the Previous Versions tab is only available when accessing a file's properties through a shared folder. If the file is stored on the local hard drive, you will not see the Previous Versions tab, even if the file is shared and VSS is enabled. See this lesson's "Practice: Advanced Backup and Restore" section for an example of using Previous Versions.

You can then choose to Restore the file to its previous location or Copy the file to a specific location.

Tip   The Shadow Copy Client software can also be downloaded from Microsoft's Web site. Information about using the Shadow Copy Client on other versions of Windows is also available on Microsoft's Web site.

Exam Tip   Unlike a true restore operation, when you restore a file with Previous Versions, the security settings of the previous version are not restored. If you restore the file to its original location and the file exists in the original location, the restored previous version overwrites the current version and uses the permissions assigned to the current version. If you copy a previous version to another location, or restore the file to its original location but the file no longer exists in the original location, the restored previous version inherits permissions from the parent folder.

If a file has been deleted, you obviously cannot go to the file's Properties dialog box to locate the Previous Versions tab. Instead, open the Properties of the parent folder, click the Previous Versions tab and locate a previous version of the folder that contains the file you want to recover. Click View, and a folder window will open, as shown in Figure 13-10, that displays the contents of the folder as of the time at which the shadow copy was made. Right-click the file and choose Copy, and then paste the file into the folder where you want the file to be re-created.

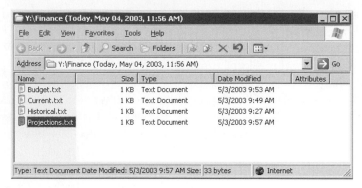

Figure 13-10   A folder's Previous Versions content list

Shadow copy, as you can see, is a useful addition to the toolset for managing file servers and shared data. With VSS, you can preserve data sets at scheduled points in time. Administrators or users can then restore deleted or corrupted files, or compare files to previous versions. As the VSS cache fills, old versions are purged and new shadow copies are added.

If a user requires data to be restored and that data is no longer available through Previous Versions, you can restore the data from backup. If the server becomes corrupted, you must restore the data from backup. Although VSS enhances the manageability and resiliency of shared files, there is no substitute for a carefully planned and verified backup procedure.

Practice: Advanced Backup and Restore

In this practice, you will schedule a backup job, execute a backup from a command prompt, and configure and use Shadow Copies Of Shared Folders.

Exercise 1: Scheduling a Backup Job

1. Log on to Server01 as Administrator.

2. Open the Backup Utility, and click the Backup tab.

3. From the Job menu, load the Finance Backup.bks selections.

4. Configure the Backup Media Or File Name: C:\Backup-Everyday.bkf.

5. Click Start Backup.

6. Click Advanced, and configure an Incremental backup type. Click OK.

7. Click Schedule.

8. In the Set Account Information dialog box, type your password and click OK.

9. Name the job Daily Incremental Backup.

10. Click Properties. Configure the job to run daily. Configure the time to be two minutes from the current time so that you can see the results of the job.

11. Click OK. You will be prompted to enter your password again.

12. Close the open dialog boxes, and close the Backup Utility.

13. Open the C:\ drive in Windows Explorer, and wait two minutes. You will see the backup job (Backup-Everyday.bkf) appear.

14. Open the Backup Utility, choose the Report command from the Tools menu and view the most recent backup log to confirm the status of the backup job. The number of files copied might be zero if you have not made changes to any of the files.

15. If the job did not run properly, open Event Viewer from the Administrative Tools folder. Examine the Application Log to identify the cause of the failure.

Exercise 2: Running a Backup from a Command Prompt

One of the easier ways to determine the correct switches to use for a command prompt backup is to schedule a backup, as you did in Exercise 1, and then examine the command that the scheduled task creates.

1. Open the Backup Utility, and click the Schedule Jobs tab.

2. Click the icon, in the calendar, representing the scheduled job.

3. Click Properties.

4. Select the command in the Run box, and press CTRL+C to copy it.

5. Click Cancel to exit the Schedule Job dialog box and close the Backup Utility.

6. Open a command prompt window.

7. Click the window menu (the icon of the command prompt in the upper-left corner of the command prompt window) and, from the Edit menu, choose Paste. The Ntbackup command with all of its switches is pasted into the command prompt. Press ENTER. The backup job is executed.

> **Note**   It is recommended that you delete the scheduled backup job at this point in the practice. You will schedule additional jobs in the "Case Scenario Exercise" section, and it will be easier to work with those jobs if the current schedule is clear. In the Backup Utility, click the Schedule Jobs tab, and then, in the calendar, click the icon representing the scheduled job. In the Scheduled Job Options dialog box, click Delete.

Exercise 3: Enabling Shadow Copies

1. Ensure that the C:\Data folder is shared and that the share permissions are configured to allow Everyone Full Control.

2. Open My Computer.

3. Right-click the C drive, and choose Properties.

4. Click the Shadow Copies tab.

5. Select the C volume, and click Enable.

6. A message will appear. Click Yes to continue.

Exercise 4: Simulating Changes to Network Files

1. Open the C:\Data\Finance folder, and open Current.txt. Modify the file's contents, and then save and close the file.

2. Delete the file C:\Data\Finance\Projections.txt.

Exercise 5: Recovering Files Using Previous Versions

1. Open the data share by clicking Start, choosing Run, and typing **server01\data**.

> **Note**   It is critical that you open the folder using its UNC, not its local path. The Previous Versions tab is available only when connected to a shared folder over the network.

2. Open the Finance folder.

3. Right-click the Current.txt file, and choose Properties.

4. Select the Previous Versions tab.

5. Select the previous version of Current.txt.

6. Click Copy, select the Desktop as the destination, and then click Copy again.

7. Click OK to close the Properties dialog box.

8. Open Current.txt from your desktop. You will see that it is the version without the changes you made in Exercise 4.

9. Return to \\Server01\Data. This time, do not open the Finance folder.

10. To recover the deleted Projections.txt file, right-click the Finance folder and click Properties.

11. Select the Previous Versions tab.

12. Select the previous version of the Finance folder, and click View.

    A window opens showing the contents of the folder as of the time that the shadow copy was made.

13. Right-click the Projections.txt file, and choose Copy.

14. Switch to the folder that shows you the current \\server01\data folder.

15. Open the Finance folder.

16. Paste the Projections.txt file into the folder. You have now restored the previous version of Projections.txt.

Lesson Review

The following questions are intended to reinforce key information presented in this lesson. If you are unable to answer a question, review the lesson materials and try the question again. You can find answers to the questions in the "Questions and Answers" section at the end of this chapter.

1. Scott Bishop is a power user at a remote site that includes 20 users. The site has a Windows Server 2003 system providing file and print servers. A tape drive is installed on the system. Because there is no local, full-time administrator at the site, you want to allow Scott to back up and restore the server. However, you want to minimize the power and the privileges that Scott obtains, limiting his capabilities strictly to backup and restore. What is the best practice to provide Scott the minimum necessary credentials to achieve his task?

   _____

   _____

2. Write the command that will allow you to fully back up the C:\Data\Finance folder to a file called Backup.bkf in a share named Backup on Server02, with the backup job name "Backup of Finance Folder." Then, write the command that will allow you to perform an incremental backup and append the backup set to the same file, with the same backup job name.

   _____

   _____

   _____

   _____

3. A user has deleted a file in a shared folder on a server. The user opens the properties of the folder and does not see a Previous Versions tab. Which of the following might be true? (Choose all that apply.)

    a. The folder is not enabled for Shadow Copy.

    b. The volume on the server is not enabled for Shadow Copy.

    c. The user doesn't have permission to view the Shadow Copy cache.

    d. The Shadow Copy Client is not installed on the user's machine.

    e. The folder is on a FAT volume.

_____

_____

_____

_____

Lesson Summary

- You must have the right to back up and restore files to use the Backup Utility or any other backup tool. The right is assigned, by default, to the Backup Operators and Administrators groups.

- The Options dialog box allows you to configure General, Backup, and Restore settings, many of which become defaults that will drive the behavior of the Backup Utility and the Ntbackup command, unless overridden by job-specific options specified in the backup job's Advanced Backup Options dialog box or in command-line switches.

- The Ntbackup command and its full complement of switches allows you to launch a backup job from a command prompt or batch file.

- Backup jobs can be scheduled to run regularly and automatically during periods of low utilization.

- Volume Shadow Copy Service (VSS) allows a user to access previous versions of files and folders in network shares. With those previous versions, users can restore deleted or damaged files or compare versions of files.

Lesson 4: Recovering from System Failure

Although Windows Server 2003 offers superior levels of stability and reliability, power supplies, cooling fans, chip sets and yes, even code, can cause a computer to fail. And when a server fails in the forest, everyone hears it fall. In a worst-case scenario, server hardware fails and cannot be recovered. To return to operations, you must have a complete backup of the server that you can restore to a new piece of hardware. This complete backup will include data stored on the server, applications, and the operating system itself. In earlier lessons in this chapter, you learned how to use the Backup Utility and the Ntbackup command to back up data. In this lesson, you will learn how to use the same utilities to back up the system so that you can return to operational status quickly in the event of such a worst-case scenario. You will also learn how to use the Recovery Console to perform surgical repairs of specific problems, including service or driver failures.

After this lesson, you will be able to

- Back up the System State
- Prepare an ASR backup set and repair a computer using Automated System Recovery
- Install and use the Windows Server 2003 Recovery Console

Estimated lesson time: 60 minutes

A Review of Recovery Options

Windows Server 2003 supports a number of methods to repair and recover from specific types of failures:

- **Data loss or corruption**   The Backup Utility and Ntbackup.exe command allow you to back up and restore data. The new Volume Shadow Copy Service allows users to access or restore previous versions of files in shared folders on servers.

- **Driver updates resulting in system instability**   Windows Server 2003 provides a new driver rollback capability of Windows Server 2003. If a driver has been updated and the system becomes unstable, that driver and any new settings that were configured can be rolled back to a previously installed version and state. Printer drivers cannot be rolled back. It is easy, using Device Manager, to disable a device that causes instability. If an application or supporting software contributes to the instability, use Add Or Remove Programs to remove the offending component.

- **Driver or service installation or update results in the inability to start the system**   Windows Server 2003, like earlier versions of Windows, provides the Last Known Good Configuration, which rolls back the active ControlSet of the system's registry to the ControlSet that was used the last time a user successfully logged on to the system. If you install or update a service or driver and the system crashes or cannot reboot to the logon screen, the Last Known Good Configuration effectively takes you back to the version of the registry that was active before the driver or service was installed. There are also a variety of Safe Mode options, which enable the system to start with specific drivers or services disabled. Safe Mode can often allow you to start an otherwise unbootable computer and, using Device Manager, disable, uninstall, or roll back a troublesome driver or service.

- **Failure of the disk subsystem**   Windows Server 2003 allows you to create redundant disk volumes by configuring mirrored (RAID-1) or RAID-5 volumes.

Each of these recovery and repair processes makes the assumption that a system can be restarted to some extent. When a system cannot be restarted, the System State, Automated System Recovery, and the Recovery Console can return the system to operational status.

System State

Windows 2000 and Windows Server 2003 introduced the concept of *System State* to the backup process. System State data contains critical elements of a system's configuration, including:

- The system's registry

- The COM+ Class Registration Database

- The boot files, including boot.ini, ntdetect.com, ntldr, bootsect.dos, and ntbootdd.sys

- System files that are protected by the Windows File Protection service

In addition, the following items are included in the System State when the corresponding services have been installed on the system:

- Certificate Services database on a certificate server

- Active Directory and the Sysvol folder on a domain controller

- Cluster service information on a cluster server

- Internet Information Services (IIS) metabase on a server with IIS installed

To back up the System State in the Backup Utility, include the System State node as part of the backup selection. The System State and its components are shown in Figure 13-11.

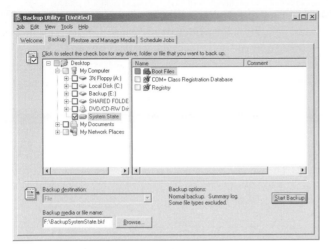

Figure 13-11   The System State

If you prefer to use the command line, use Ntbackup with the following syntax:

```
Ntbackup backup systemstate /J "backup job name" ...
```

followed by the /F switch to indicate backing up to a file, or by the appropriate /T, /G, /N, or /P switches to back up to a tape. The switches for the Ntbackup command are described fully in Lesson 3.

There are several important considerations related to backing up the System State:

- You cannot back up individual components of the System State. For example, you cannot back up the COM+ Class Registration Database alone. Because of interdependencies among System State components, you can back up only the collection of System State components as a whole.

- You cannot use Ntbackup or the Backup Utility to back up the System State from a remote machine. You must run Ntbackup or the Backup Utility on the system that is being backed up. You can, however, direct the backup to a file on a remote server, which can then transfer the file onto another backup media. Or you can purchase a third-party backup utility that can remotely back up the System State.

- The System State contains most elements of a system's configuration, but it might not include every element required to return the system to full operational capacity. It is therefore recommended that you back up all boot, system, data and application volumes when you back up the system state. The System State is a critical piece of a complete backup, but it is only one piece.

- Performing a system state backup automatically forces the backup type to Copy, although the interface might not indicate that fact. Take that fact into consideration when planning whether to include other items in your backup selection.

To restore the System State on a computer that is operational, use the Backup Utility and, on the Restore And Manage Media tab, click the System State check box. If the computer is not operational, you will most likely turn to Automated System Recovery to regain operational status.

System State on a Domain Controller

The System State on a domain controller includes the Microsoft Active Directory directory service and the Sysvol folder. You can back up the System State on a domain controller just as on any other system, using the Backup Utility or Ntbackup command. As with all backup media, it is paramount to maintain physical security of the media to which the Active Directory is backed up.

To restore the System State on a domain controller, you must restart the computer, press F8 to select startup options, and select Directory Services Restore Mode. This mode is a variation of the Safe Modes that have been supported in recent versions of Windows. In Directory Services Restore Mode, the domain controller boots but does not start Active Directory services. You can log on to the computer only as the local Administrator, using the Directory Services Restore Mode password that was specified when Dcpromo.exe was used to promote the server to a domain controller.

When in Directory Services Restore Mode, the domain controller does not perform authentication or Active Directory replication, and the Active Directory database and supporting files are not subject to file locks. You can therefore restore the System State by using the Backup Utility.

When restoring the System State on a domain controller, you must choose whether to perform a nonauthoritative (normal) or authoritative restore of the Active Directory and Sysvol folder. After restoring the System State by using the Backup Utility, you complete a nonauthoritative restore by restarting the domain controller into normal operational status. Because older data was restored, the domain controller must update its replica of the Active Directory and Sysvol, which it does automatically through standard replication mechanisms from its replication partners.

There might be occasions, however, when you do not want the restored domain controller to become consistent with other functioning domain controllers and instead want all domain controllers to have the same state as the restored replica. If, for example, objects have been deleted from Active Directory, you can restore one domain controller with a backup set that was created prior to the deletion of the objects. You must then perform an authoritative restore, which marks selected objects as authoritative and causes those objects to be replicated *from* the restored domain controllers *to* its replication partners.

To perform an authoritative restore, you must first perform a nonauthoritative restore by using the Backup Utility to restore the System State onto the domain controller. When the restore is completed and you click Close in the Backup Utility, you are prompted to restart the computer. When that occurs, you must select No. Do not allow the domain controller to restart. Then, open a command prompt and use Ntdsutil.exe to mark the entire restored database or selected objects as authoritative. You can get more information about Ntdsutil and authoritative restore by typing **ntdsutil /?** at the command prompt or by using the online references in the Help And Support Center. Chapter 3 discusses the recovery of Active Directory on domain controllers in greater detail.

> **Exam Tip**   Remember that the System State can be restored on a domain controller only by restarting the domain controller in Directory Services Restore Mode, and that Ntdsutil is used to recover deleted objects in Active Directory by marking those objects as authoritative, following a normal, or nonauthoritative, restore of the System State with the Backup Utility.

Automated System Recovery

Recovering a failed server has traditionally been a tedious task, involving reinstallation of the operating system, mounting and cataloging the backup tape, and then performing a full restore. Automated System Recovery makes that process significantly easier. Automated System Recovery requires you to create an ASR set, consisting of a backup of critical system files—including the registry—and a floppy disk listing the Windows system files that are installed on the computer. If the server ever fails, you simply restart with the Windows Server 2003 CD-ROM and select the option to perform an Automated System Recovery. The process uses the list of files on the ASR disk to restore standard drivers and files from the original Windows Server 2003 CD-ROM, and it will restore remaining files from the ASR backup set.

To create an ASR set, open the Backup Utility from the All Programs\Accessories\System Tools program group, or by clicking Start, clicking Run, and typing **Ntbackup.exe**. If the Backup And Restore Wizard appears, click Advanced Mode. Then, from the Backup Utility's Welcome tab or from the Tools menu, select ASR Wizard. Follow the instructions of the Automated System Recovery Preparation Wizard. It will request a 1.44 megabyte (MB) floppy disk to create the ASR floppy. The ASR Preparation Wizard is shown in Figure 13-12.

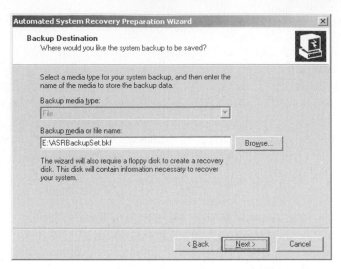

Figure 13-12   The Backup Destination page of the ASR Preparation Wizard

The backup created by the ASR Wizard includes disk configuration information for each disk in the computer, a System State backup, and a backup of files including the driver cache. The backup set is sizable. On a standard installation of Windows Server 2003, the ASR backup size will be almost 2 gigabytes (GB).

The ASR floppy disk is created by the Automated System Recovery Preparation Wizard, and it is specific to the system and the time at which the ASR set was created. You should label the ASR backup set and floppy disk carefully and keep them together.

The ASR floppy disk contains two catalogs of files on the system: Asr.sif and Asrpnp.sif. If the system does not have a floppy drive when you create the ASR set, you can create the floppy disk after running the wizard by copying these two files from the *%System-root%*\repair folder on the system to another computer that does have a floppy drive, and copying the files to the floppy disk on that second system. If you lose the floppy disk, you can restore the two files from the *%Systemroot%*\repair folder in the ASR backup set. You *must* have the ASR floppy disk to perform an Automated System Recovery. If the system does not have a floppy drive, you will need to connect one before performing the restore.

Tip   The ASR set contains the files required to start the system. It is not a comprehensive backup of the entire system. Therefore it is highly recommended that you create a complete backup, including the System State, system volume, applications and, perhaps, user data when you create your ASR set.

When you perform an Automated System Recovery, you will need the following:

- The Windows Server 2003 setup CD-ROM
- The ASR backup set
- The ASR floppy disk created at the same time as the ASR backup set

> **Tip**   You will also need any mass storage device drivers that are not part of the standard Windows Server 2003 driver set. To facilitate recovery, you should consider copying those drivers to the ASR floppy disk.

To restore a system using Automated System Recovery, restart using the Windows Server 2003 CD-ROM, just as if you were installing the operating system on the computer. If the computer requires a mass storage device driver that is not included with Windows Server 2003, press F6 when prompted and provide the driver on a floppy disk. After loading initial drivers, the system will prompt you to press F2 to perform an Automated System Recovery. Press F2 and follow the instructions on your screen. Automated System Recover will prompt you for the system's ASR floppy, which contains two catalogs, or lists, of files required to start the system. Those files will be loaded from the CD-ROM. Automated System Recovery will restore remaining critical files, including the system's registry, from the system's ASR backup set. There is a restart during the process, and if the computer requires a vendor-specific mass storage device driver, you will need to press F6 during this second restart as well. Because there is a restart, you should either remove the floppy disk after the initial text-based portion of the restore, or set the restart order so that the system does not attempt to restart from the floppy drive.

Recovery Console

The Recovery Console is a text-mode command interpreter that allows you to access the hard disk of a computer running Windows Server 2003 for basic troubleshooting and system maintenance. It is particularly useful when the operating system cannot be started, as the Recovery Console can be used to run diagnostics, disable drivers and services, replace files, and perform other targeted recovery procedures.

Installing the Recovery Console

You can start the Recovery Console by booting with the Windows Server 2003 CD-ROM and, when prompted, pressing R to choose the repair and recover option. However, when a system is down you will typically want to recover the system as quickly as possible, and you might not want to waste time hunting down a copy of the CD-ROM or waiting for the laboriously long restart process. Therefore, it is recommended that you proactively install the Recovery Console.

To install the Recovery Console, insert the Windows Server 2003 CD-ROM and type **cd-drive:\i386\winnt32 /cmdcons** on the command line. The Setup Wizard will install the 8 MB console in a hidden folder called Cmdcons, and it will modify the boot.ini file to provide the Recovery Console as a startup option during the boot process.

Removing the Recovery Console

If you ever decide to remove the Recovery Console, you must delete files and folders that are "super hidden." From Windows Explorer, choose the Folder Options command from the Tools menu. Click the View tab, select Show Hidden Files and Folders, clear Hide Protected Operating System Files, and if you are prompted with a warning about displaying protected system files, click Yes.

Then, delete the Cmdcons folder and the Cmldr file, each of which is located in the root of the system drive. You must next remove the Recovery Console startup option from Boot.ini. Open System from Control Panel, click the Advanced tab, click the Settings button in the Startup And Recovery frame, and then, in the Startup And Recovery dialog box, under System Startup, click Edit. Boot.ini will display in Notepad. Remove the entry for the Recovery Console, which will look something like this:

```
c:\cmdcons\bootsect.dat="Microsoft Windows Recovery Console" /cmdcons
```

Save the file and close Boot.ini.

Using the Recovery Console

After you have installed the Recovery Console, you can reboot the system and select Microsoft Windows Recovery Console from the startup menu. If the console was not installed or cannot be launched successfully, you can restart using the Windows Server 2003 CD-ROM and, at the Welcome To Setup page, press R to select Repair. The loading takes significantly longer from the CD-ROM, but the resulting Recovery Console is identical to that installed on the local system.

Once the Recovery Console has started, as shown in Figure 13-13, you will be prompted to select the installation of Windows to which you want to log on. You will then be asked to enter the Administrator password. You must use the password assigned to the local Administrator account, which, on a domain controller, is the password configured on the Directory Services Restore Mode Password page of the Active Directory Installation Wizard.

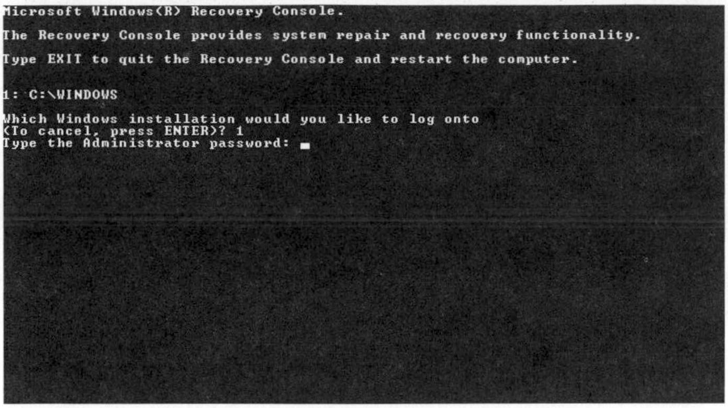

Figure 13-13   The Recovery Console

You can type **Help** at the console prompt to list the commands available in the Recovery Console, and **Help *command name*** for information about a specific command. Most are familiar commands from the standard command-line environment. Several commands deserve particular attention:

- **Listsvc**   Displays the services and drivers that are listed in the registry as well as their startup settings. This command is useful for discovering the short name for a service or driver before using the Enable and Disable commands.

- **Enable/Disable**   Controls the startup status of a service or driver. If a service or driver is preventing the operating system from starting successfully, use the Recovery Console's Disable command to disable the component, and then restart the system and repair or uninstall the component.

- **Diskpart**   Provides the opportunity to create and delete partitions by using an interface similar to that of the text-based portion of Setup. You can then use the Format command to configure a file system for a partition.

- **Bootcfg**   Enables you to manage the startup menu.

The Recovery Console has several limitations imposed for security purposes. These limitations can be modified using a combination of policies (located in the Computer Configuration\Windows Settings\Security Settings\Local Policies\Security Options node of the Local Computer Policy console) and Recovery Console environment variables.

- **Directory access**   You can view files only in the root directory, in *%Windir%* and in the \Cmdcons folder. Disable this limitation by enabling the policy Recovery Console: Allow Floppy Copy And Access To All Drives And All Folders, and using the **Set AllowAllPaths = True** command in the Recovery Console. Be sure to include the space on either side of the equal sign when typing the Set command.

- **File copy**   You can only copy files to the local hard disk, not from it. Disable this limitation by enabling the Recovery Console: Allow Floppy Copy And Access To All Drives And All Folders policy and using the **Set AllowRemovableMedia = True** command in the Recovery Console. Be sure to include the space on either side of the equal sign when typing the Set command.

- **Wildcards**   You cannot use wildcards such as the asterisk to delete files. Disable this limitation for some commands by enabling the Recovery Console: Allow Floppy Copy And Access To All Drives And All Folders policy and using the **Set AllowWildCards = True** command in the Recovery Console. Be sure to include the space on either side of the equal sign when typing the Set command.

Practice: Recovering from System Failure

In this practice, you will back up the System State and create an Automated System Recovery Set on Server02. You will also install and use the Recovery Console to troubleshoot driver or service failures. Finally, if you have access to a second physical disk drive, you will be able to perform Automated System Recovery to restore a failed server.

Exercise 1: Backing Up the System State

1. Log on to Server02 as Administrator.
2. Open the Backup Utility.
3. If the Backup And Restore Wizard appears, click Advanced Mode.
4. Click the Backup tab, and select the check box next to System State. Also click the System State label so that you can see the components of the System State listed in the other pane of the dialog box.
5. In the Backup Media Or File Name box, type a file name for the backup file, such as **C:\SystemState.bkf**.
6. Start the backup.
7. When the backup is complete, examine the file size of the System State backup file. How big is the file?

Exercise 2: Creating an ASR Set

This exercise requires a blank floppy disk and approximately 1.7 GB of free disk space. If you have a second physical disk in Server02, direct the backup to that disk so that you can perform an Automated System Recovery in Exercise 4.

1. Open the Backup Utility. If the Backup And Restore Wizard appears, click Advanced Mode.

2. Click Automated System Recovery Wizard, or choose ASR Wizard from the Tools menu.

3. Follow the prompts. Back up to a file named ASRBackup.bkf on the C drive or, if you have a second physical disk, on that volume.

4. When the backup is complete, examine the file size of ASRBackup.bkf. How big is it? How does its size compare to that of the System State backup?

Exercise 3: Installing and Using the Recovery Console

1. Insert the Windows Server 2003 CD-ROM.

2. Click Start, click Run, and then type the following command in the Open box:

```
D:\i386\winnt32.exe /cmdcons
```

where *D:* is the drive letter for your CD-ROM. The Recovery Console will be installed on the local hard disk.

3. To simulate a service in need of troubleshooting, open the Services console from Administrative Tools. Locate the Messenger service. Double-click the service, choose Automatic as the Startup Type, and click OK.

4. Restart the server.

5. When the server presents the startup boot menu, select Microsoft Windows Recovery Console.

6. When prompted, type **1** to select the installation of Windows Server 2003.

7. Type the password for the local Administrator account.

8. When the Recovery Console prompt appears (by default, C:\Windows>), type **help** to display a list of commands.

9. Type **listsvc** to display a list of services and drivers. Note that the short name of many services is not the same as the long name. However, the short name of the Messenger service is also Messenger. Confirm that its startup is set to Automatic.

10. Type **disable messenger** to disable the service. The output of the command indicates the success of the command and the original startup configuration for the service (in this case, SERVICE_AUTO_START). You should always make note of this setting so that once troubleshooting has been completed you can return the service to its original state.

11. To quit the Recovery Console, type **exit** and press ENTER.

Exercise 4: Restoring a System Using Automated System Recovery

> **Warning**   This exercise requires a second physical disk on which an ASR backup has been created in Lesson 2. This exercise will delete all data on the physical disk that contains the system and boot partition. Do not proceed if you have stored any data that you cannot afford to lose.

1. Power off your computer.

2. Restart the computer, and open the computer's BIOS. Make sure the system is configured to start from the CD-ROM.

3. Insert the Windows Server 2003 installation CD-ROM.

4. Restart Server02. Watch carefully and, when prompted, press a key to start from the CD-ROM.

5. Early in the text-mode setup phase, setup prompts you to press F2 to run an Automatic System Recovery. Press F2.

6. You will then be prompted to insert the Windows Automated System Recovery disk into the floppy drive. Insert the floppy disk you created in Exercise 2, and press any key to continue.

7. Text-mode setup prepares for Automated System Recovery and a minimal version of the operating system is loaded. This step will take some time to complete.

8. Eventually, a Windows Server 2003 Setup screen will appear.

9. Windows Server 2003 Setup partitions and formats the disk, copies files, initializes the Windows configuration, and then prepares to restart.

10. Remove the floppy disk from the disk drive, and allow the computer to restart.

    The installation will continue. When the installation completes, the computer should be restored to its previous state.

Lesson Review

The following questions are intended to reinforce key information presented in this lesson. If you are unable to answer a question, review the lesson materials and try the question again. You can find answers to the questions in the "Questions and Answers" section at the end of this chapter.

1. You're setting up a backup job on a computer running Windows Server 2003. Your want to back up the registry, startup files, and the COM+ Class Registration database. Which backup option should you select?

    a. *%Windir%*

    b. *%Systemroot%*

    c. System State

    d. None of the above. You cannot back up the registry.

2. You install a scanner on a computer running Windows Server 2003. When you try to restart your computer, the operating system will not start. Which of the following would be the least invasive recovery method to try first to restore the system to operation?

    a. Automated System Recovery

    b. Recovery Console

    c. Safe Mode

    d. Directory Services Restore Mode

3. A hard disk on a server running Windows Server 2003 has failed. You replace the disk, boot the system, initialize the disk, and create an NTFS volume on the new disk. You now want to restore that data from the last backup job from the old disk. How should you restore the data?

    a. Use the Recovery Console to copy data to the disk.

    b. Use the Backup Utility to launch the Restore Wizard.

    c. Use the ASR backup to restore the data.

    d. Use the Last Known Good Configuration option in Safe Mode to set up the new disk.

4. A file server on your network will not start. After exhausting all other options, you have decided to use Automated System Recovery (ASR) to recover the system. You created an ASR backup immediately after you installed Windows Server 2003 and another one two months ago after you installed a device driver. You perform a full backup of data files once a week. What will ASR restore? (Choose all that apply.)

    a. Data files two months ago

    b. Data files at the last full backup

    c. Disk configuration

     d. Operating system

     e. System State two months ago

     f. System State at the last full backup

Lesson Summary

■ The System State includes the registry, startup files, COM+ Class Registration Database, and other service-specific critical system files. It is wise to plan a backup strategy that coordinates backing up the System State along with the system and boot volumes.

■ Automated System Recovery uses a setup-like process to return a computer to operation, and then starts a restore operation to recover files from the ASR backup set. It is a recovery process that should be used to restore a system when other less invasive methods, such as Safe Mode or the Recovery Console, have been ineffective.

■ The Recovery Console is a text-mode command interpreter that allows you to access the hard disk of a computer running Windows Server 2003.

Case Scenario Exercise

You are asked to configure a backup strategy for the Finance Department's shared folder. The backup should occur automatically during the early-morning hours, as there are users working shifts from 4:00 A.M. to 12:00 midnight, Monday through Friday. Files in the folder change frequently—about half the files change once a week; the other half of the files change almost daily. You are told that if the server's hard drive ever fails, down time is extraordinarily costly to the company, so recovery should be as fast as possible.

1. With the knowledge that so many files change almost daily and that recovery must be as quick as possible, what type of backup job should you consider running nightly?

2. You configure a normal daily backup job to run at 12:00 midnight, after the last shift has gone home for the evening. Unfortunately, you find that the backup job is not completed by 4:00 A.M. when the morning shift arrives. How should you modify your backup strategy?

_____

_____

_____

_____

_____

Exercise 1: Create Sample Data

1. Log on to Server01 as Administrator.

2. Open My Computer and the C drive.

3. Delete the Data folder. You will be prompted to confirm the choice. You will also be informed that the folder is shared and that deleting the folder will delete the shared folder. Confirm your understanding of the warning and continue.

4. Open a command prompt window and type **cd c:**.

5. Type the command **createfiles.bat**.

 Note If you did not create the createfiles.bat file in Lesson 1, Exercise 1, complete steps 2 through 3 of Exercise 1 to create the appropriate script.

Exercise 2: Schedule the Backup Job

Configure and schedule the following backup jobs. If you need guidance to achieve these tasks, refer to the instructions in the practices in Lesson 1 and Lesson 3.

■ A normal backup job to back up the C:\Data\Finance folder to a file named C:\BackupFinance.bkf (replacing the media), every Sunday at 9:00 P.M.

■ A differential backup job to back up the same folder to the same file (appending to the media), at 12:15 A.M. on Tuesday through Saturday (that is, Monday night through Friday night).

Exercise 3: Simulate the Scheduled Jobs

Rather than waiting until Sunday night for the normal backup job to execute automatically, you will execute the backup job from a command prompt.

1. Open the Backup Utility.

2. Click the Schedule Jobs tab.

3. In the calendar, click the icon representing the Sunday night normal backup job.

4. Click Properties.

5. Select the command in the Run box, and press CTRL+C to copy it.

6. Cancel to exit the Schedule dialog boxes and close the Backup Utility.

7. Open a command prompt window.

8. Click the window menu (the icon of the command prompt in the upper left corner of the command prompt window) and, from the Edit menu, choose Paste. The Ntbackup command with all its switches is pasted into the command prompt. Press Enter.

9. The backup job is executed.

10. Open C:\Data\Finance\Projections.txt, and make changes to the file. Save and close the file.

11. Repeat steps 1 through 9, this time executing from the command prompt the *differential* backup job that is scheduled to run every night.

Exercise 4: Verify the Procedure

1. Open the Backup Utility

2. From the Tools menu, click Report.

3. Open the two most recent backup reports, and confirm that the jobs completed successfully. The normal job should have backed up four files. The differential job should have backed up one file.

4. Perform a test restore to an alternate folder location named C:\TestRestore. Restore the normal job and then the differential job. Verify that Projections.txt includes your changes. If you need guidance, refer to the practice in Lesson 2.

> **Caution**   Remember, before restoring the differential job, you must configure the Restore options (from the Tools menu, select Options) to always replace files. You might also need to catalog the file to see all the backup sets it contains.

Troubleshooting Lab

At 1:00 P.M. on Tuesday, a user in the Finance Department contacts you to let you know he accidentally deleted some files from the Finance folder. You are confident the backup procedure you established will help you recover the deleted files. However, you also want to ensure you don't roll back any files that had been changed today, after the overnight backup job was executed.

In this lab, you will simulate the workflow that creates such a scenario, and then you will recover the missing data.

Exercise 1: Create a Data Loss

1. Open the C:\Data\Finance folder.

2. Open the file Current.txt. Make some changes to the file. Save and close the file.

3. Open the Budget.txt file. Make some changes, save, and close the file.

4. Delete the Historical.txt and Projections.txt files.

Exercise 2: Plan the Recovery

Review the backup strategy you developed in the Case Scenario Exercise: a normal backup every Sunday night and a differential backup every weeknight.

How will you recover the missing data?

A normal backup includes all selected files. It is the baseline from which you begin to recover from data loss. The differential backup includes all files that have changed since the normal backup. After you have restored the normal backup, you can restore the most recent differential backup. Keep in mind, however, that some of the files (Budget and Current) have been changed by users subsequent to the overnight differential backup.

How will you prevent those newer files from being overwritten by files in the backup set?

The Options dialog box in the Backup Utility includes a Restore tab, which allows you to specify how files in the backup set are written to the destination. You can direct the Backup Utility to overwrite files only if the files on the disk are older than the files in the backup set. Files that are newer will remain.

Exercise 3: Recover the Data

1. Open the Backup Utility.

2. Choose the Options command from the Tools menu.

3. Click the Restore tab.

4. Configure restore to leave newer files untouched by selecting Replace The File On Disk Only If The File On Disk Is Older, and then click OK.

5. Select the backup media that contains your normal and differential backup.

6. Restore the normal backup to its original location.

7. Restore the differential backup to its original location.

8. Open the Current and Budget files. Because these files were newer than those on the backup set and because of the restore options you configured, they should include the changes you made in the Case Scenario Exercise.

Chapter Summary

- You must have the right to back up and restore files to use the Backup Utility or any other backup tool. The right is assigned, by default, to the Backup Operators and Administrators groups.

- The Backup Utility (Ntbackup.exe) allows you to back up and restore data from local and remote folders to local files, tape drives, removable media, or shared folders on remote servers. You cannot back up to writable CD or DVD formats.

- A backup strategy typically begins with a normal backup followed by regular incremental or differential backups. Incremental jobs create the backup more quickly; differential backups are faster to restore. Jobs can be scheduled to occur during periods of low utilization.

- Copy backups and daily backups can be used to capture files without interfering with the regular backup schedule.

- The Backup Utility will also allow you to restore backed-up data to the original location or to an alternate location. The latter is useful to test and verify restore procedures. You can control, through the Restore tab in the Options dialog box, which files are replaced during a restore.

- The Ntbackup command and its full complement of switches allows you to launch a backup job from a command prompt or batch file.

- Volume Shadow Copy Service (VSS) allows a user to access previous versions of files and folders in network shares. With those previous versions, users can restore deleted or damaged files or compare versions of files.

Exam Highlights

Before taking the exam, review the following key points and terms to help you identify topics you need to review. Return to the lessons for additional practice, and review the "Further Readings" sections in Part 2 for pointers to more information about topics covered by the exam objectives.

Key Points

■ Identify the group memberships or rights required to perform a backup or restore operation.

■ Create a backup strategy based on requirements, including the amount of time it takes to backup data and the speed with which restores must be performed.

■ Understand how to restore data under a variety of conditions, including complete and partial data loss. Compare the data loss to the backup schedule to identify the backup sets that must be restored. Integrate your knowledge of the order in which backup sets should be restored and how existing files on the hard drive should be replaced.

■ Schedule a backup job, and configure backup options.

■ Enable shadow copies of shared folders, and recover data using the Previous Versions tab of a file or folder's Properties dialog box.

■ The System State can be backed up using the Backup Utility or a command prompt, but it must be backed up locally. You cannot back up the System State on a remote machine. However, you can back up the local System State to a file on a remote machine, which can then transfer that file to another backup medium.

■ To restore the System State on a domain controller, you must restart the domain controller in Directory Services Restore Mode. The System State includes Active Directory. By restoring the domain controller's System State, you are performing a nonauthoritative restore, and the domain controller will use standard replication mechanisms to bring itself back up to date. If you want to replicate objects from the restored data to other domain controllers, you must use Ntdsutil to perform an authoritative restore before restoring the domain controller to normal operation.

■ Automated System Recovery relies on a catalog of system files stored on the ASR floppy disk to restore files from the Windows Server 2003 CD-ROM, and a comprehensive ASR backup. You prepare the ASR backup set and floppy disk by using the ASR Wizard in the Backup Utility. To perform an Automated System Recovery, restart with the Windows Server 2003 CD and press F2 when prompted.

■ The Recovery Console allows you to perform targeted repairs for certain causes of system failure. You can replace system files and disable problematic drivers or services. You can also perform a subset of other system maintenance tasks. The Recovery Console can be launched from the Windows Server 2003 CD or by installing the console on the server's hard drive using the **winnt32 /cmdcons** command.

Key Terms

Copy, daily, differential, incremental, and normal backup   These five backup types select files to back up using specific criteria. *Copy* and *normal* back up all files; *daily* backs up files that have been modified on a specified date; *differential* and *incremental* back up files with their archive attribute set. *Normal* and *incremental* backups also reset the archive attribute.

Archive attribute   An attribute that is set when a file is created or modified. Incremental and differential backups will back up files with their archive attribute set. Incremental backups also clear the archive attribute.

Volume Shadow Copy Service (VSS)   A feature of Windows Server 2003 that allows you to back up files that are locked or open.

Media pools: unrecognized, import, free, backup   The four categories of removable media. The Backup Utility will back up to media in the free and backup media pools only.

Shadow Copies of Shared Folders   A feature of Windows Server 2003 that, once configured on the server and on clients, allows users to retrieve previous versions of files without administrator intervention.

System State   A collection of critical system components, including the registry, COM+ Class Registration Database, and startup files. The System State components can be backed up using the Backup Utility or the Ntbackup command. You cannot back up the components separately.

Automated System Recovery (ASR)   A new feature that replaces the Emergency Repair process in earlier versions of Windows. Automated System Recovery returns a system to operation by reinstalling the operating system and restoring System State from an ASR backup set.

Recovery Console   A utility that provides command-line access to system files and a subset of commands to perform surgical repairs on a failed system.

Questions and Answers

Page
13-11

Lesson 1 Review

1. Which of the following locations are *not* allowed to be used for a backup of a Windows Server 2003 system? (Choose all that apply.)

    a. Local tape drive

    b. Local CD-RW

    c. Local hard drive

    d. Shared folder on a remote server

    e. Local DVD+R

    f. Local removable drive

    g. Tape drive on a remote server

    b, e, and g

2. You are to back up a Windows Server 2003 file server every evening. You perform a manual, normal backup. You will then schedule a backup job to run every evening for the next two weeks. Which backup type will complete the fastest?

    a. Normal

    b. Differential

    c. Incremental

    d. Copy

    c

3. You are to back up a Windows Server 2003 file server every evening. You perform a manual, normal backup. You will then schedule a backup job to run every evening for the next two weeks. Which backup type will provide the simplest recovery of lost data?

    a. Normal

    b. Differential

    c. Incremental

    d. Daily

    a

4. You are to back up a Windows Server 2003 file server every evening. You perform a normal backup. On the second evening, you consider whether to use incremental or differential backup. Will there be any difference in the speed or size of those two backup jobs? If the server were to fail the following day, would there be any difference in the efficiency of recovery?

On the second evening, you could use either backup type. The normal backup cleared the archive attribute. Both incremental and differential backups will, on the second evening, transfer all files created or changed on the second day. There will be no difference in the contents of the two jobs. Therefore, there will be no difference in recovery on the third day: you would have to restore the normal backup, and then the backup from the second evening.

However, incremental and differential backups treat the archive attribute on backed-up files differently: incremental turns off the attribute; differential leaves it on. So on the *next* backup, there starts to be a difference. A second incremental backup will transfer only files created or changed since the first incremental backup. However, a second differential backup will include all files created or changed since the normal backup—that is, it will include all files already copied by the first differential backup.

5. Review the steps taken during the practice. Predict the contents of the following backup jobs:

   ❑ backup-normal.bkf

   ❑ backup-diff-day1.bkf

   ❑ backup-diff-day2.bkf

   ❑ backup-inc-day2.bkf

   ❑ backup-inc-day3.bkf

Are there any differences between the contents of backup-diff-day2 and backup-inc-day2?

   ❑ backup-normal.bkf: Historical, Current, Budget and Projections

   ❑ backup-diff-day1.bkf: Current

   ❑ backup-diff-day2.bkf: Current and Budget

   ❑ backup-inc-day2.bkf: Current and Budget

   ❑ backup-inc-day3.bkf: Projections

There are no differences between backup-diff-day2 and backup-inc-day2. Both backup types will back up data that has the archive attribute set. Because a normal backup was performed on the first day, all files that have changed since the first day will have the archive attribute set.

Lesson 2 Review

1. A user has accidentally deleted the data in a Microsoft Word document and saved the document, thereby permanently altering the original file. A normal backup operation was performed on the server the previous evening. Which restore option should you select?

   a. Do not replace the file on my computer.

   b. Replace the file on disk only if the file on disk is older.

   c. Always replace the file on my computer.

   The correct answer is c. The file does exist on the server, but the file has been corrupted. You should replace the file with the copy in the backup set.

2. An executive has returned from a business trip. Before the trip, she copied files from a network folder to her hard drive. The folder is shared with other executives, who modified their files in the folder while she was away. When she returned, she moved her copy of the files to the network share, thereby updating her files with the changes she made while away, but also overwriting all the files that had been changed by other executives. The other executives are unhappy that their files have been replaced with the versions that were active when she left for her trip. Luckily, you performed a normal backup operation on the folder the previous evening. What restore option should you choose?

   a. Do not replace the file on my computer.

   b. Replace the file on disk only if the file on disk is older.

   c. Always replace the file on my computer.

   The correct answer is b. This option will not overwrite files that were changed by the executive while she was away. Those files will have a date more recent than the backup. It will, however, restore the other executives' files over the older versions she uploaded to the network.

3. You would like to test the restore procedures on your server, but would also like to avoid affecting the production copies of the backed-up data. What is the best restore location to use?

   a. Original location

   b. Alternate location

   c. Single folder

   The correct answer is b. Restoring to an alternate location will restore the folder structure and files that were backed up. You can then compare the contents of the target location with the original backed-up files to verify the success of the restore procedure.

Lesson 3 Review

1. Scott Bishop is a power user at a remote site that includes 20 users. The site has a Windows Server 2003 system providing file and print servers. A tape drive is installed on the system. Because there is no local, full-time administrator at the site, you want to allow Scott to back up and restore the server. However, you want to minimize the power and the privileges that Scott obtains, limiting his capabilities strictly to backup and restore. What is the best practice to provide Scott the minimum necessary credentials to achieve his task?

   Make Scott a member of the Backup Operators group. The Backup Operators group is assigned, by default, the privilege to back up and restore files and folders.

2. Write the command that will allow you to fully back up the C:\Data\Finance folder to a file called Backup.bkf in a share named Backup on Server02, with the backup job name "Backup of Finance Folder." Then, write the command that will allow you to perform an incremental backup and append the backup set to the same file, with the same backup job name.

   ```
   ntbackup backup "c:\data\finance" /J "Backup of Finance Folder"
   /F "\\server02\backup\backup.bkf"
   ntbackup backup "c:\data\finance" /J "Backup of Finance Folder"
   /F "\\server01\backup\backup.bkf" /a /m incremental
   ```

3. A user has deleted a file in a shared folder on a server. The user opens the properties of the folder and does not see a Previous Versions tab. Which of the following might be true? (Choose all that apply.)

   a. The folder is not enabled for Shadow Copy.

   b. The volume on the server is not enabled for Shadow Copy.

   c. The user doesn't have permission to view the Shadow Copy cache.

   d. The Shadow Copy Client is not installed on the user's machine.

   e. The folder is on a FAT volume.

   The correct answers are b, d, and e. Shadow Copy is enabled per volume, not per folder. Once Shadow Copy is enabled, any user with the client installed will see a Previous Versions tab for a file or folder that has changed. Shadow Copy is supported only on NTFS volumes.

Page
13-50
Lesson 4 Review

1. You're setting up a backup job on a computer running Windows Server 2003. Your want to back up the registry, startup files, and the COM+ Class Registration database. Which backup option should you select?

    a. *%Windir%*

    b. *%Systemroot%*

    c. System State

    d. None of the above. You cannot back up the registry.

    c

2. You install a scanner on a computer running Windows Server 2003. When you try to restart your computer, the operating system will not start. Which of the following would be the least invasive recovery method to try first to restore the system to operation?

    a. Automated System Recovery

    b. Recovery Console

    c. Safe Mode

    d. Directory Services Restore Mode

    c

3. A hard disk on a server running Windows Server 2003 has failed. You replace the disk, boot the system, initialize the disk, and create an NTFS volume on the new disk. You now want to restore that data from the last backup job from the old disk. How should you restore the data?

    a. Use the Recovery Console to copy data to the disk.

    b. Use the Backup Utility to launch the Restore Wizard.

    c. Use the ASR backup to restore the data.

    d. Use the Last Known Good Configuration option in Safe Mode to set up the new disk.

    b

4. A file server on your network will not start. After exhausting all other options, you have decided to use Automated System Recovery (ASR) to recover the system. You created an ASR backup immediately after you installed Windows Server 2003 and another one two months ago after you installed a device driver. You perform a full backup of data files once a week. What will ASR restore? (Choose all that apply.)

   a. Data files two months ago

   b. Data files at the last full backup

   c. Disk configuration

   d. Operating system

   e. System State two months ago

   f. System State at the last full backup

   c, d, and e

Page
13-52

Case Scenario Exercise

1. With the knowledge that so many files change almost daily and that recovery must be as quick as possible, what type of backup job should you consider running nightly?

   Consider normal backups. There is so much change happening to the shared folder that you are receiving less than a 50 percent benefit using a differential or incremental backup versus a normal backup; and nothing is faster to restore than a normal backup because the backup set contains all the files to restore.

2. You configure a normal daily backup job to run at 12:00 midnight, after the last shift has gone home for the evening. Unfortunately, you find that the backup job is not completed by 4:00 A.M. when the morning shift arrives. How should you modify your backup strategy?

   Create a normal backup once a week, perhaps on Sunday, and then create differential backups nightly during the week. While differential and incremental backups are both available, differential backups provide faster restore capability, as the most recent differential backup set includes all files that have been updated since the normal backup.

14 Clustering Servers

Exam Objectives in this Chapter:

- Plan services for high availability (Exam 70-296).
    - ❏ Plan a high-availability solution that uses clustering services.
    - ❏ Plan a high-availability solution that uses Network Load Balancing.

Why This Chapter Matters

As organizations are becoming increasingly dependent on their computer networks, clustering is becoming an increasingly important element of those networks. Many businesses now rely on the World Wide Web for all their contact with customers, including order taking and other revenue-producing tasks. If the Web servers go down, business stops. Understanding how clustering works, and how Microsoft Windows Server 2003 supports clustering, is becoming an important element of the network administrator's job.

Lessons in this Chapter:

Before You Begin

To perform the practices related to the objectives in this chapter, you must have

- One Windows Server 2003 (Standard, Enterprise, or Datacenter Edition) system. To perform the practice in Lesson 3, you must have the Enterprise Edition or Datacenter Edition.

- Access to the server with administrative credentials.

Lesson 1: Understanding Clustering

A cluster is a group of two or more servers dedicated to running a specific application (or applications) and connected to provide fault tolerance and load balancing. Clustering is intended for organizations running applications that must be always available, making any server downtime unacceptable. In a server cluster, each computer is running the same critical applications so that if one server fails, the others detect the failure and take over at a moment's notice. This is called *failover*. When the failed node returns to service, the other nodes take notice and the cluster begins to use the recovered node again. This is called *failback*. Clustering capabilities are installed automatically in the Windows Server 2003 operating system. In Microsoft Windows 2000 Server, you had to install Microsoft Clustering Service as a separate module.

> **After this lesson, you will be able to**
> - List the types of server clusters
> - Estimate your organization's availability requirements
> - Determine which type of cluster to use for your applications
> - Describe the clustering capabilities of the Windows Server 2003 operating systems
>
> **Estimated lesson time: 30 minutes**

Clustering Types

Windows Server 2003 supports two types of clustering: *server clusters* and *Network Load Balancing (NLB)*. The difference between the two types of clustering is based on the types of applications the servers must run and the nature of the data they use.

> **Important**   Server clustering is intended to provide high availability for applications, not data. Do not mistake server clustering for an alternative to data availability technologies, such as RAID (redundant array of independent disks) and regular system backups.

Server Clusters

Server clusters are designed for applications that have long-running in-memory states or large, frequently changing data sets. These are called *stateful applications*, and they include database servers such as Microsoft SQL Server, e-mail and messaging servers such as Microsoft Exchange, and file and print services. In a server cluster, all the computers (referred to as *nodes*) are connected to a common data set, such as a shared SCSI bus or a storage area network. Because all the nodes have access to the same application data, any one of them can process a request from a client at any time. You configure each node in a server cluster to be either active or passive. An *active node* receives and processes requests from clients, while a *passive node* remains idle and functions as a fallback, should an active node fail.

For example, a simple server cluster might consist of two computers running both Windows Server 2003 and SQL Server and that are connected to the same Network-Attached Storage (NAS) device, which contains the database files. (See Figure 14-1.) One of the computers is an active node, and one is a passive node. Most of the time, the active node is functioning normally, running the database server application, receiving requests from database clients, and accessing the database files on the NAS device. However, if the active node should suddenly fail, for whatever reason, the passive node detects the failure, immediately goes active, and begins processing the client requests, using the same database files on the NAS device.

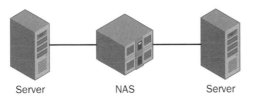

Server   NAS   Server

Figure 14-1   A simple two-node server cluster

> **See Also**   The obvious disadvantage of this two-node, active/passive design is that one of the servers is being wasted most of the time, doing nothing but functioning as a passive standby machine. Depending on the capabilities of the application, you can also design a server cluster with multiple active nodes that share the processing tasks among themselves. You learn more about designing a server cluster later in this lesson.

A server cluster has its own name and Internet Protocol (IP) address, separate from those of the individual computers in the cluster. Therefore, when a server failure occurs, there is no apparent change in functionality to the clients, which continue to send their requests to the same destination. The passive node takes over the active role almost instantaneously, so there is no appreciable delay in performance. The server cluster ensures that the application is both highly available and highly reliable because, despite a failure of one of the servers in the cluster, clients experience few, if any, unscheduled application outages.

Windows Server 2003, Enterprise Edition, and Windows Server 2003, Datacenter Edition, both support server clusters consisting of up to eight nodes. This is an increase over the Windows 2000 operating system, which supports only two nodes in the Advanced Server product and four nodes in the Datacenter Server product. Neither Windows Server 2003, Standard Edition, nor Windows 2000 Server supports server clusters at all.

> **Planning** Although Windows Server 2003, Enterprise Edition, and Windows Server 2003, Datacenter Edition, both support server clustering, you cannot create a cluster with computers running both versions of the operating system. All your cluster nodes must be running either Enterprise Edition or Datacenter Edition. You can, however, run Windows 2000 Server in a Windows Server 2003, Enterprise Edition, or Windows Server 2003, Datacenter Edition, cluster.

Network Load Balancing

Network Load Balancing (NLB) is another type of clustering that provides high availability and high reliability, with the addition of high scalability as well. NLB is intended for applications with relatively small data sets that rarely change (or which might even be read-only) and that do not have long-running in-memory states. These are called *stateless applications*, and they typically include Web, File Transfer Protocol (FTP), and virtual private network (VPN) servers. Every client request to a stateless application is a separate transaction, so it is possible to distribute the requests among multiple servers to balance the processing load.

Instead of being connected to a single data source, as in a server cluster, the servers in an NLB cluster all have identical cloned data sets and are all active nodes. (See Figure 14-2.) The clustering software distributes incoming client requests among the nodes, each of which processes its requests independently, using its own local data. If one or more of the nodes should fail, the others take up the slack by processing some of the requests to the failed server.

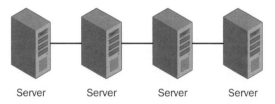

Server   Server   Server   Server

Figure 14-2 A Network Load Balancing cluster

Network Load Balancing and Replication

Network Load Balancing is clearly not suitable for stateful applications such as database and e-mail servers, because the cluster nodes do not share the same data. If one server in an NLB cluster were to receive a new record to add to the database, the other servers would not have access to that record until the next database replication. It is possible to replicate data between the servers in an NLB cluster, for example, to prevent administrators from having to copy modified Web pages to each server individually. However, this replication is an occasional event, not an ongoing occurrence.

Network Load Balancing provides scalability in addition to availability and reliability because all you have to do when traffic increases is add more servers to the cluster. Each server then has to process a smaller number of incoming requests. Windows Server 2003, Web Edition, Windows Server 2003, Standard Edition, Windows Server 2003, Enterprise Edition, and Windows Server 2003, Datacenter Edition, all support NLB clusters of up to 32 computers.

Off the Record   There is also a third type of clustering, known as *component load balancing (CLB)*, designed for middle-tier applications based on Component Object Model (COM+) programming components. Balancing COM+ components among multiple nodes provides many of the same availability and scalability benefits as Network Load Balancing. The Windows Server 2003 operating systems do not include support for CLB clustering, but it is included in the Microsoft Windows 2000 Application Center product.

Exam Tip   Be sure you understand the differences between a server cluster and a Network Load Balancing cluster, including the hardware requirements, the difference between stateful and stateless applications, and the types of clusters supported by the various versions of Windows Server 2003.

Designing a Clustering Solution

The first thing to decide when you are considering a clustering solution for your network is just what you expect to realize from the cluster—in other words, know just how much availability, reliability, or scalability you need. For some organizations, high availability means that any downtime at all is unacceptable, and clustering can provide a solution that protects against three different types of failures:

- **Software failures**   Many types of software failure can prevent a critical application from running properly. The application itself could malfunction, another piece of software on the computer could interfere with the application, or the operating system could have problems, causing all the running applications to falter. Software failures can result from applying upgrades, from conflicts with newly installed programs, or from the introduction of viruses or other types of malicious code. As long as system administrators observe basic precautions (such as not installing software updates on all the servers in a cluster simultaneously), a cluster can keep an application available to users despite software failures.

- **Hardware failures**   Hard drives, cooling fans, power supplies, and other hardware components all have limited life spans, and a cluster enables critical applications to continue running despite the occurrence of a hardware failure in one of the servers. Clustering also makes it possible for administrators to perform hardware maintenance tasks on a server without having to bring down a vital application.

- **Site failures**   In a geographically dispersed cluster, the servers are in different buildings or different cities. Apart from making vital applications locally available to users at various locations, a multisite cluster enables the applications to continue running even if a fire or natural disaster shuts down an entire site.

Estimating Availability Requirements

The degree of availability you require depends on a variety of factors, including the nature of the applications you are running; the size, location, and distribution of your user base; and the role of the applications in your organization. In some cases, having applications available at all times is a convenience; in other cases, it is a necessity. The amount of availability an organization requires for its applications can affect its clustering configuration in several ways, including the type of clustering you use, the number of servers in the cluster, the distribution of applications across the servers in the cluster, and the locations of the servers.

Real World   **High Availability Requirements**

The technical support department of a software company might need the company's customer database available to be fully productive, but it can conceivably function without it for a time. For a company that sells its products exclusively through an e-commerce Web site, however, Web server downtime means no incoming orders and therefore no income. For a hospital or police department, nonfunctioning servers can literally be a matter of life and death. Each of these organizations might be running similar applications and servicing a similar number of clients, but their availability requirements are quite different, and so should their clustering solutions be.

Availability is sometimes quantified in the form of a percentage reflecting the amount of time that an application is up and running. For example, 99% availability means that an application can be unavailable for up to 87.6 hours during a year. An application that is 99.9% available can be down for no more than 8.76 hours a year.

Achieving a specific level of availability often involves more than just implementing a clustering solution. You might also have to install fault-tolerant hardware, create an extensive hardware and software evaluation and testing plan, and establish operational policies for the entire IT department. As availability requirements increase, the amount of time, money, and effort needed to achieve them grows exponentially. You might find that achieving 95% to 99% reliability is relatively easy, but pushing reliability to 99.9% becomes very expensive indeed.

Scaling Clusters

Both server clusters and Network Load Balancing are scalable clustering solutions, meaning that you can improve the performance of the cluster as the needs of your organization grow. The two basic methods of increasing cluster performance are as follows:

- **Scaling Up**   Improving individual server performance by modifying the computer's hardware configuration. Adding random access memory (RAM) or level 2 (L2) cache memory, upgrading to faster processors, and installing additional processors are all ways to scale up a computer. Improving server performance in this way is independent of the clustering solution you use. However, you do have to consider the individual performance capabilities of each server in the cluster. For example, scaling up only the active nodes in a server cluster might establish a level of performance that the passive nodes cannot meet when they are called on to replace the active nodes. It might be necessary to scale up all the servers in the cluster to the same degree to provide optimum performance levels under all circumstances.

- **Scaling Out**   Adding servers to an existing cluster. When you distribute the processing load for an application among multiple servers, adding more servers reduces the burden on each individual computer. Both server clusters and NLB clusters can be scaled out, but it is easier to add servers to an NLB cluster.

In Network Load Balancing, each server has its own independent data store containing the applications and the data they supply to clients. Scaling out the cluster is simply a matter of connecting a new server to the network and cloning the applications and data. Once you have added the new server to the cluster, NLB assigns it an equal share of the processing load.

Scaling out a server cluster is more complicated because the servers in the cluster must all have access to a common data store. Depending on the hardware configuration you use, scaling out might be extremely expensive or even impossible. If you anticipate the need for scaling out your server cluster sometime in the future, be sure to consider this when designing its hardware configuration.

Real World   **Scalability in the Real World**

Be sure to remember that the scalability of your cluster is also limited by the capabilities of the operating system you are using. The maximum numbers of nodes supported by the Windows operating systems when scaling out a cluster are shown in Table 14-1.

Table 14-1 Number of Nodes Supported When Scaling Out a Cluster

Operating System	Network Load Balancing	Server Clusters
Windows Server 2003, Web Edition	32	Not Supported
Windows Server 2003, Standard Edition	32	Not Supported
Windows Server 2003, Enterprise Edition	32	8
Windows Server 2003, Datacenter Edition	32	8
Windows 2000 Advanced Server	32	2
Windows 2000 Datacenter Server	32	4

Table 14-2 shows the operating system limitations when scaling up a cluster.

Table 14-2 System Limitations When Scaling Up a Cluster

Operating System	Maximum Number of Processors	Maximum RAM
Windows Server 2003, Web Edition	2	2 GB
Windows Server 2003, Standard Edition	4	4 GB
Windows Server 2003, Enterprise Edition	8	32 GB (for x86-based computers), 64 GB (for Itanium-based computers)
Windows Server 2003, Datacenter Edition	64 (minimum 8-way capable machine required)	64 GB (for x86-based computers), 512 GB (for Itanium-based computers)
Windows 2000 Advanced Server	8	8 GB
Windows 2000 Datacenter Server	32	64 GB

How Many Clusters?

If you want to deploy more than one application with high availability, you must decide how many clusters you want to use. The servers in a cluster can run multiple applications, of course, so you can combine multiple applications in a single cluster deployment, or you can create a separate cluster for each application. In some cases, you can even combine the two approaches.

For example, if you have two stateful applications that you want to deploy using server clusters, the simplest method would be to create a single cluster and install both applications on every computer in the cluster, as shown in Figure 14-3. In this arrangement, a single server failure affects both applications, and the remaining servers must be capable of providing adequate performance for both applications by themselves.

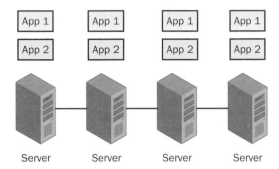

Figure 14-3   A cluster with two applications running on each server

Another method is to create a separate cluster for each application, as shown in Figure 14-4. In this model, each cluster operates independently, and a failure of one server only affects one of the applications. In addition, the remaining servers in the affected cluster only have to take on the burden of one application. Creating separate clusters provides higher availability for the applications, but it can also be an expensive solution because it requires more servers than the first method.

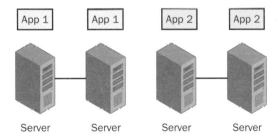

Figure 14-4   Two separate clusters running two different applications

You can also compromise between these two approaches by creating a single cluster, installing each application on a separate active node, and using one passive node as the backup for both applications, as shown in Figure 14-5. In this arrangement, a single server failure causes the passive node to take on the burden of running only one of the applications. Only if both active nodes fail would the passive node have to take on the full responsibility of running both applications. It is up to you to evaluate the odds of such an occurrence and to decide whether your organization's availability requirements call for a passive node server with the capability of running both applications at full performance levels, or whether a passive node scaled to run only one of the applications is sufficient.

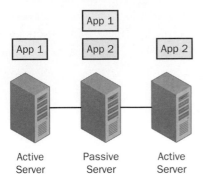

Figure 14-5   Two active nodes sharing a single passive node

Combining Clustering Technologies

The decision to use server clustering or Network Load Balancing on your clusters is usually determined by the applications you intend to run. However, in some cases it might be best to deploy clusters of different types together to create a comprehensive high-availability solution.

The most common example of this approach is an e-commerce Web site that enables Internet users to place orders for products. This type of site requires Web servers (which are stateless applications) to run the actual site and (stateful) database servers to store customer, product, and order entry information. In this case, you can build an NLB cluster to host the Web servers and a server cluster for the database servers, as shown in Figure 14-6. The two clusters interface just as though the applications were running on individual servers.

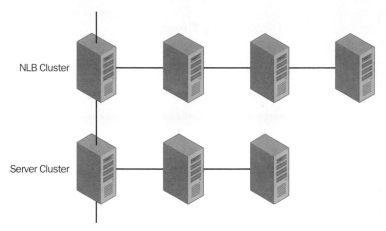

Figure 14-6   An NLB cluster interacting with a server cluster

Dispersing Clusters

Deploying geographically dispersed clusters enables applications to remain available in the event of a catastrophe that destroys a building or even a city. Having cluster servers at different sites can also enable users to access applications locally, rather than having to communicate with a distant server over a relatively slow wide area network (WAN) connection.

Geographically dispersed server clusters can be extremely complex affairs: in addition to the regular network, you have to construct a long-distance storage area network (SAN) that gives the cluster servers access to the shared application data. This usually means that you have to combine privately owned hardware and software products with WAN links for the SAN supplied by a third-party service provider.

Geographically dispersing Network Load Balancing clusters is much easier because there is no shared data store. However, in most cases, an NLB cluster that is dispersed among multiple sites is not actually a single cluster at all. Instead of installing multiple servers at various locations and connecting them all into a single cluster, you can create a separate cluster at each location and use another technique to distribute the application load among the clusters. This is possible with stateless applications. In the case of a geographically dispersed cluster of Web or other Internet servers, the most common solution is to create a separate NLB cluster at each site, and then use the Domain Name System (DNS) round robin technique to distribute client requests evenly among the clusters.

> ## Dispersing Network Load Balancing Clusters
>
> Normally, DNS servers contain resource records that associate a single host name with a single IP address. For example, when clients try to connect to an Internet Web server named www.contoso.com, the clients' DNS servers always supply the same IP address for that name. When the www.contoso.com Web site is actually a Network Load Balancing cluster, there is still only one name and one IP address, and it is up to the clustering software to distribute the incoming requests among the servers in the cluster. In a typical geographically dispersed NLB cluster, each site has an independent cluster with its own separate IP address. The DNS server for the contoso.com domain associates all the cluster addresses with the single www.contoso.com host name, and it supplies the addresses to incoming client requests in a round robin fashion. The DNS server thus distributes the requests among the clusters, and the clustering software distributes the requests for the cluster among the servers in that cluster.

Lesson Review

The following questions are intended to reinforce key information presented in this lesson. If you are unable to answer a question, review the lesson materials and try the question again. You can find answers to the questions in the "Questions and Answers" section at the end of this chapter.

Specify whether each of the following is a characteristic of server clusters, CLB clusters, or NLB clusters.

1. Used for database server clusters

_____

2. Supports clusters of up to 8 nodes in Windows Server 2003, Datacenter Edition

_____

3. Supported by Windows Server 2003, Standard Edition

_____

4. Makes stateless applications highly available

_____

5. Used for applications with frequently changing data

_____

6. Used for Web server clusters

_____

7. Not supported by Windows Server 2003, Enterprise Edition

_____

8. Requires a shared data store

_____

9. Makes stateful applications highly available

_____

10. Used for read-only applications

_____

11. Used for COM+ applications

_____

12. Supports clusters of up to 32 nodes in Windows Server 2003

_____

Lesson Summary

- A cluster is a group of servers that appears to users as a single resource, and which provides high availability, reliability, and scalability for specific applications.

- A server cluster is a group of servers running a stateful application, such as a database server, and sharing a common data store. Servers in this type of cluster can be configured as active or passive nodes.

- A Network Load Balancing cluster is a group of servers running a stateless application, such as a Web server, each of which has an identical, independent data store.

- Scaling out is the process of adding more servers to an existing cluster, while scaling up is the process of upgrading the hardware of servers already in a cluster.

- Geographically dispersed clusters have servers in different locations. If the cluster is a server cluster, it requires a long-distance storage area network to provide the common data store. NLB typically uses separate clusters at each location, with a technique like DNS round robin to distribute client requests among the clusters.

Lesson 2: Using Network Load Balancing

Of the two types of clusters supported by Windows Server 2003, Network Load Balanc-ing is the easier one to install, configure, and maintain. You can use the existing hard-ware and applications in your computers, and there is no additional software to install. You use the Network Load Balancing Manager application in Windows Server 2003 to create, manage, and monitor NLB clusters.

After this lesson, you will be able to

- Describe how Network Load Balancing works
- Understand the differences among the four NLB operational modes
- List the steps involved in deploying an NLB cluster
- Monitor NLB using Windows Server 2003 tools

Estimated lesson time: 30 minutes

Understanding Network Load Balancing

A Network Load Balancing cluster consists of up to 32 servers, referred to as hosts, each of which is running a duplicate copy of the application you want the cluster to provide to clients. Network Load Balancing works by creating on each host a *virtual network adapter* that represents the cluster as a single entity. The virtual network adapter has its own IP and media access control (MAC) addresses, independent of the addresses assigned to the physical network interface adapters in the computers. Clients address their application requests to the cluster IP address instead of to an individual server's IP address.

Off the Record   In an Ethernet or Token Ring network interface adapter, the MAC address, also known as the adapter's hardware address, is a unique six-byte hexadecimal value hard-coded into the adapter by the manufacturer. Three bytes of the address contain a code identi-fying the manufacturer, and three bytes identify the adapter itself.

NLB Clustering and DNS

Directing clients to the IP address of the cluster is a task left to the name resolution mechanism that provides clients with IP addresses. For example, if you are currently running an individual Web server on the Internet, the DNS server hosting your domain has a record associating your Web server's name with the Web server computer's IP address. If you change from the single Web server to a Network Load Balancing cluster to host your Web site, you must modify the DNS resource record for the Web site's name so that it supplies clients with the cluster IP address, not your original Web server's IP address.

When an incoming client request addressed to the cluster IP address arrives, all the hosts in the cluster receive and process the message. On each host in an NLB cluster, a Network Load Balancing service functions as a filter between the cluster adapter and the computer's TCP/IP stacks. This filter enables NLB to calculate which host in the cluster should be responsible for resolving the request. No communication between the hosts is required for this purpose. Each host performs the same calculations independently and decides whether it should process that request or not. The algorithm the hosts use to perform these calculations changes only when hosts are added or removed from the cluster.

Planning a Network Load Balancing Deployment

Before you deploy a Network Load Balancing cluster, you must create a plan for the network infrastructure that will support your cluster servers. The high availability provided by NLB will do you no good if your users can't access the servers because of a failure in a router, switch, or Internet connection. In addition, because many NLB installations provide Web and other services to Internet users, you must consider the security of your cluster servers and the rest of your internal network.

Important   Deploying a Network Load Balancing cluster is not a task to undertake casually or haphazardly. As with any major network service, the NLB deployment process must be planned carefully, tested thoroughly on a lab network, and then implemented in a pilot program before proceeding with the full production deployment.

Real World   NLB Network Design

For a high-traffic Web site with high-availability requirements, a typical network infrastructure design would consist of a Web server farm located on a perimeter network, as shown in the following figure. The perimeter network has redundant connections to the Internet, preferably with different Internet service providers (ISPs) or with one ISP that has connections to multiple Internet backbones. A firewall at each Internet access router protects the perimeter network from Internet intruders, and another firewall isolates the perimeter network from the internal network.

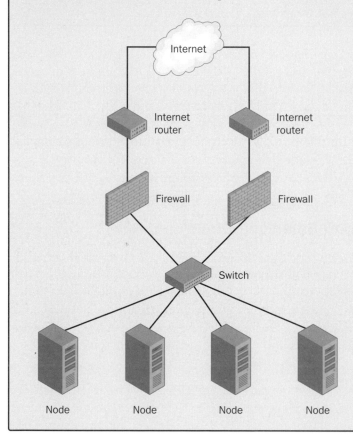

NLB Operational Modes

The servers that are going to be the hosts in your NLB cluster do not require any special hardware. There is no shared data store as in a server cluster, for example, so you do not have to build a storage area network. However, NLB imposes certain limitations on a server with a single network interface adapter in a standard configuration, and in some cases, you can benefit from installing a second network interface adapter in each of your servers.

Windows Server 2003 Network Load Balancing has two operational modes: *unicast mode* and *multicast mode*. In unicast mode, Network Load Balancing replaces the MAC address of the physical network interface adapter in each server with the MAC address of the virtual network adapter representing the cluster. The server does not use the computer's original MAC address at all, effectively transforming the computer's physical network interface adapter into a virtual network adapter. The Address Resolution Protocol (ARP) resolves both of the server's IP addresses (the IP address originally assigned to the network interface adapter and the cluster IP address) to the single MAC address for the cluster.

Off the Record   NLB does not actually modify the MAC address in the network interface adapter itself; the address assigned to the adapter by the manufacturer is permanent and cannot be changed. NLB only replaces the MAC address in the computer's memory, substituting a virtual MAC address for the physical address the system reads from the network adapter card.

NLB and ARP

The ARP is a TCP/IP protocol that resolves IP addresses into MAC or hardware addresses. To transmit to a particular IP address, a TCP/IP computer must first discover the MAC address associated with that IP address so that it can build a data-link layer protocol frame. ARP functions by transmitting a broadcast message containing an IP address to the local network. The computer using that IP address is responsible for replying with a message containing its MAC address.

In the case of an NLB cluster in unicast mode, each server in the cluster replies to ARP requests that contain either its original IP address or the cluster IP address by sending a response containing the cluster MAC address. Therefore, no computer on the network can transmit to the MAC address assigned for the NLB server's physical network interface adapter.

Because the network interface adapters of all the servers in the cluster have the same MAC address, the cluster servers cannot communicate among themselves in the normal way, using their individual MAC addresses. The servers can, however, communicate with other computers on the same subnet, and with computers on other subnets, as long as the IP datagrams don't contain the cluster MAC address.

Note   When you configure the servers in an NLB cluster to use unicast mode with a single network interface adapter, you cannot use the Network Load Balancing Manager application on one of the servers to manage the other servers in the cluster.

In some cases, this is not a problem. Dedicated Web servers hosting the same site, for example, don't often need to communicate with each other under normal conditions. However, if you determine that it is necessary for the servers in your NLB cluster to communicate with each other, there are two possible solutions:

- **Configure the cluster servers to operate in NLB multicast mode**   In multicast mode, NLB assigns a cluster MAC address to the physical network interface adapter, but it also retains the adapter's original MAC address. The cluster IP address resolves to the cluster MAC address, and the server's original IP address resolves to the original MAC address. For this configuration to function properly, the routers on the network must support the use of multicast MAC addresses.

- **Install a second network interface adapter in each server**   One of the network interface adapters becomes the network interface adapter for the cluster, with its original MAC address replaced by the cluster MAC address. Both the cluster IP address and the adapter's original IP address resolve to the cluster MAC address. The system does not use this adapter's original MAC address. Like a single adapter in unicast mode, the cluster adapter cannot communicate with the other servers in the cluster. The second adapter retains its original MAC address and assigned IP address and handles all noncluster network communications.

Tip   In a Windows Server 2003 Network Load Balancing cluster, you must configure all the servers to operate in either unicast or multicast mode. You cannot mix unicast and multicast servers in the same cluster. However, you can mix network interface adapter configurations, installing two network interface adapters in some of a cluster's servers, while leaving a single adapter in others. In the case of a unicast cluster, only the servers with multiple adapters are able to communicate with the other servers.

In summary, a server in an NLB cluster can have either one network interface adapter or multiple adapters, and it can run in either unicast or multicast mode. By combining these options, you can use four possible NLB configurations, each of which has advantages and disadvantages, as shown in Table 14-3.

Table 14-3   NLB Configuration Advantages and Disadvantages

NLB Configuration	Advantages	Disadvantages
Single network interface adapter in unicast mode	■ Requires no special hardware ■ No router incompatibility problems	■ Ordinary communications with other servers in the cluster are not possible. ■ Network performance might degrade when one network interface adapter is handling both ordinary traffic and cluster traffic.
Single network interface adapter in multicast mode	■ Requires no special hardware ■ Permits ordinary communications among cluster servers	■ Some routers do not support multicast MAC addresses. ■ Network performance might degrade when one network interface adapter is handling both ordinary traffic and cluster traffic.
Multiple network interface adapters in unicast mode	■ No router incompatibility problems ■ Permits ordinary communications among cluster servers ■ Network performance enhanced because cluster traffic and ordinary network traffic use different network interface adapters	■ Requires installation of second network interface adapter
Multiple network interface adapters in multicast mode	■ Permits ordinary communications among cluster servers ■ Network performance enhanced because cluster traffic and ordinary network traffic use different network interface adapters	■ Requires installation of second network interface adapter. ■ Some routers do not support multicast MAC addresses.

The most popular configuration for large NLB installations is to install two network interface adapters in each server and run them in unicast mode. This configuration enables the servers to function as normal participants on the network, in addition to performing their NLB server duties. There are also no problems with routers handling multicast MAC addresses and no bottlenecks caused by cluster traffic and ordinary network traffic sharing a single network interface adapter.

NLB Networking

Although the servers in a Network Load Balancing cluster do not share a single data store, as in a server cluster, and perform their own independent calculations to determine which server will service an incoming request, the servers do communicate with each other. The cluster servers must exchange information to know how many servers are in the cluster and to determine when a server has been added or removed from the cluster. This communication enables the cluster to compensate for a failed server and to take advantage of new servers in the cluster by redistributing the traffic load.

Important   A single computer, running Windows Server 2003 cannot be a member of a Network Load Balancing cluster and a server cluster at the same time, because these two clustering solutions use network interface adapters in different ways. If you want to deploy both an NLB cluster and a server cluster on your network, you must use separate servers for each cluster.

The cluster traffic between NLB servers takes the form of a *heartbeat* message that each server transmits once per second to the other servers in the cluster. If one cluster server fails, it stops transmitting its heartbeat messages, and the other servers detect the absence of the heartbeats. Once the other servers in the cluster miss five consecutive heartbeat messages from a server, they begin a process called *convergence*, in which they recalculate their traffic distribution algorithm to compensate for the missing server. In the same way, adding a new server to an NLB cluster introduces a new heartbeat to the network, which triggers a convergence in the other servers, enabling them to redistribute the traffic so that the new server receives an equal share of the load.

Note   Because all the servers in the cluster are using the same cluster MAC address, transmitting the heartbeats is simply a matter of directing the packets to that address. The servers don't need to broadcast the heartbeat messages, reducing the impact of the cluster traffic on the network.

When you deploy NLB cluster servers with a single network interface adapter in each computer, obviously all the cluster-related traffic must travel over the same network as your ordinary traffic. This is usually not a major burden because the heartbeat packets are small, less than 1,500 bytes, and they fit into a single Ethernet packet. If you decide to install multiple network interface adapters in each cluster server, you can connect both adapters to the same local area network (LAN) or construct a separate network for the cluster traffic.

Planning   If your NLB cluster consists of servers that are already isolated on a perimeter network, there is probably no need to create a separate LAN for cluster traffic. However, if you are deploying an NLB cluster on a heavily trafficked internal network, you might benefit from installing a dedicated cluster LAN.

Deploying a Network Load Balancing Cluster

Once you have planned the network infrastructure for your NLB cluster and decided on the operational mode, you can plan the actual deployment process. The basic steps in deploying NLB for a cluster of Web servers on a perimeter network are as follows:

1. Construct the perimeter network on which the Network Load Balancing servers will be located.

   Create a separate LAN on your internetwork, and isolate it from the internal network and from the Internet by using firewalls. Install the hardware needed to give the Web servers Internet access.

2. Install additional network interface adapter cards in the NLB servers if necessary.

   If you intend to use a separate network interface adapter for cluster-related communications, you must first install the second adapter card in the computer. During the Windows Server 2003 installation, you configure the network interface adapter driver for the second card just as you normally would.

3. Install Windows Server 2003 on the NLB servers.

4. Configure the TCP/IP configuration parameters for the network interface adapters on the NLB servers.

   When using two network interface adapters, you must configure them both in the normal manner, using the Internet Protocol (TCP/IP) Properties dialog box and assigning them standard IP addresses and subnet masks, just as you would configure any other computer on the network.

Important   If you are using a second network interface adapter for cluster traffic, at this point do not configure that adapter with the IP address you want to use to represent the cluster. Use a standard IP address for the subnet to which you have connected the adapter. Later, when you create the cluster, you specify the cluster IP address and NLB reconfigures the adapter's TCP/IP configuration parameters.

5. Join the NLB servers to an Active Directory domain created specifically for managing servers on the perimeter network.

6. Install the additional applications required by the NLB servers.

   For Web servers, you must install Internet Information Services (IIS), using the Add Or Remove Programs tool. At this point, you should also install any other applications that the servers need, such as the Microsoft DNS Server service.

7. Create and configure the cluster on the first host server.

   You use the Network Load Balancing Manager (shown in Figure 14-7) to create the new cluster and configure its parameters.

8. Add additional hosts to the cluster.

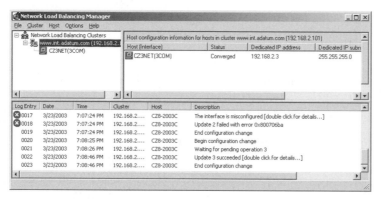

Figure 14-7   Network Load Balancing Manager

Monitoring Network Load Balancing

Once you have created and configured your Network Load Balancing cluster, several tools included in Windows Server 2003 can be used to monitor the cluster's ongoing processes.

Using Network Load Balancing Manager

When you display the Network Load Balancing Manager application, the bottom pane of the window displays the most recent log entries generated by activities in the NLB Manager. (See Figure 14-8.) These entries detail any configuration changes and contain any error messages generated by improper configuration parameters on any host in the cluster.

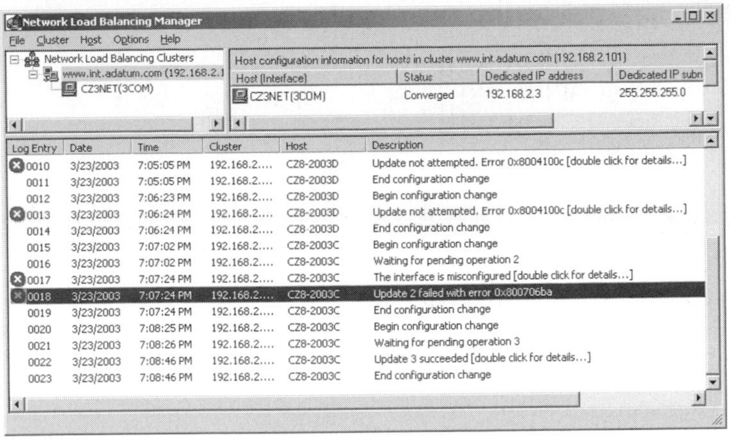

Figure 14-8   The Network Load Balancing Manager's log pane

By default, the log entries that Network Load Balancing Manager displays are not saved. To save a continuing log, you must enable logging by selecting Log Settings from the NLB Manager's Options menu. In the Log Settings dialog box, select the Enable Logging check box, and then, in the Log Filename text box, specify the name you want to use for the log file. The NLB Manager creates the file in the Documents And Settings folder's subfolder named for the account used to log on to the server.

Using Event Viewer

The Network Load Balancing Manager's log pane and log file contain information only about the NLB Manager's activities. To display log information about the Network Load Balancing service, you must look at the System log in the Event Viewer console, as shown in Figure 14-9. Entries concerning the Network Load Balancing service are labeled WLBS. (This stands for Windows Load Balancing Service, a holdover from the Windows NT name for the service.)

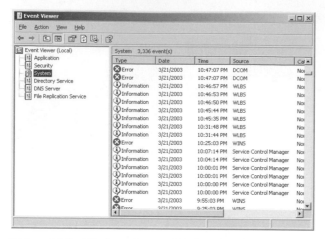

Figure 14-9 Windows Server 2003 Event Viewer

Using Nlb.exe

You can control many of an NLB cluster's functions from the Windows Server 2003 command line using a utility named Nlb.exe. Some of the program's most useful parameters are as follows:

> **Tip** Nlb.exe is the Windows Server 2003 equivalent of the Wlbs.exe program included with earlier versions of the Windows operating system. If you are accustomed to using Wlbs on your command lines, or more importantly, if you have existing scripts that use Wlbs, you can continue to use them because Windows Server 2003 includes the Wlbs.exe program as well.

- **display** Displays the configuration parameters stored in the registry for a specific cluster, plus the most recent cluster-related System log entries, the computer's IP configuration, and the cluster's current status.

- **drain** *port* Prevents a specified cluster from handling any new traffic conforming to the rule containing the port specified by the *port* variable.

- **drainstop** Disables all cluster traffic handling after completing the transactions currently in process.

- **params** Displays all the current configuration parameters for a specified cluster on the local host, as follows:

```
WLBS Cluster Control Utility V2.4 (c) 1997-2003 Microsoft Corporation.
Cluster 192.168.2.101
Retrieving parameters
Current time            = 3/19/2003 1:55:24 AM
HostName                = cz3net.int.adatum.com
ParametersVersion       = 4
CurrentVersion          = 00000204
```

```
EffectiveVersion           = 00000201
InstallDate                = 3E779B7C
HostPriority               = 3
ClusterIPAddress           = 192.168.2.101
ClusterNetworkMask         = 255.255.255.0
DedicatedIPAddress         = 192.168.2.3
DedicatedNetworkMask       = 255.255.255.0
McastIPAddress             = 0.0.0.0
ClusterName                = www.int.adatum.com
ClusterNetworkAddress      = 03-bf-c0-a8-02-65
IPToMACEnable              = ENABLED
MulticastSupportEnable     = ENABLED
IGMPSupport                = DISABLED
MulticastARPEnable         = ENABLED
MaskSourceMAC              = ENABLED
AliveMsgPeriod             = 1000
AliveMsgTolerance          = 5
NumActions                 = 100
NumPackets                 = 200
NumAliveMsgs               = 66
DescriptorsPerAlloc        = 512
MaxDescriptorAllocs        = 512
TCPConnectionTimeout       = 60
IPSecConnectionTimeout     = 86400
FilterICMP                 - DISABLED
ClusterModeOnStart         = STARTED
HostState                  = STARTED
PersistedStates            = NONE
ScaleSingleClient          = DISABLED
NBTSupportEnable           = ENABLED
NetmonAliveMsgs            = DISABLED
IPChangeDelay              = 60000
ConnectionCleanupDelay     = 300000
RemoteControlEnabled       = ENABLED
RemoteControlUDPPort       = 2504
RemoteControlCode          = 00000000
RemoteMaintenanceEnabled   = 00000000
BDATeaming                 = NO
TeamID                     =
Master                     = NO
ReverseHash                = NO
IdentityHeartbeatPeriod    = 10000
IdentityHeartbeatEnabled   = ENABLED


PortRules (1):
      VIP        Start  End  Prot  Mode      Pri Load Affinity
--------------- -----  ----- ----  --------  --- ---- --------
All               80    80   TCP   Multiple      Eql  None


Statistics:
Number of active connections      = 0
Number of descriptors allocated   = 0
```

- **query**   Displays the current state of all hosts in a specified cluster, as follows:

```
WLBS Cluster Control Utility V2.4 (c) 1997-2003 Microsoft Corporation.
Cluster 192.168.2.101
Host 3 has entered a converging state 3 time(s) since joining the cluster
   and the last convergence completed at approximately: 3/19/2003 12:06:20 AM
Host 3 converged with the following host(s) as part of the cluster:
1, 3
```

- **queryport** *port*   Displays the current status of the rule containing the port specified by the *port* variable.

```
WLBS Cluster Control Utility V2.4 (c) 1997-2003 Microsoft Corporation.
Cluster 192.168.2.101
Retrieving state for port rule 80
Rule is enabled
Packets: Accepted=0, Dropped=17
```

Exam Tip   Be sure to understand that the Nlb.exe and Wlbs.exe programs are one and the same, with identical functions and parameters.

Practice: Creating a Network Load Balancing Cluster

In this practice, you configure your Server01 computer to function as an IIS Web server and then create a Network Load Balancing cluster, enabling clients to access the Web server using a cluster name and IP address. For the purposes of this practice, you are going to create a cluster consisting of a single server.

Exercise 1: Installing IIS

In this exercise, you install Internet Information Services on your Server01 computer, and create a simple home page so that your computer can function as a Web server.

Note   If you have already installed Internet Information Services (IIS) in one of the exercises in previous chapters, you can skip to step 9.

1. Log on to Server01 as Administrator.

2. Click Start, point to Control Panel, click Add Or Remove Programs. The Add Or Remove Programs window appears.

3. Click Add/Remove Windows Components. The Windows Components Wizard appears.

4. In the Components list, click the Application Server entry (but do not select its check box) and then click Details. The Application Server dialog box appears.

5. Select the Internet Information Services (IIS) check box, and then click OK.

6. Click Next. The Configuring Components page appears as the wizard installs the new software. Insert your Windows Server 2003 CD if the wizard prompts you to do so.

7. When the Completing The Windows Components Wizard page appears, click Finish.

8. Close the Add Or Remove Programs window.

9. Click Start, point to All Programs, point to Accessories, and then click Notepad. An Untitled – Notepad window opens.

10. In the Untitled – Notepad window, type the following:

```
<html>
<title>Hello, world.</title>
<body>
<h1>Hello, world.</h1>
</body>
</html>
```

This simple Hypertext Markup Language (HTML) script will function as the contents of your newly installed Web server.

11. From the File menu, select Save As. The Save As dialog box appears.

12. Using the Save In drop-down list, browse to the C:\Inetpub\Wwwroot folder and save the file using the name **"default.htm"**—don't forget to surround the name with quotes so that the file is not saved as default.htm.txt.

13. From the File menu, select Open. The Open dialog box appears.

14. Using the Look In drop-down list, browse to the C:\Windows\System32\Drivers\Etc folder and open the file named Hosts. (To open the Hosts file, you might need to select All Files from the Files Of Type drop-down list.)

15. At the end of the Hosts file, add a line like the following:

```
192.168.0.100      www.contoso.com
```

The IP address in this Hosts file entry is the address that you will later use to represent the cluster on the network.

16. From the File menu, select Save.

17. Close Notepad.

Exercise 2: Creating a Network Load Balancing Cluster

In this exercise, you create a new cluster and configure it to balance incoming Web server traffic.

1. Click Start, point to All Programs, point to Administrative Tools, and then click Network Load Balancing Manager. The Network Load Balancing Manager window appears.

2. Click the Network Load Balancing Clusters icon in the left pane and, from the Cluster menu, select New. The Cluster Parameters dialog box appears.

3. In the IP Address text box, type **192.168.0.100**.

   This IP address will represent the entire cluster on the network. Web clients use this address to connect to the Web server cluster.

4. In the Subnet Mask text box, type **255.255.255.0**.

5. In the Full Internet Name text box, type **www.contoso.com**.

   This fully qualified domain name (FQDN) will represent the cluster on the network. Web users type this name in their browsers to access the Web server cluster.

> **Important**   Specifying a name for the cluster in the Cluster Parameters dialog box does not in itself make the cluster available to clients by that name. You must register the name you specify here in a name resolution mechanism. For an Internet Web server cluster, you must create a resource record on the DNS server hosting your domain, associating the name you specified with the cluster IP address you specified. For the purposes of this practice, you added the cluster name and IP address to the Hosts file on the computer in Exercise 1.

6. In the Cluster Operation Mode group box, click the Multicast option. Then click Next. The Cluster IP Addresses dialog box appears.

   Selecting the Multicast option on a computer with a single network interface adapter enables the computer to communicate normally with other hosts in the cluster.

7. Click Next. The Port Rules dialog box appears.

8. Click Edit. The Add/Edit Port Rule dialog box appears.

   A cluster's port rules specify which ports and which protocols the NLB service should monitor for traffic that is to be balanced among the servers in the cluster.

9. In the Port Range box, change the values of both the From and To selectors to 80.

   Port 80 is the well-known port for the Hypertext Transfer Protocol (HTTP), the application layer protocol that Web servers and clients use to communicate. By changing the Port Range values, you configure the NLB service to balance only Web traffic.

10. In the Protocols group box, click the TCP option. Then click OK.

    When defining a port rule, you can specify whether one server or multiple servers should process the traffic for that rule. You can also configure the rule's *affinity*, which specifies whether multiple requests from the same client should be processed by a single server or distributed among multiple servers.

11. In the Port Rules dialog box, click Next. The Connect dialog box appears.

12. In the Host text box, type **Server01** and then click Connect.

    The Host text box specifies the name of the server you want to add to the cluster. You can use Network Load Balancing Manager to create a cluster from any computer on the network running Windows Server 2003.

13. The Connection Status group box reads Connected, and the computer's network interfaces appear in the Interfaces Available For Configuring A New Cluster list.

14. Click Local Area Connection in the Interfaces Available For Configuring A New Cluster list, and then click Next. The Host Parameters dialog box appears.

15. Click Finish. The new cluster appears in the left pane in the Network Load Balancing Clusters list.

16. Close the Network Load Balancing Manager window. If a message box appears indicating that operations are still in progress, click Cancel and wait for the operations to finish.

Tip Optionally, you can add Server02 to the cluster by selecting Add Host from the Cluster menu.

Exercise 3: Testing the Cluster

In this exercise, you connect to the Web server using the NLB cluster IP address to prove that the NLB service is functioning.

1. Open Internet Explorer, and in the Address drop-down list, type **http://192.168.0.100** and then press ENTER. The "Hello, world" page you created earlier appears in the browser.

   This test is successful because the NLB service has created the 192.168.0.100 address you specified for the cluster.

2. Next, type **http://192.168.0.1** in the Address drop-down list, and then press ENTER. The "Hello, world" page appears again.

   This test is successful because you have configured the NLB service to operate in multicast mode. Because of this, the network interface adapter's original IP address, 192.168.0.1, remains active.

3. Now, type **http://www.contoso.com** in the Address drop-down list, and then press ENTER. The "Hello, world" page appears yet again.

   This test is successful because you added the name www.contoso.com to the computer's Hosts file earlier and associated it with the cluster IP address.

4. Close the Internet Explorer window.

Lesson Review

The following questions are intended to reinforce key information presented in this lesson. If you are unable to answer a question, review the lesson materials and try the question again. You can find answers to the questions in the "Questions and Answers" section at the end of this chapter.

1. You are the administrator of a Network Load Balancing cluster consisting of six Web servers running in unicast mode, with a single network interface adapter in each server. You are using the Network Load Balancing Manager application on one of the cluster servers to try to shut down the NLB service on one of the other servers so that you can upgrade its hardware. Why is the Manager not letting you do this?

   _____

   _____

   _____

2. Which of the following Nlb.exe commands do you use to shut down NLB operations on a cluster server without interrupting transactions currently in progress?

   a. Nlb drain

   b. Nlb params

   c. Nlb drainstop

   d. Nlb queryport

3. How long does it take a Network Load Balancing cluster to begin the convergence process after one of the servers in the cluster fails?

   _____

Lesson Summary

- Network Load Balancing works by creating a virtual network adapter with IP and MAC addresses that represent the cluster as a single unit.

- When NLB is running in unicast mode, the service replaces the network interface adapter's MAC address with the cluster MAC address, making ordinary communications between cluster servers impossible.

- When NLB is running in multicast mode, the service uses both the network interface adapter's MAC address and the cluster MAC address, enabling cluster servers to communicate normally.

- Although NLB can function with a single network interface adapter installed in each server, using multiple adapters in each server can prevent network performance degradation.

- NLB cluster servers transmit a heartbeat message once every second. If a server fails to transmit five successive heartbeats, the other servers in the cluster begin the convergence process, redistributing the incoming traffic among the remaining servers.

Lesson 3: Designing a Server Cluster

Server clusters are, by definition, more complicated than Network Load Balancing clusters, both in the way they handle applications and in the way they handle the application data. When designing a server cluster implementation, you still must evaluate your organization's high-availability needs, but you must do so in light of a server cluster's greater deployment cost and greater capabilities.

After this lesson, you will be able to

- List the shared storage hardware configurations supported by Windows Server 2003
- Understand how to partition applications
- Describe the quorum models you can use in a server cluster
- List the steps involved in creating a server cluster
- Describe the different types of failover policies you can use with server clusters

Estimated lesson time: 40 minutes

Designing a Server Cluster Deployment

As you learned in Lesson 1 of this chapter, server clusters are intended to provide advanced failover capabilities for stateful applications, particularly database and e-mail servers. Because the data files maintained by these applications change frequently, it is not practical for individual servers in a cluster to maintain their own individual copies of the data files. If this were the case, the servers would have to immediately propagate changes that clients make to their data files to the other servers, so that the server could present a unified data set to all clients at all times.

As a result, server clusters are based on a shared data storage solution. The cluster stores the files containing the databases or e-mail stores on a drive array (typically using RAID or some other data availability technique) that is connected to all the servers in the cluster. Therefore, all the application's clients, no matter which server in the cluster they connect to, are working with the same data files, as shown in Figure 14-10.

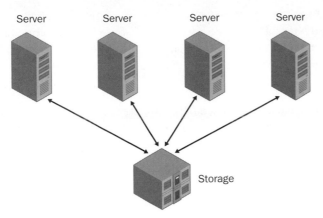

Figure 14-10   Server cluster nodes share application data

The shared data store adds significantly to the cost of building a server cluster, especially if you plan to create a geographically dispersed cluster. Unlike geographically dispersed NLB clusters, which are usually separate clusters unified by an external technology, such as round robin DNS, the hosts in server clusters must be connected to the central data store, even when the servers are in different cities. This means that you must construct a SAN connecting the various sites, as well as a standard WAN. When considering a deployment of this type of cluster, you must decide whether the impact of having your applications offline justifies the expense of building the required hardware infrastructure.

Planning a Server Cluster Hardware Configuration

The computers running Windows Server 2003 that you use to build a server cluster must all use the same processor architecture, meaning that you cannot mix 32-bit and 64-bit systems in the same cluster. Each server in the cluster must have at least one standard network connection giving it access to the other cluster servers and to the client computers that use the cluster's services. For maximum availability, having two network interface adapters in each computer is preferable, one providing the connection to the client network, and one connecting to a network dedicated to communications between the servers in the cluster.

In addition to standard network connections, each server must have a separate connection to the shared storage device. Windows Server 2003 supports three types of storage connections: Small Computer System Interface (SCSI) and two types of Fibre Channel, as discussed in the following sections.

> **Planning**   Microsoft strongly recommends that all the hardware components you use in your cluster servers for Windows Server 2003, and particularly those that make up the shared storage solution, be properly tested and listed in the Windows Server Catalog. The Windows Server Catalog can be found on the Microsoft Web site at *http://www.microsoft.com/windows /catalog/server/*.

Using SCSI

SCSI is a bus architecture used to connect storage devices and other peripherals to personal computers. SCSI implementations typically take the form of a host adapter in the computer and a number of internal or external devices that you connect to the card, using appropriate SCSI cables. In a shared SCSI configuration, however, you use multiple host adapters, one for each server in the cluster, and connect the adapters and the storage devices to a single bus, as shown in Figure 14-11.

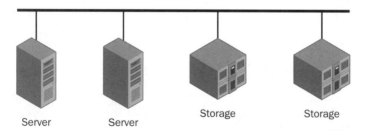

Server   Server   Storage   Storage

Figure 14-11   A cluster using a SCSI bus

Understanding SCSI

The SCSI host adapter is the component responsible for receiving device access requests from the computer and feeding them to the appropriate devices on the SCSI bus. Although you can use SCSI devices on any personal computer by installing a host adapter card, SCSI is usually associated with servers because it can handle requests for multiple devices more efficiently than other interfaces.

When the Integrated Drive Electronics (IDE) devices used in most PC workstations receive an access request from the computer's host adapter, the device processes the request and sends a response to the adapter. The adapter remains idle until it receives the response from that device. Only when that response arrives can the adapter send the next request. SCSI host adapters, by contrast, can send requests to many different devices in succession, without having to wait for the results of each one. Therefore, SCSI is better for servers that must handle large numbers of disk access requests.

Many personal computers marketed as servers have an integrated SCSI host adapter. If the computers you use for your cluster servers do not already have SCSI adapters, you must purchase and install a SCSI host adapter card for each one.

Because of the limitations of the SCSI architecture, Windows Server 2003 supports only two-node clusters using SCSI, and only with the 32-bit version of Windows Server 2003, Enterprise Edition. SCSI is not supported on Windows Server 2003, Datacenter Edition. SCSI hubs are also not supported. In addition, you cannot use SCSI for a geographically dispersed cluster, as the maximum length for a SCSI bus is 25 meters.

Real World   SCSI Clustering

SCSI is designed to support multiple devices and multiple device types on a single bus. The original SCSI standard supported up to eight devices (including the SCSI host adapter), while some newer versions of the standard can support up to 16. For the SCSI adapter to communicate with each device individually, you must configure each device on the bus with a unique SCSI ID. SCSI IDs range from 0 to 7 on the standard bus, and SCSI host adapters traditionally use ID 7. When you create a shared SCSI bus for your server cluster, you must modify the SCSI ID of one of the host adapters on the bus so that both are not using the same ID.

The other requirement for all SCSI buses is that both ends of the bus be terminated so that the signals generated by the SCSI devices do not reflect back in the other direction and interfere with new signals. A terminator uses resistors to remove the electrical signals from the cable. You must have appropriate terminators installed at the ends of your shared SCSI bus, and Microsoft recommends physical terminating devices rather than the termination circuits built into many SCSI devices.

Using Fibre Channel

Fibre Channel is a high-speed serial networking technology that was originally conceived as a general purpose networking solution, but which has instead been adopted primarily for connections between computers and storage devices. Unlike SCSI, which is a parallel signaling technology, Fibre Channel uses serial signaling, which enables it to transmit over much longer distances. Fibre Channel devices can transmit data at speeds up to 100 megabytes per second using *full duplex communications*, which means that the devices can transmit at full speed in both directions simultaneously.

> **Off the Record** The nonstandard spelling of the word "fibre" in Fibre Channel is deliberate. The designers of the technology want to avoid confusion with the term "fiber optic," because Fibre Channel connections can use copper-based as well as fiber-optic cable as a network medium.

The most common method for implementing a Fibre Channel storage solution on a server cluster is to install a Fibre Channel host adapter in each cluster server and then use them to connect the computers to one or more external storage devices. The storage devices are typically self-contained drive arrays or NAS devices, using RAID to provide high data availability.

Windows Server 2003 supports two types of Fibre Channel topologies for connecting cluster servers to storage devices: Fibre Channel arbitrated loop (FC-AL) and Fibre Channel switched fabric (FC-SW).

Fibre Channel Arbitrated Loop In the context of Windows Server 2003 server clusters, a Fibre Channel arbitrated loop is a ring topology that connects cluster servers with a collection of storage devices, as shown in Figure 14-12. The total number of devices in an arbitrated loop is limited to 126, but Windows Server 2003 limits the number of servers in an arbitrated loop cluster to two.

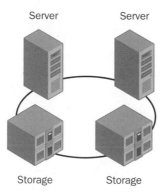

Figure 14-12 A cluster using a Fibre Channel arbitrated loop network

A Fibre Channel arbitrated loop is a shared network medium, which is one reason for the two-server limit. Data packets transmitted by one device on the loop might have to pass through other devices to reach their destinations, which lowers the overall bandwidth available to the individual devices. Compared to switched fabric, arbitrated loop is a relatively inexpensive clustering hardware technology that enables administrators to easily expand their storage capacity (although not the number of cluster nodes).

Fibre Channel Switched Fabric   The only shared storage solution supported by Windows Server 2003 that is suitable for server clusters of more than two nodes is the Fibre Channel switched fabric network. FC-SW is similar in configuration to a switched Ethernet network, in which each device is connected to a switch, as shown in Figure 14-13. Switching enables any device on the network to establish a direct, dedicated connection to any other device. There is no shared network medium as in FC-AL; the full bandwidth of the network is available to all communications.

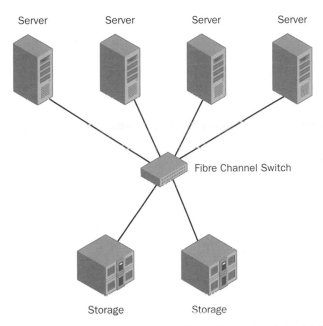

Figure 14-13   A cluster using a Fibre Channel switched fabric network

An FC-SW network that is wholly dedicated to giving servers access to data storage devices is a type of SAN. Building a SAN to service your server cluster provides the greatest possible amount of flexibility and scalability. You can add nodes to the cluster by installing additional servers and connecting them to the SAN, or you can expand the cluster's shared storage capacity by installing additional drives or drive arrays. You can also build a geographically dispersed server cluster by extending the SAN to locations in other cities.

Creating an Application Deployment Plan

The stateful applications that server clusters host usually have greater capabilities than the stateless applications used on Network Load Balancing clusters. This means that you have more flexibility in how you deploy the applications on the cluster. Windows Server 2003 can host the following two basic types of applications in a server cluster:

- **Single-instance applications**   Applications that can run on no more than one server at a time, using a given configuration. The classic example of a single-instance application is the DHCP service. You can run a DHCP server with a particular scope configuration on only one server at a time; otherwise, you risk the possibility of having duplicate IP addresses on your network. To run an application of this type in a cluster, the application can be running on only one node, while other nodes function as standbys. If the active node malfunctions, the application fails over to one of the other nodes in the cluster.

- **Multiple-instance applications**   Applications in which duplicated (or *cloned*) code can run on multiple nodes in a cluster (as in an NLB cluster) or in which the code can be *partitioned,* or split into several instances, to provide complementary services on different cluster nodes. With some database applications, you can create partitions that respond to queries of a particular type, or that furnish information from a designated subset of the database.

Deploying Single-Instance Applications

Deploying one single-instance application on a cluster is simply a matter of installing the same application on multiple nodes and configuring one node to be active, while the others remain passive until they are needed. This type of deployment is most common in two-node clusters, unless the application is so vital that you feel you must plan for the possibility of multiple server failures.

When you plan to run more than one single-instance application on a cluster, you have several deployment alternatives. You can create a separate two-node cluster for each application, with one active and one passive node in each, but this requires having two servers standing idle. You can create a three-node cluster, with two active nodes, each running one of the applications, and one passive node functioning as the standby for both applications. If you choose this configuration, the passive node must be capable of running both applications at once, in the event that both active nodes fail. A third configuration would be to have a two-node cluster with one application running on each, and each server active as a standby for the other. In this instance, both servers must be capable of running both applications.

Capacity Planning

This talk of running multiple applications on a server cluster introduces one of the most important elements of cluster application deployment: capacity planning. The servers in your cluster must have sufficient memory and enough processing capabilities to function adequately in your worst-case scenario.

For example, if your organization is running five critical applications, you can create a six-node cluster with five active nodes running the five applications and a single passive node functioning as the standby for all five. If your worst-case scenario is that all five active nodes fail, the single passive node had better be capable of running all five applications at one time with adequate performance for the entire client load.

In this example, the possibility of all five active nodes failing is remote, but you must decide on your own worst-case scenario, based on the importance of the applications to your organization.

Deploying Multiple-Instance Applications

In a multiple-instance application, more than one node in the cluster can be running the same application at the same time. When deploying multiple-instance applications, you either clone them or partition them. Cloned applications are rare on server clusters. Most applications that require this type of deployment are stateless and better suited to a Network Load Balancing cluster than to a server cluster.

Partitioning an application means that you split the application's functionality into separate instances and deploy each one on a separate cluster node. For example, you can configure a database application on a four-node server cluster so that each node handles requests for information from one fourth of the database, as shown in Figure 14-14. When an application provides a number of different services, you might be able to configure each cluster node to handle one particular service.

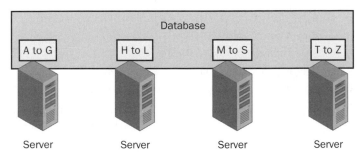

Figure 14-14   A partitioned database application

> **Note**   With a partitioned application, some mechanism must distribute the requests to the appropriate nodes and assemble the replies from multiple nodes into a single response for the client. This mechanism, like the partitioning capability itself, is something that developers must build into the application; these functions are not provided by the clustering capability in Windows Server 2003 by itself.

Partitioning by itself can provide increased application efficiency, but it does not provide high availability. Failure of a node hosting one partition renders part of the database or certain services unavailable. In addition to partitioning the application, you must configure its failover capabilities. For example, in the four-node, partitioned database application mentioned earlier, you can configure each partition to fail over to one of the other nodes in the cluster. You can also add one or more passive nodes to function as standbys for the active nodes. Adding a single passive node to the four-node cluster would enable the application to continue running at full capacity in the event of a single node failure. It would be necessary for servers to run multiple partitions at once only if multiple server failures occurred.

> **Planning**   Here again, you must decide what is the worst-case scenario for the cluster and plan your server capacity accordingly. If you want the four-node cluster to be able to compensate for the failure of three out of four nodes, you must be sure that each server is capable of running all four of the application's partitions at once.

If you plan to deploy more than one multiple-instance application on your cluster, the problem of configuring partitions, failover behavior, and server capacity becomes even more complex. You must plan for all possible failures and make sure that all the partitions of each application have a place to run in the event of each type of failure.

Selecting a Quorum Model

Every node in a server cluster maintains a copy of the cluster database in its registry. The cluster database contains the properties of all the cluster's elements, including physical components such as servers, network adapters, and shared storage devices, and cluster objects such as applications and other logical resources. When a cluster node goes offline for any reason, its cluster database is no longer updated as the cluster's status changes. When the node comes back online, it must have a current copy of the database to rejoin the cluster, and it obtains that copy from the cluster's *quorum resource*.

A cluster's quorum contains all the configuration data needed for the recovery of the cluster, and the quorum resource is the drive where the quorum is stored. To create a cluster, the first node must be able to take control of the quorum resource so that it can save the quorum data there. Only one system can have control of the quorum resource at any one time. Additional nodes must be able to access the quorum resource so that they can create the cluster database in their registries.

Selecting the location for the quorum is a crucial part of creating a cluster. Server clusters running Windows Server 2003 support the following three types of quorum models:

- **Single-node cluster** A cluster that consists of only one server. Because there is no need for a shared storage solution, the application data store and the quorum resource are located on the computer's local drive. The primary reason for creating single-node clusters is for testing and development.

- **Single-quorum device cluster** The cluster uses a single quorum resource, which is one of the shared storage devices accessible by all the nodes in the cluster. This is the quorum model that most server cluster installations use.

- **Majority node set cluster** A separate copy of the quorum is stored in each cluster node, with the quorum resource responsible for keeping all copies of the quorum consistent. Majority node set clusters are particularly well suited to geographically dispersed server clusters and clusters that do not have shared data storage devices.

 Exam Tip Be sure to understand the differences between the various quorum models supported by Windows Server 2003.

Creating a Server Cluster

Before you actually create the cluster, you must select, evaluate, and install a shared storage resource and install the critical applications on the computers running Windows Server 2003. All the computers that are to become cluster nodes must have access to the shared storage solution you have selected; you should know your applications' capabilities with regard to partitioning; and you should have decided how to deploy them. Once you have completed these tasks, you will use the Cluster Administrator tool to create and manage server clusters. (See Figure 14-15.)

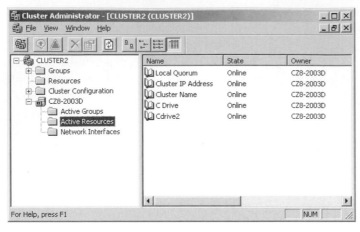

Figure 14-15   Cluster Administrator

To create a new cluster, you must have the following information available:

- The name of the domain in which the cluster will be located

- The host name to assign to the cluster

- The static IP address to assign to the cluster

- The name and password for a cluster service account

With this information in hand, you can proceed to deploy the cluster, taking the following basic steps:

1. Start up the computer running Windows Server 2003 that will be the first node in the cluster.

    At this time, the other servers you will later add to the cluster should not be running.

2. Use the Cluster Administrator application on the first server to create a new cluster.

    During this process, the New Server Cluster Wizard detects the storage devices and network interfaces on the computer and determines whether they are suitable for use by the cluster. You also supply the name and IP address for the cluster and the name and password for the cluster service account.

3. Verify that the cluster is operational and that you can access the cluster disks.

    At this point, you have created a single-node cluster.

4. Start up the computers running Windows Server 2003 that will become the other nodes in the cluster.

5. Use the Add Nodes Wizard in Cluster Administrator to make the other servers part of the cluster.

6. Test the cluster by using Cluster Administrator to stop the cluster service on each node in turn, verifying that the cluster disks are still available after each stoppage.

Once you have added all the nodes to the cluster, you can view information about the nodes in Cluster Administrator as well as manage the nodes and their resources from a central location. In addition, there are many clustering features you can use to configure how the cluster behaves under various conditions.

Understanding Cluster Resources

When managing a cluster, you frequently work with cluster resources. A cluster resource is any physical or logical element the cluster service can manage by bringing it online or offline and moving it to a different node. By default, the cluster resources supported by server clusters running Windows Server 2003 include storage devices, configuration parameters, scripts, and applications. When you deploy a third-party application on a server cluster, the application developer typically includes resource types that are specific to that application.

Some configuration tasks you can perform in Cluster Administrator are as follows:

■ **Create resource groups** A resource group is a collection of cluster resources that functions as a single failover unit. When one resource in the group malfunctions, the cluster service fails the entire group over to another node. You use the New Group Wizard to create resource groups, after which you can create new resources or move existing resources into the group.

■ **Define resource dependencies** You can configure a specific cluster resource to be dependent on other resources in the same resource group. The cluster service uses these dependencies to determine the order in which it starts and stops the resources on a node in the event of a failover. For example, when an application is dependent on a particular shared disk where the application is stored, the cluster service always brings down the application on a node before bringing down the disk. Conversely, when launching the application on a new node, the service will always start the disk before the application so that the disk is available to the application when it starts.

■ **Configure the cluster network role** For each network to which a cluster is connected, you can specify whether the cluster should use that network for client access only, for internal cluster communications only, or for both.

■ **Configure failover relationships**   For each resource the cluster manages, you can specify a list of nodes that are permitted to run that resource. With this capability, you can configure a wide variety of failover policies for your applications.

Configuring Failover Policies

By configuring the failover relationships of your cluster applications and other resources, you can implement a number of different failover policies that control which cluster nodes an application uses and when. With small server clusters, failover is usually a simple affair because you don't have that many nodes to choose from. As server clusters grow larger, however, their failover capabilities become more flexible. Some failover policies you might consider using are as follows:

■ **Failover pairs**   In a large server cluster running several applications, each application is running on one node and has one designated standby node. This makes server capacity planning simple, as the servers are never running more than one application. However, half of the cluster's processing capacity is not in use, and, in the event of multiple node failures, some applications could go offline unless an administrator intervenes.

■ **Hot-standby server**   A single node functions as the designated standby server for two or more applications. This option uses the cluster's processing capacity more efficiently (fewer servers are idle), but might not handle multiple node failures well. For capacity planning, the standby server has to support only the most resource-intensive application it might run, unless you want to plan for multiple node failures, in which case the standby must be capable of running multiple applications at once.

■ **N+I**   An expanded form of the hot-standby server policy, in which you configure a number of active nodes running different applications (N) to fail over to any one of a number of idle servers (I). As an example, you can create a six-node server cluster with four applications running on four separate nodes, plus two standby nodes that are idle. When one of the active nodes malfunctions, its application fails over to one of the standby servers. This policy is better at handling multiple server failures than failover pairs or hot-standby servers.

■ **Failover ring**   Each node in a server cluster runs an application, and you configure each application to fail over to the next node. This policy is suitable for relatively small applications because, in the event of a failure, a server might have to run two or more applications at once. In the event of multiple node failures, the application load could be unbalanced across the active nodes. For example, in a four-node cluster, if Server 1 fails, Server 2 must run its own application and that of Server 1. If Server 2 then fails, Server 3 must take on the Server 2 and Server 1 applications in addition to its own, while Server 4 continues to run only one application. This makes server capacity planning difficult.

■ **Random**   In some cases, the best policy is for the administrator not to define any specific failover relationships at all, and let the cluster service be responsible for failing over resources to other nodes in the cluster. This policy is usually preferable for smaller applications so that a single node can conceivably run multiple applications if necessary. Random failovers also place less of a burden on the cluster administrator.

Practice: Creating a Single Node Cluster

In this practice, you create a server cluster on your Server01 computer. Because you are not likely to have access to shared storage hardware that would enable you to create a multinode cluster, this will be a cluster with only one server. However, the process of creating a single node cluster is the same as the first step of creating a cluster with multiple nodes.

Exercise 1: Creating a Server Cluster

In this exercise, you use the Cluster Administrator to create a new server cluster on your Server01 computer.

> **Important**   If you have previously created a Network Load Balancing cluster on your server, as described in the Lesson 2 practice in this chapter, you must disable it before you perform this practice. To do this, open Network Load Balancing Manager, connect to the existing cluster, select the cluster you created, and from the Cluster menu, click Delete.

1. Log on to Server01 as Administrator.

2. Click Start, point to All Programs, point to Administrative Tools, and then click Cluster Administrator. The Cluster Administrator window appears, and the Open Connections To Cluster dialog box appears.

3. In the Action list, choose Create New Cluster and then click OK. The New Server Cluster Wizard appears.

4. Click Next. The Cluster Name And Domain page appears. Verify that the correct domain name is chosen in the Domain list. Type **cluster** in the Cluster Name text box, and then click Next. The Select Computer page appears.

   The name of your computer appears in the Computer Name text box.

5. Click Next. The Analyzing Configuration page appears.

   The wizard proceeds to analyze the system resources and configuration to determine whether it can create a cluster. When the process is complete, review the results. Depending on your configuration, you might notice that the Finding Common Resources On Nodes and Checking Cluster Feasibility entries are flagged with a yellow triangle containing an exclamation point. When you expand these entries, you see that the flags indicate that the wizard failed to locate a shared quorum resource and that it found only one network interface adapter in the computer. Neither of these conditions prevents you from creating the single-node cluster.

> **Note**   To create a server cluster, you must be running the Enterprise Edition or Datacenter Edition of Windows Server 2003. If you are not running these editions, the analysis of your configuration will result in errors and you won't be able to continue with the New Server Cluster Wizard.

6. Click Next. The IP Address page appears.

7. Type **192.168.0.110** in the IP Address text box, and then click Next. The Cluster Service Account page appears.

8. Type **Administrator** in the User Name text box and the password for the Administrator account in the Password text box. Then, click Next. The Proposed Cluster Configuration page appears.

   When creating an actual production cluster, you should create a new account with administrative privileges to the servers that will become your cluster nodes and use that as the cluster service account. For the purposes of this practice, you need not bother.

9. Review the configuration analysis displayed on the page, and then click Next. The Creating The Cluster page appears.

10. The wizard proceeds to create the cluster and start the cluster service.

11. When the wizard completes the process and activates the Next button, click it. The Completing The New Server Cluster Wizard page appears.

12. Click Finish.

Exercise 2: Creating a Cluster Resource

In this exercise, you create a File Share resource on your new cluster, which you will later access using the cluster name you assigned in Exercise 1.

1. From the Cluster Administrator's File menu, point to New, and then click Resource. The New Resource Wizard appears.

2. In the Name text box, type **Cdrive**.

3. In the Resource Type selector, choose File Share and then click Next. The Possible Owners page appears.

4. In the Possible Owners page, your computer appears in the Possible Owners list. Click Next. The Dependencies page appears.

5. Click Next. The File Share Parameters page appears.

6. In the Share Name text box, type **Cdrive**.

7. In the Path text box, type **C:**.

8. Click Finish. A Cluster Administrator message box appears, stating that the resource was created successfully. Click OK.

9. In Cluster Administrator's scope pane, click the Resources folder.

   The newly created Cdrive resource appears in the details pane, displaying its state as Offline.

10. Click the Cdrive icon in the details pane and, from the File menu, select Bring Online.

    The state of the Cdrive resource changes to Online.

11. Close the Cluster Administrator window.

Exercise 3: Accessing the Server Cluster

In this exercise, you access your newly created cluster using its name and IP address.

1. Click Start, point to All Programs, point to Accessories, and then click Command Prompt. A Command Prompt window appears.

2. In the Command Prompt window, type **ping 192.168.0.110** and then press ENTER.

   The Ping.exe program successfully tests the connection to the cluster IP address you specified in Exercise 1.

3. Click Start, and then select Run. The Run dialog box appears.

4. In the Open text box, type **cluster** and then click OK.

   A \\Cluster window appears, containing icons for Scheduled Tasks and for the File Share resource you created in Exercise 2.

5. Double-click the Cdrive icon. You can now access the contents of the computer's C drive using a share you created as a cluster resource.

   At this point, if your server was connected to a network with other computers running Windows Server 2003 and had the appropriate shared storage hardware, you could add other nodes to the cluster to provide failover capabilities.

Lesson Review

The following questions are intended to reinforce key information presented in this lesson. If you are unable to answer a question, review the lesson materials and try the question again. You can find answers to the questions in the "Questions and Answers" section at the end of this chapter.

1. Explain why planning server capacity is an important element of deploying a server cluster.

   _____

   _____

   _____

   _____

   _____

   _____

   _____

2. Which shared storage hardware configuration is the only possible solution for a server cluster with more than two nodes?

   _____

3. Which of the following failover policies provides the best compensation for multiple node failures?

   a. Failover pairs

   b. Hot-standby servers

   c. N+I

   d. Failover ring

Lesson Summary

- A server cluster requires a storage resource shared by the nodes in the cluster. Windows Server 2003 supports shared SCSI and Fibre Channel arbitrated loop for two-node clusters, and Fibre Channel switched fabric for server clusters with more than two nodes.

- Some of the stateful applications you can deploy in a server cluster support partitioning, which enables you to split the functionality of the application among the servers in the cluster.

- A quorum is a storage resource that contains cluster configuration data, which nodes use to create their configuration databases as they join the cluster. Server clusters running Windows Server 2003 support three quorum models: single-node cluster, single-quorum device cluster, and majority node set cluster.

■ To create and manage server clusters, you use the Cluster Administrator application. This tool enables you to create new clusters, add nodes and resources to a cluster, and control all aspects of cluster performance from a central location.

■ You can configure a cluster to use various failover policies by specifying which nodes are permitted to run various cluster resources. Some of the policies include failover pairs, hot-standby servers, N+I, and failover rings.

Case Scenario Exercise

You are the network administrator for Litware Inc., a manufacturer of specialized scientific software products, and you have already created a network design for their new office building, as described in the Case Scenario in Chapter 7. The office building is a three-story brick structure built in the late 1940s, which has since been retrofitted by various tenants with several types of network cabling. Your network design for the building calls for the installation of four LANs, each of which is connected to a fifth, backbone network.

The corporation's six Web servers running Windows Server 2003 are housed in the basement of the building on a dedicated perimeter network. The company also has a computer running both Windows Server 2003 and Microsoft SQL Server on the second floor, which is hosting the customer database used by the Sales staff. This server is currently running at near peak capacity almost all the time.

You have been directed by the home office to ensure that the company Web servers are accessible by Internet users at all times. You must also make sure that the customer database is always available to the sales staff. After informing your superiors of the database server's operational state, they have authorized you to purchase three new database servers and the additional hardware needed to connect them to the network.

You have decided to use the clustering capabilities in Windows Server 2003 to achieve both of these goals. For the Web servers, you are going to create a Network Load Balancing cluster, and to host the customer database, you are going to create a four-node server cluster. Based on this information, answer the following questions:

1. Each of the six Web servers on the perimeter network has a single network interface adapter installed. What additional hardware is absolutely required to implement the NLB cluster on the Web servers?

2. You want to be able to use Network Load Balancing Manager, running on one of the Web servers, to configure all the servers in the NLB cluster. Other than this, very little noncluster communication between the Web servers is required. Which of the following communication models should you use to make this possible with the greatest economy? Explain your answer.

   a. Single network interface adapter in unicast mode

   b. Single network interface adapter in multicast mode

   c. Multiple network interface adapters in unicast mode

   d. Multiple network interface adapters in multicast mode

   _____

   _____

3. Which of the following storage hardware configurations should you use for the four-node database server cluster? Explain your answer.

   a. Install a SCSI host adapter in each server, and connect them all to a single SCSI bus.

   b. Install a SCSI host adapter in each server, and connect them all to a SCSI hub.

   c. Install a Fibre Channel adapter in each server, and connect them in an arbitrated loop.

   d. Install a Fibre Channel adapter in each server, and connect them all to a Fibre Channel switch.

   _____

   _____

4. You have decided to partition your database server application to spread the load among the servers in the cluster. Which of the following failover policies will ensure that the entire database is constantly available without any server running multiple partitions, even if two servers fail? Explain your answer.

   a. Failover pairs. Split the database into two partitions, and assign each one to an active server. Then, configure each of the active servers to fail over to one of the two remaining servers.

   b. Hot-standby server. Split the database into three partitions, and assign each one to an active server. Then, configure each of the active servers to fail over to the one remaining server.

    c. N+I. Split the database into two partitions, and assign each one to an active server. Then, configure each of the active servers to fail over to either one of the two remaining servers.

    d. Failover ring. Split the database into four partitions, and assign each one to an active server. Then, configure each of the four servers to failover to the next server.

_____

_____

_____

_____

5. If you need to expand the server cluster, how many more servers can you add?

_____

Troubleshooting Lab

You are a network administrator who has recently installed a four-node Network Load Balancing cluster on the company internetwork. The cluster provides fault tolerance for the company's Internet Web servers. The cluster servers are located on a dedicated LAN in the building's basement data center, with routers connecting the LAN to the Internet and to the rest of the company network. When you installed the cluster, you used multicast mode on the servers so that they could communicate with each other. However, you now discover that when you try to use the Network Load Balancing Manager application on your office workstation on the third floor, you cannot connect to any of the cluster servers. For each of the following procedures, state whether it might resolve the problem and explain your answer.

1. Reconfigure the Network Load Balancing cluster servers to use unicast mode rather than multicast mode.

_____

_____

_____

_____

_____

_____

2. Install a second network interface adapter in each Network Load Balancing cluster server.

_____

_____

_____

_____

3. Replace the router connecting the Web server LAN to the company network with a computer running Windows Server 2003 that you have configured to function as a router.

_____

_____

_____

Chapter Summary

- A cluster is a group of servers that appears to users as a single resource and which provides high availability, reliability, and scalability for specific applications.

- A server cluster is a group of servers running a stateful application, such as a database server, and sharing a common data store. Servers in this type of cluster can be configured as active or passive nodes.

- A Network Load Balancing cluster is a group of servers running a stateless application, such as a Web server, each of which has an identical, independent data store.

- Network Load Balancing works by creating a virtual network adapter with IP and MAC addresses that represent the cluster as a single unit.

- When NLB is running in unicast mode, ordinary communication between cluster servers is impossible. In multicast mode, the cluster servers can communicate normally.

- Although NLB and server clusters can both function with a single network interface adapter installed in each server, using multiple adapters in each server can prevent network performance degradation.

- A server cluster requires a storage resource shared by the nodes in the cluster. Windows Server 2003 supports shared SCSI and Fibre Channel arbitrated loop for two-node clusters, and Fibre Channel switched fabric for server clusters with more than two nodes.

- In a server cluster, the quorum is a storage resource that contains cluster configuration data, which nodes use to create their configuration databases as they join the cluster.

- You can configure a cluster to use various failover policies by specifying which nodes are permitted to run various cluster resources. Some of the policies include failover pairs, hot-standby servers, N+I, and failover rings.

- To create and manage server clusters, you use the Cluster Administrator application. To manage Network Load Balancing clusters, you use Network Load Balancing Manager.

Exam Highlights

Before taking the exam, review the following key points and terms to help you identify topics you need to review. Return to the lessons for additional practice, and review the "Further Reading" sections in Part 2 for pointers to more information about topics covering the exam objectives.

Key Points

- Server clusters are for stateful applications, such as database servers, that have frequently changing data. NLB clusters are for stateless applications, such as Web servers, in which the data seldom changes.

- While both types of clusters can benefit from multiple network interface adapters, only server clusters require additional hardware, in the form of a shared storage solution that enables all the servers in the cluster to access the same application data.

- All Windows Server 2003 versions support NLB clusters, but only Enterprise Edition and Datacenter Edition support server clusters.

- To monitor Network Load Balancing, you can use the Network Load Balancing Manager itself, the Event Viewer console, and the Nlb.exe command-line utility.

- Cluster servers continually exchange heartbeat messages, which they use to determine when a node has failed or when a new server has been added to the cluster. To recover from a node failure, the remaining servers begin a process called convergence, which enables them to compensate for the loss.

Key Terms

Failover and failback   Failover is the process of shifting specific application tasks to another node in the cluster when one or more servers malfunction. Failback is the process of shifting application tasks back to their original nodes after a failed server comes back online.

Stateful and stateless applications   A stateful application is one in which the application data frequently changes or that has long-running in-memory states, such as a database server. A stateless application is one in which data changes infrequently or one that does not have long-running in-memory states.

Convergence   The process by which a cluster compensates for the failure of one or more servers. In an NLB cluster, convergence consists of redistributing the incoming client traffic among the remaining servers. In a server cluster, convergence consists of failing over the application tasks performed by the malfunctioning node to another server in the cluster.

Quorum resource   A storage device containing continually updated configuration data about a server cluster, which the cluster uses to rejoin nodes that have been offline.

Questions and Answers

Lesson 1 Review

Specify whether each of the following is a characteristic of server clusters, CLB clusters, or NLB clusters.

1. Used for database server clusters

   Server clusters

2. Supports clusters of up to 8 nodes in Windows Server 2003, Datacenter Edition

   Server clusters

3. Supported by Windows Server 2003, Standard Edition

   NLB clusters

4. Makes stateless applications highly available

   NLB clusters

5. Used for applications with frequently changing data

   Server clusters

6. Used for Web server clusters

   NLB clusters

7. Not supported by Windows Server 2003, Enterprise Edition

   CLB clusters

8. Requires a shared data store

   Server clusters

9. Makes stateful applications highly available

   Server clusters

10. Used for read-only applications

    NLB clusters

11. Used for COM+ applications

    CLB clusters

12. Supports clusters of up to 32 nodes in Windows Server 2003

    NLB clusters

Lesson 2 Review

1. You are the administrator of a Network Load Balancing cluster consisting of six Web servers running in unicast mode, with a single network interface adapter in each server. You are using the Network Load Balancing Manager application on one of the cluster servers to try to shut down the NLB service on one of the other servers so that you can upgrade its hardware. Why is the Manager not letting you do this?

   Because when cluster servers with one network interface adapter are running in unicast mode, the adapters on all the host servers are using the same cluster MAC address, making ordinary communications between the cluster servers impossible.

2. Which of the following Nlb.exe commands do you use to shut down NLB operations on a cluster server without interrupting transactions currently in progress?

   a. Nlb drain

   b. Nlb params

   c. Nlb drainstop

   d. Nlb queryport

   c

3. How long does it take a Network Load Balancing cluster to begin the convergence process after one of the servers in the cluster fails?

   Five seconds

Lesson 3 Review

1. Explain why planning server capacity is an important element of deploying a server cluster.

   Server capacity planning is the process of estimating the resources needed by each node in a cluster during a worst-case scenario. When one or more nodes in a cluster malfunction, their applications fail over to other nodes, and those nodes must be capable of running them efficiently for the applications to remain available. Depending on the failover policies you configure for the cluster, you might have to use servers that are capable of running several applications at once in the event of a node failure, and the servers must have sufficient memory, processing power, and disk space to do so.

2. Which shared storage hardware configuration is the only possible solution for a server cluster with more than two nodes?

   Fibre Channel switched fabric

3. Which of the following failover policies provides the best compensation for multiple node failures?

    a. Failover pairs

    b. Hot-standby servers

    c. N+I

    d. Failover ring

  c

Page
14-49

Case Scenario Exercise

You have decided to use the clustering capabilities in Windows Server 2003 to achieve both of these goals. For the Web servers, you are going to create a Network Load Balancing cluster, and to host the customer database, you are going to create a four-node server cluster. Based on this information, answer the following questions:

1. Each of the six Web servers on the perimeter network has a single network interface adapter installed. What additional hardware is absolutely required to implement the NLB cluster on the Web servers?

    No additional hardware is required.

2. You want to be able to use Network Load Balancing Manager, running on one of the Web servers, to configure all the servers in the NLB cluster. Other than this, very little noncluster communication between the Web servers is required. Which of the following communication models should you use to make this possible with the greatest economy? Explain your answer.

    a. Single network interface adapter in unicast mode

    b. Single network interface adapter in multicast mode

    c. Multiple network interface adapters in unicast mode

    d. Multiple network interface adapters in multicast mode

    b. Running the cluster in multicast mode enables the servers to communicate with each other without having to install a second network interface adapter in each server.

3. Which of the following storage hardware configurations should you use for the four-node database server cluster? Explain your answer.

   a. Install a SCSI host adapter in each server, and connect them all to a single SCSI bus.

   b. Install a SCSI host adapter in each server, and connect them all to a SCSI hub.

   c. Install a Fibre Channel adapter in each server, and connect them in an arbitrated loop.

   d. Install a Fibre Channel adapter in each server, and connect them all to a Fibre Channel switch.

   d. The Fibre Channel switched fabric solution is the only one that Windows Server 2003 supports for a four-node server cluster.

4. You have decided to partition your database server application to spread the load among the servers in the cluster. Which of the following failover policies will ensure that the entire database is constantly available without any server running multiple partitions, even if two servers fail? Explain your answer.

   a. Failover pairs. Split the database into two partitions, and assign each one to an active server. Then, configure each of the active servers to fail over to one of the two remaining servers.

   b. Hot-standby server. Split the database into three partitions, and assign each one to an active server. Then, configure each of the active servers to fail over to the one remaining server.

   c. N+I. Split the database into two partitions, and assign each one to an active server. Then, configure each of the active servers to fail over to either one of the two remaining servers.

   d. Failover ring. Split the database into four partitions, and assign each one to an active server. Then, configure each of the four servers to failover to the next server.

   c. To guarantee that no server ever has to run more than one partition, you must have two standby servers, so answers b and d are incorrect. Answer a is incorrect because the failure of an active server and its designated standby would cause one of the partitions to go offline.

5. If you need to expand the server cluster, how many more servers can you add?

   4

Troubleshooting Lab

You are a network administrator who has recently installed a four-node Network Load Balancing cluster on the company internetwork. The cluster provides fault tolerance for the company's Internet Web servers. The cluster servers are located on a dedicated LAN in the building's basement data center, with routers connecting the LAN to the Internet and to the rest of the company network. When you installed the cluster, you used multicast mode on the servers so that they could communicate with each other. However, you now discover that when you try to use the Network Load Balancing Manager application on your office workstation on the third floor, you cannot connect to any of the cluster servers. For each of the following procedures, state whether it might resolve the problem and explain your answer.

1. Reconfigure the Network Load Balancing cluster servers to use unicast mode rather than multicast mode.

   The cause of the problem might be that the router connecting the Web server LAN to the rest of the company network does not support the use of multicast MAC addresses. This inability would prevent the Network Load Balancing Manager on a different LAN from communicating with the Web servers. Changing the cluster servers to unicast mode would eliminate the multicast addresses, enabling the communication to take place.

2. Install a second network interface adapter in each Network Load Balancing cluster server.

   If the router connecting the Web server LAN to the company network does not support multicast MAC addresses, adding a second network interface adapter would not by itself resolve the problem because the servers would still use the same multicast address.

3. Replace the router connecting the Web server LAN to the company network with a computer running Windows Server 2003 that you have configured to function as a router.

   If the router currently connecting the Web server LAN to the company network does not support multicast MAC addresses, replacing the router with a Windows Server 2003 router would resolve the problem.

Part 2
Prepare for the Exam

15 Exam 70-292—Managing Users, Computers, and Groups (1.0)

Users need access to resources on the network to do their daily work, but they should not have access to unauthorized data. Users gain access by logging on to a computer that has access to the domain and then by being acknowledged as a member of assigned groups in the domain. Permissions to resources can only be set for users, groups, and computers that are recognized by the domain.

You can create these user, group, and computer accounts manually through tools provided in the Microsoft Windows Server 2003 interface, or their creation can be automated through command-line tools or scripts. The methods of creating user, group, and computer accounts are important for success on the exam.

Related to the creation and management of user, group, and computer accounts are the granting of permissions appropriate to the level of access needed and the management of data related to the account, such as logon scripts and user profiles.

Tested Skills and Suggested Practices

The skills that you need to master the Managing Users, Computers, and Groups objective domain on *Exam 70-292: Managing and Maintaining a Microsoft Windows Server 2003 Environment for an MCSA Certified on Windows 2000* include

- Create and manage groups.
  - ❏ Practice 1: Use manual methods to create user, group, and computer accounts. Using the Active Directory Users And Computers MMC snap-in, and the Directory Service command-line tools to create user, group, and computer accounts. Modify the properties of user accounts and test the effect of various property changes. Use the System Properties interface at a desktop computer to join computers to the domain.
  - ❏ Practice 2: Use automated methods to create user, group, and computer accounts.
  - ❏ Practice 3: Place users, groups, and computers as members of a group. Use both interface-based and command-line tools.
  - ❏ Practice 4: Identify group membership in a complex group hierarchy. Use the Directory Service command-line tools to do bulk analysis.

- Create and manage user accounts.

  ❑ Practice 1: Create four different user accounts using the Active Directory Users And Computers MMC.

  ❑ Practice 2: Create a single-user account using the Active Directory Users And Computers MMC. Configure specific settings for the user's logon hours and group membership. Create three similar accounts using the copy command.

- Troubleshoot user authentication issues.

  ❑ Practice 1: Edit the default domain policy GPO to change the password policies. Configure the Account Lockout Threshold policy to three invalid logon attempts. Set the Account Lockout Duration policy to 30 minutes.

  ❑ Practice 2: Edit the default domain policy GPO to change the password policies. Set the Enforce Password History policy to 10 passwords. Set the Minimum Password Age policy to two days. Set the Minimum Password Length policy to 10 characters.

Further Reading

This section contains a list of supplemental readings divided by objective. If you think you need additional preparation before taking the exam, study these sources thoroughly.

Objective 1.1   Microsoft Corporation. *Microsoft Windows Server 2003 Deployment Kit*. Volume: *Designing a Managed Environment*. Redmond, Washington: Microsoft Press, 2003. This volume can be found on the Microsoft Web site at: *http://www.microsoft.com/windowsserver2003/techinfo/reskit/deploykit.mspx*.

Review Chapter 4, Lesson 2, "Understanding, Creating, and Managing Groups," which focuses on the creation and management of groups.

Microsoft Corporation. Windows Server 2003 Help and Support Center: "Managing Domain Users and Groups: Using Groups."

Objective 1.2   Review Chapter 4, Lesson 1, "Creating and Modifying User Accounts," which focuses on the creation and management of user accounts.

Microsoft Corporation. Windows Server 2003 Help and Support Center: "Managing Domain Users and Groups: User and Computer Accounts."

Objective 1.3   Review Chapter 4, Lesson 3, "Planning and Troubleshooting User Authentication," which focuses on how to troubleshoot authentication issues.

Microsoft Corporation. Windows Server 2003 Help and Support Center: "Managing Domain Users and Groups: User and Computer Accounts."

Create and Manage Groups

Grouping user accounts is an efficient way to organize individual users into logical units to which permissions can be assigned. Different from organizational units (OUs), groups are security principals and can be added to the discretionary access control list (DACL or ACL) of a resource for permission assignment.

The types of groups that are available, their scope, and the combinations of nested groups that can be used depend on the functional level of the domain in which the groups reside; similarly, some groups can be converted to a different type or scope if the functional level of the domain is high enough. To support all group types, scopes, nesting, and conversion possibilities, the functional level of the domain must be Windows 2000 Native or Windows Server 2003. At the lower functional level of Windows 2000 Mixed, group nesting is limited and conversion is not possible.

Objective 1.1 Questions

1.   You're the administrator of a Windows Server 2003 domain that is currently at the domain functional level Windows 2000 mixed. Your Windows Server 2003 domain, *contoso.com*, has an external trust established with a Windows NT 4 Domain, *contoso_north*. You are planning the use of groups in your domain and need to determine what group scopes can be used in any domain in your forest.

What group scope can be used in this context as a security principal?

   A. Domain local

   B. Global

   C. Universal

   D. Domain local with a nested global group

2.   You have just raised the domain functional level of your single-domain forest, *contoso.com*, to Windows Server 2003. You want to take advantage of the security group nesting possibilities available to you.

What security group nesting is possible at this domain functional level? (Choose all that apply.)

   A. Domain local in domain local

   B. Global in domain local

   C. Universal in domain local

   D. Domain local in global

   E. Global in global

   F. Universal in global

   G. Universal in universal

   H. Global in universal

   I. Domain local in universal

3. You have just raised the domain functional level of your single-domain forest, *contoso.com*, to Windows Server 2003. You want to take advantage of the security group conversion possibilities available to you.

What security group conversion is possible at this domain functional level? (Choose all that apply.)

A. Domain local with user members; convert to global

B. Global with user members; convert to universal

C. Global with global group members; convert to universal

D. Universal group with universal group members; convert to domain local

E. Universal group with universal group members; convert to global

F. Global with user members; convert to domain local

G. Domain local with user members; convert to universal

4. You are the administrator of a Windows Server 2003 domain, *contoso.com*, that is set to domain functional level Windows 2000 mixed during a migration of your network. You are planning your use of groups during this transitional period and want to determine what group types you can create and what scopes those groups might have.

What group type and scope possibilities exist at this functional level? (Choose all that apply.)

A. Domain local group: Security type

B. Domain local group: Distribution type

C. Global group: Security type

D. Global group: Distribution type

E. Universal group: Security type

F. Universal group: Distribution type

Objective 1.1 Answers

1.   Correct Answers: B

   A. Incorrect: Domain local groups are available only for use as security principals on domain controllers in the Windows Server 2003 domain, contoso.com.

   B. Correct: Global groups are available for permission assignment in any ACL in the forest.

   C. Incorrect: Universal groups are available only as distribution groups, not security groups, in the Windows 2000 Mixed functional level.

   D. Incorrect: Domain local groups, at this functional level, are available only on domain controllers in the contoso.com domain, regardless of other groups that they might contain. The nested global group, however, is available for permission assignment.

2.   Correct Answers: A, B, C, E, G, and H

   A. Correct: Domain local groups can contain other domain local groups from the same domain.

   B. Correct: This nesting is possible regardless of the functional level.

   C. Correct: Universal groups can be placed in domain local groups.

   D. Incorrect: This nesting is not possible at any functional level.

   E. Correct: Global groups can be placed in global groups.

   F. Incorrect: This nesting is not possible at any functional level.

   G. Correct: Universal groups can be placed in universal groups.

   H. Correct: Global groups can be placed in universal groups.

   I. Incorrect: This nesting is not possible at any functional level.

3.   Correct Answers: B, D, and G

   A. Incorrect: Domain local groups cannot be converted to global groups, regardless of domain functional level.

   B. Correct: Global groups without other global groups as members can be converted to universal groups.

   C. Incorrect: The conversion of groups of this type could create a circular reference and is not permitted.

   D. Correct: There is no restriction on this type of conversion at this functional level, regardless of universal group memberships.

   E. Incorrect: The conversion of groups of this type could create a circular reference and is not permitted.

   F. Incorrect: This type of conversion is not permitted.

   G. Correct: As long as a domain local group does not have any other domain local groups as members, conversion to a universal group is permitted.

4.   Correct Answers: A, B, C, D, and F

   A. Correct: Domain local groups can be created with a group type of security but will be available only on the domain controllers in the domain in which they were created until the domain functional level is raised.

   B. Correct: Domain local groups can be created with a group type of distribution but will be available only on the domain controllers in the domain in which they were created until the domain functional level is raised.

   C. Correct: Global groups can be created with a group type of security regardless of the domain functional level.

   D. Correct: Global groups can be created with a group type of distribution regardless of the domain functional level.

   E. Incorrect: Universal groups cannot be created with a group type of security until the domain functional level is raised.

   F. Correct: Universal groups can be created with a group type of distribution regardless of the domain functional level.

Objective 1.2

Create and Manage User Accounts

You can add user accounts individually through the Active Directory Users And Computers snap-in or through the Directory Service command-line tool, Dsadd. These tools are preferred and sufficient for single accounts. Active Directory Users And Computers is also the easiest tool for managing the properties of user accounts, as it presents a common and usable interface to these properties. The Directory Service command-line tools are better suited for mass manipulation of the properties of existing collections of users such as groups, OUs, or the entire domain.

If you already have a directory or database of users, it might be more efficient to import these users into your Active Directory using Ldifde or Csvde tools.

Objective 1.2 Questions

1.   Which of the following tools allow for the creation of Active Directory security principals (user, computer, and group accounts) based on user or file input? (Choose all that apply.)

    A. Active Directory Users And Computers

    B. Active Directory Domains And Trusts

    C. Ntdsutil

    D. Ldifde

    E. Csvde

    F. Dsadd

    G. Dsquery

    H. Dsmod

2.   You are the administrator of the Windows Server 2003 domain *contoso.com*. Your company employs many temporary workers. Some of these workers are employed only once; others are employed periodically on a recurring basis.

Your goal is to automate a process that will determine which accounts have not been used within the last month and then disable them. If the accounts are needed again, you will reenable them at that time.

Which Directory Service command-line tool is the appropriate one to achieve your goal?

    A. dsquery user domainroot -inactive 4 -disabled yes

    B. dsquery user domainroot -inactive 4|dsmod user -disabled yes

    C. dsquery user domainroot -inactive 4|dsrm -q

    D. dsquery user domainroot -inactive 4|dsmove –newparent OU=disabled, DC=contoso,DC=com -q

3.   You have been given an administrative task related to user accounts in the *contoso.com* Active Directory. You need to move all accounts in the East group located in the Sales OU into the newly created East Sales OU.

Which procedure will accomplish this task?

    A. Use Active Directory Users And Computers to move the East group to the East Sales OU.

    B. Use Dsquery to get the members of the group, and then pipe (stdin) the output to the Dsmod command with the East Sales OU as the target.

    C. Use Dsquery to get the members of the group, and then pipe (stdin) the output to the Dsmove command with the East Sales OU as the target.

    D. Use Dsquery to get the members of the group, and then pipe (stdin) the output to the Dsadd command with the East Sales OU as the target.

4.   You are configuring the properties of user accounts in the Sales OU of the *contoso.com* domain. You want their home directories to be stored on the network server computer named Server01. The home directories are to be stored in a shared folder, named Home, on the server's D drive. The share name is Homedir.

In the Home folder property for each user, how will you set the home directories?

    A. D:\Home*%Username%*

    B. \\Server01\d$\Home*%Username%*

    C. \\Server01*%Homedir%**%Username%*

    D. \\Server01\Homedir*%Username%*

Objective 1.2 Answers

1.   **Correct Answers: A, D, E, and F**

   A. Correct: Active Directory Users And Computers is the primary interface tool for creating security principals.

   B. Incorrect: Active Directory Domains And Trusts is used for setting the functional level of the domain or forest and for creating and managing trust relationships. Domain accounts are not created using this tool.

   C. Incorrect: Ntdsutil is used for data restoration, metadata manipulation, and other directory service functions. Ntdsutil is not used to create security objects within Active Directory.

   D. Correct: Ldifde can create objects within Active Directory using a data file or command-line parameters for input.

   E. Correct: Csvde can create objects within Active Directory using a comma-separated-values file for input.

   F. Correct: Dsadd is a command-line tool used to add objects to the Active Directory.

   G. Incorrect: Dsquery is used to output information from Active Directory. Its output might be used for other "DS" commands, but Dsquery cannot create objects within the directory.

   H. Incorrect: Dsmod is used to modify attributes of existing Active Directory objects.

2.   **Correct Answers: B**

   A. Incorrect: This command will return a list of user accounts that have been inactive for four weeks or more and are disabled. The Dsquery command takes no action.

   B. Correct: This command will return a list of user accounts that have been inactive for four weeks or more and then pipe that output into the Dsmod command, which will disable the accounts.

   C. Incorrect: This command will return a list of user accounts that have been inactive for four weeks or more and pipe the output into the Dsrm command, which will remove the accounts.

   D. Incorrect: This command will move all accounts that have been inactive for four weeks or more into an OU named "disabled," but it will not disable the accounts.

3.   **Correct Answers: C**

   A. **Incorrect:** This action will move the group to the East Sales OU, but the user accounts will remain in the Sales OU.

   B. **Incorrect:** The Dsmod command can modify properties of a user account, but the OU is not a property of a user account.

   C. **Correct:** This action will appropriately move the accounts to an OU.

   D. **Incorrect:** This action would attempt to create new accounts in the East Sales OU and leave the old user accounts in the Sales OU. This will fail because although the OU and group are separate, they are all a part of the same domain, hence this process would fail with errors.

4.   **Correct Answers: D**

   A. **Incorrect:** This will set the home directory to the D drive on the user's computer.

   B. **Incorrect:** This setting would require explicit administrative permissions to access the root share of the D drive, which users do not have.

   C. **Incorrect:** The %Homedir% variable refers to the assigned home directory, which is being set by this property's value. The reference to the home directory will fail in this case.

   D. **Correct:** This will set the user's home directory to a folder within the Homedir share. The folder will be named with the user's logon name.

Troubleshoot User Authentication Issues

Without proper authentication, a user will be unable to access network resources and, in some cases, will not be able to log on to his or her local computer. At the root of authentication is the combination of username and password that comprises the user's credentials. If there is a mismatch between what the user believes his or her credentials to be and what the authenticating system expects, the user will not be able to connect to that resource. If that resource is the local computer, the user will not be able to log on at all.

Objective 1.3 Questions

1. A traveling user has been away from the office for several months. The laptop computer with which the user travels is not configured for dial-in access to the corporate network because it is used mostly for presentations and client documentation.

Upon returning to the office and connecting to the corporate network, the user is unable to log on to his or her computer using a local account and is presented with the Logon Failed dialog box.

What should you do?

    A. Reset the user's password in Active Directory.

    B. Reset the user's computer account in Active Directory.

    C. Use the password reset disk for that user to reset the password on the local computer.

    D. Disconnect the computer from the network and then restart the computer.

2. A user returns from an extended business trip and reconnects his or her computer to the network. The user is able to log on but is not able to connect to any network resources.

You examine the accounts associated with the user in Active Directory Users And Computers and note that the computer account for the user's laptop is marked with a red "X" icon.

What should you do to solve the problem?

    A. Reset the user's password in Active Directory.

    B. Reset the laptop computer account in Active Directory.

    C. Delete the laptop computer account from the domain, join the laptop to a workgroup, and then rejoin the laptop to the domain.

    D. Delete and recreate the laptop computer account.

3. You are the systems administrator for a medium-sized organization that runs a single Windows Server 2003 domain. The Default Domain Group Policy object has the following password policy settings:

10 Passwords Remembered

Maximum Password Age: 10 days

Minimum Password Age: 2 days

Minimum Password Length: 10 characters

A group of 40 developers who work in a department in your organization has lobbied management for a separate set of password policies specific to its members. The developers want the minimum password age set to 0 days and the maximum password age set to 28 days. Which of the following methods will allow you to alter the password policy for this group of developers?

    A. Create a child domain of the current domain and move the developers' accounts to this domain. Edit the Default Domain GPO of the child domain and implement the separate password policy requested by the developers.

    B. Create a separate OU and move the 40 developers' user accounts into this OU. Create and edit a new GPO, implementing the separate password policy requested by the developers through this GPO. Apply the GPO to the newly created OU hosting the developer's accounts.

    C. Resubnet the network and create a new site within Active Directory. Place all 40 developers' workstations onto this new subnet. Create and edit a new GPO, implementing the separate password policy requested by the developers through this GPO. Apply the GPO to the newly created site hosting the developers' computer accounts.

    D. Edit the Local GPO on each of the developer's workstations, implementing the separate password policy requested by the developers through this GPO.

4. A user reports that he or she cannot access the network by dialing in. The user can log on successfully to a local computer in the office.

You confirm that the default Remote Access policies are in place on the Routing and Remote Access Server computer. All modem devices pass diagnostic tests successfully.

What is likely the cause of the problem?

    A. The user does not have Terminal Server access enabled in his or her user account properties.

    B. The user does not have dial-in permission enabled in his or her user account properties.

    C. The user does not have a computer account in the domain for his or her remote computer.

    D. The user is not supplying the correct credentials when dialing in.

1.   Correct Answers: C

   A. Incorrect: The Logon Failed dialog box appears only if a password reset disk has been created for an account on the local computer. The domain user account is not involved in this problem.

   B. Incorrect: The Logon Failed dialog box appears only if a password reset disk has been created for an account on the local computer. The domain computer account is not involved in this problem.

   C. Correct: The password reset disk is created for local user accounts, and can be used when a user is trying to access a local computer account with the incorrect credentials, as in this case.

   D. Incorrect: The computer's connection to the network or any network interaction doesn't cause the Logon Failed dialog box to appear.

2.   Correct Answers: B

   A. Incorrect: The user's password would not affect the computer account, as the icon indicates, in Active Directory.

   B. Correct: The password between the laptop and the domain computer account has become unsynchronized and must be reset.

   C. Incorrect: This would solve the problem, but it might cause other problems if permissions are set on resources for this laptop computer. Also, this process would take much more time than a computer password reset.

   D. Incorrect: This would compound the problem by having not only unsynchronized passwords but also mismatched SIDs.

3.   **Correct Answers: A**

    A. Correct: Password policies apply domain-wide. The only method by which users can have separate password policies is if their user accounts reside in different domains. A child domain does not inherit the password policy of its parent domain.

    B. Incorrect: Password policies apply domain-wide. Password policies applied at the OU level do not override the password policies set at the domain level. If this set of steps is taken, the password policies will remain as they did before at the domain level.

    C. Incorrect: Password policies apply domain-wide. Password policies applied at the site level do not override the password policies set at the domain level. If this set of steps is taken, the password policies will remain as they did before at the domain level.

    D. Incorrect: Password policies apply domain-wide. Password policies applied at the local level do not override the password policies set at the domain level. If this set of steps is taken, the password policies will remain as they did before at the domain level.

4.   **Correct Answers: B**

    A. Incorrect: Terminal Server configuration settings are not used for dial-in permissions or access.

    B. Correct: The settings in the user account are likely prohibiting the user from accessing the network using a dial-in connection.

    C. Incorrect: This would not prohibit the user from dialing in to the network remotely.

    D. Incorrect: The user account is the same for both remote and local access, so confused credentials are unlikely.

16 Exam 70-292—Managing and Maintaining Access to Resources (2.0)

Access to resources requires proper identification and proper permissions. There is no additional configuration to be done to access files across a network than to make sure that the resource is accessible (shared) and that the user has appropriate permissions to accomplish the desired action (read, write, delete, and so on). This transactional process of analyzing the user's access token involves reading the entries on the resource's access control list (ACL) and comparing the list with the security identifiers (SIDs) on the token. If the security services governing the resource access process determine that the combination of SIDs and their permissions is sufficient to perform the requested task, permission and access is granted; if not, access to the resource is denied.

The operating system accomplishes such permission-based access based on the file system that is installed on the storage device where the resource resides. On a FAT32 file system, for example, even if the operating system version is Microsoft Windows Server 2003, permissions cannot be set at the file system level: NTFS permissions are required for this type of permission assignment.

Share permissions, however, can be set regardless of the file system on which the resources are stored. The operating system alone controls the share permissions, which are valid for any entity attempting to access the resource from across the network.

Terminal Services provides a different type of access to resources, in that it presents a local environment to the user over the network. The creation and use of this virtual local environment requires additional permissions and configuration, but the resource access to files and folders is still governed by network (share) and file system (NTFS) permissions. The understanding of these additional configuration needs and possibilities is key to the proper use of Terminal Services.

Tested Skills and Suggested Practices

The skills that you need to master the Managing and Maintaining Access to Resources objective domain on *Exam 70-292: Managing and Maintaining a Microsoft Window Server 2003 Environment for an MCSA certified on Windows 2000* include

- Troubleshoot Terminal Services
    - ❏ Practice 1: Configure Terminal Services in Remote Desktop for Administration mode in such a way that various users are allowed or denied permissions. Set properties for allowed users to control their profile paths, home directories, and whether their sessions can be controlled remotely through another Terminal Services session.
    - ❏ Practice 2: Configure Group Policy for Terminal Services users to redirect local printer and drive output to the Terminal Services session. Know the purposes and functionalities for each of these settings.

Further Reading

This section lists supplemental readings by objective. You should study these sources thoroughly before taking *Exam 70-292: Managing and Maintaining a Microsoft Windows Server 2003 Environment for an MCSA Certified on Windows 2000.*

Objective 2.1   Review Chapter 10, "Managing and Maintaining a Server Environment." This chapter discusses Remote Administration with Terminal Services, including supporting and troubleshooting.

Microsoft Corporation. Windows Server 2003 Help and Support Center. Review "Remote Assistance."

Troubleshoot Terminal Services

Terminal Services has unique permission and configuration settings compared with share permissions on other resources. The use of Terminal Services requires User Rights policy (Log On Locally, for example) for the computer on which Terminal Services is running in addition to the explicit permission to use Terminal Services. In Windows Server 2003, all these rights and permission for the use of Terminal Services are given to the Remote Desktop Users group.

The settings in Terminal Services for Remote Control, Home Directory, Application Startup, and Profile Settings should not be confused with the permissions and user rights needed to access Terminal Services.

Objective 2.1 Questions

1.   You have configured several users to be able to connect to Server01 through Terminal Services and have modified the default configuration with the Terminal Services Configuration console to allow for redirection of client printers. The goal is for all users of the Terminal Server to be able to print to print devices configured on their local computer from their Terminal Server session.

The users, however, report that they are unable to print to their locally configured print devices.

What should you do to correct the problem?

   A. Enable the Client/Server data redirection setting in Group Policy for each Terminal Server client computer.

   B. Enable the Client/Server data redirection setting in Group Policy for the Terminal Server computer.

   C. Instruct the user to install the local printer from within the user's Terminal Server session.

   D. Use a logon script for the users' Terminal Server session to add the printer.

2.   You have configured several client computers with the Terminal Service client, Remote Desktop Connection, and have configured a Terminal Server in Remote Desktop for Administration (Default) mode. When the users attempt to connect to the Terminal Server, they receive an error message stating that this system's local policy does not permit them to log on interactively.

What should you do to correct the problem?

   A. Add the users to the Remote Desktop Users group.

   B. Configure the User Right policy to Log On Locally on the Terminal Server for each user.

   C. Enable the Group Policy setting for Client/Server data redirection.

   D. Enable the Terminal Services Remote Control setting for each user.

3. A user has sent you a request, by e-mail, for a Remote Assistance session. You attempt to connect to the user's computer to establish the Remote Desktop session but cannot establish the network connection. You are able to connect to the user's computer to access the file system through the C$ share. What is the likeliest cause of the problem?

   A. Your user account is not a member of the local Administrators group on the user's computer.

   B. You do not have the Terminal Services client installed on your computer.

   C. Port 3389 is not open on the firewall between your network segment and the network segment that the user's computer is on.

   D. The user's account in Active Directory directory service is configured so as not to allow Remote Control.

4. All computer users in your company access several applications through a single Terminal Server, Server01, located on the same local area network (LAN) segment. You are running a Windows Server 2003 Active Directory and DNS, and the Terminal Server is a Windows Server 2003 server.

   At the end of business on the previous day, you renamed the Terminal Server to App1. You verified that the server was reachable using its new name through Terminal Services both as administrator and as a regular user and through Windows Explorer.

   This morning, all users report that they cannot connect to the Terminal Server. You verify that connection to the Terminal Server is possible through Windows Explorer, but that user connection through Terminal Services is not possible. You are able to connect to the Terminal Server as Administrator.

   What is the likeliest cause of the problem?

   A. The Terminal Server entry in DNS needs to be refreshed.

   B. The Terminal Server connection permissions need to be refreshed.

   C. A Terminal Services Licensing Server needs to be installed and configured.

   D. The Terminal Server needs to be restarted.

5. You attempt to connect to Server01 through the Remote Desktop for Administration client but receive a message that you cannot connect because the number of concurrent connections has been exceeded.

You can connect with the Remote Desktop for Administration client to Server02, Server03, and Server04, which are member servers in the same domain. You have administrator privileges on each of these servers.

Server01 is not physically accessible to you because it is in a remote location.

What steps should you take to resolve the problem? (Choose all that apply.)

A. Connect to Server02 with the Remote Desktop for Administration client.

B. Connect to Server01 from the Terminal Services session on Server02 with the Terminal Services Manager. Disconnect one of the Remote sessions.

C. Connect to Server01 from the Terminal Services session on Server02 with the Remote Desktop for Administration client. Disconnect one of the Remote sessions.

D. Open the Server01 Properties dialog box from Active Directory Users And Computers. Configure Server01 to deny Terminal Services connections and then reconfigure Server01 to allow Terminal Services connections.

E. Connect to Server01 from the Terminal Services session on Server02 with the Remote Desktop for Administration client. Open the System properties page for Server01 and configure Server01 to deny Remote Desktop Connections and then reconfigure Server01 to allow Remote Desktop Connections.

6. Rooslan is the administrator for an organization that has three Windows Server 2003 Terminal Servers running in application server mode. These servers have been operational for six months and have worked with the organization's 120 Windows 2000 Professional workstations. Rooslan has spent the last weekend upgrading 20 of the Windows 2000 Professional workstations to Windows XP Professional. On Monday he receives calls from the users of these upgraded workstations that they are having trouble connecting to the three Windows Server 2003 Terminal Servers. When they were using Windows 2000 Professional systems they had no such problems. Rooslan uses his Windows 2000 Professional workstation to check the servers but finds that he can connect to each server without a problem. A colleague who also uses 2000 Professional also reports to Rooslan that he has no problems with the terminal servers. Which of the following best explains what is happening?

A. Windows XP Professional workstations do not come with a built in Terminal Services client access license (CAL) like Window 2000 Professional workstations do.

B. The license server has crashed.

C. The users on the Windows XP Professional systems are using the Remote Desktop Connection client. They need to download and install the Terminal Services client.

D. The users on the Windows XP Professional systems do not have the requisite permissions to access the Terminal Servers.

7. Oksana is the administrator for an organization that has five Windows Server 2003 Terminal Servers running in application server mode. All these servers are member servers of a domain running at the functional level of Windows Server 2003. Oksana has recently upgraded the RAM and processor on one of the servers and has decided that with its increased capacity the server will be able to support more concurrent connections. She logs on to the server in question and uses the Terminal Services Configuration console, increasing the maximum connections on the server's single network adapter from 60 to 100. A week later Oksana notices that the number of concurrent connections on the newly upgraded server has never exceeded 60. Which of the following best explains what is happening?

A. These servers have the standard version of Windows Server 2003 installed. Oksana needs to install the Enterprise edition to support more than 60 concurrent connections.

B. Domain Group Policy has been configured to allow only a maximum of 60 connections.

C. The number of concurrent sessions is dependent on the bandwidth of the network rather than any setting configured. Oksana must upgrade her network to 100 megabits before more than 60 connections will be supported.

D. The Terminal Services software needs to be reinstalled before the number of concurrent connections can be increased.

8. Rooslan has been performing a security audit of the network at his organization. One of the tests that he is performing is packet sniffing data to determine if any sensitive information is being transmitted across the network in an unencrypted format. Rooslan discovers that clients in the accounting department who are using Windows XP Professional workstations to connect to a Windows Server 2003 are receiving unencrypted data from the server. Further investigation reveals that data traveling to the servers is encrypted. Which of the following actions can Rooslan take to make sure that data traveling both to and from the server is encrypted? (Choose all that apply.)

A. Configure the encryption level of the RDP-TCP Properties in the Terminal Services Configuration Console to Client Compatible.

B. Configure the encryption level of the RDP-TCP Properties in the Terminal Services Configuration Console to FIPS Compliant.

C. Configure the encryption level of the RDP-TCP Properties in the Terminal Services Configuration Console to High.

D. Configure the encryption level of the RDP-TCP Properties in the Terminal Services Configuration Console to Low.

9.   Kasia has been asked to reduce the encryption level of the RDP-TCP connection for Terminal Services from FIPS to Client Compatible on a Windows Server 2003 member server within her organization's domain. This server is located at the head office where Kasia works. The encryption level needs to be adjusted because the organization that she works for has recently purchased a small business that uses a mixture of Windows NT 4.0 workstations and Linux systems. These systems have Terminal Services client software but are unable to connect to the Windows Server 2003 Terminal Server because as they don't meet the FIPS requirements. Before the organization that Kasia works for purchased the small business, they were able to access a stand-alone Windows Server 2003 system that ran Terminal Services. Kasia modifies the default domain policy Computer Configuration, Administrative Templates, Windows Components, Terminal Services, Encryption And Security, Set Client Connection Encryption Level To Client Compatible. When she checks a day later she finds that none of the Windows NT 4.0 or Linux clients are able to connect. What is the best explanation for this?

A. Windows NT 4.0 Workstation and Linux clients cannot be properly recognized by Terminal Services licensing and hence cannot connect to a Windows Server 2003 Terminal Server.

B. The site Group Policy Object (GPO) policy at the small business is configured as Set Client Connection Encryption Level and is still set to FIPS.

C. FIPS compliance has been enabled by the System Cryptography: Use FIPS Compliant Algorithms For Encryption, Hashing, and Signing Group Policy in the default domain GPO.

D. This setting cannot be configured by Group Policy but must be done through the Terminal Services Configuration console.

10. Linton has noticed that a large number of users leave disconnected sessions idle on the five Windows Server 2003 Terminal Servers in his organization. The five servers are all in the same forest. Three are in the root domain contoso.com, and two are in the child domain sydney.contoso.com. The lingering disconnected sessions often means that other users cannot connect to the server that is Terminal Server enabled until these disconnected sessions are manually terminated. Linton wants to configure the five terminal servers so that they all end disconnected sessions after three hours. Which of the following presents the way for him to do this? (Choose all that apply.)

A. Set the domain default domain GPO for contoso.com with the Computer Configuration, Administrative Templates, Windows Components, Terminal Services, Sessions, Set Time Limit For Disconnected Sessions to 3 hours.

B. Add the machine accounts for each of the five terminal servers to a universal group named TSDISCONNECT. Create a new GPO in the domain contoso.com with the Computer Configuration, Administrative Templates, Windows Components, Terminal Services, Sessions, Set Time Limit For Disconnected Sessions to 2 hours. Apply this GPO to the contoso.com domain and set the read and apply policy only to the members of the TSDISCONNECT group.

C. Create a separate site for the three Terminal Servers in the contoso.com domain and move these servers to this site. Create a GPO with the Computer Configuration, Administrative Templates, Windows Components, Terminal Services, Sessions, Set Time Limit For Disconnected Sessions to 3 minutes. Apply this GPO to the site with the Terminal Servers.

D. Set the domain default domain GPO for Sydney.contoso.com with the Computer Configuration, Administrative Templates, Windows Components, Terminal Services, Sessions, Set Time Limit For Disconnected Sessions to 3 hours.

1. **Correct Answers: A**

    A. **Correct:** Although set to Not Configured by default, if set to Disabled, this Group Policy setting will override the Terminal Server console settings for the property of data redirection. Changing this policy from Disabled to Enabled will correct the problem.

    B. **Incorrect:** This Group Policy setting is for local computer behavior during a Terminal Services session from that computer. Enabling this setting for the Terminal Server computer would control outgoing Terminal Server sessions from that console, not incoming from the client computers as required here.

    C. **Incorrect:** This would configure a network printer connection to the local computer, which is not what the circumstance requires. Additional steps to share and set permissions for the printer from the local computer would have to be taken.

    D. **Incorrect:** This would configure a network printer connection to the local computer, which is not what the circumstance requires. Additional steps to share and set permissions for the printer from the local computer would have to be taken.

2. **Correct Answers: A**

    A. **Correct:** The Remote Desktop Users group has the appropriate configuration and rights to allow access to the Terminal Server.

    B. **Incorrect:** This setting will remove one of the barriers to the user's connecting to the Terminal Server, but there are permissions for connection to the Terminal Server itself that still must be set. Additionally, this action would allow the user to log on locally to the console as well, which might not be desired.

    C. **Incorrect:** This setting is for controlling how printer and drive redirection is accomplished within a user session, not for configuring logon access to the session itself.

    D. **Incorrect:** This setting is for controlling how Remote Control can be used on an established Terminal Services session, not for the logon access to the session itself.

3. **Correct Answers: C**

    A. **Incorrect:** This is not the case, seeing as how you are able to establish a connection to an administrative share point (C$) on the user's computer.

    B. **Incorrect:** The Terminal Services client is not involved in a Remote Assistance session. The Windows Messenger Services are responsible for handling the establishing and usage of a Remote Assistance session.

C. **Correct:** The Remote Assistance services use port 3389 to communicate. If you are unable to establish a connection to the user's computer, this is most likely the problem.

D. **Incorrect:** This setting controls whether or not Remote Control is allowed of a user's Terminal Server session, not Remote Assistance.

4.   Correct Answers: C

A. **Incorrect:** Because the computer is reachable through Windows Explorer, name resolution is not the problem.

B. **Incorrect:** The connection permissions were configured properly, as you verified after the name change on the Terminal Server, and there are no other refresh problems that would occur. These permissions are not affected by any DNS or Group Policy refreshing mechanism.

C. **Correct:** This is most likely the cause of the problem. Terminal Services will install and run properly for 120 days. After this period has expired, the Terminal Server will refuse connections until a license server is configured and available.

D. **Incorrect:** The service is not likely to be the problem because you can connect as Administrator and the service was running properly when tested after the server name change.

5.   Correct Answers: A and B

A. **Correct:** By connecting to another Terminal Server (any of the others accessible to you would suffice), you will gain access to the Terminal Services Manager console, which is how you will disconnect one of the established Terminal Services sessions to Server01, allowing you to establish another under your credentials.

B. **Correct:** The Terminal Services Manager can connect to any server in the domain that is running Terminal Services. From the Terminal Services Manager, you are able to disconnect one of the remote sessions, allowing you to establish another under your credentials.

C. **Incorrect:** If you are unable to connect to Server01 using the Remote Desktop client on your computer, the same denial of connection will occur if you attempt to connect from any other computer, regardless of whether or not that other computer is a Terminal Server.

D. **Incorrect:** This is not a valid option. The Properties dialog box of a system in Active Directory Users And Computers does not allow the configuration of Terminal Services.

E. **Incorrect:** This disabling/enabling exercise will not change any configuration on the computer, nor will it disconnect any active sessions. Because the denial of your remote connection is due to the limit on the number of sessions, the problem persists.

6. **Correct Answers: A**

   A. **Correct:** Unlike Windows 2000 Professional, which shipped with a built in Terminal Services CAL, Windows XP Professional does not. For a Windows XP Professional workstation to access Terminal Services, a Terminal Services license for that connection must be purchased and installed on the license server.

   B. **Incorrect:** If the license server had crashed, users of the Windows 2000 Professional workstations would also be reporting problems connecting to the Terminal Servers.

   C. **Incorrect:** Changing client software will not resolve the problem. The Windows XP systems cannot connect because they are unlicensed. The Windows 2000 Professional systems can connect because they are licensed.

   D. **Incorrect:** Since these same users were able to log in last week through their Windows 2000 Professional systems and made no mention of any problems, and since the question text makes no mention of any account privileges being altered, the explanation that the users do not have the requisite permissions to access the terminal server is clearly incorrect.

7. **Correct Answers: B**

   A. **Incorrect:** Theoretically, the standard version of Windows Server 2003, properly licensed, can support an unlimited number of connections. This is generally impractical given the demands that many Terminal Services sessions place on a server.

   B. **Correct:** Group Policy overrides the configuration set with the Terminal Services Configuration console. If the Computer Configuration, Administrative Templates, Windows Components, Terminal Services, Limit Number Of Connections policy has been set, it will override any locally configured setting.

   C. **Incorrect:** Although network bandwidth will definitely influence the performance of a Terminal Server, it has no limiting influence on the number of concurrent sessions that a server may support.

   D. **Incorrect:** This is simply incorrect. Unless the software has somehow become corrupted, at which point there would be no active sessions, it should not need to be reinstalled.

8.   Correct Answers: A, B, and C

A. Correct: With Windows XP Professional clients and a Windows Server 2003 terminal server, altering the encryption level to Client Compatible will result in 128-bit encryption of data sent not only from client to server but also from server to client.

B. Correct: Setting the encryption level of the RDP-TCP connection to FIPS Compliant means that data sent from client to server and from server to client will be encrypted both ways. FIPS stands for Federal Information Processing Standards and uses specified encryption algorithms by means of Microsoft's cryptographic modules.

C. Correct: High level of encryption encrypts data sent from client to server and from server to client using 128-bit encryption. For this setting to be used, the client must support 128-bit encryption; if it does not, no connection will be possible. Windows XP clients support 128-bit encrypted connections of this type.

D. Incorrect: Although setting the RDP-TCP properties to low results in 56-bit encryption being used to transmit data from the client to the server, no encryption is used to send data from the server to the client. This is the setting that the Terminal Server is currently configured with in this scenario.

9.   Correct Answers: C

A. Incorrect: Such clients can be recognized by the licensing system and appropriate licenses must be purchased for their use. The fact that these clients have already connected to a Windows Server 2003 Terminal Server should provide a hint that this answer is not correct.

B. Incorrect: Site policies are generally overridden by domain policies. Also, the site at the small business does not host the Terminal Server that Kasia is reconfiguring.

C. Correct: If the System Cryptography: Use FIPS Compliant Algorithms For Encryption, Hashing, And Signing Group Policy has been enabled in the default domain GPO, the encryption level used by Terminal Services cannot be changed by using the Computer Configuration, Administrative Templates, Windows Components, Terminal Services, Encryption And Security, Set Client Connection Encryption Level policy. Nor can it be altered by using the Terminal Services Configuration console. The system cryptography policy must be changed before the encryption level of connections to the Terminal Server can be altered.

D. Incorrect: Group Policy can be used to configure the encryption setting for Terminal Services connections. A configured Group Policy will also always override the configuration set by the Terminal Services Configuration console.

10.   Correct Answers: A and D

A. Correct: This is the answer to the first part of the question. As there are two separate domains, this step must also be performed in the child domain for all five servers to be configured to correctly terminate lingering disconnected sessions.

B. Incorrect: Although in a forest that is running at Windows Server 2003 functional level computer accounts from different domains can indeed be added to universal groups, group policies can be applied only within a single domain—not throughout a forest. The time applied is also incorrect.

C. Incorrect: The duration is set to 3 minutes rather than 3 hours. This is also not an effective use of sites, as it will involve moving these terminal servers to a separate subnet.

D. Correct: This is the answer to the second part of the question. As there are two separate domains, this step must also be performed in the root domain for all five servers to be configured to correctly terminate lingering disconnected sessions.

17 Exam 70-292—Managing and Maintaining a Server Environment (3.0)

Managing a Microsoft Windows Server 2003 system requires an awareness of what is occurring on the system. The best place to find this information is in the event logs. The three main event logs on a Windows Server 2003 system are the System, Security, and Application logs. Event log views can be filtered so that only information in which the administrator is interested is displayed.

Another part of server management is ensuring that relevant updates are downloaded and applied to the system on a timely basis. Microsoft patched many of the largest system vulnerabilities of the last few years, but systems administrators had not found the time to install those patches on servers. If administrators had found the time to install those patches, they would not have been vulnerable to such worms as Code Red and Slammer. Software Update Services (SUS) runs on Windows Server 2003 and allows an organization to use a Windows Server running on its network as the update server from which to download patches from Microsoft, rather than using Microsoft Update servers located on the Internet.

Licensing is another area that requires attention. If the company is audited for license compliance and is found wanting, the punishment for infringement can be severe. Understanding clearly how licensing works can also save a company money because a company might find better licensing options than the ones it currently uses.

Several tools exist to remotely manage servers. These include Terminal Services, Remote Assistance, the Computer Management Console, and Hypertext Markup Language (HTML) remote administration tools. Each can be used in a specific situation to perform a specific set of tasks. Administrators should be aware of the benefits and limitations of each form of remote management.

The ability to maintain a reliable file and print server infrastructure is also important. System administrators must be able to diagnose and troubleshoot problems on file and print servers as well as monitor file and print server performance to determine if anything must be done to improve that performance.

Tested Skills and Suggested Practices

The skills that you need to master the Managing and Maintaining a Server Environment objective domain on *Exam 70-292: Managing and Maintaining a Microsoft Windows Server 2003 Environment for an MCSA Certified on Windows 2000* include

- Manage Software Update Infrastructure

  - Practice 1: Install and configure the SUS add-in to generate a list of updates that you have approved and to download those updates to the SUS server. Use Group Policy to configure a Windows XP Professional system to use the SUS server as its Automatic Updates server.

  - Practice 2: Deploy a service pack using Group Policy to a Windows XP Professional system.

- Manage Servers Remotely

  - Practice 1: Install the Hypertext Markup Language (HTML) remote administration tools on a Windows Server 2003 member server and use the tools to change the server name.

  - Practice2: Log on to a remote Windows Server 2003 system using Terminal Services Remote Desktop for Administration mode.

- Manage a Web Server

  - Practice 1: Configure a second Internet Protocol (IP) address on the Ethernet adapter on a Windows Server 2003 system with Internet Information Services (IIS) installed. Configure one Web site to respond to Hypertext Transfer Protocol (HTTP) requests on the first IP address and another Web site to respond to requests on the second IP address.

  - Practice 2: Configure Web site security so that only hosts with particular IP addresses can access the Web site. Attempt to access the Web site from an allowed host and from a denied host IP address to check that the security works.

  - Practice 3: Configure two Web sites to run off a single IP address, directing content using Host Header names.

Further Reading

This section lists supplemental readings by objective. We recommend that you study these sources thoroughly before taking this exam.

Objective 3.1   Review Chapter 10, "Managing and Maintaining a Server Environment," which contains lessons about using Software Update Services and deploying service packs.

Microsoft Corporation. Windows Server 2003 Help and Support Center. Review "Deploying Software Updates."

Objective 3.2   Review Chapter 10, Lesson 1, "Remote Administration of Windows Server 2003," which provides information about managing servers remotely with the MMC, Remote Administration with Remote Desktop for Administration, and using Remote Assistance.

Microsoft Corporation. Windows Server 2003 Help and Support Center. Review "Terminal Services," "HTML Remote Administration Tools," and "Remote Assistance."

Objective 3.3   Review Chapter 10, Lesson 3, "Configuring and Managing Web Servers Using IIS," which details how to administer and secure IIS.

Microsoft Corporation. Windows Server 2003 Help and Support Center. Review "Internet Information Services."

Objective 3.1

Manage Software Update Infrastructure

Software Update Services (SUS) is an add-in to Windows Server 2003 and cannot be installed from the installation media. It must be downloaded from the Microsoft Web site. SUS enables administrators to construct an approved list of updates that can be deployed throughout their organization.

SUS works in two parts. The first part is the SUS server, which hosts a list of approved updates. The SUS server can also be configured to store updates, saving clients the bother of downloading the approved updates from the Microsoft Windows Update servers. The second part is the clients that must be configured to use the SUS server rather than the Windows Update Server. This configuration can only be done through a setting change made in Group Policy; it cannot be done from the Automatic Updates tab of the System console in Control Panel. This can be done from a local Group Policy Object (GPO) as well as those applied to sites, domains, and organizational units (OUs).

Some updates, such as service packs, can also be deployed without SUS by simply using Group Policy software installation settings. The relevant area of Group Policy is in the Computer Configuration\Software Settings node. The service pack must be extracted to a file share that is accessible to all clients on the network. In some cases, with slow wide area network (WAN) links, administrators might want to host the extracted service pack on a file share at each site and then use a site-linked GPO to point the computers at each site to their local update files rather than have all systems copy the service pack from a central location.

Objective 3.1 Questions

1. You are the systems administrator for a medium-sized organization and you are considering employing Software Update Services to manage updates provided by Microsoft for your Windows XP Professional systems. Your organization currently uses a proxy solution running on another platform that requires username and password authentication. The user and password database for the proxy is different from that used in your Windows Server 2003 domain. Given this situation, which of the following options is available to you in configuring a software update infrastructure?

   A. Because SUS cannot be configured to authenticate against a proxy, all updates must be manually downloaded by an administrator and placed on the SUS server. The Windows XP Professional machines should be configured using Group Policy to contact the SUS server for their software updates.

   B. Because SUS cannot be configured to authenticate against a proxy and Windows XP clients can, Windows XP clients should continue to contact Microsoft to download their updates.

   C. SUS can be configured to authenticate against a proxy to download a list of updates for your approval. Windows XP systems should be configured to check the SUS server to find which updates you have approved and then to automatically download those updates from the Microsoft Web site.

   D. SUS can be configured to authenticate against a proxy to download a list of updates for your approval as well as to download the updates. Windows XP systems should be configured to check the SUS server to determine which updates are approved and then to retrieve them from the SUS server.

2. You are the systems administrator for a medium-sized organization that is considering implementing SUS on all Windows XP Professional workstations and Windows Server 2003 systems companywide. Before a companywide rollout is to go ahead, a pilot program is to be implemented. You have been assigned a lab with 10 Windows XP Professional workstations, a Windows Server 2003 member server running SUS, a Windows Server 2003 domain controller, and a stand-alone Windows Server 2003 system. You wish to configure all systems except the server running SUS to use the SUS server to automatically check for, download, and install updates at 7:00 A.M. each day. Which of the following steps should you take to do this? (Choose all that apply.)

   A. Use the Automatic Updates tab in the System console from Control Panel on every Windows XP Professional workstation computer to set the update server to the address of the SUS server. Set the Windows XP workstations to automatically download and install updates at 7:00 A.M. each day.

B. Use the Automatic Updates tab in the System console from Control Panel on each Windows Server 2003 system except the SUS server to set the update server to the address of the SUS server. Set these servers to automatically download and install updates at 7:00 A.M. each day.

C. Place the Windows XP Professional workstations and the Windows Server 2003 domain controller in a separate OU named Uptest. Edit a GPO's Windows Update properties for the Uptest OU, specifying the address of the update server as the SUS server in the Specify Intranet Microsoft Update Service Location policy. Set Configure Automatic Updates Policy to automatic download and install and set the scheduled install day to Every Day and the time to 7:00 A.M. Apply this GPO to the Uptest OU.

D. On the stand-alone Windows Server 2003 system, edit the local GPO's Windows Update properties, specifying the address of the update server as the SUS server in the Specify Intranet Microsoft Update Service Location policy. Set Configure Automatic Updates Policy to automatic download and install and set the scheduled install day to Every Day and the time to 7:00 A.M. Apply this GPO to the Uptest OU.

E. On the SUS server, edit the local GPO's Windows Update properties, specifying the address of the update server as the SUS server in the Specify Intranet Microsoft Update Service Location policy. Set Configure Automatic Updates Policy to automatic download and install and set the scheduled install day to Every Day and the time to 7:00 A.M. Apply this GPO to the Uptest OU.

3. Rooslan works for a company that has a single remote office connected by Integrated Services Digital Network Basic Rate Interface (ISDN BRI) to headquarters. The remote site has a 10-megabit connection to the Internet. Headquarters has a 20-megabit connection to the Internet. The ISDN BRI connections are mostly used to carry Active Directory and distributed file system (Dfs) replication traffic. The company has a single Windows Server 2003 domain. The remote office and the headquarters are each configured as a separate site in Active Directory for replication purposes. Two Windows Server 2003 systems are running SUS. One server is located at the headquarters location and is configured to host a list of approved updates and to store those approved updates locally. The other SUS server is located at the remote site.

Primary Goal:

Rooslan wants the Windows XP Professional workstations and the Windows Server 2003 systems to download only updates that are on the approved list on the SUS server.

Secondary Goal:

Rooslan does not want to overburden the ISDN BRI connections with the transfer of updates from the SUS server located at headquarters.

Tertiary Goal:

Rooslan wants to minimize the amount of updates downloaded to headquarters through the 20-megabit Internet connection.

Which of the following will allow Rooslan to accomplish his primary, secondary, and tertiary goals? (Choose all that apply—the correct answers combine to form a completely correct solution.)

A. Rooslan should edit a GPO and configure the Windows Update properties. The Specify Intranet Microsoft Update Service Location policy should have the settings of the second SUS server for the Update Detection and Statistics fields. This Group Policy should be applied to the remote site.

B. Configure the second SUS server to retrieve a list of approved updates from the first SUS server. Also configure the second SUS server to maintain the update files on Microsoft Windows Update server.

C. Configure the first SUS server to host a list of approved updates and to download and store those approved updates.

D. Rooslan should edit a GPO and configure the Windows Update properties. The Specify Intranet Microsoft Update Service Location policy should have the settings of the first SUS server for the Update Detection and Statistics fields. This Group Policy should be applied to the headquarters site.

E. Rooslan should edit a GPO and configure the Windows Update properties. The Specify Intranet Microsoft Update Service Location policy should have the settings of the first SUS server for the Update Detection and Statistics fields. This Group Policy should be applied to the remote site.

F. Rooslan should edit a GPO and configure the Windows Update properties. The Specify Intranet Microsoft Update Service Location policy should have the settings of the second SUS server for the Update Detection and Statistics fields. This Group Policy should be applied to the headquarters site.

4.   Mick works as the network administrator for an organization that has five branch offices located across a city. The headquarters office has the only connection to the Internet and also hosts a proxy server. Headquarters has 200 Windows XP Professional workstations and several Windows Server 2003 systems. Each of the five branch offices has 150 Windows XP Professional workstations and several Windows Server 2003 systems. These branch offices are connected by ISDN BRI to the headquarters office. Currently none of the Windows systems is able to receive updates from Microsoft Windows Update because they are unable to authenticate against the proxy. Management has asked Mick to implement SUS throughout the organization so that approved updates can be installed on workstations and servers. Management also wants Mick to minimize the amount of update traffic running through the ISDN BRI lines. Which of the following methods will achieve this goal?

   A. Configure a SUS server in the headquarters location to maintain a list of approved updates and to download and store those updates from the Microsoft Windows Update. Configure a Group Policy that instructs clients to use the SUS server as their update server. Apply this GPO to the headquarters and branch-office sites.

   B. Configure a SUS server in the headquarters location to maintain a list of approved updates but maintain those updates on the Microsoft Windows Update. Configure a Group Policy that instructs clients to use the SUS server as their update server. Apply this GPO to the headquarters and branch-office sites.

   C. Configure a SUS server in the headquarters location to maintain a list of approved updates but maintain those updates on the Microsoft Windows Update. Configure a SUS server in each branch office location to maintain a list of approved updates but maintain those updates on the Microsoft Windows Update. Create a GPO and apply it at each site. The GPO should have a policy that clients are to use their local SUS server as their update server.

   D. Configure a SUS server in the headquarters location to maintain a list of approved updates and to download and store those approved updates. Configure SUS servers in each branch office to synchronize with the SUS server in the headquarters location. Configure a Group Policy that instructs clients to use the headquarters SUS server as their update server. Apply this GPO to the headquarters and branch-office sites.

   E. Configure a SUS server in the headquarters location to maintain a list of approved updates and to download and store those approved updates. Configure SUS servers in each branch office to synchronize with the SUS server in the headquarters location. Create a GPO and apply it at each site. The GPO should have a policy that clients are to use their local SUS server as their update server.

5.   Orin is the systems administrator for an academic department at the local university. The department has 40 Windows XP Professional workstations and two Windows Server 2003 systems. One of these systems is configured as a domain controller, the other as a file and print server. All department computers are members of a single Windows Server 2003 domain. Microsoft has recently released a service pack for Windows XP and, after testing it, Orin feels confident enough to deploy it to the Windows XP Professional workstations in his department. Orin extracts the service pack to a directory on the file server called \\Fileshare\newsrvpk. Which of the following methods can Orin use to install the service pack on all Windows XP Professional workstations? (Choose all that apply.)

A. Orin can visit each Windows XP Professional workstation and install the service pack from the file share.

B. Orin can create a group called Xpwkstn and put all the Windows XP Professional workstation computer accounts in this group. He can then create a GPO in which he sets up a new package in the Computer Configuration\Software Settings node using the location of the service pack .msi file on the \\Fileshare\newsrvpk share. In the Deploy Software dialog box, he should select Assign and then apply this GPO to the Xpwkstn group.

C. Orin can create a group called Xpusrs and put all those who use Windows XP Professional workstations in this group. He can then create a GPO in which he sets up a new package in the Computer Configuration\Software Settings node using the location of the service pack .msi file on the \\Fileshare\newsrvpk share. In the Deploy Software dialog box, he should select Assign and then apply this GPO to the Xpusrs group.

D. Orin can create an OU called Xpwkstn and put all the Windows XP Professional workstation computer accounts in this OU. He can then create a GPO in which he sets up a new package in the Computer Configuration\Software Settings node using the location of the service pack .msi file on the \\Fileshare\newsrvpk share. In the Deploy Software dialog box, he should select Assign and then apply this GPO to the Xpwkstn OU.

Objective 3.1 Answers

1. **Correct Answers: D**

A. Incorrect: SUS can be configured to authenticate against a proxy.

B. Incorrect: SUS can be configured to authenticate against a proxy.

C. Incorrect: Windows XP software update cannot be configured to authenticate against a proxy. In this situation the SUS server should be configured to download the updates as well so that the Windows XP systems can in turn download and install relevant updates from the SUS server.

D. Correct: Because the Windows XP client software update mechanism cannot authenticate against a proxy, they must retrieve the updates from the local SUS server. The list of updates that will be retrieved and installed will be based on the list of approved updates configured by the administrator of the SUS server.

2. **Correct Answers: C and D**

A. Incorrect: Windows XP Professional computer cannot be configured to contact an alternate update server using the System console.

B. Incorrect: Windows Server 2003 systems cannot be configured to contact an alternate update server using the System console.

C. Correct: This is the correct way to do this for computers that are members of the domain: Add them all to an OU and then apply a Group Policy with the correct update settings.

D. Correct: Because this server is not a member of the domain, this setting must be configured in the local GPO.

E. Incorrect: The SUS server was not to be configured for updating from itself; it is still meant to update from the Microsoft site.

3. **Correct Answers: A, B, C, and D**

A. Correct: This is the second part of the secondary goal and part of the primary goal. If the Group Policy pointed the clients at the first SUS server, the ISDN BRI link would be flooded by downloading updates from that server.

B. Correct: This setting will mean that clients configured to contact this SUS server will use the approved list from this server but will download the updates themselves from Microsoft Windows Update server. This is the first part of the secondary goal.

C. Correct: The first server will be able to provide update services to the headquarters site, including a list of approved updates, as well as to allow those updates to be retrieved from the server. This is part of the tertiary and primary goals.

D. Correct: This will complete the tertiary goal and is part of the primary goal. By using the first SUS server rather than the second, the headquarters clients will retrieve their update list and the updates themselves from the first SUS server. If they were pointed at the second SUS server, they would download the approved updates from Microsoft, which would not be optimal use of the headquarters connection to the Internet.

E. Incorrect: This will mean that computers at the remote site will download their updates from the first SUS server rather than from the Microsoft update servers, flooding the bandwidth of the ISDN BRI line. This would violate the secondary goal.

F. Incorrect: This will result in clients at headquarters downloading approved updates from Microsoft instead of from the first SUS server, which would violate the tertiary goal.

4. **Correct Answers: E**

A. Incorrect: Although this will allow updates to be rolled out to all clients within the organization, it will also saturate the ISDN BRI lines with update traffic because each client workstation downloads its updates from the central SUS server.

B. Incorrect: Although clients will have a list of updates, because they do not have the ability to authenticate against the proxy, they cannot download updates from the Microsoft Windows Update.

C. Incorrect: Although clients will have a list of updates, because they do not have the ability to authenticate against the proxy they cannot download updates from the Microsoft Windows Update.

D. Incorrect: Although this will allow updates to be rolled out to all clients within the organization, it will also saturate the ISDN BRI lines with update traffic because each client workstation downloads its updates from the central SUS server. Branch office computers must use their local SUS server.

E. Correct: This solution will result in rolling out updates to each computer in the organization, but it will also result in update traffic being passed only once across the ISDN BRI links. This solution meets management's criteria.

5.   **Correct Answers: A and D**

    A. **Correct:** This method will work, although it's not the most efficient way of performing this operation.

    B. **Incorrect:** Group policies cannot be applied to groups, only to sites, domains, and organizational units.

    C. **Incorrect:** Group policies cannot be applied to groups, only to sites, domains, and organizational units.

    D. **Correct:** The Group Policy will apply only to those Windows XP Professional workstations that are in the Xpwkstn OU. Because all relevant Windows XP Professional workstations have been added to this OU, however, the service pack will be deployed the next time the computers restart.

Manage Servers Remotely

Because server rooms are often loud and difficult sites from which to work, the majority of systems administrators manage their Windows Server 2003 systems remotely from their desks. Administrators might visit the server room from time to time to perform tasks such as swapping out backup tapes, but systems administrators very rarely spend the majority of their time in the same rooms as the servers they manage.

Windows Server 2003 offers several methods for remote management. The first tool is the Computer Management Console, which can be configured to connect to a remote system and perform many of the same administration tasks that can be performed on a local system. Several servers can be added to a single Computer Management Console, meaning that the administrator can use the one tool to manage multiple systems.

The second form of remote management is to use Terminal Services to remotely control the server. This gives the administrator the appearance of actually sitting in front of the server console and allows administrators to perform all management tasks as though they were actually at the server.

Another form of remote management is the HTML remote administration tool. This allows an administrator to connect to a Web service running on the Windows Server 2003 system and perform a limited set of administrative tasks. It can provide an administrative option over low-bandwidth wide area network (WAN) lines, such as those that use modems, that would render a Terminal Services connection unusable.

Remote assistance is slightly different from connecting by Terminal Services to control a server. When a remote assistance invitation is issued, an administrator working on the server can issue an invitation so that another administrator can remotely watch, or contribute to, the steps that are taken.

Objective 3.2 Questions

1. Rooslan is the senior systems administrator at a medium-sized organization. His office is located at the company headquarters in Melbourne, Australia. He has just received a telephone call from Alex, who is responsible for maintaining a server at one of the organization's branch sites in Auckland, New Zealand. The two sites are connected by means of an ISDN BRI line. Alex is about to modify some registry settings on one of the servers in Auckland and wants Rooslan to watch him remotely so that he can check that Alex completes the procedure correctly. Which of the following technologies will allow Rooslan to watch Alex modify the Auckland server's registry and talk him through any parts of the procedure that he does not understand?

   A. Remote Assistance

   B. Terminal Services Remote Administration Mode

   C. HTML Remote Administration Tools

   D. Computer Management Console

   E. REGEDT32

2. Rooslan is working from home and is using a dial-up connection to his company's RRAS server, which allows him access to Windows Server 2003 systems on the corporate LAN. It is 2:15 A.M., and the building that hosts the servers is unoccupied. Rooslan would like to initiate a disk defragmentation on the hard disk drives of several of the servers located at his office. Rooslan's home Windows XP Professional workstation is not a member of the company's Windows Server 2003 domain. Which of the following tools can Rooslan use to initiate a remote disk defragmentation?

   A. He can use the Disk Defragmenter node in his Computer Management Console in Windows XP Professional to connect to the remote systems to initiate disk defragmentation.

   B. Remote Assistance

   C. Terminal Services Remote Administration mode

   D. Using Defrag.exe from the command line of his Windows XP Professional Workstation.

3.   You want to change the name of a stand-alone Windows Server 2003 system located at a remote site on your organization's network. The system works as an FTP and WWW server and does not have a local administrator available. This server is not a member of your organization's Windows Server 2003 domain and your Windows XP Professional workstation is. Which of the following tools can you use to accomplish this task? (Choose all that apply.)

   A. Local Computer Management Console

   B. HTML Remote Administration Tools

   C. Terminal Services Remote Administration mode

   D. Active Directory Users And Computers Console

4.   You are the systems administrator for a small organization that has recently bought out a rival company. Your organization has a Windows Server 2003 domain, of which all computers are members. The rival company has six stand-alone Windows Server 2003 systems. The two networks have been integrated, and there are no firewalls between your Windows XP Professional workstation and the remote servers. Your Windows XP Professional system is a member of the domain and you have Domain Administrator privileges. You also have administrator credentials on each of the stand-alone servers. You also have the telephone numbers of staff at each site who currently have administrative privileges on each server and are logged on during business hours. Which of the following tools can you use to configure the remote stand-alone Windows Server 2003 systems to join your organization's domain? (Choose all that apply.)

   A. The Computer Management Console on your Windows XP Professional System

   B. Active Directory Users And Computers

   C. HTML Remote Administration Tools

   D. Terminal Services Remote Administration mode

   E. Remote Assistance

5.   Alex is the systems administrator of a remote satellite-tracking facility located in Outback, Australia. The facility is connected by ISDN line to a central site in Sydney. Alex is having some trouble configuring tracking software on the server and is on a support call to an administrator at the central site who is attempting to talk him through it. The administrator asks if Alex would be able to send a remote assistance invitation to him so that he can better talk Alex through the procedure. Which of the following methods will allow the administrator to receive Alex's remote assistance invitation? (Choose all that apply.)

   A. Alex can send a remote invitation to the administrator by using Windows Messenger and the Remote Assistance Wizard.

   B. Alex can e-mail a remote assistance invitation to the administrator using the Remote Assistance Wizard.

   C. Alex can create the invitation as a file and place it on an FTP server where the administrator can download it and access it

   D. Alex can run the Remote Desktop Connection client and set it to connect to the administrator's system.

   E. Alex can create the invitation as a file and place it on a file share where the administrator can access it.

Objective 3.2 Answers

1.   Correct Answers: A

A. Correct: Alex can issue a Remote Assistance invitation to Rooslan, which will enable Rooslan to view the server's screen as Alex makes the necessary registry modifications.

B. Incorrect: Although this will allow Rooslan to view the server remotely, it will not enable him to view the changes that Alex makes to the registry as they happen.

C. Incorrect: Although this technology allows Rooslan to administer the server remotely, it will not allow him to view the registry nor to watch Alex make the necessary modifications.

D. Incorrect: Although this technology allows Rooslan to administer the server remotely, it will not allow him to view the registry nor to watch Alex make the necessary modifications.

E. Incorrect: Although this technology allows Rooslan to view the registry on the remote server, it will not allow him to view the registry nor to watch Alex make the necessary modifications.

2.   Correct Answers: C

A. Incorrect: The disk defragmenter that ships with Windows XP and Windows Server 2003 cannot be used to perform remote disk defragmentation.

B. Incorrect: Because there is no one at the building that hosts the servers, Remote Assistance invitations cannot be sent.

C. Correct: This tool will allow Rooslan to connect remotely to each server and to initiate a disk defragmentation.

D. Incorrect: The Defrag.exe command cannot be used to defragment remote systems.

3.   **Correct Answers: B and C**

    A. Incorrect: Because the system is not a member of the domain, you will be unable to log on through the Local Computer Management Console to perform administrative tasks on this server.

    B. Correct: The HTML Remote Administration Tools can be used to rename a server as well as to join it to a domain. Certain servers, such as certificate servers, cannot be renamed.

    C. Correct: Terminal Services Remote Administration mode can be used to change the name of a stand-alone member server.

    D. Incorrect: This console cannot be used to change the name of a stand-alone server.

4.   **Correct Answers: C, D, and E**

    A. Incorrect: There is no way to authenticate the local Computer Management Console against the remote stand-alone servers, hence no way to alter their domain membership.

    B. Incorrect: Although you can use this to provide the stand-alone servers with computer accounts in the domain, it will not change the domain membership of those servers remotely.

    C. Correct: The HTML Remote Administration Tools can be used to alter a stand-alone Windows Server 2003 system's domain membership.

    D. Correct: You can connect to the server console in this manner and change the domain membership of the stand-alone servers.

    E. Correct: You can call one of the members of staff at each site and get them to issue you a remote assistance invitation when they are logged on to the server.

5.   **Correct Answers: A, B, C, and E**

    A. Correct: This method of delivering an invitation will work.

    B. Correct: This method of delivering an invitation will work.

    C. Correct: This method of delivering an invitation will work.

    D. Incorrect: This will not work because it does not transmit a remote administration invitation and Alex would be connecting to the administrator's system rather than the administrator connecting to the server on which Alex is working.

    E. Correct: This method of delivering an invitation will also work. Once the invitation has been copied to the administrator's local machine, he or she will be able to initiate the remote administration session.

Manage a Web Server

Internet Information Services (IIS) version 6 ships with Windows Server 2003 but is not installed by default. A version of Windows Server 2003 that is built just for serving up Web pages is also available; it is called the Web Edition. The basic functionality of IIS is to serve up Web pages, whether that is to clients connecting remotely by the Internet or to hosts connecting by the LAN. IIS, however, can be used to do far more. IIS can be used as a platform to support .NET Web services, Windows Media services, certificate services, and HTML remote administration of the Windows Server 2003 system. IIS also supports an FTP service, which can be used for file transfer between remote hosts and the server. IIS also supports a Network News Transfer Protocol (NNTP) service, allowing newsgroups to be hosted off the server, which can be read by clients such as Microsoft Outlook Express as well as other newsgroup clients.

Access to IIS can be configured in several ways. Access can be restricted or granted based upon IP address, Domain Name System (DNS) name, or Network Address. Access can also be restricted to only those hosts that have the correct certificate or by Windows authentication, limiting access only to those users who have accounts on the system or within the domain. These forms of restriction and access are not mutually exclusive; for example, clients can still be asked to provide authentication credentials even if they come from hosts that reside within an allowed network range.

The number of connections to a Web site can also be limited. This can be useful for several reasons: the first is to stop too many users from overloading the server and causing performance to suffer; the second is to reduce the Web server's impact on the Internet connection in case of a flood of traffic.

Objective 3.3 Questions

1.   Rooslan is the administrator of a Windows Server 2003 system that runs Internet Information Services. The server hosts a single Web site that contains confidential company information. This information should be accessible only by specific hosts from particular subnets within the corporate WAN. Rooslan would like to enable hosts to access the server only from the following IP address ranges:

10.10.10.1 through 10.10.10.126

10.10.10.129 through 10.10.10.190

10.10.20.225 through 10.10.20.238

10.10.30.193 through 10.10.30.254

Rooslan edits the default Web site properties, navigates to the Directory Security tab, and clicks Edit in the IP Address And Domain Name Restrictions frame. He selects Denied Access and then clicks Add to list the exceptions. Which of the following Network ID and Subnet Masks should he enter to limit access to the IP address ranges specified above? (Choose all that apply.)

   A. Network ID: 10.10.10.0, Subnet Mask: 255.255.255.128

   B. Network ID: 10.10.10.0, Subnet Mask: 255.255.255.0

   C. Network ID: 10.10.10.128, Subnet Mask: 255.255.255.64

   D. Network ID: 10.10.10.128, Subnet Mask: 255.255.255.192

   E. Network ID: 10.10.20.224, Subnet Mask: 255.255.255.224

   F. Network ID: 10.10.20.224, Subnet Mask: 255.255.255.240

   G. Network ID: 10.10.30.192, Subnet Mask: 255.255.255.192

2.   Oksana is concerned that a new Web site that she is about to launch will quickly over-load her company's connection to the Internet. The Web site will be hosted on a Windows Server 2003 system running IIS 6.0 and contains streaming media as well as files for download. Oksana has talked to the network administrator, and he has suggested that the Web site can use a maximum of 2 MB per second of the company's bandwidth without causing significant problems. Oksana would also like to limit the maximum number of users connecting to the Web site to 200 at a time. Which of the following should Oksana do to place these traffic restrictions on her Web site? (Choose all that apply.)

   A. Oksana should edit the network properties of the Windows Server 2003 system hosting the Web site and change the maximum outgoing speed to 2,048 kilobytes (KB) per second.

   B. Oksana should edit the properties of the Web site. In the Performance tab, she should select the Bandwidth Throttling check box and set the Limit The Network Bandwidth Available To This Web Site: Maximum Bandwidth (in KB per second) to 2.

   C. Oksana should edit the properties of the Web site. In the Performance Tab, she should select the Limit The Network Bandwidth Available To This Web Site check box and set the Maximum Bandwidth (in KB per second) to 2,000,000.

   D. Oksana should edit the properties of the Web site. In the Performance Tab, she should select the Limit The Network Bandwidth Available To This Web Site check box and set the Limit The Network Bandwidth Available To This Web Site: Maximum Bandwidth (in KB per second) to 2,048.

   E. Oksana should edit the properties of the Web site. In the Performance tab, she should select the Web Site Connections option and set the Connections Limited To value at 100.

   F. Oksana should edit the properties of the Web site. In the Performance tab, she should select and set the Connections Limited To value at 200.

3.   You have cleared the Enable Anonymous Access check box in Authentication Methods of the Directory Security tab of the Default Web Site properties on a stand-alone Windows Server 2003 system running IIS. Which of the following methods of authentication are available to you? (Choose all that apply.)

   A. Integrated Windows Authentication

   B. Digest Authentication

   C. Basic Authentication

   D. .NET Passport Authentication

4.   You are the Web site administrator of a Windows Server 2003 system hosted by your ISP. You want to host several Web sites off this server but your ISP is unable to allocate your hosted server more than a single public IP address. The public IP address you have been allocated is 207.46.248.234. The sites that you want to host are as follows:

www.adatum.com

www.alpineskihouse.com

www.proseware.com

www.tailspintoys.com

Each site is to contain completely unique content totally unrelated to the other sites. Which of the following steps should you take to resolve this problem? (Select two; each selection forms a part of the correct answer.)

   A. Configure the DNS server hosting the records for *www.adatum.com, www.alpineskihouse.com, www.proseware.com,* and *www.tailspintoys.com* to point these hosts' records at IP address 207.46.248.234.

   B. Configure the DNS server hosting the records for *www.adatum.com, www.alpineskihouse.com, www.proseware.com,* and *www.tailspintoys.com* to point these hosts' records at IP address 207.46.234.248.

   C. Create four separate Web sites, *www.adatum.com, www.alpineskihouse.com, www.proseware.com,* and *www.tailspintoys.com*. In the Web Site Creation Wizard, set the IP address of each Web site by typing **207.46.248.234**. For the host header of each Web site, enter the respective Web site name. In the path to the home directory for each Web site, type **c:\inetpub\wwwroot**. Disable the Default Web Site.

   D. Create four separate Web sites, *www.adatum.com, www.alpineskihouse.com, www.proseware.com,* and *www.tailspintoys.com*. In the Web Site Creation Wizard, set the IP address of each Web site by typing **207.46.234.248**. For the host header of each Web site, enter the respective Web site name. In the path to the home directory for each Web site, enter the particular directory that hosts the corresponding Web site's unique content. Disable the Default Web Site.

   E. Create four separate Web sites, *www.adatum.com, www.alpineskihouse.com, www.proseware.com,* and *www.tailspintoys.com*. In the Web Site Creation Wizard, set the IP address of each Web site by typing **207.46.248.234**. For the host header of each Web site, enter the respective Web site name. In the path to the home directory for each Web site, enter the particular directory that hosts the corresponding Web site's unique content. Disable the Default Web Site.

Objective 3.3 Answers

1.   Correct Answers: A, D, F, and G

A. **Correct:** This will allow the first set of hosts, 10.10.10.1 through 10.10.10.126, access to the Web site. 10.10.10.127 is the broadcast address for that subnet, hence not a host on the corporate WAN.

B. **Incorrect:** This will allow access to hosts, specifically in the range of 10.10.10.224 through 10.10.10.254, that should not be granted access to the Web site.

C. **Incorrect:** This is an invalid subnet mask. Subnet mask decimal quads can have the values 0, 128, 192, 224, 240, 248, 252, 254, and 255.

D. **Correct:** This will allow the second set of hosts, 10.10.10.129 through 10.10.10.190, to access the Web site. In this subnetting scheme, 10.10.10.128 is the network address and hence isn't a host address. 10.10.10.190 is the broadcast address and therefore not an addressable host.

E. **Incorrect:** This would allow hosts from 10.10.20.225 through 10.10.20.255 to access the Web site.

F. **Correct:** This will allow the third set of hosts, 10.10.20.225 through 10.10.20.238, to access the Web site. 10.10.20.224 is the network address and 10.10.20.238 is the broadcast address in this particular subnetting scheme.

G. **Correct:** This will allow the fourth set of hosts, 10.10.30.193 through 10.10.30.254, to access the Web site. 10.10.30.192 is the network address and 10.10.30.254 is the broadcast address in this particular subnetting scheme.

2.   Correct Answers: D and F

A. **Incorrect:** The bandwidth usage of network cards cannot be controlled by network properties.

B. **Incorrect:** This will limit the traffic to 2 KB rather than 2 MB.

C. **Incorrect:** This will set the allowed bandwidth to approximately 1,953 MB per second.

D. **Correct:** 2,048 KB is the same as 2 MB. This will limit the transfers from this server to 2 MB per second.

E. **Incorrect:** This will limit connections to 100 at a time rather than 200.

F. **Correct:** This will correctly set the maximum number of connections at any one time to 200.

3.   **Correct Answers: A, C, and D**

   A. **Correct:** This method is available to you and will use accounts created on the stand-alone Windows Server 2003 system.

   B. **Incorrect:** This option is available only if the Windows Server 2003 system is a member of an Active Directory environment. Because this is a stand-alone system, and therefore not a member of a domain, this option cannot be used.

   C. **Correct:** This option is available and will work with most browsers. The downside of this method is that it transmits authentication information in plaintext rather than encrypted format.

   D. **Correct:** This method of authentication is available, although it will require some further configuration on the part of the administrator.

4.   **Correct Answers: A and E**

   A. **Correct:** This is the first part of the correct answer.

   B. **Incorrect:** This is the incorrect IP address (the last two octets have been switched around).

   C. **Incorrect:** This will point all the Web sites at the same content rather than the unique content.

   D. **Incorrect:** This will set the Web site to listen on the wrong IP address. The last two octets are switched around.

   E. **Correct:** This has both the correct IP address set and points to the corresponding directory hosting the unique Web site data.

18 Exam 70-292—Managing and Implementing Disaster Recovery (4.0)

Disasters will occur. Disks will fail, files will be lost, and power supplies will fuse with a puff of smoke, a few sparks, and an acrid smell. Systems administrators should not wait for a disaster to occur before deciding on a course of action. Before disaster strikes, administrators should have planned and put in place the procedures that will restore system functionality as soon as possible.

The first step in protecting data stored on Microsoft Windows Server 2003 systems is to ensure that it is backed up correctly. Windows Server 2003 has a built-in backup application that enables the administrator to perform the vast majority of backup tasks. Critical systems should be backed up every 24 hours or more often in some cases. Backups can be written to several forms of media.

Windows Server 2003 also has a feature called Automated System Recovery (ASR) that is new to the server line of products. Automated System Recovery can be used to restore a completely non-functional system to working order. Automated System Recovery stores some configuration information on a special disk and other configuration information within the ASR backup set. Automated System Recovery restores only a system; it will not restore data that is stored on the system. Stored data must still be backed up in the normal manner.

Tested Skills and Suggested Practices

The skills that you need to successfully master the Managing and Implementing Disaster Recovery objective domain on *Exam 70-292: Managing and Maintaining a Microsoft Windows Server 2003 Environment for an MCSA Certified on Windows 2000* include

- Perform system recovery for a server.
  - ❑ Practice 1: Perform an ASR backup on a server and then use the ASR process to perform a recovery of that server.
  - ❑ Practice 2: Backup the System State data on a server with Internet Information Services (IIS) installed. Change the IIS settings. Restore the System State data and notice what has changed in the IIS settings.

Further Reading

This section lists supplemental readings by objective. We recommend that you study these sources thoroughly before taking this exam.

Objective 4.1   Review Chapter 13, "Managing and Implementing Disaster Recovery."

Microsoft Corporation. Windows Server 2003 Help and Support Center. Review "System State Data."

Microsoft Corporation. Windows Server 2003 Help and Support Center. Review "Automated System Recovery Overview."

Microsoft Corporation. Windows Server 2003 Help and Support Center. Review "Volume Shadow Copy Overview."

Microsoft Corporation. Windows Server 2003 Help and Support Center. Review "Authoritative, Primary and Normal Restores."

Perform System Recovery for a Server

When a Windows Server 2003 system crashes in a way that it cannot be fixed simply by performing a restart, other options must be explored. An option new to Windows Server 2003, Automated System Recovery (ASR), uses a combination of a Windows settings diskette, a special ASR backup set, and the Windows Server 2003 installation media to restore a system. Automated System Recovery should be used as a measure of last resort because the operating system files will be reinstalled. It is also important to note that Automated System Recovery does not back up data stored on the server, only important Windows Server 2003 files.

When recovering a domain controller, systems administrators must decide on the type of Active Directory restoration, if any, they will perform. An authoritative restore allows the Microsoft Active Directory directory service database stored on the backup set to take precedence over the Active Directory database replicated in the domain. A non-authoritative restore allows the current Active Directory database to overwrite the database from the backup set.

In some cases, the restoration of the System State data allows a server to return to operational status. The System State data includes the system's registry COM+ class registration database. The boot files and system files are protected by the Windows File Protection service. Depending on the services installed on the Windows Server 2003 system, System State data can also include the Certificate Services database, Active Directory and the Sysvol folder on a domain controller, cluster service information on a cluster server, and the Internet Information Services (IIS) metabase. If one of these areas of the operating system has been corrupted, restoring the System State data might return the server to functionality.

1. Rooslan is the systems administrator at a medium-sized organization that has 400 employees located at two sites. At 2 A.M. each day, a full backup, including System State data, is taken of the three Windows Server 2003 domain controllers on the network. One morning, Foley, a junior administrator who works for Rooslan, accidentally deleted three organizational units (OUs) from Active Directory. Foley did not discover his mistake until several hours later, by which time the mistake had replicated to the other domain controllers. No other changes have been made to the Active Directory database in the last 24 hours, so Rooslan decided to restore the System State data from the backup that was taken at 2 A.M. Which type of restore will return the three deleted OUs to the Active Directory database?

    A. Authoritative restore

    B. Nonauthoritative restore

    C. Primary restore

    D. Diligent restore

2. Rooslan has just received a panicked telephone call from Foley, a junior administrator who works for Rooslan at a medium-sized organization. Foley has accidentally deleted the OU that contained the senior management team's user accounts from the Active Directory database. Before Foley was able to do anything about this mistake, the domain controller in the domain replicated and the deletion propagated across the network. Backups are taken of all domain controller System State data at 2:30 A.M. every day. No other changes have been made to the Active Directory database today, so Rooslan tells Foley that they should prepare to do an authoritative restore of the Active Directory database on one of the domain controllers. Rooslan goes to the server room, locates the previous night's backup media, and then shuts off one of the Windows Server 2003 domain controllers. In which of the following modes should Rooslan start the Windows Server 2003 domain controller?

    A. Start the Windows Server 2003 domain controller in Last Known Good Configuration.

    B. Start the Windows Server 2003 domain controller in Safe mode.

    C. Start the Windows Server 2003 domain controller in the Recovery Console.

    D. Start the Windows Server 2003 domain controller normally.

    E. Start the Windows Server 2003 domain controller in Directory Services Restore mode.

3. You are the systems administrator of five Windows Server 2003 systems that are members of the domain. These five servers host a variety of Web sites using Internet Information Services (IIS). Each of these servers has two hard disk drives. The first disk hosts the volume that contains the operating system and program files. The second disk hosts a volume that stores all the Web site data. The Web site data and System State is backed up every 24 hours to a network file server. All the Web site settings, such as security permissions and domain access restrictions, are unique to each Web site.

This morning the hard disk drive hosting the operating system failed on one of the IIS servers. The second hard disk drive hosting the Web site data is fully operational. You get a replacement hard disk drive from the storeroom, install it into the server, and install Windows Server 2003 and the program files that had been on the server. Which of the following methods can you use to restore the functionality that existed before the crash to the Web server? (Choose all that apply.)

A. All functionality has already been restored to the server, and nothing more needs to be done.

B. Use the Backup Utility to restore the files that comprise the Web sites from the network file share to the second hard disk drive for the IIS server you are trying to restore.

C. Use Directory Services Restore mode on the IIS server to restore the System State data from the network share.

D. While logged into the IIS server you are trying to restore, copy the most recent backup across from the network file server to the local hard disk drive. Restore the System State data from this backup and restart the server if required.

E. While logged on to the IIS server you are trying to restore, use the Backup Utility to restore the System State data from the backup stored on the network location and restart the server if required.

4. Which of the following statements is true about restoring a stand-alone root certificate authority (CA) that has suffered a hard disk failure on the volume that hosts the operating system and the certificate database? (Choose all that apply.)

A. The certificate database can only be restored using the Certification Authority snap-in.

B. When restoring a CA, the IIS metabase must also be restored if it has been damaged or lost.

C. A password must be entered when restoring System State data on a server that has a stand-alone CA installed.

D. A password must be entered when restoring Private Key, CA Certificate, Certificate Database, and Certificate Database Log that has been backed up by using the Certification Authority snap-in of the Microsoft Management Console (MMC).

E. The certificate database is restored when Automated System Recover is performed.

5. A hacker has gained access to your Web server and has deleted or corrupted many of the important system files on a Windows Server 2003 system that you are responsible for administering. After spending some time using the Recovery Console, you conclude that the damage is so extensive that you must use Automated System Recovery to restore the server to its former working state. You last prepared the server for automated system recovery four days ago. Which of the following methods presents the correct way of starting Automated System Recovery?

   A. Restart in Directory Services Restore mode using the ASR disk that was created during the ASR preparation process four days ago.

   B. Restart using the Windows Server 2003 installation CD-ROM and, when prompted, insert the ASR disk that was created during the ASR preparation process four days ago.

   C. Restart in Safe mode and, when prompted, insert the ASR disk that was created during the ASR preparation process four days ago.

   D. Start in Directory Services Restore mode and, when prompted, insert the ASR disk that was created during the ASR preparation process four days ago.

   E. Start in the Recovery Console and, when prompted, insert the ASR disk that was created during the ASR preparation process four days ago.

6. Oksana is a junior systems administrator at your organization. She is responsible for administering two Windows Server 2003 systems that host Internet Information Services. Each server hosts a single Web site and each Web site has unique configuration information. This unique configuration includes individual lists of allowed and disallowed hosts as well as account access lists. Both Windows Server 2003 systems have IIS installed in its default location. Oksana telephones to inform you that a virus appears to have infiltrated one of the IIS servers. The virus has caused the deletion of 95 percent of the Web content stored on the server as well as the corruption of the IIS metabase. The system has now been cleaned with an updated virus scanner, removing all traces of infected files. However, the virus has corrupted several other areas of the system, rendering it highly unstable. Major updates to different areas of the Web site have been occurring throughout the week. Today is Friday. Oksana has performed the following disaster recovery tasks on the server in the past week.

Thursday: ASR backup

Wednesday: Incremental backup of Web site data

Tuesday: Incremental backup of Web site data

Monday: System State data backup

Sunday: Full backup of Web site data

All relevant backup media is available. Which of the following methods should Oksana use to restore the IIS metabase and the Web site data that was lost?

A. Oksana needs only to perform an Automated System Recovery.

B. Oksana must perform an Automated System Recovery. Once that is complete, she needs to restore the backup data from Wednesday.

C. Oksana needs to perform an Automated System Recovery. Once that is complete, she needs to restore Sunday's, Tuesday's, and Wednesday's backup data.

D. Oksana needs to restore Monday's backup of the System State data, Sunday's full backup, and Wednesday's incremental backup.

E. Oksana must restore Monday's backup of the System State data, Sunday's full backup, as well as Tuesday's and Wednesday's incremental backup data.

7. There has been a fire in the server room. You have lost the box that contains all the ASR disks, but the storage unit that contains the backup tapes is intact. Three of your Windows Server 2003 systems have been damaged, rendering them inoperable, and two more seem to have emerged from the fire unscathed. Each Windows Server 2003 system had its own 40 gigabyte (GB) digital audio tape (DAT) drive. A complete ASR backup on each server was performed several days ago. Each of the five Windows Server 2003 systems had a unique configuration that was different from all the others. Which of the following statements about recovering the three damaged servers using Automated System Recovery is true?

A. Once the hardware has been repaired, these servers cannot be recovered. Special files, located on an ASR disk, are unique to the server being recovered. If that disk is lost, the corresponding ASR set for that server is rendered useless.

B. Once the hardware has been repaired, these servers can be recovered. You should perform an ASR backup on one of the functional servers, creating a new disk. You can then use this ASR disk to perform the ASR process on the damaged servers.

C. Once the hardware has been repaired, these servers can be recovered. You should run the Backup Utility on one of the functional servers and use it to restore the Asr.sif and Asrpnp.sif from the functional server's ASR backup set to floppy disk. You can then use this ASR disk to perform the ASR process on the servers that had suffered damage.

D. Once the hardware has been repaired, these servers can be recovered. You should run the Backup Utility on one of the functional servers and use it to restore the Asr.sif and Asrpnp.sif from each of the damaged server's ASR backup sets to floppy disks. You can then use each formerly damaged server's corresponding ASR disk in the ASR process on that server.

8. Rooslan would like to make sure that only members of the Administrators group can restore System State data from a particular Windows Server 2003 system that contains a certificate authority database. Which of the following ways correctly describes how this can be done without removing the right of the Backup Operators group to restore other backup sets?

    A. When starting the backup, ensure that the Allow Only The Owner And The Administrator Access To The Backup Data option in the Backup Job Information dialog box is selected

    B. In the Restore And Manage Media tab, select the media properties to which the System State data is being written. Change the permissions so that only the Administrators group has access to this media.

    C. Restoration of backup sets can always be done by members of the Administrators group as well as members of the Backup Operators group. Access cannot be restricted to one group or the other.

    D. Edit the local Group Policy object, change the Backup Files And Directories policy located in the Computer Configuration\Windows Settings\Security Settings\Local Policies\User Rights Assignment container, and remove the Backup Operators group.

    E. Edit the local Group Policy object, change the Restore Files And Directories policy located in the Computer Configuration\Windows Settings\Security Settings\Local Policies\User Rights Assignment container, and remove the Backup Operators group.

9. Rooslan is the systems administrator of a Windows Server 2003 system running Internet Information Services. This server is used to issue digital certificates to third parties on the Internet. These certificates enable subscribers to access specially restricted portions of the Web site that are not available to other users who visit the site. Rooslan wants the IIS configuration and the certificate database backed up once a week. Rooslan also wants to make sure that once a week every file and folder in the C:\Inetpub folder is backed up. Finally, Rooslan wants any changes made to files or folders in this directory after the weekly backup to be backed up each day, but in a method that uses the smallest amount of space on the backup media. Which of the following backups should Rooslan perform? (Choose all that apply.)

A. A full backup each day of the week

B. A full backup once a week

C. A full backup, including System State data, once a week

D. A differential backup each day of the week

E. An incremental backup each day of the week

10. Rooslan is responsible for backing up the departmental intranet server. This server runs IIS on Windows Server 2003. The server has a single physical disk that contains a single volume formatted with the NTFS file system. A share has been created on the Wwwroot folder. Only administrators and the staff member responsible for maintaining the intranet server have access to this share. The staff member who maintains the intranet server pages has this share mapped as a separate drive by a login script. Rooslan performs an ASR backup of the server on the first of each month. Every Monday at 7 A.M., he performs a full backup of the Wwwroot folder and all its subfolders as well as backing up the System State data. On Tuesday, Wednesday, Thursday, and Friday at 8:00 A.M., he performs an incremental backup on the Wwwroot folder and all its subfolders. No backups are performed over the weekend on this server. All backups are written to DAT and are labeled with the day that the backup was taken. After lunch on Thursday, Rooslan receives a visit at his cubicle from the staff member responsible for maintaining the intranet server. Her computer was infected this morning with a virus. The virus wiped out all the documents on her hard drive as well as all the files and folders in the mapped Wwwroot folder. Rooslan goes down to the server room and locates the backup tapes from the last seven days. Which of the backup tapes will he need to use to create the most complete restoration of the Web site files? (Choose all that apply.)

A. Monday's tape

B. Tuesday's tape

C. Wednesday's tape

D. Thursday's tape

E. Friday's tape

11.   You are designing a backup strategy for a Windows Server 2003 system that runs IIS. The server has a single hard disk drive that contains a single volume. You have the following goals:

Primary Goal: To write a full backup to tape once a week.

Secondary Goals: To back up the IIS metabase on Monday, Wednesday, and Friday. To ensure that all files modified or created since the last full backup are backed up on Tuesday and Thursday.

Which of the following sets of scheduled backups will fulfill these goals? (Choose all that apply.)

   A. Full backup every Sunday at 2:00 A.M. Daily backup with System State every Monday, Wednesday, and Friday at 3:00 A.M.

   B. Full backup with System State on Monday at 2:00 A.M. Daily backup with System State on Wednesday, Friday, and Sunday at 3:00 A.M. Differential backup on Tuesday and Thursday at 3:30 A.M.

   C. Full backup with System State on Friday at 11:00 P.M. Incremental backup with System State data on Wednesday and Monday at 11:30 P.M. Differential backup on Tuesday and Thursday at 11:30 P.M.

   D. Full backup with System State on Wednesday at 11:00 P.M. Daily backup with System State on Monday and Friday at 11:00 P.M. Differential backup with System State on Tuesday and Thursday at 11:00 P.M.

   E. Incremental backup with System State data on Monday, Wednesday, and Friday at 2:00 A.M. Differential backup with System State data on Tuesday and Thursday at 2:00 A.M. Copy backup Sunday at 2:00 A.M.

12.   Oksana is designing a backup strategy for a Windows Server 2003 system that runs IIS. The server hosts a high-traffic Web site where content is updated on an almost hourly basis. Several aspects of the IIS configuration change during the week. The configuration has become so complicated that it is important that it be regularly backed up as well. Oksana's backup strategy should take into account the following conditions:

Condition 1: All the Web site data must be backed up completely at least once every two weeks.

Condition 2: The System State data must be backed up at least twice a week.

Condition 3: Any backup set except a full backup should not include files and folders that have not been altered or created in the last 24 hours. System State data is exempt from this condition.

Which of the following schedules would take into account all three of Oksana's conditions? (Choose all that apply.)

A. Full backup of selected files and folders every Monday at 11:50 P.M. Incremental backup of selected files and folders all weekdays except Monday at 11:55 P.M.

B. Full backup of selected files and folders every second Monday at 11:50 P.M. Differential backup of selected files and folders all days of the week except Monday at 11:55 P.M. System State backup every Monday, Wednesday, and Friday at 2:00 P.M.

C. Full backup of selected files and folders every second Monday at 12:05 A.M. Incremental backup of selected files and folders, including System State data, every day of the week at 11:55 P.M.

D. Full backup of selected files and folders every second Monday at 12:05 A.M. Daily backup of selected files and folders, including System State data, every day of the week at 11:59 P.M.

E. Full backup of selected files and folders every second Monday at 12:05 A.M. Copy backup of selected files and folders, including System State data, every day of the week at 11:59 P.M.

Objective 4.1 Answers

1.   **Correct Answers: A**

     A. Correct: An authoritative restore means that Active Directory objects that had originally been deleted from the Active Directory database will not be overwritten the next time the restored server replicates with other domain controllers in the domain. If an authoritative restore is not used, the deleted items will simply be removed the next time the other domain controllers in the domain replicate.

     B. Incorrect: Any Active Directory objects restored using a nonauthoritative restore that have since been deleted from the directory will be removed the next time the server replicates with other domain controllers in the domain.

     C. Incorrect: Any Active Directory objects restored using a primary restore that have since been deleted from the directory will be removed the next time the server replicates with other domain controllers in the domain.

     D. Incorrect: There is no such method as a diligent restore.

2.   **Correct Answers: E**

     A. Incorrect: Starting the domain controller in Last Known Good Configuration will not allow the Active Directory database to be restored in a way that the OU containing the senior management team's account will be recoverable.

     B. Incorrect: Starting the domain controller in Safe mode will not allow the Active Directory database to be restored in a way that the OU containing the senior management team's account will be recoverable.

     C. Incorrect: The Active Directory database cannot be recovered from the Recovery Console.

     D. Incorrect: Starting the domain controller normally will not allow the Active Directory database to be restored in a way that the OU containing the senior management team's account will be recoverable.

     E. Correct: Directory Services Restore mode is a special mode that can be used to recover the Active Directory database. From Directory Services Restore mode, the administrator can choose whether to do an authoritative or nonauthoritative restore of the Active Directory database.

3.   Correct Answers: D and E

A. Incorrect: Although the data exists, none of the Web site settings will exist. These are stored in the System State data that has to be restored.

B. Incorrect: Because the Web site files are unaffected, using the Backup Utility will not make any difference. It will simply overwrite the files that are already stored on the second disk drive with exact duplicates.

C. Incorrect: Because these servers are not domain controllers but are members of the domain, they will not have an Active Directory database, nor will the option exist to start them into Directory Services Restore mode.

D. Correct: The IIS metabase, which contains all the IIS settings, is backed up when the System State data is backed up. Although it can be restored from the network location, this will also work if the backup is copied to the local hard disk drive.

E. Correct: The IIS metabase, which contains all the IIS settings, is backed up when the System State data is backed up. As long as you are logged on to the server on which you are doing the restoration, you can use backup data stored on remote servers.

4.   Correct Answers: B, D, and E

A. Incorrect: The certificate database can be restored using the Backup Utility because the certificate database is also part of the System State data.

B. Correct: Without IIS working correctly and configured to support the CA, the certificate services Web pages will fail to load. When a CA is installed, the appropriate modifications are made to the IIS metabase.

C. Incorrect: No password is required to restore System State data. Backups and restorations can, however, be restricted to the Administrators group.

D. Correct: This is to provide a level of security so that an intruder who might have acquired the backup tapes cannot use the backup data to create his or her version of the same CA. If the database has been backed up using the System State, no password is required to access this data.

E. Correct: Automated System Recovery stores the System State data and the certificate database is part of that data.

5. **Correct Answers: B**

    A. Incorrect: The ASR disk cannot be used as a boot disk. It contains information about the system but does not contain the necessary files to start Windows Server 2003.

    B. Correct: This is the correct method of performing Automated System Recovery on a Windows Server 2003 system. The disk created in Automated System Recovery is not a boot disk; it merely stores important system configuration files, such as the disk layout, that are needed at the beginning of the recovery process. Other files are either copied from the installation media or from the ASR backup set.

    C. Incorrect: Starting in Safe mode will not initiate the ASR process.

    D. Incorrect: The ASR process cannot be initiated from Directory Services Restore mode.

    E. Incorrect: The Recovery Console cannot be used to initiate the ASR process.

6. **Correct Answers: C**

    A. Incorrect: Automated System Recovery does not restore data, although it will restore the IIS metabase and fix the files that are causing the system instability.

    B. Incorrect: Automated System Recovery does not restore data, although it will restore the IIS metabase and fix the files that are causing system instability.

    C. Correct: The Automated System Recovery will restore the files that are causing instability as well as the IIS metabase. Because the backups are incremental, each incremental backup, as well as the original full backup, must be restored to reproduce all the missing files.

    D. Incorrect: This will not fix the instability that is caused by files other than those backed up by the System State. Also, any files that were backed up in Tuesday's incremental backup will not be restored.

    E. Incorrect: Although this will restore the metabase and all the Web site data, it will do nothing about other files that are causing system instability.

7. **Correct Answers: D**

    A. Incorrect: This is not true. A new ASR disk can be generated from the corresponding ASR set on the DAT tapes for that server.

    B. Incorrect: Each server was said to have a unique configuration, which means that the information written to one server's ASR disk will be different from that written to another server's ASR disk.

    C. Incorrect: Although this process is almost correct, restoring Aas.sif and Asr-pnp.sif from the functional server's ASR backup set, rather than those files from the damaged server's ASR backup set, will mean that the ASR disk contains the wrong information to restore the damaged servers correctly.

    D. Correct: When an ASR backup set is written, the files that are written to the ASR disk are also written to the ASR backup set stored on the backup media. This means that even if the ASR disk is lost, it can be recovered from information stored in the ASR backup set.

8.   **Correct Answers: A**

    A. Correct: This is the only method of limiting which users or groups can perform a restoration of a particular backup set.

    B. Incorrect: This functionality does not exist in the Restore And Manage Media tab.

    C. Incorrect: Access can be restricted to the Administrators group by following the procedure outlined in answer A.

    D. Incorrect: This will not change the right of the Backup Operators group to restore backup sets, but it will prevent them from backing up files and folders.

    E. Incorrect: This will stop the Backup Operators group from restoring all data, not just the System State data.

9.   **Correct Answers: C and E**

    A. Incorrect: This will not back up the IIS configuration or certificate database. It also will not use the smallest amount of space on the backup media.

    B. Incorrect: This will not back up the IIS configuration or certificate database.

    C. Correct: This will back up the IIS configuration and the certificate database, as well as perform the full backup required.

    D. Incorrect: Differential backups use more space on the backup media than incremental backups do. Differential backups store all information created or modified since the last full backup.

    E. Correct: Incremental backups use the least amount of space. They back up only data that has been created or modified since the last incremental backup.

10.   **Correct Answers: A, B, C, and D**

    A. Correct: Monday's tape contains all the files in their original form. Any files that have been modified can be overwritten by restorations of tapes made later in the week.

    B. Correct: Any files that were modified between the Monday and Tuesday backups will be located on this tape.

    C. Correct: Any files that were modified between the Tuesday and Wednesday backups will be located on this tape.

    D. Correct: Any files that were modified between the Wednesday and Thursday backups will be located on this tape.

    E. Incorrect: The Friday tape has not been written yet.

11.   Correct Answers: B and D

    A. Incorrect: This will achieve the primary goal and the first of the secondary goals. It will not achieve the second secondary goal.

    B. Correct: This will achieve the primary goal and both secondary goals. The metabase is backed up when the System State data is backed up. This means that the metabase will be backed up under this scheme on Monday, Wednesday, Friday, and Sunday. Sunday isn't necessary for the primary goal, but it does not invalidate it. The differential backup on Tuesday and Thursday meets the second part of the secondary goals.

    C. Incorrect: This meets the primary goal and the first secondary goal. It does not meet the second secondary goal because the incremental backups will mean that the differential backups on Tuesday and Thursday will back up only files changed since the last incremental rather than the last full backup.

    D. Correct: The primary goal is achieved as well as both secondary goals. The key is to remember that like differential backups, daily backups do not reset the archive bit. The next backup taken after a daily or differential assumes that the file has not been backed up yet if it has been altered or is new since the time of the last backup.

    E. Incorrect: Although the incremental backup does reset the archive bit, it does not count as a full backup of the server once a week. The copy backup does not reset the archive bit and hence is functionally similar to the differential backup.

12.   Correct Answers: C and D

    A. Incorrect: This backup schedule does not meet the second condition.

    B. Incorrect: Using differential backup will not conform to the third condition.

    C. Correct: This option meets all three criteria.

    D. Correct: This option meets all three criteria. Although a daily backup does not reset the archive bit, it will back up only files or folders within the selection that have been modified that day; hence, it will meet the third condition.

    E. Incorrect: Copy backup works similarly to a differential backup in that it does not reset the archive bit, but it also copies all files, including those that have not been modified.

19 Exam 70-292— Implementing, Managing, and Maintaining Name Resolution (5.0)

The Domain Name System (DNS) is a service that resolves (or translates) host names into Internet Protocol (IP) addresses. The host names can be local, such as ServerA, or remote Fully Qualified Domain Names (FQDNs) such as *www.fabrikam.com*. Local names are typically (but not necessarily) resolved to private IP addresses such as 10.10.16.5. Remote FQDNs are resolved to registered IP addresses such as 206.73.118.10.

The significance of this last statement cannot be overemphasized. Any Web-based resource can be resolved to a registered IP address across the Internet. Resources internal to a large corporation, but not local to the resolver, can also be found by iterative queries across a large organization. You can sit at your PC and access resources on the other side of the world, and you don't need to know the IP addresses or even the physical locations. The ubiquity of DNS makes it a security hazard for organizations that want to access Internet resources and want to make their presence known on the Internet but that need to protect their internal resources. DNS has come a long way from the 1980s, with more and more sophisticated tools becoming available to set up more and more complicated structures to manage DNS. One of the key tasks of the network administrator is to make access as easy as possible for the people who need to access resources and as difficult as possible for the others.

In its initial form, DNS was a static and uninspiring service consisting of some merged hosts files and what was then known as the DNS cache (now root hints) that contained the IP addresses of a few top-level (root) servers in the DNS hierarchical structure. DNS is now dynamic, with clients registering their own resource records—including reverse lookup (PTR) resource records. The number of record types has increased beyond recognition from the simple host (A) resource records through AAAA (QuadA) IPv6 records, start-of-authority (SOA) resource records, and SRV (service) resource records.

Any Microsoft Network Infrastructure examination will focus heavily on DNS, and Exam 70-292 is no exception. You need to become familiar with components, concepts, and practices of using DNS in a Microsoft Windows Server 2003 environment. You need to know when it is appropriate to configure a DNS zone as Active Directory–integrated primary, standard primary, secondary, or stub. You should be familiar with the difference between a forward and a reverse lookup zone. You should be aware of the functions of secondary servers, caching-only servers, stub servers, and forwarders, and when it is appropriate to use each of them. You need to know how to allow dynamic updates, how to allow only secure dynamic updates, and when to use each of these functions. You should know how to disable recursion and be familiar with resource record aging and the scavenging process.

DNS works closely with the Dynamic Host Configuration Protocol (DHCP). The settings in the relevant DNS and DHCP properties dialog boxes look comparatively simple, but they combine in complex ways. You need to be able to configure settings that give the maximum possible support for dynamic updates of resource records for hosts with such legacy operating systems as Microsoft Windows 95, Microsoft Windows 98, and Microsoft NT 4.0, and such non-Microsoft operating systems as NetWare and UNIX, while still maintaining your network's security and integrity.

Tested Skills and Suggested Practices

The skills that you need to master the Managing and Maintaining a Server Environment objective domain on *Exam 70-292: Managing and Maintaining a Microsoft Windows Server 2003 Environment for an MCSA Certified on Windows 2000* include

- Install and configure the DNS Server service.
    - ❑ Practice 1: Create or obtain a configuration plan that defines primary, secondary, and stub zones. Identify a strategy for setting up an efficient DNS infrastructure that includes secondary, stub, and caching-only servers.
    - ❑ Practice 2: Install DNS on a stand-alone server and configure standard primary forward lookup zones and reverse lookup zones.
    - ❑ Practice 3: Install DNS on a second server and configure it as a secondary server for the zones created in Practice 2. Add some resource records manually on the primary server and force replication from the secondary server.
    - ❑ Practice 4: Promote one of your servers to a domain controller and configure your zones as Active Directory–integrated. Allow only secure dynamic updates. Add hosts that can register their resource records to the domain and check that their records are updated.

■ Manage DNS.

❑ Practice 1: Install DHCP on your second server. Experiment with the DNS tab in the DHCP server properties dialog box. It would be useful if you could add legacy or non-Microsoft operating system hosts to the network.

❑ Practice 2: Use the DNS console to view the contents of the server cache. Based on the cache parameters, decide whether the cache needs to be cleared. Clear it anyway.

❑ Practice 3: Modify the settings of a DNS zone. Settings include specifying the zone name and the zone type, specifying whether dynamic updates are allowed, specifying whether only secure dynamic updates are allowed (Active Directory–integrated only), specifying other DNS servers as authoritative, setting aging and scavenging parameters, and modifying security (Active Directory–integrated only).

❑ Practice 4: In the DNS console, select a forward zone. From the Action menu, select Add Other Records. Scroll through the records, using the Explain button to find out what each one does. If you do not understand the function of any record, refer to the recommended reading or to the server help files.

❑ Practice 5: In the DNS console, access the Advanced tab of the DNS server properties dialog box. Right-click each of the server options in turn and select What's This to access help information. If possible, test the effects of changing these options. (This task could be difficult on a small test network.)

Further Reading

This section contains a list of supplemental readings divided by objective. If you think you need additional preparation before taking the exam, study these sources thoroughly.

Objective 5.1   Review Chapter 8, "Implementing, Managing, and Maintaining Name Resolution."

Microsoft Corporation. *Microsoft Encyclopedia of Networking, Second Edition.* Redmond, Washington: Microsoft Press, 2002. See entries for "DNS," "Domain Name System (DNS)," and "Dynamic DNS (DDNS)."

Microsoft Corporation. *Microsoft Windows Server 2003 Deployment Guide.* Redmond, Washington. Review "DNS Overview," available on the Microsoft Web site at *http://www.microsoft.com/technet/treeview/default.asp?url=/technet/prodtechnol /windowsserver2003/proddocs/entserver/sag_DNS_und_Topnode.asp.*

Objective 5.2 Review Chapter 8, "Implementing, Managing, and Maintaining Name Resolution."

Microsoft Corporation. *Microsoft Encyclopedia of Networking, Second Edition*. Redmond, Washington: Microsoft Press, 2002. See entries for "DNS Server."

Microsoft Corporation. *Microsoft Windows Server 2003 Deployment Guide*. Redmond, Washington. Review "DNS—How to," available on the Microsoft Web site at *http://www.microsoft.com/technet/treeview/default.asp?url=/technet/prodtechnol /windowsserver2003/proddocs/entserver/sag_DNS_pro_OptimizingServersNode.asp*.

Install and Configure the DNS Server Service

A workable DNS infrastructure is the direct result of good planning and careful implementation during the installation phase. You must understand the basic guidelines for DNS installation and how to identify individuals who have rights to manage the DNS zones. You need to understand how one-to-one mapping of domains in Active Directory corresponds to and integrates with DNS. You also need to know how to verify your DNS configuration.

You are required to understand the different zone types: standard primary, Active Directory–integrated primary, secondary, and stub. You need to know the functions of primary, secondary, stub, and caching-only servers; know when to configure forwarders; know when to disable recursion; and understand the function of root hints. You also need to know how to configure aging and scavenging properties and application directory partition settings.

Objective 5.1 Questions

1.   The Active Directory domain structure of the fourthcoffee.com forest is shown in the following illustration. DC1 is the first domain controller in domain accounts.denver.fourthcoffee.com. Client1 is a client in the same domain. No changes have been made to the primary or connection-specific DNS suffixes on either PC. What is the FQDN of Client1?

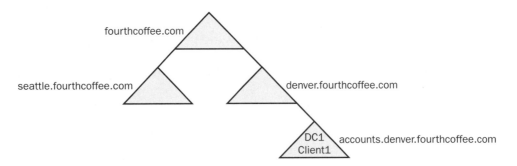

   A. client1.fourthcoffee.com

   B. client1.DC1.denver.accounts.fourthcoffee.com

   C. client1@denver.accounts.fourthcoffee.com

   D. client1.accounts.denver.fourthcoffee.com

2.   Resource1 is a multihomed Windows Server 2003 member server in the design.treyresearch.corp Active Directory domain. One of Resource1's network interface cards (NICs) is connected to a 10-MB Ethernet network, and it is configured with IP address 10.10.1.12. The second NIC is configured with IP address 10.10.2.200, and it is connected to a Gigabit Ethernet network. Active Directory–integrated DNS is implemented on the domain.

Clients on the Gigabit network need fast access to large data files on Resource1. Clients on the 10-MB network require normal file server functions. Both sets of clients access Resource1 by FQDN.

You configure a connection-specific DNS suffix of text.design.treyresearch.corp on the NIC configured with IP address 10.10.1.12. You configure a connection-specific DNS suffix of video.design.treyresearch.corp on the NIC configured with IP address 10.10.2.200. Which host (A) resource records are recorded for Resource1 in DNS? (Choose all that apply.)

   A. Resource1.text.design.treyresearch.corp: 10.10.2.200

   B. Resource1.text.design.treyresearch.corp: 10.10.1.12

    C. Resource1.video.design.treyresearch.corp: 10.10.2.200

    D. Resource1.video.design.treyresearch.corp: 10.10.1.12

    E. Resource1.design.treyresearch.corp: 10.10.2.200

    F. Resource1.design.treyresearch.corp: 10.10.1.12

3. You install DNS on a stand-alone Windows Server 2003, Enterprise Edition server. During installation, an error message reports that the DNS service has not started in a timely fashion, but when you click OK, DNS installs. You configure a standard primary forward lookup zone. You do not allow dynamic updates.

When you open the DNS console, you notice a red *x* beside the server name. You access the DNS Event Log and discover a 414 warning entry that has the error message shown in the following figure.

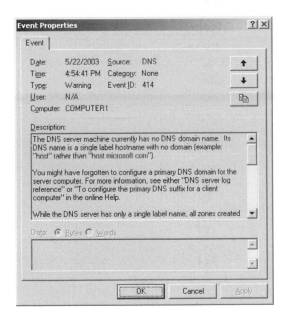

You try to start the DNS service but cannot do so. You then realize that the server has become disconnected from the network. You plug the connector back in, and now you can restart the DNS service. However, the *x* is still showing beside the DNS server, and most of the entries on the Action menu are unavailable. What should you do next?

    A. Restart the DNS service.

    B. Allow dynamic updates.

    C. Delete and recreate the zone.

    D. From the Action menu, select Refresh.

4. The Active Directory domain structure of the fourthcoffee.com forest is shown in the following illustration. DC1 through DC7 are domain controllers. The domain structure has been set up from scratch using default settings. DC1 is the first DC in the forest. DNS is Active Directory–integrated, and both forward and reverse zones have been created. The DNS Server service is installed on all DCs. All servers are Windows Server 2003, Enterprise Edition. All clients are Microsoft Windows XP Professional. Clients register their own host resource records in DNS, and DHCP registers their pointer (PTR) resource records. Which of the following statements is correct?

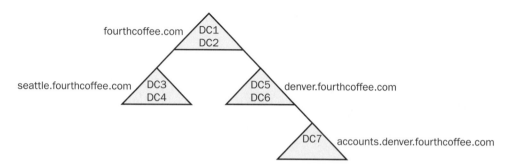

A. The zone file on DC7 contains the host resource records for all the clients in the fourthcoffee.com domain.

B. DC5 is authoritative for the denver.fourthcoffee.com DNS zone.

C. If you open the DNS console and access DC7 server properties, the SOE tab will be present but the parameters are unavailable.

D. DC1 is the only domain controller on which you can access the Security tab in the DNS server properties dialog box.

5. Litware, Inc., is a large multinational corporation with its headquarters in Chicago and large offices all over the world. The Singapore office is experiencing rapid expansion. Singapore has considerable autonomy and users in Singapore seldom access resources in Chicago. Users in Chicago access resources in Singapore sporadically. However, when they do access these resources, they need to be able to do so without undue delay.

To reduce replication traffic over WAN links, the Delegation Of Control Wizard has been used to create the child DNS zone singapore.litwareinc.com, for which the Singapore domain controllers are authoritative. Both the singapore.litwareinc.com and the litwareinc.com zones are Active Directory–integrated.

Users in Chicago report that access to resources in Singapore is becoming increasingly slow as the Singapore operation expands. How can you improve access to Singapore without unduly increasing network traffic?

A. Create a secondary DNS server for singapore.litwareinc.com in the Chicago office.

B. Install a caching-only server in Chicago.

C. Install a stub server for singapore.litwareinc.com in Chicago.

D. Configure a forwarder in Chicago to forward queries to a DNS server in Singapore.

6. Your small business has a peer-to-peer network with Windows 98 and Microsoft Windows NT 4.0 Workstation clients and a single Windows NT 4.0 file and print server. You do not use DHCP. You upgrade the server to Windows Server 2003 and decide to take advantage of DDNS. You install DNS on the server, and you configure the standard primary forward zone to use dynamic updates. You configure all PCs (including the server) to use the server's IP address as the preferred DNS server. You reboot all the clients. You find that some clients fail to register resource records in DNS. What action should you take?

A. Open the DNS console. On the Advanced tab of the server's properties dialog box, select the Always Update DNS option.

B. Configure a reverse lookup zone.

C. Manually create host (A) resource records for the Windows NT 4.0 Workstation clients.

D. Manually create host (A) resource records for the Windows 98 clients.

7. You work for Margie's Travel, which has a main office in Detroit and small branch offices in Toledo and Cleveland. DNS is implemented on a standard primary server and a standard secondary server in Detroit. All client PCs in the organization are configured to access one of these servers as their preferred DNS server, and the other as their alternative DNS server. Clients in the branch office access resources in Detroit regularly. They report that access is often slow. You do not want to increase traffic on the WAN links. How should you improve resource access for branch office staff?

A. Install a caching-only DNS server in the Cleveland and Toledo branches.

B. Install a secondary DNS server in the Cleveland and Toledo branches.

C. Install a stub DNS server in the Cleveland and Toledo branches.

D. Install a domain controller in the Cleveland and Toledo branches.

8. Proseware, Inc., has sites in several different countries. Active Directory–integrated DNS has been installed for the forest root domain, proseware.com. The DNS Server service is installed on four Windows Server 2003 domain controllers in Proseware's main facility in the United States. The servers are named Pixie, Dixie, Tom, and Jerry. They do not host any DNS zones other than proseware.com.

You are a consultant tasked with implementing Proseware's network infrastructure in Europe. You install a domain controller called London and create the Active Directory child domain europe.proseware.com. The DNS service on London is Active Directory–integrated. Authority for the europe.proseware.com DNS zone is delegated to London. You configure the Preferred DNS Server field in the TCP/IP properties dialog box for London to point to London's IP address. How can you ensure that name resolution requests originating in the europe.proseware.com domain for resources in the proseware.com domain are dealt with efficiently?

A. Configure Pixie, Dixie, Tom, and Jerry as conditional forwarders on London.

B. Configure Jerry as a master name server for London.

C. Add Pixie, Dixie, Tom, and Jerry to the root hints on London.

D. Configure Pixie, Dixie, Tom, and Jerry as alternative DNS servers on London.

9. You administer an Active Directory domain that has 200 clients. DNS is set up as a standard primary zone on a stand-alone server. Your network uses registered IP addresses. You want your DNS server to perform recursive queries on behalf of DNS clients to resolve FQDNs of external Internet sites, while still continuing to resolve internal host names. How do you configure the DNS server?

A. Configure the DNS server as a caching-only server.

B. Configure the DNS server to use forwarders.

C. Configure the DNS server as a stub server.

D. Configure the primary zone to allow dynamic updates.

10. You administer a Windows Server 2003 Active Directory domain with 100 Windows NT 4.0 Workstation clients. The clients are statically configured, and they have static entries in the DNS zone domain1.local. DNS is Active Directory–integrated and allows only secure dynamic updates. You upgrade all your clients to Windows XP Professional. You install DHCP, and you configure your clients to obtain their IP configurations and their preferred DNS server addresses automatically. DHCP is configured to always update client records in DNS.

Clients report that they can no longer access other clients by host name. You examine the DNS database and find that A resource records are not being updated, but PTR resource records are. How should you solve this problem?

   A. Reconcile the DHCP scope.

   B. Manually delete all the static A resource records. Run **Ipconfig /registerdns** on each client PC.

   C. Run **Dnscmd /ageallrecords domain1.local**.

   D. Run **Dnscmd /startscavenging**.

11. On the morning after your organization has been closed down for a two-week vacation, several users report that they cannot access an intranet Web site on your Windows Server 2003 network from the browsers on their clients running Windows XP Professional. You ping the Web server's static IP address from your own PC and the ping times out. You check the Web server PC and discover that it has become disconnected from the network.

You plug it back in and run **Ipconfig /registerdns** followed by Net stop netlogon and Net start netlogon. You can now access the Web site by typing the URL into your browser. However, the clients that previously could not access the site using their browsers still cannot access them. How do you solve this problem? (Choose all that apply).

   A. Run **Ipconfig /release** and then **Ipconfig /renew** on the Web server.

   B. Run **Ipconfig /registerdns** on each client PC that cannot access the Web site.

   C. Run **Ipconfig /flushdns** on each client PC that cannot access the Web site.

   D. Tell the users to go and have an early lunch, and everything will be OK when they come back.

12. You administer a single Windows Server 2003 Active Directory domain. DNS is installed on a domain controller and configured as a primary zone, but the zone is not stored in the Active Directory. Because clients access servers and not each other, host (A) resource records for the servers have been added to the primary zone. The network is expanding and the installation of several new servers is planned. You plan to configure dynamic updates, but management is concerned that rogue PCs could register themselves in the organization's DNS. What is the first step you should take to help implement your plan while meeting management's concerns?

   A. In the zone properties dialog box on the General tab, select Nonsecure And Secure from the Dynamic Updates list.

   B. In the zone properties dialog box on the General tab, select Secure from the Dynamic Updates list.

   C. In the DHCP console, open the server properties dialog box. On the DNS tab, select the Always Dynamically Update DNS A And PTR Records option.

   D. Convert the DNS standard primary zone to an Active Directory–integrated zone.

Objective 5.1 Answers

1. **Correct Answers: D**

   A. **Incorrect:** The FQDN consists of the client name followed by the DNS primary suffix. By default, the DNS primary suffix is the name of the domain that the client is in. Client1 is in the accounts.denver.fourthcoffee.com domain and therefore has the FQDN client1.accounts.denver.fourthcoffee.com.

   B. **Incorrect:** The FQDN does not include the name of the domain controller or controllers in that domain. Client1 is in the accounts.denver.fourthcoffee.com domain, not the DC1.accounts.denver.fourthcoffee.com domain.

   C. **Incorrect:** The at (@) symbol is used in Simple Mail Transfer Protocol (SMTP) e-mail addresses, not in FQDNs.

   D. **Correct:** Client1 is in the accounts.denver.fourthcoffee.com domain and therefore has the FQDN client1.accounts.denver.fourthcoffee.com. (Note that in Windows Server 2003 DNS, FQDNs are not case-sensitive.)

2. **Correct Answers: B, C, E, and F**

   A. **Incorrect:** The connection-specific DNS suffix text.design.treyresearch.corp is specified for the 10.10.1.0 network.

   B. **Correct:** This FQDN is on the 10.10.1.0 network.

   C. **Correct:** This FQDN is on the 10.10.2.0 network.

   A. **Incorrect:** The connection-specific DNS suffix video.design.treyresearch.corp is specified for the 10.10.2.0 network.

   B. **Correct:** Specifying a connection-specific DNS suffix does not alter the default DNS suffix. Resource1 can still be accessed on either interface using its default FQDN.

   C. **Correct:** Specifying a connection-specific DNS suffix does not alter the default DNS suffix. Resource1 can still be accessed on either interface using its default FQDN.

3. **Correct Answers: D**

   A. **Incorrect:** Starting the DNS service did not remove the x. Restarting it will not help.

   B. **Incorrect:** You cannot perform this task when the server is disabled, and it has nothing to do with enabling the server in any case.

   C. **Incorrect:** Deleting and creating zones has no effect on server status.

   D. **Correct:** Everything is in place for the DNS server to be activated. All you need to do is refresh it.

4. **Correct Answers: A**

    A. **Correct:** DNS is Active Directory–integrated, all DCs have the DNS Server service installed, and clients register their host resource records dynamically. Therefore, the zone files on all DCs contain the host resource records for all clients.

    B. **Incorrect:** The question does not mention that the Delegation Of Control Wizard has been run. Therefore, denver.fourthcoffee.com is not a DNS zone. It is important to distinguish between Active Directory domains, DNS domains, and DNS zones.

    C. **Incorrect:** If you access this tab on a standard secondary zone, the parameters are unavailable. However, DC7 does not host a standard secondary zone—it hosts an Active Directory–integrated zone, for which it is authoritative.

    D. **Incorrect:** In an Active Directory–integrated zone, you can access the Security tab from the DNS server properties dialog box of any participating DC.

5. **Correct Answers: C**

    A. **Incorrect:** This approach would speed up access, but it would also increase network traffic due to zone transfers from the master in Singapore to the secondary in Chicago. This solution is overkill for sporadic resource access.

    B. **Incorrect:** This idea might be good, but it would not solve this particular problem. A caching-only server speeds up name resolution if a server name has been resolved recently, and the results are cached. Because Chicago users access resources in Singapore only sporadically, the record of a previous query would likely time out before the query is repeated.

    C. **Correct:** Access to Singapore resources is becoming slower because as the Singapore operation expands, more DNS servers are being installed. A stub server holds records for all the authoritative name servers in the singapore.litware-inc.com zone and therefore speeds access to resources. Because the stub server receives information only when a new name server is added, the additional network traffic that is generated will be minimal.

    D. **Incorrect:** This approach would cause queries that cannot be resolved locally in Chicago to be forwarded to Singapore. Thus, traffic on the Singapore WAN link would increase and would delay the majority of resolution requests, which are not for Singapore servers. It would make sense to configure a conditional forwarder that would forward name resolution requests only for the singapore.litware-inc.com zone, but this is not what the question specifies.

6.   Correct Answers: C

   A. Incorrect: This setting is available in the DHCP server properties dialog box, not in the DNS console.

   B. Incorrect: This approach enables IP-address-to-host-name resolution. It has nothing to do with dynamic updates.

   C. Correct: Windows NT 4.0 Workstation clients cannot register resource records in DNS. In the absence of DHCP, these records need to be created manually. Another solution is to install Windows Internet Name Service (WINS), but the question does not allow for this alternative.

   D. Incorrect: Windows 98 clients can register resource records in DDNS.

7.   Correct Answers: A

   A. Correct: You should install DNS on servers in Cleveland and Toledo, and configure their root hints to point to the DNS servers in Detroit. It is probably wise for one caching-only server to access the primary server first, and for the other to access the secondary server first. No further configuration is required. Caching-only servers are not authoritative for any zone, so no zone transfer traffic will be generated. Because users in the branch offices access resources in the main office regularly, most name resolution requests will be satisfied from cache. As a result, resource access should be quicker and host name resolution traffic should decrease.

   B. Incorrect: This solution would reduce resource access delays, but at the cost of increasing zone transfer traffic over the WAN links. Because the branch offices are small, additional secondary DNS servers are not appropriate in this scenario.

   C. Incorrect: Stub servers hold resource records only for the authoritative name servers in their zone. In this case, additional DNS servers are unlikely to be installed in the main office regularly. Stub servers can be useful in large multinational organizations with delegated zones, where it is necessary for one zone to keep track of all the servers that are authoritative for the others.

   D. Incorrect: DNS is not Active Directory–integrated, so a DC would not assist in name resolution unless it were also configured as a secondary DNS server. (Refer to the explanation for answer B.) Installing DCs in Cleveland and Toledo would speed up login at the branch offices but would have no effect on name resolution, and would generate Active Directory replication traffic. Because the branch offices are small, this solution would be overkill. In any case, the question does not specify that Maggie's Travel has an Active Directory domain.

8.   Correct Answers: A

A. Correct: This solution ensures that all requests with FQDNs ending in proseware.com (except for those ending in europe.proseware.com) are passed directly to a DNS server that is authoritative for the proseware.com zone. Note that a DNS server can be configured with a number of forwarders.

B. Incorrect: Jerry and London host separate zones. You can use this configuration only if you set up London as a secondary server for the proseware.com DNS zone, which would increase replication traffic over the WAN link.

C. Incorrect: Pixie, Dixie, Tom, and Jerry do not host a root zone.

D. Incorrect: This configuration would result in London forwarding a query to one of the proseware.com servers only if it could not resolve the query. London would first attempt to resolve the query by accessing a server on its root hints file. This solution is not the most efficient way of resolving queries ending in proseware.com.

9.   Correct Answers: B

A. Incorrect: A caching-only server is not authoritative for any zone and would hold address resolution information that it obtained only from the server it uses for name resolution. It could not resolve internal name resolution requests.

B. Correct: The DNS server would then forward requests that it could not resolve from its zone file or cache to another DNS server, typically your ISP's DNS server.

C. Incorrect: A stub server holds a list of authoritative name servers only for its master zone. It cannot resolve internal name resolution requests.

D. Incorrect: This solution would allow clients to register their resource records dynamically. It would have no effect on external name resolution.

10.   Correct Answers: C

A. Incorrect: This solution repairs inconsistencies in the DHCP scope. It does not delete static DNS resource records.

B. Incorrect: This solution would work, but it involves excessive administrative effort.

C. Correct: Unlike PTR resource records, static A resource records do not age and cannot be removed automatically. The Dnscmd /ageallrecords command causes all records to age, which in effect converts static records into dynamic records. Dnscmd is a Microsoft Windows Server 2003 support tools utility. To run it, you need to install Support Tools from the sever CDROM and change to the \Program Files\Support Tools directory.

D. **Incorrect:** Scavenging removes all stale records from the DNS zone. Static records do not age and consequently are never identified as stale. You need to convert all records to dynamic.

11. **Correct Answers: C and D**

A. **Incorrect:** The Web server has a static IP address. There is no point in trying to renew its DHCP lease.

B. **Incorrect:** You have no reason to believe that the clients are not registered in DNS. No problems have been reported about clients not accessing each other.

C. **Correct:** Windows XP Professional DNS employs negative caching. The Web server has been disconnected for a length of time that is sufficient for its host resource record to have been removed from the DNS zone file. Thus, when the users tried to access the Web server's FQDN by typing in the URL, their client PCs cached that the FQDN could not be resolved. On the other hand, you "pinged" the Web server's IP address and did not, therefore, request name resolution. When the users tried to access the Web site again, the client PCs used cached information and discovered that the FQDN had been cached as invalid. Clearing the negative result from the clients' caches solves the problem.

D. **Correct:** Cache entries, including negative entries (refer to the explanation for answer C), typically time out in 45 minutes or less.

12. **Correct Answers: D**

A. **Incorrect:** This solution would expose the network to registration attempts by rogue PCs.

B. **Incorrect:** This configuration can only be done in an Active Directory–integrated primary zone.

C. **Incorrect:** This solution has no effect if DNS is not enabled to allow dynamic updates.

D. **Correct:** In the General tab of the zone properties dialog box for an Active Directory–integrated zone, you can allow only secure dynamics updates. This solution allows resource records to be updated automatically while preventing computers that do not have accounts in Active Directory from registering their details. However, you need to convert the zone to Active Directory–integrated first.

Manage DNS

This section of the exam requires that you understand how the DNS server answers queries. You should know how to ensure that DNS is working properly and that legacy desktops are updating DNS through DHCP.

You need a mastery of DNS zone settings, record settings, and server options. You should know how to allow updates, how to allow only secure updates, and how to set the Time to Live (TTL) both for zones and for individual records. You also need to know how to display the DNS cache on both servers and clients and understand the significance of negative caching. You should be aware of what server options such as round robin and disable recursion do and when they should be enabled.

You should be familiar with (at least) all the commonly used resource record types, such as A, PTR, name server (NS), SOA, and mail exchange (MX). You should know how to add records to a zone, how to monitor them, and how to delete them. You should be able to verify that both forward and reverse lookup zones are configured correctly.

Objective 5.2 Questions

1. Your DNS domain seattle.fourthcoffee.com has two mail servers, mail1 and mail2. You want mail1 to be the primary mail server and mail2 to be the secondary mail server. Which DNS resource records should you create? (Choose all that apply.)

A. @ MX 10 mail1.seattle.fourthcoffee.com.

B. @ MB 10 mail1.seattle.fourthcoffee.com.

C. @ MX 200 mail1.seattle.fourthcoffee.com.

D. @ MB 20 mail1.seattle.fourthcoffee.com.

E. @ MX 20 mail2.seattle.fourthcoffee.com.

F. @ MB 20 mail2.seattle.fourthcoffee.com.

G. @ MX 10 mail2.seattle.fourthcoffee.com.

H. @ MB 10 mail2.seattle.fourthcoffee.com.

2. You are the system administrator at Lucerne Publishing. You administer the books.lucernepublishing.com Windows Server 2003 Active Directory domain. Active Directory–integrated DNS is configured on all domain controllers in the domain. You configure a member server, ServerA, to host an internal Web site for the intranet. You want employees to access this Web site using the URL books.internal.lucernepublishing.com. What should you do?

A. Create a canonical name (CNAME) resource record called books, and specify internal.lucernepublishing.com as the target host.

B. Create a new zone called internal.lucernepublishing.com. Create a CNAME resource record called books in that new zone, and specify ServerA.books.lucernepublishing.com as the target host.

C. Create a CNAME resource record called books.internal and specify ServerA.books.lucernepublishing.com as the target host.

D. Create a CNAME resource record called internal and specify ServerA.books.lucernepublishing.com as the target host.

3. You administer a large mixed-mode Active Directory domain. All the domain controllers are Windows Server 2003, Enterprise Edition servers, but the servers are a mixture of Windows Server 2003, Windows 2000 Server, and Windows NT 4.0 Server. Client PCs are Windows XP Professional, Windows 2000 Professional, or Windows NT 4.0 Workstation. DHCP is installed on two clustered Windows Server 2003, Enterprise Edition servers. You have configured DNS to allow only secure dynamic updates.

Some hosts can be accessed by host name. Others cannot. All hosts can be accessed by IP address. What can you do to help ensure that all hosts can be accessed by host name?

A. Install NetBEUI on the hosts that cannot be accessed by host name.

B. Set DNS to allow all dynamic updates.

C. In the DNS console, on the Advanced tab of the zone properties dialog box, select the Always Update DNS option.

D. In the DHCP console, on the DNS tab of the server properties dialog box, select the Enable DNS Dynamic Updates According To The Settings Below option, and then select Always Dynamically Update DNS A And Pointer Records.

4. You have a technical support position at one of the major branch offices of Humongous Insurance. A Windows Server 2003 computer on the branch office network acts as a secondary DNS server for a master server (also Windows Server 2003) in Humongous Insurance's main office. The master server is authoritative for a single standard primary forward zone. Users in the branch office are having problems accessing resources in the main office. You suspect that some DNS resource records on the secondary server have become stale. What action should you take?

A. Open the DNS console on the secondary DNS server. Right-click the server name and select Launch Nslookup. Run the command **Set msxfr**.

B. Open the DNS console on the secondary DNS server. Right-click the server name and select Launch Nslookup. Run the command **Set nomsxfr**.

C. Open the DNS console on the primary DNS server. Access the Start Of Authority (SOA) tab in the forward zone's properties dialog box, and increment the Serial Number setting.

D. Open the DNS console on the secondary DNS server. Right-click the applicable zone and select Reload From Master.

5. Your Windows Server 2003 Active Directory domain fabrikam.com contains three Web servers that are used to host a frequently accessed intranet Web site. All three Web servers have identical content. They have static IP addresses 10.12.1.10, 10.12.1.15, and 10.12.1.20, respectively. You want employees to be able to access the intranet Web site with the single URL internal.fabrikam.com. You create three host resource records in the fabricam.com forward lookup zone as follows:

internal:10.12.1.10

internal:10.12.1.15

internal:10.12.1.20

However, when you analyze network traffic, you find that only the first of these servers is receiving Hypertext Transfer Protocol (HTTP) requests. What is likely to be the problem?

   A. Round robin is disabled on the DNS server.

   B. CNAME resource records should have been used, not host resource records.

   C. PTR resource records should have been used, not host resource records.

   D. Only Active Directory–integrated DNS supports this option.

6. You want to inspect the DNS cache on a client computer to check for negative cache entries and TTL parameters. How do you perform this task?

   A. Use the **Ipconfig /flushdns** command-line utility while logged on to the client PC.

   B. Use the **Ipconfig /displaydns** command-line utility while logged on to the client PC.

   C. Open the DNS console. In the console tree, right-click the appropriate server, and select Clear Cache.

   D. Use the **Ipconfig /registerdns** command-line utility while logged on to the client PC.

7. You administer a network that consists of a number of subnets. For historical reasons, different subnets contain different types of operating systems. Some subnets contain UNIX servers, some contain Novell NetWare servers, and some contain Windows NT 4.0 servers. There are also UNIX, NetWare, Windows 95, Windows 98, NT 4.0 Workstation, Windows 2000 Professional, and Windows XP Professional clients. All PCs have static IP configurations.

You set up an Active Directory domain with Windows Server 2003 domain controllers. You implement DHCP and configure all workstations that can do so to obtain their IP configurations automatically. You set exclusions in the DHCP scopes for clients that require static configuration. You configure Active Directory–integrated DNS zones. You configure DHCP to update DNS records for all DHCP clients. You configure DNS to allow only secure dynamic updates. Legacy Berkeley Internet Name Domain (BIND) UNIX servers are configured as secondary servers for the Active Directory–integrated DNS primary zone.

Client workstations do not require access to each other, but all clients need to be able to access all severs by host name. You find that certain servers cannot be accessed by host name. What should you do?

A. Install WINS.

B. Create Hosts file entries on all clients for all the servers that cannot currently be accessed by host name.

C. Manually enter host (A) resource records for the NetWare, UNIX, and Windows NT 4.0 servers.

D. Install NetBEUI on all client PCs.

8. You want to clear the DNS cache on a DNS server. How can you perform this task? (Choose all that apply.)

A. Use the **Ipconfig /displaydns** command-line utility while logged on to the DNS server.

B. Open the DNS console and select the appropriate server. From the Action menu, select Clear Cache.

C. Use the **Ipconfig /flushdns** command-line utility while logged on to the DNS server.

D. Open the DNS console and select the appropriate server. From the Action menu, select Scavenge Stale Resource Records.

9. For security reasons, you want to configure DNS server DNS2 so that it does not forward name requests that it cannot resolve from its own zone file. You log on to DNS2 as the local administrator. What should you do to achieve the desired result? (Choose all that apply.)

A. In the DNS console, access the DNS2 server properties dialog box. On the Advanced tab, select the Disable Recursion check box. Click OK.

B. At a command prompt, run **Dnscmd . /config /norecursion**.

C. At a command prompt, type **Dnscmd . /config /norecursion 1**.

D. At a command prompt, run **Dnscmd DNS2 /config /norecursion 1**.

10. Trey Research is a dynamic organization in an environment where rapid change is the norm. New servers are frequently added, and the names of existing resource servers are often changed to reflect new organizational structures. Active Directory–integrated DNS is hosted on all of the company's Windows Server 2003 domain controllers. There is a single forward lookup zone and a corresponding reverse lookup zone. Reverse DNS lookup is heavily used to support the security of the company's e-mail system.

Users report that sometimes name resolution fails, and they are told that a server is unavailable. At other times, they are directed to the wrong server. What can you do to improve the situation?

A. Open the DNS console. In the properties dialog box for each zone, access the Start Of Authority (SOA) tab and specify a new minimum default TTL.

B. Open the DNS console. In the General tab of the properties dialog box for each zone, click Aging. Select the Scavenge Stale Resource Records check box.

C. Open the DNS console. In the properties dialog box for each server, access the Start Of Authority (SOA) tab, and specify a new minimum default TTL.

D. Open the DNS console. For each server, from the Action menu select Set Aging/Scavenging For All Zones. Select the Scavenge Stale Resource Records check box.

11. You are a network administrator for Contoso, Inc. Contoso manufactures military equipment, and security is very important. You have converted the DNS zones on your Windows Server 2003 Active Directory domain to Active Directory–integrated zones. You suspect that Contoso is under attack from a malicious Internet user. In particular, you suspect that redirection is being used to feed incorrect data into the organization. How can you combat such an attack? (Choose all that apply.)

A. Disable recursion on all DNS servers.

B. Disable round robin on all DNS servers.

C. Ensure that all server caches are secured against pollution.

D. Allow only secure dynamic updates on all DNS zones.

12. The School of Fine Art has a standard primary DNS zone configured on a Windows Server 2003, Enterprise Edition server. Previously, name resolution was carried out by a legacy UNIX server, and this server has been reconfigured to host a secondary zone that provides backup for the Windows server. The primary server is powered down so that a second hard disk can be installed, and users report that they are having problems accessing resources. You bring the Windows server back online and the problem disappears.

You investigate and find that zone transfers are not occurring. What should you do next?

A. Disable recursion on the primary server.

B. Ensure that the BIND Secondaries check box on the primary server is selected.

C. Enable IXFR on the secondary server.

D. Enable AXFR on the primary server.

Objective 5.2 Answers

1. **Correct Answers: A and E**

   A. **Correct:** MX resource records specify mail exchange servers. The fourth parameter specifies the priority. Here, 10 is the lower of the two numbers. The lower the number, the higher the priority, so mail1 is the primary mail server.

   B. **Incorrect:** MX resource records specify mail exchange servers. Mailbox (MB) resource records indicate the DNS domain names of the hosts on which the records reside.

   C. **Incorrect:** MX resource records specify mail exchange servers. The fourth parameter specifies the priority. Here, 10 is the lower of the two numbers. The lower the number, the higher the priority; thus, mail1 would be the secondary mail server.

   D. **Incorrect:** MX resource records specify mail exchange servers. Mailbox (MB) resource records indicate the DNS domain names of the hosts on which the records reside.

   E. **Correct:** MX resource records specify mail exchange servers. The fourth parameter specifies the priority. Here, 20 is the higher of the two numbers. The lower the number, the higher the priority, so mail2 is the secondary mail server.

   F. **Incorrect:** MX resource records specify mail exchange servers. Mailbox (MB) resource records indicate the DNS domain names of the hosts on which the records reside.

   G. **Incorrect:** This record would make mail2 the primary mail exchange server. Refer to the explanation for answer E.

   H. **Incorrect:** MX resource records specify mail exchange servers. Mailbox (MB) resource records indicate the DNS domain names of the hosts on which the records reside.

2. **Correct Answers: B**

   A. **Incorrect:** No host exists called internal.lucernepublishing.com.

   B. **Correct:** This zone would map books.internal.lucernepublishing.com to ServerA.books.lucernepublishing.com. The new zone can be either standard primary or Active Directory–integrated.

C. Incorrect: This approach would map books.internal.books.lucernepublishing.com to the Web server. However, you want the Web server to be accessed as books.internal.lucernepublishing.com.

D. Incorrect: This approach would map internal.books.lucernepublishing to the Web server. However, you want the Web server to be accessed as books.internal.lucernepublishing.com.

3. Correct Answers: D

A. Incorrect: Windows Server 2003 Server does not support NetBEUI, and it cannot be installed on Windows XP Professional. Even if it were installed on the hosts that can support it, NetBEUI would not solve this problem. It cannot resolve NetBIOS names across a router, and a large domain is likely to be subnetted.

B. Incorrect: The problem is that some hosts cannot update resource records in DNS and need DHCP to perform this task for them. Allowing all dynamic updates would not solve this problem, plus it would compromise security in the domain.

C. Incorrect: This setting is a DHCP setting, and it cannot be configured from the DNS console.

D. Correct: DHCP updates resource records for Windows NT 4.0 clients that cannot register their own details in DNS, for example. Note that this solution might not be complete. Any Windows NT 4.0 server that has a static IP configuration needs to have its host (A) resource record entered manually. WINS would be a good solution in this scenario, but the question does not provide this alternative.

4. Correct Answers: D

A. Incorrect: This action enables Microsoft fast zone transfer, which uses compression and can include multiple records in a single TCP message. It does not initiate a zone transfer and cannot solve the problem described in this scenario.

B. Incorrect: This action enables Microsoft fast zone transfer, which uses compression and can include multiple records in a single TCP message. It does not initiate a zone transfer and cannot solve the problem described in this scenario.

C. Incorrect: When a zone transfer is initiated, either manually or as a scheduled operation, the master sever compares the serial numbers of the primary and secondary SOA records to determine whether the records on the secondary server need to be updated. Incrementing this number manually will not solve the problem outlined in this scenario.

D. Correct: Resource records in the secondary zone have become stale either because regular zone transfers have not occurred, or because a lot of recent changes have been made to resource records on the DNS master. This procedure initiates zone transfer manually.

5.   **Correct Answers: A**

A. **Correct:** Round robin is a server option that implements load sharing. When the same host name in resource records is associated with several IP addresses, requests for resolution of the host name result in each IP address being supplied to resolvers in turn. Round robin is enabled by default in Windows Server 2003 (for several types of resource records). Round robin has probably been disabled in this scenario.

B. **Incorrect:** The CNAME record associates a number of host names (or aliases) with the same IP address, not vice versa.

C. **Incorrect:** The PTR resource record is used to resolve IP addresses to host names, which is not what this scenario requires.

D. **Incorrect:** You implement round robin by having several host records that all have the same host name or FQDN, but different IP addresses. It makes no difference whether these records are held in an Active Directory–integrated primary zone file, a standard primary zone file, or a secondary zone file.

6.   **Correct Answers: B**

A   **Incorrect:** This solution flushes the DNS cache on the client. You want to inspect it.

B. **Correct:** This solution displays the DNS cache on the client.

C. **Incorrect:** The DNS console can be used to manage the cache on a DNS server. You cannot inspect client caches from the console.

D. **Incorrect:** This solution registers the client in DNS (assuming that DNS is set up to allow this to happen). It does not display the client's DNS cache.

7.   **Correct Answers: C**

A. **Incorrect:** The legacy UNIX and Novell NetWare servers do not register with WINS, and they require static entries. Also, you would need to set up WINS proxies for the non-Windows workstations. This approach involves excessive administrative effort. (Note that non-legacy UNIX hosts can be WINS clients.)

B. **Incorrect:** This approach involves excessive administrative effort.

C. Correct: Statically configured legacy UNIX, NetWare, and Windows NT 4.0 servers cannot update their own records in DNS, and DHCP cannot update DNS records for statically configured clients. Host resource records for servers are easily added manually. If reverse lookup is required, PTR resource records can be created automatically when host records are added. (Note that non-legacy UNIX hosts can register their host and PTR records in DDNS.)

D. Incorrect: NetBEUI cannot resolve host names across a router. Also, Windows Server 2003 Server does not support NetBEUI, and it cannot be installed on Windows XP Professional.

8. **Correct Answers: B and C**

A. Incorrect: This approach displays cache entries. It does not flush the cache.

B. Correct: This method is for flushing the cache from the DNS console. You do not need to be logged on to the specific DNS server to use this method.

C. Correct: This solution flushes the DNS cache of whatever PC you are logged on to: client or server.

D. Incorrect: This approach does not flush the cache. It removes resource records that have timed out.

9. **Correct Answers: A, C, and D**

A. Correct: Recursion enables a DNS server to forward a request that it cannot resolve from its own zone file. Selecting the Disable Recursion check box ensures that the server resolves a host name only if that host name is in the zone for which the server is authoritative.

B. Incorrect: This command needs one more parameter: 1 turns recursion off; 0 turns it on.

C. Correct: This command turns off recursion. Note that the full stop can be used in place of the server name only if you are logged on at that server.

D. Correct: This command turns off recursion. Note that the full stop can be used in place of the server name only if you are logged on at that server.

10.   **Correct Answers: A**

   A. Correct: Stale resource records are being accessed. When a record's TTL has expired, it will not be used. In this scenario, the subsequent increase in name resolution traffic that results from a smaller TTL is acceptable if fewer stale records are accessed.

   B. Incorrect: The problem is that stale records are not timing out quickly enough in cache, not that stale records with zero TTL are failing to be removed from the zone. Although selecting this check box is probably a good idea in this scenario, this solution will not solve the immediate problem.

   C. Incorrect: You can set the default TTL for a zone, or you can set the TTL for individual records. You cannot set it at server level. There is no SOA tab in the server properties dialog box.

   D. Incorrect: The problem is that stale records are not timing out quickly enough in cache, not that stale records with zero TTL are failing to be removed from the zone. Although selecting this check box is probably a good idea in this scenario, this solution will not solve the immediate problem.

11.   **Correct Answers: C and D**

   A. Incorrect: Recursion can be disabled on DNS servers that do not respond directly to clients, but receive name resolution requests from other DNS servers. Forwarders are disabled automatically if recursion is disabled. Consequently, if such a DNS server receives a name resolution request that it cannot satisfy from the zones for which it is authoritative, it returns a negative result. If all of Contoso's DNS servers had recursion disabled, no resolution of external names would be possible. This setup would certainly be secure, but it is not a good plan for a supplier of military equipment.

   B. Incorrect: Round robin is a load-balancing mechanism that allows the same FQDN to be allocated to several hosts, each with a different IP, and balances access requests between these hosts. It has no effect on network security.

   C. Correct: Redirection is when an attacker is able to redirect queries for DNS names to servers under the control of the attacker. One method of redirection is to pollute a DNS server cache with erroneous data. For example, if a query from Contoso requires resolution of the FQDN www.fabrikam.com, and a referral answer provides a resolution for fabrikam.com, the DNS server continues to use the cached data to resolve further queries for www.fabrikam.com. If all server caches are secured against pollution, such referrals are rejected. In Windows Server 2003 DNS, caches are secured against pollution by default, but in a high security environment, you should check that this setting has not been altered.

D. Correct: Redirection can be accomplished whenever an attacker has writable access to DNS data. Insecure dynamic updates allow computers that do not have computer accounts in Active Directory to register information in DNS.

12.   **Correct Answers: B**

 A. Incorrect: Recursion can be disabled on DNS servers that do not respond directly to clients but receive name resolution requests from other DNS servers. Forwarders are disabled automatically if recursion is disabled. This action has no effect on zone transfer, and it is not appropriate in this scenario.

 B. Correct: By default, Windows Server 2003 DNS servers use a fast zone transfer format. This format uses compression and can include multiple records in a single TCP message. This format is incompatible with legacy (pre–version 4.9.4) BIND-based DNS running on UNIX servers. Enabling BIND secondaries disables fast zone transfer.

 C. Incorrect: This is done by running Nslookup and using the command Set msxfr. However, this action is unnecessary in this scenario. By default, Windows Server 2003 DNS servers use IXFR, which transfers only those records that have been changed or added since the previous transfer occurred. If the secondary server does not support IXFR, the primary server automatically uses AXFR instead. IXFR cannot be enabled on a legacy BIND server, and in any case, it is the transfer format that is the problem, not the type of transfer.

 D. Incorrect: This is done by running Nslookup and using the command Set msxfr. However, this action is unnecessary in this scenario. By default, Windows Server 2003 DNS servers use IXFR, which transfers only those records that have been changed or added since the previous transfer occurred. If the secondary server does not support IXFR, the primary server automatically uses AXFR instead. IXFR cannot be enabled on a legacy BIND server, and in any case, it is the transfer format that is the problem, not the type of transfer.

20 Exam 70-292— Implementing, Managing, and Maintaining Network Security (6.0)

Few, if any, aspects of network design and implementation have received more attention—or seen more development—in the past few years than network security. The danger of external attacks from the Internet is highly publicized, and you have probably heard of such attacks as Denial of Service, Distributed Denial of Service, and Redistribution. Sophisticated hacker tools are, unfortunately, readily available on the Internet, and as the tools get more user-friendly, the attackers become more numerous. Hacking is no longer a game for the highly knowledgeable prankster. The new tools have spawned a new breed of attacker who is less knowledgeable—and a lot more destructive.

Internal attacks get much less publicity. Few organizations are willing to admit that their intranets have been hacked by malicious insiders. Yet such attacks are possibly more common and more damaging than external attacks. They are also much more difficult to guard against.

Network security tools represent one of the fastest-growing areas in the networking industry. Some remarkable tools are available. The levels of encryption currently used would have been almost unimaginable even five years ago, and the development of such protocols as Internet Protocol Security (IPSec) ensure that communications can be secured all the way from the source to the ultimate destination.

Kerberos is not a new authentication protocol, but it is a powerful one. Because it uses security certificates and timestamps, both ends of a connection can be authenticated and there can be a good level of confidence that nobody is interfering in the middle. A few configuration parameters exist in Kerberos, but these are seldom changed from their default values, and this examination does not test Kerberos configuration.

You can configure many parameters in a Microsoft Windows Server 2003 Active Directory directory service environment or, indeed, on a Windows Server 2003 stand-alone server. You can set up security groups and configure access control lists (ACLs) to protect your resources. You can determine the level of privilege of ordinary authenticated users, of various levels of administrators, and of anonymous users. You can determine how software is installed and updated and how security updates are implemented. You can set up auditing and determine who is doing what on your network.

The complexity involved in configuring a large number of available security settings could make security administration impossibly complex. Fortunately, you do not have to start from scratch. Security templates are available that allow you to set up various standard levels of security. You can also analyze a custom security setting by comparing it against standard templates. Security is always a balance. There is no point in setting up policies on your servers so strict that many of your users, particularly those with legacy client operating systems, cannot access the resources or run the software that they require to do their jobs. However, if security settings do become too restrictive, tools such as Resultant Set of Policy (RSoP) allow you to quickly identify the source of the problem.

The 70-292 certification exam does not require you to know how to design security systems. You do, however, need to know how to audit systems using security templates and how to implement predefined security settings for software and security updates. You need to be able to check that security configurations are working correctly and to troubleshoot them if they are not. You also need to be able to access and analyze security statistics.

Finally, you need to be aware that security must present a moving target. What is secure today might not be secure tomorrow, and breached security is usually worse than no security at all.

Tested Skills and Suggested Practices

The skills that you need to successfully master the Implementing, Managing, and Maintaining Network Security objective domain on *Exam 70-292: Managing and Maintaining a Microsoft Windows Server 2003 Environment for an MCSA Certified on Windows 2000* include

- Implement secure network administration procedures.
  - ❑ Practice 1: Create a security management tool by adding the Security Configuration And Analysis snap-in and the Security Templates snap-in to the Microsoft Management Console (MMC).
  - ❑ Practice 2: Use the security management tool that you created in Practice 1 to create a new database. Import a security template and analyze security. Do not use the default log; instead, specify a log file. Analyze the system security against several security templates.
  - ❑ Practice 3: Use the Secedit command-line utility to perform the same task for which you used the MMC in Practice 2.
  - ❑ Practice 4: Carry out a security analysis using the MMC and Secedit as before, but use the Runas command while logged on with an ordinary user account.
  - ❑ Practice 5: Define a new security template. Export the template and apply it to a PC other than the one on which you defined it.

■ Install and configure software update infrastructure.

❑ Practice 1: Access "Checklist: Securing Computers Using Security Configuration Manager" in the Windows Server 2003 Help And Support Center. Work through the "Preparing to Set Up Security" and the "Modifying Security Settings" procedures. Pay particular attention to the Microsoft Windows Logo Program for Software and research this topic on the Microsoft Web site (*http://www.microsoft.com/winlogo/default.mspx*).

❑ Practice 2: Install and configure Windows Update by accessing the Windows Update home page from the Microsoft Web site and clicking Personalize Windows Update. Select the Display The Link To The Windows Update Catalog Under See Also check box and click Save Settings. Ensure that you receive security updates.

❑ Practice 3: Install and configure Microsoft Software Update Services (SUS) on a server running a member of the Windows Server 2003 family on your network.

❑ Practice 4: Configure Windows Update (SUS client) on a client PC to receive Windows patches and updates from the SUS server.

Further Reading

This section contains a list of supplemental readings divided by objective. If you think you need additional preparation before taking the exam, study these sources thoroughly.

Objective 6.1 Review Chapter 9, "Planning and Implementing Server Roles and Security."

Microsoft Corporation. *Windows Server 2003 online help*. Redmond, Washington. Review "Secedit," "Analyze and Configure Security," "For Administrative Tasks, Use the Principle of Least Privilege," and "Security Configuration Manager Tools."

Microsoft Corporation. Microsoft TechNet. Review "Baseline Security Analyzer," available on the Microsoft Web site at *http://www.microsoft.com/technet/security /tools/Tools/MBSAhome.asp*.

Objective 6.2 Review all of Chapter 10, "Managing and Maintaining a Server Environment."

Microsoft Corporation. *Windows Server 2003 online help*. Redmond, Washington. Review "Windows Update," "Windows Automatic Updates," and "Windows Logo Program for Software."

Microsoft Corporation. *Microsoft Windows Server 2003 Deployment Guide*. Redmond, Washington. Review "Best Practices for Security," available on the Microsoft Web site at *http://www.microsoft.com/technet/treeview/default.asp?url=/technet /prodtechnol/windowsserver2003/proddocs/standard/sag_seconceptsbp.asp*.

Implement Secure Network Administration Procedures

You can use predefined security templates to implement particular levels of security or as a starting point for creating security policies that are customized to meet different organizational requirements. You can customize a template with the Security Templates snap-in and then use the new template to customize other computers.

You can configure individual computers by using the Security Configuration And Analysis snap-in, by using the Secedit command-line tool, or by importing a template into Local Security Policy. You can configure multiple machines by importing a template into the Security Settings extension of Group Policy. You can also use the Security Configuration And Analysis snap-in, or Secedit /analyze from command prompt, and choose a security template as a baseline for analyzing a system for potential security vulnerabilities or for policy violations.

The predefined security template types are as follows:

- Default security (Setup security.inf)

- Domain controller default security (DC security.inf)

- Compatible (Compatws.inf)

- Secure (Secure*.inf)

- Highly secure (Hisec*.inf)

- System root security (Rootsec.inf)

- Auditing of Microsoft Internet Explorer security (Iesacls.inf)

Where the wildcard (*) is used, you can apply the security template to a workstation, a server, or a domain controller (DC), with differing results. You might also receive different results by applying the same template, depending on whether the operating system was implemented by a clean installation or by an upgrade.

Even if a security template is predefined, you should not assume it is safe to use on your network. Do not apply predefined security templates to your production network without testing them first. This principle applies even more to templates that you customize yourself.

Always save a modified security template with a filename that is different from the name of the template from which you created it. Do not alter and then save standard templates. In particular, never edit the Setup security.inf template because it gives you the option to reapply the default security settings.

No user should ever be given more rights and privileges than he or she needs to do the job at hand. This principle applies particularly to the administrator. If you are using Microsoft Word to write a report, you should be logged on with your ordinary user account, not your administrator account. If you need to perform a task that requires administrator rights, you do not need to log off; instead, you can use the Runas utility. Whenever possible, you should carry out administrative tasks while logged on at your client computer with your ordinary account. If you do have to log on to a server, use an administrator level account. This standard is known as the principle of least privilege.

The examination requires that you know how to use security templates to implement baseline security and how to import a standard template to audit security settings on systems on which a customized template has been either imported or created. You should also be familiar with the principle of least privilege.

Objective 6.1 Questions

1. You are the domain administrator for the Baldwin Museum of Science. The museum has 50 computers running Windows NT 4.0 Workstation. A customized software package is installed on the clients that allows users to obtain illustrations and descriptions of the museum's exhibits. The domain's two domain controllers also act as file servers, and they have recently been upgraded to Windows Server 2003. Museum visitors who sign on for this service are given user names and passwords that allow them to log on and use this facility.

During a closure period, you upgrade all the clients to Windows XP Professional. Now users report that they cannot use the software. How should you solve the problem with the least administrative effort?

  A. Use the Security Configuration And Analysis snap-in to configure the domain controllers with the Compatible security template.

  B. Use Windows Server 2003 Group Policy to configure the client PCs with the Compatible security template.

  C. Use the Security Configuration And Analysis snap-in to configure the clients with the Compatible security template.

  D. Put all user accounts into the Power Users group on the client PCs.

2. You administer a Windows Server 2003 Active Directory domain. Your manager has become concerned with password authentication security, and she has asked you to ensure that no password policy setting for the domain is any less restrictive than those specified by the account policy settings in the Securedc.inf template. Any setting that is as restrictive, or more restrictive, should be retained. All user accounts in your domain are in either the Accounts organizational unit (OU) or the Sales OU.

You use the Security Configuration And Analysis snap-in on a domain controller and use Securedc.inf to analyze the computer settings. You find the following differences:

Policy	Database	Computer
Enforce Password History	24 passwords remembered	6 passwords remembered
Maximum Password Age	42 days	100 days
Store Password Using Reversible Encryption	Disabled	Enabled

What should you do?

A. Create a new Group Policy Object (GPO) and link it to the Sales OU and the Accounts OU. Import the Securedc.inf template into the new GPO.

B. Import the Securedc.inf template into the Domain Security Policy.

C. Create a new security template. Set Enforce Password History to 24 passwords and Maximum Password Age to 42 days. Create a new GPO and link it to the Sales OU and the Accounts OU. Import the new template into the new GPO.

D. Create a new security template. Set Enforce Password History to 24 passwords and Maximum Password Age to 42 days. Import the new template into the Domain Security Policy.

3. You are the administrator of a Windows Server 2003 Active Directory domain. Your Windows XP client PC has Windows Server 2003 Administration Tools Pack installed. You are currently logged on using your user account while using Word to write a report. A user calls and tells you that she has forgotten her password. You want to access Active Directory Users And Computers with your Domain Admin account and change the user's password. What is the recommended procedure?

A. Log off and log back on again using your Administrator account.

B. Use the Runas command at the command line.

C. From the Start menu, select All Programs, point to Administrative Tools, right click Active Directory Users And Computers, and select Runas.

D. From the Start menu, select All Programs, point to Administrative Tools, hold down the Shift key, right-click Active Directory Users And Computers, and select Runas.

4. You are experimenting with security settings on a member server running Windows Server 2003 in your Active Directory domain. You want to be able to restore the settings on the computer when you have finished. What should you do before you start and after you have finished testing the new settings? (Choose all that apply.)

   A. Before you start changing the settings, you should use the Security Templates snap-in to create a template containing the current security settings. After experimenting, you should import and apply this template using the Security Configuration And Analysis snap-in and selecting the Clear This Database Before Importing check box during the import operation.

   B. Before you start, use the Secedit /export command to export a template that contains the original security configuration. Then use Secedit /configure with the /overwrite switch to import the template into a database to restore the settings from this database.

   C. You do not need to do anything before you start. You can use Secedit /configure with the /areas switch set to SECURITYPOLICY to import the Setup security.inf template into a database and use this database to configure the original settings.

   D. Before you start, you should use Secedit /generaterollback to create a rollback template. You can then use Secedit /refreshpolicy to apply this rollback template when you are finished.

5. You administer a Windows NT 4.0 domain. Most client computers are running Windows NT 4.0 Workstation with Service Pack 3 installed. However, some clients cannot support this operating system and have Windows 98 installed instead. You upgrade your primary domain controller (PDC), backup domain controllers (BDCs), and servers to Windows Server 2003 domain controllers and member servers. You configure your domain controllers using the Hisecdc.inf template. None of the clients can access the domain controllers. You do not have a budget to upgrade client hardware or install new client operating systems at this time. You do not want to weaken the security on your domain controllers. What can you do to enable your clients to join the domain? (Choose all that apply; each answer forms part of the solution.)

   A. Upgrade your clients running Windows 98 to Windows 98, Second Edition.

   B. Create accounts in Active Directory for the client computers.

   C. Log on to each client as a local administrator and then join the domain.

   D. Upgrade the computers running Windows NT 4.0 Workstation with the latest service pack.

   E. Configure all clients to use Kerberos version 5 for authentication.

   F. Install the Active Directory Client Extensions pack on the clients running Windows 98.

6.   Company policy requires that all client machines in the Payroll department be secured using the Securews.inf template settings. You create a Payroll OU in your Windows Server 2003 Active Directory domain, put all the relevant computer accounts into this OU, create a GPO linked to the OU, and import the Securews.inf template into that GPO. All computers in the Payroll department are clients running Windows XP Professional.

You find that some clients in the Payroll department are able to access an insecure member server running Windows NT 4.0 that has no service packs installed. You have been intending to upgrade this server, but you welcome the indication that some clients are not as secure as they ought to be. What should you do to ensure that Securews.inf is applied to all the Payroll computers?

A.   Run the Convert command-line utility on the unsecured clients.

B.   Use the Security Configuration And Analysis snap-in to import the Securews.inf template on each of the unsecured clients, selecting the Clear This Database Before Importing check box during the import operation.

C.   Configure loopback policy so that clients in the Payroll OU are denied access to the insecure server.

D.   Run the Gpupdate command-line utility on the unsecured clients.

7.   You administer a Windows Server 2003 Active Directory domain that has 50 clients running Windows 2000 Professional, 20 clients running Windows NT 4.0 Workstation, and 25 clients running Windows 98, Second Edition. You want to convert all clients to Windows XP Professional. You upgrade the clients running Windows 2000 Professional but decide to do a clean installation of Windows XP Professional on the clients running Windows NT 4.0 and Windows 98. You specify the NTFS disk-filing system for all client hard disks.

You want all client computers to have the same security settings. You create an OU called Clients and move all client computer accounts into that OU. You create a GPO linked to the OU. How do you ensure that all client PCs are configured with the same security settings?

A.   Use Group Policy to apply the Compatws.inf security template to the OU.

B.   Use Secedit to apply the Compatws.inf security template to all the upgraded computers.

C.   Use Secedit to apply the Setup security.inf security template to all the upgraded computers.

D.   Use Group Policy to apply the Setup security.inf security template to the OU.

8.   You administer a Windows Server 2003 Active Directory domain for a large manufacturing company. For security reasons, the client computers used by the various design departments are subject to more stringent settings than the client computers used in other parts of the operation. A security consultant has created a security template called Secure-Design.inf that you have to apply to the client computers in all design departments.

The client computers that the managers of the design departments use are subject to the same restrictions as all other design department clients. However, separate policies outside these security requirements can be applied to the managers' computers.

The domain contains a top-level OU called Design. The Managers OU is a child of Design. You move all the clients used by design personnel into the Design OU. You create a GPO called DesignPolicy and link it to the Design OU. You import the Secure-Design.inf template to the DesignPolicy GPO.

When you test the system, you find that the design managers' computers do not have some of the security settings specified in the new template. The computers with accounts in the Design OU all have the correct security configurations. What should you do to solve the problem and to make sure the settings are applied without delay? (Choose all that apply; each answer forms part of the solution.)

A. Move all the design managers' user accounts into the Managers OU.

B. Move all the managers' computer accounts into the Design OU.

C. Select the No Override check box in the DesignPolicy GPO.

D. Run the Gpupdate command-line utility on all the managers' computers.

E. Link the Managers OU to the DesignPolicy GPO.

F. Create a DesignManagers global security group and put all the managers' user accounts into that group. Grant the group Read and Execute permissions to the DesignPolicy GPO.

Objective 6.1 Answers

1. **Correct Answers: B**

    A. **Incorrect:** Domain controllers should never be configured with the Compatible security template. In any case, the software runs on the workstations, not the domain controllers.

    B. **Correct:** This solution allows the software to run as it did before on the machines running Windows NT 4.0. An added advantage is that only one configuration change is necessary. You do not have to reconfigure each client PC.

    C. **Incorrect:** This approach would work, but you would have to configure each client individually—it could not be automated.

    D. **Incorrect:** This approach would work, but it would give the users too many rights. Also, this solution would take more administrative effort than using Group Policy.

2. **Correct Answers: D**

    A. **Incorrect:** Account policies are set at the domain level, not at the OU level.

    B. **Incorrect:** This solution enables the more restrictive settings for Enforce Password History and Maximum Password Age. However, it disables Store Password Using Reversible Encryption. This last setting is more restrictive and should be retained.

    C. **Incorrect:** This answer is incorrect for the reason given in the explanation for answer A.

    D. **Correct:** This solution enables the more restrictive settings for Enforce Password History and Maximum Password Age. Because the new template has no setting for Store Password Using Reversible Encryption, the current, more restrictive setting is retained.

3. **Correct Answers: D**

    A. **Incorrect:** This practice is inappropriate when you want to perform only one small administrative task. You could easily forget to log back on with your ordinary user account before continuing to type your report, which would violate the principle of least privilege. It also gives you extra work.

    B. **Incorrect:** You can use this command, but the syntax is complex (for example, Runas /env /profile /user:mydomain\administrator "mmc winnt\system32\filename.msc"), and you would need to know the name of the file to run. If you had this command in a batch file, running that batch file would be a sensible option.

C. **Incorrect:** On Windows XP, Runas is not available on this menu without holding down the Shift key.

D. **Correct:** This procedure accesses Runas.

4. **Correct Answers: A and B**

A. **Correct:** If you choose a setting that is not specified in the computer's original configuration, that setting will by default remain at what you changed it to when you applied the template. However, you can achieve the result you want by selecting the Clear This Database Before Importing check box during the import operation.

B. **Correct:** The /overwrite switch clears all the security settings before applying a template, so the original settings will be restored.

C. **Incorrect:** The settings that are configured on the computer when you start to experiment will not necessarily be the original default settings.

D. **Incorrect:** You can create a rollback template as described, which is used when a new template is applied. Then you must roll back this operation and restore the original settings. However, Secedit /refreshpolicy does not perform the rollback operation and has, in any case, been replaced by Gpupdate.

5. **Correct Answers: D and F**

A. **Incorrect:** Clients running Windows 98, Second Edition, do not support NT LAN Manager version 2 (NTLMv2). Highly secure Windows Server 2003 domain controllers require that clients use at least NTLMv2 authentication.

B. **Incorrect:** Computer accounts can be created either when the client joins the domain or in advance. However, if the clients cannot access the domain controllers, they cannot join the domain regardless of how their accounts are created.

C. **Incorrect:** The clients cannot access the domain controllers. It makes no difference which account is used to log on.

D. **Correct:** Computers running Windows NT 4.0 Workstation with Service Pack 4 or later can use NTLMv2 authentication and can therefore connect to a highly secure Windows Server 2003 domain controller.

E. **Incorrect:** The only Windows clients that can currently use Kerberos version 5 are clients running Windows 2000 Professional and Windows XP.

F. **Correct:** You can install the Active Directory Client Extensions pack to enable clients running Windows 98 to use NTLMv2 authentication and to access Active Directory. It needs to be installed from a Windows Server 2000 CD-ROM.

6. **Correct Answers: A**

A. Correct: The clients are in the correct OU and the correct template is applied to the appropriate OU. However, security templates can be applied only to client PCs that use the NTFS disk-filing system. Using Convert c: fs:ntfs on the unsecured (FAT-formatted) clients should solve the problem.

B. Incorrect: The template is already applied to the GPO that controls the Payroll OU settings. Importing the template on individual clients in the OU has no effect.

C. Incorrect: This solution treats the symptom, not the cause. The clients will no longer be able to access the insecure server, but the secure settings will not be applied to them.

D. Incorrect: Group Policy is automatically refreshed periodically, so the Gpupdate command is unlikely to solve the problem. You should run Gpupdate if template settings have been applied by a method other than Group Policy or if you want to ensure that changes made through Group Policy apply immediately.

7. **Correct Answers: C**

A. Incorrect: Clients that are upgraded to Windows XP Professional, rather than having a clean installation, retain the security settings that they had before they were upgraded. The Compatible security template is incremental—that is to say, it alters a security setting on the computer only if that setting clashes with a setting in the template. Thus, the upgraded computers can retain security settings that are not implemented on the computers that were cleanly installed.

B. Incorrect: A clean installation sets up and applies the Default security (Setup security.inf) template, not the Compatible template. Also, because the Compatible template is incremental, this procedure cannot guarantee consistency even among the upgraded computers. Finally, the question does not state that software outside the Windows Logo Program for Software needs to be run, so the Compatible template might not be appropriate.

C. Correct: The Default security template overrides any settings already on the computers. It is not incremental. It is also the template that is applied during a clean installation. This procedure therefore ensures that the upgraded computers will have consistent security settings and that these settings will match the security settings on the computers that had a clean installation.

D. Incorrect: You should never apply Setup security.inf using Group Policy. This template contains a large amount of data, which would move through the domain when Group Policy is periodically refreshed. You should apply this template in parts because it is so large, and the /areas switch in Secedit /configure lets you perform this task.

8.   **Correct Answers: C and D**

   A. **Incorrect:** The Managers OU is set up to hold computer accounts so that they can be configured through Group Policy. Moving user accounts into this OU would not help, and it is bad practice.

   B. **Incorrect:** This approach would ensure that the Group Policy settings applied to the design personnel's computers would also apply to the managers' computers. However, it would be difficult to assign additional policies to only the managers' computers.

   C. **Correct:** Block inheritance is set on some of the policy settings in the Managers OU, which is why some settings are not being applied. Setting No Override prevents settings that should be inherited from being blocked.

   D. **Correct:** Perform this task after you have specified No Override. This solution ensures that the changes are applied immediately, without having to wait until the next time Group Policy is refreshed.

   E. **Incorrect:** Managers is a child of Design. It is inappropriate practice to link both child and parent OUs to the same GPO.

   F. **Incorrect:** User permissions are not an issue here. This approach would not solve the problem.

Install and Configure Software Update Infrastructure

Windows Update is used to download such items as security fixes, critical updates, the latest help files, drivers, and Internet products. New content is added to the site regularly, so you can always get the most recent updates. You can configure Windows Update so that you can access the Windows Update Catalog. This strategy lets you select updates that you plan to deploy later and is of particular use to someone who administers a number of machines.

Automatic Updates is built into Windows 2000, Windows XP, and Windows Server 2003. It enables the operating system to automatically download and install critical updates from the Windows Update site. Windows Update and Automatic Updates are two separate components designed to work together to keep Windows secure. You have full control over the level of this interaction. For example, you can choose to automatically download and install updates as they become available, or you can be notified when new updates become available.

Software Update Services (SUS) lets you download a limited version of the Windows Update site and distribute updates to clients through Automatic Updates. As a result, you can control how and when updates are deployed and deliver updates to users through your intranet and inside your firewall.

Running legacy programs on Windows XP Professional, Windows Server 2003, or Windows 2000 Server or Professional typically requires that you modify the system settings that allow members of the Power Users group to run these programs. These same permissions also make it possible for Power Users to gain additional privileges on the system. Therefore, you should deploy applications that belong to the Windows Logo Program for Software. These programs can run successfully under the secure configuration that is provided by the Users group.

The other problem associated with legacy considerations occurs when clients with legacy operating systems need to have software installed and updated. If a client cannot access Active Directory, it cannot be updated through Group Policy. The Active Directory Client Extensions pack allows legacy systems to access Active Directory and make use of Group Policy.

You must be familiar with all these facilities for the examination.

Objective 6.2 Questions

1.   You want to obtain critical updates and security fixes for your PC running Windows XP Professional. You access the Windows Update site. However, you cannot find the Windows Update Catalog under See Also in the left pane. What is the problem?

    A. You have not installed and configured SUS.

    B. You have not installed and configured Automatic Updates.

    C. Transmission Control Protocol (TCP) port 80 is blocked for incoming traffic on the firewall at your Internet service provider (ISP).

    D. You need to configure the Windows Update site.

2.   You administer your company's Windows Server 2003 Active Directory domain. All client PCs run Windows XP Professional. Company policy states that employees cannot download software or software updates from the Internet. Software must be installed or upgraded on client machines automatically through Group Policy. As the domain administrator, you have been exempted from this policy so that you can download operating system upgrades, security fixes, virus definitions, and Microsoft utilities from the Windows Update site. You then want these upgrades, fixes, and so forth to be installed automatically on other users' PCs when these users log on to the domain. What do you need to do after you have downloaded the software?

    A. Install and configure SUS on your PC.

    B. Install Automatic Updates on the client computers.

    C. Create a Windows installer package.

    D. Configure Remote Installation Services (RIS) to distribute the software.

3.   You want to install an application that runs on clients running Windows XP Professional in your Active Directory domain. You do not want to add user accounts to the Power Users group on these machines, nor do you want to configure the clients using the Compatible security template. How can you find out whether an application you have chosen will run under these constraints?

    A. Consult the Microsoft Windows Catalog and look for the Designed For Windows XP logo.

    B. Obtain a VeriSign Code Signing Identity.

    C. Create a Windows installer package.

    D. Consult the Windows Catalog and look for the Compatible With Windows XP logo.

4. You are the systems administrator for a medium-sized organization, and you are considering employing Software Update Services to manage updates provided by Microsoft for your Windows XP Professional systems. Your organization currently uses a proxy solution running on another platform that requires username and password authentication. The user and password database for the proxy is different from that used in your Windows Server 2003 domain. Given this situation, which of the following options is available to you in configuring a software update infrastructure?

A. Because SUS cannot be configured to authenticate against a proxy, an administrator must manually download all updates and place them on the SUS server. The Windows XP Professional machines should be configured using Group Policy to contact the SUS server for their software updates.

B. Because SUS cannot be configured to authenticate against a proxy and Windows XP clients can, Windows XP clients should continue to contact Microsoft to download their updates.

C. SUS can be configured to authenticate against a proxy to download a list of updates for your approval. Windows XP systems should be configured to check the SUS server to find which updates you have approved and then to automatically download those updates from the Microsoft Web site.

D. SUS can be configured to authenticate against a proxy to download a list of updates for your approval as well as download the updates. Windows XP systems should be configured to check the SUS server to determine which updates are approved and then to retrieve them from the SUS server.

5. You are the systems administrator for a medium-sized organization that is considering implementing SUS on all Windows XP Professional workstations and Windows Server 2003 systems companywide. Before a companywide rollout is to go ahead, a pilot program is to be implemented. You have been assigned a lab with 10 Windows XP Professional workstations, a Windows Server 2003 member server running SUS, a Windows Server 2003 domain controller, and a stand-alone Windows Server 2003 system. You wish to configure all systems except the server running SUS to use the SUS server to automatically check for, download, and install updates at 7:00 A.M. each day. Which of the following steps should you take to do this? (Choose all that apply.)

A. Use the Automatic Updates tab in the System console from Control Panel on every Windows XP Professional workstation computer to set the update server to the address of the SUS server. Set the Windows XP workstations to automatically download and install updates at 7:00 A.M. each day.

B. Use the Automatic Updates tab in the System console from Control Panel on each Windows Server 2003 system except the SUS server to set the update server to the address of the SUS server. Set these servers to automatically download and install updates at 7:00 A.M. each day.

C. Place the Windows XP Professional workstations and the Windows Server 2003 domain controller in a separate OU named Uptest. Edit a GPO's Windows Update properties for the Uptest OU, specifying the address of the update server as the SUS server in the Specify Intranet Microsoft Update Service Location policy. Set Configure Automatic Updates Policy to automatic download and install and set the scheduled installation day to Every Day and the time to 7:00 A.M. Apply this GPO to the Uptest OU.

D. On the stand-alone Windows Server 2003 system, edit the local GPO's Windows Update properties, specifying the address of the update server as the SUS server in the Specify Intranet Microsoft Update Service Location policy. Set Configure Automatic Updates Policy to automatic download and install and set the scheduled installation day to Every Day and the time to 7:00 A.M. Apply this GPO to the Uptest OU.

E. On the SUS server, edit the local GPO's Windows Update properties specifying the address of the update server as the SUS server in the Specify Intranet Microsoft Update Service Location policy. Set Configure Automatic Updates Policy to automatic download and install and set the scheduled installation day to Every Day and the time to 7:00 A.M. Apply this GPO to the Uptest OU.

6. Rooslan works for a company that has a single remote office connected by Integrated Services Digital Network Basic Rate Interface (ISDN BRI) to headquarters. The remote site has a 10-megabit connection to the Internet. Headquarters has a 20-megabit connection to the Internet. The ISDN BRI connections are mostly used to carry Active Directory and distributed file system (DFS) replication traffic. The company has a single Windows Server 2003 domain. The remote office and the headquarters are each configured as a separate site in Active Directory for replication purposes. There are two Windows Server 2003 systems running SUS. One server is located at the headquarters location and is configured to host a list of approved updates and to store those approved updates locally. The other SUS server is located at the remote site.

Primary Goal:

Rooslan wants the Windows XP Professional workstations and the Windows Server 2003 systems to download only updates that are on the approved list on the SUS server.

Secondary Goal:

Rooslan does not want to overburden the ISDN BRI connections with the transfer of updates from the SUS server located at headquarters.

Tertiary Goal:

Rooslan wants to minimize the amount of updates downloaded to headquarters through the 20-megabit Internet connection.

Which of the following will allow Rooslan to accomplish his primary, secondary, and tertiary goals? (Choose all that apply; the correct answers combine to form a completely correct solution.)

A. Rooslan should edit a GPO and configure the Windows Update properties. The Specify Intranet Microsoft Update Service Location policy should have the settings of the second SUS server for the update detection and statistics fields. This Group Policy should be applied to the remote site.

B. Configure the second SUS server to retrieve a list of approved updates from the first SUS server. Also configure the second SUS server to maintain the update files on Microsoft Windows Update server.

C. Configure the first SUS server to host a list of approved updates and to download and store those approved updates.

D. Rooslan should edit a GPO and configure the Windows Update properties. The Specify Intranet Microsoft Update Service Location policy should have the settings of the first SUS server for the update detection and statistics fields. This Group Policy should be applied to the headquarters site.

E. Rooslan should edit a GPO and configure the Windows Update properties. The Specify Intranet Microsoft Update Service Location policy should have the settings of the first SUS server for the update detection and statistics fields. This group policy should be applied to the remote site.

F. Rooslan should edit a GPO and configure the Windows Update properties. The Specify Intranet Microsoft Update Service Location policy should have the settings of the second SUS server for the update detection and statistics fields. This Group Policy should be applied to the headquarters site.

7.   Mick works as the network administrator for an organization that has five branch offices located across a city. The headquarters office has the only connection to the Internet and also hosts a proxy server. Headquarters has 200 Windows XP Professional workstations and several Windows Server 2003 systems. Each of the five branch offices has 150 Windows XP Professional workstations and several Windows Server 2003 systems. These branch offices are connected by ISDN BRI to the headquarters office. Currently, none of the Windows systems is able to receive updates from Microsoft's Windows Update server because they are unable to authenticate against the proxy. Management has asked Mick to implement SUS throughout the organization so that approved updates can be installed on workstations and servers. Management also wants Mick to minimize the amount of update traffic running through the ISDN BRI lines. Which of the following methods will achieve this goal?

A.   Configure a SUS server in the headquarters location to maintain a list of approved updates and to download and store those updates from the Microsoft Windows Update Servers. Configure a Group Policy that instructs clients to use the SUS server as their update server. Apply this GPO to the headquarters and branch-office sites.

B.   Configure a SUS server in the headquarters location to maintain a list of approved updates but maintain those updates on the Microsoft Windows Update Servers. Configure a Group Policy that instructs clients to use the SUS server as their update server. Apply this GPO to the headquarters and branch-office sites.

C.   Configure a SUS server in the headquarters location to maintain a list of approved updates but maintain those updates on the Microsoft Windows Update Servers. Configure a SUS server in each branch-office location to maintain a list of approved updates, but maintain those updates on the Microsoft Windows Update Servers. Create a GPO and apply it each site. The GPO should have a policy that clients are to use their local SUS server as their update server.

D.   Configure a SUS server in the headquarters location to maintain a list of approved updates and to download and store those approved updates. Configure SUS servers in each branch office to synchronize with the SUS server in the headquarters location. Configure a Group Policy that instructs clients to use the headquarters SUS server as their update server. Apply this GPO to the headquarters and branch-office sites.

E.   Configure a SUS server in the headquarters location to maintain a list of approved updates and to download and store those approved updates. Configure SUS servers in each branch office to synchronize with the SUS server in the headquarters location. Create a GPO and apply it at each site. The GPO should have a policy that clients are to use their local SUS server as their update server.

8.   Orin is the systems administrator for an academic department at the local university. The department has 40 Windows XP Professional workstations and two Windows Server 2003 systems. One of these systems is configured as a Domain Controller, the other as a file and print server. All department computers are members of a single Windows Server 2003 domain. Microsoft has recently released a service pack for Windows XP and, after testing it, Orin feels confident enough to deploy it to the Windows XP Professional workstations in his department. Orin extracts the service pack to a directory on the file server called \\Fileshare\newsrvpk. Which of the following methods can Orin use to install the service pack on all Windows XP Professional workstations? (Choose all that apply.)

   A.   Orin can visit each Windows XP Professional workstation and install the service pack from the file share.

   B.   Orin can create a group called Xpwkstn and put all the Windows XP Professional workstation computer accounts in this group. He can then create a GPO in which he sets up a new package in the Computer Configuration\Software Settings node using the location of the service pack .msi file on the \\Fileshare\newsrvpk share. In the Deploy Software dialog box, he should select Assign and then apply this GPO to the Xpwkstn group.

   C.   Orin can create a group called Xpusrs and put all who use Windows XP Professional workstations in this group. He can then create a GPO in which he sets up a new package in the Computer Configuration\Software Settings node using the location of the service pack .msi file on the \\Fileshare\newsrvpk share. In the Deploy Software dialog box, he should select Assign and then apply this GPO to the Xpusrs group.

   D.   Orin can create an OU called Xpwkstn and put all the Windows XP Professional workstation computer accounts in this OU. He can then create a GPO in which he sets up a new package in the Computer Configuration\Software Settings node using the location of the service pack .msi file on the \\Fileshare\newsrvpk share. In the Deploy Software dialog box, he should select Assign and then apply this GPO to the Xpwkstn OU.

Objective 6.2 Answers

1.   Correct Answers: D

    A. Incorrect: You need to install SUS only if you are downloading updates to a server so that you can later install them to client machines from the server. This situation does not apply to this scenario.

    B. Incorrect: Automatic Updates can be configured so that a client PC can receive updates from a server on its network. In this scenario, however, you are attempting to update your PC from the Internet. Automatic Updates is installed by default on a client running Windows XP Professional.

    C. Incorrect: If this situation were the case, you could not have accessed the Windows Update site.

    D. Correct: You should select Personalize Windows Update and select the Display The Link To The Windows Update Catalog Under See Also check box.

2.   Correct Answers: C

    A. Incorrect: You would need SUS if users were permitted to access an internal Web server as if they were accessing the Internet and downloading and installing the relevant programs. However, they cannot perform this task. Software must be installed automatically through Group Policy.

    B. Incorrect: Automatic Updates is installed by default on computers running Windows XP Professional. The Windows Update site can be configured to send updates automatically to a client. However, in this scenario, clients do not receive updates or fixes by this method, but instead through Group Policy.

    C. Correct: You need to create an OU and put all the accounts of the users who need to get the update in the OU (or computer accounts if you want to install on reboot). You then create a GPO linked to the OU, download the software you want to install, create a Windows installer package, and apply that package to the GPO.

    D. Incorrect: RIS is typically used to automatically install operating systems and application software. It is not the appropriate tool in this scenario.

3.   Correct Answers: A

A. Correct: The Designed For Windows XP Logo Program for Software helps customers identify products that deliver a high-quality computing experience with the Windows XP operating system. Products that bear this logo can run on Windows XP without your having to change any security or security group settings.

B. Incorrect: This step is one that third-party software developers should take if they want to submit applications for possible inclusion in the Windows Catalog and validation through the Designed for Windows XP Logo Program for Software.

C. Incorrect: You can create a Windows installer package for many applications, not all of which will run on Windows XP under the conditions stated in the question.

D. Incorrect: No logo is associated with the Compatible With Windows XP designation, although the application is listed in the Windows Catalog. This designation is intended primarily for older applications, which the product vendor has determined will have basic functionality on Windows XP and which will not interfere with operating system or application stability. There is no guarantee that the application will run in the context of an ordinary user.

4.   Correct Answers: D

A. Incorrect: SUS can be configured to authenticate against a proxy.

B. Incorrect: SUS can be configured to authenticate against a proxy.

C. Incorrect: Windows XP software update cannot be configured to authenticate against a proxy. In this situation, the SUS server should be configured to download the updates as well so that the Windows XP systems can in turn download and install relevant updates from the SUS server.

D. Correct: Because Windows XP clients software update mechanisms cannot authenticate against a proxy, they must retrieve the updates from the local SUS server. The list of updates that will be retrieved and installed will be based on the list of approved updates configured by the administrator of the SUS server.

5.   Correct Answers: C and D

A.   Incorrect: Windows XP Professional computers cannot be configured to contact an alternate update server using the System console.

B.   Incorrect: Windows Server 2003 systems cannot be configured to contact an alternate update server using the System console.

C.   Correct: This is the correct way to do this for computers that are members of the domain: add them all to an OU and then apply a group policy with the correct update settings.

D.   Correct: Because this server is not a member of the domain, this setting must be configured in the local GPO.

E.   Incorrect: The SUS server was not meant to be configured for updating from itself; it was still meant to update from Microsoft's site.

6.   Correct Answers: A, B, C, and D

A.   Correct: This is the second part of the secondary goal and part of the primary goal. If the Group Policy pointed them at the first SUS server, the ISDN BRI link would be flooded by downloading updates from that server.

B.   Correct: This setting will mean that clients configured to contact this SUS server will use the approved list from this server but will download the updates themselves from Microsoft Windows Update servers. This is the first part of the secondary goal.

C.   Correct: The first server will be able to provide update services to the headquarters site, including a list of approved updates, as well as allow those updates to be retrieved from the server. This is part of the tertiary and primary goals.

D.   Correct: This will complete the tertiary goal and is part of the primary goal. By using the first SUS server rather than the second, the headquarters clients will retrieve their update list and the updates themselves from the first SUS server. If they were pointed at the second SUS server, they would download the approved updates from Microsoft, which would not be optimal use of the headquarters connection to the Internet.

E.   Incorrect: This will mean that computers at the remote site will download their updates from the first SUS server rather than from the Microsoft update servers, flooding the bandwidth of the ISDN BRI line. This would violate the secondary goal.

F.   Incorrect: This will result in clients at headquarters downloading approved updates from Microsoft instead of from the first SUS server, which would violate the tertiary goal.

7.   **Correct Answers: E**

   A. **Incorrect:** Although this will allow updates to be rolled out to all clients within the organization, it will also saturate the ISDN BRI lines with update traffic because each client workstation downloads its updates from the central SUS server.

   B. **Incorrect:** Although clients will have a list of updates, because they do not have the ability to authenticate against the proxy, they cannot download updates from the Microsoft Windows Update Servers.

   C. **Incorrect:** Although clients will have a list of updates, because they do not have the ability to authenticate against the proxy, they cannot download updates from the Microsoft Windows Update Servers.

   D. **Incorrect:** Although this will allow updates to be rolled out to all clients within the organization, it will also saturate the ISDN BRI lines with update traffic because each client workstation downloads its updates from the central SUS server. Branch-office computers must use their local SUS server.

   E. **Correct:** This solution will result in rolling out updates to each computer in the organization, but it will also result in update traffic only being passed once across the ISDN BRI links. This solution meets management's criteria.

8.   **Correct Answers: A and D**

   A. **Correct:** This method will work, although it is not the most efficient way of performing this operation.

   B. **Incorrect:** Group policies cannot be applied to groups, but only to sites, domains, and OUs.

   C. **Incorrect:** Group policies cannot be applied to groups, but only to sites, domains, and organizational units.

   D. **Correct:** The group policy will apply only to those Windows XP Professional workstations that are in the Xpwkstn OU. Because all relevant Windows XP Professional workstations have been added to this OU, however, the service pack will be deployed the next time the computers restart.

21 Exam 70-296—Planning and Implementing Server Roles and Server Security (1.0)

Servers are the lifeblood of a data network, and they require more protection than workstations. Servers performing different tasks also require different levels and types of security. Part of designing a network infrastructure is creating security configurations that are appropriate for each server role used on the network. The process of creating these configurations includes examining the security features provided by the operating systems that you intend to use and determining the organization's security requirements.

Tested Skills and Suggested Practices

The skills that you need to successfully master the Planning and Implementing Server Roles and Server Security objective domain on *Exam 70-296: Planning, Implementing, and Maintaining a Microsoft Windows Server 2003 Environment for an MCSE Certified on Windows 2000* include

- Configure security for servers that are assigned specific roles.
    - ❑ Practice 1: Compare the methods you can use to configure security parameters on a computer running the Microsoft Windows Server 2003 operating system, including Group Policy Objects (GPOs) and security templates, and devise scenarios for which each configuration method would be appropriate.
    - ❑ Practice 2: Examine the settings in the security templates included with Windows Server 2003 using the Security Templates snap-in. Then use the Security Configuration And Analysis snap-in to compare the secure (Securedc.inf) and highly secure (Hisecdc.inf) templates to your server and study the differences between them.

■ Plan security for servers that are assigned specific roles. Roles might include domain controllers, Web servers, database servers, and mail servers.

❑ Practice 1: Configure the security configuration for a domain controller, giving it the following different settings from the baseline: more comprehensive auditing, larger Event Logs, more restrictive assignments of user rights, and a more limited selection of services on the computer.

❑ Practice 2: Configure the security configuration for an Internet Information Services (IIS) server using Group Policy. Make your server secure, but also ensure that it is still accessible.

Further Reading

This section lists supplemental readings by objective. We recommend that you study these sources thoroughly before taking *Exam 70-296: Planning, Implementing, and Maintaining a Microsoft Windows Server 2003 Environment for an MCSE Certified on Windows 2000.*

Objective 1.1 Review Chapter 9, "Planning and Implementing Server Roles and Security."

Microsoft Corporation. *Securing Windows 2000 Server.* Review Chapter 7, Windows Server 2003 Security Guide on the Microsoft Web site at *http://www.microsoft.com /technet/security/prodtech/windows/win2003/w2003hg/sgch00.asp.*

Objective 1.2 Review Chapter 9, Lesson 2, "Planning Server Security Based on Server Roles."

Microsoft Corporation. *Securing Windows 2000 Server.* Review Chapter 7, Windows Server 2003 Security Guide on the Microsoft Web site at *http://www.microsoft.com /technet/security/prodtech/windows/win2003/w2003hg/sgch00.asp.*

Objective 1.1

Configure Security for Servers that Are Assigned Specific Roles

Servers that perform different roles have different security requirements, so it is common practice to create a security configuration for each server role and deploy it at once to all the servers performing that role. This practice minimizes the number of security configurations you have to create and saves you from having to configure each server individually.

The most common method of configuring security for servers that are assigned specific roles is to use group policies. A group policy is an Active Directory object that consists of specific settings for a collection of configuration parameters. When you associate a Group Policy Object (GPO) with an Active Directory container object, all the computers in that container receive the group policy settings. To create and modify group policies, you use the Group Policy Object Editor snap-in for Microsoft Management Console (MMC). To associate Group Policy Objects with Active Directory containers, you use the Active Directory Users And Computers console or the Active Directory Sites And Services console.

To use group policies to configure servers performing different roles, you must create different Active Directory container objects for them. You can link a Group Policy Object to a domain, site, or organizational unit (OU) object. Domain and site objects typically contain many computers performing different roles, so the best practice is to create a separate organizational unit for each role and apply a Group Policy Object that is specific to each role to each unit.

In many cases, you might find it necessary to apply more than one GPO to a particular organizational unit. Multiple assignments can be necessary because a server is performing more than one role or because you have already created a GPO to implement a baseline configuration and want to augment it with a GPO that is specific to a role. To apply multiple policies to an organizational unit, either you can link the organizational unit object to two or more GPOs or you can create a hierarchy of organizational units and allow group policy inheritance to combine the policy settings.

When you link a GPO to an organizational unit, every object in the organizational unit, including every subordinate organizational unit, inherits the group policy settings. Therefore, you can apply a GPO to one organizational unit and then create role-specific organizational units, with their own linked GPOs, beneath it. The settings in the role-specific GPOs will combine with those of the parent GPO to create a composite configuration on each computer.

Objective 1.1 Questions

1. As the network administrator of your company's new branch office, you are in the process of installing three new Web servers running Windows Server 2003 on your network. The branch office network, which is part of a single corporate domain, already has two servers functioning as domain controllers and three file and print servers. Corporate headquarters has given you a list of security configuration settings that must be used on all the company's Web servers. To deploy these configuration settings, you must use the Active Directory Users And Computers console. Which of the following procedures should you use to configure the settings on the new Web servers only?

    A. Access the GPO called Default Domain Policy and then configure the settings there.

    B. Create a new GPO containing the Web server settings and then apply it to the Computers container.

    C. Create a new organizational unit called WebSvrs and then link a new GPO containing the Web server settings to it.

    D. Create a new GPO containing the Web server settings and then apply it to the site object representing the branch office.

2. Which of the following tools do you use to change the value of a specific security configuration setting for an Active Directory domain object?

    A. Active Directory Users And Computers

    B. Active Directory Sites And Services

    C. Active Directory Domains And Trusts

    D. Group Policy Object Editor

3. Which of the following Active Directory objects can you link to a Group Policy Object? (Choose all that apply.)

    A. Domain

    B. Group

    C. Organizational unit

    D. Site

Objective 1.1 Answers

1.   Correct Answers: C

   A. Incorrect: If you configure the Web server settings in the Default Domain Policy GPO, every computer in the domain will receive those settings, not only the Web servers.

   B. Incorrect: The Computers container is not an organizational unit, site, or domain object, and therefore you cannot apply a GPO to it.

   C. Correct: By creating a new organizational unit object for the Web servers, you separate them from the rest of the Active Directory tree, enabling you to create a new GPO and apply it to only those servers by linking it to the organizational unit.

   D. Incorrect: You cannot manage GPOs for a site object using the Active Directory Users And Computers console; you must use the Active Directory Sites And Services console instead. In addition, applying a GPO to a site object would cause all the computers in the site to inherit the GPO's settings.

2.   Correct Answers: D

   A. Incorrect: You can access a domain object using the Active Directory Users And Computers console, but you cannot modify the configuration settings of a GPO associated with the domain object using that console.

   B. Incorrect: You cannot access a domain object using the Active Directory Sites And Services console.

   C. Incorrect: You cannot access a domain object using the Active Directory Domains And Trusts console.

   D. Correct: The Group Policy Object Editor console enables you to modify any of the configuration settings in the GPOs associated with a domain (or any other) object.

3.   Correct Answers: A, C, and D

   A. Correct: By linking a GPO to a domain object, you can configure security settings that affect all the objects in the domain.

   B. Incorrect: Group objects can have user and group objects as members, but they are not considered container objects and you cannot link GPOs to them.

   C. Correct: An organizational unit is a container object that can have other organizational units, computers, users, and groups as its contents. Linking a GPO to an organizational unit deploys the security settings in the GPO to all objects in the organizational unit, including subordinate containers.

   D. Correct: A site object represents a group of Active Directory objects that are connected by network connections running at approximately the same speed. Linking a GPO to a site object deploys the GPO's settings to every object at the site.

Plan Security for Servers that Are Assigned Specific Roles

Servers performing different roles have different security requirements. In many cases, you can create role-specific configurations by modifying the same parameters you set in your baseline configuration and saving them in Group Policy Objects or security templates. When planning security for specific roles, you must consider the additional security requirements of each role, both in terms of its technical vulnerabilities and of its importance to the organization.

Some of the roles for which you might have to plan security are as follows:

- **Domain controllers** On an Active Directory network, domain controllers provide essential authentication services whenever a user accesses a network resource, and therefore they must be available at all times. Securing a domain controller might call for increased physical security, such as a locked server closet, and fault-tolerant hardware, such as disk arrays and redundant power supplies, in addition to modifications to the security configuration parameters. A typical security configuration for the domain controller role might include more comprehensive auditing, larger Event Logs, more restrictive assignments of user rights, and a more limited selection of services on the computer.

- **Infrastructure servers** An infrastructure server runs network support services, such as Domain Name System (DNS), Dynamic Host Configuration Protocol (DHCP), and Windows Internet Name Service (WINS) servers. These services provide important functions to users and should remain available at all times. A security configuration for this role should protect the servers from unauthorized access, allow the required services to run, and take steps to secure them from the potential exploits that running the services opens on the computers. In addition to the security parameters found in Group Policy Objects, the services running on infrastructure servers often have their own security features, such as secure dynamic updates for DNS servers.

- **File and print servers** File and print servers are among the most common server roles and are frequently combined with other roles, such as the application or infrastructure roles, on the same computers. In addition to enabling required system services, such as the Print Spooler service, security for the file and print server role typically consists of file system permissions that allow specific users and groups the appropriate amount of access to the NTFS drives on the computer.

- **Application servers**   Application servers, including Web, database, and e-mail servers, typically have their own security features, which you can implement as part of your security configuration for that role. Internet Information Services (IIS), which provides HTTP, File Transfer Protocol (FTP), and other Internet services, is integrated into Windows Server 2003, but most server applications are separate products with built-in security features. As a result, you might not be able to implement these features using standard Windows Server 2003 mechanisms, such as GPOs, but other ways of automating the deployment of these security mechanisms might be available.

Security templates provide a mechanism for saving, manipulating, and deploying security configurations on computers running Windows Server 2003. A security template is a plain text file, with an .inf extension, that contains values for the configuration parameters found in GPOs. Storing configurations as security templates enables you to restore a computer to its previous configuration quickly and easily; compare a computer's current configuration settings to those in a template; and integrate the deployment of security configurations into scripts or batch files.

You can deploy security templates in three ways: by importing them into GPOs, by using the Security Configuration And Analysis snap-in to apply them to individual computers, and by using the Secedit.exe command line utility.

Objective 1.2 Questions

1. You are a network administrator who has been given a security template. Your supervisor wants you to check that all the Windows Server 2003 domain controllers are using the account policies, audit policies, Event Log settings, and security options stored in the template. In the case of any domain controller that is not using the same settings, you are to apply only the missing elements from the template to that computer. Which of the following procedures would enable you to perform both these tasks most efficiently?

    A. Import the security template into the Security Configuration And Analysis snap-in on each domain controller, and then use the snap-in to analyze the computer's current configuration and apply the required settings to the domain controllers that need them.

    B. Use the Active Directory Users And Computers console to apply the template to the GPO for the Domain Controllers organizational unit.

    C. Import the security template into the Security Configuration And Analysis snap-in on each domain controller, and then use the snap-in to analyze the computer's current configuration. Then you must manually configure the computer settings that need to be changed.

    D. Import the security template into the Security Configuration And Analysis snap-in on each domain controller, and then use the snap-in to analyze the computer's current configuration. Then use the Secedit.exe command-line utility to apply only the required settings to the domain controllers that need them.

2. Revoking the Add Workstations To Domain user right from the Authenticated Users group prevents the members of that group from performing which of the following tasks?

    A. Joining groups

    B. Creating computer objects

    C. Modifying file system permissions

    D. Accessing their own user objects

3.   You are the network administrator responsible for equipping 10 new employees of the Sales department for all their computing needs. After installing their workstations, you use the Active Directory Users And Computers console to create user accounts for the new employees in the Active Directory database. You also create computer objects for their workstations in the Sales organizational unit, which contains all the Sales department's computer objects. All 10 users must also be members of a group called Salespeople, which gives them access to the server resources they need. Rather than manually add each new user object to the Salespeople group, you decide to automate the process by opening the default Group Policy Object for the Sales organizational unit and adding Salespeople to the Restricted Groups folder. Then you specify the 10 new user objects as members of the Salespeople group.

Sometime later, the network help desk gets calls from dozens of other users in the Sales department, complaining that they cannot access their applications. Which of the following procedures must you perform to remedy the problem? (Choose all that apply.)

A. Add the new users to the Salespeople group using the Active Directory Users And Computers console.

B. Add the old users to the Salespeople group using the Active Directory Users And Computers console.

C. Use the Group Policy Object Editor console to remove the Salespeople group from the Restricted Groups folder.

D. Use the Group Policy Object Editor console to remove the new users from the Salespeople group in the Restricted Groups folder.

4.   After using the Security Configuration And Analysis snap-in to compare a file and print server's configuration to the Hisecws.inf security template, you decide that you need to modify some of the computer's settings to match those of the template. Which of the following procedures can you use to do this?

A. Modify the parameters you want to change in the Security Configuration And Analysis snap-in's database and apply the database to the computer.

B. Open the Security Templates snap-in, create a new template, and configure the parameters you want to change with their new settings. Then apply the template to the server using the Secedit.exe utility.

C. Open the Hisecws.inf template in the Security Templates snap-in and use it to apply the settings for the parameters you want to change.

D. Modify the parameters you want to change in the Security Configuration And Analysis snap-in's database and then use the Secedit.exe utility to apply the database file to the computer.

1. **Correct Answers: D**

    A. **Incorrect:** Although you can use the Security Configuration And Analysis snap-in to compare each domain controller's current settings to those in the template, you cannot use the snap-in to apply only part of a template to a computer.

    B. **Incorrect:** Applying the template to the Domain Controllers GPO would deploy all the configuration settings in the template to all the domain controllers on the network. This procedure does not compare the settings in the template to those on the domain controllers, nor can it apply only part of the template.

    C. **Incorrect:** Using the Security Configuration And Analysis tool to analyze the computer's settings is the proper way to determine which settings need to be modified, but manually changing them is not the most efficient way to accomplish this goal. Instead, you should use the Secedit.exe utility to apply only the Domain Controller Security Policy part of the template to the computers.

    D. **Correct:** The Security Configuration And Analysis snap-in can tell you whether each domain controller is currently configured with the same account policy and security options settings as the ones in the template, but it cannot apply only part of a template to the computer. To apply specific elements of a template, you must use the Secedit.exe utility.

2. **Correct Answers: B**

    A. **Incorrect:** Users cannot join groups of their own volition unless they have the permissions needed to modify the group object in Active Directory. The Add Workstations To Domain user right has no effect on this ability.

    B. **Correct:** By default, members of the Authenticated Users group can add up to 10 computer objects to the Computers container in the Active Directory domain. When you revoke the Add Workstations To Domain user right from the group, members are no longer able to create their own computer objects; an administrator must do it for them.

    C. **Incorrect:** The Add Workstations To Domain user right has no effect on a user's ability to modify file system permissions. To modify permissions, users must possess the appropriate permissions enabling them to do so.

    D. **Incorrect:** The ability to add workstations to the domain does not affect the users' ability to modify their own user objects. It is Active Directory permissions that make it possible for users to modify objects.

3.   **Correct Answers: A, B, and C**

    A. **Correct:** Because the procedure you used to add the new users to the Salespeople group was incorrect, you must reverse the process and add them to the group manually, using the Active Directory Users And Computers console.

    B. **Correct:** Creating a Salespeople group in the Restricted Groups folder and then adding the new users to it effectively removed all the other users from the Salespeople group. Therefore, you must add them to the group again manually.

    C. **Correct:** The Restricted Groups folder in a Group Policy Object specifies all the users who are permitted to be members of a specific group. By adding only the new users to the Salespeople restricted group, you have removed all the existing users in the Sales department from that group, which prevents them from accessing the applications they need. You must remove the Salespeople group from the Restricted Groups folder or all the users will be removed from the group the next time the server refreshes its group policies.

    D. **Incorrect:** Removing the new users from the Salespeople restricted group would leave you with no members in the group at all and would not resolve the problem.

4.   **Correct Answers: B**

    A. **Incorrect:** The database in the Security Configuration And Analysis snap-in contains settings imported from a security template, not the computer's own settings. Modifying the database would only change the template settings, which do not need to be changed.

    B. **Correct:** You can analyze the settings in a computer by using the Security Configuration And Analysis snap-in, but you can't modify the settings using that snap-in. The Security Templates snap-in enables you to create a new template containing only the security parameters you need to change. You can then apply the new template to the computer using the Secedit.exe utility.

    C. **Incorrect:** The Security Templates snap-in can only create and manage the templates themselves. You cannot use it to apply templates to a computer.

    D. **Incorrect:** You cannot use the Secedit.exe utility to apply a Security Configuration And Analysis database to a computer.

22 Exam 70-296—Planning, Implementing, and Maintaining a Network Infrastructure (2.0)

The planning phase of deploying a network infrastructure is by far the most important part of the process. When building a large network, it is crucial that you have the entire infrastructure planned before you purchase hardware or construct the network. The plan should specify elements such as the protocols the network will use and the physical topology of the network.

The Transmission Control Protocol/Internet Protocol (TCP/IP) suite is the industry standard for network communications, and creating an effective TCP/IP infrastructure is a primary element of designing and planning a network. A TCP/IP network infrastructure plan specifies how you are going to subnet your network, what Internet Protocol (IP) addresses and subnet masks you will use, what names to assign to your computers, and how the computers will resolve these names into IP addresses.

Once you have finished deploying the network and have it up and running, the focus of the administrator's job changes to maintenance and troubleshooting. Problems with TCP/IP configuration and name resolution are common, and you must be familiar with the tools and techniques that can help determine the causes of the problems and correct them.

Tested Skills and Suggested Practices

The skills that you need to successfully master the Planning, Implementing, and Maintaining a Network Infrastructure objective domain on *Exam 70-296: Planning, Implementing, and Maintaining a Microsoft Windows Server 2003 Environment for an MCSE Certified on Windows 2000* include

- Plan a host name resolution strategy, a Domain Name System (DNS) namespace design, zone replication requirements, a forwarding configuration, and DNS security. Examine the interoperability of DNS with third-party DNS solutions.

  - ❑ Practice 1: Study the online help screen for the Microsoft Windows Nslookup.exe command-line utility and learn how to send a name resolution request to a particular DNS server. (You display the online help screen for Nslookup.exe by opening the Command Prompt window, typing **nslookup** at the first command prompt, and then typing **help** at the following command prompt. You exit Nslookup.exe by typing **exit**.)

❏ Practice 2: Install the DNS Server service on a computer running Windows Server 2003, create a zone for an imaginary domain, and populate it with a series of Host (A) resource records. Then create a reverse lookup zone for the same domain and populate it with pointer (PTR) resource records corresponding to the Host (A) resource records you created earlier. Test your configuration by resolving all the host names into IP addresses and all the IP addresses into their host names.

Further Reading

This section lists supplemental readings by objective. You should study these sources thoroughly before taking *Exam 70-296: Planning, Implementing, and Maintaining a Microsoft Windows Server 2003 Environment for an MCSE Certified on Windows 2000*.

Objective 2.1   Review Chapter 7, "Planning a Host Name Resolution Strategy."

Microsoft Corporation. *Microsoft Windows Server 2003 Deployment Kit. Volume: Deploying Network Services*. Redmond, Washington: Microsoft Press, 2003. Review Chapter 3, "Deploying DNS." This volume can also be found on the Microsoft Web site at *http://www.microsoft.com/windowsserver2003/techinfo/reskit/deploykit.mspx*.

Microsoft Corporation. Microsoft Windows Server 2003 Administrator's Pocket Consultant. Redmond, Washington: Microsoft Press, 2003. Review Chapter 20, "Optimizing DNS".

Plan a Host Name Resolution Strategy

Name resolution is the process of converting a computer's name into an IP address. All TCP/IP systems communicate using IP addresses; the names are just a convenience for the user. Networks running Windows Server 2003 can use several name resolution mechanisms, but the primary one is the Domain Name System (DNS). Windows Server 2003 includes a DNS Server service that is compatible with virtually all the other DNS implementations used on the Internet. Your computers need access to a DNS server if they are connected to the Internet or if you use the Active Directory directory service. Active Directory networks nearly always have their own DNS servers, but for Internet access you can use your own DNS servers or those supplied by your Internet service provider (ISP).

To resolve Internet names, no special effort is needed beyond installing a DNS server and configuring your computers to use it. The server interacts with other DNS servers on the Internet to resolve the name of any Internet computer. To resolve your own computers' names, you must create your own DNS namespace. The DNS namespace is a hierarchy of domains, with each domain containing a number of hosts. To create your own DNS namespace, you must register a second-level domain name in one of the existing Internet top-level domains (such as com or net). Then you can create as many subdomains as you need beneath that second-level domain. The primary reason for creating subdomains is to delegate administrative responsibility for certain parts of the namespace. For example, if your organization has several offices and you want each one to manage its own DNS names, you can create a subdomain for each office.

In many cases organizations have both internal (that is, private) and external (Internet) networks, which they must keep separated. To design a DNS namespace for this type of situation, you have three alternatives:

- **Use the same domain name** By using the same domain name for your internal and external networks, you stand the risk of having computers with the same name on both networks. Microsoft strongly recommends against this option.

- **Use two domain names** Registering two different domain names for your internal and external networks eliminates the possibility of name conflicts, but you must pay two registration fees and it can cause confusion for users having to distinguish between internal and external resources.

■ **Create a subdomain** The solution that Microsoft recommends is to register a second-level domain name for your external network and then create a subdomain beneath that second-level domain for the internal network. This solution requires only one registration fee, avoids naming conflicts, and enables you to delegate authority across the internal and external domains.

To register host names in your domain, you must create a zone on your DNS server. A zone is an administrative element that contains all or part of your DNS namespace. To ensure that your zones are always available, it is a good idea to have primary and secondary zones on two separate DNS servers. A secondary zone is a copy of a primary zone. The DNS servers replicate the zone database automatically, using a process called a zone transfer. If you create Active Directory-integrated zones on a Windows Server 2003 DNS server, there is no need for zone transfers because Active Directory replicates the database automatically.

A forwarder is a DNS server that receives queries sent to it by other DNS servers that you explicitly configure to send them. You can use forwarders in a variety of ways to regulate the flow of DNS traffic on your network.

To ensure that your DNS services are always available, you should create at least one redundant server, with a copy of your zones on each redundant server. You can also protect your DNS data by securing your zone transfers. The Windows Server 2003 DNS server enables you to specify the IP addresses of the servers that you allow to participate in zone transfers. You can also use Internet Protocol Security (IPSec) to encrypt the zone data as the servers transmit it over the network. Dynamic update is a feature that enables computers to update their DNS resource records when their IP addresses change. You can configure a DNS server to permit only secure dynamic updates; in this configuration the server authenticates the computers before they can update their resource records.

Objective 2.1 Questions

1. You are designing a network running Windows Server 2003 for a new company called Fourth Coffee, which has two offices, one in New York and one in San Francisco. The company uses e-commerce Web servers to take orders from customers and has registered the fourthcoffee.com second-level domain for this purpose. Your customer does not want to register any additional domain names. At the moment, you are designing the DNS namespace for the company's internal and external networks. Because each office is going to maintain its own DNS server, you want to create a separate subdomain for each site. In accordance with the domain naming practices recommended by Microsoft, you are going to create a subdomain for the internal network and then another level of subdomains for the individual offices. Based on this information, which of the following domain names would you use for the internal network at the New York office?

    A. fourthcoffee.com

    B. fourthcoffee.ny.com

    C. int.fourthcoffee.com

    D. ny.int.fourthcoffee.com

2. Which of the following enables you to keep a copy of your DNS database files on another server?

    A. IPSec

    B. Secured dynamic updates

    C. Zone transfers

    D. A forwarder

3. You are the designer of the new network for a large company that wants no connections to the Internet whatsoever. You have created an extensive DNS namespace for the company, with multiple DNS servers at different locations. Now that the network is up and running, users are experiencing name resolution failures when they try to resolve names of computers in other offices. Which of the following options would be likely to solve the problem? (Choose all that apply.)

    A. Create an internal root.

    B. Create a secondary copy of each zone in the namespace on every DNS server.

    C. Use conditional forwarding to send the queries for each domain in the namespace to the DNS server hosting that domain.

    D. Enable secure dynamic updates to prevent DNS resource records from being corrupted.

4. Which of the following DNS server features do you *not* need to use when you create Active Directory-integrated zones? (Choose all that apply.)

   A. Primary zones

   B. Secondary zones

   C. Zone transfers

   D. Dynamic updates

5. The Active Directory domain structure of the fourthcoffee.com forest is shown in the following illustration. DC1 through DC7 are domain controllers. The domain structure has been set up from scratch using default settings. DC1 is the first domain controller in the forest. DNS is Active Directory–integrated, and both forward and reverse zones have been created. The DNS Server service is installed on all domain controllers. All servers are Windows Server 2003, Enterprise Edition, servers. All clients are Windows XP Professional. Clients register their own host resource records in DNS, and DHCP registers their pointer (PTR) resource records. Which of the following statements is correct?

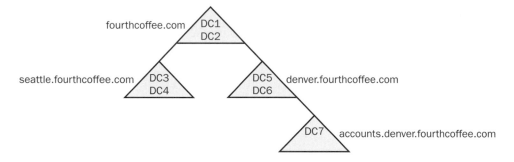

   A. The zone file on DC7 contains the host resource records for all the clients in the fourthcoffee.com domain.

   B. DC5 is authoritative for the denver.fourthcoffee.com DNS zone.

   C. If you open the DNS console and access DC7 server properties, the SOE tab will be present but the parameters are unavailable.

   D. DC1 is the only domain controller on which you can access the Security tab in the DNS server properties dialog box.

6. Litware, Inc., is a large, multinational corporation with its headquarters in Chicago and large offices all over the world. The Singapore office is experiencing rapid expansion. Singapore has considerable autonomy and users in Singapore seldom access resources in Chicago. Users in Chicago access resources in Singapore sporadically. However, when they do access these resources, they need to be able to do so without undue delay.

To reduce replication traffic over WAN links, the Delegation Of Control Wizard has been used to create the child DNS zone singapore.litwareinc.com, for which the Singapore domain controllers are authoritative. Both the singapore.litwareinc.com and the litwareinc.com zones are Active Directory–integrated.

Users in Chicago report that access to resources in Singapore is becoming increasingly slow as the Singapore operation expands. How can you improve access to Singapore without unduly increasing network traffic?

    A. Create a secondary DNS server for singapore.litwareinc.com in the Chicago office.

    B. Install a caching-only server in Chicago.

    C. Install a stub server for singapore.litwareinc.com in Chicago.

    D. Configure a forwarder in Chicago to forward queries to a DNS server in Singapore.

7. You work for Margie's Travel, which has a main office in Detroit and small branch offices in Toledo and Cleveland. DNS is implemented on a standard primary server and a standard secondary server in Detroit. All client PCs in the organization are configured to access one of these servers as their preferred DNS server and the other as their alternative DNS server. Clients in the branch office access resources in Detroit regularly. They report that access is often slow. You do not want to increase traffic on the WAN links. How should you improve resource access for branch office staff?

    A. Install a caching-only DNS server in the Cleveland and Toledo branches.

    B. Install a secondary DNS server in the Cleveland and Toledo branches.

    C. Install a stub DNS server in the Cleveland and Toledo branches.

    D. Install a domain controller in the Cleveland and Toledo branches.

8. Proseware, Inc. has sites in several countries. Active Directory–integrated DNS has been installed for the forest root domain, proseware.com. The DNS Server service is installed on four Windows Server 2003 domain controllers in Proseware's main facility in the United States. The servers are named Pixie, Dixie, Tom, and Jerry. They do not host any DNS zones other than proseware.com.

You are a consultant tasked with implementing Proseware's network infrastructure in Europe. You install a domain controller called London and create the Active Directory child domain europe.proseware.com. The DNS service on London is Active Directory–integrated. Authority for the europe.proseware.com DNS zone is delegated to London. You configure the Preferred DNS Server field in the TCP/IP properties dialog box for London to point to London's IP address. How can you ensure that name resolution requests originating in the europe.proseware.com domain for resources in the proseware.com domain are dealt with efficiently?

    A. Configure Pixie, Dixie, Tom, and Jerry as conditional forwarders on London.

    B. Configure Jerry as a master name server for London.

    C. Add Pixie, Dixie, Tom, and Jerry to the root hints on London.

    D. Configure Pixie, Dixie, Tom, and Jerry as alternative DNS servers on London.

9. You administer a network that consists of a number of subnets. For historical reasons, different subnets contain different types of operating systems. Some subnets contain UNIX servers, some contain Novell NetWare servers, and some contain Windows NT 4.0 servers. There are also UNIX, NetWare, Windows 95, Windows 98, Windows NT 4.0 Workstation, Windows 2000 Professional, and Windows XP Professional clients. All PCs have static IP configurations.

You set up an Active Directory domain with Windows Server 2003 domain controllers. You implement DHCP and configure all workstations that can do so to obtain their IP configurations automatically. You set exclusions in the DHCP scopes for clients that require static configuration. You configure Active Directory–integrated DNS zones. You configure DHCP to update DNS records for all DHCP clients. You configure DNS to allow only secure dynamic updates. Legacy Berkeley Internet Name Domain (BIND) UNIX servers are configured as secondary servers for the Active Directory–integrated DNS primary zone.

Client workstations do not require access to each other, but all clients need to be able to access all severs by host name. You find that certain servers cannot be accessed by host name. What should you do?

    A. Install WINS.

    B. Create Hosts file entries on all clients for all the servers that cannot currently be accessed by host name.

    C. Manually enter host (A) resource records for the NetWare, UNIX, and Windows NT 4 servers.

    D. Install NetBEUI on all client PCs.

10. Trey Research is a dynamic organization in an environment where rapid change is the norm. New servers are frequently added, and the names of existing resource servers are often changed to reflect new organizational structures. Active Directory–integrated DNS is hosted on all the company's Windows Server 2003 domain controllers. There is a single forward lookup zone and a corresponding reverse lookup zone. Reverse DNS lookup is heavily used to support the security of the company's e-mail system.

Users report that sometimes name resolution fails and they are told that a server is unavailable. At other times they are directed to the wrong server. What can you do to improve the situation?

    A. Open the DNS console. In the properties dialog box for each zone, access the Start Of Authority (SOA) tab and specify a new minimum default TTL.

    B. Open the DNS console. In the General tab of the properties dialog box for each zone, click the Aging button. Select the Scavenge Stale Resource Records check box.

   C. Open the DNS console. In the properties dialog box for each server, access the Start Of Authority (SOA) tab and specify a new minimum default TTL.

   D. Open the DNS console. For each server, from the Action menu select Set Aging/ Scavenging For All Zones. Select the Scavenge Stale Resource Records check box.

11. You are an enterprise administrator based at the head office of the Wingtip Toys organization in New York. You administer the wingtiptoys.com Windows Server 2003 Active Directory domain and the wingtiptoys.com Active Directory–integrated forward and reverse lookup DNS zones. Wingtip Toy's DNS zone structure mirrors its Active Directory structure, with control being delegated to the portland.wingtiptoys.com, seattle.wingtiptoys.com, and detroit.wingtiptoys.com DNS zones.

A domain administrator at Detroit has recently upgraded the DNS servers that service that zone. You suspect that this upgrade has resulted in incorrect configuration of the zone delegation. How do you verify that the zone delegation is properly configured?

   A. Run **Nslookup –querytype=ns detroit.wingtiptoys.com** server for each of the detroit.wingtiptoys.com servers. Use Nslookup to verify that the servers that are listed in the output of this command are functioning as name servers.

   B. Run **Nslookup –ls –d detroit.wingtiptoys.com** server for each of the detroit.wingtiptoys.com servers. Use Nslookup to verify that the servers that are listed in the output of this command are functioning as name servers.

   C. Use Replmon to check that replication is occurring between the wingtiptoys.com and detroit.wingtiptoys.com domains.

   D. Access the DNS object in System Monitor. Confirm that the Recursive Query Failures counter remains at zero.

12. You are planning the DNS infrastructure for a new company that is to have site offices located in five cities around the country. The head office of the company is located in Sydney with branch offices located in Melbourne, Brisbane, Adelaide, and Perth. You are interested in the following features:

The DNS servers in Melbourne and Sydney should be able to process updates to the zone file.

Only one DNS zone is required for all five sites.

Clients at each site should be able to contact a DNS server at that site to resolve their queries.

Which of the following steps should you take to implement the above features?

   A. Install a DNS server at the Melbourne and Sydney sites and configure a standard primary zone to be shared between the two servers. Install DNS servers in Brisbane, Adelaide, and Perth and configure them with secondary zones.

   B. Install a DNS server in each location. Configure the primary zone on the Melbourne server. Configure the DNS servers at the other sites to act as forwarders.

   C. Install DNS servers in each location. Configure all DNS servers as secondary servers.

   D. Install DNS servers in each location. Configure a single Active Directory Integrated Zone across all servers.

Objective 2.1 Answers

1.   Correct Answers: D

   A. Incorrect: Because fourthcoffee.com is the registered second-level domain name, Internet users will expect to use this to reach the company's Web site. Although it is possible to use the same domain name for your internal and external networks, Microsoft strongly recommends against this practice.

   B. Incorrect: This domain name would require you to register the ny.com second-level domain, which goes against the customer's wishes. The name ny.com is also already taken.

   C. Incorrect: The plan calls for you to create a subdomain for the internal network, and int.fourthcoffe.com would be an appropriate choice. However, the plan also states that you are going to create another level of subdomains for the individual offices. This additional level is not reflected in this name.

   D. Correct: To create this domain name, you create a subdomain called int, beneath fourthcoffee.com, to represent the internal network. You then create fourth-level domains to represent the offices, with names such as ny.int.fourthcoffee.com and sf.int.fourthcoffee.com.

2.   Correct Answers: C

   A. Incorrect: IPSec is a series of extensions to the IP that protects data as it is transmitted over the network. Although you can secure your DNS traffic with IPSec, you cannot use it by itself to replicate the DNS database.

   B. Incorrect: Secured dynamic updates enable DNS client computers to modify their resource records on a DNS server when their information changes. Dynamic updates do not replicate the DNS database.

   C. Correct: A zone transfer is the process by which one DNS server copies its zone database to another DNS server on the network. Zone transfers enable you to maintain redundant DNS servers on your network without having to modify each copy of the DNS database separately.

   D. Incorrect: A forwarder is a DNS server that receives queries from another DNS server. Forwarding has nothing to do with DNS database replication.

3.   Correct Answers: A, B, and C

   A. Correct: The name resolution failures are occurring because DNS servers are attempting to send queries to the root name servers on the Internet, which are inaccessible. By creating an internal root, the servers send their queries to an internal DNS server instead.

B. Correct: By creating a secondary zone on every server for each of the other zones in the namespace, each DNS server is able to resolve any name in any domain, eliminating the need to send queries to the root name servers on the Internet.

C. Correct: Conditional forwarding enables you to send queries for names in specific domains to specific DNS servers. Because each server can forward queries directly to the authoritative server for the requested domain, there is no need to send queries to the root name servers on the Internet.

D. Incorrect: Dynamic updates, whether secured or not, enable DNS clients to modify their resource records on a DNS server. Using secured dynamic updates would not prevent DNS servers from sending queries for names in other domains to the root name servers on the Internet.

4. **Correct Answers: B and C**

A. Incorrect: You must still create primary zones to host your domains, even if they are Active Directory–integrated zones.

B. Correct: When you create Active Directory–integrated zones, there is no need to create secondary zones because Active Directory takes on the responsibility of replicating the DNS data.

C. Correct: Zone transfers replicate DNS data from primary to secondary zones. When you create Active Directory–integrated zones, the directory service replicates the DNS data automatically, and there is no need for secondary zones or zone transfers.

D. Incorrect: The integration of a zone into Active Directory has no effect on the need for dynamic updates. Dynamic update can still modify a computer's DNS resource record, whether the resource record is stored in a standard zone database file or in the Active Directory database.

5. **Correct Answers: A**

A. Correct: DNS is Active Directory–integrated, all domain controllers have the DNS Server service installed, and clients register their host resource records dynamically. Therefore, the zone files on all domain controllers contain the host resource records for all clients.

B. Incorrect: The question does not mention that the Delegation Of Control Wizard has been run. Therefore, denver.fourthcoffee.com is not a DNS zone. It is important to distinguish between Active Directory domains, DNS domains, and DNS zones.

C. **Incorrect:** If you access this tab on a standard secondary zone, the parameters are unavailable. However, DC7 does not host a standard secondary zone—it hosts an Active Directory–integrated zone, for which it is authoritative.

D. **Incorrect:** In an Active Directory–integrated zone, you can access the Security tab from the DNS server properties dialog box of any participating domain controller.

6.   Correct Answers: C

A. **Incorrect:** This approach would speed up access, but it would also increase network traffic due to zone transfers from the master in Singapore to the secondary in Chicago. This solution is overkill for sporadic resource access.

B. **Incorrect:** This idea might be good, but it would not solve this particular problem. A caching-only server speeds up name resolution if a server name has been resolved recently, and the results are cached. Because Chicago users access resources in Singapore only sporadically, the record of a previous query would likely time out before the query is repeated.

C. **Correct:** Access to Singapore resources is becoming slower because as the Singapore operation expands, more DNS servers are being installed. A stub server holds records for all the authoritative name servers in the singapore litware-inc.com zone and therefore speeds access to resources. Because the stub server receives information only when a new name server is added, the additional network traffic that is generated will be minimal.

D. **Incorrect:** This approach would cause queries that cannot be resolved locally in Chicago to be forwarded to Singapore. Thus, traffic on the Singapore WAN link would increase and would delay the majority of resolution requests, which are not for Singapore servers. It would make sense to configure a conditional forwarder that would forward name resolution requests only for the singapore.litware-inc.com zone, but this is not what the question specifies.

7.   Correct Answers: A

A. **Correct:** You should install DNS on servers in Cleveland and Toledo and configure their root hints to point to the DNS servers in Detroit. It is probably wise for one caching-only server to access the primary server first and for the other to access the secondary server first. No further configuration is required. Caching-only servers are not authoritative for any zone, so no zone transfer traffic will be generated. Because users in the branch offices access resources in the main office regularly, most name resolution requests will be satisfied from cache. As a result, resource access should be quicker and host name resolution traffic should decrease.

B. Incorrect: This solution would reduce resource access delays, but at the cost of increasing zone transfer traffic over the WAN links. Because the branch offices are small, additional secondary DNS servers are not appropriate in this scenario.

C. Incorrect: Stub servers hold resource records only for the authoritative name servers in their zone. In this case additional DNS servers are unlikely to be installed in the main office regularly. Stub servers can be useful in large multinational organizations with delegated zones, where it is necessary for one zone to keep track of all the servers that are authoritative for the others.

D. Incorrect: DNS is not Active Directory–integrated, so a domain controller would not assist in name resolution unless it were also configured as a secondary DNS server. (Refer to the explanation for answer B.) Installing domain controllers in Cleveland and Toledo would speed up login at the branch offices but would have no effect on name resolution and would generate Active Directory replication traffic. Because the branch offices are small, this solution would be overkill. In any case, the question does not specify that Maggie's Travel has an Active Directory domain.

8.   Correct Answers: A

A. Correct: This solution ensures that all requests with Fully Qualified Domain Names (FQDNs) ending in proseware.com (except for those ending in europe.proseware.com) are passed directly to a DNS server that is authoritative for the proseware.com zone. Note that a DNS server can be configured with a number of forwarders.

B. Incorrect: Jerry and London host separate zones. You can use this configuration only if you set up London as a secondary server for the proseware.com DNS zone, which would increase replication traffic over the WAN link.

C. Incorrect: Pixie, Dixie, Tom, and Jerry do not host a root zone.

D. Incorrect: This configuration would result in London forwarding a query to one of the proseware.com servers only if it could not resolve the query. London would first attempt to resolve the query by accessing a server on its root hints file. This solution is not the most efficient way of resolving queries ending in proseware.com.

9.   Correct Answers: C

A. Incorrect: The legacy UNIX and Novell NetWare servers do not register with WINS, and they require static entries. Also, you would need to set up WINS proxies for the non-Windows workstations. This approach involves excessive administrative effort. (Note that nonlegacy UNIX hosts can be WINS clients.)

B. Incorrect: This approach involves excessive administrative effort.

C. Correct: Statically configured legacy UNIX, NetWare, and Windows NT 4 servers cannot update their own records in DNS, and DHCP cannot update DNS records for statically configured clients. Host resource records for servers are easily added manually. If reverse lookup is required, PTR resource records can be created automatically when host records are added. (Note that nonlegacy UNIX hosts can register their host and PTR records in DDNS.)

D. Incorrect: NetBEUI cannot resolve host names across a router. Also, Windows Server 2003 Server does not support NetBEUI, and it cannot be installed on Windows XP Professional.

10. Correct Answers: A

A. Correct: Stale resource records are being accessed. When a record's TTL has expired, it will not be used. In this scenario the subsequent increase in name resolution traffic that results from a smaller TTL is acceptable if fewer stale records are accessed.

B. Incorrect: The problem is that stale records are not timing out quickly enough in cache, not that stale records with zero TTL are failing to be removed from the zone. Although selecting this check box is probably a good idea in this scenario, this solution will not solve the immediate problem.

C. Incorrect: You can set the default TTL for a zone, or you can set the TTL for individual records. You cannot set it at server level. There is no SOA tab in the server properties dialog box.

D. Incorrect: This answer is incorrect for the reason stated in the explanation for answer B.

11. Correct Answers: A

A. Correct: The Nslookup command-line utility is used to verify zone delegation, as specified in this answer.

B. Incorrect: This command returns a full listing of the records in the detroit.wingtiptoys.com domain. It does not test DNS delegation.

C. Incorrect: Wingtiptoys.com and detroit.wingtiptoys.com are separate Active Directory domains and separate DNS zones. Zone transfer does not occur. The Replmon utility is not appropriate in this scenario.

D. Incorrect: System Monitor checks system performance. It cannot be used to check DNS delegation.

12.   Correct Answers: D

A. **Incorrect:** Only one DNS server can host a primary zone. All the DNS servers that replicate off that zone are hosting secondary zones. Servers that host secondary zones cannot process updates to the primary zone. Primary zones cannot be shared between two DNS servers.

B. **Incorrect:** If this is done, the DNS server in Sydney will be unable to process updates to the zone file. Only the server in Melbourne, as the primary DNS server, will be able to process such updates.

C. **Incorrect:** Secondary servers only host a copy of a primary zone file; they cannot process updates to a zone file.

D. **Correct:** Any DNS server configured with an Active Directory Integrated Zone can process updates. This is the only way of allowing both the Sydney and Melbourne servers to process updates to the zone file while retaining a single DNS zone. If five DNS zones were allowed, one for each site, a primary DNS server could be installed at each site and therefore updates could be processed at each site.

23 Exam 70-296—Planning, Implementing, and Maintaining Server Availability (3.0)

Servers are an essential component on most networks, and keeping them running whenever clients need them is a daunting task. Server performance can be interrupted by any number of factors, including hardware problems, software incompatibilities, accidents, theft, and natural disasters. Keeping servers available requires careful planning and continual monitoring.

Microsoft Windows Server 2003 includes tools and services that you can use to ensure that servers remain available to users. For example, Windows Server 2003 supports clusters, which are groups of connected servers that function as a single resource, sharing the performance load and providing fault tolerance. Regular backups keep servers available by enabling administrators to restore data that is lost due to a drive erasure or failure. Windows Server 2003 includes a Backup program that enables you to protect all your server files, including key elements such as the registry, Active Directory directory service databases, and cluster configuration data.

Keeping servers available is often a matter of anticipating problems that could cause a server failure. Tools such as Network Monitor and the Performance console enable you to track the performance of specific server components, to locate system bottlenecks, and to detect network service failures.

Tested Skills and Suggested Practices

The skills that you need to successfully master the Planning and Maintaining Network Security objective domain on *Exam 70-296: Planning, Implementing, and Maintaining a Microsoft Windows Server 2003 Environment for an MCSE Certified on Windows 2000* include

- Plan services for high availability; plan a high availability solution that uses clustering services; and plan a high availability solution that uses Network Load Balancing (NLB).

  - ❑ Practice 1: Using information from vendors' World Wide Web sites, catalogs, or manufacturers' product collateral, research the hardware products currently on the market that you can use to build large Network Load Balancing (NLB) and server clusters.

❑ Practice 2: Design two 10-node clusters: a 10-node server cluster for a database application and a 10-node Web server NLB cluster. Your design should include diagrams of the networks and a list of all the hardware products required to build the clusters.

■ Plan a backup and recovery strategy; identify appropriate backup types; plan a backup strategy that uses volume shadow copy; and plan system recovery that uses Automated System Recovery (ASR).

❑ Practice 1: Using the Windows Server 2003 Backup program, create backup jobs to perform differential or incremental jobs six days a week and a normal job on the seventh day.

❑ Practice 2: Perform a full system backup using the Windows Server 2003 Backup program and then practice restoring individual files, multiple files, and folders, both to their original locations and to an alternate location, using the various file overwrite options.

Further Reading

This section lists supplemental readings by objective. You should study these sources thoroughly before taking *Exam 70-296: Planning, Implementing, and Maintaining a Microsoft Windows Server 2003 Environment for an MCSE Certified on Windows 2000.*

Objective 3.1   Review Chapter 14, "Clustering Servers."

Microsoft Corporation. *Microsoft Windows Server 2003 Deployment Kit.* Volume: *Planning Server Deployments.* Redmond, Washington: Microsoft Press, 2003. Review Chapter 6, "Planning for High Availability and Scalability." This volume can also be found on the Microsoft Web site at *http://www.microsoft.com /windowsserver2003/techinfo/reskit/deploykit.mspx.*

Microsoft Corporation. *Microsoft Encyclopedia of Networking, Second Edition,* Redmond, Washington: Microsoft Press, 2002. See entries for "clustering."

Objective 3.2   Review Chapter 13, "Managing and Implementing Disaster Recovery."

Microsoft Corporation. Windows Server 2003 Online Help. Review the "Understanding Backup" pages in the Backup help file.

Plan Services for High Availability

Servers must be available to perform their functions, and, depending on how critical those functions are to your organization, you might want to take steps to ensure that your servers are up and running as much of the time as possible. One way of ensuring the high availability of your servers is to create clusters, which are groups of servers that function as a single entity. Clients access the server applications using a specially assigned cluster name and cluster Internet Protocol (IP) address, and one or more of the servers in the cluster are responsible for responding to each client request. If a server in the cluster should go offline, another server in the cluster takes over its processes, a procedure called failover. When the malfunctioning server comes back online, it can begin to perform its regular processes again, which is called failback. There are three basic types of clusters: server clusters, Component Load Balancing (CLB) clusters, and Network Load Balancing (NLB) clusters. The properties of these cluster types are specified in the following table:

	Server Cluster	**CLB Cluster**	**NLB Cluster**
Supported Applications	**Stateful** applications (database and e-mail servers)	COM+ components	**Stateless** applications (Web servers)
Number of nodes supported in Windows Server 2003, Standard Edition	0	Not supported	32
Number of nodes supported in Windows Server 2003, Enterprise Edition	8	Not supported	32
Number of nodes supported in Windows Server 2003, Datacenter Edition	8	Not supported	32
Special hardware required in Windows Server 2003	Shared storage infrastructure	N/A	None

Objective 3.1 Questions

1. A rapidly expanding company has recently extended its operations to three shifts, and as a result, the IT department must keep the company's intranet Web and Microsoft SQL Server database servers running 24 hours a day. The network administrators have decided to use Windows Server 2003 clustering to keep the servers available at all times and have purchased two additional computers for this purpose, bringing the total number of servers to four. Which of the following clustering deployments is best suited to this company's needs?

   A. A single 4-node server cluster running the Web and database applications on all four servers

   B. A single 4-node Network Load Balancing cluster running the Web and database applications on all four servers

   C. Two separate 2-node clusters: a server cluster to run the database application and a Network Load Balancing cluster to run the Web server application

   D. A single 4-node cluster, with the database application running on two of the nodes and the Web server application running on the other two

2. A server administrator for a company with a number of different clusters is told by his superiors that the 4-node Network Load Balancing cluster running the company's Internet Web servers is running at peak capacity nearly all the time and that he should design a plan to scale up the cluster to support more traffic. Which of the following actions would you be likely to see in the administrator's plan? (Choose all that apply.)

   A. Add two more servers to the cluster, bringing the total number to six.

   B. Install additional memory in all the cluster servers.

   C. Convert the NLB cluster to a server cluster.

   D. Install a second processor in each cluster server.

3.   Which of the following operating system versions is capable of hosting an 8-node Network Load Balancing cluster? (Choose all that apply.)

   A. Windows XP Professional

   B. Windows Server 2003, Standard Edition

   C. Windows Server 2003, Enterprise Edition

   D. Windows Server 2003, Datacenter Edition

4.   Which of the following operating system versions is capable of hosting an 8-node server cluster? (Choose all that apply.)

   A. Windows XP Professional

   B. Windows Server 2003, Standard Edition

   C. Windows Server 2003, Enterprise Edition

   D. Windows Server 2003, Datacenter Edition

Objective 3.1 Answers

1. **Correct Answers: C**

    A. Incorrect: A Web server is a stateless application that you cannot deploy on a server cluster. Instead, you should use a Network Load Balancing cluster for the Web server.

    B. Incorrect: A database server is a stateful application that you cannot deploy on a Network Load Balancing cluster. Instead, you should use a server cluster for the database server.

    C. Correct: You should create a server cluster to run stateful applications such as database servers and a Network Load Balancing cluster to run stateless applications such as Web servers.

    D. Incorrect: Although you can deploy multiple applications on a single cluster, all the applications must be either stateful or stateless, which dictates the types of cluster you should create. In this case, the database application is stateful and the Web server is stateless.

2. **Correct Answers: B and D**

    A. Incorrect: Scaling up a cluster is the process of increasing the existing servers' capabilities, usually by upgrading their hardware. Adding new servers to a cluster is called scaling out.

    B. Correct: Adding memory is a method of scaling up cluster servers that is likely to make them perform more efficiently and increase their overall throughput.

    C. Incorrect: Server clusters are not suitable for running stateless applications like Web servers. Server clusters and NLB clusters are parallel technologies; changing an NLB cluster to a server cluster is not necessarily an upgrade.

    D. Correct: Assuming that the servers in the cluster support multiple processors, adding a second processor is a valid method of scaling up their performance levels.

3.   **Correct Answers: B, C, and D**

A.   **Incorrect:** Windows XP is not capable of any type of clustering.

B.   **Correct:** Windows Server 2003 Standard Edition does not support server clusters, but like all Windows Server 2003 versions, it can support Network Load Balancing clusters of up to 32 nodes.

C.   **Correct:** Windows Server 2003 Enterprise Edition can support 8-node server clusters and Network Load Balancing clusters of up to 32 nodes.

D.   **Correct:** Windows Server 2003 Datacenter Edition can support 8-node server clusters and 32-node Network Load Balancing clusters.

4.   **Correct Answers: C and D**

A.   **Incorrect:** Windows XP is not capable of any type of clustering.

B.   **Incorrect:** Windows Server 2003 Standard Edition does not support server clusters. This edition can support Network Load Balancing clusters of up to 32 nodes.

C.   **Correct:** Windows Server 2003 Enterprise Edition can support 8-node server clusters and Network Load Balancing clusters of up to 32 nodes.

D.   **Correct:** Windows Server 2003 Datacenter Edition can support 8-node server clusters and 32-node Network Load Balancing clusters.

Plan a Backup and Recovery Strategy

A network backup strategy typically consists of one or more backup drives connected to a server running a network backup software program. You configure the program to execute backup jobs at times when the network is not in use so that it can protect data stored on computers all over the network without affecting normal operations. The most common storage medium used by backup drives is magnetic tape, which is available in a variety of formats that differ in capacity, data transmission speed, and the price of the drive and media. When selecting a backup medium, you should take into account the amount of data you have to back up on a daily basis. The object is typically to select a backup drive that fits all the data you must back up every day on a single tape, so that you can configure the jobs to run unattended.

To prevent having to back up all the data on your network every day, all backup software products provide a number of different backup jobs, the most common of which are as follows:

- **Full backup** Copies all the selected files to the backup medium and resets the archive bits for all the copied files

- **Incremental backup** Copies only the selected files that have archive bits and then resets those archive bits

- **Differential backup** Copies only the selected files that have archive bits without resetting those archive bits

The basic premise of incremental and differential backups is that there is no need to back up the same files every day if they have not changed. Backup software uses the archive bit stored as part of every file to determine whether that file has changed recently. Performing a full backup job copies all your files to the backup drive and resets all their archive bits to a value of 0. When an application on the computer modifies a file, the file system changes the value of the archive bit to 1. When you perform an incremental or differential backup, the backup software copies only the files with archive bit values of 1. The difference between an incremental and a differential backup is whether the backup software resets the archive bits of the files it has copied. With incremental jobs, the software does reset the archive bits; with differential jobs, it does not. Incremental backups use less storage space than differential backups, but the process of restoring an entire drive is longer and more complicated.

Windows Server 2003 includes a Backup program that enables you to protect all the files on the computer by copying them to a backup drive or to a disk file that you can move to a safe location. The version of Backup in Windows Server 2003 includes a new feature called *volume shadow copy* that enables the Backup program to protect files that are currently open and in use. This feature also has another function that can simplify the administrator's job. You can configure Windows Server 2003 to automatically maintain shadow copies of the files on a specific volume. Shadow copies capture a frequently changed file's state at one point in time. The server creates these copies on a regular schedule you specify. By default, the volume shadow copy feature creates shadow copies of each changed file twice a day, and users can access any of the previous versions of their files still stored in the shadow copy area. A user who accidentally modifies or deletes an important file can access a previous version of the file from the shadow copy area, rather than asking the backup administrator to restore a previous version from tape. You must enable the volume shadow copy feature for an entire volume, and you must specify the amount of disk space to be allotted to the shadow copies. When the disk space is full, the system automatically purges the oldest copies.

Automated System Recovery (ASR), another feature of the Windows Server 2003 Backup program, enables you to restore an entire system drive without reinstalling the operating system. With a standard backup, you can't restore a computer whose drive has been completely erased from a backup until you reinstall the operating system, because you must be able to run the Backup program to perform the restore. Automated System Recovery is a disaster recovery feature that enables you to create a backup of your operating system with a boot disk that enables you to perform a restore immediately. When you use the ASR feature to create a backup, the program prompts you for a standard backup device, such as a tape, and a floppy disk. After the backup is complete, if your system drive fails, you can simply replace the drive, insert the backup tape in it, start the computer from the floppy disk, and let the restoration of the operating system proceed automatically.

Objective 3.2 Questions

1. You are the backup administrator for a corporate network, and you are in the process of creating and scheduling your backup jobs. The company you work for has purchased a backup tape drive that uses very expensive media, and you have been ordered to keep the amount of tape used for backups to an absolute minimum. Which of the following strategies best achieves your goals?

  A. Perform a full backup every Friday night and a differential backup every Monday night through Thursday night.

  B. Perform a full backup every Friday night and an incremental backup every Monday night through Thursday night.

  C. Perform a full backup every Friday night and a volume shadow copy every Monday night through Thursday night.

  D. Perform a full backup every night.

2. Your company has recently expanded to three shifts, meaning that the network is in use 24 hours a day, 7 days a week. Your current backup strategy consists of a full backup job every Sunday and incremental jobs on Monday through Saturday. Which of the following Windows Server 2003 Backup features should you use to ensure that system backs up all open files every day?

  A. Automated System Recovery

  B. Differential backups instead of incremental backups

  C. Volume shadow copy

  D. Full backups every night, instead of incrementals

3. Which of the following magnetic tape drive types offers the greatest tape capacity and the fastest data transfer rates?

  A. Linear Tape-Open (LTO)

  B. 8 mm

  C. Digital audio tape (DAT)

  D. Digital linear tape (DLT)

4.   You have recently been named administrator of backups for your company, and you are in the process of developing a backup strategy. Your goals for this strategy are to schedule a backup job to run each night that will back up all the files modified during that day's work and to create the fastest possible recovery solution in the event of a complete server system disk failure. Which of the following strategies would enable you to achieve all these goals?

A. Perform a full backup every Friday and an incremental backup every Monday night through Thursday night.

B. Perform an ASR backup every night.

C. Perform an ASR backup once a month and perform a full backup every Friday and a differential backup every Monday night through Thursday nights.

D. Perform a full backup every night.

Objective 3.2 Answers

1. **Correct Answers: B**

   A. **Incorrect:** Although this strategy would adequately protect the network, it does not achieve the goal of using the minimum amount of tape because differential jobs back up some of the same files every night.

   B. **Correct:** Incremental backup jobs use the least amount of tape because they back up only the files that have changed since the last backup.

   C. **Incorrect:** Volume shadow copy is not a type of backup job, although it is a feature you can use for your backup jobs. Creating shadow copies of the files on your volumes is not a substitute for regular backups, because the system still stores them on the same hard drive, which can fail.

   D. **Incorrect:** Performing a full backup every night is an effective solution, but it does not fulfill the goal of using the minimum amount of tape.

2. **Correct Answers: C**

   A. **Incorrect:** Automated System Recovery is a feature that enables you to create a bootable operating system backup; it does not protect open files.

   B. **Incorrect:** Changing the incremental backups to differentials would not enable the system to back up open files. A differential backup only differs from an incremental in its treatment of the archive bits.

   C. **Correct:** Volume shadow copy enables the Windows Server 2003 Backup program to back up files that are locked open by other applications.

   D. **Incorrect:** Performing full backups instead of incrementals does nothing to enhance the backup of open files.

3.   Correct Answers: A

A. Correct: LTO drives support tape capacities of up to 200 gigabytes (GB) (uncompressed) and data transfer speeds of up to 3600 megabytes (MB) per minute, which are currently the best in the industry.

B. Incorrect: 8-mm drives support tape capacities of up to 100 GB (uncompressed) and data transfer speeds of up to 1400 MB per minute, which are exceeded by DLT and LTO drives.

C. Incorrect: DAT drives support tape capacities of up to 20 GB (uncompressed) and data transfer speeds of up to 360 MB per minute. These figures are exceeded by 8-mm, DLT, and LTO drives.

D. Incorrect: DLT drives support tape capacities of up to 160 GB (uncompressed) and data transfer speeds of up to 960 MB per minute. LTO drives have greater capacities, and LTO and 8-mm drives offer faster data transfer speeds.

4.   Correct Answers: C

A. Incorrect: This solution does back up all the files that have changed each day, but it does not provide the fastest possible recovery solution. Incremental jobs take longer to restore than differential jobs, and the lack of an ASR backup means that you must first reinstall the operating system in the event of a server system disk failure.

B. Incorrect: ASR backups provide for a fast recovery of the operating system in the event of a server system disk failure, but they only back up operating system files and are therefore not a substitute for standard backup jobs.

C. Correct: An ASR backup, in combination with daily differential backups, protects all the files changed during each day's work and also provides the fastest possible recovery. In the event of a server system disk failure, you only have to restore from the ASR backup, the most recent full backup, and the most recent differential backup.

D. Incorrect: Performing a full backup every night protects all the files that users change each day, but it does not provide the fastest recovery, since you must reinstall the operating system before you can restore files from the backup.

24 Exam 70-296—Planning and Maintaining Network Security (4.0)

Security is an essential part of the network administrator's function in almost every enterprise. As businesses become increasingly dependent on their computer networks, the threats they face become more dangerous and the attackers more ingenious. The Microsoft Windows Server 2003 family of operating systems includes a wide array of security mechanisms that can protect the network against these threats, and a competent network administrator must know how to use them properly. This chapter examines the protocols you can use to secure data as computers transmit it over the network and the tools that Windows Server 2003 provides for implementing and managing these protocols.

Tested Skills and Suggested Practices

The skills that you need to successfully master the Planning and Maintaining Network Security objective domain on *Exam 70-296: Planning, Implementing, and Maintaining a Microsoft Windows Server 2003 Environment for an MCSE Certified on Windows 2000* include

- Plan secure network administration methods.
    - ❏ Practice 1: Using the System Properties dialog box, configure a computer running Windows Server 2003 to use Remote Desktop, specifying the names of the remote users that you want to be able to access this server.
    - ❏ Practice 2: Using group policies, configure a computer running Windows Server 2003 to use Remote Assistance.
- Plan security for wireless networks.
    - ❏ Practice 1: Examine the Web sites or product literature of companies manufacturing wireless local area network (LAN) products. Make a list of network interface adapters and access points, specifying the wireless networking and security standards they support.
    - ❏ Practice 2: Design a wireless networking infrastructure for an office building that uses multiple access points and list the steps you would take to provide maximum security for the wireless transmissions.

■ Plan security for data transmission.

❑ Practice 1: Install Network Monitor on a computer running Windows Server 2003 and use it to capture a representative sampling of the network traffic generated by all the applications you commonly use. Examine the captured packets and make a list of the protocols and port numbers the applications use.

❑ Practice 2: Using the IP Security Policy Management snap-in, create a new Internet Protocol Security (IPSec) policy to encrypt all the traffic using the protocols and port numbers you listed in Practice 1.

Further Reading

This section contains a list of supplemental readings divided by objective. If you think you need additional preparation before taking the exam, study these sources thoroughly.

Objective 4.1   Review Chapter 10, "Managing and Maintaining a Server Environment."

Microsoft Corporation. *Microsoft Windows Server 2003 Deployment Kit.* Volume: *Planning Server Deployments.* Redmond, Washington: Microsoft Press, 2003. Review Chapter 4, "Hosting Applications with Terminal Server." This volume can also be found on the Microsoft Web site at *http://www.microsoft.com /windowsserver2003/techinfo/reskit/deploykit.mspx.*

Microsoft Corporation. Windows Server 2003 Online Help. Review the "I Am Managing The Use Of Remote Assistance" pages in the Remote Assistance help file, accessible from the Remote tab of the System Properties dialog box.

Objective 4.2   Review Lesson 3 in Chapter 11, "Securing Network Communication."

Microsoft Corporation. *Microsoft Windows Server 2003 Deployment Kit.* Volume: *Deploying Network Services.* Redmond, Washington: Microsoft Press, 2003. Review Chapter 11, "Deploying a Wireless LAN." This volume can also be found on the Microsoft Web site at *http://www.microsoft.com/windowsserver2003 /techinfo/reskit/deploykit.mspx.*

Objective 4.3   Review Chapter 11, "Securing Network Communication."

Microsoft Corporation. *Microsoft Windows Server 2003 Deployment Kit.* Volume: *Deploying Network Services.* Redmond, Washington: Microsoft Press, 2003. Review Chapter 6, "Deploying IPSec." This volume can also be found on the Microsoft Web site at *http://www.microsoft.com/windowsserver2003/techinfo /reskit/deploykit.mspx.*

Microsoft Corporation. *Microsoft Windows 2000 Server Resource Kit.* Volume: *Windows 2000 Server TCP/IP Core Networking Guide.* Redmond, Washington: Microsoft Press, 2000. Review Chapter 8, "Internet Protocol Security." Although written for Windows 2000, virtually this entire chapter is applicable to Windows Server 2003.

Plan Secure Network Administration Methods

Many of the administration tools included with Windows Server 2003 are capable of managing services on remote computers as well as on the local system. For example, most Microsoft Management Console (MMC) snap-ins have this capability, enabling administrators to work with systems throughout the enterprise without traveling. These are specialized tools, however, that can perform only a limited number of tasks. For comprehensive administrative access to a remote computer, Windows Server 2003 includes two tools that are extremely useful to the network administrator, called Remote Assistance and Remote Desktop.

Remote Assistance enables a user at a distant location (such as technical support or help desk personnel) to connect to another user's computer and either view all the user's activities or take over the system entirely. With Remote Assistance, users can request help from specific individuals (referred to as experts or helpers by the Windows Server 2003 software) and receive it on their own computers, without requiring an expert to travel to a user's location. To use Remote Assistance, both computers involved must be running Windows XP Professional or Windows Server 2003 and the host computer must be configured to allow remote users to access the system.

Because an expert offering assistance to another user can perform virtually any activity on the remote computer that the local user can, this feature can conceivably be a security hazard. An unauthorized user who takes control of a computer using Remote Assistance can cause practically unlimited damage. However, the Remote Assistance feature is designed to minimize the dangers and includes features that enable administrators to regulate the remote assistance process. Some of these features are as follows:

- **Invitations**   To obtain remote assistance, a user must issue an invitation and send it to an expert using either e-mail or Windows Messenger. An expert can also offer help to a user, but the user must accept it before the expert can connect. The user also maintains control over the Remote Assistance connection. Even when the expert has the ability to perform tasks on the remote computer, the user can terminate the connection at any time.

- **Configuration**   By default, Windows XP and Windows Server 2003 have Remote Assistance turned off. Before users can send invitations for remote assistance, they must turn on the feature from the Remote tab of the System Properties dialog box. By clicking Advanced in this tab, users can also specify whether the connected expert can perform tasks on the user's computer or merely observe the user's activities and can define the maximum amount of time that invitations remain open.

■ **Group policies**   Rather than configure Remote Assistance on each computer individually, network administrators can use group policies to control the Remote Assistance settings throughout the network. In the Group Policy Object Editor console, the Computer Configuration\Administrative Templates\System\Remote Assistance folder contains two policies. The Solicited Remote Assistance policy controls whether users can issue Remote Assistance invitations and whether experts can view the client computer or perform tasks remotely, specifies the maximum ticket time, and specifies the method for sending invitations. The Offer Remote Assistance policy enables you to specify the names of users or groups that can function as experts and to specify whether those experts can perform tasks or just observe.

■ **Firewalls**   Remote Assistance uses Transmission Control Protocol (TCP) port number 3389 for all its network communications. For networks that use Remote Assistance internally and are connected to the Internet, it's recommended that network administrators block this port in their firewalls to prevent users outside the network from taking control of computers requesting remote assistance. It's also possible to provide remote assistance over the Internet, which would require port 3389 to be left open.

Remote Desktop, a feature similar to Remote Assistance, is designed to give administrators access to a computer at a remote location. Remote Desktop For Administration is essentially an application of the Terminal Services service supplied with Windows Server 2003. A desktop version called Remote Desktop is included with Windows XP Professional. Windows Server 2003 allows up to two simultaneous remote desktop connections without the need for a separate license. Administrators can use Remote Desktop to manage computers that are at distant locations or are secured in a server closet or data center. Unlike Remote Assistance, Remote Desktop is designed to give a remote user complete control of a computer with no interaction at the client end. There are no invitations and no read-only capabilities. When you connect to a system using Remote Desktop, you see a separate session on the host computer, independent of the console session. You must log on to the system in the normal manner, meaning that the remote user must have a user account and the appropriate permissions to access the host system. Windows Server 2003 and Windows XP Professional also include a Remote Desktop Connection client, which you can install on a computer running an earlier version of the Windows operating system.

1. You are a network administrator who has been instructed to create a Remote Assistance strategy that will enable help desk personnel to connect to computers on the company network to provide technical support to end users. The network uses Active Directory and consists of Windows XP Professional workstations and servers running Windows Server 2003. You have already created an organizational unit called Workstations containing all the computer objects that represent the computers running Windows XP. The network is also connected to the Internet using a T-1 line. The goals of the project are to activate Remote Assistance on all the workstations without having to configure them individually and to prevent users on the Internet from taking control of workstations on the company network. To achieve these goals, you decide to perform the following procedure:

1. Create a security group in Active Directory called Remote Experts and add all the help desk operators to it.

2. Enable the Solicited Remote Assistance policy in the Group Policy Object (GPO) for the Workstations organizational unit.

3. Enable the Offer Remote Assistance policy in the GPO for the Workstations organizational unit and add the Remote Experts group to the Helpers list.

How many of the stated goals does this procedure accomplish?

A. The procedure accomplishes none of the stated goals.

B. The procedure will successfully configure the workstations to use Remote Assistance, but it does not protect the workstations from unauthorized Internet connections.

C. The procedure will successfully protect the workstations from unauthorized Internet connections, but it will not configure the workstations to use Remote Assistance.

D. The procedure accomplishes both stated goals.

2. Which of the following procedures can prevent users on the local network from making unauthorized use of the Remote Assistance feature? (Choose all that apply.)

   A. Blocking TCP port 3389 in the network's Internet firewall.

   B. Specifying the names of authorized helpers in the Offered Remote Assistance policy for Default Domain Policy GPO.

   C. Leaving the Solicited Remote Assistance policy unconfigured in the Default Domain Policy GPO.

   D. Configuring the TCP/IP client on each workstation to filter out traffic using TCP port 3389.

3. You are a network administrator who wants to be able to manage a member server at a branch office using Remote Desktop For Administration. The server is running Windows Server 2003 and your workstation is running Windows 2000 Professional. You have not been given Administrator access to the server. Which of the following tasks must you perform before you can successfully connect to the server? (Choose all that apply.)

   A. Install the Remote Desktop Connection program on the server.

   B. Install the Remote Desktop Connection program on the workstation.

   C. Add your user object to the Remote Desktop Users local group on the server.

   D. Enable Remote Assistance in the System Properties dialog box on the server.

4. Which of the following operating systems is not capable of receiving remote assistance from an expert? (Choose all that apply.)

   A. Windows XP Home Edition

   B. Windows 2000 Server

   C. Windows XP Professional

   D. Windows 2000 Professional

   E. Windows Server 2003

Objective 4.1 Answers

1.   Correct Answers: D

    A. Incorrect: Applying the two Remote Assistance policies in this way would successfully accomplish both stated goals.

    B. Incorrect: Applying the two Remote Assistance policies as specified here would enable Remote Assistance on all the workstations without needing to configure them individually, and specifying the authorized helpers would prevent unauthorized access by Internet users.

    C. Incorrect: Applying the two Remote Assistance policies in this way would successfully enable Remote Assistance on all the network workstations.

    D. Correct: Applying the two Remote Assistance policies as specified here would enable Remote Assistance on all the workstations without needing to configure them individually, and specifying the authorized helpers would prevent unauthorized access by Internet users.

2.   Correct Answers: B and D

    A. Incorrect: Configuring the firewall to block TCP port 3389 would prevent users on the Internet from using Remote Assistance to connect to computers on the private network, but it would do nothing to prevent two computers on the private network from connecting to each other using Remote Assistance.

    B. Correct: By specifying the names of the users or groups that can function as experts in the Helpers list, you prevent others not on the list from connecting to a client using Remote Assistance.

    C. Incorrect: Leaving a policy unconfigured means that the GPO does not modify the local computer settings. Individual users would therefore be able to activate the Remote Assistance feature on their computers.

    D. Correct: All the network traffic generated by the Remote Assistance feature uses TCP port 3389. Using packet filtering to block that port would prevent users from establishing any Remote Assistance connections.

3.   Correct Answers: B and C

   A. Incorrect: The Remote Desktop Connection program is a client that enables a computer running an earlier version of the Windows operating system to manage a computer running Windows XP or Windows Server 2003.

   B. Correct: Windows 2000 Professional does not include support for Remote Desktop. Therefore, you must install the Remote Desktop Connection client supplied with Windows XP and Windows Server 2003.

   C. Correct: When a user is not a member of the Administrators group on a computer to be managed with Remote Desktop, the user must be a member of the Remote Desktop Users local group on the computer.

   D. Incorrect: Remote Assistance is a separate feature that is not associated with and is not required to use Remote Desktop.

4.   Correct Answers: B and D

   A. Incorrect: Windows XP Home Edition includes the Remote Assistance client.

   B. Correct: Windows 2000 Server does not include support for Remote Assistance.

   C. Incorrect: Windows XP Professional includes the Remote Assistance client.

   D. Correct: Windows 2000 Professional does not include support for Remote Assistance.

   E. Incorrect: Windows Server 2003 includes the Remote Assistance client.

Objective 4.2

Plan Security for Wireless Networks

Wireless networking has existed for many years, but it is only recently, with the publication of the 802.11 series of standards by the Institute of Electrical and Electronic Engineers (IEEE), that wireless local area network (WLAN) technologies have become mainstream products. The 802.11b standard defines a WLAN technology running at speeds up to 11 megabits per second (Mbps). This is the first affordable wireless standard that provides performance that is comparable to that of a wired LAN. The 802.11a and 802.11g standards promise to provide wireless networking at even greater speeds, up to 54 Mbps.

WLANs can use two topologies: ad hoc and infrastructure. An ad hoc topology consists of two or more computers equipped with wireless network interface adapters that communicate directly with each other. An infrastructure topology consists of wireless computers that communicate with an access point, which provides a connection to a standard wired network. An access point is a WLAN transceiver that is also attached to the wired network, using a standard Ethernet (or other data-link layer protocol) connection. Wireless systems in an infrastructure topology can communicate with each other, but they do so through the access point; they cannot communicate directly.

Because WLAN network interface adapters and access points transmit their network packets using radio signals, they present a significant natural security risk. WLAN signals are omnidirectional, extending to the equipment's specified range. Any compatible device within transmission range can therefore transmit and receive the WLAN signals, enabling an unauthorized user to connect to the network or capture the packets transmitted by other users, compromising the data inside. Depending on your equipment's range and where you locate your access points, unauthorized users might even be able to access your WLAN from outside the building, unless you take steps to protect the network.

To provide security for a wireless network, you must first create an environment in which users are authenticated and authorized before they are able to send data to and receive it from an access point. Authentication and authorization prevent unknown users from connecting to the wireless network, but they do not prevent eavesdroppers from capturing the data packets transmitted by wireless systems. To do this, you must configure the wireless devices to encrypt all the data they transmit. The most commonly used security mechanisms on WLANs are the following:

- **IEEE 802.11 authentication**   The 802.11 standard defines two types of authentication. Open System authentication is not really an authentication at all, but rather an exchange of messages between a wireless client and an access point that specifies the user's identity. In Shared Key authentication, a wireless client verifies its identity to an access point by demonstrating its knowledge of a secret key that the access point shared with the client earlier using a secure channel. Shared Key encryption is not a particularly secure system because the access point shares the same key with all the wireless clients.

- **IEEE 802.1X authentication**   For authentication and authorization, Windows Server 2003 and Windows XP Service Pack 1 include a wireless client that is compliant with the IEEE 802.1X standard. IEEE 802.1X provides support for centralized user identification using a Remote Authentication Dial-In User Service (RADIUS) server, such as the Internet Authentication Service (IAS) included with Windows Server 2003. With this combination in place, the access points send the connection requests they receive from wireless clients to the RADIUS server, which authenticates them using an authentication protocol such as Extensible Authentication Protocol-Transport Level Security (EAP-TLS) or Protected EAP-Microsoft Challenge Handshake Authentication Protocol version 2 (PEAP-MS-CHAP v2), both of which are supported by ISA. The RADIUS server then uses remote access policies to authorize the authenticated clients. To use 802.1X on a network running the Windows operating system and using an infrastructure topology, your access points must support 802.1X and RADIUS authentication.

- **Wired Equivalent Privacy (WEP) encryption**   Included in the 802.11 standard, WEP encrypts the data transmitted on a wireless network using an encryption key that is either 40 or 104 bits long and an algorithm called RC4. When the authentication that precedes the encryption process uses EAP-TLS or PEAP-MS-CHAP v2, WEP is provided with strong cryptographic keys for each communications session, EAP-TLS using smart cards or digital certificates, and PEAP-MS-CHAP v2 using passwords only.

- **Wireless network (IEEE 802.11) policies**   The Group Policy Object Editor console contains a subheading where you can create a policy that enables you to limit a computer's wireless networking capabilities. You can restrict computers to infrastructure or ad hoc networks and specify the networks to which the computer can connect.

Objective 4.2 Questions

1.   Which of the following protocol standards defines the mechanism that Windows XP and Windows Server 2003 use to authenticate and authorize wireless network clients?

   A. IEEE 802.11a

   B. IEEE 802.11b

   C. IEEE 802.1X

   D. WEP

2.   You are adding wireless network clients to your Ethernet network in the form of laptop computers that will be deployed to the sales staff. To secure the wireless connections, you intend to use 802.1X and WEP. The laptops are also equipped with card readers, and you plan to issue smart cards to the salespeople. Which of the following authentication protocols must you use to support this security solution?

   A. PEAP-MS-CHAP v2

   B. RADIUS

   C. RC4

   D. EAP-TLS

3.   You are a network consultant who has been called in to troubleshoot a wireless networking problem. The company has a large wireless presence, with multiple access points scattered throughout a building. The access points are located so as to provide an unbroken field of coverage throughout the building, but in practice this has proven not to be so. When a wireless computer moves out of the transmission range of its native access point, it moves into the range of another access point, but it cannot connect. No matter at which access point the computer starts, it cannot connect to any of the other access points on the network. Which of the following reasons could possibly explain why this is happening? (Choose all that apply.)

   A. The wireless devices are configured to use Shared Key authentication.

   B. The construction of the building is inhibiting the wireless transmissions.

   C. The Wireless Network (IEEE 802.11) policy does not have the correct entries in the Preferred Networks list.

   D. The wireless devices are configured to use certificates for authentication, and the certificates are configured incorrectly.

4.   You have recently installed a WLAN access point on your network and equipped a number of laptop computers with wireless network interface adapters. You want all the wireless clients to be able to connect only to the access point, but not directly to each other, so that your security infrastructure will remain in effect. Which of the following steps can you use to limit the clients' connectivity in this way?

   A. Configure the wireless devices to use IEEE 802.1X and authenticate using the EAP-TLS protocol with smart cards.

   B. Configure the wireless devices to use Open System authentication.

   C. Create a Wireless Network (IEEE 802.11) policy, configure it to allow ad hoc networking only, and apply it to the computers.

   D. Create a Wireless Network (IEEE 802.11) policy, configure it to allow infrastructure networking only, and apply it to the computers.

Objective 4.2 Answers

1. **Correct Answers: C**

   A. Incorrect: The IEEE 802.11a standard defines a physical layer implementation that transmits signals at 5 gigahertz (GHz) and sends data at up to 54 Mbps using Orthogonal Frequency Division Multiplexing (OFDM). IEEE 802.11a is not used to authenticate and authorize wireless clients.

   B. Incorrect: The IEEE 802.11b standard defines a physical layer implementation that transmits signals at 2.4 GHz and sends data at up to 11 Mbps using direct sequence spread spectrum modulation. IEEE 802.11b is not used to authenticate and authorize wireless clients.

   C. Correct: IEEE 802.1X is a standard for authentication for wired Ethernet networks and wireless 802.11 networks. Windows XP and Windows Server 2003 can use IEEE 802.1X in conjunction with a RADIUS server to authenticate wireless clients using any one of several authentication protocols, including EAP-TLS and PEAP-MS-CHAP v2.

   D. Incorrect: Wired Equivalent Privacy (WEP), part of the IEEE 802.11 standard, defines the encryption that WLAN systems use to secure their transmissions. WEP is not used for authentication and authorization.

2. **Correct Answers: D**

   A. Incorrect: PEAP-MS-CHAP v2 is an authentication protocol for wireless networks that do not have access to a public key infrastructure (PKI). Without a PKI, the network cannot use certificates, and without certificates, the network cannot use smart cards for authentication.

   B. Incorrect: Remote Authentication Dial-In User Service (RADIUS) is not an authentication protocol; it is a service that provides centralized authentication for other servers on the network, using any one of several authentication protocols.

   C. Incorrect: RC4 is not an authentication protocol; it is an encryption algorithm that wireless systems use as part of their WEP implementations.

   D. Correct: EAP-TLS is the only authentication protocol supported by Windows Server 2003 that enables users to authenticate with smart cards.

3.   **Correct Answers: A and C**

    A. Correct: When you use Shared Key authentication, each client's network key is unique to its initial access point. Connecting to other access points requires a different key, which is one possible explanation for the clients' failure to connect to multiple access points.

    B. Incorrect: Environmental factors, including the construction of the building, can affect wireless transmission ranges, but the effect would not be as consistent as it is in this case. The fact that each computer can successfully connect to its initial access point, but not to any other access points, indicates that the source of the problem lies elsewhere.

    C. Correct: If the network administrator has created a Wireless Network (IEEE 802.11) policy that specifies only the native access point in the Preferred Networks list, the clients cannot connect to the other networks using different access points.

    D. Incorrect: If the certificates were configured incorrectly, the computers would not be able to authenticate themselves to any wireless network.

4.   **Correct Answers: D**

    A. Incorrect: The authentication mechanism you use does not affect which topology the computers are able to use. In this case, the client must use a smart card for authentication to the infrastructure network, but it can still connect to the other wireless computers on an ad hoc basis.

    B. Incorrect: The authentication mechanism you use does not affect which topology the computers are able to use. Despite the use of Open System authentication, the client can still connect to the other wireless computers on an ad hoc basis.

    C. Incorrect: An ad hoc network is one in which wireless computers communicate directly with each other, which is precisely what you are trying to avoid in this case.

    D. Correct: When you create a Wireless Network (IEEE 802.11) policy, you can limit the computers receiving the policy to ad hoc or infrastructure networking. By limiting the computers to infrastructure networking, you prevent them from communicating directly with each other.

Plan Security for Data Transmission

Windows Server 2003 and Windows XP Professional include three default IPSec policies, which are as follows:

- **Client (Respond Only)**   Configures the computer to use IPSec only when another computer requests its use. The computer using this policy never initiates an IPSec negotiation; it only responds to requests from other computers for secured communications.

- **Secure Server (Require Security)**   Configures the computer to require IPSec security for all communications. If the computer attempts to communicate with another computer and discovers that the second computer does not support IPSec, the computer terminates the connection.

- **Server (Request Security)**   Configures the computer to request the use of IPSec when communicating with another computer. If the other computer supports IPSec, the IPSec negotiation begins. If the other computer does not support IPSec, the systems establish a standard, unsecured IP connection.

The default IPSec policies included with Windows Server 2003 define security specifications for client and server roles that might not be appropriate for your network installation. Although a computer is not running a server operating system, the computer might actually be functioning as a server. The Client (Respond Only) IPSec policy enables computers to use IPSec in response to another computer that requests it, but they cannot initiate IPSec communications themselves. When implementing IPSec on your network, you must first examine the traffic patterns and the roles of your computers to determine which computers communicate with one another and for what reasons. Then you either assign the default IPSec policies based on this communications analysis or create IPSec policies that are better suited to your network's security requirements.

Objective 4.3 Questions

1. You are a network administrator who has recently implemented IPSec on your network, which consists of servers running Windows Server 2003 and client workstations running Windows XP Professional. You have created separate organizational units in Active Directory for the servers and the workstations and assigned the Secure Server (Require Security) IPSec policy to the Servers organizational unit and the Client (Respond Only) policy to the Workstations organizational unit. On examining the network traffic with a protocol analyzer, you notice that the users on some workstations are sharing files with each other directly, without first copying the files to a server, and that none of this traffic is being protected by IPSec. Which of the following steps can you take to secure the communications between the clients, as well as the communications between clients and servers? (Choose all that apply.)

    A. Configure the Workstations organizational unit to use the Secure Server (Require Security) IPSec policy instead of the Client (Respond Only) policy.

    B. Modify the default response rule in the Client (Respond Only) IPSec policy to include the IP addresses of the workstations.

    C. Modify the filter list in the Secure Server (Require Security) IPSec policy to include the IP addresses of the workstations.

    D. Move the computer objects from the Workstations organizational unit to the Servers organizational unit.

2. Which of the following types of traffic is not secured by the default Secure Server (Require Security) IPSec policy?

    A. TCP

    B. UDP

    C. ICMP

    D. IP

3.   You are the administrator of a network that has a number of servers running Windows Server 2003 that host a variety of data file types, some of which contain classified information needed by specific company officers and many of which do not. You have already stored the classified documents in directories that are protected using the Encrypting File System, but you also want to ensure their protection when they are transmitted over the network. You have decided to implement IPSec on the network for this purpose, but your testing has determined that encrypting all the network traffic causes a severe degradation in server performance, and there is no money in the budget for server upgrades at this time. Which of the following IPSec solutions will enable you to protect the sensitive files without encrypting all your network traffic?

   A. Configure the servers to use the Secure Server (Require Security) IPSec policy, the company officers' computers to use the Server (Request Security) policy, and the other users' computers to use the Client (Respond Only) policy.

   B. Configure the servers to use the Server (Request Security) IPSec policy and the company officers' computers to use the Secure Server (Require Security) policy.

   C. Configure the servers to use the Secure Server (Require Security) IPSec policy and the company officers' computers to use the Client (Respond Only) policy.

   D. Configure the servers and the company officers' computers to use the Client (Respond Only) IPSec policy.

Objective 4.3 Answers

1.   **Correct Answers: A and D**

   A. **Correct:** Configuring the Workstations organizational unit to use the Secure Server (Require Security) policy instead of the Client (Respond Only) policy would ensure that all communications between the client workstations are secured.

   B. **Incorrect:** The default response rule in an IPSec policy uses a dynamic filter list that you cannot modify.

   C. **Incorrect:** Modifying the Secure Server (Require Security) policy would have no effect on the client workstations when they are communicating with each other because the workstations are using the Client (Respond Only) policy.

   D. **Correct:** Moving the workstations' computer objects to the Servers organizational unit would cause them to use the Secure Server (Require Security) policy instead of the Client (Respond Only) policy, causing all workstation traffic to be protected by IPSec.

2.   **Correct Answers: C**

   A. **Incorrect:** The Secure Server (Require Security) policy protects all IP traffic, which includes TCP traffic, because TCP messages are carried in IP datagrams.

   B. **Incorrect:** The Secure Server (Require Security) policy protects all IP traffic, which includes UDP traffic, because UDP messages are carried in IP datagrams.

   C. **Correct:** The Secure Server (Require Security) policy permits systems to transmit all ICMP traffic without any IPSec negotiation or protection.

   D. **Incorrect:** The Secure Server (Require Security) policy protects all IP traffic.

3.   **Correct Answers: B**

   A. **Incorrect:** Configuring the servers to use the Secure Server (Require Security) policy would cause them to encrypt all traffic, not just the traffic containing the sensitive information.

   B. **Correct:** Configuring the servers to use the Server (Request Security) policy would cause them to initiate IPSec communications when the client computer supports IPSec. Configuring the company officers' computers to require IPSec communications ensures that all sensitive information will be encrypted.

   C. **Incorrect:** Configuring the servers to use the Secure Server (Require Security) policy would cause them to encrypt all traffic, not just the traffic containing the sensitive information.

   D. **Incorrect:** Configuring both the servers and the company officers' computers to use the Client (Respond Only) policy would result in no encryption at all because the Client (Respond Only) policy never initiates IPSec negotiations.

25 Exam 70-296—Planning, Implementing, and Maintaining Security Infrastructure (5.0)

More than ever before, security is a major element of network administration. From the very planning stages, you must consider how security concerns affect the hardware products you purchase, the software you install, and the network services you deploy. Microsoft Windows Server 2003 includes a robust collection of security features that you can use to protect your data in a variety of ways.

However, network infrastructure security is as much an administrative concern as a technological one. Proper security planning, implementation, and maintenance require input from representatives throughout the organization, as well as from IT people. To create an effective security infrastructure, you must understand what resources need to be protected, what threatens these resources, and what steps you can take to provide protection.

Tested Skills and Suggested Practices

The skills that you need to successfully master the Planning, Implementing, and Maintaining Security Infrastructure objective domain on *Exam 70-296: Planning, Implementing, and Maintaining a Microsoft Windows Server 2003 Environment for an MCSE Certified on Windows 2000* include

- Configure Active Directory directory service for certificate publication.
    - ❏ Practice 1: Install Certificate Services on a computer running Windows Server 2003 and create an enterprise root certification authority (CA).
    - ❏ Practice 2: Use the Certificates snap-in for Microsoft Management Console (MMC) to request certificates from an enterprise root CA.

■ Plan a public key infrastructure (PKI) that uses Certificate Services; identify the appropriate type of certification authority to support certificate issuance requirements; plan the enrollment and distribution of certificates; and plan for the use of smart cards for authentication.

❑ Practice 1: Design a Windows Server 2003 PKI for a large multinational corporation, using a single root CA and enabling users in every branch office to obtain certificates automatically from a local CA. All the corporation's internal users must be able to send and receive digitally signed and encrypted e-mail, and Internet users must be able to obtain digitally signed software from the company's World Wide Web servers. For each CA in the infrastructure, specify its type and its role in the PKI.

❑ Practice 2: Open the Certificate Templates snap-in in the MMC, create a duplicate of the Administrator template, display the Properties dialog box for the new template, and study the properties you can set.

■ Plan a framework for planning and implementing security; plan for security monitoring; and plan a change and configuration management framework for security.

❑ Practice 1: Make a list of resources that need protection in a typical corporation and specify what Windows Server 2003 features you could use to provide this protection.

❑ Practice 2: Make a list of the Windows Server 2003 tools you can use to monitor a network's security and, for each tool, indicate what types of threats it can detect.

■ Plan a security update infrastructure. Tools might include Microsoft Baseline Security Analyzer and Microsoft Software Update Services (SUS).

❑ Practice 1: Download the Microsoft Baseline Security Analyzer tool from the Microsoft Web site at *http://www.microsoft.com/technet/treeview/default.asp?url= /technet/security/tools/Tools/MBSAhome.asp* and use it to examine the security configuration of your computer.

❑ Practice 2: Examine the materials provided on the Microsoft Software Update Services home page at *http://www.microsoft.com/windows2000/windowsup date/sus/default.asp* and make a list of the tasks that Software Update Services (SUS) can perform, which network administrators would otherwise have to perform manually.

Further Reading

This section lists supplemental readings by objective. You should study these sources thoroughly before taking *Exam 70-296: Planning, Implementing, and Maintaining a Microsoft Windows Server 2003 Environment for an MCSE Certified on Windows 2000.*

Objective 5.1   Review Chapter 12, "Creating and Managing Digital Certificates."

Microsoft Corporation. "PKI Enhancements in Windows XP Professional and Windows Server 2003." This article is available on the Microsoft Web site at *http: //www.microsoft.com/windowsxp/pro/techinfo/planning/pkiwinxp/default.asp.*

Objective 5.2   Review Lessons 1, 2, and 3 in Chapter 12, "Creating and Managing Digital Certificates" and Lesson 3 in Chapter 4, "Managing Users, Groups, and Computers."

Microsoft Corporation. "Designing a Public Key Infrastructure." This article is available on the Microsoft Web site at *http://www.microsoft.com/technet/prodtechnol /windowsserver2003/proddocs/deployguide/adsec/part2/rkddspki.asp.*

Objective 5.3   Review Chapter 9, "Planning and Implementing Server Roles and Security."

Microsoft Corporation. *Securing Windows 2000 Server.* Review Chapter 2, "Defining the Security Landscape." Although written for the Windows 2000 Server operating systems, this article discusses many concepts that are equally applicable to Windows Server 2003. This content is available on the Microsoft Web site at *http: //www.microsoft.com/technet/security/prodtech/windows/secwin2k/02defsls.asp.*

Objective 5.4   Review Lesson 4 in Chapter 10, "Managing and Maintaining a Server Environment."

Microsoft Corporation. "Software Update Services Overview White Paper." Redmond, Washington, 2003. This white paper is available on the Microsoft Web site at *http://www.microsoft.com/windows2000/windowsupdate/sus/susoverview.asp.*

Configure Active Directory Directory Service for Certificate Publication

Windows Server 2003 Certificate Services is a flexible application that can provide many types of certificates to clients both inside and outside an organization. For internal clients, the best practice is to publish and store certificates in the Active Directory database. Because of its replicated architecture, Active Directory is available to all clients at all times and is easy to protect with regular backups.

To use Active Directory to publish and store certificates, you must configure Certificate Services to function as an enterprise certification authority. Enterprise CAs provide a number of advantages over the alternative, stand-alone CAs, including the following:

- **Active Directory storage** When an enterprise CA issues certificates, it publishes them in the Active Directory database, where they are protected from accidental loss and always available.

- **Autoenrollment** When an enterprise CA receives a certificate enrollment request from a client, it consults the information about the client stored in Active Directory and automatically determines whether to issue or deny the certificate. Stand-alone CAs, by contrast, store incoming requests in a queue, and an administrator must manually evaluate then issue or deny the certificates.

- **Certificate templates** A certificate template contains the properties that a CA uses to create a particular type of certificate, including the provider of cryptographic services and the key length. Enterprise CAs can automatically enroll clients because they use certificate templates to obtain all the settings needed to create certificates. Stand-alone CAs cannot use templates, and therefore, all the settings for certificates must be included in requests. To receive a certificate from an enterprise CA, a client must have the appropriate permissions for the template for the requested certificate type.

1.   Which of the following conditions must a user on a Windows Server 2003 network meet to obtain an Internet Protocol Security (IPSec) certificate from an enterprise CA? (Choose all that apply.)

    A. The user must have an account in Active Directory.

    B. The user must have access to the Certification Authority console.

    C. The user must have the Enroll permission for the IPSec certificate template.

    D. An administrator must manually process the user's certificate enrollment request.

2.   You are a user on a network running Windows Server 2003 Active Directory with an enterprise CA, and you need a certificate to encrypt your data files using Encrypting File System (EFS). Which of the following procedures can you use to obtain the certificate?

    A. Open the Certificates snap-in in Microsoft Management Console and request a certificate from the CA.

    B. Display the Command Prompt window and use the Certutil.exe program to request a certificate from the CA.

    C. Open the Certificate Templates snap-in in Microsoft Management Console, select the Basic EFS template, and request a certificate.

    D. Open Microsoft Internet Explorer, connect to the Certificate Services Web Enrollment Support page on the CA, and generate a certificate request.

3.   You are a network administrator for a company with an Active Directory network using servers running Windows Server 2003. The network's PKI consists of multiple enterprise CAs in various offices throughout the enterprise. After checking the security logs on the CAs at the branch offices, you discover that an unauthorized user has gained access to the Administrator account and has compromised one of the CAs. As a result, you must make sure that no certificates issued by that CA are ever used again. Which of the following tools can you use to revoke the certificates issued by the CA? (Choose all that apply.)

    A. The Certificate Templates snap-in

    B. The Certificates snap-in

    C. Certutil.exe

    D. The Certification Authority console

4.   You are designing a PKI for a small network installation. You want users to be able to obtain certificates for EFS, IPSec, and smart card logons immediately, with no administrative intervention. You have decided to deploy only one CA on the network. Which of the following CA types should you use?

   A. Enterprise root

   B. Enterprise subordinate

   C. Stand-alone root

   D. Stand-alone subordinate

Objective 5.1 Answers

1.   Correct Answers: A and C

   A.   Correct: Enterprise CAs are intended for internal users on Active Directory networks. Because an enterprise CA stores certificates in the Active Directory database and uses Active Directory information to decide whether to issue a certificate, a user must be an Active Directory client.

   B.   Incorrect: Administrators use the Certification Authority console to manage CAs and the certificates they issue. Users do not require access to this tool.

   C.   Correct: Enterprise CAs use certificate templates to create specific types of certificates, and for users to receive certificates from the CA, they must have the Enroll permission for the template representing the particular type of certificate they need.

   D.   Incorrect: Enterprise CAs support autoenrollment, which enables a CA to autonomously decide whether to issue or deny a certificate.

2.   Correct Answers: A

   A.   Correct: The Certificates snap-in enables users to view their certificates and to request certificates from an enterprise CA.

   B.   Incorrect: The Certutil.exe program is a command-line alternative to the Certification Authority console that administrators use to manage a CA. Users do not employ the Certutil.exe program to request certificates.

   C.   Incorrect: The Certificate Templates snap-in is a tool that PKI administrators use to create and configure certificate templates. Although the CA uses the templates to create certificates, users do not use this snap-in to request them.

   D.   Incorrect: The Web Enrollment Support interface for Certificate Services enables users to request certificates from stand-alone CAs. Users on a network running enterprise CAs would have to use the Certificates snap-in to manually request certificates.

3. **Correct Answers: C and D**

A. Incorrect: The Certificate Templates snap-in enables PKI administrators to create and manage certificate templates. You cannot use this tool to access, manage, or revoke the certificates that a CA creates using the templates.

B. Incorrect: The Certificates snap-in enables users to view their certificates and request new certificates from an enterprise CA. Users cannot revoke their own certificates using this tool.

C. Correct: The Certutil.exe program is a command-line utility that can perform the same tasks as the Certification Authority console. To revoke a certificate using Certutil.exe, you use the -Revoke parameter.

D. Correct: The Certification Authority console enables PKI administrators to manage the activities of a CA by viewing the certificates that it has created, processing certificate requests, and revoking certificates.

4. **Correct Answers: A**

A. Correct: Enterprise CAs support autoenrollment and are capable of issuing the specified certificate types. When deploying enterprise CAs, you must always create a root CA first.

B. Incorrect: Although an enterprise subordinate CA is capable of issuing the specified certificate types using autoenrollment, you cannot create an enterprise subordinate CA without having an enterprise root CA first.

C. Incorrect: Stand-alone CAs do not support autoenrollment and are not capable of issuing smart card logon certificates.

D. Incorrect: In addition to not supporting autoenrollment or the required certificate types, a stand-alone subordinate CA cannot be created until a stand-alone root CA exists.

Plan a Public Key Infrastructure that Uses Certificate Services

To implement a PKI using Windows Server 2003 Certificate Services, you must install at least one certification authority (CA). For a relatively small organization, a single CA might be sufficient, but for larger organizations, or if you want to provide fault tolerance and load balancing for your CAs, you can create a hierarchy of certification authorities.

The correct type of CA is an essential part of an effective PKI design. Certificate Services supports two types of CA, which are as follows:

- **Enterprise CAs** Enterprise CAs store their certificates, certificate revocation lists (CRLs), and other information in the Active Directory database. Because the CA's clients must have access to Active Directory, enterprise CAs are intended for an organization's internal users. Enterprise CAs also support autoenrollment through the use of certificate templates, eliminating the need for administrators to manually issue or deny certificates.

- **Stand-alone CAs** Stand-alone CAs store their certificates and other information as standard files on the computer's hard disk drive and are therefore intended for users external to the enterprise, such as clients connecting to the company's Web servers. Stand-alone CAs do not support autoenrollment and cannot use certificate templates, which means that the CA queues incoming certificate enrollment requests until an administrator decides whether the clients should receive the requested certificates.

For both enterprise and stand-alone CAs, you can elect to create either a root CA or a subordinate CA. The standard trust model for a PKI is called a *rooted hierarchy*. The root CA is at the top of the hierarchy and issues certificates to the subordinate CAs beneath it. These certificates grant the subordinate CAs the same degree of trustworthiness as the root CA. In large installations, the CA hierarchy consists of three layers, beginning with a root CA at the top. The second layer consists of subordinate CAs that represent different geographic locations or different types of certificates; these are also called *intermediate CAs*. The third layer consists of subordinate CAs that actually issue the end-user certificates to clients; these are called *issuing CAs*. Every certificate that an issuing CA supplies to a client contains a certificate chain leading up through the CA hierarchy to a root CA, confirming the trustworthiness of the certificate.

The process by which clients of the PKI request certificates from a CA is called *enrollment*. Enrollment can occur automatically, for example, when an application sends a certificate request to an enterprise CA and immediately receives a certificate in return, or manually, when a user explicitly requests a certificate from a CA. To send enrollment requests to an enterprise CA, you use the Certificates snap-in for MMC. To send enrollment requests to a stand-alone CA, you use the Web Enrollment Support interface provided with Windows Server 2003 Certificate Services.

A *smart card* is a portable data storage device, approximately the size of a credit card, that contains memory and, in some cases, an integrated circuit. Windows Server 2003 can use smart cards as authentication devices by storing a user's certificate and private key on the card. This enables users to log on to the network from any computer with their full privileges, as granted by the PKI. Because smart card logons are intended only for internal users with access to Active Directory, only enterprise CAs can issue smart card certificates.

Objective 5.2 Questions

1. On a network using a PKI with a three-level rooted hierarchy, which of the following types of CAs issue smart card certificates to end users?

    A. Stand-alone root

    B. Stand-alone subordinate

    C. Enterprise root

    D. Enterprise subordinate

2. You're a network consultant who has been hired to design a Windows Server 2003 PKI for a company with offices in different cities throughout the United States. The goals of the project, as specified by the client, are as follows:

    1. Provide encrypted and digitally signed e-mail communications for all company employees

    2. Provide key-based authentication for clients connecting to a company extranet from remote locations using the Internet

    3. Provide key-based authentication for roaming company employees accessing the company's wireless LAN using laptops

    4. Provide fault tolerance, so that the failure of a single CA anywhere in the enterprise cannot prevent users from requesting and receiving certificates

To address these goals, you design a PKI in the form of a rooted hierarchy, which consists of a single enterprise root CA located at the company's home office and three enterprise subordinate CAs at each of the company's branch offices. At each branch, one of the three servers functions as an intermediate CA and the other two function as issuing CAs.

Which of the following statements about this PKI design is true?

    A. This design satisfies all the goals specified by the client.

    B. This design satisfies all the goals specified by the client except number 2 because enterprise CAs cannot support external users.

    C. This design satisfies all the goals specified by the client except number 3 because Windows Server 2003 Certificate Services does not support certificates for wireless network authentication.

    D. This design satisfies all the goals specified by the client except number 4 because the use of a single root CA prevents the PKI from being fault tolerant.

3.   You are a junior network administrator who has been given the task of setting up a workstation for the company's new CFO. All high-level officers of the company are required to encrypt all their network storage and communications using EFS, IPSec, and encrypted e-mail. The company runs a number of enterprise CAs to provide certificates for these purposes. After installing Microsoft Windows XP on the workstation, you determine that you must request a Basic EFS certificate for the new user, and to do so, you log on to the computer with the new user's account, open Internet Explorer, and connect to one of the CAs using the Web Enrollment Support interface. When you attempt to request a Basic EFS certificate, the Web interface informs you that the user does not have the permissions needed. Which of the following steps can you take to resolve this problem?

    A. Use the Certificates snap-in instead of the Web Enrollment Support interface to request the certificate.

    B. Log off the new user's account, log on as Administrator, and then request the certificate again.

    C. Install a stand-alone CA on the network because enterprise CAs do not support Basic EFS certificates.

    D. Use the Certificate Templates snap-in to grant the new user the Read and Auto-enroll permissions for the Basic EFS template.

4.   When a PKI uses a three-level rooted hierarchy with enterprise CAs, to what clients do intermediate CAs issue certificates?

    A. To the root CA

    B. To other intermediate CAs

    C. To issuing CAs

    D. To end users

Objective 5.2 Answers

1.   **Correct Answers: D**

A. **Incorrect:** Stand-alone root CAs cannot issue smart card logon certificates, because this type of CA does not use Active Directory, which is required for a smart card logon.

B. **Incorrect:** Stand-alone subordinate CAs cannot issue smart card logon certificates, because this type of CA does not use Active Directory, which is required for a smart card logon.

C. **Incorrect:** In a root hierarchy, enterprise root CAs only issue certificates to other CAs, not to end users.

D. **Correct:** The issuing CAs in a rooted hierarchy are always subordinate CAs, and because only enterprise CAs use Active Directory, they are the only ones that can issue smart card logons.

2.   **Correct Answers: B**

A. **Incorrect:** Although the design does satisfy three of the four goals, it does not satisfy goal number 2 because enterprise CAs cannot support external clients.

B. **Correct:** External users cannot obtain certificates from enterprise CAs because these users do not have access to Active Directory. Therefore, because this PKI design contains only enterprise CAs, it cannot support external users, as goal number 2 requires.

C. **Incorrect:** Windows Server 2003 Certificate Services is capable of issuing certificates for wireless network authentication, so the PKI design does satisfy goal number 3.

D. **Incorrect:** In a rooted hierarchy, the root CA only issues certificates to the subordinate CAs at the next lower level. Once it has done this, a failure of the root CA server would not prevent end users from requesting and receiving certificates.

3.   Correct Answers: D

A. Incorrect: When you are working with enterprise CAs, the Certificates snap-in provides the same basic functionality as the Web Enrollment Support interface. If the user lacks the permissions to obtain a certificate from the Web interface, a request from the Certificates snap-in would fail as well.

B. Incorrect: You must request the certificate with the new user's account for that user to be able to access and use the certificate in Active Directory. Logging on as Administrator would request a certificate in the name of the Administrator account, which would be useless to the CFO.

C. Incorrect: Enterprise CAs do support Basic EFS certificates, as do stand-alone CAs.

D. Correct: For users to request certificates from an enterprise CA, they must have permission to use the templates corresponding to the certificates they need. Granting the new user account the Read and Autoenroll permissions for the Basic EFS template would make it possible for you to request and receive a certificate in the CFO's name.

4.   Correct Answers: C

A. Incorrect: CAs always issue certificates to entities that are equal to or below them in the PKI hierarchy. Therefore, an intermediate CA would never issue a certificate to a root CA, which is above it in the hierarchy.

B. Incorrect: In a rooted hierarchy, intermediate CAs always receive their certificates from root CAs, never from other intermediate CAs.

C. Correct: The function of an intermediate CA in a three-level rooted hierarchy is to issue certificates to the issuing CAs at the third level of the hierarchy. This provides the issuing CAs with a certificate chain that extends all the way up to the root CA.

D. Incorrect: In a rooted hierarchy, intermediate CAs are located at the second level, between the root CA and the issuing CAs. Intermediate CAs do not issue certificates to end users, only to the issuing CAs on the level directly below them.

Objective 5.3

Plan a Framework for Planning and Implementing Security

You must begin the security strategy for a data network long before you purchase or install any technology. Planning a security strategy for an enterprise network requires a framework of policies and procedures that dictate how your organization performs tasks such as the following:

- Estimating security risks
- Specifying security requirements
- Selecting security features
- Implementing security policies
- Designing security deployments
- Specifying security management policies

The creation of a security framework for a large organization requires input from people throughout the enterprise, not just IT personnel. The object of the security planning process is to answer questions such as the following:

- What are your organization's most valuable resources?
- What are the potential threats to your organization's resources?
- Which resources are most at risk?
- What are the consequences if specific resources are compromised?
- What security features are available to the organization?
- Which security features are best able to protect specific resources?
- How secure is secure enough?
- What is involved in implementing specific security features?
- What maintenance do the security features require?
- How will implementing specific security features affect users, administrators, and managers?

Creating a security framework is not a one-time project that ends when you have finished designing the initial security plan for your network. Security is an ongoing concern, and the responsibilities of the security design team are also ongoing. A security life cycle typically consists of three basic phases:

- **Designing a security infrastructure**   The initial planning phase consists of evaluating the organization's resources and the threats to them, selecting the security features you intend to implement, and creating an implementation plan. Windows Server 2003 security features are based on security principles such as authentication, encryption, access control, firewalls, and auditing.

- **Implementing security features**   Implementing the security features you have selected should include a phase of lab testing and a pilot deployment before you proceed with the full enterprise-wide implementation. At this time you should also create security policies that govern the use of the security features and the ways to ensure compliance with those policies.

- **Ongoing security management**   Once your security features and policies are in place, the project is not over. You must also consider what maintenance your security framework requires. Many security features are designed to gather information about network processes, and administrators must monitor them regularly to determine if a security-related incident has occurred. Auditing, for example, is a major element of Windows Server 2003 security that requires the network administrators' constant vigilance. Security strategies also must evolve over time to deal with new threats and accommodate new capabilities. Your security framework should include policies and procedures for evaluating new security information and acting on it in an organized manner.

Objective 5.3 Questions

1. Which of the following phases are part of a properly planned implementation of a security feature? (Choose all that apply.)

    A. Pilot deployment

    B. Performance simulation

    C. Lab testing

    D. Enterprise deployment

2. You are a new network administrator for a financial firm running a large Windows Server 2003 network that is spread out among buildings all over the corporate campus. Your supervisor has assigned you the task of checking the auditing information gathered by all the domain controllers on the network on a daily basis to make sure that their security has not been penetrated. There are 12 domain controllers on the network, located in 8 different buildings. Which of the following procedures will enable you to accomplish your task?

    A. Travel to each domain controller every morning and examine the auditing keys in the Windows registry.

    B. Access each domain controller from your own workstation every morning, using the C$ administrative share, and use Microsoft Notepad to view the latest entries in the audit logs.

    C. Create an MMC console containing an instance of the Event Viewer snap-in for each domain controller and use it to examine the Security logs each morning.

    D. Open the Active Directory Users And Computers console on your workstation each morning and examine the auditing logs in each domain controller's computer object.

3. To protect the users on a network running Windows Server 2003 from having their data files intercepted during transmission, you have implemented IPSec on all the network's computers. Now you want to monitor the network to make sure that all the network transmissions are actually using IPSec. Which of the following Windows Server 2003 tools can you use to do this?

    A. Network Monitor

    B. IP Security Monitor

    C. System Monitor

    D. Performance Monitor

Objective 5.3 Answers

1.   Correct Answers: A, C, and D

A. Correct: A pilot deployment is a limited implementation of a particular technology, using selected users on the live network. You should always perform a pilot deployment of a security feature before you proceed with a mass deployment on the entire network.

B. Incorrect: A performance simulation is not part of a standard technology deployment. Instead of using simulations, it is preferable to test a technology on actual equipment under conditions as near to those of the real world as possible.

C. Correct: Before implementing any new technology on a live network, you should always test it thoroughly in a lab environment first. A test lab is a network environment that is kept wholly separate from the organization's actual production network and that is used to test specific network elements.

D. Correct: The final stage of a technology implementation, after lab testing and the pilot deployment, is a full deployment throughout the enterprise.

2.   Correct Answers: C

A. Incorrect: Auditing information is not stored in the Windows registry.

B. Incorrect: Auditing information is not stored in a text file, so you cannot use Notepad to view it.

C. Correct: Windows Server 2003 stores auditing information in the Security log, which you can access using the Event Viewer console. To simplify the process of monitoring the logs on multiple computers, you can create a custom MMC console containing multiple instances of the Event Viewer snap-in, each focused on a different computer.

D. Incorrect: You cannot view auditing information in the Active Directory object for a particular computer.

3.   Correct Answers: B

A. Incorrect: By using Network Monitor to capture packets and view their contents, you can tell when IPSec has encrypted the data within the packets. However, the version of Network Monitor included with Windows Server 2003 can only capture packets that the computer running the Network Monitor program has transmitted or received, so Network Monitor can't check whether IPSec has encrypted all network transmissions.

B. Correct: The IP Security Monitor snap-in for Microsoft Management Console enables you to view the currently active IPSec policy on a computer and information such as whether computers are using a secure channel for their communications.

C. Incorrect: The System Monitor tool contains IPSec performance objects and can display statistics about IPSec operations, such as the total number of bytes sent and received using transport mode, but it cannot tell you whether all network transmissions are using IPSec.

D. Incorrect: The tool that is now called System Monitor in Windows Server 2003 was called Performance Monitor in Windows 2000. System Monitor is part of the Performance console, but there is no tool called Performance Monitor in Windows Server 2003.

Plan a Security Update Infrastructure

Security technologies are constantly changing, and network administrators must be vigilant to stay ahead of potential intruders who are continually developing new ways to exploit the weaknesses of other people's networks. Microsoft regularly releases updates and patches for its operating systems to address new security issues and eliminate potential hazards. To keep computers running Windows Server 2003 secure, you must apply new service pack and hot fix releases as needed.

When you are administering a large network, applying security updates is far more complicated than it is on a single computer. Not only must you install each update on hundreds or thousands of systems, you must also test each release carefully beforehand to ensure that it does not cause a problem that could cost you a great deal of time and production.

When planning a security update infrastructure for a medium to large network, you must address a number of problems that include the following:

- **Determining when updates are released** Microsoft frequently releases security updates that might or might not be applicable to the systems on your network. Network administrators must be aware of new releases when they occur and of the specific issues each release addresses.

- **Determining which computers need to be updated** In some cases a new security update might apply only to computers performing a specific function or using a specific application or feature. Network administrators must understand each release's specific function and determine which of their computers require the update.

- **Testing update releases on multiple system configurations** A security update that causes a malfunction might be just an annoyance on a single computer, but on a large network it could be a catastrophe. Network administrators must perform their own tests of all security updates before deploying them on the entire network.

- **Deploying update releases on large fleets** Manually installing security updates on hundreds or thousands of computers requires enormous amounts of time, effort, and expense. To deploy updates on a large network efficiently, the process must be automated.

Network administrators can use a variety of tools to address these problems. Some of these tools are as follows:

- **Microsoft Baseline Security Analyzer (MBSA)**   A graphical tool that can scan multiple computers running Windows operating systems for common security misconfigurations, such as unsuitable passwords, important security updates that have not been installed, file system and account weaknesses, and insufficient auditing policies. MBSA is useful for determining what security updates systems need, but it cannot download or deploy the actual updates themselves.

- **Microsoft Software Update Services (SUS)**   A server-based tool that enables network administrators to receive notifications when new security updates are available, download the updates, and then deploy them to the computers on the network. Software Update Services (SUS) receives notification of critical updates so that administrators don't have to check for new releases. Administrators then download the updates to the server, where they remain offline (presumably while being tested) until the administrator chooses to deploy them. When it is time to deploy the updates to the network computers, Software Update Services provides a local Windows Update server from which the other computers can download the updates without having to access the Internet.

Objective 5.4 Questions

1. Which of the following functions is Microsoft Baseline Security Analyzer able to perform? (Choose all that apply.)

   A. Download security updates from the Internet

   B. Specify which security updates have not been installed on a computer

   C. Install security updates on computers that need them

   D. Identify users with nonexpiring passwords

2. You are a network security consultant under contract to a corporation with a 700-node network running Windows Server 2003 and Windows XP Professional. The computers on the network are in various states of configuration because their operating systems were installed by the different vendors who supplied them. Your job is to examine the security configuration of all the computers on the network and determine whether any of them constitute a security risk. Which of the following procedures can achieve this goal most efficiently?

   A. Install Microsoft Baseline Security Analyzer on each computer and scan it for possible security breaches.

   B. Install Microsoft Baseline Security Analyzer on one computer and use it to scan all the computers on the network.

   C. Install Microsoft Software Update Services on one computer and use it to deploy the latest security updates to all the other computers on the network.

   D. Install Microsoft Software Update Services on each computer and use it to download the latest security updates.

3. Which of the following tools can inform you when new security updates are released, download them from the Internet, and then install them on your workstation?

   A. Windows Update

   B. Microsoft Baseline Security Analyzer

   C. Microsoft Software Update Services

   D. Security Configuration And Analysis snap-in

Objective 5.4 Answers

1. **Correct Answers: B and D**

    A. Incorrect: Microsoft Baseline Security Analyzer can scan computers for security breaches, such as missing security updates, but it cannot download the required updates from the Internet.

    B. Correct: Microsoft Baseline Security Analyzer scans computers for security updates, compares the list of installed updates to a list of available updates, and displays the results.

    C. Incorrect: Microsoft Baseline Security Analyzer can only diagnose security problems on computers; it cannot remedy them by installing missing security updates.

    D. Correct: Microsoft Baseline Security Analyzer examines the user accounts on a computer and specifies the number of users with passwords that do not expire. Nonexpiring passwords are a security hazard because the users are not compelled to change their passwords, increasing the risk that the passwords will eventually be compromised.

2. **Correct Answers: B**

    A. Incorrect: Although Microsoft Baseline Security Analyzer is the correct tool for this purpose, there is no need to install it on every computer because a single copy of the program on one computer can scan an entire network for security hazards.

    B. Correct: A copy of Microsoft Baseline Security Analyzer installed on a single computer can scan all the Windows operating systems on a network and analyze them for a variety of common security lapses.

    C. Incorrect: Microsoft Software Update Services can notify you when security updates are released and can download and install those releases, but it cannot scan a computer for security hazards.

    D. Incorrect: Microsoft Software Update Services is designed to download security updates from the Internet and deploy them to an entire network, eliminating the need to perform a manual operation on each computer. There is therefore no need to install the program on every computer.

3.   **Correct Answers: C**

   A. Incorrect: Windows Update is a Web page from which you can download and install security updates, but it does not notify you when new updates are released.

   B. Incorrect: Microsoft Baseline Security Analyzer can examine a computer and list the security updates that have not been applied to it, but it cannot download or install those updates.

   C. Correct: Microsoft Software Update Services is designed to inform administrators of new security update releases, download the new releases, and deploy them through the network.

   D. Incorrect: Security Configuration And Analysis is a tool that can compare a computer's current security policy settings to those stored in a security template and display the results. You cannot use this tool to modify the computer's security configuration in any way, including installing new security updates.

26 Exam 70-296—Planning and Implementing an Active Directory Infrastructure (6.0)

This objective domain covers the basic skills involved in the design and planning for domains and forests, as well as the skills required for installation and configuration of domain controllers. Planning is critical to the successful deployment of an Active Directory directory service network.

Planning must begin with a good understanding of the organization and its environment. The specific details surrounding an organization's environment will influence the planning and implementation of the Active Directory infrastructure for that organization. The elements involved in Active Directory planning will range from the network topology to organization charts. Although such elements as the network topology will have an impact on the way you design the Microsoft Windows Server 2003 Active Directory infrastructure, other elements will be directly affected, such as the existing Microsoft Windows NT or Microsoft Windows 2000 Active Directory domain structures.

Installation of the domain controllers is the first part of Active Directory implementation, followed by the configuration of the various elements within each domain and forest. Once you have configured Active Directory to fit in with the organization, you will then configure it to optimize Active Directory traffic. You must be familiar with the tools and techniques that will help you throughout the implementation process.

Tested Skills and Suggested Practices

The skills that you need to successfully master the Planning and Implementing an Active Directory Infrastructure objective domain on *Exam 70-296: Planning, Implementing, and Maintaining a Microsoft Windows Server 2003 Environment for an MCSE Certified on Windows 2000* include

- Plan a strategy for placement of global catalog servers.
  - ❑ Practice 1: Review several wide area network (WAN) topologies and consider the logon and authentication needs versus the traffic ramifications at each physical site in the WAN.

❑ Practice 2: Using Microsoft Network Monitor or another manufacturer's network monitoring utilities in conjunction with Performance Monitor (Perfmon), analyze the traffic during the replication process between global catalog servers.

❑ Practice 3: Implement a test network with two domains. Make certain that only one domain controller is a global catalog server. Take the global catalog server off the network. From a client station, attempt to log on the network into each domain. Bring the global catalog server back online and enable universal group membership caching on the other domain controllers. Take the global catalog server offline and attempt to log on the network from a client station again.

■ Implement an Active Directory forest and domain structure.

❑ Practice 1: Design an imaginary Active Directory forest with multiple domains. Consider which domain should be placed at the root of the forest. Document the domain trees.

❑ Practice 2: Install a test network with Windows Server 2003. Using the forest plan from Practice 1, run Dcpromo.exe to install Active Directory to create a new forest with a root domain.

❑ Practice 3: With the same network running from Practice 2, run Dcpromo.exe to install Active Directory on another server to create the first domain controller within a child domain.

❑ Practice 4: Using the same network in the previous practices, raise the functional level of each domain to Windows Server 2003, and then raise the functional level of the forest to Windows Server 2003.

❑ Practice 5: Install two domain controllers in two separate forest root domains. Raise the domain and forest functional levels to Windows Server 2003 for each domain and forest. Establish a forest trust between the two forests. Remove the forest trust and establish a one-way external trust between the two domains.

Further Reading

This section lists supplemental readings by objective. You should study these sources thoroughly before taking *Exam 70-296: Planning, Implementing, and Maintaining a Microsoft Windows Server 2003 Environment for an MCSE Certified on Windows 2000.*

Objective 6.1   Review Chapter 1, Lesson 3, "Planning an Active Directory Implementation," and Chapter 2, "Implementing an Active Directory Infrastructure."

Microsoft Corporation. *Introducing Microsoft Windows Server 2003.* Redmond, Washington: Microsoft Press, 2003. Review Chapter 3, "Active Directory," and Chapter 17, "Upgrading from Windows 2000 Server."

Microsoft Corporation. *Microsoft Windows Server 2003 Administrator's Pocket Consultant.* Redmond, Washington: Microsoft Press, 2003. Review Chapter 6, "Using Active Directory," and Chapter 7, "Core Active Directory Administration."

Microsoft Corporation. Microsoft TechNet. Redmond, Washington. Review "Understanding the Global Catalog," available on the Microsoft Web site at *http://www.microsoft.com/technet/treeview/default.asp?url=/technet/prodtechnol/windowsserver2003/proddocs/entserver/n_gc.asp.*

Objective 6.2   Review Chapter 1, Lesson 3, "Planning an Active Directory Implementation," Chapter 2, "Implementing an Active Directory Infrastructure," and Chapter 3 "Managing and Maintaining Active Directory Infrastructure."

Microsoft Corporation. *Introducing Microsoft Windows Server 2003.* Redmond, Washington: Microsoft Press, 2003. Review Chapter 17, "Upgrading from Windows 2000 Server."

Microsoft Corporation. *Microsoft Windows Server 2003 Administrator's Pocket Consultant.* Redmond, Washington: Microsoft Press, 2003. Review Chapter 6, "Using Active Directory," and Chapter 7, "Core Active Directory Administration."

Microsoft Corporation. *Microsoft Windows Server 2003 Deployment Kit, A Microsoft Resource Kit.* Redmond, Washington: Microsoft Press, 2003. Read Chapter 6, "Deploying the Windows Server 2003 Forest Root Domain," and Chapter 7, "Deploying Windows Server 2003 Regional Domains." This information can also be found on the Microsoft Web site at *http://www.microsoft.com/windowsserver2003/techinfo/reskit/deploykit.mspx.*

Microsoft Corporation. "HOW TO: Create an Active Directory Server in Windows Server 2003," available on the Microsoft Web site at *http://support.microsoft.com/default.aspx?scid=kb;EN-US;324753.*

Microsoft Corporation. "HOW TO: Manage the Application Directory Partition and Replicas in Windows Server 2003," available on the Microsoft Web site at *http://support.microsoft.com/default.aspx?scid=kb;EN-US;322669.*

Plan a Strategy for Placing Global Catalog Servers

This objective discusses the strategy for global catalog server placement. The existing network environment will help you in formulating the overall design of Active Directory, including forests, domains, and trust relationships. It will also guide you in placement of domain controllers, global catalog servers, and operations masters, as well as the configuration of the sites and site links.

Global catalog servers are Active Directory domain controllers that have been given the added functionality of holding a copy of the global catalog database. The very first domain controller installed into the root domain of the forest is always given the role of global catalog server. However, subsequent domain controllers will not automatically be designated with this role, and you will need to configure them manually.

There are certain situations in which enabling universal group membership caching makes more sense than adding a global catalog server. If you have a small branch office that contains a domain controller for a small domain and it is connected to the rest of the corporate network by a WAN link with little available bandwidth, that is an ideal situation for caching universal group memberships. In doing so, authentication and query traffic will take place locally, and replication traffic will be minimized since there will not be a large global catalog to replicate.

Objective 6.1 Questions

1. You have a Windows Server 2003 Active Directory network with seven global catalog servers. One of the Windows 2000 global catalog servers, 2KGC5, has failed, and you install a new server named GC8 to replace 2KGC5. You want to bring 2KGC5 back online, but you do not want it to be a global catalog server or a domain controller. You want to install Windows Server 2003, and you want to rename the server because your naming strategy requires member servers to be named differently from domain controllers. Which action should you take?

   A. Clear the Global Catalog check box on the NTDS Settings object within 2KGC5.

   B. Upgrade the server using the Windows Server 2003 WINNT32 command, selecting all defaults.

   C. Back up the data from the server, format the drive, and install Windows Server 2003 as a new server with a new name, making the server a member of the domain. Restore the data back to the server.

   D. Use the domain controller rename tool. Demote the domain controller to a member server using Dcpromo.exe.

2. You are planning your network strategy for a Windows Server 2003 forest. You currently have three Windows NT 4.0 domains as follows. The SALES domain encompasses all 430 members of the sales and marketing teams, who are located in 12 satellite offices, as well as users in the headquarters. The HQ domain includes all mission-critical applications, 2832 users in the headquarters, and 320 administrative users located in six of the 12 satellite offices, as well as several who work from remote sites. The RESEARCH domain incorporates the three research facilities, a testing group in the headquarters, and all seven manufacturing plants, for a total of 857 users. Which of the following documents should you refer to when planning the placement of your global catalog servers?

   A. A map of the WAN topology and traffic analysis

   B. An organization chart

   C. A map of the local area network (LAN) topology

   D. A list of administrative rights

3. You are planning a network strategy for a Windows Server 2003 forest for Fabrikam, Inc. You will be upgrading Fabrikam's current Windows NT 4.0 domains to Windows Server 2003. The domains are separated by location. There are three main offices: one in Atlanta, one in Chicago, and one in New York, each of which is a separate domain containing at least 200 or more user accounts. Remote users dial in to the Atlanta office to log on to their own domain, and all remote users regularly make use of the Atlanta printers because of a mission-critical application residing there. There is rarely any traveling between locations. Both Atlanta and Chicago have T1 lines directly connecting to the New York office but no direct connection between each other. You plan to place four global catalog servers in the offices—one in each office and a second global catalog server in the office that experiences the most global catalog usage. If you intend to upgrade each domain to Windows Server 2003 without changing the domain configuration, in which location will a global catalog server be used the most?

    A. None of the locations will require a global catalog server.

    B. Atlanta.

    C. Chicago.

    D. New York.

4. Your Windows Server 2003 Active Directory forest consists of three domains: HQ has 35,000 users, Market has 8000 users, and Sales has 300 users. The sales offices, which all belong to the Sales domain, are connected to the corporate network by slow 56 Kbps (kilobits per second) Frame Relay links. Each sales office will be given one domain controller. Which of the following will provide the users the uninterrupted ability to log on to the network without consuming too much bandwidth with replication traffic?

    A. Assign the sales offices administrative rights to their own domain controller.

    B. Assign the global catalog server role to the sales offices' domain controllers.

    C. Configure multiple backup site links for each site.

    D. Enable universal group membership caching on the sales offices' domain controllers.

Objective 6.1 Answers

1. **Correct Answers: C**

   A. Incorrect: Although this will remove the global catalog services, it will not rename the server or upgrade it, nor will it remove Active Directory and the global catalog services.

   B. Incorrect: The upgrade process will not remove the domain controller or global catalog services from 2KGC5, nor will it rename the server.

   C. Correct: This option will meet all of the objectives of bringing the server online as a member server running Windows Server 2003.

   D. Incorrect: You cannot use the domain controller rename tool unless the domain controller is running Windows Server 2003 and the domain is at the Windows Server 2003 functional level. After Dcpromo.exe removes Active Directory, the server will be a member server of the domain.

2. **Correct Answers: A**

   A. Correct: The WAN topology map and traffic analysis will determine where global catalog servers will best serve the needs of users for authentication and queries. It will also help plan for replication traffic between global catalog servers.

   B. Incorrect: An organization chart will not provide you with the available bandwidth and capacity information, which you need to plan for the traffic impact of the Active Directory domain controllers and global catalog servers.

   C. Incorrect: The LAN topology will not provide enough information for the placement of the servers.

   D. Incorrect: Administrative rights have no effect on the placement of global catalog servers.

3.   Correct Answers: B

A. **Incorrect:** Because there will be multiple domains, a global catalog server will be required in order to resolve logons, queries, and universal group membership information. In addition, the first domain controller installed in the root domain will automatically become a global catalog server.

B. **Correct:** Since the Atlanta location receives the logons, it will require either a global catalog server or universal group membership caching in order to authenticate users. This location will have the most global catalog usage because of the remote user logons and the likelihood of queries to access Atlanta printers and its mission-critical application.

C. **Incorrect:** Any global catalog servers in Chicago will experience less usage than in Atlanta, although there will probably be some usage for the rare traveler and query for the Atlanta-based resources.

D. **Incorrect:** Even though New York sits between Atlanta and Chicago because of physical connections, there is little difference between its own and Chicago's global catalog usage. New York should experience less global catalog usage than Atlanta.

4.   Correct Answers: D

A. **Incorrect:** The administrative rights to the domain controller will not ensure uninterrupted logons.

B. **Incorrect:** The global catalog server role will cause excess replication across the slow 56 Kbps links, although this option will ensure logons in the event that the WAN links fail.

C. **Incorrect:** The multiple site links will not ensure uninterrupted logons because they are logical, not actual additional physical WAN links.

D. **Correct:** Universal group membership caching will ensure that the users will be able to continue to log on even if the WAN links fail. In addition, it will ensure that there is no unnecessary global catalog replication traffic.

Implement an Active Directory Forest and Domain Structure

This objective looks at the skills of implementing an Active Directory forest and domain. The implementation of Active Directory begins with the installation of the first domain controller, which is always assigned to the root domain of the forest. A child domain is created at the point that you install the first domain controller in a domain other than the ones already existing in the forest.

Application directory partitions are a new feature for Windows Server 2003 Active Directory. Application directory partitions are basically used to overcome the challenges when using a multimaster replication scheme and applications that use a directory of information. The information contained within an application's directory can be stored and accessed locally and not included in the entire forest's replication.

In Windows Server 2003 Active Directory, the forest has optional levels, as do the domains. You have the following forest functional levels available:

- Windows 2000
- Windows Server 2003 interim
- Windows Server 2003

The default forest functional level is Windows 2000. This level supports domain controllers using the Windows NT 4, Windows 2000, and Windows Server 2003 operating systems. The next level up is Windows Server 2003 interim, which supports only Windows NT 4.0 and Windows Server 2003 operating systems. The forest functional level of Windows Server 2003 only supports domain controllers running the Windows Server 2003 operating system.

The Windows Server 2003 interim forest functional level is intended only for upgrading Windows NT 4.0 domains to become a new Windows Server 2003 forest. This level cannot be used in any other situation.

The forest features are extended when the functional level is raised to Windows Server 2003. The improvements include

- The creation of a forest trust relationship

- The faculty for renaming domains in the forest

- A new object called the InetOrgPerson, which is designated as an Internet administrator

- Global catalog replication improvements

- The ability to deactivate a schema class or attribute, creating defunct schema objects

- Improved replication, as well as the ability to replicate linked values

The four domain functional levels are

- Windows 2000 mixed

- Windows 2000 native

- Windows Server 2003 interim

- Windows Server 2003

The default functional level for a new domain is Windows 2000 mixed. This is basically the same as the Windows 2000 mixed mode domain, except that you can have Windows Server 2003 domain controllers along with Windows NT 4.0 and Windows 2000 domain controllers.

When raising the domain functional level to Windows 2000 native, you must have only Windows 2000 and Windows Server 2003 domain controllers. When running Windows 2000 native functional level, you have the added capabilities of

- Using universal security groups

- Nesting groups

- Using SID History

The Windows Server 2003 interim domain functional level is intended for upgrading a domain directly from Windows NT 4.0 to Windows Server 2003. It does not support Windows 2000 domain controllers, only those running Windows NT 4.0 and Windows Server 2003.

The Windows Server 2003 domain functional level supports only domain controllers running Windows Server 2003. Keep in mind that when you raise a domain's functional level, you cannot install any domain controllers using unsupported operating systems. For example, a Windows Server 2003 functional level domain cannot have a

Windows NT 4.0 or a Windows 2000 domain controller added to it. The additional features available within the Windows Server 2003 functional level are

- Domain controller renaming, using the domain controller rename tool
- Updating the logon timestamp
- Ability to convert groups
- Use of SID History
- Universal groups enabled for both distribution groups and security groups
- Full nesting of groups

Within an Active Directory forest, you already have an established Kerberos transitive, two-way trust relationship between each parent and child domain. Transitive means that when DomainA trusts DomainB, and DomainB trusts DomainC, then DomainA also trusts DomainC. Two-way means that when DomainA trusts DomainB, then DomainB also trusts DomainA. There are no automatic trusts with any other entity, whether another forest, an external Windows NT 4.0 domain, or a Kerberos realm. In addition, in large forests with several domains, the trust relationships must be resolved up to the root domain and back down and can cause a delay. To overcome these issues, you can establish the following types of trust relationships:

- Explicit external trusts
- Forest trusts
- Shortcut trusts

Objective 6.2 Questions

1. You are the administrator of a forest with three domain trees. Users in the sub1.child.parent.contoso.com domain complain that they have very slow access to the resources in the sub8.leaf.branch.root.contoso.local domain. Which of the following actions do you perform to help fix this problem?

   A. Enable the global catalog on three domain controllers in the sub1.child.parent.contoso.com domain.

   B. Seize the schema master role to a new domain controller.

   C. Create a shortcut trust where sub8.leaf.branch.root.contoso.local trusts sub1.child.parent.contoso.com.

   D. Create an explicit external trust where sub1.child.parent.contoso.com trusts sub8.leaf.branch.root.contoso.local.

2. You are the administrator for a Windows NT 4.0 network with three domains. You upgrade the primary domain controller (PDC) of one domain to Windows Server 2003 and automatically upgrade to Active Directory. You then upgrade a backup domain controller (BDC) in that domain to Windows Server 2003. When you upgrade the BDC, which option do you select in the Active Directory Installation Wizard?

   A. A Domain Controller In An Existing Domain In An Existing Forest

   B. A Domain Controller In A New Domain Tree In An Existing Forest

   C. A Domain Controller In A New Domain In A New Forest

   D. A Domain Controller In A Child Domain In An Existing Forest

3. Contoso Ltd.'s main office is in Seattle. Branch offices are in New York, Phoenix, and Sydney. The local administrators at each branch need to be able to control local resources. You want to prevent local administrators from managing resources in the other branch offices. You want only the main office's administrators to create and manage user objects. You want to create a structure to accomplish these goals. What should you do?

   A. Create a forest with domains in each branch office and with the root domain in the Seattle office. Each domain will contain the users and the computers for that specific office, with administrators belonging to the Domain Admins group in their respective domains.

   B. Create a forest with two domains: the root domain for the Seattle office and the child domain to be used by all other branch offices. Make the administrators members of the Domain Admins group of the child domain.

   C. Create a single domain in the forest. Develop an organizational unit (OU) structure that provides separate OUs for each branch within an overall OU. Delegate authority to each administrator to have resource management rights within the OU that represents his or her branch. Make the Seattle administrators members of the Domain Admins group.

   D. Create a single domain in the forest. Create a group named Branches. Add all the branch administrators to this group and grant it permissions to access the resources in all the branch locations.

4. Which of the following commands is used to install Active Directory on a new domain controller?

   A. Winnt

   B. Ntdsutil

   C. Adpromo

   D. Dcpromo

5. You are an administrator for a Windows Server 2003 forest that spans several cities. The New York office is planning to install an application that will be used only in that office. The application uses its own directory service that has the ability to integrate with Active Directory. The data for this application may grow to become quite large, so you want to ensure that it does not replicate throughout the network. Which command on Microsoft Management Console (MMC) do you use so that you can keep the application data from replicating beyond the New York office?

   A. Ntdsutil

   B. Winnt32

   C. Dcpromo

   D. Active Directory Sites And Services

6. At Tailspin Toys, you have three Windows NT 4.0 domains: DOMA, DOMB, and DOMC. You decide not to upgrade the domains but to install new servers in a new forest. After the forest is installed, you plan to migrate data and remove the Windows NT 4.0 servers from the network. You are able to install a server with Windows Server 2003, but when you attempt to promote it to a domain named doma.tailspintoys.com, you receive an error that the "domain name specified is already in use" on the network. What can you do to fix the problem?

   A. Change the domain name to doma.tailspintoys.local.

   B. Change the NetBIOS name of the Windows Server 2003 domain to ROOT and use root.tailspintoys.com for the DNS name.

    C. Change the domain controller's name to DOMA.

    D. Format the hard disk and reinstall Windows Server 2003 using the same name.

7. You are installing a new network for Contoso Pharmaceuticals. There are several sub-divisions within the company, including International Sales, United States Sales, Research and Development, and Headquarters. Each of these divisions requires its own domain for security, administration, or locations purposes. You have installed a forest of four domains: contoso.com, intlsales.contoso.com, ussales.contoso.com, and research.contoso.com. Which of these domain names is also the name of the forest?

    A. intlsales.contoso.com

    B. ussales.contoso.com

    C. research.contoso.com

    D. contoso.com

8. Litware, Inc., is a company in the midst of upgrading its Windows 2000 Active Directory domains and Windows NT 4.0 domains to Windows Server 2003 in a single-forest structure. The first domain you upgrade is the root domain named root.litwareinc.com. You upgrade every domain controller to Windows Server 2003 except for one in the root domain. The second domain you upgrade is a Windows NT 4.0 domain named LIT, which you change to lit.root.litwareinc.com. You upgrade the primary domain controller (PDC), but leave three backup domain controllers (BDCs) as Windows NT 4.0 BDCs for the time being. To which of the following domain functional levels can you raise lit.root.litwareinc.com?

    A. Windows 2000 mixed

    B. Windows 2000 native

    C. Windows Server 2003

    D. Windows Server 2003 interim

9. You have upgraded all three Windows 2000 domain controllers in the contoso.com domain to Windows Server 2003. You have upgraded one Windows NT 4.0 BDC in that domain to Windows Server 2003. You have removed all other Windows NT 4.0 BDCs from the domain, and you have installed a new Windows Server 2003 domain controller in the contoso.com domain. There are three member servers running Windows NT 4.0 and eight Windows 2000 Server member servers. Which domain functional level will offer the most functionality for the contoso.com domain?

    A. Windows Server 2003

    B. Windows Server 2003 interim

    C. Windows 2000 native

    D. Windows 2000 mixed

10. You have attempted to raise the functional level of a forest to Windows Server 2003, but you received an error. What must you check before you raise the forest functional level?

    A. Ensure that the domain functional level of every domain in the forest is at Windows Server 2003.

    B. Check that the schema master is running.

    C. Check to see if all the domain controllers are running Windows 2000 Server.

    D. Enable the global catalog for each domain controller.

11. You have two Windows Server 2003 forests on the network. The researchdev.local forest has several domains containing both users and resources. The contoso.com forest also has several domains containing both users and resources. The users in the researchdev.local forest must use applications and files that exist within various domains within the contoso.com forest. Which of the following actions must be accomplished before you can grant the users access?

    A. You must raise the forest functional level of both forests to Windows Server 2003 and then create a forest trust where the contoso.com forest trusts the researchdev.local forest.

    B. You must create explicit external trusts between the root domain within the researchdev.local forest and the root domain within the contoso.com forest.

    C. You must create a shortcut trust between two of the domains within the contoso.com forest.

    D. You must raise the forest functional level of both forests to Windows Server 2003 and then create a forest trust where the researchdev.local forest trusts the contoso.com forest.

Objective 6.2 Answers

1. **Correct Answers: C**

   A. **Incorrect:** The global catalog will not speed up access to resources; however, it will speed up the logon and query process for users.

   B. **Incorrect:** The schema master role is not involved in this process. Besides, you should never seize the schema master role if you can avoid it; however, you can transfer it.

   C. **Correct:** The shortcut trust is used within a forest to speed up resource access in forests with multiple domains and domain trees. Active Directory forests automatically include two-way, transitive trust relationships that follow the domain tree, parent to child, child to grandchild, and so on, as well as vice versa. When there are two domain trees, the trust relationship must be resolved up and down the tree before resources can be accessed. A shortcut trust reduces the time it takes to perform this process.

   D. **Incorrect:** The trusts within a forest are called shortcut trusts. Also, this trust relationship is in the opposite direction. In order for users in the sub1.child.parent.contoso.com domain to access resources in the sub8.leaf.branch.root.contoso.local domain, the sub8.leaf.branch.root.contoso.local domain must trust sub1.child.parent.contso.com.

2. **Correct Answers: A**

   A. **Correct:** Since this is a BDC of a domain that is already upgraded, it will automatically become a domain controller in an existing domain within an existing forest.

   B. **Incorrect:** If you select this option, you will have a second domain tree in the forest.

   C. **Incorrect:** If you select this option, you will have two separate forests.

   D. **Incorrect:** If you select this option, you will have a child domain below the root domain in a single domain tree in your forest.

3. **Correct Answers: C**

   A. **Incorrect:** This structure will permit the branch administrators to create and manage user objects in their own domain.

   B. **Incorrect:** This structure will not prevent the branch administrators from managing the resources in the other branch offices, nor will it prevent them from creating and managing user objects.

C. **Correct:** This structure will accomplish all the administrative goals: granting full administrative rights to the Seattle administrators, preventing branch administrators from creating and managing user objects, and allowing branch administrators to manage the resources only within their own branch.

D. **Incorrect:** This structure will not prevent the branch administrators from managing resources of other branches.

4.   Correct Answers: D

A. **Incorrect:** The Winnt command is used to install the Windows Server 2003 operating system.

B. **Incorrect:** The Ntdsutil command is used to configure aspects of Active Directory.

C. **Incorrect:** This is not a command within Windows Server 2003.

D. **Correct:** The Dcpromo.exe command is the Active Directory Installation Wizard and can be used to install a domain controller or to demote a domain controller to a member server.

5.   Correct Answers: A

A. **Correct:** The Ntdsutil command can be used to create and configure an application directory partition, which will store information for the application and prevent it from replicating outside the New York office.

B. **Incorrect:** The Winnt32 command is used to upgrade to the Windows Server 2003 operating system. The Winnt32 command will not make changes to the Active Directory configuration or to an application directory partition.

C. **Incorrect:** The Dcpromo command is used to install Active Directory. It will not configure additional application directory partitions.

D. **Incorrect:** The Active Directory Sites And Services console is used to configure the physical topology of Active Directory. However, this console is not used to create an application directory partition.

6.   Correct Answers: B

A. **Incorrect:** You will receive the same error with doma.tailspintoys.local as you did with doma.tailspintoys.com because it is the NetBIOS name, DOMA, which is the cause of the error.

B. **Correct:** The NetBIOS name is the only possible reason for a conflict because the existing network is using Windows NT, which doesn't use Domain Name System (DNS) names for domains.

C. Incorrect: The domain controller's name is not causing the conflict. In fact, you will cause a second NetBIOS name conflict by changing the name to DOMA.

D. Incorrect: The installation of the operating system did not cause the problem. When you use the same name, the NetBIOS conflict will occur with the original Windows NT 4.0 domain.

7. **Correct Answers: D**

A. Incorrect: The name of the forest is the name of the root domain, which is contoso.com because it is the top of the domain tree.

B. Incorrect: The name of the forest is the name of the root domain, which is contoso.com because it is the top of the domain tree.

C. Incorrect: The name of the forest is the name of the root domain, which is contoso.com because it is the top of the domain tree.

D. Correct: The root domain of the forest is the top of the domain tree. The root domain's name is given to the forest.

8. **Correct Answers: D**

A. Incorrect: The Windows 2000 mixed domain functional level is the default functional level for a new domain. You cannot raise the domain functional level to Windows 2000 mixed.

B. Incorrect: The Windows 2000 native domain functional level does not allow Windows NT 4.0 domain controllers. Because you will have Windows NT 4.0 BDCs along with the Windows Server 2003 domain controller, you cannot raise the domain functional level to Windows 2000 native.

C. Incorrect: The Windows Server 2003 domain functional level does not allow Windows NT 4.0 domain controllers, which lit.root.litwareinc.com still has.

D. Correct: The Windows Server 2003 interim domain functional level is intended for Windows NT 4.0 to Windows Server 2003 upgrades. A Windows Server 2003 Interim functional level allows Windows NT 4.0 BDCs and Windows Server 2003 domain controllers. The only type of domain controller that is not allowed in this situation is the Windows 2000 domain controller, but there is no Windows 2000 domain controller within the lit.root.litwareinc.com domain.

9. **Correct Answers: A**

A. Correct: When all the domain controllers within a domain are running Windows Server 2003, the domain functional level can be raised to Windows Server 2003, even though member servers use earlier operating systems.

B. Incorrect: This domain functional level is used only when a Windows NT 4.0 domain is in the process of upgrading directly to Windows Server 2003.

C. Incorrect: This domain functional level is used for domains that have both Windows 2000 and Windows Server 2003 domain controllers.

D. Incorrect: This domain functional level is the default and will accept Windows NT 4.0, Windows 2000, and Windows Server 2003 operating systems as domain controllers. However, the Windows 2000 mixed domain functional level offers the fewest number of capabilities of all the domain functional levels. A Windows Server 2003 domain functional level offers the highest level of functionality for the domain, and this is the best choice.

10.   Correct Answers: A

A. Correct: The forest functional level cannot be raised unless all domains have achieved the Windows Server 2003 domain functional level.

B. Incorrect: The schema master has nothing to do with the forest functional level.

C. Incorrect: The forest functional level cannot be raised unless all domain controllers are running Windows Server 2003 and the domain functional level of every domain is raised to Windows Server 2003.

D. Incorrect: The global catalog is not required to be installed on each domain controller for the forest's functional level to be raised.

11.   Correct Answers: A

A. Correct: The forest trust will enable you to grant permissions to access resources in the contoso.com forest to the users in the researchdev.local forest.

B. Incorrect: The explicit external trusts are not transitive, so this will not provide a way to grant access to resources.

C. Incorrect: The shortcut trust will not provide access to resources.

D. Incorrect: This trust relationship is one way and going in the wrong direction. If this trust is created, you can only grant permissions to users in the contoso.com forest to access resources in the researchdev.local forest.

27 Exam 70-296—Managing and Maintaining an Active Directory Infrastructure (7.0)

Active Directory directory service enables an administrator to easily manage the network. However, the Active Directory infrastructure itself requires some management and maintenance. In this domain we will review the skills that you need to manage a forest, domains, and sites. In addition, we will look at how to monitor replication, diagnose and resolve problems, and restore the files that make up Active Directory.

As an organization and its network evolve over time, new trust relationships might need to be added or old ones deleted. The more complex a forest is, the more likely that users will need to access resources outside their own domain. In order to accelerate access time, you might want to add shortcut trust relationships. New applications installed might extend the schema, while other network usage might result in the need for new objects or object attributes. Either way, the schema will require monitoring and management whenever you modify it. Forests also affect how users log on to the network through their user principal name (UPN), and that is another skill within the objective of managing an Active Directory forest.

Site management can be as simple or complex as you wish to make it. As the network grows, you need to monitor replication between the sites and evolve the site configuration to optimize the underlying network traffic.

Being able to recover from failures is invaluable during an emergency. Not only is restoration of Active Directory a critical component of disaster recovery, but also the ability to troubleshoot flexible single operations master failures and replication problems is a key ability for an Active Directory administrator.

Tested Skills and Suggested Practices

The skills that you need to successfully master the Managing and Maintaining an Active Directory Infrastructure objective domain on *Exam 70-296: Planning, Implementing, and Maintaining a Microsoft Windows Server 2003 Environment for an MCSE Certified on Windows 2000* include

- Manage an Active Directory forest and domain structure
  - ❑ Practice 1: Install a forest of at least one domain and raise the forest and domain functional levels to Microsoft Windows Server 2003. Log on as a

member of the Schema Admins group and view the schema in the Active Directory Schema console. Extend the schema by adding a new object type and attributes. You may also install an application (such as Microsoft Exchange 2000 Server or later) that will extend the schema. View the changes to the schema in the Active Directory Schema console. Using either the LDP utility or an Active Directory console, create a new object based on your schema extensions.

❑ Practice 2: Install a forest of at least one domain. Open the Active Directory Users And Computers console. Navigate to the Schema Admins group. View the permissions for this group. Create a user. Log on as that user and attempt to view and extend the schema using the Active Directory Schema console. Then log off. Add the user account as a member of the Schema Admins group. Log on as the user again and attempt to open the Active Directory Schema console. Extend the schema with a new object or attribute type.

❑ Practice 3: Install a forest of two domains with two different Domain Name System (DNS) names—for example, fabrikam.com and contoso.com. Change the UPN so that all users who log on to the forest will use the form user@fabrikam.com, even if those users are in the contoso.com domain.

❑ Practice 4: Install two forests with at least two domains apiece. Create a forest trust. Grant a user from a child domain in the first forest access to resources in a domain within the other forest. Log on as that user and attempt access to those resources. Then log off. Take the first forest's root domain offline. Log on and attempt to access the resources again. Document the response. View the trust relationships within the Active Directory Domains And Trusts console.

■ Restore Active Directory Services

❑ Practice 1: Install two domain controllers into the root domain of a new forest. Open Active Directory Users And Computers console and create an organizational unit (OU) hierarchy with at least one new user and group. Configure a site. Back up the first domain controller's system state data. Delete all the users, groups, and OUs that you created. Add a new site and Internet Protocol (IP) subnets. Perform a nonauthoritative restore on the first domain controller. Allow replication to take place and view the results.

❑ Practice 2: Install two domain controllers into the root domain of a new forest. Open Active Directory Users And Computers console. Create a new OU hierarchy with new users and groups. Back up the first domain controller's system state data. Delete all the users, groups, and OUs that you created. Add a new site and IP subnets. Perform an authoritative restore on that first domain controller, allow replication to take place, and view the results.

Further Reading

This section lists supplemental readings by objective. You should study these sources thoroughly before taking *Exam 70-296: Planning, Implementing, and Maintaining a Microsoft Windows Server 2003 Environment for an MCSE Certified on Windows 2000.*

Objective 7.1   Review Chapter 3, "Managing and Maintaining an Active Directory Implementation."

Microsoft Corporation. *Introducing Microsoft Windows Server 2003.* Redmond, Washington: Microsoft Press, 2003. Review Chapter 3, "Active Directory."

Microsoft Corporation. Redmond, Washington. Review "*HOW TO: Manage the Active Directory Schema in Windows Server 2003 Enterprise Edition,*" available on the Microsoft Web site at *http://support.microsoft.com/default.aspx?scid=kb;en-us;326310.*

Microsoft Corporation. Redmond, Washington. Review "*HOW TO: Create an External Trust in Windows Server 2003,*" available on the Microsoft Web site at *http://support.microsoft.com/default.aspx?scid=kb;en-us;816301.*

Objective 7.2   Review Chapter 3, Lesson 3, "Backing Up and Restoring Active Directory."

Microsoft Corporation. *Microsoft Windows Server 2003 Administrator's Pocket Consultant.* Redmond, Washington: Microsoft Press, 2003. Review Chapter 6, "Using Active Directory," and Chapter 7, "Core Active Directory Administration."

Manage an Active Directory Forest and Domain Structure

In this first objective of the Managing and Maintaining an Active Directory Infrastructure domain, you will be required to know how a forest interacts with external forests and domains. This objective also looks at the forest's schema management and user principal naming.

The structure of the Active Directory forest is incorporated into the trust relationships between domains both internal and external to the forest. You will need to know the types of trust relationships that you can create. In addition, you will need to know the process of creating, deleting, and troubleshooting trust relationships.

Trust relationships are intended to provide simplified management of resources across forests and domains. Because the domains and forests are separated, they can have unique and independent administration. Trust relationships ensure that network resources may still be used. The use of nontransitive trust relationships can ensure the security within each domain. You can use the Netdom command-line tool to manage computer accounts, domains, and trust relationships, plus you can use the Active Directory Domains And Trusts console for a graphical view of the forest and for trust management.

One of the reasons for having multiple forests is to be able to maintain separate schemas. The schema is a forest-wide component that has an impact on every component within the Active Directory infrastructure. You should familiarize yourself with the groups that have the ability to make changes to the Schema Admins group, as well as the rights of the Schema Admins group. The following groups will have forest-wide administrative control:

- Domain Admins of the forest root domain
- Enterprise Admins
- Schema Admins

One of the schema management tasks that you should be able to perform through the Active Directory Schema snap-in is adding an attribute to the global catalog. In addition, you should be able to view schema classes and schema attributes, extend the schema, and manage permissions to secure the schema.

Within Active Directory, user accounts use logon IDs that are concatenated with a UPN suffix, and the result appears to be the same as an e-mail address. For example, a user at Litware, Inc., would log on to the network as user@litwareinc.com. An administrator can establish the UPN name to be different for each domain or the same throughout the forest. By default, the UPN suffix is the DNS name of the domain in which the user account resides. To change the UPN name, you use the Active Directory Domains And Trusts console.

Objective 7.1 Questions

1.   As the administrator of Litware, Inc., you receive a call from the e-mail administrator to establish a trust relationship for the litwareinc.com domain in your Windows Server 2003 forest with a single Windows 2000 domain named mx.litwareinc.local. You open a ticket to document the call, taking down the appropriate name, account, password, and domain. The e-mail administrator wants to allow the users in your Windows Server 2003 forest to access and use mailboxes within mx.litwareinc.local, which is in its own forest. Which of the following actions do you take?

    A.   Create a forest trust between litwareinc.com and mx.litwareinc.local.

    B.   Create a shortcut trust between litwareinc.com and mx.litwareinc.local.

    C.   Create an explicit external trust such that mx.litwareinc.local trusts litwareinc.com.

    D.   Create an explicit external trust such that litwareinc.com trusts mx.litwareinc.local.

2.   Contoso, Ltd., is merging with Litware, Inc. Each of the companies has a Windows Server 2003 forest. The companies intend to complete a full merger in which Contoso will be the surviving company. Contoso's president calls you, the administrator of Litware's forest, and asks you to enable all the users within Contoso's forest to access the files and data within Litware's network. In addition, the president wishes to have all of Litware's users begin using Contoso's e-mail system, which is distributed across the domains within the contoso.com forest. What can you do to meet the president's request in the shortest time?

    A.   Check with Contoso's administrator to ensure that the contoso.com forest is at the Windows Server 2003 forest functional level. Create a forest trust between the root domains of the two forests and make certain that a trust relationship is going in both directions. Grant Contoso users access to Litware's files and data. Request that the Contoso administrator grant Litware users access to e-mail resources.

    B.   Perform a merger and migration of all users, resources, and data to the contoso.com forest.

    C.   Check with Contoso's administrator to ensure that the contoso.com domain is at the Windows Server 2003 domain functional level. Create an explicit external trust relationship where the root domain of the Litware forest trusts contoso.com. Grant Contoso users access to Litware's files and data. Request that the Contoso e-mail administrator grant Litware users access to e-mail resources.

    D.   Create an explicit external trust relationship where Litware's root domain trusts contoso.com. Create explicit external trust relationships for each of Litware's domains where they trust contoso.com. Make the contoso.com Enterprise Admins group a member of the Litware root domain's Domain Admins group.

3.   Fabrikam, Inc., has a Windows Server 2003 Active Directory forest. Fabrikam's research division has developed a custom expense application that integrates with Active Directory. They have added two new attributes to user and computer objects in the schema for this application. The application worked well in the research division's test forest, which consisted of one domain that the research division's programmers have extensively modified. However, when the application is installed in the root domain of the fabrikam.com forest, users in the sales.fabrikam.com and prod.fabrikam.com domains are unable to use the application. Which of the following actions should you take?

    A.   Using the Active Directory Schema console, add the two new attributes to the global catalog. Force replication and test the application as a user in each of the sales.fabrikam.com and prod.fabrikam.com domains.

    B.   Add the Domain Admins groups of both the sales.fabrikam.com and prod.fabrikam.com domains as members of the Schema Admins group.

    C.   Migrate all users to the fabrikam.com domain.

    D.   Create shortcut trusts between the root domain and sales.fabrikam.com and prod.fabrikam.com.

4.   You are the administrator of a Windows Server 2003 forest for Contoso, Ltd. You are going to roll out an upgrade to your Exchange Server systems, which will extend the schema. You want to test the rollout. Which would provide you with the most accurate experience, without interrupting the daily business activities?

    A.   Using the Active Directory Schema console, you extend the schema of the contoso.com forest with each of the attributes and objects listed in the *Microsoft Exchange 2000 Server Resource Kit.*

    B.   You remove a domain controller from the sales.contoso.com domain. With the domain controller disconnected from the network, you install Exchange Server to it and then return the domain controller to the production network.

    C.   Create a new domain in the forest. Install Exchange Server within the new domain.

    D.   Create a new forest that is not connected to the production network. Back up system state data from a production forest's domain controller and restore it to the test forest so that you have a close copy of the production forest's contents. Test the Exchange Server rollout on the forest.

5.   Contoso, Ltd., is merging with Litware, Inc. Each of the companies has a Windows Server 2003 forest. The companies intend to complete a full merger in which Contoso will be the surviving company. Users in the contoso.com forest currently log on to their own domains using their own IDs. Users in the litwareinc.com forest currently log on using UPNs of user@litwareinc.com. Contoso has three Mark Joneses whose IDs are mjones, each in a different domain—mjones in contoso.com, mjones in sales.contoso.com, and mjones in prod.contoso.com. The e-mail addresses used at Contoso are based on a different naming structure in which the three Mark Joneses have unique names including numbers and all ending in contoso.com. You have the following objectives:

■ Use UPN names in both forests

■ Make UPN names the same as the e-mail addresses used

You take the following actions:

1. You change the UPN name for the litwareinc.com forest to contoso.com in the Active Directory Domains And Trusts console.

2. You implement UPN names in the contoso.com forest so that all users log on as their ID@*contoso.com*.

Which of the following is correct? You have:

A. Achieved neither objective 1 nor objective 2

B. Achieved objective 1 but did not achieve objective 2

C. Did not achieve objective 1 but did achieve objective 2

D. Achieved both objective 1 and objective 2

Objective 7.1 Answers

1. **Correct Answers: C**

A. **Incorrect:** You will not be able to create a forest trust because one of the forests has a Windows 2000 domain (mx.litwareinc.local). Forest trusts can only be established between two Windows Server 2003 forests, which in turn require that all domains and domain controllers are running Windows Server 2003.

B. **Incorrect:** You will not be able to create a shortcut trust between litwareinc.com and mx.litwareinc.local because the two domains are in separate forests. A shortcut trust is created between two domains in the same forest.

C. **Correct:** The explicit external trust relationship occurs between the two domains. Since the resources are located in mx.litwareinc.local, it must trust litwareinc.com. Then the e-mail administrator can grant access to users so that they can use mail-boxes in the mx.litwareinc.local domain.

D. **Incorrect:** Even though this is the correct type of trust, the mx.litwareinc.local administrator would not be able to grant access to the mailboxes to the users in litwareinc.com because the direction of the trust is opposite what it needs to be.

2. **Correct Answers: A**

A. **Correct:** Forest trusts require both forests to be raised to the Windows Server 2003 forest functional level. A forest trust where Litware's forest trusts Contoso's forest will allow Contoso users to access files anywhere in the Litware forest. The trust where Contoso's forest trusts Litware's forest will enable the Contoso administrators to grant Litware users access to e-mail.

B. **Incorrect:** This action will produce the desired result, but it will be a very long and involved project.

C. **Incorrect:** The domain functional level isn't a factor in explicit external trust relationships. This particular trust relationship will not enable the Contoso users to access resources anywhere in the Litware forest, only those in the root domain. This trust relationship will not allow Contoso users in child domains to have any access at all to the Litware forest's resources. The trust relationship will allow no one in the Litware forest to have e-mail access.

D. **Incorrect:** Litware users would have no access to e-mail because none of the domains in the contoso.com forest trusts the domains within Litware's forest. Only the users in the contoso.com domain would be able to access Litware's files and data.

3. **Correct Answers: A**

    A. **Correct:** The Active Directory Schema snap-in is used for modifying the schema and adding attributes to the global catalog. Since there were new attributes added to the schema, the application might need to be able to query the local domain or global catalog to be able to function. Since the application works in the root domain, where it was installed, but is not able to function for users in the other domains, adding the two new attributes to the global catalog will allow the application to find those attributes when querying any part of Active Directory outside of the root domain.

    B. **Incorrect:** Adding the Domain Admins groups as members of the Schema Admins group will give those administrators the ability to make schema changes, reducing the security of the root domain. It will not enable the application for a standard user.

    C. **Incorrect:** This action might fix the problem, but it would override the reason that the child domains were created in the first place, making this a poor selection for a solution.

    D. **Incorrect:** There is already a parent-child trust between the root domain and each of these domains. A shortcut trust would be unnecessary because they are directly within the same domain tree. This would not fix the problem with the new expense application.

4. **Correct Answers: D**

    A. **Incorrect:** Manually extending the schema of the production forest can cause unanticipated problems. In addition, this option will not provide you with an accurate experience.

    B. **Incorrect:** Since the domain controller is not in the contoso.com root domain, it will likely not have the schema master role, and you would be prevented from installing Exchange Server in the first place. If you are able to install Exchange Server, after returning the domain controller to the network you run the risk of causing a problem to the production network. It is likely that there would be a schema conflict of some type.

    C. **Incorrect:** Since the new domain is in the production forest, you run the risk of interrupting daily business through Exchange Server's extension of the production forest's schema.

    D. **Correct:** When testing schema extensions of any type, you should use a nonproduction forest in order to avoid interrupting the daily activity of production forest users.

5.   **Correct Answers: B**

   A. **Incorrect:** You were able to meet objective 1 because you implemented UPN names in both forests. You did not achieve objective 2 because the users will not log on with their e-mail address naming scheme but with their IDs.

   B. **Correct:** You implemented UPN names in both forests but you did not change the naming scheme for the users to match their e-mail addresses.

   C. **Incorrect:** You did the opposite. You achieved objective 1 by implementing UPN names in both forests, but you did not achieve objective 2 because the names were not changed to match their e-mail addresses.

   D. **Incorrect:** You achieved objective 1 because you implemented the UPN names. However, you will have a conflict for the Mark Joneses because you did not achieve objective 2 in changing the naming scheme of IDs to match e-mail addresses.

Objective 7.2
Restore Active Directory

This objective focuses on the skills for restoring Active Directory. The nature of the Active Directory database is to be integral to the functions of a domain controller. Therefore, simply copying the Active Directory database files and restoring them will not effectively restore a domain controller to its former function. Instead, you must use a special backup and restore procedure.

The Windows Server 2003 Backup Or Restore Wizard, a graphical application, offers native backup for the system state data of a domain controller. The system state data includes the Active Directory database files, in addition to registry and configuration information. The Windows Server 2003 Backup application can also restore the system state data. There are three types of restoration methods:

- Primary restore
- Nonauthoritative restore
- Authoritative restore

The primary restore method is used when restoring Active Directory data on a stand-alone domain controller. This method is also used on the first domain controller you restore when you have a completely failed forest and you must restore the entire forest.

The nonauthoritative restore is also called the normal restore method. You should select this method when you have more than one domain controller on the network and you do not need to roll back changes that have been made to Active Directory. In this method, when replication takes place between the restored domain controller and other domain controllers on the network, the restored domain controller receives updates from its replication partners.

You use the authoritative restore when you need to roll back changes made to Active Directory. After an authoritative restore, replication partners will receive the restored data from the newly restored domain controllers. This restored data will override other changes and effectively roll back Active Directory.

Objective 7.2 Questions

1. You are the network administrator for A. Datum Corporation, a small company with 35 users. You have a single domain controller in your Active Directory forest. Your domain controller has had a hardware failure that is unrecoverable. You install a new domain controller. Which of the following actions do you take next?

   A. Perform an authoritative restore.

   B. Perform a primary restore.

   C. Perform a nonauthoritative restore.

   D. Install a second domain controller and replicate data.

2. A network administrator in another site calls you in a panic. While performing standard user changes using the Active Directory Users And Computers console, the administrator accidentally deleted an entire OU tree with hundreds of users in it. The administrator was connected to a domain controller named JAK003, and as soon as he realized his error, he disconnected JAK003 from the network. Replication has not taken place, and you have verified that fact. What do you advise the administrator to do?

   A. Perform a nonauthoritative restore on JAK003 and then reconnect JAK003 to the network so that replication can take place.

   B. Perform a primary restore.

   C. Perform an authoritative restore on JAK003 and then reconnect JAK003 to the network so that replication can take place.

   D. Reinstall the operating system on JAK003.

3. You are the network administrator for the A. Datum Corporation network. There are six domain controllers, named DC01 through DC06 in order of original installation, in the only domain of its Windows Server 2003 forest. One of the programmers in the research department was made a member of the Domain Admins group and then granted herself membership in the Schema Admins group. After that, the programmer developed a new application that was intended to integrate into Active Directory and extend the forest's schema. When the programmer tested the application, it corrupted the schema and the entire forest failed. What do you do to recover from this situation? (Choose all that apply.)

   A. Perform an authoritative restore of DC01.

   B. Perform a primary restore of DC01.

   C. Perform a primary restore of DC02 through DC06.

   D. Perform nonauthoritative restores of DC02 through DC06.

4.   You are the network administrator of a small network consisting of two sites: Dallas and Boise. Each site has two domain controllers that have full backups performed each Monday and Thursday. On Monday morning you arrive at work to a full voice mailbox and urgent messages stating that no one can log on to the network. You discover that the OU for your site, Dallas, has completely disappeared from the Active Directory Users And Computers console. You contact the Boise administrator and discover that he accidentally deleted the OU last Friday, but when there were no complaints, he figured the OU was not used, so he didn't report the change to you. How do you recover from this error?

> **A.** Perform a primary restore of Thursday's backup on one of your domain controllers.
>
> **B.** Perform an authoritative restore of last Monday's backup on one of your domain controllers.
>
> **C.** Perform a nonauthoritative restore of last Thursday's backup on one of your domain controllers.
>
> **D.** Perform an authoritative restore of last Thursday's backup on one of your domain controllers.

5.   You receive a call from a network administrator in the Los Angeles location. You are in Redmond. The administrator wants the system state data restored on a domain controller that suffered a hardware failure. The administrator has never performed a restore before and asks you to perform the restoration remotely. What do you advise the administrator?

> **A.** An administrator can restore the system state data remotely, but only as a primary restore.
>
> **B.** An administrator can restore the system state data remotely, but only in a nonauthoritative restore.
>
> **C.** The administrator must perform the restore of system state data locally in a nonauthoritative restore.
>
> **D.** The administrator must perform an authoritative restore of system state data locally.

Objective 7.2 Answers

1.   Correct Answers: B

> **A. Incorrect:** The authoritative restore is used for rolling back changes that were made to Active Directory.
>
> **B. Correct:** The primary restore is used to restore a stand-alone domain controller or the first domain controller in the restoration of an entire forest.
>
> **C. Incorrect:** Nonauthoritative restores are used when restoring a domain controller that will then receive further updates from replication partners.
>
> **D. Incorrect:** Without restoring the data to the first domain controller, there would be nothing to replicate.

2.   Correct Answers: A

> **A. Correct:** The nonauthoritative restore will restore the data to an older date on JAK003. When JAK003 is reconnected to the network, updates from other domain controllers will bring JAK003 to their own level.
>
> **B. Incorrect:** The primary restore is used only to restore a stand-alone domain controller or the first domain controller in the restoration of an entire forest. JAK003 is neither a stand-alone nor the first domain controller in the forest.
>
> **C. Incorrect:** Normally, you would perform an authoritative restore on a domain controller when you need to roll back changes made by accident. However, since JAK003 was disconnected before replication was able to take place, an authoritative restore would roll back other changes, and it is not necessary in this case.
>
> **D. Incorrect:** This is a drastic measure to take when you can perform a restore. Plus, if you reinstall the operating system without formatting the disk, the domain controller's former information might still be intact and could replicate throughout the network.

3.   Correct Answers: B and D

> **A. Incorrect:** You will need to perform a primary restore of the first domain controller of the forest, follow with nonauthoritative restores of the remaining domain controllers, and then allow replication to take place.
>
> **B. Correct:** The primary restore is used to restore a stand-alone domain controller or the first domain controller in the restoration of an entire forest, of which DC01 would be the first in the forest.

C. **Incorrect:** DC02 through DC06 would not be the first domain controllers to be recovered in the forest, so they are not candidates for a primary restore.

D. **Correct:** The nonauthoritative restores of DC02 through DC06 would follow the primary restore of DC01.

4.   Correct Answers: D

A. **Incorrect:** You are not recovering a stand-alone server or the first domain controller in a forest, so you would not select a primary restore.

B. **Incorrect:** In selecting Monday's backup, you would be losing three days' worth of Active Directory changes.

C. **Incorrect:** Nonauthoritative restores are used when restoring a domain controller. The domain controller would then receive updates from replication partners and the OU would disappear upon replication.

D. **Correct:** The authoritative restore will roll back the changes made to Active Directory to last Thursday, which is the most recent version of Active Directory backed up before the OU was deleted. The authoritative nature of the backup will force those changes to be accepted by the other domain controllers when replication next takes place.

5.   Correct Answers: C

A. **Incorrect:** An administrator cannot restore system state data remotely in any type of restoration.

B. **Incorrect:** An administrator cannot restore system state data remotely.

C. **Correct:** Since an administrator cannot perform the restore process remotely for system state data, you advise the administrator in Los Angeles to perform a nonauthoritative restore of the system state data. Nonauthoritative restores are used when restoring a domain controller that will then receive further updates from replication partners.

D. **Incorrect:** Since there is no need to roll back changes to Active Directory, you do not need to have the administrator perform an authoritative restore.

28 Exam 70-296—Planning and Implementing User, Computer, and Group Strategies (8.0)

In this domain we will review the skills required for planning and implementing security strategies related to user, computer, and group objects within Active Directory directory service. Users, computers, and groups affect the way that each user interacts with the network. The strategy that you employ will establish authentication, institute password policies, organize user objects for administration, and apply group policies.

You might consider a network to be in the form of a target of three concentric circles. The bull's-eye consists of the backbone and key systems, including directory services, secure servers, and infrastructure equipment that interconnect all the rest of the network. This is the heart of the network and should be given the highest level of security. Unauthorized access to this level of the network can disable the entire network. The next layer of the network consists mainly of the systems that provide admission to the network and share files, printers, applications, services, and other network resources. This layer requires the next highest level of security. The outer layer of the target consists of the network systems that are actually used by end users. This is the layer that provides the initial access to the network. It is this set of systems, not to mention the group and user objects that you will be creating for the initial security strategy, that will either restrict or enable access to the inner layers of the network.

You have to balance the rights and permissions granted to users with the needs and objectives of the organization. Keep in mind that when users have more rights and permissions than necessary, the network's overall security is jeopardized. Backbone systems can be penetrated and misused. By contrast, when users have fewer rights and permissions than necessary, they will not be productive. They will either have no access to the resources that enable them to do their jobs, or they will have partial access that prevents them from completing tasks.

There are two ways to organize user and computer objects so that you can apply security. You can use organizational units (OUs) to create a hierarchy that houses user, group, and computer objects, among others. You can also employ security group objects to categorize user objects for the purpose of assigning permissions. Both methods are useful in combination for applying security.

Tested Skills and Suggested Practices

The skills that you need to successfully master the Planning and Implementing User, Computer, and Group Strategies objective domain on *Exam 70-296: Planning, Implementing, and Maintaining a Microsoft Windows Server 2003 Environment for an MCSE Certified on Windows 2000* include

- Plan a user authentication strategy

  ❑ Practice 1: Install two different forests. Create a forest trust between the forests. Create a user in Forest 1 named Test. On a computer in Forest 2, attempt to log on to the network as the user Test using the user principal name (UPN) form of the user's ID. Log off and attempt to log on as Test with the standard form of the user's ID.

  ❑ Practice 2: Install a forest of at least two domains. Create a user named Test in the root domain. Log on to a computer in the child domain with the Test account using the UPN form of the user's ID. Log off and attempt to log on as Test with the standard form of the user's ID.

  ❑ Practice 3: Install a forest of at least one domain. Install certification authority services. Enable and configure authentication for smart cards. Install smart card authentication equipment. Create a user named Test and attempt to log on using the smart card.

Further Reading

This section contains a list of supplemental readings divided by objective. If you think you need additional preparation before taking the exam, study these sources thoroughly.

Objective 8.1   Review Chapter 4, "Managing Users, Groups, and Computers."

Microsoft Corporation. *Microsoft Windows Server 2003 Deployment Kit, A Microsoft Resource Kit.* Volume: *Designing and Deploying Directory and Security Services.* Redmond, Washington: Microsoft Press, 2003. Read Chapter 3, "Designing a Site Topology." This information can also be found on the Microsoft Web site at *http://www.microsoft.com/windowsserver2003/techinfo/reskit/deploykit.mspx.*

Microsoft Corporation. *Microsoft Windows Server 2003 Administrator's Pocket Consultant.* Redmond, Washington: Microsoft Press, 2003. Review Chapter 9, "Creating User and Group Accounts," specifically the section "Configuring Account Policies."

Plan a User Authentication Strategy

This objective discusses how to plan authentication for users within the network. Authentication is the process of ensuring the identity of a person or other entity and applies to smart cards and password management. User and computer objects in Active Directory correspond to users and computers that interact with the network. Since groups are granted rights that apply to other objects, they are classified along with user and computer objects as security principals. A security principal within the Active Directory domain is given a security identifier (SID) at its creation so that its identity can be authenticated.

When you plan your user authentication strategy, you need to consider the organization's requirements. For example, users should have individual accounts and passwords in order to maintain security. After a user is authenticated, the user should be able to access resources and administer other resources according to its rights and permissions either assigned individually or received through group memberships.

When you no longer need a user account, a best practice is to disable the account for a period of time, such as for six months. If the account is not needed within that period of time, you can delete it. This practice will ensure that you will not need to perform an authoritative restore of old objects in case another user requires the same authority.

Smart card authentication uses certificates during logon to authenticate the credentials of the person logging on to the network. During the smart card authentication process, a certificate (which includes a digital signature from a certification authority, or CA) is presented to the server and the server responds with its own certificate. Each computer (the local workstation and the server) can then trust the other. A smart card stores the certificate.

Objective 8.1 Questions

1. You are the network administrator for Contoso, Ltd. You have three locations: New Orleans, Houston, and Toronto, with users from two domains, contoso.com and finance.contoso.com, spanning them. Each location is configured as a separate site. You want to deploy smart cards to the Toronto location but do not want to deploy smart cards to either New Orleans or Houston. Which actions should you take?

    A. Create two OUs and apply the policy to the OUs.

    B. Apply one policy to contoso.com and the other to finance.contoso.com.

    C. Apply a policy to a local group.

    D. Apply a policy for smart card authentication to the Toronto site.

2. Litware, Inc., has had several network attacks where a hacker was able to log on to the network and access resources. You have been hired as a consultant to help Litware prevent future attacks. When you review the current network policy, you see that all users are required to change their passwords every 10 days, with a minimum password length of six characters. There are no other policies. Which of the following will best verify a user's identity at logon?

    A. Require smart card authentication at logon.

    B. Create a maximum password age of five days.

    C. Create a minimum password age of 20 days.

    D. Apply a minimum password length of five characters.

3. You have a user who insists on using the same password every time he changes his password on the network. You require users to change passwords once every 90 days. When you enforce password history for five passwords, the user immediately changes his password five times and then changes it back to the original password. How can you make certain that the user uses unique passwords?

    A. Establish a maximum password age of 30 days.

    B. Establish a minimum password age of 30 days.

    C. Establish a minimum password length of seven characters.

    D. Establish an Account Lockout policy.

4. You are installing smart cards for users in a domain. You install a certification authority (CA) and create smart cards for all users. You distribute the cards to users and install equipment. However, you discover that users are able to log on without the smart cards. What can you do?

    A. Create another smart card enrollment station.

    B. Establish an Account Lockout policy.

    C. Select the option in the user account for Smart Card Is Required For Interactive Logon.

    D. Create a universal group and add all smart card users to it.

5. Fabrikam, Inc., has a network with a single Active Directory forest consisting of two domains. In the root domain the administrator has installed a new application for the Accounting group. This application integrates with Active Directory in order to ensure that only authenticated users are able to use the application. The application uses a special user account to log on to Active Directory. Both domains have a password policy that enforces a maximum password age of 60 days, enforces complexity requirements, and requires a minimum password length of seven characters. Which of the following options should be applied to this application's user account?

    A. A Minimum Password Age of 10 days

    B. Do Not Require Kerberos Preauthentication

    C. Password Never Expires

    D. User Cannot Change Password

6. Contoso Pharmaceuticals has several pharmacies, a warehouse, and a research facility. There is a single domain, contoso.com, in the forest. You have the following objectives:

Primary objective: Ensure that all users in the Research facility have strong passwords.

Secondary objective: Create user accounts to be used by kiosks in the pharmacies that will not be able to have their passwords changed by anyone but administrators.

You take the following actions:

    1. You apply a password policy to the domain that includes the OU created to contain all users at the Research facility. The policy enforces complexity requirements, has a maximum password age of 30 days and a minimum password age of 3 days, and requires a password history of six passwords.

    2. You create a user account that will be used by all kiosks. You select the options for Password Never Expires and User Cannot Change Password on the user account.

    3. You place the kiosk user account in an OU that can be managed only by members of the Domain Admins group.

After performing these actions, you have achieved which of the following?

    A. You have achieved neither the primary nor the secondary objectives.

    B. You have achieved the primary objective but not the secondary objective.

    C. You have achieved the secondary objective but not the primary objective.

    D. You have achieved both the primary and the secondary objectives.

7. You work for Contoso, a small company that makes computer equipment for space launches. The company has a single domain named contoso.com. The company has facilities at a five-building campus out in the suburbs. Each department is housed in its own building. Each building on the company campus has its own separate logical subnet. The software development department has submitted a proposal to your office that they be exempted from the current company password policy. They want to change the policy so that instead of having to change their passwords once a week they only have to change them once every 28 days. They would also like the password history altered from the last 10 passwords to the last 6. The current password policy is specified in the default domain Group Policy Object (GPO). Your manager has asked you to look into the feasibility of granting the software development department's request. Which of the following correctly describes how this request could be implemented?

    A. That a separate site can be configured based on the TCP/IP subnet of the software development department's building. A group policy can be created and applied to this site that changes the password history to 6 and the maximum password age to 28 days. This policy must be set to No Override.

    B. That all of the user accounts from the software development department be moved into an especially created OU called SOFTDEV. A group policy can be created and applied to this OU that changes the password history to 6 and the maximum password age to 28 days. This policy must be set to Block Inheritance.

    C. Create a global security group named SOFTDEV and add all of the users from the software development department to this group. Edit the group properties and set the password history to 6 and the maximum password age to 28 days.

    D. Create a new child domain named softdev.contoso.com. Move all of the user and computer accounts from the software development department from the contoso.com domain to this new child domain. Edit the child domain's default GPO and set the password history to 6 and the maximum password age to 28 days.

8. You are the network administrator for Tailspin Toys. Tailspin Toys has a Microsoft Windows Server 2003 forest consisting of the following domains. The root domain is tailspintoys.com and the child domains are northamerica.tailspintoys.com, pacific.tailspintoys.com, europe.tailspintoys.com, and asia.tailspintoys.com. The default domain GPO for the root domain has been set with the following password policies:

Enforce Password History: 10 passwords remembered. Maximum Password Age: 20 days. Minimum Password Length: 7 characters.

The default domain GPO for the child domain pacific.tailspintoys.com has the following password policies:

Enforce Password History: 15 passwords remembered. Maximum Password Age: 25 days. Minimum Password Length: 9 characters.

The default domain GPO for the child domain asia.tailspintoys.com has the following password policies:

Enforce Password History: 20 passwords remembered. Maximum Password Age: 32 days. Minimum Password Length: 5 characters.

Given this information, which of the following statements are true? (Choose all that apply.)

A. That users in the asia.tailspintoys.com will have to change their password every 20 days.

B. That users in the pacific.tailspintoys.com domain will have to have passwords with nine or more characters.

C. That users in the tailspintoys.com domain will have a history stored of their last 15 passwords.

D. That users in the asia.tailspintoys.com domain will have a maximum password age of 32 days.

9. Wingtip Toys, a manufacturer of high-performance remote control dirigibles, has a Windows Server 2003 forest containing over 50 domains. The root domain is wingtiptoys.com. A particular tree in the forest contains the domains australia.wingtiptoys.com and its child domain melbourne.australia.wingtiptoys.com.

The root domain wingtiptoys.com has the following password policies applied in the default domain GPO:

A. Maximum Password Age: 42 days. Minimum Password Age: 1 day. Minimum Password Length: 7 characters.

The domain australia.wingtiptoys.com has the following password policies applied in the default domain GPO:

Maximum Password Age: 21 days. Minimum Password Age: 0 days. Minimum Password Length: 10 characters.

The domain melbourne.australia.wingtiptoys.com has the following password policies applied to the default domain GPO:

Maximum Password Age: 11 days. Minimum Password Age: 5 days. Minimum Password Length: 12 characters.

The forest is running at the Windows Server 2003 functional level. Oksana has a user account located in the melbourne.australia.wingtiptoys.com domain. This account has been added to a universal group created in the australia.wingtiptoys.com domain. Which of the following statements about the account is true?

A. Oksana must change her password every 11 days.

B. Oksana must change her password every 21 days.

C. The minimum length of Oksana's password is 11 characters.

D. Oksana does not have to wait to change her password once it has been changed.

10. The Windows Server 2003 domain at Fourth Coffee's organizational unit and policy structure has been configured in the following manner: The alpha OU is a child OU of the gamma OU. The beta OU is a child OU of the delta OU. The default domain GPO has the following settings: Interactive Logon: Require smart card [Enabled] and Interactive Logon: Smart card removal behavior: [Force Logoff]. Four other GPOs are in use throughout the domain. They have the following properties:

GPO DVA: Interactive Logon: Require smart card [Disabled], Interactive Logon: Smart card removal behavior: [Lock Workstation]

GPO TRI: Interactive Logon: Require smart card [Enabled], Interactive Logon: Smart card removal behavior: [Not Defined]

GPO OKS: Interactive Logon: Require smart card [Disabled], Interactive Logon: Smart card removal behavior: [Force Logoff]

GPO OZA: Interactive Logon: Require smart card [Enabled], Interactive Logon: Smart card removal behavior: [No Action]

Rooslan's user account is a member of the beta OU. Oksana's user account is a member of the alpha OU. GPO DVA has been applied to the alpha OU, GPO TRI has been applied to the beta OU, GPO OKS has been applied to the gamma OU, and GPO OZA has been applied to the delta OU.

Given this information, which of the following statements is true?

A. Oksana requires a smart card to log on to her Windows XP Professional workstation.

B. Rooslan requires a smart card to log on to his Windows XP Professional workstation.

C. If Oksana removes her smart card while using her Windows XP Professional work-station, she will be automatically logged off.

D. If Rooslan removes his smart card while using his Windows XP Professional work-station, he will automatically be logged off.

11. You are the administrator of the melbourne.wingtiptoys.com domain. Your domain has three sites located in the suburbs of Waverley, Essendon, and Cheltenham. Each of these sites has a corresponding site located in Active Directory. You have been gradually rolling out smart card authentication across the organization. Rooslan has a user account in the Technicians OU and Oksana has a user account in the Managers OU. Both have Windows XP Professional laptops with built-in smart card readers. Both travel to all three sites on a regular basis. The following group policies have been configured:

GPO ICH: Interactive Logon: Require smart card [Enabled], Interactive Logon: Smart card removal behavior: [Lock Workstation]

GPO NIH: Interactive Logon: Require smart card [Enabled], Interactive Logon: Smart card removal behavior: [Force Logoff]

GPO SAN: Interactive Logon: Require smart card [Disabled], Interactive Logon: Smart card removal behavior: [No Action]

GPO CHI: Interactive Logon: Require smart card [Disabled], Interactive Logon: Smart card removal behavior: [Not Defined]

GPO GOH: Interactive Logon: Require smart card [Not Defined], Interactive Logon: Smart card removal behavior: [Force Logoff]

GPO RUK: Interactive Logon: Require smart card [Not Defined], Interactive Logon: Smart card removal behavior: [Lock Workstation]

GPO ICH has been applied to the Waverley site, GPO NIH to the Essendon site, and GPO SAN to the Cheltenham site. GPO CHI has been applied to the Technicians OU, and GPO GOH has been applied to the managers OU. Given this information, which of the following statements are true? (Choose all that apply.)

A. When Oksana removes the smart card from her laptop's reader at the Waverley site, she is automatically logged off.

B. When Rooslan removes the smart card from his laptop's reader at the Essendon site, he is automatically logged off.

C. Oksana needs her smart card to log on when she is at the Cheltenham site.

D. Rooslan needs his smart card to log on when he is at the Waverley site.

12. You are planning a user authentication strategy for your new domain, wingtiptoys.com. Your domain has two sites, Essendon and Waverley. In planning the strategy, you have the following primary goal: accounts should be locked out after five failed logon attempts for 100 minutes. Your secondary goal for the authentication strategy is that the last 20 passwords should be remembered, that users should have to wait at least 48 hours after changing a password to change it again, and that passwords should be stored using reversible encryption. Which of the following would achieve both your primary and secondary goals?

A. Edit the default domain GPO for the wingtiptoys.com domain. Set the Enforce Password History policy to 20 passwords remembered. Set the Maximum Password Age policy to 48 hours. Set the Store Passwords Using Reversible Encryption policy to enabled. Set the Account Lockout Duration policy to 100 minutes and set the Account Lockout Threshold policy to five invalid logon attempts.

B. Create a GPO named AUTHSTRAT. Set the Enforce Password History policy to 20 passwords remembered. Set the Maximum Password Age policy to 48 hours. Set the Store Passwords Using Reversible Encryption policy to enabled. Set the Account Lockout Duration policy to 100 minutes and set the Account Lockout Threshold policy to five invalid logon attempts. Apply the AUTHSTRAT GPO to the Waverley and Essendon sites.

C. Create a GPO named AUTHSTRAT. Set the Enforce Password History policy to 20 passwords remembered. Set the Minimum Password Age policy to 48 hours. Set the Store Passwords Using Reversible Encryption policy to enabled. Set the Account Lockout Duration policy to 100 minutes and set the Account Lockout Threshold policy to five invalid logon attempts. Apply the AUTHSTRAT GPO to the Waverley and Essendon sites.

D. Edit the default domain GPO for the wingtiptoys.com domain. Set the Enforce Password History policy to 20 passwords remembered. Set the Minimum Password Age policy to 48 hours. Set the Store Passwords Using Reversible Encryption policy to enabled. Set the Account Lockout Duration policy to 100 minutes and set the Account Lockout Threshold policy to five invalid logon attempts. Apply the AUTHSTRAT GPO to the Waverley and Essendon sites.

Objective 8.1 Answers

1.   Correct Answers: D

   A.   Incorrect: Since there are two domains, you would have to configure the OU structure to match the site structure within the domains and then apply Group Policy to it. Given that this may not equate to the administrative or other requirements for the organization, this is not the appropriate action to take.

   B.   Incorrect: The policies would affect users from outside the Toronto location, requiring them to use smart card authentication when they don't need to.

   C.   Incorrect: You cannot apply a policy to a local group.

   D.   Correct: By applying the policy to the Toronto site, users will receive the correct smart card authentication policy regardless of the domain to which they belong.

2.   Correct Answers: A

   A.   Correct: Smart card authentication will require that the hacker has a smart card in addition to a user's password in order to log on.

   B.   Incorrect: The current maximum password age is 10 days, which is at the point of being difficult to manage for users. You would not get much value from changing the maximum password age to five days.

   C.   Incorrect: Making the minimum password age longer than the maximum password age will not allow users to change passwords on time.

   D.   Incorrect: This minimum password length is shorter than the minimum password length previously created, so it will not add much.

3.   Correct Answers: B

   A.   Incorrect: The user would still be able to change his password back to the original one because this will require users to change passwords only every 30 days instead of every 90 days.

   B.   Correct: This policy will make the user use the new password for at least 30 days before he can change the password again.

   C.   Incorrect: If the user is using a password that contains fewer than seven characters, this would make the user change to a new password, but only one time. The user could easily repeat the same process with a new password.

   D.   Incorrect: The Account Lockout policy will only lock out users who use the wrong password, and the user would still be able to change passwords back to the original password.

4. **Correct Answers: C**

A. Incorrect: This will only duplicate the work that you've done so far. An enrollment station will only allow you to set up a new smart card, but not to force its use.

B. Incorrect: An Account Lockout policy is not required for smart card usage.

C. Correct: This will require a user to use the smart card to log on to the network. Without selecting this option, the user will be able to log on without a smart card.

D. Incorrect: There is no need in this situation to create a universal group for smart card users.

5. **Correct Answers: C**

A. Incorrect: You cannot assign a special policy such as Minimum Password Age to a user account.

B. Incorrect: Since the application integrates with Active Directory, it probably uses the same version of Kerberos. There is no need in this case to select this option.

C. Correct: As long as you select a password with sufficient length and complexity, you should make certain the password does not expire so that the application can continue to use the user account without interruption.

D. Incorrect: This option will not prevent the Maximum Password Age policy from interrupting the application. However, this might be an additional option to select to ensure that the user account doesn't change the password.

6. **Correct Answers: D**

A. Incorrect: You have achieved both the primary and the secondary objectives, because the users at the Research facility (along with all the other users in the domain) will be given a stronger password policy, and the kiosks will use a single user account that can be managed only by Domain Admins.

B. Incorrect: You have achieved both the primary and the secondary objectives, because the users at the Research facility (along with all the other users in the domain) will be given a stronger password policy, and the kiosks will use a single user account that can be managed only by Domain Admins.

C. Incorrect: You have achieved both the primary and the secondary objectives, because the users at the Research facility (along with all the other users in the domain) will be given a stronger password policy, and the kiosks will use a single user account that can be managed only by Domain Admins.

D. Correct: You have achieved both the primary and the secondary objectives, because the users at the Research facility (along with all the other users in the domain) will be given a stronger password policy, and the kiosks will use a single user account that can be managed only by Domain Admins.

7. **Correct Answers: D**

A. **Incorrect:** Password policies can be set only at the domain level. Although it would appear from the Group Policy Editor that this task can be accomplished through a GPO applied to a site or OU, the default domain GPO controls the password policy in the domain.

B. **Incorrect:** Password policies can be set only at the domain level. Although it would appear from the Group Policy Editor that this task can be accomplished through a GPO applied to a site or OU, the default domain GPO controls the password policy in the domain.

C. **Incorrect:** Password policies can be set only at the domain level. Password policies cannot be set by editing the properties of a security group.

D. **Correct:** Password policies can be set only at the domain level. To achieve a different password policy for a group of users within an organization it is necessary to create a separate domain for them.

8. **Correct Answers: B and D**

A. **Incorrect:** Even though the domains are in a relationship through a forest, the password policy for each forest is independent of the parent or root domain. The asia.tailspintoys.com default domain GPO will specify the password policy, which means that users will have to change their password every 32 days.

B. **Correct:** Even though the domains are in a relationship through a forest, the password policy for each forest is independent of the parent or root domain. The pacific.tailspintoys.com domain has a minimum password length of nine characters, hence this statement is true.

C. **Incorrect:** Even though it is the root domain, the same rules apply. The default domain GPO is set with a password history of 10, which means that only the last 10, rather than 15, passwords will be remembered.

D. **Correct:** Even though the domains are in a relationship through a forest, the password policy for each forest is independent of the parent or root domain. The asia.tailspintoys.com domain has a maximum password age policy of 32 days.

9. **Correct Answers: A**

A. **Correct:** Even though her account is a member of a universal group, this does not influence the fact that the domain in which her account is stored is the one whose password policies will be followed. Her home domain has a maximum password age of 11 days.

B. **Incorrect:** Even though her account is a member of a universal group, this does not influence the fact that the domain in which her account is stored is the one whose password policies will be followed. Her home domain has a maximum password age of 11 days.

C. Incorrect: Even though her account is a member of a universal group, this does not influence the fact that the domain in which her account is stored is the one whose password policies will be followed. Her home domain has a minimum character length of 12, not 11, characters.

D. Incorrect: Even though her account is a member of a universal group, this does not influence the fact that the domain in which her account is stored is the one whose password policies will be followed. Her home domain has a minimum password age of 5 days.

10.   Correct Answers: B

A. Incorrect: GPO DVA, which applies to the alpha OU in which Oksana's user account resides, does not have a policy set that requires smart cards. Unless otherwise specified, the OU that the account is a member of overrides the domain and parent OU settings.

B. Correct: GPO TRI, which applies to the beta OU in which Rooslan's user account resides, does have a policy set which requires smart cards. Unless otherwise specified, the OU that the account is a member of overrides the domain and parent OU settings.

C. Incorrect: GPO DVA, which applies to the alpha OU in which Oksana's user account resides, has a policy that locks the workstation, rather than forcing a logoff. Unless otherwise specified, the OU that the account is a member of overrides the domain and parent OU settings.

D. Incorrect: Although GPO TRI applies to the beta OU in which Rooslan's user account resides, it does not have a policy setting configured for the smart card removal policy. The parent OU of the beta OU, the delta OU, has the OZA GPO applied. The OZA GPO specifies that no action should be taken when the smart card is removed.

11.   **Correct Answers: A and B**

    A. Correct: OU always overrides site policy unless no policy has been set at the OU level. GPO GOH applies to Oksana's user account and is set to force logoff if the smart card is removed.

    B. Correct: OU always overrides site policy unless no policy has been set at the OU level. GPO CHI applies to Rooslan's user account; however, no policy is defined for smart card removal. This means that the site policy holds sway (assuming no domain policy). GPO NIH applies to the Essendon site and forces a logoff if the smart card is removed.

    C. Incorrect: OU always overrides site policy unless no policy has been set at the OU level. GPO GOH applies to Oksana's user account; however, no policy has been applied with respect to smart card logins. GPO SAN applies to the Cheltenham site and does not require that a smart card be used to log in.

    D. Incorrect: OU always overrides site policy unless no policy has been set at the OU level. GPO CHI applies to Rooslan's user account; however, this GPO does not require that a smart card be used to log in.

12.   **Correct Answers: D**

    A. Incorrect: Although the default domain GPO is the area that should be addressed, answer A does not set the minimum password age to 48 hours, but the maximum password age to 48 hours.

    B. Incorrect: Password policy is set at the domain rather than the site level. This answer also sets the maximum, rather than minimum, password age to 48 hours.

    C. Incorrect: Password policy is set at the domain rather than the site level. If this were carried out, the default domain settings for these policies would still be in use in the wingtiptoys.com domain.

    D. Correct: Password policy must be set at the domain level by editing the default domain GPO. Only this answer edits the correct GPO and applies the correct policy settings as well.

29 Exam 70-296—Planning and Implementing Group Policy (9.0)

This objective domain reviews the knowledge and proficiency that you must have in planning and implementing Group Policy Objects (GPOs) throughout an Active Directory directory service network. Group Policy is an administrative tool that can manage users, computers, and domain controllers. Through sets of rules that you establish and apply to domains, sites, and organizational units (OUs), Group Policy enables you to manage detailed aspects of security, desktop configuration, software delivery, and the user environment.

One way in which Group Policy can be utilized is found in IntelliMirror. IntelliMirror takes advantage of a subset of Group Policy capabilities in order to provide a fully managed user environment. IntelliMirror enables users who roam around a network to have the same environment regardless of the computers they use. By establishing user preferences, providing software applications, and folder redirection, a user will have all the tools required no matter where the user logs on.

Tested Skills and Suggested Practices

The skills that you need to successfully master the Planning and Implementing Group Policy objective domain on *Exam 70-296: Planning, Implementing, and Maintaining a Microsoft Windows Server 2003 Environment for an MCSE Certified on Windows 2000* include

- Plan Group Policy strategy.
    - ❑ Practice 1: Install a domain controller within a root domain of a forest. Create an OU structure and add various GPOs with a variety of settings to several of the OU levels. In some OUs, add multiple GPOs. Create a user object in one of the OUs. Add the Resultant Set of Policy (RSoP) snap-in to the Microsoft Management Console (MMC) and begin the Resultant Set Of Policy Wizard to create a query in planning mode. Examine the policies applied to the user account you created.
    - ❑ Practice 2: Using the same OU structure in Practice 1, create a computer object in one of the OUs. Add the RSoP snap-in to the MMC and begin the Resultant Set Of Policy Wizard to create a query in planning mode. Examine the policies applied to the computer account you created.

❑ Practice 3: Using an imaginary organization, design a Group Policy structure for a nested OU structure in which the administrative and security policies are applicable to everyone except the administrators and in which three groups require different forms of folder redirection and distributed software.

■ Configure the user environment by using Group Policy.

❑ Practice 1: Using the Active Directory Users And Computers console on a domain controller, create an OU called Distribute. Add a GPO to Distribute that includes a policy for distributing the Terminal Services client to users in the Distribute OU. Create an OU within Distribute named Sub and then create a user within Sub named Testsw. Make certain Testsw has the rights to read the GPO and access the share with the Terminal Services client software. Log on as Testsw and document your results.

❑ Practice 2: Using the Active Directory Sites And Services console, create a GPO for your site. Configure the GPO to redirect the My Documents folder to a network share. Log on to a network workstation in that site as a user in that site and test whether the folder was redirected.

❑ Practice 3: Install a certification authority (CA) server. Using the Active Directory Users And Computers console, create an OU named Cert. Create a GPO for Cert that automatically enrolls user certificates and prompts the user during enrollment. Add a user to the Cert OU and then log on. Note your results.

Further Reading

This section lists supplemental readings by objective. You should study these sources thoroughly before taking *Exam 70-296: Planning, Implementing, and Maintaining a Microsoft Windows Server 2003 Environment for an MCSE Certified on Windows 2000*.

Objective 9.1   Review Lesson 2 in Chapter 5, "Planning, Implementing, and Troubleshooting Group Policy."

Microsoft Corporation. *Introducing Microsoft Windows Server 2003*. Redmond, Washington: Microsoft Press, 2003. Review Chapter 3, "Active Directory."

Microsoft Corporation. *Microsoft Windows Server 2003 Deployment Kit, A Microsoft Resource Kit*. Redmond, Washington: Microsoft Press, 2003. Under "Designing a Managed Environment," read Chapter 1, "Planning a Managed Environment" and Chapter 2, "Designing a Group Policy Infrastructure." This volume can also be found on the Microsoft Web site at *http://www.microsoft.com /windowsserver2003/techinfo/reskit/deploykit.mspx*.

Microsoft Corporation. Redmond, Washington. Review "Technical Overview of Windows Server 2003 Management Services," available on the Microsoft Web site at *http://www.microsoft.com/windowsserver2003/techinfo/overview/mgmtsrvcs.mspx.*

Microsoft Corporation. Redmond, Washington. Review "Introduction to Group Policy in Windows Server 2003," available on the Microsoft Web site at *http://www.microsoft.com/windowsserver2003/techinfo/overview/gpintro.mspx.*

Objective 9.2   Review Lesson 2 in Chapter 5, "Planning, Implementing, and Troubleshooting Group Policy"; and Lesson 2 in Chapter 6, "Managing the User Environment with Group Policy."

Microsoft Corporation. *Microsoft Windows Server 2003 Deployment Kit, A Microsoft Resource Kit.* Redmond, Washington: Microsoft Press, 2003. Under "Designing a Managed Environment," read Chapter 7, "Implementing User State Management." This volume can also be found on the Microsoft Web site at *http://www.microsoft.com/windowsserver2003/techinfo/reskit/deploykit.mspx.*

Microsoft Corporation. Redmond, Washington. Review "HOW TO: Install and Use RSoP in Windows Server 2003," available on the Microsoft Web site at *http://support.microsoft.com/default.aspx?scid=kb;en-us;323276.*

Plan Group Policy Strategy

This objective concentrates on the planning for Group Policy in Active Directory. Planning is a process that takes place both at the installation of Active Directory and as an ongoing response to expected changes made to the network. Networks are dynamic entities changing in response to organizational changes. Part of the planning process requires you to understand how the current configuration is functioning. You can then plan for changes that will be appropriate to the situation.

Resultant Set of Policy (RSoP) is one of the tools that can help plan for changes to Group Policy. RSoP provides for two modes:

- **Logging** For troubleshooting an existing set of policies
- **Planning** For review of existing policies and testing of a new set of policies

During the planning process, you can run the Resultant Set Of Policy Wizard to execute a query against an existing user or computer object's group policies, regardless of whether those policies are applied at the site, domain, or OU. You can also simulate the effect of new group policies on computer and user objects. This process can help to plan to avoid problems with inheritance of policies from multiple levels.

When you plan group policies, you have many options available to you. You can

- Distribute software
- Modify the registry
- Implement security settings
- Provide scripts for execution at either the startup, shutdown, logon, or logoff points

Group Policy settings are applied in the order of local policies (those configured directly on the computer itself) first. Next, site group policies are applied. Then the domain group policies, and lastly the OU group policies are applied, in order from the top node of the hierarchy to the OU containing the object. When you plan your policies, you must understand how each application can affect the next policy in line. If, for example, you have a domain-wide policy that restricts Control Panel from being accessed and then you have an OU Group Policy that allows Control Panel to be accessed, the last policy "wins" and users in that OU will be able to access Control Panel.

Every Group Policy contains a User Configuration node and a Computer Configuration node. When a user logs on to the network, that user receives the group policies in the User Configuration nodes of all the group policies that lead from the site, to domain, through each level of OU down to the one holding the user object, except in the case where the administrator has blocked or enforced inheritance of certain policies. When a computer starts up, that computer receives the group policies in the Computer Configuration nodes of all the group policies leading down to the computer object's location in the hierarchy. This means that a user might log on to two different computers and receive entirely different environments because the computer group policies are vastly dissimilar.

When you plan for user environments, you should consider the data management needs, especially regarding which folders need to be available to the user from any point in the network. This might require you to use folder redirection in your environment. You will also need to determine whether software needs to follow a user around the network or if the software needs to be statically assigned to a computer regardless of its user.

Objective 9.1 Questions

1.   You are the network administrator of A. Datum Corporation. The company has four departments, each within a separate OU in the forest root domain. Each of these OUs is a peer to the other. The company is reorganizing, and many users have moved to a different OU. These users have complained that they no longer can find their documents folders. What can be the problem?

    A. The users have moved to new locations, and they forgot to migrate their documents from their old computers.

    B. The users have changed domain controllers.

    C. The GPOs for the users' new site is overriding the GPOs that apply to the users' new OU.

    D. The GPOs for the users' new OU does not contain the correct information for folder redirection.

2.   You are the network administrator for the fabrikam.com Active Directory domain. You have three sites: Los Angeles, New York, and Miami. You have several OUs named Mkt, Svc, Prod, and Sales, and each OU contains users from two or three of the sites. You are planning the group policies for the entire network. The Miami administrator wants all the Miami users, many of whom are in the Sales OU, to redirect their My Documents folders to the MIAM02 server. The Los Angeles and New York users travel often and will need to maintain local files, and the administrators in both locations do not want to use folder redirection. What do you do to provide the correct access to the resources?

    A. Create a GPO with the correct folder redirection path to MIAM02 and apply it to the Miami site.

    B. Create a GPO with the correct folder redirection path to MIAM02 and apply it to the Sales OU.

    C. Create a GPO with the correct folder redirection path to MIAM02 and apply it to the fabrikam.com domain. Block policy inheritance to the Los Angeles and New York sites.

    D. Create a GPO with the correct folder redirection path to MIAM02 and apply it to the fabrikam.com domain. Block policy inheritance to the Mkt, Svc, and Prod OUs.

3.   You are planning to implement software distribution to your network. You need to ensure accuracy for software distribution for licensing purposes. You want to deploy application APP to all members of the Management, Executive, and Sales teams. You want to make sure that only the computers you approve of receive this software, so that a Sales team member cannot dial in to the network and be forced to accept installation of APP to that member's home computer. You want to ensure that you can add group policies that affect only the Executive team or only the Sales team in the future. How do you organize this?

   A. Create an OU hierarchy for software distribution called Swdist. Add all users of the Management, Executive, and Sales teams to this OU. Create a GPO to distribute software to the users in this OU.

   B. Create an OU hierarchy for software distribution called Swdist. Within Swdist, create separate OUs for the Management, Executive, and Sales teams. Apply a GPO to distribute software to computer objects in the Swdist OU hierarchy. Add the correct users and computers to each of the Management, Executive, and Sales OUs.

   C. Apply a GPO to each site that contains Management, Executive, and Sales team members.

   D. Apply a domain-wide GPO for distributing APP to computer objects within the domain.

4.   A. Datum Corporation has asked you to consult on a Group Policy planning project. The company currently has a set of group policies being used for folder redirection and password policies. The domain uses a single OU to house user objects and another OU to house computer objects. A. Datum Corp. wants you to create a system that will do the following:

   Primary objective: Deploy software to the Marketing team.

   Secondary objective: Avoid applying any policies to the IT group.

   Secondary objective: Apply password policy to all users.

   You create an OU hierarchy in the domain that has a single OU at the top of the tree named "All users." Within this OU, you place an IT Group OU, a Management OU, a Marketing OU, a Sales OU, a Service OU, and a Clerical OU to match the groups within A. Datum Corp. You apply a software distribution GPO to the Marketing OU. You block inheritance for the IT Group OU.

   After performing these actions, you have achieved which of the following?

   A. You have achieved neither the primary objective nor the secondary objectives.

   B. You have achieved the primary objective but neither of the secondary objectives.

    C. You have achieved the primary objective and one of the secondary objectives.

    D. You have achieved the secondary objectives but not the primary objective.

5.   You are working on a plan for a Group Policy structure that will ensure separate security settings for different users. You will not be changing the OU hierarchy. You want to test the security settings on each of the users. What is the best way to perform these tests?

    A. Use RSoP in planning mode to simulate the policies on existing users.

    B. Use RSoP in logging mode to simulate the policies on existing users.

    C. Create and test a new OU hierarchy.

    D. Create a new OU hierarchy in a test forest and then use RSoP in planning mode to simulate the policies on users.

6.   You have a new kiosk system that is being deployed to the public. Each kiosk is equipped with a computer running Microsoft Windows XP that logs on to Active Directory. You want to ensure that the kiosks are identical in all respects. Which of the following do you use? (Choose all that apply.)

    A. Enable Group Policy Loopback processing mode for the kiosks.

    B. Use a single computer account for all the kiosks to use.

    C. Place all kiosk computer accounts within the same OU.

    D. Place all kiosks within the same site.

7.   You have just been hired as a network administrator for Fabrikam, Inc. Your predecessor created local policies on all computers in the network in your Chicago location. You do not know how other locations apply group policies to computers, but the computer accounts for their computers are mingled with yours in the various OUs across the domain. Furthermore, at your site, when technicians have made changes to the computers, they have often changed the local policy settings. You want to have consistent group policies that refresh on the computer upon each startup. Which type of Group Policy should you select?

    A. Local policy

    B. Group Policy applied to OUs that contain your computer accounts

    C. Domain Group Policy

    D. Group Policy applied to the Chicago site

8. You are planning the group policies for your domain. You have six OUs in the domain. The top OU is named All. Below All, you have Computers and Users. Within Users, you have Sales, Finance, and Service. You have the following objectives:

Primary objective: You want to make certain that the Service team has a software restriction policy to prevent installation of unapproved software.

Secondary objective: You want all others to log on with the standard security policy, which is a minimum 6-character password.

Secondary objective: You want to distribute software to all computers in the company, but not to users' home computers when they dial in.

You create a domain-wide policy that requires a 6-character password. You create a software distribution policy and apply it to Computers.

After performing these actions, you have achieved which of the following?

A. You have achieved neither the primary objective nor the secondary objectives.

B. You have achieved both of the secondary objectives but not the primary objective.

C. You have achieved the primary objective and one of the secondary objectives.

D. You have achieved the primary objective and both of the secondary objectives.

1. **Correct Answers: D**

   A. **Incorrect:** The scenario did not mention that there were physical moves, so this is not likely the issue. (However, in real life a reorganization might mean a new location with new equipment.)

   B. **Incorrect:** Domain controllers are considered peers by design, so that any domain controller would be able to perform the same functions as any other domain controller.

   C. **Incorrect:** The question did not mention that there were physical moves, so you can disregard the issue of a new site.

   D. **Correct:** Since the users moved to a new OU, they would be affected by the new OU's GPOs. If the new GPOs did not contain the correct path for folder redirection, the users would appear to have "lost" their documents.

2. **Correct Answers: A**

   A. **Correct:** Applying the GPO to the site will ensure that the policy is applied to the correct set of users.

   B. **Incorrect:** Because each of the OUs contains users from more than one location, you cannot apply the GPO for folder redirection to an OU.

   C. **Incorrect:** You cannot block domain Group Policy inheritance to a site because site policies are applied first.

   D. **Incorrect:** If you perform this action, you will essentially be applying a GPO to the Sales OU, which means that all the Miami users in the Mkt, Svc, and Prod OUs will not receive the folder redirection, while all the New York and Los Angeles users in the Sales OU will receive unwanted folder redirection.

3. **Correct Answers: B**

   A. **Incorrect:** This configuration will distribute software to the correct users, but not to the correct computers. Users who dial in to the network would be able to install APP on their home computers.

   B. **Correct:** Since the computer configuration was used for distributing the software, only computer objects in the Swdist OU tree will receive the software. Furthermore, by using separate OUs for the Management, Executive, and Sales teams, you can then create new group policies that apply only to each of those teams in the future.

C. Incorrect: By applying the GPO to each site with those users, any user outside these three teams would be able to install APP.

D. Incorrect: This will distribute APP to all computers in the domain, not only to the Management, Executive, and Sales teams, which is an undesirable result.

4. Correct Answers: C

A. Incorrect: Your system will effectively deploy software to the Marketing team, which achieves the primary objective. It will also avoid applying any policies to the IT group. However, you did not create a password policy for all of the users, so you did not achieve one of the secondary objectives.

B. Incorrect: Your system will effectively deploy software to the Marketing team, which achieves the primary objective. It will also avoid applying any policies to the IT group. However, you did not create a password policy for all of the users, so you did not achieve one of the secondary objectives.

C. Correct: Your system will effectively deploy software to the Marketing team, which achieves the primary objective. It will also avoid applying any policies to the IT group. However, you did not create a password policy for all of the users, so you did not achieve one of the secondary objectives.

D. Incorrect: Your system will effectively deploy software to the Marketing team, which achieves the primary objective. It will also avoid applying any policies to the IT group. However, you did not create a password policy for all of the users, so you did not achieve one of the secondary objectives.

5. Correct Answers: A

A. Correct: You can use RSoP to either merge the tested policies with the existing ones or to exclusively test the new policies and ignore the existing ones to simulate the effect on user accounts.

B. Incorrect: RSoP's logging mode is used for troubleshooting problems with existing policies, not for simulations for planned policies.

C. Incorrect: Although creating a new OU hierarchy might be able to help determine much of the testing, it is more likely to have errors than using RSoP in planning mode. Such errors might be in upper-level GPOs that are not applied during testing or in site GPOs not being tested, and so on.

D. Incorrect: Compared to using RSoP in planning mode against existing users, this is not as fast or as accurate a method for conducting this test.

6. **Correct Answers: A and C**

   A. Correct: Kiosks are public computers that might end up under close scrutiny by any passerby. By using Group Policy Loopback processing mode, you can ensure that any user will receive only the policies that are supposed to be used on the kiosk, rather than the policy settings that might apply on a different networked computer.

   B. Incorrect: Each computer will join the domain as a separate computer account.

   C. Correct: In placing all kiosk computer accounts within the same OU, they will each receive the same set of group policies for computer configuration.

   D. Incorrect: It might be impossible to do this based on your company's physical network configuration.

7. **Correct Answers: D**

   A. Incorrect: This is the type of policy that is currently being mishandled. You should restore all local policy settings to their default state.

   B. Incorrect: Since you do not know how other administrators wish to handle Group Policy, and since your computer accounts are mingled with their computer accounts in the same OUs, you should not apply group policies to OUs.

   C. Incorrect: A domain Group Policy would affect the computer accounts managed by other administrators.

   D. Correct: After you remove the local policy, you can apply a Group Policy to the Chicago site. From that point on, computer accounts that start up in the Chicago site will automatically have the latest policies you have applied, refreshed at each startup.

8.   **Correct Answers: B**

A. Incorrect: You did not apply any policy that will restrict software installations for the Service team. However, you did create a standard security policy that will require a minimum 6-character password, and you were able to distribute software to all the computers in the company, but not to users who are using non-company equipment.

B. Correct: You did not apply any policy that will restrict software installations for the Service team. However, you did create a standard security policy that will require a minimum 6-character password, and you were able to distribute software to all the computers in the company, but not to users who are using non-company equipment.

C. Incorrect: You did not apply any policy that will restrict software installations for the Service team. However, you did create a standard security policy that will require a minimum 6-character password, and you were able to distribute software to all the computers in the company, but not to users who are using non-company equipment.

D. Incorrect: You did not apply any policy that will restrict software installations for the Service team. However, you did create a standard security policy that will require a minimum 6-character password, and you were able to distribute software to all the computers in the company, but not to users who are using non-company equipment.

Configure the User Environment by Using Group Policy

This objective centers on configuration of the user's environment through GPOs. In configuring a user's environment, you will need to have the skills to identify and specify settings for the User Configuration node within GPOs.

In the User Configuration node you have the ability to perform the following tasks (as well as many others):

- Distribute software that users will have access to regardless of the computer that they are using

- Assign user profiles and configure the desktop environment

- Apply logon and logoff scripts, and then configure whether they are hidden or visible and whether scripts run sequentially or synchronously

- Manage user certificates and enable autoenrollment

- Restrict access to files in the Windows Systemroot, to icons on the desktop or in the Start menu, and to Control Panel

- Restrict the use of software or force the use of a different application in place of Explorer.exe

- Configure how the user will interact with Microsoft Windows components such as Internet Explorer and the Windows Installer

- Establish security settings

Distributing software provides for two options—assigning the application or publishing it. If you assign an application to a user, the user has the application installed and available after first logging on. If you publish an application, the user can use Add Or Remove Programs in Control Panel to install the application. Conflicts can occur between seemingly disconnected group policies. For example, the Disable Windows Installer policy can prevent a user from installing allowed applications that use the Windows Installer method, regardless of whether the software is published or assigned. Furthermore, if you publish an application and then restrict a user from accessing Control Panel or the Add Or Remove Programs icon, the user will not be able to install the application because the user cannot access the correct icon.

Autoenrollment of certificates can be done through Group Policy for users and computers. When using autoenrollment, users do not need to be aware of the certificates that are enrolled, retrieved, or renewed. When you select autoenrollment behavior, you can establish a silent autoenrollment that requires zero user input. You can also require a user to provide input such as when users have smart cards and personal identification numbers (PINs).

Folder redirection is a key to enabling easy access to data for users. When users log on to the network, they receive the Group Policy setting that tells the computer to point to a different location for certain information. This includes

- **Application data** Information that configures an application for a specific person
- **Desktop** The data that a person saves to the desktop
- **My Documents** The information that a person would place in the My Documents folder on the desktop or when saving data to My Documents
- **Start Menu** The shortcuts and data icons that appear in the Windows Start menu

Security settings can be applied to a computer object as well as to a user object. When you deploy user-related security settings, you use the User Configuration node in Group Policy. Then you navigate to the Windows Settings section and open Security Settings. Within this Group Policy, you can edit Public Key policies, such as autoenrolling certificates, and you can restrict software. When you restrict software, you can prevent users from being able to run certain programs or to look at files in certain paths. For example, you can prevent users from accessing files in the System32 folder within Windows in order to stop them from deleting or corrupting a critical file.

There are a lot of other settings that might be considered security settings but that appear under the Administrative Templates section. These include removing icons from the desktop and Start menu, preventing access to Control Panel, and prohibiting changes to the network configuration. Password policies are applied using the Computer Configuration node in a GPO linked to the domain only.

1. You are the network administrator for Litware, Inc. Your organization has Legal, Marketing, Service, and Sales departments. Each of these departments has its own OU beneath the HQ OU, which is in the litwareinc.com domain. You have applied a folder redirection Group Policy to the HQ OU for Application Data, Desktop, My Documents, and Start Menu. In this policy all users will have their folders directed to a single, shared location. After applying this Group Policy, the Legal department users complain that they no longer have their special menu items, macros, and personal information in their Microsoft Word documents. Which policy setting is causing the problem?

   A. Application Data

   B. Desktop

   C. My Documents

   D. Start Menu

2. You have been called in to consult on a network problem being experienced by Contoso, Ltd. In the contoso.com domain, administrators have applied logon scripts and startup scripts to be executed at nearly every OU level in the hierarchy. These scripts map network drives, execute external programs, and write daily news items specific to the user's department and position. To make the scripts faster, they are set to run synchronously. A new OU named Application Service has been added below the Service OU. The Service OU is below the Corp OU and that is the top of the OU tree. The script applied to the Application Service OU is not deleting the drive mappings that the Corp OU script is making, even though the command to delete the drive mappings is in the script. The administrator has not blocked, and does not want to block, the upper script because it provides the news items that are necessary to be written at that level. What might be the best way to fix this problem?

   A. Copy the Group Policy to the lower OU and block inheritance.

   B. Force inheritance of the upper layer Group Policy.

   C. Disable the policy that runs logon scripts synchronously.

   D. Move the logon script to a different location.

3.   You are the network administrator for Contoso, Ltd., and you have a single domain named contoso.com in your forest with two locations. You have been asked to make certain that every user has the ability to install a new application named APP, which uses Windows Installer. The company does not want to install APP on any computer where the user will not use it, and the APP installation program should be available only in Control Panel. Which policy will achieve these criteria?

A. In a domain Group Policy, publish APP in the Software portion of the User Configuration node.

B. In a domain Group Policy, assign APP in the Software portion of the User Configuration node.

C. In a domain Group Policy, create a logon script in the User Configuration node that installs the APP.

D. In a site Group Policy, publish APP in the Software portion of the User Configuration node.

4.   Litware, Inc., has a single domain, litwareinc.com, in its forest. There are seven sites. The OU hierarchy has two top OUs: one named Admin for administrators and the other named Co for the remaining users. Within Co, there are three OUs named Sales, Lit, and Finance. You have the following objectives:

Primary objective: All users in the entire network require the same security settings.

Secondary objective: Users, other than Administrators, require a standard desktop and folder redirection configuration.

Secondary objective: The Lit department requires a special application that no other users should receive.

You perform the following actions:

1. You create a domain Group Policy that applies security settings.

2. You create an OU Group Policy for the Lit OU to deploy the application.

3. You create an OU Group Policy for the Co OU to apply a new logon script.

After performing these actions, you have achieved which of the following?

A. You have achieved neither the primary objective nor the secondary objectives.

B. You have achieved the primary objective but not the secondary objectives.

C. You have achieved the primary objective and one of the secondary objectives.

D. You have achieved the primary objective and both of the secondary objectives.

5.   You are the network administrator for a public library. You have 20 computers on the network that are available for users to browse the online library catalog or the Internet. You have decided to implement Group Policy settings within a single GPO on the OU containing only the public user accounts, as follows:

- Configure a Group Policy setting that restricts the user from installing new applications using Windows Installer

- Configure a Group Policy setting that restricts the user from running any file named Setup.exe

- Configure a Group Policy setting that restricts the user from accessing any files in the Windows directories

- Configure a Group Policy setting that prevents the user from changing desktop and Start menu settings

- Configure a Group Policy setting that removes the History, My Favorites, My Documents, and Network Places icons from the desktop

- Configure a Group Policy setting that restricts the user from opening Control Panel

- Configure a Group Policy setting that prohibits the user from changing Network Connection settings

Given this configuration, under what circumstances will a person using a public computer at this library be able to install a new application? (Choose all that apply.)

A. By publishing an application in a Group Policy so that it shows up in Add Or Remove Programs.

B. By logging on to the computer using a different user account in a different OU.

C. By assigning an application in a Group Policy so that it is available on the desktop.

D. By using a non-Windows Installer application, renaming the installation file from Setup.exe to something else, and executing it from the command line, the Run box, or Explorer.exe.

6.   You are the network administrator for Fabrikam, Inc. You have several users who travel from site to site and use different network workstations. You decide to implement a Group Policy to ensure that these users can access their data both on and off the network. Which of the following should you implement on an OU containing only the traveling users? (Choose all that apply.)

A. In Administrative Templates, under Network, implement the Group Policy for Offline Files.

B. In Windows Settings, under Folder Redirection, redirect the My Documents folders to a network location.

    C. In Administrative Templates, under Shared Folders, allow users to publish shares.

    D. In Administrative Templates, under Start Menu and Taskbar, remove the icons for the My Documents folder.

7. You are the network administrator for Fabrikam, Inc. You have implemented smart cards for a set of users on the network. You have placed these users in the Smart OU. You have two objectives:

Primary objective: Enable autoenrollment of certificates only for the users in the Smart OU.

Secondary objective: Require only the Smart OU users to use their smart cards during enrollment.

You implement a Group Policy for the fabrikam.com domain. In this policy you configure the Public Key autoenrollment policy so that it prompts the user for a personal identifier.

After performing these actions, you have achieved which of the following?

    A. You have achieved neither the primary objective nor the secondary objective.

    B. You have achieved the primary objective but not the secondary objective.

    C. You have achieved the secondary objective but not the primary objective.

    D. You have achieved both the primary objective and secondary objective.

8. You are the administrator of a network that has recently experienced a security incident that caused a virus to install itself into an application that is published to all users. You have written a script that will detect whether the application has been installed, as well as its version, and if the nonsecure version is being used, it will then deploy a fix to the security breach. You have replaced the files on the network share for installation so that any new installations will already have the fix. Which of the following actions do you need to perform in order to deploy the fix the fastest?

    A. Force users to log off the network and then manually run the script at each workstation.

    B. Implement a Group Policy to secure Windows Installer from being run.

    C. Implement a Group Policy to secure Add Or Remove Programs from being used.

    D. Copy the script to Sysvol. Implement a Group Policy that includes the script as a logon script.

Objective 9.2 Answers

1. **Correct Answers: A**

   A. **Correct:** The Group Policy that redirected the Application Data folder to a central location would appear to have caused changes to the Legal department's menu items and personal information for Word.

   B. **Incorrect:** The Desktop folder redirection would make users' desktops appear to be the same but would not have affected the application configuration.

   C. **Incorrect:** The users did not have a problem accessing their Word documents, just the application information that was specific to the Legal department users.

   D. **Incorrect:** The Start Menu folder redirection would not have manifested itself as a problem with a specific application's configuration.

2. **Correct Answers: C**

   A. **Incorrect:** One problem that you have with duplicating a Group Policy is that when you make changes to a Group Policy, you might not remember to make the same changes to another Group Policy.

   B. **Incorrect:** The administrator has not blocked the upper layer scripts, so forcing inheritance will not change the way that policy is being applied.

   C. **Correct:** By disabling the policy to run logon scripts synchronously, the logon scripts would execute in an order where the drive mappings would be deleted after they were made.

   D. **Incorrect:** Moving the logon script to a different location will not make a change in execution order.

3. **Correct Answers: A**

   A. **Correct:** Publishing APP in a domain Group Policy will make the APP installation available in Control Panel to all users.

   B. **Incorrect:** Assigning APP in a domain Group Policy will install APP, not make the installation available in Control Panel, as requested.

   C. **Incorrect:** By performing this action, APP will be installed rather than be made available in Control Panel, as desired.

   D. **Incorrect:** A site Group Policy will not publish the APP to all the users if you have a site defined for each of the two locations.

4.   **Correct Answers: C**

A. **Incorrect:** You were able to provide all users with security settings, meeting the primary objective. You also created a Group Policy to deploy the application to the Lit department, meeting one of the secondary objectives. However, you did not apply a Group Policy for desktop and folder redirection.

B. **Incorrect:** You were able to provide all users with security settings, meeting the primary objective. You also created a Group Policy to deploy the application to the Lit department, meeting one of the secondary objectives. However, you did not apply a Group Policy for desktop and folder redirection.

C. **Correct:** You were able to provide all users with security settings, meeting the primary objective. You also created a Group Policy to deploy the application to the Lit department, meeting one of the secondary objectives. However, you did not apply a Group Policy for desktop and folder redirection.

D. **Incorrect:** You were able to provide all users with security settings, meeting the primary objective. You also created a Group Policy to deploy the application to the Lit department, meeting one of the secondary objectives. However, you did not apply a Group Policy for desktop and folder redirection.

5.   **Correct Answers: B and D**

A. **Incorrect:** Two items are preventing the user from installing an application that was published. First, you have a policy that prevents users from installing applications using Windows Installer. Second, you have a policy that prevents a user from opening Control Panel, so the user will not be able to access Add Or Remove Programs.

B. **Correct:** By using a different user account in a different OU, the user will have different group policies that might be less restrictive for installing applications.

C. **Incorrect:** The group policies in place prevent the user from using Windows Installer and from executing Setup.exe files.

D. **Correct:** The group policies will not prevent a non–Windows Installer installation from taking place if the installation file is not named Setup.exe.

6.   **Correct Answers: A and B**

A. **Correct:** Offline Files will allow the travelers to access their data when they are not connected to the network. They will be able to synchronize the data on a local computer with the data on a network share.

B. **Correct:** Redirecting the My Documents folder will enable the user to access the user's data from any workstation connected to the network.

    C. Incorrect: Publishing shares in Active Directory will allow a user to let others search for files that are shared from that user's computer by using an Active Directory query. It will not enable access to files from any location.

    D. Incorrect: Configuring the Start menu will not enable users to access files whether they are on the network or not.

7.   **Correct Answers: A**

    A. Correct: Because you applied the Group Policy to the fabrikam.com domain, the users across the entire domain will receive the policy, not just those within the Smart OU. Therefore, you have not achieved the primary objective or the secondary objective.

    B. Incorrect: Because you applied the Group Policy to the fabrikam.com domain, the users across the entire domain will receive the policy, not just those within the Smart OU. Therefore, you have not achieved the primary objective or the secondary objective.

    C. Incorrect: Because you applied the Group Policy to the fabrikam.com domain, the users across the entire domain will receive the policy, not just those within the Smart OU. Therefore, you have not achieved the primary objective or the secondary objective.

    D. Incorrect: Because you applied the Group Policy to the fabrikam.com domain, the users across the entire domain will receive the policy, not just those within the Smart OU. Therefore, you have not achieved the primary objective or the secondary objective.

8.   **Correct Answers: D**

    A. Incorrect: A manually run script with forced logoffs will take more time than other options.

    B. Incorrect: Since future installations of the software will likely need to use Windows Installer, not to mention the script, this would hinder the deployment of the fix, rather than help it.

    C. Incorrect: Since all future installations of the software will need to use Add Or Remove Programs in Control Panel (because the application was published), this will hinder the deployment.

    D. Correct: Using a script as a logon or logoff script is one of the faster ways of deploying a script to users.

30 Exam 70-296—Managing and Maintaining Group Policy (10.0)

The Managing and Maintaining Group Policy objective domain focuses primarily on the ongoing administration of computers and users through Active Directory directory service Group Policy. In this objective we will review the methods of troubleshooting Group Policy with Resultant Set of Policy (RSoP), using the Group Policy Object Editor and the Gpresult command. We will look at maintaining software through Group Policy's software distribution capabilities. And we will discuss the application of security settings and how to troubleshoot them using various Group Policy tools and utilities.

RSoP is a tool that is helpful in simulating the effects of group policies on user or computer objects through the use of its planning mode. Planning mode can be very useful in determining what changes must be made to group policies in order to achieve a certain user or computer environment. In addition, RSoP provides for a logging mode, which is instrumental in troubleshooting group policies.

Software distribution is an ongoing effort. Not only do you need to initially create a package to distribute, but then you also need to deploy it to the users and computers that require the application. If the policy becomes corrupted, you then need to have a method for repairing the software. And finally, you should have a way to remove the software when it is no longer required to be used either for individual users, computers, or for the entire organization.

Tested Skills and Suggested Practices

The skills that you need to successfully master the Managing and Maintaining Group Policy objective domain on *Exam 70:296: Planning, Implementing, and Maintaining a Microsoft Windows Server 2003 Environment for an MCSE Certified on Windows 2000* include

- Troubleshoot issues related to Group Policy application deployment. Tools might include RSoP and the Gpresult command.
  - ❏ Practice 1: Install a domain controller within the root domain of a forest. Using the Active Directory Users And Computers console, create an organizational unit (OU) structure. Create a user object in one of the OUs at the bottom of the OU hierarchy. Create a Group Policy Object (GPO) with Group Policy to assign a software application to users at the top of the OU hierarchy.

Block inheritance at an OU between the user object and the top OU. Add the RSoP snap-in to the Microsoft Management Console (MMC) and begin the Resultant Set Of Policy Wizard to create a query. Examine the policies applied to the user account you created.

❑ Practice 2: Use the same OU structure in Practice 1. Create a computer object in one of the OUs. Create a GPO with Group Policy to assign a software application to computers at the top of the OU hierarchy. Block inheritance to computers at an OU between the computer object and the OU where the GPO was applied. Add the RSoP snap-in to the MMC and begin the Resultant Set Of Policy Wizard to create a query. Examine the policies applied to the computer account you created.

❑ Practice 3: Using the same OU structure in Practice 1, log on to a workstation that is a member of the same domain as the user object you created. Execute the command **gpresult /scope user /z >c:\mygpo.txt** and then open C:\Mygpo.txt in Microsoft WordPad to view the results.

■ Troubleshoot the application of Group Policy security settings. Tools might include RSoP as well as GPOTool, Gpupdate and Gpresult commands.

❑ Practice 1: Install two domain controllers into the root domain of a forest. Make certain that these two domain controllers are on two separate segments of the network. Create an OU structure of several OUs. Install a workstation and move its computer object into an OU. Create a user object named User-Disc in that OU. Disconnect the router between the two segments. On one of the domain controllers, use the Active Directory Users And Computers console to create a GPO for that same OU that will apply a special bitmap to the desktop wallpaper. Log on to the other segment as the user on that workstation. Execute the Gpotool command (from the Resource Kit tools) and view the results.

❑ Practice 2: Continue with the equipment and setup from Practice 1. Connect the two segments and wait 15 minutes. Execute the Gpupdate /force command from the workstation. Reboot the workstation and log on to see if the Group Policy is applied and the bitmap is used as the wallpaper.

❑ Practice 3: On a domain controller, create a set of five nested OUs. In each OU, apply a Group Policy to set a different bitmap as the wallpaper. Create a user object and move a computer object into the bottom OU. At three different OUs, either block inheritance or force inheritance of the GPO at that level. Use RSoP to see which Group Policy will "win."

Further Reading

This section contains a list of supplemental readings divided by objective. If you think you need additional preparation before taking the exam, study these sources thoroughly.

Objective 10.1   Review Chapter 6, "Managing the User Environment with Group Policy."

Microsoft Corporation. *Introducing Microsoft Windows Server 2003*. Redmond, Washington: Microsoft Press, 2003. Review Chapter 3, "Active Directory."

Crawford, Sharon, and Charlie Russel. *Microsoft Windows Server 2003 Administrator's Companion*. Redmond, Washington: Microsoft Press, 2003. Review Chapter 10, "Managing File Resources and Group Policy."

Microsoft Corporation. Redmond, Washington. Review "White Paper: Administering Group Policy by Using the Group Policy Management Console," available on the Microsoft Web site at *http://support.microsoft.com/default.aspx?scid=kb;en-us;818735*.

Microsoft Corporation. Redmond, Washington. Review "HOW TO: Assign Software to a Specific Group by Using Group Policy in the Windows Server 2003 Family," available on the Microsoft Web site at *http://support.microsoft.com /default.aspx?scid=kb;en-us;324750*.

Objective 10.2   Review Chapter 5, "Planning, Implementing, and Troubleshooting Group Policy."

Microsoft Corporation. *Introducing Microsoft Windows Server 2003*. Redmond, Washington: Microsoft Press, 2003. Review Chapter 3, "Active Directory," and Chapter 4, "Management Services."

Microsoft Corporation. Redmond, Washington. Review "HOW TO: Install and Use RSoP in Windows Server 2003," available on the Microsoft Web site at *http://support.microsoft.com/default.aspx?scid=kb;en-us;323276*.

Microsoft Corporation. *Windows Server 2003 Deployment Kit: Designing a Managed Environment*. Redmond, Washington; Microsoft Press, 2003. Review Chapter 8, "Deploying a Managed Software Environment." This chapter can also be found on the Microsoft Web site at *http://www.microsoft.com/windowsserver2003/techinfo /reskit/deploykit.mspx*.

Troubleshoot Issues Related to Group Policy Application Deployment

This objective focuses on the issues of troubleshooting GPOs for application deployment. In simple application of Group Policy, conflicts are the main challenge to application. Multiple GPOs can contain the same Group Policy with different configuration specifications. Inheritance of Group Policy can either be blocked or forced. The combination of multiple GPOs and blocked or forced inheritance can cause unexpected results.

When troubleshooting, you must first investigate the group policies that are applied, the order of their application, and whether inheritance of any of the policies is forced or blocked. The tools that you can use in this process include RSoP and the Gpresult command-line tool.

You have two options when you run RSoP. You can use either planning mode or logging mode. When troubleshooting, logging mode will provide you the exact data for an existing user and existing computer object. When you plan to deploy new Group Policy settings, you can use RSoP in planning mode to simulate the effect that loopback processing, slow network links, WMI filters, and security group memberships have on the Group Policy settings. You can also invoke RSoP to discover the results of Group Policy settings when users log on to computers in different organizational units (OUs).

Objective 10.1 Questions

1. You are the network administrator of A. Datum Corporation. The company has four departments, each within separate OUs in the forest root domain. You have had three users move to a new department. You move their user objects to a new OU that is nested below the OU for the department. When the users log on, they find that they do not receive the department's software application. Which of the following actions will help you discover the problem?

   A. Use the Group Policy Object Editor to view the group policies of the OU from which you moved the users.

   B. Use the Group Policy Object Editor to view the group policies of the OU to which you moved the users.

   C. Execute **gpresult /user** username on a domain controller.

   D. Use RSoP to look at the Group Policy results for the user objects as well as for the computer objects that the users are logging on to.

2. Litware, Inc., has three sites: London, New York, and Paris, for its single domain. Within the domain, there is an OU structure that is separated first by administrative groups and then by department. The OUs are shown in the following figure.

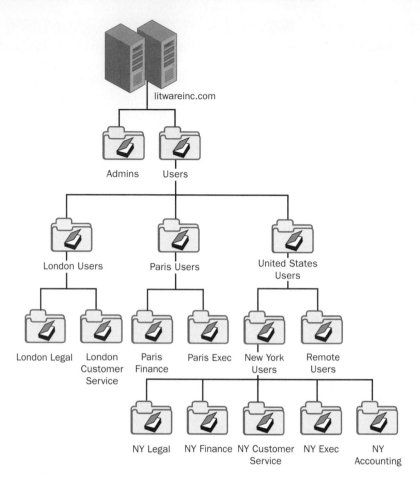

You have an application that you are deploying. The application should be available to the Accounting and Legal departments. It should not be available to anyone in the Customer Service departments or to any remote users. You want to avoid filtering out the GPO. Where do you apply the GPO for this application? (Choose all that apply.)

A. New York Legal

B. New York Accounting

C. London Legal

D. New York users

3. You are the network administrator of Contoso, Ltd. Across your three domains you have 12,000 users and 12,000 computers. There are nested OU structures in each of the domains. A user named j123@corp.contoso.com logs on to a computer that is a member of res.contoso.com. The user normally logs on to a computer that is a member of corp.contoso.com. The user is not able to find his department's software application on the computer and cannot install it. The Internet Protocol (IP) address of the user's normal computer is 172.16.88.10. The IP address of the computer that is having the problem is 172.16.72.77. The IP address of the closest domain controller is 172.16.72.8. What command do you use from the domain controller to determine the problem with the computer object?

    A. gpresult /u j123@corp.contoso.com /scope user>c:\gp.txt

    B. gpresult /s 172.16.72.77 /u corp.contoso.com\j123 /p password /scope computer /z >c:\gp.txt

    C. gpresult /s 172.16.88.10 /u corp.contoso.com\j123 /p password /scope computer /z >c:\gp.txt

    D. gpotool /u j123@corp.contoso.com /scope user >c:\gp.txt

4. You are the network administrator for Contoso, Ltd. You have three domains. The root domain, contoso.com, is used only for administrators and has very few group policies placed on it. You want to make certain that all users in the corp.contoso.com domain are not able to change the files in the C:\Windows\System32 directory, so you apply a Group Policy software restriction policy to the corp.contoso.com domain. When you log on to the domain as a test user in the All OU, the Group Policy works. When you log on to the domain as a test user in the All\Research\Dev OU, the Group Policy no longer works, and you are able to view and change the files in the C:\Windows\System32 directory. You have the following objectives:

Primary objective: Use the correct tool to discover the problem.

Secondary objective: Use the correct tool to fix the problem.

You use RSoP to query the test user object in the All\Research\Dev OU. You then use the Group Policy Object Editor to fix the Group Policy application.

After performing these actions, you have achieved which of the following?

    A. You have achieved both the primary and the secondary objectives.

    B. You have achieved the primary objective but not the secondary objective.

    C. You have achieved the secondary objective but not the primary objective.

    D. You have achieved neither the primary objective nor the secondary objective.

5.   You are the administrator of Litware, Inc.'s network. In the litwareinc.com domain, you have five OUs in the following order: All is at the top of the tree. Within All are Exec and Corp. Within Corp are HQ and Branches. You create the following group policies:

Pol1: Defines the security policy for password length, complexity, and account lockout.

Pol2: Defines desktop and Control Panel restrictions.

Pol3: Defines software distribution for an application called App.

You have applied Pol1 to litwareinc.com. You have applied Pol2 to HQ. You have applied Pol3 to Corp. Before you applied these group policies, another administrator had configured other GPOs as well as inheritance blocking and forcing.

How do you best simulate the results of your new GPOs when you've added them to the old GPOs?

A. Use the Group Policy Object Editor to view all the group policies.

B. Run the Gpotool command.

C. Configure auditing on Event Viewer.

D. Use RSoP to perform a query.

6.   You are troubleshooting Group Policy for a user who travels between multiple sites in your company. At his normal site, the user's stand-alone computer has an IP address of 172.16.88.100 and the domain controller at that site has an IP address of 172.16.88.1. The user is able to install a special application named App1 from Add Or Remove Programs. However, when the user travels from his normal location, sometimes the software is not available. The user has consistent problems at one site, where the user uses a computer with an IP address of 172.16.12.12. The domain controller at that location is 172.16.12.1. You suspect that there is a problem with forced inheritance at one of the sites. To test your theory, which of the commands should you perform from your location, where your computer's IP address is 172.16.1.253?

A. gpresult /s 172.16.1.253 /u corp.contoso.com\j123 /p password /z >c:\gp.txt

B. gpresult /s 172.16.12.1 /u corp.contoso.com\j123 /p password /z >c:\gp.txt

C. gpresult /s 172.16.12.12 /u corp.contoso.com\j123 /p password /z >c:\gp.txt

D. gpresult /s 172.16.88.100 /u corp.contoso.com\j123 /p password /z >c:\gp.txt

7.   You have created a Group Policy for deploying Microsoft Office XP to users across the domain. To conserve disk space, you do not want the computers in the warehouse, which are used for a special database application, to have Office XP on them. These computers are housed in the Warehouse OU. You do want all the rest of the networked computers to have Office XP available at all times. Which of the following should you choose for the fastest deployment?

   A. Assign the Group Policy to users in the domain and block inheritance in the Warehouse OU.

   B. Assign the Group Policy to computers in the domain and block inheritance in the Warehouse OU.

   C. Publish the Group Policy to users in the domain and block inheritance in the Warehouse OU.

   D. Publish the Group Policy to computers in the domain and block inheritance in the Warehouse OU.

8.   You are running a Microsoft Windows 2000 Active Directory domain. You have several Windows Server 2003 member servers in the domain, and you are planning to upgrade to Windows Server 2003. You have applied a new Group Policy that deploys a new application to a test OU in your domain. You have the following objectives:

   Primary objective: You want to simulate the effect of this Group Policy on other OUs.

   Secondary objective: You want to test how inheritance blocking can be used on a group of users so that they will never receive this Group Policy.

   You create a test OU structure that mirrors your actual OU structure. You link the same OUs in the test structure to the GPOs of their peers in the actual OU structure.

   You intend to use RSoP in planning mode.

   Which of the following can you achieve?

   A. Both the primary and secondary objectives

   B. The primary objective but not the secondary objective

   C. The secondary objective but not the primary objective

   D. Neither the primary nor secondary objectives

Objective 10.1 Answers

1.   Correct Answers: D

A. Incorrect: The users' former OU will not have any affect on the user objects that have moved.

B. Incorrect: Simply looking at the group policies attached to the OU where the users have moved to will give you only a partial picture of the configuration that a user or computer object should receive.

C. Incorrect: Although this will show the user object's Group Policy results, it will show the domain controller's group policies rather than the Group Policy results for the computer object that the users are logging on to.

D. Correct: This will show you what policy will "win" for both the user objects and the computer objects and better enable you to discover the problem.

2.   Correct Answers: A, B, and C

A. Correct: You should apply the GPO to each OU for both the Legal and the Accounting departments.

B. Correct: You should apply the GPO to each OU for both the Legal and the Accounting departments.

C. Correct: You should apply the GPO to each OU for both the Legal and the Accounting departments.

D. Incorrect: If you apply the GPO to New York users, you will have to filter out the New York Customer Service users from receiving it because they would automatically inherit the GPO from New York users. Since you want to avoid filtering, this is not the correct choice.

3.   Correct Answers: B

A. Incorrect: This command does not look at the computer object. In addition, the syntax of this command is incorrect. The correct syntax of this Gpresult command would be gpresult /u corp.contoso.com\j123 >c:\gp.txt.

B. Correct: This command will provide the Group Policy results for the computer object with the problems, executed with the permissions of the user j123.

C. Incorrect: This command will provide the Group Policy results for the computer object that does not have the problems, so it would not indicate the problem.

D. Incorrect: You would not want to use the Gpotool command because it looks at replication problems for group policies, plus this is the incorrect syntax for the Gpotool command.

4.   Correct Answers: A

    A. Correct: RSoP is the correct troubleshooting tool to use when determining the Group Policy application. Group Policy Object Editor can be used to make changes to group policies.

    B. Incorrect: RSoP is the correct troubleshooting tool to use when determining the Group Policy application. Group Policy Object Editor can be used to make changes to group policies.

    C. Incorrect: RSoP is the correct troubleshooting tool to use when determining the Group Policy application. Group Policy Object Editor can be used to make changes to group policies.

    D. Incorrect: RSoP is the correct troubleshooting tool to use when determining the Group Policy application. Group Policy Object Editor can be used to make changes to group policies.

5.   Correct Answers: D

    A. Incorrect: This is one of the most time-consuming ways of looking at the group policies, and it will not simulate the results.

    B. Incorrect: Gpotool is useful for determining if there is a replication problem with group policies, not for simulating Group Policy results.

    C. Incorrect: Event Viewer auditing will not simulate the results of Group Policy application.

    D. Correct: RSoP will provide you with the results of the policies that are applied to user and computer objects in a graphical interface. You have the ability to receive a text file using the Gpresult command as well.

6.   Correct Answers: C

    A. Incorrect: You need to direct your command to the IP address where the user has consistent problems, which would be 172.16.12.12.

    B. Incorrect: You need to direct your command to the IP address where the user has consistent problems, which would be 172.16.12.12.

    C. Correct: You need to direct your command to the IP address where the user has consistent problems, which would be 172.10.12.12.

    D. Incorrect: You need to direct your command to the IP address where the user has consistent problems, which would be 172.16.12.12.

7.   **Correct Answers: B**

   A. Incorrect: If a user who is not in the Warehouse OU logs on to the Warehouse computers, Office XP will be installed.

   B. Correct: This will correctly install Office XP on all computers in the domain upon startup, except for any computers in the Warehouse OU.

   C. Incorrect: If a user who is not in the Warehouse OU logs on to the Warehouse computers and then selects Office XP installation from Add Or Remove Programs in Control Panel, Office XP will be installed.

   D. Incorrect: This will prevent the Warehouse computers from receiving Office XP; however, it will not install Office XP on all the rest of the network computers.

8.   **Correct Answers: D**

   A. Incorrect: To achieve your objectives, you must run RSoP, which requires you to have a Windows Server 2003 domain controller. You do not have the necessary tools to achieve either of these objectives.

   B. Incorrect: To achieve your objectives, you must run RSoP, which requires you to have a Windows Server 2003 domain controller. You do not have the necessary tools to achieve either of these objectives.

   C. Incorrect: To achieve your objectives, you must run RSoP, which requires you to have a Windows Server 2003 domain controller. You do not have the necessary tools to achieve either of these objectives.

   D. Correct: To achieve your objectives, you must run RSoP, which requires you to have a Windows Server 2003 domain controller. You do not have the necessary tools to achieve either of these objectives.

Troubleshoot the Application of Group Policy Security Settings

This objective discusses the troubleshooting process for Group Policy security settings. When security settings are deployed, it is important that they are applied correctly. Like all group policies, conflicts from overriding group policies can cause inconsistent results with group policies that include security settings. In addition, when other issues interfere with replication, group policies might be applied inconsistently across the domain.

You can discover replication issues with group policies through the Gpotool command-line tool. In addition, you can use Gpupdate to refresh the group policies on a local workstation when you suspect that the user or workstation has not received the latest group policies.

In order to determine whether there is a Group Policy inheritance conflict, you can use RSoP. The Group Policy Management Console can access RSoP data to obtain the same results. For a command-line tool option, you can use the Gpresult command.

Objective 10.2 Questions

1. You have added a new GPO to litwareinc.com that follows the default domain policy to prevent users from installing nonapproved software through software restrictions. You discover that the policy is not applied consistently to all users throughout the domain. What should you do to discover whether the problem is caused by blocked inheritance?

    A. Configure each computer's local policy to require software restrictions for local users.

    B. Use RSoP to query each OU containing users.

    C. Run the Gpresult command on your computer.

    D. Run the Gpotool command on your computer.

2. Litware, Inc. has three sites for its single domain: London, New York, and Paris. Within the domain there is an OU structure that is separated by administrative groups and then by department. Users in London are required to use software restrictions that prevent them from installing any software or using Windows Installer. These group policies are applied, but not all London users receive them. Which tool is best used for determining the problem? (Choose all that apply.)

    A. RSoP

    B. Gpresult

    C. GPMC

    D. Gpupdate

3. You are the administrator of the contoso.com domain. In contoso.com, you have 38 sites. You do not have any site-attached GPOs. You have deployed a new Group Policy that prevents users from accessing their Windows and System32 directories. Two months later, you find out that a user has corrupted the operating system by deleting files from these directories. You investigate the problem and find out that all the users at that same site have not received the new Group Policy, even though their user objects are in the same OUs as users in other locations who are receiving the Group Policy. Which of the following tools do you use to determine the problem?

    A. RSoP

    B. Gpresult

    C. Group Policy Object Editor

    D. The Gpotool command

4. You are the administrator of the litwareinc.com domain. You have three sites: Detroit, Minneapolis, and Los Angeles. You have created a Group Policy named SecurityPol that restricts software installation and Control Panel access. In your network, you want administrators to be able to have full access to everything. In addition, executives and management require full access to their workstations and laptops. You have the following OU configuration in your single domain: All Users is at the top of the OU tree. Within All Users are the Administrators, Executives, and Corp OUs. Within Corp, you have the Management, Research, Finance, Legal, Service, and Sales OUs. You do not want to filter group policies. Which of the following is one of the containers to which you should apply SecurityPol?

    A. The litwareinc.com domain

    B. The All Users OU

    C. The Research OU

    D. The Detroit site

5. You have just been hired at Contoso, Ltd. as the new network administrator. You are reviewing the files on the former administrator's hard disk. One is a text file that lists Computer Settings, applied group policies, group policies that were filtered out, and security settings that the computer was a member of. Which tool did the former administrator use to create this text file?

    A. GPMC

    B. The Gpresult command

    C. The Gpotool command

    D. D.The Gpupdate command

6. You have deployed a security policy to all users by applying it to the domain. You imported a security template and then edited it to create the GPO. After using the security policy for a while, you decide that you would like to change the requirements back to the template's defaults. Which is the fastest way to apply this change?

    A. Configure each computer separately with a new Group Policy.

    B. Delete the existing GPO. Create a new GPO by importing the template and apply it to the domain.

    C. Edit the individual policies within the GPO.

    D. Use the Gpupdate command to refresh the Group Policy defaults.

7.   Your network requires a more secure workstation policy. You have the following objectives:

Primary objective: Use a security template to increase security for workstations.

Secondary objective: Apply the security template to workstations but not to member servers or domain controllers.

You perform the following actions:

1. You run the Group Policy Object Editor on a GPO at the domain level.

2. You navigate through Computer Settings to Windows Settings and then right-click Security Settings.

3. You select Import Policy.

4. You select Hisecws.inf and click Open.

5. You save this policy and apply it to the domain.

After performing these actions, you have achieved which of the following?

   A. You have achieved both the primary and secondary objectives.

   B. You have achieved the primary objective but not the secondary objective.

   C. You have achieved the secondary objective but not the primary objective.

   D. You have achieved neither the primary nor the secondary objectives.

8.   You are the network administrator for Litware, Inc. Another administrator has called you because she is unable to install software on workstations when logging on with the administrator account. You have recently applied a software restriction policy to the entire domain. Which of the following can be changed to allow the administrator to bypass software restrictions?

   A. Move all administrators to a new domain.

   B. Delete the software restriction policy and apply it to the OUs instead.

   C. Redeploy the software restriction policy as a site-attached policy.

   D. Change the policy so that it is applied to All Users Except Administrators.

Objective 10.2 Answers

1.   Correct Answers: B

A. Incorrect: Not only is this time-consuming, but it will not help you discover the problem affecting domain users.

B. Correct: By querying each OU, you can determine whether the users in that OU have had the Group Policy blocked.

C. Incorrect: The Gpresult command will look only at one computer and user object, and the question does not state whether you have been affected by the inconsistent application of the Group Policy or not.

D. Incorrect: The Gpotool command will tell you whether there is a problem with replication of the Group Policy, and although that might be a cause of the problem, it will not tell you whether inheritance of the domain controller Group Policy has been blocked.

2.   Correct Answers: A, B, and C

A. Correct: Resultant Set of Policy has the ability to display the group policies to see where the problem might lie.

B. Correct: Gpresult is a command-line tool that can display Group Policy results. It displays the results in a text file that might not be as easy to view as the RSoP graphical tool.

C. Correct: GPMC is able to integrate the RSoP data in addition to the Group Policy Object Editor tool, making it easy to research and troubleshoot Group Policy application from a single console.

D. Incorrect: Gpupdate is used to trigger a refresh of the Group Policy on a computer. It will not help you discover the root of a problem.

3.   Correct Answers: D

A. Incorrect: Given the symptoms of the problem, the likelihood is that the site has not received the Group Policy through replication. RSoP will not help you with a replication problem.

B. Incorrect: Since the security policy is not distributed to a single site, it is likely that there is a replication problem. Gpresult will not help with replication issues.

C. Incorrect: The Group Policy Object Editor will not help detect a problem with Group Policy replication.

D. Correct: The Gpotool command is used to discover a problem with replication of the Group Policy.

4.   **Correct Answers: C**

A. Incorrect: SecurityPol should not be assigned to the domain because it would be applied to the Administrators, Management, and Executives OUs.

B. Incorrect: SecurityPol should not be assigned to the All Users OU because Administrators, Management, and Executives are all OUs nested within it.

C. Correct: The Research OU is one of the three OUs to which you should apply SecurityPol. In addition, you should apply SecurityPol to the Finance, Legal, Service, and Sales OUs.

D. Incorrect: The SecurityPol should not be assigned to a single site because Administrators, Executives, and Management OU users might be located there and would receive the policy.

5.   **Correct Answers: B**

A. Incorrect: The Group Policy Management Console is a graphical tool.

B. Correct: The Gpresult command can create a text file that lists only computer settings.

C. Incorrect: The Gpotool command is used to discover replication problems with Group Policy.

D. Incorrect: The Gpupdate command is used to refresh the group policies on the local computer.

6.   **Correct Answers: B**

A. Incorrect: Configuring each computer separately will be time-consuming.

B. Correct: This method will be the fastest for deploying the defaults that are in the security template.

C. Incorrect: This method would be slower than importing the security template defaults.

D. Incorrect: The Gpupdate command will not pull in the defaults from the security template. The Gpupdate command will only refresh the policies on a local workstation.

7.   **Correct Answers: B**

A.   **Incorrect:** You achieved the primary objective because the security template increased security on workstations. You did not achieve the secondary objective because by applying the template to the domain, you included member servers and domain controllers. You should separate domain controllers and member servers into OUs outside the OU structure that contains computer objects. You should apply this GPO to the highest OU that contains computer objects so that it can be inherited by lower level OUs.

B.   **Correct:** You achieved the primary objective because the security template increased security on workstations. You did not achieve the secondary objective because by applying the template to the domain, you included member servers and domain controllers. You should separate domain controllers and member servers into OUs outside the OU structure that contains computer objects. You should apply this GPO to the highest OU that contains computer objects so that it can be inherited by lower level OUs.

C.   **Incorrect:** You achieved the primary objective because the security template increased security on workstations. You did not achieve the secondary objective because by applying the template to the domain, you included member servers and domain controllers. You should separate domain controllers and member servers into OUs outside the OU structure that contains computer objects. You should apply this GPO to the highest OU that contains computer objects so that it can be inherited by lower level OUs.

D.   **Incorrect:** You achieved the primary objective because the security template increased security on workstations. You did not achieve the secondary objective because by applying the template to the domain, you included member servers and domain controllers. You should separate domain controllers and member servers into OUs outside the OU structure that contains computer objects. You should apply this GPO to the highest OU that contains computer objects so that it can be inherited by lower level OUs.

8. **Correct Answers: D**

A. **Incorrect:** This will not fix the problem. There will still be administrative accounts in the domain that will be restricted.

B. **Incorrect:** It is possible that user accounts within the OU hierarchy are actually administrators who need the rights to install software, so applying the policy to the OUs will not necessarily fix the problem.

C. **Incorrect:** Site-attached policies can affect administrators. This would not avoid the problem.

D. **Correct:** This is an option that is available to prevent software restrictions from affecting the administrators within the domain.

Glossary

Special characters

.inf   The filename extension for files that contain device information, scripts to control hardware operations, or security template information.

10Base-T   Short name for an Ethernet physical layer specification that uses unshielded twisted-pair (UTP) cables in a star topology. The "10" refers to the network's speed of 10 Mbps, the "base" refers to the network's baseband transmissions, and the "T" refers to the use of twisted-pair cable. The maximum cable segment length for a 10Base-T network is 100 meters.

802.11   Refers to a family of Institute of Electrical and Electronics Engineers (IEEE) specifications for wireless networking.

802.11a   An extension to 802.11 that applies to wireless local area networks (WLANs) and provides up to 54 Mbps in the 5 GHz band.

802.11b   (also called *Wi-Fi*) An extension to 802.11 that applies to wireless LANs and provides 11 Mbps transmission (with a fallback to 5.5, 2, and 1 Mbps) in the 2.4 GHz band. 802.11b is a 1999 ratification to the original 802.11 standard, allowing wireless functionality comparable to Ethernet.

802.11g   An extension to 802.11 that applies to wireless LANs and provides 54 Mbps transmission in the 2.4 GHz band. 802.11g is backward compatible with 802.11b, allowing the two to work together.

802.1X authentication   An Institute of Electrical and Electronics Engineers (IEEE) standard for port-based network access control that provides authenticated network access to Ethernet networks and wireless 802.11 local area networks (LANs).

A

access control   A security mechanism that determines which operations a user, group, service, or computer is authorized to perform on a computer or on a particular object.

access control entry (ACE)   An entry in an object's discretionary access control list (DACL) that grants or denies a permission to a security principal (user, group, computer, or inetOrgPerson). An ACE is also an entry in an object's system access control list (SACL) that specifies the security events to be audited for a user or group.

access control list (ACL)   The mechanism for limiting access to certain items of information or to certain controls based on users' identity and their membership in various predefined groups.

access point   A hardware device, used on wireless local area networks (LANs) that use the infrastructure topology, that provides an interface between a cabled network and wireless devices. The access point is connected to a standard network using a cable and also has a transceiver enabling it to communicate with wireless computers and other devices. See also *infrastructure topology*.

access token or security access token   A collection of security identifiers (SIDs) that represent a user and that user's group memberships. The security subsystem compares SIDs in the token to SIDs in an access control list (ACL) to determine resource access.

account lockout   A security feature that prevents a user account from logging on if a number of failed logon attempts occur within a specified amount of time, based on security policy lockout settings. After an account is locked, users cannot use it to log on.

account   *See* user account.

ACE   *See* access control entry (ACE).

ACK (acknowledgment)   A message transmitted to indicate that data has been received correctly. The Transmission Control Protocol (TCP) requires that the recipient acknowledge successful receipt of data.

ACL   *See* access control list (ACL).

Active Directory   The enterprise directory service included with the Microsoft Windows Server 2003 operating system. The Active Directory service is a hierarchical directory service that consists of objects that represent users, computers, groups, and other network resources. The objects are arranged in a tree display that consists of hierarchical layers ranging upward from organizational units, to domains, to trees, and to forests. Objects are composed of attributes that contain information about the resource the object represents. See also *directory service*.

Active Directory–integrated zone   A primary Domain Name System (DNS) zone that is stored in Active Directory so that it can use multimaster replication and Active Directory security features.

Active Directory Service Interfaces (ADSI)   A Component Object Model (COM)-based directory service model that allows ADSI-compliant client applications to access a wide variety of distinct directory protocols, including Windows Directory Services and Lightweight Directory Access Protocol (LDAP), while using a single, standard set of interfaces. ADSI shields the client application from the implementation and operational details of the underlying data store or protocol.

Active Directory quota   For domain controllers running Windows Server 2003, a feature that determines the number of objects that can be owned in a given directory partition by a security principal.

ActiveX   A loosely defined set of technologies that allows software components to interact with each other in a networked environment.

ActiveX component   Reusable software component that adheres to the ActiveX specification and can operate in an ActiveX–compliant environment.

ad hoc topology   A type of communication used on wireless local area networks (LANs) in which devices equipped with wireless network interface adapters communicate with each other at will. Compare with *infrastructure topology*.

address   A precise location where a piece of information is stored in memory or on disk. Also, the unique identifier for a node on a network. On the Internet, the code by which an individual user is identified. The format is *username@hostname*, where username is your user name, logon name, or account number, and hostname is the name of the computer or Internet provider you use.

address (A) resource record   A resource record (RR) used to map a DNS domain name to a host Internet Protocol version 4 (IPv4) address on the network.

Address Resolution Protocol (ARP)   A TCP/IP and AppleTalk protocol used to resolve the IP addresses of computers on a LAN into the hardware (or media access control [MAC]) addresses needed to transmit data-link layer frames to them.

administrative credentials   Logon information that is used to identify a member of an administrative group. Groups that use administrative credentials include Administrators, Domain Admins, and DNS Admins. Most system-wide or domain-wide tasks require administrative credentials.

Administrators group   On a local computer, a group whose members have the highest level of administrative access to the local computer.

ADSI   *See* Active Directory Service Interfaces.

Advanced Configuration Power Interface (ACPI)   An industry specification, defining power management on a range of computer devices. ACPI compliance is necessary for devices to take advantage of Plug and Play and power management capabilities.

agent   A program that performs a background task for a user and reports to the user when the task is done or when some expected event has taken place.

AH   *See* IP Authentication Header (AH).

alert   A function that detects when a predefined counter value rises above or falls below the configured threshold and notifies a user by means of the Messenger service.

algorithm   In cryptography, a mathematical process that is used in cryptographic operations such as the encryption and digital signing of data. An algorithm is commonly used with a cryptographic key to enhance security.

allocation unit   The smallest unit of managed space on a hard disk or logical volume. Also called a *cluster*.

analog   Related to a continuously variable physical property, such as voltage, pressure, or rotation. An analog device can represent an infinite number of values within the range the device can handle. See also *digital*.

anonymous FTP   A way to use an FTP program to log on to another computer to copy files when you do not have an account on that computer. When you log on, enter anonymous as the user name and your e-mail address as the password to gain access to publicly available files. See also *File Transfer Protocol (FTP)*.

answer file   A file that contains answers to questions that should be automated during installation. When used to automate Active Directory installation, the answer file must contain all of the parameters that the Active Directory Installation Wizard needs to install Active Directory.

APIPA   *See* Automatic Private IP Addressing (APIPA).

application directory partition   An Active Directory partition that stores application-specific data that can be dynamic (subject to Time to Live restrictions). Application directory partitions can store any type of object except security principles and are not replicated to the global catalog. The replication scope of an application directory partition can be configured to include any set of domain controllers in the forest.

Archive (A) attribute   An attribute of each file that is used by backup utilities to determine whether or not to back up that file. The Archive attribute is set to TRUE whenever a file is created or modified. Differential and incremental backup jobs will back up files only if their archive attribute is TRUE.

ARP   *See* Address Resolution Protocol (ARP).

ARPANET (Advanced Research Projects Agency Network)   A pioneering wide area network (WAN) commissioned by the Department of Defense, ARPANET was designed to facilitate the exchange of information between universities and other research organizations. ARPANET, which became operational in the 1960s, is the network from which the Internet evolved.

ASCII (American Standard Code for Information Interchange)   A coding scheme that assigns numeric values to letters, numbers, punctuation marks, and certain other characters. By standardizing the values used for these characters, ASCII enables computers and computer programs to exchange information.

ASR   *See* Automated System Recovery (ASR).

attribute   A characteristic. In Windows file management, it is information that shows whether a file is read-only, hidden, compressed, encrypted, ready to be backed up (archived), or should be indexed. In Active Directory, a unit of information that makes up an object in a directory service, such as Active Directory.

audit policy   A policy that determines the security events to be reported to the network administrator.

auditing   A process that tracks network activities by user accounts, and a routine element of network security.

authentication   The process for verifying that an entity or object is who or what it claims to be. Examples include confirming the source and integrity of information, such as verifying a digital signature or verifying the identity of a user or computer. See also *trust relationship*.

authentication   Verification of the identity of a user or computer process. In Windows Server 2003, Windows 2000, and Windows NT, authentication involves comparing the user's security identifier (SID) and password to a list of authorized users on a domain controller.

Authentication Header (AH)   A header that provides authentication, integrity, and antireplay for the entire packet (the Internet Protocol [IP] header and the data payload carried in the packet).

authentication protocol   The protocol by which an entity on a network proves its identity to a remote entity. Typically, identity is proved with the use of a secret key, such as a password, or with a stronger key, such as the key on a smart card.

authoritative restore   A type of restore operation performed with the Ntdsutil.exe utility on an Active Directory domain controller in which the objects in the restored directory are treated as authoritative, replacing (through replication) all existing copies of those objects. Authoritative restore is applicable only to replicated System State data, such as Active Directory data, and File Replication service data. See also *non-authoritative restore*.

authoritative server   A DNS server that has been designated as the definitive source of information about the computers in a particular domain. When resolving a computer's DNS name into its IP address, DNS servers consult the authoritative server for the domain in which that computer is located. Whatever information the authoritative server provides about that domain is understood by all DNS servers to be correct. See also *Domain Name System (DNS)*.

authorization   A process that verifies that the user has the correct rights or permissions to access a resource.

autochanger   A hardware device consisting of one or more backup drives, a media array, and a robotic mechanism that inserts media into and removes it from the drives. Used to perform automated backups of large amounts of data.

autoenrollment   The process by which a computer automatically requests and receives a digital certificate from a certification authority, with no manual interaction from the user.

Automated System Recovery (ASR)   A feature of Windows Server 2003 that allows an administrator to return a failed server to operation efficiently.

Automatic Updates   A client-side component that can be used to keep a system up to date with security rollups, patches, and drivers. Automatic Updates is also the client component of a Software Update Services (SUS) infrastructure, which allows an enterprise to provide centralized and managed updates.

AXFR   *See* full zone transfer (AXFR).

B

Background Intelligent Transfer Service (BITS)   A service used to transfer files between a client and a Hypertext Transfer Protocol (HTTP) server. BITS intelligently uses idle network bandwidth, and will decrease transfer requests when other network traffic increases.

backup domain controller (BDC)   In a Windows NT domain, a computer that stores a backup of the database that contains all the security and account information from the primary domain controller (PDC). A BDC also authenticates logons and can be promoted to a PDC when necessary. In a Windows Server 2003 or Windows 2000 domain, BDCs are not required; all domain controllers are peers, and all can perform maintenance on the directory.

backup media pool   A logical set of backup storage media used by Windows Server 2003 and Windows 2000 Server Backup.

Backup Operators group   A type of local or global group that contains the user rights you need to back up and restore files and folders.

bandwidth   In communications, the difference between the highest and lowest frequencies in a given range. In computer networks, bandwidth is the amount of data that can be transmitted across a communications channel in a specific amount of time. Greater bandwidth indicates faster data-transfer capability and is expressed in bits per second (bps).

Bandwidth Allocation Protocol (BAP)   A Point-to-Point Protocol (PPP) control protocol that is used on a multiprocessing connection to dynamically add and remove links.

BAP   *See* Bandwidth Allocation Protocol (BAP).

base schema   A basic set of schema classes and attributes shipped with Windows Server 2003. There are nearly 200 schema classes and more than 900 schema attributes provided in the base schema.

basic disk   A physical disk that is configured with partitions. The disk's structure is compatible with previous versions of Windows and with several non-Windows operating systems.

basic input/output system (BIOS)   On PC-compatible computers, the set of essential software routines that test hardware at startup, start the operating system, and support the transfer of data among hardware devices. The BIOS is stored in read-only memory (ROM) so that it can be executed when the computer is turned on.

basic service area (BSA)   The operational range of a group of wireless networking devices.

basic service set (BSS)   A group of wireless networking devices within operational range of each other.

batch program   An ASCII (unformatted text) file that contains one or more operating system commands. A batch program's filename has a .cmd or .bat extension. When you type the filename at the command prompt, or when the batch program is run from another program, its commands are processed sequentially. Also called *batch files*.

Berkeley Internet Name Domain (BIND)   An implementation of Domain Name System (DNS) written and ported to most available versions of the UNIX operating system. The Internet Software Consortium maintains the BIND software.

BIND   *See* Berkeley Internet Name Domain (BIND).

bind   To associate two pieces of information with one another.

binding   A process by which software components and layers are linked together allowing communication between the components. When a network component is installed, the binding relationships and dependencies for the components are established.

BIOS   *See* basic input/output system (BIOS).

bit   Short for binary digit: either 1 or 0 in the binary number system.

bits per second (bps)   A measure of the speed at which a device can transfer data.

boot volume   The volume that contains the Microsoft Windows Server 2003 operating system and its support files.

bounded media   A type of network medium in which the signals are confined to a restricted space, such as the inside of a cable. Compare with *unbounded media*.

bps   *See* bits per second (bps).

bridgehead server   A domain controller in a site, designated automatically by the knowledge consistency checker (KCC) as the contact point for exchange of directory information between this site and other sites. See also *preferred bridgehead server*.

broadcast address   An address that is destined for all hosts on a particular network segment.

broadcast domain   A group of computers connected in such a way that if one computer transmits a broadcast message, all the other computers will receive it.

broadcast message   A network message sent from a single computer that is distributed to all other devices on the same segment of the network as the sending computer.

broadcast network   A network that supports more than two attached hosts and has the ability to address a single message to all the attached hosts. Ethernet is an example of a broadcast network.

Browser service   The service that maintains a current list of computers and provides the list to applications when needed. Also called the Computer Browser service.

browsing   The process of creating and maintaining an up-to-date list of computers and resources on a network or part of a network by one or more designated computers running the Computer Browser service.

BSA *See* basic service area (BSA).

BSS *See* basic service set (BSS).

built-in groups The default security groups installed with the operating system. Built-in groups have been granted useful collections of rights and built-in abilities.

built-in user account A user account used to perform administrative tasks or to gain access to network resources.

byte A unit of information consisting of eight bits. In computer processing or storage, a byte is equivalent to a single character, such as a letter, numeral, or punctuation mark.

C

CA *See* certificate authority (CA).

cache For Domain Name System (DNS) and Windows Internet Name Service (WINS), a local information store of resource records for recently resolved names of remote hosts. Typically, the cache is built dynamically as the computer queries and resolves names. It also helps optimize the time required to resolve queried names.

Caching A process used to enhance performance by retaining previously accessed information in a location that provides faster response than the original location. Hard disk caching is used by the File and Print Sharing for Microsoft Networks service. The Remote Desktop Connection client can cache previously viewed screen shots from the terminal server on its local hard disk to improve performance of the Remote Desktop Protocol (RDP) connection.

caching-only server A DNS sever that does not host any DNS zones but that forwards name resolution requests and stores the results in its cache.

callback security A form of network security in which a remote access server calls a user back at a preset number after the user has made an initial connection and has been authenticated.

catalog An index of files in a backup set.

catalog service An information store that contains selected information about every object in every domain in the directory, and which is used for performing searches across an enterprise. The catalog service provided by Active Directory is called the global catalog.

certificate   A digital document that is commonly used for authentication and to secure information on open networks. A certificate securely binds a public key to the entity that holds the corresponding private key. Certificates are digitally signed by the issuing certification authority (CA) and can be managed for a user, computer, or service. See also *certification authority (CA)*; *public key infrastructure (PKI)*.

certification authority (CA)   An entity responsible for establishing and vouching for the authenticity of public keys belonging to subjects (usually users or computers) or other certification authorities. Activities of a CA can include binding public keys to distinguished names through signed certificates, managing certificate serial numbers, and handling certificate revocation.

certificate revocation list (CRL)   A list of certificates that have been revoked, rendering them unusable. Certification authorities publish their CRLs at regular intervals, so that authenticating systems can check the validity of certificates.

certificate rule   A software restriction policies rule that recognizes software that is digitally signed by an Authenticode software publisher certificate.

Certificate Services   A software service that issues certificates for a particular certification authority (CA).

certificate trust list   A signed list of root certification authority certificates that an administrator considers reputable for designated purposes, such as client authentication or secure e-mail. See also *certification authority (CA)*.

child domain   For the Domain Name System (DNS), a domain located in the namespace tree directly beneath another domain (the parent domain). For example, example.microsoft.com is a child domain of the parent domain, microsoft.com. A child domain is also called a subdomain.

child object   An object that resides in another object. For example, a file is a child object that resides in a folder, which is a parent object. See also *parent object*.

client   A program designed to communicate with a server program on another computer, usually to request and receive information. The client provides the interface with which the user can view and manipulate the server data. A client can be a module in an operating system, which enables the user to access resources on the network's other computers, or a separate application, such as a World Wide Web browser or e-mail reader.

Client Access License (CAL)   The legal right to connect to a service or application. CALs can be configured per server or per device/per user.

client/server networking   A computing model in which data processing tasks are distributed between clients, which request, display, and manipulate information, and servers, which supply and store information.

cluster   A set of computers joined together in such a way that they behave as a single system. Clustering is used for network load balancing as well as fault tolerance. In data storage, a cluster is the smallest amount of disk space that can be allocated for a file.

Cluster service   The collection of software on each node that manages all cluster-specific activity.

codec   Technology that *compresses* and *decompresses* data, particularly audio or video. Codecs can be implemented in software, hardware, or a combination of both.

COM   *See* Component Object Model (COM).

COM+   *See* Component Object Model (COM+).

common name (CN)   The primary name of an object in a Lightweight Directory Access Protocol (LDAP) directory, such as Active Directory. The CN must be unique within the container or organizational unit (OU) in which the object exists.

Component Object Model (COM)   An object-based programming model designed to promote software interoperability; it allows two or more applications or components to easily cooperate with one another, even if they were written by different vendors, at different times, in different programming languages, or if they are running on different computers running different operating systems.

Component Object Model (COM+)   An object-based programming model that allows two or more applications or components to easily cooperate with one another, even if the applications or components are written by different vendors.

computer account   An account that is created by a domain administrator and that uniquely identifies the computer on the domain. The Microsoft Windows Server 2003 computer account matches the name of the computer joining the domain.

Computer Configuration node   A node within Group Policy that contains the settings used to set group policies applied to computers, regardless of who logs onto them. Computer configuration settings are applied when the operating system initializes.

computer name   A unique name of up to 15 uppercase characters that identifies a computer to the network. The name cannot be the same as any other computer or domain name in the network.

configuration container   *See* configuration partition.

configuration partition   An Active Directory partition containing the replication topology and related metadata that is replicated to every domain controller in the forest. Directory-aware applications store information in the configuration container that applies to the entire forest.

connection object   An Active Directory object that represents a replication connection from one domain controller to another. The connection object is a child of the replication destination's NTDS Settings object and identifies the replication source server, contains a replication schedule, and specifies a replication transport. Connection objects are created automatically by the knowledge consistency checker (KCC), but they can also be created manually. Connections generated automatically must not be modified by the user unless they are first converted into manual connections.

connectionless   A type of protocol that transmits messages to a destination without first establishing a connection with the destination system. Connectionless protocols are used primarily for transactions that consist of a single request and reply. The Internet Protocol (IP) and the User Datagram Protocol (UDP) are both connectionless protocols.

connection-oriented   A type of protocol that transmits a series of messages to a destination to establish a connection before sending any application data. Establishing the connection ensures that the destination system is active and ready to receive data. Connection-oriented protocols are typically used to send large amounts of data, such as entire files, which must be split into multiple packets and which are useless unless every packet arrives at the destination without error. The Transmission Control Protocol (TCP) is a connection-oriented protocol.

console   A framework for hosting administrative tools, such as Microsoft Management Console (MMC). A console is defined by the items in its console tree, which might include folders or other containers, World Wide Web pages, and other administrative items.

console tree   The window pane in a Microsoft Management Console (MMC) that displays the items contained in the console. The items in the console tree and their hierarchical organization determine the capabilities of a console.

container   An Active Directory object that has attributes and is part of the Active Directory namespace. Unlike other objects, it does not usually represent anything concrete; it is a package for a group of objects and other containers.

contiguous namespace   A namespace where the name of the child object in an object hierarchy always contains the name of the parent domain. A tree is a contiguous namespace.

counters The individual system attributes or processes monitored by the Performance console in Windows Server 2003.

credentials A set of information that includes identification and proof of identification that is used to gain access to local and network resources.

CRL *See* certificate revocation list (CRL).

cross-link trust *See* shortcut trust.

cross-reference object An object in which Active Directory stores information about directory partitions and external directory services. An example of an external directory service is another LDAP-compliant directory.

cryptography The processes, art, and science of keeping messages and data secure. Cryptography is used to enable and ensure confidentiality, data integrity, authentication (entity and data origin), and nonrepudiation.

D

data encryption *See* encryption.

Data Encryption Standard (DES) A commonly used, highly sophisticated algorithm developed by the U.S. National Bureau of Standards for encrypting and decoding data An encryption algorithm that uses a 56-bit key and maps a 64-bit input block to a 64-bit output block. The key appears to be a 64-bit key, but 1 bit in each of the 8 bytes is used for odd parity, resulting in 56 bits of usable key. *See also* *encryption*.

datagram A term for the unit of data used by the Internet Protocol (IP) and other network layer protocols. Network layer protocols accept data from transport layer protocols and package it into datagrams by adding their own protocol headers. The protocol then passes the datagrams down to a data-link layer protocol for further packaging before they are transmitted over the network.

dedicated connection A communications channel that connects two or more geographic locations. Dedicated connections are private or leased lines, rather than on-demand connections.

dedicated domain In a forest of multiple domains, a domain that does not contain any user or many computer accounts and is dedicated to the operations associated with enterprise management. This domain is created to serve as the forest root domain.

default gateway   The router on the local network used by a TCP/IP client computer to transmit messages to computers on other networks. To communicate with other networks, TCP/IP computers consult their routing tables for the address of the destination network. If they locate the address, they send their packets to the router specified in the table entry, which relays them to the desired network. If no specific entry for the network exists, the computer sends the packets to the router specified in the default gateway entry, which the user (or a DHCP server) supplies as one of the basic configuration parameters of the TCP/IP client.

default groups   Groups that have a predetermined set of user rights or group membership. There are four categories of default groups: groups in the Builtin folder, groups in the Users folder, special identity groups, and default local groups. All of the default groups are security groups and have been assigned common sets of rights and permissions that you might want to assign to the users and groups that you place into the default groups.

delegated subdomain   A separate Domain Name System (DNS) subdomain set up in the established DNS namespace.

Delegation of Control Wizard   A wizard that steps you through the process of assigning administrative permissions at the domain, OU, or container level.

Denial of Service (DoS) attack   An attack in which an intruder exploits a weakness or a design limitation of a network service to overload or halt the service so that the service is not available for use.

DES   *See* Data Encryption Standard (DES).

details pane   The pane in the Microsoft Management Console (MMC) that displays the details for the selected item in the console tree. The details can be a list of items or they can be administrative properties, services, and events that are acted on by a console or snap-in.

device driver   A program that enables a specific device, such as a modem, network interface adapter, or printer, to communicate with an operating system, such as Microsoft Windows Server 2003.

DHCP   *See* Dynamic Host Configuration Protocol (DHCP).

DHCP service   A service that enables a computer to function as a DHCP server and configure DHCP-enabled clients on a network. DHCP runs on a server, enabling the automatic, centralized management of IP addresses and other TCP/IP configuration settings for network clients.

differential backup   A type of backup job that uses a filter that causes it to back up only the files that have changed since the last full backup job. Compare with *incremental backup*.

Diffie-Hellman key agreement protocol   A cryptographic mechanism that allows two parties to establish a shared secret key without having any preestablished secrets between them. Diffie-Hellman is frequently used to establish the shared secret keys that are used by common applications of cryptography, such as Internet Protocol Security (IPSec). It is not normally used for data protection.

digital   A system that encodes information numerically, by using digits such as 0 and 1, in a binary context. Computers use digital encoding to process data. A digital signal is a discrete binary state, either on or off. See also *analog*.

digital line   A communication line that carries information only in binary-encoded (digital) form. To minimize distortion and noise interference, a digital line uses repeaters to regenerate the signal periodically during transmission.

digital signature   An attribute of a driver, application, or document that identifies the creator of the file. Microsoft's digital signature is included in all Microsoft-supplied drivers, providing assurance as to the stability and compatibility of the drivers with Windows Server 2003 and Windows 2000 Server.

directory   An information source (for example, a telephone directory) that contains information about people, computer files, or other objects. In a file system, a directory stores information about files. In a distributed computing environment (such as a Microsoft Windows Server 2003 domain), the directory stores information about objects such as printers, fax servers, applications, databases, and other users.

directory database   The physical storage for each replica of Active Directory. The directory database is also called the store.

directory partition   *See* naming context.

directory service   A database containing information about network entities and resources, used as a guide to the network and as an authentication resource by multiple users. See also *Active Directory*.

directory service log   A log in Event Viewer in which Active Directory records events, including errors, warnings, and information that Active Directory generates.

directory services restore mode   A boot option that allows restores of Active Directory on a domain controller.

distinguished name (DN)   A name that uniquely identified an object by using the relative distinguished name for the object, plus the names of container objects and domains that contain the object. The distinguished name identifies the object as well as its location in a tree. Every object in Active Directory has a distinguished name. A typical distinguished name might be: CN=MyName,CN=Users,DC=microsoft,DC=com. This identifies the MyName user object in the microsoft.com domain.

Distributed File System (DFS)   A service that allows system administrators to organize distributed network shares into a logical namespace, enabling users to access files without specifying their physical location and providing load sharing across network shares.

distribution group   A group that is used solely for e-mail distribution and is not security enabled. See also *security group*.

DMZ   *See* perimeter network.

DN   *See* distinguished name (DN).

DNS   *See* Domain Name System (DNS).

DNS client   A client computer that queries DNS servers in an attempt to resolve DNS domain names. DNS clients maintain a temporary cache of resolved DNS domain names.

DNS server   A computer that runs DNS server programs containing name-to-IP address mappings, IP address-to-name mappings, information about the domain tree structure, and other information. DNS servers also attempt to resolve client queries. A DNS server is also called a DNS name server.

DNS suffix   For DNS, a character string that represents a domain name. The DNS suffix shows where a host is located relative to the DNS root, specifying a host's location in the DNS hierarchy. Usually, the DNS suffix describes the latter portion of a DNS name, following one or more of the first labels of a DNS name.

DNS zone   In a DNS database, a contiguous portion of the DNS tree that is administered as a single, separate entity by a DNS server. The zone contains resource records for all the names within the zone.

domain   In Active Directory, a collection of computer, user, and group objects defined by the administrator. These objects share a common directory database, security policies, and security relationships with other domains. In DNS, a domain is any tree or subtree within the DNS namespace. Although the names for DNS domains often correspond to Active Directory domains, DNS domains should not be confused with Active Directory domains.

domain controller   In an Active Directory forest, a server that contains a writable copy of the Active Directory database, participates in Active Directory replication, and controls access to network resources. Administrators can manage user accounts, network access, shared resources, site topology, and other directory objects from any domain controller in the forest. See also *Active Directory*; *authentication*; *directory*; *forest*.

domain controller locator (Locator)   An algorithm running in the context of the Netlogon service that enables a client to locate a domain controller.

domain functional level   A way to enable domain-wide Active Directory features within your network environment. Four domain functional levels are available: Windows 2000 Mixed (default), Windows 2000 Native, Windows Server 2003 interim, and Windows Server 2003.

domain hierarchy   A tree structure of parent and child domains.

domain local group   A security or distribution group that can contain universal groups, global groups, other domain local groups from its own domain, and accounts from any domain in the forest. Domain local security groups can be granted rights and permissions on resources that reside only in the same domain where the domain local group is located.

domain model   A grouping of one or more domains that have administration and communication links between them, set up to manage users and resources.

domain name   The name given by an administrator to a collection of networked computers that share a common directory. Part of the DNS naming structure, domain names consist of a sequence of name labels separated by periods. See also *domain*; *Domain Name System (DNS)*.

Domain Name System (DNS)   A hierarchical, distributed database that contains mappings of DNS domain names to various types of data, such as IP addresses. DNS enables the location of computers and services by user-friendly names, and it also enables the discovery of other information stored in the database. See also *domain*; *domain name*.

domain namespace   The database structure used by the Domain Name System (DNS).

domain naming master   The one domain controller assigned to handle the addition or removal of domains in a forest. See also *Flexible Single Operations Master*.

domain partition   An Active Directory partition that describes the logical structure of the deployment, including data such as domain structure or replication topology. This data is common to all domains in a forest and is replicated to all domain controllers in a forest.

domain suffix   For DNS, an optional parent domain name that can be appended to the end of a relative domain name used in a name query or host lookup. The domain suffix can be used to complete an alternate fully qualified DNS domain name to be searched when the first attempt to query a name fails.

domain tree   In DNS, the inverted hierarchical tree structure that is used to index domain names. Domain trees are similar in purpose and concept to the directory trees used by computer filing systems for disk storage. When a domain tree has one or more branches, each branch can organize domain names used in the namespace into logical collections.

In Active Directory, a hierarchical structure of one or more domains, connected by transitive, bidirectional trusts, that forms a contiguous namespace. Multiple domain trees can belong to the same forest.

domain user account   Allows a user to log on to the domain to gain access to network resources.

driver   *See* device driver.

DWORD   A data type consisting of four bytes in hexadecimal.

Dynamic Host Configuration Protocol (DHCP)   A TCP/IP service protocol that offers dynamic leased configuration of host IP addresses and distributes other configuration parameters to eligible network clients. DHCP uses a client/server model where the DHCP server centrally manages IP addresses that are used on the network.

dynamic update   Enables clients with dynamically assigned Internet Protocol (IP) addresses to register directly with a server running the Domain Name System (DNS) service and update their DNS resource records automatically. Dynamic updates eliminate the need for other Internet naming services, such as Windows Internet Name Service (WINS), in a homogeneous environment.

dynamic-link library (DLL)   A program module that contains executable code and data that can be used by various programs. A program uses the DLL only when the program is active, and the DLL is unloaded when the program closes.

E

EAP   *See* Extensible Authentication Protocol (EAP)

effective permissions   The permissions that result from the evaluation of group and user permissions allowed, denied, inherited, and explicitly defined on a resource. The effective permissions determine the actual access for a security principal.

EFS   *See* encrypting file system (EFS).

Encapsulating Security Payload (ESP)   An Internet Protocol Security (IPSec) protocol that provides confidentiality, in addition to authentication and integrity. ESP can be used alone, in combination with Authentication Header (AH), or nested with the Layer2 Tunneling Protocol (L2TP).

encapsulation   The method used to pass data from one protocol over a network within a different protocol. Data from one protocol is wrapped with the header of a different protocol.

Encrypting File System (EFS)   A feature of NTFS that enables users to encrypt files and folders on an NTFS volume disk to keep them safe from access by intruders.

encryption   The process of making information indecipherable to protect it from unauthorized viewing or use, especially during transmission or when the data is stored on a transportable magnetic medium. A key is required to decode the information. See also *data encryption standard (DES)*.

enrollment   The process by which a user or computer obtains a certificate from a certification authority.

enterprise certification authority   A certification authority (CA) that is fully integrated with Active Directory.

entire zone transfer (AXFR)   The standard query type supported by all DNS servers to update and synchronize zone data when the zone has been changed. When a DNS query is made using AXFR as the specified query type, the entire zone is transferred as the response.

environment variable   A string of environment information, such as a drive, path, or filename, associated with a symbolic name.

ephemeral port   A Transmission Control Protocol (TCP) or User Datagram Protocol (UDP) port number of 1024 or higher, chosen at random by a TCP/IP client computer during the initiation of a transaction with a server. Compare with *well-known port*.

ESP   *See* IP Encapsulating Security Payload (ESP).

Ethernet   Common term used to describe Institute of Electrical and Electronic Engineers (IEEE) 802.3, a data-link layer LAN protocol developed in the 1970s, which is now the most popular protocol of its kind in the world. Ethernet runs at 10 Mbps, is based on the Carrier Sense Multiple Access with Collision Detection (CSMA/CD) Media Access Control (MAC) mechanism, and supports a variety of physical layer options, including coaxial, unshielded twisted pair (UTP), and fiber-optic cables. More recent revisions of the protocol support speeds of 100 Mbps (Fast Ethernet) and 1,000 Mbps (gigabit Ethernet).

event   Any significant occurrence in the system, or an application that requires users to be notified or an entry to be added to a log.

Event Log service   A service that records events in the system, security, application, and other logs. Events recorded by the Event Log service can be viewed by using the Event Viewer.

event logging   The Microsoft Windows Server 2003 process of recording an audit entry in the audit trail whenever certain events occur, such as services starting and stopping or users logging on and off and accessing resources. You can use Event Viewer to review Windows Server 2003 events.

explicit trust   A trust created manually.

extended partition   A nonbootable portion of a hard disk that can be subdivided into logical drives. There can be only a single extended partition per hard disk.

Extensible Authentication Protocol (EAP)   An extension to the Point-to-Point Protocol (PPP) that allows for arbitrary authentication mechanisms to be employed for the validation of a PPP connection.

Extensible Markup Language (XML)   An abbreviated version of the Standard Generalized Markup Language (SGML), it allows the flexible development of user-defined document types and provides a non-proprietary, persistent, and verifiable file format for the storage and transmission of text and data both on and off the Web.

extensions   Snap-ins that provide additional administrative functionality to another snap-in.

external trust   A trust that must be explicitly created between two Active Directory domains that are in different forests or between an Active Directory domain and a Windows NT 4.0 or earlier domain. The trust is nontransitive and can be one- or two-way. See also *shortcut trust*; *forest trust*; *realm trust*.

extranet   A limited subset of computers or users on a public network, typically the Internet, that can access an organization's internal network.

F

failback   The ability of a cluster to redistribute its application load when a failed node is restored to the cluster.

failover   An operation that automatically switches to a standby database, server, or network if the primary system fails or is temporarily shut down for servicing. In server clusters, the process of taking resources off one node in a prescribed order and restoring them on another node.

fault tolerance   The ability of a system to ensure data integrity when an unexpected hardware or software failure occurs.

FDDI   *See* Fiber Distributed Data Interface (FDDI).

Fiber Distributed Data Interface (FDDI)   A data-link layer LAN protocol running at 100 Mbps and designed for use with fiber-optic cable. Typically used for backbone networks, FDDI uses the token-passing Media Access Control (MAC) mechanism and supports a double-ring topology that provides fault tolerance in the event of a system disconnection or cable failure.

fiber optic   A type of network medium that uses cables made of glass or plastic that transmit signals in the form of light pulses.

Fibre Channel   A high-speed serial networking technology used primarily for connections between computers and storage devices.

File Replication Service (FRS)   The service responsible for ensuring consistency of the SYSVOL folder on domain controllers. FRS will replicate, or copy, any changes made to a domain controller's SYSVOL to all other domain controllers. FRS can also be used to replicate folders in a Distributed File System (DFS).

File Transfer Protocol (FTP)   An application layer TCP/IP protocol designed to perform file transfers and basic file management tasks on remote computers. FTP is a mainstay of Internet communications. FTP is unique among TCP/IP protocols in that it uses two simultaneous TCP connections. One, a control connection, remains open during the entire life of the session between the FTP client and the FTP server. When the client initiates a file transfer, a second connection is opened between the two computers to carry the transferred data. This connection closes when the data transfer concludes.

firewall   A hardware or software product designed to isolate part of an internetwork to protect it against intrusion by outside processes.

flexible single master operations (FSMO)   Active Directory operations that are not permitted to occur at different places in the network at the same time.

folder   A grouping of files or other folders, graphically represented by a folder icon, in both Microsoft Windows Server 2003 and Apple Macintosh environments. Also called a *directory*.

folder redirection   An extension within Group Policy that allows administrators to redirect the following special folders to network locations: Application Data, Desktop, My Documents, My Pictures, and Start Menu.

forest   One or more Active Directory domains that share the same class and attribute definitions (schema), site and replication information (configuration), and forest-wide search capabilities (global catalog). Domains in the same forest are linked with two-way, transitive trust relationships.

forest functional level   A way to enable forest-wide Active Directory features within your network environment. Three forest functional levels are available: Windows 2000 (default), Windows Server 2003 interim, and Windows Server 2003.

forest root domain   The first domain created in a new forest. The forest-wide administrative groups, Enterprise Admins and Schema Admins, are located in this domain. As a best practice, new domains are created as children of the forest root domain.

forest trust   A trust that must be explicitly created by a systems administrator between two forest root domains. This trust allows all domains in one forest to transitively trust all domains in another forest. A forest trust is transitive between two forests only and can be one-way or two-way. See also *shortcut trust*; *external trust*; *realm trust*.

forward lookup   In Domain Name System (DNS), a query process in which the friendly DNS domain name of a host computer is searched to find its Internet Protocol (IP) address.

forwarder   A DNS server designated by other internal DNS servers to be used to forward queries for resolving external or offsite DNS domain names.

FQDN   *See* fully qualified domain name (FQDN).

frame   Unit of data constructed, transmitted, and received by data-link layer protocols, such as Ethernet and Token Ring. Data-link layer protocols create frames by packaging the data they receive from network layer protocols inside a header and footer. Frames can be different sizes, depending on the protocol used to create them.

frame relay   A type of wide area networking technology in which two or more locations install their own leased lines to connect to a service provider's frame relay network, called a cloud. The devices connected to the cloud can then establish connections with the other connected systems.

FSMO   *See* Flexible Single Master Operation (FSMO).

FTP   *See* File Transfer Protocol (FTP).

full zone transfer (AXFR)   The standard query type supported by all Domain Name System (DNS) servers to update and synchronize zone data when the zone has been changed. When a DNS query is made using AXFR as the specified query type, the entire zone is transferred as the response.

fully qualified domain name (FQDN)   An unambiguous DNS domain name that indicates its location in the domain namespace with absolute certainty. Fully qualified domain names differ from relative names in that they can be stated with a trailing period (.)—for example, host.example.microsoft.com.—to qualify their position in relation to the root of the name space.

G

gateway   On a Transmission Control Protocol/Internet Protocol (TCP/IP) network, the term gateway is often used synonymously with the term router, referring to a network layer device that connects two networks and relays traffic between them as needed, such as the default gateway specified in a TCP/IP client configuration. However, gateway is also used to refer to an application layer device that relays data between two different services, such as an e-mail gateway that enables two separate e-mail services to communicate with each other.

GBps   Gigabytes per second, a unit of measurement typically used to measure the speed of data storage devices.

Global Catalog   Contains a full replica of all Active Directory objects in its host domain plus a partial replica of all directory objects in every domain in the forest. A Global Catalog contains information about all objects in all domains in the forest; a single query to the Global Catalog produces the information about where the object can be found.

Global Catalog server   A domain controller that holds a copy of the Global Catalog for the forest.

global group   A security or distribution group that can contain users, groups, and computers from its own domain as members. Global security groups can be granted rights and permissions for resources in any domain in the forest. See also *local group*; *group*.

globally unique identifier (GUID)   A 128-bit number that is guaranteed to be unique. GUIDs are assigned to objects when the objects are created. The GUID never changes, even if you move or rename the object. Applications can store the GUID of an object and use the GUID to retrieve that object regardless of its current distinguished name.

glue chasing   In DNS, queries to resolve delegation name server (NS) resource records that do not have corresponding glue address (A) resource records in the same zone.

glue record   In DNS, a delegation resource record used for locating the authoritative DNS servers for a delegated zone. These records are used to glue zones together and provide an effective delegation and referral path for other DNS servers to follow when resolving a name.

GPO   *See* Group Policy Object (GPO).

Group Policy   The component within Active Directory that enables directory-based change and configuration management of user and computer settings, including security and user data. You use Group Policy to define configurations for groups of users and computers. With Group Policy, you can specify policy settings for registry-based policies, security, software installation, scripts, folder redirection, remote installation services, and Internet Explorer maintenance. See also *Group Policy Object.*

Group Policy Object (GPO)   A collection of Group Policy settings. GPOs are essentially the documents created by the Group Policy snap-in. GPOs are stored at the domain level and affect users and computers contained in sites, domains, and organizational units. In addition, each computer running Microsoft Windows Server 2003 has exactly one group of settings stored locally, called the local GPO.

group scopes   An indicator of where in the network the group can be used to assign permissions to the group. The three group scopes are global, domain local, and universal. See also *global group*; *domain local group*; *universal group*.

group type   An indicator of how a group is used. There are two group types: security and distribution. Both types of groups are stored in the database component of Active Directory, which allows you to use them anywhere in your network. See also *security group*; *distribution group*.

GUID   *See* globally unique identifier (GUID).

GUID partition table (GPT)   The storage location for disk configuration information for disks used in 64-bit versions of Windows.

H

handshaking   A series of signals acknowledging that communication can take place between computers or other devices. A hardware handshake is an exchange of signals over specific wires (other than the data wires), in which each device indicates its readiness to send or receive data. A software handshake consists of signals transmitted over the same wires used to transfer data, as in modem-to-modem communications over telephone lines.

hash   A fixed-size result that is obtained by applying a one-way mathematical function (sometimes called a *hash algorithm*) to an arbitrary amount of data. If there is a change in the input data, the hash changes. The hash can be used in many operations, including authentication and digital signing. Also called a *message digest*.

hash algorithm   An algorithm that produces a hash value of some piece of data, such as a message or session key. Typical hash algorithms include MD2, MD4, MD5, and SHA-1. Also called a *hash function*.

hash message authentication code (HMAC)   A type of checksum calculation used by IP Security (IpSec) systems to ensure that data is not modified during transmission over the network.

hash rule   A software restriction policies rule that recognizes specific software based on the hash of the software.

headless server   A server without a monitor, keyboard, mouse, or video card, which is administered remotely.

hexadecimal   A base-16 number system represented by the digits 0 through 9 and the uppercase or lowercase letters A (equivalent to decimal 10) through F (equivalent to decimal 15).

hierarchical name space   A namespace, such as the Domain Name System (DNS) and Active Directory service, that has a tiered structure that allows names and objects to be nested inside each other.

hive   One of five sections of the registry. Each hive is a discrete body of keys, subkeys, and values that record configuration information for the computer. Each hive is a file that can be moved from one system to another but can be edited only by using the Registry Editor.

Home folder   A folder (usually on a file server) that administrators can assign to individual users or groups. Administrators use home folders to consolidate user files onto specific file servers for easy backup. Home folders are used by some programs as the default folder for the Open and Save As dialog boxes. Home folders may also be referred to as home directories.

hop   A unit of measurement used to quantify the length of a route between two computers on an internetwork, indicated by the number of routers that packets must pass through to reach the destination end system. Distance vector routing protocols like the Routing Information Protocol (RIP) use the number of hops as a way to compare the relative efficiency of routes.

host   Any device on the network that uses TCP/IP. A host is also a computer on the Internet you might be able to log on to.

host ID   The portion of the IP address that identifies a computer within a particular network ID.

host name   The DNS name of a device on a network. These names are used to locate computers on the network. To find another computer, its host name must either appear in the Hosts file or be known by a DNS server.

Hosts file   An ASCII text file used by TCP/IP computers to resolve host names into IP addresses.

hotfix   A small Microsoft software update, released between service packs, that is designed to address a specific issue.

HTTP   *See* Hypertext Transfer Protocol (HTTP).

hub   A hardware component to which cables running from computers and other devices are connected, joining all the devices into a network. In most cases, the term hub refers to an Ethernet multiport repeater, a device that amplifies the signals received from each connected device and forwards them to all the other devices simultaneously. See also *multiport repeater*.

hypertext   A system of writing and displaying text that enables the text to be linked in multiple ways, available at several levels of detail. Hypertext documents can also contain links to related documents, such as those referred to in footnotes.

Hypertext Transfer Protocol (HTTP)   Application layer protocol that is the basis for World Wide Web communications. Each HTTP transaction requires a separate TCP connection.

I

IANA   *See* Internet Assigned Numbers Authority (IANA).

IAS   *See* Internet Authentication Services (IAS).

ICMP   *See* Internet Control Message Protocol (ICMP).

identity store   A database of security identities, or security principals. Active Directory is the identity store for a Windows Server 2003 domain.

IEEE   *See* Institute of Electrical and Electronic Engineers (IEEE).

IETF   *See* Internet Engineering Task Force (IETF).

IGMP   *See* Internet Group Management Protocol (IGMP).

IIS   *See* Internet Information Services (IIS).

IMAP   *See* Internet Message Access Protocol (IMAP).

implicit trust   A trust created automatically. In Active Directory replication, the set of connections that domain controllers use to replicate information among themselves. In Windows Server 2003 domains, native mode is referred to as *Windows 2000 native*, and it is one of three domain functional levels available.

in-addr.arpa domain   A special top-level DNS domain reserved for reverse mapping of IP addresses to DNS host names.

incremental backup   A type of backup job that employs a filter that causes it to back up only the files that have changed since the last backup job. Compare with *differential backup*.

incremental zone transfer (IXFR)   An alternate query type that some Domain Name System (DNS) servers can use to update and synchronize zone data when a zone is changed. When IXFR is supported between DNS servers, servers can keep track of and transfer only incremental changes of resource records between each version of the zone.

infrastructure master   The domain controller assigned to update group-to-user references whenever group memberships are changed and to replicate these changes to any other domain controllers in the domain. At any time, there can be only one infrastructure master in a particular domain. The infrastructure master should not be located on the same computer as the Global Catalog if there is more than one domain controller in the forest.

infrastructure server   A computer that runs network services, such as DNS server, DHCP server, or Windows Internet Name Service (WINS).

infrastructure topology   A type of communication used on wireless local area networks (LANs) in which devices equipped with wireless network interface adapters communicate with a standard cabled network using a network access point. Compare with ad hoc topology. See also *access point*.

inheritance   The process through which permissions are propagated from a parent object to its children. Inheritance is at work in Active Directory and on disk volumes formatted with NTFS.

inherited permissions   Permissions propagated to a child object from a parent object.

instance   The most granular level of performance counter. A performance object, such as LogicalDisk, has counters, such as % Free Space. That counter may have instances, representing specific occurrences of that counter, for example the free space on disk volume C:\ and disk volume D:\.

Institute of Electrical and Electronics Engineers (IEEE)   Founded in 1963. IEEE is an organization composed of engineers, scientists, and students, best known for developing standards for the computer and electronics industry.

Integrated Services Digital Network (ISDN)   A dial-up communications service that uses standard telephone lines to provide high-speed digital communications.

IntelliMirror   A set of change and configuration management features based on Active Directory that enables management of user and computer data and settings, including security data. IntelliMirror also provides limited ability to deploy software to Windows 2000 and later workstations or servers.

intermediate system   On a TCP/IP network, a router that relays traffic generated by an end system from one network to another. The end systems in a TCP/IP transmission are identified by the Source IP Address and Destination IP Address fields in the IP header. All the other systems (that is, routers) involved in the transmission are known as intermediate systems.

International Organization for Standardization (ISO)   An organization, founded in 1946, that consists of standards bodies from over 75 countries, such as the American National Standards Institute (ANSI) from the United States. The ISO is responsible for the publication of many computer-related standards, the best known of which is "The Basic Reference Model for Open Systems Interconnection," commonly known as the OSI reference model.

International Telecommunications Union-Telecommunication (ITU-T)   The Telecommunication Standards Section of the International Telecommunications Union (ITU) responsible for telecommunication standards. Its responsibilities include standardizing modem design and operations and standardizing protocols for networks and facsimile transmission. ITU is an international organization within which governments and the private sector coordinate global telecom networks and services.

Internet Assigned Numbers Authority (IANA)   The organization responsible for the assignment of unique parameter values for the TCP/IP protocols, including IP address assignments for networks and protocol number assignments. The "Assigned Numbers" Requests for Comments (RFC) document (currently RFC 1700) lists all the protocol number assignments and many other unique parameters regulated by the IANA.

Internet Authentication Service (IAS)   The Microsoft implementation of Remote Authentication Dial-In User Service (RADIUS), an authentication and accounting system used by many Internet Service Providers (ISPs). When a user connects to an ISP using a username and password, the information is passed to a RADIUS server, which checks that the information is correct, and then authorizes access to the ISP system.

Internet Control Message Protocol (ICMP) A network layer TCP/IP protocol that carries administrative messages, particularly error messages and informational queries. ICMP query messages request information (or simply a response) from other computers, and are the basis for TCP/IP utilities like Ping, which is used to test the ability of one computer on a network to communicate with another.

Internet Engineering Task Force (IETF) An open community of network designers, operators, vendors, and researchers concerned with the evolution of Internet architecture and the smooth operation of the Internet. Internet standards are developed in IETF Requests for Comments (RFCs), which are a series of notes that discuss many aspects of computing and computer communication, focusing on networking protocols, programs, and concepts.

Internet Group Management Protocol (IGMP) A protocol that enables network devices to support Internet Protocol (IP) multicasting by registering hosts in specific multicast groups.

Internet Information Services (IIS) Software services that support Web site creation, configuration, and management, along with other Internet functions. Microsoft Internet Information Services include Network News Transfer Protocol (NNTP), File Transfer Protocol (FTP), and Simple Mail Transfer Protocol (SMTP).

Internet Key Exchange (IKE) A protocol that establishes the security association and shared keys necessary for two parties to communicate by using Internet Protocol Security (IPSec).

Internet Message Access Protocol (IMAP) An application layer TCP/IP protocol used by e-mail clients to download mail messages from a server. E-mail traffic between servers and outgoing e-mail traffic from clients to servers use the Simple Mail Transfer Protocol (SMTP). See also *Post Office Protocol 3 (POP3)*.

Internet Printing Protocol (IPP) A protocol that allows a client to send a job to a printer over the Internet or an intranet. The communication between the client and the printer is encapsulated in HTTP.

Internet Protocol (IP) The primary network layer protocol in the TCP/IP suite. IP is the protocol that is ultimately responsible for end-to-end communications on a TCP/IP internetwork, and it includes functions such as addressing, routing, and fragmentation.

Internet Protocol multicasting The extension of local area network multicasting technology to a TCP/IP network. Hosts send and receive multicast datagrams, the destination fields of which specify IP host group addresses rather than individual IP addresses. A host indicates that it is a member of a group by means of the Internet Group Management Protocol (IGMP).

Internet Protocol Security (IPSec)   A set of industry-standard, cryptography-based protection services and protocols. IPSec protects all protocols in the TCP/IP protocol suite and Internet communications by using Layer2 Tunneling Protocol (L2TP).

Internet Protocol version 6 (IPv6)   A new version of Internet Protocol supported in Windows Server 2003.

Internet zone rule   A software restriction policies rule that recognizes software based on the zone of the Internet from which the software is downloaded.

Internetwork Packet Exchange (IPX)   A network protocol native to NetWare that controls addressing and routing of packets within and between local area networks (LANs). IPX does not guarantee that a message will be complete (no lost packets).

interrupt request (IRQ)   One of a set of possible hardware interrupts, identified by a number. The number of the IRQ determines which interrupt handler will be used.

intersite replication   The replication traffic that occurs between sites.

intranet   A TCP/IP network owned by a private organization that provides services such as Web sites only to that organization's users.

intrasite replication   The replication traffic that occurs within a site.

IP address   A 32-bit address used to identify a node on an Internet Protocol (IP) internetwork. Each node on the IP internetwork must be assigned a unique IP address, which is made up of the network ID and a unique host ID. This address is typically represented in dotted-decimal notation, with the decimal value of each octet separated by a period, for example, 192.168.7.27. You can configure the IP address statically or dynamically through DHCP.

IP Authentication Header (AH)   One of the two protocols used by IPSec to protect data as it is transmitted over the network. AH provides authentication, anti-replay, and data integrity services, but it does not encrypt the data. See also *IP Encapsulating Security Payload (ESP)*.

IP Encapsulating Security Payload (ESP)   One of the two protocols used by IP Security (IPSec) to protect data as it is transmitted over the network. ESP provides encryption, authentication, anti-replay, and data integrity services. See also *IP Authentication Header (AH)*.

IP Security protocol (IPSec)   A set of Transmission Control Protocol/Internet Protocol (TCP/IP) protocol extensions designed to provide encrypted network layer communications. For computers to communicate using IPSec, they must share a public key.

IP   *See* Internet Protocol (IP).

IPSec policy   A collection of configuration settings containing rules, filter lists, and filter actions, which defined what network traffic IP Security (IPSec) should secure and how IPSec should secure it.

IPSec   *See* IP Security protocol (IPSec).

IPv6   New version of the Internet Protocol (IP) that expands the IP address space from 32 to 128 bits. See also *Internet Protocol (IP)*.

IPX   *See* Internetwork Packet Exchange (IPX).

IPX/SPX/NetBIOS Compatible Transport Protocol (NWLink)   The Microsoft implementation of the Internetwork Packet Exchange/Sequenced Packet Exchange (IPX/SPX) protocol used on NetWare networks. NWLink allows connectivity between Windows-based computers and NetWare networks running IPX/SPX. NWLink also provides Network Basic Input Output System (NetBIOS) functionality and the Routing Information Protocol (RIP).

ISDN   *See* Integrated Services Digital Network (ISDN).

ISO   *See* International Organization for Standardization (ISO).

iterative query   A query made to a DNS server for the best answer the server can provide without seeking further help from other DNS servers. Also called a *non-recursive query*.

ITU   *See* International Telecommunications Union (ITU).

IXFR   *See* incremental zone transfer (IXFR).

K

KB   Kilobyte, equal to 1000 bytes.

Kbps   Kilobits per second, a unit of measurement typically used to measure network transmission speed.

KCC   *See* knowledge consistency checker (KCC).

KDC   *See* Key Distribution Center (KDC).

Kerberos   An identity-based security system developed by MIT that authenticates users at logon. It works by assigning a unique key, called a *ticket*, to each user who logs on to the network. The ticket is then embedded in messages to identify the sender of the message. The Kerberos security protocol is the primary authentication mechanism in Windows Server 2003 and Windows 2000 Server.

Kerberos V5   An Internet standard security protocol for handling authentication of user or system identity. With Kerberos V5, passwords that are sent across network lines are encrypted, not sent as plain text. Kerberos V5 includes other security features as well.

kernel   The part of the executive (or operating system) that manages the processor. The kernel performs thread scheduling and dispatching, interrupt and exception handling, and multiprocessor synchronization.

Key Distribution Center (KDC)   A network service that supplies session tickets and temporary session keys used in the Kerberos V5 authentication protocol.

key   In Registry Editor, a folder that appears in the left pane of the Registry Editor window. A key can contain subkeys and entries. For example, Environment is a key of HKEY_CURRENT_USER. In IP Security (IPSec), a value used in combination with an algorithm to encrypt or decrypt data. Key settings for IPSec are configurable to provide greater security.

knowledge consistency checker (KCC)   A built-in service that runs on all domain controllers and automatically establishes connections between individual machines in the same site, called connection objects.

L

LAN   *See* local area network (LAN).

Layer 2 Tunneling Protocol (L2TP)   A protocol used to establish virtual private network connections across the Internet. See also *virtual private network (VPN)*.

Layer 2 Tunneling Protocol/Internet Protocol Security (L2TP/IPSec)   A virtual private network (VPN) connection method that provides session authentication, address encapsulation, and strong encryption of private data between remote access servers and clients. L2TP provides address encapsulation and user authentication, and Internet Protocol Security (IPSec) provides computer authentication and encryption of the L2TP session.

layering   The coordination of various protocols in a specific architecture that enables the protocols to work together to ensure that the data is prepared, transferred, received, and acted on as intended.

LDAP   *See* Lightweight Directory Access Protocol (LDAP).

Lightweight Data Interchange Format (LDIF)   An ASCII file format used to transfer data between LDAP directory services.

Lightweight Directory Access Protocol (LDAP)   The primary access protocol for Active Directory. LDAP version 3 is defined by a set of Proposed Standard documents in Internet Engineering Task Force (IETF) RFC 2251.

Lmhosts   An ASCII text file used by TCP/IP computers running Windows operating systems to resolve NetBIOS names into IP addresses. An Lmhosts file is a list of the NetBIOS names assigned to computers on the network and their corresponding IP addresses. Lmhosts files can also contain special entries used to preload the computer's NetBIOS name cache or to identify the domain controllers on the network.

load balancing   A technique used to scale the performance of a server-based program (such as a Web server) by distributing its client requests across multiple servers within the cluster.

local area network (LAN)   A group of connected computers, usually located close to one another (such as in the same building or the same floor of the building) so that data can be passed among them.

local computer   A computer that you can access directly without using a communications line or a communications device, such as a network card or a modem.

local group   A security group that can be granted permissions and rights to only those resources on the computer on which the group resides. Local groups contain local user accounts from the computer on which the group is created. Local groups cannot be members of any other group. See also *global group*.

local Group Policy Object   A Group Policy Object (GPO) stored on each computer whether the computer is part of an Active Directory environment or a networked environment. Local GPO settings can be overwritten by nonlocal GPOs and are the least influential if the computer is in an Active Directory environment. In a non-networked environment (or in a networked environment lacking a domain controller), the local GPO's settings are more important because they are not overwritten by nonlocal GPOs.

local user account   For Microsoft Windows Server 2003, a user account a domain provides for a user whose global account is not in a trusted domain. A local account is not required where trust relationships exist between domains.

local user profile   A computer-based record about an authorized user that is created automatically on the computer the first time a user logs on to a workstation or server computer.

log file   A file that stores messages generated by an application, service, or operating system. These messages are used to track the operations performed. Log files are usually plain text (ASCII) files and often have a .log extension.

logical printer   The representation of a physical printer. A logical printer is created on a Windows computer and includes the printer driver, printer settings, print defaults, and other configuration information that controls when and how a print job is sent to the printer.

logon script Typically a batch file set to run when a user logs on or logs off a system. A logon script is used to configure a user's initial environment. A logoff script is used to return a system to some predetermined condition. Either script can be assigned to multiple users individually or through Group Policy.

M

MAC *See* Media Access Control (MAC).

mandatory user profile A user profile that is not updated when the user logs off. It is downloaded to the user's desktop each time the user logs on and is created by an administrator and assigned to one or more users to create consistent or job-specific user profiles. Only members of the Administrators group can change profiles.

master boot record (MBR) The first sector on a hard disk where the computer gets its startup information. The MBR contains the partition table for the computer and a small program called the master boot code.

master file table (MFT) A special system file on an NTFS volume that consists of a database describing every file and subdirectory on the volume.

master server An authoritative Domain Name System (DNS) server for a zone. Master servers can vary and are either primary or secondary masters, depending on how the server obtains its zone data.

MB Megabyte, equal to 1000 kilobytes or 1,000,000 bytes.

Mbps Megabits per second, a unit of measurement typically used to measure network transmission speed.

MD5 *See* Message Digest 5 (MD5).

media In networking, a term used to describe the hardware mechanism for carrying data that computers and other network devices use to send information to each other. In computers, a term used to describe a means of storing data permanently, such as a hard or floppy disk.

Media Access Control (MAC) A method by which computers determine when they can transmit data over a shared network medium. The MAC mechanism implemented in the data-link layer protocol prevents data collisions from occurring during data transmission or permits them to occur in a controlled manner. The MAC mechanism is the defining characteristic of a data-link layer LAN protocol. The two most common MAC mechanisms in use today are Carrier Sense Multiple Access with Collision Detection (CSMA/CD), which is used by Ethernet networks, and token passing, which is used by Token Ring and Fiber Distributed Data Interface (FDDI) networks, among others.

media pool   A logical collection of removable media sharing the same management policies.

member server   A server that is joined to a domain but is not a domain controller in the domain. Member servers typically function as file servers, application servers, database servers, Web servers, certificate servers, firewalls, or remote access servers. See also *domain controller*, *global group*, *local group*.

Message Digest 5 (MD5)   A 128-bit hashing scheme developed by RSA Security Inc. and used by various Point-to-Point (PPP) vendors for encrypted authentication.

metadata   Information about the properties of data, such as the type of data in a column (numeric, text, and so on) or the length of a column.

metric   A number used to indicate the cost of a route in the Internet Protocol (IP) routing table that enables the selection of the best route among possible multiple routes to the same destination.

Microsoft Software Update Services (SUS)   An intranet version of the Microsoft Windows Update Web site that notifies administrators when new software updates are released and deploys them to the computers on the internal network.

minimal routing   The process of routing Internet Protocol (IP) using only the default routing table entries created by the operating system. Compare with *static routing, dynamic routing*.

minimum TTL   In DNS, a default Time to Live (TTL) value that is set in seconds and used with all resource records in a zone. This value is set in the start-of-authority (SOA) resource record for each zone. By default, the DNS server includes this value in query responses. It is used to inform recipients how long they can store and use resource records, which are provided in the query answer, before they must expire the stored records' data. When TTL values are set for individual resource records, those values override the minimum TTL.

mirror   1. Two partitions on two hard disks (also called RAID-1) configured so that each will contain identical data to the other. If one disk fails, the other contains the data and processing can continue. 2. A File Transfer Protocol (FTP) server that provides copies of the same files as another server. Some FTP servers are so popular that other servers have been set up to mirror them and spread the FTP load to more than one site.

mixed mode   In a Windows 2000 domain, the default domain mode setting. Mixed mode enables Windows NT–based backup domain controllers to coexist with Windows 2000–based domain controllers. Mixed mode does not support universal groups or the nesting of groups. In Windows Server 2003 domains, mixed mode is referred to as *Windows 2000 mixed*, and it is one of three domain functional levels available.

modifications   .mst files that allow you to customize Windows Installer packages (which have the .msi extension). Modifications are also called *transforms*. The Microsoft Windows Installer package format provides for customization by allowing you to "transform" the original package using authoring and repackaging tools.

multibyte   A character set that can consist of both 1-byte and 2-byte characters. A multibyte-character string can contain a mixture of 1-byte and 2-byte characters. Windows Server 2003 DNS uses the Unicode Transformation Format 8 (UTF-8) encoding scheme described in Request for Comments (RFC) 2044 to interpret and transform multibyte characters into 1-byte characters of 8-bit length.

multicast   A network transmission with a destination address that represents a group of computers on the network. Transmission Control Protocol/Internet Protocol (TCP/IP) multicast addresses are defined by the Internet Assigned Numbers Authority (IANA) and represent groups of computers with similar functions, such as all the routers on a network. Compare with *broadcast* and *unicast*.

multicasting   The process of sending a message simultaneously to more than one destination on a network.

multihomed computer   A computer that has multiple network adapters or that has been configured with multiple IP addresses for a single network adapter.

multimaster replication   A replication model in which any domain controller accepts and replicates directory changes to any other domain controller. This differs from other replication models in which one computer stores the single modifiable copy of the directory and other computers store backup copies. See also *domain controller; replication*.

multiplexing   Any one of several techniques used to simultaneously transmit multiple signals over a single cable or other network medium. Multiplexing works by separating the available bandwidth of the network medium into separate bands, by frequency, wavelength, time, or other criteria, and transmitting a different signal in each band.

multitasking   Computer legerdemain by which tasks are switched in and out of the processor so quickly that it appears they are all happening at once. The success of a multitasking system depends on how well the various tasks are isolated from one another.

multithreading   The simultaneous processing of several threads inside the same program. Because several threads can be processed in parallel, one thread does not have to finish before another one can start.

N

name resolution   The process of having software translate between names that are easy for users to work with and numerical IP addresses, which are difficult for users but necessary for TCP/IP communications. Name resolution can be provided by software components such as DNS or WINS.

name server (NS) resource record   A resource record used in a zone to designate the DNS domain names for authoritative DNS servers for the zone.

namespace   A set of unique names for resources or items used in a shared computing environment. For MMC, the namespace is represented by the console tree, which displays all the snap-ins and resources that are accessible to a console. For DNS, namespace is the vertical or hierarchical structure of the domain name tree.

naming context   A contiguous subtree of Active Directory that is replicated as a unit to other domain controllers in the forest that contain a replica of the same subtree. In Active Directory, a single server always holds at least three naming contexts: schema (class and attribute definitions for the directory), configuration (replication topology and related metadata), and domain (the subtree that contains the per-domain objects for one domain). The schema and configuration naming contexts are replicated to every domain controller in a specified forest. A domain naming context is replicated only to domain controllers for that domain. A naming context is also called a directory partition.

NAT   *See* network address translation (NAT).

native mode   In Windows 2000 domains, the domain mode in which all domain controllers in a domain are running Windows 2000 and a domain administrator has switched the domain operation mode from mixed mode to native mode. Native mode supports universal groups and nesting of groups. In native mode, domain controllers running Windows NT 4.0 or earlier are not supported.

negative caching   In DNS, client caching of failed responses to a query. Negative caching improves the response time for successive queries for the same name.

Net Logon service   A service that accepts logon requests from any client and provides authentication from the Security Accounts Manager (SAM) database of accounts.

NetBEUI   *See* NetBIOS Extended User Interface (NetBEUI).

NetBIOS   *See* network basic input/output system (NetBIOS).

NetBIOS Enhanced User Interface (NetBEUI) A small and fast protocol that requires little memory but can be routed only by using *token ring* routing. Remote locations linked by routers cannot use NetBEUI to communicate.

NetBIOS name A 16-byte name of a process using Network Basic Input Output System (NetBIOS). The NetBIOS name is a name that is recognized by Windows Internet Name Service (WINS), which maps the name to an IP address.

Netlogon service A user-mode service that runs in the Windows security subsystem. The Netlogon service passes the user's credentials through a secure channel to the domain database and returns the domain security identifiers and user rights for the user. In addition, the Netlogon service performs a variety of other functions related to the user logon process, such as periodic password updates for computer accounts and domain controller discovery.

netmask ordering A method DNS uses to give ordering and preference to IP addresses on the same network when a requesting client queries for a host name that has multiple host address (A) type resource records. This is designed so that the client program will attempt to connect to a host using the closest (and fastest) IP address available.

Network Access Server (NAS) A server that accepts Point-to-Point Protocol connections and places them on the network served by NAS.

network adapter A device that connects your computer to a network. Sometimes called an *adapter card* or *network interface card*.

Network Address Translation (NAT) A technology that enables a local-area network (LAN) to use one set of Internet Protocol (IP) addresses for internal traffic and a second set of addresses for external traffic.

Network Basic Input Output System (NetBIOS) An application programming interface (API) that can be used by programs on a LAN. NetBIOS provides programs with a uniform set of commands for requesting the lower-level services required to manage names, conduct sessions, and send datagrams between nodes on a network.

Network Load Balancing (NLB) A type of clustering designed for stateless applications, such as Web servers, in which each node has a duplicate copy of the server data and incoming client requests are distributed among the cluster nodes.

NLB *See* network load balancing (NLB).

node For tree structures, a location on the tree that can have links to one or more items below it. For local area networks (LANs), a device that is connected to the network and is capable of communicating with other network devices.

nonauthoritative restore   A restore operation performed on an Active Directory domain controller in which the objects in the restored directory are not treated as authoritative. The restored objects are updated with changes held in other domain controllers in the restored domain. See also *authoritative restore*.

nonauthoritative restore   When a domain controller's System State is restored, Active Directory is restored. When the domain controller is restarted, the information in the directory, which is only as recent as the date of the backup set, is brought up to date through normal replication processes between the restored domain controller and its replication partners.

nontransitive trust   A trust that is bound by the domains in the trust relationship.

notify list   A list maintained by the primary master for a zone of other Domain Name System (DNS) servers that should be notified when zone changes occur. The notify list consists of IP addresses for DNS servers configured as secondary masters for the zone. When the listed servers are notified of a change to the zone, they initiate a zone transfer with another DNS server and update the zone.

Ntds.dit   The filename of the Active Directory database.

NTFS file system   The native file system for Windows Server 2003, Windows 2000, and Windows NT. Supports long filenames, a variety of permissions for sharing files to manage access to files and folders, and a transaction log that allows the completion of any incomplete file-related tasks if the operating system is interrupted.

NWLink   *See* IPX/SPX/NetBIOS Compatible Transport Protocol.

O

object   An entity such as a file, folder, shared folder, printer, or Active Directory object described by a distinct, named set of attributes. See also *attribute*; *container object*; *parent object*; *child object*.

object attributes   The characteristics of objects in the directory.

object class   A logical grouping of objects.

object identifier (OID)   A globally unique identifier (GUID), which is assigned by the Directory System Agent (DSA) when the object is created. The GUID is stored in an attribute, the object GUID, which is part of every object. The object GUID attribute cannot be modified or deleted. When storing a reference to an Active Directory object in an external store (for example, a database), you should use the object GUID because, unlike a name, it will not change.

octet   A data unit consisting of eight bits.

offline files   A feature that provides users with access to redirected folders even when they are not connected to the network.

Open System authentication   A null authentication method used by wireless local area networks (WLANs) using the IEEE 802.11 standard that consists solely of messages in which one system identifies itself to another and the other system replies. There is no exchange of passwords, keys, or any other type of credential, and there is no way for a device configured to use Open System authentication to refuse authentication to another system.

Operations Master   *See* Floating Single Master Operation (FSMO).

operations master role   A domain controller that has been assigned one or more special roles in an Active Directory domain. The domain controllers assigned these roles perform operations that are single master (not permitted to occur at different places on the network at the same time). The domain controller that controls the particular operation owns the operations master role for that operation. The ownership of these operations master roles can be transferred to other domain controllers.

organizational unit (OU)   An Active Directory container object used within a domain. An OU is a logical container into which you can place users, groups, computers, and other OUs. It can contain objects only from its parent domain. An OU is the smallest scope to which you can apply a Group Policy or delegate authority.

OU   *See* organizational unit (OU).

owner   In Microsoft Windows Server 2003, the person who controls how permissions are set on objects and grants permissions to others.

P

packet   The largest unit of data that can be transmitted over a data network at any one time. Messages generated by applications are split into pieces and packaged into individual packets for transmission over the network. Each packet is transmitted separately and can take a different route to the destination. When all the packets arrive at the destination, the receiving computer reassembles them into the original message. This is the basic functionality of a packet switching network.

packet filtering   Prevents certain types of network packets from either being sent or received. This strategy can be employed for security reasons (to prevent access from unauthorized users) or to improve performance by preventing unnecessary packets from going over a slow connection.

page   A document, or collection of information, available over the Web. A page can contain text, graphics, video, and sound files. Also can refer to a portion of memory that the virtual memory manager can swap to and from a hard disk.

paging   A virtual memory operation in which pages are transferred from memory to disk when memory becomes full.

parent domain   For the Domain Name System (DNS), a domain that is located in the namespace tree directly above another derivative domain name (child domain). For example, microsoft.com is the parent domain for example.microsoft.com, a child domain.

parent object   The object in which another object resides. A parent object implies relation. For example, a folder is a parent object in which a file, or child object, resides. An object can be both a parent and a child object. See also *child object*; *object*.

parent-child trust   The two-way, transitive trust relationship created when a domain is added to an Active Directory tree. The Active Directory installation process automatically creates a transitive trust relationship between the domain you are creating (the new child domain) and the parent domain. These trust relationships make all objects in the domains of the tree available to all other domains in the tree. The trust is transitive and two-way. See also *tree-root trust*.

partial replica   A read-only replica of a directory partition that contains a subset of the attributes of all objects in the partition. Each Global Catalog contains partial replicas of all domains in the forest. The attributes contained in a partial replica are defined in the schema as the attributes whose attributeSchema objects have the isMemberOfPartialAttributeSet attribute set to TRUE. See also *Global Catalog*.

partition   A portion of a physical disk that functions as though it were a physically separate disk. Partitions can be created only on basic disks.

password   A security measure used to restrict logon names to user accounts and access to computer systems and resources. A password is a unique string of characters that must be provided before a logon name or an access is authorized.

Password Authentication Protocol (PAP)   A simple plaintext authentication scheme for authenticating Point-to-Point Protocol (PPP) connections. The user name and password are requested by the remote access server and returned by the remote access client in plaintext.

path   A sequence of directory (or folder) names that specifies the location of a directory, file, or folder within the directory tree. Each directory name and file name within the path (except the first) must be preceded by a backslash (\).

path rule   A software restriction policies rule that recognizes software based on the location in which the software is stored.

Pathping.exe   A Microsoft Windows Server 2003 command-line utility that displays the path through an internetwork to a particular destination and computes packet-loss percentages for each hop on the path.

PDC emulator   A domain controller that holds the PDC emulator operations master role in Active Directory. The PDC emulator services network clients that do not have Active Directory client software installed, and it replicates directory changes to any Windows NT backup domain controllers (BDCs) in the domain. The PDC emulator handles password authentication requests involving passwords that have recently changed and not yet replicated. At any time, the PDC emulator master role can be assigned to only one domain controller in each domain.

PDC   *See* primary domain controller (PDC).

PEAP   *See* Protected Extensible Authentication Protocol (PEAP).

performance alert   A Microsoft Windows Server 2003 feature that detects when a predefined counter value rises above or falls below the configured threshold and notifies a user by means of the Messenger service.

performance counter   In System Monitor, a data item associated with a performance object. For each counter selected, System Monitor presents a value corresponding to a particular aspect of the performance defined for the performance object.

Performance Logs And Alerts   A tool that give you the ability to create counter logs, trace logs, and system alerts automatically from local or remote computers.

performance object   In System Monitor, a logical collection of counters that is associated with a resource or service that can be monitored.

performance object instance   In System Monitor, a term used to distinguish between multiple performance objects of the same type on a computer.

perimeter network   A network separated from an organization's primary production network by a firewall, to prevent outside traffic from infiltrating the private network. Also known as a DMZ.

permissions inheritance   A mechanism that allows a given access control entry (ACE) to be copied from the container where it was applied to all children of the container. Inheritance can be combined with delegation to grant administrative rights to a whole subtree of the directory in a single update operation.

PKI   *See* public key infrastructure (PKI).

pointer (PTR) resource record   A resource record used in a reverse lookup zone created within the in-addr.arpa domain to designate a reverse mapping of a host Internet Protocol (IP) address to a host Domain Name System (DNS) domain name.

Point-to-Point Protocol (PPP)   A data-link layer TCP/IP protocol used for wide area network (WAN) connections, especially dial-up connections to the Internet and other service providers. PPP includes support for multiple network layer protocols, link-quality monitoring protocols, and authentication protocols. PPP is used for connections between two computers only.

Point-to-Point Tunneling Protocol (PPTP)   Networking technology that supports multiprotocol virtual private networks (VPNs), enabling remote users to access corporate networks securely across the Internet or other networks by dialing into an ISP or by connecting directly to the Internet. PPTP tunnels, or encapsulates, Internet Protocol (IP), Internetwork Packet Exchange (IPX), or NetBIOS Extended User Interface (NetBEUI) traffic inside IP packets.

policy   The mechanism by which computer settings are configured automatically, as defined by the administrator. Depending on context, this can refer to a Microsoft Windows Server 2003 group policy, a remote access server (RAS) policy, a Microsoft Windows NT 4.0 system policy, or a specific setting in a Group Policy Object (GPO).

POP3   *See* Post Office Protocol 3 (POP3).

port   From a computer system perspective, a physical connection point on a computer where you can connect devices that pass data into and out of a computer. For example, a printer is typically connected to a parallel port (also called an LPT port), and a modem is typically connected to a serial port (also called a COM port). From a network perspective, a port is a numbered communication channel through which information passes from one computer system to another. Terminal Services traffic, for example, communicates on port 3389.

Power Users group   A group whose members can manage accounts, resources, and applications that are installed on a workstation, stand-alone server, or member server. This group does not exist on domain controllers.

PPP   *See* Point-to-Point Protocol (PPP).

PPTP   *See* Point-to-Point Tunneling Protocol (PPTP).

preferred bridgehead server   A domain controller in a site, designated manually by the administrator, that is part of a group of bridgehead servers. Once designated, preferred bridgehead servers are used exclusively to replicate changes collected from the site. An administrator may choose to designate preferred bridgehead servers when there is a lot of data to replicate between sites, or to create a fault-tolerant topology. If one preferred bridgehead server is not available, the KCC automatically uses one of the other preferred bridgehead servers. If no other preferred bridgehead servers are available, replication does not occur to that site. See also *bridgehead server.*

preshared key   An Internet Protocol Security (IPSec) technology in which a shared, secret key is used for authentication in IPSec policy.

primary domain controller (PDC)   In a Windows NT domain, the server that authenticates domain logons and maintains the security policy and master database for a domain. In a Windows 2000 or Windows Server 2003 domain, running in mixed mode, one of the domain controllers in each domain is identified as the PDC emulator master for compatibility with down-level clients and servers.

primary master   An authoritative Domain Name System (DNS) server for a zone that can be used as a point of update for the zone. Only primary masters can be updated directly to process zone updates, which include adding, removing, or modifying resource records that are stored as zone data. Primary masters are also the first sources used for replicating the zone to other DNS servers.

primary partition   A portion of the hard disk that's been marked as a potentially bootable logical drive by an operating system. MS-DOS can support only a single primary partition. Master boot record disks can support four primary partitions. Computers with the Intel Itanium processor use a GUID partition table that supports up to 128 primary partitions.

primary zone   A copy of the zone that is administered locally.

primary zone database file   The master zone database file. Changes to a zone, such as adding domains or hosts, are performed on the server that contains the primary zone database file.

principle of least privilege   The security guideline that a user should have the minimum privileges necessary to perform a specific task. This helps to ensure that, if a user is compromised, the impact is minimized by the limited privileges held by that user.

private key   The secret half of a cryptographic key pair that is used with a public key algorithm. Private keys are typically used to decrypt a symmetric session key, digitally sign data, or decrypt data that has been encrypted with the corresponding public key.

process   The virtual address space and the control information necessary for the execution of a program.

profile   Loaded by the system when a user logs on, the profile defines a user's environment, including network settings, printer connections, desktop settings, and program items.

promiscuous mode   Operational mode available in some network interface adapters that causes the adapter to read and process all packets transmitted over the local area network (LAN), not just the packets addressed to it. Protocol analyzers use promiscuous mode to capture comprehensive samples of network traffic for later analysis.

Protected Extensible Authentication Protocol (PEAP)   A standards-based authentication method, used by Microsoft Windows 2000 and later versions of the operating system, that uses digital certificates to verify the user's identity.

protocol   A documented format for the transmission of data between two networked devices. A protocol is essentially a "language" that a computer uses to communicate, and the other computer to which it is connected must use the same language for communication to take place.

proxy server   An application layer firewall technique that enables TCP/IP client systems to access Internet resources without being susceptible to intrusion from outside the network. Administrators can also configure the proxy server to cache Internet information for later use and to restrict access to particular Internet sites. See also *firewall*. Compare with *network address translation (NAT)*.

public key encryption   A method of encryption that uses two encryption keys that are mathematically related. One key is called the *private key* and is kept confidential. The other is called the *public key* and is freely given out to all potential correspondents. In a typical scenario, a sender uses the receiver's public key to encrypt a message. Only the receiver has the related private key to decrypt the message. The complexity of the relationship between the public key and the private key means that, provided the keys are long enough, it is computationally infeasible to determine one from the other. Also called *asymmetric encryption*.

public key infrastructure (PKI)   The term generally used to describe the laws, policies, standards, and software that regulate or manipulate certificates and public and private keys. In practice, it is a system of digital certificates, certification authorities, and other registration authorities that verify and authenticate the validity of each party involved in an electronic transaction. Standards for PKI are still evolving, even though they are being widely implemented as a necessary element of electronic commerce.

public key The nonsecret half of a cryptographic key pair that is used with a public key algorithm. Public keys are typically used when encrypting a session key, verifying a digital signature, or encrypting data that can be decrypted with the corresponding private key.

publish To make data available for replication.

Q

query A specific request for data retrieval, modification, or deletion.

quorum A storage resource in a cluster that contains all the configuration data needed for the recovery of the cluster. To create a cluster, the first node must be able to take control of the quorum resource, so that it can save the quorum data there.

R

RAS *See* Remote Access Server (RAS).

RDN *See* relative distinguished name (RDN).

realm A set of security principles, in a non-Windows networked environment, that are subject to Kerberos authentication.

realm name An identifying prefix or suffix appended to a user name to enable appropriate routing and authentication during a remote logon process.

realm trust A trust that must be explicitly created by a systems administrator between a non-Windows Kerberos realm and an Active Directory domain. This trust provides interoperability between the Active Directory domain and any realm used in Kerberos version 5 implementations. The trust can be transitive or non-transitive and one-way or two-way. See also *shortcut trust*; *external trust*; *forest trust*.

Recovery Console A command-line interface that provides limited access to the system for troubleshooting purposes.

recursive query A query made to a DNS server in which the requester asks the server to assume the full workload and responsibility for providing a complete answer to the query. The DNS server then uses separate iterative queries to other DNS servers on behalf of the requester to assist in completing an answer for the recursive query.

redirector A network client component that determines whether a resource requested by an application is located on the network or on the local system, and then sends the request either to the local input/output system or to the networking protocol stack. A computer can have multiple redirectors to support different networks, such as a network running Microsoft Windows and a network running Novell NetWare.

redundant array of independent disks (RAID) A range of disk management and striping techniques to implement fault tolerance.

refresh interval An interval of time used by secondary masters of a zone to determine how often to check whether their zone data needs to be refreshed. This interval is set in the start-of-authority (SOA) resource record for each zone.

registry path rule A software restriction policies rule that recognizes software based on the location of the software as it is stored in the registry.

relative distinguished name (RDN) The part of an object's distinguished name that is an attribute of the object itself. For most objects, this is the Common Name attribute. For security principals, the default common name is the security principal name. For the distinguished name CN=MyName,CN=Users,DC=Microsoft,DC=com, the relative distinguished name of the MyName user object is CN=MyName. The relative distinguished name of the parent object is CN=Users.

relative ID master The domain controller assigned to allocate sequences of relative IDs to each domain controller in its domain. Whenever a domain controller creates a security principal (user, group, or computer object), the domain controller assigns the object a unique security ID (SID). The SID consists of a domain SID that is the same for all SIDs created in a particular domain and a relative ID that is unique for each SID created in the domain. At any time, there can be only one relative ID master in a particular domain.

relative identifier (RID) The part of the security identifier (SID) that is unique to each object.

remote access Part of the integrated Routing And Remote Access service that provides remote networking for telecommuters, mobile workers, and system administrators who monitor and manage servers at multiple branch offices.

Remote Access Server (RAS) Any computer running Microsoft Windows Server 2003 that is configured to accept remote access connections.

Remote Assistance A feature that allows a novice user to use Windows Messenger to request personal, interactive help from an expert user. When the help request is accepted and the remote session negotiated, the expert is able to view and, if allowed by the novice, control the desktop.

Remote Authentication Dial-In User Service (RADIUS)   A security authentication system used by many Internet service providers (ISPs).

remote computer   A computer that can be accessed only by using a communications line or a communications device, such as a network interface adapter or a modem.

Remote Desktop   A Microsoft Windows Server 2003 and Microsoft Windows XP feature that enables an administrator to connect to a computer at a distant location and remotely operate the console.

Remote Desktop for Administration (RDA)   A technology based on Terminal Services that allows up to two remote connections to a server for remote administration purposes. In Windows 2000, this was known as Terminal Server in Remote Administration mode.

Remote Installation Services (RIS)   Allows clients to boot from a network server and use special preboot diagnostic tools installed on the server to automatically install a client operating system.

remote procedure call (RPC)   A message-passing facility that allows a distributed application to call services that are available on various computers on a network. Used during remote administration of computers.

remote user   A user who dials in to the server over modems and telephone lines from a remote location.

Removable Storage Management (RSM) system   A feature of Windows Server 2003 that interfaces with robotic changers and media libraries, enables multiple applications to share local libraries and tape or disk drives, and controls removable media within a single-server system.

replica   In Active Directory replication, one instance of a logical Active Directory partition that is synchronized by means of replication between domain controllers that hold copies of the same directory partition. *Replica* can also refer to an instance of an object or attribute in a distributed directory. In the File Replication service (FRS), a computer that has been included in the configuration of a specific replica set.

replication   The process of copying data from a data store or file system to multiple computers to synchronize the data. The Active Directory service provides multiple master replication of the directory between domain controllers within a given domain. The replicas of the directory on each domain controller can be written to, enabling administrators to apply updates to any replica of a given domain. The replication service automatically copies the changes from a given replica to all other replicas. See also *multiple master*.

replication availability   A schedule assigned to the site link that indicates when the link is available for replication.

replication frequency   A value assigned to the site link that indicates the number of minutes Active Directory should wait before using a connection to check for replication updates.

replication partner   A domain controller that acts as a replication source for a given domain controller. The KCC determines which servers are best suited to replicate with each other, and generates the list of domain controllers that are candidates for replication partners from the list of domain controllers in the site on the basis of connectivity, history of successful replication, and matching of full and partial replicas. A domain controller has some number of direct replication partners with whom it replicates for a given directory partition. The other domain controllers in the site replicate transitively with this domain controller.

Request for Comments (RFC)   A document published by the Internet Engineering Task Force (IETF) that contains information about a topic related to the Internet or to the Transmission Control Protocol/Internet Protocol (TCP/IP) suite. For example, all TCP/IP protocols have been documented and published as RFCs and eventually might be ratified as Internet standards. Some RFCs are only informational or historical, however, and are not submitted for ratification as a standard. After they are published and assigned numbers, RFCs are never changed. If a new version of an RFC document is published, it is assigned a new number and cross-indexed to indicate that it renders the old version obsolete.

resolver   Another name for the DNS client found on every TCP/IP computer. Whenever the computer attempts to access a TCP/IP system using a DNS name, the resolver generates a DNS Request message and sends it to the DNS server specified in the computer's TCP/IP client configuration. The DNS server then takes the necessary steps to resolve the requested name into an IP address and returns the address to the resolver in the client computer. The resolver can then furnish the IP address to the TCP/IP client, which uses it to transmit a message to the destination. See also *Domain Name System (DNS)*.

resource record (RR)   The standard database record used in a zone to associate Domain Name System (DNS) domain names to related data for a given type of network resource, such as a host Internet Protocol (IP) address.

Resultant Set Of Policy (RSoP)   The sum of the policies applied to the user or computer, including the application of filters (security groups, WMI) and exceptions (No Override, Block Policy Inheritance).

retry interval   The time, in seconds, after the refresh interval expires, used by secondary masters of a zone to determine how often to try and retry contacting its source for zone data to see whether its replicated zone data needs to be refreshed. This interval is set in the start-of-authority (SOA) resource record for each zone.

reverse lookup   A DNS query for a hostname based on a known IP address.

reversible encryption   A mechanism that stores an encrypted password in such a way that the original password can be unencrypted and retrieved. Some applications require the unencrypted password so that they can perform certain tasks.

RFC   *See* Request for Comments (RFC).

Rivest Shamir Adleman (RSA) cryptographic algorithms   A widely used set of public key algorithms that were published by RSA Data Security, Inc. The RSA cryptographic algorithms are supported by the Microsoft Base Cryptographic Service Provider and the Microsoft Enhanced Cryptographic Service Provider.

roaming user profile   A server-based user profile that is downloaded to the local computer when a user logs on, and is updated both locally and on the server when the user logs off. A roaming user profile is available from the server when logging on to a workstation or server computer. When logging on, the user can use the local user profile if it is more current than the copy on the server.

root certificate authority   The most trusted certificate authority (CA), which is at the top of a certification hierarchy. The root CA has a self-signed certificate. Also called the *root authority.*

root domain   The domain at the top of the DNS namespace hierarchy, represented as a period (.).

root hints   DNS data stored on a DNS server that identifies the authoritative DNS servers for the root zone of the DNS namespace. The root hints are stored in the file Cache.dns, located in the WINDOWS\System32\Dns folder.

root name server   One of a handful of servers that represent the top of the Domain Name System (DNS) namespace by supplying other DNS servers with the Internet Protocol (IP) addresses of the authoritative servers for all the top-level domains in the DNS. See also *Domain Name System (DNS)*; *authoritative server.*

round robin   A simple mechanism used by DNS servers to share and distribute loads for network resources. Round robin is used to rotate the order of resource records (RRs) returned in a response to a query when multiple RRs of the same type exist for a queried DNS domain name.

router   A network hardware device (or computer-installed software package) that handles the connection between two or more networks. Routers look at the destination addresses of the packets passing through them and decide which route to use to send them.

Routing and Remote Access   A Windows Server 2003 service that enables the computer to function as a router, connecting two local area networks (LANs) together, or connecting a LAN to a wide area network (WAN) The Routing and Remote Access service (RRAS) also includes additional features, such as network address translation (NAT), Routing Information Protocol (RIP), and Open Shortest Path First (OSPF).

routing   The process of forwarding a packet through an internetwork from a source host to a destination host on different local area networks.

RRAS   *See* Routing and Remote Access service (RRAS).

RSoP   *See* Resultant Set of Policy (RSoP).

Run As   A feature that provides users with a secondary logon capability. By using Run As, users can run applications or commands in a different security context without having to log off. Run As prompts the user for different credentials before running the application or command.

S

safe mode   A method of starting Windows operating systems using basic files and drivers only, without networking. This allows you to start your computer when a problem prevents it from starting normally.

SAM   *See* Security Accounts Manager (SAM).

SAN   *See* storage area network (SAN).

schema   A set of definitions of the object classes and attributes that can be stored in Active Directory. Like other objects in Active Directory, schema objects have an access control list (ACL) to limit alterations to only authorized users.

schema master   The domain controller assigned to control all updates to the schema within a forest. At any time, there can be only one schema master in the forest.

schema partition   A partition in Active Directory that defines the objects that can be created in the directory and the attributes those objects can have. This data is common to all domains in a forest and is replicated to all domain controllers in a forest.

SCSI   *See* Small Computer System Interface (SCSI).

secondary master   An authoritative Domain Name System (DNS) server for a zone that is used as a source for replicating the zone to other servers. Secondary masters update their zone data only by transferring zone data from other DNS servers. They do not have the ability to perform zone updates.

secondary zone   A read-only copy of a DNS zone that is transferred from an authoritative DNS server to another DNS server to provide redundancy.

second-level domain   A DNS domain name that is rooted hierarchically at the second tier of the domain namespace, directly beneath the top-level domain names. Top-level domain names include .com and .org. When DNS is used on the Internet, second-level domains are usually names that are registered and delegated to individual organizations and businesses.

secure dynamic update   The process in which a DNS client submits a dynamic update request to a DNS server and the DNS server performs the update only if the client is authenticated.

Secure Hash Algorithm (SHA-1)   An algorithm that generates a 160-bit hash value from an arbitrary amount of input data. SHA-1 is used with the Digital Signature Algorithm (DSA) in the Digital Signature Standard (DSS), among other places.

secure zone   A DNS zone that is stored in Active Directory and to which access control list (ACL) security features are applied.

Security Accounts Manager (SAM)   A Windows service used during the logon process. SAM maintains user account information, including the list of groups to which a user belongs.

Security Association (SA)   A combination of identifiers, which together define Internet Protocol Security (IPSec) that protects communication between sender and receiver. An SA is identified by the combination of a Security Parameters Index (SPI), destination IP address, and security protocol (Authentication Header [AH] or Encapsulation Security Payload [ESP]). An SA must be negotiated before secured data can be sent.

security descriptor   A data structure that contains security information associated with a protected object. Security descriptors include information about who owns the object, who may access it and in what way, and what types of access will be audited. See also *access control list*.

security group   A group that can be used to administer permissions for users and other domain objects.

security ID   *See* security identifier (SID).

security identifier (SID)   A unique number that identifies a user, group, or computer account. Every account on the network is issued a unique SID when the account is first created. Internal processes in Windows refer to an account's SID rather than the account's user or group name.

security log   An event log containing information on security events that are specified in the audit policy.

security principal   An identity that can be given permission to a resource. A security principal is an object that includes a security identifier (SID) attribute. Windows Server 2003 supports four security principals: users, groups, computers, and the InetOrgPerson object.

security template   A physical representation of a security configuration; a single file where a group of security settings is stored. Locating all security settings in one place eases security administration. Each template is saved as a text-based .inf file. This allows you to copy, paste, import, or export some or all of the template attributes.

selective authentication   A method of setting the scope of authentication differently for outgoing and incoming external and forest trusts. Selective trusts allow you to make flexible access control decisions between external domains in a forest.

server cluster   A type of clustering in which two or more servers are joined together to service stateful applications, such as database servers. In a server cluster, the nodes are all connected to a shared data storage device, and the application load can be distributed among the servers using a variety of criteria.

server message block (SMB)   The protocol developed by Microsoft, Intel, and IBM that defines a series of commands used to pass information between network computers. The redirector packages SMB requests into a network control block (NCB) structure that can be sent over the network to a remote device. The network provider listens for SMB messages destined for it and removes the data portion of the SMB request so that it can be processed by a local device.

service   A program, routine, or process that performs a specific system function to support other programs, particularly at a low (close to the hardware) level.

service (SRV) resource record   A DNS resource record used to identify computers that host specific services, specified in RFC 2782. SRV resource records are used to locate domain controllers for Active Directory.

service pack   A software update package provided by Microsoft for one of its products. A service pack contains a collection of fixes and enhancements packaged into a single self-installing archive file.

service-dependent filtering   A type of packet filtering used in firewalls that limits access to a network based on the port numbers specified in packets' transport layer protocol headers. See also *firewall; port; packet filtering.*

session key   In Internet Protocol Security (IPSec), a value that is used in combination with an algorithm to encrypt or decrypt data that is transferred between computers. A session key is created for every pair of computers to provide enhanced security on computers that have multiple simultaneous active sessions.

Shared Key authentication   An authentication method, used by wireless local area networks (WLANs) using the Institute of Electrical and Electronic Engineers (IEEE) 802.11 standard, that is based on a security key that an external process shares with both systems.

shared system volume   A folder structure that exists on all domain controllers. It stores public files that must be replicated to other domain controllers, such as logon scripts and some of the Group Policy objects (GPOs), for both the current domain and the enterprise. The default location for the shared system volume is *%systemroot%*\Sysvol.

sharepoint   A centralized location for key folders on a server or servers, which provides users with an access point for storing and finding information and administrators with an access point for managing information.

shortcut trust   A trust that must be explicitly created by a systems administrator between two domains that are logically distant from each other in a forest or tree hierarchy. The purpose of a shortcut trust is to optimize the interdomain authentication process by shortening the trust path. All shortcut trusts are transitive and can be one- or two-way. A shortcut trust is also known as a cross-link trust. See also *external trust; forest trust; realm trust; trust path.*

SID   *See* security identifier (SID).

Simple Network Management Protocol (SNMP)   A network protocol used to manage TCP/IP networks. In Windows, the SNMP service is used to provide status information about a host on a TCP/IP network.

single-master replication   A type of replication where one domain controller is the master domain controller and operations are not permitted to occur at different places in a network at the same time. In Active Directory, one or more domain controllers can be assigned to perform single-master replication. Operations master roles are special roles assigned to one or more domain controllers in a domain to perform single-master replication. See also *operations master role.*

site   One or more well-connected (highly reliable and fast) TCP/IP subnets. A site allows administrators to configure Active Directory access and replication topology quickly and easily to take advantage of the physical network. When users log on, Active Directory clients locate Active Directory servers in the same site as the user. See also *subnet*; *well connected*.

site link   A link between two sites that allows replication to occur. Each site link contains the schedule that determines when replication can occur between the sites that it connects. See also *site link cost*; *replication availability*; *replication frequency*.

site link bridge   The linking of more than two sites for replication using the same transport. When site links are bridged, they are transitive; that is, all site links for a specific transport implicitly belong to a single site link bridge for that transport. A site link bridge makes disjoint networks possible. All site links within the bridge can route transitively, but they do not route outside of the bridge.

site link cost   A value assigned to the site link that indicates the cost of the connection in relation to the speed of the link. Higher costs are used for slow links, and lower costs are used for fast links.

site topology   A logical representation of a physical network.

Small Computer System Interface (SCSI)   A bus architecture used to connect storage devices and other peripherals to personal computers. SCSI implementations typically take the form of a host adapter in the computer, and a number of internal or external devices that you connect to the card, using appropriate SCSI cables.

smart card   A credit card–sized device that is used with an access code to enable certificate-based authentication and single sign-on to the enterprise. Smart cards securely store certificates, public and private keys, passwords, and other types of personal information. A smart card reader attached to the computer reads the smart card.

SMB   *See* server message block (SMB).

SMTP   *See* Simple Mail Transfer Protocol (SMTP).

snap-in   A tool that can be added to a console supported by the Microsoft Management Console (MMC). You can add a snap-in extension to extend the function of a snap-in.

sniffer   An application or device that can read, monitor, and capture network data exchanges and read network packets. If the packets are not encrypted, a sniffer provides a full view of the data inside the packet.

SNMP   *See* Simple Network Management Protocol (SNMP).

software distribution point In Software Installation, a network location from which users are able to get the software that they need.

software restriction policies A collection of policy settings that define what software can run on a computer, based on the default security level for a Group Policy Object (GPO). Exceptions to the default security level can then be defined by certificate rules, hash rules, path rules, registry path rules, and Internet zone rules. See also *certificate rule*; *hash rule*; *path rule*; *registry path rule*; *Internet zone rule*.

Software Update Services (SUS) A server-based technology that centralizes the acquisition and approval of security rollups and critical updates for distribution to network clients running the Automatic Updates client.

special identity groups Groups that are installed with the operating system. Membership in these groups is controlled by the operating system.

stand-alone certification authority A certification authority (CA) that is not integrated with Active Directory.

Stand-alone server A computer that runs Windows 2000 or Windows Server 2003 but does not participate in a domain. A stand-alone server has only its own database of users, and it processes logon requests by itself.

start-of-authority (SOA) resource record A record that indicates the starting point or original point of authority for information stored in a zone. The SOA resource record (RR) is the first RR created when adding a new zone. It also contains several parameters used by other computers that use DNS to determine how long they will use information for the zone and how often updates are required.

stateful application An application that has long-running in-memory states or large, frequently changing data sets, such as a database server, making it suitable for server clustering.

stateless application An application with relatively small data sets that rarely change (or may even be read-only), and that do not have long-running in-memory states, such as a Web or FTP server, which is suitable for Network Load Balancing.

storage area network (SAN) A dedicated local area network (LAN) that connects servers with storage devices, often using the Fibre Channel protocol, reducing the storage-related traffic on the user network.

stub zone A copy of a zone that contains only the resource records required to identify the authoritative DNS servers for that zone. A DNS server that hosts a parent zone and a stub zone for one of the parent zone's delegated child zones can receive updates from the authoritative DNS servers for the child zone.

subnet A group of computers on a TCP/IP network that share a common network identifier.

subnet mask   A TCP/IP configuration parameter that specifies which bits of the IP address identify the host and which bits identify the network on which the host resides. When the subnet mask is viewed in binary form, the bits with a value of 1 are the network identifier and the bits with a value of 0 are the host identifier.

SUS   *See* Microsoft Software Update Services (SUS).

switch   A data-link layer network connection device that looks like a hub, but forwards incoming packets only to the computers for which they are destined. Switches essentially eliminate the need to share the medium on Ethernet networks by providing each computer with a dedicated connection to its destination. Contrast with a *hub*, which forwards incoming packets through all its ports.

symmetric encryption   An encryption algorithm that requires the same secret key to be used for both encryption and decryption. Because of its speed, symmetric encryption is typically used when a message sender needs to encrypt large amounts of data. Also called *secret key encryption*.

synchronous   A form of communication that relies on a timing scheme coordinated between two devices to separate groups of bits and transmit them in blocks called frames. Special characters are used to begin the synchronization and periodically check its accuracy.

System State   In Backup, a collection of system-specific data maintained by the operating system that must be backed up as a unit. It is not a backup of the entire system. The System State data includes the registry, COM+ Class Registration database, system files, boot files, and files under Windows File Protection. For servers, the System State data also includes the Certificate Services database (if the server is operating as a certificate server). If the server is a domain controller, the System State data also includes Active Directory and the Sysvol directory.

system volume   The volume that contains the hardware-specific files needed to load Windows on x86-based computers with a basic input/output system (BIOS). The system volume can be, but does not have to be, the same volume as the boot volume. See also *basic input/output system (BIOS)*.

SystemRoot   The path and folder where the Windows system files are located. The value %SystemRoot% can be used in paths to replace the actual location. To identify the SystemRoot folder on a computer, type **%SystemRoot%** at a command prompt.

Systems Management Server (SMS)   A Microsoft product that includes inventory collection, software deployment, and diagnostic tools. SMS automates the task of upgrading software, allows remote problem solving, provides asset management information, and monitors software use, computers, and networks.

SYSVOL   The folder on a domain controller that contains group policies and logon scripts. SYSVOL is replicated between domain controllers by the file replication service (FRS).

T

T-1   A dedicated telephone connection, also called a leased line, running at 1.544 Mbps. A T-1 line consists of twenty-four 64-Kbps channels, which can be used separately, in combinations, or as a single data pipe.

TCP/IP   *See* Transmission Control Protocol/Internet Protocol (TCP/IP).

Telecommunications Network Protocol (Telnet)   An application layer Transmission Control Protocol/Internet Protocol (TCP/IP) client/server protocol used to remotely control a computer at another location.

Telnet   *See* Telecommunications Network Protocol (Telnet).

temporary user profile   A profile issued any time an error condition prevents a user's profile from being loaded. Temporary profiles are deleted at the end of each session. Changes made to a user's desktop settings and files are lost when the user logs off.

terminal   A device that allows you to send commands to another computer. At a minimum, this usually means a keyboard, a display screen, and some simple circuitry. You will usually use terminal software in a personal computer—the software pretends to be, or emulates, a physical terminal and allows you to type commands to another computer.

Terminal Services   The underlying technology that enables Remote Desktop for Administration, Remote Assistance, and Terminal Server.

thread   An executable entity that belongs to one (and only one) process. In a multitasking environment, a single program can contain several threads, all running at the same time.

ticket   A set of identification data for a security principal, issued by a domain controller for purposes of user authentication. Two forms of tickets in Windows are Ticket Granting Tickets (TGTs) and service tickets.

Ticket Granting Service (TGS)   A Kerberos V5 service provided by the Kerberos V5 Key Distribution Center (KDC) service that issues service tickets that allow users to authenticate to services in a domain.

Ticket Granting Ticket (TGT)   A credential issued to a user by the Key Distribution Center (KDC) when the user logs on. The user must present the TGT to the KDC when requesting session tickets for services. Because a TGT is normally valid for the life of the user's logon session, it is sometimes called a *user ticket*.

Time to Live (TTL)   A numeric value included in packets sent over TCP/IP-based networks that each router decrements before forwarding the packet. If TTL is decremented to zero, the router drops the packet. For DNS, TTL values are used in resource records within a zone to determine how long requesting clients should cache and use this information when it appears in a query response answered by a DNS server for the zone.

time-out error   A condition where a response is not received in the expected time. When this condition occurs, the software assumes that the data has been lost and requests that it be resent.

timestamp   A certification specifying that a particular message existed at a specific time and date. In a digital context, trusted third parties generate a trusted timestamp for a particular message by having a timestamping service append a time value to a message and then digitally signing the result.

TLS   *See* Transport Layer Security (TLS).

token ring   A type of computer network in which the computers connected in a ring. A *token,* which is a special bit pattern, travels around the ring. To communicate to another computer, a computer catches the token, attaches a message to it, and the token continues around the network, dropping off the message at the designated location.

tombstone   In Active Directory, an object that is removed from the directory but not yet deleted.

top-level domains   Domain names that are rooted hierarchically at the first tier of the domain namespace directly beneath the root (.) of the DNS namespace. On the Internet, top-level domain names such as .com and .org are used to classify and assign second-level domain names (such as microsoft.com) to individual organizations and businesses according to their organizational purpose.

topology   The physical layout of computers, cables, switches, routers, and other components of a network. *Topology* also refers to the underlying network architecture, such as Ethernet or Token Ring.

transforms   *See* modifications.

transitive trust   The standard trust between Windows Server 2003 domains in a domain tree or forest. Transitive trusts are always two-way trusts. When a domain joins a domain tree or forest, a transitive trust relationship is established automatically.

Transmission Control Protocol/Internet Protocol (TCP/IP)   A set of networking protocols used on the Internet that provide communications across interconnected networks that consist of computers with diverse hardware architectures and various operating systems. TCP/IP includes standards for how computers communicate and conventions for connecting networks and routing traffic.

transport mode   An IPSec operational mode that protects data transmissions from end system to end system. See *tunnel mode.*

trap   A message generated by a Simple Network Management Protocol (SNMP) agent and transmitted immediately to the network management console, indicating that an event requiring immediate attention has taken place.

tree   A tree in Active Directory is just an extension of the idea of a directory tree. It's a hierarchy of objects and containers that demonstrates how objects are connected, or the path from one object to another. Endpoints on the tree are usually objects.

tree-root domain   The highest-level domain in the tree; child and grandchild domains are arranged under it. Typically, the domain you select should be the one that is most critical to the operation of the tree.

tree-root trust   The two-way, transitive trust relationship that is established when you add a new tree to an Active Directory forest. The Active Directory installation process automatically creates a transitive trust relationship between the domain you are creating (the new tree root) and the forest root. A tree-root trust can be set up only between the roots of two trees in the same forest. The trust is transitive and two-way. See also *parent-child trust.*

triple DES (3DES)   An implementation of Data Encryption Standard (DES) encryption that employs three iterations of cryptographic operations on each segment of data. Each iteration uses a 56-bit key for encryption, which yields 168-bit encryption for the data. Although 3DES is slower than DES because of the additional cryptographic calculations, its protection is far stronger than DES.

Trojan horse   A program that masquerades as another common program in an attempt to receive information.

trust path   A series of trust links from one domain to another, established for the purpose of passing authentication requests.

trust relationship   A logical relationship established between domains to allow pass-through authentication, in which a trusting domain honors the logon authentications of a trusted domain. User accounts and global groups defined in a trusted domain can be given rights and permissions in a trusting domain, even though the user accounts or groups don't exist in the trusting domain's directory. See also *authentication; domain; parent-child trust; tree-root trust; shortcut trust; external trust.*

trust relationship   A security term meaning that one workstation or server trusts a domain controller to authenticate a user logon on its behalf. It also means a domain controller trusts a domain controller in another domain to authenticate a logon.

TTL   *See* Time to Live (TTL).

tunnel   A logical connection over which data is encapsulated. Typically, both encapsulation and encryption are performed and the tunnel is a private, secure link between a remote user or host and a private network.

tunnel mode   An IPSec operational mode designed to secure wide area network (WAN) communications by protecting data transmissions from gateway to gateway. See *transport mode*.

tunnel server   A server or router that terminates tunnels and forwards traffic to the hosts on the target network.

tunneling   A technique for transmitting data over a network by encapsulating it within another protocol.

tunneling protocol   A communication standard used to manage tunnels and encapsulate private data. Data that is tunneled must also be encrypted to be a virtual private network (VPN) connection. Two commonly used tunneling protocols are the Point-to-Point Tunneling Protocol (PPTP) and Layer2 Tunneling Protocol (L2TP).

U

UCS Transformation Format 8 (UTF-8)   A character set for protocols evolving beyond the use of ASCII. The UTF-8 protocol provides for support of extended ASCII characters and translation of UCS-2, an international 16-bit Unicode character set. UTF-8 enables a far greater range of names than can be achieved using ASCII or extended ASCII encoding for character data.

UDP   *See* User Datagram Protocol (UDP).

unbounded media   A type of network medium in which the signals are not confined to a restricted space, such as wireless radio signals. Compare with bounded media.

UNC   *See* Universal Naming Convention (UNC).

unicast   A network transmission addressed to a single computer. Compare with *broadcast*; *multicast*.

Unicode   A character encoding standard developed by the Unicode Consortium that represents almost all of the written languages of the world. The Unicode character repertoire has multiple representation forms, including UTF-8, UTF-16, and UTF-32. Most Windows interfaces use the UTF-16 form.

universal group   A security or distribution group that can contain users, groups, and computers from any domain in its forest as members. Universal security groups can be granted rights and permissions on resources in any domain in the forest. See also *domain local group*; *forest*; *global catalog*.

Universal Naming Convention (UNC) name   The full name of a resource on a network. It conforms to the *servername**sharename* syntax, where servername is the name of the server and sharename is the name of the shared resource. UNC names of directories or files can also include the directory path under the share name, with the following syntax: *servername**sharename**directory**filename*.

Universal Plug and Play (UPnP)   A standard that enables a network-attached device such as a PC, peripheral, or wireless device to acquire an IP address and then, using Internet and Web protocols such as HTTP, announce its presence and availability on the network.

universal serial bus (USB)   An interface between a computer and add-on devices that enables simplified connection and plug-and-play detection of those devices. USB ports support multiple devices per port.

UPN   *See* user principal name (UPN).

user account   In Active Directory, an object that consists of all the information that defines a domain user, which includes user name, password, and groups in which the user account has membership. User accounts can be stored in Active Directory or on your local computer.

User Datagram Protocol (UDP)   A Transmission Control Protocol (TCP) complement that offers a connectionless datagram service that guarantees neither delivery nor correct sequencing of delivered packets (much like Internet Protocol [IP]).

user principal name (UPN)   A user account name (sometimes referred to as the user logon name) and a domain name identifying the domain in which the user account is located. The format is as follows: someone@example.com (as for an e-mail address).

user principal name (UPN) suffix   The part of the UPN to the right of the @ character. The default UPN suffix for a user account is the DNS domain name of the domain that contains the user account. Alternative UPN suffixes may be added to simplify administration and user logon processes by providing a single UPN suffix for all users. The UPN suffix is only used within the Active Directory forest, and it is not required to be a valid DNS domain name. See also *domain*; *domain name*; *Domain Name System (DNS)*; *forest*; *user account*; *user principal name (UPN)*.

user profiles   Information about user accounts. See also *profile*.

user right   A logon right or privilege that allows a user to perform a system task, such as logging on locally or restoring files and folders. Because user rights are system-specific, they override permissions on an individual resource.

V

virtual private network (VPN)   A technique for connecting to a network at a remote location using the Internet as a network medium. A user can dial in to a local Internet service provider (ISP) and connect through the Internet to a private network at a distant location, using a protocol like the Point-to-Point Tunneling Protocol (PPTP) to secure the private traffic.

volume shadow copy   A Microsoft Windows Server 2003 feature that provides multiple copies of files in a shared folder, made at specific times, enabling users to retrieve copies of files as they existed at a previous time. This enables users to recover files that they accidentally deleted or overwrote.

Volume Shadow Copy Service (VSS)   A service that creates snapshot backups of files, allowing a backup utility to back the snapshot regardless of whether the original file is locked or open.

VPN   *See* virtual private network (VPN).

VPN server   A computer that accepts virtual private network (VPN) connections from VPN clients. A VPN server can provide a remote access VPN connection or a router-to-router VPN connection.

W

WAN   *See* wide area network (WAN).

Web server   A computer that is maintained by a system administrator or Internet service provider (ISP) and that responds to requests from a user's Web browser.

Web-Based Enterprise Management (WBEM)   A set of management and Internet standard technologies developed to unify the management of enterprise computing environments. Microsoft's implementation of WBEM is the Windows Management Instrumentation.

WEP   *See* Wired Equivalent Privacy (WEP).

wide area network (WAN)   A network that spans a large geographical area using long-distance point-to-point connections, rather than shared network media as with a local area network (LAN). The Internet is the ultimate example of a WAN. Compare with *local area network (LAN)*.

Wi-Fi   Another name for wireless networking technologies defined by the Institute for Electrical and Electronic Engineers (IEEE) 802.11 standards.

Windows Installer package   A file containing explicit instructions about the installation and removal of specific applications. The company or developer who produces the application provides the Windows Installer package .msi file and includes it with the application. See also *Windows Installer Service*.

Windows Installer Service   A component of Windows operating systems that standardizes the way applications are installed on multiple computers. Windows Installer Service implements all the proper Setup rules in the operating system itself by using the Windows Installer package file to install the application. See also *Windows Installer package*.

Windows Internet Name Service (WINS)   A service supplied with Microsoft Windows server operating systems that registers the Network Basic Input/Output System (NetBIOS) names and Internet Protocol (IP) addresses of the computers on a local area network (LAN) and resolves NetBIOS names into IP addresses for its clients as needed.

Windows Management Instrumentation (WMI)   A programming interface that provides access to the hardware, software, and other components of a computer. WMI is the Microsoft implementation of Web-Based Enterprise Management Initiative to establish standards of data in Enterprise Management.

WINS   *See* Windows Internet Name Service (WINS).

Wired Equivalent Privacy (WEP)   A feature of the Institute of Electrical and Electronic Engineers (IEEE) 802.11 wireless networking standard that defines a method for encrypting data transmitted by wireless devices.

workgroup   A simple grouping of computers, intended only to help users find such things as printers and shared folders within that group. Workgroups in Windows do not offer the centralized user accounts and authentication offered by domains.

X

X.500   A standard for a directory service established by the International Telecommunications Union (ITU). The same standard is also published by the International Standards Organization/International Electro-technical Commission (ISO/IEC). The X.500 standard defines the information model used in the directory service. All information in the directory is stored in entries, each of which belongs to at least one object class. The actual information in an entry is determined by attributes that are contained in that entry.

X.509   A document published by the International Telecommunications Union (ITU) that defines the structure of digital certificates.

Z

zone   In a DNS database, a manageable unit of the DNS database that is administered by a DNS server. A zone stores the domain names and data of the domain with a corresponding name, except for domain names stored in delegated subdomains.

zone database file   The file where name-to-IP-address mappings for a zone are stored.

zone transfer   The process by which Domain Name System (DNS) servers interact to maintain and synchronize authoritative name data. When a DNS server is configured as a secondary master for a zone, it periodically queries another DNS server configured as its source for the zone. If the version of the zone kept by the source is different, the secondary master server will pull zone data from its source DNS server to synchronize zone data.

Index

J–K

L

how to:

Make sure your training doesn't end here.

Want to help your Windows Server™ 2003 knowledge stay sharp? Subscribe to TechNet, the definitive resource IT professionals rely on to plan, deploy, manage, and support Microsoft® products. Enhance your career development with monthly technology updates direct from the source — all in a portable package of CDs or DVDs that goes wherever the job takes you.

Subscribe now and get 20% off our yearly rate.*

www.microsoft.com/technet/buynow/keeplearning
or call 1-800-344-2121
Use promotion code: T20001

Microsoft **TechNet know how.**

Microsoft

CONFIDENT.
INTELLIGENT.
SECURE.

She must be a Microsoft Certified Professional.
She must have just tested with Pearson VUE.

MCSA/MCSE certification on Microsoft Windows Server 2003 validates your technical expertise and enhances your credibility in the marketplace. Simply put, it helps position you as a strategic asset to employers.

At Pearson VUE, scheduling your exam is easy and convenient. Your exam results are securely and accurately merged with the Microsoft database — and your exam will be ready when you are.

Test with Pearson VUE

Visit www.PearsonVUE.com or call 1-800-TEST-REG
(North America only) to schedule your exam.

Pearson VUE has 3400+ test centers in 130 countries. For a toll-free phone number in your area or the location of a test center near you, visit www.PearsonVUE.com.

PEARSON
VUE

Focused on your future

Microsoft
CERTIFIED
Exam Provider

MEASUREUP
Know what you know
Official practice exam provider
of Pearson VUE

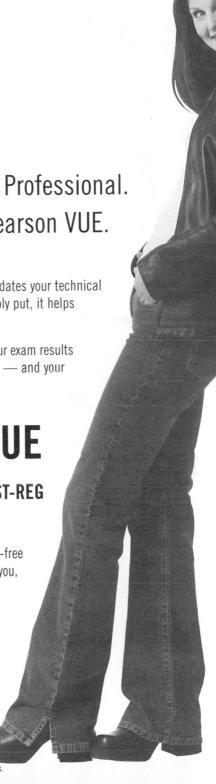

Get a **Free**
e-mail newsletter, updates,
special offers, links to related books,
and more when you

register online!

Register your Microsoft Press® title on our Web site and you'll get a FREE subscription to our e-mail newsletter, *Microsoft Press Book Connections.* You'll find out about newly released and upcoming books and learning tools, online events, software downloads, special offers and coupons for Microsoft Press customers, and information about major Microsoft® product releases. You can also read useful additional information about all the titles we publish, such as detailed book descriptions, tables of contents and indexes, sample chapters, links to related books and book series, author biographies, and reviews by other customers.

Registration is easy. Just visit this Web page and fill in your information:

http://www.microsoft.com/mspress/register

Microsoft

- -

Proof of Purchase

Use this page as proof of purchase if participating in a promotion or rebate offer on this title. Proof of purchase must be used in conjunction with other proof(s) of payment such as your dated sales receipt—see offer details.

MCSA/MCSE Self-Paced Training Kit (Exams 70-292 and 70-296): Upgrading Your Certification to Microsoft® Windows Server™ 2003

0-7356-1971-9

CUSTOMER NAME

Microsoft Press, PO Box 97017, Redmond, WA 98073-9830

System Requirements

To complete the exercises in Part 1, your computer must have the following minimum configuration. All hardware should be in the Windows Server Catalog at *http://www.microsoft.com/windows/catalog/server/* and should meet the requirements listed at *http://www.microsoft.com/windowsserver2003/evaluation/sysreqs/*.

- Windows Server 2003, Enterprise Edition (A 180-day evaluation edition of Windows Server 2003, Enterprise Edition, is included on the CD-ROM.)

- Minimum CPU: 133 MHz for x86-based computers (733 MHz is recommended) and 733 MHz for Itanium-based computers

- Minimum RAM: 128 MB (256 MB is recommended.)

- Disk space for setup: 2.0 GB for x86-based computers and 2.0 GB for Itanium-based computers

- Display monitor capable of 800 x 600 resolution or higher

- CD-ROM drive

- Microsoft Mouse or compatible pointing device

Uninstall Instructions

The time-limited release of Microsoft Windows Server 2003, Enterprise Edition, will expire 180 days after installation. If you decide to discontinue the use of this software, you will need to reinstall your original operating system. You might need to reformat your drive.